CW00347505

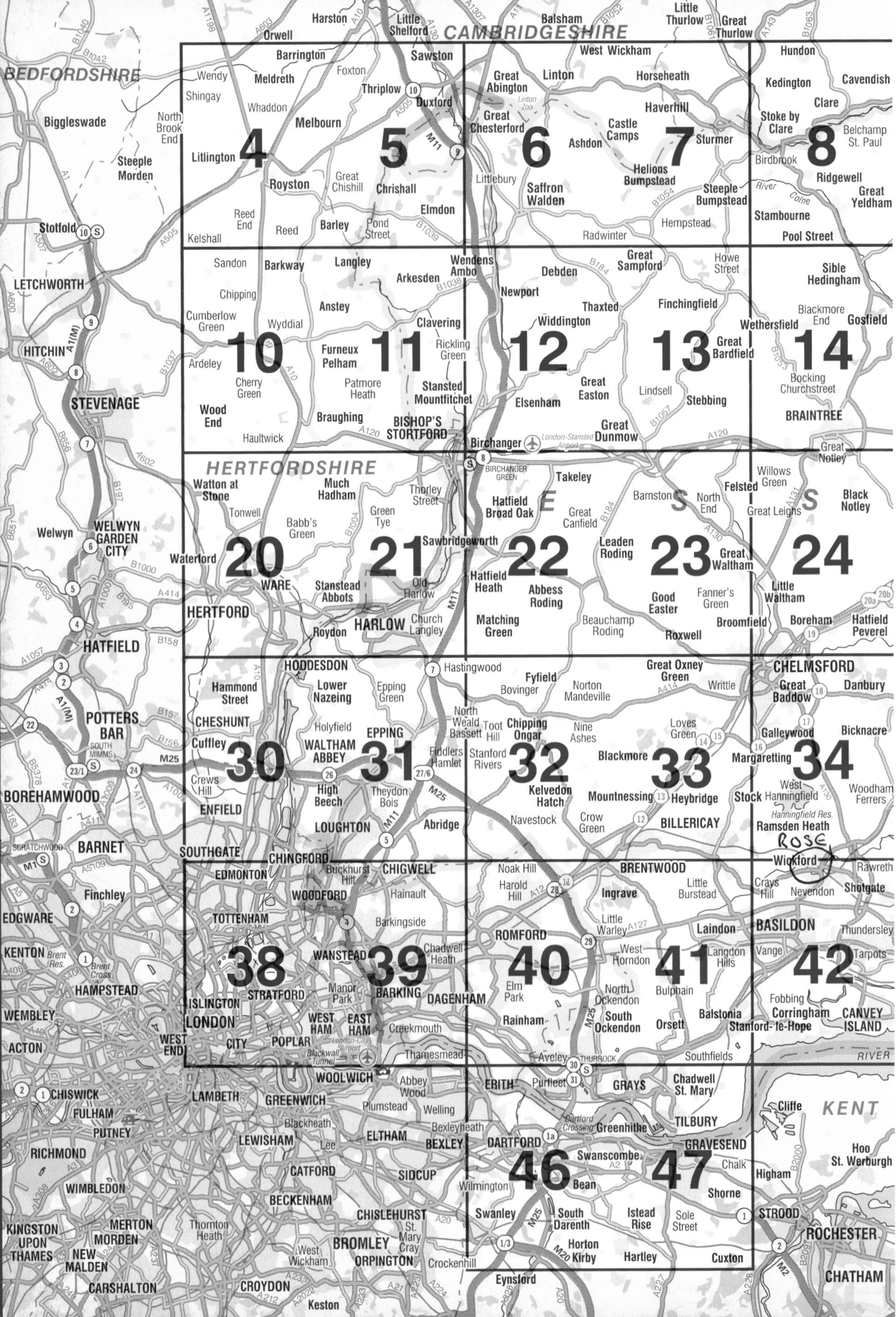

CAMBRIDGESHIRE
BEDFORDSHIRE
HERTFORDSHIRE
KENT
Harston
Orwell
Little Shelford
Balsham
Little Thurlow
Great Thurlow
Barrington
Sawston
West Wickham
Hundon
Wendy
Meldreth
Foxton
Thriplow
Duxford
Great Abington
Linton
Horseheath
Kedington
Cavendish
Shingay
Whaddon
Melbourn
Great Chesterford
Haverhill
Clare
Biggleswade
North Brook End
Castle Camps
Stoke by Clare
Belchamp St. Paul
Litlington
4
5
6
Ashdon
7
Sturmer
8
Steeple Morden
Helions Bumpstead
Birdbrook
Royston
Great Chishill
Chrishall
Littlebury
Saffron Walden
Steeple Bumpstead
Ridgewell
Great Yeldham
River Colne
Reed End
Elmdon
Stambourne
Stotfold
Reed
Barley
Pond Street
Hempstead
Kelshall
Radwinter
Pool Street
Sandon
Barkway
Langley
Wendens Ambo
Great Sampford
Howe Street
Sible Hedingham
Arkesden
Debden
LETCHWORTH
Chipping
Newport
Anstey
Thaxted
Finchingfield
Blackmore End
Gosfield
Cumberlow Green
Wyddial
Clavering
Widdington
Wethersfield
HITCHIN
Furneux Pelham
Rickling Green
10
11
12
13
Great Bardfield
14
Ardeley
Cherry Green
Patmore Heath
Great Easton
Lindsell
Bocking Churchstreet
STEVENAGE
Stansted Mountfitchet
Elsenham
Stebbing
Wood End
Braughing
BISHOP'S STORTFORD
Great Dunmow
BRAINTREE
Haultwick
Birchanger
London-Stansted Airport
BIRCHANGER GREEN
Great Notley
Willows Green
Watton at Stone
Much Hadham
Thorley Street
Takeley
Felsted
Barnston
North End
Black Notley
Tonwell
Green Tye
Hatfield Broad Oak
Great Canfield
Great Leighs
Babb's Green
Welwyn
WELWYN GARDEN CITY
Sawbridgeworth
Leaden Roding
Great Waltham
Waterford
20
21
22
23
24
WARE
Stanstead Abbots
Old Harlow
Hatfield Heath
Abbess Roding
Good Easter
Fanner's Green
Little Waltham
HERTFORD
Broomfield
Boreham
Hatfield Peverel
HARLOW
Church Langley
Matching Green
Beauchamp Roding
Roydon
Roxwell
HATFIELD
HODDESDON
Hastingwood
Great Oxney Green
CHELMSFORD
Fyfield
Lower Nazeing
Epping Green
Bovinger
Norton Mandeville
Writtle
Great Baddow
Danbury
Hammond Street
POTTERS BAR
CHESHUNT
Holyfield
EPPING
North Weald Bassett
Toot Hill
Chipping Ongar
Nine Ashes
Loves Green
Galleywood
Bicknacre
SOUTH MIMMS
Cuffley
WALTHAM ABBEY
Fiddlers Hamlet
Stanford Rivers
30
31
32
Blackmore
33
Margaretting
34
Crews Hill
High Beech
Theydon Bois
Kelvedon Hatch
Mountnessing
Heybridge
Stock
West Hanningfield
Woodham Ferrers
BOREHAMWOOD
ENFIELD
Abridge
Navestock
Crow Green
BILLERICAY
Hanningfield Res.
LOUGHTON
Ramsden Heath
SCRATCHWOOD
BARNET
ROSE
SOUTHGATE
CHINGFORD
Noak Hill
BRENTWOOD
Wickford
Rawreth
EDMONTON
Buckhurst Hill
CHIGWELL
Harold Hill
Little Burstead
Crays Hill
Nevendon
Shotgate
Finchley
WOODFORD
Hainault
Ingrave
EDGWARE
TOTTENHAM
Barkingside
Little Warley
Laindon
BASILDON
Thundersley
ROMFORD
KENTON
Brent Res.
Chadwell Heath
West Horndon
Langdon Hills
Vange
Tarpots
WANSTEAD
38
39
40
41
42
Brent Cross
HAMPSTEAD
STRATFORD
Manor Park
BARKING
Elm Park
North Ockendon
Bulphan
Fobbing
WEMBLEY
ISLINGTON
DAGENHAM
Corringham
CANVEY ISLAND
LONDON
WEST HAM
EAST HAM
Rainham
South Ockendon
Orsett
Balstonia
Stanford-le-Hope
ACTON
Creekmouth
WEST END
CITY
POPLAR
London-City Airport
Blackwall Tunnel
Thamesmead
Aveley
THURROCK
Southfields
RIVER
WOOLWICH
Abbey Wood
ERITH
Purfleet
GRAYS
Chadwell St. Mary
CHISWICK
LAMBETH
GREENWICH
FULHAM
Plumstead
Welling
Cliffe
Blackheath
Dartford Crossing
Greenhithe
TILBURY
PUTNEY
Bexleyheath
LEWISHAM
Lee
ELTHAM
BEXLEY
DARTFORD
GRAVESEND
Hoo St. Werburgh
RICHMOND
Swanscombe
Chalk
CATFORD
SIDCUP
46
47
Higham
Wilmington
Bean
Shorne
WIMBLEDON
BECKENHAM
CHISLEHURST
Swanley
South Darenth
Istead Rise
Sole Street
STROOD
KINGSTON UPON THAMES
MERTON
MORDEN
Thornton Heath
St. Mary Cray
ROCHESTER
NEW MALDEN
BROMLEY
West Wickham
ORPINGTON
Horton Kirby
Hartley
Cuxton
Crockenhill
CHATHAM
CARSHALTON
CROYDON
Eynsford
Keston
M11
M25
M1
M20
M2
A1(M)
A1
A10
A120
A130
A12
A13
A127
A2
A20
A414
A505
A602
A1307
B1038
B184
B1054
B1057

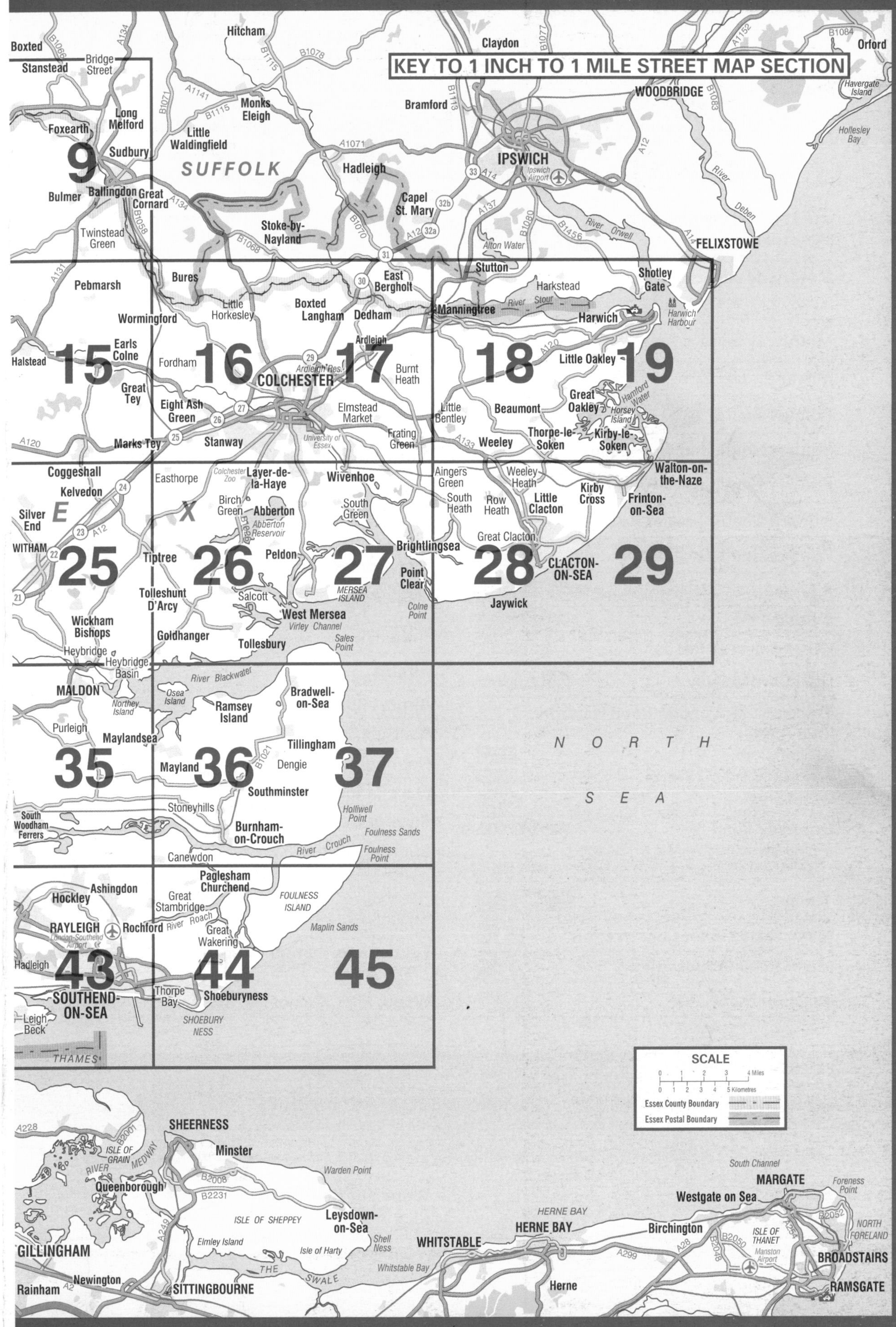

KEY TO 1 INCH TO 1 MILE STREET MAP SECTION
Boxted
Stanstead
Bridge Street
Hitcham
Claydon
Orford
Havergate Island
WOODBRIDGE
Hollesley Bay
Long Melford
Monks Eleigh
Bramford
Foxearth
Little Waldingfield
SUFFOLK
Hadleigh
IPSWICH
Ipswich Airport
Sudbury
9
Bulmer
Ballingdon
Great Cornard
Capel St. Mary
River Deben
River Orwell
Alton Water
Twinstead Green
Stoke-by-Nayland
FELIXSTOWE
Pebmarsh
Bures
East Bergholt
Stutton
Shotley Gate
Harkstead
River Stour
Wormingford
Little Horkesley
Boxted
Langham
Dedham
Manningtree
Harwich
Harwich Harbour
Halstead
15
Earls Colne
Fordham
16
Ardleigh
17
18
Little Oakley
19
Great Tey
COLCHESTER
Ardleigh Res.
Burnt Heath
Great Oakley
Hamford Water
Horsey Island
Eight Ash Green
Elmstead Market
Little Bentley
Beaumont
Thorpe-le-Soken
Kirby-le-Soken
Marks Tey
Stanway
University of Essex
Frating Green
Weeley
Coggeshall
Easthorpe
Colchester Zoo
Layer-de-la-Haye
Wivenhoe
Aingers Green
Weeley Heath
Walton-on-the-Naze
Kelvedon
South Heath
Row Heath
Little Clacton
Kirby Cross
Frinton-on-Sea
Silver End
E
X
Birch Green
Abberton
Abberton Reservoir
South Green
WITHAM
Great Clacton
Brightlingsea
25
Tiptree
26
Peldon
27
28
CLACTON-ON-SEA
29
Point Clear
Tolleshunt D'Arcy
Salcott
Mersea Island
Jaywick
Colne Point
West Mersea
Virley Channel
Wickham Bishops
Goldhanger
Tollesbury
Sales Point
Heybridge
Heybridge Basin
River Blackwater
MALDON
Osea Island
Bradwell-on-Sea
Northey Island
Ramsey Island
Purleigh
Maylandsea
Tillingham
NORTH SEA
35
Mayland
36
Dengie
37
Southminster
Stoneyhills
South Woodham Ferrers
Holliwell Point
Burnham-on-Crouch
Foulness Sands
River Crouch
Foulness Point
Canewdon
Paglesham Churchend
Ashingdon
Hockley
Great Stambridge
Foulness Island
RAYLEIGH
Rochford
River Roach
London-Southend Airport
Great Wakering
Maplin Sands
Hadleigh
43
44
45
SOUTHEND-ON-SEA
Thorpe Bay
Shoeburyness
Leigh Beck
Shoebury Ness
Thames
SCALE
0 1 2 3 4 Miles
0 1 2 3 4 5 Kilometres
Essex County Boundary
Essex Postal Boundary
SHEERNESS
Isle of Grain
River Medway
Minster
Warden Point
Queenborough
South Channel
MARGATE
Foreness Point
Westgate on Sea
Isle of Sheppey
Leysdown-on-Sea
HERNE BAY
Birchington
North Foreland
Isle of Thanet
GILLINGHAM
Elmley Island
Isle of Harty
Shell Ness
WHITSTABLE
Manston Airport
BROADSTAIRS
The Swale
Whitstable Bay
Newington
Rainham
SITTINGBOURNE
Herne
RAMSGATE

REFERENCE TO 1 INCH TO 1 MILE STREET MAP SECTION

Symbol	Example
Motorway	M11
Motorway Junction Numbers — Unlimited Interchange 8, Limited Interchange 9	
Motorway Service Area	S THURROCK
Mileages - between Motorway Junctions	4
Primary Route	A12
Primary Route Junction Numbers	16
Primary Route Service Area	S Babraham
North & South Circular Roads	
Primary Route Destination	HARLOW
A Road	A128
B Road	B1033
Other Selected Roads	
Dual Carriageway	
Transport for London Road Network (Red Route)	
Primary Route	
North & South Circular Roads	
A Road	
One Way Road (Motorway, Primary Route & A Road only - Traffic flow indicated by a heavy line on the driver's left)	
Tunnel	
Major Road Under Construction	
Major Road Proposed	
Junction Name	GALLOWS CORNER

Symbol	Example
Toll	TOLL
Ferry	
Railway and Croydon Tramlink	
Level Crossing and Tunnel	
Railway Station	COLCHESTER
London Underground Station	UPMINSTER
Docklands Light Railway Station and Tramlink Stop	SOUTH QUAY
Local Authority Boundary	
Posttown & London Postal District Boundaries	
Postcode Boundary	
Map Continuation	
for 1 Inch to 1 Mile Street Mapping (Blue Pages)	5
to 3 Inches to 1 Mile Street Mapping (Red Pages)	89 or 205
Airport	LONDON - STANSTED AIRPORT
Airport Runway	
Built-up Area	
National Grid Reference	580
Place of Interest	• Audley End
River or Canal	
Sporting Venues — Cricket, Rugby, Football, Stadium, Golf Course 18 Hole, 9 Hole	
Tourist Information Centre — Open all year, Open Summer only	
Wood, Park, Cemetery, Etc.	

SCALE 1 Inch (2.54 cm) to 1 Mile; 1.58 cm to 1 Kilometre — 0, ½, 1, 2 Miles; 0, 1, 2, 3 Kilometres — 1:63,360

The following features are shown only in those areas of Essex not covered by 3 Inches to 1 Mile Street Mapping (Red Pages)

Building	**Church or Chapel** †
Car Park - selected	**Post Office** ★

A-Z ESSEX

CONTENTS

1 inch to 1 mile Street Map section Blue Pages

Key to Map Pages.........................Inside front cover

Reference to Maps...2

Map Pages..4-47

Postcode Map...**48**

3 inches to 1 mile Street Map section Red Pages

Key to Map Pages.........................Inside back cover

Reference to Maps...49

Map Pages..50-230

Index to Streets, Towns, Villages and selected Places of Interest..................................**231-316**

Index to Hospitals, Health Centres and Hospices..................................**317-319**

Geographers' A-Z Map Company Ltd.

Head Office : Fairfield Road, Borough Green, Sevenoaks, Kent TN15 8PP Telephone : 01732 781000 (General Enquiries & Trade Sales)
Showrooms : 44 Gray's Inn Road, London WC1X 8HX Telephone 020 7440 9500 (Retail Sales)
www.a-zmaps.co.uk

4
A
B
C
D
E
1
2
3
4
5
6
7
530
32
34
36
38
250
48
46
44
42
240
38
36
East Hatley
Arrington
Wimpole Hall
Wimpole Park
Orwell
Barrington
Croydon
Bookcroft Bunnery
New Wimpole
Wendy
Shingay
Whaddon
Meldreth
Shepreth
Docwra's Manor Gardens
Crossing House Garden
Willers Wildlife
Dyer's Green
Chiswick End
Melbourn
Kneesworth
Royston
SG8
Abington Pigotts
North Brook End
Bassingbourn
Steeple Morden
Litlington
Morden Green
Gatley End
Baldock
SG7
Odsey
The Thrift
Morden Grange Plantation
Church Hill
Therfield Heath
Museum
Seven Rides Plantation
Therfield
Kelshall
Reed End
Reed
Dane End
Chapel Green
Barkway
Newsells
Newsells Park
Cooper Green
Smith's End
Rokey Wood
Lords Wood
Reed Wood
Earls Wood
Philpott's
DANGER AREA
River Cam or Rhee
River Mel
Cat Ditch
SOUTH CAMBRIDGESHIRE
NORTH HERTFORDSHIRE
A1198
A603
B1042
A10
A505
B1039
B1368
ERMINE WAY
CAMBRIDGE ROAD
OLD NORTH ROAD
BALDOCK ROAD
LONDON RD.
MELBOURN RD.
NEWMARKET ROAD
ROYSTON ROAD
COOMBE ROAD
STATION ROAD
THE JOINT
MALTON LANE
HIGH ST.
CHURCH ST.
WENDY ROAD
LOWER ROAD
HIGH RD.
CROYDON ROAD
CHESTNUT LANE
WHADDON ROAD
FEN ROAD
BROOK ROAD
NORTH END
SOUTH END
SPRING LANE
NORTH BROOK END
LITLINGTON
CHEYNEY ST.
ABINGTON ROAD
ROOKS NEST LANE
BARKWAY RD.
ASHWELL & MORDEN
SHEPRETH
MELDRETH
ROYSTON
10
9
18

F
G
H
J
K
5
A10
Harston
Newton
Sawston
Pampisford
Whittlesford
Foxton
Thriplow
Fowlmere
Heathfield
Cambridge
CB2
Duxford
Imperial War Museum
Duxford Airfield
M11
A505
A1301
A11
Hinxton
Stump Cross
Ickleton
Watermill
Fowlmere Aerodrome
CB10
Gt. Chesterford
Flint Cross
Anthonyhill Plantation
Saffron Walden
Heydon
Crawley End
Broad Green
Chrishall
Elmdon
Strethall
Howe Wood
Littlebury
Catmere End
Littlebury Green
Park Wood
Great Chishill
Windmill
Barley
CB11
Monkshole Wood
Shaftenhoe End
Little Chishill
Little Chishill Wood
Building End
Pond Street
Bridge Green
Rockell's Wood
Green Wood
Pondbottom Wood
Cross Leys
Duddenhoe End
Rough Wood
High Wood
Clanver End
West End
Messop's Grove
Oaks Bushes
Killems Green
Nuthampstead Airfield
Langley
Norton End
B1368
B1039
B1383
B184
M11
202
9
10
11
18
1
2
3
4
5
6
7

6
A
B
C
D
E
1
2
3
4
5
6
7
A11
Babraham
A1307
A505
M11
CB2
CB1
CB11
CB10
Cambridge
Saffron Walden
Sawston
Pampisford
Little Abington
Great Abington
Hildersham
Linton
Balsham
Balsham Wood
Borley Wood
Vineyard
Linton Zoo
Hinxton
Watermill
Ickleton
Stump Cross
Great Chesterford
Little Chesterford
Hadstock
Hadstock Wood
Hadstock Common
Thirty Three Acre Covert
Bartlow
Home Wood
Steventon End
Ashdon
Church End
Shadwell Wood
Nun Wood
Chesterford Park
Emanuel Wood
Little Walden
Springwell
Protection Plantation
Pond Plantation
Grimsditch Wood
Long Grove
Little Hales Wood
Hales Wood
Water End
Littlebury
Howe Wood
Catmere End
Littlebury Green
Northend
Robins' Grove
Pounce Wood
Audley End
Ring Hill
The Oaks
Brand's Hill
Cornwallis Hill
Green Wood
Sewards End
Stocking Green
Maple End
School
Cole End
Wimbish
Crowney Wood
West End
Sparrows End
Wendens Ambo
Brakey Ley Wood
Shortgrove Park
Peverel's Wood
Purton End
Tye Green
Castle
Cemy.
SOUTH CAMBRIDGESHIRE
UTTLESFORD
B1052
B1053
B1383
B184
B1039
A1301
202
190
218
227
12
9
18
550
52
54
56
58
50
48
46
44
42
40
38
36

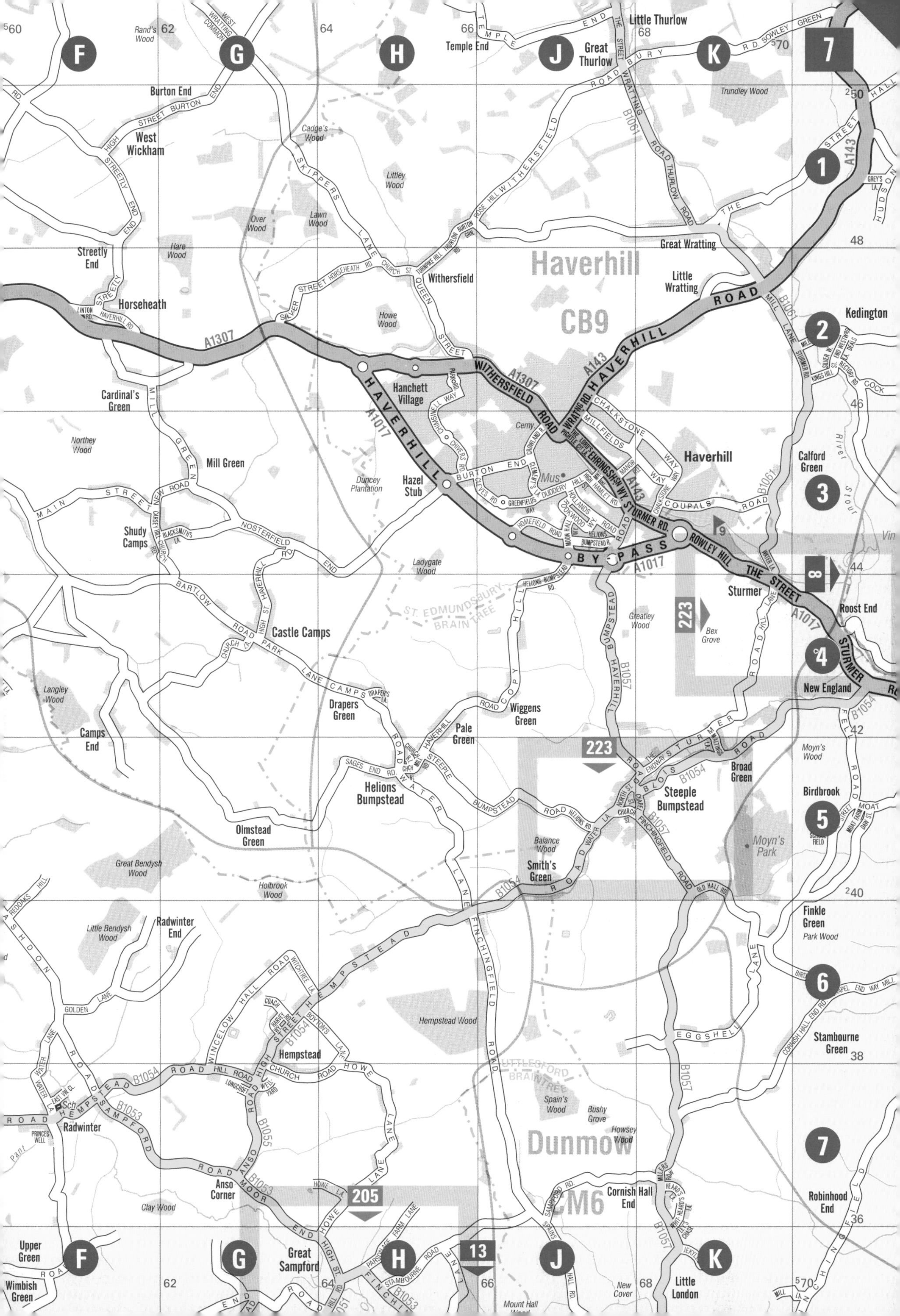

7
F
G
H
J
K
Little Thurlow
Great Thurlow
Temple End
West Wickham
Burton End
Streetly End
Horseheath
Withersfield
Haverhill
CB9
Great Wratting
Little Wratting
Kedington
Hanchett Village
Hazel Stub
Cardinal's Green
Mill Green
Shudy Camps
Castle Camps
Calford Green
Sturmer
Roost End
New England
Drapers Green
Wiggens Green
Pale Green
Helions Bumpstead
Steeple Bumpstead
Broad Green
Birdbrook
Camps End
Olmstead Green
Smith's Green
Finkle Green
Radwinter End
Hempstead
Radwinter
Anso Corner
Great Sampford
Upper Green
Wimbish Green
Cornish Hall End
Little London
Stambourne Green
Robinhood End
Dunmow
CM6
A1307
A1017
A143
B1061
B1057
B1054
B1053
B1055
223
205
13

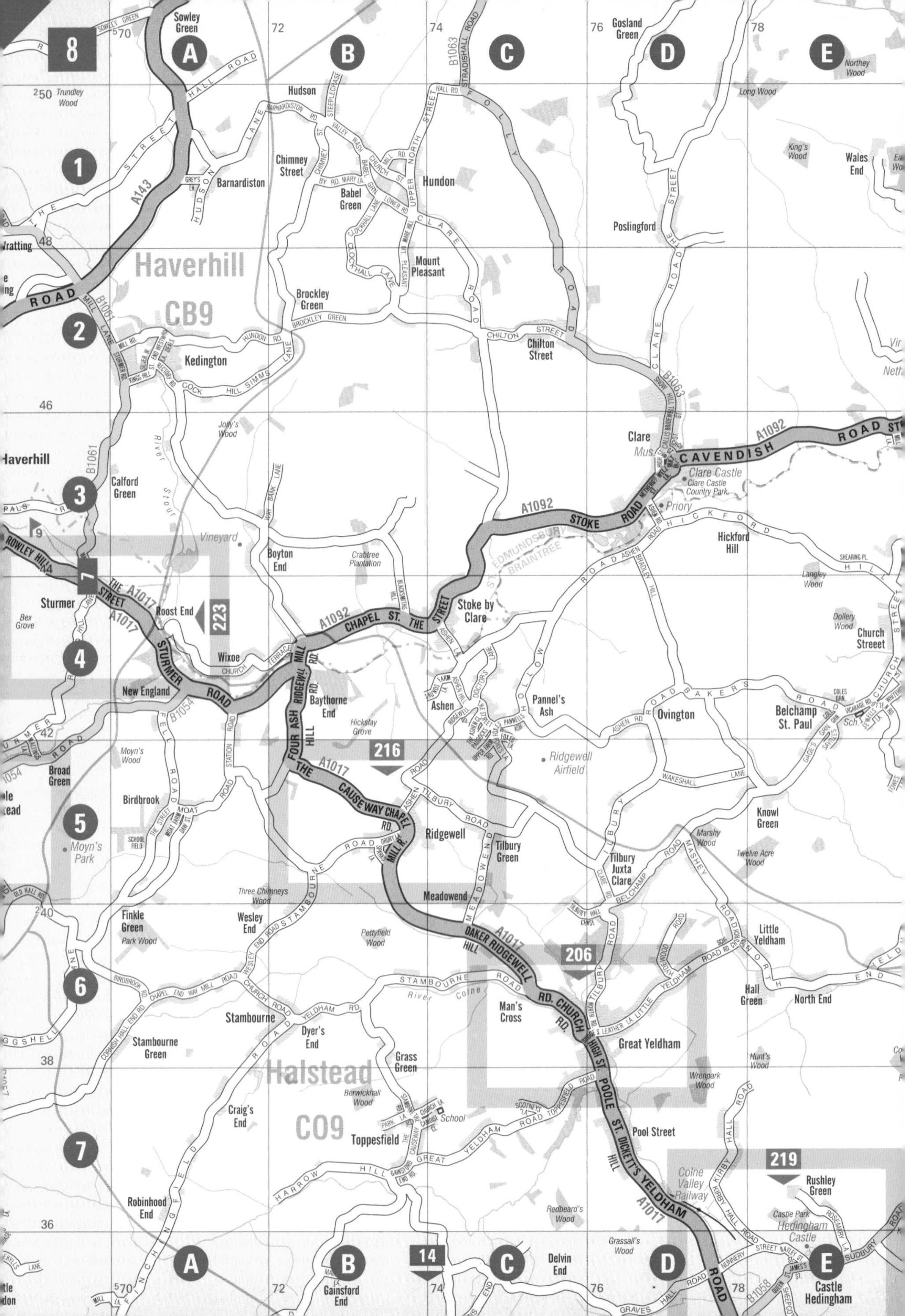
8
A
B
C
D
E
1
2
3
4
5
6
7
72
74
76
78
50
48
46
42
40
38
36
570
Haverhill
CB9
Halstead
CO9
Sowley Green
Trundley Wood
Hudson
Barnardiston
Chimney Street
Babel Green
Hundon
Mount Pleasant
Brockley Green
Kedington
Gosland Green
Northey Wood
Long Wood
King's Wood
Wales End
Poslingford
Chilton Street
Clare
Clare Castle
Clare Castle Country Park
Priory
Hickford Hill
Langley Wood
Dollery Wood
Church Streeet
Calford Green
Jolly's Wood
Vineyard
Boyton End
Crabtree Plantation
Stoke by Clare
Sturmer
Bex Grove
Roost End
Wixoe
New England
Baythorne End
Hickslay Grove
Ashen
Pannel's Ash
Ovington
Belchamp St. Paul
Ridgewell Airfield
Broad Green
Moyn's Wood
Birdbrook
Moyn's Park
Ridgewell
Tilbury Green
Knowl Green
Marshy Wood
Twelve Acre Wood
Tilbury Juxta Clare
Three Chimneys Wood
Meadowend
Finkle Green
Park Wood
Wesley End
Pettyfield Wood
Little Yeldham
Hall Green
North End
Man's Cross
Stambourne
Stambourne Green
Dyer's End
Grass Green
Great Yeldham
Hunt's Wood
Berwickhall Wood
Wrenpark Wood
Craig's End
Toppesfield
School
Pool Street
Colne Valley Railway
Rushley Green
Robinhood End
Redbeard's Wood
Castle Park
Hedingham Castle
Grassall's Wood
Gainsford End
Delvin End
Castle Hedingham
223
216
206
219
14
A143
A1092
A1017
B1061
B1063
B1054
B1058
CAVENDISH ROAD
STOKE ROAD
CHAPEL ST.
THE STREET
STURMER ROAD
FOUR ASH HILL
RIDGEWELL RD.
THE CAUSEWAY
CHAPEL RD.
MILL RD.
OAKER HILL
RIDGEWELL RD.
CHURCH RD.
HIGH ST.
POOLE ST.
DICKETT'S HILL
YELDHAM ROAD
ROWLEY HILL
STRADISHALL ROAD
FOLLY ROAD
CLARE ROAD
THE STREET
HUDSON LANE
MILL LANE
HUNDON RD.
SIMMS LANE
COCK HILL
BROCKLEY GREEN
HICKFORD HILL
ASHEN ROAD
BRADLEY HILL
HOLLOW ROAD
BAKER'S ROAD
WAKESHALL LANE
TILBURY ROAD
ASHEN ROAD
BELCHAMP ROAD
MASHEY ROAD
MEADOWEND
STAMBOURNE ROAD
YELDHAM RD.
TOPPESFIELD ROAD
GREAT YELDHAM ROAD
HARROW HILL
FINCHINGFIELD ROAD
GRAVES HALL ROAD
KIRBY HALL ROAD
HALL ROAD
SUDBURY ROAD
ST. EDMUNDSBURY
BRAINTREE
River Stour
River Colne
Vratting
Haverhill
Sturmer

9
F
G
H
J
K
1
2
3
4
5
6
7
Fenstead End
Alpheton
Aveley Wood
Lavenham
A134
Bridge Street
Lineage Wood
Spelthorn Wood
Fern Hill
Brook Street
Stanstead
Stanstead Great Wood
Bar Wood
Kentwell Hall
Glemsford
Court Wood
Cavendish
LOWER ROAD
MELFORD RD.
WINDMILL HILL
WESTGATE ST.
HIGH STREET
A1092
B1065
B1066
B1064
River Stour
River Glem
Melford Hall
Long Melford
LONG MELFORD BY-PASS
BULL LANE
Acton Place
Acton
Pentlow
Foxearth
Liston Garden
Liston
Cuckoo Tye
Sudbury
Bradfield's Wood
CO10
Temple End
Rodbridge Corner
Newman's Green
Great Waldingfield
Borley
Borley Green
HALL ROAD
MELFORD ROAD
SPRINGLANDS WY.
NORTHERN RD.
Belchamp Otten
Heaven Wood
Gainsborough's House
NEWTON ROAD
A131
B1115
B1508
Cornard Tye
Sudbury (Belchamp Water) Airfield
Puttock End
Belchamp Walter
Bulmer
Ballingdon
BALLINGDON HILL
Great Cornard
Bath Wood
Middleton
195
Gestingthorpe
Bulmer Tye
Parsonage Wood
Home Wood
Gt. Cornard Country Park
Little Cornard
Henny Street
Audley End
Little Henny
Great Henny
Workhouse Green
Butler's Wood
Waldegrave Wood
Paradise Centre Gardens
Twinstead
Twinstead Green
Wickham St. Paul
Long Gardens
CO8
Lamarsh
15
Catley Cross
Alphamstone
Parkhill Wood
Longspring Wood
Ashground
B1058
18

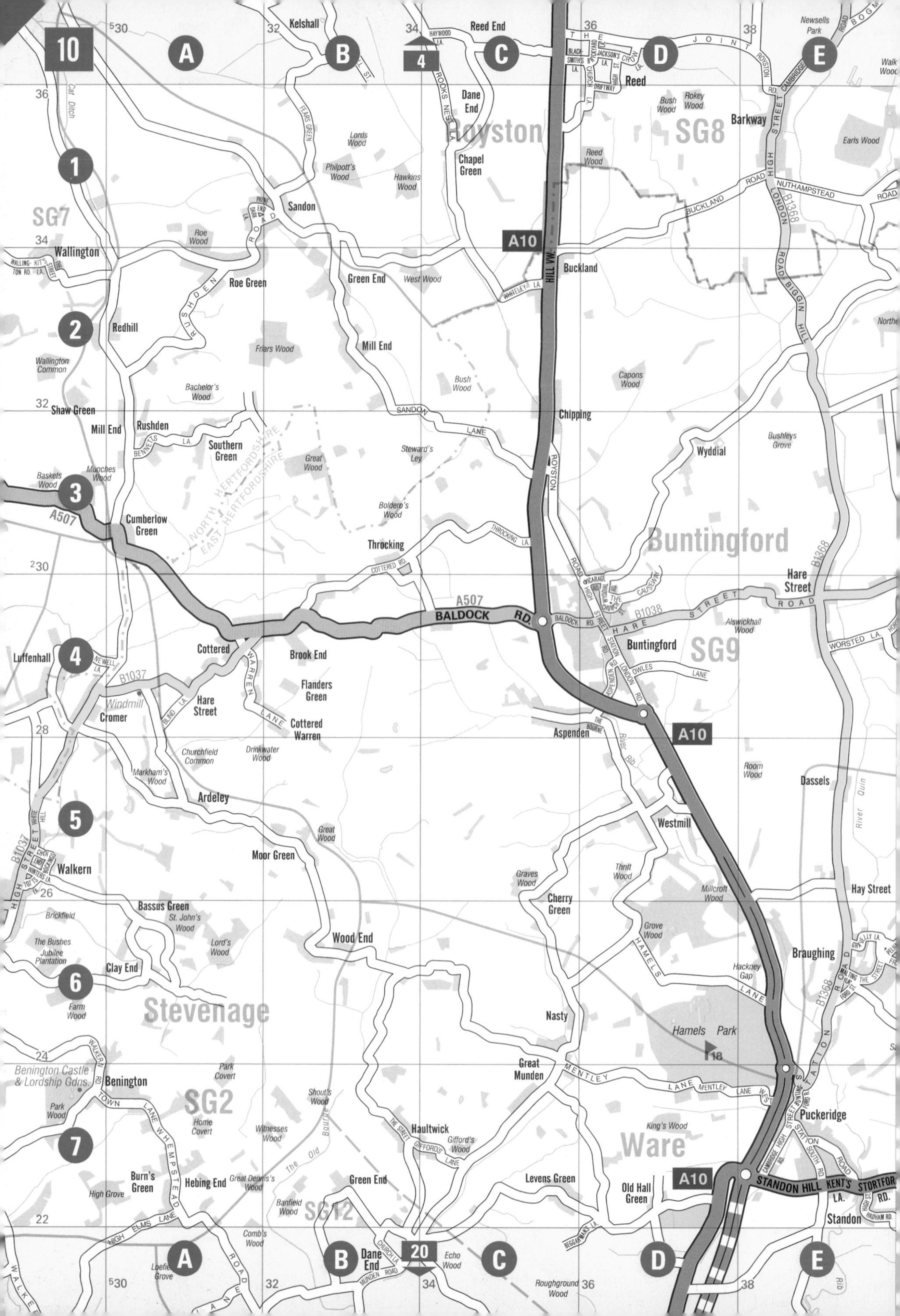
10
A
B
C
D
E
4
20
A10
A507
B1037
B1038
B1368
BALDOCK RD.
SG7
SG8
SG9
SG2
SG12
Royston
Buntingford
Stevenage
Ware
Kelshall
Reed End
Reed
Dane End
Chapel Green
Barkway
Newsells Park
Lords Wood
Philpott's Wood
Hawkins Wood
Bush Wood
Rokey Wood
Reed Wood
Earls Wood
Sandon
Roe Wood
Wallington
Roe Green
Green End
West Wood
Buckland
Redhill
Wallington Common
Friars Wood
Mill End
Capons Wood
Bachelor's Wood
Bush Wood
Shaw Green
Mill End
Rushden
Southern Green
Chipping
Steward's Ley
Great Wood
Wyddial
Bushleys Grove
Baskets Wood
Munches Wood
NORTH HERTFORDSHIRE
EAST HERTFORDSHIRE
Boldero's Wood
Cumberlow Green
Throcking
Hare Street
Cottered
Brook End
Buntingford
Alswickhall Wood
Luffenhall
Flanders Green
Hare Street
Windmill
Cromer
Cottered Warren
Aspenden
Churchfield Common
Drinkwater Wood
Markham's Wood
Ardeley
Room Wood
Dassels
Westmill
Great Wood
Walkern
Moor Green
Thrift Wood
Graves Wood
Cherry Green
Millcroft Wood
Hay Street
Brickfield
Bassus Green
St. John's Wood
Grove Wood
Wood End
The Bushes
Jubilee Plantation
Lord's Wood
Clay End
Braughing
Hackney Gap
Farm Wood
Nasty
Hamels Park
Benington Castle & Lordship Gdns.
Benington
Park Covert
Great Munden
Park Wood
Home Covert
Shout's Wood
Witnesses Wood
Haultwick
Gifford's Wood
King's Wood
Puckeridge
Burn's Green
Hebing End
Great Dennis's Wood
Green End
Levens Green
Old Hall Green
High Grove
Banfield Wood
Standon
Comb's Wood
Dane End
Echo Wood
Loefield Grove
Roughground Wood
STANDON HILL
KENT'S STORTFORD
River Quin
The Old Bourne

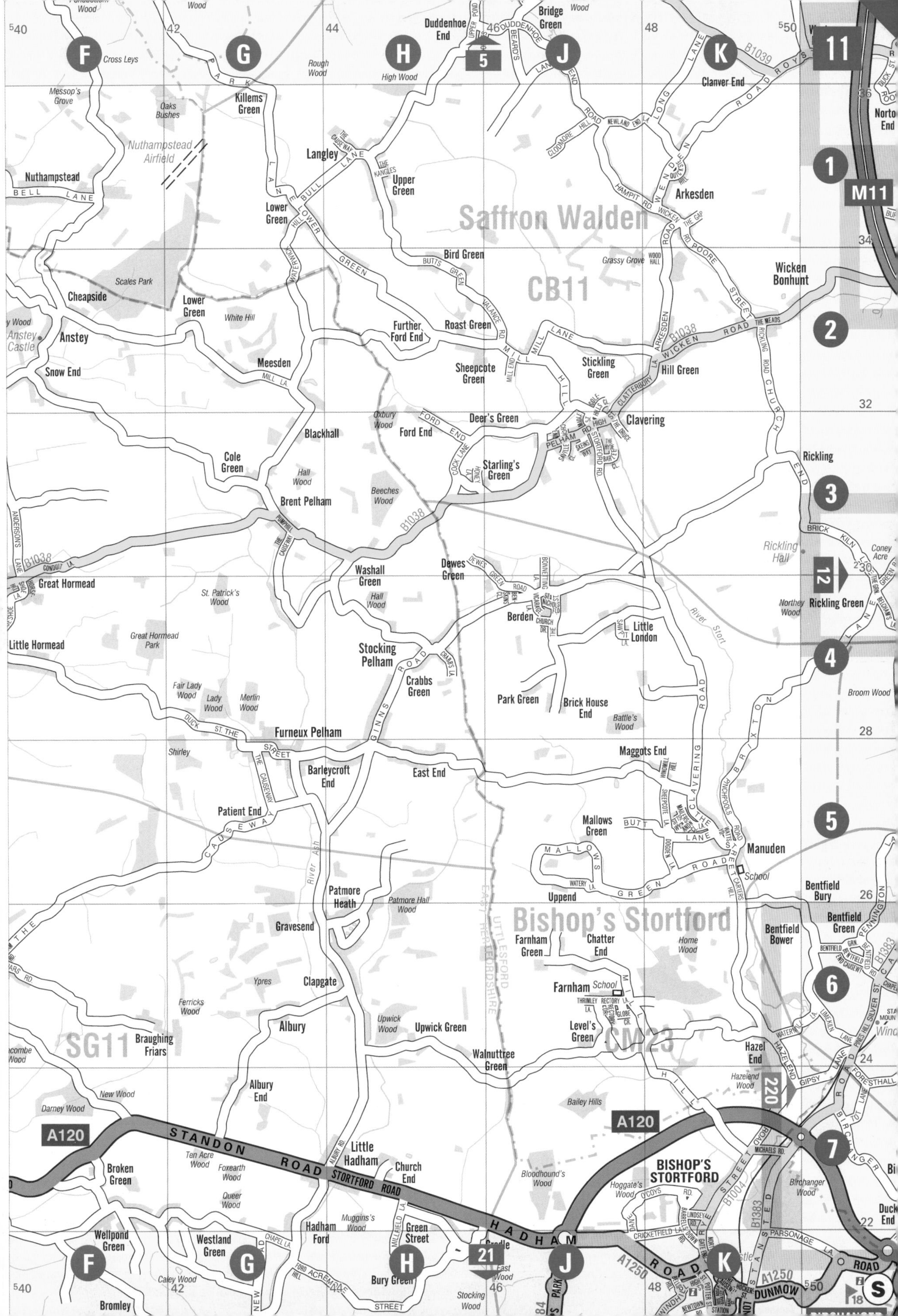

11
12
5
21
220
F
G
H
J
K
1
2
3
4
5
6
7
540
42
44
46
48
550
36
34
32
30
28
26
24
22
M11
A120
B1038
B1039
B1383
B1004
A1250
Saffron Walden
CB11
Bishop's Stortford
CM23
SG11
BISHOP'S STORTFORD
Cross Leys
Messop's Grove
Oaks Bushes
Nuthampstead Airfield
Nuthampstead
BELL LANE
Rough Wood
High Wood
Duddenhoe End
Bridge Green
Clanver End
Norton End
Killems Green
Langley
Upper Green
Lower Green
Arkesden
Bird Green
Grassy Grove
Wicken Bonhunt
Scales Park
Cheapside
Lower Green
White Hill
Further Ford End
Roast Green
Anstey
Anstey Castle
Snow End
Meesden
Sheepcote Green
Stickling Green
Hill Green
Clavering
Deer's Green
Oxbury Wood
Ford End
Blackhall
Starling's Green
Rickling
Cole Green
Hall Wood
Beeches Wood
Brent Pelham
Rickling Hall
Coney Acre
Great Hormead
Washall Green
Dewes Green
Hall Wood
St. Patrick's Wood
Northey Wood
Rickling Green
Berden
Little London
Little Hormead
Great Hormead Park
Stocking Pelham
Crabbs Green
Park Green
Brick House End
Broom Wood
Fair Lady Wood
Lady Wood
Merlin Wood
Battle's Wood
Furneux Pelham
Shirley
Maggots End
Barleycroft End
East End
Patient End
Mallows Green
Manuden
School
Patmore Heath
Patmore Hall Wood
Uppend
Bentfield Bury
Bentfield Green
Bentfield Bower
Gravesend
Farnham Green
Chatter End
Home Wood
Ypres
Clapgate
Farnham
Ferricks Wood
Albury
Upwick Wood
Upwick Green
Level's Green
Braughing Friars
Walnuttree Green
Hazel End
Hazelend Wood
New Wood
Albury End
Darney Wood
Bailey Hills
STANDON ROAD
STORTFORD ROAD
HADHAM ROAD
DUNMOW ROAD
Little Hadham
Ten Acre Wood
Foxearth Wood
Broken Green
Church End
Queer Wood
Bloodhound's Wood
Hoggate's Wood
Birchanger Wood
Duck End
Wellpond Green
Westland Green
Hadham Ford
Muggins's Wood
Green Street
Cradle End
East Wood
Caley Wood
Bury Green
Stocking Wood
Bromley
River Ash
River Stort
UTTLESFORD
EAST HERTFORDSHIRE

12
Wendens Ambo
West End
Sparrows End
Audley End
Clanver End
Norton End
M11
Shortgrove Park
Brakey Ley Wood
Peverel's Wood
Purton End
Cole End
Crowney Wood
Wimbish
Tye Green
Carver Barracks
Howe Wood
Saffron Walden
Elder Street
Howlett End
Newport
Debden Water
Rowney Wood
Wicken Bonhunt
Horseley End
Cabbage Wood
Debden
Smiths Green
Spring Close
CB11
Rook End
Debden Green
Priors Hall Barn
Widdington
Mole Hall Wildlife Park
Littley Wood West
Littley Wood East
Rickling
Hamperden End
Broom Wood
Prior's Wood
Quendon
Cutlers Green
Coney Acre
Rickling Hall
Little Henham
River Cam or Granta
Rickling Green
Quendon Wood
Cherry Green
Home Wood
Northey Wood
Catherine Grove
Reservoir
Armigers
Broom Wood
Ugley
Henham
Woodend Green
Sucksted Green
Hawland Wood
Bishop's Stortford
Old Mead
Chickney
Ugley Green
Pledgdon Green
Broxted
Manuden
Alsa Wood
Elsenham
Lady Wood
Pledgdon Wood
Tilty
Bentfield Bury
Brick End
Bentfield Bower
Bentfield Green
Fuller's End
Gaunt's End
Eastend Wood
Stansted Mountfitchet
CM22
Molehill Green
Broxted Hill
Castle & Mus.
Stansted Park
Windmill
Tye Green
The Lays
Broxted Common Wood
Hazel End
Hazelend Wood
Terminal
Stansted Airport
Burton End
Stansted
Mill End
Bamber's Green
Digby Wood
CM24
Birchanger
Birchanger Wood
CM23
LONDON-STANSTED AIRPORT
ESTIMATED COMPLETION EARLY 2004
Fanns Wood
Canfield Spring
A120
Duck End
Start Hill
Prior's Wood
Takeley Street
Brewer's End
Takeley
Smith's Green
Little Canfield
Tilekin Green
Street Coppice
Little Canfield
Runnel's
DUNMOW ROAD
STORTFORD

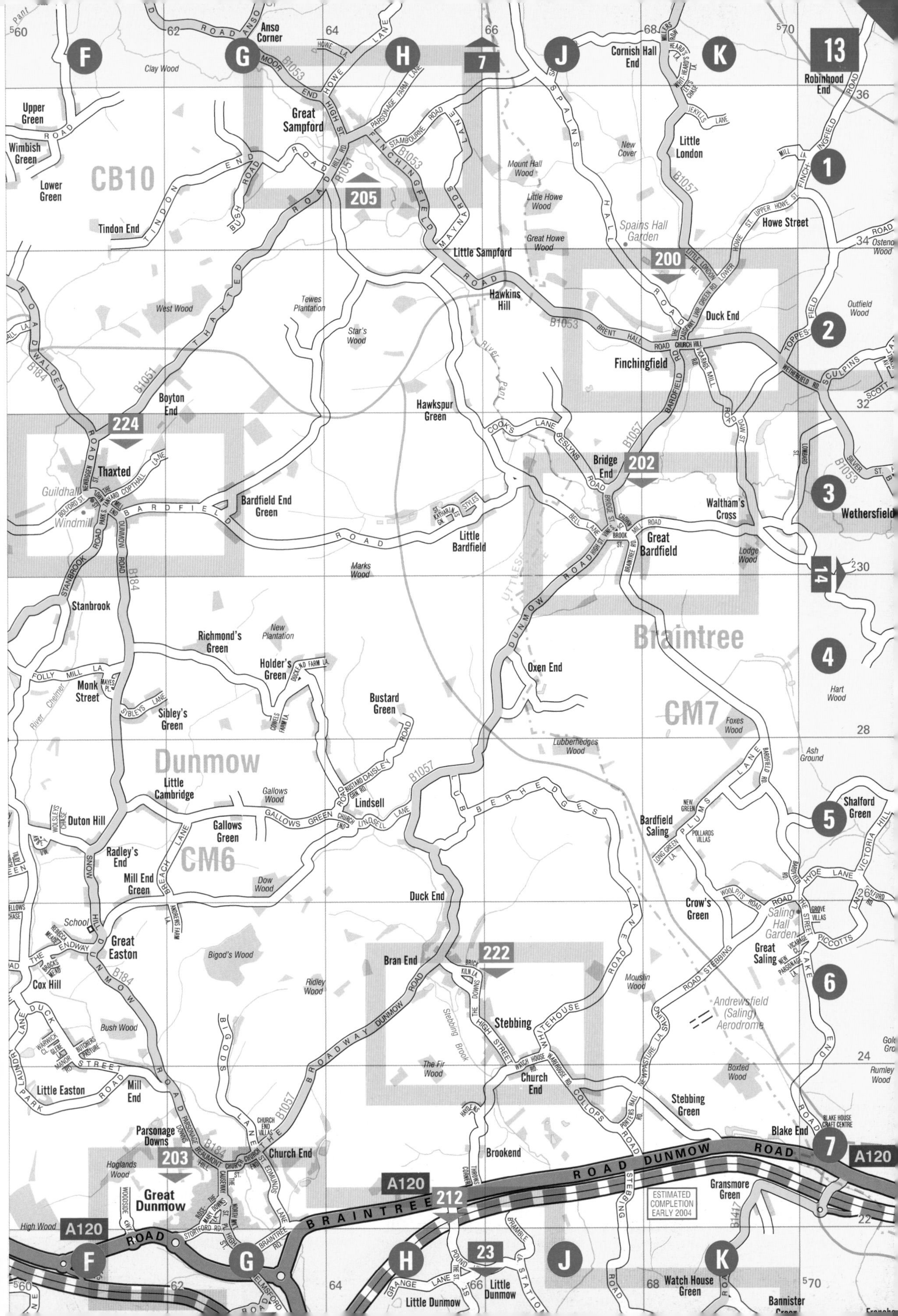
13
7
14
200
202
205
224
203
222
212
23
A120
CB10
CM6
CM7
Braintree
Dunmow
Anso Corner
Cornish Hall End
Robinhood End
Upper Green
Wimbish Green
Lower Green
Great Sampford
Little London
Tindon End
Howe Street
Little Sampford
Spains Hall Garden
Hawkins Hill
Duck End
Finchingfield
Boyton End
Hawkspur Green
Thaxted
Bridge End
Bardfield End Green
Little Bardfield
Waltham's Cross
Great Bardfield
Wethersfield
Stanbrook
Richmond's Green
Holder's Green
Oxen End
Monk Street
Sibley's Green
Bustard Green
Little Cambridge
Lindsell
Shalford Green
Duton Hill
Gallows Green
Bardfield Saling
Radley's End
Mill End Green
Crow's Green
Great Easton
Great Saling
Cox Hill
Bran End
Stebbing
Little Easton
Mill End
Church End
Stebbing Green
Blake End
Parsonage Downs
Great Dunmow
Brookend
Gransmore Green
Little Dunmow
Watch House Green
Bannister Green
Clay Wood
West Wood
Tewes Plantation
Star's Wood
Mount Hall Wood
Little Howe Wood
Great Howe Wood
New Cover
Outfield Wood
Marks Wood
New Plantation
Lodge Wood
Hart Wood
Foxes Wood
Lubberhedges Wood
Ash Ground
Gallows Wood
Dow Wood
Bigod's Wood
Ridley Wood
Mouslin Wood
Bush Wood
The Fir Wood
Boxted Wood
Rumley Wood
Hoglands Wood
High Wood
Andrewsfield (Saling) Aerodrome
Saling Hall Garden
River Pant
River Chelmer
Stebbing Brook
Guildhall
Windmill
School
ESTIMATED COMPLETION EARLY 2004
BLAKE HOUSE CRAFT CENTRE
THAXTED ROAD
BRAINTREE ROAD
DUNMOW ROAD
LUBBERHEDGES LANE
WHITEHOUSE ROAD
BROADWAY
GALLOWS GREEN ROAD
BARDFIELD ROAD
TINDON END
BRENT HALL ROAD
SPAINS HALL ROAD
FINCHINGFIELD ROAD
B1051
B1053
B1057
B184
B1417

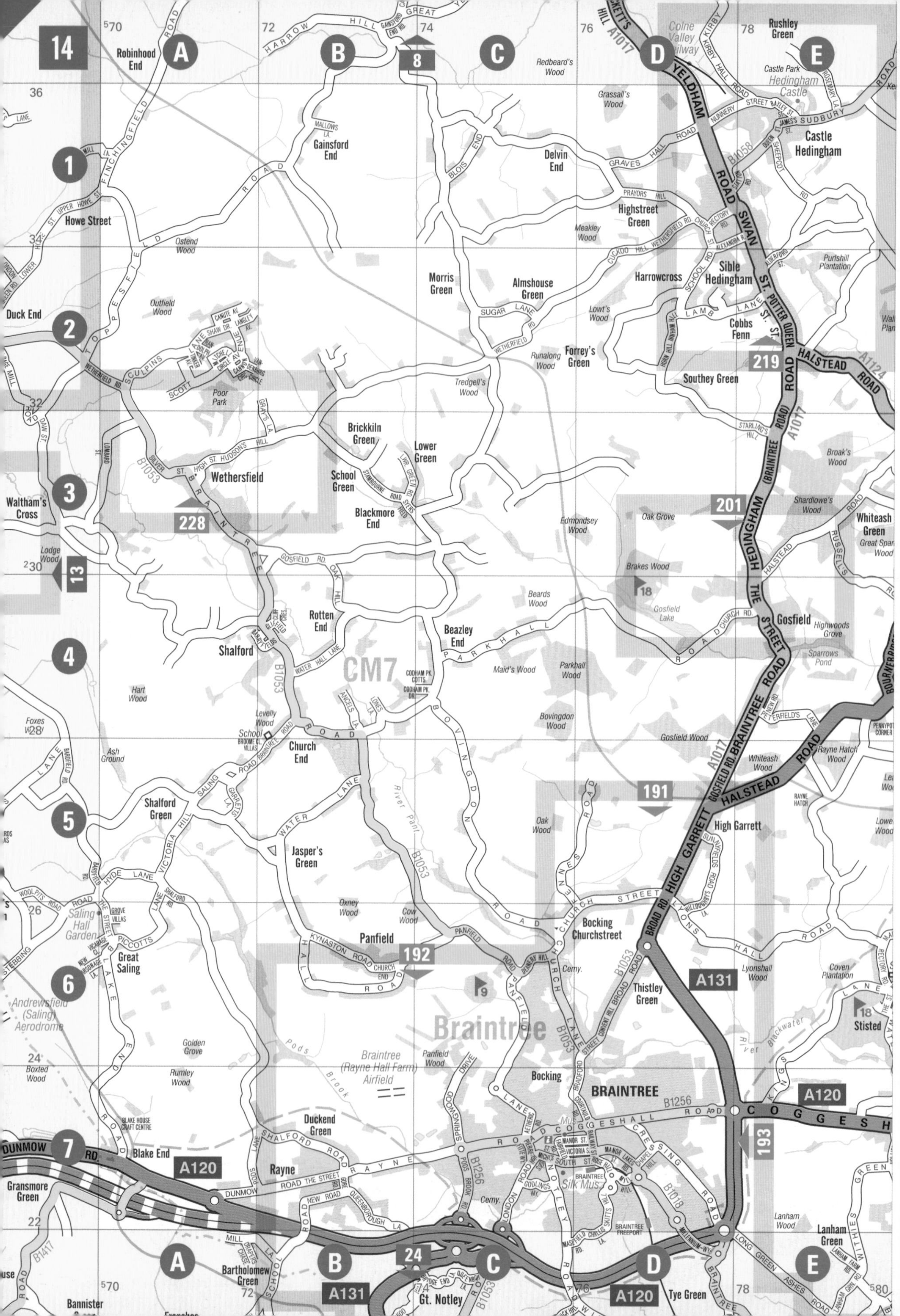

Robinhood End
Gainsford End
Redbeard's Wood
Colne Valley Railway
Rushley Green
Castle Park
Hedingham Castle
Castle Hedingham
Grassall's Wood
Delvin End
Howe Street
Highstreet Green
Meakley Wood
Ostend Wood
Sible Hedingham
Harrowcross
Purlshill Plantation
Morris Green
Almshouse Green
Cobbs Fenn
Lowt's Wood
Duck End
Outfield Wood
Runalong Wood
Forrey's Green
Southey Green
Poor Park
Tredgell's Wood
Brickkiln Green
Lower Green
Broak's Wood
Wethersfield
School Green
Waltham's Cross
Blackmore End
Shardlowe's Wood
Whiteash Green
Oak Grove
Edmondsey Wood
Lodge Wood
Brakes Wood
Gosfield Lake
Beards Wood
Gosfield
Highwoods Grove
Rotten End
Beazley End
Shalford
Sparrows Pond
CM7
Maid's Wood
Parkhall Wood
Hart Wood
Levelly Wood
Bovingdon Wood
Foxes Wood
School
Church End
Gosfield Wood
Ash Ground
Rayne Hatch Wood
Whiteash Wood
Oak Wood
Shalford Green
High Garrett
Jasper's Green
River Pant
Saling Hall Garden
Oxney Wood
Cow Wood
Bocking Churchstreet
Great Saling
Panfield
Thistley Green
Lyonshall Wood
Coven Plantation
Andrewsfield (Saling) Aerodrome
Cemy.
Stisted
Braintree
River Blackwater
Golden Grove
Braintree (Rayne Hall Farm) Airfield
Panfield Wood
Boxted Wood
Rumley Wood
Bocking
BRAINTREE
Duckend Green
Blake House Craft Centre
Mus.
Blake End
Rayne
Silk Mus.
Gransmore Green
Lanham Wood
Lanham Green
Bartholomew Green
Braintree Freeport
Tye Green
Gt. Notley
Bannister
YELDHAM ROAD
SWAN ST.
HALSTEAD ROAD
HEDINGHAM ROAD
THE STREET
BRAINTREE ROAD
HIGH GARRETT
COGGESHALL ROAD
DUNMOW RD.
A1017
A1124
A131
A120
B1053
B1058
B1256
B1018
B1417
8
13
18
9
24
191
192
193
201
219
228

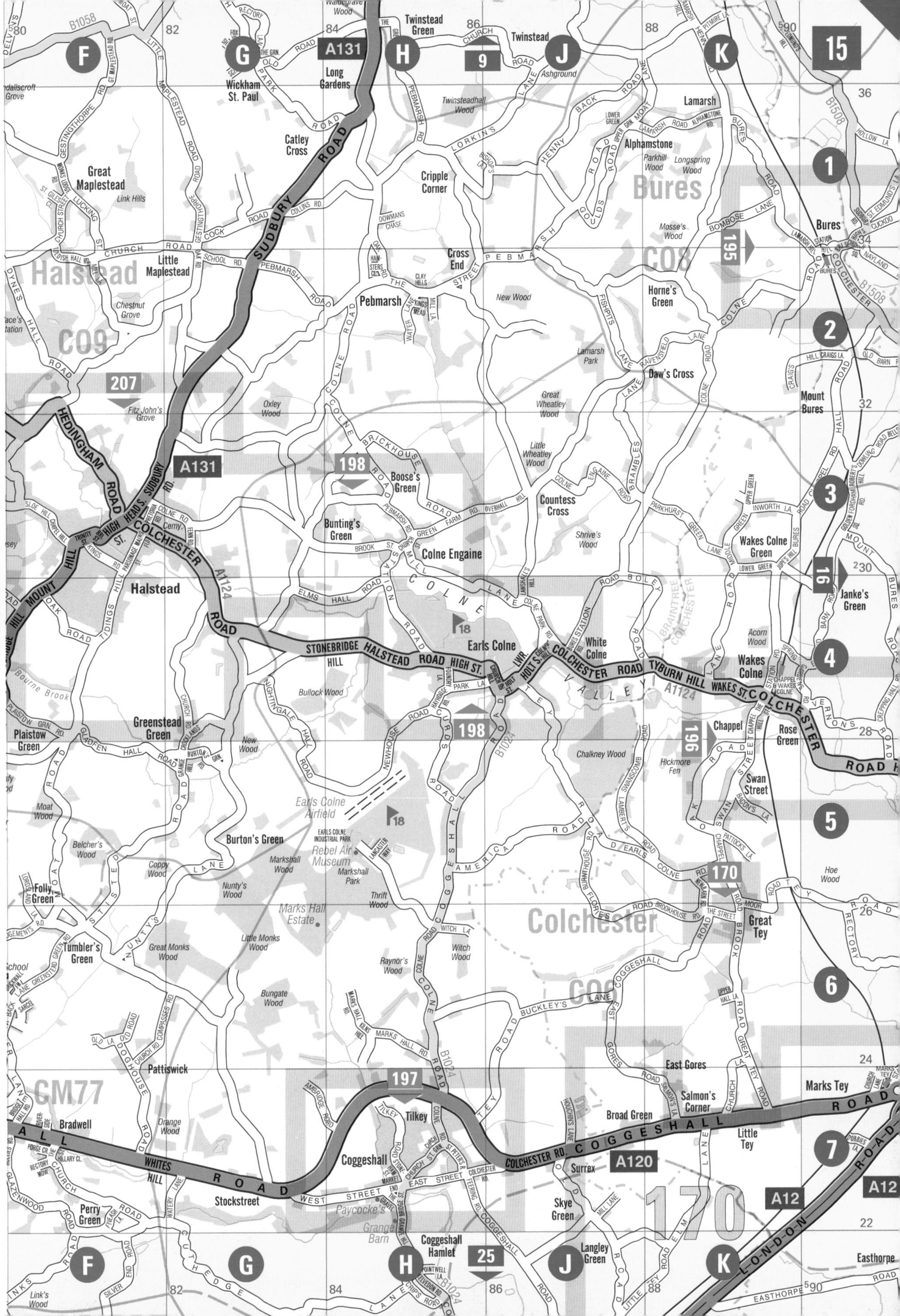
15
F
G
H
J
K
1
2
3
4
5
6
7
Twinstead Green
Twinstead
Ashground
Wickham St. Paul
Long Gardens
Catley Cross
Great Maplestead
Link Hills
Little Maplestead
Halstead
Chestnut Grove
CO9
207
Fitz John's Grove
A131
Lamarsh
Alphamstone
Parkhill Wood
Longspring Wood
Bures
Mosse's Wood
CO8
195
Horne's Green
Lamarsh Park
Daw's Cross
Mount Bures
Cripple Corner
Cross End
Pebmarsh
New Wood
Oxley Wood
Great Wheatley Wood
Little Wheatley Wood
198
Boose's Green
Bunting's Green
Colne Engaine
Countess Cross
Shrive's Wood
Wakes Colne Green
16
Janke's Green
Earls Colne
White Colne
Acorn Wood
Wakes Colne
Chappel
Rose Green
196
Hickmore Fen
Swan Street
Chalkney Wood
Bullock Wood
Greenstead Green
Plaistow Green
New Wood
Moat Wood
Belcher's Wood
Earls Colne Airfield
Rebel Air Museum
Markshall Park
Burton's Green
Coppy Wood
Nunty's Wood
Folly Green
Marks Hall Estate
Thrift Wood
Colchester
170
Great Tey
Hoe Wood
Tumbler's Green
Great Monks Wood
Little Monks Wood
Witch Wood
Raynor's Wood
Bungate Wood
CO6
Pattiswick
CM77
Bradwell
Orange Wood
197
Tilkey
Coggeshall
East Gores
Salmon's Corner
Broad Green
Marks Tey
Little Tey
A120
Surrex
Skye Green
Stockstreet
Perry Green
Paycocke's
Grange Barn
Coggeshall Hamlet
25
Langley Green
A12
Easthorpe
Link's Wood
82
84
86
88
590
36
34
32
230
28
26
24
22

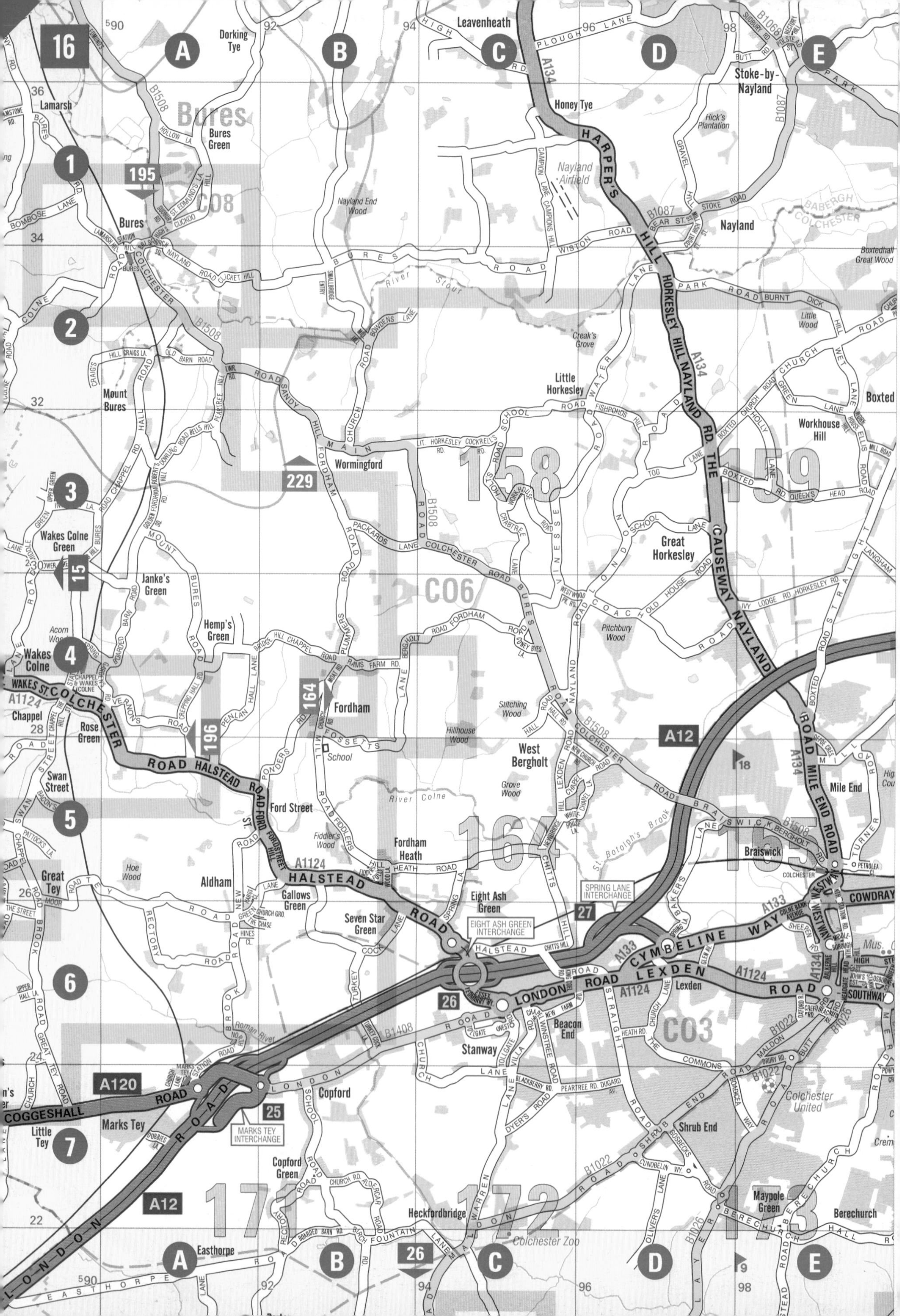

16
Leavenheath
Dorking Tye
Bures
Lamarsh
Bures Green
Stoke-by-Nayland
Honey Tye
Hick's Plantation
Nayland Airfield
Nayland
Nayland End Wood
Boxtedhall Great Wood
Little Wood
Creak's Grove
Little Horkesley
Mount Bures
Wormingford
Boxted
Workhouse Hill
Great Horkesley
Wakes Colne Green
Janke's Green
Hemp's Green
Pitchbury Wood
Acorn Wood
Wakes Colne
Fordham
Stitching Wood
Hillhouse Wood
West Bergholt
Chappel
Rose Green
Swan Street
Ford Street
Grove Wood
Mile End
Braiswick
Great Tey
Hoe Wood
Aldham
Fiddler's Wood
Fordham Heath
Gallows Green
Seven Star Green
Eight Ash Green
SPRING LANE INTERCHANGE
EIGHT ASH GREEN INTERCHANGE
Lexden
Stanway
Beacon End
CO3
Copford
Marks Tey
MARKS TEY INTERCHANGE
Little Tey
Shrub End
Colchester United
Copford Green
Maypole Green
Berechurch
Heckfordbridge
Easthorpe
Colchester Zoo
CO6
CO8
158
159
164
165
171
172
173
195
196
229
A12
A120
A134
A1124
A133

17
18
Withermarsh Green
Holton St. Mary
Lattinford Hill
Bentley
Thorington Street
Higham
FOUR SISTERS INTERCHANGE
Four Sisters
East End
Lodge Gardens
East Bergholt
STRATFORD ST. MARY INTERCHANGE
Stratford St. Mary
The Haugh
Brantham
Cophedge Wood
Ash Wood
Dedham Vale Family Farm
Flatford Mill
Cattawade
Dedham
Toy Mus.
Boxted Cross
The Grove
Hornestreet
Langham
Langham Moor
Langham Wick
Parney Heath
Lamb Corner
Dedham Heath
Munnings Art Mus.
Manningtree
Mistley
Lawford
Colchester
Ardleigh Heath
Foxash Estate
CROWN INTERCHANGE
Ardleigh
Manningtree
CO11
CO4
Ardleigh Reservoir
Little Bromley
Highwoods
Fox Street
CO7
Burnt Heath
Parson's Heath
Bromley Cross
COLCHESTER
Crockleford Heath
Great Bromley
Elmstead
Churn Wood
Cowey Green
Greenstead
Elmstead Market
Raven's Green
The Hythe
Hare Green
University of Essex
Beth Chatto Gardens
Balls Green
Bourne Mill
Old Heath
Frating Green
CO2
Wivenhoe
Elmstead Heath
DANGER AREA
Frating
Great Bentley
Blackheath
Rowhedge
Alresford
160
161
162
166
167
168
174
175
176
A12
A120
A137
A133
A1232
A134
B1029
B1070
B1068
B1027
B1028
B1025
B1035
B1352
29
30
31
27

18
Bentley
The Heath
Holbrook
East End
Stutton
Lower Holbrook
Harkstead
Upper Street
Brantham
Cattawade
Alton Water (Reservoir)
Holbrook Bay
Seafield Bay
Stutton Ness Dovehouse Point
RIVER
BABERGH
TENDRING
Mistley Towers
Copperas Bay
Jacques Bay
Manningtree
Mistley
New Mistley
Wrabness
Stour Wood
Lawford
163
Mistley Heath
Bradfield
Bradfield Heath
Manningtree
17
Little Bromley
Horsleycross Street
CO11
Wix
204
Great Oakley
A120
Goose Green
Horsley Cross
Stones Green
169
Tendring Green
Little Bentley
Goose Green
Colchester
Hare Green
Raven's Green
Beaumont
Balls Green
A133
CO7
Tendring
Clacton-on-Sea
Thorpe Green
CO16
Crematorium
177
Great Bentley
178
Weeley
179
Thorpe-le-Soken
28
A133
Weeleyhall Wood

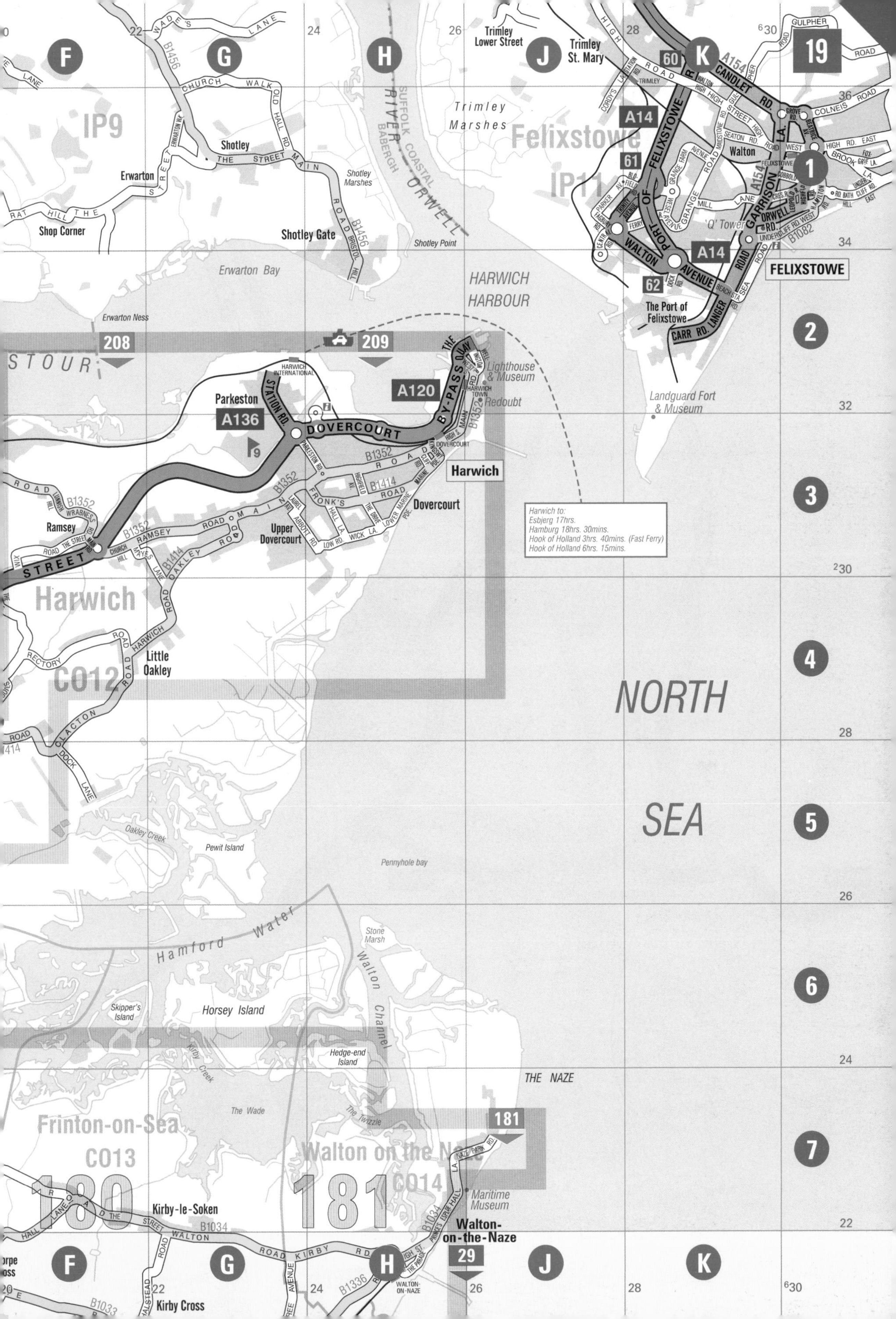
19
Trimley Lower Street
Trimley St. Mary
Trimley Marshes
Felixstowe
IP11
Walton
'Q' Tower
FELIXSTOWE
The Port of Felixstowe
Landguard Fort & Museum
IP9
Shotley
Erwarton
Shop Corner
Shotley Gate
Shotley Marshes
Shotley Point
Erwarton Bay
Erwarton Ness
HARWICH HARBOUR
RIVER ORWELL
STOUR
208
209
Parkeston
A136
A120
DOVERCOURT
Lighthouse & Museum
Redoubt
Harwich
Dovercourt
Upper Dovercourt
Ramsey
Harwich
Little Oakley
CO12
Harwich to:
Esbjerg 17hrs.
Hamburg 18hrs. 30mins.
Hook of Holland 3hrs. 40mins. (Fast Ferry)
Hook of Holland 6hrs. 15mins.
NORTH
SEA
Oakley Creek
Pewit Island
Pennyhole bay
Hamford Water
Stone Marsh
Walton Channel
Skipper's Island
Horsey Island
Hedge-end Island
Kirby Creek
THE NAZE
The Wade
The Twizzle
Frinton-on-Sea
CO13
Walton on the Naze
CO14
181
180
Maritime Museum
Kirby-le-Soken
Walton-on-the-Naze
29
Kirby Cross
F
G
H
J
K
1
2
3
4
5
6
7

Burn's Green
Hebing End
Great Dennis's Wood
Green End
Levens Green
Old Hall Green
Standon
Banfield Wood
Dane End
Comb's Wood
Echo Wood
Loefield Grove
Roughground Wood
Whempstead
Arbury Wood
Cock's Wood
Colliers End
Potter's Green
Plashes Wood
Latchford
Longcroft Wood
Bromley Common
The Rookery
Nearer Wood
Standon Green End
ESTIMATED COMPLETION EARLY 2004
Blackey Mead Wood
Bardolphspark Wood
Sacombe
Sacombe Green
Church Wood
Salmonsley Wood
Barwick
Round Wood
Biggin's Wood
Low Wood
Home Wood
Sutes Woods
WATTON-AT-STONE
High Cross
Tyler's Hill
Woodhall Park
Sidehill Wood
Great Southey Wood
Round Wood
Sawtrees Wood
Watton at Stone
Furzeground Wood
Riding Wood
Youngsbury
Steere Wood
King Edward's Gorse
Lord's Wood
Widow Bushes
Wadesmill
Ware
Wade's Wood
Tonwell
Stapleford
Thundridge
Buckney Wood
Baker's End
Cold Christmas
Chapmore End
Row Wood
Babbs Green
Hanbury Manor
Flowersash Wood
Jubilee Plantation
Bramfield
Priest Wood
Wareside
SG14
St. John's Wood
Oak Wood
Waterford
Ware
SG12
Cowshed Corner
Priory & Gdns.
Mus.
Young Wood
Selebroom Wood
Scott's Grotto
Widbury Wood
Easneye Wood
Long Wood
HERTFORD EAST
Mus.
Chisel Shelf
HERTFORD
Great Amwell
Stanstead Abbots
Hertingfordbury
Birch Green
Staines Green
Hertford
Golding's Wood
St. Margarets
Hertford Heath
Hailey
Letty Green
Balls Wood
Dells Wood
Rye House Gatehouse
Broadgreen Wood
Woollensbrook
Rye Park
SG13
Weepings Wood
Box Wood
Hoddesdon
Goose Green
The Lynch
Little Berkhamsted
Hoddesdonpark Wood
Bayford
Highfield Wood
Hoddesdon
Museum
Spitalbrook
Dobb's Weir
Bayford Wood
Brickendon
Cowheath Wood
Broxbourne
Broxbourne Wood
Epping Green
A602
A10
A119
A1170
A414
B158
B1004
B1000
B1502
B1197
B181
B194
SG11
EN11
52
30
10
18

Bishop's Stortford
Much Hadham
Sawbridgeworth
Harlow
Little Hadham
Hadham Ford
Church End
Green Street
Bury Green
Wellpond Green
Westland Green
Broken Green
Bromley
Cradle End
Much Hadham
Hadham Cross
Kettle Green
Nobland Green
Perry Green
Green Tye
South-end
Allen's Green
Trims Green
Spellbrook
Thorley
Thorley Street
Latchmore Bank
Latchmore Common
Little Hallingbury
Wright's Green
Gaston Green
Mott's Green
Hockerill
Duck End
Widford
Helham Green
Hunsdon
Hunsdonbury
High Wych
Gilston
Pye Corner
Temple Fields
Eastwick
Old Harlow
Lower Sheering
Sheering
Churchgate Street
Mark Hall North
Mark Hall South
Little Parndon
Netteswell
Roydon
Eastend
Pinnacles
Hare Street
The High
Harlow Tye
Housham Tye
Hobb's Cross
Church Langley
New Way
Threshers Bush
Tilegate Green
Potter Street
Foster Street
Brays Grove
Tye Green
Great Parndon
Katherines
Halls Green
Passmores
Kingsmoor
Latton Bush
Roydon Hamlet
Broadley Common
Sumners
Stewards
Hastingwood
M11
A120
A414
A1184
A1169
A1025
A1250
A1060
B1004
B180
B181
B183
B1383
B1133
CM17
CM18
CM19
CM20
CM21
CM23
SG10

22
A120
M11
Birchanger
Duck End
Start Hill
LONDON-STANSTED AIRPORT
12
THREMHALL AV.
220
221
Takeley Street
Brewer's End
Takeley
Smith's Green
ESTIMATED COMPLETION EARLY 2004
A120
DUNMOW ROAD STORTFORD
Little Canfield
BIRCHANGER GREEN
BISHOP'S STORTFORD
Hockerill
Tilekiln Green
224
Hope End Green
Hatfield Forest (Country Park)
Bedlar's Green
Great Hallingbury
Hallingbury Street
Bush End
Puttock's End
Bishop's Stortford
Hellman's Cross
Latchmore Bank
Howe Green
Latchmore Common
Little Hallingbury
Wright's Green
Woodside Green
Taverners Green
Great Canfield
Church End
CM22
206
213
Gaston Green
Mott's Green
21
Hatfield Broad Oak
Needham Green
Hatfield Heath
The Heath
Ardley End
CHELMSFORD ROAD STORTFORD
A1060
Aythorpe Roding
Roundbush Green
212
Lower Sheering
Sheering
210
Keeres Green
White Roding
Leaden Roding
Parvilles
Newman's End
Manwood Green
Nether Street
M11
The Mores
Churchgate Street
Matching
Harlow
Matching Tye
Abbess Roding
Abbess End
Matching Green
Harlow Tye
Housham Tye
Carter's Green
CM17
Hobb's Cross
Woodend
Beauchamp Roding
New Way
Loyter's Green
Ongar
Threshers Bush
Blackcat
Little Laver
CM5
Foster Street
Tilegate Green
Magdalen Laver
High Laver
Birds Green
Norwood End
200
Moreton Mill
Newhouse
Miller's Green
32
Moreton
Fyfield
Willingale

Great Dunmow
Church End
Brookend
Blake End
Hoglands Wood
High Wood
A120
BRAINTREE ROAD
DUNMOW ROAD
ESTIMATED COMPLETION EARLY 2004
23
Gransmore Green
Watch House Green
199
203
212
Little Dunmow
Bannister Green
Frenches Green
Pharisee Green
Felsted
Cock Green
Dunmow
Baconend Green
CM6
Bacon End
Barnston
Causeway End
Cobler's Green
Thistley Green
191
Wellstye Green
A130
Philpot End
North End
Hounslow Green
Garnetts Wood
Bishop's Green
Hartford End
High Roding
Ford End
Littley Green
Ringtail Green
24
Rolphy Green
CM3
High Easter
Stagden Cross
Pleshey
Pleshey Castle
Howe Street
56
57
Great Waltham
Breeds
Minnow End
Clatterford End
Broad's Green
Little Waltham
Tye Green
Chelmsford
Blatche's Wood
Margaret Roding
Good Easter
Chignall Smealy
Fanner's Green
Sparrowhawk Wood
Blasford Hill
Four Wantz
Farmbridge End
Mashbury
Partridge Green
Broomfield
A1060
Beech Wood
Chalk End
Nightingale Wood
Bushy Wood
Berners Wood
Pepper's Green
CM1
Parsonage Green
Berners Roding
Chignall St. James
217
Boyton Cross
CHELMSFORD
58
59
Roxwell
Shellow Bowells
Skreens Park
33
ROXWELL ROAD
West Park
Admiral's Park
VICTORIA
River Chelmer
River Can
River Ter

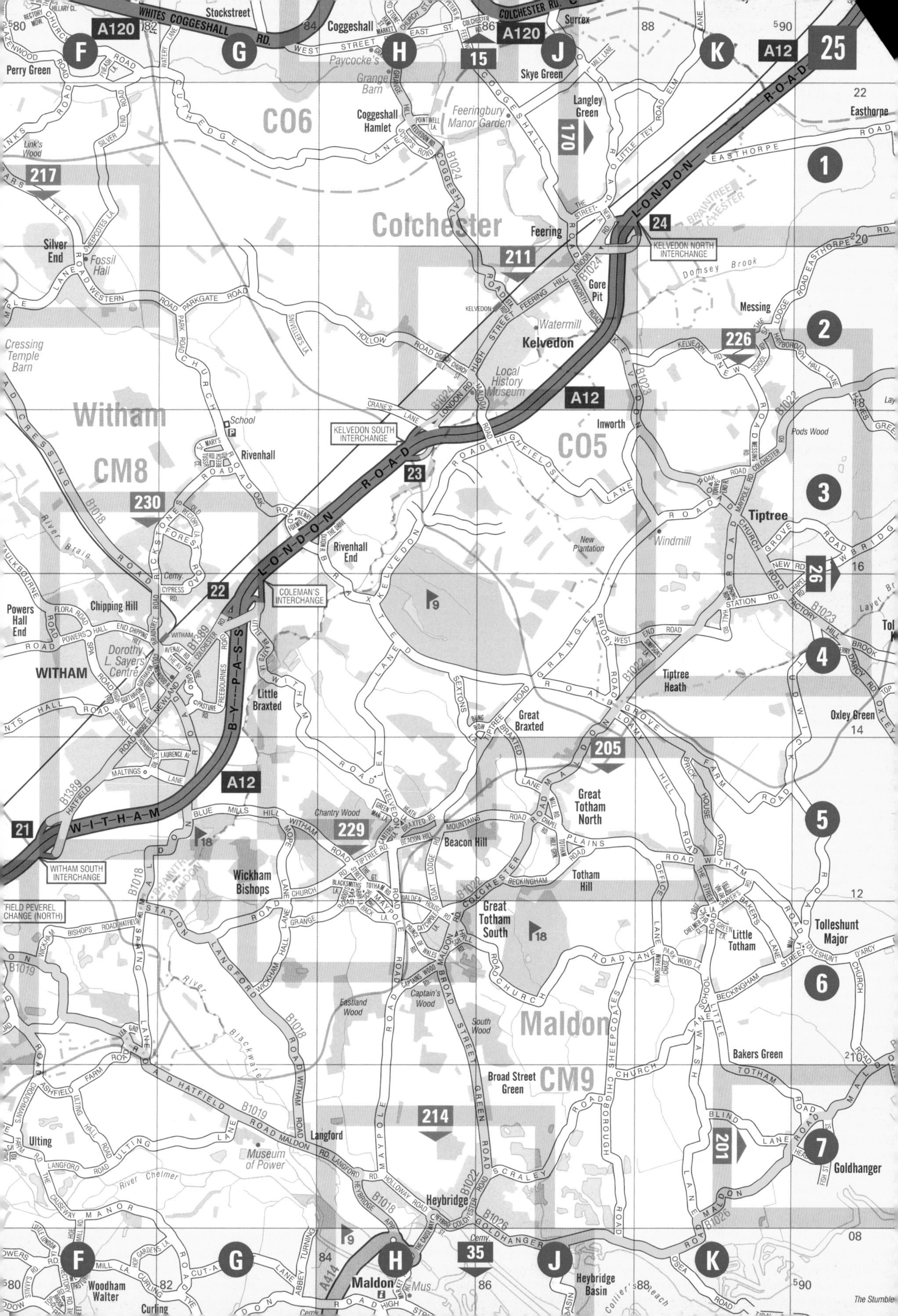

25
Coggeshall
Coggeshall Hamlet
Stockstreet
Surrex
Skye Green
Perry Green
Paycocke's
Grange Barn
Feeringbury Manor Garden
CO6
Langley Green
Easthorpe
Link's Wood
Silver End
Fossil Hall
Colchester
Feering
Kelvedon North Interchange
Gore Pit
Messing
Watermill
Kelvedon
Local History Museum
Cressing Temple Barn
Witham
Inworth
Pods Wood
Kelvedon South Interchange
CO5
CM8
Rivenhall
Tiptree
Windmill
New Plantation
Rivenhall End
Coleman's Interchange
Chipping Hill
Powers Hall End
WITHAM
Dorothy L. Sayers Centre
Little Braxted
Tiptree Heath
Great Braxted
Oxley Green
Great Totham North
Chantry Wood
Beacon Hill
Witham South Interchange
Wickham Bishops
Totham Hill
Great Totham South
Little Totham
Tolleshunt Major
Eastland Wood
Captain's Wood
South Wood
Maldon
Bakers Green
Broad Street Green
CM9
Ulting
Langford
Museum of Power
Goldhanger
River Chelmer
River Blackwater
Heybridge
Woodham Walter
Curling
Maldon
Heybridge Basin
The Stumble

26
16
36
25
201
225
226
227
172
A
B
C
D
E
1
2
3
4
5
6
7
171
172
173
A12
London Road
Easthorpe
Copford Green
Heckfordbridge
Colchester Zoo
Maypole Green
Berechurch
Porters Green
Hardy's Green
Sanfordhall Green
Birch
Chest Wood
CO2
Layer-de-la-Haye
Abberton
Abberton Reservoir
Messing
Birch Green
Smythe's Green
Layer Breton
Layer Wood
Pods Wood
Layer Marney
Layer Marney Tower
Tiptree
Peldon
Stafford's Corner
Long Wood
Layer Brook
CO5
Little Wigborough
Tolleshunt Knights
Great Wigborough
Oxley Green
Salcott Creek
Abbot's Hall Saltings
Copthall Saltings
Salcott-cum-Virley
Feldy Marshes
Quince's Corner
Old Hall Marshes
Salcott Channel
Little Ditch
Pennyhole Fleet
Joyce's Head
Tolleshunt D'Arcy
Old Hall Creek
Tolleshunt Major
Little Totham
Tollesbury Fleet
North Channel
South Channel
Great Cob Island
Tollesbury
Woodrolfe Creek
Shinglehead Point
Maldon
CM9
Tollesbury Wick Marshes
Bakers Green
Goldhanger
Mill Creek
Mill Point
River Blackwater
Pewet Island
Gore Saltings
Goldhanger Creek
The Stumble

Wivenhoe
Elmstead Heath
Alresford
Frating
Blackheath
Rowhedge
High Park Corner
Fingringhoe
Roman River
South Green
Langenhoe
Thorrington
Tide Mill
Alresford Creek
CO7
Colchester
DANGER AREA
Fingringhoe Marsh
Fingringhoe Ranges
Geedon Saltings
Geedon Creek
Langenhoe Marsh
Rat Island
Wick Marsh
RIVER COLNE
COLCHESTER TENDRING
Brightlingsea
Hurst Green
Pyefleet Channel
Pewit Island
Reeveshall Marsh
Maydays Marsh
Broad Fleet
Brightlingsea
Cindery Island
Martello Tower & Museum
Point Clear
MERSEA ISLAND
East Mersea
Cudmore Grove Country Park
Ray Island
Blue Row
Strood Channel
Brightlingsea Reach
Mersea Flats
Ray Creek
Lee-over Sands
Colne Point
West Mersea
Cobmarsh Island
Besom Fleet
Virley Channel
NORTH SEA
Bradwell Power Station
Visitor Centre
Sales Point
Tip Head
St. Peter's Flat
Gunners Creek
Downhall
East End
F G H J K
1 2 3 4 5 6 7
02 04 06 08 610
220 18 16 14 12 210 08
174 175 176 182
17 28 37 174 228

28
A
B
C
D
E
1
2
3
4
5
6
7
610
12
14
16
18
220
18
16
14
12
210
08
Great Bentley
Weeley
Thorpe-le-Soken
Crematorium
Colchester
CO7
CO16
CO15
Thorrington
Aingers Green
South Heath
Weeley Heath
Weeleyhall Wood
Row Heath
Maldon Wood
Little Clacton
Cook's Green
Riddles Wood
St. Osyth Heath
Hartley Wood
Burrsville Park
Brightlingsea
Hurst Green
Point Clear
St. Osyth
St. Osyth Priory
St. Osyth Park
St. Osyth Marsh
Flag Creek
Ray Creek
Holland Brook
Picker's
Cindery Island
Colne Point
Lee-over-Sands
Seawick
Jaywick
Rush Green
Clacton Airfield
Great Clacton
Clacton-on-Sea
CLACTON-ON-SEA
A133
B1027
B1029
B1033
B1414
B1441
B1442
B1369
B1032
LITTLE CLACTON BY-PASS
ROAD
HOLLAND ROAD
CENTENARY WAY
LONDON RD.
ST. JOHN'S ROAD
CLACTON RD.
PUMP HILL
BYPASS ROAD
COLCHESTER ROAD
HOLLYBUSH HILL
POINT CLEAR
MARINE PARADE W.
MARINE PARADE EAST
KINGS PARADE
WEST ROAD
JAYWICK LANE
BROOKLANDS
BROADWAY
177
178
179
183
184
185
188
189
27
SUNDAY BOOT SALE

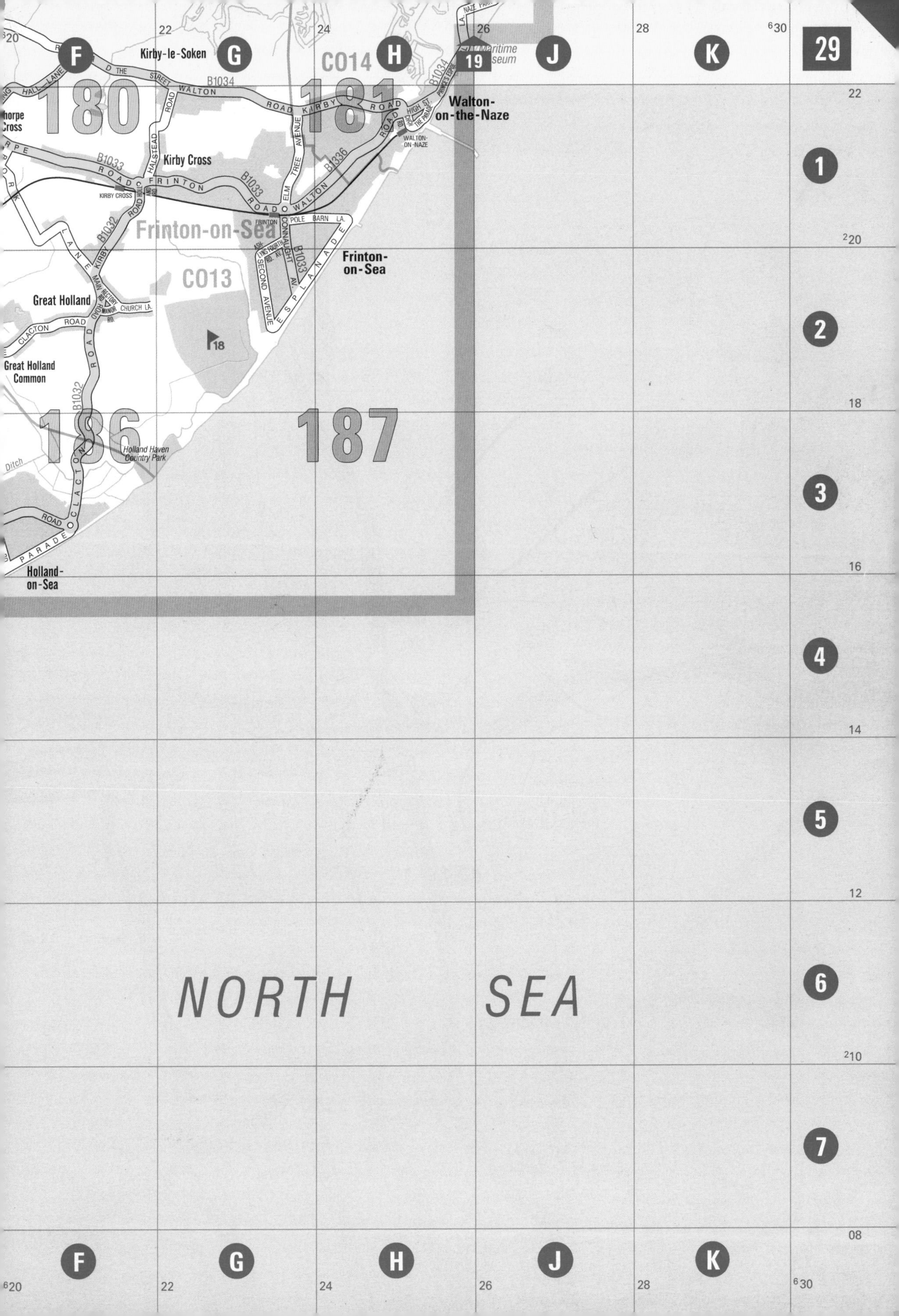
Kirby-le-Soken
CO14
Maritime Museum
19
Walton-on-the-Naze
Walton-on-Naze
180
181
Thorpe Cross
Kirby Cross
Kirby Cross
B1034
B1033
B1336
B1032
Walton Road
Kirby Road
Frinton Road
Holland Road
Halstead Road
Elm Tree Avenue
Pole Barn La.
Connaught Av.
Second Avenue
Esplanade
Frinton
Frinton-on-Sea
Frinton-on-Sea
CO13
18
Great Holland
Church La.
Clacton Road
Kirby Lane
Great Holland Common
186
187
Holland Haven Country Park
Ditch
Clacton Road
Parade
Holland-on-Sea
NORTH SEA
F
G
H
J
K
1
2
3
4
5
6
7
620
22
24
26
28
630
22
220
18
16
14
12
210
08

30
A
B
C
D
E
1
2
3
4
5
6
7
20
52
62
76
90
38
Bayford
Bayford Wood
Hertford
SG13
Blackfan Wood
Brickendon
Cowheath Wood
Broxbourne Wood
Hoddesdonpark Wood
Highfield Wood
Hoddesdon
Museum
Spitalbrook
The Lynch
Dobb's Weir
Little Berkhamsted
Epping Green
Tylers Causeway
Ashen Grove
Calves Grove
The Warren
Paradise Wildlife Park
Broxbourne
Carneles Green
Baas Hill
Nazeing Glass Works
Keysers Estate
Lower Nazeing
Wormley West End
Wormley Wood
Derry's Wood
EAST HERTFORDSHIRE
BROXBOURNE
EN10
Wormley
Thunderfield Grove
Hell Wood
Turnford
Newgate Street
Northaw Great Wood
Grimes Bottom
Home Wood
Hammond Street
Cheshunt Park
Flamstead End
Holyfield Hall Farm
Hayes Hill Farm
Holyfield
Galleyhill Wood
Lucas End
Rosedale
Waltham Cross
Cheshunt
Goff's Oak
EN7
Churchgate
Cuffley
Potters Bar
Bury Green
Fishers Green
Aimes Green
Waltham
EN8
EN6
Bowyer's Water
Royal Gunpowder Mills
Barvin Park
Cattlegate
Cattlins
Home Wood
M25
A10
ENFIELD
Waltham Cross
Holdbrook
Waltham Abbey
Crews Hill
Whitewebbs Museum
Whitewebbs Wood
Whitewebbs Park
Bulls Cross
Bullsmoor
Freezy Water
Botany Bay
Clay Hill
Enfield
EN2
Forty Hall
Forty Hill
Hilly Fields Park
ENFIELD CHASE
Enfield Wash
Albany Park
Enfield Lock
Ride Wood
TRENT PARK
(Country Park)
EN3
Chase Side
Brimsdown
Sewardstone
Enfield Town
EN1
Enfield Highway
Durants Park
King George's Reservoir
World's End
Town Park
Bush Hill Park
Grange Park
Bush Hill Park
Sewardstonebury
Oakwood Park
Oakwood
Ponders End
Jubilee Park
The Hawk Wood
Chingford Plain
Grovelands Park
Winchmore Hill
Lower Edmonton
William Girling Reservoir
Chingford Green
Osidge
Southgate
Palmers Green
Edmonton
Chingford
Ridgeway Park
Friday Hill
A1170
A121
A1055
A1010
A105
A110
A111
A112
A1005
A1004
A1037
A1009
B156
B157
B176
B198
B194
B137
B154
B169
B160
B146

HARLOW
Harlow
Epping
Loughton
Chigwell
Romford
Abbey
CM18
CM17
CM16
EN9
IG10
IG7
RM4
31
32
26
27
39
21
M11
M25
A414
A113
A121
A104
A1168
A1169
B181
B1393
B172
B170
B175
Halls Green
Katherines
Great Parndon
Potter Street
Foster Street
Tilegate Green
Roydon Hamlet
Broadley Common
Sumners
Kingsmoor
Stewards
Latton Bush
Hastingwood
Ada Cole Memorial Stables
Nazeing
Harknett's Gate
Jack's Hatch
Rye Hill
Crematorium
Parndon Wood
Mark Bushes
Bumble's Green
Nazeing Gate
Nazeing Long Green
Epping Green
Epping Upland
Thornwood Common
North Weald Airfield
North Weald Bassett
Tyler's Green
Museum
The Lower Forest
Roughtalley's Wood
Deerpark Wood
Claverhambury
Stocking Grove
Orange Field Plantation
Cobbin's Brook
Gernon Bushes
Coopersale Common
Birching Coppice
High Wood
Ongar Park Wood
Colliers Hatch
Mount Wood
Hawkshill Wood
Gravelpit Wood
Tawney Common
Woodhatch
Rookery Wood
Bell Common
Coopersale Street
Gaynes Park
Knightslar Wood
Northlands Wood
Upshire
Copped Hall
Ivy Chimneys
Stewards Green
Fiddlers Hamlet
Mount End
Beachet Wood
Copthall Green
Warren Wood
Wood Green
Stable Shaw
Barber's Wood
Long Plantation
Icehouse Plantation
Theydon Bois
Theydon Mount
Stapleford Tawney
Bob's Barn Woo
Theydon Garnon
Hobbs Cross
Shales More
Redoak Wood
Birch Wood
Debden Green
Gaunt's Wood
Great Monk Wood
Little Monk Wood
High Beach
Cemy.
River Roding
Passing Brid
Long Shaw
Stapleford Tawney Airfield
BBC Essex Garden
Broadfield Shaw
Abridge
Debden
Curtismill Green
Deerbarn Wood
Great Wood
Lambourne
Bentleyfield Wood
Stapleford Abbotts
Hill Wood
Warren Hill
Buckhurst Hill
High Wood
Lambourne End
Bournebridge
Nuper's Hatch
Chigwell Row
Hainault Forest (Country Park)
Havering-atte-Bower
Lord's Bushes
Woodford
F
G
H
J
K
1
2
3
4
5
6
7
40
42
44
46
48
550
08
06
04
02
200
98
196
94

32
22
200
31
40
11
A
B
C
D
E
1
2
3
4
5
6
7
A414
A128
A113
M25
A12
B184
B181
B175
A1023
CM16
CM5
CM14
CM15
RM4
66
67
68
80
81
82
94
95
96
Tilegate Green
Magdalen Laver
High Laver
Moreton Mill
Newhouse
Nor Wood
Norwood End
Birds Green
Miller's Green
Willingale
Hastingwood
Moreton
Pedlars End
Fyfield
Witney Green
Clatterford End
Ongar
Cannon's Green
Tyler's Green
Bovinger
Epping
Bobbingworth
Lower Bobbingworth Green
Blake Hall Gdns. & Mus.
Shelley
North Weald Bassett
Norton Mandeville
Norton Heath
High Ongar
Greensted Green
Saxon Wooden Church
Chipping Ongar
Greensted
Ongar Castle
King Street
Toot Hill
Marden Ash
Nine Ashes
Colliers Hatch
Clatterford End
Paslow Wood Common
Tawney Common
Woodhatch
Littlebury
Stanford Rivers
Stondon Massey
Clapgate
Little End
Hare Street
Tip's Cross
Hook End
Theydon Mount
Stapleford Tawney
Beacon Hill
Kelvedon Hatch
Doddinghurst
Fox Hatch
Kelvedon Common
Passingford Bridge
Navestock
Navestock Side
Bentley
Brentwood
Curtismill Green
Crow Green
Sabine's Green
Romford
Horseman Side
Coxtie Green
Stapleford Abbotts
Waterhales
Pilgrims Hatch
Watton's Green
Nuper's Hatch
St. Vincent's Hamlet
Weald Park (Country Park)
Bournebridge
South Weald
Old Macdonalds Farm Park
Havering-atte-Bower
Noak Hill
Dagnam Park
The Round House

F
G
H
J
K
33
23
217
Roxwell
Shellow Bowells
Skreens Park
ROXWELL ROAD
A1060
CHELMSFORD
Admiral's Park
West Park
CM1
Newney Green
Great Oxney Green
Writtle
Chelmsford
Wall's Green
Pigstye Green
Cooksmill Green
Radley Green
Little Oxney Green
Lady Grove
Edney Common
Highwood
Loves Green
ONGAR ROAD
A414
Widford
PRINCES RD.
A1114
Moulsham
Crematorium
Museum
Writtle Wood
Hylands Park Gardens
Hylands Park
South Wood
Moulsham Thrift Wood
CM2
69
70
71
72
Horsfrithpark Wood
Little Edney Wood
Great Edney Wood
Writtle Deer Park
Baker's Wood
King Wood
High Woods
Writtlepark Wood
Bosmore Wood
Chapel Wood
THREE MILE HILL
Galleywood
Galleywood Common
GALLEYWOOD / STOCK INTERCHANGE
34
FURZE HILL INTERCHANGE
WEBBS FARM INTERCHANGE
15
14
16
A12
Parsons Spring
Barrow Wood
Birch Spring
Coppice Wood
Parkponds Wood
Deerslade Wood
Box Wood
Handley Green
Elkins Green
College Wood
Stoneymore Wood
Blackmore
Millgreen Common
Ingatestone
Bell Grove
Beggar Hill
Fryerning Wood
Mill Green
The Grove
Margaretting
Crondon
Margaretting Tye
Temple Wood
CM4
Portsmoorhall Wood
Hay Green
Woodbarns Spring
Green Street
Fryerning
Pound Wood
Rook Wood
Forest Wood
83
84
85
86
Ingatestone
Tye Green
Long Wood
Little Wood
Swan Wood
Swallows Cross
INGATESTONE BY-PASS
TRUELOVES INTERCHANGE
13
Ingatestone Hall
Buttsbury
White's Wood
Stock
Blythhedges Wood
Windmill
Heybridge
Lodge Wood
Long Wood
Mountnessing
Kiln Common
Padham's Green
MARYLANDS INTERCHANGE
Home Wood
Harespring Wood
Queen's Park Country Park
Forty Acre Plantation
Queen's Park
12
Arnold's Wood
Canterbury Tye Spring
Billericay
Lake Meadows
Ramsden Heath
Meepshole Wood
Hutton
Gooseberry Green
Norsey Wood
97
98
99
CM13
CM12
CM11
Devil's Wood
RAYLEIGH ROAD
LONDON ROAD
Shenfield
Hutton Mount
Havering's Grove
Sunnymede
Moses Spring Wood
BRENTWOOD
Tye Common
BILLERICAY
41
Little Bladen's Wood
South
A129
A128
B1002
B1007

34
A
B
C
D
E
24
60
61
Springfield
Chelmer Village
CHELMSFORD
Admiral's
West Park
Moulsham
Crematorium
Museum
Widford
Great Baddow
Sandon
SANDON INTERCHANGE
Lower Green
72
73
74
Moulsham Thrift Wood
Galleyend
Galleywood
Galleywood Common
GALLEYWOOD / STOCK INTERCHANGE
HOWE GREEN INTERCHANGE
Howe Green
Butt's Green
Thorn Wood
Mead's Grove
Bicknacre
Chelmsford
East Hanningfield
CM2
Crondon
Margaretting Tye
Temple Grove
Temple Wood
Forest Wood
West Hanningfield
86
87
88
Woodham Ferrers
RHS Garden Hyde Hall
Swan Wood
Blythhedges Spring Wood
Blythhedges Wood
Windmill
Ingatestone
Stock
CM4
Hanningfield Reservoir
Hounden Wood
Coalhill
Rettendon
Kiln Common
Visitor Centre
South Hanningfield
Billericay
Foxearth Wood
Gorse Wood
Forty Acre Plantation
Thrift Wood
Brock Hill
Rettendon Shaw
CM11
Downham
Morrgarden Wood
Ramsden Heath
Meepshole Wood
Rectory Wood
100
101
Wickford
Devil's Wood
CHELMSFORD BASILDON
Moses Spring Wood
Runwell
SS11
Memorial Park
Ramsden Bellhouse
Battlesbridge
Wickford
Rawreth
Holybreds Wood
Little Baddow
Scrub Wood
Bassett's Wood
Long Spring Wood
Blake's Wood
Woodham Walter Common
Hall Wood
Lingwood Common
Bellhill Wood
Danbury
Runsell Green
Danbury Country Park
Woodhill
Horne Row
Danbury Common
Gay Bowers
A12
A138
A1060
A1114
A414
A130
A132
A1245
A129
B1007
B1009
B1418
MALDON ROAD
MAIN ROAD
PRINCES RD.
PARKWAY
CHELMER RD.
42

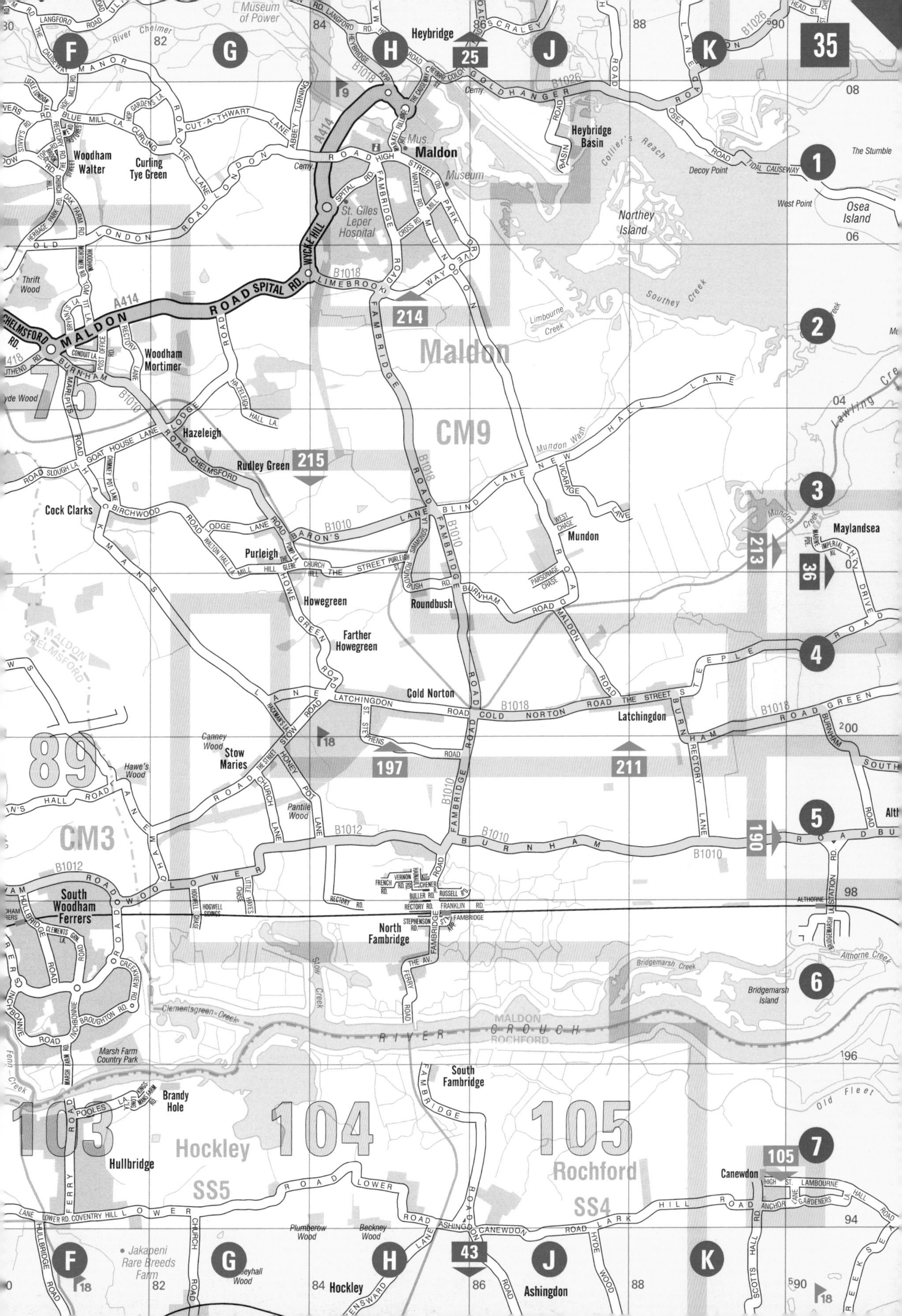
35
Museum of Power
River Chelmer
Heybridge
25
Heybridge Basin
Collier's Reach
Decoy Point
Tidal Causeway
The Stumble
West Point
Osea Island
Northey Island
Southey Creek
Limbourne Creek
Maldon
Mus.
Museum
St. Giles Leper Hospital
Woodham Walter
Curling Tye Green
Cut-A-Thwart Lane
Thrift Wood
Woodham Mortimer
Chelmsford Rd.
Maldon Road
Spital Rd.
Wycke Hill
Limebrook Way
214
Mundon Wash
New Hall Lane
CM9
Hazeleigh
Rudley Green
215
Cock Clarks
Purleigh
Blind Lane
Baron's Lane
Mundon
Maylandsea
213
36
Mundon Creek
Lawling Creek
Howegreen
Roundbush
Farther Howegreen
Cold Norton
Latchingdon
Maldon Chelmsford
89
Canney Wood
Stow Maries
Hawe's Wood
197
211
Pantile Wood
CM3
B1012
B1010
B1018
Burnham Road
190
Althorne
South Woodham Ferrers
North Fambridge
Bridgemarsh Creek
Bridgemarsh Island
Althorne Creek
Stow Creek
Clementsgreen Creek
River Crouch
Maldon
Rochford
Marsh Farm Country Park
Fenn Creek
South Fambridge
Old Fleet
Brandy Hole
103
104
105
Hullbridge
Hockley
SS5
Rochford
SS4
Canewdon
105
Plumberow Wood
Beckney Wood
Ashingdon
43
Jakapeni Rare Breeds Farm
Hockley
F
G
H
J
K
1
2
3
4
5
6
7

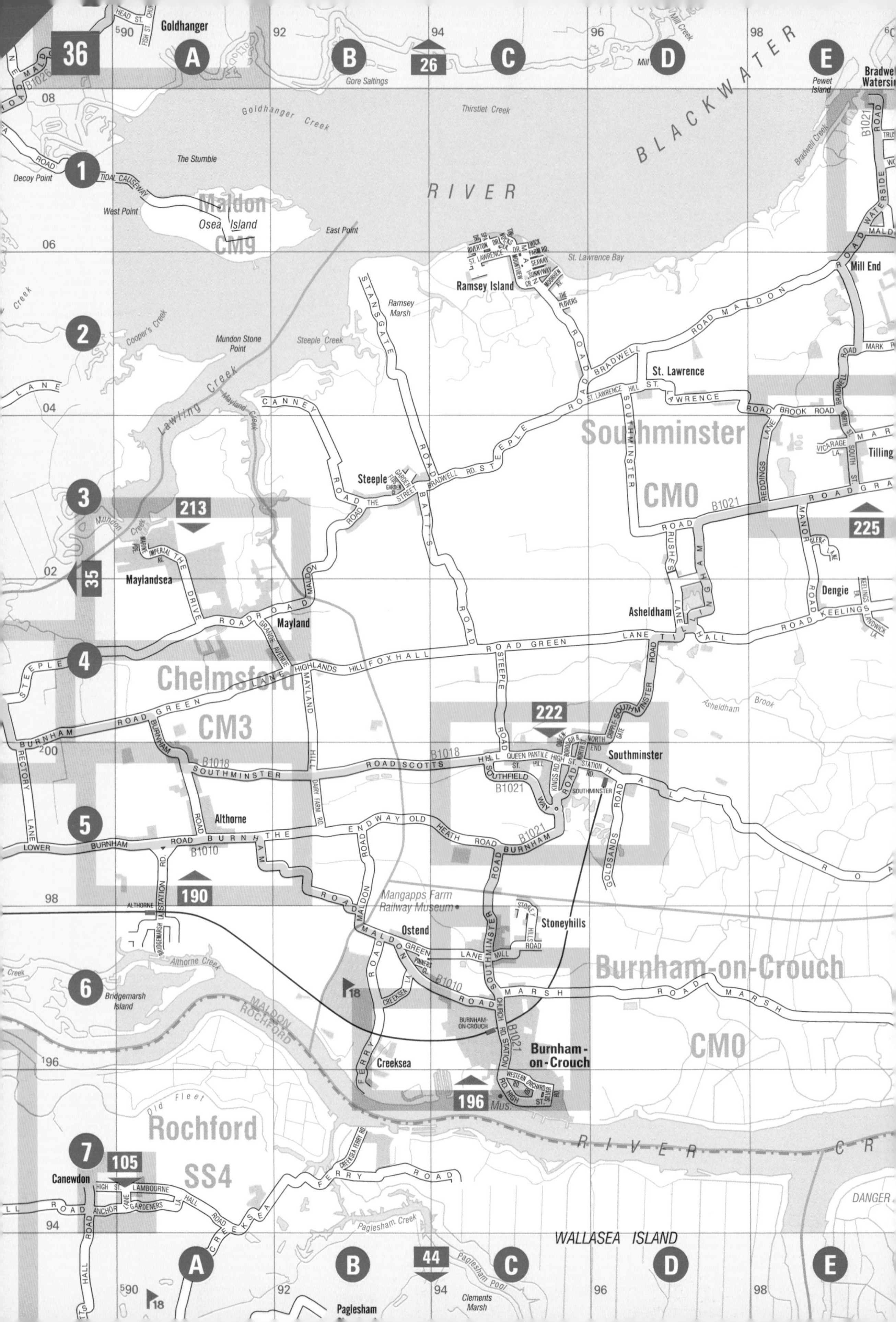
36
26
Goldhanger
Gore Saltings
Mill Creek
Pewet Island
Bradwell Waterside
BLACKWATER
RIVER
Goldhanger Creek
Thirstlet Creek
The Stumble
Decoy Point
West Point
Maldon
Osea Island
CM9
East Point
St. Lawrence Bay
Ramsey Island
Ramsey Marsh
Steeple Creek
Mundon Stone Point
Cooper's Creek
Lawling Creek
Mayland Creek
Bradwell Creek
Mill End
St. Lawrence
Southminster
CM0
Tillingham
Steeple
213
225
Maylandsea
35
Mayland
Dengie
Asheldham
Chelmsford
CM3
222
Asheldham Brook
Southminster
Althorne
190
Mangapps Farm Railway Museum
Ostend
Stoneyhills
Burnham-on-Crouch
18
Bridgemarsh Island
Althorne Creek
CM0
Creeksea
Burnham-on-Crouch
196
Mus.
Rochford
SS4
Old Fleet
RIVER CROUCH
Canewdon
105
DANGER
WALLASEA ISLAND
Paglesham Creek
Paglesham Pool
44
Clements Marsh
Paglesham
B1018
B1021
B1010
B1026

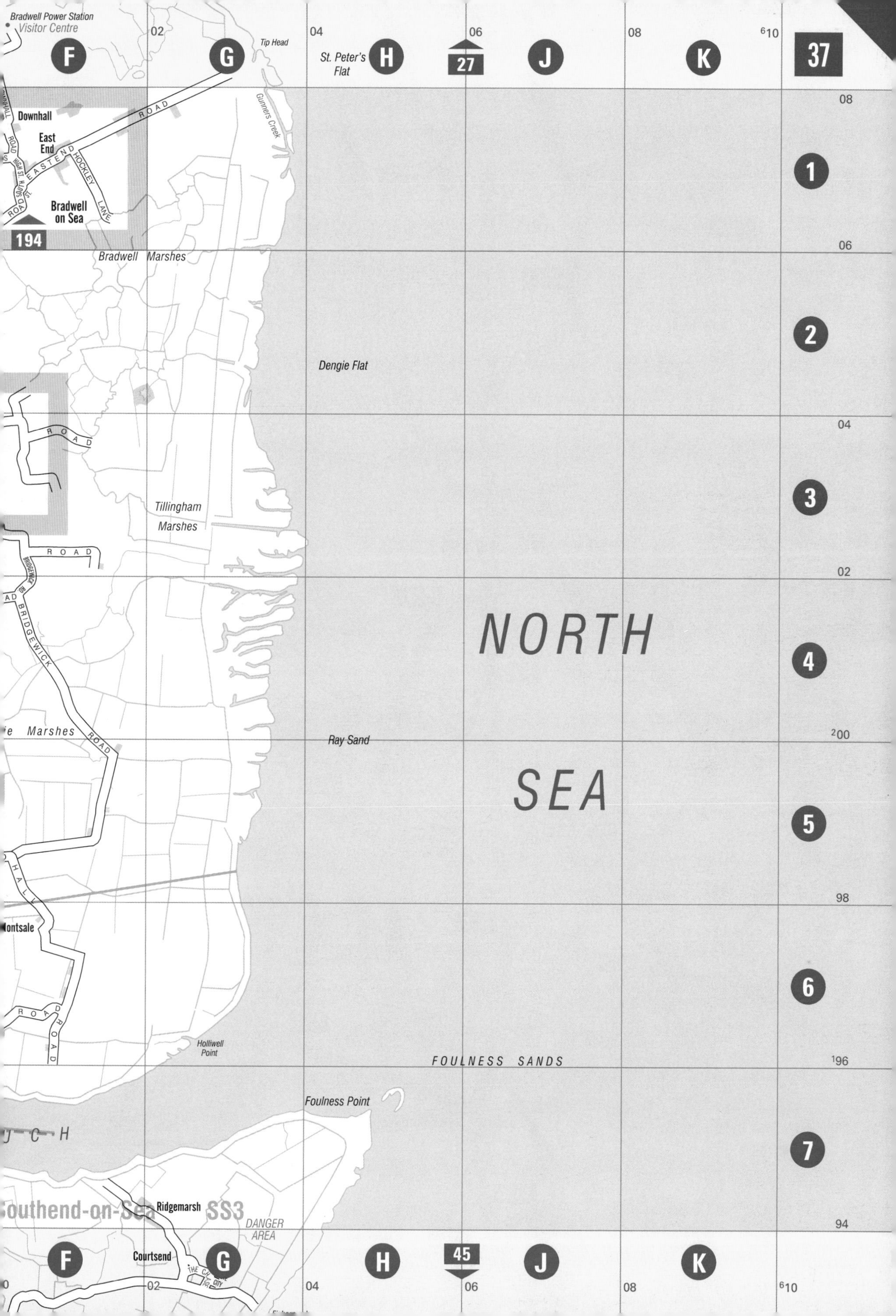
Bradwell Power Station
Visitor Centre
F
G
H
J
K
Tip Head
St. Peter's Flat
27
02
04
06
08
610
08
Gunners Creek
Downhall
East End
EAST END
ROAD
HOCKLEY LANE
HIGH ST.
Bradwell on Sea
194
1
06
Bradwell Marshes
2
Dengie Flat
04
3
Tillingham Marshes
ROAD
BRIDGEWICK RD
BRIDGEWICK ROAD
02
NORTH
SEA
4
Marshes
Ray Sand
200
5
HALL
98
6
ROAD
Holliwell Point
FOULNESS SANDS
196
Foulness Point
7
Southend-on-Sea
Ridgemarsh
SS3
DANGER AREA
94
Courtsend
45
THE CHASE
CITY
10
02
04
06
08
610

A
B
C
D
E
1
2
3
4
5
6
7
Oakwood
Osidge
Southgate
Palmers Green
Arnos Park
Bowes Park
Bounds Green
Muswell Hill
Alexandra Park
Hornsey
Cranley Gardens
Queen's Wood
Crouch End
Upper Holloway
Holloway
Tufnell Park
Lower Holloway
Barnsbury
Highbury
Camden Town
Islington
Finsbury
Clerkenwell
Marylebone
Bloomsbury
Holborn
St. Pancras
West End
St. James's
St. James's Pk.
Buckingham Palace
Southwark
The Borough
Newington
Bermondsey
Rotherhithe
Wapping
Shadwell
Whitechapel
Spitalfields
Stepney
Limehouse
Poplar
Millwall
London Arena
Mile End
Bow Common
Bromley
Bow
Old Ford
South Hackney
Victoria Park
Globe Town
Bethnal Green
Shoreditch
Haggerston
Hoxton
De Beauvoir Town
Dalston
Hackney
Homerton
Hackney Wick
Kingsland
Canonbury
Stoke Newington
Finsbury Park
Harringay
Stroud Green
Hornsey Vale
Stamford Hill
Shacklewell
Lower Clapton
Upper Clapton
Clapton Park
Lea Bridge
Hackney Marsh
Walthamstow Marshes
Springfield Park
Warwick Reservoirs
Reservoirs
Lockwood Reservoir
Banbury Reservoir
Walthamstow
Higham Hill
William Morris Gallery
Upper Walthamstow
Chingford
Chingford Mount
Chingford Hatch
South Chingford
Highams Park
Hale End
Larkswood Park
Ridgeway Park
Friday Hill
William Girling Reservoir
Leyton
Leyton Orient
Leytonstone
Cann Hall
Temple Mills
Stratford
Stratford New Town
Stratford Marsh
Mill Meads
Canning Town
Millennium Dome
Tottenham
Tottenham Hotspur
Tottenham Hale
South Tottenham
West Green
Noel Park
Wood Green
Edmonton
Upper Edmonton
Lower Edmonton
Pymmes Park
Groveland Park
Jubilee Park
City
Arsenal
A10
A406
A10
A1
A503
A107
A503
A1
A102
A12
A12
A11
A13
A100
A200
A101
A202
A501
A10
A406
NORTH CIRCULAR ROAD
GREAT CAMBRIDGE JUNCTION
ANGEL EDMONTON
HALL LANE
KENNINGHALL
CROOKED BILLET
WOOD STREET
THE BELL
BLACKHORSE LANE
TOTTENHAM HALE GYRATORY
SEVEN SISTERS
MANOR HOUSE
NAG'S HEAD
HIGHBURY CORNER
KINGS CROSS
ANGEL
OLD ST
ALDGATE
TOWER HILL
LEA INTERCHANGE
HACKNEY WICK
OLD FORD
BOW INTERCHANGE
CANNING TOWN
GREEN MAN ROUNDABOUT
THE HIGHWAY
COMMERCIAL ROAD
EAST INDIA DOCK RD.
MILE END ROAD
BOW ROAD
SEVEN SISTERS ROAD
HOLLOWAY ROAD
CAMDEN ROAD
EUSTON RD.
PENTONVILLE RD.
CITY RD.
EMBANKMENT
THAMES
ROTHERHITHE TUNNEL
BLACKWALL TUNNEL
LEA VALLEY VIADUCT
FOREST ROAD
FOREST RD.
LEA BRIDGE RD.
CLAPTON COMMON
KINGSLAND RD.
STAMFORD HILL
HIGH ROAD
GREEN LANES
LORDSHIP LANE
THE ROUNDWAY
MERIDIAN WAY
WATERMEAD WAY
HERTFORD RD.
SOUTHEND ROAD
NEW ROAD
CHINGFORD MNT. RD.
OLD CHURCH RD.
STRAND
PICCADILLY
REGENT ST.
VICTORIA ST.
WHITEHALL
WATERLOO RD.
SOUTHWARK ST.
JAMAICA RD.
TOWER BRIDGE RD.
ST. PAUL'S RD.
BALLS POND RD.
GRAHAM RD.
MARE ST.
HACKNEY RD.
BETHNAL GREEN RD.
CAMBRIDGE HEATH RD.
BURDETT RD.
GROVE RD.
BLACKWALL TUNNEL NORTHERN APP.
MANCHESTER RD.
WESTFERRY RD.
MANOR RD.
WEST HAM LANE
LEYTON RD.
LEYTONSTONE RD.
HIGH ST.
WOODFORD RD.
WHIPPS CROSS RD.
HOE ST.
LEA BRIDGE RD.
RUCKHOLT RD.
CHURCH RD.
HORNSEY RD.
ARCHWAY RD.
JUNCTION RD.
KENTISH TOWN RD.
HAMPSTEAD RD.
FORTESS RD.
YORK WAY
CALEDONIAN RD.
UPPER ST.
ESSEX RD.
NEW NORTH RD.
GOSWELL RD.
OLD ST.
FARRINGDON RD.
ROSEBERY AV.
THEOBALDS R.
BISHOPSGATE
LONDON WALL
CABLE ST.
WAPPING HIGH ST.
LOWER RD.
REDRIFF RD.
THE BOURNE
BOURNE HILL
HEDGE LANE
ALDERMANS HILL
BOWES RD.
BOUNDS GREEN RD.
HIGH RD.
WOOD GREEN
HIGH ST.
PRIORY RD.
MUSWELL HILL
STROUD GRN. RD.
CROUCH HILL
TURNPIKE LA.
WEST GREEN RD.
AMHURST PK.
FERRY LA.
BRIDGE RD.
LEA BRIDGE ROAD
A1009
A110
A112
A1
A503
A104
A11
A5200
A400
A40
A4
A3211
A3036
A301
A3212
A1203
A1206
A1205
A1208
A1200
A1201
A105
A1080
A109
A111
A1010
A1055
A112
A114
A106
A1006
A115
A1011
A504
A5203
A5201
A103
B106
B138
B150
B152
B153
B155
B137
B179
B160
B161
B164
B125
B126
B140
B118
B135
B113
B112
B108
B104
B105
B111
B515
B502
B504
B154
B205
30
32
34
36
38
84
88
90
92
94
18
Cemy.

39
31
40
F
G
H
J
K
1
2
3
4
5
6
7
92
93
107
108
109
123
124
125
140
141
M11
A12
A13
A406
A1400
A1020
A117
Buckhurst Hill
Lord's Bushes
Woodford Wells
Woodford Green
Woodford
Woodford Bridge
Hospital Hill Wood
Chigwell
Chigwell Row
Grange Hill
Hainault
Hainault Forest (Country Park)
Lambourne End
Bournebridge
Havering-atte-Bower
Collier Row
Rise Park
Mawney
Marks Gate
Fairlop
Fairlop Waters
Fullwell Cross
Clayhall
Clayhall Park
Barkingside
Aldborough Hatch
Redbridge
Gants Hill
Gants Hill
Newbury Park
Little Heath
Chadwell Heath
St. Chad's Park
Seven Kings
Seven Kings Park
Valentines Park
Cranbrook
Snaresbrook
Wanstead
Redbridge Roundabout
Charlie Brown's Roundabout
Aldersbrook
Wanstead Flats
City of London Cemetery
Manor Park
Little Ilford
Ilford
Goodmayes
Goodmayes Park
Becontree
Becontree Heath
Rush Green
Central Park
Crowlands
ROMFORD
Romford
Dagenham
Dagenham & Redbridge
Parsloes Park
Mayesbrook Park
Loxford
Fair Cross
Barking Park
South Park
BARKING
Plashet
Plashet Park
Upton
Upton Park
West Ham
West Ham Utd.
Wallend
East Ham
Central Park
Old Dagenham Park
Goresbrook Park
Ripple Rd. Junction
Goresbrook Interchange
Movers Lane
Barking
Creekmouth
Barking Creek
Beckton
Beckton District Park
Custom House
Docklands
Canning Town
ExCeL
London City Airport
North Woolwich
Silvertown
Thames Flood Barrier
Woolwich
Woolwich Ferry
Visitor Centre
Gallions Reach
Thamesmead
Erith Marshes
Hornchurch Marshes
River Thames
Moby Dick
Eastern Avenue
Romford Road
London Road
Whalebone Lane
High Road
Longbridge Road
Ripple Road
Alfreds Way
Barking Road
Woodford Road
Cranbrook Road
Heathway
New Road
Rainham Road
Green Lane
Wood Lane
Porters Avenue
Thames Road
Royal Albert Way
Eastern Way
Manor Way
Gateway

40
Nuper's Hatch
Bournebridge
Pygro Wood
Noak Hill
St. Vincent's Hamlet
Weald Park (Country Park)
South Weald
Front Park
The Oaks
Havering-atte-Bower
The Round House
Pyrgo Park
Foxburrow Wood
Havering Park (Country Park)
Bower Wood
Dagnam Park
Hatters Wood
Harold Hill
Bedfords Park
Chase Cross
Collier
Rise Park
Gallows Corner
Harold Park
Harold Wood
Great Warley
Tylers Common
Brook Street
Brook Street Interchange
Brentwood Museum
Warley
Holden's Wood
Ellen's Wood
Foxburrow Wood
Coombe Wood
Codham Hall Wood
Raphael Park
Romford
Mawney
Mawney Park
Moby Dick
Gidea Park
Squirrel's Heath
Lodge Farm Park
Harold Wood Park
ROMFORD
Ardleigh Green
Haynes Park
Emerson Park
Heath Park
Hylands Park
Crowlands
Hornchurch
St. Andrew's Park
Museum
Cranham
Upminster
Windmill
Beacontree Heath
Rush Green
Central Park
St. Leonards Hamlet
Harrow Lodge Park
Upminster Park
Dagenham & Redbridge
Dagenham
Elm Park
Hacton
Parklands
Corbets Tey
Cemy. Crematorium
North Ockendon
Old Dagenham Park
Hornchurch Country Park
South Hornchurch
Rainham
Dovers Corner
Chandlers Corner
Belhus Woods Country Park
Cemetery
Hornchurch Marshes
Rainham
Belhus Park
South Ockendon
River Thames
Wennington
Rainham Marshes
Aveley
Brannett's Wood
Wennington Marshes
Aveley Marshes
Thurrock
M25
A12
A127
A13
A1306
A124
A118
A125
B1335
B1421
B187
B186
Havering
Thurrock
Brentwood
RM1
RM3
RM4
RM5
RM7
RM10
RM11
RM12
RM13
RM14
RM15
94
95
110
111
112
126
127
128
142
143
144
A
B
C
D
E
1
2
3
4
5
6
7

41
33
42
47
F
G
H
J
K
1
2
3
4
5
6
7
Shenfield
Hutton Mount
BRENTWOOD
Havering's Grove
BILLERICAY
Sunnymede
Devil's Wood
Moses Spring Wood
Tye Common
James's Wood
Bluntswall Wood
Thrift Wood
Hall Wood
Frith Wood
Billericay
South Green
Little Bladen's Wood
Laindon Common
Little Burstead
Great Burstead
CM11
Crays Hill
Ingrave Common
Harts Wood
Kent's Wood
Ingrave
Thorndon Park
Barleylands Farm Mus.
Cemetery
Noak Hill
River Crouch
The Forest Country Park
Herongate
Parkhill Wood
CM12
Broomhills
113
114
115
Brentwood
Little Warley
Thorndon Country Park
Lady Spring Wood
Friern Manor Wood
Steeple View
Noak Bridge
Pipps Hill
BASILDON
Gloucester Park
Ghyllgrove
Mill Wood
A127
Childerditch
Southfields
Devonshire Park
SS15
Laindon
CM13
West Horndon
Basildon
Lee Chapel North
Great Berry
Langdon Hills
Kirks Wood
Long Wood
Lee Chapel South
Kingswood
BASILDON
THURROCK
SS16
Hall Wood
Westley Heights Country Park
Gravelhill Wood
Dry Street
Coombe Wood
Martinhole Wood
129
130
131
One Tree Hill Country Park
Northlands Wood
The Park
Bulphan
A13
(STANFORD-LE-HOPE BY-PASS)
Balstonia
Corringham
Horndon on the Hill
Mar Dyke
ORSETT FEN
Reservoir
Grays
Orsett
Orsett Park
Stanford-le-Hope
145
146
147
Baker Street
RM16
Mardyke Country Park
Stanford-le-Hope
Mucking
SS17
MUCKING MARSHES
North Stifford
Walton Hall Farm Museum
Orsett Heath
Grays
A1089
Chadwell St. Mary
Linford
Muckingford
A128
A129
A176
A1235
A1321
A1014
A1013
B1007
B148
B1036
B188
B1420
A1013
B1007
60
62
64
66
68
570
94
92
190
88
86
84
82
180

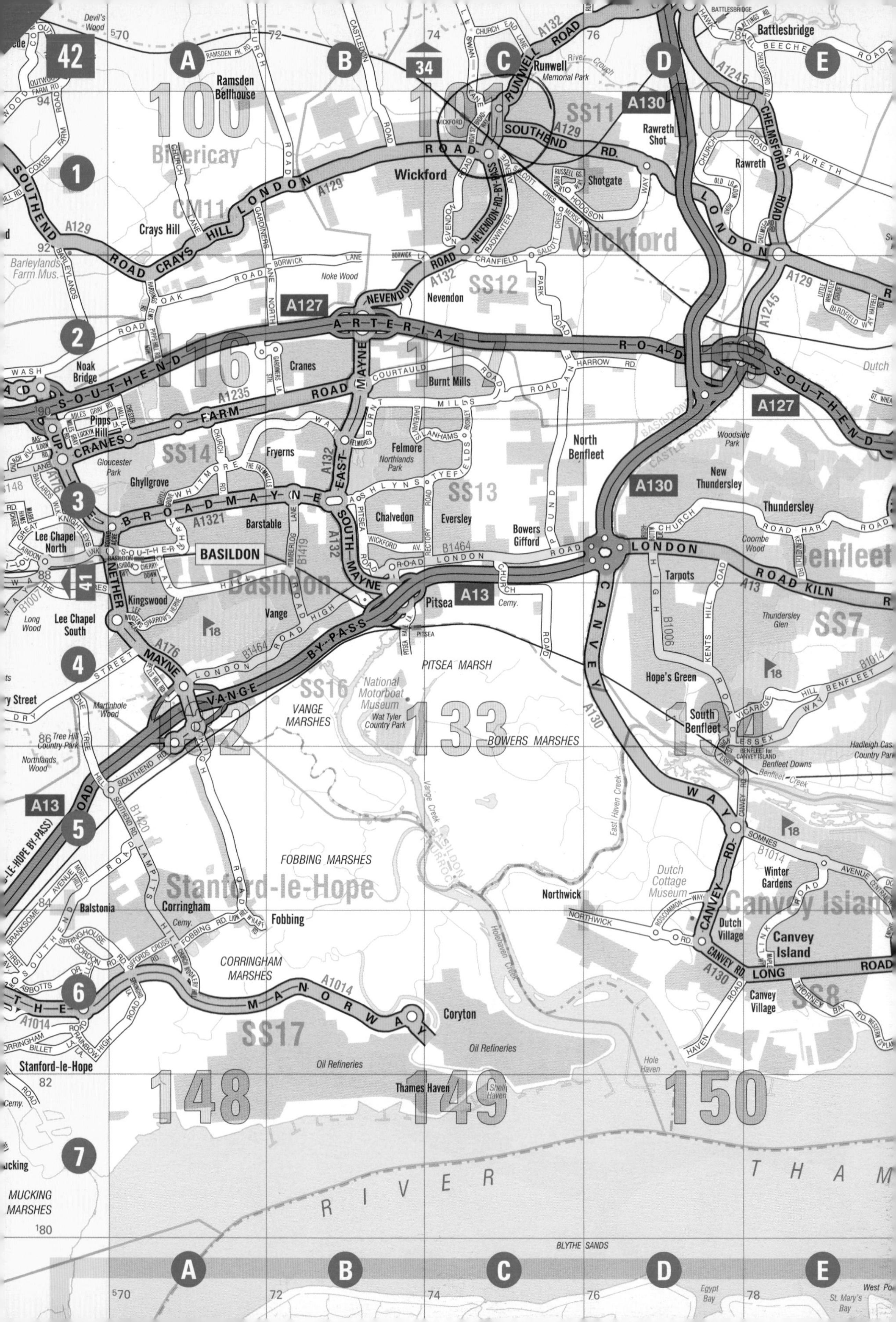
42
34
41
A
B
C
D
E
1
2
3
4
5
6
7
100
101
102
116
117
118
132
133
134
148
149
150
Ramsden Bellhouse
Billericay
CM11
Crays Hill
Barleylands Farm Mus.
Runwell
Runwell Memorial Park
River Crouch
SS11
A130
Rawreth Shot
Battlesbridge
Wickford
Shotgate
Rawreth
Nevendon
SS12
Noke Wood
A127
ARTERIAL ROAD
SOUTHEND ROAD
Noak Bridge
Cranes
Burnt Mills
Pipps Hill
SS14
Fryerns
Felmore
Northlands Park
North Benfleet
Woodside Park
New Thundersley
Thundersley
Gloucester Park
Ghyllgrove
BROADMAYNE
SS13
Chalvedon
Eversley
Bowers Gifford
Barstable
Lee Chapel North
BASILDON
Basildon
Kingswood
Vange
Pitsea
A13
Tarpots
Coombe Wood
Benfleet
SS7
Lee Chapel South
Long Wood
Thundersley Glen
Hope's Green
PITSEA MARSH
SS16
National Motorboat Museum
Wat Tyler Country Park
VANGE MARSHES
BOWERS MARSHES
South Benfleet
Hadleigh Castle Country Park
Benfleet Downs
Benfleet Creek
Martinhole Wood
Tree Hill Country Park
Northlands Wood
Vange Creek
East Haven Creek
FOBBING MARSHES
Stanford-le-Hope
Balstonia
Corringham
Fobbing
Northwick
Dutch Cottage Museum
Dutch Village
Winter Gardens
Canvey Island
Canvey Village
SS8
CORRINGHAM MARSHES
MANORWAY
A1014
Coryton
Holehaven Creek
SS17
Oil Refineries
Thames Haven
Shell Haven
Hole Haven
MUCKING MARSHES
RIVER THAMES
BLYTHE SANDS
Egypt Bay
St. Mary's Bay
570
72
74
76
78
94
92
90
88
86
84
82
180

Hullbridge
Hockley
Ashingdon
Rochford
Rayleigh
Hawkwell
Stroud Green
Great Stambridge
Ballards Gore
Canewdon
Eastwood
Eastwoodbury
Noblesgreen
Daws Heath
Hadleigh
Leigh-on-Sea
Westcliff-on-Sea
Prittlewell
Chalkwell
Southchurch
Southend-on-Sea
SOUTHEND-ON-SEA
LONDON-SOUTHEND AIRPORT
Hockley Woods
Belfairs Park
Hadleigh Castle
Hadleigh Marsh
Two Tree Island
Leigh Sand
Chalkwell Ooze
Southend Flat
Southend Pier
Canvey Point
Chapman Sands
Newlands
Leigh Beck
Sea Life Centre
Jakapeni Rare Breeds Farm
A127
A13
A1015
A1159
A129
B1013
B1014
B1015
B1016
43
44
35
103
104
105
120
121
135
136
137
151
SS0
SS1
SS2
SS4
SS5
SS9
F
G
H
J
K
1
2
3
4
5
6
7

44
A
B
C
D
E
36
43
Canewdon
WALLASEA ISLAND
Rochford
Paglesham Churchend
Clements Marsh
Ballards Gore
SS4
Paglesham Eastend
RIVER ROACH
FOULNESS
Great Stambridge
DANGER AREA
POTTON ISLAND
Barling Marsh
New England Island
HAVENGORE ISLAND
RUSHLEY ISLAND
Barling
Little Wakering
Stonebridge
SS3
Sharpness Head
Havengore Head
Haven Point
Southend-on-Sea
Great Wakering
Samuel's Corner
Wakering Stairs
Bournes Green
North Shoebury
SS2
SS1
Southchurch
Thorpe Bay
Shoeburyness
Gunners Park
Black Grounds
Pig's Bay
SHOEBURY NESS
SOUTHEND-ON-SEA
Sea Life Centre
Friars Pk.
138
139
1
2
3
4
5
6
7
590
92
94
96
98
94
92
190
88
86
84
82
180

600
02
04
06
08
610
F
G
H
37
J
K
Ridgemarsh
DANGER AREA
Courtsend
WHITE CITY
Churchend
Fisherman's Head
ISLAND
Eastwick Head
DANGER AREA
Rugwood Head
Asplins Head
The Broomway
MAPLIN SANDS
NORTH SEA
94
1
92
2
190
3
88
4
86
5
84
6
82
7
180

A
B
C
D
E
1
2
3
4
5
6
7
RAINHAM MARSHES
WENNINGTON MARSHES
Wennington
Aveley
THURROCK
Thurrock Lakeside
Chafford Hundred
West Thurrock
Purfleet
AVELEY MARSHES
RIVER THAMES
Erith
Belvedere
Lessness Heath
Frank's Park
Northumberland Heath
North End
Slade Green
DARTFORD MARSHES
CRAYFORD MARSHES
DARTFORD CROSSING
DARTFORD TUNNEL
QUEEN ELIZABETH II BRIDGE
Channel Tunnel Rail Link (Under Construction - Estimated Completion 2006)
LITTLEBROOK INTERCHANGE
TOLL
Barnehurst
Barnes Cray
Bexleyheath
Joyce Green
Temple Hill
Greenhithe
Crayford
DARTFORD
Bexley
Hall Place
BLACK PRINCE INTERCHANGE
Stone
Horns Cross
Knockhall
New Town
West Hill
Bluewater
Old Bexley
DARTFORD HEATH
Dartford Heath
PRINCES RD. INTERCHANGE
DARENTH INTERCHANGE
Fleet Downs
Darenth Wood
Darenth Country Park
Bean
Coldblow
Joydens Wood
Hawley
Wilmington
Darenth
Ladies Wood
Lane End
Lords Wood
Beacon Wood Country Park
Sidcup
Chalk Wood
Gattons Plantation
Hextable
Sutton at Hone
St. John's Jerusalem
Green Street Green
Grubb Street
Swanley Village
Newbarn Park
South Darenth
Hockenden
Swanley
Bourne Wood
Farningham Wood
Horton Kirby
Churchdown Wood
Crockenhill
SWANLEY INTERCHANGE
Farningham
Fawkham
Pennis Wood
Horton Wood
Parkfield Wood
Fawkham Green
Crown Wood
Lullingstone Roman Villa
Eynsford
Olivers Shaw
West Yoke
M25
M20
A2
A13
A20
A282
A206
A226
A225
A2018
A2000
A223
A220
A207
A296
A1306
A1090
B2173
B2174
B2186
B258
B260
B255
B262
B186
B1335
153
152
154
DA1
DA2
DA4
DA5
DA6
DA7
DA14
BR8
RM19
RM20

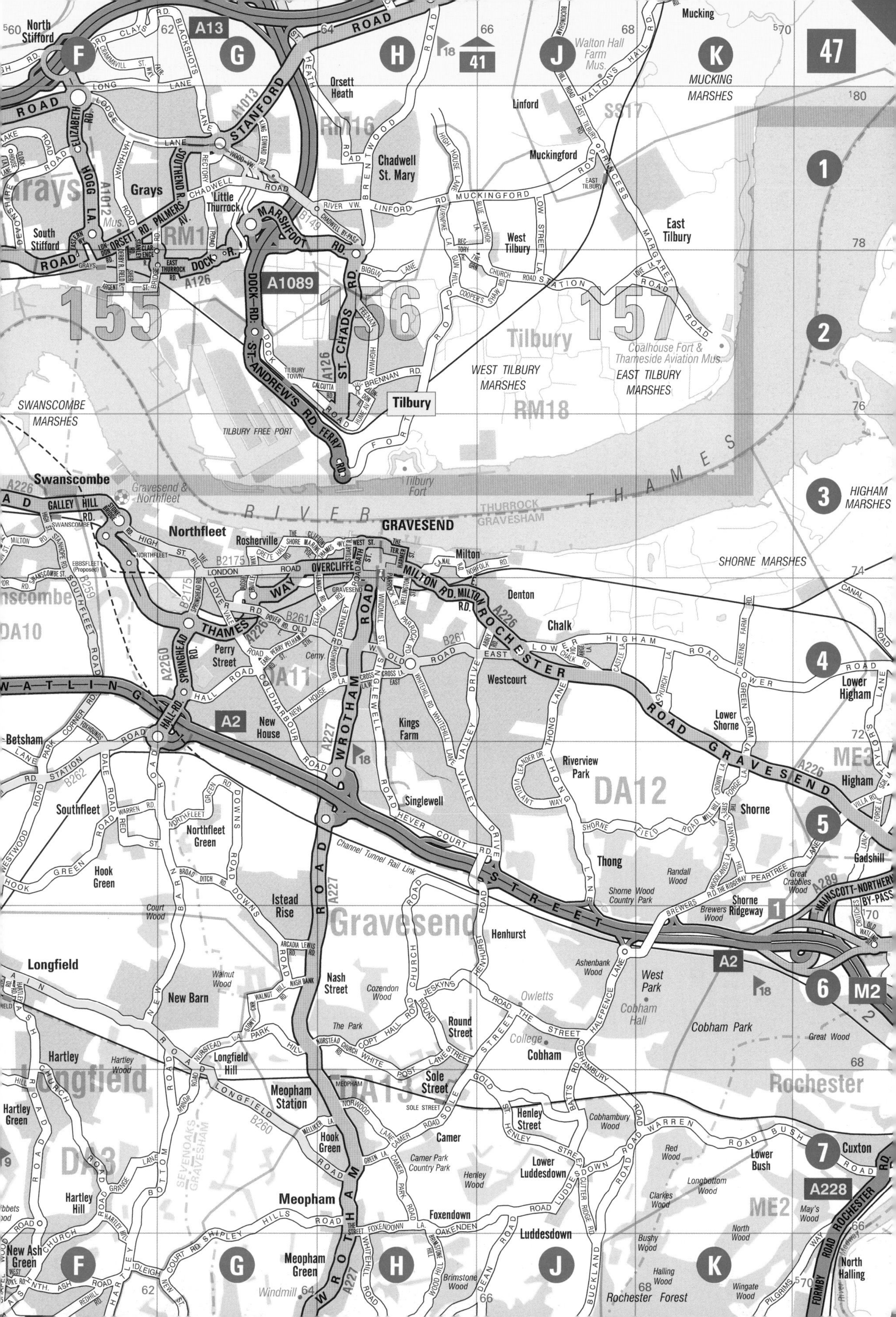
North Stifford
Orsett Heath
Chadwell St. Mary
Linford
Mucking
Walton Hall Farm Mus.
MUCKING MARSHES
Muckingford
East Tilbury
West Tilbury
Grays
Little Thurrock
South Stifford
155
156
157
Tilbury
Coalhouse Fort & Thameside Aviation Mus.
WEST TILBURY MARSHES
EAST TILBURY MARSHES
SWANSCOMBE MARSHES
TILBURY FREE PORT
Tilbury Fort
RIVER THAMES
HIGHAM MARSHES
Swanscombe
Gravesend & Northfleet
Northfleet
Rosherville
GRAVESEND
Milton
SHORNE MARSHES
Denton
Chalk
Perry Street
Westcourt
Lower Higham
Betsham
New House
Kings Farm
Riverview Park
DA12
Lower Shorne
Higham
Southfleet
Singlewell
Shorne
Northfleet Green
Hook Green
Thong
Gadshill
Channel Tunnel Rail Link
Istead Rise
Gravesend
Henhurst
Shorne Ridgeway
Longfield
Nash Street
West Park
Cobham Hall
Cobham Park
New Barn
Round Street
Cobham
Hartley
Longfield Hill
Longfield
Sole Street
Rochester
Meopham Station
Henley Street
Hartley Green
Hook Green
Camer
Cuxton
Lower Luddesdown
Lower Bush
Hartley Hill
Meopham
Foxendown
Luddesdown
New Ash Green
Meopham Green
North Halling
Rochester Forest
A2
M2
A13
A1089
A228
A226
A227
A289
41
18

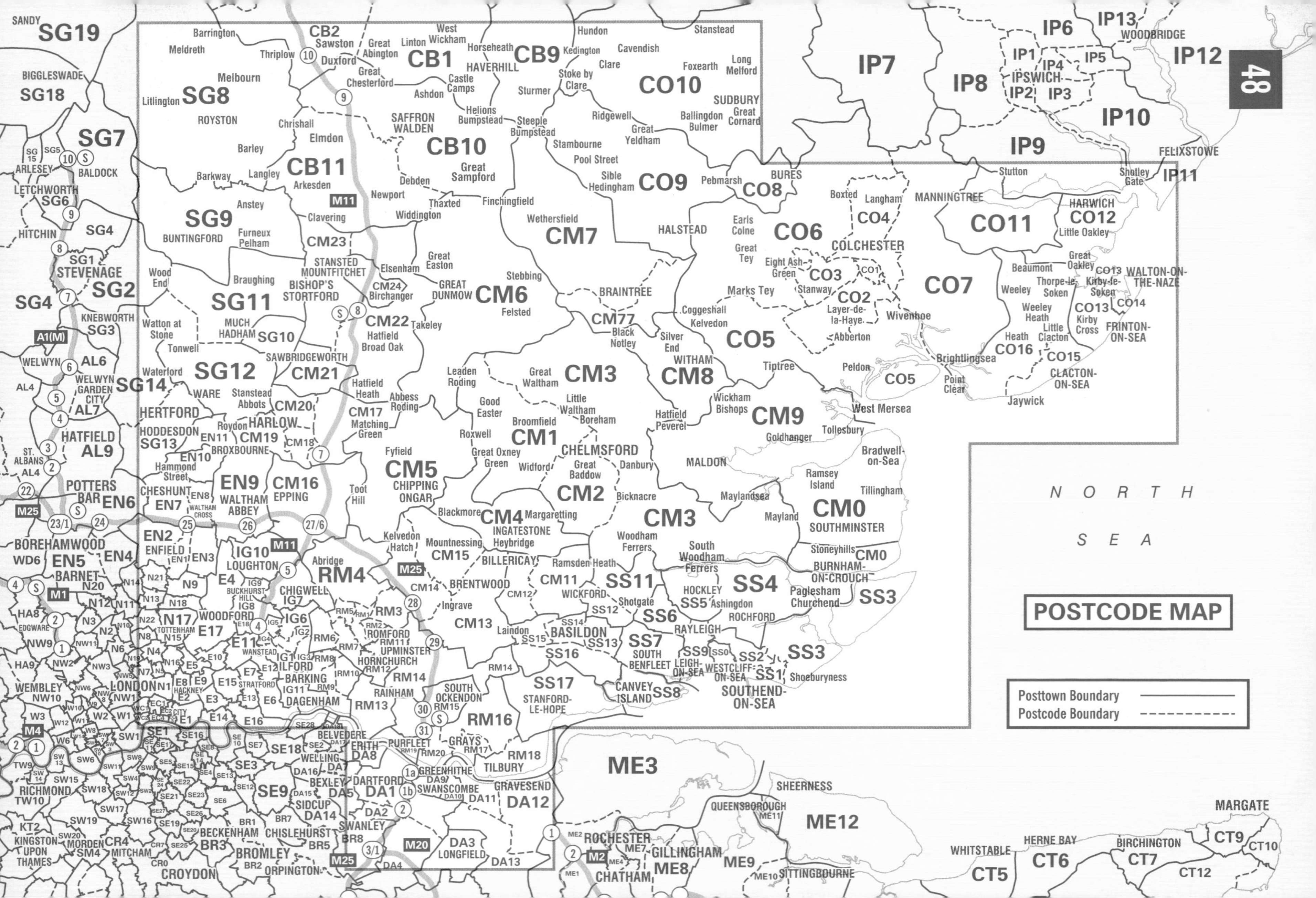
POSTCODE MAP
Posttown Boundary
Postcode Boundary
NORTH SEA
SG19
SG18
SG7
SG8
SG9
SG11
SG12
SG14
SG4
SG2
CB1
CB9
CB10
CB11
CB2
CO10
CO9
CO8
CO6
CO5
CO7
CO11
CO12
IP7
IP8
IP9
IP10
IP12
IP6
IP13
IP11
CM7
CM6
CM3
CM8
CM9
CM1
CM2
CM5
CM4
CM0
CM77
CM22
CM21
CM23
CM16
CM15
CM13
SS4
SS3
SS11
SS6
SS7
SS16
SS17
RM4
RM16
EN9
EN6
EN5
EN4
EN2
ME3
ME12
ME8
CT5
CT6
CT7
CT9
DA1
DA12
SE9
SANDY
BIGGLESWADE
BALDOCK
LETCHWORTH
HITCHIN
STEVENAGE
KNEBWORTH
WELWYN
WELWYN GARDEN CITY
HATFIELD
ST. ALBANS
POTTERS BAR
BOREHAMWOOD
BARNET
ROYSTON
BUNTINGFORD
SAFFRON WALDEN
HAVERHILL
SUDBURY
HALSTEAD
BRAINTREE
WITHAM
COLCHESTER
MANNINGTREE
HARWICH
WALTON-ON-THE-NAZE
FRINTON-ON-SEA
CLACTON-ON-SEA
IPSWICH
WOODBRIDGE
FELIXSTOWE
BISHOP'S STORTFORD
STANSTED MOUNTFITCHET
GREAT DUNMOW
MUCH HADHAM
SAWBRIDGEWORTH
HARLOW
WARE
HERTFORD
HODDESDON
BROXBOURNE
CHESHUNT
WALTHAM ABBEY
EPPING
CHIPPING ONGAR
INGATESTONE
CHELMSFORD
MALDON
SOUTHMINSTER
BURNHAM-ON-CROUCH
BILLERICAY
BRENTWOOD
WICKFORD
BASILDON
RAYLEIGH
ROCHFORD
HOCKLEY
LEIGH-ON-SEA
WESTCLIFF-ON-SEA
SOUTHEND-ON-SEA
CANVEY ISLAND
STANFORD-LE-HOPE
SOUTH OCKENDON
GRAYS
TILBURY
PURFLEET
ROMFORD
UPMINSTER
HORNCHURCH
RAINHAM
DAGENHAM
BARKING
ILFORD
CHIGWELL
LOUGHTON
WOODFORD
ENFIELD
LONDON
WEMBLEY
EDGWARE
RICHMOND
KINGSTON UPON THAMES
MORDEN
MITCHAM
CROYDON
BECKENHAM
BROMLEY
CHISLEHURST
ORPINGTON
SIDCUP
BEXLEY
WELLING
ERITH
BELVEDERE
DARTFORD
GREENHITHE
SWANSCOMBE
SWANLEY
LONGFIELD
GRAVESEND
ROCHESTER
CHATHAM
GILLINGHAM
SITTINGBOURNE
QUEENSBOROUGH
SHEERNESS
WHITSTABLE
HERNE BAY
BIRCHINGTON
MARGATE
M11
M25
M20
M2
M1
M4
A1(M)

REFERENCE TO 3 INCHES TO 1 MILE STREET MAP SECTION

Motorway M11

A Road A12

Under Construction

Proposed

B Road B184

Dual Carriageway

One Way Street

Traffic flow on A Roads is indicated by a heavy line on the driver's left

Junction Names RIPPLE ROAD JUNCTION

Restricted Access

Pedestrianized Road

Track & Footpath

Residential Walkway

Railway Tunnel Level Crossing

Stations:

National Rail Network

Docklands Light Railway DLR

Underground Station Symbol is the registered trade mark of Transport for London

Heritage Station

Posttown & London Postal District Boundaries

Postcode Boundary (within Posttowns)

Local Authority Boundary

Built Up Area HIGH STREET

Map Continuation For 3 Inches to 1 Mile Street Mapping (Red Pages) 166

Map Continuation To 1 Inch to 1 Mile Street Mapping (Blue Pages) 34

Airport

Car Park (Selected) P

Church or Chapel †

Cycleway (Selected)

Fire Station

Hospital H

House Numbers A & B Roads only 51 22 19 48

Information Centre

National Grid Reference 563

Park & Ride North Station P+

Police Station

Post Office

Toilets
with facilities for the Disabled
without Disabled Facilities
for the Disabled only

Educational Establishment

Hospital or Hospice

Industrial Building

Leisure or Recreational Facility

Place of Interest

Public Building

Shopping Centre and Market

Other Selected Buildings

SCALE approx. 3 Inches (7.94 cm) to 1 Mile

0 ¼ ½ ¾ Mile

0 250 500 750 Metres 1 Kilometre

1:20,267 or 4.93 cm to 1km

A
B
C
21
D
E
F
G
44
545
46
1
2
3
4
5
6
7
8
9
215
14
13
12
11
Much Hadham
Mole Wood
SG10
Lawns Wood
High Trees
Actons Farm Cottages
Actons Farm
Maplecroft Wood
Battles Wood
Carters Cottage
Carters
Stonards
Fryars Farm Cottage
Fryars
Great Pennys Farm
Hoskins Cottages
Gangies
Gangies Hill
Hoskins Farm
Crumps
Noons Bungalow
Noons Cottages
Bonny's Row
Club House
The Grove
MANOR OF GROVES GOLF & COUNTRY CLUB
The Manor of Groves
Cricket Grd.
Jeffs
Alexander Cotts.
Peace Cotts.
Mabletts
HIGH WYCH LANE
Bakers Farm
Playing Field
Sludge Beds
Filter Beds
Sawbridgeworth
High Wych Jun. & Inf. School
HIGH WYCH
High Wych Grange
Church Plantation
CM21
Keeper's
Brook
Golden Grove
Sayes Coppice
New Plantation
Sayes Park Farm
Sayes Park Cottages
Sayes Park Lodge
WYCH
Overhall Farm
Golden Hill
Golden
Gibson's Shaw
Dairy Cottages
CHANNOCKS
Channock's Fm. Cottages
Channocks Farm
Rectory Plantation
Fox Earths
Reservoir (Covered)
Depot
Home Wood
Cumberland Lodge
THE STABLES
Baker's Belt
The Old Rectory
Gilston Park House
Little Park
High Gilston School Cottages
Redricks Farm Cottages
REDRICKS
Redericks Farm
Pole Hole Farm
HIGH ROAD
Weir
Pole Hill
Harlow
Warehouse
Gilston
EASTWICK
The Mount
The Chase
Pye Corner
Hollingson Meads
Latton Island
Latton Lock
RIVER STORT (Navigation)
Templefields House
Fiddlers Bridge
CM20
MEAD PARK INDUSTRIAL ESTATE
ROSELEY COTTAGES
CARTER PL.
Eastwick
Eastwick Lodge Farm
Burntmill Corner
Honeymead Marsh
Works
ROMAN ROUNDABOUT
Temple Fields
ST. JAMES CENTRE
EASTWICK RD.
A414
Gilston House
Terlings Park
QUEENSGATE CENTRE
ASTRA CENTRE
Ford
River Stort
FIFTH AV.
ALLENDALE AV.
Harlow Outdoor Cen. for Outdoor Learning
Town Park
Marshgate Spring
HARLOW
SOUTH PLACE
Mill Stream
Road Safety Training Ground
Harlow Town
EDINBURGH
HOWARD
THE OAKS RETAIL PARK
Mark Hall North
Tany's Dell Prim. Sch.
Parndon Lock
Parndon Mill
Harcamlow Way
Field Ho.
Offs.
Playground
Putting Green
Netteswell Cross
NETTESWELL
Moat
PARNDON MILL LANE
BURNT MILL INDUSTRIAL ESTATE
Spurriers
GLEBELANDS
TANY'S DELL
MARK HALL MOORS
Mark Hall Gardens
Mus.
ELIZABETH WAY
Ram Gorse
RIVERMILL
Harlow Ski Cen.
Cricket Ground
Pets Corner
Nursery
54
Burnt Mill School
Prim. Sch.
ALTHAM GROVE
THE CHANTRY
FIRST AVENUE
MANDELA AVENUE
THE HORNBEAMS
Adult Community

H
J
K
21
L
M
N
47
48
49
50
SAWBRIDGEWORTH
Sawbridgeworth
Mandeville Primary School
Claylane Farm
Little Heazleys
Football Grd.
Rec. Ground
Reedings Jun. Sch.
The New House
Tennis Courts
Play. Flds.
Great Hyde Hall
North Cottage
South Lodge
Chalks Farm
Quickbury Lodge
Quickbury Cottages
Quickbury Farm
LOWER SHEERING
THE RIVERS HOSPITAL
The Gardens Nursing Home
Rowney Bois Riding Stables
Rowney Wood
Bonnyvale
New House Farm
Bishop's Stortford
Nursery Wood
The Osier Bed
PISHIOBURY PARK
EAST HERTFORDSHIRE
EPPING FOREST
Playing Fields
Feakes Lock
Landing Stage
Union Wood
Rowneybury
Alston Oak
Ashplant
RIVER STORT (Navigation)
CM22
Chapel Field
Pincey
Garage Cottage
The Cottages
Ashlands
Durrington Hall
Aylmers Farm
Sheering Hall Cotts.
Sheering Hall
Pond Bay
Harlow Mill Bri.
Harlow Lock
Wyldwood Farm
SARBIR INDUSTRIAL ESTATE
Depots
Works
Harlow Mill
EPPING FOREST
HARLOW
The House
The Cottage
Ealing Bridge
Gibberd Garden
Campions
The Coach House
Little Campions
Mayfield Farm
The Mores
Harlowbury
CM17
M11
M11 MOTORWAY
Moorhall Wood
Old Harlow
Harlowbury Primary School
Playing Field
Morgan Farm
Garden Cottage
The Bothie
St. Stephen's Cottages
Cricket Ground
Sports Ground
Norman Booth Leisure Cen.
Nursery
Churchgate C.E. Prim. Sch.
Feltimores Farm
Feltimores
Feltimores Cottages
Moor Hall Farm
EAST PARK
Mark Hall School
St. Nicholas School (Hillingdon House)
Bridge Cottages
Harlow Tye
Reformatory Cotts.
The Kennels
Essex Cottages
Playing Field
Thatched Cottages
Rosslyn
Muttons Row
The Bungalow
Spiers Farm
55
LONDON ROAD
CAMBRIDGE ROAD
BONKS HILL
HARLOW ROAD
SHEERING ROAD
GILDEN WAY
MOOR HALL ROAD
MATCHING ROAD
ROAD
B183
A1184
A414
1
2
3
4
5
6
7
8
9
210
22
G
H
J
K
L
M
N

A
B
C
20
D
E
F
G
37
38
39
540
11
210
09
08
07
1
2
3
4
5
6
7
8
9
Ware
SG12
Gravel Pit
Ryegate Farm
A414
Rye Meads Nature Reserve
Rye Meads
Toll House Stream
Rye House Nature Reserve
Rye House Gatehouse
Tanks
Sewage Works
Conveyor
EAST HERTFORDSHIRE
EPPING FOREST
BROXBOURNE
Roydon Leisure Park
Mill Stream
Lock
Hailey
WARE RD.
WARE
ST. MARGARET'S ROAD
BEECHFIELD
CAXTON
CRANBOURNE
The Cranbourne Prim. Sch.
Sports Cen.
The John Warner Sch.
Play. Fld.
NURSERY ROAD
WALLERS
MURCHISON RD.
Forres Prim. Sch.
Recreation Ground
WHITLEY
Eng. Wks.
Works
Recreation Ground
Caravan Park
Stadium
Hoddesdon
Rye House
Riverfields
River Stort (Navigation)
Kart Race Track
ROYDON PARK
LEE VALLEY PARK
Rye Park Rec. Grd.
EN11
Burford Ho.
Ryelands Prim. Sch.
Warehouse
The Grove
Glen Faba
HERTFORD RD.
A10
DINANT LINK RD.
STORTFORD ROAD
Depot
Adult Ed. Cen.
TRIDENT INDUSTRIAL ESTATE
Power Station
Electricity Transformer Station
Downe Hall
Hailes Farm
Burles Fm.
GLEN FABA ROAD
LOW
NETHERHALL
Warehouse
Works
CHARLTON
Electricity Transformer Station
THE HASLEMERE ESTATE
WATERSIDE INDUSTRIAL ESTATE
Netherhall Common
Nether Hall (remains of)
Netherhall Farm
HODDESDON
River Lynch
Admirals Walk Lake
Dobb's Weir Bridge
Dobbs Weir
DOBB'S WEIR ROAD
Flood-Relief Channel
Netherhall Nursery
GREEN HAM
Poplars Farm
Gladwyn Farm
Nursery
Nurseries
Clay Hill
A1170
Spitalbrook
LEE VALLEY CARAVAN PK.
Boating Lake
Broxbourne
Gas Station
Nazeing Mead
Essex Schs. Sailing Club
Sand & Gravel Works
R. Lee Navigation
MEADGATE ROAD
Nurseries
LEE VALLEY PARK
EN10
Broxbourne
Works
STATION ROAD
BROXBOURNE
Rec. Grd.
War Mem.
CARTHAGENA ESTATE
SEDGE GREEN
Shottentons Farm
NAZEING NEW ROAD
B194
Lee Valley Leisure Pool
Picnic Area
Boating Lake
Boat Ho. Club
Keysers Estate
LEE VALLEY PARK
NURSERY ROAD
Sports Ground
NORTH STREET
PECK'S HILL
62
HILLGROVE BUSINESS PARK
SHOOTERS DRIVE
Spinny Nursery
Stonyfield Nursery
Brook Farm
Nursery

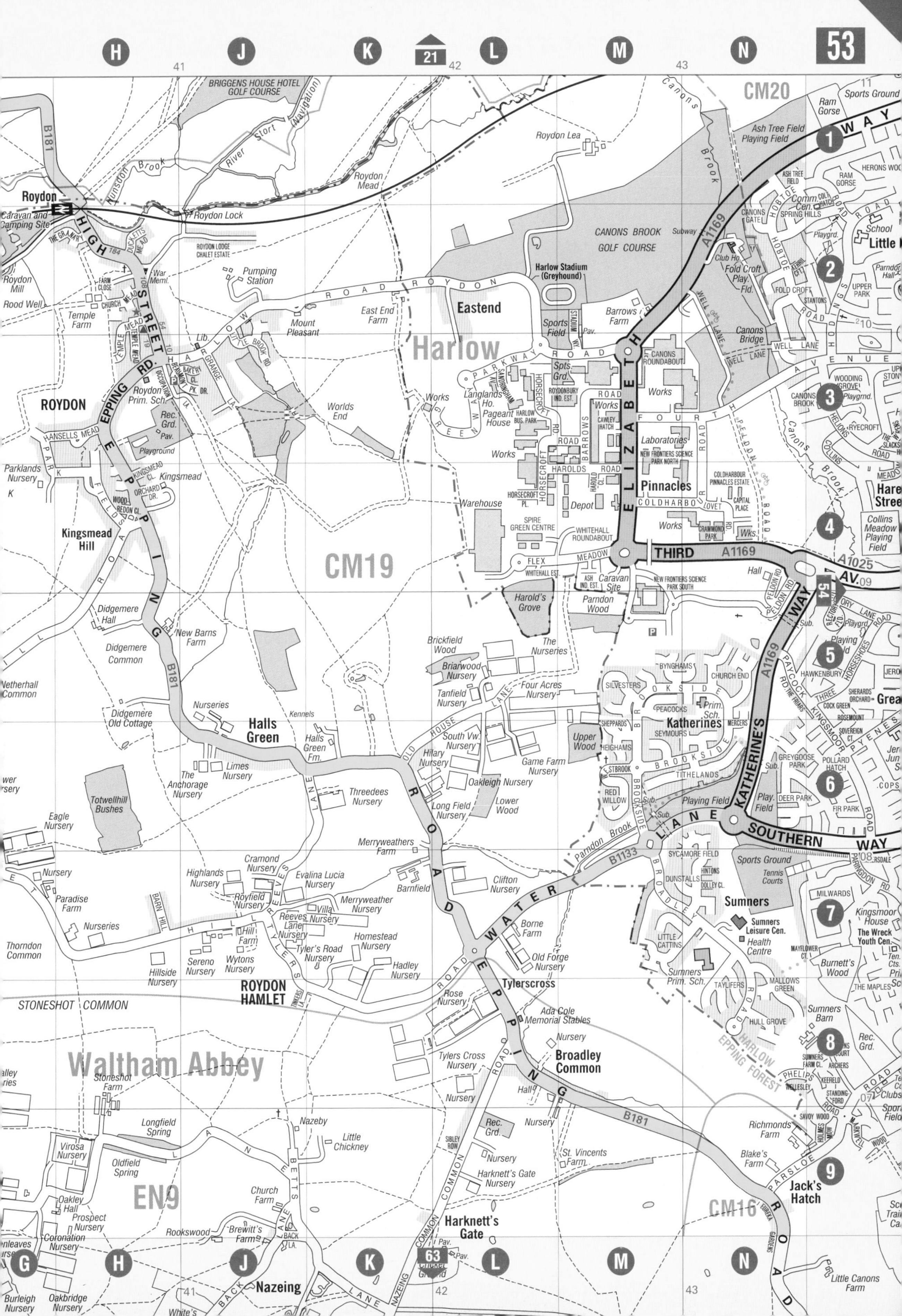

53
H
J
K
21
L
M
N
41
42
43
BRIGGENS HOUSE HOTEL GOLF COURSE
CM20
Sports Ground
Ram Gorse
Ash Tree Field Playing Field
Roydon Lea
River Stort (Navigation)
Hunsdon Brook
Roydon Mead
Roydon
Caravan and Camping Site
Roydon Lock
ROYDON LODGE CHALET ESTATE
HIGH STREET
B181
Roydon Mill
Rood Well
Temple Farm
War Meml.
Pumping Station
CANONS BROOK GOLF COURSE
Harlow Stadium (Greyhound)
Eastend
East End Farm
Mount Pleasant
Barrows Farm
Sports Field
Fold Croft Play. Fld.
Canons Bridge
Harlow
ROYDON ROAD
ELIZABETH WAY
A1169
Little
School
ROYDON
EPPING RD.
Roydon Prim. Sch.
Rec. Grd.
Playground
Worlds End
Works
Langlands Ho.
Pageant House
Laboratories
NEW FRONTIERS SCIENCE PARK NORTH
Pinnacles
COLDHARBOUR PINNACLES ESTATE
FOURTH AVENUE
Parklands Nursery
Kingsmead
Kingsmead Hill
Warehouse
SPIRE GREEN CENTRE
WHITEHALL ROUNDABOUT
Depot
CM19
THIRD AVENUE
A1169
A1025
Collins Meadow Playing Field
Harold's Grove
Caravan Site
Parndon Wood
NEW FRONTIERS SCIENCE PARK SOUTH
54
Didgemere Hall
New Barns Farm
Didgemere Common
Brickfield Wood
The Nurseries
Briarwood Nursery
Tanfield Nursery
Four Acres Nursery
Katherines
KATHERINE'S WAY
Didgemere Old Cottage
Nurseries
Halls Green
Kennels
Halls Green Fm.
Upper Wood
OLD HOUSE LANE
South Vw. Nursery
Hilary Nursery
Game Farm Nursery
Oakleigh Nursery
Limes Nursery
The Anchorage Nursery
Totwellhill Bushes
Threedees Nursery
Long Field Nursery
Lower Wood
Playing Field
Play. Field
SOUTHERN WAY
Eagle Nursery
Merryweathers Farm
Parndon Brook
B1133
Sports Ground
Tennis Courts
Sumners
Sumners Leisure Cen.
Health Centre
Nursery
Paradise Farm
Highlands Nursery
Cramond Nursery
Evalina Lucia Nursery
Barnfield
Clifton Nursery
WATER LANE
Royfield Nursery
Villa Nursery
Merryweather Nursery
Borne Farm
Kingsmoor House
The Wreck Youth Cen.
Burnett's Wood
Thorndon Common
Hill Farm
Reeves Lane Nursery
Tyler's Road Nursery
Homestead Nursery
Old Forge Nursery
Sumners Prim. Sch.
Hillside Nursery
Sereno Nursery
Wytons Nursery
Hadley Nursery
ROYDON HAMLET
Tylerscross
STONESHOT COMMON
Rose Nursery
Ada Cole Memorial Stables
Sumners Barn
HARLOW EPPING FOREST
Waltham Abbey
Tylers Cross Nursery
Broadley Common
Stoneshot Farm
Hall
Nursery
EPPING ROAD
Rec. Grd.
Longfield Spring
Nazeby
Little Chickney
Richmonds Farm
Virosa Nursery
Oldfield Spring
St. Vincents Farm
Blake's Farm
Jack's Hatch
EN9
Church Farm
Harknett's Gate Nursery
CM16
Oakley Hall
Prospect Nursery
Coronation Nursery
Rookswood
Brewitt's Farm
Harknett's Gate
63
Little Canons Farm
G
Burleigh Nursery
Oakbridge Nursery
Nazeing
White's

Harlow Town
Mark Hall North
Parndon Lock
Parndon Mill
Harcamlow
Moat
Field Ho.
Edinburgh Way
Burnt Mill
Pets Corner
Nursery
Netteswell Cross
Putting Green
Playground
Tany's Dell Prim. Sch.
Mark Hall Gardens
Mus.
Elizabeth Way
A1169
Fifth Av.
Allendale Av.
A1019
Sports Ground
Ram Gorse
Ash Tree Field
Playing Field
Harlow Ski Cen.
Cricket Ground
Stand
Adult Community College
Harlow Sports Centre
Sports Hall
Burnt Mill School
Prim. Sch.
First Avenue
Mandela Avenue
Harlow Pool & Fitness Cen.
Comm. Cen.
Cooks Spinney
Stow Play Fld.
Mark Hall South
Schools
Little Parndon
Hall
School
Rectory Wood
Super market
Depots
Netteswell
CM20
Vicarage
Wood
Fold Croft Play. Fld.
Oak Wood
Parndon Hall
Princess Alexandra Hospital
Health Cen.
Comm. Cen.
Post Office
Harvey Centre (Shop. Cen.)
The High
The Dashes Play. Fld.
Harlow College
The Downs Prim. Sch.
Health Cen.
Play. Field
Markhall
Canons Bridge
Well Lane
Fourth Avenue
HARLOW
Mag. Ct.
Town Hall
Crown Gate
Play. Fld.
Long Ley
Playground
Todd Brook
Gravelpit Springs
The Moors
Heliport
Netteswell Plantation
Second Avenue
A1025
Latton Farm
Puffers Green
Canons Brook
School
Play Flds.
Hare Street
Collins Meadow Playing Field
St. Mark's West Essex Catholic Sch.
Visitors Cen.
Bushy Fair Playing Field
Third Av.
Third
Harlow Museum
Playing Field
Harlow
Tye Green
School
Brays Grove
53
Katherine's Way
Passmores Comp. Sch.
Harlow Fields Sch.
Playing Field
Schools
Great Parndon
Prim. Sch.
Abbotsweld Prim. Sch.
Passmores
Catholic Sch.
Jerounds Jun. & Inf. Schs.
Playing Field
Comm. Cen.
Rec. Grd.
Goldings Farm
Tye Green Village
CM19
Southern Way
Health Cen.
Playing Field
Latton Bush
Sports Ground
Tennis Courts
Stewards
Stewards Pool
Stewards School
Intergrated Support Cen.
Sumners
Sumners Leisure Cen.
Health Centre
Kingsmoor House
The Wreck Youth Cen.
Schools
Latton Green Prim. Sch.
Burnett's Wood
KINGSMOOR
Maund's Wood
Prim. Sch.
CM18
Caravan Park
Nursery
Sumners Barn
Rec. Grd.
Kennels
Riddings House
Harlow
Epping Forest
Clubs
Sports Field
Playing Field
Dorrington Farm
Riddings Spring
Richmonds Farm
Parndon Wood (Nature Reserve)
Blake's Farm
Jack's Hatch
Risden's Wood
Parndon Wood Crematorium & Cemetery
Resr. (covered)
Water Tower
Rye Hill Common
Epping Road
CM16
Scout Training Camp
Rye Hill Reservoir (covered)
Moat
Latton Priory Farm
Hospital Wood
64
Rye Hill
Little Canons Farm
Rivetts Farm
Green

55
H
J
K
L
M
N
G
1
2
3
4
5
6
7
8
9
22
32
51
65
47
48
49
50
11
10
09
08
07
Gilden Way
B183
First Avenue
Mandela Avenue
East Park
Sch.
Sub.
Churchgate C.E. Prim. Sch.
Hobbs
St. Nicholas School (Hillingdon House)
Feltimores Farm
Feltimores Cottages
Chalk
Harlow Tye
Moor Hall Farm
Chalk Lane
Reformatory Cottage
Harlow Tye
Lane
Mark Hall School
Playing Field
The Kennels
Essex Hunt Cottages
Bridge Cottages
Thatched Cottages
Mutton Row
Rosslyn
The Bungalow
Spiers Farm
Cross
M11
M11 Motorway
Franklins Farm
London Road
Old London Road
A414
Mark Hall Sports Ground
Tennis Courts
Bowling Green
Sports Ground
Works
Gravelpit Spring
Newpond Spring
New Hall Farm
Roundhouse
The Chase
Braggowens
Ley
Gt. Augur
Hubbard's Hall
Hubbard's Hall Farm
Highlands
Elm Cottage
Hobbs Cross
Mead Cott.
Hobbs Cross Cott.
Wyses Barn
Hobbs Cross House
Head Road
Hobbs Cross
Brenthall Wood
Barnsley Wood
Barnsley Cottage
Reservoir
Church Langley Prim. Sch.
Comm. Cen.
Health Cen.
Perry Spring
Superstore
Ashworth Place
Mallards Rise
Challinor
Ruston Grove
Denby Grange
Old Hall Rise
Ridgeways
Doulton Cl.
Roffey Hall Cottages
Roffey Hall Farm
Burrs Farm
CM17
Church Langley Way
Church Langley
Elwood
Doulton
Chelsea Gdns.
Davenport
Threshers
Threshers Bush
New Way Lane
Bush Hall Farm
Barkers
Workers Rd.
Green Lane Cottages
Boar
Grave Yard
All Saints Cottage
Foster Street Cottages
Shoe Lane
Foster Street
Green
Kingsdon Lane
Oaklands Dr.
Abbeydale Cl.
Belfield Gdns.
Westbury Rise
Albert Gdns.
Coalport Close
Burley Hill
Kitchen Hall
Wheeldon Grange
Malkin Drive
Fullers Mead
Wayside Farm
Second Av.
Latton
Campbell Close
Pinewood Cl.
Carters Mead
Nightingales
Perry Spring
Lion Lane
Potter Street
Wrights Ct.
Brenthall Towers
Red Lion Crescent
Potters Field
Health Cen.
Southern Way
Larkswood
Mandeville Cl.
Chapel Fields
Hillside
Jack Stevens Cl.
The Sweyns
Playgrd.
Harlow Common
Hoggs Farm
Searles Farm
Works
Foster Street
Brent Ho. Fm.
Horn & Horseshoe Lane
Crabbs Farm
Greenways
Works
Mill Street
Windyridge
Church Road
Priory Court
Road
Latton Street
Harlow
Mill House Farm
Moat
Wynters Armourie
Wynters Farm
Road
Newhouse
A414
London Road
Park Av.
Shonks Farm
Sewage Pump. Sta.
Wyntersbrook
Wynter's Grange
The Retreat
CM5
Harlow Park
Underpass
Nursery
Hastingwood
Hastingwood
Piggery
Latton Park
Sewalds Hall Farm
Junction 7
St. Clare Hospice
Hastingwood Farm
Paris Hall Farm
Moat
Shonks Brook
Rundell's Grove
Glovers Farm
Gloves La.
Canes
Nursy
Canes Cottages
Rundells
B1393
M11
A414
Canes Wood
Canes Cottages
Canes
Lane
Horseshoes Farm
Depot

A
B
C
23
D
E
F
G
Pleshey
Post Bridge
Park Farm
The Bushet
Oak Hall
Dropshots
Earthwork
Bull's Corner
Mount House
Sewage Works
Pleshey Bridge
Folly Farm
Pleshey Castle (Remains of)
Cricket Grd.
Lodge Farm
Pleshey Lodge
De Lancey Cottages
Walthambury Farm
Waltham Bury
Reservoir
Weir
Deadman's Bank
Bury Hall
Bury Lodge
Fitzjohn's Farm
Fitzjohn's Wood
High Houses
Cobblers Hall Cottages
Meads Cottages
Israel's Bungalows
Garnett's Farm
Israel's Farm
Murray Cottages
Wart Cottages
Bards Hall
Chelmsford
The Chalet
Breed's Farm
Humphrey's Farm
Moat
Breeds
Rest Harrow
Jobbers Orchard
Blatche's Wood
Mansion Cottage
Fanner's Green
Sand & Gravel Pit
The Bungalow
Fanner's Farm
Margaret Woods Farm
Walnut Tree Farm
Border Wood
Beadles Hall
Chignall Smealy
Cricket Ground
Hawthorne Cottages
The Bells
Whitelead Cottages
Hoddock's Wood
Chignall Smealy Church
Dyers Hall Farm
CM1
Langleys Farm
Maple View
Howletts Hall
Ford
58
Woodhall Farm
Greenfields
Gray's Farm
Playing Field

57
23
24
59
H
J
K
L
M
N
G
1
2
3
4
5
6
7
8
9
570
71
72
215
14
13
12
11
ESSEX REGIMENT WAY
A130
BRAINTREE ROAD
B1007
STRAWBROOK HILL
ROAD
A131
ROMAN ROAD
CM3
Hill House
Hill House Farm
Chalk Farm
Mill House
Weir
RIVER CHELMER
Fitzandrews Farm
Cobbs
Rectory Farm Ho.
Parsonage Bridge
Rectory Farm
Waltham House
Boat House
LUCK'S LA.
PARSONAGE LANE
HYDE
CHATHAM HALL
BRIDGE CROFT
Howe Street
Straights
Park Farm
Howe Street Plantation
West Lodge
Waterfall
Pav.
Cricket Grd.
Brook
Great Waltham
Great Waltham Guildhall
Langleys
DEER PARK
Wallops
Weir
South Lodge
CHELMSFORD
Whites Plantation
CHERRY GARDEN ROAD
GLEBE MDW.
BROOK MEAD
LANE
Prim. Sch.
Hall
STREET
HATCHFIELD
DANNATTS BAKERS MEAD
Recreation Ground
South House Farm
Minnow End
Broad's Green
LARKS LANE
Larks Lodge
Ball's Farm
Walnut Tree Cottages
Sparrowhawk Wood
Sports Ground
Pavilion
Partridge Green Farm
The New House
WOODHOUSE
Partridge Green Cotts.
Staff Houses
THE LINDEN CEN.
The Christopher Unit
WOODLANDS
Puddings Wood
BROOMFIELD HOSPITAL
Playing Fields
Tennis Cts.
Chelmer Valley High Sch.
Playground
CHURCH AVENUE
BROOMHALL ROAD
JUBILEE
Hyde Hall Lane
HALL
Bailey's Farm
Chatham Green
Recreation Ground
Chathamhall Spring
Chatham Hall Lodge
Great Stonage Farm
LANE
Little Stonage Farm
SCURVY HALL LANE
East Lodge
Cresseners
Chatham Hall
The Bungalow
Albion House
Reservoir
Little Waltham C.E. Prim. Sch.
Tufnell Hall
Football Field
Works
Pav.
Cricket Ground
Brooklands
Playing Field
SHEEPCOTES
CHURCH HILL
RECTORY CL.
Winckford Bridge
THE STREET
CHAPEL DR.
SORRELL CL.
WINCKFORD CL.
BROOK HILL
Little Waltham
WHEELER'S HILL
BACK LANE
Waltham Nursery
Weir
ROAD
MAIN ROAD
Ash Tree Corner
Little Waltham Lodge
MANOR
CHELMER AV.
ROMAN RD.
Hall
Fish Pond
Merefields
RIVER CHELMER
Rolphs Farm
Montpelier Farm
Thorley's Farm
Blasford Hill
Lodge
LANE
COURT
Wood House
Croxton's Mill Cottage
Croxton's Mill
Weir
ROAD
HOSPITAL APP.
Broomfield
THE MILLAR
THE WINDMILLS
CONSTANCE CL.
NASH DR.
COURT
MANDEVILLE
AYLETTS
WARREN CL.
Butler's Farm
Sheepcotes Wood
Stonage Wood
Titelands Spring
Sheepcotes Cottage
LANE
Sheepcotes Farm
Shuttleworth Farm
LEIGHS RD.
CRANHAM RD.
Wheeler's Farm
WHEELER'S HILL
Power's Farm
THE REGIMENT WAY GOLF CENTRE
Club House
PRATTS FARM LANE
Pratt's Farm
Pratt's Cottages
Little Belstead's Farm
PRATTS FARM LANE
BACK LANE
Blenheim Cottage
Quagmire
Sand & Gravel Pit
CHANNELS GOLF COURSE
Belsteads
Club Ho.
Newland Grove Nature Reserve
BELSTEADS FARM
Sports Field

56
23
33
71
Langleys Farm
Maple View
Howletts Hall
Woodhall Farm
Playing Field
Hall
Gray's Farm
Greenfields
Woodside
Bushy Wood
Chignal Hall Chase Cottages
CHIGNAL HALL RD.
Chignal Hall
Stevens Farm
Chignall St. James
Hardoak
MASHBURY
Nurseries
THE GREEN
Broomwood Lodge
Broom Wood
Beaumont Otes
Sand & Gravel Pit
Chobbing's Farm
HOLLOW
Brittons Hall Farm
Brittons
The Blue House
CM1
River Can
Brickbarns Cottages
Pengymill
Brickbarns Farm
CHIGNALL ROAD
Superstore
Comm. Cen.
College Wood
Melbourne Park
Playing Field
School
Reed's Spring
River Can
New Barns
Roxwell Brook
ROXWELL
Two Bridge
Warren Cottages
Warren House
One Bridge
A1060
Reservoir
The Hickerage
Thieves' Corner
Cattle Breeding Centre
Manor Cottage
Manor House
Warren Cotts.
The Orchards
OLD ROXWELL ROAD
Cader Idris
Whitesmiths
Stradella
Reeds Farm
Warren Farm
Sports Ground
Reeds Cottage
Orchard House
Warren Bridge
WATERING LANE
Ten. Cts.
Writtle College
RIVER CAN
Weir
West
Sturgeons Farm
Spinney House
FOX BURROWS LANE
Pavilion
Sports Ground
Sturgeons Cottages
Lordship Farm
Tennis Courts
LAWFORD LANE
Moat
Reservoir
Writtle College
Barn
COW
VICTORIA
Daws Farm
WRITTLE
Hassenbrook
Great Oxney Green
BACK ROAD
Recreation Ground
Lib.
ST. JOHN'S RD.
Writtle Bridge
Writtle Grn.
Aubyns
Skeggs Farm
Mill Mound
Mill House
Hylands School
GREEN
BRIDGE ST

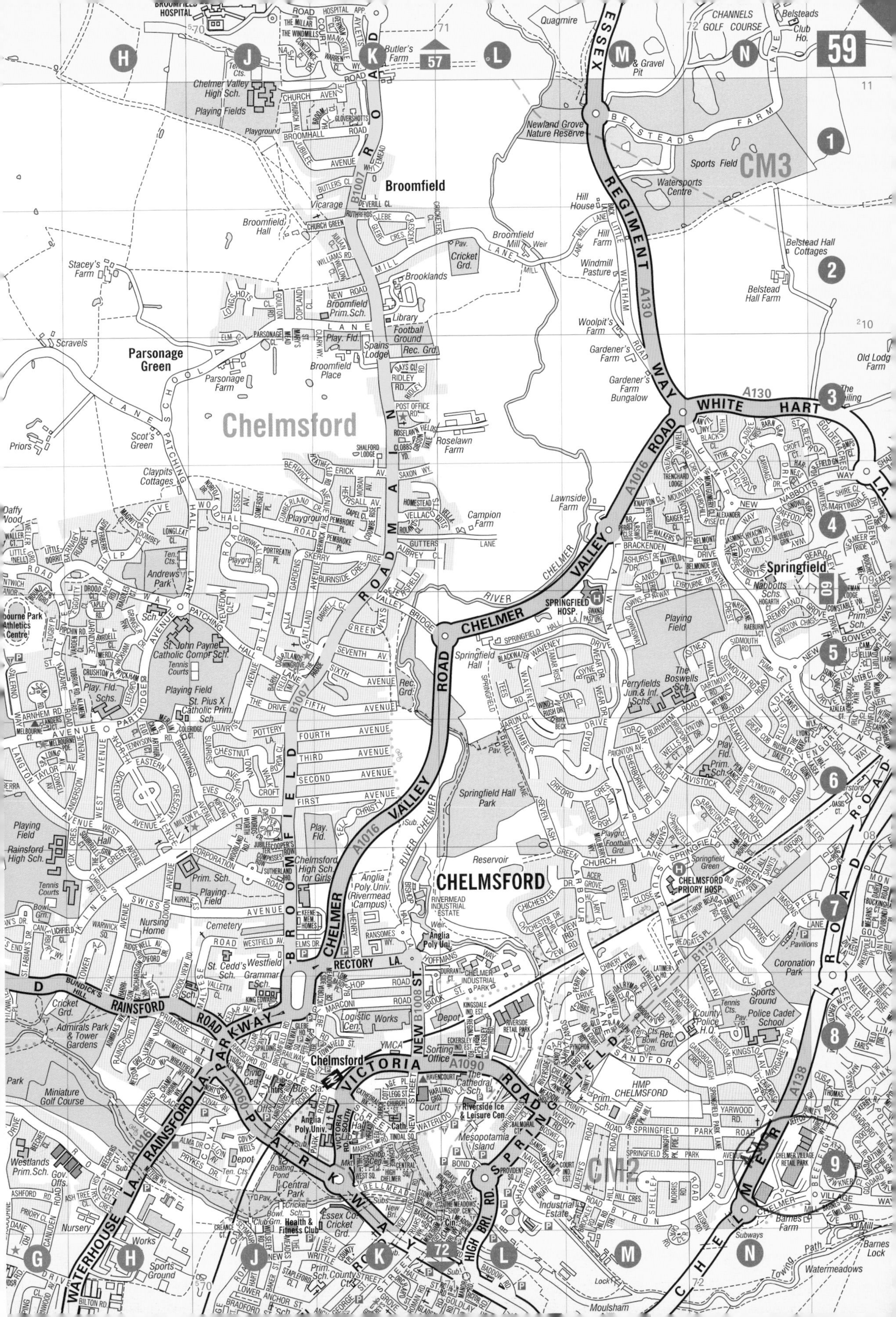
Broomfield Hospital
Chelmer Valley High Sch.
Playing Fields
Butler's Farm
57
Quagmire
ESSEX REGIMENT WAY
Sand & Gravel Pit
CHANNELS GOLF COURSE
Belsteads Club Ho.
Newland Grove Nature Reserve
BELSTEADS FARM
Sports Field
CM3
Watersports Centre
Broomfield
Vicarage
Broomfield Hall
CHURCH GREEN
Hill House
Hill Farm
Broomfield Mill
Weir
Belstead Hall Cottages
Belstead Hall Farm
Stacey's Farm
Cricket Grd.
Brooklands
Windmill Pasture
MILL LANE
Broomfield Prim.Sch.
Library
Football Ground
Rec. Grd.
Play. Fld.
Spains Lodge
Broomfield Place
Woolpit's Farm
Gardener's Farm
Gardener's Farm Bungalow
Old Lodge Farm
Scravels
Parsonage Green
Parsonage Farm
SCHOOL LANE
PATCHING LANE
Scot's Green
Priors
Chelmsford
Roselawn Farm
WHITE HART
A130
A1016
Claypits Cottages
Campion Farm
Lawnside Farm
Daffy Wood
Andrews Park
Springfield
Nabbotts Schs.
Melbourne Park Athletics Centre
St. John Payne Catholic Comp. Sch.
Tennis Courts
Playing Field
St. Pius X Catholic Prim. Sch.
Play. Fld. Schs.
SPRINGFIELD HOSP.
Springfield Hall
Playing Field
The Boswells Sch.
Perryfields Jun.& Inf. Schs.
CHELMER VALLEY ROAD
RIVER CHELMER
Rec. Grd.
Springfield Hall Park
Play. Fld. Prim. Sch.
Playing Field
Rainsford High Sch.
Tennis Courts
Bowl. Grn.
Prim. Sch.
Playing Field
Nursing Home
Cemetery
Chelmsford High Sch. for Girls
Anglia Poly.Univ. (Rivermead Campus)
RIVERMEAD INDUSTRIAL ESTATE
Reservoir
CHELMSFORD
Springfield Green
CHELMSFORD PRIORY HOSP.
Pavilions
Coronation Park
St. Cedd's Sch.
Westfield Grammar Sch.
Anglia Poly.Univ.
CHELMER INDUSTRIAL PARK
RAINSFORD ROAD
PARKWAY
Cricket Grd.
Admirals Park & Tower Gardens
Logistic Cen.
Works
Depot
RIVERSIDE RETAIL PARK
Sports Ground
Police Cadet School
County Police H.Q.
Rec. Grd.
YMCA
Sorting Office
VICTORIA ROAD
A1090
Chelmsford
Bus Sta.
Civic Cen.
The Cathedral Sch.
Riverside Ice & Leisure Cen.
HMP CHELMSFORD
Prim. Sch.
Miniature Golf Course
Park
Anglia Poly.Univ.
Cath.
Mesopotamia Island
Westlands Prim.Sch.
Gov. Offs.
Depot
Boating Pond
Central Park
CM2
Industrial Estate
CHELMER VILLAGE RETAIL PARK
Barnes Farm
Barnes Lock
Mill
Nursery
Works
Sports Ground
Health & Fitness Club
Essex Co. Cricket Grd.
Prim. Sch.
County Ct.
72
Subways
Towing Path
Watermeadows
Lock
Moulsham
WATERHOUSE LA.
RAINSFORD LA.
A1060
PARKWAY
HIGH BRI. RD.
SPRINGFIELD ROAD
CHELMER ROAD
A138
A1137
B1007
B1008
B1137
BROOMFIELD ROAD
MAIN ROAD
NEW ST.
H J K L M N
G H J K L M N
1 2 3 4 5 6 7 8 9
60
11
10
09
08
07
70
71
72

CHANNELS GOLF COURSE
Sports Field
Belstead Hall Cottages
Belstead Hall Farm
Park Farm Cottage
Walter Hall
Rose Cottage
New Hall Farm
Fish Pond
New Hall Sch.
Riding School
Wilderness
Orchard Cotts.
Lodge
Burial Ground
Old Lodge Farm
The Sheiling
Bulls Lodge Cottages
Bulls Lodge
Bulls Lodge Dairy
The Grove
Brick House Farm
Lionfield Cottages
Millmead Cotts.
Tyrell Cottage
Genfield
South Barn Nurseries
WHITE HART LANE
CM1
Springfield
Gate House
Service Area
Car Auctions
Superstore
Junction 19
BOREHAM INTERCHANGE
Boreham House
Boreham Hall
Boreham Hall Cottages
COLCHESTER ROAD
Sorting Office
White Hart Cottages
Sheepcotes
Warehouse
Chelmsford
Chelmer & Blackwater Navigation
Stonham's Lock
CM2
Dairy Farm Cotts.
Cuton Hall
DUKES PARK INDUSTRIAL ESTATE
Chelmer Village
Pavilions
Coronation Park
Sports Ground
Police Cadet School
Barnes Farm Jun. & Inf. Schs.
Superstore
Brookend
Cuton Lock
Weir
Reservoir
Phillow's Farm
Whitwell's Farm
Phillow's Farm Cottages
Hammond's Cottages
Hammond's Farm
HURREL
Storms Way
Sewage Works
Pease Hall
Reservoir
Prentice's Farm
Barnes Farm
Subways
Towing Path
Watermeadows
RIVER CHELMER
Chelmer & Blackwater Navigation
Sandford Lock
Sandford Mill Bridge
Rumbold's Farm
Rumbold's
Sandon Brook
GRACE'S
A12
A130
A138
B1137

INSET
Hatfield Peverel
HATFIELD PEVEREL INTERCHANGE (NORTH)
HATFIELD PEVEREL INTERCHANGE (SOUTH)
Junc. 20a
Junc. 20b
A12
B1137
B1019
THE STREET
MALDON ROAD
HATFIELD PEVEREL
Chelmsford CM3
BOREHAM
Hatfield Peverel Green
Strutt Memorial Recreation Ground
Inf. & Jun. Schs.
Crabb's Hill Farm
Stratford House
Cricket Ground
Shepherds Cottage
Hatfield Peverel Lodge
Sewage Works
Crabb's Bridge
Round Wood
Brewhouse Wood
Bishop's Wood
Sandpit Wood
Long Wood
Gauging Weir
The Priory
Priory Farm
Nounsley
Barnards & Gate Farm
Bridge Farm
Middlefield
Jenkins Farm
Reservoir
Reservoirs
Bovingtons Farm
Ivy Barn Cottages
Ivy Barn Farm
Langlea
Annerlea Cottage
Burial Ground
Mowden Hall
Fairfield House
Chase Cottages
Fairfields Farm
Bridgefields
SPORTSMANS LANE
NOUNSLEY ROAD
ULTING ROAD
Titbeech House
The Grove
Church Hills
Hatfield Bury Farm
Hatfield Bury
Mortiers
Depots
Hatfield Bridge
Hatfield Place
Benning Hall
Mathcot
Nursery
Roselea
Culvert's Cottages
Old Hall
Mulberries
Res.
LITTLE BADDOW
CM3
Coleraines
Vica Cottages
Chelmer Cottage
Tofts Lodge
Tofts
Walter's Cottage
The Return
Warren Farm
Bassett's Wood
Scrub Wood
Hollybred Wood
Poultry Houses
Holybreds Farm
Little Baddow Hall
Little Baddow Hall Farm
Little Baddow Mill House
Little Baddow Lock
Willow Shade
Puddocks Tail
The Hoppet
The Forge
Cuckoos
Chestnut Cott.
Broomhill
Jimmy's Field
May Cotts.
Bright House
Three Gables
Rectory Wood Cottage
The Hornets Nest
Robjohns Fld.
Heather Hills
The Warren
Pillow Mound
The Rodney
Froggs Hall
Berries
Herons
Pyne Cottage
Gibbs
Duke's Orchard
Ollands
Lordlands
The Bungalow
Burghfields Farm
Admirals
Poultry Ho.
Wood Ways
Sparrows
Rec.
Belle Vue Farm
Elm Green Preparatory Sch.
Little Bowers
Cortina
Mushroom Farm
Dunromin
Rec. Grd.
Birkenshaw
Oaklands
Pheasanthouse Farm
Birch Wood
Blakeswood Hill
Openways
Knole Cottage
Long Wood
Old Riffhams
Longwood Chase
Blakes Wood Nature Reserve
Cherrytree Cott.
Pheasanthouse Wood Nature Reserve
Water Hall
Waterhall Meadows Nature Reserve
Long Spring Wood
New Lodge
Great Graces Farm
Little Graces Farm
Good Graces
Chase Cottages
Jays Glen
The White House
Dolphins
Fuzzy Chats
Willowfield
Firtree Wood
Poor's Piece Nature Reserve
Riffhams
MALDON
CHELMSFORD
HOLYBREAD ROAD
COLAM LANE
SPRING ELMS LANE
THE RIDGE
CHAPEL LANE
NEW LODGE CHASE
GRACES LANE
RIFFHAMS LANE
FIR TREE LANE
POSTMAN'S LANE
COMMON LANE
PARSONAGE LANE
MILL LANE
NORTH HILL
TOFTS CHASE
RYSLEY
HIGH PASTURE
THE RYE FIELD
OAKLANDS WAY
24
25
34
74
H J K L M N G

BROXBOURNE
Lee Valley Leisure Pool
Keysers Estate
Boating Lake
Works
Nurseries
NAZEING NEW ROAD
LEE VALLEY PARK
Broxbourne
HILLGROVE BUSINESS PARK
Marshgate Fm.
Pumping Station
NAZEING ROAD
B194
LOWER NAZEING
Sports Ground
SHOOTERS DRIVE
WESTERN ROAD
Brook Farm
Spinny Nursery
Stonyfield Nursery
Nazing Prim. Sch.
Mansion Ho. Fm.
Mulberries
Ninnings
Old House Farm
PERRY HILL
Perry Hill Farm
Sewage Works
Flood Relief Channel
Nurseries
Clayton Hall Country Park
Paynes Farm
Nursery
Clayton Hill
EN10
Nazeing Marsh
BROXBOURNE
EPPING FOREST
King's Weir
SLIPE LANE
Sand & Gravel Pit
PAYNES LANE
ST. LEONARDS ROAD
LAUNDRY
Waltham Abbey
EN9
Netherkidders Farm
The New House
CEMETERY LANE
St. Lawrence Farm
Lee Valley Regional Park
Towing Path
Lock
Sailing Club
Weir
COLEMAN'S LANE
Coleman's Shaw
LOUGHALL LANE
Holyfield Hall Farm
WALTHAM
Denver Lodge Farm
Marsh Hill House
MARSH HILL
Holyfield Marsh
Electricity Transformer Station
Greenview
Galley Hill
GALLEYHILL WOOD
RIVER LEE NAVIGATION
Breaker's Yard
Gate Cottages
Hayes Hill Farm
Hayes Hill
Hayes Hill Cottages
Works
Seventy Acres
Broadgate Springs
Galley Wood House
Aimes Green
CLAVERHAMBURY ROAD
Nursery
Stubbings Cottages
Woodside
HOLYFIELD
North Lodge Farm
Grubb's Hill
PUCK LANE
RIVER LEE COUNTRY PARK
Holy Field
Homefield Wood
Monkhams Cottage
Aimesgreen Farm
Sluice
FISHERS GREEN LA.
Fishers Green
Holyfield Farm
Monkhams Hall
Stable Lodge
CROOKED MILE
Turnershill Marsh
Hooks Marsh
Hooksmarsh Ditch
Kennel Wood
CLAYGATE LANE
MONKHAMS
Eagle Lodge
Poultry Farm
BREACH
GALLEY HILL
Dallance Farm
LONG WALK
Lock
Sluice
Powdermill
Hall Marsh
Nursery
Arboretum
Brook
A B C D E F G
1 2 3 4 5 6 7 8 9
37 38 39 540
06 05 04 03 02
52 30 76

Jack's Hatch
Harknett's Gate Nursery
Church Farm
Oakley Hall
Prospect Nursery
Coronation Nursery
Rookswood
Brewitt's Farm
Harknett's Gate
Cricket Ground
Nazeing
Little Canons Farm
White's Wood
Burleigh Nursery
Oakbridge Nursery
Nazeing Brook
Lodge Farm
Little Canons Cottages
NAZEING GOLF COURSE
NAZEINGWOOD COMMON
West View
Summers Farm
Curtis Farm
Convalescent Home
Nursery
The Old Farm
Epping Green House
Epping Green
Club House
Belchers Farm
Bumble's Green
Nazeing Gate
Sturtsbury Farm
Epping Long Green
Epping Upland C.of.E Prim Sch.
Mamelons Farm
Rec. Ground
Copy Wood
Vicarage
Beverley Pig Farm
Nazeing Long Green
Epping
Hunter's Hall Farm
Great Riddens Pond
Longfield Shaw
Harold's Park Farm
CM16
Nabhill Grove
Hunter's Hall Cottages
Galleyhill Green
The Springs
Parvills
Gills
Orange Wood
DEERPARK WOOD
Ballhill Wood
Gills Farm
The Manor House
Claverhambury
Orange Peel
Orange Field Plantation
Sewage Works
Woodyers Farm
Piggery
Reevesgate Farm
Gills Plantation
Longcroft Grove
Stocking Grove
Cobbin's Brook
Scatterbushes Wood
Shooting Lodge
Cobbinsend Farm
Maynards Farm
Spratt's Hedgerow Wood
Spratt's Hedgerow
Maple Springs
Playground
BREACH BARNS MOBILE HOME PARK
Playing Field
Pond Field Plantation
Fernhall Farm
Fernhall Wood
Little Rookery Wood
Rookery Wood
Nursery
Willows
Brookmeadow Wood
Fitches Plantation
Newhouse Farm
Obelisk
Nicholls Farm
Lodge Farm
Home Farm
Cobbin
53
64
77
G H J K L M N
1 2 3 4 5 6 7 8 9
41 42 43
02 03 04 05 06

Jack's Hatch
Scout Training Camp
Crematorium & Cemetery
Hospital Wood
CM19
Little Canons Farm
HARLOW
EPPING FOREST
Long Green
Severs Green
Gibbon's Bush Farm
Little Canons Cottages
Little Marles Farm
West View
Epping Long Green
Water Tower
Rye Hill Reservoir (covered)
Resr. (covered)
RYE HILL COMMON
Moat
Rye Hill
Latton Priory Farm
Rivetts Farm
CM18
RYE HILL ROAD
Marles Farm
Summers Farm
Marles Farm Cottages
The Old Farm
Epping Green
Shingle Hall
Hill Farm
Orchard Farm
Rose Farm
Sewage Works
Cobbin's Brook
Epping Upland C.of.E Prim Sch.
Vicarage
Hayleys Manor Farm
Crabbs Green House
Currance Cottages
Currance House
Pinch Timber Farm Cottages
Pinch Timber Farm
Hayleys Manor Farm Cottages
Epping Upland
EPPING UPLAND
Chambers Manor Cotts.
War Memorial
Walton
Moat
Takeleys
Piggery
Chambers Manor Farm
Epping CM16
Hunter's Hall Cottages
Gills
Orange Wood
Cobbin's Bridge
Gills Farm
Sewage Wks.
Orange Peel
Orange Field Plantation
LINDSEY ST
Wintry Wood
Wintry Park Farm
Bury Farm
Lindsey Street Farm
Shaftesbury Farm
Electricity Sub Station
Rec. Grd.
Hall
Shooting Lodge
Pond Field Plantation
Jenkins's Plantation
Epping Infants Sch.
Council Offs.
Scout Hall
The Thatch Cottage
Rec. Grd.
Little Rookery Wood
Tennis Courts
St. John's C. of E. Sch.
Epping Jun. Sch.
Lib.
Fitches Plantation
Cemetery
Sports Grd.
Spts. Grd.
Spts. Cen.
EPPING
Wood House
Paris Hall
New Farm
EPPING ROAD
BURY LANE
HIGH STREET
PALMERS HILL
B181
B182
B1393

54
63
78

Harlow
CM17
Thornwood
THORNWOOD COMMON
NORTH WEALD AIRFIELD
Wealdgullet
NORTH WEALD BASSETT
COOPERSALE
COOPERSALE STREET
Colliers Hatch
M11 MOTORWAY
CANES LANE
A414
NORTH WEALD GOLF COURSE
Club House
Delved Bridge
Cripsey Brook
Weald Hall
Wealdhall Coppice
Weald Hall Farm
Moat
HALL LANE
Golf Driving Range
Sewage Works
Depot
Tanks
Rifle Range
RAYLEY LA.
VICARAGE LANE
Nursery
Chase Farm
New House Farm
Thornwood Common
Weald Place
Esgors
LONDON ROAD
B1393
HIGH ROAD
Rundells
Canes Cottages
Canes
Canes Wood
Tawneys
The Herb Farm
Seed Mill
Cross Keys
WINTRY WOOD
STUMP ROAD
The Lower Forest
The Lake
Epping Plain
EPPING PLAIN
Brickfield Cottages
Park Place
Toll House
The Poplars
B181
Club House
NORTH WEALD VILLAGE PAR 3
ROUGHTALLEY'S WOOD
Forest Cottage
Timber Yard
Gernon Bushes Nature Reserve
Cricket Ground
Coopersale & Theydon Garnon C.E. Prim. Sch.
ST. MARGARET'S HOSPITAL
Ansons Farm
Coopersale Cottage
Coopersale Farm
Coopersale House
Posternlane Spring
Hawkshill Wood
Redyn's Wood
BIRCHING COPPICE
MOUNT WOOD
High Wood
Ongar Park Wood
Mount Wood Cottage
Forty Acres
Ongar Down
Mount Quarter
GRAVELPIT WOOD
Carisbrooke Farm
Cold Hall Farm
Old House
Moat House
Tawney Hatch
Fyrth Tawney
Mount Farm
ROMAN ROAD
EPPING ROAD
Bowling Green
GAYNES PARK ESTATE
55
79
99

Weald Bridge
Weald Bridge Cottage
Bridge House
Depot
Moat
Ashlyns
Bovinger Lodge
Bowlers Green
Ashlyns Cottages
Candelab Farm
NORTH WEALD GOLF COURSE
Wyldingtree Farm
Piggery
Great Notts
Hobban's Farm
Nursery
Hall Wood
Slough House Farm
New House Farm
Nursery
Bovinger
Sayers Farm
Nursery
Reynkyns Wood
Bantham & Ongar Bowls Club
Tyler's Green
Spinney Lodge
Silver Wings
Lower Bobbingworth Green
A414
HIGH RD.
EPPING
Playing Field
St. Andrew's C.of E. Prim. School
Tyler's Farm
Comm. Cen.
Telephone Exchange
MARCONI BUNGALOWS
Chase Farm
Epping
Sewage Works
THORNBROOK
Waterloo Bridge
Skips Corner
Dewley Wood
B181
CM16
Kerr's Cottages
Keeper's Cottage
NORTH WEALD BASSETT
Bowling Green
Perrills
Springbank
Ongar Radio Station
Miller's Grove
Hall
The Cottage
Ongar Park Hall
Dolman's Spring
Greensted House
Ongar Park Lodge
Little Thorbens
Greensted Green
Cold Hall Farm
Hardings Farm
Greensted Wood
Wood
Clunes House
Wealds Farm
TOOT HILL
Ongar Park Wood
Hall
Widow's Farm
Steers Farm
Does Farm
Four Winds
Clatterford End
High Tawney
Old House
Freemans Farm
Newhouse
Tawney Hatch
Moat House
Play. Fld.
Burrows Farm
Colliers Hatch
Club House
Gladdens
Fyrth Tawney
Mount Farm
TOOTHILL

32
65
80

H
J
K
32
L
M
200
N
54
55
56
New Farm
NEWHOUSE LA.
MORETON BRIDGE ROAD
MORETON
Cripsey Brook
Cross Lees Farm
Sports Ground
ABBEY CL.
FOREST DRIVE
ELMBRIDGE HALL
ROAD
1
Upper Herons
HERONS LANE
06
Herons Farm
Moat
2
Wood Farm
Bundish Spring
Bundish Hall
Bundish Hall Cottages
Moat
Bobbingworth
GAINSTHORPE
LANE
Bovinger Hall
Rectory
Round Spring
Fairview
ONGAR ROAD
B184
Folyats
Folyats Cottages
3
Long Walk
Blake Hall War Museum & Blake Hall Gardens
Shelley Common
Tumulus
Shelley
CHURCH
Hall
CHURCH LA. COTTS
Research Station
Little Forest Hall Cottage
05
Bott's Cottages
Boarded Barns Farm
Lodge
STONY LANE
A414
The Warren
4
Bridge Farm
Clark's Spring
West Lodge
Ongar
CM5
Shelley Bridge
Lodge
Bilsdens Cottages
Water End Farm
Bilsdens
BROOKFIELDS
ROAD
ONGAR WAR MEM. HOSP.
ABIGAIL CT.
COLES
FINCH CT.
Bowl. Gn.
Pav.
Ongar Leisure Centre
68
River Roding
5
Forest Lodge
Cripsey Brook
CRIPSEY AVENUE
SHORTLANDS AV.
QUEENSWAY
Playgrd.
ST. PETER'S
SHELLEY CL.
QUEENSWAY
HERON CT.
CLARE MS.
ONGAR ENTERPRISE CENTRE
FYFIELD
Shelley Prim. Sch.
SPRINGFIELD CL.
AUKINGFORD GRN.
ORCHARD END
Depot
The Wantz Farm
Weir
HIGH ONGAR ROAD
High Ongar Bridge
04
LANE
The Rosary
ROAD
Ackingford Bridge
THE FOUR WANTZ
HIGH ONGAR RD.
A414
CHELMSFORD ROAD
Mulberry Ho.
GREAT STONY PARK
THE PAVILIONS
THE GREAT LAWN
Education Centre
THE STREET
6
PENSON'S LANE
MARK'S AV.
BOWES DRIVE
MAYFLOWER
THE JOHNS
WAY
RODING GDS.
High Ongar Prim. Sch.
HIGH ONGAR
MILL GRO.
Village Hall
New Barns Cottages
HIGH STREET
A128
CHURCHILL
ONSLOW
Club House
Pav.
Rec. Grd.
Playing Field
LOVE LA.
Clatterford End
Clatterford Bridge
FRANK BRETTON HOUSE
BANSONS WY.
Hall
SHAKLETONS
MILLFIELD
7
Ongar Wood
BANSON'S CT.
Lib.
BANSON'S YD.
Health Cen.
BANSON'S LA.
Ongar Castle (site of)
Castle Farm
Greensted Hall
The Avenue
Westlands
03
Hall Farm
Greensted Church
East Lodge
Superstore
Greensted
CHURCH LA.
ST. MARTINS
CASTLE ST.
CHIPPING ONGAR
Draper's Corner
GREENSTED ROAD
FAIRBANK CL.
MILLBANK AV.
GLEBE RD.
FAIRFIELD ROAD
RODNEY RD.
Rectory
Greensted Croft
Ongar Bridge
STANLEY PL.
BUSHEY LEA
CROSSBOW CL.
Cripsey Brook
River Roding
8
Lodge Farm
TURNERS CL.
COOPERS HILL
LONG FIELDS
Chipping Ongar Primary School
WOODLAND WAY
GREEN WLK.
PARK LAND
LANDVIEW GDS.
CLOVERLEY ROAD
THE ELMS
CLIFTON
MARDEN ASH
Works
MILL LANE
EPPING FOREST
BRENTWOOD
Newhouse Farm
ST. JAMES' AV.
KETTLEBURY WAY
A128
BRENTWOOD
STONDON ROAD
ONGAR ROAD
9
Hallsford Farm House
Clay Pit
A113
STANFORD RIVERS RD.
HUNTERS CHASE
02
Kettlebury Spring
G
H
J
K
81
L
M
N
54
55
56
HALLSFORD BRIDGE INDUSTRIAL ESTATE
Gray's Farm
ROAD

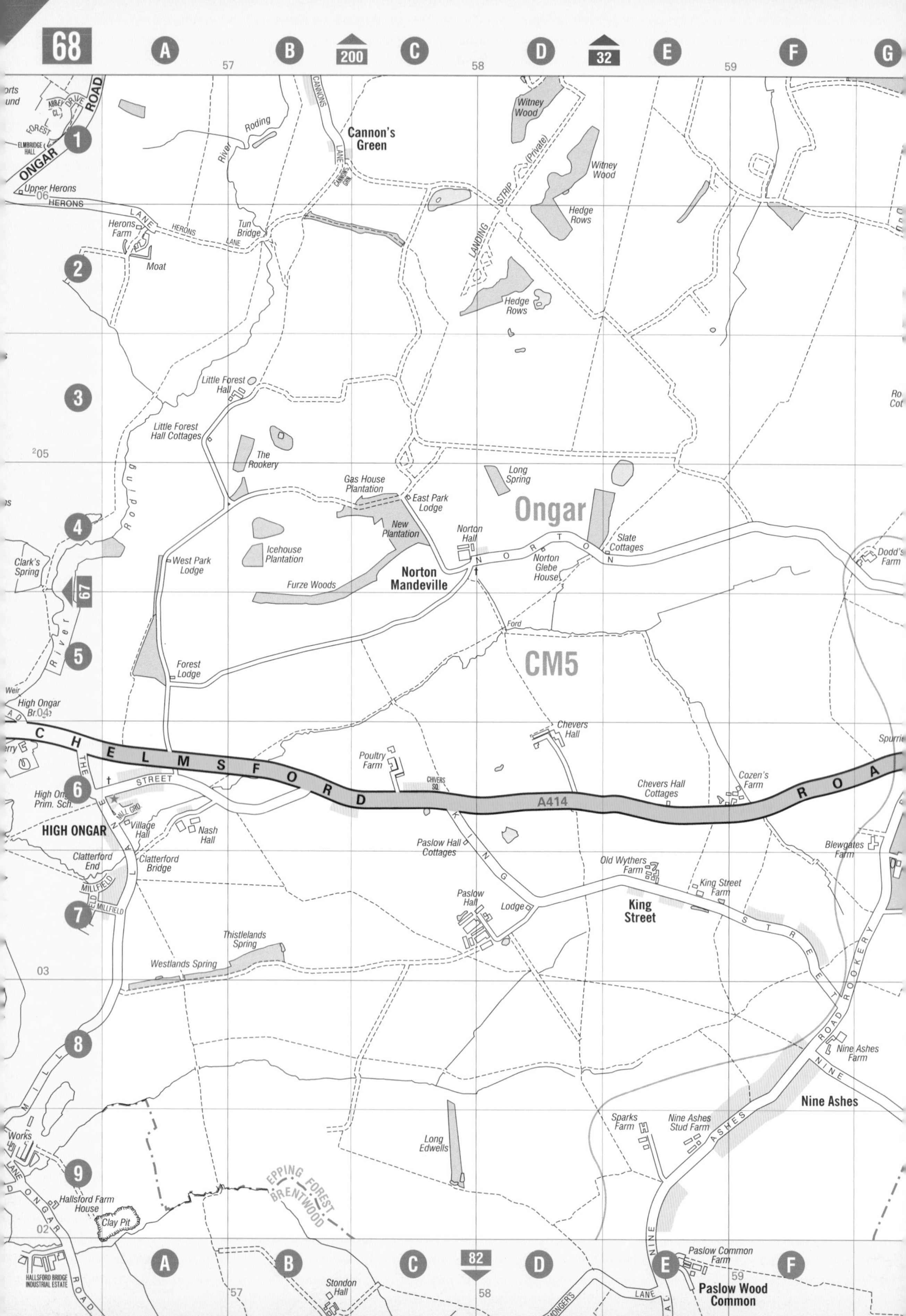
A
B
200
C
D
32
E
F
G
57
58
59
Cannon's Green
Witney Wood
Witney Wood
Hedge Rows
Hedge Rows
Upper Herons
Herons Farm
Moat
Tun Bridge
Little Forest Hall
Little Forest Hall Cottages
The Rookery
Gas House Plantation
East Park Lodge
Long Spring
Ongar
New Plantation
Norton Hall
Slate Cottages
Norton Glebe House
Dodd's Farm
West Park Lodge
Icehouse Plantation
Furze Woods
Norton Mandeville
Clark's Spring
Ford
Forest Lodge
CM5
Weir
High Ongar Br.
Chevers Hall
C H E L M S F O R D R O A D
A414
Poultry Farm
Cozen's Farm
Chevers Hall Cottages
High Ongar Prim. Sch.
HIGH ONGAR
Village Hall
Nash Hall
Paslow Hall Cottages
Blewgates Farm
Clatterford End
Clatterford Bridge
Old Wythers Farm
King Street Farm
Paslow Hall
Lodge
King Street
Thistlelands Spring
Westlands Spring
Nine Ashes Farm
Nine Ashes
Sparks Farm
Nine Ashes Stud Farm
Long Edwells
Works
EPPING FOREST
BRENTWOOD
Hallsford Farm House
Clay Pit
HALLSFORD BRIDGE INDUSTRIAL ESTATE
Stondon Hall
82
Paslow Common Farm
Paslow Wood Common
67
1
2
3
4
5
6
7
8
9
06
05
04
03
02

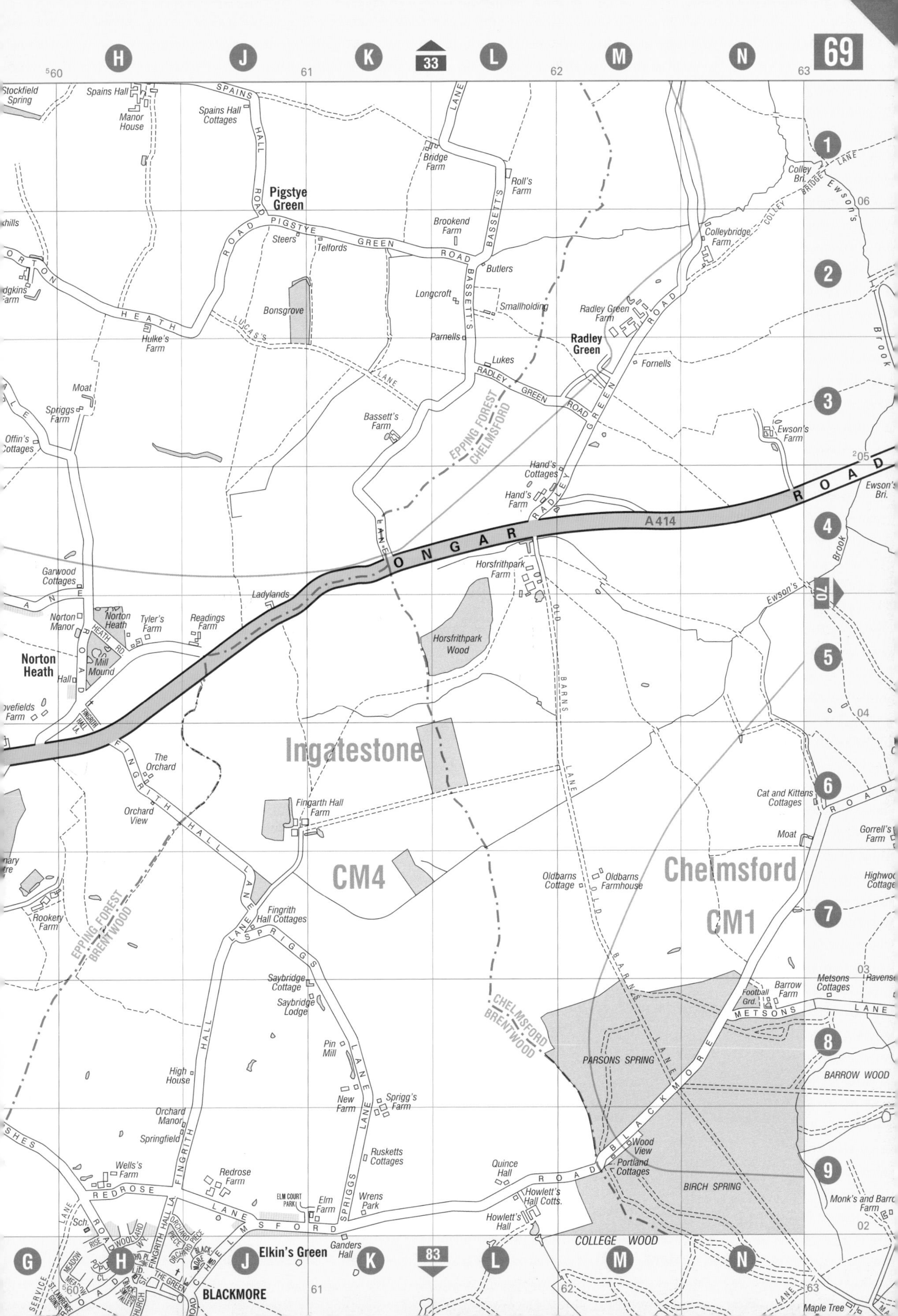
H
J
K
33
L
M
N
Spains Hall
Manor House
Spains Hall Cottages
Pigstye Green
Bridge Farm
Roll's Farm
Brookend Farm
Steers
Telfords
Butlers
Longcroft
Smallholding
Bonsgrove
Hulke's Farm
Parnells
Lukes
Radley Green Farm
Radley Green
Fornells
Colley Bri.
Colleybridge Farm
Moat
Spriggs Farm
Offin's Cottages
Bassett's Farm
Ewson's Farm
Hand's Cottages
Hand's Farm
Ewson's Bri.
ONGAR ROAD
A414
Garwood Cottages
Norton Manor
Norton Heath
Tyler's Farm
Readings Farm
Ladylands
Horsfrithpark Farm
Horsfrithpark Wood
Mill Mound
Hall
Ingatestone
The Orchard
Orchard View
Fingarth Hall Farm
CM4
Chelmsford
CM1
Cat and Kittens Cottages
Moat
Gorrell's Farm
Oldbarns Cottage
Oldbarns Farmhouse
Rookery Farm
Fingrith Hall Cottages
EPPING FOREST
BRENTWOOD
CHELMSFORD
Saybridge Cottage
Saybridge Lodge
Pin Mill
Football Grd.
Barrow Farm
Metsons Cottages
PARSONS SPRING
BARROW WOOD
High House
New Farm
Sprigg's Farm
Orchard Manor
Springfield
Rusketts Cottages
Quince Hall
Wood View
Portland Cottages
BIRCH SPRING
Monk's and Barrow Farm
Wells's Farm
Redrose Farm
Elm Farm
Wrens Park
Howlett's Hall Cotts.
Howlett's Hall
Elkin's Green
Ganders Hall
COLLEGE WOOD
BLACKMORE
Maple Tree
SPAINS HALL ROAD
PIGSTYE GREEN ROAD
BASSETT'S LANE
NORTON HEATH ROAD
LUCAS'S LANE
RADLEY GREEN ROAD
FINGRITH HALL LANE
SPRIGGS LANE
OLD BARNS LANE
BLACKMORE ROAD
METSONS LANE
REDROSE LANE
CHELMSFORD ROAD
G
83
1
2
3
4
5
6
7
8
9
70

A
B
C
D
E
F
G
33
84
69
63
64
565
66
06
205
04
03
02
1
2
3
4
5
6
7
8
9
Blow's Farm
Moor Hall
Moat
Sand & Gravel Pit
Sand & Gravel Pit
CHAPEL LA
LANE
BRIDGE
Colley Bri.
EWSON'S
COLLEY
olleybridge Farm
Star House
Cooksmill Green
Armswick
Wellington House
Home Farm
Cooksmill Nursery
Bush House
Range Cottage
Grove House
Prospect Cottages
Little Oxney Gree
Red House
Reservoir
Longfield
Whitehaven
Depot
Little Moor Hall
Ladygrove
Ingatestone
Brainwood Farm
Landview House
Lady Grove
CM4
Ewson's Farm
ONGAR ROAD
A414
Hawkin Smith's Farm
WYSE'S
ROAD
Lee Cottages
THE CAUSEWAY
Ewson's Bri.
Brook
Ewson's
Lee Farm
Lee Wood
Phillips Farm
Bramwood Farm
Argents Nurseries
CM1
Vicarage
HIGHWOOD ROAD
Playing Field
Montague Farm
Depot
Edney Common
Woodside Cottages
NATHAN'S
Fithlers Hall Farm
Highwood
SPARROWS CL
Writtle Park Cottages
Jordan's Farm
Moat
Moat
Ward's Farm
Loves Green
Franklin's Island
Moat
Wards Cottage
Highwood Prim. Sch.
BUCKNELLS MEAD
Playing Field
Little Edney Wood
Writtle Park Farm
Cat and Kittens Cottages
Depot
The Forge
Gorrell's Farm
Awes Farm
INGATESTONE
Great Edney Wood
Moat
Writtle Park House
POOL'S LANE
Roseville
Highwood Cottages
Mayfield House
BLACKMORE
Baker's Wood
CHALK HILL
WRITTLE DEER PARK
Coptfold Hall
Football Grd.
Barrow Farm
Metsons Cottages
Ravenscraig
COCK LANE
COCK LA
Writtlepark Wood
COPTFOLD
METSONS LANE
The Entire Farm
ELLIS WOOD
Hockley Shaw
Furness Wood
Bosmore Wood
Budds Farm
BARROW WOOD
Furness Farm
Finches Spring
HALL
Highwood Cottage
High Woods
Parkponds Wood
Keeper's Cottage
Redindyke Farm
Coppice Wood
Chatterbox Wood
IVY BARN LANE
Wells and Sheds
James's Spring
BIRCH SPRING
Poultry Houses
Whitegates
DRIVE
Monk's and Barrow's Farm
CHELMSFORD
BRENTWOOD
BARN
CM4
Deerslade Wood
Handley Green Farm
Dawes Farm
Handley Green
Long Meadow
Stoneymere Wood
Well Wood
Box Wood
Maple Tree
LANE

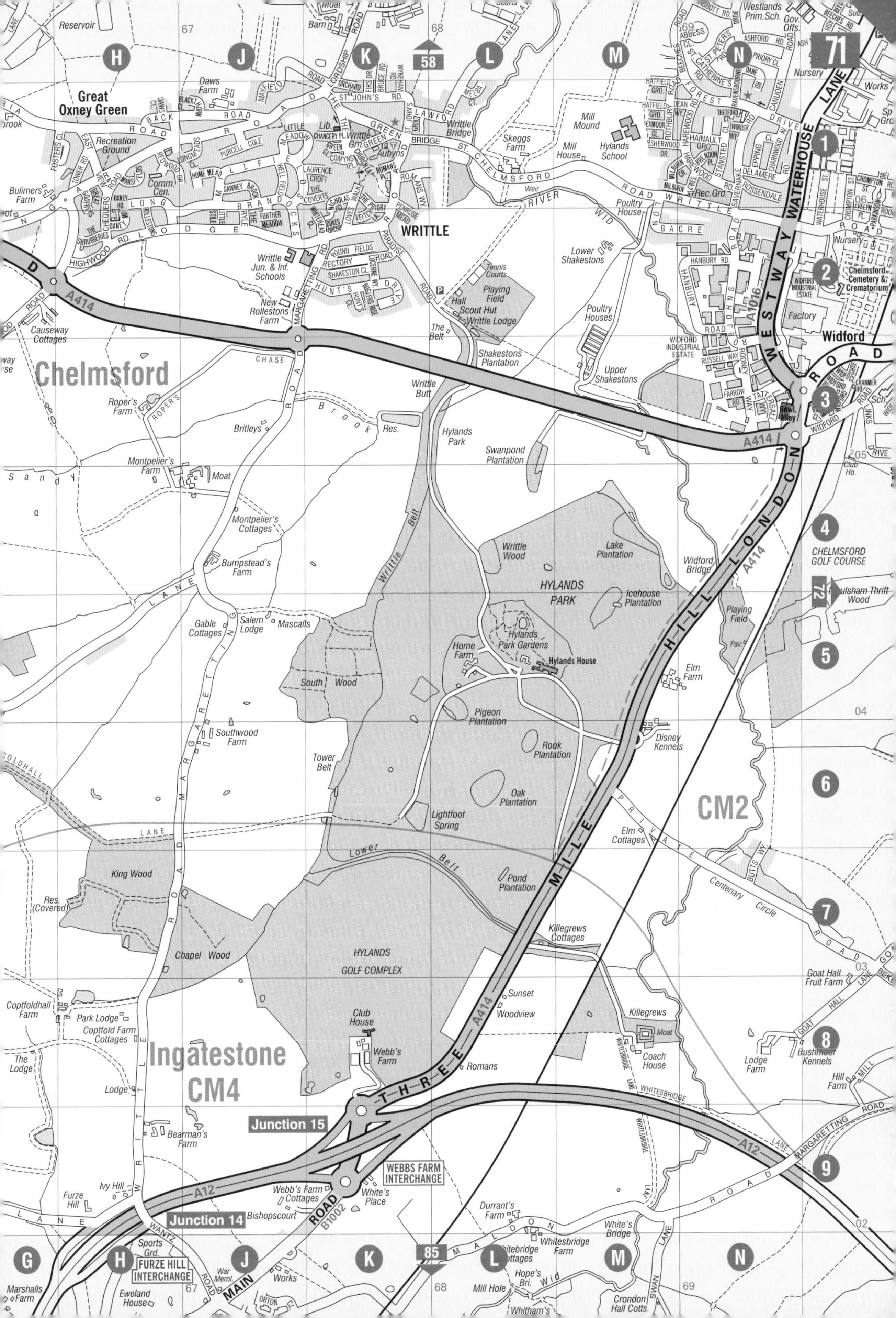
71
58
85
72
Great Oxney Green
WRITTLE
Chelmsford
Widford
Hylands Park
HYLANDS PARK
Hylands House
Hylands Park Gardens
Ingatestone CM4
CM2
HYLANDS GOLF COMPLEX
Junction 15
Junction 14
WEBBS FARM INTERCHANGE
FURZE HILL INTERCHANGE
CHELMSFORD GOLF COURSE
Chelmsford Cemetery & Crematorium
Writtle Jun. & Inf. Schools
Hylands School
WIDFORD INDUSTRIAL ESTATE
THREE MILE HILL
LONDON ROAD
WESTWAY
WATERHOUSE LANE
MARGARETTING ROAD
A414
A12
A1016
B1002
King Wood
Chapel Wood
South Wood
Writtle Wood
Lake Plantation
Icehouse Plantation
Pigeon Plantation
Rook Plantation
Oak Plantation
Pond Plantation
Swanpond Plantation
Shakestons Plantation
Lightfoot Spring
Tower Belt
Writtle Belt
Lower Belt
Killegrews
Killegrews Cottages
Webb's Farm
Club House
Disney Kennels
Elm Farm
Elm Cottages
Centenary Circle
Bumpstead's Farm
Montpelier's Farm
Montpelier's Cottages
Roper's Farm
Britleys
Southwood Farm
Salem Lodge
Mascalls
Gable Cottages
Coptfoldhall Farm
Park Lodge
Coptfold Farm Cottages
The Lodge
Bearman's Farm
Ivy Hill
Furze Hill
Webb's Farm Cottages
White's Place
Bishopscourt
Durrant's Farm
Whitesbridge Farm
White's Bridge
Mill Hole
Crondon Hall Cotts.
Eweland House
Marshalls Farm
Lodge Farm
Goat Hall Fruit Farm
Hill Farm
Bushwood Kennels
Moulsham Thrift Wood
Widford Bridge
Playing Field
Upper Shakestons
Lower Shakestons
Poultry Houses
Poultry House
Mill Mound
Mill House
Skeggs Farm
Writtle Bridge
Recreation Ground
Comm. Cen.
Causeway Cottages
Bulimers Farm
Reservoir
New Rollestons Farm
Writtle Lodge
Scout Hut
Writtle Butt
Factory
Sunset
Woodview
Romans
Coach House
Moat
Sports Grd.
War Meml.
Works
Hope's Bri.

72
CHELMSFORD
CM1
Chelmsford
Moulsham
Widford
GREAT BADDOW
GALLEYWOOD
Galleyend
WATERHOUSE LA.
WESTWAY
LONDON ROAD
NEW LONDON ROAD
PARKWAY
PRINCES ROAD
CHELMER ROAD
BADDOW ROAD
BEEHIVE LANE
GALLEYWOOD ROAD
STOCK ROAD
WOOD STREET
ARMY & NAVY FLYOVER
00:10 - 14:30 EAST TO WEST
14:40 - 00:00 WEST TO EAST
A1016
A1060
A1114
A138
A12
B1007
B1009
Chelmsford Cemetery & Crematorium
ST. JOHN'S HOSPITAL
CHELMSFORD GOLF COURSE
Moulsham Thrift Wood
Chelmsford College
John Shennan Playing Field
Moulsham High Sch.
Moulsham Jun. & Infs. Schools
Superstore
Oaklands Park
Essex Co. Cricket Grd.
Health & Fitness Club
Central Park
Industrial Estate
Moulsham Mill
Meadgate Farm
Barnes Farm
Watermeadows
Noakes Park & Baddow Rec. Grd.
Marconi Athletic & Social Club
Great Baddow High Sch.
Beehive Lane Prim. School
Mildmay Jun. & Infs. Schs.
Chelmer Park
Thriftwood Sch.
Lathcoats Farm
Appletrees
Riding School
Carlton House
Deadman's Well
Great Seabrights
Seabrights House
Little Seabrights Cottages
Lawn Cemetery
Reservoir
Willow Cottage
Canon-Leys Farm
Parklands Farm
Baddow Park Farmhouse
Baddow Park Farm
GALLEYWOOD COMMON
Race Course (dis.)
White House
Goat Hall Fruit Farm
Bushmoor Kennels
Lodge Farm
Hill Farm
Wood Farm
Byron Hall
Pond's Farm
Glebe Farm Cottages
Bexfield Farm
Bexfields
Lady Grove
The Chase
Centenary Cir.
A B C D E F G
1 2 3 4 5 6 7 8 9
59
71
86

Long Spring Wood
Storms Way
Prentice's Farm
Reservoir
Pease Hall
Sewage Works
SANDFORD
RIVER CHELMER
Chelmer & Blackwater Navigation
Sandford Lock
Sandford Mill Bridge
Water Works
Reservoirs
Mill Cottages
Manor Farm
Rumbold's Farm
Rumbold's
HAMMONDS
GRACE'S WALK
CM3
Sandon Brook
Hall Wood
Old Hare Wood
Playing Field
Potash Cotts.
The White House
MALDON ROAD
A1060
A414
MAIN ROAD
Weir
Sandon Bridge
Lower Lodge
Grace's Cross
SANDON INTERCHANGE
Junction 18
A12
Brick Kiln Cottage
Sandon Lodge
Bridge Farm
HULLS LANE
WOODHILL ROAD
Sandon
Sandon Place
The Sandons Sch.
Recreation Ground
Baddow Hall Jun. & Inf. Schs.
Tennis Court
Sandon Centre
Hall Playing Field
The Rectory
Playing Fields
Lower Green
Plumping Bridge
Sand & Gravel Pit
Mayes Farm
Barn House
Police Kennels
Dealtrees Farm
Mayfield Farm
A1114
Depot
Pitt Place
Tennis Club
CM2
Hotel
Park Studios
Brookside Dairy
The Briars
Crack Willows
Spare Bridge
Sandon Hall
Pontlands Farm
Electronics Research Laboratories
Chamberlains Farm
BLIND LA.
SPOREHAMS LANE
Sporhams Orchard
Butt's Green Livery
Farm Cottage
BUTTS GREEN
HOWE GREEN INTERCHANGE
Junction 17
Gingerbreadhall Bridge
Poplars
St. Swithins Cottages
Howe Farm
White Lodge Farm
Kellythorpe
Butt's Green Farm
Butt's Green
The Turnpike
Great Mascalls Cottages
Moat
Great Mascalls
Whiss-Stocks
A130
EAST HANNINGFIELD
Gravel Hill Farm
Greensmiths Farm
Howe Green
Three Oaks
Orchard View
Southlands Cottage
Southlands Farm
Grove Farm
Mill Hill House
Mill Hill Farm
Little Mascalls Farm
Great Sir Hughes Cottages
Little Sir Hughes
West Chase
Corrina
Reservoir
Great Sir Hughes
Rowlands
Riddens Court
The Paddock
Pelham Lodge
Great Claydons Farm
The Lodge
Cricket Grd.
Little Claydons Bungalow
Little Claydons
Great Claydons
Bluebell Wood
OLD SOUTHEND ROAD
60
74
87
G H J K L M N
1 2 3 4 5 6 7 8 9

Long Spring Wood
Lodge
GRACE'S WALK
NEW LODGE CHASE
Great Graces Farm
Little Graces Farm
Blakes Wood Nature Reserve
61
Old Riffhams
Chase Cottages
Jays Glen
The White House
Good Graces
GRACES LANE
Riffhams Farm
Riffhams
Long Wood
Longwood Chase
Knole Cottage
Openways
Cherrytree Cott.
Alcina
Dolphins
Fuzzy Chats
Willowfield
Pheasanthouse Wood Nature Reserve
FIR TREE LANE
Firtree Wood
Poor's Piece Nature Reserve
Rose Bungalow
Ling Wood
LINGWOOD COMMON NATURE RESERVE
Hall Wood
Weir
Clark's Farm
Timber Yard
Saw Mill
Scrubs Wood Nature Reserve
Weatheroak
Old Hare Wood
Factory
Sand & Gravel Pit
St. Clere's Hall
Clovers
Bellhill Wood
Elm Green Farm
Elm Green
CM3
MAIN ROAD
A414
The Main Lodge
BELL HILL
Danbury Park Prim. Sch.
DANBURY COUNTRY PARK
MALDON ROAD
Reservoir (covered)
Prim. Sch.
Lib.
Ind. Est.
Playing Field
Works
Danbury Palace
Anglia Polytechnic University
Home Farm
CM2
DANBURY
PENNY ROYAL ROAD
Hitchcock's Meadows Nature Reserve
Danecourt
Woodhill Lodge
Woodhill House
Woodhill Common
Woodhill
Danbury Common
Reservoir
Ludgores Farm
Horne Row
Reservoir
Paternoster Farm
Ball's Farm
Danbury Common Nature Reserve
Gay Bowers Farm
Manor Farm
Chamberlains Farm
Chamberlains Farm Cottages
Chelmsford
Backwarden Nature Reserve
Reservoirs
Sporhams Orchard
Farm Cottage
Sporhams Farm
Thorn Farm
Hillbroom Cottage
Orchard End
Res.
Ford
Poplar Farm
Hillcrest
Overshot Bri.
Overshot Farm
Springate Farm
Butt's Green Farm
Thorn Wood
Kellythorpe
Butt's Green
The Turnpike
Little Gibcracks
Peartree Farm
Compasses Farm
Cemetery
The Priory Prim. Sch.
Willow Lodge
Gibcracks
Hillcrest
CM2
Grove Farm
Days Hill Cottages
Works
Badgers
Mead's Grove
Remains of Priory (Augustinian founded 1175)
Horseshoe Farm
WHITE
Mill Hill House
Mill Hill Farm
Great Gibcracks
Broadoaks Farm
Saint Giles
Priory Farm
BICKNACRE
The Old Convent Moor House
South Gibcracks
PRIORY ROAD
MAIN ROAD B1418
Cricket Grd.
Pav.
Great Claydons Farm
Salesfrith Cottages
Salesfrith Farm
Playing Field
The Lodge
88
Common Farm
Old Common Farm
Great Claydons
Crossfield House
Highfields Farm
THRIFT WOOD NATURE RESERVE

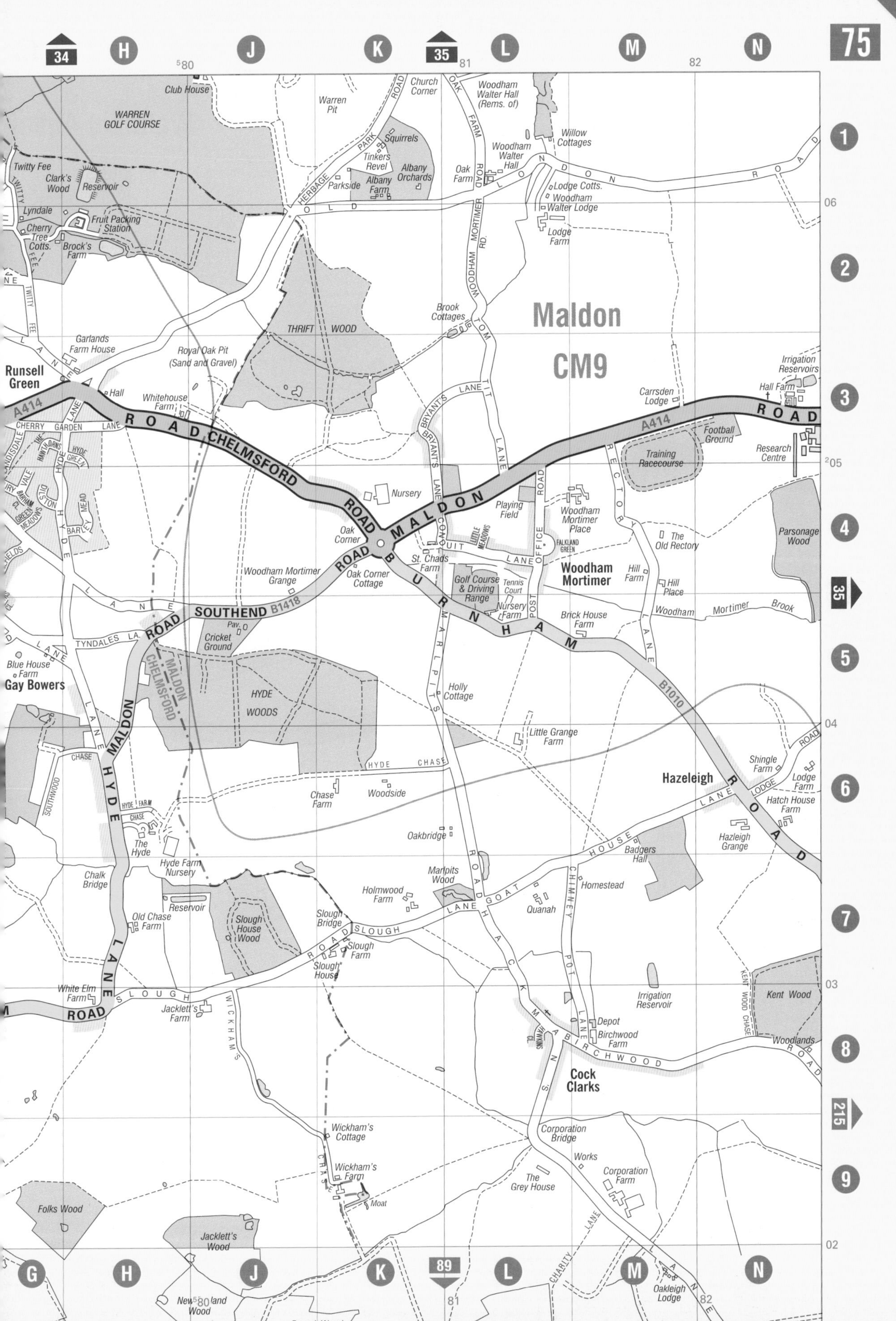
34
35
H
J
K
L
M
N
580
81
82
1
2
3
4
5
6
7
8
9
06
05
04
03
02
Club House
WARREN GOLF COURSE
Warren Pit
Church Corner
Woodham Walter Hall (Rems. of)
Willow Cottages
Squirrels
Tinkers Revel
Albany Orchards
Albany Farm
Parkside
Woodham Walter Hall
Oak Farm
Lodge Cotts.
Woodham Walter Lodge
Lodge Farm
Twitty Fee
Clark's Wood
Reservoir
Lyndale
Cherry Tree Cotts.
Fruit Packing Station
Brock's Farm
OLD
LONDON ROAD
HERBAGE PARK ROAD
OAK FARM ROAD
WOODHAM MORTIMER RD.
Brook Cottages
THRIFT WOOD
Maldon
CM9
Garlands Farm House
Runsell Green
Royal Oak Pit (Sand and Gravel)
Hall
Whitehouse Farm
Irrigation Reservoirs
Hall Farm
Carrsden Lodge
A414
ROAD CHELMSFORD ROAD
CHERRY GARDEN LANE
Football Ground
Training Racecourse
Research Centre
Nursery
MALDON
Playing Field
Woodham Mortimer Place
Parsonage Wood
Oak Corner
The Old Rectory
FALKLAND GREEN
St. Chads Farm
Woodham Mortimer
Hill Farm
Hill Place
Woodham Mortimer Grange
Oak Corner Cottage
Golf Course & Driving Range
Tennis Court
Nursery Farm
Woodham Mortimer Brook
SOUTHEND ROAD
B1418
Brick House Farm
TYNDALES LA.
Pav.
Cricket Ground
BURNHAM ROAD
B1010
Blue House Farm
Gay Bowers
MALDON CHELMSFORD
HYDE WOODS
Holly Cottage
Little Grange Farm
HYDE CHASE
Shingle Farm
Lodge Farm
Hazeleigh
Chase Farm
Woodside
Hatch House Farm
The Hyde
Oakbridge
HOUSE LANE
Hazleigh Grange
Badgers Hall
Hyde Farm Nursery
Chalk Bridge
Marlpits Wood
Homestead
Holmwood Farm
Quanah
Reservoir
Old Chase Farm
Slough House Wood
Slough Bridge
SLOUGH
GOAT LANE
Slough Farm
Slough House
Irrigation Reservoir
White Elm Farm
Jacklett's Farm
Kent Wood
KENT WOOD CHASE
Depot
Birchwood Farm
Woodlands
ROAD
SLOUGH
HYDE LANE
BIRCHWOOD ROAD
Cock Clarks
WICKHAM'S CHASE
215
Wickham's Cottage
Corporation Bridge
Works
Wickham's Farm
The Grey House
Corporation Farm
Moat
Folks Wood
Jacklett's Wood
G
89
CHARITY LANE
Oakleigh Lodge
Newland Wood
Round Wood

Waltham Abbey
EN9
WALTHAM CROSS
WALTHAM ABBEY
LEE VALLEY REGIONAL PARK
Royal Gunpowder Mills
Visitor Cen.
Hall Marsh
Waltham Marsh
Cheshunt Marsh
Arboretum
Tree Nursery
Nurseries
Abbey Fish Ponds
Harold's Bri.
Waltham Abbey
Abbey Gdns.
King Harold Sch.
Spts Cen.
Playing Field
Recreation Ground
Football Ground
Cemetery
Town Mead
Waltham Abbey Swim. Pool
King George's Field
The Leverton Infant & Junior Sch.
Honeylands
M25 MOTORWAY
A121
STATION RD.
CROOKED MILE
B194
RAMMEY MARSH
Enfield
EN3
Meridian Park
COUNTRY PARK
Warehouse
Quinton Hill Farm
The Downing Nursery
Beechview Nursery
Felicia Nursery
Providence Nursery
Normandy Nursery
Aveylane Farm
High Beech Nurseries
Pynest Green
Avey Cottages
Kennels
Piggery
Round Hills
BEECH HILL PARK
The Grange
Sewardstone Nursery
Chandlers Farm
Mott Street Nursery
Thompson's Wood
Sewardstone Hall
Kingsfield Nurseries
Barnfield Riding Stables
Netherhouse Nursery
Netherhouse Farm
Beechside Nursery
E4
Enfield Island Village
Manor Farm
High Beech C. of E. Primary School
Oak Farm
Aldergrove Wood
KING GEORGE'S RESERVOIR
SEWARDSTONE
Hannah Nursery
Fouracres Nursery
Northfield Nursery
Northcroft Nursery
Chapelfield Nursery
Marshfield Nursery
Luthers Farm
Woodlands Nursery
Barn Hill
Day's Farm
Pumping Station
Overflow Channel
WATERWAYS BUSINESS CENTRE
MOLLISON AVENUE
A1055
SEWARDSTONE ROAD
A112
MOTT STREET
LIPPITTS HILL
PEPPER ALLEY
GREEN LANE
BLIND LANE
AVEY LANE
EPPING FOREST
BROXBOURNE
ENFIELD
RIVER LEE NAVIGATION
Cattlegate Flood Relief Channel
Rammey Marsh Flood Relief Channel
Poultry Farm
Dallance Farm
Eagle Lodge
Oaklands Farm
Nursing Home
62
90
30

Fernhall Wood
Little Rookery Wood
Rookery Wood
Nursery
Brookmeadow Wood
Willows
63
Newhouse Farm
Fitches Plantation
Obelisk
Nicholls Farm
Lodge Farm
Cobbin Pond
Home Farm
Obelisk Farm
Copped Hall Gardens
WARLIES PARK
Nurseries
Warlies Gardens
Copped Hall
Epping
Home Farm
Warlies Park House
The Temple
Burgess Farm
Copped Hall Green
West Hill
Pickhill Farm
Temple Hill
CM16
Cricket Ground
Warlie's Lodge
UPSHIRE
The Selvage
Upshire Prim. Sch.
HORSESHOE HILL
CROWN HILL
Sergeants Green
Warlies Park Farm
COPTHALL GREEN
Raveners Farm
M25 MOTORWAY
M25
Oxleys Wood
The Warren
Warren Wood
Nursery
Woodgreen Farm
Potkiln Wood
Brambly Shaw
Crown Hill Farm
Ambresbury
Woodgreen Potteries
Southend Farm
WOOD GREEN
Upshire Hall
Woodredon House
Conybury Wood
78
Woodredon Farm
St. Thomas's Quarters
Long Running
HONEY LANE
Skillet Hill Farm
Sudbury Farm
Stable Shaw
WOODRIDDEN HILL
CM16
Forest Lodge
Riding School
Jack's Hill
Junction 26
A121
B172
B1393
EPPING ROAD
Lord Padgets Wood
Prayer Halls
Cemetery
Honey Lane Plain
Wake Arms Roundabout
Poplar Shaw
Oak Hill
Tile Hill Farm
Honey Lane Quarters
Sunshine Plain
Dulsmead Hollow
Copley Plain
Riding School
Deershelter Plain
HIGH BEECH GOLF COURSE
Wake Valley Pond
Furze Ground
Wake Valley
Debden House Camp Site
Club House
Riding School
Rushey Plain
Great Monk Wood
Broadstrood Plain
Bowling Green
Youth Hostel
Epping Forest Nature Reserve
Loughton
Epping Forest Conservation Centre
Mount Pleasant
Court Hill
Golding's Hill Ponds
LOUGHTON GOLF COURSE
HIGH BEECH
Hall
Bellringer's Hollow
Manor House
Little Monk Wood
Little Goldings Estate
Club House
Blackweir Pond
Wallsgrove House
IG10
Paul's Nursery
Blackweir Hill
Baldwins Hill
Arewater Green
The Vicarage
Dairy Farm
Loughton Camp
Kate's Cellar
Baldwins Pond
91
Shelleys Hill
Riding School
Dryad's Hall
Hillyfields
NEW ROAD
GOLDINGS HILL
A104
EPPING NEW ROAD
EPPING FOREST
CLAY RIDE
GREGSON'S RIDE
DEBDEN ROAD

EPPING
Fitches Plantation
Home Farm
Wood House
Paris Hall
New Farm
Griffin's Wood
Creeds Farm
Bell Common
New House Farm
Ladderstile Farm
Millhouse Farm
Sports Ground
Cemetery
Ivy Chimneys Prim. Sch.
Ivy Chimneys
Epping
CM16
M25 MOTORWAY
M25
HIGH ROAD
B1393
Park Cottages
The Warren
Warren Wood
EPPING THICKS
Ambresbury Banks
Theydon Towers
Bowlands Meadow
Great Gregories Farm
Gardners Farm
Coopersale School
Farm Bungalow
Club House
Little Gregories
THEYDON BOIS GOLF COURSE
Piercing Hill
PIERCING HILL
Long Running
Wansfell College
Genesis Slade
Junction 6 (M11)
B172
COPPICE ROW
Oak Hill
Oak Hill Farm
Theydon Plain
The Coppice
Theydon Bois Prim. Sch.
Playing Field
Birch Hall
Birch Hall Farm
Cricket Ground
THEYDON BOIS
Theydon Bois
ABRIDGE
Parsonage Farm
Blunts Farm
Blunts Chase
Copley Plain
Furze Ground
Redoak Wood
Birch Wood
Thrifts Hall
Thrifts Hall Farm
Council Depot
Springhouse Cottages
COOPERSALE
Debden House Camp Site
DEBDEN GREEN
Loughton
Ripley Grange
Gaunt's Wood
The Boundary
Cemetery
M11 MOTORWAY
ABRIDGE ROAD
Theydon Hall Cottages
Theydon Hall Farm
Theydon Hall
Mossford Green Nurseries
LOUGHTON GOLF COURSE
IG10
Davenant Foundation School
Playing Field
Club House
ARWATER GREEN
Prim. Sch.
M11
Long Shaw
Piggotts Farm Cottages
Piggotts Farm

64
77
92

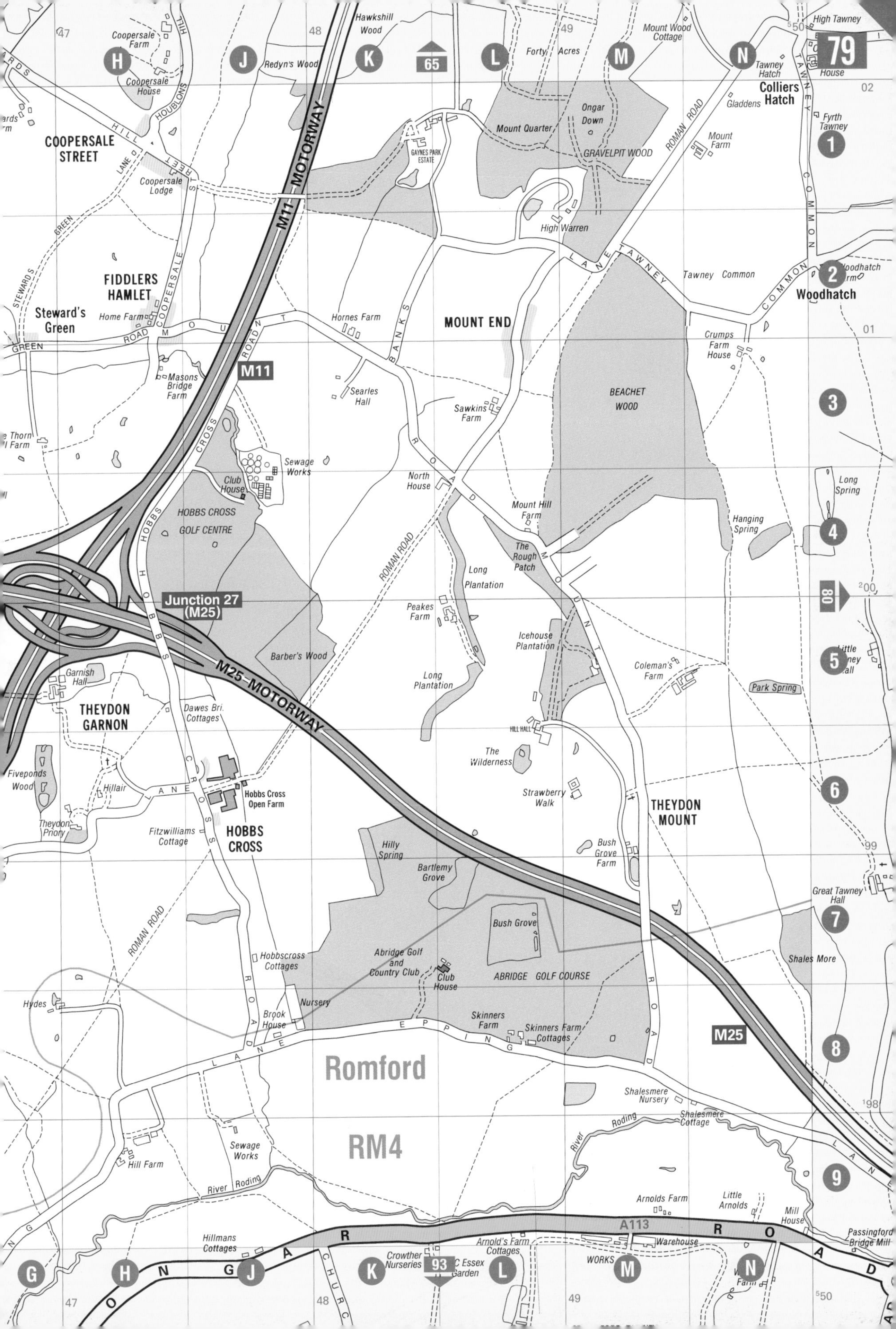

Coopersale Farm
Coopersale House
COOPERSALE STREET
Coopersale Lodge
FIDDLERS HAMLET
Steward's Green
Home Farm
Masons Bridge Farm
Redyn's Wood
Hawkshill Wood
65
Forty Acres
Mount Wood Cottage
High Tawney
Tawney Hatch
House
Colliers Hatch
Gladdens
Fyrth Tawney
Mount Farm
Ongar Down
Mount Quarter
GRAVELPIT WOOD
GAYNES PARK ESTATE
High Warren
M11 MOTORWAY
ROMAN ROAD
TAWNEY LANE
Tawney Common
Woodhatch Farm
Woodhatch
COMMON
MOUNT ROAD
Hornes Farm
MOUNT END
Crumps Farm House
BEACHET WOOD
M11
Searles Hall
Sawkins Farm
Sewage Works
Club House
HOBBS CROSS GOLF CENTRE
North House
Mount Hill Farm
Long Spring
Hanging Spring
The Rough Patch
Long Plantation
Junction 27 (M25)
80
Peakes Farm
Icehouse Plantation
Barber's Wood
Coleman's Farm
Little Tawney Hall
Park Spring
Garnish Hall
M25 MOTORWAY
Long Plantation
THEYDON GARNON
Dawes Bri. Cottages
HILL HALL
The Wilderness
Fiveponds Wood
Hillair
Hobbs Cross Open Farm
Strawberry Walk
THEYDON MOUNT
Theydon Priory
Fitzwilliams Cottage
HOBBS CROSS
Hilly Spring
Bartlemy Grove
Bush Grove Farm
Great Tawney Hall
Bush Grove
Hobbscross Cottages
Abridge Golf and Country Club
Club House
ABRIDGE GOLF COURSE
Shales More
Hydes
Nursery
Brook House
Skinners Farm
Skinners Farm Cottages
M25
EPPING LANE
Romford
RM4
Shalesmere Nursery
Shalesmere Cottage
River Roding
Sewage Works
Hill Farm
River Roding
Arnolds Farm
Little Arnolds
Mill House
A113
Passingford Bridge Mill
Hillmans Cottages
Crowther Nurseries
93
C Essex Garden
Arnold's Farm Cottages
Warehouse
WORKS
ONGAR ROAD
CHURCH
47
48
49
550
02
01
200
99
198

High Tawney
Old House
Moat House
Colliers Hatch
Gladdens
Fyrth Tawney
Four Winds
Freemans Farm
66
Club House
Blake's Farm
TOOTHILL GOLF COURSE
End
Burrows Farm
Coleman's Farm
Stewart's Farm
Nickerlands
Woodhatch Farm
Woodhatch
Common
Caravan Park
KNIGHTSLAND WOOD
Northlands Wood
Cessland's Farm
Ongar
CM5
CM16
Long Spring
Hanging Spring
Well Eaves
The Old Rectory
Barn Cottage
ICEHOUSE WOOD
Berwick Farm
79
Little Tawney Hall
Bell's Farm
Howfields
The Grove
Twentyacre Wood
Berwick Ham
Murrells Farm
Park Spring
Garden Cottage
The Old Rectory
Traceys Farm
Tracey's Tiger
Tenacre Wood
The Moors
Dog Kennel Spring
Tenacre Cottage
Stonyrocks Plantation
STAPLEFORD TAWNEY
Bob's Barn Wood
Langford Bottom
Wayletts
Bob's Barn
Romford
Great Tawney Hall
Lawns
Shales More
RM4
Railmead Plantation
Mitchells Farm
Shonks Mill Bridge
River Roding
M25 MOTORWAY
Passingford Bridge
Suttons
Sutton's Farm
Playing Field
Howletts Hall
M25
Mill House
Passingford Bridge Mill
ONGAR ROAD
LONDON ROAD
PASSINGFORD BRIDGE
94
Dabbs Farm
Waters Farm
BERWICK LANE
SCHOOL ROAD
TOOT HILL ROAD
OLD RECTORY
SHONKS

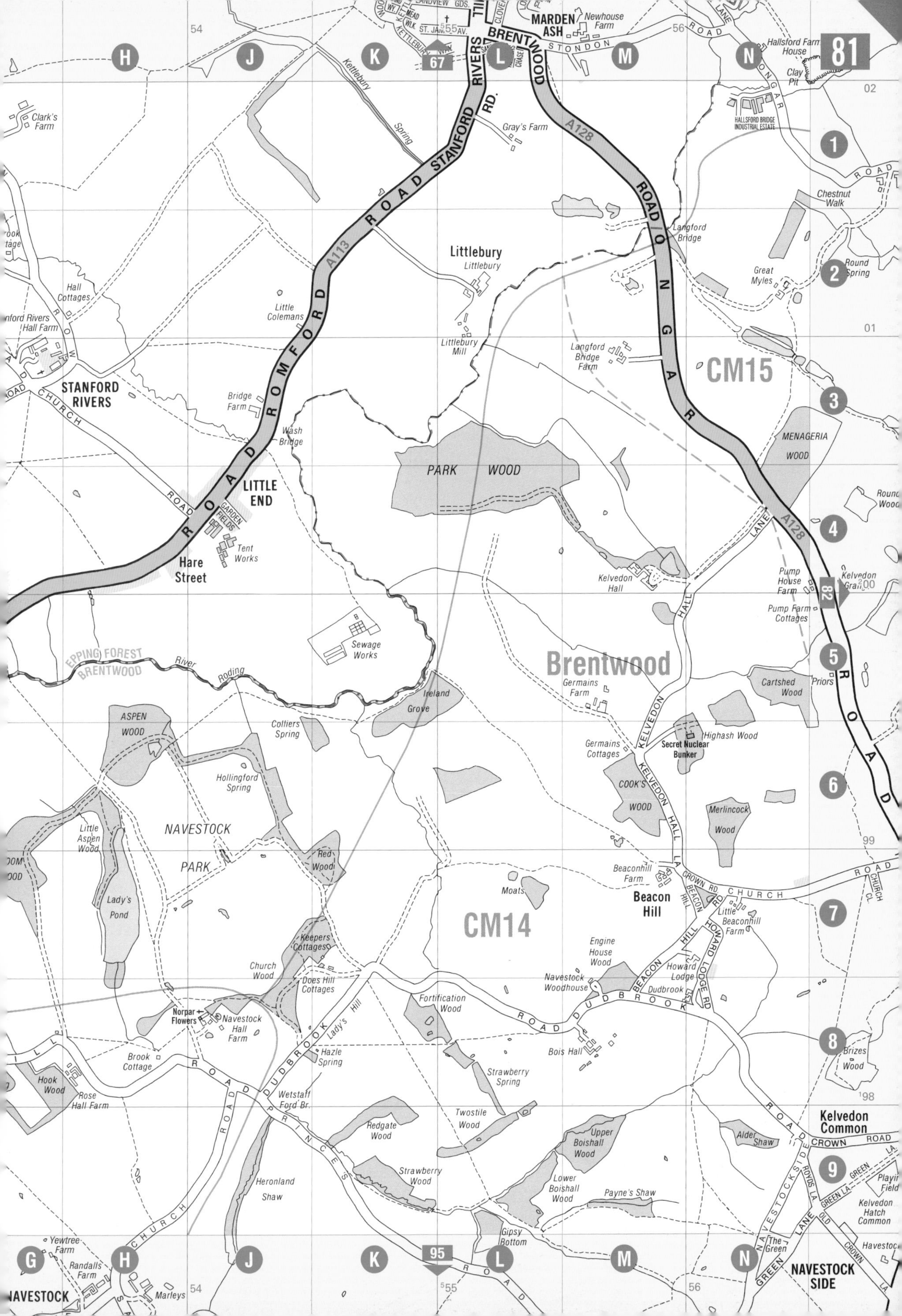

MARDEN ASH
Newhouse Farm
BRENTWOOD
STONDON
ROAD
Hallsford Farm House
Clay Pit
HALLSFORD BRIDGE INDUSTRIAL ESTATE
ONGAR
67
Kettlebury Spring
Clark's Farm
Gray's Farm
A128
ROMFORD ROAD STANFORD RIVERS RD.
A113
Chestnut Walk
Littlebury
Langford Bridge
Round Spring
Great Myles
Hall Cottages
Little Colemans
Littlebury Mill
Langford Bridge Farm
CM15
STANFORD RIVERS
CHURCH ROAD
Bridge Farm
Wash Bridge
MENAGERIA WOOD
PARK WOOD
LITTLE END
GARDEN FIELDS
Tent Works
Hare Street
Kelvedon Hall
Pump House Farm
Pump Farm Cottages
82
Sewage Works
EPPING FOREST
BRENTWOOD
River Roding
Brentwood
Germains Farm
Priors
Cartshed Wood
Ireland Grove
ASPEN WOOD
Colliers Spring
Germains Cottages
Secret Nuclear Bunker
Highash Wood
Hollingford Spring
COOK'S WOOD
KELVEDON HALL LANE
Merlincock Wood
NAVESTOCK PARK
Little Aspen Wood
Red Wood
Beaconhill Farm
CROWN RD
CHURCH
Moats
Beacon Hill
Lady's Pond
CM14
Little Beaconhill Farm
Keepers Cottages
Engine House Wood
Church Wood
Does Hill Cottages
Navestock Woodhouse
BEACON HILL
HOWARD LODGE RD
Howard Lodge
Dudbrook
Fortification Wood
Norpar Flowers
Navestock Hall Farm
DUDBROOK ROAD
Lady's Hill
Bois Hall
Brizes Wood
Brook Cottage
Hazle Spring
Strawberry Spring
Hook Wood
Rose Hall Farm
Wetstaff Ford Br.
Twostile Wood
Kelvedon Common
CROWN ROAD
Redgate Wood
Upper Boishall Wood
Alder Shaw
PRINCES ROAD
Heronland Shaw
Strawberry Wood
Lower Boishall Wood
Payne's Shaw
NAVESTOCKSIDE
GREEN LA
Kelvedon Hatch Common
CHURCH ROAD
Gipsy Bottom
The Green
GREEN LANE
Yewtree Farm
Randalls Farm
Marleys
95
NAVESTOCK SIDE
NAVESTOCK
54
55
56
02
01
00
99
98
H J K L M N
G H J K L M N
1 2 3 4 5 6 7 8 9

82
Ongar
CM5
Stondon Hall
Stondon Hall Farm
Little Myles
Chestnut Walk
CHURCH WOOD
Round Spring
Great Myles
Stondon Massey House
COURTFIELD WOOD
Stondon Manor
MENAGERIA WOOD
Clapgate
STONDON MASSEY
Stondon Place
Round Wood
Kelvedon Grange
Pump House Farm
Pump Farm Cottages
Priors Wood
Bushy Wood
Willow Tree Farm
POLE'S WOOD
Mellow Purgess Farm
Oak Wood
Cartshed Wood
Chivers
The Coppice
Grove Side
Long Chase
Hatch Farm
Radio Station
CM14
KELVEDON HATCH
Brizes
Brizes Wood
Moat
Doddinghurst Common
Kelvedon Common
Alder Shaw
Playing Field
Kelvedon Hatch Common
Havestock
NAVESTOCK SIDE
The Green
Club Ho.
Kennels
Cow Farm
Camping & Caravaning Site
Alders Wood
BENTLEY GOLF COURSE & COUNTRY CLUB
FOX HATCH
Furze Wood
Red House Farm
Dagwood Farm
Cowes Farm
Place Farm
Waterworks Spring
Fish Ponds
CHURCH WOOD
Brentwood
Barfield Farm
Deal Tree Farm
Soaphouse Farm
Tip's Cross
Brook Farm
Whipple Farm
Stondon Green
Tel.Ex.
Pickett's Wood
Hunters Moon
Fox Farm
Fagg's Farm
Paslow Common Farm
Paslow Wood Common
Ashling's Farm
Copyhold Farm
Twites Farm
EPPING FOREST
BRENTWOOD
Hook End Farm
Blackmore House
Springfield
HOOK END
DODDINGHURST
Doddinghurst C. of E. Jun. & Inf. Schs.
Play. Field
Peartree Farm
Mushroom Farm
Moat
Park Farm
Play. Fld.
ONGAR ROAD
STONDON ROAD
NINE ASHES ROAD
BLACKMORE ROAD
HOOK END ROAD
BACK ROAD
SCHOOL ROAD
CHURCH ROAD
CHURCH LANE
DAGWOOD LANE
WARREN LANE
FROG STREET
CROWN ROAD
BLACKMORE
A128
68
96
81
57
58
59

Blackmore
Ingatestone
CM4
CM15
Elkin's Green
Fryerning Wood
College Wood
Portsmoorhall Wood
Beggar Hill
Green Street
Hay Green
Wyatt's Green
Swallows Cross
Peartree Green
Mountnessing
Blackmore Wood
Long Wood
Woodbarns Spring
Little Woodbarns
Remains of Thoby Priory (Augustinian)
Thoby Priory Farm
Mountnessing Post Mill
69
97
84

84
70
83
98
A
B
C
D
E
F
G
1
2
3
4
5
6
7
8
9
63
64
565
66
02
01
200
99
98
Monk's Barrow's
Deerslade Wood
Whitegates
Poultry Houses
Handley Green Farm
Dawes Farm
Handley Green
Maple Tree Farm
Stoneymere Wood
Long Meadow
Box Wood
Well Wood
Moore's Ditch
Potter Row Farm
Millgreen Common
Handley Barns
Bushey Wood
Glasshouse
Woodside Cotts
Brick House Farm
Beggar Hill
The Grange
Harding's Farm
Mill Green Park
Whitehouse Farm
Millgreen Wood
Mill Green
Osborne's Wood
Lyndsey's Farm
The Grove
Fryerning (Mill Green) Postmill
Redcote
Field House
High Point
Pennyfields
Delamas
The Grange
Maisonette
Lodge
Little Hyde Farm
Playing Field
Fryerning
Murcock's Farm
Fryerning Hall
Oakwood
Cemetery
Ingatestone Inf. Sch.
Seymour Field
Pav.
Ray Farm
Waskett's
Church Hill Cottages
Longview Cottage
Anglo European Sch.
Green Street Green
Ingatestone
Cornishe's Cottages
Dodd's Farm
Little Raysons
Orchard Farm
C. of E. Junior Sch.
INGATESTONE
Fair Field
Fairacres
Dunstead's Farm
Lib.
Ingatestone
CM4
Lodge
Sewage Works
Adam & Powis's Farm
Weir
Kettles Place
Junction 13
TRUELOVES INTERCHANGE
Remains of Thoby Priory (Augustinian)
Kennels
Ingatestone Hall Farm
Ingatestone Hall
Thoby Priory Farm
Heybridge
Playground
Bacons Farm
New Cottages
Moat
Tilehurst
Nurseries
Mountnessing Post Mill
Playing Field
Tennis Court
Lodge Wood
Kitchen Wood
MOUNTNESSING
Valentine
Keepers Cottage
Padhams Green
Ford
Bakers Farm
CM15
CM13
Bellman's Farm
Westlands Farm
Shoulder Hall
Drury's Farm
Mountnessing C. of E. Prim. School
Rose Cottage
Jordans Farm
Begrums Farm
Hillrise Farm
MAPLETREE LANE
MILL GREEN ROAD
INGATESTONE RD.
IVY BARN LANE
IVY BARN DRIVE
DOG KENNEL LANE
HARDING'S LANE
HYDE LANE
LITTLE HYDE RD.
LITTLE HYDE LANE
MILL LANE
BACK LANE
HILL LANE
BEGGAR HILL
BLACKMORE ROAD
FRYERNING LANE
GREEN STREET
BAG LANE
TRUELOVES LANE
A12 BY-PASS
INGATESTONE BY-PASS
B1002
HIGH STREET
ROMAN ROAD
NEW ROAD
DOCKLANDS AV.
PARK DRIVE
PINE DRIVE
PINE CLOSE
STOCK LANE
HALL LANE
STATION LANE
AVENUE ROAD
BRIDGE
BURNTHOUSE LANE
PADHAM'S GREEN ROAD
THOBY LANE
LAUNDRY LA.
CHURCH LANE
OLD CHURCH RD.
MARSH LA.
MOUNTNESSING RD.
MOUNTNESSING BY-PASS
THE HILLWAY

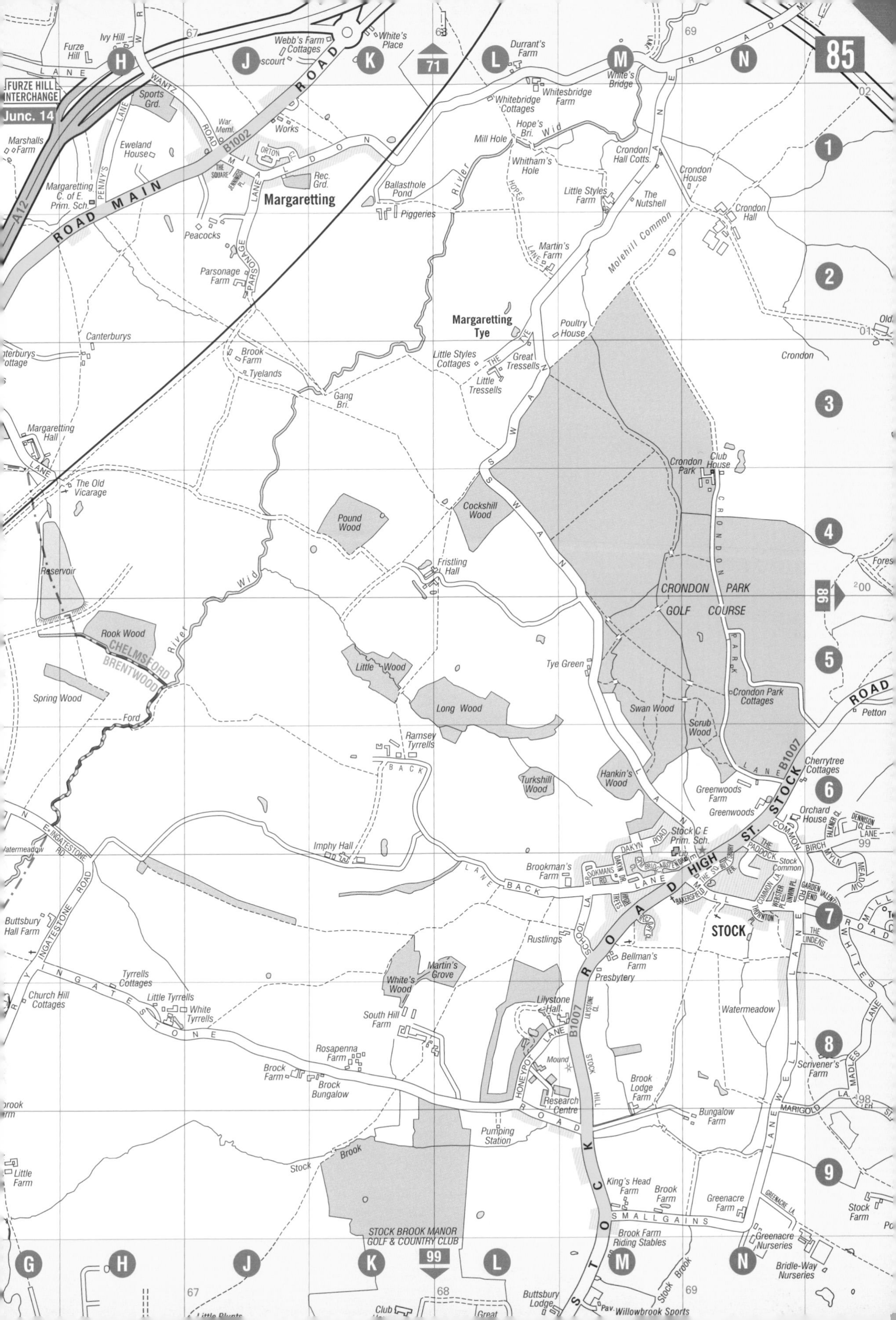
FURZE HILL INTERCHANGE
Junc. 14
Furze Hill
Ivy Hill
Webb's Farm Cottages
White's Place
Durrant's Farm
White's Bridge
71
Sports Grd.
Marshalls Farm
Eweland House
Works
War Meml.
Whitebridge Cottages
Whitesbridge Farm
Hope's Bri.
Mill Hole
Whitham's Hole
Crondon Hall Cotts.
Crondon House
Crondon Hall
Margaretting C. of E. Prim. Sch.
Rec. Grd.
Margaretting
Ballasthole Pond
Piggeries
Little Styles Farm
The Nutshell
Molehill Common
Peacocks
Parsonage Farm
Martin's Farm
MAIN ROAD
B1002
A12
Margaretting Tye
Poultry House
Canterburys
Brook Farm
Tyelands
Little Styles Cottages
Great Tressells
Little Tressells
Crondon
Gang Bri.
Margaretting Hall
The Old Vicarage
Cockshill Wood
Pound Wood
Crondon Park
Club House
Reservoir
Fristling Hall
CRONDON PARK GOLF COURSE
86
Rook Wood
CHELMSFORD
BRENTWOOD
River Wid
Little Wood
Tye Green
Spring Wood
Long Wood
Crondon Park Cottages
Swan Wood
Scrub Wood
Petton
Ford
Ramsey Tyrrells
BACK LANE
Turkshill Wood
Hankin's Wood
Cherrytree Cottages
Greenwoods Farm
Greenwoods
Orchard House
Stock C E Prim. Sch.
Imphy Hall
Brookman's Farm
HIGH ST.
STOCK ROAD
B1007
Stock Common
INGATESTONE ROAD
Buttsbury Hall Farm
Rustlings
STOCK
Bellman's Farm
Presbytery
Martin's Grove
White's Wood
Tyrrells Cottages
Church Hill Cottages
Little Tyrrells
White Tyrrells
South Hill Farm
Lilystone Hall
Watermeadow
Scrivener's Farm
Rosapenna Farm
Mound
Brock Farm
Brock Bungalow
Research Centre
Brook Lodge Farm
Bungalow Farm
MARIGOLD LA.
Pumping Station
Stock Brook
Little Farm
King's Head Farm
Brook Farm
Greenacre Farm
Stock Farm
SMALLGAINS
STOCK BROOK MANOR GOLF & COUNTRY CLUB
Brook Farm Riding Stables
Greenacre Nurseries
Bridle-Way Nurseries
99
Buttsbury Lodge
Willowbrook Sports
G H J K L M N
1 2 3 4 5 6 7 8 9
67 68 69

86
A
B
C
D
E
F
G
1
2
3
4
5
6
7
8
9
72
85
100
Wood Farm
Byron Hall
Pond's Farm
Glebe Farm Cottages
STOCK ROAD
B1007
A12
Lady Grove
The Chase
GALLEYWOOD/STOCK INTERCHANGE
Junction 16
Works
Gay Bowers Farm
Peveril Hall
Crondon Hall
Temple Grove
Long Leys
BAKERS LANE
TEMPLETON PARK
TEMPLE GROVE CARAVAN PARK
Depot
Little Peverels
The Red House
Tanfield Tye Cottage
The Villa
Tanfield Tye Cottages
Oldbarn
TEMPLE FARM TRADING ESTATE
Crondon
Temple Wood
CM2
Works
Forest Lodge Cottages
Ship Cotts.
Forest Lodge
West Hanningfield Hall
Elm's Farm
WEST HANNINGFIELD ROAD
SHIP
Westholme
HALL LANE
South View
Chase Farm
Stone
Foxburrow Wood
Clovile Hall
Willowdene
FOXBOROUGH
The Cedars
Wantz Corner
Forest Wood
Daylands Farm
ROAD
BLIND
CRONDON PARK GOLF COURSE
Ashridge
CHASE
Hicks Farm
HOLIDAY HILL
Foxborough Farm
Kent's Farm
KENTS FARM LANE
Farrow's Farm
Garden Fields
Brickhouse Farm
Brookside
Tristans
Crondon Park Cottages
Granville
STOCK ROAD
Brooklands
Slough House Farm
Uplands
Petton
Harvard
Keelings
Ravenstor
LOWER
MOWN
Cherrytree Cottages
Holes Place Farm
Sweetdrops
Blythhedges Spring Wood
Greenwoods
Orchard House
Blythhedges Wood
Ingatestone
STOCK
COMMON
BIRCH
LANE
DENNISON CL
Stock Common
Steel's Farm
CM4
MEADOWGATE
LEATHERBOTTLE HILL
Stock Towermill
App's Farm
SEAMANS
LANE
STOCK
THE LINDENS
WHITE'S
ROAD
GREAT PRESTONS LANE
Great Prestons
The Plantation
Watermeadow
Albards
Scrivener's Farm
Whiteholme
MADLES
Little Bishop's Wood
MARIGOLD
PETER ST
Jetty
Kiln Common
BRITTONS
BROOMWOOD
Billericay
CM11
Bishop's Farm
THE CHASEWAY
Bishop's Lodge
DOWSETT LA.
Whitelilies Farm
HAWKSWOOD ROAD
Greenacre Farm
Stock Farm
Cloyna Poultry Farm
Great Bishop's Wood
HANNINGFIELD RESERVE
BIRD SANCTUARY
SMALLGAINS
GREENACRE LA
DOWSETT LANE
Greenacre Nurseries
Bridle-Way Nurseries
Woodholm
FURZE LANE
GOATSMOOR LANE
Broom Wood
Oak Hall
Broomwood
Fremnells
Longcroft

Riddens Court
Great Sir Hughes
Reservoir
73
Rowlands
The Paddock
Pelham Lodge
Little Claydons Bungalow
Little Claydons Farm
Great Claydons
The Lodge
Bluebell Wood
Downhouse Farm
Tanfield Tye
Silos
Claydons Farm
Claydons Manor
Moat
Bushy Wood
Glebe Cottages
Hill Farm
Ford
A130
Lone Farm
Tudor Farm
Tinsley Farm
Sun View
Elm Bank
Raescroft
Orchard End
Good Gracious
Haryesters Farm
Patten's Farm
Dunnock Cottage
Chelmsford
Charvilles
Helmons Farm
Link House Farm
Doylands Farm
St. Peter's C.E. Prim. Sch. South & West Hanningford
West Hanningfield
Playing Fields
Barnard's Farm
The Rectory
Sandon Brook
Pumping Station
Reservoir
East Hanningfield Lodge
Canon Barns
Tank
Tanks
Water Works
Bloodlands
Silver Ash
Highlands Farm
Ralph's Farm
Blair Court
Old Barn Bungalow
Hilltop House
Tank
CM3
Hounden Wood
HANNINGFIELD RESERVOIR
Lacey's Farm
Rettendon Great Common
Morlands Ind. Est.
Bromley Lodge
Chelsfield
Hall Farm
Ridgemount
Rickstones Farm
Hobbit's Hole
Bearmains
Romans Farm
Works
Rawling's Farm
South Hanningfield Tye
Landing Stage
Hanningfield Reservoir Visitor Centre
Nature Trail
South Hanningfield
Horse Bri.
Mark's Farm
Coalhill
Claydons Farm
101
Stacey's Farm
Well Wood
88

BICKNACRE
EAST HANNINGFIELD
Rettendon
Chelmsford
CM3
Great Claydons Farm
Cricket Grd.
The Lodge
Great Claydons
Crossfield House
Highfields Farm
Sumptners Farm
Common Farm
Old Common Farm
Salesfrith Cottages
Salesfrith Farm
The Gables
Claydons Farm
Moat
Claydons Manor
Play. Fld. Hall
East Hanningfield C. of E. Prim. Sch.
Rough Hill Farm
Back Butt's
Leigham's Farm
Leighams
Niagara
The Spinney
Foxes Close
Hounds Hill Farm
Playing Field
THRIFT NATURE
B1418
MAIN RD.
Hill Farm
Huntingdon's Farm
Windmill Farm
Rails Farm
Industrial Estate
Willis Farm
Dunnock Cottage
Woodham Lodge Farm
Fultons Farm
Woodham Lodge
Rosewarne House
Quilter's Farm
Rosehill Hatchery
Hillberry
Depot
Creephedge Ho.
Barrack Cottages
Rose Hill Farm
White Cottage
Reservoir
Paprill's Farm
Great Reddings
Hall Cottages
East Hanningfield Hall
Lodge Farm Cottages
Barn Meade
The Firs
East Hanningfield Lodge
Hill View
Green Hanger
The Bungalow
New Cottages
RHS Garden Hyde Hall
Bramley
RETTENDON LITTLE COMMON
Little Timbers
Buckhatch Farm
Inglenook
Silver Ash
Highlands Farm
Brook Field
South Lodge
Vale Farm
Bartletts
Ralph's Farm
Blair Court
Bartlett's Farm
Buckhatch Nurseries
Old Barn Bungalow
Brecon
Hilltop House
Herds Farm
The Willows
Hill House
Wheeler's Farm
Brunwins Farm
Millhill Farm
Potter's Farm
Lappage's Farm
Rettendon Great Common
Pound Farm
Rawling's Farm
Mark's Farm
Playing Fld.
Playing Fie
CHELMSFORD ROAD
BACK LANE
THE COMMON (MAIN RD.)
BICKNACRE ROAD
OLD CHURCH ROAD
MAIN ROAD
RETTENDON ROAD
CREEPHEDGE LANE
LEIGHAMS ROAD
WOODHAM LODGE
HYDE HALL RD.
HANNINGFIELD
BUCKHATCH
POTTERS LANE
SOUTHEND ROAD
MAIN ROAD
EAST
WORKHOUSE LA.
SOUTH HANNINGFIELD
MARKS LA.
OLD BARN LANE
BENNETTS AV.
A130
A B C D E F G
1 2 3 4 5 6 7 8 9
76 77 78 79
02 01 200 99 98
74 87 102

Folks Wood
Jacklett's Wood
New England Wood
Round Wood
Squeaking-gate Wood
Great Wood
Corporation Farm
The Grey House
Oakleigh Lodge
Seven Acre Farm
Prentice's Farm
Emberson's Wood
Brook Farm
Emberson Lodge
Cank Wood
Hobclerk's Farm
The Bungalow
Ash Cotts.
Dyers Farm
Flambird's Farm
Brazils Farm
Nuttings
Charity Farm
Broadacres
Chapel Row
White's Farm
Reservoir
Old Rectory Lodge
Hollands Farm
Blacklands
St. Mary's C. of E. Prim. Sch.
Birkett Hall
Edwin's Hall Cottages
Hawe's Wood
Hill Farm
Woodham Ferrers
Edwin's Hall Farm
Moats
Edwin's Hall
Eastham
Town Farm
Reservoir (covered)
Happy Valley
Cattle Grid
Wellinditch
Mill Hill
Edwinshall Wood
Ilgar's Manor
Ilgar's Manor Cottages
Research Station
Bushy Hill
Morris Farm
Hamberts Farm
Nurseries
Garden of Remembrance
Hogwell Farm
Saltcoats
Woodham Ferrers
Woodham Fenn Nature Reserve
SOUTH WOODHAM FERRERS
Schools
William De Ferrers Sports Cen.
Sewage Works
Elmwood Prim. Sch.
CROWS LANE
CHARITY LANE
MALDON
CHELMSFORD
MAIN ROAD
EDWIN'S HALL ROAD
BURNHAM ROAD
WOODHAM ROAD
LWR. BURNHAM RD.
B1418
B1012
A132
75
35
103

A
B
C
76
D
E
F
G
1
2
3
4
5
6
7
8
9
97
96
95
94
93
30
38
106
37
38
39
40
Playing Field
Fouracres Nursery
Northfield Nursery
Northcroft Nursery
Chapelfield Nursery
Marshfield Nursery
Luthers Farm
Amesbury Mead Farm
SEWARDSTONE
Woodlands Nursery
Caravan Park
Santa Maria Nursery
Sewardstone Lodge
MILL LANE
Clock House Riding Stables
Picks Farm
Gilwellbury
Barn Hill
BLIND LANE
Aldergrove
Day's Farm
LIPPITTS HILL
Fernhill Wood
THE ELMS
Police Training Camp
Pipers Farm
Three Horseshoes Farm
THE OWL CARAVAN SITE
Springfield Farm
Lippittshill Lodge
DAWS HILL
Carrolls Farm
KING GEORGE'S RESERVOIR
Enfield
EN3
ENFIELD
EPPING FOREST
GILWELL PARK
GILWELL LA
Club Ho.
WEST ESSEX GOLF COURSE
Ludgate Water
Caravan Site
Ludgate House
Almshouse Plain
The White Cottage
Reservoir (covered)
Kennels
Bury Wood
Ludgate Plain
Peartree Plain
Yardley Hill
Bury Farm
Filter Beds
SEWARDSTONEBURY
River Lea (or Lee) Diversion
Valley Golf Course
WOODMAN LA.
HORNBEAM LA
Woodman's Glade
Cuckoo Pits
Bury Wood
Cuckoo Brook
Hawkswood School & Centre
The Hawk Wood
EPPING FOREST
WALTHAM FOREST
Yardley Prim. Sch.
Nursery
King George's Sailing Club
HAWKWOOD CRESCENT
HAWKDENE
EPPING GLADE
EPPING WAY
SEWARDSTONE ROAD
ROYAL EPPING FOREST & CHINGFORD PUBLIC GOLF COURSE
LEA VALLEY ROAD
A110
A112
Chingford Plain
Pole Hill Obelisk
Recreation Ground
EPPING
Horse Ride
FOREST VIEW ROAD
The Hawk Wood
Club Ho.
Queen Elizabeth's Hunting Lodge
WILLIAM GIRLING RESERVOIR
E4
RANGER'S ROAD
Playing Field
KINGS HEAD HILL
MAIDA AV.
CONNAUGHT
MORNINGTON
FREDERICA RD
The Warren
Club
Tennis Courts
Bowl. Grn.
Warren Pond
Barn Hoppet
Chingford
STATION ROAD
A1069
COLLEGE GDNS
Council Offs.
Chingford Sch.
RIDGEWAY
THE GREEN
KINGS ROAD
CHINGFORD GREEN
VICTORIA
Cricket Ground
Club
Playing Field
WALTHAM WAY
A1037
MANSFIELD HILL
Playground
Mansfield Park
CHINGFORD
FAVERSHAM AV.
WHITEHALL RD
Whitehall Plain
THE B169
Ridgeway Putting Park Green
MAYFIELD
ELMFIELD
Pimp Hall Nurseries
Pimp Hall Park
Friday Hill
FRIDAY HILL
B146
B160
ROSSLYN AV.
Playing Field
Bluehouse Grove
Playing Field
Hatch Forest
Hatch Grove
HERIOT AV.
WELLINGTON AV.
LEADALE AVENUE
CHINGFORD AVENUE
SIMMONS LANE
WITTENHAM WAY
CHURCH ROAD
Chingford Mount Cemetery
PRIORY AVENUE
Old Peoples Cen.
GUNNERS GR.
COLVIN GDNS
CRESCENT
LARKSHALL ROAD
Football Ground
Pav.
WOODFORD GOLF COURSE
OLD CHURCH ROAD
TEMPLETON AVENUE
HATCH LA.
Schs.
The Lops
NEW ROAD
A1099
CHINGFORD MOUNT
Suffield Hatch
Greens Health & Fitness
Larkswood
CHINGFORD LANE
HALL LANE

EPPING FOREST
Loughton
IG10
LOUGHTON
Buckhurst Hill
IG9
BUCKHURST HILL
Chigwell
IG7
CHIGWELL
WOODFORD WELLS
IG8
RODING VALLEY MEADOWS NATURE RESERVE
LORD'S BUSHES
M11 MOTORWAY
77
92
107

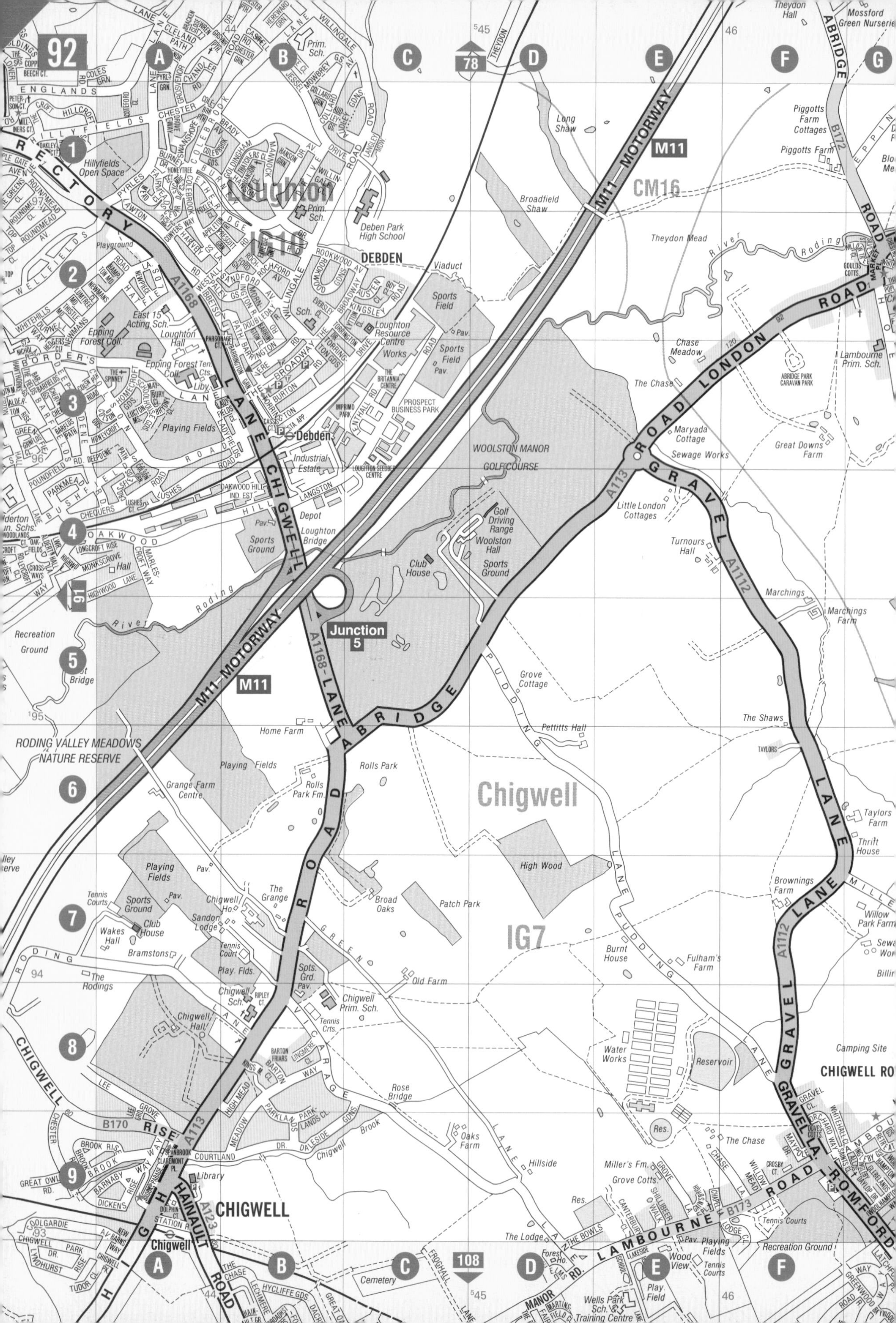

92
A
B
C
D
E
F
G
78
108
91
1
2
3
4
5
6
7
8
9
Loughton
IG10
DEBDEN
CM16
Chigwell
IG7
CHIGWELL
CHIGWELL RO
M11
M11 MOTORWAY
M11–MOTORWAY
Junction 5
A1168
A1168–LANE
A113
A1112
A123
B170
B172
B173
RECTORY
LANE
CHIGWELL
LANE
ABRIDGE
ROAD
LONDON ROAD
GRAVEL LANE
GRAVEL LA.
ROMFORD
LAMBOURNE RD.
PUDDING LANE
HAINAULT ROAD
HIGH RD.
VICARAGE LANE
GREEN LANE
RODING LANE
CHIGWELL RISE
LEE GROVE
ABRIDGE ROAD
MANOR RD.
Hillyfields Open Space
Playground
East 15 Acting Sch.
Epping Forest Coll.
Loughton Hall
Epping Forest Coll.
Liby
Playing Fields
Debden
Industrial Estate
Depot
Loughton Bridge
Sports Ground
Hall
Recreation Ground
Bridge
River Roding
RODING VALLEY MEADOWS NATURE RESERVE
Prim. Sch.
Deben Park High School
Sch.
Loughton Resource Centre
Works
Viaduct
Sports Field
Pav.
PROSPECT BUSINESS PARK
Long Shaw
Broadfield Shaw
Theydon Mead
Theydon Hall
Mossford Green Nurseries
Piggotts Farm Cottages
Piggotts Farm
Chase Meadow
The Chase
ABRIDGE PARK CARAVAN PARK
Lambourne Prim. Sch.
Maryada Cottage
Sewage Works
Great Downs Farm
WOOLSTON MANOR GOLFCOURSE
Golf Driving Range
Woolston Hall
Sports Ground
Club House
Little London Cottages
Turnours Hall
Marchings
Marchings Farm
Grove Cottage
Pettitts Hall
The Shaws
TAYLORS
Taylors Farm
Thrift House
Brownings Farm
Willow Park Farm
Home Farm
Rolls Park
Rolls Park Fm.
Grange Farm Centre
Playing Fields
High Wood
Patch Park
Broad Oaks
The Grange
Chigwell Ho.
Sandon Lodge
Tennis Court
Play. Flds.
Spts. Grd.
Old Farm
Chigwell Prim. Sch.
Tennis Crts.
Chigwell Sch.
Chigwell Hall
Tennis Courts
Sports Ground
Club House
Wakes Hall
Bramstons
The Rodings
Burnt House
Fulham's Farm
Water Works
Reservoir
Res.
Camping Site
Rose Bridge
Oaks Farm
Hillside
Miller's Fm.
Grove Cotts
The Chase
Tennis Courts
Recreation Ground
Playing Fields
Wood View
Tennis Courts
Play. Field
Wells Park Sch. & Training Centre
The Lodge
Forest Ho.
THE BOWLS
Cemetery
Library
Chigwell
Chigwell Brook

93
79
94
109
Romford
RM4
ABRIDGE
Lambourne
LAMBOURNE END
Crabtree Hill
Bournebridge
STAPLEFORD ABBOTTS
STAPLEFORD TAWNEY AIRFIELD
HAINAULT FOREST (COUNTRY PARK)
HAINAULT FOREST GOLF COURSE
EPPING FOREST
HAVERING
EPPING FOREST REDBRIDGE
WEDDRELL'S PLAIN
A113
B175
River Roding
Hillmans Cottages
Crowther Nurseries
BBC Essex Garden
Arnold's Farm Cottages
Arnolds Farm
Little Arnolds
Mill House
Passingford Bridge Mill
Warehouse
WORKS
Waters Farm
Pryors
Lower Wood
Lambourne Place
Patch Park
Foxburrow Wood
Hammonds
Ape's Grove
Lodge
Alder Wood
New Fm.
North Lodge
Jubilee Plantation
Great Wood
Mutton Corner
Lambourne Hall
Church Cotts.
Soapley's Wood
Lodge
Halfmoon Wood
Knoll's Wood
Woodside Farm
Kirton's Fm.
Gordon Cotts.
Church Farm
Old Rectory Farm
Battles Hall
Stapleford Abbotts Prim. Sch.
Bishop's Moat
Conduit Wood
Belmont Fm.
Grove House
Dews Hall Farm
Clark's Wood
The Bungalow
Bishop's Hall
Lodge
Farm
St. John's Farm
High House Farm
Woodlands Fm.
Lambourne Park Farm
Park Square
Gallman's End Farm
Hook Lane Nurseries
Isabella Cottages
Tuttleby Cotts.
Blackbush Farm
Priors
Playing Fields
Sports Ground
Pav.
Mansfield Outdoor Centre
Blue House Farm
Knolls Hill Farm
Nursery
Augusta Cottages
Bournebridge Farm
Crown Park Farm
Hop Pole Farm
The Camelot
Lambourne Well
Bourne Bridge
Harmes Farm
Three Cornered Plain
Cavill's Walk
Spurgate Plain
Spurgate Brook
Banks Farm
Lambourne Sq.
Taylor's Plain
Sheepcotes
Lodge
Sandhills
Oster Bed
Cabin Plain
Cabin Hill
Mile Plantation
Sheep Water
Foreberry Wood North
Lower Sandhills
Roes Well
Park Farm
Visitor Centre
Fox Burrows
Foreberry Wood South
The Lake
HAVERING
WELLINGTONIA
CLOCKHOUSE
PINEWOOD
ONGAR ROAD
CHURCH LANE
FEATHERBED LANE
NEW NORTH ROAD
HOOK LANE
MANOR ROAD
BOURNEBRIDGE LANE
STAPLEFORD ROAD
GUTTERIDGE LA
LAMBOURNE ROAD
FOX BURROW ROAD

94
80
93
110
M25
M25 MOTORWAY
PASSINGFORD BRIDGE
Passingford Bridge Mill
ONGAR A113 RD.
LONDON ROAD
EPPING LANE
Waters Farm
Hammonds
Woodside Farm
Kirton's Fm.
Gordon Cotts.
Battles Hall
STAPLEFORD ROAD
B175
ALBYNS LANE
The Lodge
Rookery Wood
Bons Farm
Church Wood
Albyns Hall
Albyns Manor
North East Lodge
Grafton Farm
River Roding
BRENTWOOD
EPPING FOREST
Green Farm Cotts.
Green Farm
Curtismill Green
Landend Cottage
Thatched Cottage
Rose Cottages
Willow Cottage
Lady Abdy's Walk
CHURCH TERRACE
Deerbarn Wood
Bentleyfield Wood
Church Farm
Old Rectory Farm
CURTIS MILL LANE
Bourne Brook
Brook Farm
Brook Farm Bungalow
Horsemans Lodge
Jenkins Farm
The Harrow
Curtis Mill Cottage
Willow Tree Cottage
Dabbs Farm
Howletts Hall
MURTHERING LANE
Stapleford Abbotts Prim. Sch.
STAPLEFORD ABBOTTS
Belmont Fm.
Grove House
Stapleford Hall Fm.
Rose Cottage
High House Farm
GUTTERIDGE LA.
Mitchell's Farm
Woodlands Fm.
Tyseahill Farm
Olives Farm
Spring Farm
NAVESTOCK COMMON
Moat
Watton Farm
Dycotts
STAPLEFORD ABBOTS GOLF COURSE
Watton's Green
Works
THE PRIORS GOLF COURSE
THE PADDOCKS
RM4
High Willows
Ashwood Farm
Stocks Farm
Tysea Hill
Skips Corner Farm
Club House
TYSEA HILL
HORSEMAN
GOATSWOOD
Asheton Fm.
Stapleford Common
Nursery
THE DRIVE
Brook Farm
Stapleford Farm
Twinoaks Farm
Nuper's Hatch
Nuper's Farm
Lyngs Farm
Pinchback Bridge
Bournebridge Farm
BOURNEBRIDGE LANE
Bournebridge
Bourne Bridge
Butcher's Farm
Nursery
Greenacres Farm
ROAD OAK HILL ROAD
Boyland's Oak Farm
TOWNELEY COTTS.
Spencers Farm
Pygro Wood
Romford
Straights Plantation
Lodge
Palace Plantation
Sandpits Plantation
Hilly Park
Witch Hill Plantation
EPPING FOREST
HAVERING
Osier Bed
Home Farm
Horseshoe Farm
Tench Pond Plantation
Wilderness
Play. Fld.
Bower Farm
BOWER FARM
Dame Tipping C. of E. Prim. School
South Park Plantation
PYRGO PARK
Foxburrow Wood
Pheasant Wood
SAMANTHA M.
RD
ROWLAND WLK.
NORTH ROAD
ST. FRANCIS HOSPICE
Round House Farm
HAVERING-ATTE-BOWER
Riding Stables
The Round House
Avenue Wood
AVENUE
WELLINGTONIA
ELMER AV.
THE GN.
BROXHILL ROAD
Ckt. Grd
Pav.
Playing Field
ORANGE TREE HILL
HAVERING COUNTRY PARK
CLOCKHOUSE
Pine Wood
Poultry Farm
Orange Tree
Bower Farm
PINEWOOD ROAD
Bower
Bower Wood
Tennis Courts
A
B
C
D
E
F
G
1
2
3
4
5
6
7
8
9
550
51
52
53
97
96
95
94
93

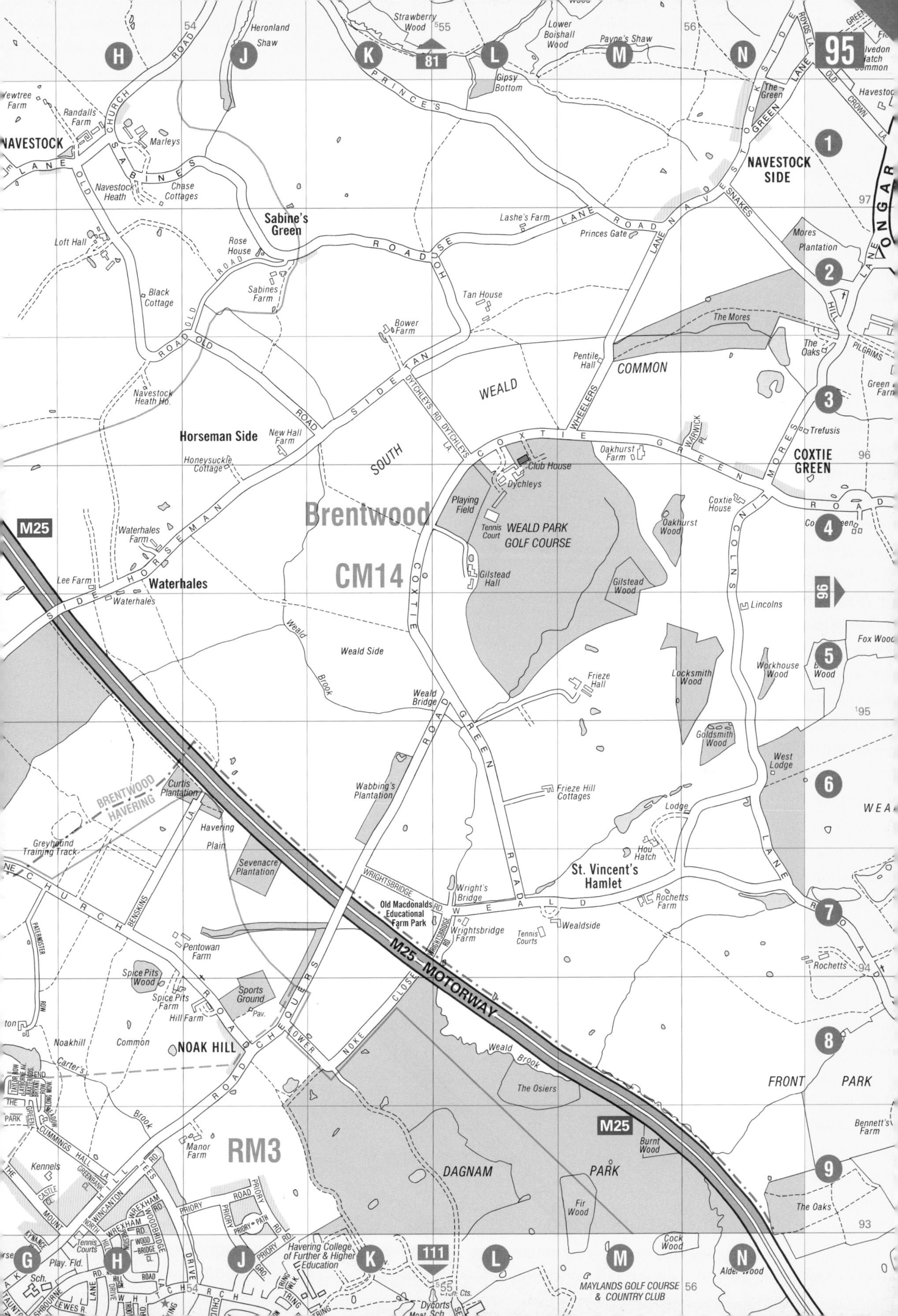
Strawberry Wood
81
Heronland Shaw
Lower Boishall Wood
Payne's Shaw
Gipsy Bottom
NAVESTOCK
Randalls Farm
Marleys
Navestock Heath
Chase Cottages
Sabine's Green
Loft Hall
Rose House
Sabines Farm
Black Cottage
Navestock Heath Ho.
Horseman Side
New Hall Farm
Honeysuckle Cottage
Waterhales Farm
Waterhales
Lee Farm
M25
Brentwood
CM14
SOUTH
WEALD
COMMON
Lashe's Farm
Princes Gate
Tan House
Bower Farm
Pentile Hall
The Mores
Mores Plantation
NAVESTOCK SIDE
The Green
The Oaks
Trefusis
COXTIE GREEN
Green Farm
Oakhurst Farm
Club House
Dychleys
Playing Field
Tennis Court
WEALD PARK GOLF COURSE
Coxtie House
Oakhurst Wood
Gilstead Hall
Gilstead Wood
Lincolns
96
Fox Wood
Weald Side
Frieze Hall
Locksmith Wood
Workhouse Wood
Goldsmith Wood
West Lodge
Weald Bridge
Wabbing's Plantation
Frieze Hill Cottages
Lodge
Hou Hatch
St. Vincent's Hamlet
Rochetts Farm
Rochetts
Wealdside
Tennis Courts
Old Macdonalds Educational Farm Park
Wright's Bridge
Wrightsbridge Farm
BRENTWOOD
HAVERING
Curtis Plantation
Havering Plain
Greyhound Training Track
Sevenacre Plantation
Pentowan Farm
Spice Pits Wood
Spice Pits Farm
Hill Farm
Sports Ground
Pav.
Noakhill Common
NOAK HILL
M25 MOTORWAY
Weald Brook
The Osiers
FRONT PARK
Bennett's Farm
Burnt Wood
Manor Farm
RM3
Kennels
DAGNAM PARK
Fir Wood
The Oaks
Cock Wood
Havering College of Further & Higher Education
111
Tennis Courts
Play. Fld.
Sch.
MAYLANDS GOLF COURSE & COUNTRY CLUB
Alder Wood
Dycorts

96
82
95
112
NAVESTOCK SIDE
BENTLEY
COXTIE GREEN
CROW GREEN
PILGRIMS HATCH
Brentwood
BRENTWOOD
SOUTH WEALD
CM14
WEALD COUNTRY PARK
BENTLEY GOLF COURSE & COUNTRY CLUB
FRONT PARK
M25 MOTORWAY
ONGAR ROAD
A128
A12
A1023
BRENTWOOD BY-PASS
LONDON ROAD
HIGH STREET
WEALD ROAD
Havestock
Alders Wood
Camping & Caravaning Site
Mores Plantation
The Mores
The Oaks
Nursery
Green Lane Farm
Trefusis
Pilgrim's Hall
Ashwells Farm
Millfield
Wishfields Farm
Sumner's Farm
Days Farm
Clay Hall
Kennels
Brick House Wood
Canterbury Tye Farm
Gents Farm
Hullett's Farm
Coxtie Green Farm
Playing Field
Depot
Larch Wood
Fox Wood
Shepherds Spinney
Broom Wood
Langton's Wood
The Forest
Foxdown Cottage
West Lodge
The Park
Sandpit Cottage
Cricket Grd.
Rochetts
Keeper's Cottage
Halfway House Farm
Reservoir
Calcott Hall Farm
The Spinney
High Wood
Larkin's Playing Flds.
Brentwood Radio Station
Bishops Hall Park
The Brentwood Centre
Little Highwood Hosp.
Highwood Hosp.
Sawyer's Hall Farm
The Hedley Walter High Sch.
St. Peter's C. of E. Prim. Sch.
Vicarage
Vicarage Wood
Bennett's Farm
Colmar
Offices
Cemy.
Warehouse
Gasholder Station
Lower Vicarage Wood
Alder Wood
Hotel
Tennis Cts.
Spts. Grd.
Superstore
Brentwood

97
MOUNTNESSING
Long Wood
83
Chelmwood Farm
America Farm
Thoby Farm
Fox Earth Wood
River Wid
Heard's Farm
Drury's Farm
Mountnessing C. of E. Prim. School
Hillrise Farm
Icehouse Wood
Fitzwalter's
Moat
HOME WOOD
Palmer's Farm
Palmer's Farm Cottages
HALL LANE
Howe's Farm
Blue House
Chainbridge Farm
Junction 12
MOUNTNESSING
A12 BY-PASS
ROMAN ROAD
LOWER ROAD
B1002
Arnold's Farm
Keepers Cottage
Marylands
MARYLANDS INTERCHANGE
A1023
Arnold's Wood
Arnold's Shaw
Brickley Shaw
Canterbury Tye Spring
Wynbarns Farm
Shenfield High Sch. & Sports Centre
Play. Fld.
Ind. Est.
Prospect Works
Long Ridings Prim. Sch.
HUTTON
Poplars Hall
Shenfield Hall
Shenfield Hall Farm
Hall Wood
Tennis Courts
St. Mary's C. of E. Prim. Sch.
CHELMSFORD ROAD
RAYLEIGH ROAD
HUTTON ROAD
A129
Shenfield
Lib.
Coll.
Fire Brigade H.Q.
Willowbrook Prim. Sch.
Hutton Play. Flds.
Hutton Prim. Sch.
Comm. Cen.
CM15
Playing Field
SHENFIELD
HUTTON MOUNT
Sports Ground
Ckt. Grd.
HALL GREEN LANE
RIDGEWAY
Playing Field
St. Martins School
Sports Grd.
Brentwood Lawn Ten. Club
THE ESSEX NUFFIELD HOSP.
BRENTWOOD COMMUNITY HOSPITAL
Brentwood Preparatory School
Sports Ground
Running Track
Brentwood Sch. Sports Cen.
Scout Camp
THRIFT WOOD
Playing Field
Hogarth Prim. Sch.
The Endeavor Sch.
South Hove
Brindles Farm
Hall Wood
Hall Wood
CM13
Sewage Works
Brentwood High Sch.
Play. Fld.
Shenfield Common
Three Arch Bridge
A128
Seven Arch Bridge
Ingrave Hall
Birches Wood
Sutton Shaw
Ingrave Common
113
Min. Golf Course
Club House
King George's Playing Field
Highfield Wood
Council Off.

MOUNTNESSING
Valentine
Keepers Cottage
Bakers Farm
Drury's Farm
Mountnessing C. of E. Prim. School
Hillrise Farm
ROMAN ROAD
MOUNTNESSING BY-PASS
A12
CHURCH LANE
Begrums Farm
Rose Cottage
Jordans Farm
OLD CHURCH RD.
MARSH LANE
CHURCH ROAD
BURNTHOUSE LA.
84
Padhams Green
PADHAMS GREEN ROAD
Westlands Farm
Ford
Shoulder Hall
Harespring Wood
Arnold's Farm
Moat
ARNOLDS FARM LANE
LOWER ROAD
OLD ROAD
OLD CHURCH LANE
Mountnessing Hall
CHURCH ROAD
MOUNTNESSING ROAD
Wardroper's
Lawness
Arnold's Shaw
Brickley Shaw
ROAD
Ind. Est.
PROSPECT WY.
Works
TALLON RD.
KESTREL PARK
HUTTON
Clapgate Wood
Sewage Works
Cock Wood
Brentwood
River Wid
Little Cowbridge Grange
BLUEBELL WOOD
THE LINKS
Collins Farm
MOUNT PLEASANT AV.
SUN BAY AV.
OAKWOOD AV.
GOODWOOD AVENUE
Studd Farm
CM13
Round Wood
RAYLEIGH ROAD
A129
CHELMER
LONSDALE AV.
RANDALLS DR.
DELTA RD.
CEDAR RD.
CEDAR CL.
FAIRVIEW
HUTTON DRIVE
VILLAGE
Willowbrook Prim. Sch.
Poultry House
Great Cowbridge Grange Farm
Bushwood Farm
NORTH DRIVE
Hutton Manor
Ellices Farm
HUTTON CT.
The Willows
Martines
Haveringsgrove Bridge
LONDON ROAD
Hutton Village Nursing Home
Humes Farm
Nursery
Havering's Grove
CHASE
MARGETH WORKS
Shipmans Shaw
BOUNDARY DR.
KINGSLEY RD.
HALL ROAD
SHELLEY
Sports Ground
Ckt. Grd.
Pav.
Lodge
Hutton Hall
Moat
GREEN LANE
AVENUE
CLIFTON WAY
CHURCH LANE
FOXES GRO.
TALLY-HO DR.
HUNTERS
The Coppice
Church Shaw
Blunts Wall Farm
BLUNTS
Creasey's Farm
James's Wood
South Hove
Bluntswall Wood
BRENTWOOD BASILDON
Bluntswall Shaws
Hall
Wood
Primstock
Elmshaws Farm
COMMON
Sewage Works
Little Bladen's Wood
Sutton Shaw
Ninges Corner
TYE
Bladen's Wood
114
Sudbury's Farm
SUDBURYS FARM ROAD
Salmon's Farm
Four Acres
Sudbury's Bungalow
Babshole Farm
Highfield Wood
Long Shaw
The Willows
Richdean Farm
A B C D E F G
1 2 3 4 5 6 7 8 9
63 64 565 66
97 96 95 94 93

H
J
K
L
M
N
85
115
100
1
2
3
4
5
6
7
8
9
G
67
68
69
97
96
95
94
93
Ingatestone
CM4
CM12
CM11
Billericay
BILLERICAY
Queen's Park
Gooseberry Green
Sunnymede
South Green
Tye Common
STOCK BROOK MANOR GOLF & COUNTRY CLUB
Club House
King's Head Farm
Brook Farm
Greenacre Farm
Brook Farm Riding Stables
Greenacre Nurseries
Bridle-Way Nurseries
Willowbrook Sports Ground
Buttsbury Lodge
Great Blunts Fm.
Little Blunts
North Nook
Hillside Farm
Buckwyns Farm
Hannikins Farm Recreation Ground
Queen's Park Country Park
Community Centre
Recreation Ground
Brightside Prim. Sch.
Oaklands Farm
Foxfield House
Springfield
FORTY ACRE PLANTATION
Ramsden Heath Reservoir (Covered)
NORSEY WOOD NATURE RESERVE
Great Fox Hill
Tylde Hall Farm
Ramsden Hall School
Poplar Plantation
Moses Spring Wood
Outwood Farm
Mayflower High School
Playing Field
Buttsbury Jun. Sch.
Buttsbury Inf. Sch.
Boating Lake
Lake Meadows Rec. Grd.
Miniature Golf Course
Billericay Swimming Pool
Health Cen.
Sunnymede Junior & Infants Schools
Sewage Works
Hummerstone
Hillcroft
Oak Hill Farm
White Farm
Boyce Farm
Rosedene
Cox's Farm
Nursery
Brier Mount
Southend Farm
St. Peter's Catholic Prim. Sch.
Factory
Snails Hall
Common Land
Mill House
Gatwick House
The Billericay Sch. & Sports Hall
Langhams
The Kennels
The Frith
Frith Wood
THE BURSTEAD GOLF COURSE
Curd Farm
Kingsmans Farm
Quilters Jun & Inf. Schs.
Billericay Town FC (New Lodge)
Reservoir
STOCK ROAD
SOUTHEND ROAD
NOAK HILL ROAD
LAINDON ROAD
HIGH STREET
NORSEY ROAD
OUTWOOD COMMON ROAD
COXES FARM RD.
A129
A176
B1007

Ingatestone
CM4
Billericay
CM11
HANNINGFIELD RESERVOIR
HANNINGFIELD RESERVE BIRD SANCTUARY
Cloyna Poultry Farm
Great Bishop's Wood
Bishop's Lodge
Whitelilies Farm
Greenacre Nurseries
Bridle-Way Nurseries
Woodholme
Broom Wood
Oak Hall
Broomwood Cottage
Heathfield
Longcroft
Fremnells
Crowsheath Farm
Pumping Sta.
Little Abbott's
Crowsheath Wood Nature Reserve
Cock Wood
Bridleway Cottage
Oaklands Farm
OAKLANDS FARM IND. EST.
Common Farm
Hilltop Nursery
Ramsden Back Common
Tippler's Bridge
FORTY ACRE PLANTATION
Works
Sports Field
Allen's Farm
Downham
Ramsden Heath Reservoir (Covered)
Hunt's Farm
Heath Farm
Lodge Farm
Barn Farm
Chitham's Farm
Moat
Ramsden Heath
Rec. Grd.
Poultry Houses
WINDSOR TRADING ESTATE
Greenacres Farm
Rectory Wood
Downham C.E. Prim. Sch.
Fylde Hall Farm
Ramsden Hall School
Cox Green
MEEPSHOLE WOOD
De Beauvoir Farm
Langdale Farm
Sewage Works
Parsonage Farm
De-Beauvoir Farm
Parsonage
Pump Hill
Poplar Plantation
Devil's Wood
Crays Wood
Moses Spring Wood
Kent Hill
CHELMSFORD
BASILDON
Amberwood
Outwood Farm
Barrenleys Wood
Claypitshills Wood
Ramsden Park Farm
Hall
The Grange
Sewage Works
Hummerstone
RAMSDEN BELLHOUSE
Hillcroft
Recreation Ground
Oak Hill Farm
White Farm
Boyce Farm
Rosedene
Cox's Farm
Nursery
Brier Mount
Parsonage Farm
River Crouch
Playing Field
Crays Hall Farm
WOOLSHOTS COTTS.
Woolshot's Farm
St. Peter's Catholic Prim. Sch.
Crays Hall Cottages
HILL FARM COTTS.
Gurnard's
THE CHASEWAY
BROOMWOOD
LANE
GOAT'S MOOR
HEATH ROAD
COMMON ROAD
DOWNHAM ROAD
SCHOOL ROAD
CROWSHEATH LANE
HAWKSWOOD ROAD
MILL LANE
PARK LANE
CHURCH ROAD
DE BEAUVOIR CHASE
RAMSDEN PARK ROAD
ORCHARD AVENUE
HOMESTEAD ROAD
GLEBE
OUTWOOD FARM ROAD
COXES FARM ROAD
CHURCH LANE
WOOLSHOTS RD.
LONDON ROAD
WINDSOR ROAD
OAK ROAD
MOUNT VIEW
BALMORAL
DURLEY
86
99
116

101
South Hanningfield
Coalhill
Chelmsford
CM3
Brock Hill
Wickford
SS11
RUNWELL
RUNWELL HOSPITAL
WICKFORD
SS12
SHOTGATE
Hawk's Wood
Well Wood
Scrub Wood
Foxearth Wood
Harrow Wood
Middle Wood
Moorgarden Wood
Gorse Wood
Sandpit Wood
Pitfield Shaw
Reservoir (covered)
Barn Hall Open Space
Memorial Park (Rec. Ground)
River Crouch
Pumping Station
Gas Pipeline Station
87
117
102

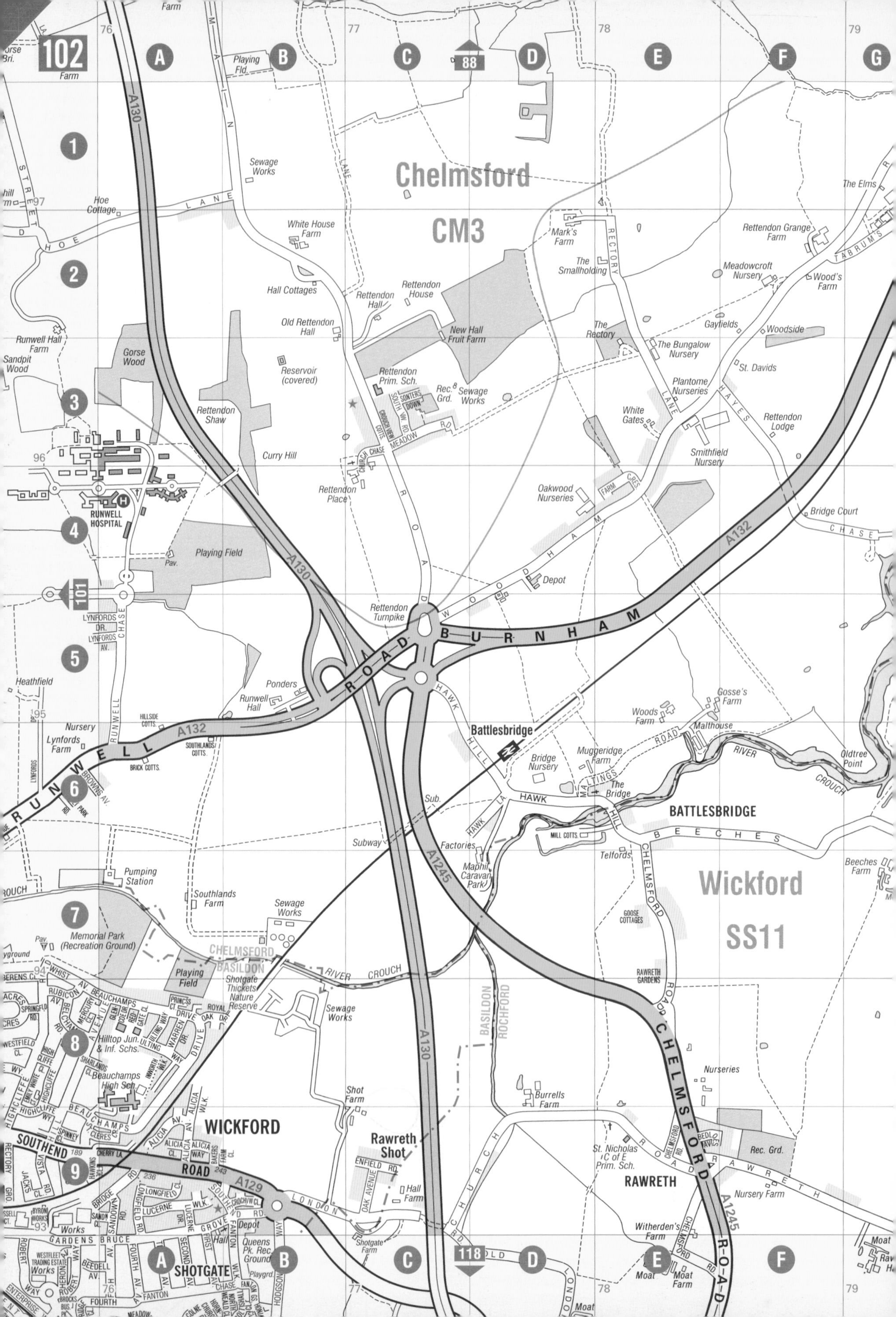

Chelmsford
CM3
Wickford
SS11
WICKFORD
BATTLESBRIDGE
RAWRETH
SHOTGATE
Battlesbridge
Rawreth Shot
RUNWELL HOSPITAL
Runwell Hall Farm
Sandpit Wood
Gorse Wood
Rettendon Shaw
Curry Hill
Playing Field
Hoe Cottage
Sewage Works
White House Farm
Hall Cottages
Old Rettendon Hall
Rettendon Hall
Rettendon House
New Hall Fruit Farm
Reservoir (covered)
Rettendon Prim. Sch.
Rec. Grd.
Rettendon Place
Rettendon Turnpike
Mark's Farm
The Smallholding
The Rectory
The Bungalow Nursery
Plantome Nurseries
White Gates
Oakwood Nurseries
Depot
Smithfield Nursery
Rettendon Lodge
St. Davids
Woodside
Gayfields
Meadowcroft Nursery
Wood's Farm
Rettendon Grange Farm
The Elms
Bridge Court
Ponders
Runwell Hall
Heathfield
Nursery
Lynfords Farm
Bridge Nursery
Muggeridge Farm
The Bridge
Woods Farm
Gosse's Farm
Malthouse
Oldtree Point
Telfords
Factories
Maphill Caravan Park
Subway
Pumping Station
Southlands Farm
Memorial Park (Recreation Ground)
Shotgate Thickets Nature Reserve
Hilltop Jun. & Inf. Schs.
Beauchamps High Sch.
Shot Farm
Hall Farm
Burrells Farm
St. Nicholas C of E Prim. Sch.
Nurseries
Nursery Farm
Witherden's Farm
Moat Farm
Beeches Farm
Queens Pk. Rec. Ground
Works
A130
A132
A1245
A129
BURNHAM ROAD
RUNWELL ROAD
SOUTHEND ROAD
CHELMSFORD ROAD
HOE LANE
RECTORY LANE
HAYES CHASE
BEECHES ROAD
HAWK HILL
RIVER CROUCH
CHELMSFORD BASILDON
BASILDON ROCHFORD
88
101
118

103
SOUTH WOODHAM FERRERS
Woodham Ferrers
Woodham Fenn Nature Reserve
Sewage Works
Tabrum's Farm
Elmwood Prim. Sch.
William De Ferrers Sports Cen.
Schools
Collingwood Prim. Sch.
Chetwood Prim. Sch.
Eyott's Farm
Eyott Sailing Club
Chelmsford
CM3
MARSH FARM COUNTRY PARK
Marsh Farm
Nursery
Hayes Farm
HAYES FARM CARAVAN PARK
Long Reach
Boatbuilding Yard
RIVER CROUCH
CHELMSFORD
ROCHFORD
Recreation Ground
Kingsmans Farm
Brandy Hole
104
Clementsgreen Creek
Hawbush Creek
Saltcoats
Riverside Jun. & Inf. Schs.
HULLBRIDGE
Reservoir
Hockley
SS5
Highlands
Pickerels Farm
The Mousery
Boxes
Sewage Works
Malyons
Little Malyons
Cracknell's Farm
Sheepcotes Farm
Barton's Farm
Mount View
Jakapeni Rare Breeds Farm
Moat House
Madingley Lodge
Vicarage Farm
Wadham Park Farm
Nursery
Hockley Hall
Mill Hill
Rayleigh
SS6
Club House
HANOVER GOLF COURSE & COUNTRY CLUB
Moat
Trenders Hall
Pengelly
Lubard's Lodge
Res.
Murrells Hall
Blounts Farm
Blounts Wood
Lakes
89
119
A132 ROAD
LOWER ROAD
COVENTRY HILL
WATERY LANE
HULLBRIDGE ROAD
FERRY ROAD
CHURCH ROAD
BLOUNTSWOOD ROAD
MURRELLS LANE
KINGSMANS FARM ROAD
LONG LANE
POOLES LANE
CREEKVIEW ROAD
MALDON ROAD
CHELMSFORD ROAD

A
B
C
35
D
E
F
G
83
84
585
North Fambridge
West Wick Marina
Powneys Cottage
White House
Whitehouse Farm
Kennett's Farm
Manor Farm
Post Moor Cottage
Slipways
Tidal Ponds
Stow Creek
Clementsgreen Creek
MALDON
CHELMSFORD
Hawbush Creek
Brandyhole Reach
RIVER
CHELMSFORD
ROCHFORD
Brandy Hole
Kingsmans Farm
Brandy Hole
103
Shellfish Packing Station
South Fambridge
Brickhouse Farm
Beckney Farm
New Bungalow
Uguess
Hockley
SS5
Lovedown
HOCKLEY MOBILE HOMES
Sheepcotes Farm
Nursery
Reservoir
Lowlands Farm
Nursery
New Hall
Beckney Wood Ho.
New Hockley Hall Farm
Lower Hockley Hall
Lower Hockley Hall Farm
Cherry Tree Farm
Barton's Farm
Horseshoe Farm
Betts Farm
Plumberow Wood
Plumberow Mount
Beckney Wood
Northcroft
New Hall Farm
Reservoir
Long Ridings
Reservoir
Madingley Lodge
Vicarage Farm
Wadham Park Farm
Nursery
The Old Vicarage
Hockleyhall Wood
Crabtree Wood
Hockley Hall
Mill Hill
Woodlands Nurseries
Trinity Wood
Clydesdale
Covertside
Mount View
Highfield
Homefield Farm
Playing Field
HOCKLEY
Plumberow Prim. Sch.
Greensward College
Marylands Wood
Community Centre
Bett's Wood
Hockley Prim. Sch.
Nurseries
Nurseries
Murrells Hall
Blounts Farm
Nursery
Hockley
Bines Cottage
120
LOWER ROAD
CHURCH ROAD
MURRELLS LANE
ST. PETERS RD.
WADHAM PK. AVENUE
MERTON RD.
FOLLY CHASE
ROSILIAN DR.
PLUMBEROW AVENUE
BECKNEY AV.
WOOD AVENUE
ETHELDORE AV.
BRANKSOME AV.
PEACH RUSSET WY.
ORCHARD AV.
TONBRIDGE RD.
MALVERN RD.
HARROGATE DR.
HARROGATE RD.
LEAMINGTON RD.
PULPITS CL.
CHELTENHAM RD.
CORNHILL AVENUE
OAK WALK
GREENSWARD LANE
HAMILTON GDNS.
ROSSLYN RD.
MARYLANDS AVENUE
MERRYFIELDS AV.
BRACKEN DALE CL.
SOUTHVIEW
BROAD WALK
BROADLANDS RD.
CHESTNUT
WILLOW
BROAD WALK
WESTMINSTER DR.
BUCKINGHAM
ELDON WAY
ELDON WAY IND. EST.
LOWER ROAD
GRANVILLE RD.
CLARENDON RD.
WOODSIDE RD.
WELLINGTON RD.
CAVENDISH RD.
OAKFIELD RD.
NEW PK. RD.
NEW HALL ROAD
VINCENT ROAD
LANE
CROUCH VIEW CRES.
TRINITY WOOD
FERRY ROAD
CHURCH RD.
THE AVENUE
RUTLAND RD.
ROBERTS RD.
BRABANT RD.
FAMBRIDGE RD.
BLUE HO. FARM CHASE
FAMBRIDGE ROAD
PEMBERTON FLD.
ST. THOMAS RD.
MAIN RD.
SPUR
THE DOME VILLAGE
APPLEYARD AV.
BLENHEIM CL.
PLUMBEROW MT.
MAPLE LEAF CL.
WESTBOURNE CL.
SOUTHBOURNE
BEACHES CL.
BRINKWITH CL.
HAMPTON CL.
CAERNARVON CL.
MOUNT AV.
SELBOURNE
POPLARS
RACHEL CL.
REGENCY CL.
SUDELEY GDS.
MARLBOROUGH
97
96
95
94
93
1
2
3
4
5
6
7
8
9

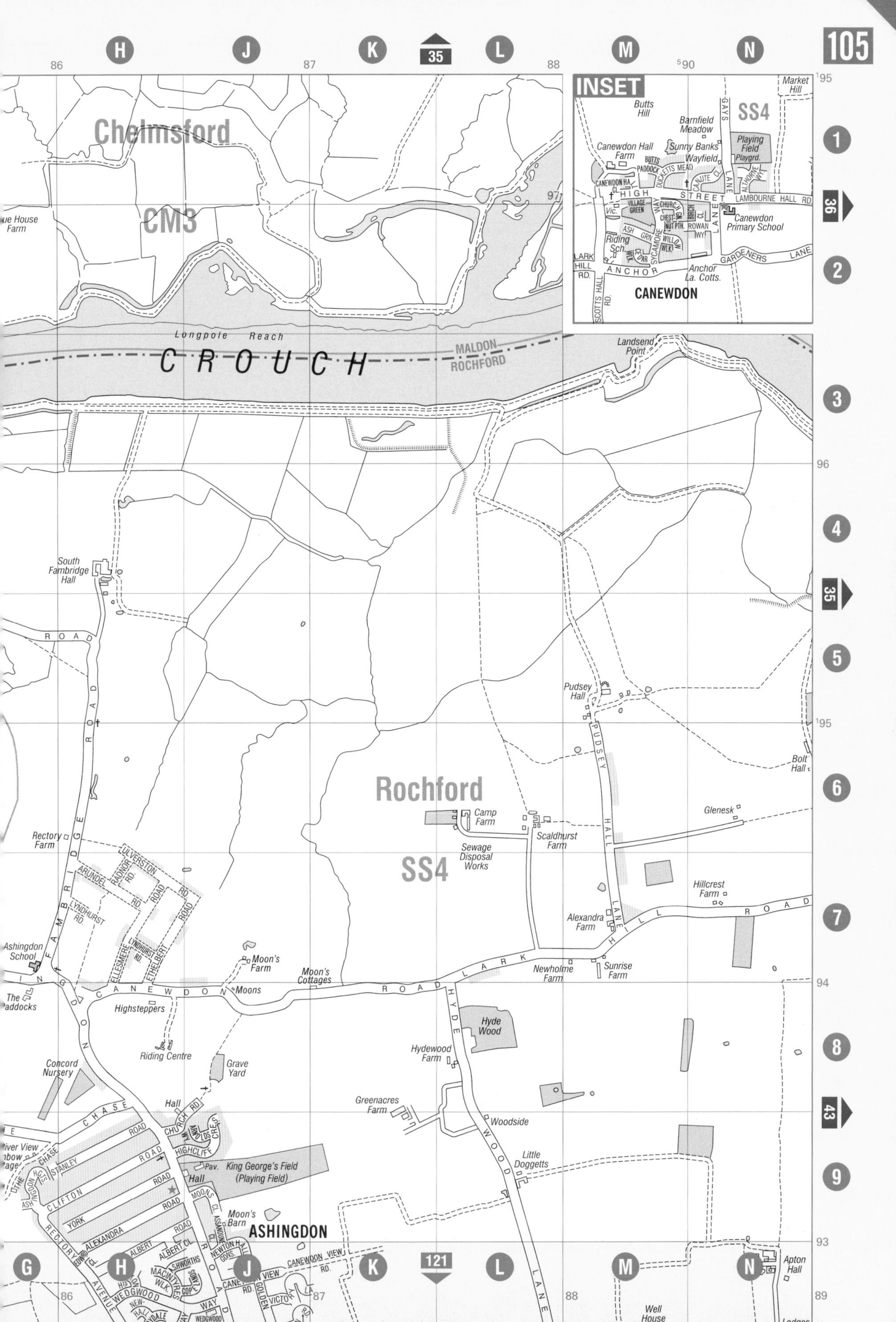

H
J
K
35
L
M
N
86
87
88
90
95
INSET
Butts Hill
Barnfield Meadow
SS4
Canewdon Hall Farm
Sunny Banks
Playing Field
Playgrd.
Wayfield
HIGH STREET
LAMBOURNE HALL RD.
Canewdon Primary School
VILLAGE GREEN
Riding Sch.
Anchor La. Cotts.
ANCHOR
GARDENERS LANE
LARK HILL RD.
SCOTTS HALL RD.
CANEWDON
Chelmsford
CM3
House Farm
Longpole Reach
CROUCH
MALDON
ROCHFORD
Landsend Point
96
South Fambridge Hall
ROAD
FAMBRIDGE ROAD
Pudsey Hall
PUDSEY HALL LANE
Bolt Hall
Rochford
Camp Farm
Glenesk
Sewage Disposal Works
Scaldhurst Farm
SS4
Rectory Farm
ULVERSTON RD.
ARUNDEL
RADNOR RD.
LYNDHURST RD.
Hillcrest Farm
Alexandra Farm
HILL ROAD
Ashingdon School
Moon's Farm
Moon's Cottages
LARK
Newholme Farm
Sunrise Farm
The Paddocks
CANEWDON ROAD
Moons
Highsteppers
HYDE WOOD LANE
Hyde Wood
Hydewood Farm
Riding Centre
Grave Yard
Concord Nursery
CHASE
Hall
Greenacres Farm
Woodside
Little Doggetts
King George's Field (Playing Field)
Pav.
Moon's Barn
ASHINGDON
STANLEY
CLIFTON
YORK
ALEXANDRA
RECTORY AVENUE
CANEWDON VIEW RD.
93
G
121
Apton Hall
89
Well House
Lodges
1
2
3
4
5
6
7
8
9
36
35
43

106
A
B
C
D
E
F
G
1
2
3
4
5
6
7
8
9
90
38
122
WOODFORD GOLF COURSE
CHINGFORD MOUNT
Suffield Hatch
CHINGFORD HATCH
E4
Larkswood Playing Fields
Larkswood Leisure Centre
Larks Wood
Larkswood Park
SOUTH CHINGFORD
Ainslie Wood Nature Reserve
Rolls Sports Grd.
HIGHAMS PARK
Highams Park
HIGHAMS PARK INDUSTRIAL ESTATE
HALE END
The Highams Park
Boating Lake
Woodford Side
Woodford Green Prim. Sch.
Sports Grd.
Woodford High Sch. for Girls
Rugby Football Grd.
Cedar Lodge
EPPING FOREST
Walthamstow Stadium (Greyhound)
The Peter May Centre
Playing Field
LLOYD PARK
Chapel End
E17
WATERWORKS CORNER
Walthamstow Forest
Reservoir (Covered)
Gillbert's Slade
Waltham Forest Pool & Track
Chestnuts Sports Ground
WALTHAMSTOW
Town Hall
Civic Cen.
THORPE COOMBE HOSP
Wood St. Walthamstow
UPPER WALTHAMSTOW
Boating Pond
Community Hall
Nature Reserve
Sports Ground Forest Sch.
Round Pond
Eagle Pond
Snaresbrook Crown Court
Hollow Pond (Boating Lake)
Walthamstow Central
Walthamstow Queens Rd
WHIPPS CROSS UNIVERSITY HOSP.
SOUTH WOODFORD
Snaresbrook House
Sports Ground
NEW ROAD
CHINGFORD LANE
SOUTHEND ROAD
WOODFORD NEW ROAD
WHIPPS CROSS ROAD
HOE ST
FOREST RD.
LEA BRIDGE ROAD
CHINGFORD ROAD
LARKSHALL RD.
WINCHESTER ROAD
HOLLYBUSH HILL
HIGH ROAD WOODFORD GREEN

107
H
J
K
L
M
N
G
1
2
3
4
5
6
7
8
9
91
108
123
LORD'S BUSHES
Knighton Wood
WOODFORD WELLS
Roding Valley
Buckhurst Hill
IG9
Chigwell
IG7
Playing Fields
Cedar Park
West Hatch High School
CHIGWELL GOLF COURSE
Club House
Old Loughtonians Hockey Club
New Barns Farm
Luxborough
Chigwell Sewage Works
REDBRIDGE
EPPING FOREST
M11 MOTORWAY
M11
Woodford Green
WOODFORD GREEN
IG8
Woodford
WOODFORD
Ashton Playing Fields
Running Track
Ray Park
Sports Ground
Ray Lodge Prim. Sch.
Football Grd.
Dartnalls Playing Field
River Roding
Winn Bridge
Woodbridge High Sch.
MANOR ROAD
CHIGWELL ROAD
HIGH ROAD
WOODFORD BRIDGE
Roding Prim. Sch.
Claybury Hall
Forest House
Orchard House
Kennels
Redbridge Av. Ho.
Health Club
Claybury Hospital Woods Nature Reserve
Hospital Hill Wood
Cocked Hat Plantation
Egg Clump
Ash Plantation
Cemetery
Playing Field
Sewage Works
Junction 4
SOUTHEND RD.
A406
A1009
A113
A1400
B173
A104
A12
A123
B192
NORTH CIRCULAR ROAD
CHARLIE BROWN'S ROUNDABOUT
Superstore
WOODFORD TRADING ESTATE
South Woodford
E18
Hatton School
P.D.S.A. (Veterinary Centre)
RODING BUPA HOSPITAL
Beal High Sch.
Recreation Ground
Playground
CLAYHALL
IG5
Ilford
CLAYHALL PARK
Tennis Courts
Bowl. Grn.
Sports Cen.
High Sch.
IG4
IG2
GANTS HILL
Gants Hill
Nightingale Prim. Sch.
Wanstead Youth Cen.
SNARESBROOK
E11
SOUTH WOODFORD TO BARKING RELIEF ROAD
REDBRIDGE ROUNDABOUT
Redbridge
EASTERN AVENUE
CRANBROOK ROAD
WOODFORD AVENUE
BEEHIVE LANE
REDBRIDGE
Sports Ground
Garden of Rest

108
CHIGWELL
Chigwell
Library
VICARAGE
92
The Lodge
Miller's Fm.
Grove Cotts
LAMBOURNE ROAD
Pav. Playing Fields
Tennis Courts
Recreation Ground
EPPING FOREST
REDBRIDGE
Cemetery
Wood View
Play. Field
Wells Park Sch. & Training Centre
Grange Hill
CHIGWELL GOLF COURSE
Club House
HAINAULT ROAD
MANOR ROAD
FENCEPIECE ROAD
A123
A113
B173
HIGH ROAD
Limes Farm Inf. & Jun. Schools
GRANGE HILL
Depot
Manford Prim. Sch.
Coppice Prim. Sch.
HAINAULT
Hainault Forest High Sch.
IG7
Hainault
Works
Forest Road Playing Field
Hainault Recreation Ground
Bowl. Grn.
Club House
North View Caravan Site
Sports Ground
Playing Field
Fairlop Oak Recreation Ground
Powerleague Soccer Cen.
IG6
FAIRLOP
Fairlop Sailing Centre
Forest Farm
Forest Farm Cottages
Fairlop
Redbridge Sports Centre
Oakfield Sch Sports Centre
Oakfield Playing Field
Fairlop Lodge
Fairlop Lake
Slipways
FAIRLOP WATERS COUNTRY PARK
Golf Driving Range
FAIRLOP WATERS GOLF COURSE
Nature Reserve
Lagoon
Farm Cottages
Hainault Farm
Seven Kings Water
Claybury Hospital Woods Nature Reserve
Hospital Hill Wood
Hospital Hill
Forest House
Health Club
107
IG8
Fairlop Prim. Sch.
Playing Field
FULLWELL CROSS
King Solomon High Sch.
Swim. Pool
IG5
Ilford High Sch.
CLAYHALL AVENUE
Garden of Rest
Cemetery
Green Elms
Barkingside Rec. Grd.
BARKINGSIDE
Aldborough Hall Equestrian Centre
PAINTERS RD
Ilford Jewish Prim. Sch.
Ilford
Barnardos
Barnardos Village
Barkingside
Football Ground
Aldborough Hall Farm
IG2
ALDBOROUGH HATCH
Aldborough Ho. Farm
Aldborough House
Fullwood Prim. Sch.
Superstore
Oaks Park High Sch.
KING GEORGE HOSPITAL
North Residence
South Residence
IG3
GOODMAYES HOSPITAL
LITTLE HEATH
GANTS HILL
CRANBROOK ROAD
NEWBURY PARK
Newbury Park
124
EASTERN AV. A12
Gants Hill
Retail Park
Park Playing Field
War Mem.
Sports Ground
Bowling Green
Playing Field
Tennis Courts
SEVEN KINGS
BARLEY LANE
B177
A B C D E F G
1 2 3 4 5 6 7 8 9

H
J
K
L
M
N
93
HAINAULT FOREST (COUNTRY PARK)
Visitor Centre
Fox Burrows
The Lake
Refreshments
Old Hainault Oak
Dog Kennel Hill
HAINAULT FOREST GOLF COURSE
Reservoirs (Covered)
Club Ho.
Golf Driving Range
Riding School
Nursery
FIVE OAKS LANE
Hainault Lodge
HAINAULT INDUSTRIAL ESTATE
Works
Hog Hill
RM4
Foreberry Wood South
Lower Park Farm
Willoughby's Hill
Havering Park
Pinewood Prim. Sch.
HAVERING
Churchpath Plantation North
1
2
3
4
5
6
7
8
9
RM5
Clockhouse Jun. & Inf. Schools
Health Cen.
Comm. Cen.
COLLIER ROW
Havering Lodge
Forest Farm
Cold Blow Farm
ROMFORD ROAD B174
HOG HILL RD.
COLLIER ROW RD.
Recreation Ground
Gobions Farm
WHALEBONE LANE
Romford
Marks Gate
Football Grd.
Bowling Alley
Nursery
Whites Farm
Furze Cottage
Furze House Farm
Crownfield Jun. & Inf. Schs.
REDBRIDGE
BARKING and DAGENHAM
HAVERING
Mawney
RM6
RM7
Mill Farm
Warehouse
King Georges Field
MAWNEY PARK
Red House Farm
Hainault House
Willow Farm
Playing Field
Little Heath Sch.
Sports Ground
Jun. Sch.
Chadwell Heath Cemetery
Comm. Cen.
Infant Sch.
Moat
Warren Farm
A12
EASTERN AVENUE
MOBY DICK
Warren Park Golf Centre
Club House
Rec. Ground
Warren Sports Centre
Warren Jun. Sch.
Playing Field
Redbridge College
Grove Prim. Sch.
ST. CHAD'S PARK
Crown Farm
Sports Ground
Crown Cottages
LONDON ROAD
G
125
CHADWELL
47
48
49
50

110
HAVERING-ATTE-BOWER
ST. FRANCIS HOSPICE
Round House Farm
94
Pheasant Wood
Avenue Wood
HAVERING COUNTRY PARK
Pine Wood
Poultry Farm
Orange Tree Inn
Bower Farm
Bower House
Churchpath Plantation North
Kiln Wood
Nursery
Playing Field
Bower Wood
RM4
Upper Bedfords Farm
Broxhill Common
Bedfords
Deer Park
Larch Wood
BEDFORDS PARK
Nursery
St. Ursula's R.C. Jun. & Inf. Schs.
Tennis Courts
Bower Park School
CHASE CROSS
Pinewood Prim. Sch.
Havering Grange
Immanuel Sch.
Clockhouse Jun. & Inf. Schools
Health Cen.
Comm. Cen.
RM5
COLLIER ROW
Play Grd.
Romford
Sunnyside Farm
Sports Grd.
Hilldene Prim. Sch.
RISEBRIDGE GOLF COURSE
Club House
Lawns Rec. Grd.
Rise Park Jun. & Inf. Schs.
RISE PARK
Sports Ground
Gallows Corner
Sports Ground
ROMFORD GOLF COURSE
Marshalls Park Lower Sch.
RM1
RAPHAEL PARK
Fish Ponds
Warehouse
King Georges Field
MAWNEY PARK
Bus Depot
Prim. Schs.
Lake
County Court
Town Hall
GIDEA PARK
RM2
Gidea Park
RM7
Superstore
Cottons Park
Comm. Cens.
THE BREWERY
ROMFORD
Prim. Sch.
Playing Field
HEATH PARK
126
EASTERN AVENUE
EASTERN AVENUE EAST
A12
A118
A125
B175
B174
B1459
HAVERING ROAD
ORANGE TREE HILL
COLLIER ROW LANE
MAIN ROAD
NORTH STREET
SOUTH STREET
LONDON ROAD
WATERLOO RD.
ST. EDWARDS WAY
MERCURY GDS.
THURLOE GDS.
BEDFORDS ROAD
LOWER BEDFORDS ROAD
CHASE CROSS ROAD
MAWNEY ROAD

DAGNAM
PARK
Fir Wood
Cock Wood
Alder Wood
The Oaks
M25 MOTORWAY
M25
BROOK ST. INTERCHANGE
Junc. 28 (M25)
Grove Farm
The Grove
Putwell Bridge
Junc. 11 (A12)
MAYLANDS GOLF COURSE & COUNTRY CLUB
CM14
Duck Wood Community Nature Reserve
Club House
Maylands
Maylands Cottage
Sports Grd.
Havering College of Further & Higher Education
Hatters Wood
Dycorts Sch.
Kingswood Sch.
Pyrgo Priory Prim. Sch.
Central Park
Central Park Swim. Pool
Long Wood
Sage Wood
Min. Golf Course
HAROLD HILL
Health Cen.
THE DAVID CROMPTON LODGE
Comm. Centre
RM3
Mead Sch.
Football Ground
HAROLD PARK
Harold Court Prim. Sch.
Roman Road
Paine's Brook
ELMS INDUSTRIAL ESTATE
BATES INDUSTRIAL ESTATE
HAVERING
BRENTWOOD
Sewage Disposal Works
Ingrebourne
COLCHESTER ROAD
A12
HAROLD HILL IND. EST.
Guardian Bus. Cen.
Factory
Wks.
Superstore
Farringdon Cen.
The Grange
GALLOWS CORNER
Harold Wood
HAROLD WOOD
HAROLD WOOD HOSPITAL
Bleasend Farm
The Chase
Garden Centre
Tylers Hall
TYLERS COMMON
Cissbury Lodge Farm
Ivy Lodge Farm
Ely Cott.
WARLEY
SHEPHERDS HILL
Cockabourne Bridge
Miniature Golf Course
Pages Farm
Montrose
Tomkyns Manor
Riding Stables
Four Wantz Works
Four Wantz Cottages
Emanuel Cottage
Greathouse
Chalkfield
Burnside
HAROLD WOOD PARK
Redden Ct. Sch.
Upminster
RM14
Tyes Cottage
Harold Wood Prim. Sch.
Prospect Farm
Ingrebourne Farm
Cornlands Farm
Abattoir
Great Tomkyns Farm
Upminster Lodge
Upminster Lodge Farm
SOUTHEND ARTERIAL ROAD
A127
Squirrel's Heath
Sunset Play. Fld.
The Campion School
Playing Field
College
Hotel
Mount Pleasant Farm
The Rosary
Grasslands
ARDLEIGH GREEN
HAYNES PARK
Miniature Golf Course
Hornchurch
RM11
THE WITHERINGS
Chapmans Farm
Lillyputts Equestrian Centre
EMERSON
95
112
127
54
55
56
93
92
91
90
89
H J K L M N G
1 2 3 4 5 6 7 8 9

BROOK STREET INTERCHANGE
Junction 11 (A12)
Junction 28 (M25)
M25 MOTORWAY
BRENTWOOD BY-PASS
BROOK STREET
CM14
WARLEY
MASCALLS PARK
Brentwood Museum
The Duchess of Kent Social Centre
HARTSWOOD BUPA HOSP.
Brentwood Park Ski & Snowboarding Centre
Spring Health Leisure Club
Headley Common
Warley Prim. Sch.
GREAT WARLEY
GREAT WARLEY STREET
WARLEY ROAD
Brentwood
TYLERS COMMON
BRENTWOOD
HAVERING
Sewage Disposal Works
Top Plantation
Boyles Court Farm
Jackson's Wood
Coombe Wood
Foxburrow Wood
The Squirrels Nursing Home
Barrack Reservoir (disused)
Upminster
RM14
SOUTHEND ARTERIAL ROAD
A127
Junction 29
Hazle Ceramics Workshop
Codham Hall
Latchet's Shaw
Oak Royal Nurseries
Woodlands School
Chapmans Farm
Upminster Lodge Farm
Great Tomkyns Farm
Abattoir
Cornlands Farm
Tylers Hall
Garden Centre
Putwell Bridge
Grove Farm
Alder Wood
Lower Vicarage Wood
The Oaks
Jax Folly
Gladstone

Ingrave Common
Brentwood Golf Centre
Octagon Lodge
Dairy Farm
Ingrave
Salmond's Farm
Thorndon Hall
Thorndon Country Park
Club House
Visitors Centre
Chantry Chapel & Mausoleum
Countryside Centre
The Country Forest Park
Kent's Wood
Saw Mill
Lodge
Devil's Head Plantation
Little Warley Common
Brentwood Hard Court Tennis Club
Long Plantation
New Hall Pond
Thorndon Park Golf Course
Herongate
CM13
Hatch House
Horse Pond
Hatch Farm
Childerditch Wood
Childerditch Pond
Little Warley Lodge
Home Farm
Home Park
Little Warley
Clapgate Farm
Village Hall
Roses Farm
Menagerie Plantation
Country Park
The Rookery
The Old Shop
Old Hall Pond
Warley Park Golf Course
Virginia Nursery
Childerditch
Hill Farm
Pigeon Mount
Mill Wood
Octagon Plantation
Childerditch Industrial Park
Childerditch Hall
Jury Hill
Barrett's Shaw
Thick Shaw
Glencar
Broadfields
Woodside Farm
Hollow Bottom Shaw
Straight Path Shaw
East Horndon
Warley Hall Wood
Clearview Health & Racquet Club
Round Shaw
Little Warley Hall
West Horndon Prim. Sch.
Play. Field.
Nuttys Farm
Hall Lane Farm
Prettigate Farm
Smallholding
West Horndon
Engineering Works
Highfield Wood
Heatleys
Ingrave Hall
Sewage Works
Birches Wood
Three Arch Bridge
Seven Arch Bridge
Shenfield Common
Brentwood High Sch. Play. Fld.
Harts Wood
Min. Golf Course
Bowling Greens
King George's Playing Field
Club House
Brentwood Road
Ingrave Road
Arterial Road
Thorndon Avenue
Childerditch Lane
Hall Lane
Little Warley Hall Lane
A128
A127

97
114
129

Brentwood
CM13
HERONGATE
EAST HORNDON
SOUTH ESSEX GOLF & COUNTRY CLUB
SOUTHEND ARTERIAL ROAD
A127
A128
B148
BRENTWOOD ROAD
BILLERICAY ROAD
TILBURY ROAD
DUNTON ROAD
BOTNEY HILL ROAD
SUDBURYS FARM ROAD
TYE COMMON ROAD
HATCHES FARM ROAD
LANE
NIGHTINGALE LANE
WEST DUNTON ROAD
CHURCH ROAD
STATION AVENUE
MERRYLANDS CHASE
BASILDON
BRENTWOOD
Little Bladen's Wood
Bladen's Wood
Sutton Shaw
Highfield Wood
Long Shaw
Round Wood
Sudbury's Farm
Babshole Farm
Four Acres
Salmon's Farm
Sudbury's Bungalow
The Willows
Richdean Farm
Little Burstead Common
Hatches
Botneyhill Wood
Chase Farm
Moat
Heron Hall
Heron Hall Farm
Botney Hill Farm
St. Margaret's Farm
Res. (Cov.)
Fouchers Farm
Parkhill Wood
Heron Ct. Farm
Pav.
Football Ground
Mount Thrift
Spearshill Wood
Park House
The Green
Dog Wood
Barn Wood
Park Farm
Heron Court Farm
Lady Spring Wood
Stonyhill Wood
Cockridden
Cockridden Farm
Club House
Gravelpit Wood
Old Hall Pond
Octagon Plantation
Eastlands Spring
Friern Manor Wood
Mill Wood
Green Meadows Nurseries
Thick Shaw
Meadow House
Brookman's Fm.
Clyde Lodge Fm.
Friern Manor
Glencar
East Horndon Hall
Hollow Bottom Shaw
Broadfields
Woodside Farm
Straight Path Shaw
Warehouse
The Old Rectory
Dunton Hills
Play. Field.
Rectory
Works
Dunton Hall
Old Mill Cottages
98
113
130

Billericay
Basildon
CM11
CM12
SS15
South Green
Great Burstead
Little Burstead
Noak Hill
Steeple View
Laindon
Southfields
Lee Chapel North
Pipps Hill
The Burstead Golf Course
Noak Hill Golf Course
Devonshire Park
Barleylands Farm Museum & Visitors Centre
Automobile Research Centre
Vehicle Test Track
Southend Arterial Road
Noak Hill Road
Southend Road
Wash Road
Dunton Road
New Road
Church Street
Laindon Common Road
St. Nicholas Lane
Mayne Crest
West Mayne
Durham Road
Cranes Farm Rd.
Laindon Link
River Crouch
Millhouse Jun.& Inf. Schs.
James Hornsby High Sch.
Markhams Chase Leisure Centre
Merrylands Prim. Sch.
Bluehouse Jun. & Inf. Schs.
St. Anne Line R.C. Jun. & Inf. Schs.
St. Peter's Catholic Prim. Sch.
99
116
131

116
A
B
C
D
E
F
G
100
115
132
Billericay
CM11
SS15
SS14
CRAYS HILL
NOAK BRIDGE
PIPPS HILL
CRANES
FRYERNS
GHYLLGROVE
BARSTABLE
LEE CHAPEL NORTH
BASILDON
SOUTHEND ROAD
LONDON ROAD
CRAYS HILL
A129
A127
A1235
A176
A1321
B1419
CRANES FARM ROAD
BROADMAYNE
MAYNE
SOUTHERNHAY
TIMBERLOG
GLOUCESTER PARK
Football Grd.
Running Track
Cycle Track
Bowling Greens
Tennis Courts
Gloucester Park Swim. Pool
Tractor Works
Rugby Football Grd.
Sports Ground
Football Grd.
Superstore
MAYFLOWER RETAIL PARK
Basildon House
Works
Warehouse
PIPPS HILL INDUSTRIAL ESTATE
Playing Field
Pipps Hill Country Club
David Lloyd Leisure
Hollywood Bowl
Cin.
Hotel
FESTIVAL LEISURE PARK
Holy Cross Recreation Ground
De La Salle School
Willow Prim. Sch.
Ghyllgrove Nursing Home
Whitmore Park
Whitmore Jun. & Inf. Schs.
Golf Driving Range
Rec. Grd.
Resr.
Barleylands Farm Museum & Visitors Centre
Barleylands
Council Depot
White's Farm
Gurnard's Farm
Crays Hall Farm
Crays Hall Cottages
Parsonage Farm
River Crouch
Woolshot's Farm
Playing Field
Crays Hill Prim. Sch.
Southlands Farm
The Chestnuts & Caravan Site
Whites Bridge Farm
White's Bridge
Great Barns
Nutton's Wood
Woodfield Farm
Dale Farm
Bury Farm
Pylon Nurseries
Woodland Nursery
Great Wasketts Farm
Summer Hill Farm
Summerhill Nurseries
Pippshill
Harding's Elms
Laindon Ponds
Portsea House Farm
Moat
Factory
Orchard View
Grange Poultry Farm
Beverley Farm Kennels
Brooklands
Ely House
Ruskin Lodge
Mopsies Park
Fairview School
Hypermarket
Bus Sta.
Basildon
St. Anne Line R.C. Jun. & Inf. Schs.
Offices
Rec. Gnd.
Open Space
LAINDON
Play. Grd.
Nursery
Brier Mount
570
71
72
93
92
91
90
89

117
WICKFORD
SHOTGATE
Wickford
NEVENDON
SS12
SS11
SS13
BURNT MILLS
FELMORE
Basildon
Chalvedon
PITSEA
NORTH BENFLEET
Bowers Gifford
Eversley
NEVENDON ROAD
A132
A127
ARTERIAL ROAD
EAST MAYNE
SOUTH MAYNE
LONDON ROAD
BURNT MILLS ROAD
COURTAULD ROAD
CRANFIELD PARK ROAD
SALCOTT CRESCENT
POUND LANE
Noke Wood
Doeshill Farm
Nevendon Manor
Great Bromfords
Great Broomfields
Cotswold Farm
Sappers Farm
Newlands Farm
Cranfield House
Fanton Hall
Pantile Farm
Pumping Station
Bradfield's Farm
Tiffaynes Farm
North Benfleet Hall
ST. ANDREW'S CLARE HOUSE
Nevendon Bushes
FELMORE PARK EAST
NORTHLANDS PARK
Felmore Farm
Football Ground
Eversley Leisure Centre
Recreation Ground
Louisa Cottage
Little Chalvedon Hall
Sadlers Hall Farm
Pitsea Leisure Cen.
Howard Park
Sewage Works
Recycling Plant
Recreation Ground
White House Farm
Playing Field
Ravenstone
Sports Centre
Bell Farm
Longfield
Grays Farm
Phoenix Ho.
Supermkt.
Carlton Ct.
101
118
133

118
102
117
134
SHOTGATE
RAWRETH
SS11
SS12
SS13
Wickford
Basildon
NORTH BENFLEET
New Thundersley
THUNDERSLEY
SOUTHEND ARTERIAL ROAD
CHELMSFORD ROAD
LONDON ROAD
A130
A129
A127
A1245
A13
Doublegate Lane Bridge
Dollymans Farm
Chichester Hall
Rawreth Barn
Fanton Hall
Morbec Farm
Annwood Lodge
Carpenters Farm
Bonvilles Farm
Lychgate Farm
North Benfleet Hall
Woodside Park
Woodside Cemetery
Kingston Primary School
Robert Drake Prim. Sch.
Glenwood School
The Montgomerie Jun. & Inf. Schs.
Thundersley Jun. & Inf. Schs.
Our Lady of Ransom R. C. Prim. Sch.
Sports Ground
Reservoir
Coombe Wood

119
103
120
135
Hockley
SS5
Rayleigh
RAYLEIGH
SS6
Benfleet
SS7
Daws Heath
HANOVER GOLF COURSE & COUNTRY CLUB
Blounts Wood
Sweyne Park
The Sweyne Park Sch.
The Fitzwimarc School
Rayleigh Castle
Rayleigh Tower Mill
Fairview Playing Fld.
Cemetery
Hardwick Ho.
Weir
Rayleigh Indoor Karting Stadium
Wyburns Prim. Sch.
Acacia Nurseries
Lynwood Nurseries
Eastwood Nurseries
Heath Nurseries
Tile Wood
Starvelarks Wood
Little Haven Nature Reserve
LITTLE HAVEN CHILDREN'S HOSPICE
Reservoir
Cottage Plantation
Claydons Farm
POUND WOOD
Pound Wood Nature Reserve
Cedar Hall School
The Deanes School
Solby Wood Farm
Brook Farm
Great Common
Great Wheatley
Kingley Wood
Lower Wyburns Farm
Tylerset Farm
Garrolds Farm
Cosy Nook Farm
Highcroft
The Thatch
Oakwood Resrs.
Bullwood Hall
H.M. Young Offenders Institute
Whitbreds Wood
Turret Farm
Northlands Farm
Home Farm
Blounts Farm
Murrells Hall
Stevens Farm
Fisher's Farm
Brierley
Sandy Lodge
Lubard's Lodge
Grove Jun. & Inf. Schools
Playing Field
Rawreth Industrial Estate
Superstore
Eastern Elec. Board Offs.
SOUTHEND ARTERIAL ROAD
EASTWOOD ROAD
HIGH ROAD
HOCKLEY ROAD
RAYLEIGH ROAD
LONDON ROAD
A129
A1015
A127
B1013
ROCHFORD
CASTLE POINT
80
81
82
89
90
91
92
93

HOCKLEY
Hockley
HAWKWELL
Rayleigh
SS6
Leigh-on-Sea
SS9
Noblesgreen
EASTWOOD
HOCKLEY WOODS
Great Bull Wood
Beeches Wood
Whitbreds Wood
H.M. Young Offenders Institute Bullwood Hall
Parson's Snipe
Gustedhall Wood
Potash Wood
The Scrubs
Primrose Wood
EDWARDS HALL PARK
New England Wood
Clements Hall Leisure Centre
Recreation Ground
Greensward College
Marylands Wood
Bett's Wood
Folly Wood
MAIN ROAD
SOUTHEND RD.
RAYLEIGH RD.
SOUTHEND ARTERIAL ROAD
EASTWOOD RD.
PRINCE AV.
HALL ROAD
B1013
A1015
A127
104
119
136

ASHINGDON
Rochford
SS4
ROCHFORD
Southend-on-Sea
SS2
LONDON-SOUTHEND AIRPORT
Passenger Terminal
ROCHFORD HUNDRED GOLF COURSE
Eastwoodbury
Stroud Green
King George's Field (Playing Field)
Little Doggetts
Apton Hall
Well House
Old Rectory
Wood Sloppy
Great Brays
Margam
Shepherd's Grove
Playing Field
The King Edmund Sch.
Doggetts
Little Stambridge Hall
Poultry Houses
Hawkwell Hall Farm
River Roach
Holt Farm Jun. & Inf. Schs.
Doggetts Prim. Sch.
Recreation Ground
Coombes Farm
Winters
Castle Point & Rochford Community College
Cricket Ground
Stambridge Mills
Broomhills
Mill Head
Boat Yard
Purdey's Farm
PURDEYS IND. ESTATE
Fleet Hall
Crowstone Preparatory School
Sutton Ford Bri.
Sutton Hall
New Hall
Temple Farm
Temple Cotts.
Smither's Farm
Pelham's Farm
The Glebe
Glebe Cottage
Rochford Hall
The Rectory
Club Ho.
New House
Brick Works
Cherry Orchard
Harrier House
Flights Leisure Centre
AVIATION WAY IND. AREA
Avro Adult Training Centre
EASTWOODBURY COTTAGES
SOUTHEND AIRPORT RETAIL PARK
Warners Bridge
Sports Ground
Club House
Sewage Works
Nursery
CHERRY ORCHARD WAY
B1013
SUTTON ROAD
STAMBRIDGE ROAD
APTON HALL ROAD
HYDE WOOD LANE
ASHINGDON ROAD
RECTORY ROAD
HALL ROAD
SOUTHEND ROAD
SHOPLAND RD.
LITTLE STAMBRIDGE HALL LANE
MILL LANE
105
137
43

A
B
C
D
E
F
G
1
2
3
4
5
6
7
8
9
88
87
86
85
84
37
38
39
40
106
38
WHIPPS CROSS UNIVERSITY HOSP.
Hollow Pond (Boating Lake)
Epping Forest
Playing Field
WHIPPS CROSS ROAD
A114
HOLLYBUSH HILL
NEW WANSTEAD
A1199
A113
GREEN MAN ROUNDABOUT
BUSH
A114
E11
LEYTONSTONE
Leytonstone
Leytonstone High Rd.
HIGH ROAD LEYTONSTONE
A11
GAINSBOROUGH RD.
BUSHWOOD
The Avenue
Horse Ride
Playing Field
HARROW ROAD
B161
LAKE HOUSE ROAD
DAMES ROAD
Cann Hall
West Ham Cemetery
Cemetery
St. Patrick's R.C. Cemetery
HIGH RD. LEYTONSTONE
CANN HALL RD.
Maryland
WATER LANE
ROMFORD ROAD
A118
EARLHAM GROVE
FOREST LANE
Forest La. Pk.
WEST HAM PARK
THE GROVE
BROADWAY
WEST HAM LA.
VICARAGE LA.
LEYTON
E10
Leyton Midland Rd.
HIGH RD. LEYTON
FRANCIS RD.
GROVE GREEN RD.
A12
A106
CATHALL RD.
Leyton
Leyton Orient F.C. (Matchroom Stadium)
Sidmouth Park
Coronation Gdns.
WARREN RD.
LEYTON GRN. RD.
LEYTON ROAD
A112
MAJOR R.
CHOBHAM RD.
ORIENT WAY
A1006
LEA BRIDGE RD.
A104
Running Track
Dagenham Brook
MARKET PAVILION
NEW SPITALFIELDS MARKET
WALTHAM FOREST
Recreation Ground
R. LEE or LEA
Dressing Rooms
Temple Mills
Temple Mills Play. Flds.
Cricket Ground
RUCKHOLT RD.
HOMERTON RD.
B112
LEA INTERCHANGE
EAST CROSS ROUTE
Eastway Cycle Circuit
Camp Site
Football Ground
Container Terminal
STRATFORD NEW TOWN
Channelsea River
Kingsway International Christian Centre
Arena Field Rec. Grd.
HACKNEY WICK
Hackney Wick
E9
NEWHAM
HACKNEY
CHANNEL TUNNEL RAIL LINK (UNDER CONSTRUCTION)
Cold Stores
Freight Terminal
Warehouses
E15
Stratford
Stratford (Low Level)
STRATFORD
CARPENTER'S ROAD
A115
Stratford Marsh
Sun Wharf
E3
TOWER HAMLETS
Lee Navigation
Waterworks River
ANGEL LANE
GREAT EASTERN RD.
A11
HIGH ST.
Arts Cen.
Thtre.

SNARESBROOK
GANTS HILL
WANSTEAD
REDBRIDGE
REDBRIDGE ROUNDABOUT
Redbridge
EASTERN AVENUE
SOUTH WOODFORD-TO-BARKING RELIEF ROAD
WANSTEAD GOLF COURSE
The Basin (Fish Pond)
Reservoir Wood
Shoulder of Mutton Pond
Heronry Pond
Perch Pond
WANSTEAD PARK
The Temple
The Heronry
Lincoln Island
Rook Island
River Roding
ILFORD GOLF COURSE
Ilford
IG1
IG4
CRANBROOK
VALENTINES PARK
Valentines High Sch.
The Ornamental Pond
The Lake
Bowling Green
Ilford Cricket Club
ALDERSBROOK
WANSTEAD FLATS
Sewage Works
CITY OF LONDON CEMETERY
City of London Crematorium
NORTH CIRCULAR ROAD
ILFORD
Cranbrook Coll.
MANOR PARK
THE MANOR PARK CEMETERY
Manor Park
Wanstead Park
FOREST GATE
E7
E12
E6
Woodgrange Park
Woodgrange Park Cemetery
ROMFORD ROAD
LITTLE ILFORD
Little Ilford Park
PLASHET
Jewish Cemetery
PLASHET PARK
The Shrewsbury Cen.
East Ham
UPTON
BARKING
River Roding
REDBRIDGE
NEWHAM

124
GANTS HILL
Gants Hill
NEWBURY PARK
108
GOODMAYES HOSPITAL
A
B
C
D
E
F
G
1
2
3
4
5
6
7
8
9
EASTERN AVENUE
A12
CRANBROOK
Valentines High Sch.
The Ornamental Pond
VALENTINES PARK
The Lake
Ilford Cricket Club
Cranbrook Coll.
Newbury Park
SEVEN KINGS PARK
Sports Ground
Playing Field
SEVEN KINGS
Seven Kings
IG2
Ilford
Council Depot
Factory
Depot
HIGH ROAD
A118
GREEN LANE
A1083
Goodmayes
GOODMAYES
GRIGGS APP.
WINSTON WY.
Ilford
ILFORD HILL
Cricklefield Stadium
Ilford Pools
Cemetery
IG1
ILFORD
Gordon Fields Prim. Sch.
SOUTH PARK
The Lake
IG3
Mayespark Prim. Sch.
GOODMAYES PARK
LONGBRIDGE
University of East London (Barking Campus)
Barking & East Ham United (Mayesbrook Park)
Mayesbrook Park Arena
LITTLE ILFORD
Little Ilford Park
BARKING RELIEF ROAD
SOUTH WOODFORD TO BARKING RELIEF ROAD
A406
ILFORD LANE
A123
LOXFORD
Loxford Park
Loxford Sch. of Science & Technology
Woodlands Jun. & Inf. Schs.
Hyleford (Home for the Elderly)
FAIR CROSS
BARKING PARK
Swimming Pool
Bowling Greens
The Lake
LONGBRIDGE ROAD
A124
Barking
Barking Abbey Comp. Sch.
Leisure Centre
Manor Jun. & Inf. Schs.
MAYESBROOK PARK
Boating Lake
Eastbury Comp. Sch.
IG11
BARKING HOSPITAL
Upney
FANSHAWE AV.
BARKING NORTHERN RELIEF RD.
Barking
BARKING
RODING TRADING ESTATE
ABBEY RETAIL PARK
LONDON RD.
ABBEY RD.
NORTH CIRCULAR ROAD
WALLEND
Sports Ground
Gasholder
Health Cen.
VICARAGE FIELD SHOPPING CEN.
RIPPLE RD.
140
Barking Abbey
A123
RIPPLE ROAD JUNCTION
AVENUE
LODGE
A1153
Cemetery

109
126
141
H
J
K
L
M
N
G
1
2
3
4
5
6
7
8
9
47
48
49
50
84
85
86
87
88
CHADWELL HEATH
Chadwell Heath
Romford
RM6
RM7
RM8
RM9
RM10
BECONTREE HEATH
BECONTREE
Becontree
Dagenham
DAGENHAM
Dagenham Heathway
Dagenham East
OLD DAGENHAM PARK
PARSLOES PARK
CENTRAL PARK
CASTLE GREEN
Crowlands
Crown Farm
Crown Cottages
ST. CHAD'S PARK
Warren Sports Centre
St. Edward's C. of E. Comp. School
Westlands Playing Field
Sports Ground
CROWLANDS HEATH GOLF COURSE
Crowlands Sports Ground
Romford Stadium (Greyhound)
Fords Sports Ground
Wood Lane Sports Centre
Aqua Driving Range
Dagenham Civic Centre
Miniature Golf Course
Football Ground
All Saints R.C. Comp. Sch. & Tech. Coll.
Robert Clack Sch.
CHADWELL HEATH INDUSTRIAL PARK
ELDENWALL INDUSTRIAL ESTATE
Mayfield Sch. & Coll.
Superstore
Warehouse
Valence Ho. Mus & Gall.
VALENCE PARK
BECONTREE DAY HOSP.
Sydney Russell Comp. Sch.
Dagenham & Redbridge F.C. (Victoria Rd.)
Pondfield Park
Pondfield Rec. Grd.
Goresbrook Park
William Ford C of E Jun. Sch.
MORLAND ROAD DAY HOSP.
Sports Arena
Goresbrook Leisure Centre
THE LEYS
Wantz Stream
HIGH ROAD
LONDON ROAD
WHALEBONE LANE NORTH
WHALEBONE LANE SOUTH
WOOD LANE
RAINHAM ROAD NORTH
RAINHAM ROAD
RUSH GRN. RD.
HEATHWAY
BENNETT'S CASTLE LANE
VALENCE AVENUE
BECONTREE AVENUE
AVENUE
WOOD ROAD
PORTERS AVENUE
BALLARDS RD.
GORESBROOK ROAD
RAINHAM ROAD SOUTH
BARKING and DAGENHAM
HAVERING
A118
A1112
A1083
A124
A1240
A1153
B178
B191

ROMFORD
Romford
Oldchurch Hosp.
Romford Ice Rink
Oldchurch Park
Romford Cemetery
Crowlands Sports Ground
RUSH GREEN
RUSH GREEN ROAD
HORNCHURCH ROAD
HEATH PARK
Hylands Park
RM1
RM7
RM10
RM12
RM13
Romford
Dagenham
Rainham
CENTRAL PARK
Barking College
Eastbrookend Country Park
Eastbrook End Cemetery
Hook's Hall Farm
The Chase Nature Reserve
The Millennium Centre
Eastbrook Comp. Sch.
Dagenham & Redbridge F.C. (Victoria Rd.)
Dagenham East
Pondfield Park
St. Leonards Hamlet
Hornchurch Sports Centre
The Albany School
Harrow Lodge
Elm Park
ELM PARK
Bretons Outdoor Recreation Centre
Scargill Jun. & Inf. Schools
Brittons Sch.
Dagenham Beam Bridge
Nason Waters Centre
SOUTH HORNCHURCH
OLD DAGENHAM PARK
Gas Transmission Station
Sports Arena
Fords Sports Ground
Wood Lane Sports Centre
Miniature Golf Course
Romford Stadium (Greyhound)
Driving Tuition Course
A B C D E F G
1 2 3 4 5 6 7 8 9
110
125
142

127
H
J
K
L
M
N
111
128
143
RM11
RM14
EMERSON PARK
HORNCHURCH
Hornchurch
UPMINSTER
Upminster
UPMINSTER PARK
CORBETS TEY
HACTON
HAYNES PARK
UPMINSTER GOLF COURSE
HIGH STREET
UPMINSTER ROAD
ST. MARY'S LANE
OCKENDON ROAD
AVELEY ROAD
CORBETS TEY RD
HALL LANE
HACTON LANE
WINGLETYE LANE
NORTH STREET
STATION LANE
SUTTONS LANE
POND ROAD
BERWICK POND RD.
PARK FARM ROAD
HARWOOD HALL LANE
GERPINS LA.
LITTLE GAYNES LANE
Emerson Pk.
Hornchurch
Upminster
Upminster Bridge
Emerson Park School
Playing Field
Lillyputts Equestrian Centre
Upminster Court
Upminster Playing Field
Hall Lane Miniature Golf Course
Sports Ground
Queens Theatre
Langton Gds.
Arts Cen.
Coun. Offs.
St. Andrew's Park
Smock Mill
Hornchurch Stadium
Cemetery
The Dell
Mill Cott.
Branfil Jun. & Inf. Schools
Hacton Junior Mixed & Inf. Sch.
The Sanders Draper Sch.
Suttons Prim. Sch.
Ingrebourne Centre
ST. GEORGES HOSPITAL
Suttons Parkway
Gaynes Parkway
Hacton Parkway
River Ingrebourne
Gaynes School
South Essex Crematorium
Redcrofts Farm
Corbets Tey School
Parklands Open Space
Harwood Hall
The Lodge
West Lodge
Great Sunnings
Gay's Cottages
Sullens Farm
Lodge Farm
Park Corner Farm
Rainham Lodge Farm
Central Cottages
Central Farm
New House
Llantrisant Oaks
Greenacres
Refuse Transfer Station
Gerpins Farm
Berwick Cottages
Runway Wood
Airfield Wood
Chapmans Farm
Goodrington Sch.
Tower Jun. Sch.
Tower Inf. Sch.
Upminster Cemetery
Bush Farm
Hall Cottages
54
55
56
84
85
86
87
88
A124
B187
B1421

UPMINSTER
CRANHAM
NORTH OCKENDON
Upminster
RM14
Clay Tye Hill
SOUTHEND ARTERIAL ROAD
A127
Junction 29
M25 MOTORWAY
M25
BRENTWOOD
HAVERING
ST. MARY'S LANE
B187
OCKENDON ROAD
B1421
CLAY TYE ROAD
B186
OCKENDON ROAD NORTH
WARLEY STREET
DENNISES LANE
PEA LANE
PIKE LANE
STUBBERS LANE
SUNNINGS LANE
CHURCH LANE
FEN LANE
Upminster Hall Playing Fields
Hall Mead School
Hall Lane Miniature Golf Course
Museum
Club House
Tennis Courts
Coopers Coy & Coborn Sch.
Sports Grd.
The James Oglethorpe Prim. Sch.
CRANHAM GOLF COURSE
Club House
Franks Wood
Franks Farm
Westbury Farm
Cranham Court
Broadfields Farm
Cranham Hall
Cranham Farm
Cranham Marsh (Nature Reserve)
Spring Wood
Middle Wood
Bonus Wood
Hobbs Hole
South Essex Crematorium
Upminster Cemetery
Gaynes School
Redcrofts Farm
Great Sunnings
Gay's Cottages
Sullens Farm
Russells Lake
Stubbers Lodge
Stubbers Adventure Centre
Coys Lake
Caravan Site
Dennises Cottages
Manor Farm
Manor Farm Cottages
Bridge Cottages
Cranham Place
Remembrance Cottages
Rectory
Hall Farm
Moat
Kennels
White Post Farm
Claynes House
Clay Tye Farm
Elec. Grid Sta
Puddle Dock
Jax Folly
Gladstone Cottages
Upminster Trading Park
Tabrams Farm
Folkes Farm
Oak Royal Nurseries
Chapmans Farm
Bush Farm
Bramble Farm
Home Farm Cottage
Redcrofts
Groves Farm Cottages
Depot
Upminster Court
Playing Field
Pavilion
112
127
144

129
SOUTH
Clearview Health & Racquet Club
Warley Hall
Hall Lane Farm
Prettigate Farm
Smallholding
Abattoir
Orchard Farm
WARLEY HALL LANE
113
CHILDERDITCH LANE
Nuttys Farm
Engineering Works
WEST HORNDON
HORNDON INDUSTRIAL PARK
West Horndon Prim. Sch.
Play. Field.
THORNDON AVENUE
CADOGAN AVENUE
ROAD
Hall
PETRESFIELD WY.
SANDERSON CL.
DUNMOW GS
CLAVERING GS.
FRESHWELL GS.
West Horndon
Lower Shaw
BRENTWOOD
THURROCK
ST. MARY'S LANE
Brentwood
DUNNINGS LANE
MARY'S
Monks Farm
Little Tillingham Hall
CM13
Old England
Moat Tillingham Hall
Field House
Sewage Works
Bury Farm
THURROCK HAVERING
130
CHINA LANE
Slough House
Fairplay Farm
Bullens & Herds
Hatch Farm
LANE
Blankets Farm
Mar Dyke
Caylock's Farm
Home Farm
Stone Hall
FEN LANE
Corner Farm
TOP MEADOW GOLF COURSE
Club House
FEN LANE
Fen Farm
FARROW LANE
Mar Dyke
Judds Farm
Bulphan Fen
Castles Farm
Moat
The Downes
South Ockendon
Stringcock Fen
Groves Cottages
Groves Barns
RM15
145
G H J K L M N
1 2 3 4 5 6 7 8 9
560 61 62 63
88 87 86 85 84

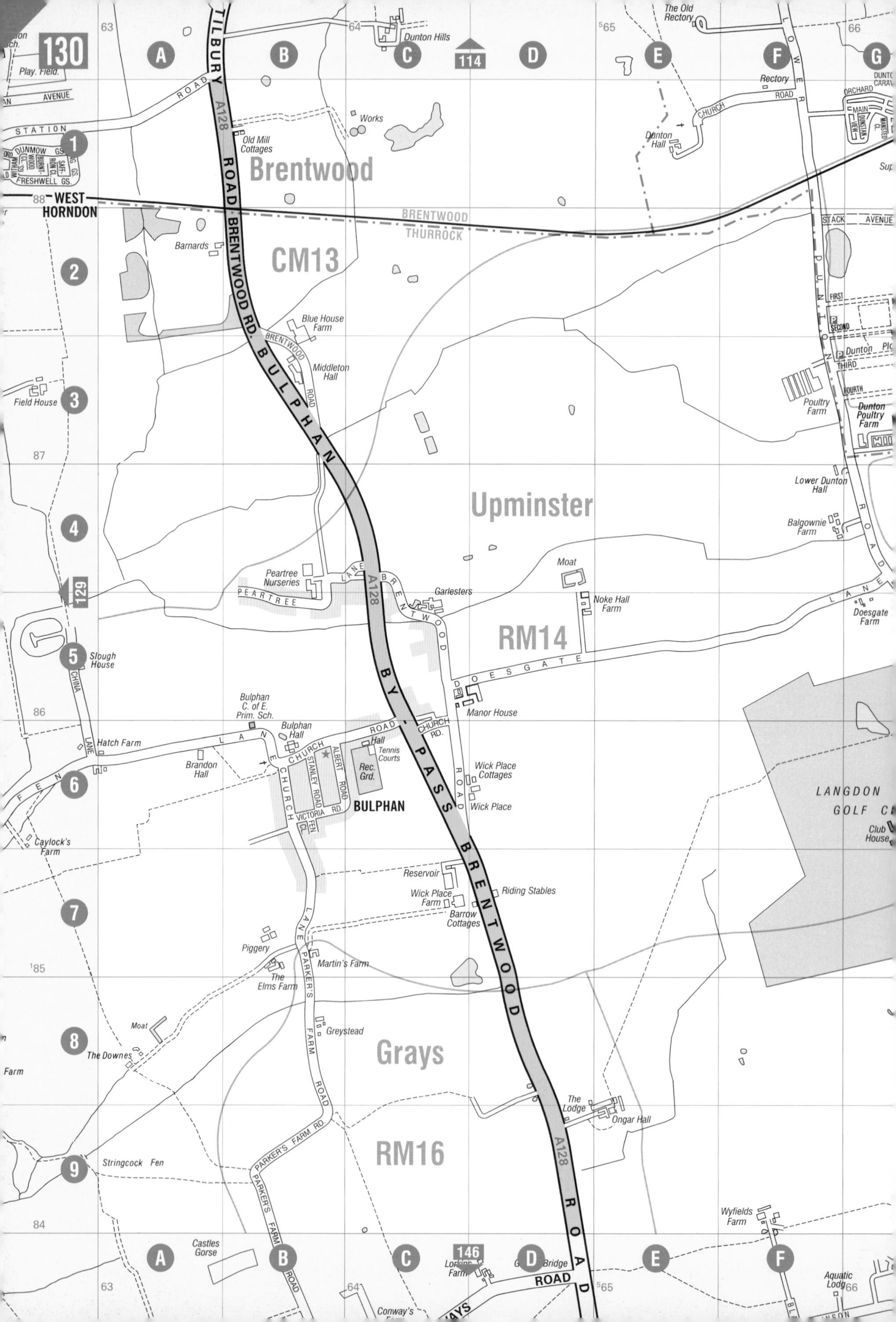
130
114
146
129
A
B
C
D
E
F
G
1
2
3
4
5
6
7
8
9
Brentwood
CM13
Upminster
RM14
Grays
RM16
BULPHAN
WEST HORNDON
BRENTWOOD
THURROCK
TILBURY ROAD
BRENTWOOD RD.
BULPHAN BY-PASS
BRENTWOOD ROAD
A128
The Old Rectory
Dunton Hills
Rectory
Dunton Hall
Works
Old Mill Cottages
Barnards
Blue House Farm
Middleton Hall
Field House
Poultry Farm
Dunton Poultry Farm
Lower Dunton Hall
Balgownie Farm
Moat
Noke Hall Farm
Doesgate Farm
Garlesters
Peartree Nurseries
Slough House
Manor House
Bulphan C. of E. Prim. Sch.
Bulphan Hall
Hatch Farm
Brandon Hall
Hall
Tennis Courts
Rec. Grd.
Wick Place Cottages
Wick Place
Caylock's Farm
Reservoir
Wick Place Farm
Riding Stables
Barrow Cottages
Piggery
Martin's Farm
The Elms Farm
Greystead
The Downes
Farm
The Lodge
Ongar Hall
Stringcock Fen
Castles Gorse
Wyfields Farm
Aquatic Lodge
Conway's
LANGDON GOLF C
Club House
STATION ROAD
AVENUE
Play. Field.
DUNMOW GS.
FRESHWELL GS.
CHURCH ROAD
LOWER DUNTON ROAD
ORCHARD
STACK AVENUE
FIRST
SECOND
THIRD
FOURTH
Dunton
PEARTREE LANE
DOESGATE LANE
CHINA LANE
FEN LANE
CHURCH LANE
CHURCH RD.
STANLEY ROAD
ALBERT ROAD
VICTORIA RD.
FEN CL.
WICK PLACE ROAD
PARKER'S FARM ROAD
PARKER'S FARM RD.
PARKER'S LANE
ROAD
63
64
565
66
88
87
86
185
84

MANDEVILLE WAY
LAINDON
LEE CHAPEL NORTH
LAINDON LINK
SS15
Laindon
B1036
LANGDON HILLS
Rec. Grd.
Gt. Berry Prim. Sch.
Marks Hill Nature Reserve
Reservoir (covered)
Long Wood
Kirks Wood
Lee Chapel Prim. Sch.
LEE CHAPEL SOUTH
Basildon
BASILDON
THURROCK
B1007
NEW LANE WAY
LEE CHAPEL LANE
Nature Trail
Westley Hall
Westley Heights
Langdon Hills Country Park
Riding School
Dry Street Farm
Hall Wood
Ckt. Gnd.
Langdon Hill
Hall Farm
Gravelhill Wood
Coombe Wood
WESTLEY HEIGHTS COUNTRY PARK
Northlands Farm
OLD CHURCH HILL
Rectory
SS16
LITTLE MALGRAVES INDUSTRIAL ESTATE
GOLDSMITHS
The Park
One Tree Hill
Kennels
One Tree Hill Country Park
Oak Park
Old Hill
Great Sutton Wood
Northlands Wood
DUNTON ROAD
KIRKHAM ROAD
Sutton Hall Farm
Tyelands Poultry Farm
SOUTH HILL
Great Malgraves
NORTH HILL (LAINDON RD.)
Subway
Stanford-le-Hope
SS17
Brooklyn Farm
Wrens Park Farm
A13 (STANFORD-LE-HOPE BY-PASS)
ARTERIAL ROAD
Arden Hall
Rose Valley
Maplecroft
Greenacre Farm
BALSTONIA
115
132
147
H J K L M N
1 2 3 4 5 6 7 8 9
G H J K L M N
67 68 69
84 85 86 87 88

132
A
B
C
D
E
F
G
1
2
3
4
5
6
7
8
9
116
131
148
BASILDON
LEE CHAPEL NORTH
LEE CHAPEL SOUTH
KINGSWOOD
VANGE
BARSTABLE
CORRINGHAM
BALSTONIA
FOBBING
Stanford-le-Hope
SS14
SS16
SS17
BROADMAYNE
LAINDON LINK
B1007
NETHER MAYNE
A176
LONDON ROAD
B1464
VANGE BY-PASS
A13
ARTERIAL ROAD (STANFORD-LE-HOPE BY-PASS)
SOUTHEND ROAD
B1420
LAMPITS HILL
HIGH ROAD
CLAY HILL ROAD
TIMBERLOG LANE
B1419
GORDON ROAD
CHERRYDOWN EAST
DRY STREET
ONE TREE HILL
MARSH LANE
MILL LANE
MILL LANE NORTH
INGLEFIELD ROAD
WHITEHALL LA.
PATRICIA DRIVE
GREATHOUSE CHASE
WATERWORKS LANE
MOORES AVENUE
LION HILL
WHARF RD.
Gloucester Park Swim. Pool
Basildon
Bus Dep.
Hypermarket
Open Space
Woodlands School
Kingswood Jun. & Inf. Sch.
Lee Chapel Prim. Sch.
St. Luke's Hospice
Basildon College
Basildon Sports Centre
BASILDON HOSPITAL
BASILDON GOLF COURSE
Nature Trail
Club Ho.
Tompkins Farm
Superstore
Vange Prim. Sch.
Bardfield Jun. & Inf. Schs.
Riding School
Dry Street Farm
Hawkesbury Manor
BASILDON
THURROCK
Vange Mission
Marsh Farm
Hotel
Hovels Farm
Martinhole Wood
Water Works
Brook House Farm
Reservoir (covered)
Sludge Beds
One Tree Hill
Kennels
One Tree Hill Country Park
Oak Park
Corringham Park Farm
Cawder Hall
Whitehall Farm
Subway
Oakway Lodge
Gable Hall School
Rec. Grd.
Curtis's Farm
Fobbing Hall
Old Clay Pits
Gouldings

PITSEA
Pitsea Leisure Cen.
Pitsea Swim Pool
Chalvedon Sch. & Sixth Form Coll.
Northlands Jun. & Inf. Schs.
Playing Field
Recreation Ground
117
Sports Ground
Bowers Gifford
Sadlers Hall Farm
Howard Park
RECTORY
LONDON ROAD
B1464
A13
A132
A130
HIGH ROAD
MAYNE
SOUTH
BY-PASS
CANVEY WAY
Community Centre
Cemetery
Basildon and District Crematorium
The Gables
Little Bowers
Bowers Hall
St. Margaret's C of E Prim. Sch.
Lyndhurst
Football Grd.
Blue Ho. Fm.
Superstore
Pitsea
SS13
Basildon
Essex Horse and Pony Protection Society
Works
Pitsea Marsh
Pitsea Creek
REFUSE TIP
Timberman's Creek
Sewage Works
National Motorboat Museum
Picnic Area
Wat Tyler Country Park
Pitseahall Fleet
Old Dock
VANGE CREEK
Pitsea Wharf
BOWERS MARSHES
Great Mussels
JOTMANS LANE
Fobbing Creek
Fobbing Horse
Flood Barrier
BASILDON
CASTLE POINT
Canvey Island
SS8
Sewage Works
Northwick
NORTHWICK ROAD
Oil Refinery
134
149
G H J K L M N
1 2 3 4 5 6 7 8 9
73 74 575 76
88 87 86 185 84

118
THUNDERSLEY
Kingston Primary School
Coombe Wood
LONDON ROAD
A13
Sadlers Hall Farm
Tarpots
The Appleton Sch.
Recreation Ground
SS13
CANVEY WAY
A130
Reservoir (covered)
Jotmans Hall
Reservoir
Thundersley Glen
Guideacres
Benfleet
SOUTH BENFLEET
SS7
BOYCE HILL GOLF COURSE
Club House
Hilltop Farm
Hope's Green
South Benfleet Playing Fields
Benfleet Marsh
Sewage Works
Creekside Playing Fields
Playing Fields
Reeds Hill Farm
HADLEIGH
Benfleet Downs
Rayview
Benfleet for Canvey Island
FERRY RD.
Flood Barrier
BENFLEET CREEK
BOWERS MARSHES
133
Basildon
SS16
EAST HAVEN CREEK
Waterside Cottages
Waterside Farm
SOMNES
B1014
Golf Driving Range
Club House
CASTLE POINT
Miniature Railway
Athletics Track
Waterside Farm Sports Centre
Playing Field
Sports Ground
All Weather Pitch
Great Russell Head
Canvey Island
SS8
Winter Gardens
The Cornelius Vermuyden School
Sewage Works
Monkswick
Little Russells Head
Dutch Village
Dutch Cottage Museum
Poultry Houses
Oil Refinery
NORTHWICK ROAD
ROSCOMMON WAY
150

136
A
B
C
D
E
F
G
1
2
3
4
5
6
7
8
9
83
84
85
86
87
88
120
135
43
Garrolds Farm
Oakwood Resrs.
Grange Farm
The Grange
Heath Mount
Thatch
Depot
Forest Keepers Hut
Factory
Oak Wood Park
SOUTHEND
ARTERIAL
ROAD
A127
EASTWOOD
Eastwood Park
Bowling Green
The Eastwood Sch.
Factory
Play. Fld.
Health Cen.
Liby.
RAYLEIGH
RD.
A1015
PRINCE
AV.
Eastwood Jun. & Inf. Schs.
Kingsdown School
Play Field
Melrose Nurseries
Fairways Prim. Sch.
CASTLE POINT
SOUTHEND-ON-SEA
BELFAIRS PARK
BELFAIRS PARK GOLF COURSE
Club House
Belfairs Sports Grd.
Playground
Prittle Brook
Belfairs High School
Belfairs Swim Cen.
Track
Trotting Track
The St. Christopher Sch.
Blenheim Prim. Sch.
Blenheim Park
Play. Fld.
St. Thomas More High Sch. for Boys
Leigh-on-Sea
SS9
Westcliff High Schs.
Playing Field
Tennis Courts
Sports Grd.
Darlinghurst Prim. Sch.
R.C. Prim. Sch.
Rec. Grd.
LONDON ROAD
A13
LEIGH-ON-SEA
Leigh Schs. Cem.
Pav. Chalkwell Park
Belton Hills
Leigh-on-Sea
Depot
Skate Park
Playing Field
Golf Range
Superbowl
Leigh Heritage Cen. & Mus.
Bell Wharf
Leigh Cliffs
Essex Yacht Club
Chalkwell
Bowling Greens
Chalkwell Oaze
Leigh Marsh
LEIGH NATIONAL NATURE RESERVE
Two Tree Island
MARSH END SAND
Leigh Swatch
Crow

Eastwoodbury
Avro Adult Training Centre
Warners Bridge
Sports Grd.
Club House
Temple Farm
Temple Gate Cotts.
Smither's Farm
ROCHFORD
SOUTHEND-ON-SEA
Fossett's Farm
SS2
Sutton Road Cemetery
Jewish Cemy.
Southend-on-Sea Crematorium
Recreation Ground
Sports Ground
Jones Meml. Rec. Grd.
Superstore
WELLESLEY BUPA HOSPITAL
Scout H. Q.
Temple Sutton Prim. Sch.
The Victory Sports Ground
Cecil Jones High Sch.
Southend-on-Sea
PRINCE AVENUE
A127
PRIORY CRES.
EASTERN AVENUE
A1159
MANNERS WAY
VICTORIA AVENUE
Cuckoo Corner
Priory Park
Prittlewell Priory Mus.
Prittlewell Priory
Priory Lodge
Bowling Greens
Southend High School for Boys
Play. Fld.
Earls Hall Jun.& Inf. Schs.
SOUTHEND HOSPITAL
The Prittlewell Sch.
Chase Sports & Fitness Centre
PRITTLEWELL
Prittlewell Brook
Lancaster Sch.
Timber Yard
Southend United FC (Roots Hall)
Prittlewell
EAST STREET
WEST ST.
Westborough
Westcliff-on-Sea
SS0
WESTBOROUGH ROAD
LONDON ROAD
A13
WEST ROAD
B1015
Palace Theatre
Civic Cen.
Law Cts.
Arts & Tech. Coll.
P.O. Sorting Office
Govt. Offs.
VICTORIA
QUEENS WAY
Cinema
Superstore
SOUTHCHURCH ROAD
Training Centre
SUTTON ROAD
NORTH AVENUE
CENTRAL AVENUE
CHALKWELL
Westcliff
Fair Havens Hospice
SOUTHEND CENTRAL
County Ct.
Warriors Swim. Cen.
The Royals Shop. Cen.
Bus Sta.
QUEENSWAY
Catholic Cen.
Burial Ground
Westcliff Casino
Cliffs Pav.
Gall.
The Cliffs
Bandstand
CLIFFTOWN
Cliffs Lift
The Shrubbery
Paddling Pool
WESTCLIFF-ON-SEA
First Aid Post
Southend Flat
Marine Gardens
Peter Pan's Amusement Park
Jetty
Pier Museum
Kursaal Bowl
Sealife Cen.
Putting Green
SOUTHEND-ON-SEA
PIER
Hard
ESPLANADE
MARINE PARADE
WESTERN ESPLANADE
86
87
88
89
88
87
86
85
84
H J K L M N
G H J K L M N
1 2 3 4 5 6 7 8 9
121
138
43

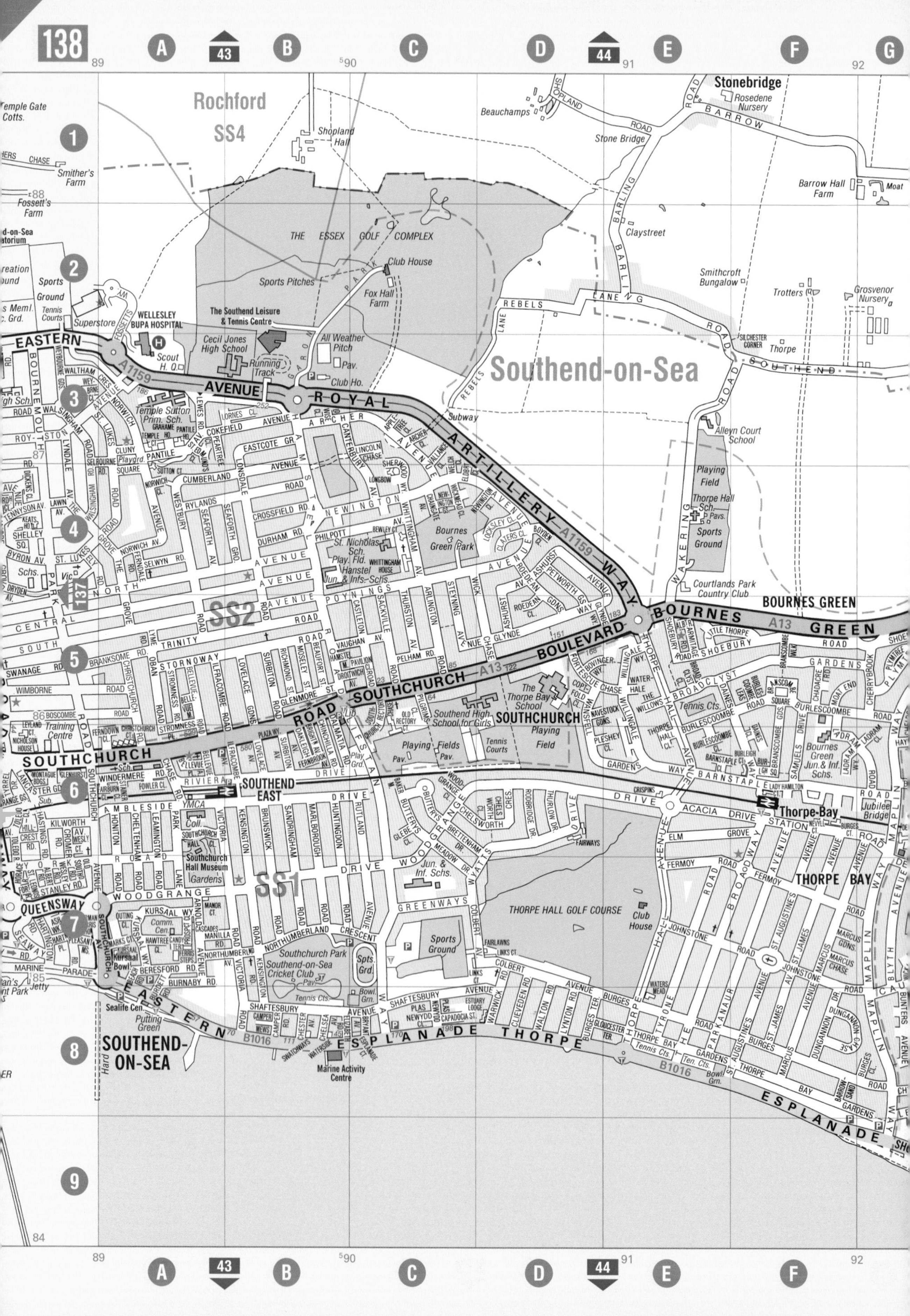

138
A
43
B
C
D
44
E
F
G
Rochford
SS4
Shopland Hall
Beauchamps
Stonebridge
Rosedene Nursery
Stone Bridge
BARROW
Barrow Hall Farm
Moat
Claystreet
Smithcroft Bungalow
Trotters
Grosvenor Nursery
Silchester Corner
Thorpe
Temple Gate Cotts.
Smither's Farm
Fossett's Farm
THE ESSEX GOLF COMPLEX
Club House
Sports Pitches
Fox Hall Farm
The Southend Leisure & Tennis Centre
All Weather Pitch
Pav.
Club Ho.
Cecil Jones High School
Running Track
WELLESLEY BUPA HOSPITAL
Superstore
Sports Ground
Scout H.Q.
Southend-on-Sea
REBELS LANE
BARLING ROAD
WAKERING ROAD
Subway
Alleyn Court School
Playing Field
Thorpe Hall Sch.
Sports Ground
Courtlands Park Country Club
BOURNES GREEN
EASTERN AVENUE
A1159
ROYAL ARTILLERY WAY
Temple Sutton Prim. Sch.
Bournes Green Park
St. Nicholas Sch.
Play. Fld.
Hanstel Jun. & Infs. Schs.
SS2
SOUTHCHURCH BOULEVARD
A13
SOUTHCHURCH ROAD
The Thorpe Bay School
SOUTHCHURCH
Playing Field
Southend High School for Girls
Playing Fields
Tennis Courts
Training Centre
Tennis Cts.
Bournes Green Jun.& Inf. Schs.
SOUTHEND EAST
Thorpe Bay
Jubilee Bridge
YMCA
Coll.
Southchurch Hall Museum
Gardens
SS1
Jun. & Inf. Schs.
THORPE HALL GOLF COURSE
Club House
THORPE BAY
QUEENSWAY
Kursaal Bowl
Comm. Cen.
Southchurch Park
Southend-on-Sea Cricket Club
Spts. Grd.
Sports Ground
Bowl. Grn.
Sealife Cen.
Putting Green
Jetty
SOUTHEND-ON-SEA
Marine Activity Centre
EASTERN ESPLANADE
B1016
THORPE ESPLANADE
89
90
91
92
84

BARKING
Upney
BARKING HOSPITAL
124
39
A B C D E F G
1 2 3 4 5 6 7 8 9
84 83 82 81 80
44 545 46
NORTH CIRCULAR RD.
ABBEY RD.
ST. PAUL'S RD.
RIPPLE ROAD
RIPPLE ROAD JUNCTION
Barking Abbey (Rem. of)
Superstore
Langdon School
Cemetery
Barking Industrial Park
Ripplesi
Greatfields Park
EAST HAM & BARKING BY-PASS
A13
A123
A406
A1020
ALFREDS WAY
MOVERS LANE
RIVER ROAD
THAMES ROAD
Newlands Park
Library
Health Cen.
Thames View Jun. Sch.
Youth Centre
Jun. & Inf. Sch.
Hand Trough Creek
Cuckold's Haven
Refuse & Sewage Works
Showcase Cinema
Hollywood Bowl Barking
Powerleague Soccer Cen.
Refuse Transfer Station
Lagoon
BARKING and DAGENHAM
NEWHAM
Beckton Sewage Treatment Works
Barking Creek
Barking
IG11
CREEKMOUTH
Thameside Community Nature Reserve
Thameside Park City Fm.
Warehouses
Works
GATEWAY RETAIL PARK
BECKTON TRIANGLE RETAIL PK.
Greenway
ROYAL DOCKS ROAD
THE LONDON INDUSTRIAL PARK
GALLIONS REACH SHOPPING PARK
Superstore
Sewage Treatment Works
Tanks
Gas Works
E6
Winsor Park
Barking Creek Flood Barrier
Jetty
Pier
Barking or False Point
RIVER
BARKING REACH
Docklands Light Railway Depot
Engine Shed
Margaret or Tripcock Ness
Gallions Reach
DLR
GALLIONS ROUNDABOUT
WOOLWICH MNR. WY.
ROYAL ALBERT WY
A1020
CYPRUS
ROYAL ALBERT DOCK
ALBERT BASIN
Gallions Point Marina
Thames House
Newham Coll. of Further Education (Royal Docks Campus)
E16
KING GEORGE V DOCK
Drawbridge
A117
Custom House
WOOLWICH MANOR WAY
NEWHAM GREENWICH
Gallions Reach
SE28
Twin Tumps
THAMESMEAD CENTRAL
Thamesmere Leisure Cen.
Library & Comm. Hall
Superstore
Pumping Station
THAMESIDE
Tor
A2041
A2016
Woolwich Poly. Sch.
Waterfield Canal
Play. Fld.
Ecumenical Cen.
Butts Wood
THAMESMEAD
Birchmere Park
HARROW MANORWAY
WOOLWICH ROAD
Gallions Point
GALLIONS REACH
WOOLWICH REACH
Royal Victoria Gdns.
Hoba Wharf
THAMESMEAD WEST
Gallions Park
Gallions Lake
Broadwater
WESTERN WAY
CENTRAL WAY
EASTERN WAY
PLUMSTEAD MARSHES
Thamesmead South West
HMP BELMARSH
Crown Ct. & Magistrates Ct.

141
CASTLE GREEN
Goresbrook Leisure Centre
RIPPLE ROAD
A13
Goresbrook Park
RM10
HEATHWAY
A1240
NEW ROAD
A1306
BALLARDS
GORESBROOK INTERCHANGE
Superstore
MOTOR WORKS
Dagenham Dock
CHANNEL TUNNEL RAIL LINK
(UNDER CONSTRUCTION)
Dagenham RM9
A13 GATEWAY
Dagenham Breach
Oil Storage Depot
Coal Depot
ACTIVE WORKINGS
Horse Shoe Corner
Power Station
Motor Works
FORD INDUSTRIAL PARK
HORNCHURCH MARSHES
Car Compound
No.8 Jetty
No.7 Jetty
Thunderer Jetty
Landing Stage
Pontoon
THAMES
Cross Ness
Abbey Sluice
BARKING and DAGENHAM
BEXLEY
Hornchurch Shoot
REACH
Thamesmead North
RIVERSIDE GOLF COURSE
Club Ho.
Driving Range
SEWAGE WORKS
Belvedere DA17
Playing Field
Football Ground
CARLYLE RD.
HARROW MANOR WY.
THAMESMEAD SOUTH
Southmere Lake
Lakeside Centre
Erith DA18
ERITH MARSHES
A2016
THAMESMEAD EAST
BRONZE AGE WY.
PICARDY MANORWAY
SE2
Thamesmead Community College
Thamesmead Adult Education Centre
EASTERN INDUSTRIAL ESTATE
Abbey Wood Pk.
Superstore
1 2 3 4 5 6 7 8 9
G H J K L M N
47 48 49 50
84 83 82 81 80
125
142

142
126
141
152
Dagenham
RM10
SOUTH HORNCHURCH
Rainham
RM13
RAINHAM
RM9
HORNCHURCH MARSHES
RAINHAM MARSHES
Belvedere
DA17
RIVER
THAMES
ERITH REACH
HAVERING
BEXLEY
SOUTH DAGENHAM RD.
RAINHAM RD.
NEW ROAD
A1306
A125
A13
B1335
A2016
THAMES AVENUE
MARSH WAY
FERRY LANE
COLDHARBOUR LANE
GATEWAY
WENNINGTON
BROADWAY
UPMINSTER RD.
EASTERN WAY
BRONZE AGE WAY
PICARDY MANORWAY
CHANNEL TUNNEL RAIL LINK (UNDER CONSTRUCTION)
DOVERS CORNER
Sewage Works
Rainham Steel Mills
Car Compound
Silt Lagoons
Hornchurch Shoot
Old Man's Head
Frog Island
Jenningtree Point
Ingrebourne River
Beam River
Parsonage Farm
Albyns Farm
Farmhouse Wood
Nason Waters Centre (Adult Training)
Chafford Sports Complex
Southall Bridge
Newtons Corner
Dagenham Beam Bridge
Occupation Centre
FORD INDUSTRIAL PARK
MOTOR WORKS
DENVER INDUSTRIAL ESTATE
ALBRIGHT INDUSTRIAL ESTATE
Rainham Hall

Upminster
RM14
South Ockendon
RM15
Purfleet
RM19
AVELEY
WENNINGTON
HORNCHURCH COUNTRY PARK
Abbey Wood
Berwick Pond
Berwick Ponds Farm
Berwick Cottages
Berwick Manor
Berwick Manor Farm
Berwick Manor Cottages
Gerpins Farm
Refuse Transfer Station
Llantrisant Oaks
Damyn's Hall
Damyn's Hall Cottages
Bush Farm
Landfill Site
White Post Corner
Ayletts Cotts.
Redbrick Cotts.
Sand & Gravel Pits
Jewish Cemetery
Warwick Wood
White Post Wood
Hunt's Hill Cottages
Hunt's Hill Farm
Sand & Gravel Pit
Romford Lodge
Visitors Cen.
Running Water Wood
Common Watercourse
THURROCK
HAVERING
Bretts Cottages
Bretts Farm
Works
Moat
Kenningtons
The Orchard
Kennington's Cottages
Moor Hall
Kennington Park (Belhus Woods Country Park)
Kenningtons Prim. Sch.
BELHUS PARK
The Aveley Sch.
Playing Field
Tennis Courts
Mill Fld.
Jun. & Inf. School
Tennis Courts
Spring Farm Park
Pavilion
South Hall Farm
East Hall Farm
Landthorpe House
Halldare Cottages
Wennington Hall
The Willows
Whitehouse Cottage
Depot
Willow Cottage
Easter Farm
Works
Ponds Farm
PURFLEET INDUSTRIAL PARK
THURROCK COMMERCIAL CENTRE
PURFLEET INDUS. PARK
Warehouses
Bowling Green
Pav.
Sports Ground
Tennis Courts
Fanns Farm
Tel. Ex.
Playing Field
Tennis Courts
MARSHES
AVELEY MARSHES
PURFLEET RIFLE RANGES
Reservoir
NEW ROAD
A1306
A13
B1335
GATEWAY
THAMES
LONDON ROAD
SANDY LANE
WENNINGTON ROAD
ROMFORD ROAD
AVELEY BY-PASS
WARWICK LANE
LAUNDERS LANE
BERWICK POND ROAD
GERPINS LANE
BRAMBLE LANE
NORTH ROAD
EAST HALL LANE
CHURCH LANE
PURFLEET ROAD
HIGH STREET
MILL ROAD
127
153
144
H J K L M N
G H J K L M N
1 2 3 4 5 6 7 8 9
54 55 56
84 83 82 81 80

Upminster
RM14
South Ockendon
RM15
RM20
SOUTH OCKENDON
AVELEY
Ockendon
BELHUS PARK
BELHUS PARK GOLF COURSE
BELHUS WOOD COUNTRY PARK
M25 MOTORWAY
Junction 30
Thurrock Service Area
Arena Essex
Speedway Circuit
MARDYKE VALLEY
BRANNETT'S WOOD
MILLARD'S GARDEN
Davy Down (Visitors Centre)
Lakeside Karting Cen.
Motor Sports Complex
Caravan Site
Purfleet FC
Bush Farm
Bramble Farm
Freeman's Shaw
Sand & Gravel Pit
Cockhide
Whitehall Wood
Little Brickkiln Wood
Brickkiln Wood
Running Water Wood
Romford Lodge
Oak Wood
Ash Plantation
Bonnygate Wood
Hangman's Wood
Low Well Wood
Brickbarn Wood
Combe Wood
Dennises Cottages
Kemps
Moat
Kenningtons
Bretts Cottages
Garden Centre
Buckles Farm
Benyon Prim. Sch.
Ockenden Leisure Centre
The Ockendon Sch.
Woodacre Sch.
Dilkes Prim. Sch.
Shaw Prim. Sch.
Holy Cross R.C. Prim. Sch.
The Aveley Sch.
Aveley Prim. Sch.
Kenningtons Prim. Sch.
Belhus Park Leisure Centre
Golf Driving Range
Rugby & Football Pitches
Sports Ground
Playing Field
DENNISES LANE
BRAMBLE LANE
ROMFORD ROAD
STIFFORD ROAD
B1335
A13
A126
A1306
B186
ARTERIAL ROAD
THAMES
GATEWAY
BY-PASS
SOUTH ROAD
NORTH ROAD
PILGRIMS LANE
HIGH STREET
128
143
154

Groves Cottages
Groves Barns
Stringcock
129
Dyke
ORSETT FEN
South Ockendon Hall
Moat
Mar Dyke
Hobletts
Depot
ROAD
Great Mollands
Works
Little Mollands Farm
MOLLANDS LANE
Grange Farm
GRANGEWATER'S RECREATION AREA
(Water Sports)
Little Palmer's Shaw
Great Palmer's Shaw
BRIDGE ROAD
Mar Dyke
GREEN LANE
Old Rectory
Whitfields
STIFFORD CLAYS ROAD
Orsett Smock Mill
Stifford Clays
A13
RM16
Bloomfields Farm
William Edwards Sch.
Playing Field
Little Wellhouse Farm
Greygoose Farm Cottage
Greygoose Farm
Hotel
NORTH STIFFORD
Jun. & Inf. Schs.
Health Cen.
THURROCK COMMUNITY HOSPITAL
Rec. Grd.
Grays
A1012
A1306 ROAD
LONG LANE
Deneholm Prim. Sch.
Thurrock Athletics Stadium
King George's Field
Civic Hall
Blackshots Leisure Centre
Cycle Speedway
Thurrock Rugby C
ELIZABETH RD.
GRAYS
155
LODGE LA.
STANFORD
A1013 ROAD
Hangmans Wood
CHAFFORD HUNDRED
The Grays Sch.
146

Stringcock Fen
Upminster
RM14
Castles Gorse
Fen Covert
ORSETT FEN
Hobletts
Lorkins Farm
Golden Bridge
Conway's Farm
Parker's Farm
CONWAYS ROAD
BRENTWOOD ROAD
Gorwyn's Plantation
Snake Spinney
New Covert
Sticking Hill
Sticking Hill Covert
Long Covert
Wyfields Farm
Aquatic Lodge
BLACK ROBINSON
Kennels
Avondale
BUSH LANE
Home Farm
Fox Holes
Well Wood
ORSETT PARK
Cherry Orchard Farm
Orsett Hall
Linsteads Farm
Orsett Fruit Farm
The Decoy
Old Hall Farm
Poplars Farm
FEN LANE
GREEN LANE
Orsett House
ORSETT
ORSETT HOSPITAL
Loft Hall
Old Rectory
Larch Plantation
Whitfields
HIGH ROAD
BAKER STREET
Orsett C.E. Prim. Sch.
Mill House
Barringtons Farm
STIFFORD CLAYS ROAD
Orsett Smock Mill
Grays
RM16
Riding School
A13
STANFORD ROAD
Southfields
Old Kennels Farm
Club Ho.
Five Chimney Cottages
Nevilles Farm
Whitecroft's Farm
ORSETT GOLF COURSE
Walnut Tree Cottages
Caravan Site
Heath Place
Thurrock Rugby Club
Brook Farm
Rec. Grd.
Cycle Speedway
Old House Wood
Ashen Shaw
Thurrock Athletics Stadium
Playing Field
Torells Sch.
ORSETT HEATH
Subway
Recreation Ground
Civic Hall
Blackshots Leisure Centre
DANEHOLES ROUNDABOUT
School Play. Fld.
Hangmans Wood
Terrels Heath
GRANGEWOOD AV.
ORSETT HEATH
A1013
A1089
A128
B188
130
145
156

131
157
148
HORNDON ON THE HILL
Stanford-le-Hope
SS17
BALSTONIA
STANFORD-LE-HOPE
Stanford le -Hope
MUCKING
LINFORD
MUCKINGFORD
MUCKING MARSHES
ST. CLERE'S GOLF COURSE
Stanford Warren Nature Reserve
Walton Hall Farm Museum
Arden Hall
Greenacres Farm
Horndon House
Saffron Garden Cottages
Saffron Gardens
Cholley's Farm
Rose Valley
Maplecroft Farm
Arden Hall Cotts.
Gas Valve Compound
Club House
St. Cleres Hall Cottages
Thames Haven Junction
Sewage Works
Cemetery
Hassenbrook School
Corringham Leisure Cen.
Bluehouse Farm
Gobians Quarry
Heronrys Shaw
Turners Farm
Sutton's Farm
Merrie Loots Farm
Collingwood Farm
Active Workings
Mucking Creek
STANHOPE INDUSTRIAL PARK
A13
A1014
A1013
B1007
THE MANORWAY
ARTERIAL (STANFORD-LE-HOPE BY-PASS) ROAD
BUCKINGHAM HILL ROAD
WALTON'S HALL LANE
MUCKING WHARF ROAD

148
132
147
47
Stanford-le-Hope
SS17
CORRINGHAM
BALSTONIA
FOBBING
STANFORD -LE-HOPE
The Billet
THE MANORWAY
A1014
B1420
OIL REFINERIES
Stanford Le Hope Marshes
Earls Hope
Mucking Creek
Active Workings
Jetty
RIVER
Corringham Hall
Cobblers Mede Lake
Corringham Prim. Sch.
Sports Ground
Old Clay Pits
Fobbing Hall
Curtis's Farm
Old Hall
Oak Farm
Old Garlands
Great Garlands Farm
Football Pitch
Corringham Leisure Cen.
Graham James Prim. Sch.
STANHOPE INDUSTRIAL PARK
Depot
Tennis Courts
LAMPITS HILL
CORRINGHAM HILL
SPRINGHOUSE ROAD
HIGH ROAD
RAINBOW LANE
LION HILL
FOBBING ROAD
ROOKERY HILL
THAMES HAVEN ROAD
GIFFORDS CROSS ROAD
MANOR WAY
CHURCH ROAD

MARSHES
THE MANORWAY
A1014
Manorway
Fleet
SHELL HAVEN
Oozedam
Salt
Fleet
Depot
Coryton
OIL STORAGE DEPOT
Power Station
Shellhaven
Creek
Thames Haven
Shelly Bay
Jetty
Jetties
Shell Haven
Coryton Wharves
Horseshoe Bay
OIL REFINERY
Holehaven Creek
Upper Horse
CASTLE POINT
THURROCK
Canvey Island
SS8
Tanks
Oil Refinery
Chimney
Northwick
Works
NORTHWICK
ROAD
THAMES
THURROCK
133
150
H
J
K
L
M
N
G
1
2
3
4
5
6
7
8
9
73
74
75
76
84
83
82
81
80

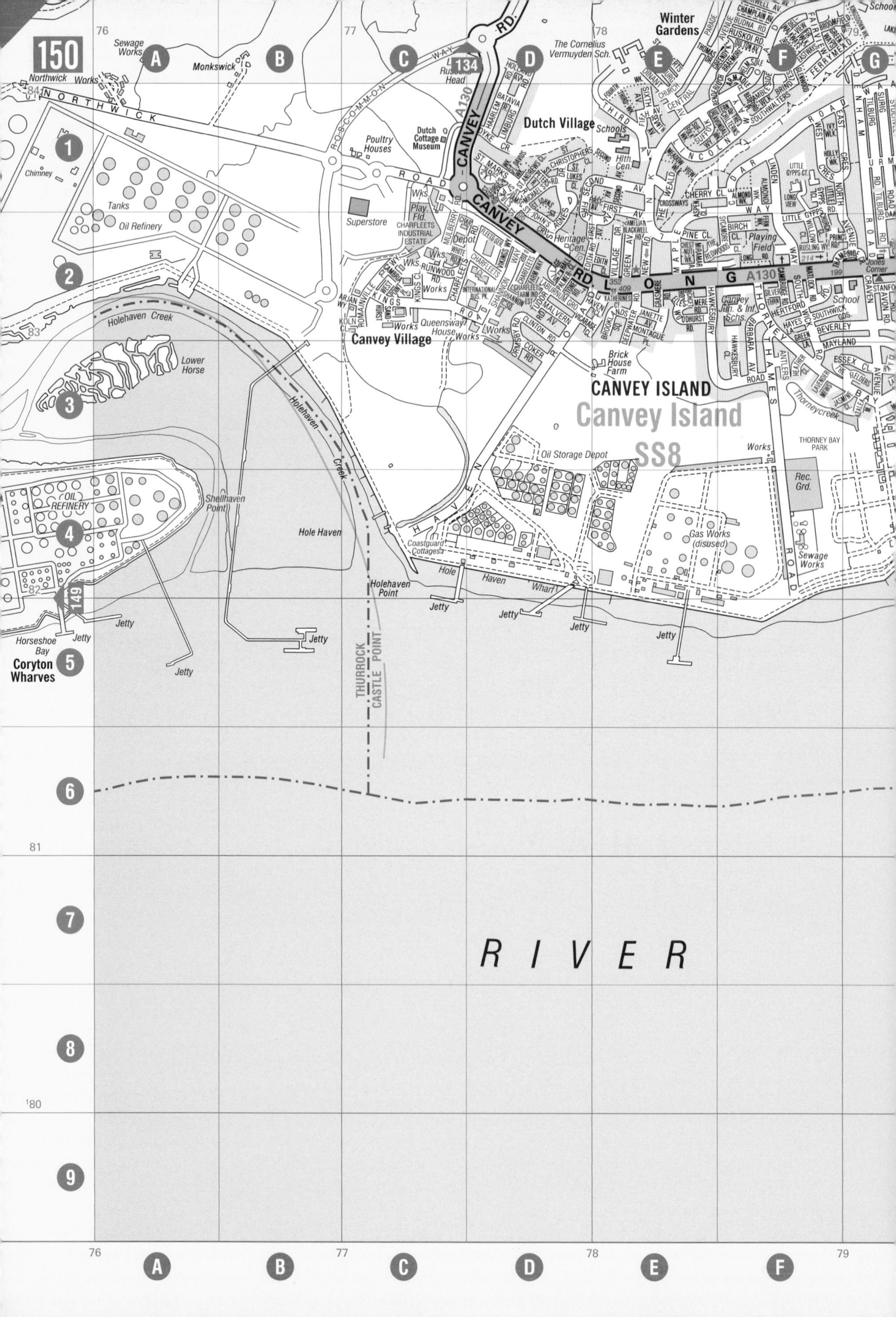
CANVEY ISLAND
Canvey Island
SS8
Canvey Village
Dutch Village
Winter Gardens
Coryton Wharves
Horseshoe Bay
Holehaven Creek
Hole Haven
Holehaven Point
Lower Horse
Shellhaven Point
Oil Refinery
Oil Storage Depot
Gas Works (disused)
Sewage Works
Northwick
Monkswick
Thorney Bay Park
Brick House Farm
Dutch Cottage Museum
Poultry Houses
Superstore
Canvey Jun. & Inf. Schs.
The Cornelius Vermuyden Sch.
Coastguard Cottages
THURROCK
CASTLE POINT
R I V E R
A130
134
149

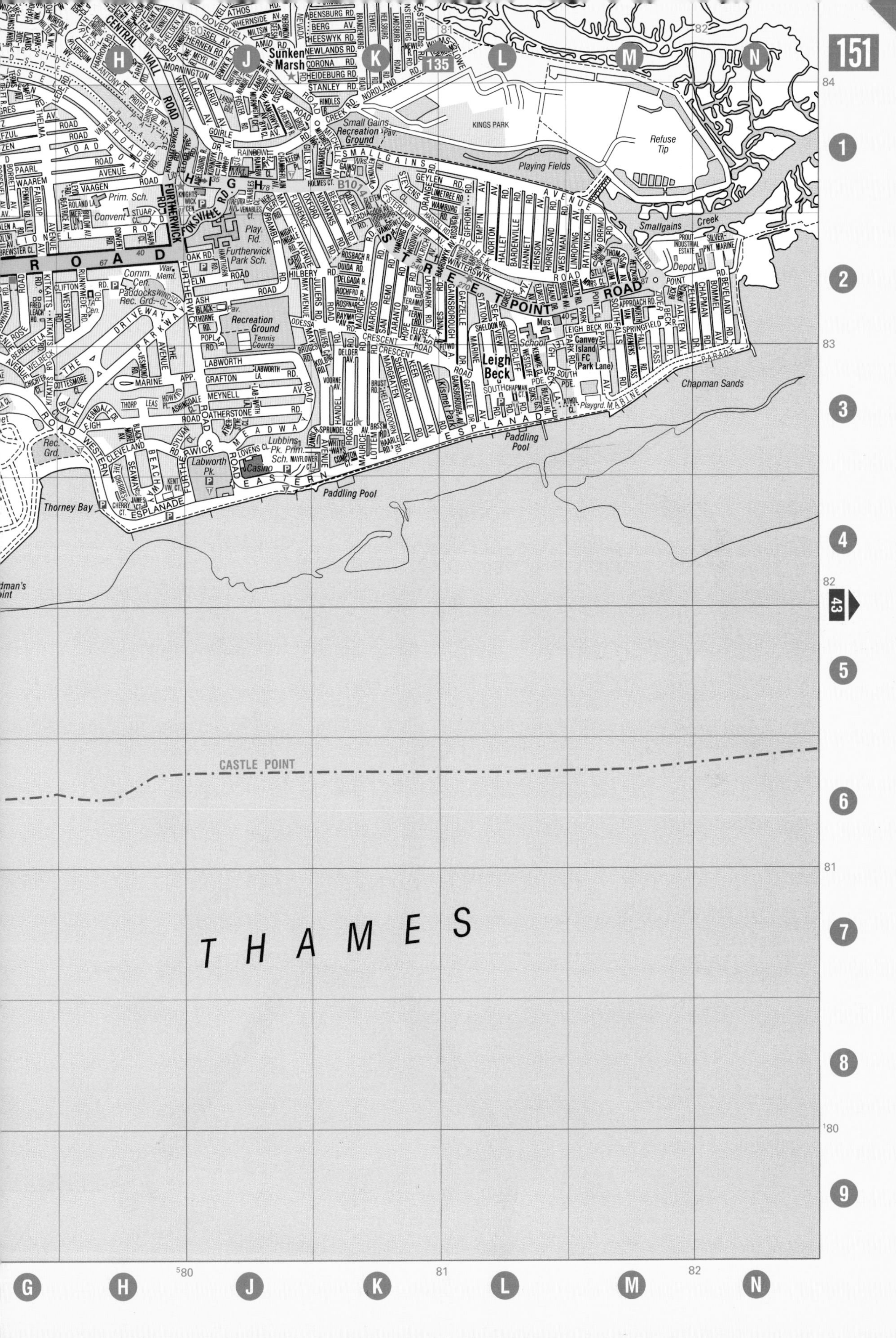

Sunken Marsh
Small Gains Recreation Ground
KINGS PARK
Refuse Tip
Playing Fields
Smallgains Creek
CENTRAL WALL ROAD
FURTHERWICK ROAD
HIGH STREET
FOKSVILLE RD.
Furtherwick Park Sch.
Recreation Ground
Tennis Courts
Labworth Pk.
Casino
Lubbins Pk. Prim. Sch.
Leigh Beck
Canvey Island FC (Park Lane)
POINT ROAD
Prout Industrial Estate
Depot
Chapman Sands
Paddling Pool
Kismet Park
EASTERN ESPLANADE
MARINE PARADE
Thorney Bay
Prim. Sch.
Convent
Comm. Cen.
Paddocks Rec. Grd.
Rec. Grd.
THE PARKWAY
CASTLE POINT
THAMES
135
43
G
H
J
K
L
M
N
1
2
3
4
5
6
7
8
9

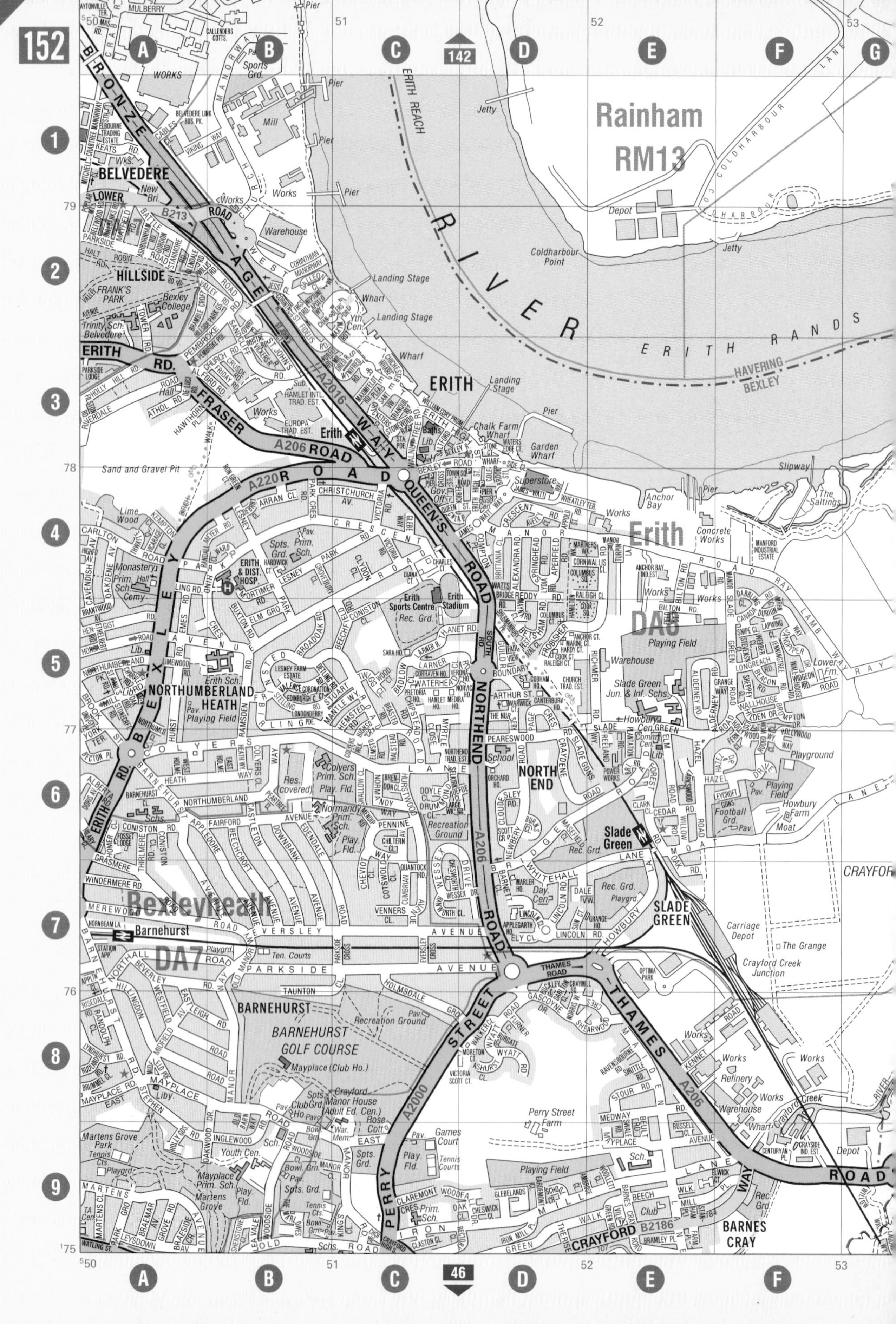
152
142
46
Rainham
RM13
RIVER
ERITH REACH
ERITH RANDS
HAVERING
BEXLEY
BELVEDERE
LOWER
HILLSIDE
ERITH
Erith
DA8
NORTHUMBERLAND HEATH
NORTH END
SLADE GREEN
Slade Green
Bexleyheath
DA7
Barnehurst
BARNEHURST
BARNEHURST GOLF COURSE
CRAYFORD
BARNES CRAY
Coldharbour Point
Erith Sports Centre
Erith Stadium
ERITH & DIST. HOSP.
Crayford Creek
Perry Street Farm
Martens Grove Park
Mayplace Prim. Sch.
BRONZE AGE WAY
FRASER ROAD
BEXLEY ROAD
QUEEN'S ROAD
NORTHEND ROAD
THAMES ROAD
PERRY STREET
A206
A220
A2016
A2000
B213
B2186

AVELEY MARSHES
PURFLEET RIFLE RANGES
Purfleet
RM19
South Ockendon
RM15
AVELEY
THAMES
LONG REACH
PURFLEET
Crayford Ness
The Saltings
DARENT INDUSTRIAL PARK
THAMESIDE IND. EST.
Flood Barrier
DARTFORD SALT MARSHES
MARSHES
Dartford
DA1
Joyce Green Farm
Power Station
LITTLEBROOK BUSINESS CENTRE
LITTLEBROOK INTERCHANGE
Junc. 1a
DARTFORD FRESH MARSHES
JOYCE GREEN
RIVERSIDE INDUSTRIAL ESTATE
CROSSWAYS 25 BUSINESS PARK
QUEEN ELIZABETH DISTRIBUTION PARK
PURFLEET THAMES TERMINAL
BEACON HILL INDUSTRIAL ESTATE
CHANNEL TUNNEL RAIL LINK (UNDER CONSTRUCTION)
UNIVERSITY WAY
A206
A13
A1306
A1090
A282
A2026
Oil Storage Depot
Beacon Hill
Watt's Wood
Mar Dyke
Playing Field
Sports Ground
Fanns Farm
Reservoir
EDISON'S PARK
QUEEN ELIZABETH II BRIDGE
DARTFORD TUNNEL
143
154
46

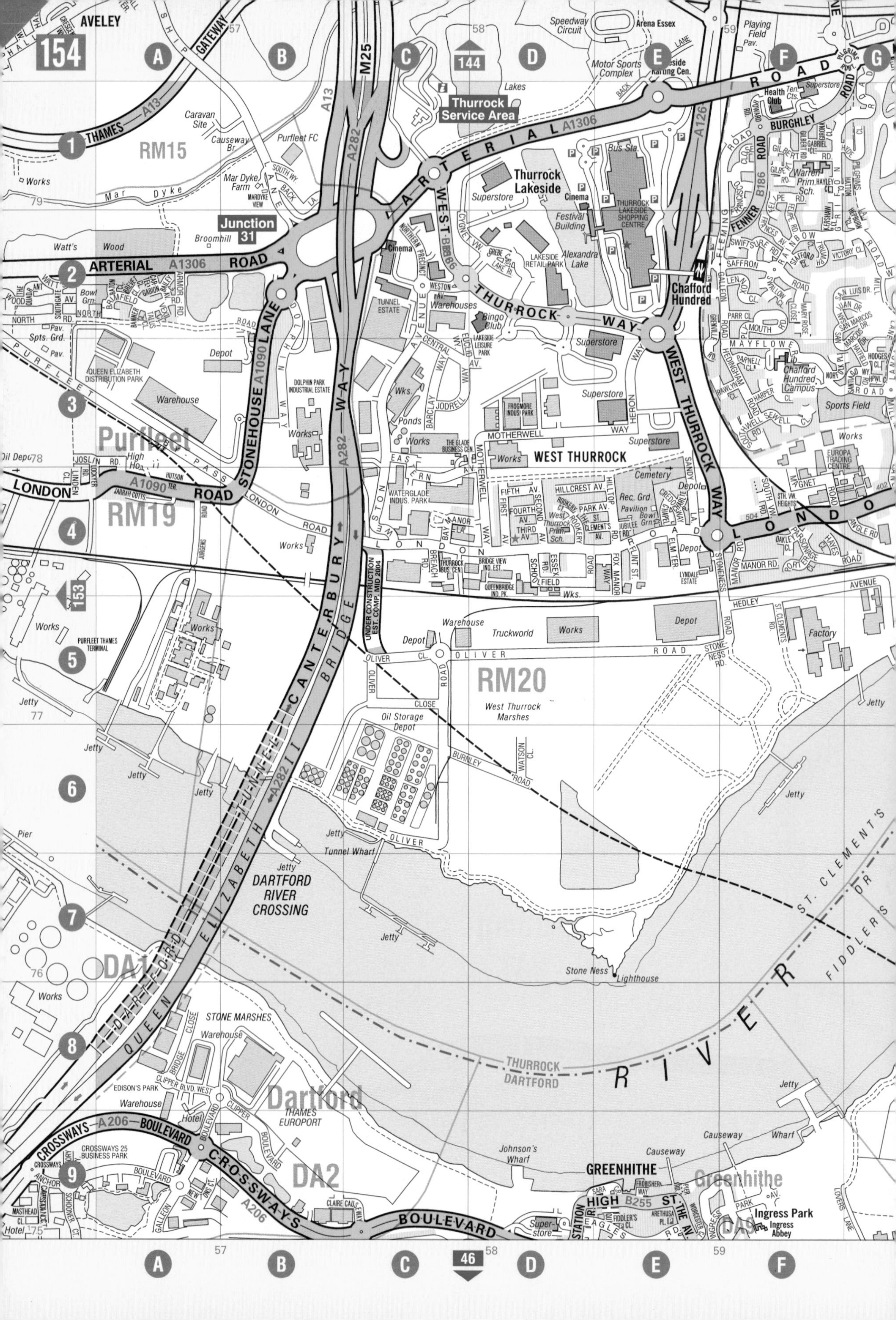
154
AVELEY
A
B
C
D
E
F
G
144
153
46
1
2
3
4
5
6
7
8
9
M25
Speedway Circuit
Arena Essex
Playing Field
Motor Sports Complex
Lakes
Thurrock Service Area
THAMES
A13
GATEWAY
SHIP
RM15
Caravan Site
Causeway Br.
Purfleet FC
Works
Mar Dyke
Mar Dyke Farm
MARDYKE VIEW
Junction 31
Broomhill
Watt's Wood
ARTERIAL
A1306
ROAD
A282
Thurrock Lakeside
Superstore
Cinema
THURROCK LAKESIDE SHOPPING CENTRE
Festival Building
Alexandra Lake
LAKESIDE RETAIL PARK
Bus Sta.
Chafford Hundred
A126
Health Club
BURGHLEY
B186
FENNER
SAFFRON
MAYFLOWER
Chafford Hundred Campus
Sports Field
Warren Prim. Sch.
NORTH
Pav.
Spts. Grd.
QUEEN ELIZABETH DISTRIBUTION PARK
Warehouse
Depot
STONEHOUSE
LANE
A1090
DOLPHIN PARK INDUSTRIAL ESTATE
TUNNEL ESTATE
Warehouses
Bingo Club
LAKESIDE LEISURE PARK
THURROCK
WAY
WEST THURROCK WAY
Superstore
FROGMORE INDUS. PARK
MOTHERWELL
WEST THURROCK
THE GLADE BUSINESS CEN.
WATERGLADE INDUS. PARK
Cemetery
Rec. Grd.
Pavilion
EUROPA TRADING CENTRE
Purfleet
High Ho.
LONDON
ROAD
RM19
JARRAH COTTS
HUTSON TER.
LONDON ROAD
PURFLEET BY-PASS
CANTERBURY
BRIDGE
UNDER CONSTRUCTION EST. COMP. MID 2004
THURROCK BUS. CEN.
BRIDGE VIEW IND. EST.
QUEENBRIDGE IND. PK.
LYNDALE ESTATE
HEDLEY AVENUE
Works
PURFLEET THAMES TERMINAL
Warehouse
Depot
Truckworld
Factory
OLIVER ROAD
RM20
West Thurrock Marshes
Oil Storage Depot
BURNLEY ROAD
Jetty
Pier
Tunnel Wharf
DARTFORD RIVER CROSSING
QUEEN ELIZABETH II TUNNEL
DARTFORD
Stone Ness
Lighthouse
ST. CLEMENT'S
FIDDLER'S
RIVER
THURROCK
DARTFORD
DA1
STONE MARSHES
Warehouse
EDISON'S PARK
CLIPPER BLVD. WEST
Dartford
THAMES EUROPORT
Hotel
CROSSWAYS
A206
BOULEVARD
CROSSWAYS 25 BUSINESS PARK
DA2
Johnson's Wharf
Causeway
Causeway Wharf
GREENHITHE
Greenhithe
HIGH
B255
ST.
Ingress Park
Ingress Abbey
Super-store
STATION
DA9
57
58
59
76
77
78
79
75

GRAYS
CHAFFORD HUNDRED
RM16
Grays
SOUTH STIFFORD
LITTLE THURROCK
RM17
THAMES
Tilbury
RM18
TILBURY DOCKS
Gravesend
DA11
Swanscombe
DA10
NORTHFLEET HOPE
THURROCK GRAVESHAM
Broadness Salt Marshes
Swanscombe Marshes
Botany Marshes
Northfleet Hope Container Terminal
Rail Container Terminal
Grain Terminal
TILBURY FREE PORT
Rolling Lift Bridge
Tilbury Ness
CHANNEL TUNNEL RAIL LINK (ESTIMATED COMPLETION 2006)
Thurrock Yatch Club
The Beach
Boating Pool
Lighthouse
Radar Sta.
Grays Park
Stifford Prim. Sch.
Grays New Cemetery
145
156
47

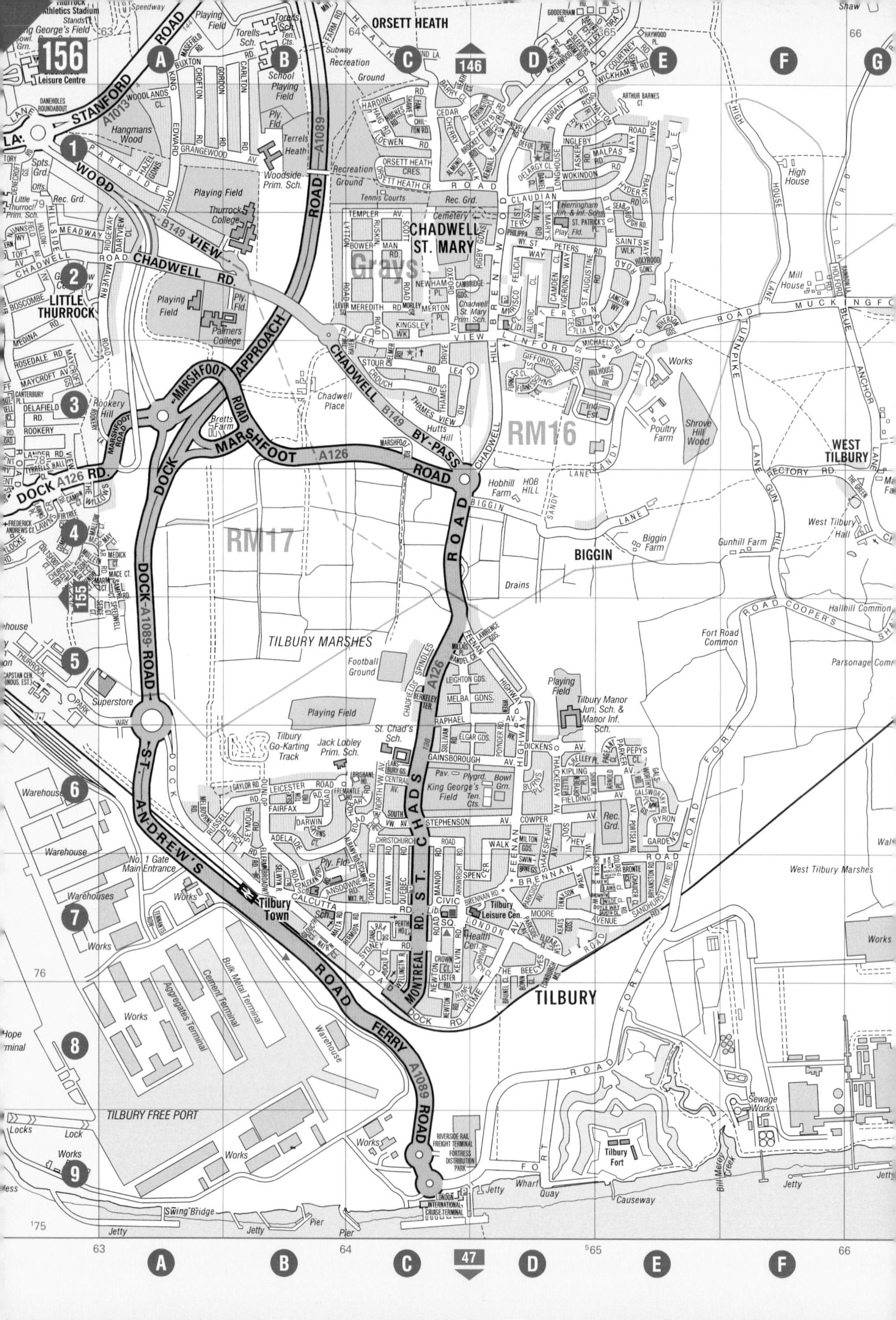
ORSETT HEATH
146
CHADWELL ST. MARY
Grays
LITTLE THURROCK
RM16
RM17
WEST TILBURY
BIGGIN
TILBURY MARSHES
TILBURY
TILBURY FREE PORT
Tilbury Fort
West Tilbury Marshes
STANFORD ROAD
A1013
A1089
B149
A126
DOCK APPROACH ROAD
MARSHFOOT ROAD
CHADWELL BY-PASS
ST. CHADS ROAD
DOCK ROAD
ST. ANDREW'S ROAD
FERRY ROAD
FORT ROAD
Tilbury Town
London International Cruise Terminal
Riverside Rail Freight Terminal
Fortress Distribution Park
Aggregates Terminal
Cement Terminal
Bulk Metal Terminal
Sewage Works
Hangmans Wood
Shrove Hill Wood
Thurrock College
Palmers College
Superstore
Tilbury Manor Jun. Sch. & Manor Inf. Sch.
Tilbury Go-Karting Track
Football Ground
King George's Field
Tilbury Leisure Cen.
Swing Bridge
Causeway
Bill Meroy Creek
63
64
65
66
75
76
77
78
79
A
B
C
D
E
F
G
1
2
3
4
5
6
7
8
9
155
47

MUCKING MARSHES
LINFORD
MUCKINGFORD
Stanford-le-Hope
SS17
Merrie Loots Farm
Gobions
Rec. Grd.
Pump. Sta.
Becksland
East Tilbury
Old Counter Wall
Sewage Works
Pav. Ten. Cts. Plygd.
Thomas Bata Memorial Park
East Tilbury Jun. & Inf. Schs.
THAMES INDUSTRIAL PARK
Sports Ground
Factory
EAST TILBURY MARSHES
EAST TILBURY
West Cotts.
Condovers Cotts.
Low Street
Industrial Estate
Barvills Farm
Goshem's Farm
Coalhouse Battery (Dismantled)
Tilbury
RM18
Buckland
Bowaters Farm
Mariner Cotts.
Castle Farm
Church Green
Coalhouse Fort & Thameside Aviation Museum
East Tilbury Marshes
Valve Compound
Water Tower
Coalhouse Point
THE LOWER HOPE
Jetty
RIVER THAMES
Tilbury Power Station
Wharf
THURROCK
Jetty
LOW STREET LANE
COAL ROAD
STATION ROAD
LOVE LANE
GRASS RD.
PRINCESS MARGARET ROAD
CORONATION AV.
QUEEN MARY AV.
PRINCESS AV.
GLOUCESTER AV.
FARM RD.
BATA AV.
THOMAS BATA
ROAD
ALEXANDRA
QUEEN ELIZABETH
KING GEORGE VI AV.
TORRIDGE
STRATHMORE
SEVERN
WALDON
HAYLE WAY
SOLWAY
COLNE
AVENUE
BURE
CLYDE
TWEED
TRENT
ARUN
ORWELL
FROME
TYNE
WELLAND
COLNE CT.
LINLEY CL.
GORDON CL.
NORTHUMBERLAND RD.
SOMERSET
DORSET
ESSEX GDS.
EAST TILBURY ROAD
DEVON CRES.
STAFFORD CL.
LOWER MEADOW
REDBROOKE CT.
STENNING AV.
BRINDLES CL.
BEECHCROFT AV.
DRIVE
HALT
68
69
67
79
78
77
76
75
147
47
G H J K L M N
1 2 3 4 5 6 7 8 9

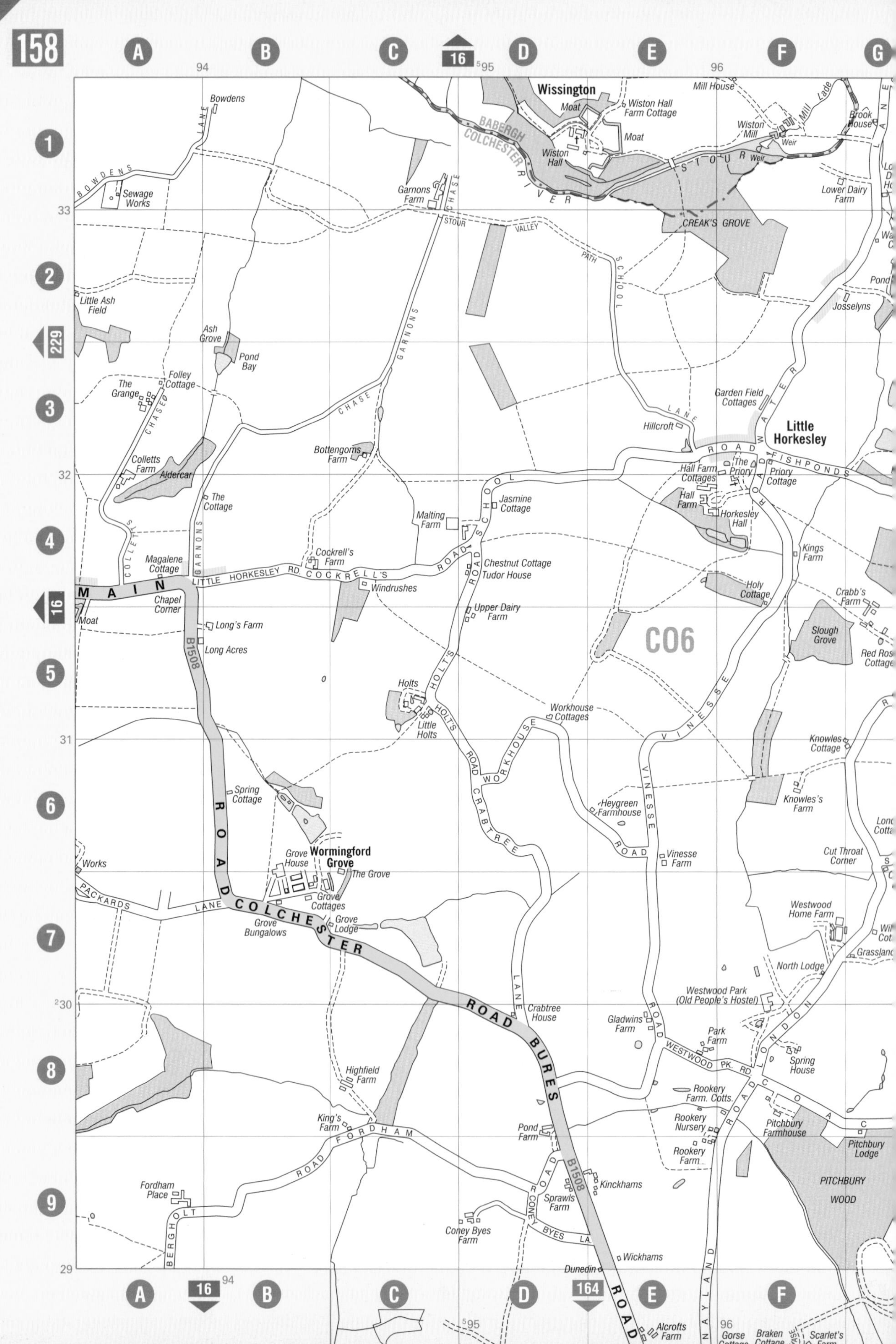

16
229
16
16
164

H
J
K
16
L
M
N
97
98
99
600
Windyridge Cottages
Windyridge
Kings Yard
Burnt Dick Hill Cottages
Valley Yard
Boxted C of E Prim. Sch.
Cemetery
Parsonage Farm
Little Wood
Boxted Hall Cottages
Boxted Hall
The Bungalow
Knights Tourney
Whitepark Farm
The Nurseries
Kerseys
Kerseys Lodge
Pond House
South Lodge
Rectory Grove
Greenfields
The Chantry
Broad Acres
War Mem.
Play Fld.
Chantry Lodge
Pav.
Reservoirs
Ridgnalls
Potter's Farm
Potter's Cottage
Greenfield Cottages
Orchard Farm
Carter's Farm
Brook Farm
Carter's Vineyards
HILL FARM INDUSTRIAL ESTATE
Nursery
Ridgnalls Lodge
Little Thatches
Thatch Cottage
Mouse Hall
Horkesley Green
Brook Cottages
High Bank
Boxted Lodge
Martins
Coveneys
Baytrees House
Holly Lodge Farm
Reservoir
Elm Croft
Line Cottages
EAST SIDE
Oakfield
Baytrees
Wheatlands
Rookery Lodge
Workhouse Hill
The Ramblers
Rowleigh
Peartree Cottage
The Cottage
Blossoms
Orchard Cottage
Mount Hall
Newhey
Abattoir
Emdon
The Grove
Nevards Farm
Tye Green
Barritts Farm
Thatchers Cottages
160
Scarfe's Corner
Enfield's Farm
CO4
Nevards
Noakes Farm
Freads Corner
Hospytts
The Cedars
Lodge Farm
Preen View
New Enfield's Farm
Old Ellis Farmhouse
Poultry Houses
Powers Court
Reservoir (covered)
Depot
The Bungalow
Altyre House
Altyre Cottage
Mill House
Lodge Farm Cottage
Tye Cottage
The Croft
Frost's Grove
The Old Queen's Head
Four-acres
Heathfield
Rose House
Chapel Cottage
Colchester
Harrow Corner
Harrow Wood
Oakwood
Classford Lodge
Gardens Cottages
Breewood Hall
Rose Cottage
Nursery
Priory Hall Farm
Breewood
New Barn House
Redhouse Farm
Oldhouse Farm
White House
Nursery
The Spinney
The Cottage
Horkesley Plantation
Cumberland House
Shrublands
THE CRESCENT
BLACKBROOKE COTTS.
GLEBELANDS
Spratt's Marsh
Farthings
Fairways
Hither Woodthorpes
Nursery
Woodside Farm
Nursery
Fruit Farm
Little Simons
Old House Farm
GREAT HORKESLEY
Bapton
Gaen Trees
Blackbrook Farm
Pucks Croft
Kennels
Ponders Farm
Pondereeter House
Blacksmith's Corner
Blue Stones
Nursery
Tile House Farm
Great Horkesley Manor
Whitehouse Farm
The Haven
Bishop William Ward C of E Prim. Sch.
Cuckoo Cottages
Cuckoo Farm
A12
Terrace Hall
165
The Mullions
Poultry Houses
Woodhouse Farm
Kiln House
Moorlands Farm
Playing Field
Club House
Resr.
HORKESLEY HILL
NAYLAND ROAD
A134
THE CAUSEWAY
ROMAN ROAD
BOXTED CHURCH ROAD
BOXTED ROAD
QUEEN'S HEAD ROAD
HORKESLEY ROAD
IVY LODGE ROAD
ACCOMMODATION ROAD
BOXTED ROAD
LANGHAM ROAD
SEVERALLS LANE
PEPPER'S RD.
CHAPEL RD.
MILL ROAD
ELLIS ROAD
WORKHOUSE HILL
WET LANE
HOLLY LANE
BROAD LANE
LINCOLN LANE
OLD HOUSE ROAD
OLD HOUSE LANE
PARSONAGE ROAD
CHURCH STREET
PARK ROAD
BURNT DICK HILL
Black Brook
Salary Brook
1
2
3
4
5
6
7
8
9
33
32
31
30
29
G

160
A
B
C
D
E
F
G
17
01
02
03
Boxted C of E Prim. Sch.
Cemy.
Knights Tourney
Parsonage Farm
CHURCH STREET
PARSONAGE
CHURCH ROAD
COOKS ROAD
ASH WOOD
Rivers Hall
Moat
Tennis Cts.
SKY HALL HILL
Plumb's Farm
WATER LANE
Alderton's Cottages
Whale Bone House
Martin's Farm
The Bungalow
The White House
Whalebone Corner
Sports Ground
RECTORY ROAD
Glebe House
Glebe Farm
Pond House
Rose Cottage
Vine Cottage
CARTERS HILL
CROSS COTTS.
Dullingham
Hill Farm
HILLCREST COTTAGES
Furze Lodge
Springfield Farm
NIGHTINGALE HILL
Piggeries
PRIORY LANE
HILL FARM INDUSTRIAL ESTATE
WHITE ARCH PL.
DEDHAM ROAD
SONGERS COTTAGES
Homedale Cottages
Homedale Farm
Boxted Cross
King George's Field
Pav.
Perrymans
Works
Black Brook
Spike's Grove
Godfreys
Nightingale Farm
Greyhound Hill Farm
Sewage Works
HOBBS' DR.
DAFFIELD DR.
BOXTED
Songers
The Old Mill House
Thatchways
Piggery
Hornestreet
The Grove
Grove Cottage
Boxted Lodge
Hope Cottages
Oak Apple Farm
Bardles Barn
Grove Farm
The Grove
EAST SIDE
Plains Farm
HUNDRED LANE
HIGH STREET
Serenity
Gaywoods
Pungford Cottages
Line Cottages
CAGE LANE
OLD CHAPEL ROAD
Six Acres
Wenlock
Gridleys
WHITEHOUSE CL.
GREYHOUND ROAD
Homestead Sch.
SPENCERS PIECE
Playing Field
Langham Prim. Sch.
Perry Grove
PERRY
Rowleigh
NEWMAN DR.
SCHOOL ROAD
ST. MARGARET'S CROSS
LANGHAM
Peartree Cottage
Cottage
Blossoms
Newhey
Abattoir
Langham Moor
Blacksmith's Corner
Rec. Grd.
School Farm
Mott's Farm
MILL ROAD
159
Emdon
Broomfield Farm
Mountain Ash
Langham Wick
Thatchers Cottages
Piggeries
Field Nursery
Wheatcroft
MOOR ROAD
ORCHARD COTTAGES
BIRCHWOOD
Nevards
Noakes Farm
CHAPEL
Wenlocks
C04
Chaplin's Farmhouse
New Homestead
Poultry House
Powers Court
Chapel Farm
CHAPEL LA.
PARK LANE
WICK TER.
Works
Rose House
St. Ives Farm
Malting Farm
Ashdene
Four-acres
Heathfield
STRAIGHT ROAD
Park Lane Farm
The Thatched Cottage
New House
Reservoir
Park Farm
WICK LANE
ROMAN
Priory Hall Farm
Nursery
OLD HOUSE LANE
Rose Cottage
Oaklands
Oldhouse Farm
Malting Farm Cottage
Elkst
New Da
BIRCH WOOD
Willow Farm
Reservoir
Oak Bury
Windyridge
Reservoir
Cumberland House
LANGHAM
East View
Poultry House
Silver Birches
The Bungalow
Fox Earth
Nevada
Poultry House
Blue Barns Farm
Holly Tree Farm
A12
IPSWICH ROAD
Fruit Farm
Bapton
LODGE LANE
Langham Lodge
WICK
LANGHAM ROAD
SEVERALLS
Runkins Corner
LANGHAM LODGE LA.
TURNPIKE CLOSE
Salary Brook
Kiln Wood
Whitehouse Farm
Croft Stud
CROWN INTERCHANGE
Junction 29
Severalls Hall
CONNAUGHT HOUSE
OLD IPSWICH RD.
CROWN LANE
White House Farm
Gatehouse Farm
Chestnuts
Bridge House
29
THE CRESCENT
THE CENTRE
Playing Field
Tennis Cts.
Sports Club
FLOOD
COLCHESTER BUSINESS PARK
166
WAY
Depot
Sandpit Lodge
NORTH
Whinstone
Playing Field
Club House
MILL ROAD
SEVERALLS LA.
NEWCOMEN
SEEDBED CENTRE
CROWN CT
CLOUGH RD.
A120
33
32
31
230
600
1
2
3
4
5
6
7
8
9

H
J
K
17
L
M
N
Stratford Bridge
BABERGH
COLCHESTER
RIVER STOUR
Dedham Vale Family Farm
Dedham Hall
Lodge
Gun Hill Place
The Rookery
Bridges Farm
Works
Princel House
Bell Cottage
DEDHAM
Craft Cen. & Toy Mus.
Football Grd.
The Duchy Field
The Rose House
Sunnyside Farm
Poultry Houses
Rookery Farm
Lower Park
The Flemish House
Hallfields Farm
Hallfields Cotts.
Pound Farm
Uplands
Monk's Farm
Boxhouse Farm
Fruit Packing Station
Monk's Lane Farm
Two Acres
Almhouses
Coles Oak House
Dedham C.of E. Prim. Sch.
Playground
Arley Grange
The Lecture House
Shelley Glebe Farm
Park Farm
Castle Cottages
East House
Blackbrook
Kiddles Cottage
Greenfield Orchard
Brook Farm
Meadowbrook
Hunters Moon
Castle House (Sir Alfred Munnings Art Museum)
Heavy Horse Centre
Barretts
Parkside
Kiddles Farm
Grove Hill House
Grove Cottage
May's Barn
Cuckoo Cottage
Perry House
Stone Cottage
Parney Heath
Hill House
Lamb Corner
Frostwood House
Dedham Heath
Blomfields
The Cottage
Heath Court
Lamb Cottage
Stud Farm
Birchwood Farm Cotts.
Rye Cottages
Little Paddocks
Cross Vale
Lufkins
Heath Farm
Birchwood Farm
Colchester
CO7
The Cottage
Great Hickle House
COLCHESTER
TENDRING
Malting Farm
Cranmore
Goodhall
God's House Farm
Birchhall Corner
The Bungalow
Rookery Farm
Goodhall Farm
Greenacres
Oatlands
Clarke's Farm
Old Barn Farm
Sideways Cottage
Fieldside
Ardleigh Heath
Goodhall Cottages
Rookery Bungalow
Whaley Farm
Benson Stud
Oak Tree Corner
Bloomfield's Farm
Rookery Cottage
Pyghtle Poultry Farm
Badliss Hall
Blachernae
Reservoir
Home Farm
Cemetery
Fountain Farm
St. Mary's C of E Prim. Sch.
Glebe Corner
Piggeries
Cowmans Cottage
ARDLEIGH
Glebe Cottages
New Hall
Reservoir (covered)
Recreation Ground
Garden Centre
Guide Post Farm
Chilver's Cottage
Lodge Farm
The Manor House
Bovill's Hall
Elm Park
ARDLEIGH RESERVOIR
IPSWICH ROAD
COLCHESTER ROAD
HARWICH ROAD
ARDLEIGH ROAD
DEDHAM ROAD
STATION ROAD
GROVE HILL
SHOEBRIDGE'S HILL
HIGH STREET
MILL LA.
LONG ROAD
WEST LONG ROAD
HUNTER'S CHASE
ROOKERY CHASE
MALTING FARM LANE
FEN LANE
LITTLE BROMLEY ROAD
MANNINGTREE ROAD
EAST LANE
THE HEATH
CROWN STREET
CASTLE HILL
COGGESHALL ROAD
PENNYPOT
BIRCHWOOD ROAD
A12
A137
B1029
162
167
G
1
2
3
4
5
6
7
8
9
04
05
06
29
30
31
32
33

A
B
C
D
E
F
G
17
168
07
08
09
33
32
31
30
29
1
2
3
4
5
6
7
8
9
Sluice Valve
Hubletts
Bridge Cottage Info. Cen.
Flatford Bridge Cottage
Valley Farm
Flatford Mill (Field Centre)
Moat
Judas Gap
Barrage
RIVER STOUR
VALLEY PATH
HOGS LA.
DAZELEY'S LA.
Lighterman's Piece
West Green Cotts.
BERGHOLT
BRANTHAM MILL IND. EST.
Lock (dis.)
Pound Farm
Hallfields Cotts.
DEDHAM
MANNINGTREE
Dedham Old River
BABERGH
COLCHESTER
Lower Barn Farm
ROAD
Colchester
CO7
MANNINGTREE RD.
JUPES
COLCHESTER TENDRING
Hall Fleet
Manningtree
Heavy Horse Centre
Barretts
Cuckoo Cottage
Stour House
HILL
EAST
MILL
The Rookery
Lawford Hall
Lawford Park
Frostwood House
Jupes Hill House
Shirburn Mill
The Cottage
Heath Court
Hill Farm
DEDHAM
Broom Knolls
Lodge
LONG
LANE
BARGATE
Lufkins
Aldercar
Humberland's
Heath Farm
The Cottage
Bargate Lane Farm
Charity Farm
Abbots Manor
The Mount
Lawford Place
WIGNALL
ROAD
STREET
COX'S HILL
IPSWICH
A137
LAWFORD
Great Hickle House
Burn
Shir
FOXWOOD CL.
Tye Hill
Rec. Grd.
SCHOOL LANE
Bromley Corner
Lawford C. of E. Prim. Sch.
Resr.
Play. Fld.
HARWICH
TILE
Glanfields
Lower Farm
Tile Barn
BARN LANE
Lawford House
Foxash Estate
Wisdom's Farm
Grange Farm Cottages
WOOD BARN LANE
DOWN
Grange Farm
Lawfordhouse Farm
Aldhams Cottage
Badliss Hall
Res.
Reservoir
Wormseywood Farm
Hungerdowns
FARM
HUNGERDOWN
Riddlesdale Farm
Hollylodge Farm
Bounds Farm
LITTLE BROMLEY LANE
Lower Barn
GRANGE BARN LANE
Spinks's Farm
BROMLEY
Badley Hall
MORROW LANE
ARDLEIGH ROAD
CHESHOP RD.
Little Broml

Manningtree
CO11
MANNINGTREE
MISTLEY
Mistley
New Mistley
Mistley Heath
Cattawade
SEAFIELD BAY
RIVER STOUR
Sewage Works
Decoy Pond
Marsh Farm
Palfrey Farm
Sports Ground
Works
Cattawade Bridge
Cattawade Creek
Hook Shoal
Norman's Reach
Middlebridge Creek
Manningtree Channel
Hopping Bridge
Swimming Pool
Mistley Towers
Mistley Quay
Baltic Wharf
Depot
Lower Park
Mistley Place Pk. Environmental & Animal Rescue Cen.
The Dormy Ho.
Recreation Ground
Mistley Lodge
Round Clump
Oldhall
Laundry Wood
Long Plantation
Dairy Wood
Dairy House
Riding School
Mistley Wood
Mistley Hall
Pedler's Corner
School Wood
FURZE HILL
Tennis Courts
Playing Field
Village Hall
Waiftfleet Creek
Lowercraft Fleet
Uppercraft Fleet
The Oven
Home Farm
Lynwood
St. Mary's Church (Rems. of)
Church Farm
Smithy
Dovehouse Farm
Aldhams Farm
Stacie's Farm
Ford Farm
Beech Plantation
Irrigation Reservoir
Round Clump
Brickkiln Grove
Old Mount
Reservoir
Dickley Hall
Mast
Chequers Wood
Rose Farm
Chequers Farm
Highfields Prim. Sch.
Manningtree Sports Cen.
Manningtree High Sch.
Lawford Hill
HARWICH ROAD
B1352
B1035
B1070
A137
CLACTON ROAD
STEAM MILL ROAD
HIGH STREET
THE WALLS
NEW ROAD
SHRUBLAND
SKIP HATCH
CHEQUERS ROAD
HEATH ROAD
WINDMILL RD.
GREEN LANE
COLCHESTER ROAD
Stour Prim. Sch.
18
169

INSET
Quilters Green
FORDHAM
CO6
Fordham Hall
Aldercar
Stitching Wood
Hillhouse Wood
West Bergholt Hall
Hall Farm Cottages
Cook's Hall
Spring Wood
Grove Wood
The Old Rectory
Poole's Farm
Cook's Mill
Great Porter's Farm
WEST BERGHOLT
Colchester
Fordham Heath
New Bridge
Newbridge Mill
Sewage Works
River Colne
EIGHT ASH GREEN
Iron Latch Meadow Nature Reserve
Chitts Hills
CO3
SPRING LANE INTERCHANGE
Seven Star Green
Stanway Depot
Junction 26
EIGHT ASH GREEN INTERCHANGE
Beacon End
Lexden
Lexden Earthworks
STANWAY
TOLLGATE ROUNDABOUT
THE TOLLGATE CENTRE
WESTSIDE CENTRE
Superstore
HALSTEAD ROAD
LONDON ROAD
A12
A1124
B1508
B1408
158
172
16

165
159
166
173
H
J
K
L
M
N
G
1
2
3
4
5
6
7
8
9
GREAT HORKESLEY
Woodhouse Farm
Poultry Houses
Kiln House
Woodside
Terrace Hall
America Hall
The Mullions
Moorlands Farm
Cuckoo Farm
Ward C of E Prim. Sch.
A12
NAYLAND ROAD
A134
Black Brook
Chapman's Farm
Severalls House
Oak House
Chestnut Villa
Maplehurst Villa
Birchwood Villa
Sports Ground
Social Club
Mile End
MILE END ROAD
Playing Field
Club House
HIGH WOODS COUNTRY PARK
Armoury Bungalows
Armoury Farm
Armoury Bungalow
The Armoury
B1508
COLCHESTER GOLF COURSE
Braiswick Farm
Myland Lodge
Church Farm
Hall
COLCHESTER GENERAL HOSPITAL
OAKS HOSPITAL
CO4
Kingswood Cen.
Gainsborough Wing
Bowling Green
Club House
Braiswick
BRAISWICK
BERGHOLT ROAD
West Ho. Wood Nature Res.
Ramparts Farm
St. Botolph's Brook
Spring Grove
Works
Superstore
North Station
COLCHESTER
Subway
Baker's Bridge
Lexden Lodge Farm
Moat
Lexden Lodge
Moat Farm Cottages
LEXDEN WOOD GOLF COURSE
Club House
Westhouse Farm
Red Brick Cottages
Lexden Bridge
The Bridge Ho.
Playing Fields
River Colne
Sheepen Bridge
Junction 27
COLNE BANK AVENUE
COWDRAY AVENUE
(COLCHESTER BY-PASS RD.)
A133
Colchester Leisure World
Megabowl
Depot
Colchester & East Essex Cricket Club
Riverside
Pond
St. Helena School
Playing Field
COLCHESTER
CAMVLODVNVM (Roman Town)
Colchester Institute
COLCHESTER RETAIL PARK
Sheepen Farm
Kingswode Hoe School
Avenue of Remembrance
(COLCHESTER BY-PASS)
Maltings Farm
Nature Reserve
Lexden Springs
Spring Lane Park
LEXDEN ROAD
A1124
St. Mary's School
Royal Grammar School
ESSEX HOSPL.
Dutch Quarter
Castle Park
Castle Museum
HIGH ST.
EAST HILL
Art Gall.
Colchester Town
MAGDALEN ST.
SOUTHWAY
St. John's Abbey Gate
Le Cateau Barracks
CO2
B1025
MERSEA RD.
B1026
B1022
Playing Field
LEXDEN PARK
St. Benedicts Catholic College
Colchester High Sch. for Girls
The Philip Morant Sch. & Sixth Form College
Cavalry Barracks
Colchester Garrison Athletics Stadium
Miniature Rifle Range
Sports Ground
Meeanee Barracks
Hyderabad Barracks
MALDON ROAD
BUTT ROAD

Junction 29
A12
160
165
174
A B C D E F G
1 2 3 4 5 6 7 8 9
Severalls Hall
Bridge House
Connaught House
White House Farm
Gatehouse Farm
Chestnuts
Playing Field
Sports Club
Whitehouse
Playing Field
Club House
The Vineyard
Sandpit Lodge
Depot
Colchester Business Park
Seedbed Centre
Plains Farm
A120
Harvey's Farm
Wyldberry Farm
Ashfield
Brunel Ct. Ind. Est.
Severalls Ind. Est.
Works
Factory
Depot
Playing Field
The Gilberd School
Brinkley Grove
Factory
Bullock Wood
Fen Farm
Wyldberry Farm
A137
Tendring
Colchester
High View
Fox Street
Heathcote Farm
Highwoods
Superstore
Comm. Cen.
School
Parson's Heath
Buildings Farm
St. Johns Farm Cottage
Shaw's Farm
St. Helena Hospice
HIGH WOODS COUNTRY PARK
Magdalen Wood
Colchester
IPSWICH ROAD
A1232
HEATH COLCHESTER
CO4
Friar's Grove
Play Field
Schs.
Welshwood Park
Parsons Heath C. of E. Prim. Sch.
Crockleford Mill
The Cowdray Centre
Works
Colne Vw Retail Pk.
Depot
Mason Works
St. Anne's Prim. Sch.
Welsh Wood
Roach Vale Prim. Sch.
Sports Grd.
COWDRAY (COLCHESTER BY-PASS ROAD) AVENUE
A133
Colchester Leisure World
Megabowl
Depot
COLCHESTER
CAMVLODVNVM (Roman Town)
By-Pass Nurseries
Recreation Ground
HARWICH ROAD
A137
Hazlemere Jun. & Inf. Schs.
Sir Charles Lucas Arts College
Crockleford Bridge
Colchester & East Essex Ckt. Club
Castle Park
Nursery
Ash Plantation
Tennis Courts
Playing Field
Castle Park
Castle Museum
St. James C of E Prim. Sch.
Pump. Sta.
East Bridge
Superstore
Greenstead
Mus.
HIGH ST. EAST HILL EAST
A1232
ST. ANDREW'S AVENUE
A133
The Minories Art Gall.
Colonial
Roller world
Works
St. Andrew's Jun. & Inf. Schs.
Avon Way House
Colchester Town
Saw Hill
CO1
Tennis Courts
Bowling Green
Hythe
Superstore
Greenstead Roundabout
MAGDALEN ST. BARRACK ST.
A134
HYTHE HILL
Works
Salary
Home
St. John's Abbey Gate
Officers Club
Tennis Courts
Gasholder
CO2
Works
Clingoe Hill Wood
Home Farm House
(COLCHESTER BY-PASS RD.)
A133
ST. ANDREW'S
Pav.
Cricket Ground
Meeanee Barracks
Hyderabad Barracks
Recreation Ground
Warehouses
Gasholder
The Hythe
CAUSEWAY
A134
COLNE
Superstore
Salary Bri.
Salarybrook Farm
West Lodge
WIVENHOE PARK
Ponds
Football Grd.
TA
Range
MERSEA RD
B1025

ARDLEIGH
ARDLEIGH STATION
Reservoir (covered)
Guide Post Farm
Chilver's Cottage
Lodge Farm
White Walls
Recreation Ground
Garden Centre
New Hall
The Manor House
Bovill's Hall
Elm Park
Trapstreet
Hillhouse Farm
Water Works
Res. (covered)
Ardleigh Sailing Club
De Bois Hall
Redbury Farm
Bowling Green
George Hall
Springhead Corner
Martells Pit
Sand & Gravel Pit
Morrow Lane Farm
Old Shields Farm
Vinces Farm
Nichols Corner
Chancery Farm
Burnt Heath
Park Farm
Spinney House Farm
Bromley Cross
John De Bois Hill
Copeland
Spring Valley Mill
John De Bois Bridge
Spring Vale
Hull Farm
Moze Hall
Subway
Slough Farm
Park Farm Cottages
Ardleigh Park
Holly Lodge
The Hollies
Crockleford Hall
Wall's Wood
Woodland
Nursery
Green Island
Park Corner
Colliersword Farm
Morants
Crockleford Heath
CO7
The Broomhangings
Hammonds Farm
Cherry Tree Farm
Nursery
Broom Grove
Strawberry Grove
Broomhangings Farm
Chapel Grove
Glebelands Stud
Whitehouse Farm
A120
Elmstead
Elmstead Hall
Churn Wood
Peacock Farm
Allen's Farm
Mount Pleasant
Parsonage Farm
Thousand Acres
Whitmore Terrace
Pyecat's Corner
Turnip Lodge
Ball's Farm
Money Wood
Colleer's Farm
The Strip
Wivenhoe New Park
Elmstead Prim. Sch.
Vicarage
Cricket Grd.
Fruit Farm
ELMSTEAD MARKET
Blossomwood Farm
Brick & Tile Cottages
Brook Cottages
Tye House
Tye Farm
Park Farm
Fen Farm
White Barn
WIVENHOE PARK CORNER
A137
B1029
A133
B1027
HARWICH ROAD
COLCHESTER ROAD
FRATING ROAD
STATION ROAD
BROMLEY ROAD
COLCHESTER ROAD
CLACTON ROAD
BROMLEY ROAD
161
168
175
H J K L M N
G H J K L M N
1 2 3 4 5 6 7 8 9
04 05 06
25 26 27 28 29

LITTLE BROMLEY RD
Badley Hall
Lower Barn
BARN LANE
Spinks's Farm
ROAD
GRANGE ROAD
LITTLE BROMLEY ROAD
ARDLEIGH ROAD
ARDLEIGH
Little Bromley
MORROW LANE
Morrow Lane Farm
Norman's Farm
Jenning's Farm
Cattsgreen Farm
Waterhouse Farm
Old Shields Farm
Waterhouse Cottages
Vinces Farm
Nichols Corner
WATERHOUSE LANE
BACK LANE
FRATING ROAD
Burnt Heath
MILL LANE
Chancery Farm
BRIAR ROAD
Little Bromley Hall
The Old Rectory
CHURCH
Lilleys Farm
LILLEYS LANE
Walnut Tree
Townlands
Hazels
Spinney House Farm
ARDLEIGH ROAD
Bromley Cross
CARRINGTONS ROAD
BARLON ROAD
SPRATTS LANE
Manning Grove
The Hollies
Holly Lodge
COLCHESTER ROAD
Pond Farm
Carringtons Farm
LITTLE BROMLEY ROAD
Morants
Newhouse
Blue Gate Farm
Bromley
MOREBARN ROAD
HALL ROAD
B1029
Sparling's Hall
Badley Hall
Bush Farm
Brook
Fish Pond
Seven Rivers Cheshire Home
Red House
BADLEY
Colchester
CO7
Great Bromley
St. George's C. of E. Prim. Sch.
A120
Elmstead
HALL RD
BROOK
Brook Farm
SPRINGHILL CL.
Elmstead Hall
MARY
STONE
Sewage Works
ST. PARSONS
Manor Farm
Boudge Hill Wood
Football Field
Cowey Green
Parsonage Farm
Kennel Bungalow
Michaelmas House
Park Cottages
Hamilton Lodge
Copley Dene
CAMP ROAD
NORTH LANE
Wright Far
Money Wood
Cricket Ground
Hall
BACK LANE WEST
HILL
Lodge Farm
Cold Hall
Vicar
Pav.
Cricket Grd.
Reservior
Strutt's Farm
Dairy Farm
FAIRFIELD
MARY LANE STH.
CHASE ROAD WEST
Rec. Grd.
ASH GRD.
BACK LANE EAST
MEADOW CL.
Fruit Farm
Mill Wood
Broughton
FRATING
Greshams Farm
HALL CHASE
The Hollies
Portlands Farm
Nurseries
Pig
ELMSTEAD MARKET
ORCHARD CL.
JOHNSON DR.
OLD SCH. LA.
HATCHCROFT
HATCHARD CL.
CHURCH ROAD
Hall
CHAPEL LA.
THE CHASE
HARWICH ROAD
COLD
Caravan Park
Mill Farm
BROMLEY
CLACTON ROAD
A133
Market Field Sch.
Oak House Farm
Grove House
BRUNDELLS ROAD
White Barn
Bottles
FINCH
Balls Green
CHAPEL

162
167
176

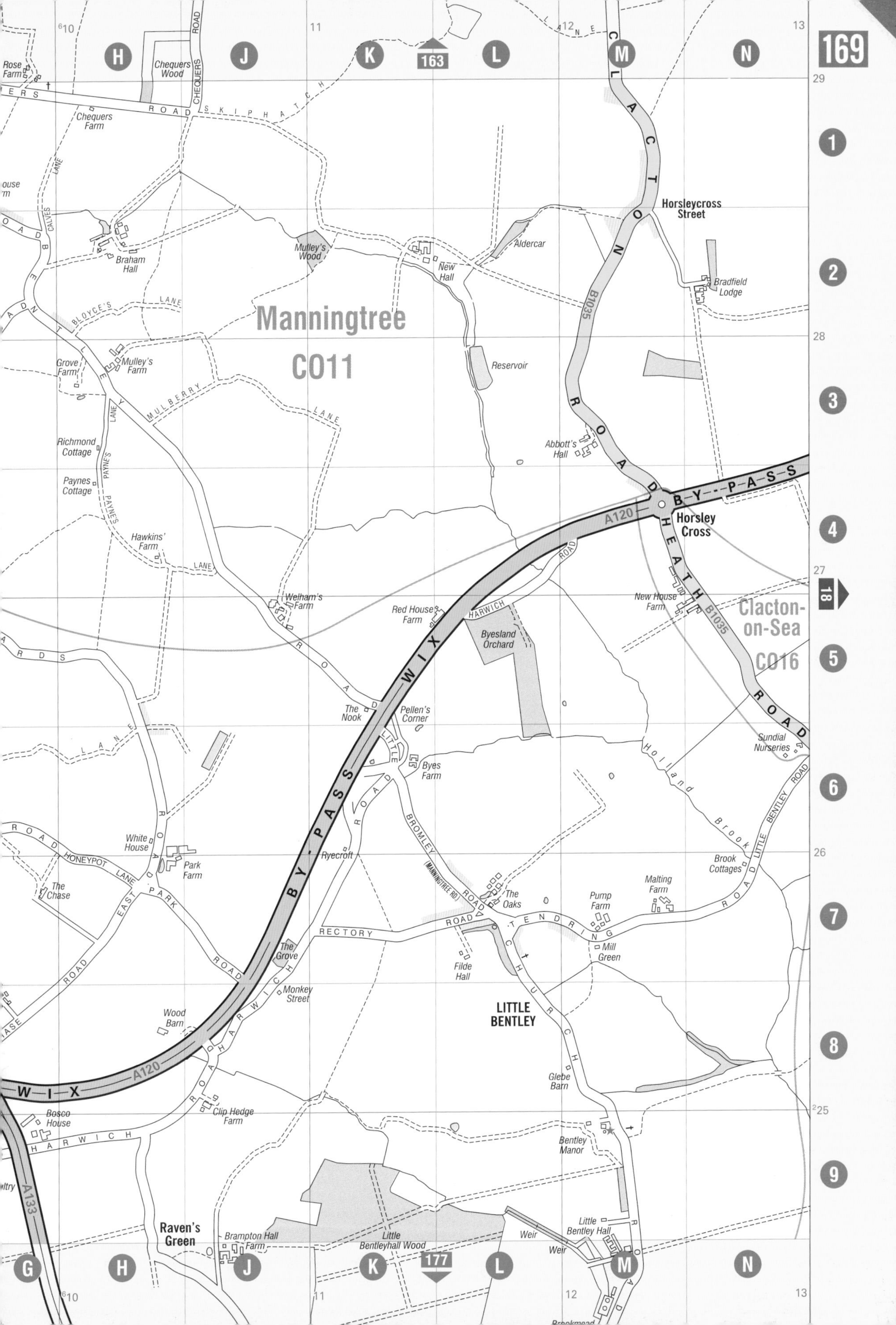
163
Manningtree
CO11
Clacton-on-Sea
CO16
Chequers Wood
Chequers Farm
Rose Farm
Braham Hall
Mulley's Wood
New Hall
Aldercar
Horsleycross Street
Bradfield Lodge
Grove Farm
Mulley's Farm
Reservoir
Richmond Cottage
Paynes Cottage
Abbott's Hall
Hawkins' Farm
Horsley Cross
Welham's Farm
Red House Farm
Byesland Orchard
New House Farm
The Nook
Pellen's Corner
Byes Farm
Sundial Nurseries
White House
Park Farm
Ryecroft
The Chase
The Oaks
Brook Cottages
Malting Farm
Pump Farm
Mill Green
The Grove
Filde Hall
Monkey Street
LITTLE BENTLEY
Wood Barn
Glebe Barn
Bosco House
Clip Hedge Farm
Bentley Manor
Little Bentley Hall
Weir
Raven's Green
Brampton Hall Farm
Little Bentleyhall Wood
177
18
CHEQUERS ROAD
SKIPHATCH
LANE
CLACTON ROAD
B1035
CALVES LANE
BLOYCE'S LANE
MULBERRY LANE
PAYNE'S LANE
A120
WIX BY-PASS
HARWICH ROAD
HEATH ROAD
Holland Brook
LITTLE BENTLEY ROAD
BROMLEY ROAD
(MANNINGTREE RD)
TENDRING ROAD
RECTORY ROAD
CHURCH
HONEYPOT LANE
EAST PARK ROAD
A133
G H J K L M N
1 2 3 4 5 6 7 8 9
10 11 12 13
25 26 27 28 29

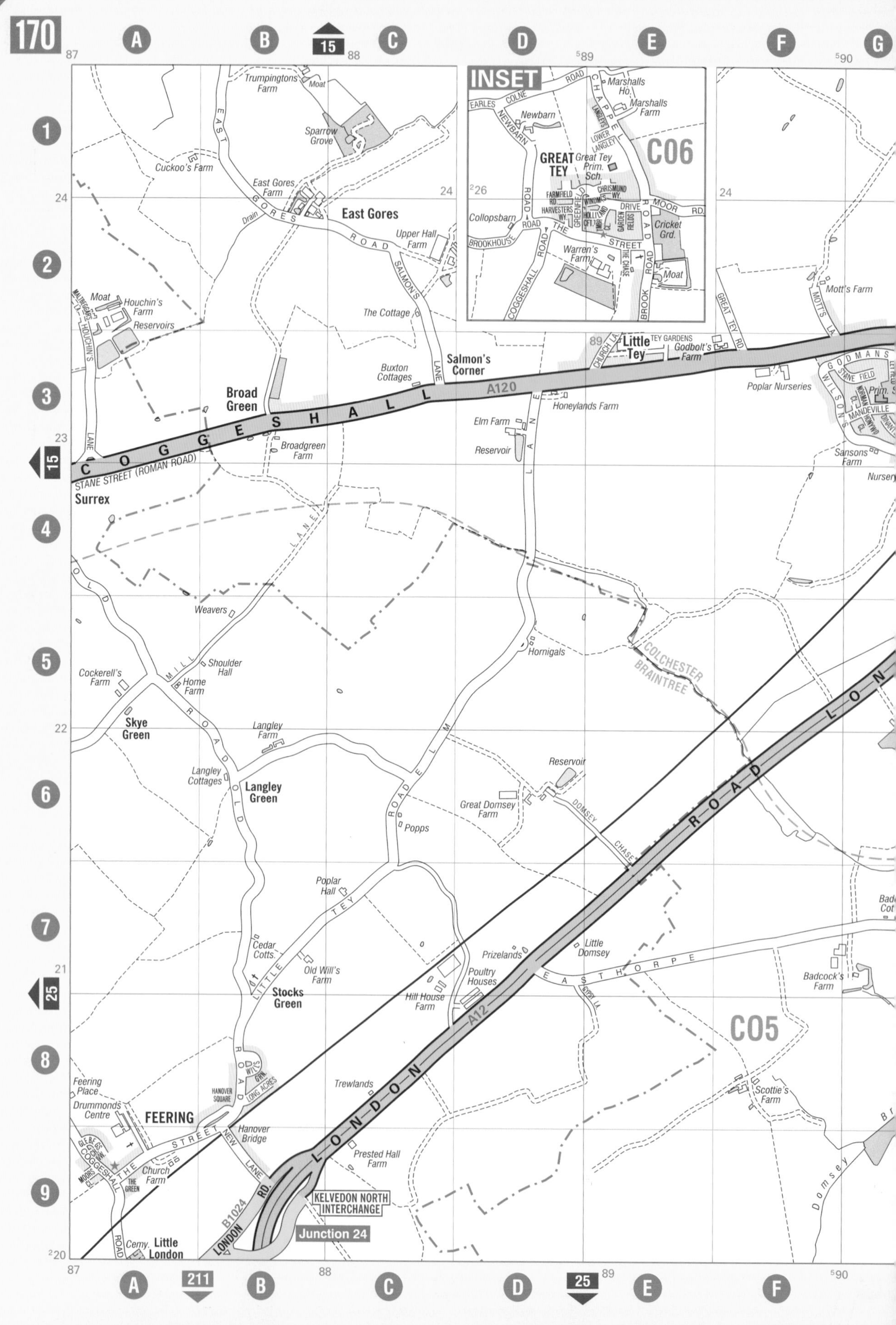
A
B
15
C
D
E
F
G
87
88
589
590
INSET
Trumpingtons Farm
Moat
Sparrow Grove
Cuckoo's Farm
East Gores Farm
EAST
GORES
ROAD
East Gores
Drain
Upper Hall Farm
SALMON'S
LANE
The Cottage
Salmon's Corner
Buxton Cottages
Moat
Houchin's Farm
Reservoirs
MALTINGS CT.
HOUCHIN'S
LANE
Broad Green
COGGESHALL ROAD
A120
STANE STREET (ROMAN ROAD)
Broadgreen Farm
Surrex
OLD
MILL
ROAD
LITTLE
LANE
Weavers
Shoulder Hall
Home Farm
Cockerell's Farm
Skye Green
Langley Farm
Langley Cottages
Langley Green
ELM
LANE
Popps
Poplar Hall
TEY
Cedar Cotts.
Old Will's Farm
Stocks Green
Hornigals
COLCHESTER
BRAINTREE
Reservoir
Great Domsey Farm
DOMSEY
CHASE
Elm Farm
Reservoir
Honeylands Farm
Little Tey
TEY GARDENS
CHURCH LA.
Godbolt's Farm
GREAT TEY RD
Mott's Farm
MOTT'S LA.
Poplar Nurseries
GODMANS
STANE FIELD
WILSONS
MANDEVILLE
Prim. S
Sansons Farm
Nursery
LONDON ROAD
A12
Prizelands
Little Domsey
Poultry Houses
Hill House Farm
EASTHORPE
GYPSY LA.
Badcock's Farm
CO5
Scottie's Farm
Trewlands
Prested Hall Farm
Domsey Brook
Feering Place
Drummonds Centre
FEERING
HANOVER SQUARE
LONG ACRES
WILLS GRN.
Hanover Bridge
NEW LANE
THE STREET
Church Farm
THE GREEN
GLEBE GDNS.
COGGESHALL
MOORE CL.
ROAD
Cemy.
Little London
B1024
LONDON RD.
KELVEDON NORTH INTERCHANGE
Junction 24
EARLES COLNE ROAD
CHAPPEL
Marshalls Ho.
Marshalls Farm
Newbarn
NEWBARN ROAD
LANGLEYS
LOWER LANGLEY
GREAT TEY
Great Tey Prim. Sch.
CO6
FARMFIELD RD.
GREENFIELD
CHRISMUND WY.
WINDMILL
HARVESTERS WY.
HOLLY CFT.
GARDEN FIELDS
DRIVE
MOOR RD.
Collopsbarn
BROOKHOUSE ROAD
THE STREET
Cricket Grd.
Warren's Farm
THE CHASE
COGGESHALL ROAD
BROOK ROAD
Moat
226
24
23
22
21
220
1
2
3
4
5
6
7
8
9
25
211

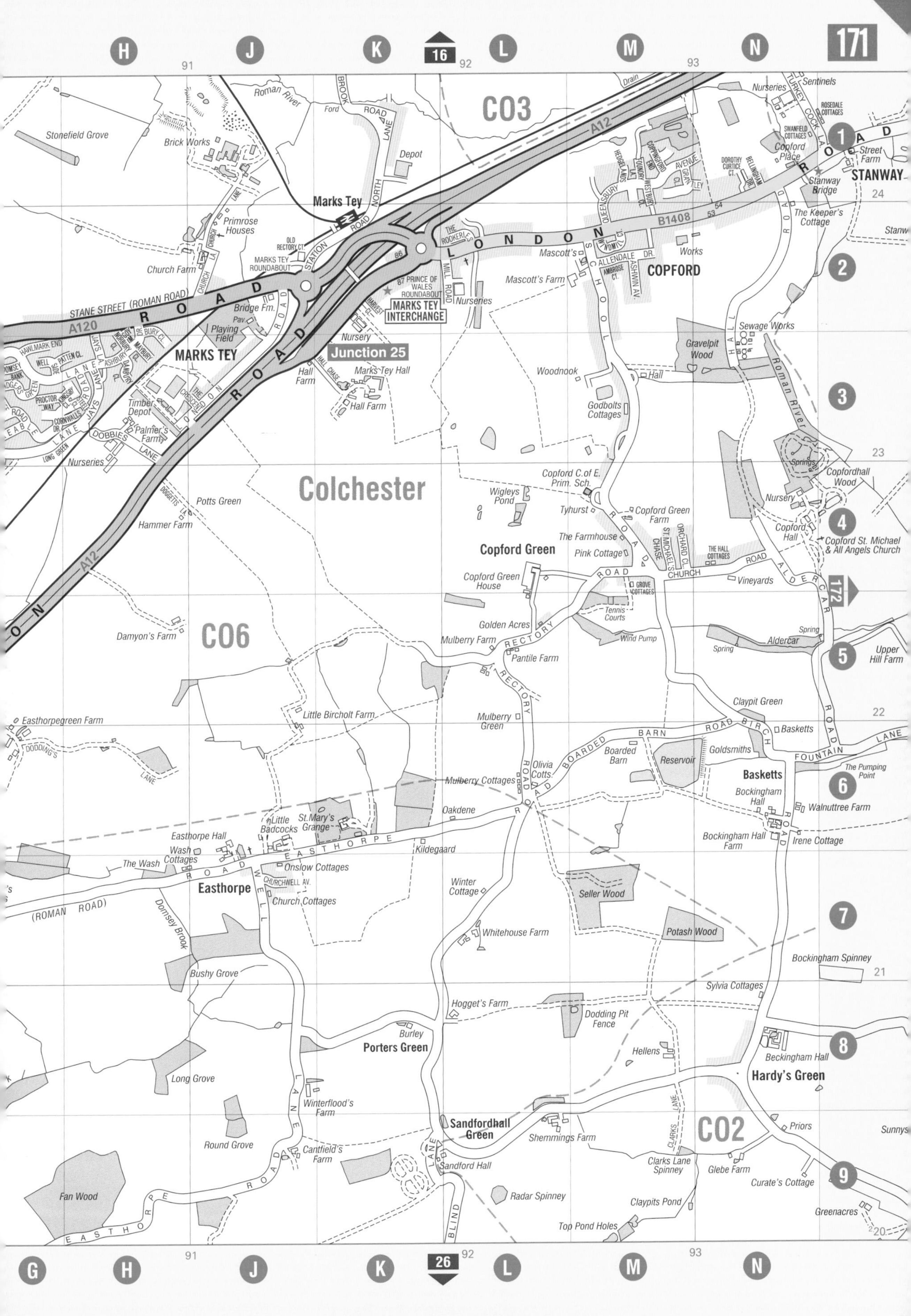

H
J
K
16
L
M
N
CO3
Stonefield Grove
Brick Works
Roman River
Depot
Marks Tey
Primrose Houses
Church Farm
STANE STREET (ROMAN ROAD)
A120
A12
B1408
LONDON ROAD
MARKS TEY ROUNDABOUT
PRINCE OF WALES ROUNDABOUT
MARKS TEY INTERCHANGE
Junction 25
MARKS TEY
Bridge Fm.
Playing Field
Nursery
Marks Tey Hall
Hall Farm
Timber Depot
Palmer's Farm
Nurseries
Mascott's
Mascott's Farm
Works
COPFORD
Sentinels
Nurseries
Copford Place
Stanway Bridge
STANWAY
Street Farm
The Keeper's Cottage
Sewage Works
Gravelpit Wood
Woodnook
Godbolts Cottages
Colchester
Potts Green
Hammer Farm
Copford C.of E. Prim. Sch.
Wigleys Pond
Tyhurst
Copford Green Farm
The Farmhouse
Pink Cottage
Copford Green
Copford Green House
Copfordhall Wood
Nursery
Copford Hall
Copford St. Michael & All Angels Church
Vineyards
172
Golden Acres
Mulberry Farm
Pantile Farm
Tennis Courts
Wind Pump
Aldercar
Upper Hill Farm
Damyon's Farm
CO6
Easthorpegreen Farm
Little Bircholt Farm
Mulberry Green
Claypit Green
Basketts
Boarded Barn
Reservoir
Goldsmiths
Basketts
The Pumping Point
Olivia Cotts.
Mulberry Cottages
Bockingham Hall
Walnuttree Farm
Oakdene
Easthorpe Hall
Little Badcocks
St.Mary's Grange
Bockingham Hall Farm
Irene Cottage
Wash Cottages
The Wash
Kildegaard
Onslow Cottages
Easthorpe
Church Cottages
(ROMAN ROAD)
Winter Cottage
Seller Wood
Potash Wood
Domsey Brook
Whitehouse Farm
Bockingham Spinney
Bushy Grove
Sylvia Cottages
Hogget's Farm
Dodding Pit Fence
Burley
Porters Green
Hellens
Beckingham Hall
Hardy's Green
Long Grove
Winterflood's Farm
Sandfordhall Green
Shemmings Farm
CO2
Priors
Round Grove
Cantfield's Farm
Sandford Hall
Clarks Lane Spinney
Glebe Farm
Curate's Cottage
Fan Wood
Radar Spinney
Claypits Pond
Greenacres
Top Pond Holes
G
H
J
26
K
L
M
N

A
B
C
D
E
F
G
1
2
3
4
5
6
7
8
9
94
95
96
24
23
22
21
20
Moat
Wyvern Farm
STANE STREET
TOLLGATE ROUNDABOUT
(ROMAN RD.)
ROAD
164
Evergreen House
Superstore
TOLLGATE
WEST
Beacon End
Lib. Hall
Prim. Sch.
Play. Fld.
Playing Field
Grymes Dyke
Lexden Earthworks
Playing Field
Lexden King George Field
St. Teresa's R.C. Prim. Sch.
HEATH
Nurseries
Sentinels
ROSEMARY ALMSHOUSES
ROSEDALE COTTAGES
WESTSIDE CENTRE
THE TOLLGATE CENTRE
The Heath Sch.
Play. Fld.
Copford Place
B1408
LONDON
Street Farm
School
STANWAY
Stanway Bridge
Tudor Barn
Rooks End
CHURCH
The Stanway Sch.
New Farm Lodge
Playing Field
Fiveways Prim. Sch.
Playing Field
PEARTREE BUSINESS CENTRE
FIVEWAYS RETAIL PARK
Depot
OAKLANDS
AVENUE
DUGARD
The Keeper's Cottage
Robin Hill
Airlie
Stanway Rectory
Oldhouse Farm
Stirling Lodge
LANE
Digomy Corner
PEARTREE ROAD
Works
Works
Depot
FIVE WAYS
Sewage Works
Tye Grove
HALL
Roman River
The Bungalow
Stanway Green
Dyke
Wiseman's Farm
Bell House Farm
DYER'S
Springs
Copfordhall Wood
Nursery
Furze Hill
CO3
Ware Depot
Brickwall Farm
Copford Hall
Copford St. Michael & All Angels Church
ROAD
Vineyards
171
Hanging Wood
Well House
ROAD
B1022
Iron Age & Roman Settlement
Spring
Aldercar
ALDERCAR ROAD
Upper Hill Farm
CO6
Warren Plantation
Priory Lodge
Springfield
MALDON
WARREN
Lexden Earthworks
Claypit Green
Baskets
GOL GROVE
The Bungalow
Stanway Hall Farm
COLCHESTER ZOO
Butcher's Wood
Oliver's Thicks
FOUNTAIN
Fountain Cottage
Basketts
The Pumping Point
Reservoir
Bockingham Hall
Walnuttree Farm
Heckfordbridge
ROAD
Bridge Covert
Ram Plantation
Irene Cottage
Lukes Farm
Eldred Cottages
Aldercar
Baymill
Cansdale's Garden
Olivers Spinney
Heckford House
Te Whare
Parc Gwyn
North Lodge
Keeper's Cottage
The Sandpit
Birch Wood
Bockingham Spinney
B1022
Sylvia Cotts.
Whitehorse Plantation
INSET
Hill Farm
LEAS
LANE
CHEST WOOD
Theodor
Cricket Ground
Sewage Works
Recreation Ground
Cook's Wood
Beckingham Hall
Hardy's Green
Football Ground
BIRCH GREEN
Mill Lodge
Mill Ho.
King Edward Cotts.
Priors
Sunnyside
SCHOOL
HILL
CO2
The Nest
Woodhouse Farm
LAYER-DE-LA-HAY
Stamps Farm
Curate's
Heath Farm
Great Billet Wood
The Old Rectory
Greenacres
Birch
Stamps & Crows
Farthing Garden
The Hangings
Brickwall Farm
The Bailey Meadow
LOWER ROAD
Bushes House
GARLANDS RD.
BIRCH
ROAD

26

173
Lexden
Lexden Park
St. Benedicts Catholic College
The Philip Morant Sch. & Sixth Form College
Colchester High Sch. for Girls
Le Cateau Barracks
St. John's Abbey Gate
Cavalry Barracks
Colchester Garrison Athletics Stadium
Miniature Rifle Range
Abbey Field
Goojerat Barracks
Colchester United FC (Layer Rd.)
West End Sports Ground
Shrub End Sports Ground
Shrub End
Alderman Blaxill Sch.
Gosbecks Prim. Sch.
Prettygate Jun. & Inf. Sch.
Recreation Ground
Kirkee & McMunn Barracks
Colchester Cemetery
Colchester Crematorium
Thomas, Lord Audley School
Monkwick Jun. & Inf. Schs.
Monkwick Sports Centre
Roman Way Camp
Roman Barracks
Berechurch
Montgomery Jun. & Inf. Schs.
Colchester
Cheshunt Field
Gosbeck's Farm
Maypole Green
Maypole Farm
CO2
Berechurch Hall
Berechurch Hall Camp
Blackheath
Lethe Grove
Birch Grove Golf Course
Birch Grove Farm
Kingsland Farm
Walnut Cottage
Sodoms
Olivers Orchard
Walk Wood
Olivers Copse
Roman River
Needles Eye Wood
Miniature Rifle Range
Charity Wood
Berechurch Poultry Farm
Kingsford Farm
King's Ford Grove
Fridaywood Farm
Friday Wood
Bounstead Grove
Layer Mill Mushroom Farm
Mill House
Mill Grove
Bounstead Bridge
Bounstead Hill Poultry Farm
Chestnut Farm
Little Billets
The Folley House
Malting Green
Lower End
Electricity Sub. Station
Park Farm
Charlotte's Grove
Rock Farm House
Layer Brook
LAYER ROAD
MALDON ROAD
BUTT ROAD
DRURY ROAD
BERECHURCH HALL ROAD
ROMAN WAY
CHERRY TREE LANE
ABBERTON ROAD
BOUNSTEAD ROAD
G H J K L M N
1 2 3 4 5 6 7 8 9
165
174
26

MAGDALEN ST.
BARRACK ST.
HYTHE HILL
166
HYTHE QUAY
CAUSEWAY
COLNE
A134
COLCHESTER-BY-PASS ROAD
ST. ANDREW'S
A133
Clingoe Hill Wood
Home Farm House
Salary Brook
Salary Bri.
Salarybrook Farm
Superstore
Works
Gasholder
Warehouses
Recreation Ground
Worsnop Ho.
The Hythe
Woodlands
Scarletts Distillery Pond
CO1
CO4
WIVENHOE PARK
West Lodge
Ponds
UNIVERSITY OF ESSEX
Univ. of Essex Sports Cen.
Tennis Courts
BOUNDARY ROAD
St. George's Infant School
Bourne Pond
Bourne Mill
Cricket Ground
Meeanee Barracks
Hyderabad Barracks
Colchester Cemetery
War Memorial
Colchester Crematorium
Thomas, Lord Audley School
Monkwick Jun. & Inf. Schs.
Monkwick Spts. Cen.
Playing Field
Depot
Warehouse
Timber Yard
Whitehall Ind. Est.
Grange Farm
Indikart Racing Club
Grange Way Business Park
Sewage Works
Sludge Lagoon
RIVER COLNE
HYTHE MARSHES
Old Heath
Old Heath Prim. Sch.
MIDDLEWICK RANGES
Middlewick
CO2
Cleavelands
Cleavelands Farm
The Bungalow
Donyland Farm
Donyland Lodge
Birch Brook
Birch Grove
Battleswick Farm
Success
Birchbrook Cottage
ROWHEDGE
Birchwood House
Depot
Donyland House
St Lawrence Prim. Sch.
Rec. Grd.
Colchester
Berechurch
Blackheath
BLACKHEATH
MERSEA (ROMAN HILL) ROAD
B1025
Sports Ground
Lethe Grove
Roman Hill Farm
Roman Hill House
Ball Grove
DONYLAND HEATH
Semaphore Cottage
The Lodge
Lawn Cottage
Moat
East Donyland Hall
Fish Ponds
DONYLAND WOODS
CO5
ROMAN RIVER
Fingringhoe Bridge
Mill
The Vicarage
Fingringhoe C.of E. Prim. Sch.
Fingringhoe
Tennis Courts
Fingringhoe Hall
West House Farm
Pig's Foot Green
The Forge
UPPER HAYE LANE
FURNEAUX LANE
FINGRINGHOE ROAD
INSET
Oxley House
Oxley Hill Farm
Manwood Farm
The Maltings
ABBERTON
Rectory
The Gate Farm
Grange Farm
The Grange
View Park
Tudhoe Farm
Cricket Grd.
Fairlands House
Green Acres
Uppershotts
Langenhoe
Glebe House
Captains Field
Langenhoe Prim. Sch.
MERSEA RD.
COLCHESTER RD.
PELDON RD.
CO5
173
26
27
A
B
C
D
E
F
G
1
2
3
4
5
6
7
8
9

CLACTON AVENUE
A133
COLCHESTER ROAD
CLACTON ROAD
167
Blossomwood Farm
Brick & Tile Cottages
Park Farm
Tye House
Brook Cottages
Tye Farm
ELMSTEAD MARKET
Market Field Sch.
Fen Farm
Beth Chatto Gardens
White Barn Farm
BROMLEY ROAD
Wivenhoe Park Corner
COLCHESTER B1027
BRIGHTLINGSEA ROAD
Wivenhoe House
Ten. Cts.
Playing Fields
Pavilions
COLCHESTER TENDRING
ELMSTEAD ROAD
Club Ho.
Football Grd.
B1027
Broad Lanes
Sixpenny Brook
Grove Farm
Reservoir
Reservoirs
Palegate Wood
Park Farm
Park Farm South
Park Wood
Keelars Tye
Keelars Farm
Birds Farm
Englishes Farm
Elmstead Heath
SCHOOL ROAD
B1028
Broomgrove Junior & Infant Schools
Cross Farm
C07
WIVENHOE
Wivenhoe Cross
Cricket Grd.
Pav.
The Old Rectory
Piggeries
Works
The Grove
Gravel Pit Grove
Cemy.
Prospect House
KEELARS LANE
176
Reservoir
THE AVENUE
B1028
HIGH STREET
WIVENHOE WOOD
King George's Field
Rec. Grd.
Wivenhoe
STATION ROAD
Black Horse Corner
Sunnymead Farm
ALRESFORD ROAD
Millfields Primary School
Heath Farm
COCKAYNES LANE
ALRESFORD
Cockaynes Wood
Cockaynes
Ballast Quay Farm
Ballast Quay House
Sewage Works
Alresford
Wivenhoe Sailing Club
Slipways
Hard
Warehouses
WIVENHOE ROAD
MARSH FARM LA.
Sixpenny Brook
Marsh Farm
Lodge
Church Farm
Alresford Prim. Sch.
Hall
RIVER
The Mount
Ballast Quay Farm
FERRY RD.
Fingringhoe Common
Alresford Grange
BALLAST QUAY ROAD
Wks.
Picketts
High Park Corner
BROOK HALL ROAD
Lower Brickhouse Farm
Holmwood Farm
COLNE
Oldhall Wood
Alresford Lodge
FORD LANE
Elmstead Row
04
605
06
20
21
22
23
24
G H J K L M N
1 2 3 4 5 6 7 8 9
27

176
ELMSTEAD MARKET
168
175
182
Alresford
ALRESFORD
Elmstead Heath
Colchester
CO7
Frating
Frating Green
Balls Green
Hare Green
THORRINGTON
CLACTON ROAD
A133
FRATING HILL
MAIN ROAD
BROMLEY ROAD
FRATING ROAD
FRATING RD.
B1029
GREAT BENTLEY ROAD
ST. OSYTH ROAD
TENPENNY HILL
B1027
BRIGHTLINGSEA RD.
STATION ROAD
STATION RD.
SCHOOL LANE
CHURCH ROAD
RECTORY ROAD
WIVENHOE ROAD
FORD LANE
CHURCH RD.
COCKAYNES ROAD
FINCH LANE
THE CHASE
HARWICH ROAD
Beth Chatto Gardens
White Barn Farm
Bottles Hall
Rolts Nursery
Blue Barn
Reservoirs
Elmstead Brook
Park Farm
Park Farm South
Park Wood
Grove Farm
Reservoir
Fratinghall Wood
Captains Wood
Frating Brook
Tenpenny Brook
Hill Farm
Frating Lodge
Frating Hall
Blue Gates
Hockley Farm
Hockley Place
Hockley Wood
Tenpenny Farm
Elmstead Row
Brook Farm
Reeves Grove
Tenpenny Bridge
Tenpenny Hill
Sewage Works
Stable Wood
Thorrington Plantation
Tenpenny Heath
Scout Camp
Scout Hut
Hall Farm
Alresford Hall
Oldhall Wood
The Quarters
Hart Wood
Crestland Wood
Recreation Ground
Alresford Prim. Sch.
Church Farm
Oak House Farm
Grove House
Morehams Hall
Spring Farm
Kennels
Gordon House
Holly Farm
FRATING PARK CARAVAN SITE
Mannings
The Cedars Farm
Ivy Lodge
Slough House Farm
Burr's Farm
Lufkins Farm
Goldacre Farm
Poplars Chase Farm
The Talbots
Whitehouse Farm
Nurseries
Thorington Cross
Works
Village Hall
Glebe Farm
Rosslyn
Thors Park
Mill Wood
Broomfield Plantation
Plumpton's Farm
Landing Stage
Caravan Park
Mill Farm
The Hollies
Portlands Farm
Greshams Farm
Market Field Sch.
White Barn
Cockaynes
24
23
22
21
20
07
08
09

Raven's Green
Brampton Hall Farm
Little Bentleyhall Wood
169
Weir
Little Bentley Hall
Brookmead Cottages
Paynes Farm
Ravens Green
Crabtree Cottages
Ellington
Crabtree Farm
Lone Barn
ROWHERNS LANE
Rowherns
Warren's Farm
Spring Cottage
Gurnhams
CHURCH ROAD
Clacton-on-Sea
CO16
Shair Wood
A133
ROAD
High Barn
Fisher's Farm
The Woodlands
178
SHAIR LANE
Reservoirs
Brook
The Grange
Admiral's Farm
Alder Car
Heckford House
Green Corner
Sturrick Farm
GREAT BENTLEY
MOORS CLOSE
Moorlands
Bentley Green
Eden Farm
Risby's Farm
Green Lane Farm
Brook Farm
WEELEY ROAD
SWALLOWS ROW
Hill House Farm
The Hall
Playing Field
Prim. Sch.
Great Bentley
Works
Tye Farm
Weeley
THORRINGTON ROAD
St.Mary's Farm
LOVER'S LANE
THE TYE ROAD
Jubilee Cottage
Frating Abbey
Bentley Brook
Tye Homestead
Moynes Grove
Coppice Farm
Lodge Plantation
Reservoir
WEELEY RD.
AINGERS GREEN ROAD
Aingers Green
Moynes Farm
Abbey Wood
ABBEY FARM ROAD
High Barns
Thicket Grove
WOOD GREEN ESTATE
Carpenter's Farm
College Farm
183
Pound Farm
Thorrington Hall
Brook
COLES BROOK RD
WICK ROAD
Stockets Grove
St.Osyth

A
B
C
D
E
F
G
13
14
15
16
18
184
177
24
23
22
21
20
1
2
3
4
5
6
7
8
9
Hall Farm House
LONG LANE
The Hall
SCHOOL RD.
The Grange
THE STREET
THORPE ROAD
HOLLY VW. CL.
Tendring
Tendring Grove
Brook
Hannam's Hall
Yewtree Farm
Brookside Cottage
B1035
Simon's Wood
Holland
Brook Lane
Hill Farm
New Hall
New Hall Farm
The Mill
Hollywood Farm
CROW LANE
The Plantation
Manor House
Barker's Hall
Hollywood
Lodge
The Rookery
Cricket Ground
Home Wood
The Spinney
White House
Pav.
HILLHOUSE LANE
Ford
Hillhouse Farm
Hillands Wood
BRADLEYHALL LANE
Brett's Hall
Pestles Hall
Shair Wood
Nursery
Chiltern Farm
Hawk Farm
Holland Brook
COLCHESTER ROAD
A133
Fisher's Farm
SHAIR LANE
The Woodlands
Elizabeth Cottage
Weeley Crematorium
Far Thorpe Green
Saxon Lodge Kennels
Nurseries
COLCHESTER ROAD
THORPE ROAD
B1033
Council Offices
Brook Farm
Clacton-on-Sea
CO16
Ash Farm
WEELEY
WOODLANDS RISE
MT. PLEASANT
HILLTOP CRES.
HILLTOP RISE
KATE DANIELS HO.
HILLTOP CR.
WEELEY BY-PASS
B1441
Green Lane Farm
SWALLOW'S ROW
Nursery
ST. ANDREW'S RD.
FIRST AV.
THORNBERRY AV.
ALEXANDRA RD.
SECOND AVENUE
Roger's Grove
Risby's Farm
WILLOW WLK.
Sewage Works
Weeley Brook
Island Grove
WEELEY BRIDGE HOLIDAY PARK
Weeley
LITTLE CLACTON ROAD
Pav.
Play. Fld.
Hall
Station Nurseries
St.Andrew's C. of E. Prim. Sch.
Hall Farm
Tye Farm
THE TYE ROAD
Weeley Brook
Reedlands
HALL LANE
Gutteridge Hall
GUTTERIDGE
Ten. Ct.
Rectory
CHURCH RD.
Pond Farm
Gutteridge Wood
Nursery
Weeleyhall Wood Nature Reserve
Colchester
CO7
Cole's Farm
FIELDS
Tye Homestead
MILL ROAD
ROXBURGHE RD.
Willow Farm
Twycross
Moynes Grove
WENLOCK RD.
MILL LANE
MILL CL.
Coppice Farm
Edgewood House
GREEN LANE
Weeley Heath
Oakhurst
Res.
BOTANY
Botany Farm
Moynes Farm
The Cottage
Norwood Lodge
Depot
Kidbys Nurseries
VICTORIA RD.
WICK ROAD
BENTLEY ROAD
Maldon Wood Cottage
HIGHBIRCH ROAD
CLACTON BY-PASS
RECTORY ROAD
WEELEY ROAD
CONNAUGHT RD.
KEMPTON PK.
College Farm
Stockets Grove
Simplebirch Wood
Airstrip
St.Osyth
HONEYPOT
LANE

H
J
K
L
M
N
18
17
19
Pond Farm
Wasses Corner
Betty Dent's Corner
Barker's Farm
Beaumonthall Wood
HARWICH ROAD
B1414
Lower Barn Farm
Quay Farm
Beaumont Cut
Hard
Beaumont Bridge
Kingshead
Landermere
Landermere Hall
TENDRING ROAD
B1035
Cyprus Cottage
Valley Farm
GOLDEN LANE
Thorpe Green
Thorpe Green House
The Spinney
Green Farm
Whitehall Farm
White Hall
B1033
Mill House
Vicarage
Comarques
Playing Field
Thorpe Lodge
WALTON ROAD
New Hall
THORPE-LE-SOKEN
HIGH STREET
LANDERMERE
Schools
ABBEY ST.
FRINTON ROAD
Elm Farm
Folly Farm
Barnard's Farm
Play. Fld.
Lodge
Grange Farm
Bradewick Nurseries
Rose Farm
Rose Hill
Thorpecross Farm
FARM LANE
DAMANT'S
Damons Farm
Thorpe Cross
Holland Brook
Cradle Bridge
Thorpe Hall
STATION ROAD
Pit (Dis.)
Weeley Lodge
Navigation Beacons
Thorpe Maltings
Thorpe-le-Soken
Hall Row
Alder Car
THORPE PARK LANE
Rice Bridge
Leys Farm
Thorpe Park
Porklane Grove
Lower Botany Farm
Woodlands
Pig Street
St.Chad's Nurseries
Brickkiln Grove
HARWICH ROAD
Poultry Houses
Playing Field
Crackstakes Farm
TAN LANE
Little Clacton Lodge
Clacton Grove Farm
FEVERILLS RD.
G
H
J
K
L
M
N
185
180
1
2
3
4
5
6
7
8
9

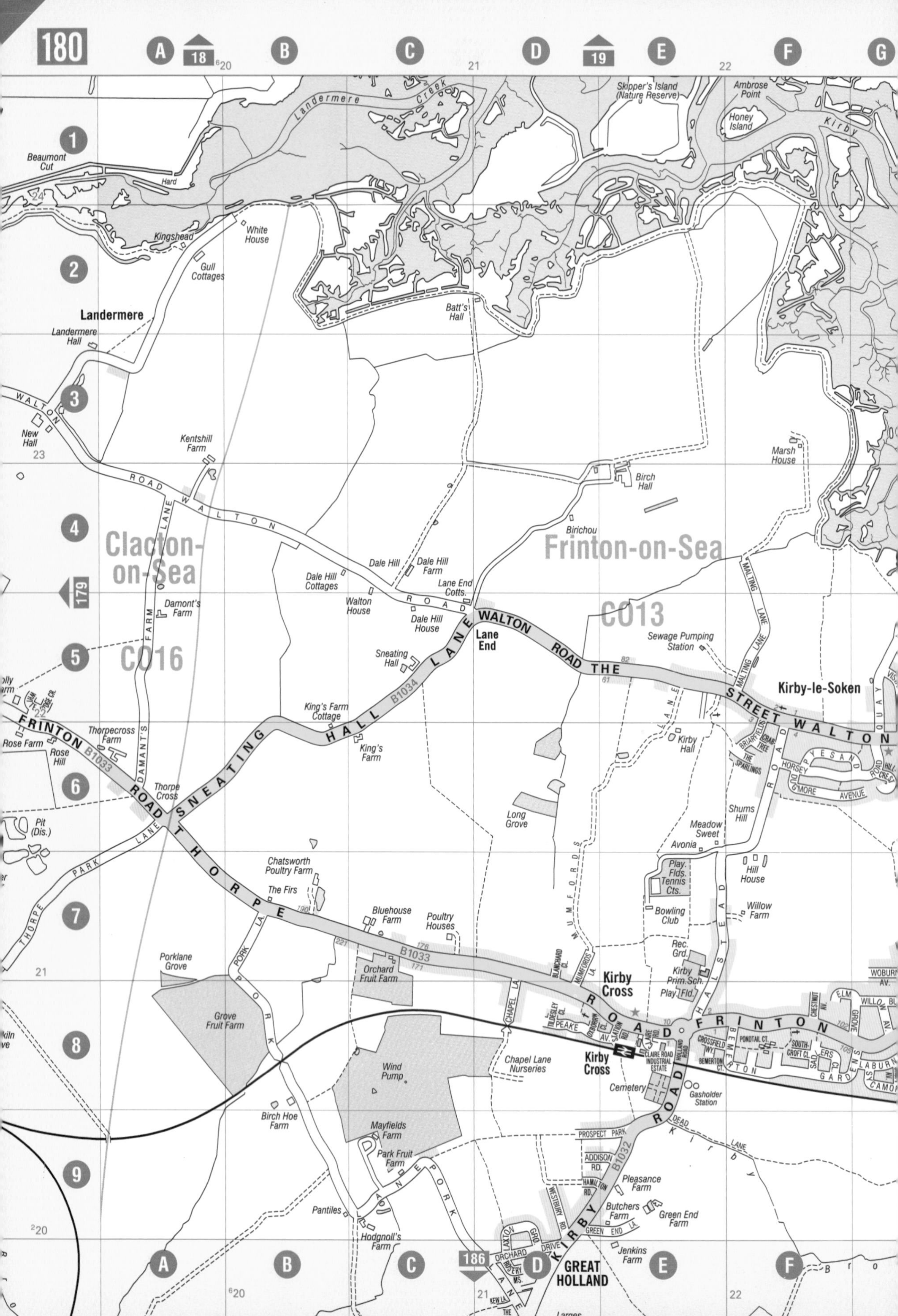

A B C D E F G
18
19
Skipper's Island (Nature Reserve)
Ambrose Point
Honey Island
Landermere Creek
Kirby
Beaumont Cut
Hard
Kingshead
White House
Gull Cottages
Landermere
Landermere Hall
Batt's Hall
WALTON ROAD
New Hall
Kentshill Farm
Marsh House
Birch Hall
Birichou
Clacton-on-Sea
Frinton-on-Sea
Dale Hill
Dale Hill Farm
Dale Hill Cottages
Lane End Cotts.
Walton House
Dale Hill House
Damont's Farm
CO16
CO13
Lane End
Sewage Pumping Station
MALTING LANE
Sneating Hall
Kirby-le-Soken
THE STREET WALTON
King's Farm Cottage
SNEATING HALL LANE
B1034
Thorpecross Farm
Rose Farm
Rose Hill
FRINTON ROAD
B1033
Kirby Hall
BRIARFIELDS
CRAB TREE
THE SPARLINGS
HORSEY
PYESAND
DUNMORE AVENUE
King's Farm
Thorpe Cross
DAMANT'S FARM LANE
Pit (Dis.)
Long Grove
Shums Hill
Meadow Sweet
Avonia
THORPE PARK LANE
THORPE ROAD
Chatsworth Poultry Farm
The Firs
MUMFORDS LANE
Play. Flds. Tennis Cts.
Hill House
Bowling Club
Willow Farm
Bluehouse Farm
Poultry Houses
Rec. Grd.
Porklane Grove
PORK LANE
Orchard Fruit Farm
BLANCHARD CL.
MUMFORDS LA.
Kirby Cross
Kirby Prim. Sch.
Play. Fld.
HALSTEAD ROAD
WOBURN AV.
Grove Fruit Farm
CHAPEL LA.
TILBURY CL.
PEAKE AV.
OXBORROW CL.
STATION RD.
CLAIRE RD.
FRINTON ROAD
CHESTNUT AV.
ELM GROVE
WILLOW AV.
CROSSFIELD WY.
PONDTAIL CT.
SOUTHCROFT CL.
BEMERTON CT.
BEMERTON GARDENS
LABURNUM AV.
CAMOMILE
Wind Pump
Chapel Lane Nurseries
Kirby Cross
CLAIRE ROAD INDUSTRIAL ESTATE
HOLLAND ROAD
Cemetery
Gasholder Station
Birch Hoe Farm
Mayfields Farm
PROSPECT PARK
DEAD LANE
Kirby Brook
Park Fruit Farm
PORK LANE
ADDISON RD.
HAMILTON RD.
B1032
Pleasance Farm
Pantiles
Hodgnoll's Farm
WESTBURY RD.
KIRBY ROAD
Butchers Farm
Green End Farm
GREEN END LA.
LAXTON GRO.
ORCHARD DRIVE
MAYBERRY MS.
Jenkins Farm
186
GREAT HOLLAND
KEW LA.
THE CRESCENT
LANE
Larges
Brook
1 2 3 4 5 6 7 8 9
179

H
J
K
19
L
M
N
INSET
The Naze Tower
Tower Breakwater
The Naze
CO14
Breakwater
Mabel Greville Breakwater
Jubilee Beach
HORSEY ISLAND
New Decoy Pond
Salt Fleet
Walton Channel
HEDGE-END ISLAND
Boathouse Creek
Landing Place
THE WADE
The Twizzle
Coles Creek
Landing Stage
Titchmarsh Marina
Horseshoe
Peter's Point
Kirby Quay
Willow Caravan Park
Iron Foundry
Sole Creek
Naze Marine Holiday Park
Walton Mere (Boating Lake)
Sewage Works
Club House
The Columbine Centre
Putting Green
Swim. Pool
Rec. Grd.
Playing Field
Prim. Sch.
Walton-on-the-Naze
CO14
MARTELLO CARAVAN PARK
Martello Tower
MARTELLO HOLIDAY PARK
Putting Green
Brick Barn Farm
Devereux Farm
B1034
ROAD KIRBY
ROAD HIGH
PRINCE'S ESPLANADE
Albion Breakwater
WALTON-ON-THE-NAZE
Marine Breakwater
Central Beach
Walton Pier
Ten Pin Bowling Centre
New Walton Pier
Winchester Breakwater
Lifeboat Landing Stage
Walton-on-the-Naze
Mott Cemy.
Southcliffe Trailer Pk.
Pavilion Breakwater
B1336
Prim. Sch.
TRIANGLE SHOP CEN.
Tennis Cts.
Playing Field
Tendring Technology College (Upper School)
Park Playing Field
Tennis Cts.
Bowl. Grns.
Pedlars Wood
Turpin's Gro
Burnt House Breakwater
B1033
ROAD WALTON
Frinton-on-Sea
CONNAUGHT
NORTH SEA
Sandy Hook Breakwater
Play. Fld.
FRINTON-ON-SEA
Wittonwood Farm
Pumping Station
G
H
J
187
K
L
M
N

Colchester
CO7
BRIGHTLINGSEA
THORRINGTON
Hurst Green
Point Clear
BRIGHTLINGSEA ROAD
CHURCH ROAD
B1029
Alresford Creek
Brightlingsea Creek
RIVER COLNE
TENDRING
COLCHESTER
Thicks Wood
Mill Wood
Hart Wood
Broomfield Plantation
Plumpton's Farm
Thorrington Tide Mill
Church Docks (disused)
Gatehouse Farm
Rook Wood
Moverons Farm
Ford Farm
Gravesend
Brightlingsea Hall
Little Clump
Big Clump
Road Clump
Little Wapping Hill
Big Wapping Hill
Upper Wedge
Lower Wedge
Long Plantation
The Link
The Belt
Samson's Corner
The Grove
Depot
Oakwood
Superstore
Morses Farm
Morses Wood
Crocky Grove
Lowermarsh Farm
Poultry House
Colthouse
Playing Field
Stranger's Corner
Queech
Sewage Works
Lodge Farm
Lodge Wood
Wick's Wood
Football Grd.
Recreation Ground
Recreation Grd.
Furze Hill
Lakeside Caravan Park
Western Prom.
Boating Lake
Swim. Pool
Breakwaters
Bateman's Tower
Westmarsh Point
Outfall
Landing Stages
St.Osyth Stone Point
Sports Centre
Martello Tower & East Essex Aviation Museum
The Orchards Holiday Village
Cindery Island
Underwood's Hard
Mill Farm
Ivy House
Glebe Farm
Tenpenny Heath
Scout Camp
Scout Hut
The Quarters
Thors Park
Rosslyn
Mill Dam
The Leat
Points
Sixpenny Brook
Tenpenny Brook

Aingers Green
South Heath
Clacton-on-Sea
CO16
ST. OSYTH
HOLLYBUSH HILL
FLAG HILL
COLCHESTER ROAD
BY-PASS
B1027
Thorringtonhall Wood
Saltwater Bridge
Dial Corner
Lady Wood
Deadlane Grove
Martin's Grove
Riddles Wood
Millton Wood
Stockets Grove
St.Osyth Wick
South Heath Farm
Kellands Farm
Frowick Hall Farm
Dines Farm
Bentley Country Park
Hill House
Colne Villa
Eastmarsh Point
Wellwick Wharf
Flag Creek
Shangri-la Caravan & Camping Park
Wellwick Farm
Lodges
Conduit House (remains of)
Nun's Wood
Kitchen Pond
Breeches Pond
Dolphin Pond
Engine Pond
Seal Pond
ST.OSYTH PARK
St. Osyth Priory (Rems. of Abbey)
Convalescent Home
Priory Farm
The Bury
Rec. Grd.
MILL STREET
Lamb Farm Cottages
Lamb Farm
St.Osyth Cemetery
Park Farm Cottages
Pump Hill Farm
Folly Farm
St. Osyth C of E Prim. Sch.
Marsh Farm
Cottage Farm
Hill Cottages
Hillside
Thorrington Creek
Marsh Farm House
Lower Farm
East End Green Farm
Lynch Creek
Fred's Hard
Cushion Island
Pound Farm
Thorrington Hall
High Barns
Thicket Grove
Carpenter's Farm
Abbey Wood
Reservoir
The Lodge
Saltwater Brook Cottages
Dialhouse
Weirs
Weir
Sandhall
177
184

178
188
183
College Farm
Stockets Grove
St.Osyth Wick
Simplebirch Wood
Bowshots Wood
Maldon Wood Cottage
Norwood Lodge
Maldon Wood
High Birch
Airstrip
Kidbys Nurseries
Row Heath
Rowheath Farm
Ideal Nurseries
Reservoirs
Millton Wood
Violet Grove
Woodland Farm
Ampers Wick Farm
Bush Wood
Jaggards
Welches
Crosslands Farm
St. Osyth Heath
Borgue House
Little Ampers Wick
Hartleywood Farm
Poultry Houses
Heath Farm
The Leys
Lower Heath Farm
Newhouse Farm
Weir
Riddles Wood
The Stackyd
Sandhayes
Kiln Cottage
High Grove
Hartley Grove
Greenview
Meadowview Holiday Park
Gidea Hall
Bovill's Hall
Moat
Hartley Wood
Long Grove
Elcombe Farm
CO16
Bocking Elm
Park Farm Cottages
Park Farm
Earls Hall Farm
Hodges
St.Osyth Cemetery
Lower Farm
ST. OSYTH
Bush Paddock
Nursery
Dutchess Farm
Coppin's Hall Wood
Depot
Folly Farm
Pump Hill Farm
Red House Cotts.
Playing Field
Chester Chalet & Caravan Camp (Silver Down Touring Pk.)
Poultry Houses
St. Osyth C of E Prim. Sch.
St.Osyth Lodge Farm
Rouses Farm
Wick Lodge
Rush Green
Playing Fields
Prim. Sch.
BY-PASS
PUMP HILL
ST. JOHN'S ROAD
B1027
A133
B1441
LITTLE CLACTON ROAD
HIGH BIRCH ROAD
FROWICK LANE
HEATH ROAD
RECTORY ROAD
HONEYPOT LA.
BENTLEY ROAD
CLACTON ROAD
LODGE FARM LANE
EARLS HALL DRIVE
JAYWICK LANE
ASDA CO15 3TH
BULL HILL ROAD

Playing Field
HARWICH ROAD
Poultry Houses
Crackstakes Farm
179
Little Clacton Lodge
Holland Brook
Clacton Grove Farm
Hunter's Bridge
Parkgate Farm
Dairy House
Kinfauns
Kennels
Street Farm
Reedland's Farm
Sentinels
Cook's Green
Bond's Farm
THE STREET
LITTLE CLACTON
HOLLAND ROAD
Swallow Farm
Sunbeam Farm
Parkgate Corner
Cook's Green Farm
Rayners Farm
Bridge Cottages
Vicarage
Nurseries
Piggeries
GT. HOLLAND COMMON RD.
Fan Bridge
Oak House Farm
Clacton-on-Sea
Willow Farm
CENTENARY WAY
MORRISONS
Superstore
OAKWOOD BUSINESS PARK
CLACTON FACTORY SHOPPING VILLAGE
STEPHENSON RD. WEST
Montana Nurseries
White House
Woodville Farm
Recreation Ground
Foot's Farm
CRUSADER BUSINESS PARK
GORSE LANE INDUSTRIAL ESTATE
Depot
Factory
Works
Chota Ghur
Langford Nursery
Langford Lodge
Highfield Holiday Park
Tumbrils
186
The Grove
Treasure Holt Farm
Pond House
TESCO
BROOK FARM CARAVAN PARK
HIGHLANDS CHALET PARK
CASTLE HILL PARK
Burrsville Park
Smythie's Farm
Brook Farm Riding Centre
Cemetery
Jun. Sch.
Infant Sch.
Picker's Ditch
CO15
Reservoir (Covered)
Valley Farm Camping Ground
Bowling Green
Tennis Courts
Sports Ground
FRINTON RD.
ST. JOHN'S RD.
VALLEY ROAD
HOLLAND ROAD
Great Clacton
Playing Field
Colbayns High School
Swim Pool
Rec. Sch. Grd.
Vic. Fruit Farm
Factories
Recreation Ground
CLACTON-ON-SEA
Putting Greens
Clacton Leisure Cen.
Clacton High Sch.
Windsor School
Nurs. Home
Sports Grd.
Clacton
Health Cen.
189
NORTH SEA
MARINE PARADE EAST
KINGS PARADE
G H J K L M N
1 2 3 4 5 6 7 8 9
17 18 19 20

A
B
C
D
E
F
G
180
185
Frinton-on-Sea
CO13
Clacton-on-Sea
CO15
GREAT HOLLAND
Great Holland Common
HOLLAND HAVEN COUNTRY PARK
HOLLAND HAVEN
HOLLAND-ON-SEA
Pantiles
Hodgnoll's Farm
Pleasance Farm
Green End Farm
Butchers Farm
Jenkins Farm
The Rosery
Larges Farm
Hunter's Bridge
Sand & Gravel Pit
The Mill House
Great Holland Mill (Provender)
Great Holland Pits Nature Reserve
Seven Acres Farm
Beckwith Farm
The Old Rectory
The Warren
Holland Wood
Hollandhall Wood
Great Holland Nurseries
Great Holland Hall
Village Hall
Manor Farm
Council Cottages
Dairy House Farm
Vesey Farm
Elm Todd
Bridge Cottages
Fan Bridge
Great Holland Lodge
Lodge Farm
Sladburys Cottage
Sladbury's Old House
Depot
Factory
Tumbrils
Sladburies
Pond House
Treasure Holt Farm
Sheep Wash
Chevaux de fr Point
Breakwater
Pumping Station
Outfall
Gas Meter House
Holland Bridge
Smythie's Farm
Brook Farm Riding Centre
Boat Compound
Library
Haven Gds.
York Mansions
Sports Grd.
KIRBY ROAD
MAIN RD.
ROAD
B1032
CLACTON ROAD
FRINTON ROAD
HOLLAND RD.
GT. HOLLAND COMMON RD.
LITTLE HOLLAND
SLADBURYS LANE
MANOR RD.
CHURCH LANE
RECTORY RD.
ORCHARD DRIVE
LAXTON GRO.
WESTBURY RD.
GREEN END LA.
KEW LA.
THE CRESCENT
THE CLOSE
MILL LANE
SHORT LANE
LONG LANE
WOOD LANE
POND HOUSE LA.
Picker's Ditch
BROOK
MANOR WAY
THE ESPLANADE
KINGS PARADE
KINGS PROMENADE
FLEETWOOD
NORMAN
MERRILEES CRES.
NANSEN ROAD
STRATFORD ROAD
KENT'S AV.
HUCKLESBURY AV.
NORFOLK
DORSET CL.
OAKWOOD AV.
BOULEVARD
AVENUE
BRIARWOOD
AYLESBURY
DRIVE
SUSSEX GDNS.
PEMBROKE GDNS.
HAVEN AV.
SUNDALE CL.
VIKING WY.
SAXON WY.
BRIGHTON
EDISON RD.
INGARFIELD RD.
PRIMROSE
MANCHESTER
NOTTINGHAM
KENILWORTH RD.
YORK ROAD
PRINCES ROAD
QUEENSWAY
KINGS AVENUE
PRESTON
COLCHESTER
CHELMSFORD
BRENTWOOD
WINDERMERE
IPSWICH ROAD
BEDFORD
SALISBURY
SALISBURY CT.
MADEIRA
DULWICH
HOWARD RD.
HAZLE AVENUE
LYNDHURST RD.
MERE RD.
TURPINS CL.
TURPINS GS.
SEAFIELDS
SEA
HILLSIDE CR.
HOLLAND LANE
CANTERBURY
CLIFF ROAD
HEREFORD
REC. Grd.
FERNWOOD AV.
CHASE
BOSCOMBE CT.
BOURNEMOUTH RD.
KINGS CT.
MAPLIN CT.
QUEEN'S CT.
GUNFLEET CT.
Play. Fld.
Sch.
129
226
339
377
316
100
28
29
620
21
22
20
19
18
17
16
1
2
3
4
5
6
7
8
9

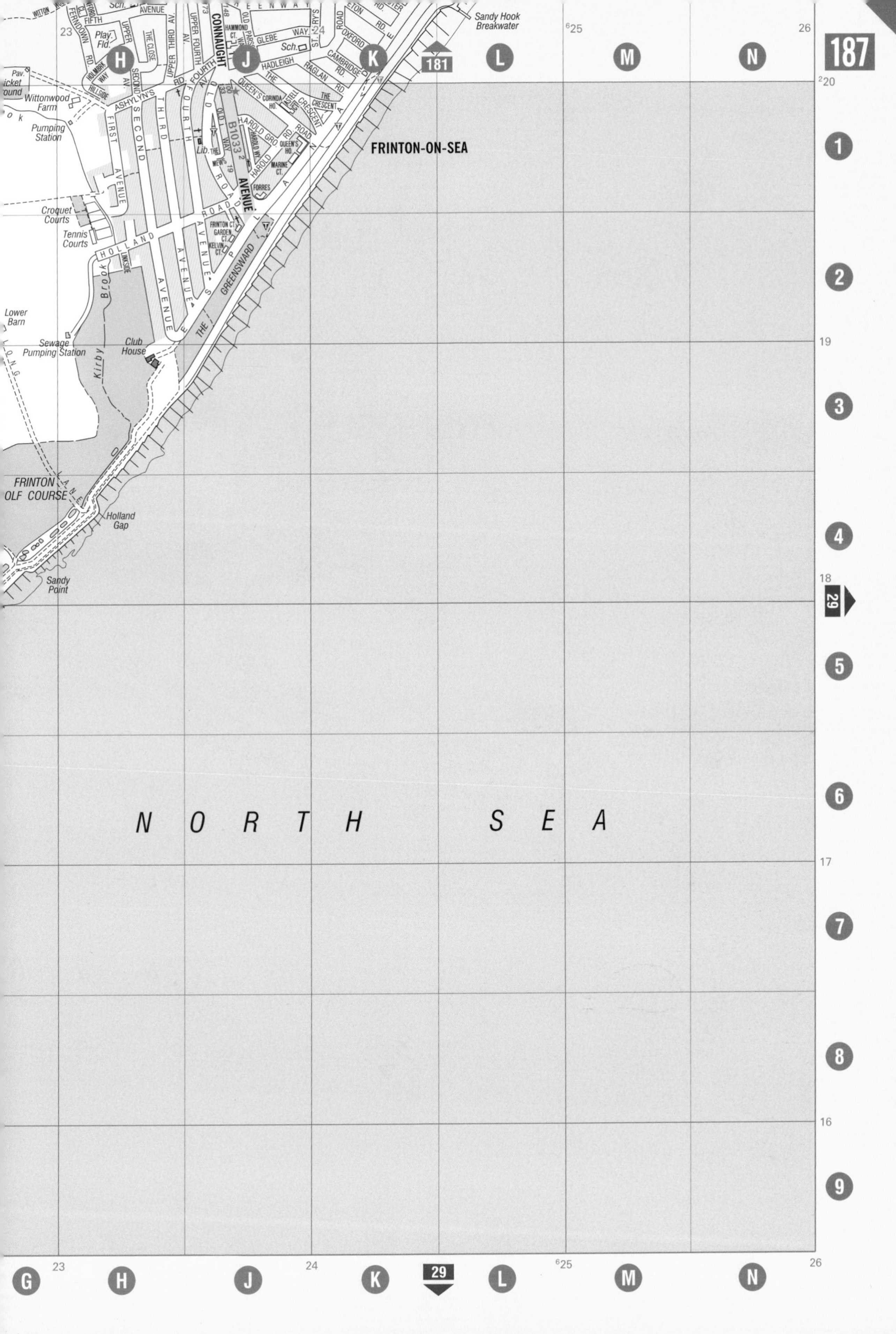
FRINTON-ON-SEA
NORTH SEA
Sandy Hook Breakwater
Wittonwood Farm
Pumping Station
Croquet Courts
Tennis Courts
Lower Barn
Sewage Pumping Station
Club House
FRINTON GOLF COURSE
Holland Gap
Sandy Point
Kirby Brook
CONNAUGHT AVENUE
THE GREENSWARD
B1033
HOLLAND ROAD
ASHYLYN'S RD
FIRST AVENUE
SECOND AVENUE
THIRD AVENUE
FOURTH AVENUE
UPPER FOURTH AV.
UPPER THIRD AV.
UPPER FIFTH
FERNDOWN RD
THE CLOSE
GLEBE WAY
HADLEIGH
OXFORD RD.
CAMBRIDGE RD.
RAGLAN RD
THE CRESCENT
HAROLD GRO
HAROLD RD
QUEEN'S RD
FORRES
MARINE CT.
FRINTON CT
GARDEN CT.
KELVIN CT.
LINKSIDE
Lib.
Sch.
Play. Fld.
181
29
H J K L M N
G H J K L M N
1 2 3 4 5 6 7 8 9
23 24 25 26
20 19 18 17 16

184
28
Clacton-on-Sea
CO16
Rush Green
JAYWICK
Seawick
St.Osyth Lodge Farm
Rouses Farm
Daltes Farm
Wick Lodge
Playing Fields
Football Ground
Pavilions
Chester Chalet & Caravan Camp (Silver Down Touring Pk.)
Poultry Houses
Playing Field
Botany Barn Farm
Cross House
Tinker's Hall
MILLERS BARN GOLF COURSE
Club House
Sackett's Grove Caravan Park
Prim. Sch.
Sewage Works
Cockett Wick Farm
West Clacton House
CLACTON-ON-SEA AIRFIELD
CLACTON GOLF COURSE
Hall & Library
Health Cen.
Marsh Cott.
Seawick Holiday Centre
Hutleys East Caravan Park
St. Osyth Beach Holiday Park
Decoy Pond
Go-Kart Track
Tower Caravan Park
Martello Tower
Martello Tower (No 3)
Lion Point
PROMENADE
BROOKLANDS
LOTUS WAY
WEST ROAD
RUSH GREEN ROAD
GOLF GREEN ROAD
CROSSWAY
MEADOW WAY
PARK SQUARE WEST
PARK SQUARE EAST
TUDOR GREEN
BOTANY LANE
DALTES LANE
COCKETT WICK LANE
BEACH ROAD
LODGE FARM LANE
ROUSES LANE
N O R

28

CLACTON-ON-SEA
THE SEA
Clacton Leisure Cen.
Playing Field
Clacton High Sch.
Windsor School
Clacton
Health Cen.
MAYFIELD CEN.
Lib.
T.H.
Off.
Cinema
Educ. Cen.
Works
Warehouse
Oakwood Infants Sch.
Alton Park Jun. Sch.
Play.Fld.
Leas Sch. Clacton
Reservoir (Covered)
Depot
WATERGLADE RETAIL PARK
HOSPICE
Mag. Ct.
Offs.
West Cliff Theatre
CLACTON & DISTRICT HOSP.
Colchester Institute
Clacton Pier
RNLI Lifeboat Station
Pavilion
Landing Stage
Coach Park
Coastguard Station
Martello Tower (No 2)
CARNARVON RD.
HIGH STREET
HOLLAND ROAD
WELLESLEY RD.
OLD ROAD
PARADE
PROMENADE
MARINE PARADE
KINGS PDE
CO15
185
28
H
J
K
L
M
N
G
1
2
3
4
5
6
7
8
9
11
12
13
14
15
17
18
19

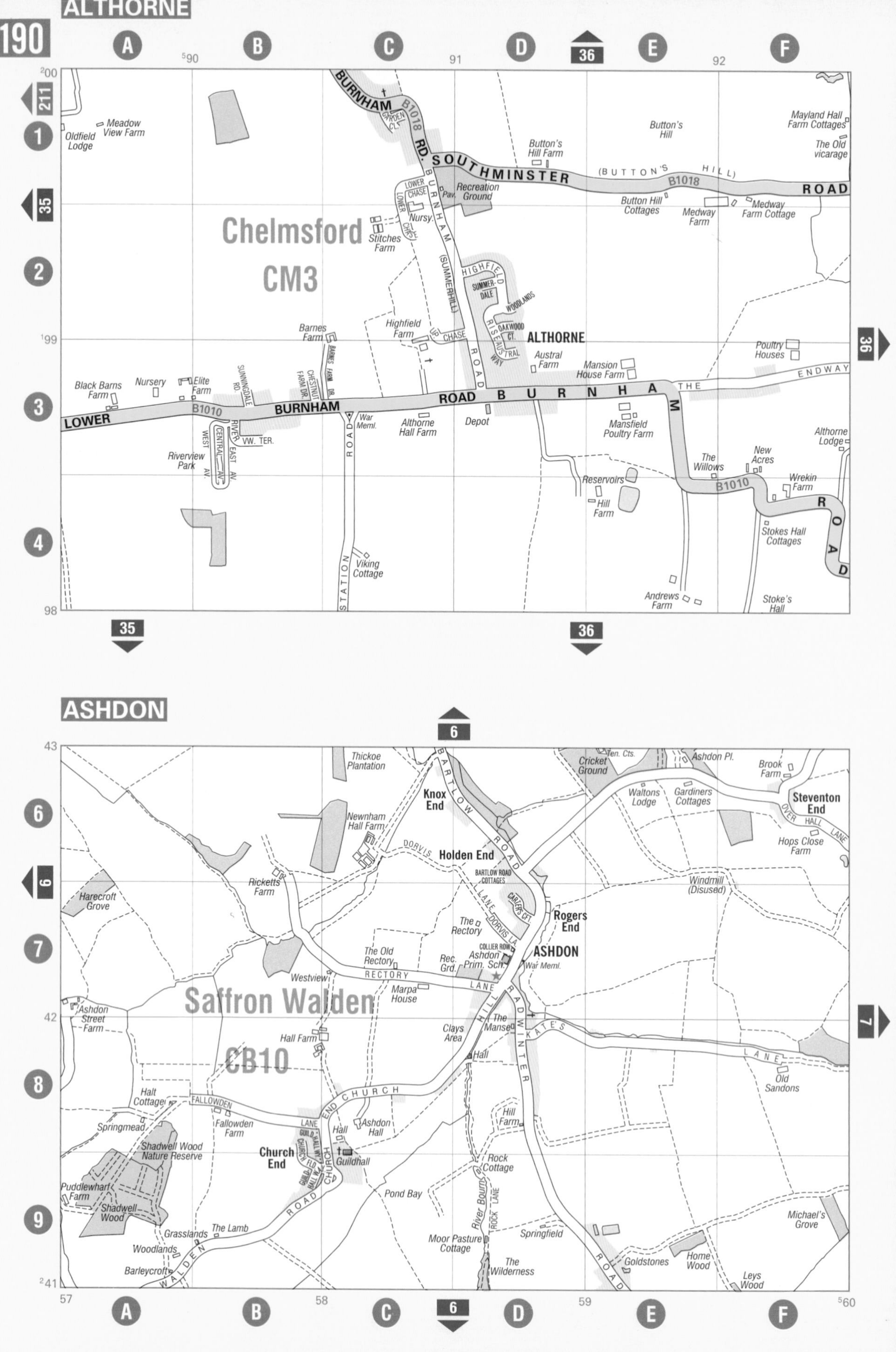
ALTHORNE
Chelmsford
CM3
Oldfield Lodge
Meadow View Farm
Button's Hill Farm
Button's Hill
Mayland Hall Farm Cottages
The Old vicarage
SOUTHMINSTER ROAD
(BUTTON'S HILL)
B1018
BURNHAM RD.
Recreation Ground
Button Hill Cottages
Medway Farm
Medway Farm Cottage
Stitches Farm
Nursy.
HIGHFIELD RISE
SUMMERDALE
WOODLANDS
OAKWOOD CT.
AUSTRAL WAY
Barnes Farm
Highfield Farm
Austral Farm
Mansion House Farm
Poultry Houses
THE ENDWAY
Black Barns Farm
Nursery
Elite Farm
LOWER BURNHAM ROAD
B1010
War Meml.
Althorne Hall Farm
Depot
Mansfield Poultry Farm
Althorne Lodge
Riverview Park
VW. TER.
The Willows
New Acres
Wrekin Farm
Reservoirs
Hill Farm
Stokes Hall Cottages
Viking Cottage
STATION ROAD
Andrews Farm
Stoke's Hall
ASHDON
Saffron Walden
CB10
Thickoe Plantation
Cricket Ground
Ten. Cts.
Ashdon Pl.
Brook Farm
Knox End
Newnham Hall Farm
Waltons Lodge
Gardiners Cottages
Steventon End
OVER HALL LANE
Holden End
Hops Close Farm
BARTLOW ROAD
BARTLOW ROAD COTTAGES
DORVIS LANE
Ricketts Farm
Windmill (Disused)
Harecroft Grove
The Rectory
Rogers End
The Old Rectory
Rec. Grd.
COLLIER ROW
Ashdon Prim. Sch.
War Meml.
RECTORY LANE
Westview
Marpa House
Ashdon Street Farm
Hall Farm
Clays Area
The Manse
KATE'S LANE
RADWINTER ROAD
Hall
Old Sandons
Halt Cottage
FALLOWDEN LANE
Fallowden Farm
END CHURCH HILL
Hill Farm
Springmead
Hall
Ashdon Hall
Shadwell Wood Nature Reserve
Church End
GUILD HALL WAY
Guildhall
Rock Cottage
Puddlewharf Farm
Pond Bay
Shadwell Wood
CHURCH END ROAD
Michael's Grove
River Bourn
ROCK LANE
The Lamb
Grasslands
Springfield
Moor Pasture Cottage
Woodlands
Goldstones
Home Wood
The Wilderness
Barleycroft
WALDEN ROAD
Leys Wood

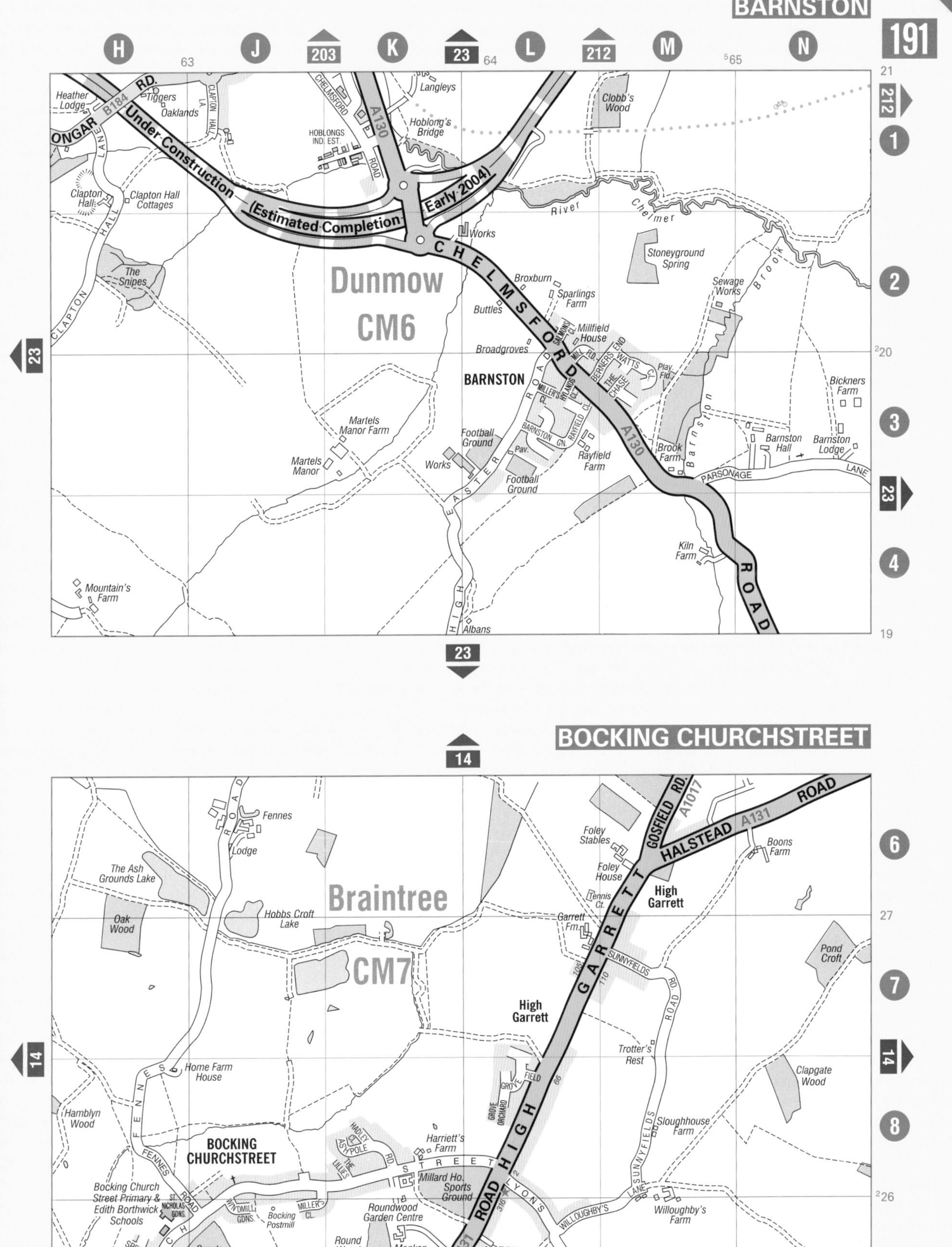
Heather Lodge
ONGAR B184 RD.
Tiggers
Oaklands
CLAPTON HALL LA
CHELMSFORD ROAD
HOBLONGS IND. EST.
A130
Langleys
Hoblong's Bridge
Clobb's Wood
Under Construction (Estimated Completion Early 2004)
Clapton Hall
Clapton Hall Cottages
River Chelmer
Works
CHELMSFORD ROAD
Stoneyground Spring
The Snipes
Dunmow CM6
Broxburn
Sparlings Farm
Buttles
Sewage Works
Brook
CLAPTON
Millfield House
Broadgroves
SALMONS CL.
MILL FLD.
BERNERS END
WATTS CL.
THE CHASE
Play. Fld.
BARNSTON
MILLER'S CL.
RYLANDS CL.
Bickners Farm
Martels Manor Farm
Football Ground
BARNSTON GN.
RAYFIELD CL.
Barnston Hall
Barnston Lodge
Martels Manor
Pav.
Works
Rayfield Farm
Brook Farm
Barnston
PARSONAGE LANE
Football Ground
A130
EASTER HIGH ROAD
Kiln Farm
ROAD
Mountain's Farm
Albans
BOCKING CHURCHSTREET
Fennes
ROAD
GOSFIELD RD. A1017
HALSTEAD A131 ROAD
Lodge
Foley Stables
Boons Farm
The Ash Grounds Lake
Foley House
Braintree
High Garrett
Tennis Ct.
Oak Wood
Hobbs Croft Lake
Garrett Fm.
GARRETT
SUNNYFIELDS
Pond Croft
CM7
High Garrett
ROAD
Trotter's Rest
Clapgate Wood
FENNES
Home Farm House
GROVE FIELD
GROVE ORCHARD
HIGH
Hamblyn Wood
SUNNYFIELDS
Sloughhouse Farm
BOCKING CHURCHSTREET
HADLEY CL.
ASHPOLE RD
THE LILLIES
Harriett's Farm
STREET
FENNES ROAD
Millard Ho. Sports Ground
LYONS
Bocking Church Street Primary & Edith Borthwick Schools
ST. NICHOLAS GDNS.
WINDMILL GDNS.
Bocking Postmill
MILLER'S CL.
Roundwood Garden Centre
ROAD
WILLOUGHBY'S LANE
Willoughby's Farm
Bocking Hall
SPENCER SQ.
CHURCH
Sports Ground
Round Wood
Monken Hadley
A131
Tennis Courts
HALL ROAD
BOVINGDON RD.
Works
CAMERON CL.
KINGSBRIDGE CL.
CHAPEL HILL
KINGSTON WY
DOREWARDS AV.
DEANS WLK.
CHURCH LA
BROAD
Bramble Wood

PANFIELD
Panfield Hall
Towerlands Equestrian Centre
TOWERLANDS GOLF COURSE
Reservoir
Matthew's Farm
Park Farm
Piggeries
Kynaston's Farm
Noakes House
Lightwater Cottage
Lightwaters Farm
Perry Childs Farm
The White House
Panfield Farm
The Old Smithy
Community Centre
Playground
Gardeners Cottage
Oak Cottage
Panfield Wood
Braintree
Braintree Airfield (Rayne Hall Farm)
Sewage Works
Pods Brook
Bowling Green
Club House
BRAINTREE ENTERPRISE CEN.
Tabor High Sch.
Leisure Centre
Running Track
Playing Field
Reservoir (Covered)
SPRINGWOOD INDUSTRIAL ESTATE
ST.MICHAEL'S HOSPITAL
Rayne Lodge
Poultry Houses
Gould's Farm
Gould's Farm House
Duckend Green
The Cottage
The Pines
Pump House
Rayne Hall
Rayne Hall Farm
War Memorial
Clap Bridge
RAYNE
Rayne Prim. Sch.
Havering's Farm
Works
Pav.
Hall
Sports Ground
Depot
Rayne Sta. Cen.
STANE STREET (ROMAN RD.)
FLITCH WAY
Gatewoods Farm
Hatchery
Little Sandyhurst
CM77
Greensleeves
Naylinghurst
Braintree Green
Fairy Hall
Wenas Farm
Tyeponds
Springett
Payling Cottages
Stanford Farm
Little Bishops
Two Hoots
Lakes Farm
Cottage Acre
Queenborough Meadow
The Commons
A120
A131
All Views
Villa Farm
Reservoir
Little Common Farm
Common Farm
Spinners
Little Common
Manorcroft
BRAINTREE
UTTLESFORD
Great Notley Country Park
The Discovery Centre
Concord Farm
Bartholomew Green
GREAT NOTLEY
Cemetery
Millhouse
Bridge Farm
Piggery
Hill House Farm
Hill House Cottage
Ludham Hall
RAYNE ROAD B1256
PODS BROOK RD.
PANFIELD B1053
Prim. Sch.
Ford

14
24
204

H
J
K
14
L
191
M
N
76
77
78
1
2
3
4
5
6
7
8
9
25
24
23
22
21
14
24
Lyons Hall
Doreward's Hall
Cemetery
Essex Traffic Police
Thistley Green
Playing Field
Lyonshall Wood
Highfield Stile Farm
Works
Boleyn's Farm
Boleyns
Braintree College
Bradford Bri.
Sewage Works
Blackwater
Bocking
Darby's Hole
Bocking Hole
Great Bradfords Jun. & Inf. Schs.
CM7
Public Gardens
Tennis Courts
St. Francis R.C. Prim. Sch.
Howard Hall
Recreation Ground
Tennis Courts
BRAINTREE
Playing Fields
Prim. Sch.
Kingsmead Caravan Park
Moat
Hatches Farm
Gainsford
COGGESHALL RD.
Baytree Cottage
A120
The Leys
Superstore
HOSP.
Offs.
Court
Art Gall.
Mus.
Libr.
Court
SOUTH STREET
RAILWAY ST.
MANOR ST.
LAKES RD.
COGGESHALL ROAD
B1256
A131
B1053
BROAD
CONVENT HILL
CHURCH LANE
BRADFORD ST.
Ind. Estate
Gasholder Station
Chapel Hill Prim. Sch.
Braintree Town FC (Cressing Rd. Stadium)
King George's Field
Ley Wood
Comm. Cen.
The Leywood Centre
Pyefleet Lodge
Templeborder Wood
Braintree
The Riverside Centre
Hoppit Bridge
Works
Marsh Farm
Playing Field
Alec Hunter High Sch.
Playing Field
BRAINTREE FREEPORT DESIGNER OUTLET VILLAGE
Braintree Freeport
Weirs
Factory
Works
Sewage Works
Number Ten Bowling Alley
Cineworld
BRAINTREE RETAIL PARK
MILLENNIUM WAY
B1018
Slough House Farm
GALLEY ROUNDABOUT
Cressing Lodge
Depots
Galley's Corner
Hoppit House
Sandiacres
LONG GREEN
BRAINTREE RD.
BRAINTREE ROAD
John Ray Jun. & Inf. Schs.
Playing Field
Notley High Sch.
Notley Sports Centre
Play. Fld.
Playing Field
A120
NOTLEY ROAD
Hayeswood Farm
PARK FARM INDUSTRIES
Park Farm
Buck Fm.
Cricket Ground
Wright's Farm
River Brain
G
H
76
J
K
24
77
L
194
M
78
N

BLACK NOTLEY

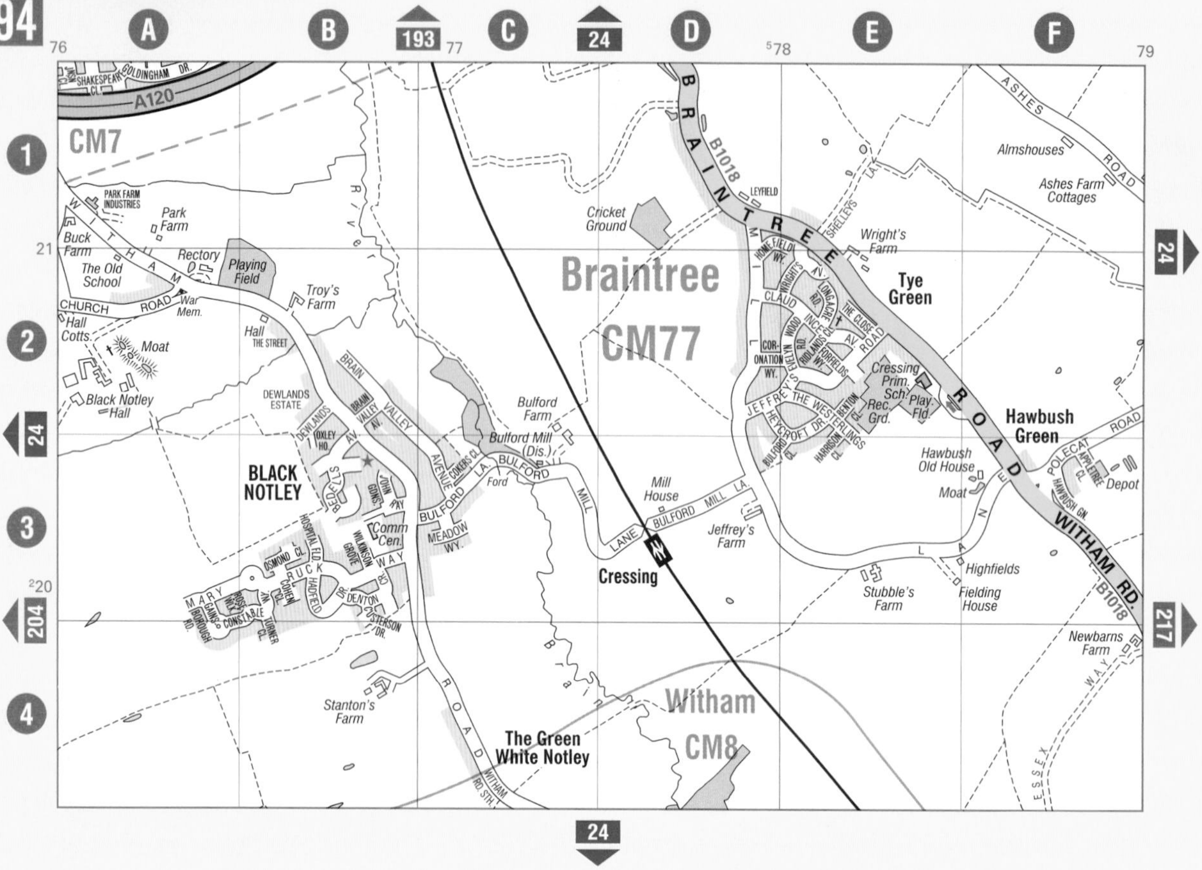

193
24
24
24
24
204
217
24

A B C D E F

1 2 3 4

76 77 578 79 21 220

SHAKESPEARE
GOLDINGHAM DR.
A120
CM7
PARK FARM INDUSTRIES
Park Farm
Buck Farm
WITHAM
The Old School
Rectory
Playing Field
CHURCH ROAD
War Mem.
Troy's Farm
Hall Cotts.
Hall
THE STREET
Moat
Black Notley Hall
DEWLANDS ESTATE
DEWLANDS
OXLEY HO.
BRAIN VALLEY AV.
BRAIN VALLEY AVENUE
BLACK NOTLEY
JOHN RAY
GOINGS
BEDELLS
HOSPITAL FLD.
OSMOND CL.
WILKINSON GROVE
Comm Cen.
BUCK WAY
HADFIELD
COHEN CL.
MARY RUCK WAY
GAINS
CONSTABLE
TURNER CL.
BOROUGH RD.
DENTON
PATERSON DR.
River
COKERS CL.
BULFORD LA.
BULFORD
MEADOW WY.
Ford
Bulford Mill (Dis.)
Bulford Farm
MILL LANE
Cricket Ground
Braintree
CM77
Mill House
BULFORD MILL LA.
Cressing
Jeffrey's Farm
Stanton's Farm
ROAD
WITHAM RD. STH.
The Green
White Notley
Brain
Witham
CM8
BRAINTREE ROAD
B1018
LEYFIELD
MILL
SHELLEYS LA.
HOME FIELD WY.
WRIGHTS AV.
CLAUDE
LONG ACRE
INCE
THE CLOSE
ROAD
RIDLANDS RD.
FAIRFIELDS
CORONATION WY.
EVELYN WOOD RD.
JEFFREY'S
THE WESTERLINGS
DENTON CL.
HEYCROFT DR.
BULFORD CL.
HARRISON CL.
Cressing Prim. Sch.
Rec. Grd.
Play. Fld.
Wright's Farm
Tye Green
Hawbush Green
Hawbush Old House
Moat
LANE
Highfields
Stubble's Farm
Fielding House
ASHES ROAD
Almshouses
Ashes Farm Cottages
POLECAT ROAD
APPLETREE CL.
HAWBUSH GN.
Depot
WITHAM RD.
B1018
Newbarns Farm
ESSEX WAY

BRADWELL-ON-SEA

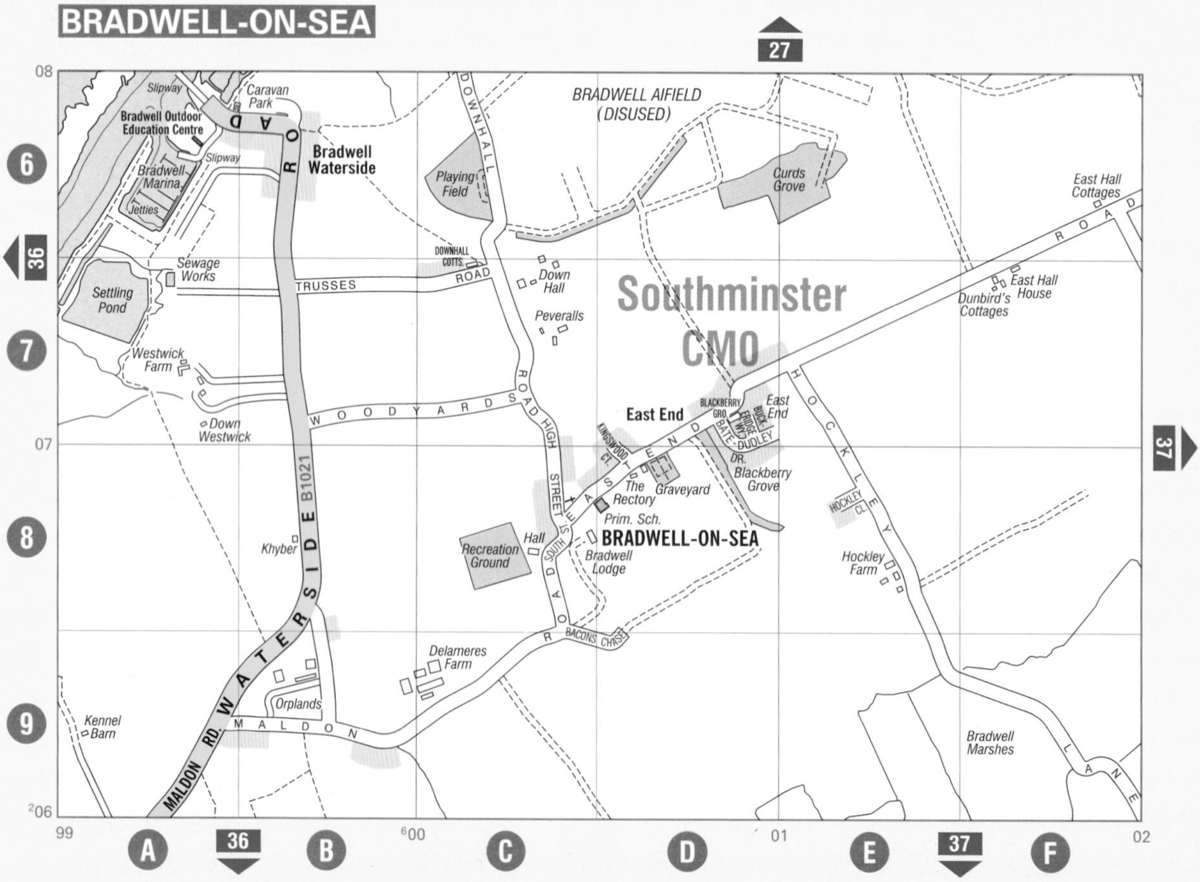

27
36
37
36
37

6 7 8 9

08 07 206 99 600 01 02

Slipway
Caravan Park
Bradwell Outdoor Education Centre
ROAD
Bradwell Waterside
Slipway
Bradwell Marina
Jetties
Sewage Works
Settling Pond
TRUSSES ROAD
DOWNHALL COTTS.
DOWNHALL
Playing Field
BRADWELL AIFIELD (DISUSED)
Curds Grove
Down Hall
Peveralls
Southminster
CM0
East Hall Cottages
ROAD
East Hall House
Dunbird's Cottages
Westwick Farm
WOODYARDS ROAD
Down Westwick
HIGH STREET
East End
BLACKBERRY GRO.
BUCK FIELD
KINGSWOOD CL.
EAST END
DUDLEY
East End
Blackberry Grove
The Rectory
Graveyard
Prim. Sch.
BRADWELL-ON-SEA
Hall
Recreation Ground
Bradwell Lodge
SOUTH ROAD
BACONS CHASE
HOCKLEY LANE
HOCKLEY CL.
Hockley Farm
Khyber
WATERSIDE
B1021
Delameres Farm
Orplands
Kennel Barn
MALDON RD.
MALDON
Bradwell Marshes

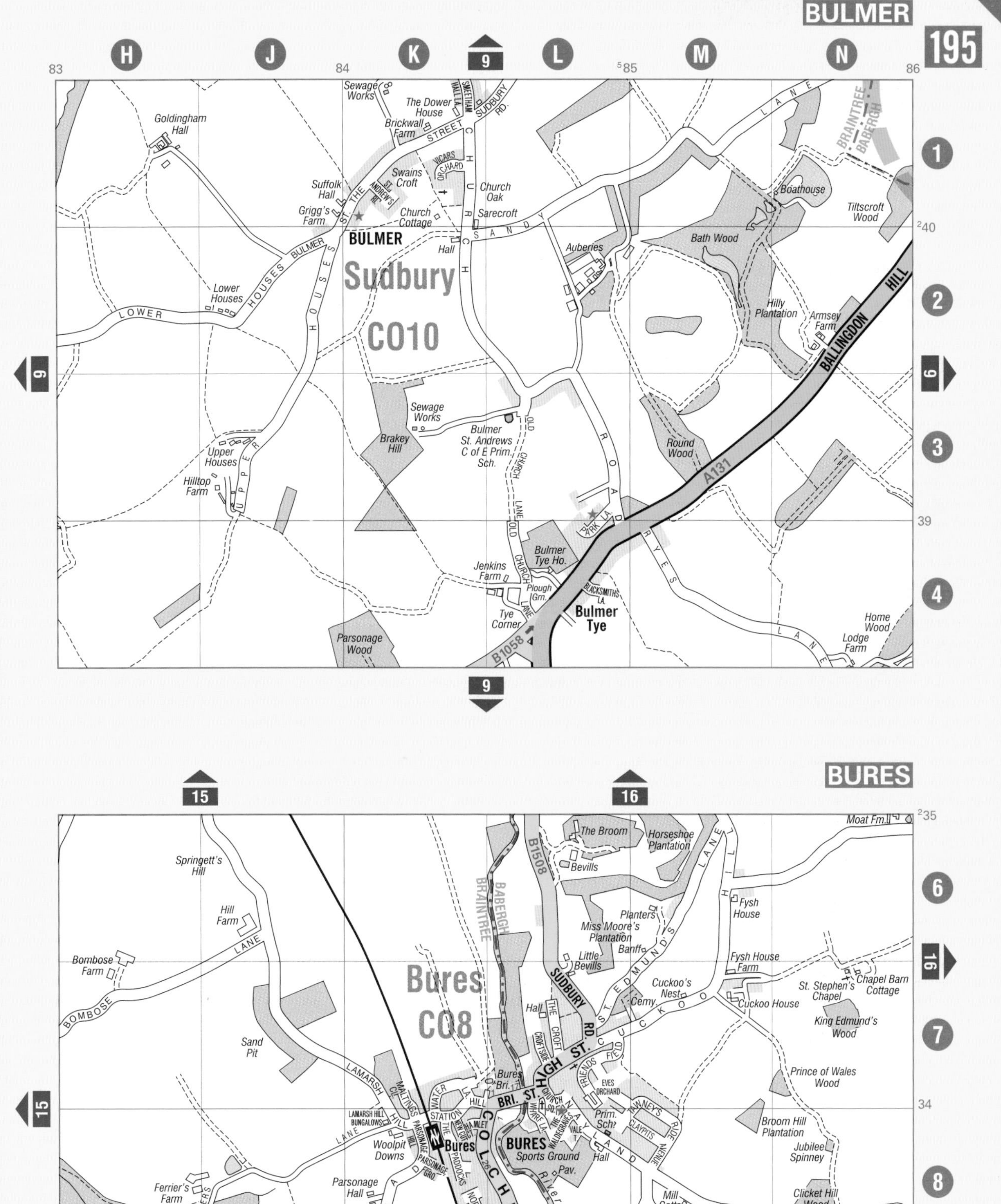
Goldingham Hall
Sewage Works
The Dower House
Brickwall Farm
SMEETHAM HALL LA.
SUDBURY RD.
STREET
BRAINTREE
BABERGH
Suffolk Hall
Grigg's Farm
Swains Croft
VICARS' ORCHARD
ST. ANDREW'S RD.
Church Oak
Church Cottage
Sarecroft
BULMER
Hall
SANDY
Boathouse
Tiltscroft Wood
Bath Wood
Auberies
Sudbury
CO10
Lower Houses
LOWER
HOUSES
BULMER
Hilly Plantation
Armsey Farm
BALLINGDON HILL
Sewage Works
Bulmer St. Andrews C of E Prim. Sch.
Brakey Hill
Upper Houses
Hilltop Farm
UPPER
OLD CHURCH LANE
ROAD
Round Wood
A131
PARK LA.
RYES
Bulmer Tye Ho.
Jenkins Farm
Plough (Grn.)
BLACKSMITHS LA.
Bulmer Tye
Tye Corner
B1058
Parsonage Wood
Home Wood
Lodge Farm
LANE
BURES
Moat Fm.
The Broom
Horseshoe Plantation
B1508
Bevills
Springett's Hill
Hill Farm
Fysh House
Planters
Miss Moore's Plantation
Banff
Little Bevills
Fysh House Farm
Bombose Farm
BOMBOSE
LANE
Bures
CO8
SUDBURY RD.
ST. EDMUND'S
Cuckoo's Nest
Cemy.
Cuckoo House
St. Stephen's Chapel
Chapel Barn Cottage
King Edmund's Wood
Sand Pit
Hall
THE CROFT
CROFTSIDE
HIGH ST.
CUCKOO
FRIENDS FIELD
EVES ORCHARD
Prince of Wales Wood
LAMARSH HILL
MALTINGS CL.
WATER
Bures Bri.
BRI. ST.
CHURCH SQ.
NAYLAND
LAMARSH HILL BUNGALOWS
STATION HILL
Bures
BURES Sports Ground
Pav.
Prim. Sch.
CLAYPITS
NEWEY'S RIDE
AVENUE
Broom Hill Plantation
Jubilee Spinney
Woolpit Downs
PARSONAGE HILL
PARSONAGE GRO.
PADDOCKS
NORMANDIE WY.
CAMBRIDGE WY.
COLCHESTER ROAD
Ferrier's Farm
FERRIERS
Parsonage Hall
ROAD
River Stour
Mill Cotts.
Nether Hall
Bures Mill
BABERGH
COLCHESTER
Clicket Hill Wood
CLICKET HILL
Sewage Works
Baker's Hall
COLNE
Brook House
Brook House Farm
Brook House Cottage

BURNHAM-ON-CROUCH

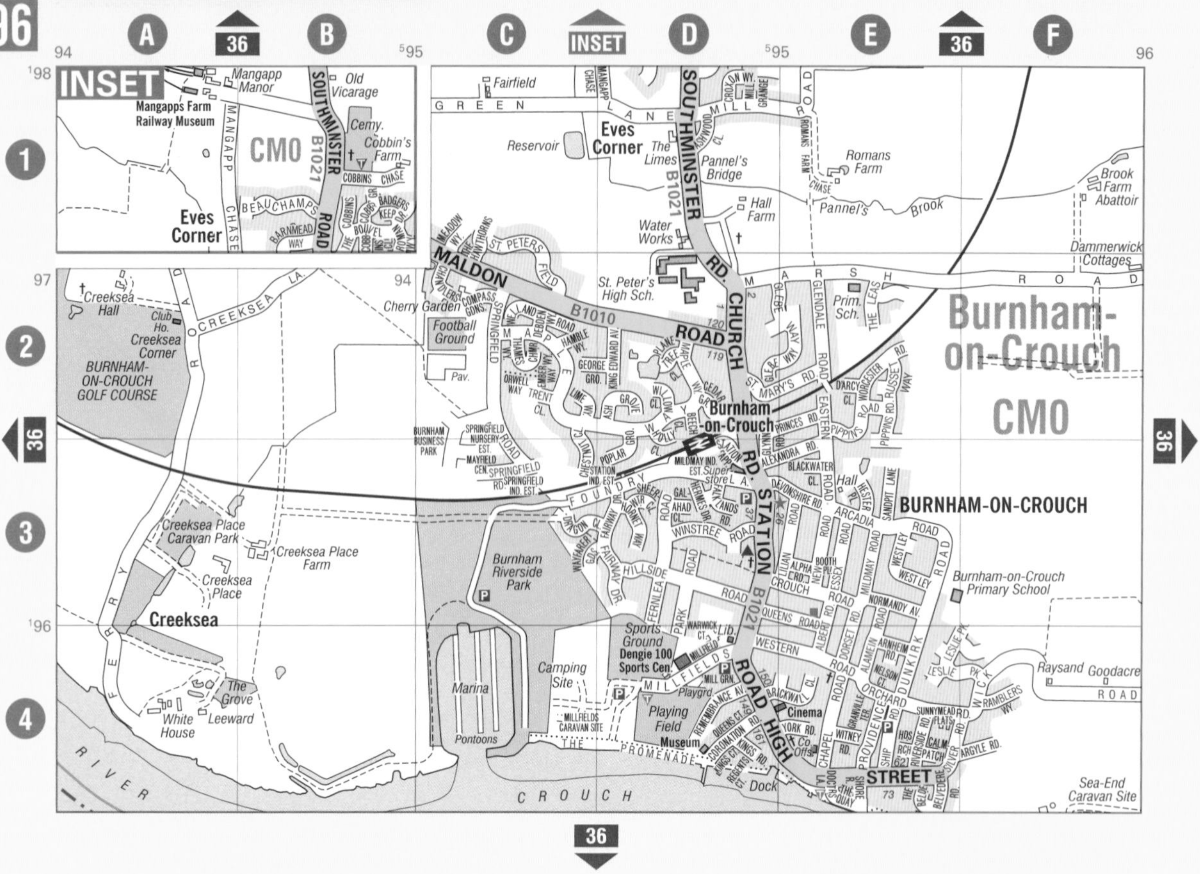

CHAPPEL & WAKES COLNE

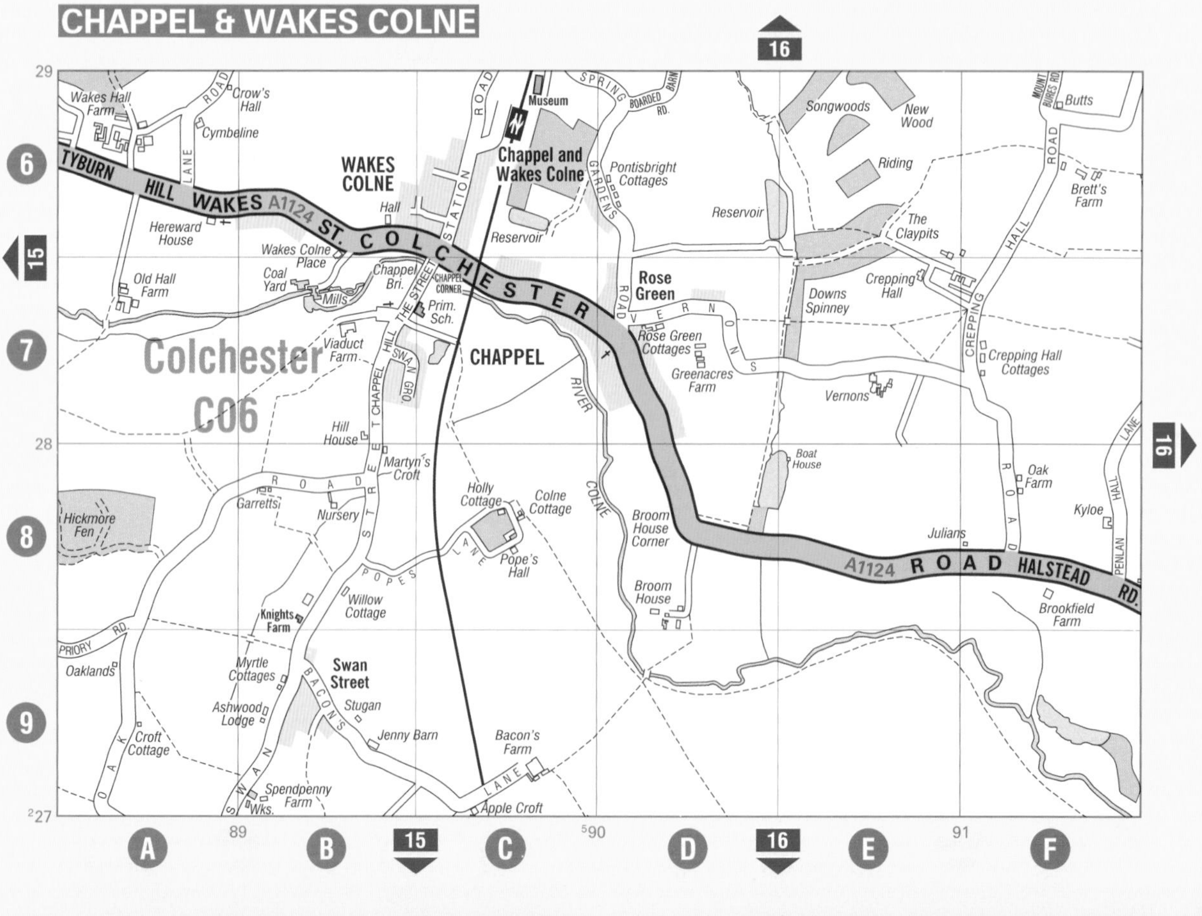

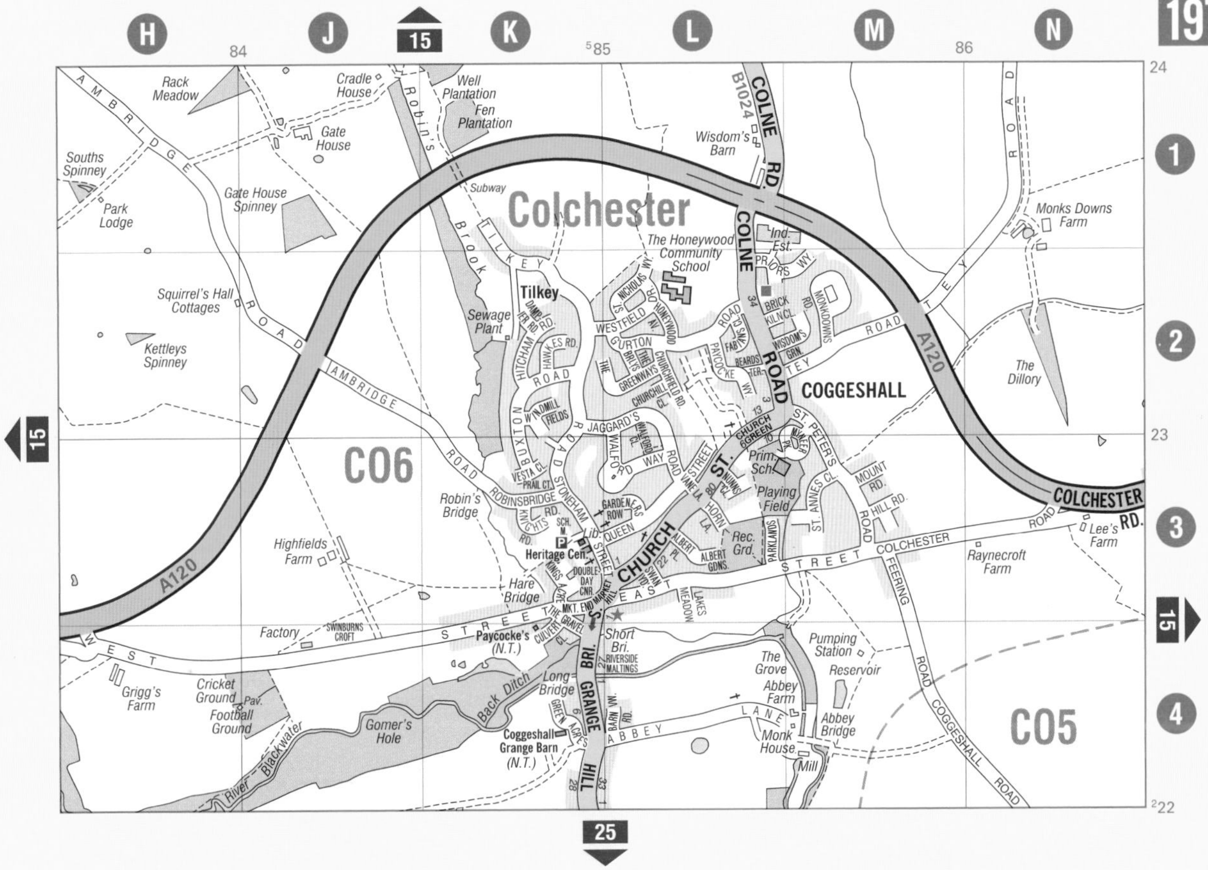

15
25
15
15

215
35
35
211
35
35

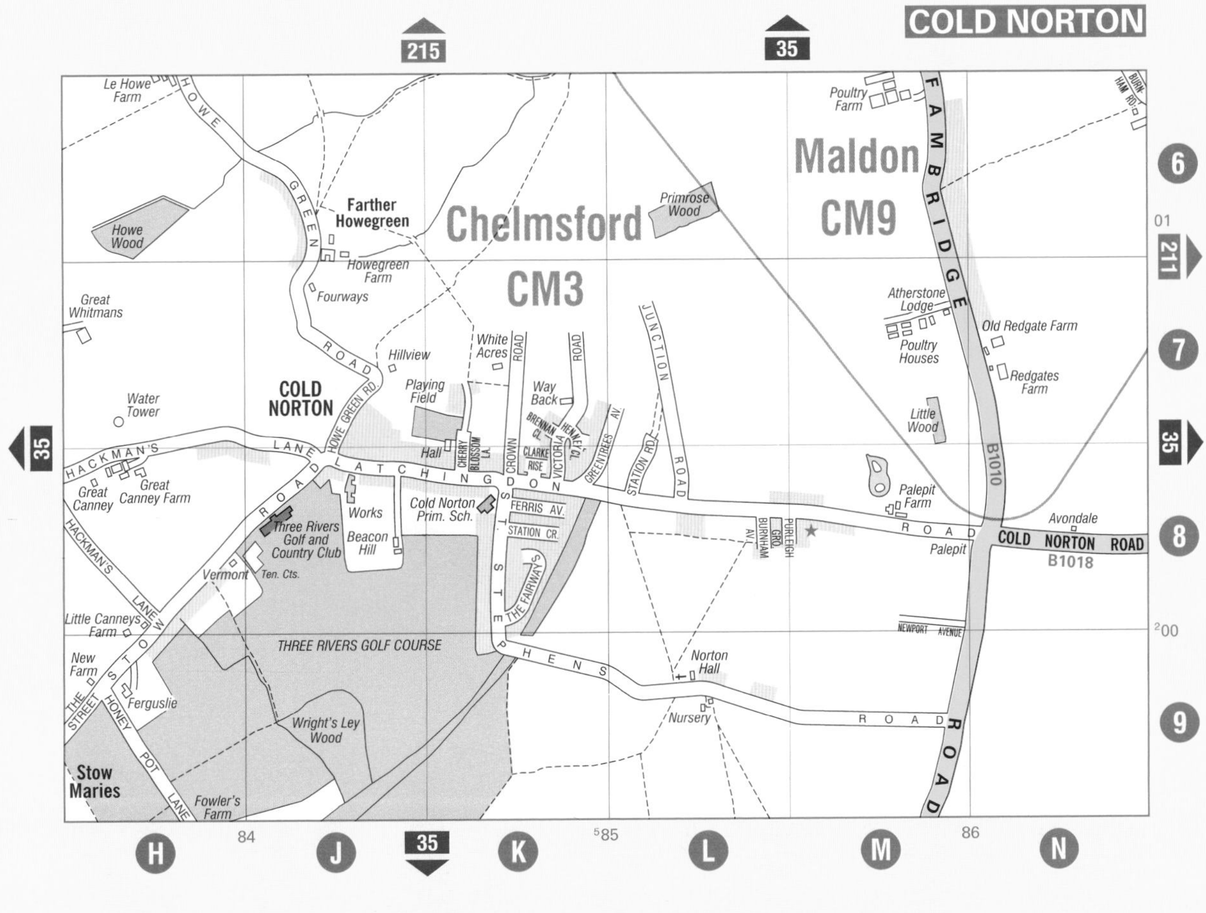

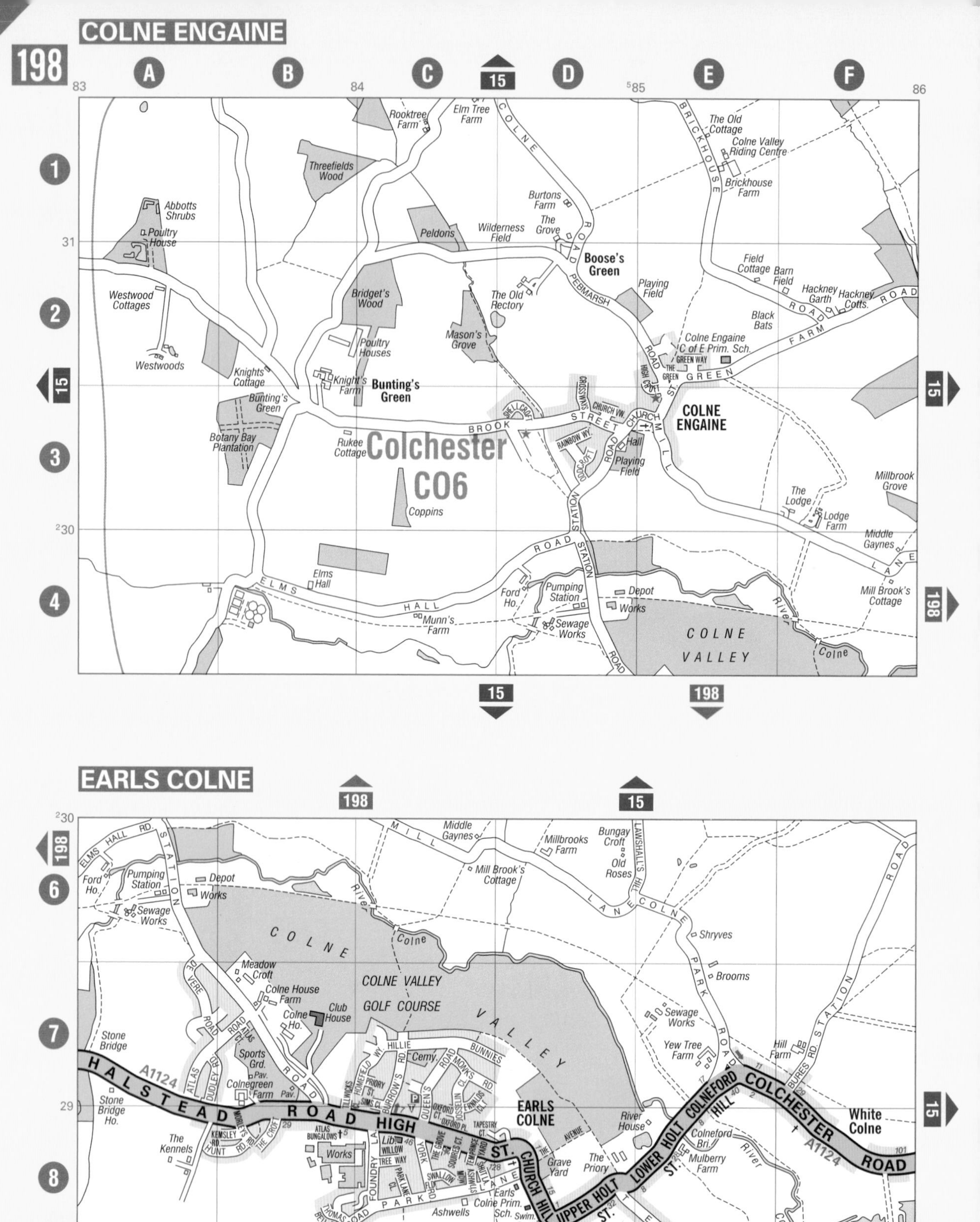
A
B
C
D
E
F
83
84
585
86
15
1
2
3
4
31
230
Abbotts Shrubs
Poultry House
Westwood Cottages
Westwoods
Threefields Wood
Rooktree Farm
Elm Tree Farm
Peldons
Bridget's Wood
Poultry Houses
Knight's Farm
Bunting's Green
Knights Cottage
Bunting's Green
Botany Bay Plantation
Rukee Cottage
Colchester
CO6
Coppins
Mason's Grove
The Old Rectory
Wilderness Field
Burtons Farm
The Grove
Boose's Green
Playing Field
COLNE ROAD
PEBMARSH ROAD
BRICKHOUSE
The Old Cottage
Colne Valley Riding Centre
Brickhouse Farm
Field Cottage
Barn Field
Hackney Garth
Hackney Cotts.
Black Bats
FARM ROAD
Colne Engaine C of E Prim. Sch.
GREEN WAY
THE GREEN
HIGH CROFT
GREEN ST.
COLNE ENGAINE
CROSSWAYS
CHURCH VW.
SHELLCROFT
BROOK STREET
CHURCH ROAD
MILL
RAINBOW WY.
OLDCROFT
Hall
Playing Field
STATION ROAD
Millbrook Grove
The Lodge
Lodge Farm
Middle Gaynes
LANE
Mill Brook's Cottage
ELMS HALL
Elms Hall
Munn's Farm
Ford Ho.
Pumping Station
Sewage Works
Depot
Works
COLNE VALLEY
River Colne
198
EARLS COLNE
198
15
230
6
7
8
9
29
28
ELMS HALL RD.
STATION
Ford Ho.
Pumping Station
Depot
Works
Sewage Works
MILL
Middle Gaynes
Mill Brook's Cottage
Millbrooks Farm
Bungay Croft
Old Roses
LAWSHALL'S HILL
LANE COLNE
River Colne
COLNE VALLEY
Shryves
Brooms
PARK ROAD
Meadow Croft
Colne House Farm
Colne Ho.
Club House
COLNE VALLEY GOLF COURSE
DE VERE ROAD
Stone Bridge
HALSTEAD ROAD
A1124
ATLAS
DUDLEY
Sports Grd.
Pav.
Colnegreen Farm
Stone Bridge Ho.
The Kennels
KEMSLEY RD.
HUNT RD.
THE CROFT
HILLIE
BUNNIES
Cemy.
PRIORY ST.
ATLAS BUNGALOWS
Works
Lib.
WILLOW
TREE WAY
HIGH ST.
YORK
QUEEN'S RD.
OXFORD CT.
OXFORD PL.
TAPESTRY CT.
THE GROVE
SQUIRES CT.
PARK LANE
SWALLOW
FOUNDRY LA.
PARK LANE
EARLS COLNE
THE AVENUE
Grave Yard
CHURCH HILL
Earls Colne Prim. Sch.
Swim. Pool
Ashwells
Pound Green
THOMAS BELL RD.
HAYHOUSE ROAD
Hayhouse Farm
Ash Bottom
CURDS ROAD
NEWHOUSE
Holly Cottage
Colchester
CO6
ROAD
COGGESHALL ROAD
B1024
Tilekiln Farm
UPPER HOLT ST.
The Priory
River House
LOWER HOLT ST.
COLNEFORD HILL
Colneford Bri.
Mulberry Farm
LOWEFIELDS
Sewage Works
Yew Tree Farm
Hill Farm
BURES RD.
STATION ROAD
COLCHESTER ROAD
A1124
White Colne
River Colne
Mill Race
Peek's Corner
ROAD
Chalkney Wood Nature Reserve
A
585
B
C
86
D
E
87
F

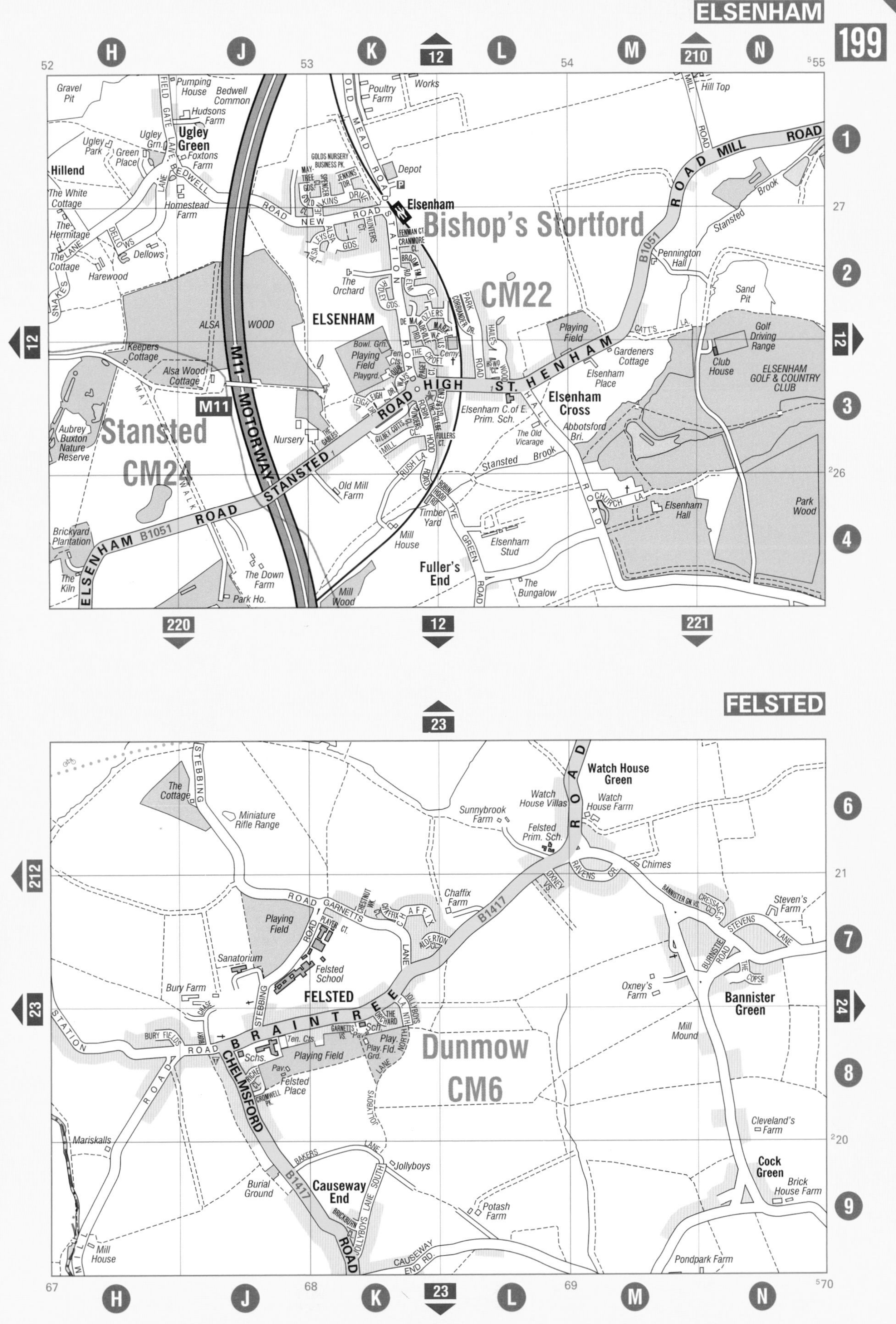
ELSENHAM
Gravel Pit
Pumping House
Bedwell Common
Hudsons Farm
Ugley Green
Foxtons Farm
Hillend
The White Cottage
Homestead Farm
The Hermitage
Dellows
Harewood
Poultry Farm
Works
Depot
Elsenham
Bishop's Stortford
The Orchard
ELSENHAM
CM22
Hill Top
MILL ROAD
Pennington Hall
Stansted Brook
Sand Pit
Golf Driving Range
Club House
ELSENHAM GOLF & COUNTRY CLUB
Playing Field
Gardeners Cottage
Elsenham Place
Elsenham Cross
Abbotsford Bri.
ALSA WOOD
Keepers Cottage
Alsa Wood Cottage
M11
M11 MOTORWAY
Aubrey Buxton Nature Reserve
Stansted CM24
Nursery
HIGH ST.
Elsenham C.of E. Prim. Sch.
The Old Vicarage
Old Mill Farm
Timber Yard
Mill House
Elsenham Stud
Elsenham Hall
Park Wood
Brickyard Plantation
The Kiln
ELSENHAM ROAD
STANSTED ROAD
The Down Farm
Park Ho.
Mill Wood
Fuller's End
The Bungalow
FELSTED
The Cottage
Miniature Rifle Range
Watch House Green
Watch House Villas
Watch House Farm
Sunnybrook Farm
Felsted Prim. Sch.
Chimes
Chaffix Farm
Steven's Farm
Playing Field
Sanatorium
Felsted School
Bury Farm
FELSTED
BRAINTREE ROAD
Oxney's Farm
Bannister Green
Mill Mound
Dunmow CM6
Playing Field
Felsted Place
CHELMSFORD ROAD
Cleveland's Farm
Mariskalls
Jollyboys
Causeway End
Burial Ground
Cock Green
Brick House Farm
Potash Farm
Mill House
Pondpark Farm
CAUSEWAY END RD.

200
FINCHINGFIELD
A
B
C
D
E
F
13
67
68
69
570
34
33
232
1
2
3
4
14
228
Lodge
SPAINS
The Warren
Fish Ponds
Darielay Farm
Lodge
Mill End
HALL
LITTLE LONDON HILL
B1057
LOWER HOWE STREET
Howe Hall Farm
Howe Hall
Fancy Covert
Fancy Cottage
The Round House
Braintree
CM7
WALFORDS
LANE
The Thicket
Spinney Cottages
Spinney Lodge
BRENT
B1053
Brent Hall
The Moors
Duck End
ROAD
LOWER GREEN RD.
HALL
LANE
FINCHINGFIELD
THE CAUSEWAY
Finchingfield Windmill
COACHMANS MEAD
ROAD
CHURCH
HILL
Guildhall
THE PIGHTLE
VICARAGE
Sch.
KEMPE RD
Moat
Highbank
TOPPESFIELD ROAD
Justice's Hill
Tom's Grove
TOM'S
WINSEY CHASE
STEPHEN MARSHALL AV.
WINSEY
THE HOPGROUNDS
Great Biggins Farm
Gatward's Farm
B1053
WETHERSFIELD RD.
Sports Ground
Hall
WINCEY CLOSE
B1057
Brook
MILL ROAD
Moat
Little Winsey
BARDFIELD RD.
Penmon
Finchingfield
The Mill House
Dynes Cottage
FYFIELD
22
32
6
7
8
9
08
207
Nor Wood
Norwood End
NORWOOD
PERRYFIELD
Rose Cottages
LANE
ROAD
B184
Green's Farm
Rose Bank
Diggins Farm
Diggins Cottages
GREEN
Pickerells
Malting Farm
Tannerwhites
Works
Three Acre Farm
Nockholds Farm
Piggery
Gang Bridge
Ongar
CM5
BIRDS
Clarks Farm
River Roding
Roding Vale Nurseries
Stables and Kennels
Alders Farm
ROAD
END
Lampetts
Poultry Farm
DUNMOW
Radar House
MORETON
FYFIELD
ROAD
Fyfield Hall
The Parsonage House
White Chicks Farm
Rectory
Pennyfeathers
QUEEN ST.
WALKER AV.
Sch.
WILLINGALE
CANNONS LANE
ROAD
B184
Sports Field
Pav.
Mill Lodge
The Mill House
Mill
Witney Green
Dunstans Farm
Clatterford End
Sports Ground
ONGAR
67
556
68
57
32
58

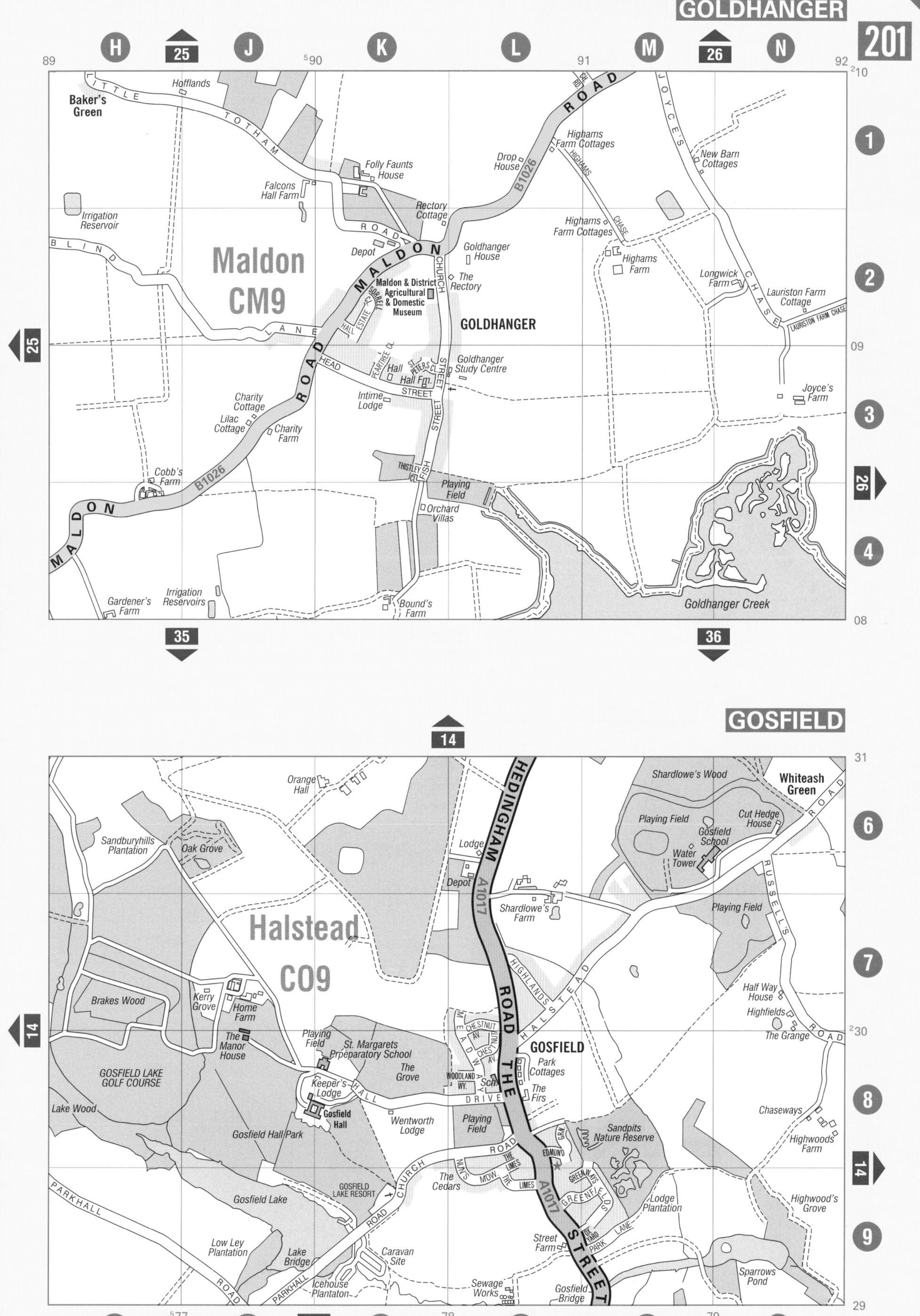
H
25
J
K
L
M
26
N
89
590
91
92
210
Baker's Green
Hofflands
LITTLE TOTHAM ROAD
Folly Faunts House
Falcons Hall Farm
Irrigation Reservoir
BLIND LANE
Maldon CM9
Depot
Rectory Cottage
Drop House
Highams Farm Cottages
HIGHAMS CHASE
New Barn Cottages
JOYCE'S CHASE
Goldhanger House
The Rectory
Highams Farm
Longwick Farm
Lauriston Farm Cottage
LAURISTON FARM CHASE
Maldon & District Agricultural & Domestic Museum
GOLDHANGER
SORREL CL
HALL ESTATE
MALDON ROAD
B1026
CHURCH STREET
HEAD STREET
PEARTREE CL
ST. PETERS CL
Hall
Hall Fm.
Goldhanger Study Centre
Intime Lodge
Charity Cottage
Lilac Cottage
Charity Farm
Joyce's Farm
09
THISTLEY CL
FISH STREET
Playing Field
Cobb's Farm
Orchard Villas
Gardener's Farm
Irrigation Reservoirs
Bound's Farm
Goldhanger Creek
08
35
36
1
2
3
4
GOSFIELD
14
31
Orange Hall
Shardlowe's Wood
Whiteash Green
Sandburyhills Plantation
Oak Grove
Playing Field
Cut Hedge House
Gosfield School
Water Tower
Lodge
HEDINGHAM ROAD
A1017
Depot
Shardlowe's Farm
RUSSELLS ROAD
Playing Field
Halstead CO9
HIGHLANDS
HALSTEAD ROAD
Brakes Wood
Kerry Grove
Home Farm
Half Way House
Highfields
The Grange
230
The Manor House
Playing Field
St. Margarets Prpeparatory School
CHESTNUT AV.
MEADWAY
GOSFIELD
Park Cottages
GOSFIELD LAKE GOLF COURSE
The Grove
WOODLAND WY.
Sch
The Firs
Keeper's Lodge
HALL DRIVE
Lake Wood
Gosfield Hall
Wentworth Lodge
Playing Field
Sandpits Nature Reserve
Chaseways
Gosfield Hall Park
EDMUND
Highwoods Farm
PARKHALL ROAD
CHURCH ROAD
NUNS MDW.
THE LIMES
The Cedars
GREENWAYS
GREENFIELDS
GOSFIELD LAKE RESORT
Gosfield Lake
Lodge Plantation
Highwood's Grove
Low Ley Plantation
Lake Bridge
Caravan Site
Street Farm
PARK LANE
THE STREET
Sparrows Pond
Icehouse Plantation
Sewage Works
Gosfield Bridge
29
577
78
79
6
7
8
9

GREAT BARDFIELD

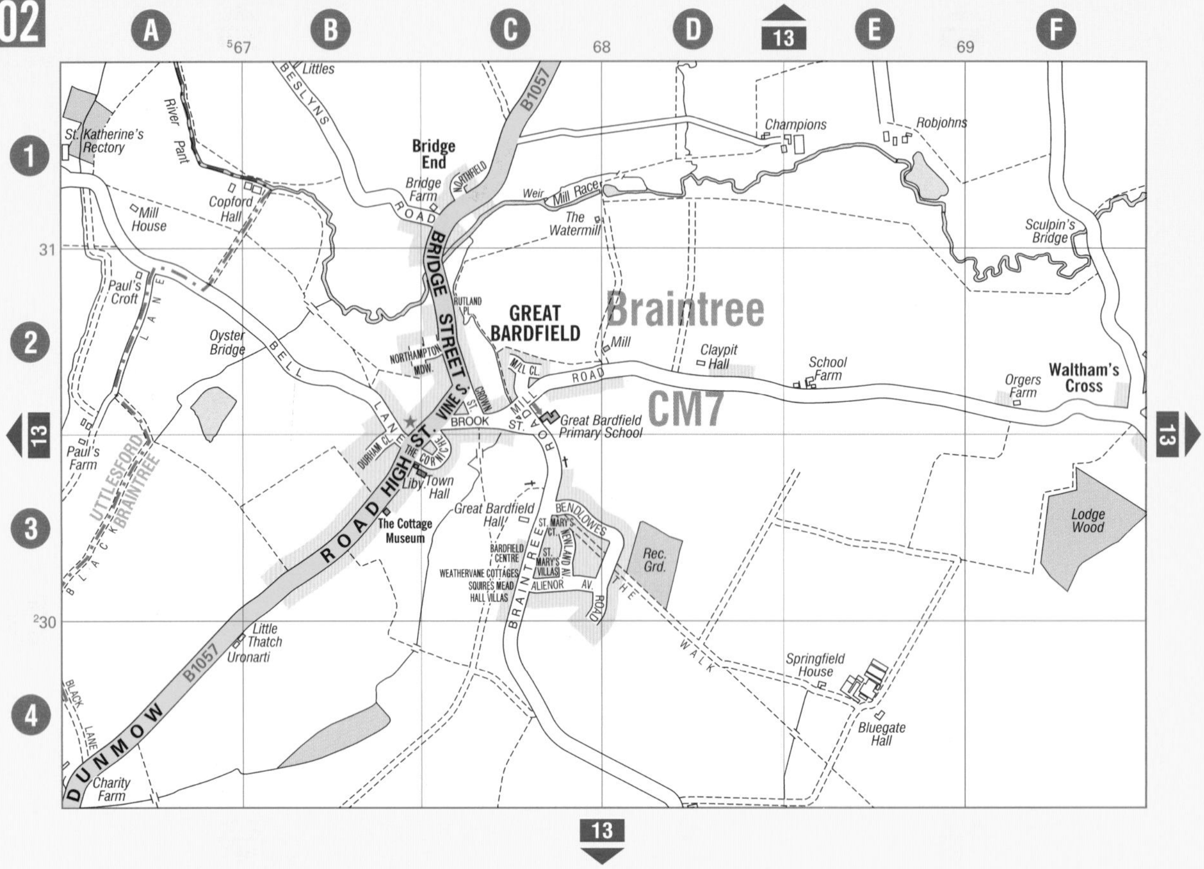

GREAT CHESTERFORD

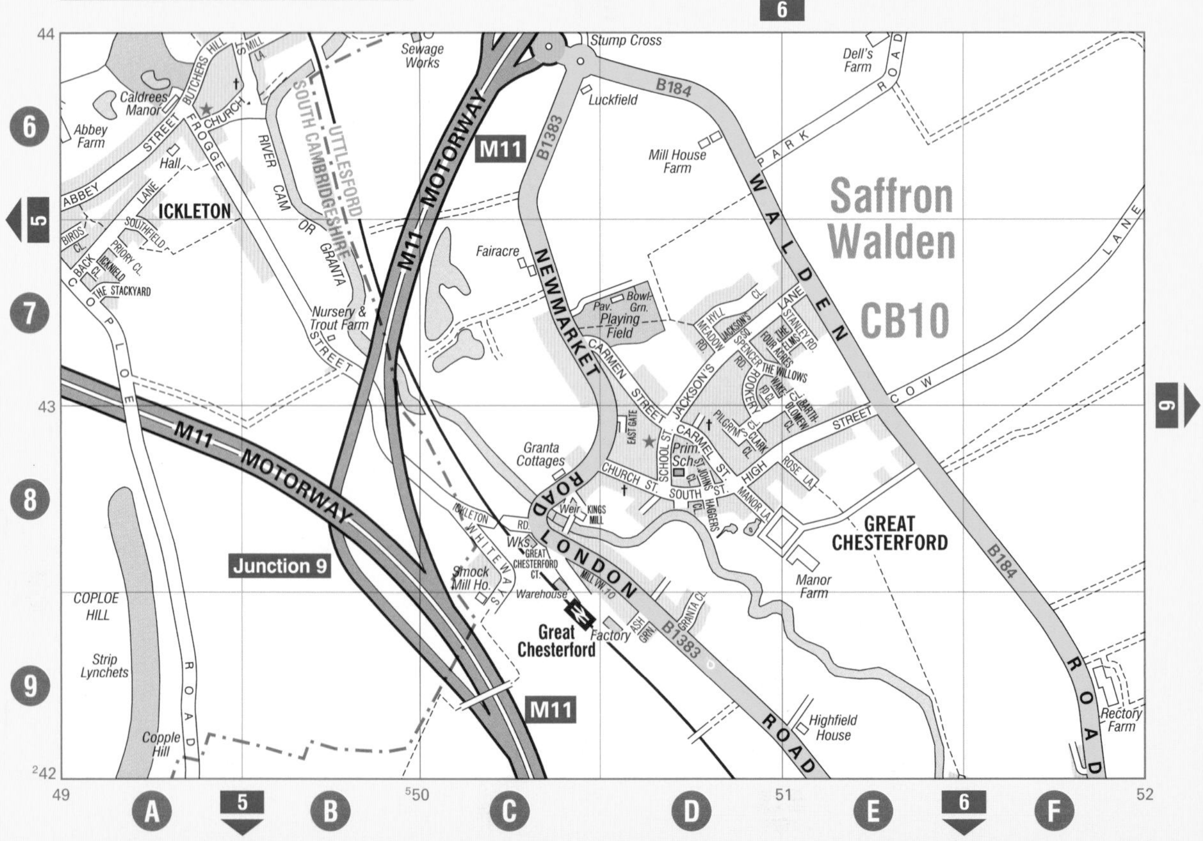

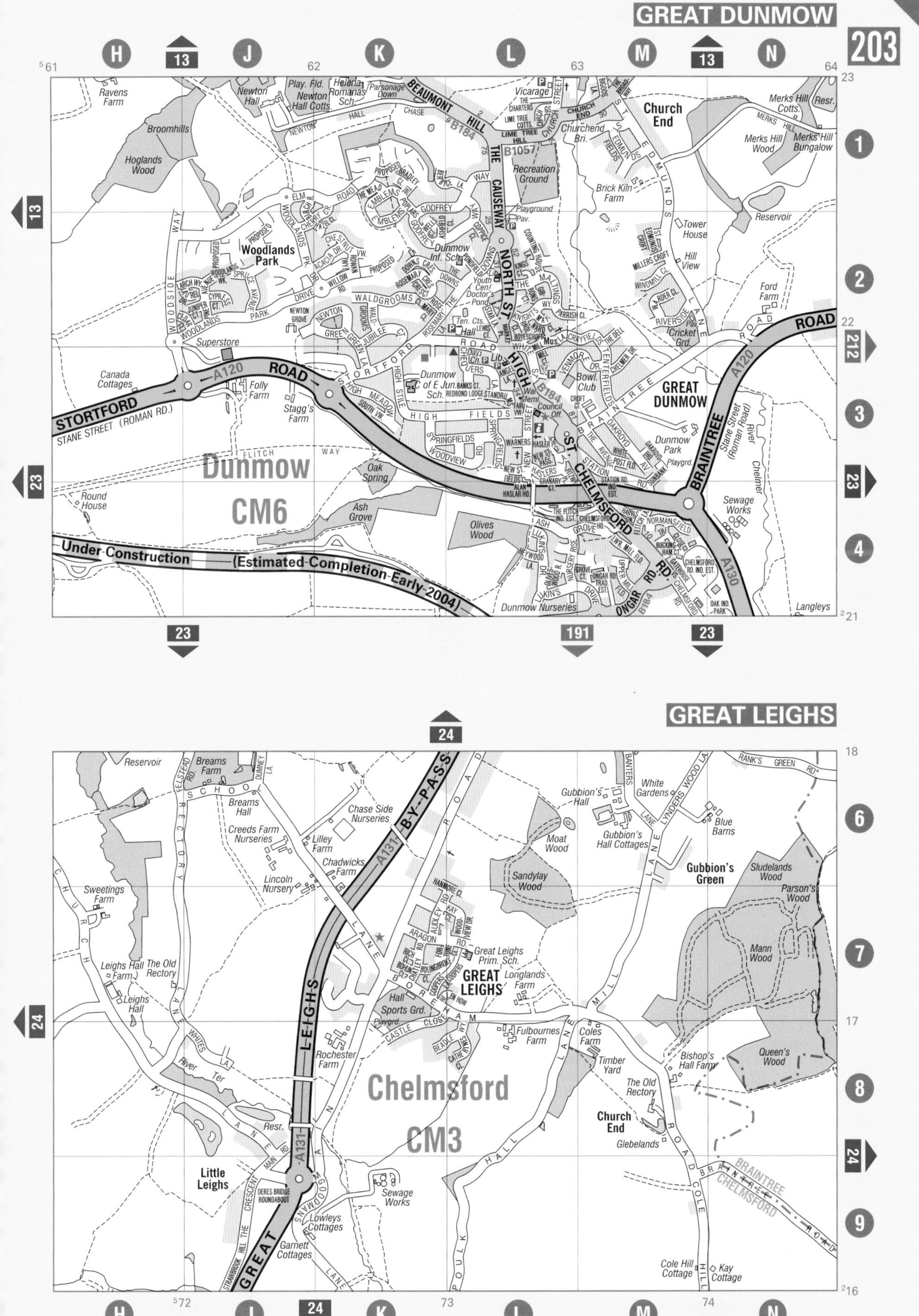
GREAT DUNMOW
Ravens Farm
Newton Hall
Play. Fld.
Newton Hall Cotts.
Helena Romanas Sch.
Parsonage Down
BEAUMONT HILL
Vicarage
Church End
Merks Hill Cotts.
Merks Hill Wood
Merks' Hill Bungalow
Broomhills
Hoglands Wood
Recreation Ground
Brick Kiln Farm
Reservoir
Tower House
Hill View
Woodlands Park
Dunmow Inf. Sch.
Youth Cen/ Doctor's Pond
Ford Farm
THE CAUSEWAY
NORTH ST.
HIGH ST.
Superstore
Canada Cottages
Folly Farm
Stagg's Farm
STORTFORD ROAD
STANE STREET (ROMAN RD.)
Dunmow C of E Jun. Sch.
Council Off.
GREAT DUNMOW
Bowl. Club
Cricket Grd.
BRAINTREE ROAD
Dunmow Park
Stane Street (Roman Road)
River Chelmer
Dunmow
CM6
Round House
Oak Spring
Ash Grove
Olives Wood
Sewage Works
Under Construction (Estimated Completion Early 2004)
Dunmow Nurseries
ONGAR RD.
Langleys
GREAT LEIGHS
Reservoir
Breams Farm
Breams Hall
Creeds Farm Nurseries
Chase Side Nurseries
Lilley Farm
Chadwicks Farm
Lincoln Nursery
Sweetings Farm
LEIGHS BY-PASS
Gubbion's Hall
White Gardens
Blue Barns
Moat Wood
Gubbion's Hall Cottages
Sandylay Wood
Gubbion's Green
Sludelands Wood
Parson's Wood
Mann Wood
Great Leighs Prim. Sch.
GREAT LEIGHS
Longlands Farm
Leighs Hall Farm
The Old Rectory
Leighs Hall
Hall Sports Grd.
Fulbournes Farm
Coles Farm
Timber Yard
Bishop's Hall Farm
Queen's Wood
Rochester Farm
River Ter
Chelmsford
CM3
The Old Rectory
Church End
Glebelands
Resr.
Little Leighs
DERES BRIDGE ROUNDABOUT
Sewage Works
Lowleys Cottages
Garnett Cottages
BRAINTREE CHELMSFORD
Cole Hill Cottage
Kay Cottage

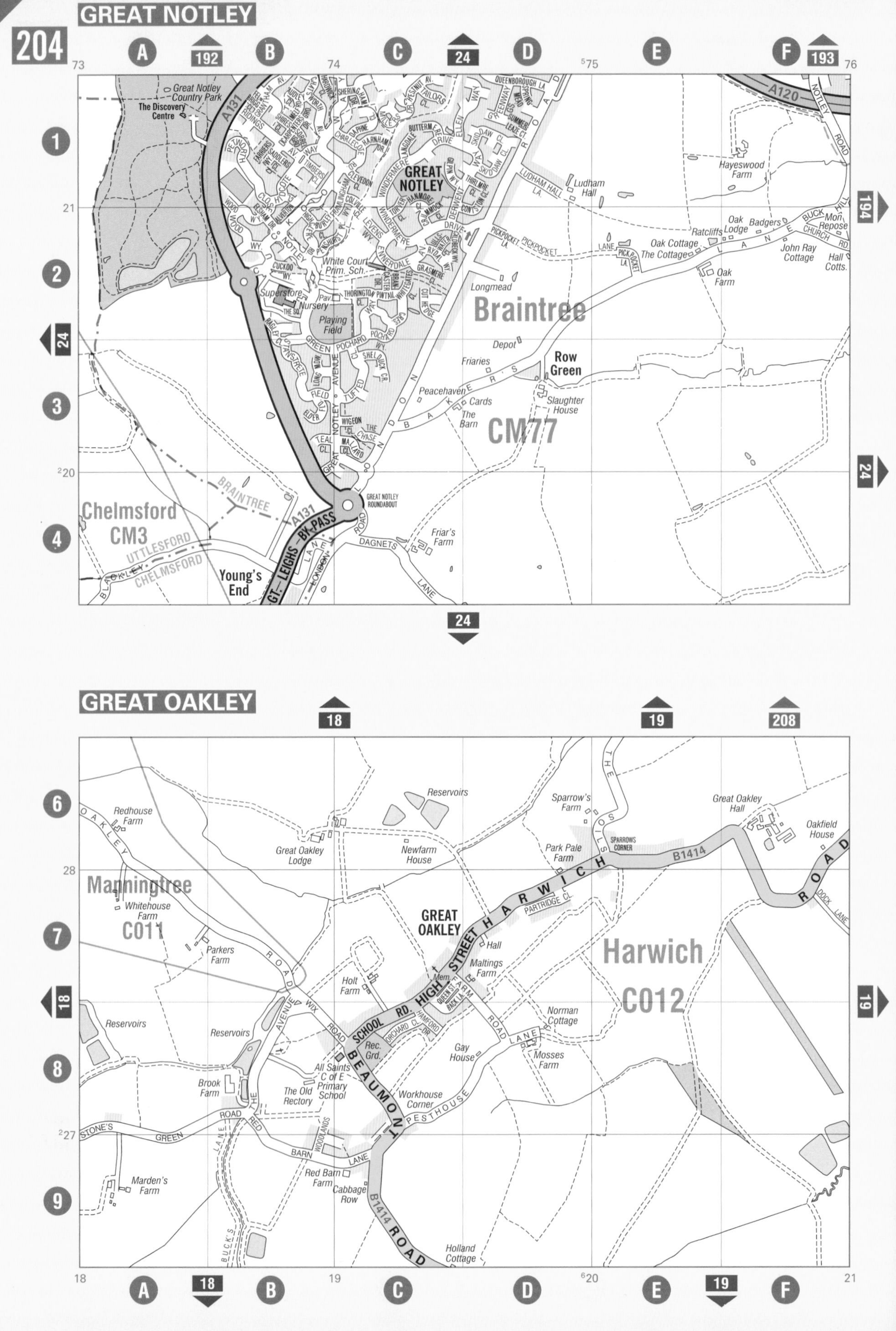
GREAT NOTLEY
204
A
B
C
D
E
F
192
24
193
194
Great Notley Country Park
The Discovery Centre
A131
A120
GREAT NOTLEY
Braintree
CM77
Superstore
Nursery
White Court Prim. Sch.
Playing Field
Longmead
Depot
Friaries
Row Green
Peacehaven
Cards
The Barn
Slaughter House
Ludham Hall
Hayeswood Farm
Oak Lodge
Badgers
Mon Repose
Ratcliffs
Oak Cottage
The Cottage
John Ray Cottage
Hall Cotts.
Oak Farm
Friar's Farm
GREAT NOTLEY ROUNDABOUT
Chelmsford CM3
BRAINTREE
UTTLESFORD
CHELMSFORD
Young's End
GT. LEIGHS BY-PASS
BLACKLEY
DAGNETS LANE
GREAT OAKLEY
18
19
208
Reservoirs
Redhouse Farm
Great Oakley Lodge
Newfarm House
Sparrow's Farm
Great Oakley Hall
Oakfield House
Park Pale Farm
SPARROWS CORNER
B1414
HARWICH ROAD
Manningtree CO11
Whitehouse Farm
Parkers Farm
GREAT OAKLEY
Hall
Maltings Farm
Harwich CO12
Holt Farm
Mem.
SCHOOL RD.
HIGH STREET
Norman Cottage
Rec. Grd.
All Saints C of E Primary School
Gay House
Mosses Farm
Brook Farm
The Old Rectory
Workhouse Corner
BEAUMONT ROAD
PESTHOUSE LANE
STONE'S GREEN ROAD
RED BARN LANE
Red Barn Farm
Cabbage Row
Marden's Farm
Holland Cottage
BUCK'S LANE

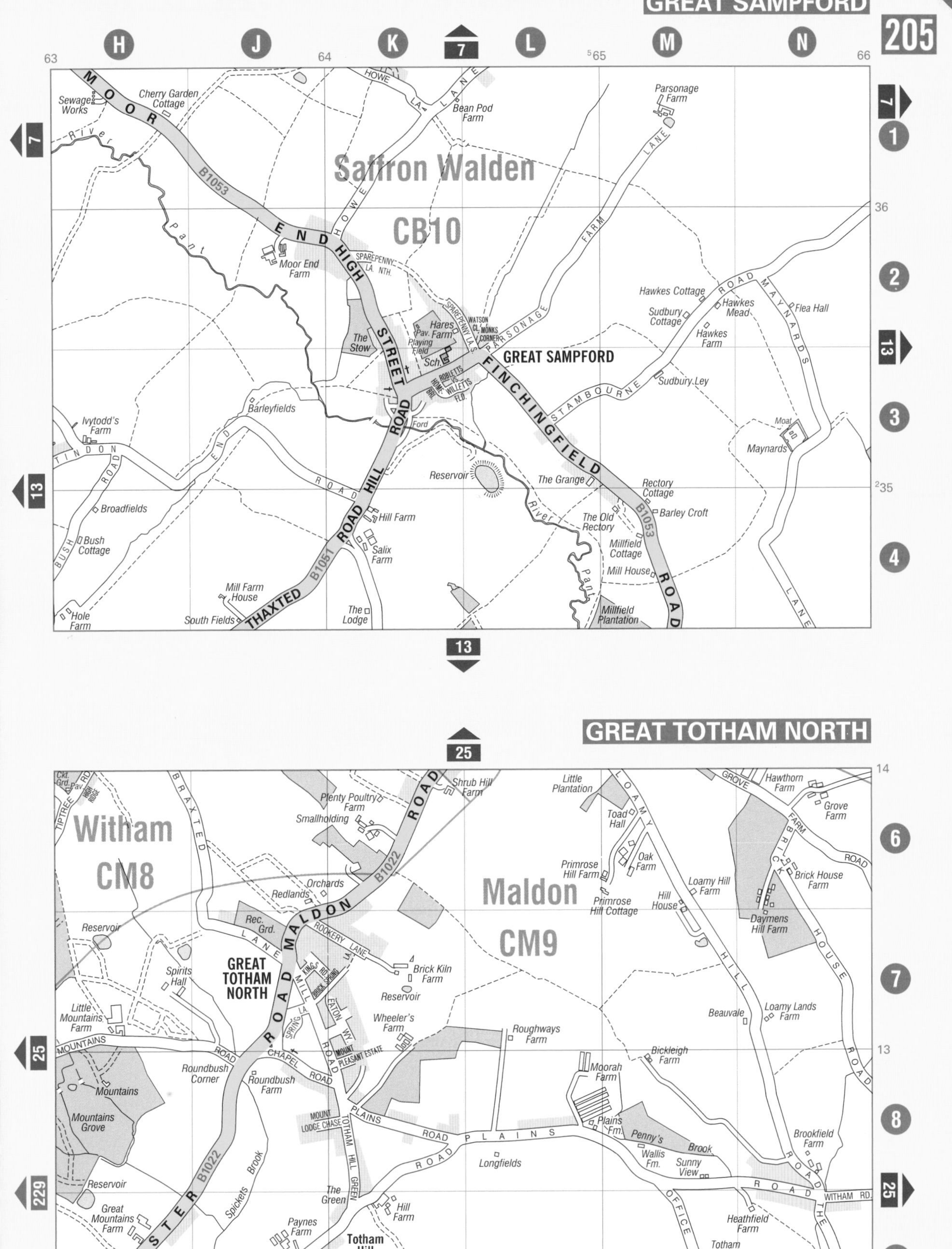

H J K L M N
7 13 25 229
1 2 3 4 6 7 8 9

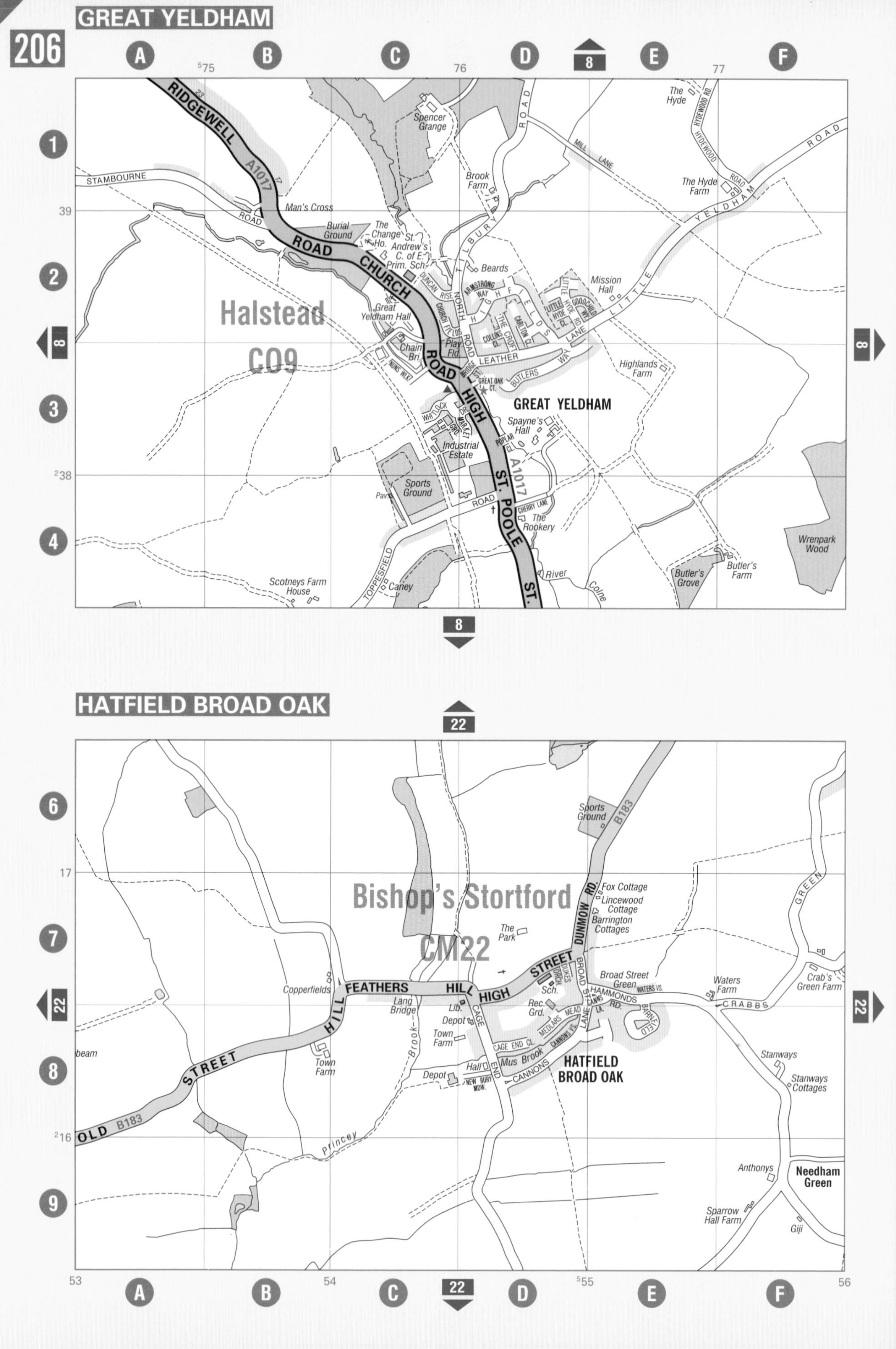
GREAT YELDHAM
Halstead
CO9
GREAT YELDHAM
RIDGEWELL
A1017
ROAD
CHURCH
HIGH
ST. POOLE ST.
STAMBOURNE ROAD
Man's Cross
Burial Ground
The Change Ho.
St. Andrew's C. of E. Prim. Sch.
Great Yeldham Hall
Chain Bri.
Play Fld.
Spencer Grange
Brook Farm
TILBURY ROAD
Beards
MILL LANE
The Hyde
HYDEWOOD RD.
HYDEWOOD ROAD
The Hyde Farm
LITTLE YELDHAM ROAD
Mission Hall
LEATHER LANE
Highlands Farm
BUTLERS WAY
Spayne's Hall
Industrial Estate
Sports Ground
Pavn.
CHERRY LANE
The Rookery
River Colne
Butler's Grove
Butler's Farm
Wrenpark Wood
Scotneys Farm House
TOPPESFIELD ROAD
Caney
HATFIELD BROAD OAK
Bishop's Stortford
CM22
HATFIELD BROAD OAK
Sports Ground
B183
DUNMOW RD.
Fox Cottage
Lincewood Cottage
Barrington Cottages
The Park
HIGH STREET
FEATHERS HILL
HILL
Copperfields
Lang Bridge
Lib.
Depot
Town Farm
Sch.
Rec. Grd.
Broad Street Green
HAMMONDS RD.
WATERS VS.
Waters Farm
CRABBS GREEN
Crab's Green Farm
BARNFIELD
CAGE END
CAGE END CL.
MEDLARS MEAD
CANNONS LANE
Mus Brook
Hall
Depot
NEW BURY MDW.
Town Farm
STREET
OLD B183
Princey Brook
Stanways
Stanways Cottages
Anthonys
Needham Green
Sparrow Hall Farm
Giji
beam

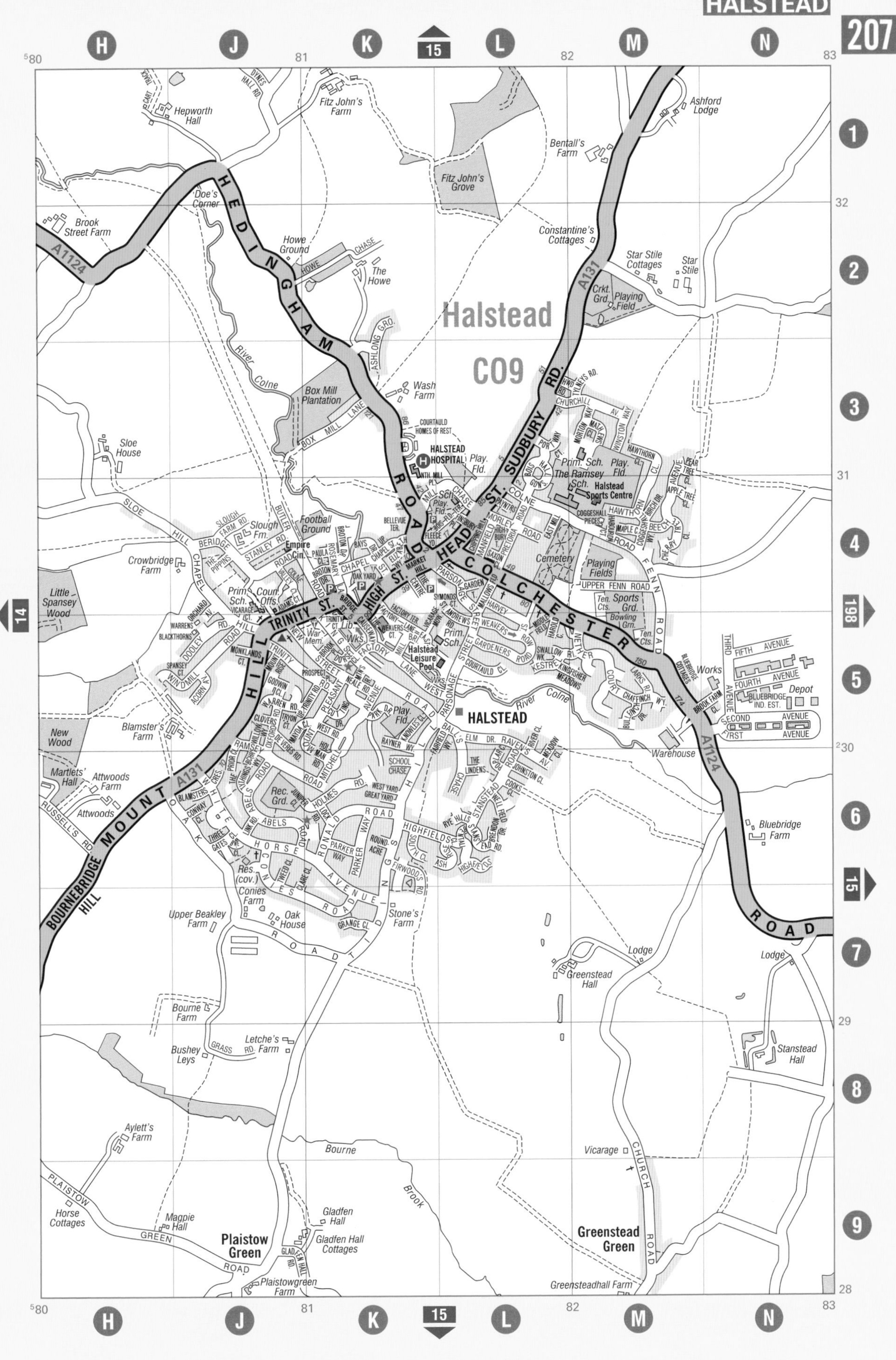
Halstead
CO9
HALSTEAD
HEDINGHAM ROAD
SUDBURY RD.
COLCHESTER ROAD
HEAD ST.
HIGH ST.
TRINITY ST.
MOUNT HILL
BOURNEBRIDGE HILL
A1124
A131
Hepworth Hall
Fitz John's Farm
Fitz John's Grove
Ashford Lodge
Bentall's Farm
Brook Street Farm
Doe's Corner
Howe Ground
The Howe
Constantine's Cottages
Star Stile Cottages
Star Stile
Playing Field
River Colne
Box Mill Plantation
Wash Farm
Sloe House
HALSTEAD HOSPITAL
Halstead Sports Centre
Slough Fm.
Football Ground
Crowbridge Farm
Little Spansey Wood
Cemetery
Playing Fields
Halstead Leisure Pool
Works
Depot
BLUEBRIDGE IND. EST.
Warehouse
New Wood
Blamster's Farm
Martlets' Hall
Attwoods Farm
Attwoods
Bluebridge Farm
Conies Farm
Upper Beakley Farm
Oak House
Stone's Farm
Lodge
Greenstead Hall
Bourne Farm
Letche's Farm
Bushey Leys
Stanstead Hall
Aylett's Farm
Bourne Brook
Vicarage
CHURCH ROAD
Horse Cottages
Magpie Hall
Gladfen Hall
Gladfen Hall Cottages
Plaistow Green
Greenstead Green
Plaistowgreen Farm
Greensteadhall Farm
H J K L M N
1 2 3 4 5 6 7 8 9
14
15
198

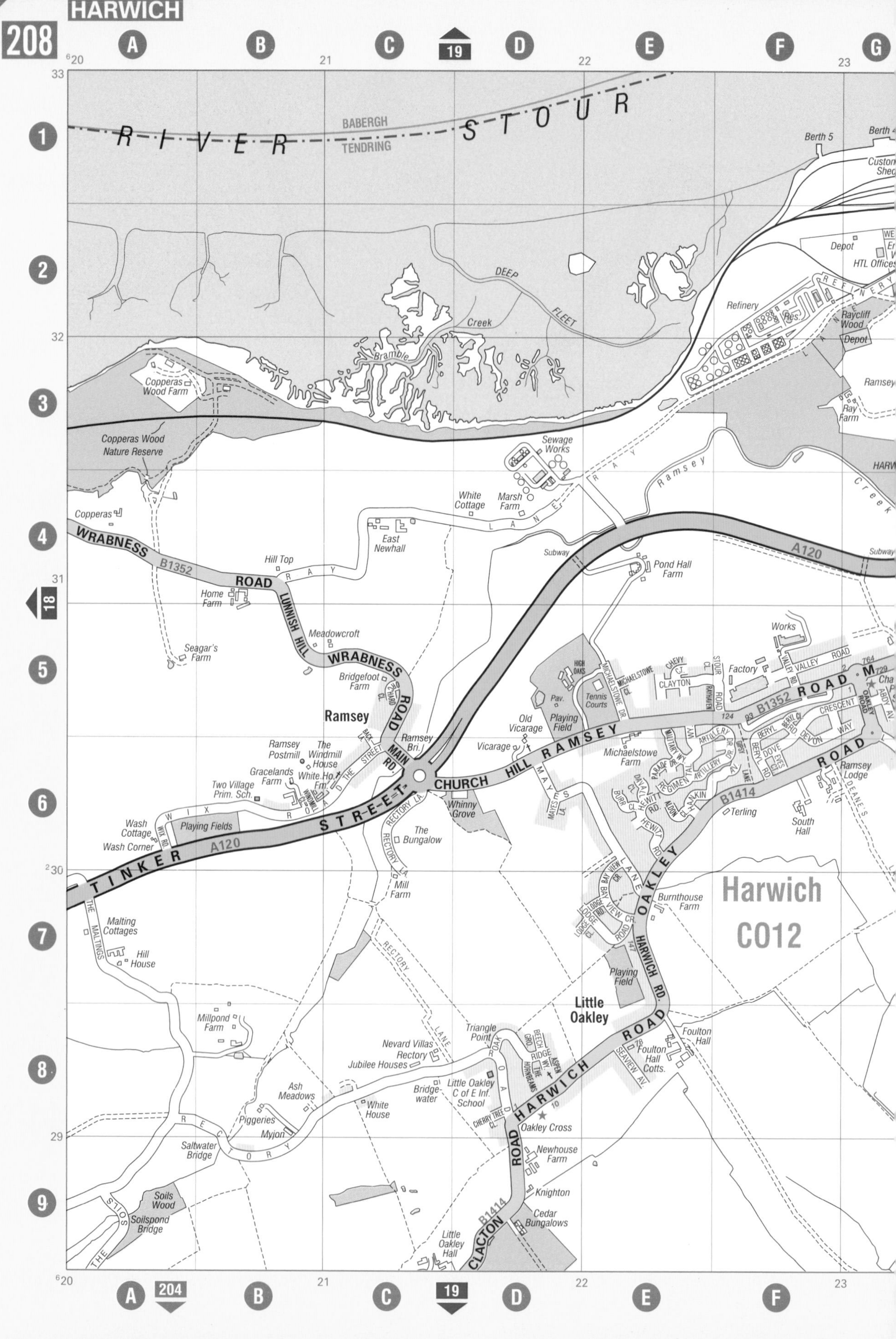
A
B
C
D
E
F
G
19
18
204
RIVER STOUR
BABERGH
TENDRING
Berth 5
Berth 4
Depot
HTL Offices
DEEP FLEET
Creek
Bramble
Refinery
Res.
REFINERY LANE
Raycliff Wood
Depot
Ramsey
Ray Farm
Ramsey Creek
Copperas Wood Farm
Copperas Wood Nature Reserve
Sewage Works
RAY LANE
White Cottage
Marsh Farm
Copperas
WRABNESS B1352 ROAD
East Newhall
Subway
A120
Pond Hall Farm
Hill Top
RAY
Home Farm
LUNNISH HILL
Meadowcroft
Seagar's Farm
WRABNESS ROAD
Bridgefoot Farm
Works
VALLEY ROAD
Factory
CLAYTON
Tennis Courts
Pav.
Playing Field
B1352 ROAD
CRESCENT
Ramsey
Old Vicarage
Vicarage
RAMSEY
Ramsey Postmill
The Windmill House
Gracelands Farm
White Ho. Fm.
THE STREET
MAIN RD.
Ramsey Bri.
CHURCH HILL
Michaelstowe Farm
Two Village Prim. Sch.
WIX ROAD
Whinny Grove
Ramsey Lodge
Wash Cottage
Wash Corner
Playing Fields
STREET
A120
RECTORY LA.
The Bungalow
B1414
Terling
South Hall
TINKER
Mill Farm
OAKLEY
Burnthouse Farm
Harwich CO12
THE MALTINGS
Malting Cottages
Hill House
RECTORY LANE
HARWICH RD.
Playing Field
Little Oakley
Millpond Farm
Triangle Point
Foulton Hall
Nevard Villas
Rectory
Jubilee Houses
HARWICH ROAD
Foulton Hall Cotts.
Ash Meadows
Bridge-water
Little Oakley C of E Inf. School
White House
Oakley Cross
Piggeries
Myjon
RECTORY
Saltwater Bridge
Newhouse Farm
Soils Wood
Soilspond Bridge
Knighton
Cedar Bungalows
CLACTON ROAD
Little Oakley Hall
20
21
22
23
29
30
31
32
33
1
2
3
4
5
6
7
8
9

Harwich to :
Esbjerg 17hrs.
Hamburg 18hrs. 30mins.
Hook of Holland (Fast Ferry) 3hrs. 40mins.
Hook of Holland 6hrs. 15mins.
HARWICH HARBOUR
Harwich International
Parkeston
DOVERCOURT
Dovercourt
HARWICH
Harwich Town
DOVERCOURT BAY
Upper Dovercourt
NORTH SEA
Middle Beach
South Hall Creek
LONG BANK

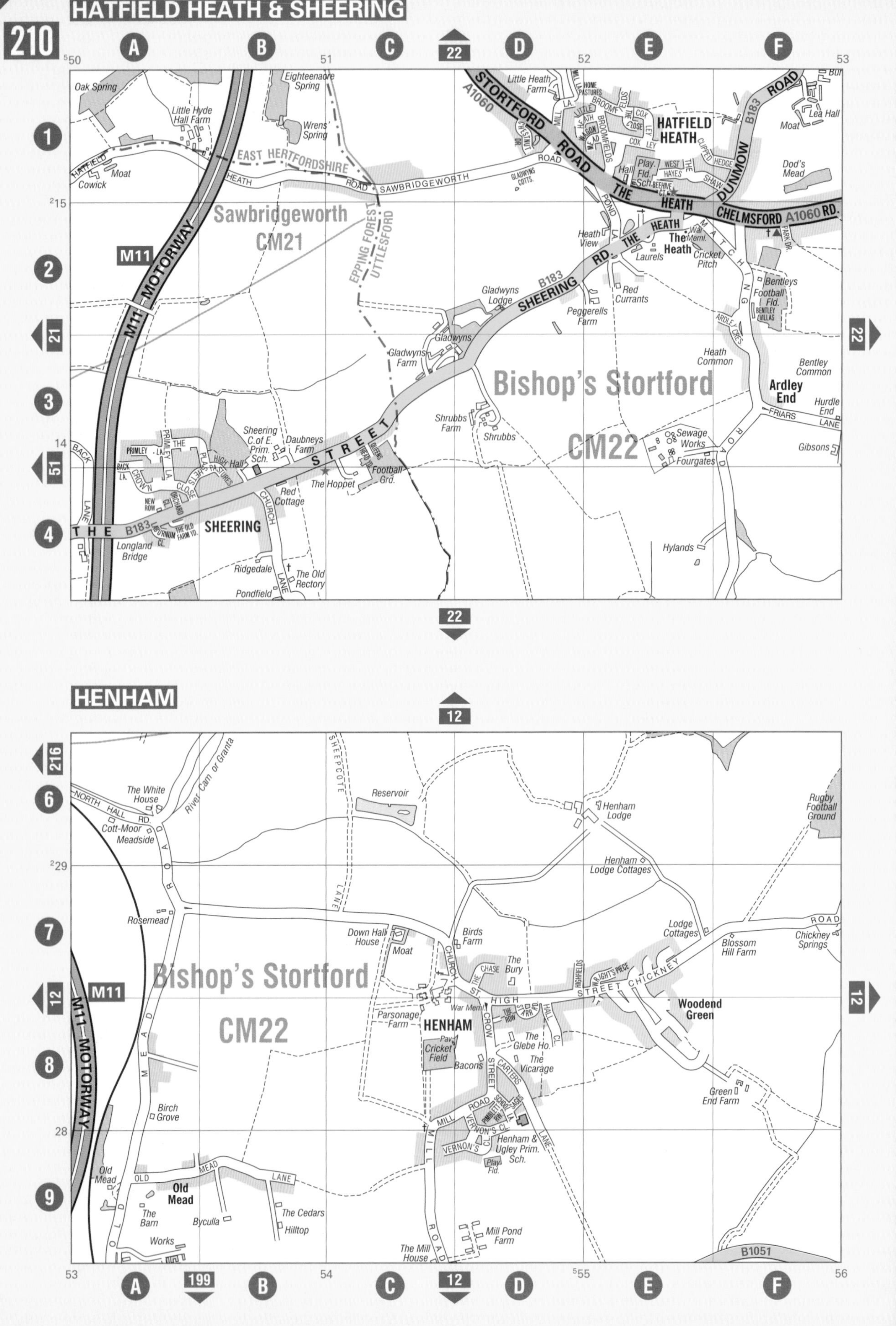

210
HATFIELD HEATH & SHEERING
Oak Spring
Eighteenacre Spring
Little Hyde Hall Farm
Wrens' Spring
Little Heath Farm
HATFIELD HEATH
Lea Hall
Moat
Cowick
EAST HERTFORDSHIRE
SAWBRIDGEWORTH ROAD
STORTFORD ROAD
A1060
THE HEATH
CHELMSFORD RD.
DUNMOW ROAD
B183
Dod's Mead
Sawbridgeworth
CM21
EPPING FOREST
UTTLESFORD
M11
M11 MOTORWAY
Heath View
The Heath
Laurels
War Meml.
Cricket Pitch
Red Currants
Peggerells Farm
Gladwyns Lodge
Gladwyns
Gladwyns Farm
SHEERING RD.
Bentleys Football Fld.
Heath Common
Bentley Common
Bishop's Stortford
Ardley End
Hurdle End
FRIARS LANE
Shrubbs Farm
Shrubbs
CM22
Sewage Works
Fourgates
Gibsons
Sheering C.of E. Prim. Sch.
Daubneys Farm
STREET
The Hoppet
Football Grd.
Red Cottage
SHEERING
CHURCH LANE
Longland Bridge
Ridgedale
The Old Rectory
Pondfield
Hylands
THE B183
HENHAM
The White House
NORTH HALL RD.
Cott-Moor
Meadside
River Cam or Granta
Reservoir
Henham Lodge
Henham Lodge Cottages
Rugby Football Ground
Rosemead
Down Hall House
Moat
Birds Farm
The Bury
Lodge Cottages
Blossom Hill Farm
Chickney Springs
Bishop's Stortford
CM22
M11
M11 MOTORWAY
Parsonage Farm
HENHAM
Cricket Field
Bacons
The Glebe Ho.
The Vicarage
Woodend Green
Green End Farm
Birch Grove
Henham & Ugley Prim. Sch.
Old Mead
OLD MEAD LANE
The Cedars
Hilltop
The Barn
Byculla
Works
Mill Pond Farm
The Mill House
B1051

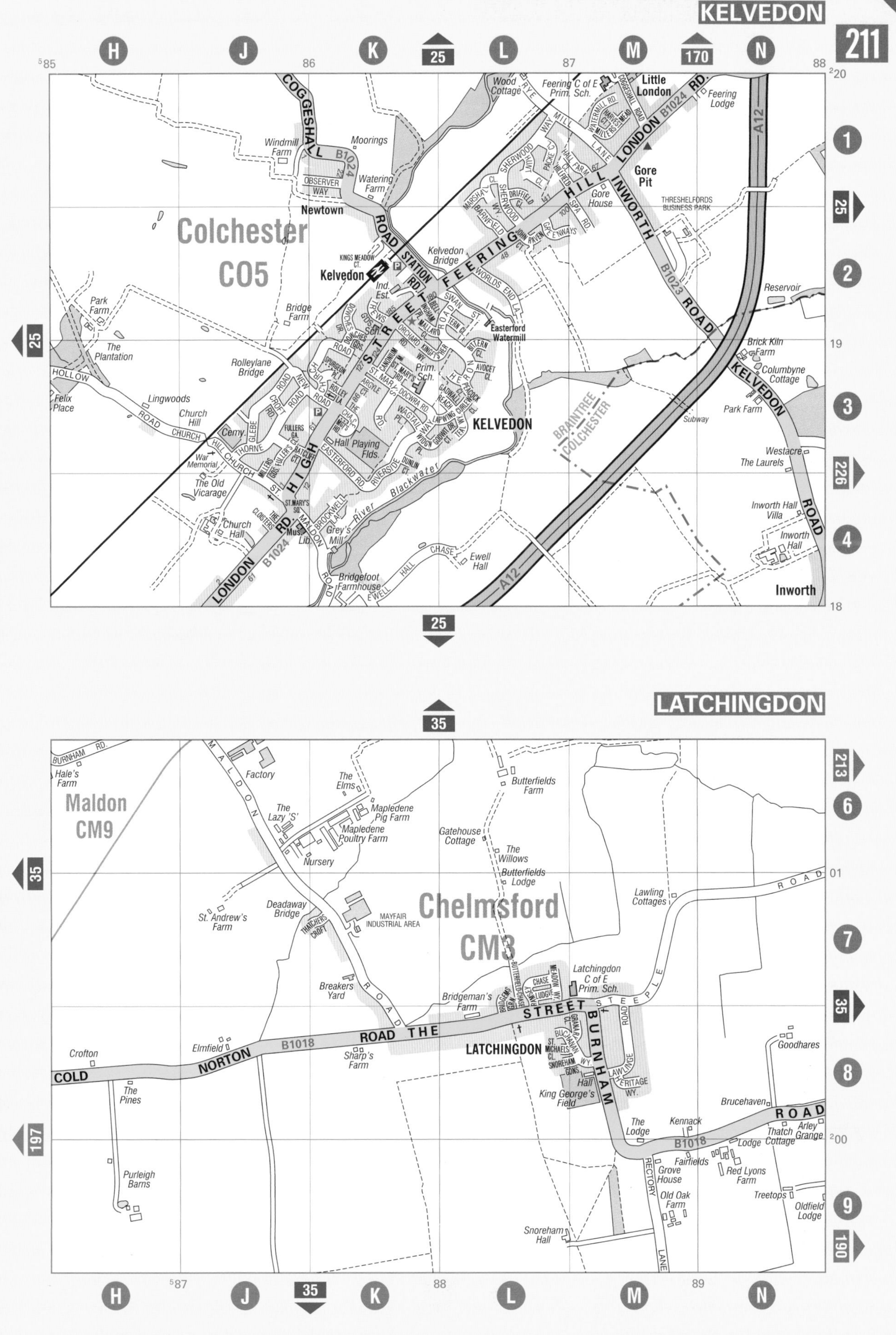
KELVEDON
Colchester
CO5
Kelvedon
Feering C of E Prim. Sch.
Little London
Gore Pit
Gore House
THRESHELFORDS BUSINESS PARK
Newtown
Windmill Farm
Moorings
Watering Farm
Kelvedon Bridge
Park Farm
The Plantation
Rolleylane Bridge
Bridge Farm
Lingwoods
Church Hill
Felix Place
Easterford Watermill
Reservoir
Brick Kiln Farm
Columbyne Cottage
Park Farm
Westacre
The Laurels
Inworth Hall Villa
Inworth Hall
Inworth
Ewell Hall
Bridgefoot Farmhouse
Grey's Mill
The Old Vicarage
War Memorial
Church Hall
Playing Flds.
BRAINTREE
COLCHESTER
LATCHINGDON
Maldon
CM9
Chelmsford
CM3
Hale's Farm
Factory
The Elms
Butterfields Farm
The Lazy 'S'
Mapledene Pig Farm
Mapledene Poultry Farm
Nursery
Gatehouse Cottage
The Willows
Butterfields Lodge
St. Andrew's Farm
Deadaway Bridge
MAYFAIR INDUSTRIAL AREA
Lawling Cottages
Latchingdon C of E Prim. Sch.
Breakers Yard
Bridgeman's Farm
Crofton
Elmfield
Sharp's Farm
LATCHINGDON
Goodhares
The Pines
King George's Field
Brucehaven
The Lodge
Kennack
Arley Grange
Thatch Cottage
Lodge
Grove House
Fairfields
Red Lyons Farm
Purleigh Barns
Old Oak Farm
Treetops
Oldfield Lodge
Snoreham Hall
COLD NORTON ROAD
THE STREET
BURNHAM ROAD
STEEPLE ROAD
MALDON ROAD
RECTORY LANE

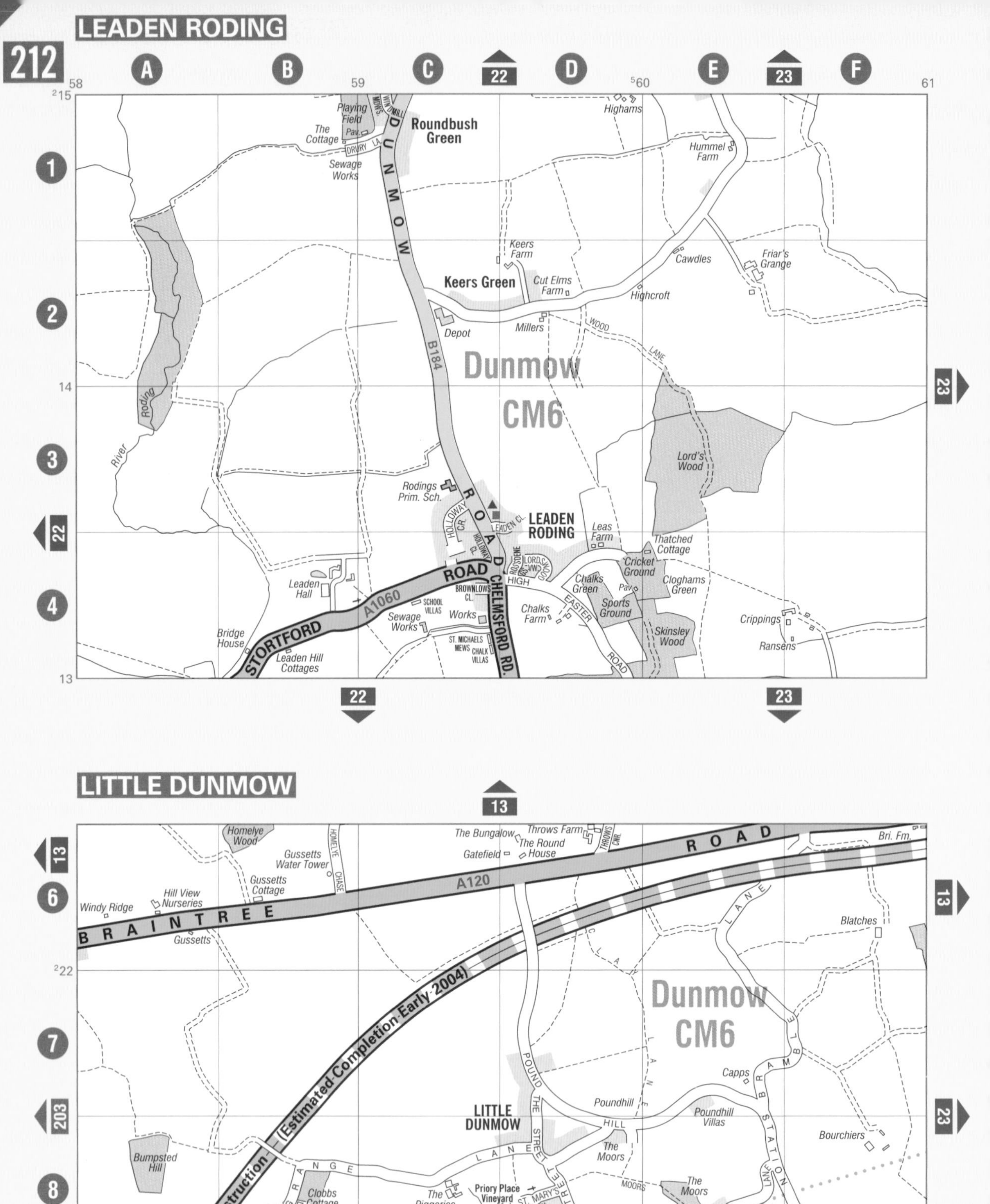
LEADEN RODING
Roundbush Green
Playing Field
The Cottage
Sewage Works
Drury La.
Highams
Hummel Farm
Keers Farm
Cawdles
Friar's Grange
Keers Green
Cut Elms Farm
Highcroft
Depot
Millers
Wood Lane
Dunmow CM6
Dunmow Road
B184
River Roding
Lord's Wood
Rodings Prim. Sch.
Holloway Cr.
Leaden Cl.
LEADEN RODING
Leas Farm
Thatched Cottage
Cricket Ground
Leaden Hall
Stortford Road
A1060
High
Chalks Green
Pav.
Cloghams Green
Easter Road
Sports Ground
Chalks Farm
Sewage Works
Works
School Villas
Brownlows Cl.
Chelmsford Rd.
Skinsley Wood
Crippings
Ransens
Bridge House
Leaden Hill Cottages
St. Michaels Mews
Chalk Villas
LITTLE DUNMOW
Homelye Wood
Gussetts Water Tower
The Bungalow
Throws Farm
The Round House
Gatefield
Bri. Fm.
Road
A120
Braintree
Gussetts Cottage
Hill View Nurseries
Windy Ridge
Gussetts
Blatches
Clay Lane
Dunmow CM6
(Estimated Completion Early 2004)
Under Construction
Pound the Street
Capps
Bramble
Poundhill
Little Dunmow
Hill
Poundhill Villas
Station
Bourchiers
Bumpsted Hill
Grange Lane
The Moors
Clobbs Cottage
The Piggeries
Priory Place Vineyard
St. Mary's Pl.
Street
Moors
Gypsy Lane
Fitzwalter Road
Mildmay Cl.
Avenue
Bayleys
Baynard
Clobb's Wood
Brook
Priory Bridge
Sewage Works
Brick House
River Chelmer

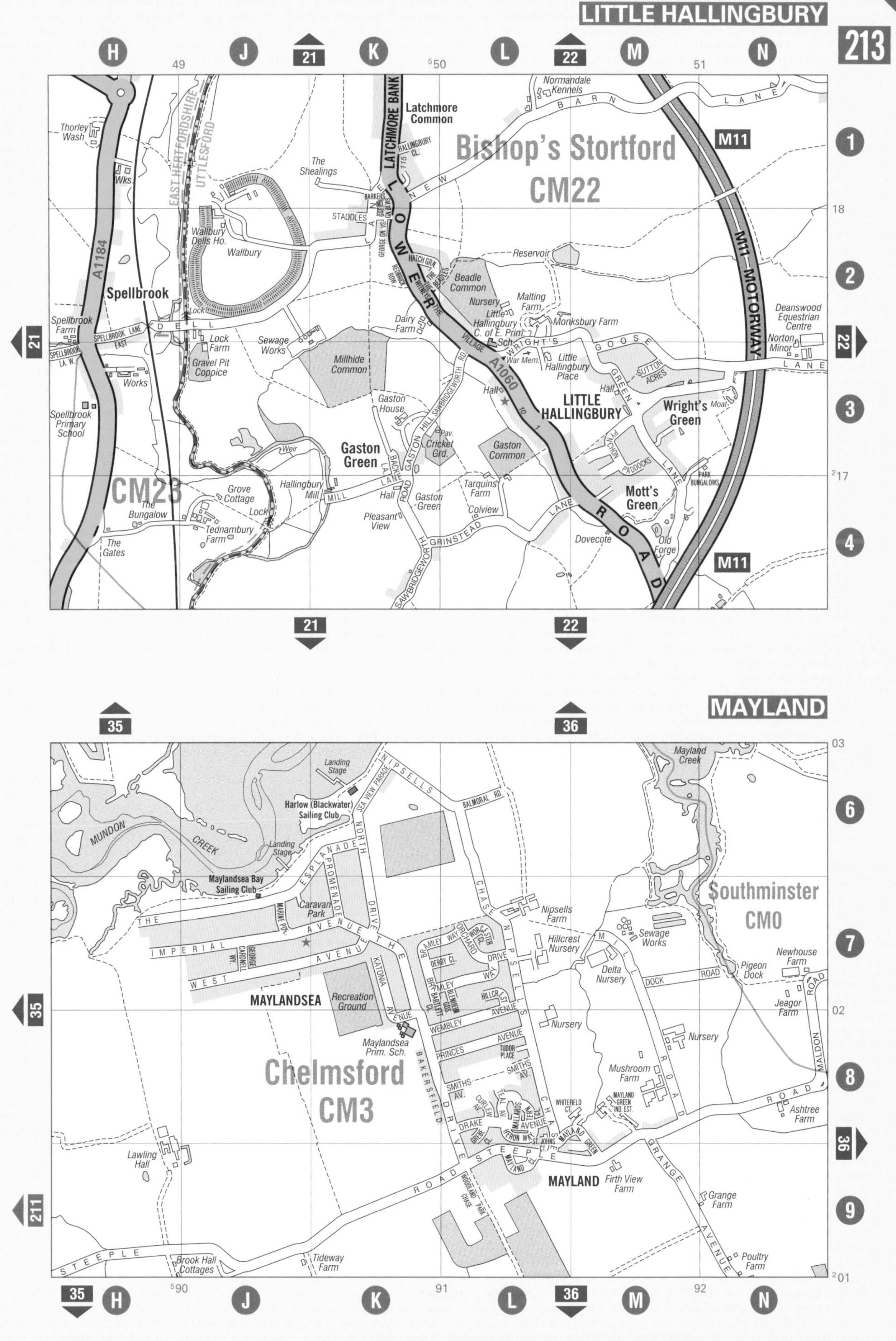
LITTLE HALLINGBURY
Bishop's Stortford CM22
Latchmore Common
Normandale Kennels
Thorley Wash
Wks.
The Shealings
Staddles
Wallbury Dells Ho.
Wallbury
Reservoir
Spellbrook
Beadle Common
Nursery
Malting Farm
Monksbury Farm
Little Hallingbury C. of E. Prim. Sch.
Spellbrook Farm
Dairy Farm
Sewage Works
Lock Farm
Gravel Pit Coppice
Millhide Common
War Mem.
Little Hallingbury Place
Deanswood Equestrian Centre
Norton Minor
Works
Spellbrook Primary School
Gaston House
Hall
Wright's Green
Moat
Gaston Green
Cricket Grd.
Gaston Common
Weir
Grove Cottage
Hallingbury Mill
Tarquins Farm
Mott's Green
CM23
The Bungalow
Lock
Gaston Green
Colview
Pleasant View
Tednambury Farm
The Gates
Dovecote
Old Forge
M11
M11 MOTORWAY
A1184
A1060
LATCHMORE BANK
LOWER ROAD
BARN LANE
GOOSE LANE
DELL LANE
SPELLBROOK LANE EAST
SPELLBROOK LA. W.
MILL LANE
GRINSTEAD LANE
SAWBRIDGEWORTH RD
GASTON HILL
BACK LANE
WRIGHT'S GREEN
SUTTON ACRES
PARK BUNGALOWS
PADDOCKS
EAST HERTFORDSHIRE
UTTLESFORD
MAYLAND
Mayland Creek
Landing Stage
Harlow (Blackwater) Sailing Club
MUNDON CREEK
Maylandsea Bay Sailing Club
Caravan Park
Southminster CM0
Nipsells Farm
Hillcrest Nursery
Sewage Works
Newhouse Farm
Pigeon Dock
Delta Nursery
Jeagor Farm
MAYLANDSEA
Recreation Ground
Nursery
Maylandsea Prim. Sch.
Mushroom Farm
Chelmsford CM3
Ashtree Farm
Lawling Hall
MAYLAND
Firth View Farm
Grange Farm
Brook Hall Cottages
Tideway Farm
Poultry Farm
THE ESPLANADE
IMPERIAL AVENUE
WEST AVENUE
THE AVENUE
NORTH DRIVE
PROMENADE
SEA VIEW PARADE
NIPSELLS CHASE
BALMORAL RD.
MILL ROAD
DOCK ROAD
MALDON ROAD
GRANGE AVENUE
STEEPLE ROAD
BAKERSFIELD DRIVE
WEMBLEY AVENUE
PRINCES AVENUE
TUDOR PLACE
SMITHS AV.
DRAKE AVENUE
HERON WAY
WHITEFIELD CT.
MAYLAND GREEN
ST. JOHNS CT.
WOODLAND PARK CHASE
KATONIA AVENUE
DERBY CL.
BRAMLEY WAY
ORCHARD DRIVE
WORCESTER CL.
HILLCREST AVENUE
MARINE PDE.
GEORGE WY.
CARDINELL

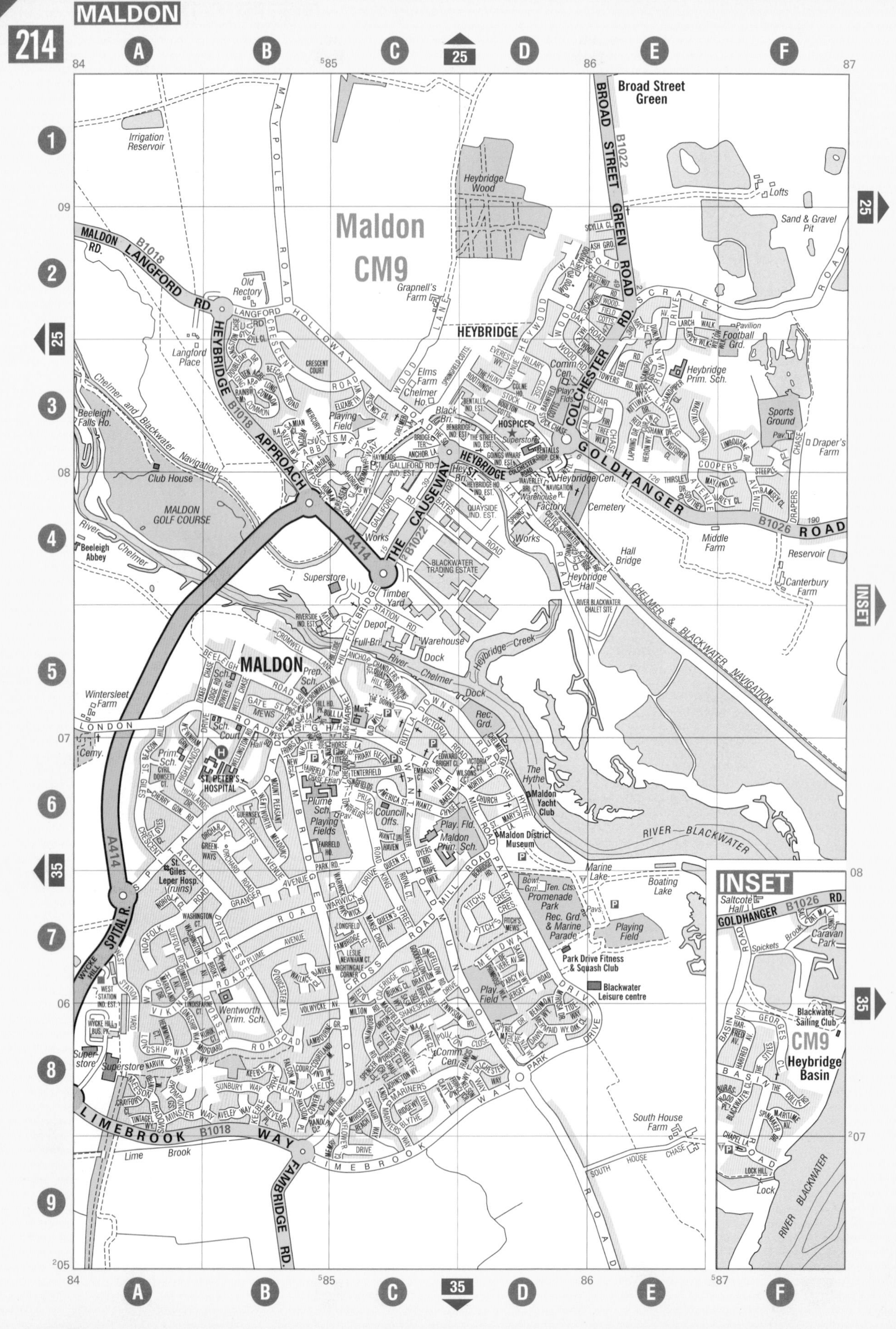
Broad Street Green
Irrigation Reservoir
Heybridge Wood
Maldon CM9
Lofts
Sand & Gravel Pit
MALDON RD.
LANGFORD RD.
B1018
Old Rectory
Grapnell's Farm
HEYBRIDGE
Langford Place
Chelmer and Blackwater Navigation
Beeleigh Falls Ho.
Elms Farm
Chelmer Ho.
Playing Field
HOSPICE
Superstore
Heybridge Prim. Sch.
Sports Ground
Draper's Farm
Football Grd.
Pavilion
Club House
MALDON GOLF COURSE
HEYBRIDGE APPROACH
THE CAUSEWAY
COLCHESTER RD.
GOLDHANGER ROAD
B1026
Heybridge Cen.
Cemetery
Middle Farm
Reservoir
Canterbury Farm
Beeleigh Abbey
River Chelmer
BLACKWATER TRADING ESTATE
Superstore
Timber Yard
Heybridge Hall
Hall Bridge
CHELMER & BLACKWATER NAVIGATION
Depot
Warehouse
Dock
Heybridge Creek
River Chelmer
MALDON
Wintersleet Farm
LONDON RD.
Cemy.
Prep. Sch.
Mus.
Rec. Grd.
ST. PETER'S HOSPITAL
Prim. Sch.
The Hythe
Maldon Yacht Club
Plume Sch.
Playing Fields
Council Offs.
Play. Fld.
Maldon Prim. Sch.
Maldon District Museum
RIVER BLACKWATER
A414
St. Giles Leper Hosp. (ruins)
SPITAL R.
Marine Lake
Boating Lake
Promenade Park
Rec. Grd. & Marine Parade
Playing Field
Park Drive Fitness & Squash Club
Blackwater Leisure centre
Wentworth Prim. Sch.
Play. Field
Comm. Cen.
Superstore
LIMEBROOK WAY
B1018
Lime Brook
FAMBRIDGE RD.
South House Farm
SOUTH HOUSE CHASE
INSET
Saltcote Hall
GOLDHANGER RD.
Caravan Park
Blackwater Sailing Club
CM9
Heybridge Basin
Lock
RIVER BLACKWATER
A B C D E F
1 2 3 4 5 6 7 8 9
84 85 86 87
25 35

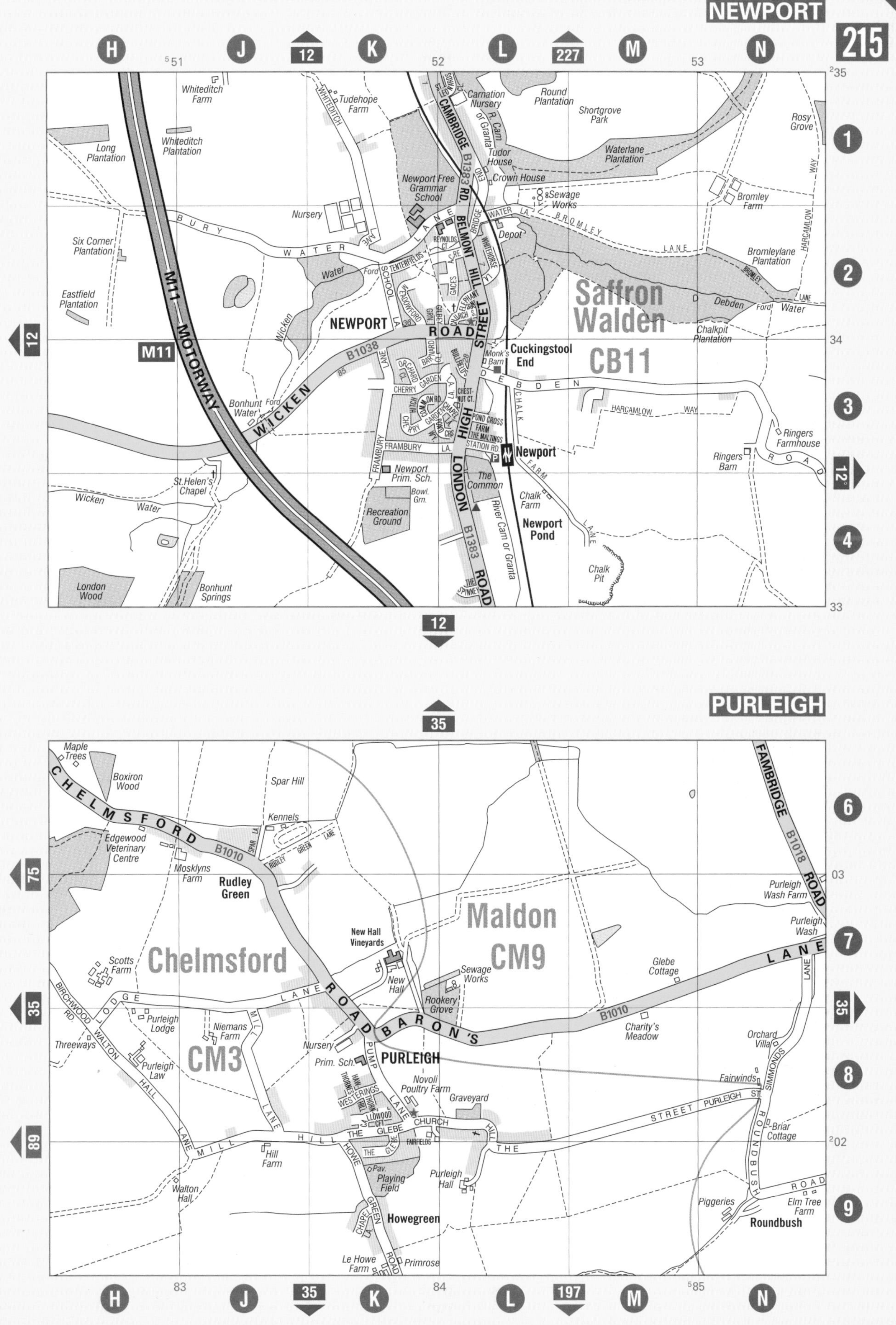
NEWPORT
Saffron Walden
CB11
Cuckingstool End
Newport Pond
Whiteditch Farm
Tudehope Farm
Carnation Nursery
Round Plantation
Shortgrove Park
Rosy Grove
Long Plantation
Whiteditch Plantation
Tudor House
Crown House
Waterlane Plantation
Newport Free Grammar School
Sewage Works
Bromley Farm
Nursery
Six Corner Plantation
Depot
Bromleylane Plantation
Eastfield Plantation
Debden
Water
Chalkpit Plantation
M11 MOTORWAY
Monk's Barn
Bonhunt Water
Ringers Farmhouse
Ringers Barn
Newport Prim. Sch.
St.Helen's Chapel
The Common
Wicken Water
Chalk Farm
Bowl. Grn.
Recreation Ground
Chalk Pit
London Wood
Bonhunt Springs
CAMBRIDGE RD.
HIGH STREET
LONDON ROAD
WICKEN ROAD
BURY WATER LANE
BROMLEY LANE
HARCAMLOW WAY
DEBDEN ROAD
FRAMBURY LA.
PURLEIGH
Maple Trees
Boxiron Wood
Spar Hill
Kennels
Edgewood Veterinary Centre
Mosklyns Farm
Rudley Green
Chelmsford
Maldon
CM9
CM3
New Hall Vineyards
New Hall
Scotts Farm
Sewage Works
Rookery Grove
Glebe Cottage
Purleigh Wash Farm
Purleigh Wash
Purleigh Lodge
Niemans Farm
Charity's Meadow
Threeways
Purleigh Law
Nursery
Prim. Sch.
Orchard Villa
Novoli Poultry Farm
Fairwinds
Graveyard
Briar Cottage
Hill Farm
Playing Field
Purleigh Hall
Walton Hall
Piggeries
Elm Tree Farm
Howegreen
Roundbush
Le Howe Farm
Primrose
CHELMSFORD ROAD
BARON'S LANE
FAMBRIDGE ROAD
PURLEIGH STREET
MILL HILL
CHURCH HILL
WALTON HALL LANE
BIRCHWOOD RD.
HOWE GREEN ROAD
ROUNDBUSH ROAD

QUENDON & RICKLING GREEN

RIDGEWELL

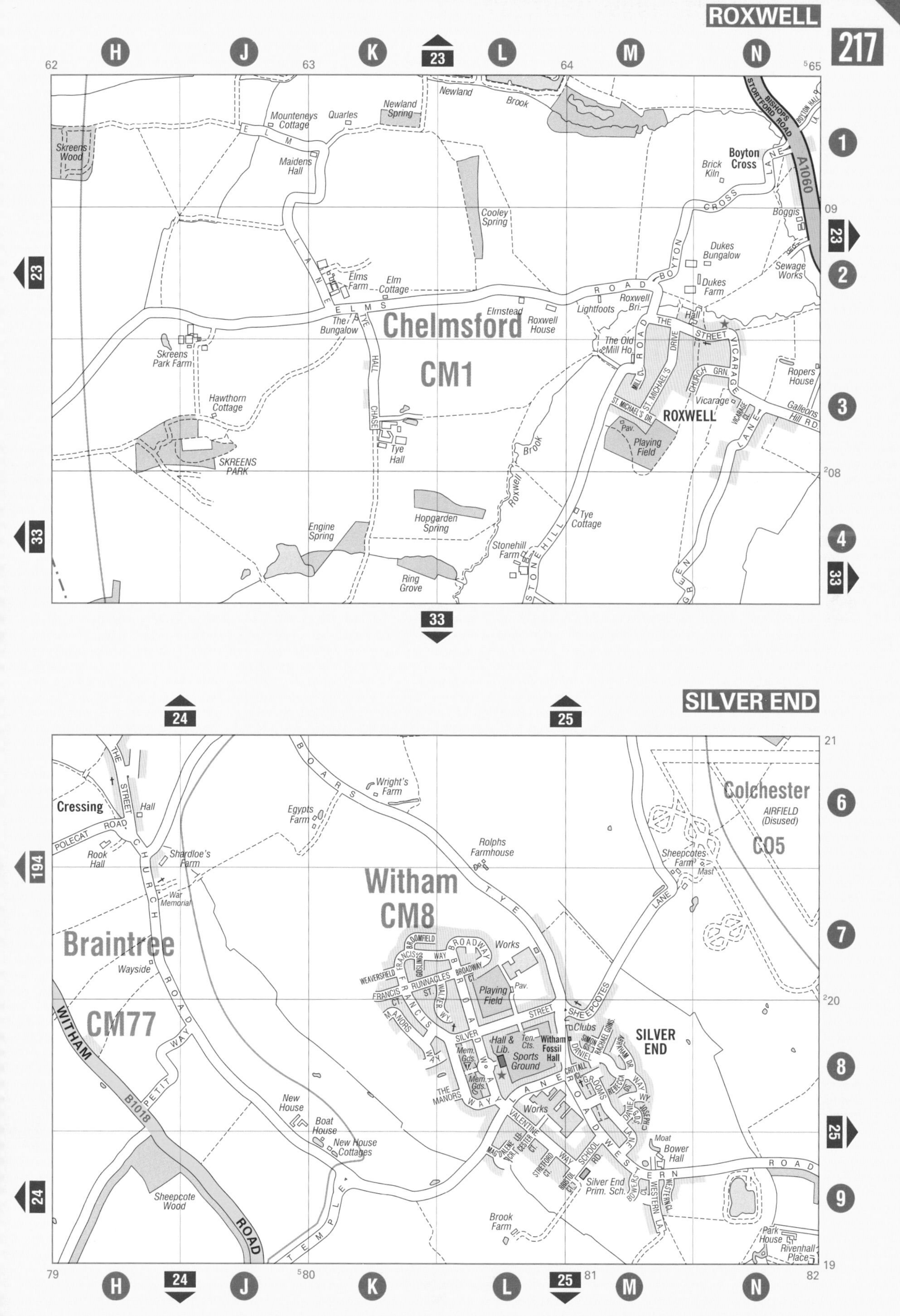
Chelmsford
CM1
ROXWELL
Boyton Cross
Skreens Wood
Mounteneys Cottage
Quarles
Newland Spring
Newland
Brook
Maidens Hall
ELM LANE
ELMS
Cooley Spring
Elms Farm
Elm Cottage
ROAD
BOYTON
CROSS
LANE
Dukes Bungalow
Dukes Farm
Brick Kiln
Boggis
Sewage Works
BISHOPS STORTFORD ROAD
A1060
BOYTON HALL LA.
The Bungalow
Elmstead
Roxwell House
Lightfoots
Roxwell Bri.
Hall
THE STREET
VICARAGE
The Old Mill Ho.
Skreens Park Farm
TYE HALL CHASE
MILL RD.
ST. MICHAEL'S DRIVE
CHURCH GRN.
ST. MICHAEL'S DR.
Vicarage
VICARAGE CL.
Ropers House
Galleons Hill RD.
Hawthorn Cottage
Pav.
Playing Field
Tye Hall
SKREENS PARK
Roxwell Brook
Tye Cottage
Hopgarden Spring
Engine Spring
Stonehill Farm
STONEHILL
Ring Grove
GREEN
62
63
64
565
09
208
SILVER END
Colchester
CO5
AIRFIELD (Disused)
Witham
CM8
Braintree
CM77
Cressing
THE STREET
Hall
POLECAT ROAD
Rook Hall
CHURCH ROAD
Shardloe's Farm
War Memorial
BOARS TYE
Wright's Farm
Egypts Farm
Rolphs Farmhouse
Sheepcotes Farm
Mast
Wayside
WITHAM ROAD
B1018
PETIT WAY
BROOMFIELD
BROADWAY
Works
FRANCIS WAY
GOSLINGS
WEAVERSFIELD
RUNNACLES ST.
BROADWAY CT.
Playing Field
Pav.
FRANCIS CT.
WALTER WY.
MANORS
SILVER STREET
SHEEPCOTES LANE
Clubs
Hall & Lib.
Ten. Cts.
Witham Fossil Hall
Sports Ground
Mem. Gds.
SIMON GD.
RACHAEL GDNS
ABRAHAM DR.
DANIEL
SILVER END
THE MANORS
WAY LANE
CRITTALL CL.
GROOMS
REBECCA GDS.
DANIEL GDS.
JOSEPH WY.
VALENTINE WAY
Works
New House
Boat House
New House Cottages
SCHOOL RD.
STRETFORD CT.
BRISTOL CT.
Silver End Prim. Sch.
Moat
Bower Hall
WESTERN ROAD
BOWERS CL.
WESTERN CL.
WESTERN LA.
Sheepcote Wood
ROAD
TEMPLE
Brook Farm
Park House
Rivenhall Place
21
220
19
79
580
81
82

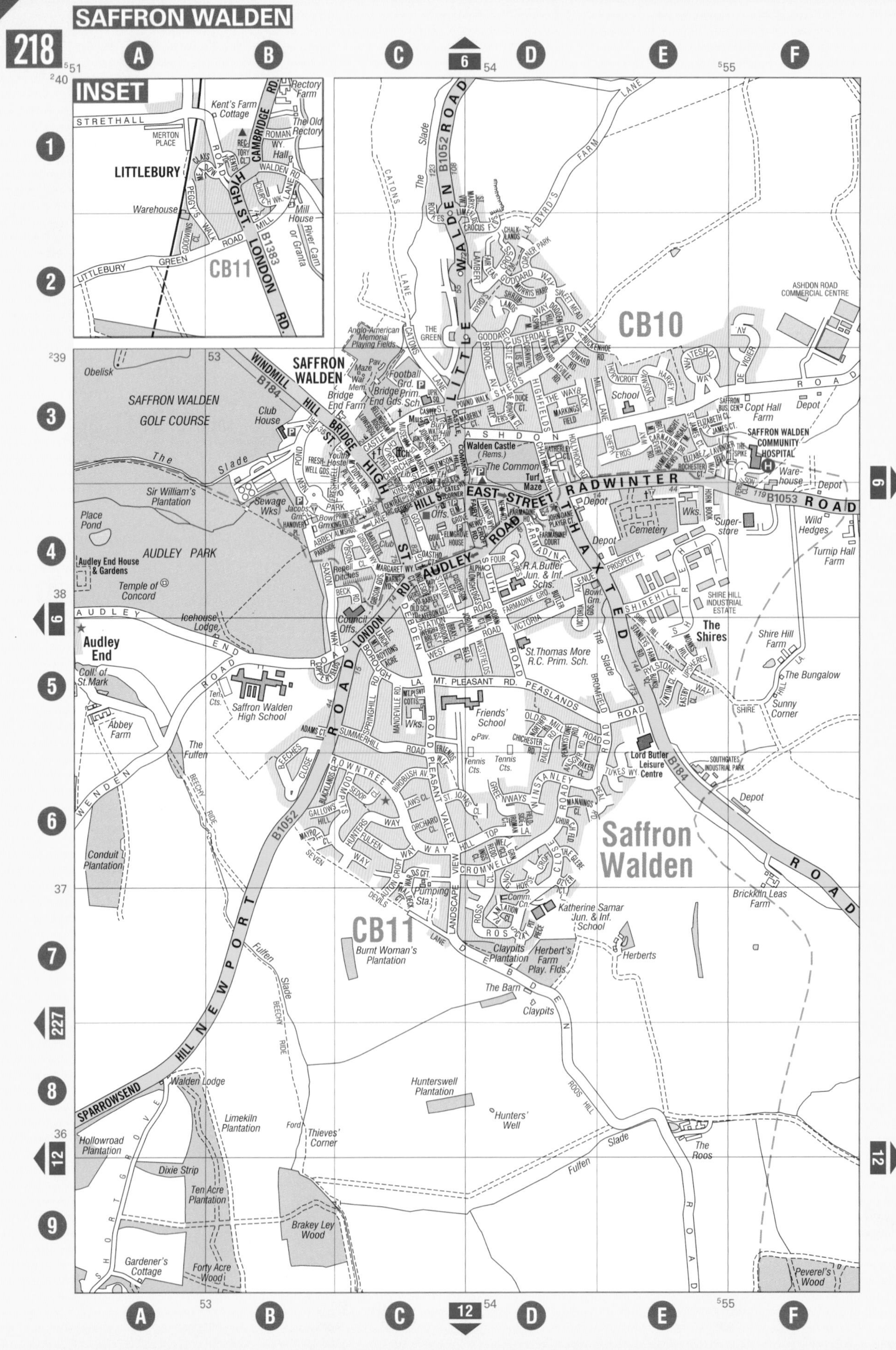
INSET
LITTLEBURY
Kent's Farm Cottage
Rectory Farm
The Old Rectory
MERTON PLACE
STRETHALL
CAMBRIDGE RD.
HIGH ST. LONDON RD.
B1383
Warehouse
Mill House
River Cam or Granta
LITTLEBURY GREEN ROAD
CB11
SAFFRON WALDEN
Obelisk
SAFFRON WALDEN GOLF COURSE
Club House
The Slade
Sir William's Plantation
Place Pond
AUDLEY PARK
Audley End House & Gardens
Temple of Concord
AUDLEY END ROAD
Icehouse Lodge
Audley End
Coll. of St.Mark
Abbey Farm
The Fulfen
WENDEN
Conduit Plantation
Saffron Walden High School
Sewage Wks.
WINDMILL HILL
BRIDGE ST.
HIGH ST.
B184
Youth Hostel
Anglo-American Memorial Playing Fields
Football Grd.
Bridge End Farm
Bridge End Gds.
Prim. Sch.
Mus.
Walden Castle (Rems.)
The Common
Turf Maze
Council Offs.
LONDON ROAD
B1052
NEWPORT
HILL
SPARROWSEND
Walden Lodge
Limekiln Plantation
Hollowroad Plantation
Dixie Strip
Ten Acre Plantation
Gardener's Cottage
Forty Acre Wood
Brakey Ley Wood
Thieves' Corner
Ford
Hunterswell Plantation
Hunters' Well
Fulfen Slade
The Roos
ROOS HILL
Peverel's Wood
SHORT GROVE
BEECHY RIDE
DEBDEN ROAD
Burnt Woman's Plantation
CB11
The Barn
Claypits
Claypits Plantation
Herbert's Farm Play. Flds
Herberts
Katherine Semar Jun. & Inf. School
Pumping Sta.
DEVILS LANE
LANDSCAPE VIEW
PLEASANT VALLEY
Friends' School
Tennis Cts.
MT. PLEASANT RD.
PEASLANDS ROAD
St.Thomas More R.C. Prim. Sch.
R.A.Butler Jun. & Inf. Schs.
EAST STREET
RADWINTER ROAD
B1053
THAXTED ROAD
AUDLEY ROAD
Cemetery
Depot
Wks.
Super-store
SHIRE HILL INDUSTRIAL ESTATE
The Shires
Lord Butler Leisure Centre
SOUTHGATES INDUSTRIAL PARK
Saffron Walden
Shire Hill Farm
The Bungalow
Sunny Corner
Turnip Hall Farm
Wild Hedges
Brickkiln Leas Farm
SAFFRON WALDEN COMMUNITY HOSPITAL
Ware-house
Copt Hall Farm
ASHDON ROAD COMMERCIAL CENTRE
CB10
DE VIGIER AV.
WHITESHOT WAY
School
LITTLE WALDEN ROAD
B1052
CATONS LANE
The Slade
BYRD'S FARM LANE
The Green
GODDARD WAY
ASHDON ROAD
WINSTANLEY ROAD
CROMWELL RD.
SUMMERHILL ROAD
ROWNTREE WAY
SEVEN DEVILS
A B C D E F
1 2 3 4 5 6 7 8 9
6 12 227
53 54 55 36 37 38 239 240

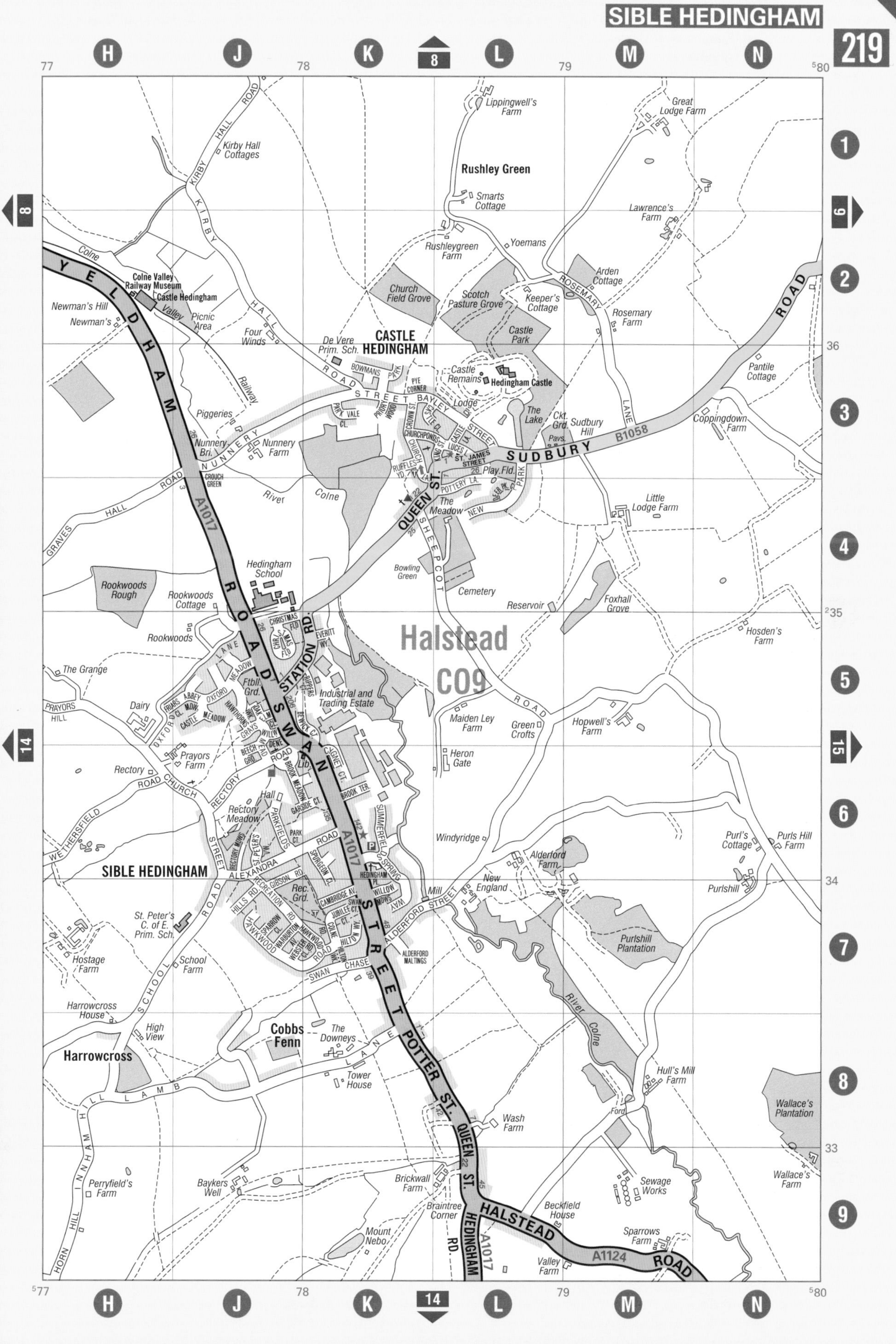
Lippingwell's Farm
Great Lodge Farm
Kirby Hall Cottages
Rushley Green
Smarts Cottage
Lawrence's Farm
Rushleygreen Farm
Yoemans
Colne Valley Railway Museum
Castle Hedingham
Newman's Hill
Newman's
Picnic Area
Church Field Grove
Scotch Pasture Grove
Keeper's Cottage
Arden Cottage
Rosemary Farm
Four Winds
De Vere Prim. Sch.
CASTLE HEDINGHAM
Castle Park
Castle Remains
Hedingham Castle
Pantile Cottage
Piggeries
The Lake
Ckt. Grd.
Sudbury Hill
Coppingdown Farm
Nunnery Bri.
Nunnery Farm
SUDBURY ROAD
B1058
Play. Fld.
River Colne
The Meadow
Little Lodge Farm
Hedingham School
Bowling Green
Cemetery
Rookwoods Rough
Rookwoods Cottage
Reservoir
Foxhall Grove
Rookwoods
Halstead CO9
Hosden's Farm
The Grange
Industrial and Trading Estate
Dairy
Maiden Ley Farm
Green Crofts
Hopwell's Farm
Prayors Farm
Heron Gate
Rectory
Rectory Meadow
Windyridge
Purl's Cottage
Purls Hill Farm
Alderford Farm
SIBLE HEDINGHAM
Rec. Grd.
New England
Purlshill
St. Peter's C. of E. Prim. Sch.
Mill
Purlshill Plantation
Hostage Farm
School Farm
Alderford Maltings
Harrowcross House
Cobbs Fenn
The Downeys
High View
Harrowcross
Tower House
Hull's Mill Farm
Wash Farm
Wallace's Plantation
Ford
Perryfield's Farm
Baykers Well
Brickwall Farm
Sewage Works
Wallace's Farm
Braintree Corner
Beckfield House
Mount Nebo
Sparrows Farm
Valley Farm
YELDHAM ROAD
SWAN STREET
POTTER ST.
QUEEN ST.
HALSTEAD ROAD
A1017
A1124
HEDINGHAM RD.

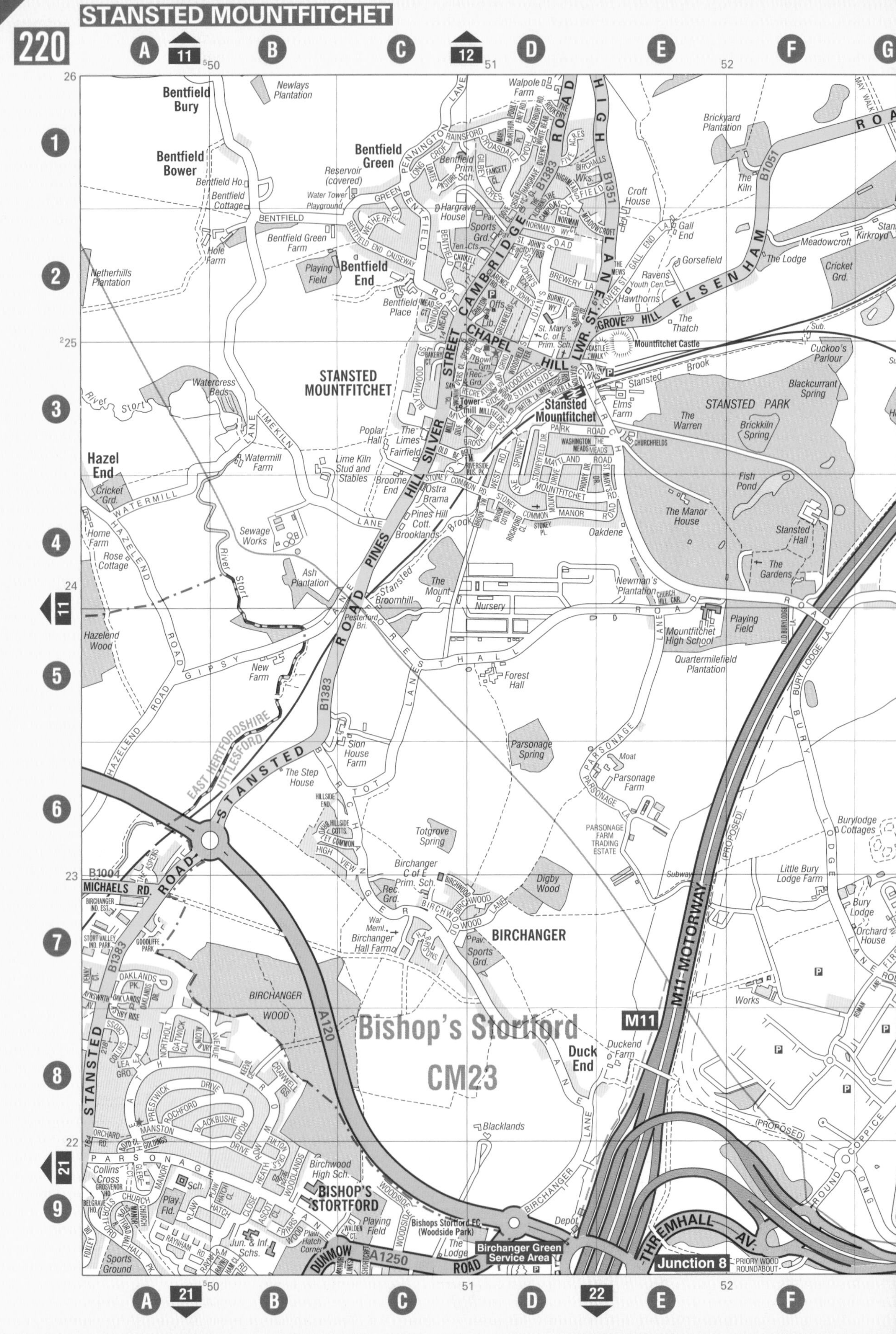
Bentfield Bury
Bentfield Bower
Bentfield Green
Bentfield End
Newlays Plantation
Netherhills Plantation
Watercress Beds
River Stort
Hazel End
Watermill Farm
Lime Kiln Stud and Stables
Sewage Works
Ash Plantation
Hazelend Wood
New Farm
STANSTED MOUNTFITCHET
Stansted Mountfitchet
Mountfitchet Castle
Walpole Farm
Croft House
Gall End
Gorsefield
Ravens Youth Cen.
Hawthorns
The Thatch
Brickyard Plantation
The Kiln
The Lodge
Meadowcroft
Kirkroyd
Cricket Grd.
Cuckoo's Parlour
Blackcurrant Spring
STANSTED PARK
The Warren
Brickkiln Spring
Fish Pond
The Manor House
Stansted Hall
The Gardens
Oakdene
Newman's Plantation
Mountfitchet High School
Playing Field
Quartermilefield Plantation
Forest Hall
The Mount
Nursery
Broomhill
Pesterford Bri.
Parsonage Spring
Parsonage Farm
PARSONAGE FARM TRADING ESTATE
Sion House Farm
The Step House
Totgrove Spring
Birchanger C of E Prim. Sch.
Digby Wood
BIRCHANGER
Birchanger Hall Farm
BIRCHANGER WOOD
Bishop's Stortford
CM23
Duck End
Duckend Farm
Blacklands
Little Bury Lodge Farm
Burylodge Cottages
Bury Lodge
Orchard House
Works
M11-MOTORWAY
M11
Junction 8
PRIORY WOOD ROUNDABOUT
THREMHALL AV.
Birchanger Green Service Area
Bishops Stortford FC (Woodside Park)
Birchwood High Sch.
BISHOP'S STORTFORD
Playing Field
Jun. & Inf. Schs.
Sports Ground
Collins Cross
A120
A1250
B1383
B1351
B1051
B1004
EAST HERTFORDSHIRE
UTTLESFORD
STANSTED ROAD
DUNMOW ROAD
PARSONAGE LANE
BIRCHANGER LANE
FORESTHALL LANE
PINES HILL
SILVER STREET
CAMBRIDGE ROAD
CHAPEL HILL
ELSENHAM ROAD
HIGH LANE
GIPSY LANE
HAZELEND ROAD
BURY LODGE LA.

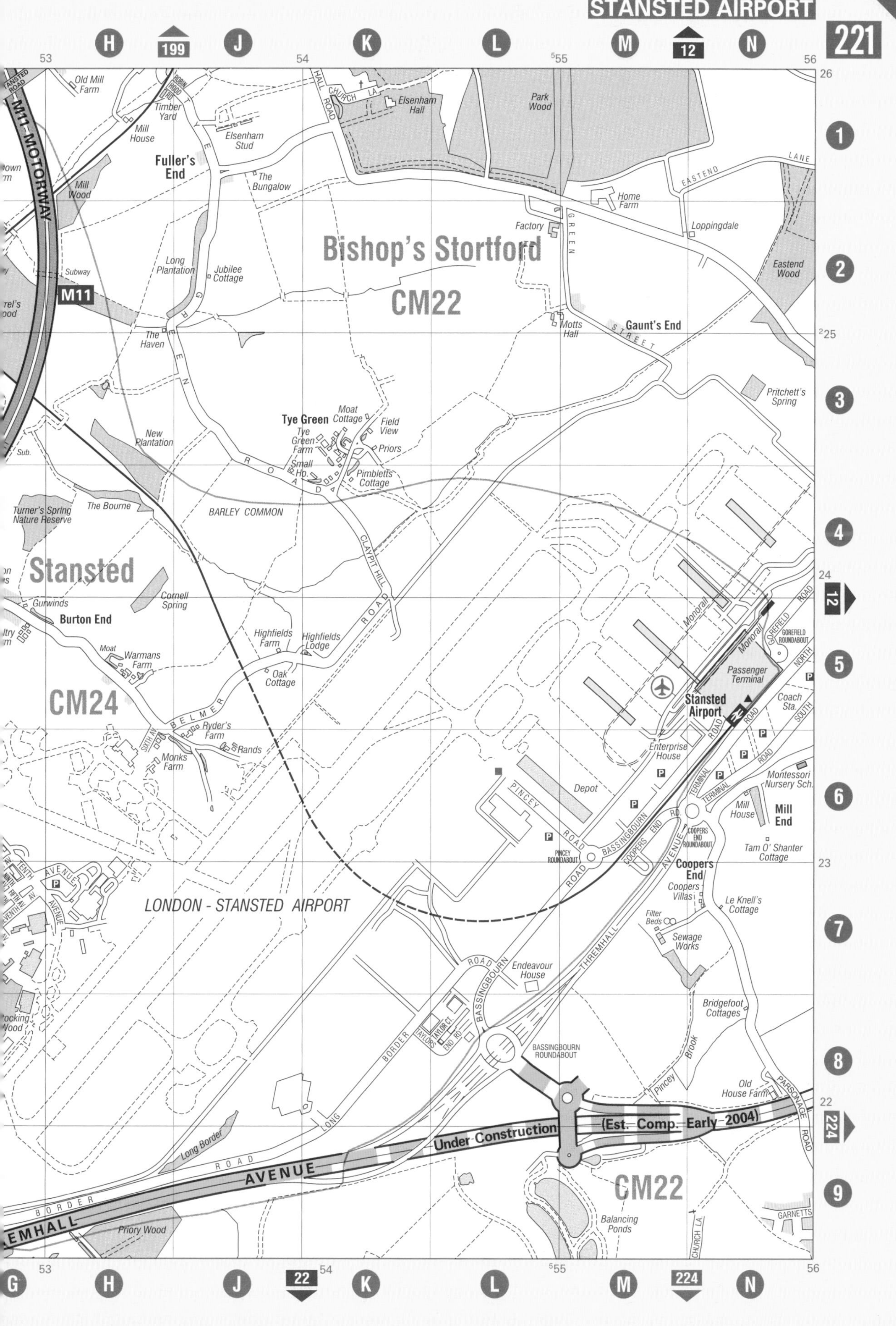
Old Mill Farm
Timber Yard
Mill House
Elsenham Stud
Elsenham Hall
Park Wood
Fuller's End
The Bungalow
Mill Wood
M11 MOTORWAY
Home Farm
Factory
Loppingdale
Bishop's Stortford
CM22
Long Plantation
Jubilee Cottage
Subway
M11
Eastend Wood
The Haven
Motts Hall
Gaunt's End
Pritchett's Spring
Tye Green
Moat Cottage
Field View
Tye Green Farm
Priors
New Plantation
Small Ho.
Pimbletts Cottage
Turner's Spring Nature Reserve
The Bourne
BARLEY COMMON
Stansted
Cornell Spring
Gurwinds
Burton End
Highfields Farm
Highfields Lodge
Monorail
Moat
Warmans Farm
Oak Cottage
Passenger Terminal
CM24
Stansted Airport
Coach Sta.
Ryder's Farm
Rands
Monks Farm
Enterprise House
Depot
Montessori Nursery Sch.
Mill House
Mill End
Pincey Roundabout
Coopers End Roundabout
Tam O' Shanter Cottage
Coopers End
Coopers Villas
LONDON - STANSTED AIRPORT
Le Knell's Cottage
Filter Beds
Sewage Works
Endeavour House
Bridgefoot Cottages
Bassingbourn Roundabout
Old House Farm
Under Construction
(Est. Comp. Early 2004)
Long Border
CM22
Balancing Ponds
Priory Wood
AVENUE
Garnetts

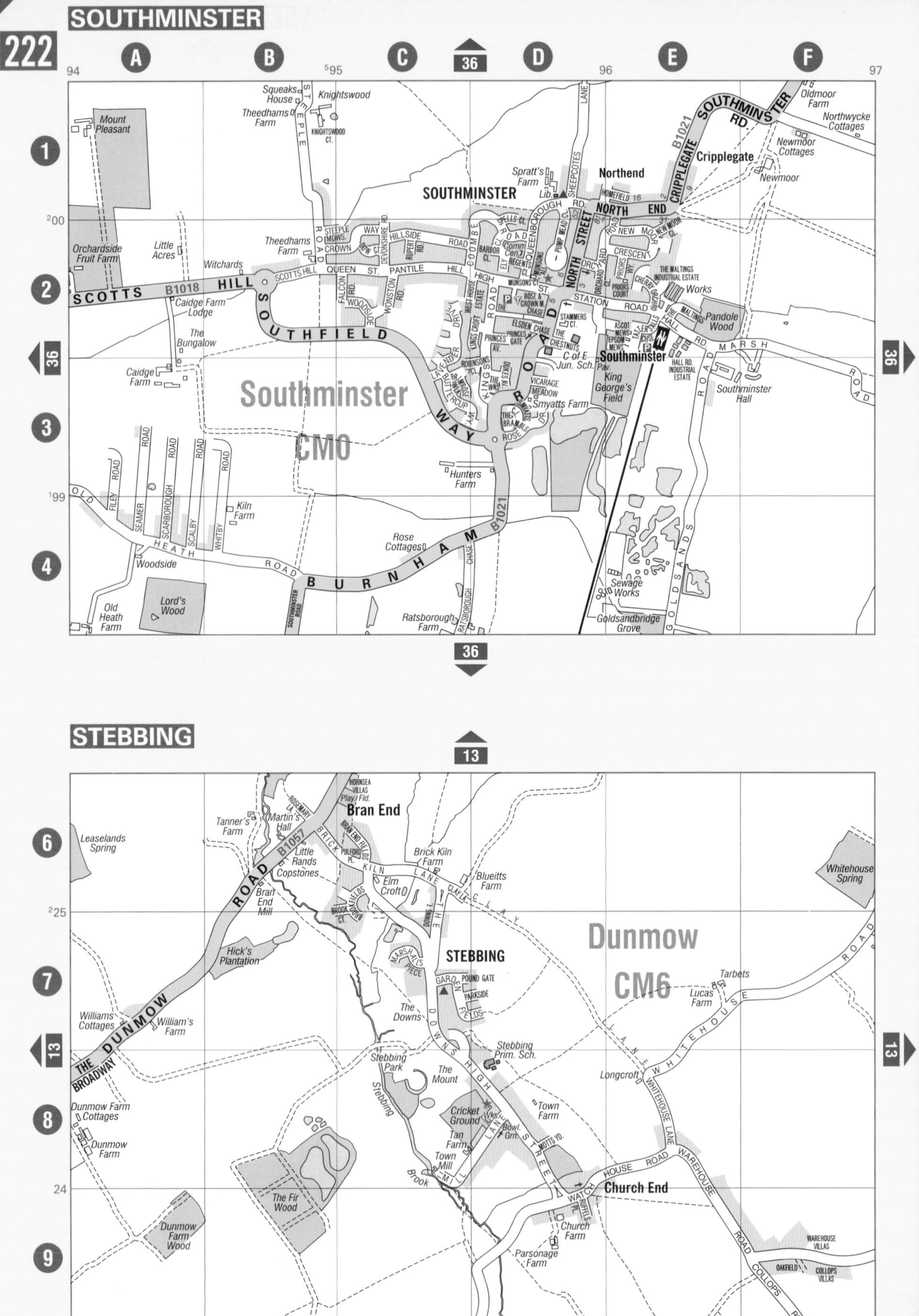
SOUTHMINSTER
Southminster
CM0
Northend
Cripplegate
Scotts Hill
Southfield Way
Burnham Road
Queen St.
Pantile Hill
High St.
North Street
North End
Station Road
Queenborough Rd.
Steeple Road
Old Heath Road
Goldsands Road
Marsh Road
Southminster Rd.
Crown
Hillside
Way
Devonshire Rd.
Falcon Rd.
Woodside
Wonston Rd.
Rupert Rd.
Coombe
New Moor Crescent
Orchard Rd.
Filey Road
Seamer Road
Scarborough Road
Scalby Road
Whitby Road
Mount Pleasant
Orchardside Fruit Farm
Little Acres
Witchards
Caidge Farm Lodge
The Bungalow
Caidge Farm
Squeaks House
Knightswood
Theedhams Farm
Spratt's Farm
Lib.
Oldmoor Farm
Northwycke Cottages
Newmoor Cottages
Newmoor
The Maltings Industrial Estate
Works
Pandole Wood
Southminster Hall
Hall Rd. Industrial Estate
King George's Field
C of E Jun. Sch.
Smyatts Farm
Vicarage Meadow
Hunters Farm
Kiln Farm
Woodside
Lord's Wood
Old Heath Farm
Rose Cottages
Ratsborough Farm
Ratsborough Chase
Sewage Works
Goldsandbridge Grove
STEBBING
Stebbing
Dunmow
CM6
Bran End
Tanner's Farm
Martin's Hall
Little Rands
Copstones
Bran End Mill
Brick Kiln Lane
Brick Kiln Farm
Elm Croft
Blueitts Farm
Clay Lane
Hick's Plantation
Leaselands Spring
Williams Cottages
William's Farm
The Dunmow Road
The Broadway
Dunmow Farm Cottages
Dunmow Farm
Dunmow Farm Wood
The Fir Wood
Marshalls Piece
The Downs
Garden Fields
Pound Gate
Parkside
Stebbing Park
The Mount
Stebbing Prim. Sch.
Cricket Ground
Bowl. Grn.
Tan Farm
Town Mill
Mill Lane
Stebbing Brook
High Street
Town Farm
Motts Yd.
Watch House Road
Church End
Church Farm
Parsonage Farm
Longcroft
Whitehouse Lane
Whitehouse Road
Warehouse Road
Lucas Farm
Tarbets
Whitehouse Spring
Warehouse Villas
Oakfield
Collops Villas
Collops Rd.

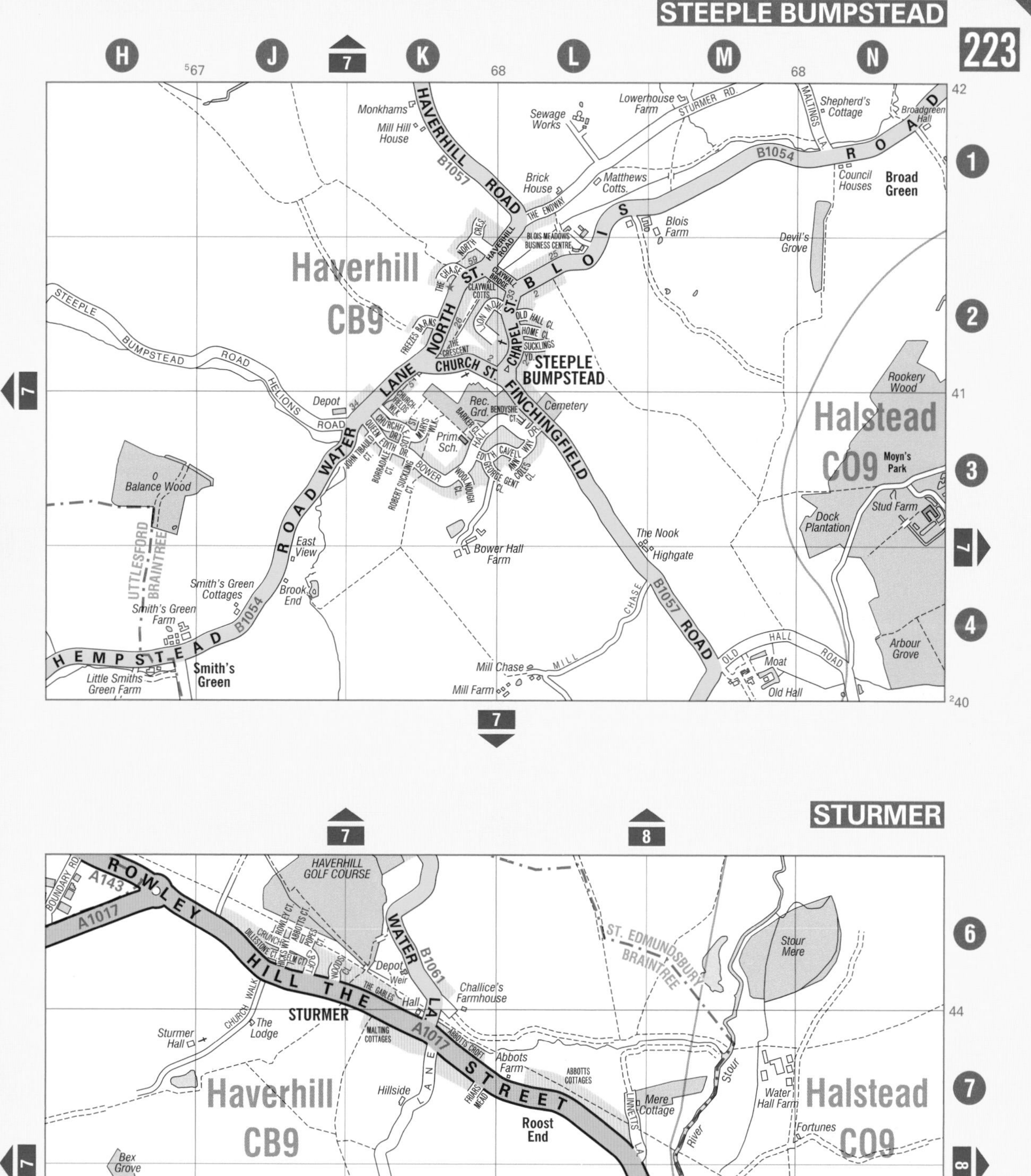

STURMER

7
8
BOUNDARY RD.
A143
ROWLEY
A1017
HAVERHILL GOLF COURSE
WATER LA.
B1061
ROWLEY CT.
ABBOTTS CT.
CRUNCH WY.
DILLESTONE CT.
HICKS WY.
ELM CT.
POPES CT.
LOFTS CT.
WOODS CL.
Depot
Weir
THE GABLES
Hall
Challice's Farmhouse
ST. EDMUNDSBURY
BRAINTREE
Stour Mere
6
44
CHURCH WALK
The Lodge
Sturmer Hall
STURMER
HILL THE STREET
A1017
ABBOTTS CROFT
MALTING COTTAGES
Abbots Farm
ABBOTTS COTTAGES
Stour
Water Hall Farm
7
Haverhill
CB9
Hillside
LANE
FRIARS MEAD
STREET
Roost End
LINNETTS LA.
Mere Cottage
River
Halstead
CO9
Fortunes
Bex Grove
8
Homefield
STURMER
Pitt House
FORDWATER
Weir
Craig Holme
Dutch Cottage
Watsoe Bri.
Fordwater Cottage
243
Watsoe House
Nursery
Depot
Wixoe Mill
Weir
9
ROAD HILL
Walton's Farm
New England
A1017
B1054
ROAD
STURMER
Upper House
Sunnybank
H
69
J
7
K
570
L
8
M
71
N

TAKELEY

THAXTED

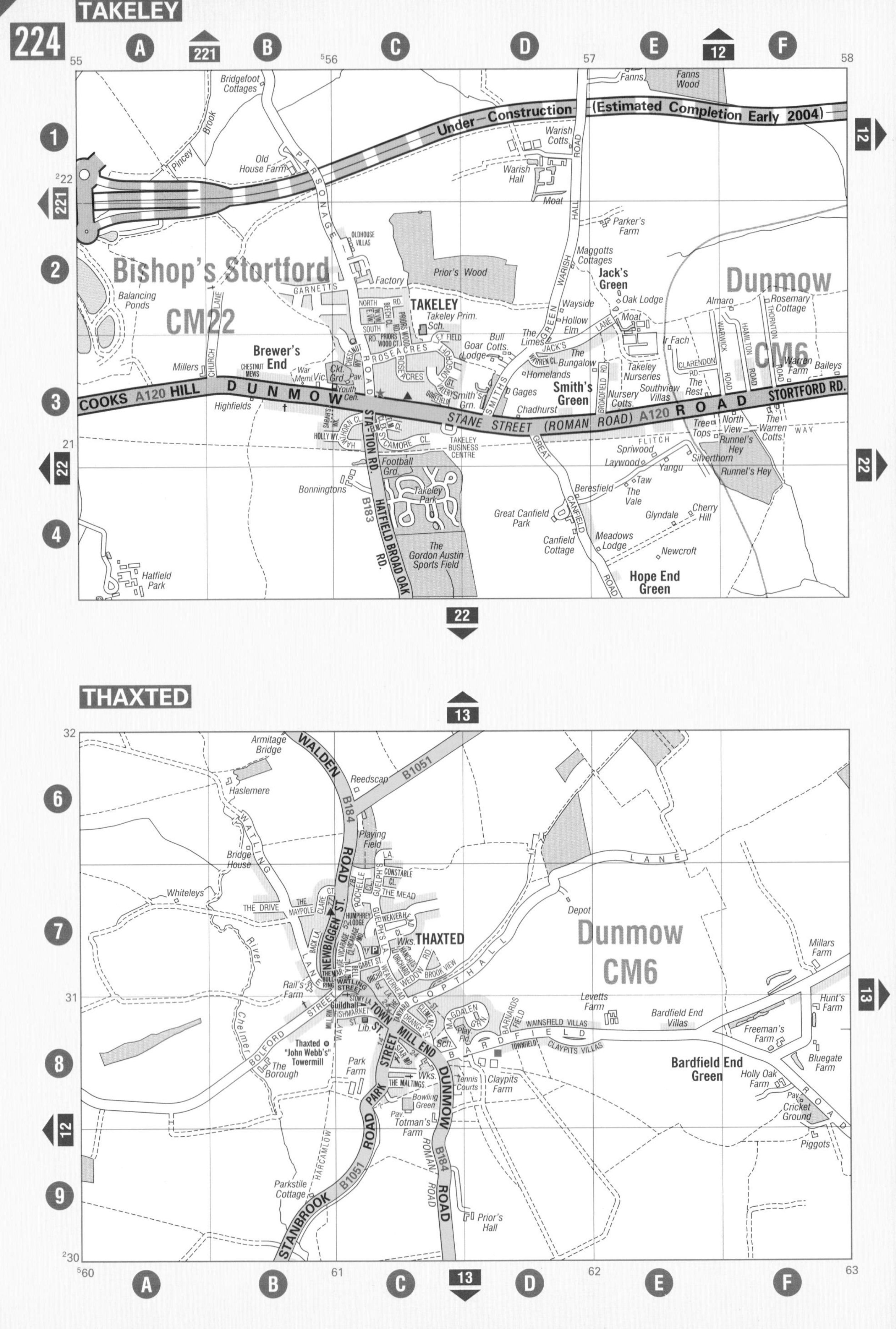

TILLINGHAM
Southminster
CM0
Blackbirds
Sewage Works
Brick House Farm
The Pightle
East Hyde
Brook Cottage
Poultry Houses
Tillingham Hall Farms
Tillingham Hall
Mark Farm Cottage
Shingleford
Dots and Melons
Leggatts
Leggatts Cottages
Reservoirs
Recreation Ground
Prim. Sch.
Stows Farm
Vicarage
Air Strip
Reddings Farm
Reddings
The Haven
Dengie Council Houses
The Cottage
White Horse Farm
Slate Cottage
Primley Lodge
Old Schoolhouse
Bacons
Dengie
Midlands
Bridgemans Farm Cottages
Bridgemans Farm
Jerry's Farm
BRADWELL RD. NORTH ST.
SOUTH STREET
B1021
TILLINGHAM ROAD
GRANGE ROAD
MARSH ROAD
STOWE'S LANE
VICARAGE LANE
ST. LAWRENCE RD.
BROOK ROAD
REDDINGS LANE
MANOR ROAD
CHAPEL LA.
MARLBOROUGH AV.
BAKERY CL.
ENGLEFIELDS
BIRCH RD.
CASEY LA.
MILL CL.
WESSLEY CL.
CHANCEL CL.
THE SQ.
ST. NICHOLAS RD.
TOLLESBURY
Maldon
CM9
The Rookery
Carrington Farm
Garland's House
Garlands Farm
Prentice Hall Farm
Cemetery
Recreation Ground
De Bohuns
Bohuns Hall
Poultry House
Great Downs
Bus Depot
Sewage Works
Oyster Business Centre
Works
Hall
Club
Tennis Court
Yacht Harbour
Boatbuilding Yard
Woodrolfe Farm
Wick Farm
Mell Farm
Marsh House Farm
Tollesbury Fleet
Woodrolfe Creek
TOLLESBURY WICK MARSHES
TOLLESBURY RD. WEST STREET HIGH ST. EAST ST.
B1023
BACK ROAD
ROAD NORTH
STATION ROAD
WOODROLFE ROAD
WOODROLFE FARM LANE
MELL ROAD
WYCKE LANE
PRENTICE HALL LANE
THISTLY ROAD
CHURCH ST.
ELYSIAN GARDENS
ST. JOHN'S CT.
THE CHASE
CHURCHACRE
KENTS GRASS
SCEPTRE CL.
THURSTABLE RD.
THURSTABLE WAY
MALLARD CL.
WATERWORKS RD.
ESTUARY M.
HUNTS FARM CL.
ORCHARD CL.
KINGS WALK
DARWEN
CRESCENT RD.
MONKS WLK.
Prim. Sch.
Play. Fld.
War Mem.
The Green

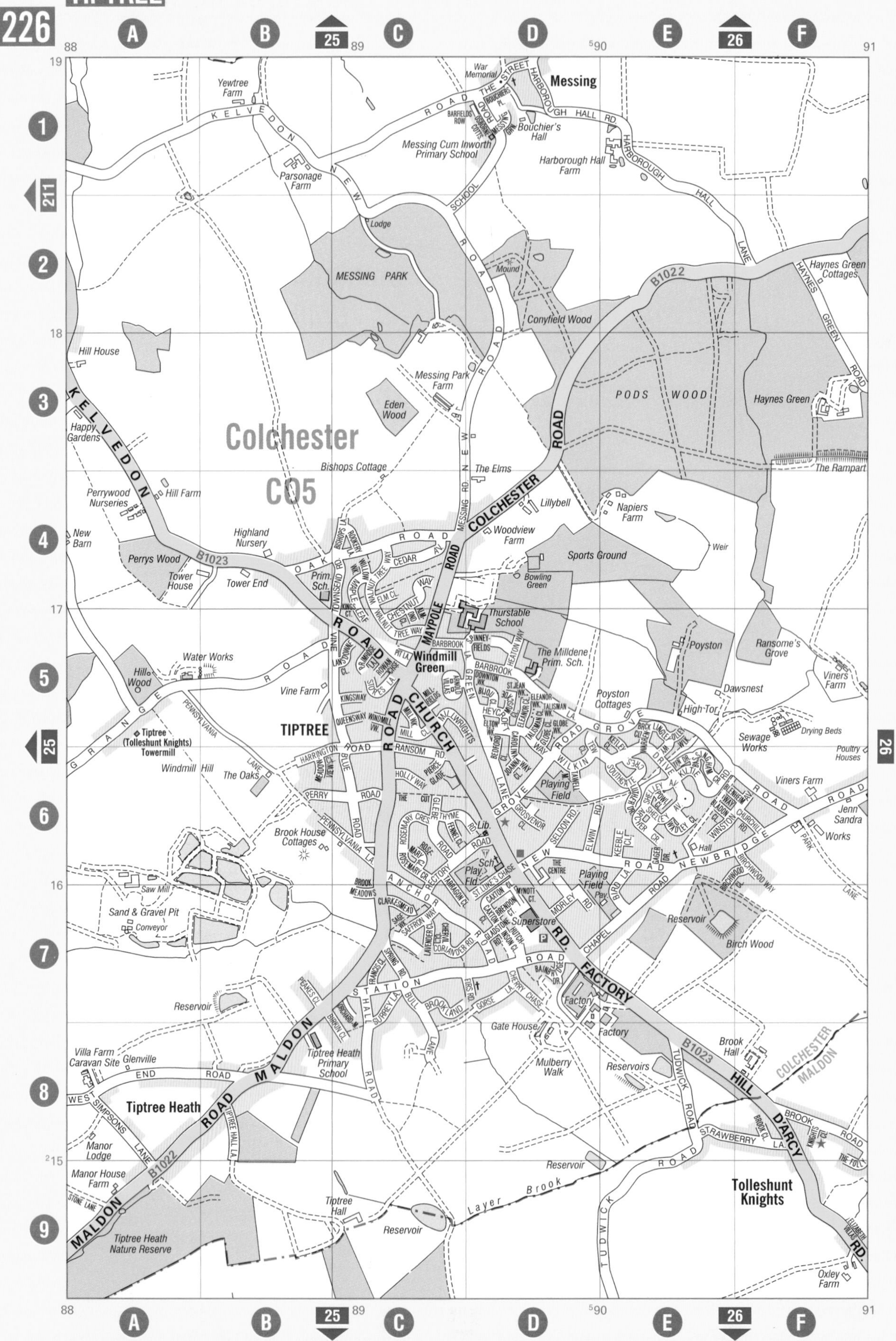
A
B
C
D
E
F
25
26
211
Messing
War Memorial
Yewtree Farm
KELVEDON ROAD
HARBOROUGH HALL RD.
Bouchier's Hall
Messing Cum Inworth Primary School
Harborough Hall Farm
Parsonage Farm
NEW ROAD
SCHOOL ROAD
Lodge
MESSING PARK
Mound
B1022
Haynes Green Cottages
HAYNES GREEN ROAD
Conyfield Wood
Hill House
Messing Park Farm
Eden Wood
PODS WOOD
Haynes Green
The Rampart
Happy Gardens
Colchester
CO5
Bishops Cottage
The Elms
COLCHESTER ROAD
Perrywood Nurseries
Hill Farm
Lillybell
Napiers Farm
New Barn
Highland Nursery
Woodview Farm
Weir
Perrys Wood
B1023
OAK ROAD
CEDAR AV.
Sports Ground
Bowling Green
Tower House
Tower End
Prim. Sch.
MAYPOLE ROAD
Thurstable School
Poyston
Ransome's Grove
Water Works
Hill Wood
Windmill Green
BARBROOK
The Milldene Prim. Sch.
Vine Farm
Dawsnest
Viners Farm
Poyston Cottages
High Tor
Tiptree (Tolleshunt Knights) Towermill
TIPTREE
CHURCH ROAD
GROVE ROAD
Sewage Works
Drying Beds
Poultry Houses
RANSOM RD.
Windmill Hill
The Oaks
Playing Field
Viners Farm
Jenn Sandra
Works
Brook House Cottages
Lib.
Sch.
Play. Fld.
Playing Field
NEWBRIDGE ROAD
Hall
Saw Mill
Sand & Gravel Pit
Conveyor
ANCHOR ROAD
Superstore
Reservoir
Birch Wood
STATION ROAD
FACTORY RD.
Factory
Reservoir
Gate House
Tiptree Heath Primary School
Mulberry Walk
Reservoirs
Brook Hall
COLCHESTER MALDON
Villa Farm Caravan Site
Glenville
END ROAD
MALDON ROAD
Tiptree Heath
TUDWICK ROAD
B1023
HILL
D'ARCY RD.
BROOK ROAD
STRAWBERRY LA.
Manor Lodge
Manor House Farm
Reservoir
Tolleshunt Knights
Tiptree Hall
Layer Brook
Reservoir
Tiptree Heath Nature Reserve
Oxley Farm
88
89
90
91
19
18
17
16
15
1
2
3
4
5
6
7
8
9

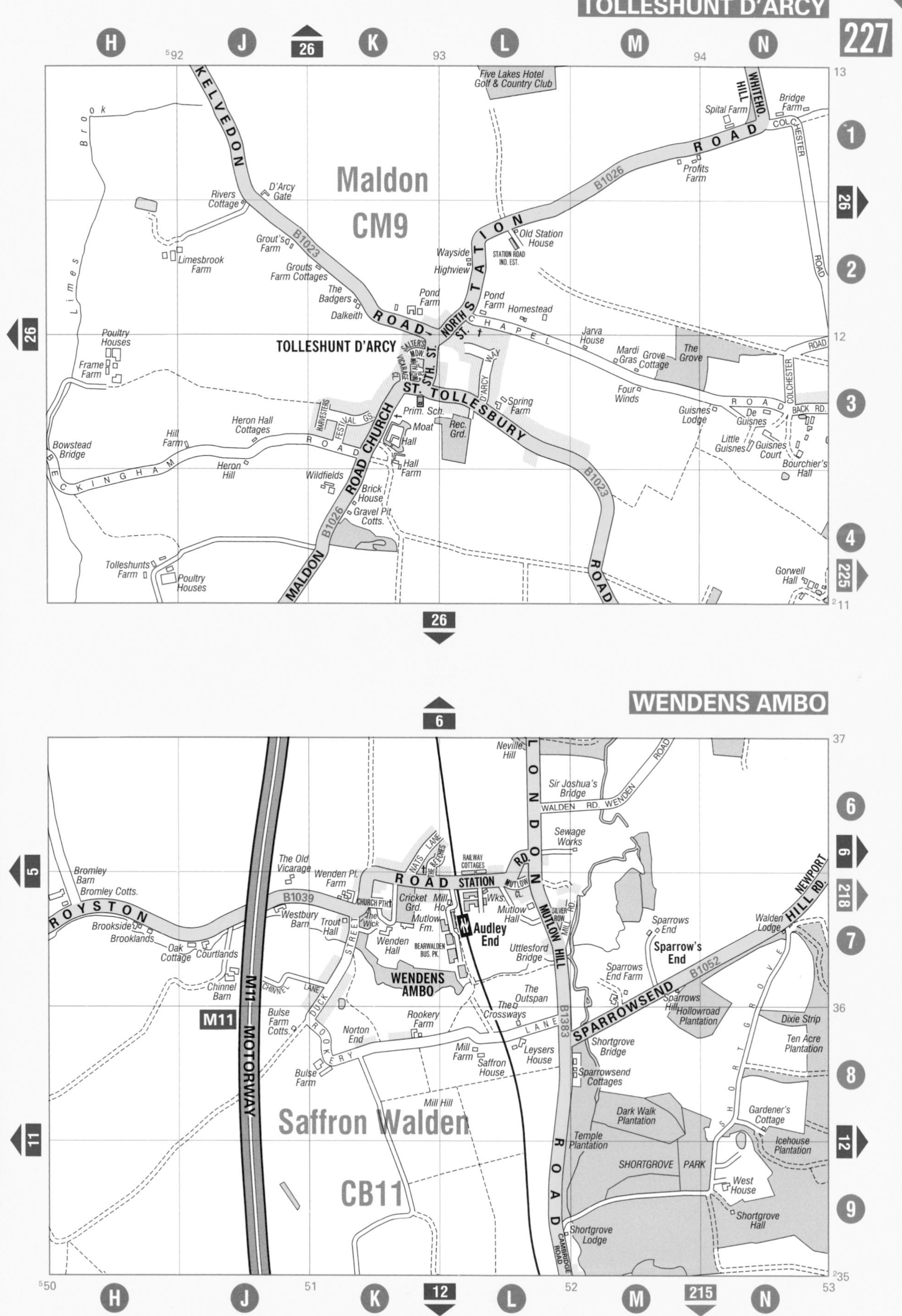
TOLLESHUNT D'ARCY
Maldon
CM9
TOLLESHUNT D'ARCY
KELVEDON
ROAD
B1023
B1026
STATION
ROAD
NORTH ST.
STH. ST.
ST.
TOLLESBURY
CHURCH
ROAD
MALDON
ROAD
CHAPEL
ROAD
BECKINGHAM
ROAD
COLCHESTER
ROAD
WHITEHO. HILL
BACK RD.
Five Lakes Hotel Golf & Country Club
Spital Farm
Bridge Farm
Profits Farm
D'Arcy Gate
Rivers Cottage
Grout's Farm
Grouts Farm Cottages
Limesbrook Farm
The Badgers
Dalkeith
Pond Farm
Wayside
Highview
Old Station House
STATION ROAD IND. EST.
Pond Farm
Homestead
Jarva House
Mardi Gras
Grove Cottage
The Grove
Four Winds
Guisnes Lodge
De Guisnes
Little Guisnes
Guisnes Court
Bourchier's Hall
Poultry Houses
Frame Farm
Bowstead Bridge
Hill Farm
Heron Hall Cottages
Heron Hill
Wildfields
Prim. Sch.
Moat
Hall
Hall Farm
Rec. Grd.
Spring Farm
Brick House
Gravel Pit Cotts.
Tolleshunts Farm
Poultry Houses
Gorwell Hall
HARVESTERS
FESTIVAL GS
VICARAGE CL.
SALTER'S MDW.
D'ARCY WAY
Limes Brook
WENDENS AMBO
Saffron Walden
CB11
WENDENS AMBO
Audley End
Sparrow's End
ROYSTON
B1039
M11 MOTORWAY
M11
STATION ROAD
LONDON ROAD
MUTLOW HILL
B1383
SPARROWSEND HILL
B1052
NEWPORT HILL RD.
WALDEN RD.
WENDEN ROAD
CAMBRIDGE ROAD
SHORTGROVE
DUCK STREET
ROOKERY LANE
CHINNEL LANE
LANE
NATS LANE
THE BEECHES
CHURCH PTH.
MUTLOW CL.
SILVER ROW
MILL RD.
RAILWAY COTTAGES
Neville Hill
Sir Joshua's Bridge
Sewage Works
Bromley Barn
Bromley Cotts.
Brookside
Brooklands
Oak Cottage
Courtlands
Chinnel Barn
The Old Vicarage
Wenden Pl. Farm
Westbury Barn
Trout Hall
The Wick
Cricket Grd.
Mill Ho
Mutlow Fm.
Wks.
Mutlow Hall
Wenden Hall
BEARWALDEN BUS. PK.
Uttlesford Bridge
The Outspan
The Crossways
Rookery Farm
Norton End
Bulse Farm Cotts.
Bulse Farm
Mill Farm
Saffron House
Leysers House
Mill Hill
Sparrows End
Sparrows End Farm
Sparrows Hill
Hollowroad Plantation
Walden Lodge
Dixie Strip
Ten Acre Plantation
Shortgrove Bridge
Sparrowsend Cottages
Dark Walk Plantation
Gardener's Cottage
Temple Plantation
SHORTGROVE PARK
Icehouse Plantation
West House
Shortgrove Hall
Shortgrove Lodge

WEST MERSEA

WETHERSFIELD

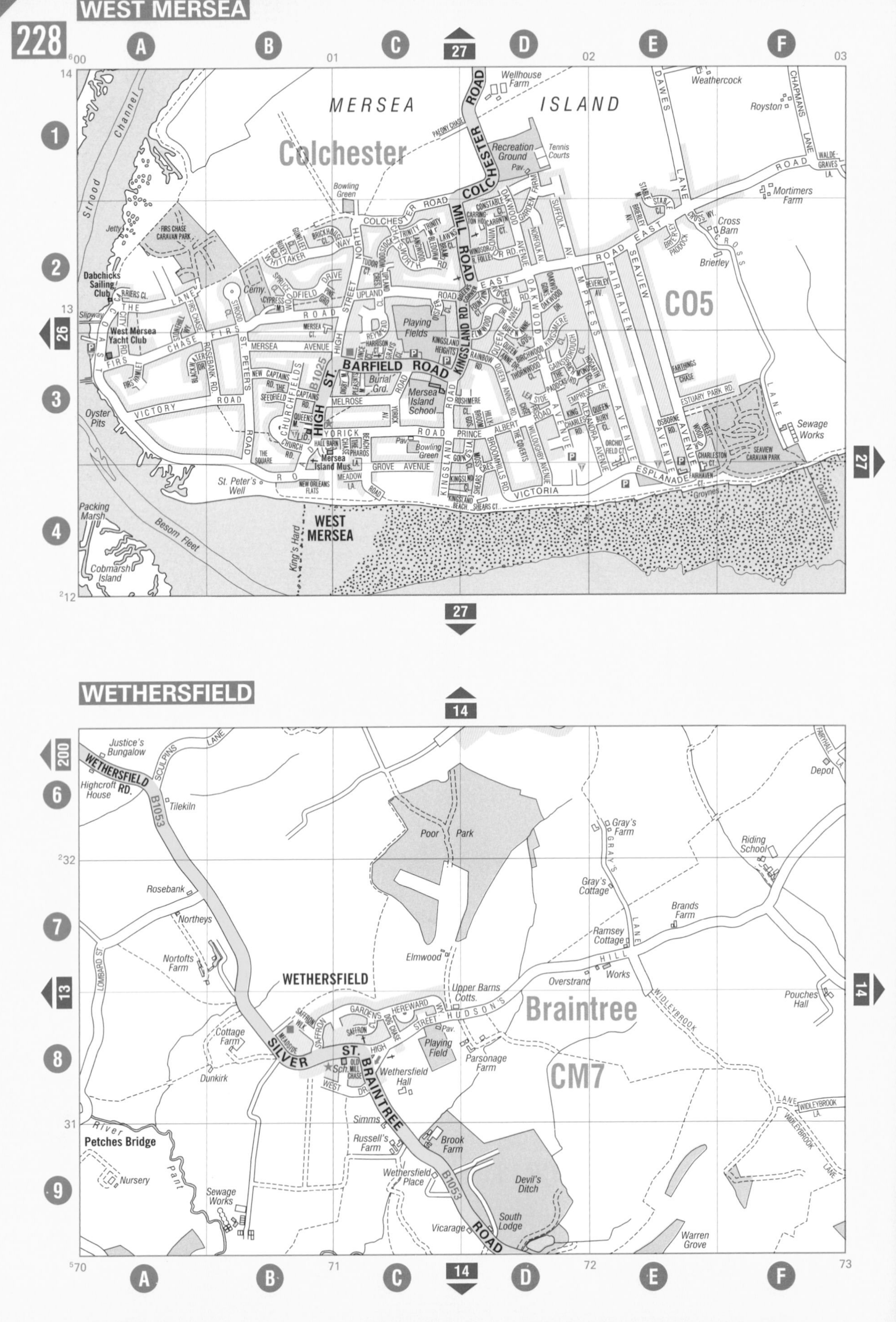

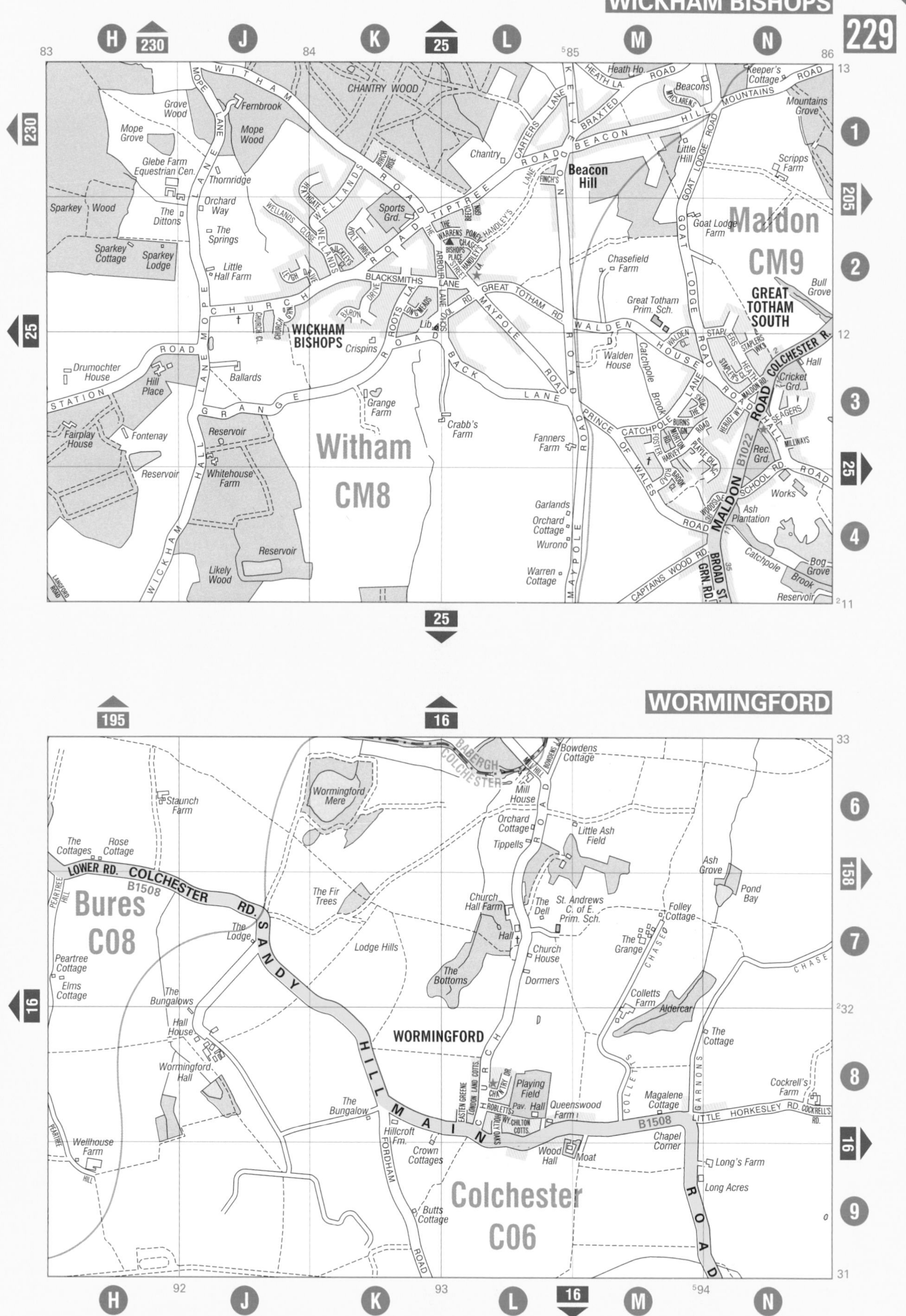
H
J
K
L
M
N
230
25
205
83
84
85
86
13
12
11
1
2
3
4
WITHAM ROAD
CHANTRY WOOD
Grove Wood
Fernbrook
Mope Grove
Mope Wood
MOPE LANE
Glebe Farm Equestrian Cen.
Thornridge
Orchard Way
Sparkey Wood
The Dittons
The Springs
Sparkey Cottage
Sparkey Lodge
Little Hall Farm
WELLANDS ROAD
WELLANDS CLOSE
BIRCH RISE
Sports Grd.
TIPTREE ROAD
CARTERS LANE
Chantry
BEACON HILL
Beacon Hill
HEATH LA.
Heath Ho.
ROAD
Beacons
MACLARENS
BRAXTED
MOUNTAINS ROAD
Keeper's Cottage
Mountains Grove
Little Hill
GOAT LODGE ROAD
Scripps Farm
Goat Lodge Farm
Maldon
CM9
HANDLEY'S LANE
FINCH'S
BLACKSMITHS LANE
CHURCH ROAD
CHURCH CL.
WICKHAM BISHOPS
Crispins
ROOTS LA.
Lib.
SCHOOL RD.
GREAT TOTHAM RD.
MAYPOLE ROAD
Chasefield Farm
Great Totham Prim. Sch.
GREAT TOTHAM SOUTH
Bull Grove
WALDEN HOUSE ROAD
Walden House
WALDEN CL.
STAPLERS
HEATH
COLCHESTER R.
Hall
Cricket Grd.
Drumochter House
STATION ROAD
Hill Place
Ballards
GRANGE ROAD
Grange Farm
BACK LANE
Crabb's Farm
Catchpole Brook
CATCHPOLE LANE
SEAGERS
MILLWAYS
Fairplay House
Fontenay
Reservoir
Whitehouse Farm
Witham
CM8
Fanners Farm
PRINCE OF WALES ROAD
Rec. Grd.
B1022
MALDON ROAD
SCHOOL RD.
Works
WICKHAM HALL LANE
Garlands
Orchard Cottage
Wurono
Warren Cottage
Ash Plantation
Likely Wood
CAPTAINS WOOD RD.
BROAD ST. GRN. RD.
Catchpole Brook
Bog Grove
LANGFORD ROAD
WORMINGFORD
195
16
158
92
93
94
33
32
31
6
7
8
9
BABERGH
COLCHESTER
Bowdens Cottage
Wormingford Mere
Staunch Farm
Mill House
Orchard Cottage
Little Ash Field
Tippells
The Cottages
Rose Cottage
LOWER RD.
COLCHESTER RD.
B1508
Bures
CO8
The Fir Trees
Ash Grove
Pond Bay
Church Hall Farm
The Dell
St. Andrews C. of E. Prim. Sch.
Folley Cottage
The Lodge
SANDY HILL
Lodge Hills
Hall
Church House
The Grange
CHASE
Peartree Cottage
Elms Cottage
The Bottoms
Dormers
The Bungalows
Colletts Farm
Aldercar
Hall House
WORMINGFORD
The Cottage
Wormingford Hall
CHURCH ROAD
Playing Field
Pav.
Hall
Queenswood Farm
Magalene Cottage
Cockrell's Farm
The Bungalow
MAIN ROAD
Hillcroft Fm.
FORDHAM ROAD
Crown Cottages
Wood Hall
Moat
B1508
LITTLE HORKESLEY RD.
Chapel Corner
GARNONS ROAD
Wellhouse Farm
Long's Farm
Long Acres
Colchester
CO6
Butts Cottage

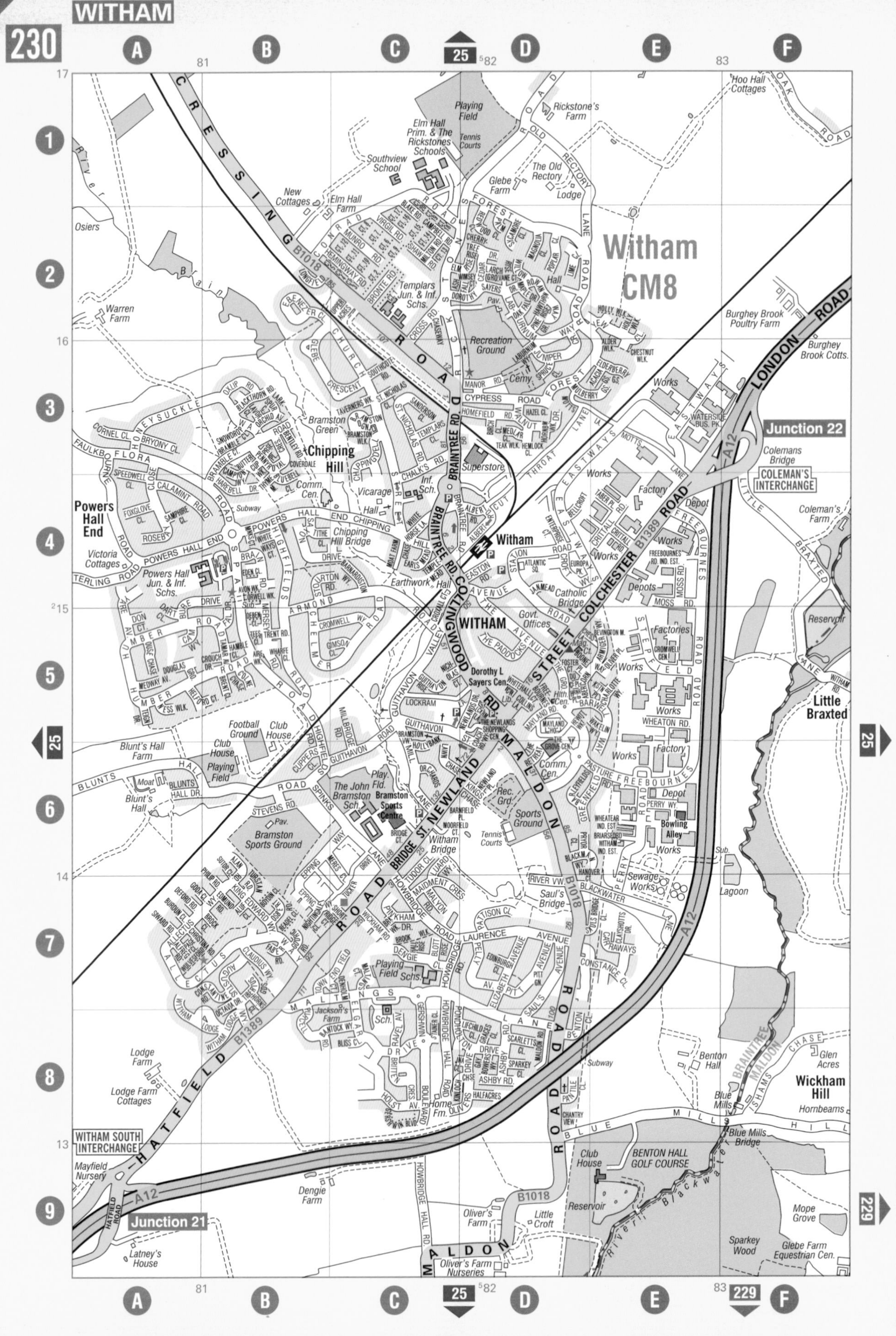
Witham
CM8
WITHAM
Chipping Hill
Powers Hall End
Little Braxted
Wickham Hill
Junction 22
COLEMAN'S INTERCHANGE
Junction 21
WITHAM SOUTH INTERCHANGE
BENTON HALL GOLF COURSE
Recreation Ground
Bramston Sports Ground
Superstore
Dorothy L Sayers Cen.
Templars Jun. & Inf. Schs.
Powers Hall Jun. & Inf. Schs.
Elm Hall Prim. & The Rickstones Schools
Southview School
The John Bramston Sch.
Bramston Sports Centre
CRESSING ROAD
LONDON ROAD
COLCHESTER ROAD
HATFIELD ROAD
MALDON ROAD
NEWLAND ST.
BRAINTREE RD.
COLLINGWOOD RD.
A12
B1018
B1389

INDEX

Including Streets, Places & Areas, Industrial Estates, Selected Flats & Walkways, Junction Names, Stations and Selected Places of Interest.

HOW TO USE THIS INDEX

1. Each street name is followed by its Postal District and then by its Locality abbreviation(s) and then by its map reference; e.g. **Aalten Av.** SS8: Can I . . . .2M **151** is in the Southend-on-Sea 8 Postal District and the Canvey Island Locality and is to be found in square 2M on page **151**. The page number is shown in bold type.

2. A strict alphabetical order is followed in which Av., Rd., St., etc. (though abbreviated) are read in full and as part of the street name; e.g. **Abbey Flds.** appears after **Abbeyfield Ho.** but before **Abbeygate St**.

3. Streets and a selection of flats and walkways too small to be shown on the maps, appear in the index with the thoroughfare to which it is connected shown in brackets; e.g. **Abbots Ct.** *RM3: H Wood . . . .5K **111** (off Queen's Pk. Rd.)*

4. Addresses that are in more than one part are referred to as not continuous.

5. Places and areas are shown in the index in **BLUE TYPE** and the map reference is to the actual map square in which the town centre or area is located and not to the place name shown on the map; e.g. **ABBEY FIELD 2N 173**

6. An example of a selected place of interest is Anstey Castle 2F 11

7. Junction names are shown in the index in **BOLD TYPE**; e.g. **ANGEL 6A 38**

8. An example of a station is **Alexandra Palace Station (Rail)** . . . .2A 38. Included are Rail **(Rail)**, London Underground **(Tube)** and Docklands Light Railway **(DLR)** Stations.

9. Streets that appear on the 3 inches to 1 Mile Street Mapping red pages and 1 Inch to 1 Mile Street Mapping blue pages are given two references: e.g **Abbot's Rd**. CO2: Colc . . . .3A **174** (7F **17**) is to be found in square 3A on page **174** on the 3 inches to 1 Mile Street Mapping and in square 7F on page **17** on the 1 inch to 1 Mile Street Mapping.

GENERAL ABBREVIATIONS

All. : Alley
App. : Approach
Arc. : Arcade
Av. : Avenue
Bk. : Back
Blvd. : Boulevard
Bri. : Bridge
B'way. : Broadway
Bldg. : Building
Bldgs. : Buildings
Bungs. : Bungalows
Bus. : Business
Cvn. : Caravan
C'way. : Causeway
Cen. : Centre
Chu. : Church
Circ. : Circle
Cir. : Circus
Cl. : Close
Comn. : Common
Cnr. : Corner
Cott. : Cottage
Cotts. : Cottages
Ct. : Court
Cres. : Crescent
Cft. : Croft
Dr. : Drive
E. : East
Ent. : Enterprise
Est. : Estate
Fld. : Field
Flds. : Fields
Gdn. : Garden
Gdns. : Gardens
Gth. : Garth
Ga. : Gate
Gt. : Great
Grn. : Green
Gro. : Grove
Hgts. : Heights
Ho. : House
Ind. : Industrial
Info. : Information
Intl. : International
La. : Lane
Lit. : Little
Lwr. : Lower
Mnr. : Manor
Mans. : Mansions
Mkt. : Market
Mdw. : Meadow
Mdws. : Meadows
M. : Mews
Mt. : Mount
Mus. : Museum
Nth. : North
No. : Number
Pal. : Palace
Pde. : Parade
Pk. : Park
Pas. : Passage
Pav. : Pavilion
Pl. : Place
Pct. : Precinct
Prom. : Promenade
Res. : Residential
Ri. : Rise
Rd. : Road
Rdbt. : Roundabout
Shop. : Shopping
Sth. : South
Sq. : Square
Sta. : Station
St. : Street
Ter. : Terrace
Twr. : Tower
Trad. : Trading
Up. : Upper
Va. : Vale
Vw. : View
Vs. : Villas
Vis. : Visitors
Wlk. : Walk
W. : West
Yd. : Yard

LOCALITY ABBREVIATIONS

Abb : **Abberton**
Ab R : **Abbess Roding**
Abgtn : **Abington**
Ab P : **Abington Pigotts**
Abr : **Abridge**
Act : **Acton**
Abry : **Albury**
Aldh : **Aldham**
A Grn : **Allens Green**
Alph : **Alphamstone**
Alp : **Alpheton**
Alr : **Alresford**
Alth : **Althorne**
Anst : **Anstey**
Ard : **Ardeley**
A'lgh : **Ardleigh**
A'den : **Arkesden**
Arr : **Arrington**
Anw : **Arwarton**
Ash : **Ash**
A'dn : **Ashdon**
Ashel : **Asheldham**
Ashen : **Ashen**
Aspen : **Aspenden**
Ass : **Assington**
A End : **Audley End**
Ave : **Aveley**
Ayt R : **Aythorpe Roding**
Bab : **Babraham**
B'shm : **Balsham**
Bar S : **Bardfield Saling**
Bark : **Barking**
B'wy : **Barkway**
Bar : **Barley**
Barl M : **Barling Magna**
B'dstn : **Barnardiston**
Barn : **Barnet**
Barns : **Barnston**
Barr : **Barrington**
Bart : **Bartlow**
Bas : **Basildon**
Bass : **Bassingbourn**
Bat : **Battlesbridge**
B'frd : **Bayford**
Bayf : **Bayfordbury**
Bay E : **Baythorne End**
Bean : **Bean**
Beau R : **Beauchamp Roding**
Bee : **Beeleigh**
Bel O : **Belchamp Otten**
Bel P : **Belchamp St Paul**
Bel W : **Belchamp Walter**
Belv : **Belvedere**
Ben : **Benfleet**
B'tn : **Benington**
B'ley : **Bentley**
Ber : **Berden**
Bex : **Bexley**
Bexh : **Bexleyheath**
Bick : **Bicknacre**
Bill : **Billericay**
B'ch : **Birch**
Bchgr : **Birchanger**
Bir G : **Birch Green**
Bird : **Birdbrook**
Bis S : **Bishop's Stortford**
B'hth : **Blackheath**
B'more : **Blackmore**
Bla E : **Blackmore End**
Bla N : **Black Notley**
Blue : **Bluewater**
Bore : **Boreham**
Bor : **Borley**
Boxt : **Boxted**
Brad : **Bradfield**
Brad S : **Bradwell-on-Sea**
Brain : **Braintree**
B'fld : **Bramfield**
Bran : **Brantham**
Brau : **Braughing**
Bre P : **Brent Pelham**
Brtwd : **Brentwood**
Brick : **Brickendon**
B'sea : **Brightlingsea**
Broom : **Broomfield**
Brox : **Broxbourne**
Broxt : **Broxted**
Buck H : **Buckhurst Hill**
Bkld : **Buckland**
Bulm : **Bulmer**
Bulp : **Bulphan**
Bunt : **Buntingford**
Bures : **Bures**
Bur C : **Burnham-on-Crouch**
Bur E : **Burton End**
Cwdn : **Canewdon**
Can I : **Canvey Island**
Cas C : **Castle Camps**
Cas H : **Castle Hedingham**
Caven : **Cavendish**
Chad H : **Chadwell Heath**
Chaf H : **Chafford Hundred**
Chap E : **Chapmore End**
Chap : **Chappel**
Chelm : **Chelmsford**
Chesh : **Cheshunt**
Ches : **Cheshut**
Chig S : **Chignall Smealy**
Chig J : **Chignal St James**
Chig : **Chigwell**
Chipp : **Chipping**
Chip : **Chipping Ongar**
Chris : **Chrishall**
Clac S : **Clacton-on-Sea**
Clare : **Clare**
Clav : **Clavering**
Clot : **Clothall**
Cobh : **Cobham**
Cock C : **Cock Clarks**
Cogg : **Coggeshall**
Colc : **Colchester**
Cold N : **Cold Norton**
Col G : **Cole Green**
Col R : **Collier Row**
Coln E : **Colne Engaine**
Cook G : **Cooksmill Green**
Coop : **Coopersale**
Cop : **Copford**
Corn T : **Cornard Tye**
Corn H : **Cornish Hall End**
Corr : **Corringham**
Cot : **Cottered**
Cray : **Crayford**
Cray H : **Crays Hill**
Crock : **Crockenhill**
Cro : **Cromer**
Croy : **Croydon**
Cuff : **Cuffley**
Cux : **Cuxton**
Dag : **Dagenham**
Dan : **Danbury**
D End : **Dane End**
Dart : **Dartford**
Deb : **Debden**
Deb G : **Debden Green**
Ded : **Dedham**
Deng : **Dengie**
Dodd : **Doddinghurst**
D'ham : **Downham**
Dun E : **Dunddenhoe End**
Dun : **Dunton**
Dut H : **Duton Hill**
Dux : **Duxford**
E Col : **Earls Colne**
E Ber : **East Bergholt**
E Han : **East Hanningfield**
Ethpe : **Easthorpe**
E Mer : **East Mersea**
E Til : **East Tilbury**
E'wck : **Eastwick**
Ed C : **Edney Common**
Eig G : **Eight Ash Green**
Elm : **Elmdon**
Elms : **Elmstead**
Else : **Elsenham**
Enf : **Enfield**
Epp : **Epping**
E Grn : **Epping Green**
Epp Up : **Epping Upland**
Eri : **Erith**
Eyns : **Eynsford**
F'std : **Fairstead**
Farnh : **Farnham**
F'ham : **Farningham**
Fau : **Faulkbourne**
Fawk : **Fawkham**
Fee : **Feering**
Felix : **Felixstowe**
Fels : **Felsted**
Fid : **Fiddlers Hamlet**
F'fld : **Finchingfield**
Fing : **Fingringhoe**
Fob : **Fobbing**
For : **Fordham**
Fou I : **Foulness Island**
Fow : **Fowlmere**
Fox : **Foxearth**
Foxt : **Foxton**
Frat : **Frating**
Frin S : **Frinton-on-Sea**
Fry : **Fryerning**
Fur P : **Furneux Pelham**
Fy'd : **Fyfield**
Gall : **Galleywood**
Gest : **Gestingthorpe**
Gil : **Gilston**
Glem : **Glemsford**
G Oak : **Goffs Oak**
Gold : **Goldhanger**
Good E : **Good Easter**
Gosf : **Gosfield**
Grav : **Gravesend**
Grays : **Grays**
Gt Ab : **Great Abington**
Gt Amw : **Great Amwell**
Gt Bad : **Great Baddow**
Gt Bar : **Great Bardfield**
Gt Ben : **Great Bentley**
Gt Br : **Great Braxted**
Gt Bro : **Great Bromley**
Gt Can : **Great Canfield**
Gt Che : **Great Chesterford**
Gt Chi : **Great Chishill**
Gt Cor : **Great Cornard**
Gt D : **Great Dunmow**
Gt Eas : **Great Easton**
Gt Hal : **Great Hallingbury**
Gt Hen : **Great Henny**
Gt Hol : **Great Holland**
Gt Hork : **Great Horkesley**
Gt Hor : **Great Hormead**
Gt L : **Great Leighs**
Gt Map : **Great Maplestead**
Gt N : **Great Notley**

Gt Oak : **Great Oakley**
Gt Sal : **Great Saling**
Gt Sam : **Great Sampford**
Gt Tey : **Great Tey**
Gt Tot : **Great Totham**
Gt W : **Great Wakering**
Gt Wal : **Great Waldingfield**
Gt Walt : **Great Waltham**
Gt War : **Great Warley**
Gt Wig : **Great Wigborough**
Gt Wra : **Great Wratting**
Gt Yel : **Great Yeldham**
Grnh : **Greenhithe**
G'std G : **Greenstead Green**
G'sted : **Greensted**
Had : **Hadleigh**
Hads : **Hadstock**
Hail : **Hailey**
Hall : **Halling**
Hals : **Halstead**
Hare S : **Hare Street**
Hark : **Harkstead**
H'low : **Harlow**
H Wood : **Harold Wood**
Hars : **Harston**
Hart : **Hartford**
Har E : **Hartford End**
Hley : **Hartley**
Har : **Harwich**
H'wd : **Hastingwood**
Hat O : **Hatfield Broad Oak**
Hat H : **Hatfield Heath**
Hat P : **Hatfield Peverel**
Haul : **Haultwick**
H'hll : **Haverhill**
Hav : **Havering-Atte-Bower**
Haz : **Hazeleigh**
Hel B : **Helions Bumpstead**
Hpstd : **Hempstead**
Hen : **Henham**
Heron : **Herongate**
Hert H : **Hertford Heath**
Hert : **Hertingfordbury**
H'bri : **Heybridge**
Hey B : **Heybridge Basin**
Hey : **Heydon**
High : **Higham**
H Bee : **High Beech**
H Cro : **High Cross**
High E : **High Easter**
H Lav : **High Laver**
H Ong : **High Ongar**
High R : **High Roding**
Hghwd : **Highwood**
H Wych : **High Wych**
Hdshm : **Hildersham**
Hxtn : **Hinxton**
Hock : **Hockley**
Hod : **Hoddesdon**
Holb : **Holbrook**
Hol S : **Holland-on-Sea**
Hook E : **Hook End**
Horn : **Hornchurch**
Horn H : **Horndon-on-the-Hill**
H'hth : **Horseheath**
Hor X : **Horsley Cross**
Hort K : **Horton Kirby**
Howe G : **Howe Green**
Hull : **Hullbridge**
Hun : **Hunsdon**
Hut : **Hutton**
I'tn : **Ickleton**
Ilf : **Ilford**
Ing : **Ingatestone**
Ingve : **Ingrave**
Inw : **Inworth**
Ist R : **Istead Rise**
Jay : **Jaywick**
Ked : **Kedington**
Kel : **Kelshall**
K'dn : **Kelvedon**
Kel C : **Kelvedon Common**
Kel H : **Kelvedon Hatch**
King : **Kingsford**
Kir S : **Kirby-le-Soken**
Lain : **Laindon**
Lmsh : **Lamarsh**
Lang H : **Langdon Hills**
L'hoe : **Langenhoe**
L'frd : **Langford**
L'ham : **Langham**
Lang L : **Langley Lower Green**
Lang U : **Langley Upper Green**
Latch : **Latchingdon**
Lav : **Lavenham**
Law : **Lawford**
Lay B : **Layer Breton**
Lay H : **Layer-de-la-Haye**
Lay M : **Layer Marney**
Lea R : **Leaden Roding**
L'hth : **Leavenheath**
Lee S : **Lee-over-Sands**
Lgh S : **Leigh-on-Sea**

Lndsl : **Lindsell**
Linf : **Linford**
Lin : **Linton**
Lis : **Liston**
Lit : **Litlington**
L Bad : **Little Baddow**
L Bar : **Little Bardfield**
L Ben : **Little Bentley**
L Berk : **Little Berkhamsted**
L Brax : **Little Braxted**
L Bro : **Little Bromley**
L Bur : **Little Burstead**
L'bry : **Littlebury**
Lit Gr : **Littlebury Green**
L Can : **Little Canfield**
L Ches : **Little Chesterford**
Lit C : **Little Chishill**
L Cla : **Little Clacton**
L Cor : **Little Cornard**
L Dun : **Little Dunmow**
L Eas : **Little Easton**
L Had : **Little Hadham**
L Hall : **Little Hallingbury**
L Hen : **Little Henny**
L Hork : **Little Horkesley**
L Hor : **Little Hormead**
Lit L : **Little Laver**
L L'gh : **Little Leighs**
L Map : **Little Maplestead**
L Oak : **Little Oakley**
L Sam : **Little Sampford**
L She : **Little Shelford**
L Tey : **Little Tey**
L Tot : **Little Totham**
Lit W : **Little Wakering**
L Wal : **Little Walden**
L Walt : **Little Waltham**
L War : **Little Warley**
L Wig : **Little Wigborough**
L Wra : **Little Wratting**
L Yel : **Little Yeldham**
Lon : **London**
Stan Apt : **London Stansted Airport**
Long : **Longfield**
Long H : **Longfield Hill**
L Mel : **Long Melford**
Lou : **Loughton**
Ludd : **Luddesdown**
Mag L : **Magdalen Laver**
Mal : **Maldon**
Man : **Manuden**
Mar R : **Margaret Roding**
Marg : **Margaretting**
M Tey : **Marks Tey**
Mash : **Mashbury**
Mat G : **Matching Green**
Mat T : **Matching Tye**
Maw : **Mawney**
May : **Mayland**
Mee : **Meesden**
Mel : **Melbourn**
Meld : **Meldreth**
Meop : **Meopham**
Mess : **Messing**
Mdltn : **Middleton**
Mill G : **Mill Green**
Mist : **Mistley**
M'ton : **Moreton**
M Bur : **Mount Bures**
Mount : **Mountnessing**
M Hud : **Much Hadham**
Mun : **Mundon**
Nasty : **Nasty**
Nave : **Navestock**
N'side : **Navestockside**
Nay : **Nayland**
Naze : **Nazeing**
New Ash : **New Ash Green**
New E : **New England**
New S : **Newgate Street**
Newp : **Newport**
New : **Newton**
Nine A : **Nine Ashes**
Noak H : **Noak Hill**
N'thaw : **Northaw**
N Ben : **North Benfleet**
N End : **North End**
N Fam : **North Fambridge**
N'fleet : **Northfleet**
N'flt G : **Northfleet Green**
N Ock : **North Ockendon**
N Stif : **North Stifford**
N Wea : **North Weald**
Nor H : **Norton Heath**
Nuth : **Nuthampstead**
Odsey : **Odsey**
Old G : **Old Hall Green**
Orp : **Orpington**
Ors : **Orsett**
Orw : **Orwell**
Ovtn : **Ovington**
Pag : **Paglesham**
Pam : **Pampisford**

Pan : **Panfield**
Pans : **Panshanger**
Peb : **Pebmarsh**
Pel : **Peldon**
Pent : **Pentlow**
Pil H : **Pilgrims Hatch**
Pits : **Pitsea**
Ples : **Pleshey**
P Bay : **Point Clear Bay**
Pos : **Poslingford**
Puck : **Puckeridge**
Purf : **Purfleet**
Pur : **Purleigh**
Quen : **Quendon**
Rad G : **Radley Green**
R'ter : **Radwinter**
Rain : **Rainham**
Rams B : **Ramsden Bellhouse**
Rams H : **Ramsden Heath**
R'sy : **Ramsey**
Raw : **Rawreth**
Ray : **Rayleigh**
Rayne : **Rayne**
Reed : **Reed**
Ret C : **Rettendon Common**
R'lng : **Rickling**
Rick G : **Rickling Green**
Ridg : **Ridgewell**
Riven : **Rivenhall**
Roch : **Rochester**
R'fd : **Rochford**
Romf : **Romford**
Rhdge : **Rowhedge**
Rox : **Roxwell**
Roy : **Roydon**
R'ton : **Royston**
Runw : **Runwell**
Rush : **Rushden**
Rush G : **Rush Green**
Rye P : **Rye Park**
Sac : **Sacombe**
Saf W : **Saffron Walden**
St La : **St Lawrence**
St O : **St Osyth**
Salc : **Salcott**
S'don : **Sandon**
Saw : **Sawbridgeworth**
Saws : **Sawston**
Sew E : **Sewards End**
Shalf : **Shalford**
Srng : **Sheering**
Shenf : **Shenfield**
Shepr : **Shepreth**
Shin W : **Shingay Cum Wendy**
Shoe : **Shoeburyness**
Shorne : **Shorne**
S'ly : **Shotley**
Shudy C : **Shudy Camps**
Sib H : **Sible Hedingham**
Sidc : **Sidcup**
Sil E : **Silver End**
Sole S : **Sole Street**
S Dar : **South Darenth**
Sth A : **Southend Airport**
Sth S : **Southend-on-Sea**
S'fleet : **Southfleet**
S Han : **South Hanningfield**
S'min : **Southminster**
S Ock : **South Ockendon**
S Wea : **South Weald**
S Fer : **South Woodham Ferrers**
Spel : **Spellbrook**
Stamb : **Stambourne**
Stam : **Stambridge**
Stdn : **Standon**
Stan H : **Stanford-le-Hope**
S'std : **Stanstead**
Stan A : **Stanstead Abbotts**
Stan M : **Stansted Mountfitchet**
S'way : **Stanway**
Stfrd : **Stapleford**
Stap A : **Stapleford Abbotts**
Stap T : **Stapleford Tawney**
Steb : **Stebbing**
Stpl : **Steeple**
Stpl B : **Steeple Bumpstead**
Stpl M : **Steeple Morden**
Stock : **Stock**
Stoc P : **Stocking Pelham**
Stoke C : **Stoke by Clare**
Stok : **Stoke-by-Nayland**
Ston M : **Stondon Massey**
Sto G : **Stones Green**
Stow M : **Stow Maries**
Strat M : **Stratford St Mary**
Stret : **Strethall**
Stur : **Sturmer**
Stut : **Stutton**
Sud : **Sudbury**
S at H : **Sutton at Hone**
Swan : **Swanley**
Swans : **Swanscombe**
Tak : **Takeley**

Temp I : **Temple Farm Industrial Estate**
Ten : **Tendring**
Terl : **Terling**
Thax : **Thaxted**
Ther : **Therfield**
They B : **Theydon Bois**
They G : **Theydon Garnon**
They M : **Theydon Mount**
Thor : **Thorley**
Thorn : **Thornwood**
T Sok : **Thorpe-le-Soken**
Thorr : **Thorrington**
Thri : **Thriplow**
Thro : **Throcking**
Thund : **Thundersley**
Thun : **Thundridge**
Thurl : **Thurlow**
Til : **Tilbury**
Til C : **Tilbury Juxta Clare**
T'ham : **Tillingham**
Tilty : **Tilty**
Tip : **Tiptree**
Tol : **Tollesbury**
Tol D : **Tolleshunt D'Arcy**
Tol K : **Tolleshunt Knights**
Tol M : **Tolleshunt Major**
Ton : **Tonwell**
Toot : **Toot Hill**
Top : **Toppesfield**
T Mary : **Trimley St Mary**
Trimms : **Trimms Green**
Turn : **Turnford**
T'std : **Twinstead**
Tye G : **Tye Green**
Ugley : **Ugley**
U Grn : **Ugley Green**
Ult : **Ulting**
Upm : **Upminster**
Van : **Vange**
Vir : **Virley**
Wad : **Wadesmill**
Wak C : **Wakes Colne**
Walk : **Walkern**
Wall : **Wallington**
Wal A : **Waltham Abbey**
Wal X : **Waltham Cross**
Walt : **Walton-on-the-Naze**
Ware : **Ware**
W'side : **Wareside**
War : **Warley**
W'frd : **Waterford**
Wat S : **Watton at Stone**
Wee : **Weeley**
Wee H : **Weeley Heath**
Wen L : **Wenden Lofts**
Wen A : **Wendens Ambo**
Wen : **Wennington**
W Ber : **West Bergholt**
Wclf S : **Westcliff-on-Sea**
W Han : **West Hanningfield**
W H'dn : **West Horndon**
W Mer : **West Mersea**
W'mll : **Westmill**
W Thur : **West Thurrock**
W Til : **West Tilbury**
W W'ck : **West Wickham**
W Wra : **West Wratting**
Weth : **Wethersfield**
Whad : **Whaddon**
Whi C : **White Colne**
Whi N : **White Notley**
Whi R : **White Roding**
Whitt : **Whittlesford**
Wick B : **Wicken Bonhunt**
W'fd : **Wickford**
W Bis : **Wickham Bishops**
Wick P : **Wickham St Paul**
Widd : **Widdington**
Wid : **Widford**
Will : **Willingale**
Will G : **Willows Green**
Wim : **Wimbish**
Wimp : **Wimpole**
Wthm : **Witham**
Wthfld : **Withersfield**
W'hoe : **Wivenhoe**
Wix : **Wix**
Wixoe : **Wixoe**
Wfd G : **Woodford Green**
Wdhm F : **Woodham Ferrers**
Wdhm M : **Woodham Mortimer**
Wdhm W : **Woodham Walter**
Wmgfd : **Wormingford**
Wmly : **Wormley**
Wrab : **Wrabness**
Writ : **Writtle**
Wy G : **Wyatts Green**
Wyd : **Wyddial**

A

Aalten Av. SS8: Can I 2M **151**
ABBERTON 8B **174** (2E **26**)
Abberton Rd. CO2: Abb, Lay H 9J **173** (1D **26**)
CO5: Fing, L'hoe 8C **174** (2F **27**)
Abberton Wlk. RM13: Rain 1D **142**
Abbess Cl. CM1: Chelm 9G **58**
ABBESS END 6D **22**
ABBESS RODING 6D **22**
Abbey Cl. CM5: Fy'd 1N **67**
RM1: Romf 1E **126**
SS5: Hull 6K **103**
Abbey Ct. EN9: Wal A 4B **76**
Abbey Cres. CO16: T Sok 5L **179**
Abbeydale Cl. CM17: H'low 4H **55**
Abbeydale Ct. E17: Lon 7D **106**
ABBEY FIELD 2N **173**
Abbeyfield Ho. SS7: Had 3J **135**
Abbey Flds. CM3: E Han 2B **88**
Abbeygate St. CO2: Colc 9N **165**
Abbey Ho. CB10: Saf W 4C **218**
Abbey La. CB10: Saf W 4B **218**
CO6: Cogg 4L **197**
E15: Lon 6E **38**
Abbey Mead Ind. Est. EN9: Wal A 4C **76**
(not continuous)

Abbey Mdw. CO9: Sib H . . . 5J 219
Abbey M. E17: Lon . . . 9A 106
Abbey Mills EN9: Wal A . . . 3B 76
Abbey Pk. Ind. Est. IG11: Bark . . . 2B 140
Abbey Retail Pk. IG11: Bark . . . 9A 124
Abbey Rd. CM12: Bill . . . 7H 99
DA12: Grav . . . 4H 47
IG2: Ilf . . . 9C 108
IG11: Bark . . . 1A 140 (5G 39)
SS5: Hull . . . 7K 103
Abbey Sports Cen. . . . 1B 140
Abbey St. CB10: I'tn . . . 6A 202 (4K 5)
CO16: T Sok . . . 5L 179 (7E 18)
SE1: Lon . . . 7B 38
Abbey Turning CM9: Bee, Mal . . . 1G 35
Abbey Vw. CM6: Dut H . . . 5F 13
EN9: Wal A . . . 3B 76 (4D 30)
Abbey Wharf Ind. Est. IG11: Bark . . . 3C 140
Abbey Wood La. RM13: Rain . . . 2H 143
Abbots Cl. CM15: Shenf . . . 7K 97
CO11: Wix . . . 4D 18
CO15: Clac S . . . 7J 185
RM13: Rain . . . 2G 143
Abbots Ct. RM3: H Wood . . . 5K 111
(off Queen's Pk. Rd.)
SS15: Bas . . . 6N 115
Abbotsford Gdns. IG8: Wfd G . . . 4G 106
Abbotsford Rd. IG3: Ilf . . . 4F 124
Abbots Gdns. CO16: St O . . . 9A 184
Abbotsleigh Rd. CM3: S Fer . . . 2K 103
Abbotsmead CM9: Mal . . . 3B 214
Abbots Ride CM11: Bill . . . 6L 99
Abbot's Rd. CO2: Colc . . . 3A 174 (7F 17)
Abbots Wlk. SS3: Shoe . . . 6G 139
Abbotsweld CM18: H'low . . . 6C 54
Abbot's Wick La. CO5: Gt Wig . . . 4C 26
Abbotswood SS7: Thund . . . 1J 135
Abbotswood Gdns. IG5: Ilf . . . 7M 107
Abbott Rd. CO12: Har . . . 5H 209 (3G 19)
E14: Lon . . . 7E 38
(not continuous)
Abbotts Cl. RM7: Maw . . . 7N 109
SE28: Lon . . . 7H 141
SS9: Lgh S . . . 1D 136
Abbotts Cotts. CB9: Stur . . . 7L 223
Abbotts Ct. CB9: Stur . . . 6J 223
Abbotts Cres. E4: Lon . . . 1D 106
Abbotts Cft. CB9: Stur . . . 7K 223
Abbotts Dr. EN9: Wal A . . . 3G 77
SS17: Stan H . . . 3M 147 (6K 41)
Abbotts Hall Chase SS17: Stan H . . . 3N 147
Abbotts La. CO6: Eig G . . . 8B 164
SG12: Wid . . . 4F 21
Abbotts Pk. Rd. E10: Lon . . . 2C 122
Abbotts Pl. CM2: Chelm . . . 8M 59
Abbs Cross RM11: Horn . . . 3G 127
Abbs Cross Gdns. RM12: Horn . . . 3G 127
Abbs Cross La. RM12: Horn . . . 5G 126 (4B 40)
Abdy Av. CO12: Har . . . 5G 208
Abels Rd. CO9: Hals . . . 6J 207
Abenberg Way CM13: Hut . . . 8L 97
Abensburg Rd. SS8: Can I . . . 9K 135
Abercorn Gdns. RM6: Chad H . . . 1G 124
Abercorn Ho. CM3: Bore . . . 3F 60
Abercorn Way CM8: Wthm . . . 5D 230
Abercrombie Way CM18: H'low . . . 4B 54 (7H 21)
Aberdeen Gdns. SS9: Lgh S . . . 4N 135
Aberdour Rd. IG3: Ilf . . . 5G 124
Abigail Ct. CM5: Chip . . . 5L 67
Abigail M. RM3: H Wood . . . 6K 111
Abingdon Ct. SS13: Bas . . . 6H 117
Abinger Cl. CO16: Clac S . . . 7G 185
IG11: Bark . . . 6F 124
Abington Ct. RM14: Upm . . . 3N 127
ABINGTON PIGOTTS . . . 3A 4
Abington Rd. SG8: Ab P, Lit . . . 3A 4
Abraham Ct. RM14: Upm . . . 4L 127
Abraham Dr. CM8: Sil E . . . 8M 217
Abram's La. SG8: Chris . . . 5H 5
Abreys SS7: Thund . . . 8G 119
ABRIDGE . . . 2G 92 (6J 31)
Abridge Gdns. RM5: Col R . . . 3M 109
Abridge Pk. Cvn. Pk.
RM4: Abr . . . 3F 92
Abridge Rd.
CM16: Abr, Lou, They B . . . 7D 78 (5H 31)
IG7: Abr, Chig . . . 5C 92 (7H 31)
RM4: Abr . . . 8F 78 (6J 31)
Abridge Way IG11: Bark . . . 2G 141
Acacia Av. CO4: Colc . . . 7E 166
RM12: Horn . . . 4D 126
Acacia Bus. Cen. E11: Lon . . . 5E 122
Acacia Ct. EN9: Wal A . . . 4G 77
(off Lamplighters Cl.)
Acacia Dr. CM6: Gt D . . . 2K 203
CM9: Mal . . . 6A 214
RM14: Upm . . . 6L 127
SS1: Sth S . . . 6E 138 (5A 44)
Acacia Gdns. CM8: Wthm . . . 3E 230
RM14: Upm . . . 2C 128
Acacia Rd. E11: Lon . . . 4E 122
SS13: Pits . . . 7M 117
Acacias Ct. EN11: Hod . . . 5A 52
(off Brocket Rd.)
Accommodation Rd. CO4: Boxt . . . 9L 159
Accrington Ho. RM3: Romf . . . 2H 111
(off Montgomery Cres.)
Acer Av. RM13: Rain . . . 3H 143
Acer Gro. CM1: Chelm . . . 7M 59
Achilles Way CM7: Brain . . . 3K 193
Achnacone Dr. CO4: Colc . . . 4K 165
Acland Av. CO3: Colc . . . 8H 165
Acland Ct. CO3: Colc . . . 8H 165
Acle Cl. IG6: Ilf . . . 4A 108
Aconbury Rd. RM9: Dag . . . 1G 140
Acorn Av. CM7: Brain . . . 6F 192
CO9: Hals . . . 5J 207
Acorn Cen., The IG6: Ilf . . . 3G 108
Acorn Cl. CM9: Mal . . . 3B 214
CO4: Colc . . . 3D 166
CO12: Har . . . 6J 209
E4: Lon . . . 2B 106
Acorn Ct. E6: Lon . . . 9L 123
IG2: Ilf . . . 1D 124
Acorn M. CM18: H'low . . . 5E 54
Acorn Pl. CO4: Colc . . . 1C 166
SS16: Lang H . . . 1K 131
Acorns, The IG7: Chig . . . 1D 108
SS5: Hock . . . 9D 104
Acorn St. SG12: Hun . . . 5F 21
Acorn Trad. Est. RM20: Grays . . . 4G 155
Acorn Wlk. CO7: Thorr . . . 9F 176
Acreland Grn. CM3: Ples . . . 4G 23
Acremore St. SG11: L Had . . . 1G 21
Acre Rd. RM10: Dag . . . 9N 125
Acres Av. CM5: Chip . . . 5K 67
Acres End CM1: Chelm . . . 7G 58
Acres, The SS17: Stan H . . . 2A 148
Acre Vw. RM11: Horn . . . 8J 111
ACTON . . . 3K 9
Acton La. CO10: Act, Sud . . . 4K 9
ACTON PLACE . . . 3K 9
Ada Cole Memorial Stables . . . 8L 53 (1G 31)
Adalia Cres. SS9: Lgh S . . . 3A 136
Adalia Way SS9: Lgh S . . . 4A 136
Adams Bus. Cen. SS14: Bas . . . 6G 116
Adams Ct. CB11: Saf W . . . 5B 218
CO9: Hals . . . 4J 207
Adam's Elm Ho. SS9: Lgh S . . . 4D 136
Adams Glade SS4: R'fd . . . 1J 121
Adams Ho. CM20: H'low . . . 2C 54
(off Post Office Rd.)
Adams Rd. SS17: Stan H . . . 4N 147
Adam Way SS11: W'fd . . . 8M 101
Adderley Rd. CM23: Bis S . . . 1K 21
Addison Ct. CM16: Epp . . . 1F 78
Addison Gdns. RM17: Grays . . . 2M 155
Addison Rd. CO13: Gt Hol . . . 9D 180
E11: Lon . . . 1G 123
E17: Lon . . . 9B 106
IG6: Ilf . . . 5B 108
Adelaide Dr. CO2: Colc . . . 5A 174
Adelaide Gdns. RM6: Chad H . . . 9K 109
SS7: Ben . . . 5D 134
Adelaide Rd. E10: Lon . . . 5B 122
IG1: Ilf . . . 4A 124
RM18: Til . . . 6B 156
Adelaide St. CO12: Har . . . 2H 209
Adeliza Cl. IG11: Bark . . . 9B 124
Adelphi Cres. RM12: Horn . . . 4E 126
Adelsburg Rd. SS8: Can I . . . 1J 151
Aden Rd. IG1: Ilf . . . 2B 124
Adingtons CM20: H'low . . . 1E 54
Admiral Ct. IG11: Bark . . . 2G 141
Admirals Cl. E18: Lon . . . 8H 107
Admirals Ct. E6: Lon . . . 6A 140
(off Trader Rd.)
Admirals Lodge RM1: Romf . . . 8D 110
Admirals Wlk. CM1: Chelm . . . 8H 59
CO7: W'hoe . . . 6H 175
EN11: Hod . . . 7A 52
SS3: Shoe . . . 8H 139
Adnams Wlk. RM13: Rain . . . 8E 126
Adomar Rd. RM8: Dag . . . 5J 125
Adstock Way RM17: Grays . . . 2J 155
Advice Av. RM16: Grays . . . 9K 145
Aetheric Rd. CM7: Brain . . . 5G 193 (7C 14)
Affleck Rd. CO4: Colc . . . 8E 166
Afflets Ct. SS14: Bas . . . 7D 116
(off Moat Fld.)
Afton Dr. RM15: S Ock . . . 6E 144
Agar Gro. NW1: Lon . . . 5A 38
Agar Rd. CO14: Walt . . . 6M 181
Agate Rd. CO15: Clac S . . . 2J 189
Agincourt Rd. CO15: Clac S . . . 9H 185
Agister Rd. IG7: Chig . . . 2F 108
Agnes Av. IG1: Ilf . . . 6N 123
SS9: Lgh S . . . 4A 136
Agnes Gdns. RM8: Dag . . . 6J 125
Aidan Cl. RM8: Dag . . . 6K 125
Aileen Wlk. E15: Lon . . . 9F 122
Ailsa Rd. SS0: Wclf S . . . 6H 137
AIMES GREEN . . . 8F 62 (3F 31)
Aimes Grn. SS13: Bas . . . 7K 117
(off Porters)
Ainger Rd. CO12: Har . . . 5G 209
AINGERS GREEN . . . 9L 177 (1A 28)
Aingers Grn. Rd.
CO7: Gt Ben . . . 9L 177 (1A 28)
Ainsley Av. RM7: Romf . . . 1N 125
Ainslie Wood Cres. E4: Lon . . . 2B 106
Ainslie Wood Gdns. E4: Lon . . . 1B 106
Ainslie Wood Nature Reserve . . . 2B 106
Ainslie Wood Rd. E4: Lon . . . 2A 106
Aintree Cres. IG6: Ilf . . . 6B 108
Aintree Gro. RM14: Upm . . . 5K 127
Airborne Cl. SS9: Lgh S . . . 1D 136
Airborne Ind. Est. SS9: Lgh S . . . 1D 136
Aire Dr. RM15: S Ock . . . 4E 144
Aire Wlk. CM8: Wthm . . . 5B 230
Airey Neave Ct. RM17: Grays . . . 9K 145
Airfield Pathway RM12: Horn . . . 9G 126
Airfield Way
RM12: Horn . . . 8F 126 (5B 40)
Airlie Gdns. IG1: Ilf . . . 3A 124
Airthrie Rd. IG3: Ilf . . . 4G 124
Aisher Rd. SE28: Lon . . . 7H 141
Aisne Rd. CO2: Colc . . . 2L 173
Ajax Cl. CM7: Brain . . . 3K 193
Akenfield Cl. CM3: S Fer . . . 1L 103
Alamein Rd. CM0: Bur C . . . 4E 196
CM1: Chelm . . . 5H 59
CO2: Colc . . . 4K 173
Alanbrooke Rd. CO2: Colc . . . 4D 174
Alan Cl. DA1: Dart . . . 9G 153
SS9: Lgh S . . . 9D 120
Alander M. E17: Lon . . . 8C 106
Alan Dr. CO16: L Cla . . . 4H 185
Alan Gdns. RM7: Rush G . . . 2M 125
Alan Gro. SS9: Lgh S . . . 9D 120
Alan Haslar Ho. CM6: Gt D . . . 4L 203
Alan Rd. CM8: Wthm . . . 6B 230
Alan Way CO3: Colc . . . 2G 173
Albany Av. SS0: Wclf S . . . 5K 137
Albany Chase CO15: Clac S . . . 9M 185
Albany Cl. CM1: Chelm . . . 6G 58
CO6: W Ber . . . 3F 164
Albany Ct. CM16: Epp . . . 9E 64
E10: Lon . . . 2A 122
Albany Gdns. E. CO15: Clac S . . . 9M 185
Albany Gdns. W. CO15: Clac S . . . 9L 185
Albany Ri. SS6: Ray . . . 6M 119
Albany Rd. CM15: Pil H . . . 5E 96
CO6: W Ber . . . 3F 164
E10: Lon . . . 2A 122
E12: Lon . . . 6K 123
RM6: Chad H . . . 1L 125
RM12: Horn . . . 3E 126
RM18: Til . . . 6C 156
SS6: Ray . . . 6N 119
SS12: W'fd . . . 1L 117
Albany St. NW1: Lon . . . 6A 38
Albany, The IG8: Wfd G . . . 1F 106
Albany Vw. IG9: Buck H . . . 7G 91
Alba Rd. CM17: H'low . . . 2H 55
Albemarle App. IG2: Ilf . . . 1A 124
Albemarle Cl. RM17: Grays . . . 9K 145
Albemarle Gdns. CM7: Brain . . . 3L 193
IG2: Ilf . . . 1A 124
Albemarle St. CO12: Har . . . 2M 209
Alberta Rd. DA8: Eri . . . 6A 152
Albert Av. E4: Lon . . . 1A 106
Albert Cl. RM16: Grays . . . 1M 155
SS4: R'fd . . . 1H 121
SS6: Ray . . . 4M 119
Albert Ct. E7: Lon . . . 6G 123
Albert Cres. E4: Lon . . . 1A 106
Albert Dr. SS15: Lain . . . 9L 115
Albert Gdns. CM17: H'low . . . 4J 55
CO6: Cogg . . . 3L 197
CO15: Clac S . . . 1L 189
Albert Ho. E18: Lon . . . 7H 107
(off Albert Rd.)
SE28: Lon . . . 9B 140
(off Erebus Dr.)
Albertine Cl. CO3: S'way . . . 9D 164
Albertine St. CM17: H'low . . . 2H 55
Albert M. SS0: Wclf S . . . 6K 137
Albert Pl. CO6: Cogg . . . 3L 197
SS1: Sth S . . . 7A 138
(off Beach Rd.)
Albert Rd. CM0: Bur C . . . 4E 196
CM3: S Fer . . . 1J 103
CM7: Brain . . . 5J 193
CM8: Wthm . . . 4D 230
CO7: B'sea . . . 7F 182
DA17: Belv . . . 1A 46
E10: Lon . . . 4C 122
E16: Lon . . . 9A 140 (7G 39)
E17: Lon . . . 9A 106
E18: Lon . . . 7H 107
IG1: Ilf . . . 5A 124
IG9: Buck H . . . 8K 91 (1F 39)
N10: Lon . . . 2A 38
RM1: Romf . . . 9D 110 (3A 40)
RM8: Dag . . . 3M 125
RM14: Bulp . . . 6B 130
SS1: Sth S . . . 5E 138
(Armitage Rd.)
SS1: Sth S . . . 7N 137
(York Rd.)
SS4: R'fd . . . 1H 121
SS6: Ray . . . 4M 119
SS7: Thund . . . 9B 118
Albert Sq. E15: Lon . . . 7E 122
Albert St. CM14: War . . . 2F 112
CO1: Colc . . . 7M 165
CO12: Har . . . 2M 209
Albert Ter. IG9: Buck H . . . 8L 91
Albert Wlk. E16: Lon . . . 9A 140
Albert Whicher Ho. E17: Lon . . . 8C 106
Albion Cl. RM7: Romf . . . 1B 126
Albion Ct. CM2: Chelm . . . 1C 72
CM12: Bill . . . 7J 99
Albion Dr. E8: Lon . . . 6C 38
Albion Gro. CO2: Colc . . . 1A 174
Albion Hill IG10: Lou . . . 4J 91
Albion Ho. E16: Lon . . . 8A 140
(off Church St.)
Albion Pk. IG10: Lou . . . 4K 91
Albion Rd. DA6: Bexh . . . 3A 46
E17: Lon . . . 7C 106
N16: Lon . . . 5B 38
SS0: Wclf S . . . 5K 137
SS7: Ben . . . 2C 134
Albion St. CO5: Rhdge . . . 6G 174
Albion Ter. E4: Lon . . . 3B 90
Albra Mead CM2: Chelm . . . 7C 60
Albright Ind. Est. RM13: Rain . . . 4D 142
Albrighton Cft. CO4: Colc . . . 3C 166
ALBURY . . . 6G 11
ALBURY END . . . 7G 11
Albury M. E12: Lon . . . 4J 123
Albury Rd. SG11: L Had . . . 7H 11
Albyns SS16: Lang H . . . 2L 131
Albyns Cl. RM13: Rain . . . 9E 126
Albyns La. RM4: Stap T . . . 1A 94 (6A 32)
Alcester Ho. RM3: Romf . . . 2H 111
(off Northallerton Way)
Alconbury CM23: Bis S . . . 8A 220
Alcorns, The CM24: Stan M . . . 1D 220
Alcotes SS14: Bas . . . 1G 133
Aldborough Ct. IG2: Ilf . . . 9E 108
(off Aldborough Rd. Nth.)
ALDBOROUGH HATCH . . . 8E 108 (3H 39)
Aldborough Rd. RM10: Dag . . . 8A 126
RM14: Upm . . . 4K 127
Aldborough Rd. Nth. IG2: Ilf . . . 9E 108 (3H 39)
Aldborough Rd. Sth. IG3: Ilf . . . 3D 124 (4H 39)
Aldeburgh Cl. CO16: Clac S . . . 9F 184
Aldeburgh Gdns. CO4: Colc . . . 3B 166
Aldeburgh Pl. IG8: Wfd G . . . 1G 107
Aldeburgh Way CM1: Chelm . . . 6M 59
Alder Av. RM14: Upm . . . 6K 127
Alderbury Lea CM3: Bick . . . 9F 74
Alderbury Rd. CM24: Stan M . . . 1D 220
Aldercar Rd. CO6: Cop . . . 4N 171 (7B 16)
Alder Cl. EN11: Rye P . . . 3B 52
SS15: Lain . . . 6M 115
Alder Dr. CM2: Chelm . . . 4C 72
RM15: S Ock . . . 4F 144
Alderford Maltings CO9: Sib H . . . 7K 219
Alderford St. CO9: Sib H . . . 7K 219 (2E 14)
Aldergrove Wlk. RM12: Horn . . . 8G 126
Alderleys SS7: Thund . . . 9G 119
Alderman Av. IG11: Bark . . . 3F 140
Alderman Howe Lodge CO4: Colc . . . 3B 166
(off Tynedale Sq.)
Aldermans Hill N13: Lon . . . 1A 38
SS5: Hock . . . 2A 120 (1G 43)
Alderman Wlk. SS17: Stan H . . . 9N 131
Alderney Gdns. SS11: W'fd . . . 6K 101
Alderney Rd. DA8: Eri . . . 5E 152
Alders Av. IG8: Wfd G . . . 3E 106
ALDERSBROOK . . . 4H 123 (4F 39)
Aldersbrook La. E12: Lon . . . 5M 123
Aldersbrook Rd. E11: Lon . . . 4H 123 (4F 39)
E12: Lon . . . 4J 123 (4F 39)
Alders Cl. E11: Lon . . . 4H 123
Aldersey Gdns. IG11: Bark . . . 8C 124
Aldersgate St. EC1: Lon . . . 7B 38
Aldersgrove EN9: Wal A . . . 4E 76
Alders Wlk. CM21: Saw . . . 2K 51
Alderton Cl. CM6: Fels . . . 7K 199
CM15: Pil H . . . 4E 96
IG10: Lou . . . 3N 91
Alderton Hall La. IG10: Lou . . . 3N 91
Alderton Hill IG10: Lou . . . 4L 91 (7G 31)
Alderton M. IG10: Lou . . . 3N 91
Alderton Ri. IG10: Lou . . . 3N 91
Alderton Rd. CO4: Colc . . . 7C 166
RM16: Ors . . . 6G 146
Alderton Way IG10: Lou . . . 4M 91
Alder Wlk. CM8: Wthm . . . 3E 230
IG1: Ilf . . . 7B 124
Alderwood Cl. RM4: Abr . . . 2G 93
Alderwood Dr. RM4: Abr . . . 2G 93
Alderwood Way SS7: Ben . . . 3J 135
ALDGATE . . . 7B 38
Aldgate East Station (Tube) . . . 7B 38
Aldgate Station (Tube) . . . 7B 38
ALDHAM . . . 5A 16
Aldham Dr. RM15: S Ock . . . 5F 144
Aldham Gdns. SS6: Ray . . . 4F 118
Aldingham Ct. RM12: Horn . . . 7F 126
(off Easedale Dr.)
Aldingham Gdns. RM12: Horn . . . 7E 126
Aldington Cl. RM8: Dag . . . 3H 125
Aldis M. EN3: Enf . . . 7A 76
Aldon Cl. CO12: Har . . . 6E 208
Aldria Rd. SS17: Stan H . . . 9N 131
Aldriche Way E4: Lon . . . 3C 106
Aldridge Av. EN3: Enf . . . 8A 76
Aldridge Cl. CM2: Chelm . . . 7B 60
Aldrin Cl. SS17: Stan H . . . 3N 147
Aldrin Way SS9: Lgh S . . . 9F 120
Aldworth Rd. E15: Lon . . . 9E 122
Aldwych WC2: Lon . . . 7A 38
Aldwych Av. IG6: Ilf . . . 8B 108
Aldwych Cl. RM12: Horn . . . 4E 126
Aldwych Station (Tube) . . . 7A 38
Alec Kay Ct. CO2: Colc . . . 4K 173
(off Layer Rd.)
Alefounder Cl. CO4: Colc . . . 9E 166
Alethea Farm Pl. CO9: Til C . . . 8F 216
Alexander Ct. CM1: Chelm . . . 4N 59
Alexander La. CM13: Hut . . . 5L 97
CM15: Shenf . . . 4K 97 (7F 33)
Alexander M. CM2: S'don . . . 8L 73
Alexander Rd. CM7: Brain . . . 4G 193
SS16: Lang H . . . 3K 131
(not continuous)
Alexandra Av. CO5: W Mer . . . 3D 228
Alexandra Cl. RM16: Grays . . . 9D 146
Alexandra Ct. SS1: Sth S . . . 7L 137
SS2: Sth S . . . 5L 137
Alexandra Dr. CO7: W'hoe . . . 3J 175
Alexandra Ho. IG8: Ilf . . . 4N 107
Alexandra M. CM7: Brain . . . 5J 193
Alexandra Palace Station (Rail) . . . 2A 38
Alexandra Pal. Way N8: Lon . . . 3A 38
Alexandra Pk. Rd. N10: Lon . . . 2A 38
N22: Lon . . . 2A 38
Alexandra Rd. CM0: Bur C . . . 3D 196
CM14: Brtwd . . . 9F 96
CM17: H'low . . . 2H 55
CO3: Colc . . . 9M 165
CO9: Sib H . . . 6J 219 (1D 14)
CO12: Har . . . 2M 209
CO15: Clac S . . . 1J 189

Alexandra Rd. CO16: Wee 5D 178
DA8: Eri. 4D 152
E10: Lon 5C 122
E18: Lon 7H 107
RM1: Romf 1D 126
RM6: Chad H. 1K 125
RM13: Rain. 1D 142
RM18: Til 7B 156
SS1: Sth S. 7L 137
SS3: Gt W 4K 139
SS4: R'fd. 1H 121
SS6: Ray 4L 119
SS7: Ben. 4D 134
SS9: Lgh S 6D 136
Alexandra St. CO12: Har 2M 209
SS1: Sth S. 7M 137 (5K 43)
Alexandra Ter. CO3: Colc. 9M 165
Alexandra Way RM18: E Til 2K 157
Alexandria Dr. SS6: Ray. 3G 119
Alfells Rd. CO7: Elms 1M 175
Alford Rd. DA8: Eri 3A 152
Alfreda Av. SS5: Hull 5K 103
Alfred Gdns. SS11: W'fd. 7L 101
Alfred Ho. *E12: Lon* 9L 123
(off Tennyson Av.)
Alfred Prior Ho. E12: Lon. 6N 123
Alfred Rd. CM14: Brtwd 8G 96
E15: Lon 7F 122
IG9: Buck H. 8K 91
RM15: Ave 8N 143
Alfred's Gdns. IG11: Bark. 2D 140
Alfred St. RM17: Grays 4M 155
Alfreds Way IG11: Bark. 3A 140 (6H 39)
Alfreds Way Ind. Est. IG11: Bark 1F 140
Alfred Ter. CO14: Walt. 6M 181
Alfreg Rd. CM8: Wthm 7A 230
Algars Way CM3: S Fer. 9K 89
Algers Cl. IG10: Lou. 4K 91
Algers Rd. IG10: Lou 4K 91
Alghers Mead IG10: Lou. 4K 91
Alibon Gdns. RM10: Dag 7M 125
Alibon Rd. RM9: Dag 7L 125
RM10: Dag. 7M 125
Alicia Av. SS11: W'fd 9A 102
Alicia Cl. SS11: W'fd 9A 102
Alicia Wlk. SS11: W'fd. 8A 102
Alicia Way SS11: W'fd 9A 102
Alienor Av. CM7: Gt Bar 3C 202
Alkerden La. DA9: Grnh, Swans 3E 46
Allandale SS7: Thund. 8G 118
Allandale Rd. RM11: Horn. 2D 126
Allanson Ct. *E10: Lon.* 4A 122
(off Leyton Grange Est.)
Allectus Way CM8: Wthm. 7A 230
Allenby Cres. RM17: Grays. 3L 155
Allenby Dr. RM11: Horn 3J 127
Allen Ct. *E17: Lon.* 1A 122
(off Yunus Khan Cl.)
Allendale Av. CM20: H'low. 9B 50
(not continuous)
Allendale Dr. CO6: Cop 2M 171
Allen Rd. RM13: Rain. 2G 143
Allens Cl. CM3: Bore 2G 60
ALLEN'S GREEN 3H 21
Allens Rd. CM11: Rams H 3C 100
Allensway SS17: Stan H. 3A 148
Allen Way CO16: P Bay. 4K 27
Allerton Cl. SS4: R'fd. 1H 121
Alley Dock SS9: Can I, Lgh S 6C 136
Alleyndale Rd. RM8: Dag. 4H 125
Alleyne Way CO15: Jay. 4E 188
Alleyn Pl. SS0: Wclf S 5J 137
Allfields CO12: Har. 5H 209
Allington Ct. CM11: Bill 9L 99
Allis M. *CM17: H'low* 2H 55
(off Tatton St.)
Allison Cl. EN9: Wal A 2G 76
Alliston Way SS17: Stan H 2A 148
Allmains Cl. EN9: Naze 4H 63
Allnutts Rd. CM16: Epp. 3F 78
Alloa Rd. IG3: Ilf. 4F 124
All Saints Av. CO3: Colc 2H 173
All Saints Cl. CM1: Chelm 7N 59
CM15: Dodd 6E 82
IG7: Chig 9F 92
All Saints Station (DLR) 7D 38
All Saints Twr. E10: Lon 2B 122
Allysum Wlk. CM12: Bill. 3H 99
Alma Av. E4: Lon 4C 106
RM12: Horn. 6J 127
Alma Cl. SS7: Had 4M 135
SS12: W'fd 1H 117
Alma Dr. CM1: Chelm. 9H 59
Alma Link CM12: Bill. 6J 99
Alma Rd. EN3: Enf 7C 30
SS7: Had. 4N 135
Alma Sq. *CO11: Mist.* 4J 163
(off Kiln La.)
Alma St. CO7: W'hoe 6H 175
E15: Lon 8D 122
Almere SS7: Ben 2D 134
Almond Av. SS5: Hull 4L 103
SS12: W'fd 9K 101
Almond Cl. CO5: Tip. 5C 226
CO7: W'hoe. 4J 175
CO15: Clac S. 1G 188
RM16: Grays. 1C 156
Almonds Av. IG9: Buck H 8G 90
Almond Wlk. SS8: Can I 1F 150
Almond Way CO4: Colc. 7E 166
ALMSHOUSE GREEN 2C 14
Almshouses *CM17: H'low.* 8K 51
(off Gilden Cl.)
IG10: Lou. 9M 77
Alnwick Cl. SS16: Lang H 1H 131
Alp Ct. SS3: Gt W 3L 139
Alpha Cl. CM7: Brain. 6J 193
SS13: Pits. 9N 117
Alpha Ct. EN11: Hod 4A 52
ALPHAMSTONE 1J 15
Alphamstone Rd. CO8: Alph. 1K 15
Alpha Pl. CB11: Saf W. 4D 218
Alpha Rd. CM0: Bur C. 3E 196
CM13: Hut. 5N 97
CO16: St O 4K 27
E4: Lon 9A 90
SS13: Pits. 9N 117
ALPHETON 1K 9
Alpine Rd. E10: Lon 4B 122
Alport Av. CO2: Colc 2K 173
Alracks SS15: Lain 9N 115
ALRESFORD 6A 176 (7J 17)
Alresford Grn. SS12: W'fd 1M 117
Alresford Rd. CO7: Alr, W'hoe. 5K 175 (7H 17)
Alresford Station (Rail) 6N 175 (1J 27)
Alsa Bus. Pk. CM24: Stan M 5A 12
Alsa Gdns. CM22: Else. 2K 199
Alsa Leys CM22: Else 2K 199
Alsa St. CM24: Stan M 5A 12
Alston Ct. SS0: Wclf S 5H 137
Altar Pl. SS15: Lain 8L 115
Altbarn Cl. CO4: Colc 2C 166
Altbarn Rd. CO2: Colc 9D 166
Altham Gro. CM20: H'low 1E 54
ALTHORNE 2D 190 (5A 36)
Althorne Cl. SS13: Bas 6J 117
Althorne Gdns. E18: Lon. 8F 106
Althorne Station (Rail) 6A 36
Althorne Way RM10: Dag 4M 125
SS4: Cwdn 1N 105
Althorpe Cl. SS5: Hock. 1C 120
Altmore Av. E6: Lon. 9M 123
Alton Dr. CO3: Colc 9J 165
Alton Gdns. SS2: Sth S. 1K 137
Alton La. IP9: Stut 1C 18
Alton Pk. Rd. CO15: Clac S. 2H 189 (4D 28)
(Link Rd.)
CO15: Clac S 3E 188
(Richmond Dr.)
Alton Rd. CO15: Clac S 2J 189
Aluf Cl. CM8: Wthm 7B 230
Aluric Cl. RM16: Grays. 2D 156
Alverstoke Rd. RM3: Romf. 4J 111
Alverstone Rd. E12: Lon 6N 123
Alverton Cl. CM77: Gt N. 2B 204
Alverton Way CO4: Colc 4B 166
Alvis Av. CO15: Jay. 6C 188
Alwen Gro. RM15: S Ock 6E 144
Alwyne Av. CM15: Shenf. 5K 97
Alyssum Cl. CM1: Chelm 5B 60
Alyssum Wlk. CO4: Colc. 8D 166
Amanda Cl. IG7: Chig 3C 108
Amanda M. RM7: Romf 9A 110
Amarells Rd. CO16: L Cla. 1G 185
Amberden SS15: Lain 1M 131
Amber La. IG6: Ilf 4A 108
Amberley Cl. CO7: W'hoe. 5K 175
Amberley Rd. E10: Lon 2A 122
IG9: Buck H. 7J 91
Amberley Way RM7: Maw 8N 109
Amberry Ct. *CM20: H'low.* 2C 54
(off Netteswell Dr.)
Ambleside CM16: Epp. 1F 78
Ambleside Av. RM12: Horn. 7F 126
Ambleside Cl. E10: Lon 2B 122
Ambleside Ct. CO15: Clac S. 1L 189
Ambleside Dr. SS1: Sth S. 6A 138
Ambleside Gdns. IG4: Ilf 8L 107
SS5: Hull. 6K 103
Ambleside Wlk. SS8: Can I. 1F 150
Ambridge Rd. CO6: Cogg 1H 197 (7G 15)
(not continuous)
Ambrose Av. CO3: Colc, S'way. 2G 172
Ambrose Cl. DA1: Cray. 9D 152
Ambrose Ct. CO6: Cop. 2M 171
Amcotes Pl. CM2: Chelm 2D 72
Ameland Rd. SS8: Can I. 8G 134
Amelia Blackwell Ho. *SS8: Can I.* 2E 150
(off Link Rd.)
America Rd. CO6: E Col 5H 15
America St. CM9: Mal 6C 214
Amersham Av. SS16: Lang H. 1H 131
Amersham Cl. RM3: Romf 3K 111
Amersham Dr. RM3: Romf 3J 111
Amersham Rd. RM3: Romf. 3J 111
Amersham Wlk. RM3: Romf 3K 111
Amery Gdns. RM2: Romf. 7H 111
Amesbury EN9: Wal A. 2G 76
Amesbury Cl. CM16: Epp 1E 78
Amesbury Dr. E4: Lon. 5B 90
Amesbury Rd. CM16: Epp. 1E 78
RM9: Dag 9J 125
Amethyst Rd. E15: Lon. 6D 122
Amhurst Pk. N16: Lon 4B 38
Amhurst Rd. E8: Lon 5B 38
N16: Lon. 5B 38
Amhurst Wlk. SE28: Lon. 8F 140
Amidas Gdns. RM8: Dag 6G 124
Amid Rd. SS8: Can I 9J 135
Amies Ct. CO2: Colc 1A 174
Amity Rd. E15: Lon. 9F 122
Amos Hill CO10: Gt Hen 7H 9
Amoss Rd. CM2: Gt Bad 2G 73
Ampers End SS14: Bas 1E 132
Ampleforth Rd. SE2: Lon 9G 141
Ampthill Ho. *RM3: Romf* 2H 111
(off Montgomery Cres.)
Amwell Ct. EN9: Wal A 3F 76
EN11: Hod. 4A 52
Amwell End SG12: Ware. 4C 20
Amwell Hill SG12: Gt Amw 5D 20
Amwell La. SG12: Gt Amw, Stan A 5D 20
Amwell St. EN11: Hod. 4A 52 (7D 20)
(not continuous)
WC1: Lon 6A 38
Amwell Vw. IG6: Chig, Ilf. 2G 108
Ancels La. CM7: Shalf 4B 14
Anchorage *SS8: Can I.* 4H 151
(off Western Esplanade)
Anchorage Hill CM9: Mal 5C 214
Anchorage, The SS3: Gt W 2M 139
Anchor Bay Ind. Est. DA8: Eri. 4E 152
Anchor Blvd. DA2: Dart 9N 153
Anchor Cvn. Pk. CO16: L Cla 3H 185
Anchor Cl. IG11: Bark. 3G 140
Anchor Ct. DA8: Eri. 5D 152
Anchor Dr. RM13: Rain 3F 142
Anchor End CO11: Mist 4M 163
Anchor Hill CO7: W'hoe 7H 175
Anchor Ho. CO2: Colc. 4L 173
Anchor La. CM6: Ab R 6C 22
CM9: Mal. 3C 214
CO7: Ded. 4N 161
CO11: Mist 4M 163
SG12: Ton, Wad, W'mll. 3B 20
SS4: Cwdn 2M 105 (7K 35)
Anchor Reach CM3: S Fer. 3L 103
Anchor Rd. CO5: Tip 6C 226
CO15: Clac S. 1H 189
E12: Lon 4K 123
Anchor St. CM2: Chelm 1C 72
Anders Fall SS9: Lgh S 9F 120
Anderson Av. CM1: Chelm 6H 59
Anderson Cl. CM23: Man 5K 11
Anderson Ho. IG11: Bark 1C 140
Anderson Rd. IG8: Wfd G 7K 107
Andersons SS17: Stan H. 2A 148
Anderson's La. SG9: Gt Hor 3F 11
Anderson Way DA17: Belv 9N 141
Andover Cl. CO15: Clac S 7L 185
Andrea Av. RM16: Grays. 9K 145
Andrew Cl. CM7: Brain. 3H 193
IG6: Ilf. 3C 108
SS17: Stan H 1M 147
Andrews Cl. IG9: Buck H. 8J 91
Andrews Farm La. CM6: Gt Eas. 6G 13
Andrewsfield Aerodrome 6K 13
Andrew's La. EN7: Chesh 3B 30
(not continuous)
Andrews Pl. CM1: Chelm 9H 59
Andromeda Ct. RM3: Romf 4G 111
Andwell Cl. SE2: Lon 9G 141
Andyk Rd. SS8: Can I 2L 151
Anemone Ct. CO4: Colc 5K 165
Anerley Rd. SS0: Wclf S. 6J 137
ANGEL 6A 38
Angel Cl. SS16: Van 3E 132
Angel Ct. CO1: Colc 8N 165
ANGEL EDMONTON. 1C 38
Angel Ga. CO12: Har 1N 209
Angel La. CM6: Gt D. 3L 203
E15: Lon. 8D 122 (5E 38)
Angel Rd. N18: Lon 1C 38
Angel Road Station (Rail) 1C 38
Angel Station (Tube) 6A 38
Angel Way RM1: Romf. 9C 110
Anglefield CO15: Clac S 2K 189
Angle Grn. RM8: Dag 3H 125
Angle Rd. RM20: Grays 4G 154
Anglesea Rd. CO7: W'hoe. 6J 175
Anglesey Dr. RM13: Rain 4E 142
Anglesey Gdns. SS12: W'fd 2N 117
Angle Side CM7: Brain 6K 193
Anglia Cl. CO2: Colc 3J 173
Anglia Ct. *RM8: Dag* 3J 125
(off Spring Cl.)
Anglian Ind. Est. IG11: Bark. 4E 140
Anglian Rd. E11: Lon 5D 122
Anglia Polytechnic University
Hoffman's Way 7K 59
Park Rd. 9J 59
Anglia Way CM7: Brain. 6K 193
Anjou Grn. CM1: Chelm 4B 60
Annabell Av. RM16: Ors 6F 146
Annalee Gdns. RM15: S Ock 5E 144
Annalee Rd. RM15: S Ock 5E 144
Anna Neagle Cl. E7: Lon 6G 123
Annan Way RM1: Romf 5C 110
Ann Coles Cl. CB9: Stpl B. 3L 223
Anne Boleyn Dr. SS4: R'fd 8L 121
Anne Boleyn Mans. SS13: Pits 1J 133
Anne Cl. CO7: B'sea 7E 182
Anne Nastri Ct. *RM2: Romf* 9F 110
(off Heath Pk. Rd.)
Annett Cl. SS12: W'fd. 2A 118
Anne Way IG6: Ilf 3B 108
Annie Taylor Ho. *E12: Lon* 6N 123
(off Walton Rd.)
Annifer Way RM15: S Ock 5E 144
Annonay Wlk. *CM2: Chelm.* 9L 59
(off Spingfield Rd.)
Annwood Lodge Bus. Pk. SS12: Ray 5D 118
Ansgar Rd. CB11: Saf W. 6D 218
ANSO CORNER 7G 7
Anson Chase SS3: Shoe 6J 139
Anson Cl. CM3: S Fer. 2M 103
CO12: Har 5J 209
RM7: Maw 6N 109
Anson Pl. SE28: Lon. 9C 140
Anson Way CM7: Brain 4L 193
Anso Rd. CB10: Hpstd 7G 7
Anstead Dr. RM13: Rain 2E 142
ANSTEY. 2F 11
Anstey Castle 2F 11
Anstey Cl. SS9: Lgh S 8C 120
Antelope Av. RM16: Grays 1K 155
Anthony Cl. CM11: Bill. 1M 115
CO4: Colc 4D 166
Anthony Dr. SS17: Stan H. 1N 147
Antlers SS8: Can I. 3F 150
Antlers Hill E4: Lon 4B 90
Antonio Wlk. CO4: Colc. 8F 166
Antonius Way CO4: Colc. 1B 166
Anton Rd. RM15: S Ock 5E 144
Antony Cl. SS8: Can I. 9H 135
Antrim Rd. SS3: Shoe 7H 139
Anvil Way CM1: Chelm. 3N 59
CM12: Bill 3K 99
Anworth Cl. IG8: Wfd G 3H 107
Anzio Cres. CO2: Colc. 4K 173
Apeldoorn SS7: Thund 8B 118
Aperfield Rd. DA8: Eri 4D 152
Apollo Cl. RM12: Horn 4F 126
Apollo M. CO2: Colc 5K 173
Apollo Pl. E11: Lon. 5E 122
Apollo Way DA8: Eri 2B 152
Appleby Cl. E4: Lon 3C 106
Appleby Dr. RM3: Romf 2G 110
SS16: Lang H 1H 131
Appleby Grn. RM3: Romf. 2G 110
Appleby St. EN7: Chesh 2B 30
Apple Ct. CM1: Chelm 9H 59
Appledene Cl. SS6: Ray. 3K 119
Appledore SS3: Shoe 5G 139
Appledore Av. DA7: Bexh 6A 152
Appledore Cl. RM3: Romf 5G 111
Appleford Ct. SS13: Pits. 9K 117
Applegarth Dr. IG2: Ilf. 8E 108
Applegarth Ho. DA8: Eri. 7D 152
Applegarth Rd. SE28: Lon 8G 141
Apple Ga. CM14: Pil H 4C 96
Apple Rd. E11: Lon. 5E 122
Applerow SS9: Lgh S 9E 120
Appleton Cl. CM19: H'low 4B 54
DA7: Bexh 7A 152
Appleton Rd. IG10: Lou 2A 92
SS7: Ben. 3B 134
Appleton Way RM12: Horn. 3H 127
Appletree Cl. CM15: Dodd 8G 82
CM77: Tye G 3F 194
Apple Tree Cl. CO9: Hals. 4M 207
Appletree Cl. SS2: Sth S 3C 138
Apple Tree Cres. CM15: Dodd 8F 82
Appletree Wlk. CM7: Brain 7J 193
Apple Tree Way SS11: W'fd 8N 101
Apple Way CM2: Gt Bad 4E 72
Appleyard Av. SS5: Hock 8D 104
Appold St. DA8: Eri. 4D 152
Approach Rd. CM11: Cray H. 2E 116
SS8: Can I 2M 151
Approach, The CO15: Jay. 4E 188
RM14: Upm 5M 127
SS6: Ray 4J 119
April Pl. CM21: Saw 1L 51
Apton Hall Rd. SS4: Cwdn 1M 121 (1K 43)
Apton Rd. CM23: Bis S. 1K 21
Aquiline Ho. CO15: Clac S 4H 189
Arabia Cl. E4: Lon 6D 90
Araglen Av. RM15: S Ock. 5E 144
Aragon Cl. CO15: Jay. 4D 188
IG10: Lou 5L 91
RM5: Col R. 3N 109
SS2: Sth S. 2K 137
Aragon Ct. IG6: Ilf. 4B 108
Aragon Dr. IG6: Ilf. 4B 108
Aragon Rd. CM3: Gt L 7K 203
Arakan Cl. CO2: Colc. 5J 173
Arandora Cres. RM6: Chad H. 2G 124
Arbor Rd. E4: Lon. 9D 90
Arbour Cl. CM14: War. 2F 112
Arbour La. CM1: Chelm 7M 59 (1A 34)
CM8: W Bis 2K 229 (5H 25)
Arbour Way CO4: Colc 3C 166
RM12: Horn. 7F 126
Arbutus Cl. CM2: Chelm. 4C 72
Arcade Pl. RM1: Romf 9C 110
Arcade, The E17: Lon. 8A 106
IG11: Bark. 9B 124
RM3: Romf. 2H 111
(off Farnham Rd.)
SS11: W'fd 8L 101
Arcadian Gdns. SS7: Had 2J 135
Arcadia Rd. CM0: Bur C 3E 196
DA13: Ist R 6G 47
SS8: Can I. 2K 151
Arcany Rd. RM15: S Ock 4E 144
Archates Av. RM16: Grays 1K 155
Archer Av. SS2: Sth S. 3B 138
Archer Cl. SS2: Sth S 3C 138
Archer Cres. CO5: Tip. 6E 226
Archer Rd. SS15: Lain 7K 115
Archers CM19: H'low 8A 54
Archers Cl. CM12: Bill. 8J 99
Archers Ct. RM15: S Ock 5E 144
Archers Flds. SS13: Bas 6J 117
Archers Fields Cl. SS13: Bas 6H 117
Archers Way CM2: Gall. 8D 72
Archery Flds. CO15: Clac S. 8L 185
Archibald Rd. RM3: H Wood 5L 111
Archibald Ter. SS15: Lain. 8K 115
Archway RM3: Romf. 3F 110
Archway Station (Tube) 4A 38
ARDELEY 5A 10
Arden Cl. CO4: Colc 4C 166
SE28: Lon 6J 141
Arden Cres. RM9: Dag 9H 125
Arden M. E17: Lon 9B 106
Arderne Cl. CO12: Har 5H 209
ARDLEIGH 8L 161 (4H 17)
Ardleigh SS16: Bas. 1N 131

Ardleigh Cl. RM11: Horn 7H **111**
Ardleigh Ct. CM15: Shenf 6J **97**
CO7: A'lgh 8L **161**
Ardleigh Gdns. CM13: Hut 5A **98**
ARDLEIGH GREEN 8G **110** (3B **40**)
Ardleigh Grn. Rd. RM11: Horn 9H **111** (3B **40**)
ARDLEIGH HEATH 7K **161** (3H **17**)
Ardleigh Ho. IG11: Bark 1B **140**
Ardleigh M. IG1: Ilf 5A **124**
Ardleigh Rd. CO7: A'lgh, Ded 4K **161** (3H **17**)
CO7: A'lgh, Gt Bro 3A **168** (5J **17**)
CO11: L Bro 1C **168** (4J **17**)
Ardleigh Sailing Club 2H **167**
Ardley Cres. CM22: Hat H 2F **210**
ARDLEY END 3F **210** (4B **22**)
Ardley Way SS6: Ray 3K **119**
Ardmore La. IG9: Buck H 6H **91**
Ardmore Pl. IG9: Buck H 6H **91**
Ardmore Rd. RM15: S Ock 4E **144**
Ardwell Av. IG6: Ilf 9B **108**
Arena Essex 9E **144**
Arethusa Pl. DA9: Grnh 9E **154**
AREWATER GREEN 9M **77**
Argent Ct. SS15: Lain 8H **115**
Argent St. RM17: Grays 4H **155** (2F **47**)
Argent Way EN7: Chesh 2B **30**
Argus Cl. RM7: Maw 5N **109**
Argyle Ct. CO5: K'dn 3K **211**
Argyle Gdns. RM14: Upm 4A **128**
Argyle Rd. CM0: Bur C 4F **196**
CO16: T Sok 4K **179**
(not continuous)
E15: Lon 6E **122**
IG1: Ilf 4N **123**
Argyll Ho. SS0: Wclf S 7J **137**
Argyll Rd. CM2: Chelm 6B **60**
RM17: Grays 3K **155**
SS0: Wclf S 6J **137**
Ariel Cl. CO4: Colc 8E **166**
Arisdale Av. RM15: S Ock 5E **144** (6E **40**)
Arjan Way SS8: Can I 2C **150**
Ark Av. RM16: Grays 1K **155**
ARKESDEN 1K **11**
Arkesden Rd. CB11: A'den, Clav 2K **11**
Ark La. SS4: R'fd 6E **120**
Arkwright Rd. RM18: Til 7C **156**
Arkwrights CM20: H'low 2E **54**
(not continuous)
Arlington Gdns. IG1: Ilf 3N **123**
RM3: H Wood 5J **111**
Arlington M. *EN9: Wal A* *3C 76*
(off Sun St.)
Arlington Rd. IG8: Wfd G 5G **107**
SS2: Sth S 5C **138**
Arlington Sq. CM3: S Fer 3J **103**
Arlington Way CM12: Bill 3H **99**
Armada Cl. SS15: Lain 1M **131**
Armada Ct. RM16: Grays 2K **155**
Armadale SS8: Can I 9F **134**
Armada Way E6: Lon 5A **140**
(Gallions Reach Shop. Pk.)
E6: Lon 7A **140**
(Woolwich Mnr. Way)
Armagh Rd. SS3: Shoe 7H **139**
Armath Pl. SS16: Lang H 2H **131**
Armidale Wlk. CO2: Colc 4A **174**
ARMIGERS 4E **12**
Armiger Way CM8: Wthm 5E **230**
Armitage Rd. SS1: Sth S 5E **138**
Armonde Cl. CM3: Bore 2F **60**
Armond Rd. CM8: Wthm 5B **230**
Armor Rd. RM19: Purf 2A **154**
Armoury Rd. CO6: W Ber 3G **164**
Armstead Wlk. RM10: Dag 9M **125**
Armstrong Av. IG8: Wfd G 3E **106**
Armstrong Cl. CM3: Dan 2F **74**
RM8: Dag 2J **125**
SS17: Stan H 3N **147**
Armstrong Rd. SS7: Thund 8D **118**
Armstrong Way CO9: Gt Yel 2D **206**
Army & Navy Flyover CM2: Chelm 1D **72**
Arncroft Ct. IG11: Bark 3G **141**
Arne Cl. SS17: Stan H 2M **147**
Arne Ct. SS15: Lain 7L **115**
Arne M. *SS15: Lain* *7L 115*
(off Basildon Dr.)
Arneways Av. RM6: Chad H 7J **109**
Arnheim Rd. CM0: Bur C 4E **196**
Arnhem Av. RM15: Ave 8N **143**
Arnhem Gro. CM7: Brain 3G **193**
Arnhem Rd. CM1: Chelm 5G **59**
Arnold Av. SS1: Sth S 7A **138**
SS16: Lang H 1J **131**
Arnold Av. E. EN3: Enf 8A **76**
Arnold Cen., The SS14: Bas 5G **116**
Arnold Dr. CO4: Colc 9E **166**
Arnold Pl. RM18: Til 6E **156**
Arnold Rd. CO15: Clac S 2H **189** (4D **28**)
EN9: Enf 5C **76**
RM9: Dag 9L **125**
Arnolds Av. CM13: Hut 4M **97**
Arnolds Cl. CM13: Hut 4M **97**
Arnolds Farm La.
CM13: Mount 2A **98** (6G **33**)
Arnold's La. DA4: S at H 5C **46**
Arnolds Way SS4: R'fd 9J **105**
Arnold Vs. CO5: Tip 5C **226**
Arnold Way CM2: Gall 7D **72**
Arnos Grove Station (Tube) 1A **38**
Arnott Cl. SE28: Lon 8H **141**
Arnsberg Way DA7: Bexh 3A **46**
Arnstones Cl. CO4: Colc 7C **166**
Arran Cl. DA8: Eri 4B **152**
Arran Ct. SS12: W'fd 1N **117**
Arran Dr. E12: Lon 3K **123**
Arras Rd. CO2: Colc 3L **173**
ARRINGTON 1B **4**
Arrivals and Departures Terminal 2G **209**
(Harwich International)
Arrowhead Ct. E11: Lon 1D **122**
Arrow Rd. CO4: Colc 8F **166**
Arrowsmith Cl. IG7: Chig 2E **108**
Arrowsmith Path IG7: Chig 2E **108**
Arrowsmith Rd. IG7: Chig 2D **108**
Arsenal F.C. (Highbury) 5A **38**
Arsenal Station (Tube) 4A **38**
Arterial Av. RM13: Rain 4F **142**
Arterial Rd. RM16: N Stif 9G **144** (1E **46**)
RM19: Purf, W Thur 2M **153** (1C **46**)
RM20: W Thur 1C **154** (1E **46**)
SS17: Horn H 2L **147** (6K **41**)
Artesian Cl. RM11: Horn 1D **126**
Artesian Wlk. E11: Lon 5E **122**
Arthur Barnes Ct. RM16: Grays 1E **156**
Arthur Ct. CM1: Chelm 6H **59**
Arthur Horsley Wlk. *E7: Lon* *7F 122*
(off Twr. Hamlets Rd.)
Arthur Rd. RM6: Chad H 1H **125**
Arthur St. CO2: Colc 9N **165**
DA8: Eri 5D **152**
RM17: Grays 4M **155**
Arthur Toft Ho. *RM17: Grays* *4L 155*
(off New Rd.)
Arthy Cl. CM3: Hat P 2L **61**
Artillery Barracks Folley CO2: Colc 9M **165**
Artillery Cl. IG2: Ilf 1B **124**
Artillery Dr. CO12: Har 6E **208**
Artillery Ho. E15: Lon 8E **122**
Artillery St. CO1: Colc 9B **166**
Artisan Cl. E6: Lon 6A **140**
Artisans Dwellings *CB10: Saf W* *4D 218*
(off New Rd.)
Arun RM18: E Til 2L **157**
Arun Cl. CM1: Chelm 6L **59**
Arundel Cl. CM12: Bill 2L **99**
E15: Lon 6E **122**
Arundel Dr. IG8: Wfd G 4G **107**
SS17: Corr 1B **148**
Arundel Gdns. IG3: Ilf 4F **124**
SS0: Wclf S 3F **136**
SS6: Ray 2H **119**
Arundel M. CM12: Bill 2L **99**
Arundel Rd. DA1: Dart 9G **153**
RM3: H Wood 4K **111**
SS4: R'fd 7H **105**
SS7: Thund 8B **118**
SS11: W'fd 7K **101**
Arundel Way CM12: Bill 2L **99**
Arwen Gro. CM3: S Fer 2J **103**
Asbury Cl. CO4: Colc 7D **166**
Ascension Rd. RM5: Col R 3A **110**
Ascent Pk. CM20: H'low 7F **50**
Ascham Dr. E4: Lon 4B **106**
Ascot Cl. CM23: Bis S 9B **220**
IG6: Ilf 3D **108**
SS7: Thund 8H **119**
Ascot Gdns. RM12: Horn 6J **127**
Ascot Gro. SS14: Bas 9F **116**
Ascot M. CM0: S'min 2E **222**
Ashanti Cl. SS3: Shoe 6K **139**
Ashbeam Cl. CM13: Gt War 3F **112**
Ashbourne Av. E18: Lon 8H **107**
Ashbourne Rd. RM3: Romf 1G **111**
Ashbridge Rd. E11: Lon 2E **122**
Ashbrook Rd. RM10: Dag 5N **125**
Ash Bungs. CM7: Brain 5G **192**
Ashburnham Gdns. RM14: Upm 3M **127**
Ashburnham Rd. DA17: Belv 2A **152**
SS1: Sth S 6L **137**
Ashburton Av. IG3: Ilf 7D **124**
Ashbury Dr. CO6: M Tey 3H **171**
Ashbury Gdns. RM6: Chad H 9J **109**
Ashby Cl. RM11: Horn 3L **127**
RM16: Ors 6G **146**
Ashby Ri. CM23: Bis S 8A **220**
Ashby Rd. CM8: Wthm 8D **230**
Ash Cl. CM3: Hat P 2L **61**
CM15: Pil H 4C **96**
CO7: B'sea 6D **182**
CO15: Clac S 1G **188**
RM5: Col R 4N **109**
Ashcombe SS4: R'fd 4J **121**
Ashcombe Cl. SS9: Lgh S 9A **120**
Ashcombe Way SS6: Ray 5M **119**
Ash Ct. CO12: Har 5G **209**
SS3: Shoe 8K **139**
Ashdene Cl. SS5: Hull 6L **103**
ASHDON 7D **190** (4E **6**)
Ashdon Cl. CM13: Hut 5M **97**
IG8: Wfd G 3H **107**
RM15: S Ock 6E **144**
Ashdon Rd. CB10: R'ter 6F **7**
CB10: Saf W 3D **218** (6C **6**)
Ashdon Rd. Commercial Cen.
CB10: Saf W 2F **218**
Ashdon Way SS16: Bas 1B **132** (3A **42**)
Ashdown Cl. CM77: Gt N 8D **192**
SS17: Corr 9A **132**
Ashdown Cres. SS7: Had 2L **135**
Ashdown Wlk. RM7: Maw 5N **109**
Ashdown Way CO4: Colc 8D **166**
ASHELDHAM 4D **36**
ASHEN 6F **216** (4C **8**)
Ashen Cl. CO10: Ashen 4C **8**
Ashendene Rd. SG13: B'frd 1A **30**
Ashen Hill CO10: Ashen 4C **8**
Ashen La. CO10: Stoke C 4C **8**
Ashen Rd. CO9: Ridg 7D **216** (5B **8**)
CO10: Clare 3D **8**
CO10: Ovtn 4D **8**
Ashes Cl. CO14: Walt 6J **181**
Ashes Rd. CM77: Tye G 1F **194** (1E **24**)
Ash Fall CM8: Wthm 2C **230**
Ashfield SS6: Ray 4F **118**
Ashfield Cl. CM6: Gt D 2K **203**
Ashfield Farm Rd. CM9: Ult 7F **25**
Ashfields IG10: Lou 1M **91**
SS13: Pits 8K **117**
Ashford Av. CM14: Brtwd 9E **96**
Ashford Ct. RM17: Grays 3N **155**
Ashford Rd. CM1: Chelm 9G **59**
E6: Lon 9N **123**
E18: Lon 6H **107**
Ash Grn. CB10: Gt Che 9D **202**
CM11: Bill 6M **99**
SS4: Cwdn 2M **105**
Ash Gro. CM0: Bur C 2D **196**
CM2: Chelm 3D **72**
CM6: Gt D 4L **203**
CM9: Mal 2E **214**
CO2: Colc 6A **174**
CO7: Gt Bro 9F **168**
CO7: W'hoe 3J **175**
Ashgrove Rd. IG3: Ilf 3E **124**
Ash Groves CM21: Saw 2M **51**
Ash Ind. Est. CM19: H'low 4M **53**
Ashingdale Cl. SS8: Can I 3H **151**
ASHINGDON 3J **121** (1J **43**)
Ashingdon Cl. E4: Lon 9C **90**
Ashingdon Hgts. SS4: R'fd 9G **105**
Ashingdon Rd.
SS4: Hock, R'fd 7G **104** (1J **43**)
Ashlands Ct. RM18: E Til 2L **157**
Ash La. RM1: Romf 3E **110**
RM11: Horn 8K **111**
Ashleigh Cl. SS8: Can I 8G **134**
Ashleigh Ct. EN9: Wal A 4G **77**
EN11: Hod 6A **52**
SS8: Can I 8G **134**
Ashleigh Dr. SS9: Lgh S 6E **136**
Ashleigh Gdns. RM14: Upm 5A **128**
Ashley Av. IG6: Ilf 6A **108**
Ashley Cl. SS17: Corr 1B **148**
Ashley Gdns. CO3: Colc 9K **165**
RM16: Grays 8M **145**
Ashley Grn. CM3: E Han 2B **88**
Ashley Gro. IG10: Lou 2L **91**
Ashley Rd. CO12: Har 4J **209**
E4: Lon 3A **106**
E7: Lon 9J **123**
Ashlin Rd. E15: Lon 6D **122**
Ashlong Gro. CO9: Hals 3K **207**
Ashlyn Gro. RM11: Horn 7H **111**
Ashlyns SS13: Pits 8H **117** (3B **42**)
Ashlyns La. CM5: Chip, Mag L 1D **66** (1A **32**)
Ashlyns Rd. CM16: Epp 9E **64**
Ashmans Row CM3: S Fer 2K **103**
Ashmeads IG10: Lou 2M **91**
Ashmole Dr. CO13: Frin S 8J **181**
Ashmour Gdns. RM1: Romf 6B **110**
Ash Pole Rd. CM7: Brain 8K **191**
Ash Ri. CO9: Hals 6L **207**
Ash Rd. CO7: Alr 6A **176**
DA3: Ash, Long 6F **47**
E15: Lon 7E **122**
SS7: Had 4L **135**
SS8: Can I 2J **151**
Ashtead Cl. CO16: Clac S 7F **184**
Ashton Gdns. RM6: Chad H 1K **125**
Ashton Ga. RM3: Romf 4H **111**
Ashton Pl. CM2: Chelm 8B **60**
Ashton Rd. E15: Lon 7D **122**
RM3: Romf 4H **111**
Ash Tree Cl. CM1: Chelm 9H **59**
Ashtree Ct. *EN9: Wal A* *4G 77*
(off Horseshoe Cl.)
Ash Tree Ct. SS4: Stam 2K **43**
Ash Tree Cres. CM1: Chelm 9H **59**
Ash Tree Fld. CM20: H'low 1N **53**
Ash Tree Wlk. SS14: Bas 1G **132**
Ashurst Av. SS2: Sth S 5D **138**
Ashurst Cl. CO5: Rhdge 6F **174**
DA1: Cray 8D **152**
Ashurst Dr. CM1: Chelm 4M **59**
IG2: Ilf 1A **124**
IG6: Ilf 9B **108**
(Hamilton Av.)
IG6: Ilf 8B **108**
(Horns Rd.)
Ashvale Dr. RM14: Upm 4B **128**
Ashvale Gdns. RM5: Col R 2B **110**
RM14: Upm 4B **128**
Ashville Rd. E11: Lon 4D **122**
Ash Wlk. RM15: S Ock 3G **144**
SS1: Sth S 7N **137**
Ash Way CO3: S'way 3G **173**
SS5: Hock 8E **104**
Ashway SS17: Corr 9C **132**
Ashwell & Morden Station (Rail) 6A **4**
Ashwells Mdw. CO6: E Col 8C **198**
Ashwells Rd. CM15: Pil H 2A **96** (6D **32**)
Ashwin Av. CO6: Cop 2M **171**
Ashwood SS7: Thund 8B **118**
Ashwood Av. RM13: Rain 4F **142**
Ashwood Cl. CM0: Bur C 1D **196**
Ashwood Rd. E4: Lon 9D **90**
Ashworth Pl. CM17: H'low 3J **55**
Ashworths SS4: R'fd 1H **121**
SS8: Can I 8G **134**
Ashylyn's Rd. CO13: Frin S 1H **187** (2G **29**)
Askews Farm La. RM17: Grays 3H **155**
Askwith Rd. RM13: Rain 3B **142**
Aspen Cl. SS8: Can I 1E **150**
Aspen Ct. CM13: Brtwd 9K **97**
SS15: Lain 6L **115**
ASPENDEN 4C **10**
Aspenden Rd. SG9: Aspen 4D **10**
(not continuous)
Aspen Gro. RM14: Upm 6L **127**
Aspens, The CM23: Bis S 6A **220**
EN9: Wal A *5J 77*
(off Woodbine Cl.)
Aspen Way CO4: Colc 7D **166**
CO12: L Oak 8D **208**
E14: Lon 7D **38**
RM15: S Ock 3G **145**
Aspin M. CB10: Saf W 2D **218**
Asquith Av. SS7: Had 9H **119**
Asquith Cl. RM8: Dag 3H **125**
Asquith Dr. CO4: Colc 2C **166**
Asquith Gdns. SS7: Had 8J **119**
Assandune Cl. SS4: R'fd 9J **105**
Astell Ct. CO13: Frin S 1J **187**
Aster Cl. CO16: Clac S 9G **184**
Aster Ct. CM1: Chelm 5A **60**
Asthall Gdns. IG6: Ilf 8B **108**
Astins Ho. E17: Lon 8B **106**
Astley RM17: Grays 4J **155**
Astley Rd. CO15: Clac S 1H **189**
Aston Ct. IG8: Wfd G 3G **106**
Aston M. RM6: Chad H 2H **125**
Aston Rd. SS15: Lain 9K **115**
Astor Av. RM7: Romf 1A **126**
Astra Cen. CM20: H'low 8F **50**
Astra Cl. RM12: Horn 8F **126**
Atcost Rd. IG11: Bark 5F **140**
Athelstan Cl. RM3: H Wood 6K **111**
Athelstan Gdns.
SS11: W'fd 7L **101**
Athelstan Rd. CO3: Colc 1K **173**
RM3: H Wood 5K **111**
Athena Est. CM20: H'low 8G **51**
Athenaeum Lawn Tennis Club *1E 124*
(off Aldborough Rd. Sth.)
Atherstone Cl. SS8: Can I 3J **151**
Atherstone Rd. SS8: Can I 3J **151**
Atherton End CM21: Saw 1K **51**
Atherton Gdns. RM16: Grays 2E **156**
Atherton Ho. *RM3: Romf* *4J 111*
(off Leyburn Cres.)
Atherton Leisure Cen. 8F **122**
Atherton M. E7: Lon 8F **122**
Atherton Rd. E7: Lon 8F **122**
IG5: Ilf 6L **107**
Athlone Ct. E17: Lon 7D **106**
Athol Cl. SS8: Can I 3M **151**
Atholl Rd. CM2: Chelm 6A **60**
IG3: Ilf 2F **124**
Athol Rd. DA8: Eri 3A **152**
Athos Rd. SS8: Can I 9J **135**
Atkinson Ct. *E10: Lon* *2B 122*
(off Kings Cl.)
Atkins Rd. E10: Lon 1B **122**
Atlanta Blvd. RM1: Romf 1C **126**
Atlantic Sq. CM8: Wthm 4D **230**
Atlantis Cl. IG11: Bark 3G **140**
Atlas Bungs. CO6: E Col 8B **198**
Atlas Ct. CO6: E Col 7B **198**
Atlas Rd. CO6: E Col 7A **198**
DA1: Dart 8K **153**
Atlas Wharf E9: Lon 8A **122**
Atridge Chase CM12: Bill 4J **99**
Attlee Ct. RM17: Grays 1K **155**
Attlee Dr. DA1: Dart 3C **46**
Attlee Gdns. CO1: Colc 9A **166**
Attlee Rd. SE28: Lon 7G **141**
Attlee Ter. E17: Lon 8B **106**
Attwood Cl. CO4: Colc 2B **166**
Attwoods Cl. CM2: Gall 7C **72**
Atwell Cl. E10: Lon 1B **122**
Aubretia Cl. RM3: H Wood 5J **111**
Aubrey Buxton Nature Reserve 3H **199**
Aubrey Cl. CM1: Chelm 4K **59**
Aubrey Rd. E17: Lon 7A **106**
Auckland Av. RM13: Rain 3D **142**
Auckland Cl. CM1: Chelm 6G **58**
RM18: Til 7C **156**
Auckland Rd. E10: Lon 5B **122**
IG1: Ilf 3A **124**
Audleigh Pl. IG7: Chig 3N **107**
Audley Ct. CM77: Gt N 1B **204**
Audley Cl. CB11: Saf W 4C **218**
E18: Lon 8F **106**
AUDLEY END
CB11 4A **218** (7B **6**)
CO9 7F **9**
Audley End House & Gardens 4A **218** (6B **6**)
Audley End Rd.
CB11: A End, Saf W 4A **218** (6B **6**)
Audley End Station (Rail) 7L **227** (7A **6**)
Audley Gdns. EN9: Wal A 4C **76**
IG3: Ilf 4E **124**
IG10: Lou 1B **92**
(not continuous)
Audley Rd. CB11: Saf W 4C **218** (6B **6**)
CM3: Gt L 7K **203**
CO3: Colc 1K **173**
Audleys Cl. SS2: Sth S 1K **137**
Audley Way CO13: Frin S 8K **181**
SS14: Bas 9B **116**
Audrey Rd. IG1: Ilf 5A **124**
Audries Est. CO14: Walt 6K **181**
Augustine Ct. EN9: Wal A 3B **76**
Augustine Way CM3: Bick 8F **74**
Augustus Cl. CO4: Colc 1B **166**
Augustus Way CM8: Wthm 7B **230**
Aukingford Gdns. CM5: Chip 5K **67**
Aukingford Grn. CM5: Chip 5K **67**
Auriel Av. RM10: Dag 8B **126**
Aurum Ct. SS15: Lain 8H **115**

Austen Cl. CM7: Brain 8J 193
IG10: Lou 2C 92
RM18: Til 7E 156
SE28: Lon 8G 141
Austen Dr. CM4: Stock 7M 85
Austen Gdns. DA1: Dart 9K 153
Austin Av. CO15: Jay 6C 188
Austral Dr. RM11: Horn 2H 127
Austral Way CM3: Alth 3D 190
Auton Cft. CB11: Saf W 7C 218
Autoway CO4: Colc 2C 166
Autumn Cl. CO16: Clac S 8G 184
Avebury Rd. E11: Lon 3D 122
SS0: Wclf S 5K 137
AVELEY 8A 144 (7D 40)
Aveley By-Pass RM15: Ave 7N 143 (7D 40)
Aveley Cl. DA8: Eri 4D 152
RM15: Ave 8A 144
Aveley La. CO10: Lav, S'std 1J 9
Aveley Mans. IG11: Bark 9A 124
(off Whiting Av.)
Aveley Rd. RM1: Romf 8B 110
RM14: Upm 8M 127 (5C 40)
Aveley Way CM9: Mal 8B 214
Aveline Rd. CO7: A'lgh 9L 161
Aveling Pk. Rd. E17: Lon 6A 106
Avelon Rd. RM5: Col R 3B 110
RM13: Rain 1E 142
Avenue Cl. RM3: H Wood 4K 111
Avenue Ga. IG10: Lou 5J 91
Avenue Ind. Est. RM3: H Wood 6H 111
Avenue Lodge RM17: Grays 3M 155
Avenue Rd. CM2: Gt Bad 3E 72
CM4: Ing 6C 84
CM8: Wthm 4D 230 (4G 25)
CM14: War 1F 112
CM16: They B 7C 78
DA8: Eri 5A 152
DA17: Belv, Eri 2A 152
E7: Lon 6H 123
EN11: Hod 7D 52
IG8: Wfd G 3J 107
N14: Lon 7A 30
RM3: H Wood 4K 111
RM6: Chad H 2G 125
SS0: Wclf S 6L 137
SS7: Ben 3E 134
SS9: Lgh S 6D 136
Avenue Ter. SS0: Wclf S 6K 137
Avenue, The CM3: Dan 3F 74
CM3: N Fam 1F 104 (6H 35)
CM6: Gt D 3M 203
CM7: Brain 5H 193
CM8: Wthm 5D 230 (4G 25)
CM12: Bill 6H 99
CM13: Brtwd 3H 113 (2F 41)
CM15: Kel H 9B 82
CO3: Colc 9K 165
CO6: E Col 8D 198
CO6: W Ber 4E 164
CO7: W'hoe 5H 175 (7G 17)
CO12: Gt Oak 8B 204 (5E 18)
CO15: Clac S 6M 185
DA9: Grnh 9E 154 (3E 46)
E4: Lon 3D 106 (2E 38)
E11: Lon 1H 123
EN9: Naze 4J 63
IG9: Buck H 8J 91
IG10: Lou 5K 91
RM1: Romf 8B 110
RM12: Horn 4G 127
SS5: Hull 5K 103
SS7: Had 3L 135
SS8: Can I 3H 151
SS14: Bas 6H 117
SS17: Fob 9E 132
Avery Gdns. IG2: Ilf 9M 107
Avey La. EN9: Lou, Wal A 6D 76 (5E 30)
IG10: H Bee 8G 76
Aviation Way SS2: Sth A 8G 121
Aviation Way Ind. Area SS2: Sth S 8G 121
Avignon Cl. CO2: Colc 2B 174
Avila Chase CM2: Gall 9C 72
Avington Wlk. SS7: Thund 9F 118
Avoca Ter. SS0: Wclf S 4J 137
(off Fairfax Dr.)
Avocet Cl. CO5: K'dn 3L 211
CO5: W Mer 2D 228
CO13: Frin S, Walt 8H 181
Avocet Way CM9: Mal 3E 214
Avon Cl. SS4: R'fd 2H 121
Avon Ct. E4: Lon 7C 90
IG9: Buck H 7H 91
Avondale Cl. IG10: Lou 6M 91
SS6: Ray 5M 119
Avondale Ct. E11: Lon 3E 122
E18: Lon 5H 107
Avondale Cres. IG4: Ilf 9K 107
Avondale Dr. IG10: Lou 6M 91
SS9: Lgh S 2E 136
Avondale Gdns. SS17: Stan H 1N 147
Avondale Rd. CO15: Clac S 1L 189
E17: Lon 2A 122
SS6: Ray 5M 119
SS7: Ben 3D 134
SS16: Van 2H 133
Avondale Wlk. SS8: Can I 1E 150
Avonfield Ct. E17: Lon 7D 106
Avon Grn. RM15: S Ock 6E 144
Avon Rd. CM1: Chelm 6E 58
E17: Lon 7D 106
RM14: Upm 1A 128 (3D 40)
SS8: Can I 2G 150
Avontar Rd. RM15: S Ock 4E 144 (6E 40)
Avon Wlk. CM8: Wthm 4B 230
Avon Way CO4: Colc 9E 166 (6G 17)
E18: Lon 7G 107
SS3: Shoe 7H 139
SS14: Bas 8G 116
Avon Way Ho. CO4: Colc 9F 166
Avril Way E4: Lon 2C 106
Avro Rd. SS2: Sth S 9J 121
Axe St. IG11: Bark 1B 140
(not continuous)
Ayerst Ct. E10: Lon 2C 122
Aylesbeare SS3: Shoe 6H 139
Aylesbury Cl. E7: Lon 8F 122
Aylesbury Dr. CO15: Hol S 7C 186
SS16: Lang H 1H 131
Aylesbury M. SS15: Bas 5A 116
Aylets Fld. CM18: H'low 7D 54
Aylett Cl. SS8: Can I 1J 151
Aylett Rd. RM14: Upm 4N 127
Ayletts CM1: Broom 9K 57
SS14: Bas 9G 117
Aylmer Rd. E11: Lon 3F 122
RM8: Dag 5K 125
Ayloffe Rd. CO4: Colc 6C 166
RM9: Dag 8L 125
Ayloffs Cl. RM11: Horn 8H 111
Ayloffs Wlk. RM11: Horn 9H 111
Aylsham La. RM3: Romf 1G 111
Aylsham Rd. EN11: Rye P 4C 52
Aynsley Gdns. CM17: H'low 3H 55
Aynsworth Av. CM23: Bis S 7A 220
Ayr Grn. RM1: Romf 5C 110
Ayron Rd. RM15: S Ock 4E 144
Ayr Way RM1: Romf 5C 110
AYTHORPE RODING 4E 22
Aythorpe Roding Windmill 4E 22
Azalea Av. SS12: W'fd 9K 101
Azalea Cl. IG1: Ilf 7A 124
Azalea Ct. CM1: Chelm 5A 60
CO4: Colc 7D 166
IG8: Wfd G 3E 106
Azalea M. SS8: Can I 3G 150
Azalea Way CO16: Clac S 9F 184
Aztec Ho. IG6: Ilf 5B 108

B

Baardwyk Av. SS8: Can I 2L 151
BAAS HILL 1C 30
Baas Hill EN10: Brox 1C 30
Baas La. EN10: Brox 1D 30
Babbacombe Gdns. IG4: Ilf 8L 107
BABBS GREEN 3E 20
BABEL GREEN 1B 8
Babel Grn. CO10: Pos 1B 8
Babington Rd. RM8: Dag 7H 125
RM12: Horn 3F 126
BABRAHAM 1A 6
Babraham Rd. CB2: Saws 1K 5
Back Hill CB1: Hads 3C 6
IP9: Holb 1D 18
Back La. CB10: I'tn 7A 202
CM1: Broom 2M 59
CM3: E Han 2A 88 (4D 34)
CM3: Har E 3J 23
CM3: L Walt 6L 57 (5A 24)
CM3: Ples 2A 56 (4J 23)
CM4: Fry, Mill G 4C 84 (4H 33)
CM4: Stock 6K 85 (5K 33)
(not continuous)
CM6: Thax 7B 224
CM8: W Bis 3L 229 (6H 25)
CM15: Kel H 6D 82
CM21: Saw, Srng 3M 51 (4K 21)
(not continuous)
CM22: L Hall 3K 213
CM22: Saw, Srng 3M 51 (4K 21)
CM77: Tye G 6F 15
CO3: Colc 8F 164
CO12: Gt Oak 8C 204
CO12: R'sy 6C 208
EN9: Naze 1J 63 (1F 31)
RM6: Chad H 2J 125
RM16: N Stif 8F 144
RM19: Purf 1B 154
RM20: W Thur 1E 154
SS4: R'fd 6L 121
Back La. E. CO7: Gt Bro 8F 168
Back La. W. CO7: Gt Bro 8E 168
Backnang Sq. CM2: Chelm 9L 59
(off Springfield Rd.)
Back Rd. CB1: Lin 2C 6
CM1: Writ 1H 71
CM9: Tol, Tol D 6J 225 (6C 26)
CO7: A'lgh, Gt Bro 2A 168 (4J 17)
Backwarden Nature Reserve 6D 74
Bk. Waterside La. CO7: B'sea 8E 182
BACON END 2F 23
BACONEND GREEN 2F 23
Bacon Link RM5: Col R 3N 109
Bacons Chase CM0: Brad S 9C 194
Bacon's La. CO6: Chap 9B 196 (5K 15)
Bacon Ter. RM8: Dag 7G 125
Badburgham Ct. EN9: Wal A 3F 76
Baddeley Cl. EN3: Enf 7A 76
Baddow Cl. IG8: Wfd G 3J 107
RM10: Dag 1M 141
Baddow Ct. CM2: Gt Bad 4H 73
Baddow Hall Av. CM2: Gt Bad 3H 73
Baddow Hall Cres. CM2: Gt Bad 3H 73
Baddow Pl. Av. CM2: Gt Bad 4H 73
Baddow Rd. CM2: Chelm 1C 72 (2A 34)
(not continuous)
Baden Powell Cl. RM9: Dag 1K 141
Baden Powell Dr. CO3: Colc, S'way 3G 173
Baden Rd. IG1: Ilf 7A 124
Bader Way RM13: Rain 8E 126
Badger Cl. IG2: Ilf 1B 124
Badger Gro. CM7: Brain 5K 193
Badger Hall Av. SS7: Ben 2G 135
Badgers Cl. CM2: Gall 9C 72
SS0: Wclf S 2G 137
Badgers Grn. CO6: M Tey 3G 171
Badgers Holt CO3: S'way 9E 164
(off Hedgerows)
Badgers Keep CM0: Bur C 1B 196
Badgers Mt. RM16: Ors 9B 146
SS5: Hock 2B 120
Badgers, The SS16: Lang H 2J 131
Badgers Way SS7: Ben 2G 135
Badley Hall Rd. CO7: Gt Bro 6D 168 (5K 17)
Badlis Rd. E17: Lon 7A 106
Badlow Cl. DA8: Eri 5C 152
Badminton Rd. CO15: Jay 5E 188
Bag La. CM4: Fry, Ing 5A 84 (5G 33)
Bagleys Spring RM6: Chad H 8K 109
Bagshaw Rd. CO12: Har 3M 209
Bailey Bri. Rd. CM7: Brain 4G 192
Bailey Cl. E4: Lon 1C 106
RM19: Purf 2A 154
Bailey Dale CO3: S'way 2D 172
Bailey Rd. SS9: Lgh S 4A 136
Bailey, The SS6: Ray 5J 119
Baillie Cl. RM13: Rain 4F 142
Bainbridge Dr. CO5: Tip 7D 226
Bainbridge Rd. RM9: Dag 6L 125
Baines Cl. CO3: Colc 1G 173
Baird Cl. E10: Lon 3A 122
Bairny Wood App. IG8: Wfd G 3H 107
Baker Av. CM3: Hat P 3L 61
Baker M. CM9: Mal 6C 214
Bakers Av. E17: Lon 1B 122
Bakers Cl. CM3: S Fer 9K 89
Bakers Ct. CM14: Brtwd 9F 96
CO1: Colc 6M 165
SS14: Bas 5H 117
BAKER'S END 3E 20
Bakers Farm Cl. SS11: W'fd 9A 102
Bakersfield CM3: May 8K 213
CM4: Stock 7N 85
BAKER'S GREEN 1H 201 (6K 25)
Bakers La. CM2: W Han 2C 86 (4A 34)
Baker's La. CM3: Dan 3E 74
Bakers La. CM4: Ing 5D 84
CM6: Fels 9J 199
Baker's La. CM9: Tol M 6K 25
Bakers La. CM16: Epp 9E 64
Baker's La. CM77: Bla N 3C 204 (1C 24)
CO3: Colc 6H 165 (6D 16)
CO4: Colc 6H 165
Bakers La. SG8: Bar 6E 4
Bakers Mead CM3: Gt Walt 5H 57
Bakers Mdw. CM15: Dodd 7F 82
Bakers M. CM4: Ing 5D 84
Baker's Rd. CO10: Bel P, Ovtn 4D 8
BAKER STREET 6A 146 (7G 41)
Baker St. CM2: Chelm 1B 72
EN2: Enf 6B 30
RM16: Ors 6A 146 (7G 41)
Bakers Vs., The CM16: Epp 9E 64
Bakers Wlk. CM21: Saw 2K 51
Bakery Cl. CM0: T'ham 3K 225
CM19: Roy 3J 53
Bakery Ct. CM24: Stan M 3C 220
Balaam St. E13: Lon 6F 39
Baldock Rd. SG7: Kel, R'ton 7A 4
SG9: Bunt 4C 10
Baldocks Rd. CM16: They B 5D 78
Baldock St. SG8: R'ton 5C 4
SG12: Ware 4C 20
Baldwins Hill IG10: Lou 1M 91
Baldwyn's Pk. DA5: Bex 4A 46
Bale Cl. CO3: S'way 2F 172
Balfe Ct. CO4: Colc 9E 166
Balfour Cl. SS12: W'fd 2M 117
Balfour Rd. IG1: Ilf 4A 124
RM17: Grays 2M 155
Balgonie Rd. E4: Lon 7D 90
Balgores Cres. RM2: Romf 7F 110
Balgores La. RM2: Romf 7F 110 (3B 40)
Balgores Sq. RM2: Romf 8F 110
Balkerne Cl. CO1: Colc 8M 165
Balkerne Gdns. CO1: Colc 8M 165
Balkerne Gate 8M 165
Balkerne Hill CO3: Colc 8M 165 (6E 16)
Balkerne Pas. CO1: Colc 8M 165
Ball All. CO1: Colc 8N 165
Ballards Cl. RM10: Dag 1N 141
BALLARDS GORE 1A 44
Ballards Rd. RM10: Dag 2N 141 (6K 39)
Ballards Wlk. SS15: Lain 8N 115 (3K 41)
Ballast Quay Rd. CO5: Fing 8H 175 (1G 27)
CO7: W'hoe 6J 175
(not continuous)
BALLINGDON 5J 9
Ballingdon Hill
CO10: Bulm, Sud 2N 195 (6H 9)
Ballingdon St. CO10: Sud 5J 9
Balliol Av. E4: Lon 1E 106
Ball La. CO2: B'hth 9N 173 (1F 27)
Ball's Chase CO9: Hals 5L 207
BALLS GREEN 1F 176 (6K 17)
Balls Pond Rd. N1: Lon 5B 38
Balmerino Av. SS7: Had 9J 119
Balmoral Av. CO15: Clac S 1H 189
SS17: Corr 1B 148
SS17: Stan H 2N 147
Balmoral Cl. CM11: Bill 7N 99
Balmoral Ct. CM2: Chelm 9L 59
Balmoral Gdns. IG3: Ilf 3E 124
SS5: Hock 1B 120
Balmoral Ho. SS0: Wclf S 6K 137
(off Balmoral Rd.)
Balmoral Rd. CM3: May 6L 213
CM15: Pil H 5E 96
E7: Lon 6J 123 (5F 39)
E10: Lon 4B 122
RM2: Romf 9F 110
RM12: Horn 5H 127
SS0: Wclf S 6K 137
Balmoral Ter. SS0: Wclf S 4J 137
(off Fairfax Dr.)
Balmoral Trad. Est. IG11: Bark 5E 140
BALSHAM 1E 6
Balsham Rd. CB1: Lin 2D 6
BALSTONIA 1A 148 (5K 41)
Balstonia Dr. SS17: Stan H 9N 131
Baltic Av. SS1: Sth S 6M 137
Balton Way CO12: Har 5H 209
Bamber Ho. IG11: Bark 1C 140
BAMBER'S GREEN 7D 12
Bamford Ct. E15: Lon 7B 122
(off Clays La.)
Bamford Rd. IG11: Bark 8B 124
Bamford Way RM5: Col R 2N 109
Bampton Rd. RM3: Romf 4J 111
Bancroft Av. IG9: Buck H 8G 91
Bancroft Chase RM12: Rush G 4D 126
Bancrofts Rd. CM3: S Fer 9L 89
Bandhills Cl. CM3: S Fer 9K 89
Banes Down EN9: Naze 1E 62
Bangles, The CB11: Elm 6J 5
Banister Cl. CO16: Clac S 8G 185
Bankart La. CM2: Chelm 7A 60
Bank Bldgs. E4: Lon 3D 106
(off Avenue, The)
Bankfoot RM17: Grays 3J 155
Bank Pas. CO1: Colc 8M 165
Bank Pl. CM14: Brtwd 8F 96
Banks Ct. CM6: Gt D 3L 203
Bankside Cl. CM3: S Fer 8L 89
Bankside Pk. IG11: Bark 3F 140
Bankside Rd. IG1: Ilf 7B 124
Banks La. CM16: Fid, They M 3K 79 (4K 31)
Bank Station (Tube, DLR) 7B 38
Bank St. CM7: Brain 5H 193
Banks Way E12: Lon 6N 123
Bannatyne's Health & Raquet Club 1F 154
Bannatyne's Health Club 3A 106
Bann Cl. RM15: S Ock 7E 144
Banner Cl. RM19: Purf 2A 154
Bannister Dr. CM13: Hut 5M 97
BANNISTER GREEN 7N 199 (1K 23)
Bannister Grn. SS12: W'fd 1M 117
Bannister Grn. Vs. CM6: Fels 7M 199
Banson's Ct. CM5: Chip 7L 67
Banson's La. CM5: Chip 7L 67
Banson's Way CM5: Chip 7L 67
Banson's Yd. CM5: Chip 7L 67
Banters La. CM3: Gt L 6M 203 (2B 24)
Bantham & Ongar Bowls Club 3B 66
Bantock Way CM8: Wthm 8B 230
Banyards RM11: Horn 8J 111
Banyard Way SS4: R'fd 3H 121
Barbara Av. SS8: Can I 2F 150
Barbara Cl. SS4: R'fd 5K 121
Barbel Cl. EN8: Wal X 4A 76
Barbel Rd. CO4: Colc 6F 166
Barberry Cl. RM3: Romf 4G 111
Barbican Station (Tube) 7A 38
Barbour Gdns. CO2: Colc, King 4G 173
Barbour Grn. SS12: W'fd 2L 117
Barbrook La. CO5: Tip 5C 226
Barbrook Way CM3: Bick 9E 74
Barclay Cl. CM2: Gt Bad 3H 73
Barclay Ct. EN11: Hod 6A 52
Barclay Oval IG8: Wfd G 1G 107
Barclay Path E17: Lon 9C 106
Barclay Rd. E11: Lon 3F 122
(not continuous)
E17: Lon 9C 106
SS13: Pits 6M 117
Barclay Way RM20: W Thur 3C 154
Bardell Cl. CM1: Chelm 5H 59
Bardenville Rd. SS8: Can I 2L 151
Bardeswell Cl. CM14: Brtwd 8F 96
Bardfield SS16: Van 1F 132
Bardfield Av. RM6: Chad H 7J 109
Bardfield Cen. CM7: Gt Bar 3C 202
Bardfield Cotts. CM15: Dodd 5E 82
BARDFIELD END GREEN 8E 224 (3G 13)
Bardfield Rd. CM6: Thax 8D 224 (3F 13)
CM7: Bar S 5K 13
CM7: F'fld 4C 200 (2K 13)
CO2: Colc 5A 174
BARDFIELD SALING 5K 13
Bardfield Way CO13: Frin S 8J 181
SS6: Ray 4G 118 (2E 42)
Barfield Rd. CO5: W Mer 3C 228 (5F 27)
E11: Lon 3F 122
Barfields IG10: Lou 3N 91
Barfields Gdns. IG10: Lou 3N 91
Barfields Path IG10: Lou 3N 91
Barfields Row CO5: Mess 1C 226
Bargate La. CO7: Ded 5A 162 (3J 17)
CO11: Law 5A 162
Barge Ho. Rd. E16: Lon 9A 140
Barge Pier Rd. SS3: Shoe 9J 139
Barham Cl. RM7: Maw 6N 109
Baring St. N1: Lon 6B 38
Bark Burr Rd. RM16: Chaf H 9J 145
Barker Cl. CB9: Stpl B 3K 223
CO11: Law 4G 163
Barkers La. CO16: T Sok 1H 179

Barkers Mead CM22: L Hall 1K 213
BARKING 9B 124 (5H 39)
Barking Abbey 1B 140
Barking Abbey School Leisure Cen. 8F 124
Barking & East Ham United (Mayesbrook Pk.) 7F 124
Barking Bus. Cen. IG11: Bark 3F 140
Barking Ind. Pk. IG11: Bark 1E 140
Barking Northern Relief Rd.
IG11: Bark 9A 124 (5G 39)
Barking Rd. E6: Lon 7E 38
E13: Lon 7E 38
E16: Lon 7E 38
BARKINGSIDE 7B 108 (3G 39)
Barkingside Station (Tube) 7C 108 (3H 39)
Barking Station (Rail & Tube) 9B 124 (5H 39)
Barkis Cl. CM1: Chelm 4F 58
Barkstead Rd. CO4: Colc 6C 166
BARKWAY 1E 10
Barkway Rd. SG8: R'ton 5D 4
Barkway St. SG8: R'ton 5C 4
Barkwood Cl. RM7: Romf 9A 110
Barlee Cl. CB11: Clav 3J 11
Barle Gdns. RM15: S Ock 6E 144
BARLEY 6F 5
Barley Cl. CM22: Hat H 4C 22
SS16: Lang H 3J 131
Barleycorn Way RM11: Horn 1K 127
Barley Ct. CB11: Saf W 4C 218
Barley Cft. CM18: H'low 7D 54
BARLEYCROFT END 5G 11
Barley Fld. CM15: Kel H 7C 82
Barleyfields CM8: Wthm 6D 230
Barleyfields Cl. RM6: Chad H 1G 125
Barleylands Farm Mus. & Vis. Cen. 2A 116 (1K 41)
Barleylands Rd.
CM11: Bas, Bill 2N 115 (2K 41)
SS15: Bas 2N 115 (2K 41)
Barley La. IG3: Ilf 2F 124 (4J 39)
RM6: Chad H 2F 124
Barley Mead CM3: Dan 4H 75
Barley Rd. SG8: Bar 6F 5
(Barley)
SG8: Bar 6F 5
(Great Chishill)
Barley Way CO3: S'way 1E 172
BARLING 3B 44
Barling Rd.
SS3: Barl M, Gt W, Lit W 2E 138 (3A 44)
Barlon Rd. CO7: Gt Bro, L Bro 4E 168 (5K 17)
Barlow's Reach CM2: Chelm 7B 60
Barlow Way RM13: Rain 5B 142
Barnaby Rudge CM1: Chelm 4H 59
Barnaby Way IG7: Chig 9A 92
SS15: Lain 8M 115
Barnard Acres EN9: Naze 2E 62
Barnard Cl. CB11: Newp 3K 215
SS16: Van 4F 132
Barnard Gro. E15: Lon 9F 122
BARNARDISTON 1A 8
Barnardiston Rd. CB9: B'dstn, Pos 1B 8
CO4: Colc 6C 166
Barnardiston Way CM8: Wthm 4C 230
Barnardo Dr. IG6: Ilf 8B 108
Barnardos Village IG6: Ilf 7B 108
Barnard Rd. CM2: Gall 8C 72
CM21: Saw 1K 51
SS9: Lgh S 4A 136
Barnards Av. SS8: Can I 1K 151
Barnards Ct. CB10: Saf W 3C 218
Barnards Fld. CM6: Thax 8D 224
Barnard's Yd. CB11: Saf W 4C 218
Barncombe Cl. SS7: Thund 9D 118
Barn Ct. CM21: Saw 1K 51
Barncroft Cl. CO4: Colc 4B 166
IG10: Lou 4N 91
Barncroft Grn. IG10: Lou 4N 91
Barncroft Rd. IG10: Lou 4N 91
BARNEHURST 8A 152 (3A 46)
Barnehurst Av. DA7: Bexh 6A 152
DA8: Bexh, Eri 6A 152
Barnehurst Cl. DA8: Eri 6A 152
Barnehurst Rd.
DA7: Bexh 7A 152 (2A 46)
Barnehurst Station (Rail) 7A 152 (2A 46)
Barn End La. DA2: Dart, Swan 5B 46
Barnes Cl. E12: Lon 6K 123
Barnes Ct. IG8: Buck H, Wfd G 2K 107
BARNES CRAY 9E 152 (3B 46)
Barnes Cray Rd. DA1: Cray 9E 152
Barnes Farm Dr. CM3: Alth 3C 190
Barnes Ho. IG11: Bark 1C 140
Barnes Mill Rd. CM2: Chelm 9A 60
Barnes Rd. IG1: Ilf 7B 124
Barnet Pk. Rd. SS11: Runw 6N 101
Barnett Cl. DA8: Eri 7D 152
Barneveld Av. *SS8: Can I 2L 151*
(off Winterswyk Av.)
Barnfield CM16: Epp 7F 64
CM22: Hat O 8E 206
CO5: Fee 2L 211
CO11: Mist 4J 163
SS11: W'fd 8M 101
Barnfield Cl. EN9: Naze 1F 62
EN11: Rye P 3A 52
Barnfield Cotts. CM9: Mal 3D 214
Barnfield M. CM1: Chelm 5J 59
Barnfield Pl. CM8: Wthm 6C 230
Barnfield Rd. CO6: Gt Hork 1K 165
Barnfields CO3: S'way 9D 164
Barn Grn. CM1: Chelm 3N 59
Barn Hall Av. CO2: Colc 2B 174
Barn Hall Cotts. SS11: W'fd 6J 101
Barnhall Rd. CM9: Tol K 4A 26
Barnham Dr. SE28: Lon 8E 140
(not continuous)
Barn Hill CM19: Roy 7H 53
Barn La. CO11: L Bro 9D 162
Barnmead CM5: Toot 8D 66
Barn Mead CM7: Brain 6M 193
CM15: Dodd 6F 82
CM16: They B 6D 78
Barnmead CM18: H'low 5C 54
Barnmead Gdns. RM9: Dag 7L 125
Barnmead Rd. RM9: Dag 7L 125
Barnmead Way CM0: Bur C 1B 196
BARNSBURY 5A 38
Barnsbury Rd. N1: Lon 6A 38
Barns Ct. CM19: H'low 8A 54
Barnsley Rd. RM3: Romf 4K 111
Barns Rd. CM11: Cray H 2D 116
Barnstaple Cl. SS1: Sth S 6E 138
Barnstaple Path RM3: Romf 2G 111
Barnstaple Rd. RM3: Romf 2G 111
SS1: Sth S 6E 138
BARNSTON 3L 191 (2H 23)
Barnston Grn. CM6: Barns 3L 191
Barnston Way CM13: Hut 4M 97
Barn, The RM17: Grays 2L 155
Barn Vw. Rd. CO6: Cogg 4L 197
Barnwell Dr. SS5: Hock 1C 120
Barnwell Rd. DA1: Dart 8K 153
Barnyard, The SS16: Lang H 2J 131
Baron Ct. SS2: Temp I 1L 137
Baron Gdns. IG6: Ilf 7B 108
Baronia Cft. CO4: Colc 4C 166
Baron Rd. CM3: S Fer 1L 103
RM8: Dag 3J 125
Barons Ct. IG1: Ilf 4C 124
Barons Ct. Rd. SS6: Ray 2J 119
Baron's La. CM9: Mun, Pur 8K 215 (3G 35)
Barons Way SS16: Lang H 2K 131
Baronswood Way CO2: Colc 4K 173
Barpack St. CO11: Brad 1D 150
Barrack La. CM3: Gt Walt 4F 56 (5K 23)
CO7: Gt Ben 2M 183
CO12: Har 3N 209
CO16: Gt Ben 2M 183
Barrack Rd. CM1: Good E 5H 23
Barrack Sq. CM2: Chelm 9K 59
Barrack St. CO1: Colc 9B 166 (6F 17)
Barra Glade SS12: W'fd 2N 117
Barras Cl. EN3: Enf 7A 76
Barr Cl. CO7: W'hoe 5J 175
Barrell Cl. CO7: Frat 3F 176
Barrels Down Rd. CM23: Bis S 7K 11
Barrett Cl. RM3: Romf 4F 110
Barrett Rd. E17: Lon 8C 106
Barrie Pavement SS12: W'fd 2L 117
BARRINGTON 1E 4
Barrington Cl. CM2: Gt Bad 4J 73
CO16: L Cla 3G 184
IG5: Ilf 5M 107
IG10: Lou 2B 92
SS3: Shoe 5J 139
SS14: Bas 7G 116
Barrington Ct. CM13: Hut 6M 97
Barrington Gdns. CO15: Clac S 8N 185
SS14: Bas 7G 116
Barrington Grn. IG10: Lou 3B 92
Barrington Pl. CM4: Ing 6D 84
Barrington Rd. CO2: Colc 1A 174
E12: Lon 8N 123
IG10: Lou 3B 92
SG8: Orw 1D 4
Barringtons Cl. SS6: Ray 4K 119
Barron's Cl. CM5: Chip 6K 67
Barrow Hall Rd.
SS3: Gt W, Lit W 1E 138 (3A 44)
Barrow Hill CO10: Act 3K 9
Barrow La. EN7: Chesh, G Oak 4B 30
Barrowsand SS1: Sth S 8F 138
Barrows Rd. CM19: H'low 3M 53
Barry Cl. RM16: Grays 1C 156
Barry Ct. RM5: Col R 2B 110
Barryfields CM7: Shalf 4A 14
Barrymore Wlk. SS6: Ray 5M 119
BARSTABLE 9F 116 (3A 42)
Barstable Rd. SS17: Stan H 3M 147
Bartholomew Cl. CB10: Gt Che 8E 202
Bartholomew Dr. RM3: H Wood 6H 111
BARTHOLOMEW GREEN 9A 192 (1B 24)
Bartholomew Ho. IG8: Ilf 4A 108
Bartholomew Way BR8: Swan 6A 46
Bartlett Cl. CM3: May 7K 213
Bartlett Ho's. *RM10: Dag 9N 125*
(off Vicarage Rd.)
Bartletts SS6: Ray 7N 119
Bartley Cl. SS7: Thund 9B 118
Bartley Rd. SS7: Thund 9B 118
BARTLOW 3E 6
Bartlow End SS13: Bas 7J 117
Bartlow Gdns. RM5: Col R 5B 110
Bartlow Rd. CB1: Cas C 4G 7
CB1: Hads 3D 6
CB1: Lin 2D 6
CB10: A'dn, Bart 6C 190 (3E 6)
Bartlow Rd. Cotts. CB10: A'dn 6D 190
Bartlow Side SS13: Bas 7J 117
Barton Av. RM7: Rush G 3N 125
Barton Cl. CM3: S Fer 8K 89
IG7: Chig 8B 92
Barton Friars IG7: Chig 8B 92
Barton Mdws. IG6: Ilf 8A 108
Barton Rd. RM12: Horn 3E 126
Bartram Av. CM7: Brain 5L 193
Barwell Way CM8: Wthm 5D 230
BARWICK 2E 20
Barwick La. SG11: H Cro 2D 20
Barwick Rd. E7: Lon 6H 123
Baryta Cl. SS17: Stan H 4L 147
Baryta Ct. *SS9: Lgh S 5D 136*
(off Rectory Gro.)
Basedale Rd. RM9: Dag 9G 124
BASILDON 9C 116 (3A 42)
Basildon & District Crematorium
SS13: Pits 2M 133
Basildon Av. IG5: Ilf 5N 107
Basildon Bowl 9B 116
Basildon Bus. Cen. SS14: Bas 7B 116
Basildon Cen., The SS14: Bas 9B 116
Basildon Dr. SS15: Lain 8L 115
Basildon Ri. SS15: Lain 7N 115
Basildon Rd. SS15: Lain 7N 115 (3K 41)
Basildon Sports Cen. 3A 132
Basildon Station (Rail) 1B 132 (3A 42)
Basildon Trad. Cen. SS14: Bas 7A 116
Basil M. *CM17: H'low 2H 55*
(off Chase, The)
Basing Ho. *IG11: Bark 1C 140*
(off St Margarets)
Basin Rd. CM9: Hey B 8F 214 (1J 35)
BASKETTS 6N 171
Bassenthwaite Rd. SS7: Thund 9E 118
Bassett Gdns. CM16: N Wea 5N 65
Bassett Ho. RM9: Dag 1G 141
Bassett Rd. E7: Lon 6K 123
Bassetts La. CM3: L Bad, Wdhm W 7E 24
Bassett's La. CM5: Will 2L 69 (2F 33)
BASSINGBOURN 4B 4
Bassingbourn Rd.
CM24: Stan Apt 8L 221 (7C 12)
SG8: Bass, Lit 4A 4
Bassingbourn Rdbt. CM22: Tak 8L 221
Bassingham Cres. CO5: Tip 6E 226
BASSUS GREEN 6A 10
Bastable Av. IG11: Bark 2D 140 (6H 39)
Bata Av. RM18: E Til 3K 157
Batavia Rd. SS8: Can I 1D 150
Bate-Dudley Dr. CM0: Brad S 7D 194
Bateman Cl. IG11: Bark 8B 124
Bateman Rd. CO7: B'sea 5D 182 (3K 27)
E4: Lon 3A 106
Bateman's La. CO16: L Cla 1F 184
Batemans M. CM14: War 1E 112
Bates Bus. Cen. RM3: H Wood 4L 111
Bates Ind. Est. RM3: H Wood 4L 111
(not continuous)
Bates Rd. CM9: Mal 4C 214
RM3: H Wood 4L 111
Bath Hill IP11: Felix 1K 19
Bath Rd. E7: Lon 8K 123
RM6: Chad H 1K 125
BATH SIDE 2M 209
Bath St. CO7: W'hoe 6H 175
DA11: Grav 3H 47
EC1: Lon 6B 38
Bathurst Cl. CO2: Colc 5A 174
Bathurst Rd. IG1: Ilf 3A 124
Baton Cl. RM19: Purf 2A 154
Battery Rd. SE28: Lon 9D 140
Battisford Dr. CO16: Clac S 9E 184
Battis, The RM1: Romf 1C 126
Battle Ct. CM5: Chip 8L 67
Battle Rd. DA8: Eri 2A 152
DA17: Belv, Eri 2A 152 (1A 46)
BATTLESBRIDGE 6D 102 (7E 34)
Battlesbridge Station (Rail) 6D 102 (7D 34)
Battlesbrook Rd. CO2: Colc 4D 174
Battleswick SS14: Bas 6F 116
Batt's Rd. CM0: Stpl 3B 36
DA13: Cobh, Ludd 7J 47
Bawdsey Av. IG2: Ilf 8E 108
Bawdsey Cl. CO16: Clac S 1F 188
Bawn Cl. CM7: Brain 4H 193
Bawtree Way CO3: Colc 1H 173
Baxter Av. SS2: Sth S 5L 137
Baxter Gdns.
RM3: Noak H, Romf 8G 95
Baxter Rd. IG1: Ilf 7A 124
Baxters CM3: Dan 3G 74
Bayard Av. CO7: B'sea 6E 182
Bay Cl. SS8: Can I 3H 151
BAYFORD 7A 20
Bayford La. SG13: B'frd 7A 20
Bayford Station (Rail) 7A 20
Bayham St. NW1: Lon 6A 38
Bayleys Mead CM13: Hut 8M 97
Bayley St. CO9: Cas H 3K 219 (1E 14)
Bayliss Av. SE28: Lon 7J 141
Bay Mnr. La. RM20: W Thur 4C 154
Baymans Wood CM15: Shenf 8H 97
Baynard Av. CM6: Fels 9E 212
Baynards Cres. CO13: Walt 8H 181
Bay Rd. CO12: Har 3M 209
Bays Dr. CO9: Hals 4K 207
BAYTHORNE END 4B 8
Bay Tree Cl. CM77: Rayne 6B 192
IG6: Ilf 4A 108
Baytree Ho. E4: Lon 6B 90
Bay Vw. *CM0: St La 2C 36*
(off Mountview Cres.)
Bay Vw. Cres.
CO12: L Oak, R'sy 7E 208
Baywood Sq. IG7: Chig 1G 108
BBC Essex Garden 1L 93 (6K 31)
Beach Av. SS9: Lgh S 5F 136
Beach Ct. SS0: Wclf S 7H 137
SS3: Gt W 3N 139
Beach Cres. CO15: Jay 6D 188
Beachcroft Av. CO13: Walt 8G 180
Beachcroft Rd. E11: Lon 5E 122
Beaches Cl. SS5: Hock 1F 120
Beach Ho. Gdns. SS8: Can I 3L 151
Beach Rd. CO5: W Mer 3C 228
CO12: Har 4L 209
CO15: Clac S 2K 189
CO16: St O 6A 188 (4B 28)
SS1: Sth S 7A 138
SS3: Shoe 9K 139
SS8: Can I 1K 151
Beach's Dr. CM1: Chelm 8F 58
Beach Sta. Rd. IP11: Felix 2K 19
Beach Way CO15: Jay 6D 188
Beachway SS8: Can I 3H 151
Beachy Dr. *CM0: St La 2C 36*
(off Moorhen Av.)
Beachy Rd. E3: Lon 9A 122
Beacon Cl. CO7: B'sea 7D 182
BEACON END 9E 164 (6C 16)
Beaconfield Av. CM16: Epp 8E 64
Beaconfield Rd. CM16: Epp 8E 64
Beaconfield Way CM16: Epp 8E 64
Beacon Hgts. CO16: St O 4K 27
BEACON HILL
CM14 7M 81 (5C 32)
CM8 1M 229 (5H 25)
Beacon Hill
CM8: Gt Tot, W Bis 1M 229 (5H 25)
CM9: Mal 6A 214
CM14: Kel H 7N 81 (5C 32)
RM19: Purf 3M 153
Beacon Hill Av. CO12: Har 3N 209
Beacon Hill Ind. Est. RM19: Purf 3M 153
Beacon Hill Rd.
CM14: Kel C, Kel H 8M 81 (5C 32)
Beacon Rd. DA8: Eri 5F 152
Beaconsfield Av. CO3: Colc 9M 165 (6E 16)
Beaconsfield Rd. CO15: Clac S 1K 189
E10: Lon 4C 122
Beaconsfield Ter. RM6: Chad H 1J 125
Beacons, The IG10: Lou 8N 77
Beacontree Av. E17: Lon 5D 106
BEACONTREE HEATH 3M 125 (4K 39)
Beacontree Rd. E11: Lon 3F 122
Beacon Way CO3: S'way 9D 164
CO16: St O 4K 27
Beadel Cl. CM8: Wthm 7B 230
Beadle's Pde. RM10: Dag 8A 126
Beadles, The CM22: L Hall 2K 213
Beadle Way CM3: Gt L 8K 203
Beadon Dr. CM7: Brain 7J 193
Beads Hall La. CM15: Pil H 3E 96
Beal Rd. IG1: Ilf 4N 123
Beam Av. RM10: Dag 1N 141
Beambridge SS13: Pits 9H 117
Beambridge Ct. SS13: Pits 9H 117
Beambridge M. SS13: Pits 9H 117
Beambridge Pl. SS13: Pits 9H 117
Beaminster Gdns. IG6: Ilf 6A 108
Beamish Cl. CM16: N Wea 4A 66
Beams Cl. CM11: Bill 8L 99
Beams Way CM11: Bill 8L 99
Beam Vs. RM9: Dag 2A 142
Beamway RM10: Dag 9B 126
BEAN 4E 46
Beanfield Rd.
CM21: H Wych, Saw 1F 50 (4J 21)
Bean La. DA2: Bean 4E 46
Beansland Gro. RM6: Chad H 6K 109
Bear Cl. RM7: Romf 1N 125
Beard's La. CB11: Dun E 7J 5
Beardsley Dr. CM1: Chelm 4N 59
Beardsley Ter. *RM8: Dag 7G 125*
(off Fitzstephen Rd.)
Beards Ter. CO6: Cogg 2L 197
Bearing Cl. IG7: Chig 1F 108
Bearing Way IG7: Chig 1F 108
Bearsted Dr. SS13: Pits 1K 133
Bear St. CO6: Nay 1D 16
Bearwalden Bus. Pk. CB11: Wen A 7K 227
Beatrice Av. IP11: Felix 1K 19
SS8: Can I 1H 151
Beatrice Cl. SS5: Hock 1C 120
Beatrice Ct. IG9: Buck H 8K 91
Beatrice Littlewood Ho. *SS8: Can I 2G 151*
(off Kitkatts Rd.)
Beatrice Rd. CO14: Walt 4N 181
CO15: Clac S 2J 189
E17: Lon 9A 106
Beatty Gdns. CM7: Brain 4L 193
Beatty La. SS14: Bas 9F 116
Beatty Ri. CM3: S Fer 2M 103
Beattyville Gdns. IG6: Ilf 8N 107
Beauchamp Rd. E7: Lon 9H 123
BEAUCHAMP RODING 6E 22
Beauchamps CM0: Bur C 1B 196
Beauchamps Cl. CM1: Chelm 3A 60
Beauchamps Dr. SS11: W'fd 9N 101
Beaufort Cl. CM16: N Wea 6M 65
E4: Lon 3B 106
RM7: Maw 8A 110
RM16: Chaf H 1J 155
Beaufort Gdns. CM7: Brain 4J 193
IG1: Ilf 3N 123
Beaufort Rd. CM2: Chelm 7B 60
CM12: Bill 6H 99
Beaufort St. SS2: Sth S 5B 138
Beaulieu Blvd. CM1: Chelm 4A 60
Beaulieu Dr. EN9: Wal A 3B 76
Beauly Way RM1: Romf 5C 110
Beaumaris Dr. IG8: Wfd G 4K 107
BEAUMONT 6D 18
Beaumont Av. CO7: B'sea 6F 182
CO15: Clac S 1H 189
Beaumont Cl. CO4: Colc 3M 165
CO14: Walt 7J 181
RM2: Romf 6G 110
Beaumont Cres. RM13: Rain 8E 126

Beaumont Gdns. CM13: Hut 5M 97
Beaumont Hill CM6: Gt D 1K 203 (7G 13)
Beaumont Ho. E10: Lon 2B 122
Beaumont Pk. CM3: Dan 4C 74
Beaumont Pk. Dr. CM19: Roy 3H 53
Beaumont Pl. CM7: Brain 5K 193
Beaumont Rd. CO12: Gt Oak 8C 204 (5E 18)
E10: Lon 2B 122
(not continuous)
EN7: Brox 2B 30
Beaumont Wlk. CM1: Chelm 6F 58
Beaumont Way CM9: Mal 8D 214
Beaver Cl. CO3: S'way 8F 164
Beaver Rd. IG6: Ilf 2H 109
Beaver Twr. SS9: Lgh S 9D 120
BEAZLEY END 4C 14
Beazley End SS12: W'fd 1M 117
Bebington Cl. CM12: Bill 5J 99
Beccles Ct. SS11: W'fd 8L 101
Beccles Dr. IG11: Bark 8D 124
Beche Rd. CO2: Colc 1B 174
Bechervaise Ct. E10: Lon 3B 122
(off Leyton Grange Est.)
Becker Rd. CO3: S'way 2F 172
Beckers Grn. Rd. CM7: Brain 7M 193
Becket Cl. CM13: Gt War 3F 112
SS4: R'fd 2J 121
Beckett Dr. SS17: Stan H 1M 147
Becketts SS15: Lain 9J 115
Becketts Ct. CM1: Chelm 8J 59
(off Glebe Rd.)
Becketts Ho. IG1: Ilf 5N 123
Becket Way CM3: S Fer 3L 103
Beck Farm Cl. SS8: Can I 2M 151
Beckford Rd. CO11: Mist 4M 163
Beckingham Rd. CM9: Gt Tot 9H 205 (5J 25)
CM9: Tol D, Tol M 4H 227 (6A 26)
Beckingham St. CM9: Tol M 6K 25
Beckney Av. SS5: Hock 7D 104
Beck Rd. CB11: Saf W 4C 218
SS8: Can I 2M 151
BECKTON 7G 39
Beckton Park Station (DLR) 7G 39
Beckton Rd. E16: Lon 7E 38
Beckton Station (DLR) 7G 39
Beckton Triangle Retail Pk. E6: Lon 4A 140
BECONTREE 5K 125 (4K 39)
Becontree Av. RM8: Dag 6G 124 (4J 39)
Becontree Cl. CO15: Clac S 5K 185
Becontree Station (Tube) 8J 125 (5J 39)
Bective Rd. E7: Lon 6G 123
Becton Pl. DA8: Eri 6A 152
Bedale Rd. RM3: Romf 2L 111
Beddington Rd. IG3: Ilf 2E 124
Bedells Av. CM77: Bla N 3B 194
Bede Rd. RM6: Chad H 1H 125
Bedford Cl. CM7: Brain 4K 193
CO5: Tip 6D 226
SS6: Ray 6K 119
Bedford Gdns. RM12: Horn 4G 127
Bedford Pl. SS8: Can I 1F 150
Bedford Rd. CO4: Colc 3N 165
CO15: Hol S 8N 185
E17: Lon 6A 106
E18: Lon 6G 106
IG1: Ilf 5A 124
RM17: Grays 3L 155
SS15: Lain 9K 115
Bedfords Hill CM1: Good E 5G 23
Bedford Sq. W1: Lon 7A 38
BEDLAR'S GREEN 1A 22
Bedloes Av. SS11: Raw 9E 102
Bedonwell Rd. DA7: Bexh 2A 46
Bedwell Ct. RM6: Chad H 2J 125
(off Broomfield Rd.)
Bedwell Rd.
CM22: Else, U Grn 1J 199 (5B 12)
Beecham Ct. SS15: Lain 7L 115
Beech Av. CM7: Brain 3H 193
CM13: Brtwd 9J 97
CO7: W'hoe 5H 175
CO9: Hals 4M 207
IG9: Buck H 8H 91
RM14: Upm 5M 127
SS6: Ray 4K 119
Beech Cl. CM0: Bur C 2D 196
CM22: Tak 2C 224
IG10: Lou 2A 92
RM12: Horn 5F 126
Beechcombe SS17: Corr 9C 132
Beech Ct. IG1: Ilf 5N 123
(off Riverdene Rd.)
SS14: Bas 1F 132
Beechcroft Av. DA7: Bexh 6B 152
SS17: Linf 2J 157
Beechcroft Rd. E18: Lon 6H 107
SS8: Can I 2E 150
Beech Dr. CM21: Saw 4H 51
Beechenlea La. BR8: Swan 6B 46
Beechers Ct. CM1: Chelm 9H 59
Beeches Cl. CB11: Saf W 6B 218
CM1: Chelm 9G 59
Beeches Rd. CM1: Chelm 9G 58
CM9: Mal 3B 214
SS11: Raw 6E 102 (7E 34)
Beeches, The CB11: Wen A 6K 227
CM14: Brtwd 9E 96
CO11: Law 5H 163
E12: Lon 9L 123
EN9: Wal A 5J 77
(off Woodbine Cl.)
RM18: Til 7D 156
Beechfield CM21: Saw 2L 51
EN11: Hod 1A 52
Beechfield Gdns. RM7: Rush G 2A 126
Beechfield Rd. DA8: Eri 5C 152
Beechfield Wlk. EN9: Wal A 5D 76
Beech Gdns. RM10: Dag 9A 126
Beech Grn. CM8: W Bis 2L 229
Beech Gro. CO3: S'way 6A 164
CO9: Sib H 6J 219
CO12: L Oak 8D 208
IG6: Ilf 3D 108
RM15: Ave 8N 143
Beech Hall Cres. E4: Lon 4D 106
Beech Hall Rd. E4: Lon 4C 106
Beech Hill CO3: Colc 9H 165
Beech Hill Gdns. EN9: Wal A 7H 77
Beech Ho. CM13: Hut 5M 97
E17: Lon 7D 106
Beech La. CB2: Pam 1K 5
IG9: Buck H 8H 91
Beech Lodge SS3: Shoe 7K 139
Beechmont Gdns. SS2: Sth S 2K 137
Beech Pl. CM16: Epp 1E 78
Beech Ri. CM3: Hat P 3L 61
Beech Rd. CM5: Will 1E 32
CM8: Riven 3G 25
SS5: Hull 6L 103
SS7: Had 4K 135
SS14: Bas 1F 132
Beech St. EC2: Lon 7B 38
RM7: Romf 8A 110
Beech Tree Glade E4: Lon 7F 90
Beech Wlk. DA1: Cray 9E 152
Beechwood Cl. CO2: Colc 4L 173
Beechwood Dr. IG8: Wfd G 2F 106
Beechwood Gdns. IG5: Ilf 9M 107
RM13: Rain 5F 142
Beechwood Pk. E18: Lon 7G 106
Beechy Ride CB11: A End, Saf W 6A 218
CB11: Newp 7B 218
Beecroft Art Gallery 7K 137 (5J 43)
Beecroft Cres. SS8: Can I 8G 135
Beedell Av. SS0: Wclf S 5J 137
SS11: W'fd 1N 117
Beehive Chase CM15: Hook E 5G 82
Beehive Ct. CM22: Hat H 1E 210
CO1: Colc 9A 166
(off Kendall Rd.)
IG2: Ilf 1M 123
RM3: H Wood 4K 111
Beehive La. CM2: Gall 7C 72 (3A 34)
IG1: Ilf 1M 123
IG4: Ilf 9M 107 (3G 39)
SS14: Bas 9C 116
Beeleigh Abbey 4A 214
Beeleigh Av. SS16: Bas 4L 131
Beeleigh Cl. CO2: Colc 5A 174
SS2: Sth S 3K 137
Beeleigh Cross SS14: Bas 8F 116
Beeleigh E. SS14: Bas 7F 116
Beeleigh Link CM2: Chelm 8A 60
Beeleigh Rd. CM9: Mal 5B 214
Beeleigh W. SS14: Bas 8E 116
Beesfield La. DA4: F'ham 7C 46
BEGGAR HILL 2N 83 (4G 33)
Beggar Hill CM4: Fry 2N 83 (4G 33)
Beggarman's La. SG11: Old G 1C 20
Begonia Cl. CM1: Chelm 5A 60
Begonia Pl. CO16: Clac S 9G 185
Beke Hall Chase Nth. SS6: Ray 3E 118
Beke Hall Chase Sth. SS6: Ray 3E 118
Bekeswell La.
CM2: Chelm, Gall 8A 72 (3K 33)
Bekeswell Pl. CM2: Gall 8D 72
Bel-Air Chalet Est. CO16: St O 5B 28
BELCHAMP OTTEN 5F 9
Belchamp Rd. CO9: Til C 5D 8
BELCHAMP ST PAUL 4E 8
Belchamps Rd. SS11: W'fd 8N 101
Belchamps Way SS5: Hock 2D 120
BELCHAMP WALTER 5G 9
Belcham's La.
CB11: Quen, Rick G 3B 216 (4A 12)
Belcher Rd. EN11: Hod 4A 52
Belchers La. EN9: Naze 3J 63
Belcon Ind. Est. EN11: Hod 5C 52
Beldams Cl. CO16: T Sok 5L 179
Beldowes SS16: Van 1E 132
Belfairs Cl. SS9: Lgh S 4C 136
Belfairs Ct. SS9: Lgh S 9A 120
(off Southend Arterial Rd.)
Belfairs Dr. RM6: Chad H 2H 125
SS9: Lgh S 4C 136
Belfairs Pk. Cl. SS9: Lgh S 1B 136
Belfairs Pk. Dr. SS9: Lgh S 1A 136
Belfairs Swimming Cen. 4B 136
Belfield Gdns. CM17: H'low 4H 55
Belfry Rd. E12: Lon 4K 123
Belgrave Av. RM2: Romf 7G 111
Belgrave Cl. CM2: Gt Bad 3E 72
SS6: Ray 3H 119
SS9: Lgh S 8A 120
Belgrave Hgts. E11: Lon 3G 123
Belgrave Ho. CM23: Bis S 9A 220
Belgrave Rd. CM12: Bill 4J 99
E10: Lon 3C 122
E11: Lon 4G 122
E17: Lon 9A 106
IG1: Ilf 3M 123
SS9: Lgh S 9A 120
Belgrave Ter. IG8: Wfd G 9G 90
Belhus Pk. Leisure Cen. 6B 144
Belhus Wood Country Pk. 3A 144
Bellamy Cl. CO13: Walt 8G 181
Bellamy Rd. E4: Lon 3B 106
Bell Av. RM3: Romf 5F 110
Bell Cl. CO2: Colc 4D 174
BELL COMMON 2C 78 (4H 31)
Bell Comn. CM16: Epp 2D 78
Bell Cnr. RM14: Upm 4N 127
Bell Ct. CM3: Ret C 8A 88
Bellcroft CM8: Wthm 4D 230
Bellermine Cl. SE28: Lon 8E 140
Bellestaines Pleasaunce E4: Lon 8A 90
Belle Vue CM2: Chelm 1B 72
Bellevue Av. SS1: Sth S 6A 138
Bellevue M. SS2: Sth S 5A 138
Bellevue Pl. SS1: Sth S 6A 138
Bellevue Rd. CM12: Bill 6H 99
Belle Vue Rd. CO1: Colc 6M 165
CO7: W'hoe 6H 175 (7H 17)
E17: Lon 6D 106
RM5: Col R 3A 110
Bellevue Rd. RM11: Horn 3K 127
SS2: Sth S 5A 138
Bellevue Ter. CO9: Hals 4K 207
Bell Farm Av. RM10: Dag 5A 126
Bell Farm Cotts. CM16: Epp 2D 78
Bell Farm Grn. CM12: Bill 8K 99
Bellfield SS16: Van 3F 132
Bellfield Av. CO7: B'sea 5E 182
Bellfield Cl. CO7: B'sea 5F 182
Bellflower Path RM3: Romf 4G 111
Bell Gdns. E10: Lon 3A 122
(off Church Rd.)
Bell Hill CM3: Dan 3C 74
CM11: Bill 8K 99
Bell Hill Cl. CM12: Bill 8K 99
Bell Ho. RM17: Grays 4J 155
SS3: Gt W 3M 139
Bellhouse Cres. SS9: Lgh S 1C 136
Bellhouse La. CM14: Pil H 4B 96
SS9: Lgh S 2C 136 (4G 43)
Bell Ho. Rd. RM7: Rush G 3A 126
Bellhouse Rd. SS9: Lgh S 1C 136
Bellingham Bldgs. CB10: Saf W 3C 218
Bellingham Ct. IG11: Bark 3G 141
Bellingham Dr. CO6: Cop 1N 171
Bellingham La. SS6: Ray 5K 119
Bellingham Pl. CO5: K'dn 2K 211
Bell La. CM6: Thax 7C 224
CM7: Gt Bar 2B 202 (3J 13)
CM7: Pan 1C 192
EN3: Enf 5C 30
EN10: Brox 1D 30
EN11: Hod 5A 52
SG8: Nuth 1F 11
Bellmaine Av. SS17: Corr 1A 148
Bellmead CM1: Chelm 9K 59
Bell Mead CM4: Ing 6D 84
CM21: Saw 2K 51
Bell Reeves Cl. SS17: Stan H 3L 147
Bells Chase CM2: Gt Bad 4F 72
Bells Cl. CB11: Saf W 5D 218
Bells Hill CM23: Bis S 1K 21
CO8: M Bur 3A 16
Bells Hill Rd. SS16: Van 4C 132 (4A 42)
Bells La. CO10: Glem 1G 9
Bells Rd. CO10: Bel W 5F 9
Bell St. CM2: Gt Bad 4G 73
CM21: Saw 2K 51 (4K 21)
BELL, THE 7A 106 (3D 38)
Bell Wlk. SS0: Sth S 2J 137
Belmans Ct. CO12: Har 5H 209
Belmarsh Rd. SE28: Lon 9D 140
Belmer Rd. CM24: Bur E 5J 221 (7B 12)
Belmonde Dr. CM1: Chelm 4N 59
Belmont Av. RM14: Upm 4K 127
SS12: W'fd 9J 101
Belmont Cl. CM1: Chelm 4N 59
E4: Lon 2D 106
IG8: Wfd G 1H 107
SS12: W'fd 9J 101
Belmont Cres. CO4: Colc 4C 166
Belmont Hill CB11: Newp 2L 215 (1B 12)
Belmont Pk. Rd. E10: Lon 1B 122
Belmont Pl. CO1: Colc 1C 174
Belmont Rd. DA7: Bexh 2A 46
IG1: Ilf 5B 124
N15: Lon 3B 38
N17: Lon 3B 38
RM12: Horn 5H 127
RM17: Grays 4J 155
Belsize Av. CO15: Jay 6B 188
Belsteads Farm La. CM3: L Walt 1M 59 (6A 24)
Belstedes SS15: Lain 9M 115
Beltinge Rd. RM3: H Wood 6K 111
Belton Bri. SS9: Lgh S 6C 136
Belton Cnr. SS9: Lgh S 6C 136
Belton Gdns. SS9: Lgh S 6B 136 (5G 43)
Belton Rd. E7: Lon 9H 123
E11: Lon 6E 122
Belton Way E. SS9: Lgh S 6B 136 (5G 43)
Belton Way W. SS9: Lgh S 6A 136 (5G 43)
Beltwood Rd. DA17: Belv 2A 152
Belvawney Cl. CM1: Chelm 5G 58
BELVEDERE 1A 152 (1A 46)
Belvedere Av. IG5: Ilf 6A 108
SS5: Hock 1B 120
Belvedere Cl. CM3: Dan 3F 74
Belvedere Ct. CM2: Chelm 2A 72
Belvedere Ind. Est. DA17: Belv 8A 142
Belvedere Link Bus. Pk. DA8: Eri 1A 152
Belvedere Pl. CM9: Mal 8B 214
Belvedere Rd. CM0: Bur C 4E 196
CM3: Dan 3F 74
CM14: Brtwd 9C 96
SE2: Lon 8H 141
Belvedere Station (Rail) 7K 39
Belvedere, The CM0: Bur C 4E 196
Belvoir, The CM4: Ing 6C 84
Bembridge Cl. CO15: Clac S 5K 185
Bemerton Ct. CO13: Walt 8E 180
Bemerton Gdns. CO13: Walt 8F 180
Benbow Dr. CM3: S Fer 2L 103
Benbridge Ind. Est. CM9: Mal 3C 214
Bendalls Ct. CO11: Law 4J 163
Benderloch SS8: Can I 1E 150
Bendish Point SE28: Lon 9B 140
(off Erebus Dr.)
Bendish Rd. E6: Lon 9L 123
Bendlowes Rd. CM7: Gt Bar 3C 202
Bendyshe Ct. CB9: Stpl B 3L 223
Benedict Ct. RM6: Chad H 1L 125
Benedict Dr. CM1: Chelm 9G 58
Benets Rd. RM11: Horn 3L 127
Benfield Way CM7: Brain 6K 193
Benfleet for Canvey Island Station (Rail)
6D 134 (5D 42)
Benfleet Pk. Rd. SS7: Ben 3B 134
Benfleet Rd. SS7: Ben, Had 4G 134 (4E 42)
Bengal Rd. IG1: Ilf 6A 124
Bengeo Gdns. RM6: Chad H 1H 125
Bengeo St. SG14: Hart 5B 20
Benham Wlk. SS13: Bas 7K 117
Benhurst Av. RM12: Horn 6F 126
BENINGTON 7A 10
Benington Castle 7A 10
Benjamin Cl. RM11: Horn 1E 126
Ben Jonson Rd. E1: Lon 7C 38
Bennett Cl. CM7: Brain 8J 193
CO14: Walt 6K 181
Bennett Ct. CO4: Colc 9E 166
Bennett Rd. RM6: Chad H 1K 125
Bennetts Av. CM3: Ret C 6N 87
Bennett's Castle La. RM8: Dag 4H 125 (4J 39)
Bennett's La. CM6: Barns, N End 2H 23
Bennetts La. SG9: Rush 3A 10
Bennett Way CM3: Hat P 2L 61
Bennington Rd. IG8: Wfd G 4E 106
Bennions Cl. RM12: Horn 8H 127
Bennison Dr. RM3: H Wood 6H 111
Benrek Cl. IG6: Ilf 5B 108
Ben Sainty Ct. CM8: Wthm 5D 230
(off Collingwood Rd.)
Benskins Cl. CM23: Ber 4J 11
Benskins La. RM4: Noak H 7H 95
Benson Rd. RM17: Grays 4L 155
Bensusan Ct. CO2: Colc 3J 173
(off Iceni Way)
Bentall Cl. CO9: Hals 6L 207
Bentalls SS14: Bas 6B 116
Bentalls Cl. SS2: Sth S 2M 137
Bentalls Ind. Est. CM9: Mal 3D 214
Bentalls Shop. Cen. CM9: Mal 3D 214
BENTFIELD BOWER 1A 220 (6K 11)
BENTFIELD BURY 1A 220 (5A 12)
BENTFIELD END 2C 220
Bentfield End C'way.
CM24: Stan M 2C 220 (6A 12)
Bentfield Gdns. CM24: Stan M 2C 220
BENTFIELD GREEN 1C 220 (6A 12)
Bentfield Grn. CM24: Stan M 2B 220 (6A 12)
Bentfield Rd. CM24: Stan M 1C 220 (6A 12)
Bentham Rd. SE28: Lon 7G 140 (7J 39)
Ben Tillet Cl. IG11: Bark 9F 124
Bentleigh Ct. CO1: Colc 8C 166
BENTLEY
CM15 1A 96 (6D 32)
IP9 1A 18
Bentley Av. CO15: Jay 6C 188
Bentley Dr. CM17: H'low 4H 55
IG2: Ilf 1B 124
Bentley La. IP9: Stut 1B 18
Bentley Rd. CM8: Wthm 3B 230
CO7: Gt Ben, Wee H 9A 178 (1B 28)
CO7: L Ben 2G 169 (4K 17)
CO11: L Ben, L Bro 2G 169 (4K 17)
CO16: Wee, Wee H 9A 178 (1C 28)
Bentleys, The SS2: Sth S 8F 120
Bentley Vs. CM22: Hat H 2F 210
Bentley Way IG8: Buck H, Wfd G 8G 90
Benton Cl. CM8: Wthm 8D 230
CM77: Tye G 2E 194
Benton Gdns. SS17: Stan H 9A 132
Benton Rd. IG1: Ilf 3C 124 (4H 39)
Bentonwood SS7: Had 1J 135
Bentry Cl. RM8: Dag 4K 125
Bentry Rd. RM8: Dag 4K 125
Benvenue Av. SS9: Lgh S 9E 120
Benyon Path RM15: S Ock 3F 144
Berberis Cl. SS16: Lang H 2H 131
Berberis Ct. IG1: Ilf 8A 124
Berberis Wlk. CO4: Colc 8E 166
Berbice La. CM6: Gt D 1K 203
BERDEN 4J 11
Berdens SS16: Van 1E 132
BERECHURCH 5A 174 (7E 16)
Berechurch Hall Rd. CO2: Colc 5J 173 (7D 16)
Berechurch Rd. CO2: Colc 5L 173 (7E 16)
Berecroft CM18: H'low 8C 54
Beredens La. CM13: Gt War 7C 112
Berefield Way CO2: Colc 5N 173
Berens Cl. SS11: W'fd 7N 101
Beresford Cl. SS7: Had 2K 135
Beresford Ct. CM12: Bill 3H 99
Beresford Dr. IG8: Wfd G 1J 107
Beresford Gdns. RM6: Chad H 9K 109
SS7: Had 2J 135
Beresford Mans. SS1: Sth S 7A 138
(off Beresford Rd.)
Beresford Rd. E4: Lon 7E 90
E17: Lon 5B 106
SS1: Sth S 7A 138
Berg Av. SS8: Can I 9K 135
Bergen Ct. CM9: Mal 8B 214
(off Midguard Way)
Bergholt Av. IG4: Ilf 9L 107

Bergholt Rd. CO4: Colc 5L 165 (5E 16)
CO6: For, W Ber 9A 158 (4B 16)
CO11: Bran 1G 162 (2K 17)
IP9: B'ley 1A 18
Beridge Rd. CO9: Hals 4J 207
Beriffe Pl. CO7: B'sea 6E 182
Berkeley Av. IG5: Ilf 6N 107
RM5: Col R 4A 110
Berkeley Cl. RM11: Horn 4M 127
Berkeley Dr. CM12: Bill 3J 99
RM11: Horn 3L 127
Berkeley Gdns. SS9: Lgh S 5N 135
Berkeley La. SS8: Can I 3G 151
Berkeley Rd. CO15: Clac S 9K 185
E12: Lon 7L 123
Berkeley St. W1: Lon 7A 38
Berkeley Ter. RM18: Til 5C 156
Berkely Dr. CM2: Chelm 9A 60
Berkhamsted La. SG13: L Berk 1A 30
Berkley Cl. CO4: Colc 3C 166
Berkley Hill SS17: Corr 1N 147
Berkshire Cl. SS9: Lgh S 1B 136
Berkshire Rd. E9: Lon 8A 122
Berkshire Way RM11: Horn 9L 111
Berman's Cl. CM13: Hut 8L 97
BERMONDSEY 7C 38
Bermondsey Station (Tube) 7C 38
Bermondsey St. SE1: Lon 7B 38
Bermuda Rd. RM18: Til 7C 156
Bernal Cl. SE28: Lon 7J 141
Bernard Cl. CO13: Walt 8H 181
Bernard Gro. EN9: Wal A 3B 76
Bernard Rd. RM7: Rush G 2A 126
Bernards Cl. IG6: Ilf 4C 108
Bernard St. WC1: Lon 6A 38
Berners End CM6: Barns 3L 191
BERNERS RODING 7F 23
Berners Wlk. SS14: Bas 7F 116
Bernice Cl. RM13: Rain 4G 142
Bernside CM7: Brain 6H 193
Bernwell Rd. E4: Lon 9E 90
Berridge Ho. CM9: Mal 7D 214
Berrimans Cl. CO4: Colc 9D 166
Berrybank Cl. E4: Lon 8C 90
Berry Cl. RM10: Dag 7M 125
RM12: Horn 7G 127
SS12: W'fd 1J 117
SS16: Lang H 1K 131
Berryfield Cl. E17: Lon 8B 106
Berryfield Cotts. CO1: Colc 8B 166
Berry La. SS16: Lang H 1K 131
Berryman Cl. RM8: Dag 5H 125
Berrys Arc. *SS6: Ray 5K 119*
(off High St.)
Berry Va. CM3: S Fer 2L 103
Bersham La. RM17: Grays 2J 155
Berther Rd. RM11: Horn 2H 127
Berthold M. EN9: Wal A 3B 76
Berthons Gdns. *E17: Lon 9D 106*
(off Wood St.)
Bertram Av. CO16: L Cla 4H 185
Bertrand Way SE28: Lon 7G 141
Berwick Av. CM1: Chelm 4J 59
Berwick Cl. EN8: Wal X 4A 76
Berwick La. CM5: Chip, Stap T 3C 80 (4A 32)
Berwick Pond Cl. RM13: Rain 2H 143
Berwick Pond Rd. RM13: Rain 1J 143 (6C 40)
RM14: Rain 9K 127 (5C 40)
Berwick Rd. RM13: Rain 2H 143
Berwood Rd. SS17: Corr 2A 148
Beryl Rd. CO12: Har 5F 208
Besant Ct. *SE28: Lon 8G 141*
(off Titmuss Av.)
Beslyns Rd. CM7: Gt Bar 1B 202 (3J 13)
Betchworth Rd. IG3: Ilf 4D 124
Bethany St. CO7: W'hoe 7H 175
Beth Chatto Gardens 1A 176 (6J 17)
Bethell Av. IG1: Ilf 2N 123
BETHNAL GREEN 6C 38
Bethnal Grn. Rd. E1: Lon 6B 38
Bethnal Green Station (Rail & Tube) 6C 38
Bethune Rd. N16: Lon 4B 38
Betjeman Cl. CM7: Brain 8J 193
SS6: Ray 4M 119
Betjeman M. SS2: Sth S 4M 137
Betjeman Way CM5: Chip 5K 67
Betony Cres. CM12: Bill 3H 99
Betony Rd. RM3: Romf 3G 111
Betoyne Av. E4: Lon 1E 106
Betoyne Cl. CM11: Bill 6M 99
BETSHAM 5F 47
Betsham Rd. DA8: Eri 5D 152
DA13: S'fleet 5E 46
Betterton Rd. RM13: Rain 3C 142
Betts Grn. Rd. CO16: L Cla 9H 179
Betts La. EN9: Naze 9J 53 (1F 31)
Bett's La. SS5: Hock 1C 120
Betty Brooks Ho. E11: Lon 5D 122
Betula Wlk. RM13: Rain 3H 143
Beulah Path E17: Lon 9C 106
Beulah Pl. EN9: Wal A 3L 77
Beulah Rd. CM16: Epp 8F 64
E17: Lon 9B 106
RM12: Horn 5G 127
Beult Rd. DA1: Cray 9E 152
Bevan Av. IG11: Bark 9F 124
Bevan Ho. RM16: Grays 9N 145
Bevan Way RM12: Horn 6K 127
Beveland Rd. SS8: Can I 2N 151
Beveridge Ct. *SE28: Lon 7G 140*
(off Saunders Way)
Beverley Av. CO5: W Mer 2E 228
SS8: Can I 2F 150
Beverley Cl. RM11: Horn 2K 127
RM16: Ors 6F 146
Beverley Cres. IG8: Wfd G 5H 107
Beverley Dr. CO13: Walt 7H 181
Beverley Gdns. EN7: Chesh 3C 30
RM11: Horn 2K 127
SS2: Sth S 2K 137
Beverley M. E4: Lon 3D 106
Beverley Ri. CM11: Bill 7L 99
Beverley Rd. CO3: Colc 9L 165
DA7: Bexh 7A 152
E4: Lon 3D 106
RM9: Dag 6K 125 (5K 39)
Bevil Ct. EN11: Hod 2A 52
Bevile Ho. RM17: Grays 5L 155
Bevington M. CM8: Wthm 5E 230
Bevin Wlk. SS17: Stan H 3M 147
Bewick Ct. CO9: Sib H 5J 219
Bewley Ct. SS2: Sth S 4C 138
Bexhill Cl. CO15: Clac S 4G 189
Bexhill Dr. RM17: Grays 4H 155
BEXLEY 3A 46
Bexley Av. CO12: Har 6H 209
Bexley Gdns. RM6: Chad H 9G 108
Bexley High St. DA5: Bex 4A 46
Bexley Rd. DA8: Eri 6A 152 (2A 46)
(not continuous)
Bexley Station (Rail) 4A 46
Beyers Gdns. EN11: Hod 2A 52
Beyers Prospect EN11: Hod 1A 52
Beyers Ride EN11: Hod 2A 52
Bibby Cl. SS17: Corr 2B 148
Bickenhall SS3: Shoe 6H 139
Bickerton Point CM3: S Fer 1M 103
Bickley Rd. E10: Lon 2B 122
BICKNACRE 8F 74 (3E 34)
Bicknacre Rd. CM3: Dan 4D 74 (2E 34)
CM3: E Han 2C 88 (4D 34)
Biddenden Ct. SS13: Pits 9K 117
Bideford Cl. RM3: Romf 5G 111
SS0: Wclf S 1F 136
BIGGIN 4D 156
Biggin Hill SG9: Anst 2E 10
Biggin La. RM16: Grays 4D 156 (2H 47)
Bight, The CM3: S Fer 2M 103
Bignell Cft. CO4: Colc 3C 166
Bignold Rd. E7: Lon 6G 123
Bigods La. CM6: Gt D 1M 203 (6G 13)
Bijou Cl. CO5: Tip 5D 226
Bilberry End CB1: Hads 3D 6
BILLERICAY 6J 99 (7J 33)
Billericay Rd. CM12: Bill 4A 114
CM13: Bill, Heron 4A 114 (2G 41)
Billericay Station (Rail) 6J 99 (7J 33)
Billericay Swimming Pool 5J 99
Billericay Town F.C. (New Lodge) 7G 99
Billers Chase CM1: Chelm 4B 60
Billet Cl. RM6: Chad H 7J 109
Billet La. RM11: Horn 3H 127 (4B 40)
SS9: Lgh S 6C 136
SS17: Stan H 4M 147 (6K 41)
Billet Rd. E17: Lon 5A 106 (2C 38)
RM6: Chad H 7G 109 (3J 39)
BILLET, THE 4A 148
Billing Cl. RM9: Dag 9H 125
Bilsdale Cl. CO4: Colc 3C 166
Bilton Rd. CM1: Chelm 1A 72
DA8: Eri 5E 152
SS7: Had 3L 135
Bilton Way EN3: Enf 5D 30
Bincote Rd. EN2: Enf 6A 30
Bingham Cl. RM15: S Ock 6E 144
Bingley Rd. EN11: Hod 5C 52
Binley Rd. CM2: Chelm 9N 59
Binsey Wlk. SE2: Lon 9H 141
(not continuous)
BIRCH 9B 172 (1C 26)
Birchalls CM24: Stan M 1D 220
Bircham Rd. SS2: Sth S 4M 137
BIRCHANGER 7C 220 (7A 12)
Birchanger Ind. Est. CM23: Bis S 7A 220
Birchanger La. CM23: Bchgr 6B 220 (7A 12)
Birch Av. CO7: Gt Ben 6K 177
CO12: Har 4K 209
Birch Cl. CM7: Brain 6E 192
CM8: Wthm 3D 230
CO7: B'sea 7D 182
CO15: Clac S 1G 188
IG9: Buck H 9K 91
RM7: Maw 7N 109
RM15: S Ock 4G 144
SS4: Cwdn 2N 105
SS6: Ray 4J 119
SS7: Thund 8B 118
SS8: Can I 2F 150
Birch Ct. RM6: Chad H 1H 125
Birch Cres. RM11: Horn 8J 111
RM15: S Ock 3G 144
Birchdale SS5: Hull 5K 103
Birchdale Gdns.
RM6: Chad H 2J 125
Birchdale Rd. E7: Lon 7J 123
Birchdene Dr. SE28: Lon 8F 140
Birch Dr. CO9: Hals 4M 207
Birche Cl. SS9: Lgh S 2D 136
Birches, The CM13: Brtwd 9H 97
CM16: N Wea 5N 65
CO13: Walt 8H 181
E12: Lon 6L 123
EN9: Wal A 4F 76
SS7: Thund 7C 118
Birches Wlk. CM2: Gall 8B 72
Birch Gdns. CM0: T'ham 2K 225
RM10: Dag 5A 126
BIRCH GREEN
CO2 . . . . 8D 172 (2C 26)
SG14 . . . . 6A 20
Birch Grn. SS12: W'fd 9L 101
Birch Gro. E11: Lon 6E 122
Birch La. CM4: Stock 6A 86
Birchmere Bus. Site SE28: Lon 9F 140
Birch Ri. CM8: W Bis 1K 229
Birch Rd. CM0: T'ham 2K 225
CM6: Gt D 2J 203
CO2: B'ch, Lay H 9E 172 (1C 26)
CO6: Cop 6N 171 (1B 26)
RM7: Maw 7N 109
Birch St. CO2: B'ch, Lay B 8D 172 (2C 26)
Birch Vw. CM16: Epp 8G 64
Birch Wlk. DA8: Eri 4A 152
Birchway CO2: B'ch 9D 172
Birchwood CM23: Bchgr 7C 220
EN9: Wal A 4E 76
SS7: Thund 8B 118
Birchwood Cl. CM13: Gt War 3F 112
CO5: Tip 6E 226
CO5: W Mer 3D 228
Birchwood Dr. SS9: Lgh S 4F 136
Birchwood Rd. BR8: Swan 6A 46
CM3: Cock C, Pur 8M 75 (3F 35)
CO4: L'ham 4F 160 (3G 17)
CO7: A'lgh, Ded 5G 161 (3G 17)
DA2: Dart 6A 46
SS17: Corr 9C 132
Birchwood Way CO5: Tip 6F 226
BIRDBROOK 5A 8
Birdbrook Cl. CM13: Hut 5L 97
RM10: Dag 9A 126
Birdbrook Rd. CO9: Bay E, Stamb 6A 8
Birdbush Av. CB11: Saf W 6C 218
BIRD GREEN 2H 11
Bird La. CM13: Gt War 7F 112 (3E 40)
CO5: Tip 7E 226
RM14: Upm 9A 112 (3D 40)
Birds Cl. CB10: I'tn 7A 202
CM11: Rams H 3D 100
Birds Farm Av. RM5: Col R 4N 109
BIRDS GREEN 7E 22
Birds Grn. CM5: Fy'd, Will 7D 200 (1D 32)
Birk Beck CM1: Chelm 6L 59
Birkbeck Gdns. IG8: Wfd G 8G 90
Birkbeck Rd. CM13: Hut 5N 97
IG2: Ilf 9C 108
RM7: Rush G 3B 126
Birkdale Av. RM3: H Wood 4K 111
Birkdale Cl. SE28: Lon 6J 141
Birkdale Ri. CM3: Hat P 2M 61
Birkin Cl. CO5: Tip 7B 226
Birling Rd. DA8: Eri 5B 152
Birs Cl. SS11: W'fd 7L 101
Biscay SS2: Sth S 8F 120
Bishop Hall La. CM1: Chelm 7K 59
Bishop Ho. SS2: Sth S 9G 120
Bishop Rd. CM1: Chelm 8K 59
CO2: Colc 3H 173
Bishops Av. CM7: Brain 5K 193
RM6: Chad H 1H 125
Bishops Cl. E17: Lon 8B 106
SS13: Bas 5H 117
Bishops Ct. *SS8: Can I 2K 151*
(off Maurice Rd.)
Bishops Court Gdns. CM2: Chelm 7N 59
Bishopsfield CM18: H'low 6C 54
Bishopsgate EC2: Lon 7B 38
BISHOP'S GREEN 3G 23
Bishop's Hall Rd. CM15: Pil H 5E 96
Bishops La. CO5: Tip 4C 226
Bishop's La. CO9: Peb 1J 15
Bishops Pk. Way CM23: Bis S, Thor 1J 21
Bishops Pl. CM8: W Bis 2L 229
Bishops Rd. SS12: W'fd 4L 117
SS17: Stan H 2A 148
BISHOP'S STORTFORD 1K 21
Bishop's Stortford F.C. (Woodside Pk.) 9C 220
Bishop's Stortford Local History Mus. 1K 21
Bishops Stortford Mus. 1K 21
Bishops Stortford Rd.
CM1: Rox 1N 217 (6G 23)
Bishop's Stortford Station (Rail) 1K 21
Bishopsteignton SS3: Shoe 6G 138
Bishop's Way E2: Lon 6C 38
Bishop Wlk. CM15: Brtwd 8J 97
Bisley Cl. CO16: Clac S 7F 184
Bisterne Av. E17: Lon 7D 106
Bittern Cl. CO5: K'dn 3L 211
Blackacre Rd. CM16: They B 7D 78
Blackall Ind. Est CM3: S Fer 8M 89
Blackberry Gro. CM0: Brad S 7D 194
Blackberry Rd. CO3: S'way 2D 172 (7C 16)
Blackborne Rd. RM10: Dag 8M 125
Black Boy La. CO11: Wrab 3E 18
N15: Lon 3B 38
Black Bread Cl. CM7: Brain 5M 193
Blackbrooke Cotts. CO6: Gt Hork 7K 159
Blackbrook Hill
CO7: Ded, L'ham 3H 161 (2G 17)
Blackbrook Rd. CO6: Gt Hork 9K 159
Black Buoy Hill CO7: W'hoe 7H 175
Blackbush Av. RM6: Chad H 9J 109
Blackbushe CM23: Bis S 8A 220
Black Bush La. SS17: Horn H 1F 146 (6H 41)
Blackbush Spring CM20: H'low 2F 54
BLACKCAT 7C 22
Blackdown SS0: Wclf S 5L 137
Blackfriars Bri. SE1: Lon 7A 38
Blackfriars Rd. SE1: Lon 7A 38
Blackfriars Station (Rail & Tube) 7A 38
Blackgate Rd. SS3: Shoe 7L 139
BLACKHALL 3G 11
BLACKHEATH 6A 174 (1E 26)
Blackheath CO2: Colc 6A 174 (1F 27)
Blackheath Chase SS16: Bas 6M 131
BLACKHORSE LANE 3C 38
Blackhorse La. CM16: N Wea 4B 66
(not continuous)
E17: Lon 2C 38
Blackhorse Rd. E17: Lon 3C 38
Blackhorse Road Station (Rail & Tube) 3C 38
Blackhouse La. CO10: Gt Cor, L Cor 6K 9
Blacklands Cl. CB11: Saf W 6B 218
Black La. CM7: Gt Bar, L Bar 3A 202
Blackley La.
CM3: Gt N, Will G 4A 204 (2B 24)
Black Lion Ct. CM17: H'low 8H 51
Black Lion St. *CM17: H'low 8H 51*
(off Market St.)
Blacklock CM2: Chelm 8B 60
Blackman Way CM8: Wthm 6D 230
BLACKMORE 1H 83 (4E 32)
Blackmore Av. SS8: Can I 3H 151
Blackmore Cl. RM17: Grays 3L 155
Blackmore Ct. EN9: Wal A 3G 77
BLACKMORE END 3B 14
Blackmore Mead CM4: B'more 1J 83
Blackmore Rd. CM1: B'more 9M 69 (3G 33)
CM4: B'more 3F 82 (4E 32)
(Tip's Cross)
CM4: B'more, Hghwd 9M 69 (3G 33)
(High Woods)
CM4: Fry 3K 83 (4F 33)
CM15: B'more, Dodd, Hook E,
Kel H, Ston M 8B 82 (5D 32)
IG9: Buck H 6L 91
Blackmores SS15: Lain 9H 115
Blackmore Wlk. SS6: Ray 5N 119
BLACK NOTLEY 3B 194 (1D 24)
BLACK PRINCE INTERCHANGE 3A 46
Blackshots La. RM16: Grays 7M 145 (7G 41)
Blackshots Leisure Cen. 9N 145
Blacksmith Cl. CM1: Chelm 3N 59
CM12: Bill 3K 99
Blacksmiths All. CM4: B'more 1H 83
Blacksmiths Cl. CB2: Bab 1A 6
RM6: Chad H 1H 125
Blacksmiths Hill CO10: Stoke C 4B 8
Blacksmiths Ho. *E17: Lon 8A 106*
(off Gillards M.)
Blacksmiths La. CB1: Shudy C 3G 7
CM8: W Bis 2K 229 (5H 25)
CO10: Bulm 4L 195
Blacksmith's La. CO12: Har 4H 209
RM13: Rain 1D 142
SG8: Reed 7C 4
Blacksmiths Way CM21: H Wych 3F 50
Blackstock Rd. N4: Lon 4A 38
N5: Lon 4A 38
Blackthorn Av. CO4: Colc 8E 166
Blackthorn Cl. CM1: Writ 1J 71
Blackthorn Ct. *E11: Lon 6D 122*
(off Hall Rd.)
SS16: Lang H 2J 131
Blackthorne Dr. E4: Lon 1D 106
Blackthorne Rd. SS8: Can I 2J 151
Blackthorn Rd. CM8: Wthm 3B 230
CO12: Har 4H 209
RM16: Grays 8L 145
SS5: Hock 8E 104
Blackthorns CO9: Hals 5H 207
Blackthorn Way CM14: War 2G 112
Blackwall Station (DLR) 7E 38
Blackwall Tunnel SE10: Lon 7E 38
Blackwall Tunnel Northern App.
E14: Lon 6E 38
E3: Lon 6E 38
Blackwall Tunnel Southern App.
SE10: Lon 7E 38
Blackwater CM14: Brtwd 7E 96
SS7: Thund 2F 134
Blackwater Av. CO4: Colc 5E 166
Blackwater Cl. CM0: Bur C 3E 196
CM1: Chelm 5L 59
CM9: Hey B 8F 214
E7: Lon 6F 122
RM13: Rain 5B 142
SS3: Shoe 5J 139
Blackwater Dr. CO5: W Mer 3A 228
Blackwater La. CM8: Wthm 7E 230
Blackwater Leisure Cen. 7E 214
Blackwater Sailing Club 8F 214
Blackwater Trad. Est. CM9: Mal 4C 214
Blackwater Way CM7: Brain 4J 193
SS14: Bas 8G 116
Blackwell Dr. CM7: Brain 4E 192
Blackwood Chine CM3: S Fer 2L 103
Bladon Cl. CM7: Brain 1G 193
CO5: Tip 6E 226
Blaine Dr. CO13: Frin S 7H 181
Blake Av. IG11: Bark 1D 140
Blakeborough Dr. RM3: H Wood 6J 111
Blake Cl. CO11: Law 4G 163
RM13: Rain 1D 142
Blake Ct. CM3: S Fer 2L 103
Blake Dr. CM7: Brain 4L 193
CO16: Clac S 7H 185
BLAKE END 7A 14
Blake End CM77: Rayne 7A 14
Blake End Rd. CM6: Rayne 7A 14
CM7: Gt Sal 6A 14
Blake Gdns. DA1: Dart 9K 153
Blake Hall Cres. E11: Lon 3G 123
Blake Hall Dr. SS11: W'fd 1A 118
Blake Hall Rd.
CM5: Chip, N Wea 4E 66 (2B 32)
E11: Lon 2G 123 (4F 39)
Blake Hall War Mus. & Gardens 3H 67 (2B 32)
Blake House Craft Cen. 7A 14
Blake Rd. CM8: Wthm 2C 230

Blakes Ct. CM21: Saw 2K 51
Blakes Wood Nature Reserve 9K 61
Blake Way RM18: Til 7E 156
Blamsters Cres. CO9: Hals 6J 207
Blanchard Cl. CO13: Walt 7D 180
Blanchard Gro. EN3: Enf 8B 76
Blanchard M. RM3: H Wood 4K 111
Blandford Cl. RM7: Maw 8M 109
Blandford Cres. E4: Lon 6C 90
Blaney Cres. E6: Lon 3A 140
BLASFORD HILL 8K 57 (6A 24)
Blatches Chase SS9: Lgh S 9E 120
SS9: Sth S 7F 120
Bledlow Cl. SE28: Lon 7H 141
Blenheim Av. IG2: Ilf 1N 123
Blenheim Chase
SS9: Lgh S 3C 136 (4G 43)
Blenheim Cl. CM3: Dan 8F 74
CM7: Brain 1G 193
CM21: Saw 4H 51
RM7: Maw 8A 110
RM14: Upm 3B 128
SS5: Hock 8D 104
Blenheim Ct. IG8: Wfd G 4H 107
RM12: Horn 7G 126
SS11: W'fd 2A 118
Blenheim Cres. SS9: Lgh S 3D 136
Blenheim Dr. CO2: Colc 6A 174
Blenheim Gdns. CM3: May 7L 213
RM15: Ave 8M 143
Blenheim M. SS9: Lgh S 3D 136
Blenheim Pk. Cl. SS9: Lgh S 2E 136
Blenheim Rd. CM15: Pil H 5D 96
CO15: Clac S 2H 189
E15: Lon 6E 122
Blenheim Way CM16: N Wea 6M 65
CO5: Tip 6E 226
Blessing Way IG11: Bark 3H 141
Blewbury Ho. SE2: Lon 9H 141
(Tavy Bri.)
SE2: Lon 9J 141
(Tilehurst Point)
Blewitts Cotts. *RM13: Rain* 3D 142
(off New Rd.)
Blickling Rd. CM77: Gt N 8E 192
Bligh Way ME2: Roch 6K 47
Blind La. CM2: S'don 6M 73
CM2: W Han 4F 86 (4B 34)
CM9: Gold, L Tot 2H 201 (7K 25)
CM9: Mun 3H 35
CM9: Tol D 5A 26
CM12: Bill, L Bur 2D 114
CO5: B'ch, Ethpe 9L 171 (1A 26)
CO6: Eig G 7B 164
CO7: B'sea 6E 182
EN9: Wal A 3J 77
IG10: Lou 1E 90
SG2: Ard, Cro 4A 10
Blindman's La. EN8: Chesh 3C 30
Bliss Cl. CM8: Wthm 8C 230
Blithbury Rd. RM9: Dag 8G 125
Blockhouse Rd. RM17: Grays 3M 155
Blofield Rd. IP11: Felix 1K 19
Blois End CO9: Sib H 1C 14
Blois Mdws. Bus. Cen. CB9: Stpl B 1L 223
Blois Rd. CB9: Stpl B 2L 223 (5K 7)
Blomville Rd. RM8: Dag 5K 125
Bloom Cl. CO13: Frin S 8J 181
Bloomfield Av. CO13: Walt 7H 181
Bloomfield Cres. IG2: Ilf 1A 124
Bloomfields, The IG11: Bark 8B 124
BLOOMSBURY 7A 38
Bloomsbury St. WC1: Lon 7A 38
Blooms Hall La. CO10: S'std 1H 9
Blossom Cl. RM9: Dag 1L 141
Blott Ri. CM8: Wthm 7C 230
Blountswood Rd. SS5: Hock, Hull 7M 103
(not continuous)
Blower Cl. SS6: Ray 4M 119
Bloyce's La. CO11: L Bro 2H 169
Blue Anchor La. RM18: W Til 2F 156 (1H 47)
Bluebell Av. CO16: Clac S 9G 184
E12: Lon 7K 123
Bluebell Cl. CM8: Wthm 4B 230
RM7: Rush G 4C 126
Bluebell Grn. CM1: Chelm 4N 59
Bluebell Way CO4: Colc 5K 165
IG1: Ilf 8A 124
Bluebell Wood CM12: Bill 4F 98
Blueberry Cl. IG8: Wfd G 3G 107
Bluebird La. RM10: Dag 9M 125
Bluebird Way SE28: Lon 9C 140
Bluebridge Cotts. CO9: Hals 5M 207
Bluebridge Ind. Est. CO9: Hals 5N 207
Bluegate Pk. CM14: Brtwd 9E 96
Bluehouse Av. CO16: Clac S 9E 184
Blue Ho. Farm Chase CM3: N Fam 1G 104
Bluehouse Rd. E4: Lon 8E 90
Bluemans CM16: N Wea 3B 66
Bluemans End CM16: N Wea 3B 66
Blue Mill La. CM9: Wdhm W 1F 35
Blue Mills Hill
CM8: W Bis, Wthm 8D 230 (5G 25)
Blue Rd. CO5: Tip 6C 226
BLUE ROW 4G 27
BLUEWATER 4D 46
Bluewater Parkway DA9: Blue, Grnh 4D 46
Blunden Cl. RM8: Dag 3H 125
Blunts Hall Dr. CM8: Wthm 6A 230
Blunts Hall Rd. CM8: Wthm 6A 230 (4E 24)
Blunts Wall Rd. CM12: Bill 7F 98
Blyford Rd. CO16: Clac S 9E 184
Blyth Av. SS3: Shoe 7G 138
Blythe Ct. *CO7: W'hoe* 6H 175
(off Station Rd.)
Blythe La. *CO7: W'hoe* 6H 175
(off High St.)
Blythe Rd. EN11: Hod 7D 52
SS17: Stan H 1N 147
Blythe Way CM9: Mal 8C 214
Blyth Rd. SE28: Lon 7H 141
Blyth's Mdw. CM7: Brain 5H 193
Blyth's Way CM77: Rayne 6B 192
Blythswood Rd. IG3: Ilf 3F 124
Blyth Wlk. RM14: Upm 1B 128
Blyth Way SS7: Thund 8C 118
Blythwood Gdns. CM24: Stan M 3C 220
Blyton Cl. SS12: W'fd 2L 117
Boadicea Way CO2: Colc 2J 173 (7E 16)
Boar Cl. IG7: Chig 2F 108
Boarded Barn Rd.
CO6: Chap, Wak C 6D 196 (4A 16)
CO6: Cop 6M 171 (1B 26)
Boardman Av. E4: Lon 4B 90
Boar Head Rd. CM17: H'low 4M 55 (7K 21)
Boars Tye Rd. CM8: Sil E 6K 217 (1F 25)
Bobbing Cl. SS4: R'fd 5L 121
BOBBINGWORTH 2G 66 (2B 32)
Bobbingworth Mill CM5: Chip 3E 66 (2B 32)
Bobbits Way CO7: W'hoe 6J 175
Bober Ct. CO2: Colc 7B 174
Bobs La. RM1: Romf 4E 110
BOCKING 3H 193 (7C 14)
BOCKING CHURCHSTREET 9H 191 (6D 14)
Bocking End CM7: Brain 5H 193
Bockingham Grn. SS13: Bas 7H 117
Bocking Pl. CM7: Brain 5H 193
Bockings SG2: Walk 5A 10
BOCKING'S ELM 8F 184
Bocking's Gro. CO16: Clac S 8F 184
Bodell Cl. RM16: Grays 1L 155
Bodiam Cl. SS13: Pits 9J 117
Bodley Cl. CM16: Epp 9E 64
Bodmin Rd. CM1: Chelm 6M 59
Bogmoor Rd. SG8: B'wy, Bar 7E 4
Bogs Gap La. SG8: Stpl M 4A 4
Bohemia Chase SS9: Lgh S 1B 136
Bohun Cl. CM3: Gt L 7K 203
Bois Fld. Ter. CO9: Hals 4L 207
Bois Hall Gdns. CO9: Hals 3L 207
Boley Dr. CO15: Clac S 8L 185
Boleyn Cl. CM12: Bill 3J 99
E17: Lon 8A 106
IG10: Lou 5L 91
RM16: Chaf H 1J 155
SS9: Lgh S 8B 120
Boleyn Ct. IG9: Buck H 7G 91
Boleyn Gdns. CM13: Brtwd 9K 97
RM10: Dag 9A 126
Boleyn Rd. E7: Lon 9G 123
N16: Lon 5B 38
Boleyns Av. CM7: Brain 2H 193
Boleyn Way CM3: Bore 2G 60
CO15: Jay 4D 188
IG6: Ilf 3B 108
Boley Rd. CO6: Whi C 4J 15
Bolford St. CM6: Thax 8B 224 (3F 13)
Bolingbroke Cl. CM3: Gt L 7K 203
Bolls La. CO2: Lay H 9F 172
Bolney Dr. SS9: Lgh S 8B 120
Bolt Cellar La. CM16: Epp 9D 64
Bolton Rd. E15: Lon 8F 122
Boltons, The IG8: Wfd G 1G 107
Bolton St. W1: Lon 7A 38
Bombose La. CO8: Bures, Lmsh 7H 195 (1K 15)
Bommel Av. SS8: Can I 2N 151
Bonchurch Av. SS9: Lgh S 4C 136
Bonchurch Ct. RM19: Purf 3N 153
Bondfield Wlk. DA1: Dart 9K 153
Bond St. CM2: Chelm 9L 59
E15: Lon 7E 122
RM17: Grays 4M 155
Bonham Cl. CO15: Clac S 8L 185
Bonham Gdns. RM8: Dag 4J 125
Bonham Rd. RM8: Dag 4J 125
Bonington Chase CM1: Chelm 5N 59
Bonington Rd. RM12: Horn 7H 127
Bonks Hill CM21: Saw 3J 51 (4J 21)
Bonner Rd. E2: Lon 6C 38
Bonner Wlk. RM16: Chaf H 1J 155
Bonnett M. RM11: Horn 3J 127
Bonningtons CM13: Brtwd 9L 97
Bonnygate SS14: Bas 8E 116
Bookcroft Bunnery 1A 4
Boomes Ind. Est. RM13: Rain 4D 142
Boone Pl. CM8: Wthm 5D 230
Boons Cl. CM3: Bore 3F 60
BOOSE'S GREEN 2D 198 (3H 15)
Bootham Cl. CM12: Bill 7H 99
Bootham Rd. CM12: Bill 7H 99
Booth Av. CO4: Colc 8C 166
Boothby Ct. E4: Lon 9C 90
Booth Cl. SE28: Lon 8G 141
Booth Pl. CM0: Bur C 3E 196
Booth's Ct. CM13: Hut 5M 97
Borda Cl. CM1: Chelm 6J 59
Border's La. IG10: Lou 3N 91 (6G 31)
BOREHAM 3F 60 (7D 24)
Boreham Cl. E11: Lon 3C 122
SS11: W'fd 1B 118
Boreham Ind. Est. CM3: Bore 1G 61
BOREHAM INTERCHANGE 4D 60 (7C 24)
Boreham Rd. CM3: Gt L 7K 203 (3B 24)
CM3: L Walt 4B 24
Borges Gdns. CO4: Colc 3L 165
BORLEY 4H 9
Borley Ct. RM16: Ors 6F 146
BORLEY GREEN 4H 9
Borley Rd. CO10: Lis, L Mel 4H 9
Borman Cl. SS9: Lgh S 9F 120
Borough High St. SE1: Lon 7B 38
Borough La. CB11: Saf W 5C 218 (7B 6)
Borough Rd. SE1: Lon 7A 38
Borough Station (Tube) 7B 38
BOROUGH, THE 7B 38
Borradale Ct. CB9: Stpl B 3K 223
Borrett Av. SS8: Can I 1G 151
Borrowdale Cl. IG4: Ilf 8L 107
SS7: Thund 9F 118
Borrowdale Rd. SS7: Thund 9F 118
(not continuous)
Borthwick M. E15: Lon 6E 122
Borthwick Rd. E15: Lon 6E 122
Borwick La. CM11: Cray H 3F 116 (2B 42)
(not continuous)
Bosanquet Rd. EN11: Rye P 3C 52
Boscawen Gdns. CM7: Brain 4L 193
Boscombe Av. E10: Lon 2D 122
RM11: Horn 2H 127
RM17: Grays 2N 155
SS12: W'fd 8G 101
Boscombe Ct. CO15: Hol S 7C 186
Boscombe Rd. SS2: Sth S 5N 137
Bosgrove E4: Lon 8C 90
Boston Av. SS2: Sth S 5L 137
(not continuous)
SS6: Ray 3G 119
Boston Rd. E17: Lon 1A 122
Boswell Av. SS4: R'fd 2J 121
Boswells Dr. CM2: Chelm 9L 59
Bosworth Cl. SS5: Hock 3E 120
Bosworth Cres. RM3: Romf 3G 111
Bosworth Ho. *DA8: Eri* 3C 152
(off Saltford Cl.)
Bosworth Rd. RM10: Dag 5M 125
SS9: Lgh S 8B 120
Botanical Way CO16: St O 8M 183
BOTANY BAY 5A 30
Botany Dr. CM7: Brain 5M 193
Botany La. CO16: Clac S, Jay, St O 1B 188
CO16: L Cla, Wee H 9F 178
Botany Rd. DA11: N'fleet 9K 155
Botany Way RM19: Purf 3M 153
Botelers SS16: Bas 2N 131
Boteley Cl. E4: Lon 8D 90
Botney Hill Rd. CM12: L Bur 3E 114 (2H 41)
Bouchers Mead CM1: Chelm 4A 60
Bouchiers Pl. CO5: Mess 1D 226
Bouchier Wlk. RM13: Rain 8E 126
Boudicca Wlk. CO7: W'hoe 3J 175
Bouldrewood Rd. SS7: Ben 1B 134
Boulevard, The IG8: Ilf 3N 107
SS4: R'fd 4L 121
Boulter Gdns. RM13: Rain 8E 126
Boulton Cotts. CM9: Mal 3D 214
Boulton Rd. RM8: Dag 4K 125
Boult Rd. SS15: Lain 7L 115
Bounces Rd. N9: Lon 1C 38
Boundary Cl. IG3: Ilf 6D 124
Boundary Ct. CM16: Epp 2C 78
Boundary Dr. CM13: Hut 6A 98
Boundary Rd. CB9: Stur 6H 223
CO4: Colc 1E 174 (6G 17)
CO7: Colc 1E 174
E13: Lon 6F 39
E17: Lon 2A 122 (4D 38)
IG11: Bark 2B 140
(Gascoigne Rd.)
IG11: Bark 1C 140
(King Edwards Rd.)
RM1: Romf 1E 126
RM14: Upm 5L 127
SS9: Lgh S 7A 120
Boundary St. DA8: Eri 5D 152
Bounderby Gro. CM1: Chelm 4G 59
BOUNDS GREEN 2A 38
Bounds Grn. Rd. N11: Lon 2A 38
N22: Lon 2A 38
Bounds Green Station (Tube) 2A 38
Bounstead Hill
CO2: B'hth, Lay H 9K 173 (1E 26)
Bounstead Rd.
CO2: B'hth, Colc, Lay H 8L 173 (1E 26)
Bourchier Av. CM7: Brain 3M 193
Bourchier Way CO9: Hals 6J 207
Bourn Bri. Rd. CB1: Abgtn 1B 6
Bourne Av. SS15: Lain 7J 115
BOURNEBRIDGE 7N 93 (7K 31)
Bournebridge Cl. CM13: Hut 6A 98
Bournebridge Hill CO9: Hals 7H 207 (4E 14)
Bournebridge La. RM4: Stap A 6L 93 (7K 31)
Bourne Cl. CO9: Hals 6J 207
SS15: Lain 7J 115
Bourne Ct. CM77: Brain 7M 193
CO2: Colc 2A 174
IG8: Wfd G 7K 107
Bourne End RM11: Horn 2L 127
Bourne Gdns. E4: Lon 1B 106
Bourne Hill N13: Lon 1A 38
Bourne Ho. IG9: Buck H 9K 91
Bourne Mill 2B 174 (7F 17)
Bournemouth Pk. Rd.
SS2: Sth S 3N 137 (4K 43)
Bournemouth Rd. CO15: Hol S 7C 186
Bourne Rd. CO2: Colc 2A 174 (7F 17)
CO6: W Ber 4E 164
DA5: Bex 4A 46
E7: Lon 5F 122
BOURNES GREEN 5E 138 (4A 44)
Bournes Grn. Chase
SS1: Shoe, Sth S 5E 138 (4A 44)
SS3: Sth S 5E 138
Bourne, The N14: Lon 7A 30
SG9: Aspen 4D 10
SG12: Ware 4C 20
Bouvel Dr. CM0: Bur C 1B 196
Bouverie Rd. CM2: Chelm 2C 72
Bovey Way RM15: S Ock 5E 144
Bovingdon Rd. CM7: Brain, Shalf 9H 191 (4C 14)
BOVINGER 3E 66 (2B 32)
Bovinger Way SS1: Sth S 5D 138
BOW 6D 38
Bowbank Cl. SS3: Shoe 5K 139
Bow Church Station (DLR) 6D 38
BOW COMMON 6D 38
Bow Comn. La. E3: Lon 6D 38
Bowden Dr. RM11: Horn 3J 127
Bowdens La. CO6: Wmgfd 6L 229 (2B 16)
Bowdon Rd. E17: Lon 2A 122
Bower Cl. RM5: Col R 4B 110
Bower Ct. CM16: Epp 2F 78
E4: Lon 7C 90
(off Ridgeway, The)
Bower Farm Rd. RM4: Hav 9A 94
Bower Gdns. CM9: Mal 5B 214
Bower Hall Dr. CB9: Stpl B 3K 223
Bower Hall La. CO5: W Mer 4G 27
Bower Hill CM16: Epp 1F 78 (4J 31)
Bower Hill Ind. Est. CM16: Epp 2F 78
Bower La. DA4: Eyns 7C 46
SS14: Bas 7F 116
Bowerman Rd. RM16: Grays 2C 156
Bowers RM11: Horn 9H 111
Bowers Cl. CM8: Sil E 9M 217
Bowers Ct. Dr. SS13: Pits 1N 133
BOWERS GIFFORD 9N 117 (3C 42)
Bowers Pk. Cotts. SS13: Pits 1M 133
Bowers Rd. SS7: Ben 1D 134
Bower Ter. CM16: Epp 2F 78
Bower Va. CM16: Epp 2F 78
Bowes Dr. CM5: Chip 6K 67
Bowe's Ho. IG11: Bark 9A 124
BOWES PARK 2A 38
Bowes Park Station (Rail) 2A 38
Bowes Rd. CO7: W'hoe 5J 175
N11: Lon 1A 38
RM8: Dag 6H 125
Bowfell Dr. SS16: Lang H 2J 131
Bowhay CM13: Hut 8K 97
Bow Ind. Pk. E15: Lon 9A 122
BOW INTERCHANGE 6E 38
Bowland Rd. IG8: Wfd G 3J 107
Bowlers Cft. SS14: Bas 5G 116
BOWLERS GREEN 1E 66
Bowls, The IG7: Chig 9D 92
Bowman Av. SS9: Lgh S 9A 120
Bowmans Pk. CO9: Cas H 3K 219
Bowmont Cl. CM13: Hut 5L 97
Bown Cl. RM18: Til 8D 156
Bowness Way RM12: Horn 7E 126
Bow Rd. E3: Lon 6D 38
Bow Road Station (Tube) 6D 38
Bowsers La. CB10: L Wal 4C 6
Bow St. E15: Lon 7E 122
WC2: Lon 7A 38
Box Cl. SS15: Lain 6M 115
Boxford Cl. SS6: Ray 4F 118
Boxhouse La. CO7: Ded 2H 161 (2H 17)
(not continuous)
Box La. IG11: Bark 2G 141
Box Mill La. CO9: Hals 3K 207
Boxmoor Rd. RM5: Col R 2A 110
Boxoll Rd. RM9: Dag 6L 125
BOXTED 3A 160 (2E 16)
Boxted Av. CO16: Clac S 9F 184
Boxted Chu. Rd.
CO6: Boxt, Gt Hork 4J 159 (3D 16)
Boxted Cl. IG9: Buck H 7L 91
BOXTED CROSS 3B 160 (2F 17)
Boxted Rd.
CO4: Boxt, Colc, Gt Hork 2L 165 (4E 16)
CO6: Boxt, Gt Hork 5J 159 (3D 16)
Boyce Grn. SS7: Ben 4D 134
Boyce Hill Cl. SS9: Lgh S 1A 136
Boyce Rd. SS3: Shoe 6M 139
SS17: Stan H 2L 147
Boyce Vw. Dr. SS7: Ben 4C 134
Boyd Cl. CM23: Bis S 9A 220
Boyd Ct. SS12: W'fd 2M 117
Boyden Cl. SS2: Sth S 4D 138
Boyden Ho. E17: Lon 7C 106
Boydin Cl. CM8: Wthm 7B 230
Boyescroft CM6: Gt D 2L 203
Boyles Ct. CO2: B'hth 7B 174
Boyne Dr. CM1: Chelm 5M 59
Boyne Rd. RM10: Dag 5M 125
Boyton Cl. SS7: Thund 1G 134
BOYTON CROSS 1N 217 (7H 23)
Boyton Cross La. CM1: Rox 2M 217 (7H 23)
BOYTON END
CM6 2G 13
CO10 3A 8
Boyton Hall La. CM1: Rox 1N 217
Boytons SS15: Lain 9N 115
Boytons Acre CB11: Saf W 5C 218
Boyton's La. CB10: Hpstd 6G 7
Boyton Vineyard 3A 8
Brabant Rd. CM3: N Fam 1F 104
Brabner Gdns. CM11: Rams H 4D 100
Bracelet Cl. SS17: Corr 9A 132
Brace Wlk. CM3: S Fer 3L 103
Bracken Cl. IG10: Lou 9A 78
Bracken Ct. IG6: Ilf 3E 108
Brackendale CM11: Bill 5M 99
Brackendale Av. SS13: Pits 2J 133
Brackendale Cl. SS5: Hock 9D 104
Brackendale Ct. SS13: Pits 2K 133
Brackendale Gdns. RM14: Upm 6N 127
Bracken Dell SS6: Ray 5L 119
Brackenden Dr. CM1: Chelm 4M 59

Bracken Dr. IG7: Chig . . . 3A 108
Bracken Ind. Est. IG6: Ilf . . . 4D 108
Bracken M. E4: Lon . . . 7C 90
RM7: Romf . . . 1N 125
Brackens Dr. CM14: War . . . 2F 112
(not continuous)
Brackens, The CO4: Colc . . . 4B 166
Bracken, The E4: Lon . . . 8C 90
Bracken Way CO5: Abb . . . 9B 174
SS7: Thund . . . 9G 119
Brackley Cres. SS13: Bas . . . 6H 117
Brackley Sq. IG8: Wfd G . . . 4K 107
Bradbourne Rd. RM17: Grays . . . 4L 155
Bradbourne Way SS13: Pits . . . 1K 133
Bradbrook Cotts. CO6: W Ber . . . 3G 165
Bradbury Dr. CM7: Brain . . . 5F 192
Bradd Cl. RM15: S Ock . . . 3F 144
Braddock Cl. RM5: Col R . . . 3A 110
Braddy Ct. CO5: K'dn . . . 3K 211
(off Rolley La.)
BRADFIELD . . . 3C 18
Bradfield Dr. IG11: Bark . . . 7F 124
BRADFIELD HEATH . . . 4B 18
Bradfield Ho. IG8: Ilf . . . 3N 107
Bradfield Rd. CO11: Wix . . . 4C 18
Bradford Bury SS9: Lgh S . . . 9B 120
Bradford Ct. CM7: Brain . . . 4J 193
Bradford Rd. IG1: Ilf . . . 3C 124
Bradford St. CM2: Chelm . . . 1B 72
CM7: Brain . . . 4H 193 (7D 14)
Brading Av. CO15: Clac S . . . 6L 185
Brading Cres. E11: Lon . . . 4H 123
Bradleigh Av. RM17: Grays . . . 3L 155
Bradley Av. SS7: Thund . . . 1F 134
Bradley Cl. CM6: Gt D . . . 1K 203
SS7: Thund . . . 1F 134
SS8: Can I . . . 9G 134
Bradley Comn. CM23: Bchgr . . . 6B 220
Bradley Grn. SS13: Bas . . . 6K 117
Bradleyhall La. CO16: T Sok . . . 3G 178 (7D 18)
Bradley Ho. IG8: Wfd G . . . 4G 107
Bradley Link SS7: Thund . . . 1F 134
Bradley M. CB10: Saf W . . . 3E 218
Bradley Rd. EN9: Enf . . . 5C 76
Bradley Way SS4: R'fd . . . 6K 121 (2J 43)
Bradshawe Rd. RM16: Grays . . . 8K 145
BRADWELL . . . 7F 15
Bradwell Av. RM10: Dag . . . 4M 125
Bradwell Cl. E18: Lon . . . 8F 106
RM12: Horn . . . 8F 126
Bradwell Ct. CM7: Brain . . . 8M 193
CM13: Hut . . . 5M 97
(off Bradwell Grn.)
Bradwell Grn. CM13: Hut . . . 5M 97
Bradwell Ho. SS11: W'fd . . . 9N 101
BRADWELL ON SEA . . . 8C 194 (1F 37)
Bradwell Outdoor Education Cen. . . . 6A 194
Bradwell Power Station Vis. Cen. . . . 7F 27
Bradwell Rd. CM0: Brad S, St La . . . 2D 36
CM0: Stpl . . . 3C 36
CM0: T'ham . . . 1K 225 (2E 36)
IG9: Buck H . . . 6L 91
BRADWELL WATERSIDE . . . 6B 194 (7E 26)
Brady Av. IG10: Lou . . . 1B 92
Brady Ct. RM8: Dag . . . 3J 125
Bradymead E6: Lon . . . 6A 140
Braemar Av. CM2: Chelm . . . 2C 72
DA7: Bexh . . . 9A 152
Braemar Cres. SS9: Lgh S . . . 4N 135
Braemar Gdns. RM11: Horn . . . 1L 127
Braemar Wlk. SS13: Pits . . . 9J 117
Braemore SS8: Can I . . . 9F 134
Braemore Cl. CO4: Colc . . . 4D 166
Braeside Cres. DA7: Bexh . . . 9A 152
Bragg Cl. RM8: Dag . . . 8G 124
Braggon's Hill CO10: Glem . . . 1G 9
Braggowens Ley CM17: H'low . . . 2H 55
Braham St. E1: Lon . . . 7B 38
Brain Rd. CM8: Wthm . . . 4B 230
BRAINTREE . . . 5H 193 (7C 14)
BRAINTREE AIRFIELD
RAYNE HALL FARM . . . 4D 192 (6B 14)
Braintree Av. IG4: Ilf . . . 8L 107
Braintree District Mus. . . . 5H 193 (7C 14)
Braintree Ent. Cen. CM7: Brain . . . 3F 192
Braintree Foyer, The CM7: Brain . . . 6H 193
(off St Michael's Rd.)
Braintree Freeport Designer Outlet Village
CM7: Brain, Tye G . . . 7L 193
Braintree Freeport Station (Rail)
. . . 7K 193 (7D 14)
Braintree Leisure Cen. . . . 4F 192
Braintree Retail Pk. CM7: Tye G . . . 7L 193
Braintree Rd. CM3: Gt L . . . 9N 203
CM3: Gt Walt, L Walt . . . 5K 57 (5A 24)
CM3: Terl . . . 4D 24
CM6: Fels . . . 8J 199 (1J 23)
CM6: Gt D, L Dun, Steb . . . 6A 212 (1G 23)
CM7: Gt Bar . . . 3C 202 (3J 13)
CM7: Shalf . . . 5B 14
(Church End)
CM7: Shalf, Weth . . . 8C 228 (3A 14)
(Wethersfield)
CM8: Wthm . . . 4C 230 (4F 25)
(not continuous)
CM77: Tye G . . . 9M 193 (1D 24)
CO9: Gosf . . . 4E 14
RM10: Dag . . . 5M 125
Braintree Station (Rail) . . . 6J 193 (7D 14)
Braintree Town F.C. (Cressing Road Stadium)
. . . 6L 193
Braintree Town Hall Centre & Art Gallery
. . . 5H 193
Brain Valley Av. CM77: Bla N . . . 2B 194
BRAISWICK . . . 5K 165 (5E 16)
Braiswick CO4: Colc . . . 4J 165 (5D 16)
Braiswick La. CO4: Colc . . . 3L 165
Braiswick Pl. SS15: Lain . . . 7K 115
Braithwaite Av. RM7: Rush G . . . 2M 125
Braithwaite Dr. CO4: Colc . . . 5M 165
Bramall Cl. E15: Lon . . . 7F 122
Bramble Cl. SS9: Lgh S . . . 8A 120
Bramble Ct. CM8: Wthm . . . 3B 230
IG6: Chig . . . 3E 108
Bramble Cres. SS7: Had . . . 1N 135 (3G 43)
Bramble Cft. DA8: Eri . . . 2A 152
Brambledown CO5: W Mer . . . 2C 228
Bramble Hall La. SS7: Had . . . 1N 135
Bramble La.
CM6: Fels, L Dun, Steb . . . 7E 212 (7J 13)
RM14: Upm . . . 1N 143 (6D 40)
Bramble Ri. CM20: H'low . . . 2B 54
Bramble Rd. CM8: Wthm . . . 3B 230
SS7: Had . . . 9L 119 (3F 43)
SS8: Can I . . . 2J 151
SS9: Lgh S . . . 8A 120
Brambles CO14: Walt . . . 7K 181
Brambles La. CO6: Whi C . . . 3J 15
Brambles, The CM0: S'min . . . 3D 222
CM7: Brain . . . 5G 193
CO3: S'way . . . 3G 173
IG7: Chig . . . 3B 108
SS15: Lain . . . 7J 115
Bramble Tye SS15: Bas . . . 6A 116
Bramblings, The E4: Lon . . . 1D 106
Bramerton Rd. SS5: Hock . . . 1C 120
BRAMFIELD . . . 4A 20
Bramfield La.
SG14: B'fld, Stfrd, W'frd . . . 4A 20
Bramfield Rd. SG14: Hart . . . 4A 20
Bramfield Rd. E. SS6: Ray . . . 5N 119
Bramfield Rd. W. SS6: Ray . . . 5M 119
Bramley Cl. CM7: Brain . . . 7J 193
CO3: Colc . . . 8J 165
CO7: Alr . . . 6A 176
IG8: Wfd G . . . 4J 107
Bramley Ct. E4: Lon . . . 7C 90
(off Ridgeway, The)
SS7: Had . . . 4M 135
Bramley Cres. IG2: Ilf . . . 1N 123
Bramley Gdns. SS15: Lain . . . 7L 115
Bramley Pl. CM2: Gt Bad . . . 3E 72
DA1: Cray . . . 9E 152
Bramley Rd. N14: Lon . . . 7A 30
Bramleys SS17: Stan H . . . 2M 147
Bramley Shaw EN9: Wal A . . . 3F 76
Bramleys, The CO6: Cogg . . . 2L 197
SS4: R'fd . . . 2J 121
Bramley Way CM3: May . . . 7K 213
Brampstead SS15: Lain . . . 9J 115
Brampton Cl. SS0: Wclf S . . . 2F 136
SS17: Corr . . . 9B 132
Bramshill Cl. IG7: Chig . . . 2D 108
Bramston Cl. CM2: Gt Bad . . . 2G 73
IG6: Ilf . . . 3E 108
Bramston Grn. CM8: Wthm . . . 3C 230
Bramston Link SS15: Lain . . . 8G 115
Bramston Sports Cen. . . . 6C 230
Bramston Vw. CM8: Wthm . . . 5C 230
Bramston Wlk. CM8: Wthm . . . 3C 230
Bramston Way SS15: Lain . . . 9G 114 (3J 41)
Bramwoods Rd. CM2: Gt Bad . . . 2F 72
Brancaster Dr. CM77: Gt N . . . 2C 204
Brancaster Pl. IG10: Lou . . . 2M 91
Brancaster Rd. E12: Lon . . . 6M 123
IG2: Ilf . . . 1D 124
Brancepeth Gdns. IG9: Buck H . . . 8G 90
Branch Rd. IG6: Ilf . . . 2G 109
SS7: Had . . . 4L 135
Brand Ct. CM7: Brain . . . 1H 193
Brand Dr. CO5: L'hoe . . . 9B 174
Brandenburg Rd. SS8: Can I . . . 9K 135
Brandesbury Sq. IG8: Ilf . . . 4N 107
Brandon Cl. CM12: Bill . . . 3J 99
RM16: Chaf H . . . 9J 145
Brandon Groves Av. RM15: S Ock . . . 3F 144
Brandon Rd. CM7: Brain . . . 6F 192
E17: Lon . . . 8C 106
Brands Hatch Rd. DA3: Fawk . . . 7E 46
Brandville Gdns. IG6: Ilf . . . 8A 108
BRANDY HOLE . . . 4N 103 (7G 35)
BRAN END . . . 6C 222 (6H 13)
Bran End Flds. CM6: Steb . . . 6C 222
Branfill Rd. RM14: Upm . . . 4M 127
Branksome Av. SS5: Hock . . . 8D 104
SS12: W'fd . . . 9G 100
SS17: Stan H . . . 2M 147 (6K 41)
Branksome Cl. SS17: Stan H . . . 2L 147
Branksome Rd. SS2: Sth S . . . 5N 137
Branscombe Cl. CO13: Frin S . . . 9H 181
Branscombe Gdns. SS1: Sth S . . . 6F 138
Branscombe Sq. SS1: Sth S . . . 5F 138
Branscombe Wlk. SS1: Sth S . . . 5F 138
Branstone Ct. RM19: Purf . . . 3M 153
Branston Rd. CO15: Clac S . . . 1G 189
BRANTHAM . . . 1A 18
Brantham Hill CO11: Bran . . . 2A 18
Brantham Mill Ind. Est
CO11: Law . . . 1F 162
Brantwood Av. DA8: Eri . . . 5A 152
Brantwood Cl. E17: Lon . . . 7B 106
Brantwood Gdns. IG4: Ilf . . . 8L 107
Brantwood Rd. N17: Lon . . . 2C 38
Brasted Rd. DA8: Eri . . . 5C 152
Brathertons Ct. CM12: Bill . . . 5H 99
BRAUGHING . . . 6E 10
BRAUGHING FRIARS . . . 6F 11
Braxted Cl. SS4: R'fd . . . 3H 121
Braxted La. CM8: Gt Br . . . 6H 205 (4J 25)
CM9: Gt Tot . . . 6H 205
Braxted Rd. CM8: Gt Br, Riven . . . 3H 25
CM8: L Brax, W Bis . . . 1M 229 (5H 25)
CO5: Tip . . . 3H 25
Braxteds SS15: Lain . . . 9J 115
Braybrooke SS14: Bas . . . 9C 116
Braybrooke Gdns. CB11: Saf W . . . 5C 218
Bray Ct. SS3: Shoe . . . 5J 139
Brayers M. SS4: R'fd . . . 6L 121
BRAYS GROVE . . . 4F 54 (7J 21)
Brays La. SS4: Cwdn, R'fd . . . 2J 121 (1J 43)
Brays Mead CM18: H'low . . . 5E 54
Bray Springs EN9: Wal A . . . 4E 76
Braziers Cl. CM2: Gall . . . 7D 72
Breach Barns La. EN9: Wal A . . . 9F 62
Breach Barns Mobile Home Pk.
EN9: Wal A . . . 9H 63
Breachfield Rd. CO2: Colc . . . 4K 173
Breach La. CM6: Gt Eas . . . 5F 13
RM9: Dag . . . 3M 141
Breach Rd. RM20: W Thur . . . 4C 154
Bread and Cheese Hill
SS7: Ben, Thund . . . 1E 134
Bread and Cheese La. EN7: Chesh . . . 2B 30
EN10: Brox, Chesh . . . 2B 30
Break Egg Hill CM11: Bill . . . 5M 99
(not continuous)
Breakmoor Hill CO10: Mdltn . . . 6J 9
Bream Ct. CO4: Colc . . . 6F 166
Breamore Ct. IG3: Ilf . . . 4F 124
Breamore Rd. IG3: Ilf . . . 4E 124
Breams Fld. SS16: Lang H . . . 2L 131
Bream St. E3: Lon . . . 9A 122
Brecknock Rd. NW5: Lon . . . 5A 38
Brecon SS0: Wclf S . . . 5K 137
Brecon Cl. SS13: Pits . . . 7K 117
Bredo Ho. IG11: Bark . . . 3G 141
Bree Av. CO6: M Tey . . . 3G 171
BREEDS . . . 6F 56 (5K 23)
Breeds Rd. CM3: Gt Walt . . . 6F 56 (5K 23)
Bree Hill CM3: S Fer . . . 2J 103
Bremer M. E17: Lon . . . 8B 106
Brempsons SS14: Bas . . . 8B 116
Brendans Cl. RM11: Horn . . . 3J 127
Brendon SS15: Lain . . . 1M 131
Brendon Cl. DA8: Eri . . . 6C 152
Brendon Ct. CO5: Tip . . . 7D 226
Brendon Dr. CO9: Hals . . . 6L 207
Brendon Gdns. IG2: Ilf . . . 9D 108
Brendon Pl. CM1: Chelm . . . 1N 71
Brendon Rd. RM8: Dag . . . 3L 125
Brendon Way SS0: Wclf S . . . 1F 136
Brennan Cl. CM3: Cold N . . . 7K 197
Brennan Rd. RM18: Til . . . 7D 156 (2H 47)
Brent Av. CM3: S Fer . . . 8J 89
Brent Cl. CM8: Wthm . . . 5B 230
CO13: Frin S . . . 7J 181
Brent Hall Rd. CM7: F'fld . . . 2A 200 (2J 13)
Brenthall Towers
CM17: H'low . . . 5H 55
Brentleigh Ct. CM14: Brtwd . . . 9D 96
BRENT PELHAM . . . 3G 11
Brent, The DA1: Dart . . . 4C 46
BRENTWOOD . . . 8G 96 (1E 40)
Brentwood By-Pass
CM14: Brtwd, Pil H, S Wea . . . 1A 112 (1D 40)
CM15: Brtwd, Pil H, Shenf . . . 5F 96
Brentwood Cathedral . . . 8G 97
Brentwood Cen., The . . . 5F 96
Brentwood Hard Court Tennis Club . . . 4H 113
Brentwood Lawn Tennis Club . . . 7G 97
Brentwood Mus. . . . 1F 112 (1E 40)
Brentwood Pk. Ski & Snowboarding Cen.
. . . 4E 112
Brentwood Pl. CM15: Brtwd . . . 7G 96
Brentwood Rd. CM5: Chip . . . 9L 67 (3C 32)
CM13: Heron, Ingve, W H'dn . . . 1K 113 (1F 41)
CM13: W H'dn . . . 2B 130 (4G 41)
CO15: Hol S . . . 7N 185
RM1: Romf . . . 1D 126 (3A 40)
RM2: Romf . . . 1F 126
RM14: Bulp . . . 4C 130 (5H 41)
RM16: Ors . . . 2D 156 (1H 47)
Brentwood School Sports Cen. . . . 8G 97
Brentwood Station (Rail) . . . 9F 96 (1E 40)
Brentwood Theatre . . . 7G 97
Bressey Gro. E18: Lon . . . 6F 106
Bressingham Gdns. CM3: S Fer . . . 1J 103
Bretons SS15: Lain . . . 9N 115
Bretons Outdoor Recreation Cen. . . . 8D 126
Bretten Cl. CO16: Clac S . . . 9E 184
Brettenham Av. E17: Lon . . . 5A 106
Brettenham Dr. SS1: Sth S . . . 6C 138
Brettenham Rd. E17: Lon . . . 6A 106
Brett Gdns. RM9: Dag . . . 9K 125
Bretts Bldgs. CO1: Colc . . . 9A 166
Brevet Cl. RM19: Purf . . . 2A 154
BREWER'S END . . . 3B 224 (1C 22)
Brewers Rd.
DA12: Cobh, Shorne . . . 6K 47
Brewers Yd. CM0: S'min . . . 2D 222
(off Burnham Rd.)
Brewery La. CM24: Stan M . . . 2D 220
Brewery Rd. CB2: Saws . . . 1K 5
EN11: Hod . . . 5A 52
(not continuous)
N7: Lon . . . 5A 38
Brewery, The RM1: Romf . . . 9C 110
Brewery Yd. CM24: Stan M . . . 2D 220
Brewood Rd. RM8: Dag . . . 8G 125
Brewster Cl. SS8: Can I . . . 2G 151
Brewster Rd. E10: Lon . . . 3B 122
Brian Bishop Cl. CO14: Walt . . . 6L 181
Brian Cl. CM2: Chelm . . . 4C 72
RM12: Horn . . . 6F 126
Brian Rd. RM6: Chad H . . . 9H 109
Briar Cl. CM11: Bill . . . 9M 99
IG9: Buck H . . . 8K 91
SS5: Hock . . . 3E 120
Briardale Av. CO12: Har . . . 4H 209
Briarfields CO13: Kir S . . . 6F 180
Briarleas Gdns. RM14: Upm . . . 2B 128
Briar Mead SS15: Lain . . . 7K 115
Briar Rd. CO7: Gt Bro . . . 3A 168 (5J 17)
RM3: Romf . . . 4G 111
Briarsford Witham Ind. Est. CM8: Wthm . . . 6E 230
Briars, The CM15: Kel H . . . 9B 82
CM18: H'low . . . 6D 54
Briars Wlk. RM3: H Wood . . . 6K 111
Briarswood CM1: Chelm . . . 4M 59
SS8: Can I . . . 9G 134
Briar Vw. CM11: Bill . . . 9M 99
Briarwood CM15: Kel H . . . 7C 82
Briarwood Av. CO15: Hol S . . . 7C 186
Briarwood Cl. SS9: Lgh S . . . 1C 136
Briarwood Dr. SS9: Lgh S . . . 1C 136
Briarwood End CO4: Colc . . . 4B 166
Briary, The SS12: W'fd . . . 9J 101
Briceway SS17: Corr . . . 2A 148
Brickburn Cl. CM6: Fels . . . 9K 199
Brick Cotts. SS11: Runw . . . 6A 102
Brick Ct. RM17: Grays . . . 4K 155
(off Jetty Wlk.)
Brickcroft Hoppit CM17: H'low . . . 2H 55
BRICK END . . . 6D 12
Brickenden Ct. EN9: Wal A . . . 3F 76
BRICKENDON . . . 1B 30
Brickendon Ct. EN11: Hod . . . 6A 52
Brickendon La. SG13: Brick, Hart . . . 6B 20
(not continuous)
Brickfield Cl. SS16: Van . . . 4E 132
Brickfield Rd. CM16: Coop . . . 8J 65
SS16: Van . . . 4E 132
Brickfields SS7: Thund . . . 8F 118
Brickfields Rd. CM3: S Fer . . . 1L 103
Brickfields Way SS4: R'fd . . . 6M 121
Brickhouse Cl. CO5: W Mer . . . 2B 228
BRICK HOUSE END . . . 4J 11
Brickhouse La. CM3: Bore . . . 2F 60
Brick Ho. Rd. CM9: Tol M . . . 6N 205 (5K 25)
Brickhouse Rd. CO6: Coln E . . . 1E 198 (3H 15)
Brick Kiln Cl. CO6: Cogg . . . 2L 197
BRICKKILN GREEN . . . 3B 14
Brickkiln Green CM7: Bla E . . . 3B 14
Brick Kiln La.
CB11: R'lng, Rick G . . . 1A 216 (3A 12)
CM6: Steb . . . 6B 222 (6H 13)
CO6: Gt Hork . . . 1J 165
CO7: Thorr . . . 9D 176
Brick Kiln Rd. CM2: S'don . . . 3K 73 (2C 34)
CO1: Colc . . . 6M 165
Brick Kiln Way CM7: Brain . . . 6M 193
Brick La. E1: Lon . . . 6B 38
Brickmakers La. CO4: Colc . . . 5N 165
Brickman's Hill CO11: Brad . . . 3B 18
Brick Row SG8: Chris . . . 6H 5
Brickspring La. CM9: Gt Tot . . . 7J 205
Brickstock Furze CM15: Shenf . . . 7K 97
Brick St. CO3: S'way . . . 6C 164
Brickwall Cl. CM0: Bur C . . . 4D 196
Brickwall Farm CM77: Tye G . . . 6F 15
Brickyard La. SG8: Reed . . . 7D 4
Bridewell St. CO10: Clare . . . 3D 8
Bridge Av. RM14: Upm . . . 5L 127
Bridge Brook Cl. CO4: Colc . . . 6D 166
Bridge Cl. CM13: Brtwd . . . 9H 97
DA2: Dart . . . 8A 154
RM7: Rush G . . . 1C 126
SS3: Shoe . . . 7J 139
Bridgecote La. SS15: Bas . . . 5A 116
Bridge Cotts. SS3: Shoe . . . 6H 139
Bridge Ct. CM8: Wthm . . . 6C 230
RM17: Grays . . . 4L 155
(off Bridge Rd.)
Bridge Cft. CM3: Gt Walt . . . 2H 57
BRIDGE END . . . 1C 202 (3J 13)
Bridge End CB11: Newp . . . 2L 215
E17: Lon . . . 5C 106
Bridge End Gardens . . . 3C 218 (6B 6)
Bridge End La. CM77: Gt N . . . 8E 192 (1C 24)
Bridgefield Cl. CO4: Colc . . . 8C 166
BRIDGE GREEN . . . 7J 5
Bri. Hall Rd. CM77: Tye G . . . 7F 15
Bridge Hill CM16: Epp . . . 3E 78 (4H 31)
CO6: For . . . 4B 16
Bridge Ho. Cl. SS12: W'fd . . . 9K 101
Bridgemans Grn. CM3: Latch . . . 8L 211
Bridgemarsh La. CM3: Alth . . . 6A 36
Bridgend Cl. CM3: S Fer . . . 9L 89
Bridge Pde. CM12: Bill . . . 5H 99
Bridge Rd. CM5: M'ton . . . 1B 32
DA8: Eri . . . 7D 152 (2A 46)
E6: Lon . . . 9M 123
E15: Lon . . . 9D 122 (6E 38)
N22: Lon . . . 2A 38
RM13: Rain . . . 4E 142 (6A 40)
RM17: Grays . . . 4L 155 (2F 47)
SS3: Fou I, Gt W . . . 4D 44
SS11: W'fd . . . 9A 102
BRIDGE STREET . . . 1K 9
Bridge St. CB10: Saf W . . . 3C 218 (6B 6)
CM1: Writ . . . 1K 71 (1K 33)
CM7: F'fld . . . 3C 200
CM7: Gt Bar . . . 2C 202 (3J 13)
CM8: Wthm . . . 6C 230 (5F 25)
CO6: Cogg . . . 4K 197 (7H 15)
CO8: Bures . . . 7L 195 (1A 16)
CO9: Gt Yel . . . 3D 206 (6C 8)
CO9: Hals . . . 4K 207 (3F 15)
SG8: Whad . . . 2C 4
SS15: Bas . . . 5N 115

Bridge St. Rd. CO10: Alp . . . 1K 9
Bridge Ter. CM9: Mal . . . 3C 214
E15: Lon . . . 9D 122
Bridgeview Ct. IG6: Ilf . . . 3C 108
Bridge Vw. Ind. Est. RM20: W Thur. . . . 4D 154
Bridge Wlk. IG1: Ilf. . . . 4A 124
(in Exchange, The)
Bridgeway IG11: Bark . . . 9E 124
Bridgeways EN11: Hod . . . 6B 52
Bridgewick Rd. CM0: Deng. . . . 3F 37
Bridgwater Cl. RM3: Romf. . . . 2H 111
Bridgwater Dr. SS0: Wclf S . . . 1E 136 (3H 43)
Bridgwater Rd. RM3: Romf . . . 2G 111
Bridgwater Wlk. RM3: Romf . . . 2H 111
Bridle Cl. EN11: Hod . . . 1A 52
Bridle Path, The IG8: Wfd G. . . . 4E 106
Bridle Wlk. CO3: S'way. . . . 9E 164
(off Stirrup M.)
Bridleway CM11: Bill . . . 2M 99
Bridle Way EN11: Hod . . . 2A 52
Bridle Way Nth. EN11: Hod. . . . 1A 52 (6D 20)
Bridle Way Sth. EN11: Hod. . . . 2A 52 (6D 20)
Bridle Way, The SS16: Bas . . . 3N 131
Bridon Cl. CM3: E Han . . . 3B 88
(off Ashley Grn.)
Bridport Av. RM7: Romf. . . . 1N 125
Bridport Rd. CM1: Chelm. . . . 6M 59
N18: Lon. . . . 2B 38
Bridport Way CM7: Brain. . . . 3M 193
Brierley Av. CO5: W Mer. . . . 2E 228
Brierley Cl. RM11: Horn. . . . 1G 126
Brierley Paddock CO5: W Mer . . . 2E 228
Brierley Rd. E11: Lon. . . . 6D 122
Brigadier Way SS3: Shoe . . . 8K 139
Brighstone Ct. RM19: Purf . . . 3M 153
Bright Cl. CO16: Clac S . . . 7H 185
BRIGHTLINGSEA . . . 7E 182 (3K 27)
Brightlingsea Mus. . . . 7E 182 (3K 27)
Brightlingsea Open Air Swimming Pool . . . 8D 182
Brightlingsea Rd.
CO7: B'sea, Thorr . . . 3C 182 (2J 27)
CO7: Elms, W'hoe . . . 1H 175 (7H 17)
Brightlingsea Sports Cen. . . . 5D 182
Brighton Av. SS1: Sth S . . . 6B 138
Brighton Rd. CO15: Hol S. . . . 7C 186
SS0: Sth S. . . . 6L 137
Brights Av. RM13: Rain. . . . 4F 142
Brightside CM12: Bill . . . 4G 99
CO13: Walt . . . 7H 181
Brightside Cl. CM12: Bill . . . 4G 99
Brightwell Av. SS0: Wclf S . . . 4J 137
Brimfield Rd. RM19: Purf. . . . 2A 154
BRIMSDOWN. . . . 6D 30
Brimsdown Av. EN3: Enf. . . . 6D 30
SS15: Lain. . . . 9K 115
Brimsdown Station (Rail) . . . 6D 30
Brimstone Ct. CM7: Gt N . . . 8G 193
Brimstone Hill DA13: Meop . . . 7H 47
Brimstone Ho. E15: Lon . . . 9E 122
(off Victoria St.)
Brimwade Cl. CO11: Bran. . . . 1J 163
Brindles RM11: Horn . . . 8J 111
SS8: Can I. . . . 1F 150
Brindles Cl. CM13: Hut . . . 8M 97
SS17: Linf . . . 2J 157
Brindley Rd. CO15: Clac S. . . . 5M 185
Brindwood Rd. E4: Lon. . . . 9A 90
Bringey, The CM2: Gt Bad . . . 4H 73
Brinkley Cres. CO4: Colc . . . 6D 166
Brinkley Gro. Rd. CO4: Colc . . . 2A 166 (4F 17)
Brinkley La. CO4: Colc. . . . 2B 166 (4F 17)
Brinkley Pl. CO4: Colc . . . 4N 165
Brinkworth Cl. SS5: Hock. . . . 1E 120
Brinkworth Rd. IG5: Ilf . . . 7L 107
Brinsmead Rd. RM3: H Wood . . . 6L 111
Brisbane Ho. RM18: Til . . . 6C 156
Brisbane Rd. E10: Lon . . . 4B 122
IG1: Ilf. . . . 2A 124
Brisbane Way CO2: Colc. . . . 5A 174
Briscoe Cl. E11: Lon. . . . 4F 122
Briscoe Rd. RM13: Rain. . . . 2G 143
SS13: Pits . . . 8J 117
Brise Cl. CM7: Brain . . . 7J 193
Bristol Cl. SS6: Ray . . . 2J 119
Bristol Ct. CM8: Sil E. . . . 9M 217
Bristol Hill IP9: S'ly . . . 1H 19
Bristol Ho. IG11: Bark. . . . 9F 124
(off Margaret Bondfield Av.)
Bristol Rd. CO1: Colc . . . 7A 166
E7: Lon . . . 8J 123
SS2: Sth S. . . . 9J 121
Bristowe Av. CM2: Gt Bad . . . 4H 73
Bristowe Dr. RM16: Ors . . . 6F 146
Britannia Cen., The IG10: Lou. . . . 3C 92
Britannia Cl. CM11: Bill . . . 6K 99
Britannia Ct. CO7: W'hoe . . . 5H 175
SS13: Bas . . . 6L 117
Britannia Cres. CO7: W'hoe. . . . 5H 175
Britannia Gdns. SS0: Wclf S . . . 6H 137
Britannia Lodge SS0: Wclf S . . . 6H 137
Britannia Rd. CM14: War . . . 2F 112
IG1: Ilf. . . . 5A 124
SS0: Wclf S. . . . 6H 137
British Legion Rd. E4: Lon . . . 8F 90
Britric Cl. CM6: Fels . . . 9F 212
Brittain Rd. RM8: Dag . . . 5K 125
Brittania Cl. DA8: Eri . . . 4D 152
Brittany Way CO2: Colc. . . . 2B 174
(not continuous)
Britten Cl. CO4: Colc. . . . 9E 166
SS16: Lang H . . . 1J 131
Britten Cres. CM2: Gt Bad . . . 2G 72
CM8: Wthm. . . . 8C 230
Britton Ct. SS6: Ray . . . 6K 119
Brittons La. CM4: Stock . . . 9A 86
Brixham Cl. CO15: Clac S. . . . 4G 188
SS6: Ray. . . . 2K 119
Brixham Gdns. IG3: Ilf . . . 7D 124
Brixton La. CB11: Man, Rick G, Ugley
. . . 4B 216 (4A 12)
CM23: Man, Ugley . . . 5K 11
Broad Cl. SS5: Hock. . . . 1D 120
Broadclyst Av. SS9: Lgh S . . . 1C 136
Broadclyst Cl. SS1: Sth S. . . . 5E 138
Broadclyst Gdns. SS1: Sth S . . . 5E 138
Broad Ditch Rd. DA13: Ist R, N'flt G . . . 5G 47
Broadfield CM6: High R . . . 3F 23
CM20: H'low. . . . 2D 54
Broadfield Cl. RM1: Romf . . . 9D 110
Broadfield Rd. CM22: Tak. . . . 3E 224
Broadfields CM21: H Wych . . . 3G 50
CO7: W'hoe . . . 2J 175
Broadfield Way IG9: Buck H . . . 9J 91
Broadgate EN9: Wal A. . . . 3F 76
BROAD GREEN
CB9 . . . 1N 223 (5K 7)
CO6 . . . 3B 170 (7J 15)
SG8 . . . 6H 5
Broad Grn. SG13: B'frd. . . . 7A 20
SS14: Bas. . . . 8D 116
BROADGREEN WOOD . . . 7A 20
Broadhope Av. SS17: Stan H . . . 5L 147
Broadhurst Av. IG3: Ilf. . . . 6E 124
Broadhurst Gdns. IG7: Chig . . . 1B 108
(not continuous)
Broadhurst Wlk. RM13: Rain . . . 8E 126
Broadlands RM17: Grays . . . 3J 155
SS7: Thund . . . 9F 118
Broadlands Av. SS5: Hock . . . 9E 104
SS6: Ray. . . . 4K 119
Broadlands Rd. SS5: Hock . . . 1E 120
Broadlands Way CO4: Colc. . . . 6B 166
Broad La. CO6: Boxt, Gt Hork . . . 7J 159
DA2: Dart . . . 5B 46
N15: Lon. . . . 3B 38
Broadlawn SS9: Lgh S . . . 2B 136
BROADLEY COMMON . . . 8M 53 (1G 31)
Broadley Rd. CM19: H'low . . . 7M 53
Broadmayne SS14: Bas. . . . 9B 116 (3A 42)
Broadmead Cen. IG8: Wfd G. . . . 4J 107
(off Navestock Cres.)
Broadmead Ct. IG8: Wfd G. . . . 3G 106
Broad Mdw. CM15: Kel H . . . 8C 82
Broadmead Rd. CO4: Colc . . . 6E 166
IG8: Wfd G . . . 3G 106 (2F 39)
(not continuous)
Broadmere Cl. CO15: Hol S . . . 6B 186
Broad Oak IG8: Wfd G . . . 2H 107
Broadoak Chase CM9: Gt Tot . . . 5J 25
Broad Oak Cl. E4: Lon . . . 2A 106
Broad Oakes Cl. CB10: Wim. . . . 1D 12
Broadoak Rd. DA8: Eri . . . 5B 152
Broadoaks CM16: Epp. . . . 1E 78
Broad Oaks SS12: W'fd . . . 1M 117
Broadoaks Cres. CM7: Brain . . . 4M 193
Broad Oaks Pk. CO4: Colc . . . 4D 166
Broad Oak Way SS6: Ray . . . 5L 119
Broad Pde. SS5: Hock . . . 1E 120
Broad Rd. CM7: Brain. . . . 9K 191
(Bradford St.)
CM7: Brain. . . . 2J 193 (6D 14)
(Highfield Stile Rd.)
CO9: Wick P . . . 7G 9
Broad Sanctuary SW1: Lon . . . 7A 38
BROAD'S GREEN. . . . 7G 57 (5K 23)
Broadstone Rd. RM12: Horn . . . 4E 126
Broad St. CM22: Hat O . . . 7D 206 (3C 22)
RM10: Dag . . . 9M 125 (5K 39)
BROAD STREET GREEN. . . . 1E 214 (7J 25)
Broad St. Grn. Rd.
CM9: Gt Tot, Mal . . . 1E 214 (6H 25)
Broad St. Mkt. RM10: Dag. . . . 9M 125
Broadstrood CO16: St O. . . . 8M 183
IG10: Lou . . . 8N 77
Broadview Av. RM16: Grays. . . . 9N 145
Broad Wlk. CM20: H'low . . . 2C 54
Broadwalk E18: Lon . . . 7F 106
Broadwalk SS5: Hock . . . 1E 120
Broadwalk SS12: W'fd . . . 2M 117
Broad Wlk. Nth., The CM13: Brtwd . . . 9K 97
(not continuous)
Broad Wlk. Sth., The CM13: Brtwd . . . 1K 113
Broadwater Grn. SS15: Lain. . . . 9H 115
Broadwater Rd. SE28: Lon. . . . 7H 39
Broadway BR8: Crock . . . 7A 46
CM8: Sil E. . . . 7L 217
CO10: Glem. . . . 1G 9
CO15: Jay . . . 6D 188 (5C 28)
E15: Lon. . . . 9D 122 (5E 38)
IG11: Bark. . . . 1B 140
RM2: Romf . . . 6E 110
RM13: Rain . . . 4E 142 (6A 40)
RM17: Grays . . . 4M 155
RM18: Til . . . 7B 156
Broad Way SS5: Hock. . . . 9E 104
Broadway SS9: Lgh S . . . 6D 136 (5H 43)
Broadway Av. CM17: H'low . . . 8G 51
Broadway Cl. IG8: Wfd G. . . . 3H 107
Broadway Ct. CM8: Sil E. . . . 7L 217
Broadway Gdns. IG8: Wfd G. . . . 3H 107
Broadway Link SS13: Pits. . . . 1J 133
Broadway Mkt. E2: Lon . . . 6C 38
IG6: Ilf. . . . 6C 108
(Forest Rd.)
IG6: Ilf. . . . 6B 108
(Greystone Gdns.)
Broadway Nth. SS13: Pits. . . . 1J 133
Broadway Pde. E4: Lon . . . 3C 106
RM12: Horn. . . . 6F 126
(off Broadway, The)
Broadway Superbowl. . . . 6E 136
Broadway, The CM6: Gt D . . . 1M 203 (7G 13)
CM6: Steb . . . 8A 222 (7G 13)
E4: Lon . . . 3D 106
IG8: Wfd G . . . 3H 107
IG10: Lou. . . . 3B 92 (6H 31)
N8: Lon. . . . 3A 38
N9: Lon. . . . 1C 38
RM8: Dag . . . 3L 125
RM12: Horn . . . 6F 126 (5B 40)
SS1: Sth S . . . 7F 138 (5A 44)
SS11: W'fd. . . . 8L 101 (1C 42)
SS15: Lain. . . . 8K 115
Broadway W. SS9: Lgh S . . . 6C 136 (5G 43)
Brock Cl. CM8: Wthm . . . 7B 230
CO5: Tip . . . 5E 226
Brockdish Av. IG11: Bark . . . 7E 124
Brockenhurst Dr. SS17: Stan H. . . . 5L 147
Brockenhurst Gdns. IG1: Ilf . . . 7B 124
Brockenhurst Way CM3: Bick . . . 9F 74
Brocket Cl. IG7: Chig . . . 1E 108
Brocket Rd. EN11: Hod . . . 5A 52 (7D 20)
RM16: Grays. . . . 1C 156
Brocket Way IG7: Chig . . . 2D 108
Brock Grn. RM15: S Ock. . . . 6E 144
Brockham Cl. CO16: Clac S. . . . 7F 184
Brockham Dr. IG2: Ilf . . . 1A 124
BROCK HILL . . . 3J 101 (6B 34)
Brock Hill SS11: Runw . . . 2H 101 (6B 34)
Brock Hill Dr. SS11: Runw . . . 5K 101
Brockles Mead CM19: H'low . . . 7B 54
Brockley Cres. RM5: Col R. . . . 4A 110
BROCKLEY GREEN . . . 2B 8
Brockley Grn. CO10: Pos . . . 2B 8
Brockley Gro. CM13: Hut . . . 7K 97
Brockley Rd. CM2: Chelm . . . 9M 59
Brocks Bus. Pk. SS11: W'fd. . . . 1N 117
Brocksford Av. SS6: Ray . . . 6M 119
Brocks Mead CM6: Gt Eas. . . . 6F 13
Brocksparkwood CM13: Brtwd . . . 9L 97
Brockton Cl. RM1: Romf . . . 8D 110
Brockway Cl. E11: Lon . . . 4E 122
Brockwell La. CO5: K'dn. . . . 4K 211
Brockwell Wlk. SS12: W'fd. . . . 1L 117
Brodie Rd. E4: Lon . . . 7C 90
SS3: Shoe . . . 6L 139
Brodie Wlk. SS12: W'fd . . . 2N 117
Brograve Cl. CM2: Gall . . . 7E 72
BROKEN GREEN . . . 7F 11
Broman's La. CO5: E Mer . . . 4J 27
Bromefield Ct. EN9: Wal A. . . . 3G 76
Bromfelde Rd. CM11: Cray H. . . . 2D 116
Bromfield CB11: Saf W. . . . 5D 218
Bromfield Rd. CM1: Chelm. . . . 8J 59
Bromfords Cl. SS12: W'fd . . . 2J 117
Bromfords Dr. SS12: W'fd . . . 2J 117
Bromhall Rd. RM8: Dag. . . . 8G 124
BROMLEY
E3 . . . 6D 38
SG11 . . . 1F 21
Bromley RM17: Grays. . . . 4J 155
Bromley-by-Bow Station (Tube) . . . 6D 38
Bromley Cl. CO16: Clac S. . . . 9H 185
BROMLEY CROSS . . . 3A 168 (5J 17)
Bromley La. CB11: Newp . . . 2L 215
(not continuous)
Bromley M. SS6: Ray. . . . 4G 118
Bromley Rd. CO4: Colc . . . 6E 166 (5G 17)
CO7: A'lgh . . . 6E 166 (5G 17)
CO7: Elms . . . 1N 175 (6J 17)
CO7: Frat . . . 2F 176 (7K 17)
CO11: Law, L Bro . . . 6F 162 (3K 17)
E10: Lon . . . 1B 122
E17: Lon . . . 7A 106
Brompton Cl. CM12: Bill . . . 3J 99
Brompton Dr. DA8: Eri. . . . 5F 152
Brompton Gdns. CM9: Mal . . . 8A 214
Bronte Cl. CM7: Brain . . . 8J 193
E7: Lon . . . 6G 123
IG2: Ilf. . . . 8N 107
RM18: Til. . . . 7E 156
Bronte Gro. DA1: Dart. . . . 9K 153
Bronte M. SS2: Sth S . . . 4N 137
Bronte Rd. CM8: Wthm . . . 2C 230
Bronze Age Way DA8: Eri . . . 1A 152 (1A 46)
DA17: Belv. . . . 9N 141 (1A 46)
Brook Av. RM10: Dag . . . 9N 125
Brook Cl. CM7: Brain . . . 6E 192
CM9: Gt Tot . . . 4M 229
CM9: Wdhm W . . . 1F 35
CO5: Tip. . . . 8F 226
RM2: Romf. . . . 5D 110
SS4: R'fd . . . 7M 121
Brook Cotts. CM24: Stan M . . . 4D 220
Brook Ct. E11: Lon . . . 5E 122
E15: Lon . . . 7B 122
(off Clays La.)
IG11: Bark. . . . 1E 140
Brook Cres. E4: Lon. . . . 1A 106
Brookdale Av. RM14: Upm . . . 5L 127
Brookdale Cl. RM14: Upm. . . . 5M 127
Brookdale Rd. E17: Lon . . . 7A 106
Brook Dr. SS12: W'fd . . . 2K 117
SS17: Fob . . . 5D 132
Brooke Av. CB10: Saf W . . . 3D 218
BROOKEND . . . 7J 13
BROOK END. . . . 4B 10
Brook End CM21: Saw. . . . 2J 51
SG8: Stpl M. . . . 4A 4
Brook End Rd. CM2: Chelm . . . 8C 60 (1B 34)
Brook End Rd. Nth. CM2: Chelm . . . 7B 60
Brook End Rd. Sth.
CM2: Chelm . . . 8C 60
Brooke Rd. E17: Lon. . . . 8C 106
RM17: Grays. . . . 3K 155
Brooker Rd. EN9: Wal A . . . 4C 76
(not continuous)
Brooke Sq. CM9: Mal . . . 7C 214
Brooke Trad. Est. RM11: Horn . . . 2D 126
Brook Farm Cvn. Pk.
CO15: Clac S. . . . 6H 185
Brook Farm Cl. CO9: Hals . . . 5N 207
Brookfield CM16: Thorn . . . 4H 65
Brookfield Av. E17: Lon . . . 8C 106
Brookfield Cl. CM13: Hut. . . . 5M 97
Brookfield La. W. EN8: Chesh . . . 3C 30
(not continuous)
Brookfield Path IG8: Wfd G . . . 3E 106
Brookfield Rd. CO16: L Cla . . . 2G 184
Brookfields CM5: Chip . . . 4K 67
CM6: Steb. . . . 7C 222
CM21: Saw . . . 2J 51
SS9: Lgh S . . . 1C 136
Brookfields Cl. SS9: Lgh S. . . . 1C 136
Brook Gdns. E4: Lon. . . . 1B 106
Brook Hall Rd. CO5: Fing . . . 8H 175 (1G 27)
Brookhampton St. CB10: Dux, I'tn. . . . 3K 5
Brook Hill CM3: L Walt . . . 6K 57 (5A 24)
CM6: N End . . . 2J 23
Brookhouse Gdns. E4: Lon . . . 1E 106
Brookhouse Rd. CO6: Gt Tey. . . . 2D 170 (6K 15)
Brookhurst Cl. CM2: Chelm . . . 8M 59
Brooking Cl. RM8: Dag. . . . 5H 125
Brooking Rd. E7: Lon . . . 7G 123
Brookland CO5: Tip. . . . 7C 226
Brooklands CO1: Colc. . . . 9A 166
CO15: Jay. . . . 6C 188 (5C 28)
SS6: Ray. . . . 4K 119
SS12: W'fd . . . 9J 101
Brooklands App. RM1: Romf . . . 8B 110
Brooklands Av. SS9: Lgh S. . . . 9D 120
Brooklands Cl. RM7: Romf. . . . 8B 110
Brooklands Gdns. CO15: Jay . . . 6C 188
RM11: Horn . . . 1G 127
Brooklands La. RM7: Romf . . . 8B 110
(not continuous)
Brooklands Pk. SS15: Lain. . . . 9H 115
Brooklands Rd. CO11: Bran . . . 1H 163
RM7: Romf. . . . 8B 110
Brooklands Sq. SS8: Can I . . . 2E 150
Brooklands Wlk. CM2: Chelm. . . . 2B 72
Brook La. CM2: Chelm . . . 9C 60
CM2: Gall . . . 7E 72 (3A 34)
CM15: Dodd, Wy G . . . 7F 82
(not continuous)
CM21: Saw . . . 2J 51
IP11: Felix. . . . 1K 19
Brooklane Fld. CM18: H'low . . . 6G 54
Brook Lodge CO3: Colc. . . . 9K 165
RM7: Romf. . . . 8B 110
(off Medora Rd.)
Brooklyn Av. IG10: Lou. . . . 3L 91
Brooklyn Ct. CO12: Har. . . . 4L 209
(off Brooklyn Rd.)
IG10: Lou . . . 3L 91
Brooklyn Dr. SS6: Ray . . . 2K 119
Brooklyn M. CO12: Har . . . 4L 209
Brooklyn Rd. CO12: Har . . . 4L 209
Brookman's Av. RM16: Grays . . . 8M 145
Brookmans Cl. RM14: Upm . . . 2B 128
Brookmans Rd. CM4: Stock. . . . 7M 85
Brook Mead CM3: Gt Walt . . . 4G 57
SS15: Lain. . . . 8K 115
Brook Mdw. CO9: Sib H. . . . 6J 219
Brook Mdw. Cl. IG8: Wfd G . . . 3E 106
Brook Mdws. CO5: Tip . . . 6C 226
Brookmeadow Way
EN9: Wal A . . . 9H 63
Brook Pde. IG7: Chig . . . 9A 92
Brook Path IG10: Lou . . . 3L 91
Brook Pl. CO9: Hals . . . 5K 207
Brook Ri. IG7: Chig. . . . 9N 91
Brook Rd. CB2: New. . . . 1G 5
CM0: T'ham . . . 1H 225 (2E 36)
CM14: Brtwd. . . . 9C 96
CM16: Epp . . . 3F 78 (4J 31)
CM21: Saw . . . 3J 51
CM24: Stan M. . . . 3D 220
CO5: Tip, Tol K . . . 8F 226 (4A 26)
CO6: Aldh, M Tey . . . 1K 171 (6A 16)
CO6: Gt Tey, L Tey . . . 2E 170 (6K 15)
IG2: Ilf . . . 1D 124 (3H 39)
IG9: Buck H, Wfd G . . . 8G 90 (1E 38)
IG10: Lou . . . 3L 91
RM2: Romf. . . . 6D 110
SG8: Bass . . . 4B 4
SS6: Ray . . . 7J 119
SS7: Ben. . . . 5C 134
Brook Rd. Ind. Est. SS6: Ray. . . . 7K 119
Brookscroft E17: Lon . . . 7B 106
(off Forest Rd.)
Brookscroft Rd. E17: Lon . . . 5B 106
(not continuous)
Brooks Ho. CM14: Brtwd. . . . 7F 96
Brookside CM11: Bill. . . . 2L 99
CM19: H'low. . . . 6M 53
EN9: Wal A . . . 2E 76
EN11: Hod. . . . 5A 52
IG6: Ilf. . . . 3B 108
RM11: Horn. . . . 9J 111
SS5: Hock . . . 3E 120
SS8: Can I. . . . 9G 135
SS11: Runw . . . 6N 101
Brookside Av. SS3: Gt W . . . 4N 139
Brookside Cen. SS2: Temp I. . . . 1L 137
Brookside Cl. CM11: Bill. . . . 2L 99
CO2: Colc . . . 2B 174
Brookside Ind. Est. SS0: Wclf S. . . . 4J 137
Brooksies CB11: Dun E. . . . 7H 5
Brooks Malting CO11: Mist. . . . 4J 163

BROOK STREET
CM14 1C 112 (1D 40)
CO10 1G 9
Brook St. CM1: Chelm 8K 59
CM6: L Dun 9D 212 (1H 23)
CM7: Gt Bar 2C 202 (3J 13)
CM14: Brtwd 2A 112 (1D 40)
CO1: Colc 8B 166 (6F 17)
CO6: Coln E 3C 198 (3H 15)
CO7: Ded 1M 161 (2H 17)
CO7: Gt Bro 6D 168 (5K 17)
CO7: W'hoe 6H 175
CO10: Glem 1G 9
CO11: Mist 4J 163 (3A 18)
DA8: Eri 5A 152
DA17: Belv, Eri 1A 46
BROOK ST. INTERCHANGE 1A 112 (1D 40)
Brook Ter. CO9: Sib H 6K 219
Brookvale CO16: St O 9M 183 (4B 28)
Brook Vw. CM2: S'don 4K 73
CM6: Thax 7C 224
CM24: Stan M 4D 220
Brook Wlk. CM8: Wthm 7C 230
(not continuous)
SS0: Wclf S 4F 136
Brook Way IG7: Chig 9N 91
RM13: Rain 5F 142
Broome Cl. CM11: Bill 3M 99
Broome Gro. CO7: W'hoe 4H 175
Broome Pl. RM15: Ave 8A 144
Broome Rd. CM11: Bill 3M 99
Broome Way CO15: Jay 6D 188
Broom Farm Rd. CM22: Else 2K 199
BROOMFIELD 3K 59 (6A 24)
Broomfield CM8: Sil E 7K 217
CM20: H'low 9G 50
SS7: Had 2K 135
Broomfield Av. IG10: Lou 5M 91
N13: Lon 1A 38
SS6: Ray 4G 118
SS9: Lgh S 1E 136
Broomfield Cl. RM5: Col R 4B 110
Broomfield Ct. CM1: Broom 9H 57
Broomfield Cres. CO7: W'hoe 4H 175
Broomfield Grn. SS8: Can I 9F 134
Broomfield La. N13: Lon 1A 38
Broomfield Rd. CM1: Chelm 7J 59 (1A 34)
RM6: Chad H 2J 125
Broomfields CM22: Hat H 1E 210
SS13: Pits 9H 117
Broomfields Ct. SS13: Pits 9H 117
Broomfields M. SS13: Pits 9H 117
Broomfields Pl. SS13: Pits 9H 117
Broomhall Cl. CM1: Broom 1K 59
Broomhall Rd. CM1: Broom 1J 59
Broomhill Ct. IG8: Wfd G 3G 107
Broomhill Rd. IG3: Ilf 4F 124
IG8: Wfd G 3G 106 (2F 39)
(not continuous)
BROOMHILLS 4J 115 (2J 41)
Broomhills Chase CM12: L Bur 2H 115
Broomhills Ind. Est. CM7: Brain 6E 192
Broomhills Rd. CO5: W Mer 3D 228 (5F 27)
Broomhill Wlk. IG8: Wfd G 3F 106
Broom Rd. SS5: Hull 6L 103
Broomstick Hall Rd. EN9: Wal A 3E 76 (4E 30)
Broom Way CO5: Abb 9B 174
Broomways SS3: Gt W 3N 139
Broomwood Gdns. CM15: Pil H 5D 96
Broomwood La. CM4: Rams H 9B 86 (6A 34)
CM11: Rams H 9B 86
Broseley Gdns. RM3: Romf 1J 111
Broseley Rd. RM3: Romf 1J 111
Broton Dr. CO9: Hals 4K 207
(not continuous)
Brougham Cl. SS3: Gt W 2L 139
Brougham Glades CO3: S'way 1E 172
Broughton Cl. CO2: Colc 2K 173
Broughton Rd. CM3: S Fer 2L 103 (6F 35)
SS7: Had 4M 135
Browne Cl. CM14: Brtwd 7E 96
RM5: Col R 2N 109
Browning Av. SS2: Sth S 4M 137
Browning Cl. CO3: Colc 9G 164
E17: Lon 8C 106
RM5: Col R 4L 109
Browning Rd. CM7: Brain 8J 193
CM9: Mal 8C 214
CO11: Bran 1H 163
DA1: Dart 9K 153
E11: Lon 2F 122
E12: Lon 7M 123 (5G 39)
EN2: Enf 5B 30
Brownings Av. CM1: Chelm 6H 59
Browning Wlk. RM18: Til 7E 156
Brownlea Gdns. IG3: Ilf 4F 124
Brownlow Bend SS14: Bas 9E 116
Brownlow Cross SS14: Bas 9E 116
Brownlow Grn. SS14: Bas 9E 116
Brownlow Rd. E7: Lon 6G 123
N11: Lon 2A 38
Brownlows Cl. CM6: Lea R 4C 212
Browns Av. SS11: Runw 6N 101
Brownsea Dr. SS12: W'fd 2A 118
Brownsea Way CO3: Colc 2H 173
Brown's End Rd. CM6: Broxt 6D 12
Browns Rd. E17: Lon 7A 106
Brownswood Rd. N4: Lon 4A 38
BROXBOURNE 1D 30
Broxbourne Av. E18: Lon 8H 107
Broxbourne Rd. E7: Lon 5G 122
Broxbourne Station (Rail) 8A 52 (1D 30)
Broxburn Dr. RM15: S Ock 7D 144
Broxburn Pde. RM15: S Ock 7E 144
Broxhill Cen. RM3: Romf 1F 110
Broxhill Rd. RM4: Hav 9C 94 (1A 40)
BROXTED 5D 12
Broxted Dr. SS12: W'fd 1M 117
Broxted End SS12: W'fd 1M 117
BROXTED HILL 6E 12
Broxted M. CM13: Hut 5M 97
Broxted Rd. CM6: Gt Eas 6E 12
Bruce Av. RM12: Horn 4G 127
Bruce Gro. CM2: Chelm 3B 72
N17: Lon 2B 38
SS11: W'fd 1A 118
Bruce Grove Station (Rail) 2B 38
Bruce Rd. CM1: Writ 1K 71
Bruces Wharf Rd. RM17: Grays 4K 155
Bruff Cl. CO4: Colc 5M 165
Bruff Dr. CO14: Walt 7K 181
Bruges Cl. CO12: Har 6J 209
Bruges Rd. SS8: Can I 3J 151
Brummel Cl. DA7: Bexh 8A 152
Brundells Rd. CO7: Gt Bro 1F 176
Brundish SS13: Pits 1H 133
Brundon La. CO10: Sud 5J 9
Brunel Cl. RM1: Romf 8C 110
RM18: Til 8D 156
Brunel Ct. CO4: Colc 1C 166
Brunel Ct. Ind. Est. CO4: Colc 2C 166
Brunel Rd. CM7: Brain 7J 193
CO15: Clac S 5M 185
IG8: Wfd G 2M 107
SE16: Lon 7C 38
SS7: Thund 8D 118
SS9: Lgh S 8B 120
Brunel Way CM3: S Fer 1J 103
CO4: Colc 1C 166
Brunswick Av. RM14: Upm 2B 128
Brunswick Ct. *EN11: Hod 6A 52*
(off Rawdon Dr.)
RM14: Upm 2C 128
Brunswick Gdns. IG6: Ilf 4B 108
Brunswick Ho. Cut CO11: Mist 5M 163
Brunswick Pl. SS6: Ray 2H 119
Brunswick Rd. E10: Lon 3C 122
EN3: Enf 8A 76
SS1: Sth S 6B 138
Brunswick St. E17: Lon 9C 106
Brunwin Rd. CM77: Rayne 6B 192
Brunwins Cl. SS11: W'fd 8N 101
Brussels Cl. CO12: Har 6K 209
Brussum Rd. SS8: Can I 3K 151
Brust Rd. SS8: Can I 3K 151
Bruton Av. SS0: Wclf S 1F 136
Bruton St. W1: Lon 7A 38
Bryanstone M. CO3: S'way 1F 172
Bryanston Rd. RM18: Til 7E 156
Bryant Av. RM3: H Wood 5H 111 (2B 40)
SS1: Sth S 8C 138
Bryant Link CM2: Chelm 7C 60
Bryant Row RM3: Romf 8G 95
Bryant's La. CM9: Wdhm M 3K 75 (2F 35)
Bryant St. E15: Lon 9D 122
Bryce Rd. RM8: Dag 6H 125
Brydges Rd. E15: Lon 7D 122
Bryn Farm Cl. SS14: Bas 7D 116
Bryony Cl. CM8: Wthm 3A 230
IG10: Lou 3A 92
Buchanan Cl. RM15: Ave 8N 143
Buchanan Gdns. SS12: W'fd 2L 117
Buchanan Way CM3: Latch 8L 211
Buchan Cl. CM7: Brain 8J 193
Buckbean Path RM3: Romf 4G 111
Buckenhoe Rd. CB10: Saf W 2D 218
Buckeridge Way CM0: Brad S 7D 194
Buckerills SS13: Pits 1H 133
Buckfast Av. CO13: Walt 8G 180
Buckhatch La. CM3: E Han, Ret C 7C 88 (5D 34)
Buck Hill CM77: Bla N 9H 193 (1C 24)
Buckhurst Ct. *IG9: Buck H 8K 91*
(off Albert Rd.)
BUCKHURST HILL 8J 91 (1F 39)
Buckhurst Hill Ho. IG9: Buck H 8H 91
Buckhurst Hill Station (Tube) 8K 91 (1F 39)
Buckhurst Ter. IG9: Buck H 7K 91
Buckhurst Way IG9: Buck H 1K 107 (1F 39)
Buckingham Cl. RM11: Horn 1H 127
Buckingham Ct. CM2: Chelm 7A 60
CM6: Gt D 4M 203
Buckingham Dr. CO4: Colc 8E 166
Buckingham Hill Rd.
SS17: Ors, Stan H 7H 147 (7J 41)
Buckingham Palace 7A 38
Buckingham Rd. E10: Lon 5B 122
E11: Lon 9J 107
E15: Lon 7F 122
E18: Lon 5F 106
IG1: Ilf 4C 124
N22: Lon 2A 38
SS5: Hock 1C 120
SS15: Lain 7N 115
Buckingham Sq. SS11: W'fd 2A 118
BUCKLAND 2C 10
Buckland SS3: Shoe 5G 139
Buckland Ga. CM3: S Fer 2J 103
Buckland Rd. DA13: Ludd 7J 47
E10: Lon 4C 122
SG9: B'wy 1D 10
Bucklebury Heath CM3: S Fer 2K 103
Bucklers Ct. CM14: War 2F 112
Buckles La. RM15: S Ock 5F 144
Buckley Cl. DA1: Cray 7D 152
SS17: Corr 9A 132
Buckleys CM2: Gt Bad 3G 72
Buckleys Cl. CM8: W Bis 2K 229
Buckley's La. CO6: Cogg 6J 15
Bucknells Mead CM1: Hghwd 6C 70
Buckrell Rd. E4: Lon 8D 90
Bucks All. SG13: L Berk 1A 30
Buck's La. CO12: Gt Oak 9B 204
Buck Wlk. E17: Lon 8D 106
Buckwins Sq. SS13: Bas 6L 117
Buckwoods Rd. CM7: Brain 7H 193
Buckwyns CM12: Bill 2G 98
Buckwyns Chase CM12: Bill 2H 99
Buckwyns Ct. CM12: Bill 4H 99
Buddleia Ct. CO7: W'hoe 4G 175
Budna Rd. SS8: Can I 9F 134
Budoch Ct. IG3: Ilf 4F 124
Budoch Dr. IG3: Ilf 4F 124
Buffett Way CO4: Colc 9E 166
Buglers Ri. CM1: Writ 2K 71
Buick Av. CO15: Jay 6B 188
BUILDING END 7G 5
Building End Rd. SG8: Chris 7G 5
Bulbecks Wlk. CM3: S Fer 3K 103
Bulford Cl. CM77: Tye G 3D 194
Bulford La. CM77: Bla N 3C 194 (1D 24)
Bulford Mill La. CM77: Tye G 3C 194 (1D 24)
Bullace Cl. CO4: Colc 4D 166
Bullbanks Rd. DA17: Belv 2A 152
Bull Cl. RM16: Chaf H 9J 145
SS16: Van 1F 132
Bullen Wlk. CM2: Gall 7D 72
Buller Rd. CM3: N Fam 5H 35
IG11: Bark 9D 124
SS15: Lain 8K 115
Bull Farm Cotts. SS13: Pits 1L 133
Bullfields CB11: Newp 3L 215
CM21: Saw 1K 51
Bullfinch Cl. CO4: Colc 7F 166
CO12: Har 6G 209
Bullfinch Dr. CO9: Hals 5M 207
Bull Hill Rd. CO15: Clac S 8K 185
Bull La. CB11: Lang L, Lang U 1G 11
CM9: Mal 5C 214
CO5: Tip 7C 226
CO10: L Mel 3J 9
N18: Lon 1B 38
RM10: Dag 5N 125
SS5: Hock 1B 120
SS6: Ray 5K 119 (2F 43)
Bullocks La. CM22: Tak 1D 22
Bullock's La. SG13: Hart 6B 20
Bullock Wood Cl. CO4: Colc 3D 166
Bullring, The CM6: Thax 7B 224
BULLS CROSS 5C 30
Bull's Cross EN2: Enf 5C 30
Bulls Cross Ride EN2: Enf 5C 30
Bullsmill Rd. SG14: W'frd 4A 20
BULLSMOOR 5C 30
Bullsmoor La. EN1: Enf 5C 30
EN3: Enf 5C 30
Bullwood App. SS5: Hock 2A 120
Bullwood Hall La. SS5: Hock 2N 119
Bullwood Rd. SS5: Hock 2C 120
BULMER 1K 195 (5G 9)
Bulmer Rd. CO10: Sud 5J 9
Bulmer St. CO10: Bulm 2J 195 (6G 9)
BULMER TYE 4L 195 (6H 9)
Bulmer Wlk. RM13: Rain 2G 142
Bulow Av. SS8: Can I 2H 151
BULPHAN 6B 130 (5G 41)
Bulphan By-Pass
CM13: Bulp, W H'dn 3B 130 (4G 41)
RM14: Bulp 3B 130 (4H 41)
Bulphan Cl. SS12: W'fd 1M 117
Bulphan Vw. CM13: Dun 1G 130
Bulrush Cl. CM7: Brain 7K 193
Bulwark Rd. SS3: Shoe 6J 139
Bulwer Ct. E11: Lon 3D 122
Bulwer Ct. Rd. E11: Lon 3D 122
Bulwer Rd. E11: Lon 2D 122
BUMBLE'S GREEN 3H 63 (2F 31)
Bumbles Grn. La. EN9: Naze 4H 63
Bumfords La. CM3: Hat P 7E 24
Bumpstead Rd. CB9: H'hll 4J 7
Bunce's La. IG8: Wfd G 4F 106
Bundick's Hill CM1: Chelm 8H 59 (1K 33)
Bungalows, The E10: Lon 1C 122
IG6: Ilf 5D 108
Bung Row CM8: Gt Br 4H 25
Bunhill Row EC1: Lon 6B 38
Bunkers Hill DA14: Sidc 4A 46
Bunters Av. SS3: Shoe 8G 138
Buntingbridge Rd. IG2: Ilf 9C 108
Bunting Cl. CM2: Chelm 5C 72
BUNTINGFORD 4D 10
Buntingford Ct. CO2: Colc 5A 174
Buntingford Rd. SG11: Puck 7E 10
Bunting La. CM11: Bill 7L 99
BUNTING'S GREEN 3C 198 (3H 15)
Bunyan Rd. CM7: Brain 5G 193
(not continuous)
Burchell Rd. E10: Lon 3B 122
Burches SS14: Bas 6N 115
Burches Mead SS7: Thund 8G 118
Burches Rd. SS7: Thund 6E 118
Burchett Way RM6: Chad H 1L 125
Burchwall Cl. RM5: Col R 4A 110
Burden Way E11: Lon 4H 123
Burdett Av. SS0: Wclf S 6K 137
Burdett Rd. E3: Lon 6D 38
SS1: Sth S 8A 138
Burdetts Rd. RM9: Dag 1L 141
Burdun Cl. CM8: Wthm 7A 230
Bure RM18: E Til 1L 157
Bure Dr. CM8: Wthm 5A 230
Buren Av. SS8: Can I 2L 151
BURES 7L 195 (1A 16)
BURES GREEN 1A 16
Bures Rd. CO6: L Hork, W Ber 8D 158 (4C 16)
CO6: Wak C 3K 15
Bures Rd. CO6: Whi C 7F 198 (4J 15)
CO8: Bures, Nay 2B 16
CO8: Lmsh 1K 15
Bures Rd. CO10: Gt Cor 5K 9
Bures Station (Rail) 8K 195 (2A 16)
Burfield Cl. SS9: Lgh S 9E 120
Burfield Rd. SS9: Lgh S 9E 120
Burford Cl. IG6: Ilf 8B 108
RM8: Dag 5H 125
Burford Gdns. EN11: Rye P 4B 52
Burford M. EN11: Hod 4A 52
Burford Pl. EN11: Hod 4A 52
Burford St. EN11: Hod 5A 52 (7D 20)
Burgate Cl. CO16: Clac S 9E 184
DA1: Cray 8D 152
Burge Rd. E7: Lon 6K 123
Burges Cl. RM11: Horn 1K 127
SS1: Sth S 8G 138
Burges Ct. SS1: Sth S 6F 138
Burges Rd. E6: Lon 9L 123 (5G 39)
SS1: Sth S 8E 138
Burgess Av. SS17: Stan H 4N 147
Burgess Ct. CM15: Brtwd 7G 96
E6: Lon 9N 123
Burgess Fld. CM2: Chelm 7A 60
Burgess Rd. E6: Lon 9N 123
E15: Lon 6E 122
Burges Ter. SS1: Sth S 8D 138
Burghley Cl. CM77: Gt N 2B 204
Burghley Rd. E11: Lon 3E 122
RM16: Chaf H 1F 154
Burghley Way CM2: Chelm 2D 72
Burghstead Cl. CM12: Bill 7J 99
Burghstead Ct. *CM12: Bill 7J 99*
(off Burghstead Cl.)
Burgoyne Hatch CM20: H'low 2F 54
Burgundy Gdns. SS13: Pits 7J 117
Burland Rd. CM15: Brtwd 7G 96
RM5: Col R 3A 110
Burleigh Cl. CM12: Bill 3K 99
Burleigh Ct. SS0: Wclf S 6H 137
SS1: Sth S 6F 138
Burleigh Rd. EN1: Enf 6B 30
Burleigh Sq. SS1: Sth S 6F 138
Burlescoombe Cl. SS1: Sth S 6E 138
Burlescoombe Leas SS1: Sth S 5F 138
Burlescoombe Rd. SS1: Sth S 5E 138
Burley Cl. E4: Lon 2A 106
Burley Hill CM17: H'low 4J 55
Burlington Av. RM7: Romf 1N 125
Burlington Ct. SS13: Bas 7J 117
Burlington Gdns. RM6: Chad H 2K 125
SS5: Hull 7M 103
SS7: Had 3M 135
Burlington Pl. IG8: Wfd G 9H 91
Burlington Rd. CO3: Colc 9M 165
Burmanny Cl. CO15: Clac S 1G 189
Burnaby Rd. SS1: Sth S 7A 138
Burne Av. SS12: W'fd 1H 117
Burnell Ga. CM1: Chelm 4B 60
Burnells Way CM24: Stan M 2D 220
Burnell Wlk. CM13: Gt War 3F 112
Burnett Pk. CM19: H'low 8A 54
Burnett Rd. DA8: Eri 4H 153
IG6: Ilf 4A 108
Burney Dr. IG10: Lou 1A 92
(not continuous)
Burnham Av. CM3: Cold N 8L 197
Burnham Bus. Pk. CM0: Bur C 2C 196
Burnham Cl. CO14: Walt 6L 181
Burnham Ct. CO15: Clac S 4G 189
Burnham Cres. DA1: Dart 9G 153
E11: Lon 1J 107
BURNHAM-ON-CROUCH 3D 196 (6C 36)
Burnham-on-Crouch & District Mus.
4D 196 (7C 36)
Burnham-on-Crouch Station (Rail)
3D 196 (6C 36)
Burnham Riverside Pk. 3C 196
Burnham Rd. CM0: S'min 4C 222 (5C 36)
CM1: Chelm 6M 59
CM3: Alth 1C 190 (5A 36)
CM3: Haz 4K 75 (3G 35)
CM3: Latch 8M 211 (4K 35)
CM3: S Fer 5C 102 (6F 35)
CM9: Mun 6H 211 (4J 35)
CM9: Wdhm M 4K 75 (2F 35)
DA1: Dart 9G 153 (3B 46)
RM7: Romf 7B 110
RM9: Dag 9G 124
SS5: Hull 6L 103
SS9: Lgh S 5B 136
SS11: Bat, Ret C, S Fer 5C 102 (7D 34)
Burnham Trad. Est. DA1: Dart 9H 153
Burnley Rd. RM20: W Thur 6C 154
Burnsall Cl. CB11: Saf W 5E 218
Burns Av. CO3: Colc 9G 164
RM6: Chad H 2H 125
SS13: Pits 1J 133
Burns Cl. CM9: Mal 7C 214
CM11: Bill 5K 99
DA8: Eri 6D 152
E17: Lon 8C 106
Burns Cres. CM2: Chelm 2C 72
BURN'S GREEN 7A 10
Burns Grn. CM9: Gt Tot 3M 229
Burnside CM21: Saw 2J 51
SS8: Can I 9G 135
Burnside Av. E4: Lon 3A 106
Burnside Cres. CM1: Chelm 4K 59
Burnside Ind. Est. IG6: Ilf 2G 108
Burnside Rd. CM6: Fels 7N 199
RM8: Dag 4K 125
Burnside Ter. CM17: H'low 9L 51
Burns Pl. RM18: Til 6D 156

Burns Way CM13: Hut 5N 97
Burnt Dick Hill CO4: Boxt. 1K 159 (2E 16)
BURNT HEATH 3A 168 (5J 17)
Burnthouse La.
CM4: Ing, Mount 8B 84 (5G 33)
Burnthouse Rd. CO6: Gt Tey 5J 15
Burnt Mill CM20: H'low 9C 50
(Edinburgh Way)
CM20: H'low 1B 54
(Elizabeth Way)
Burnt Mill Cl. CM20: H'low 9B 50
Burnt Mill Ind. Est.
CM20: H'low 9B 50
Burnt Mill La. CM20: H'low 9B 50 (6H 21)
BURNT MILLS 5K 117 (2C 42)
Burnt Mills Rd. SS12: N Ben 7H 117
SS13: Bas 7H 117 (3B 42)
Burnt Oak Lodge SS7: Lgh S 4N 135
Burntwood CM14: Brtwd 9F 96
Burntwood Av. RM11: Horn 1H 127
Burntwood Cl. CM12: Bill 6H 99
CM13: W H'dn 1N 129
Burnway RM11: Horn 2J 127
Burr Cl. CO12: R'sy 6E 208
SS16: Lang H 1G 131
Burrell Towers E10: Lon 2A 122
Burr Hill Chase SS2: Sth S, Wclf S 3K 137
Burrow Cl. IG7: Chig 2E 108
Burrow Grn. IG7: Chig 2E 108
Burrow Rd. IG7: Chig 2E 108
Burrows Chase EN9: Enf 5D 76
Burrows Cl. CO11: Law 4G 163
CO16: Clac S 7H 185
Burrow's Rd. CO6: E Col 7C 198
Burrows Way SS6: Ray 6J 119
Burrs Rd. CO15: Clac S 8K 185 (3E 28)
BURRSVILLE PARK 6L 185 (3E 28)
Burr's Way SS17: Corr 1C 148
Burrswood Pl. CM9: Hey B 8F 214
Burses Way CM13: Hut 6L 97
Burslem Av. IG6: Ilf 3F 108
Burstall Cl. CO16: Clac S 9F 184
Burstead Dr. CM11: Bill 9M 99
Burton Cl. SS17: Corr 9A 132
Burton Dr. EN3: Enf 7A 76
BURTON END
CM24 5H 221 (7B 12)
CB1 1G 7
Burton End CB1: W W'ck 1G 7
CB9: H'hll 3H 7
Burton Grn. CB9: Wthfld 1H 7
Burton La. EN7: G Oak 3B 30
Burton Pl. CM2: Chelm 7A 60
Burton Rd. E18: Lon 7H 107
IG10: Lou 3B 92
BURTON'S GREEN 5G 15
Burton's Grn. Rd. CO9: G'std G 5G 15
Burtons Mill CM21: Saw 1L 51
(Leat Cl.)
CM21: Saw 1L 51
(Mill La.)
Burwell Av. SS8: Can I 9F 134
Burwood Ct. CM2: Chelm 1D 72
Burwood Gdns. RM13: Rain 3D 142
Bury Chase CM6: Fels 8J 199
Bury Cl. CO1: Colc 7A 166
CO6: M Tey 2H 171
Bury Farm La. CM11: Cray H 4E 116
Bury Flds. CM6: Fels 8H 199
Bury Gdns. CB11: Elm 6J 5
BURY GREEN
EN7 4C 30
SG11 1H 21
Bury Grn. Rd. EN7: Chesh 3C 30
(not continuous)
Bury La. CB11: Elm 6J 5
CM3: Gt Walt 4F 56 (5K 23)
CM3: Hat P 2K 61 (6E 24)
(not continuous)
CM16: Epp 7C 64 (3H 31)
SG8: Chris 6H 5
Bury Lodge La.
CM24: Bur E, Stan Apt,
Stan M 5F 220 (7B 12)
Bury Rd. CB9: Thurl 1K 7
CM3: Ples 3A 56 (4H 23)
CM16: Epp 1D 78
CM17: H'low 8H 51
CO10: Lav 1K 9
E4: Lon 2D 90 (6E 30)
RM10: Dag 7N 125
Buryside Cl. IG2: Ilf 8E 108
Bury St. N9: Lon 7B 30
Bury, The CO16: St O 9M 183 (4B 28)
Bury Water La. CB11: Newp 2J 215 (1A 12)
Burywoods CO4: Colc 4J 165
Bush Cl. IG2: Ilf 9C 108
Bushell Way CO13: Walt. 8H 181
Bush Elms Rd. RM11: Horn 2E 126
BUSH END 2C 22
Bushey Av. E18: Lon 7F 106
Bushey Cl. CM3: S Fer 1L 103
E4: Lon 9C 90
Bushey Ct. *DA8: Eri.* *6E 152*
(off Hazel Rd.)
Bushey Cft. CM18: H'low 5D 54
Bushey Lea CM5: Chip 8L 67
CM7: Brain 5M 193
Bush Fair CM18: H'low 5E 54
Bushfields IG10: Lou 4N 91
Bushgrove Rd. RM8: Dag 6J 125
Bush Hall Rd. CM12: Bill 3K 99
Bush Hill N21: Lon 7B 30
BUSH HILL PARK 7B 30
Bush Hill Park Station (Rail) 7B 30
Bush Hill Rd. N21: Lon 7B 30
Bush Ho. *CM18: H'low* *5E 54*
(off Bush Fair)
Bush Rd. CB10: L Sam 4H 205 (1G 13)
E11: Lon 2F 122 (4E 38)
IG9: Buck H 1K 107
ME2: Cux 7K 47
Bushway RM8: Dag 6J 125
Bushwood E11: Lon 3F 122
Bushy Mead SS15: Lain 7K 115
Business Cen., The RM3: Romf 4H 111
BUSTARD GREEN 4H 13
Bustard Grn. Rd. CM6: Lndsl 5H 13
Busway SS13: Bas 7J 117
Butcher Row CB10: Saf W 4C 218
E1: Lon 7C 38
Butchers Hill CB10: I'tn 6A 202 (4K 5)
Butchers La. CO14: Walt 7L 181
(not continuous)
TN15: Fawk 7E 46
Butchers Pasture CM6: L Eas 6F 13
Bute Rd. IG6: Ilf 9A 108
Butler Cl. CB11: Saf W 4D 218
Butler Ct. *RM8: Dag.* *4M 125*
(off Gosfield Rd.)
Butler Rd. CO9: Hals 4J 207
RM8: Dag 6G 124
Butlers Cl. CM1: Broom 1K 59
Butlers Dr. E4: Lon 8C 76
Butlers Gro. SS16: Lang H 3K 131
Butler's Hall La. CM23: Thor 2J 21
Butlers La. CB10: Saf W 5D 6
CO11: Wrab 3D 18
Butlers Way CO9: Gt Yel 3D 206
Butler Wlk. RM17: Grays 2N 155
Butneys SS14: Bas 8C 116
Buttell Cl. RM17: Grays 3N 155
Butterbur Chase CM3: S Fer 2J 103
Buttercross La. CM16: Epp 9F 64
Buttercup Cl. CM12: Bill 4J 99
RM3: H Wood 5H 111
Buttercup Wlk. CM8: Wthm 3B 230
Buttercup Way CM0: S'min 3C 222
Butterfield Chase CM3: Latch 7L 211
Butterfield Rd. CM3: Bore 3F 60
Butterfields E17: Lon 9C 106
Butteridges Cl. RM9: Dag 1L 141
Buttermere CM77: Gt N 1C 204
Buttermere Cl. E15: Lon 6D 122
Buttersweet Ri. CM21: Saw 3K 51
Butterworth Gdns. IG8: Wfd G 3G 107
Butterys SS1: Sth S 6C 138
Buttfield Cl. RM10: Dag 8N 125
Butt La. CM9: Mal 6C 214
CM23: Man 5J 11
Buttleys La. CM6: L Can 1F 23
Buttondene Cres. EN10: Brox 1B 62
Button Rd. RM17: Grays 2J 155
Button's Hill CM3: Alth, May 1E 190
Button St. BR8: Swan 6B 46
Butt Rd. CO2: Colc 1L 173
CO3: Colc 1L 173 (6E 16)
CO6: Stok 1E 16
BUTTSBURY 7H 85 (5J 33)
Buttsbury CM4: Ing 9F 84 (6H 33)
Buttsbury Rd. IG1: Ilf 7B 124
Buttsbury Ter. CM4: Stock 7N 85
BUTT'S GREEN 7N 73 (3D 34)
Butts Grn. CB11: Clav 2H 11
Butt's Grn. Rd. CM2: S'don 6N 73 (3C 34)
Butts Grn. Rd. RM11: Horn 1H 127 (3B 40)
Butts La. CM3: Dan 3E 74 (2E 34)
CM13: L War 6J 113
SS17: Stan H 4K 147 (7K 41)
Butts Paddock SS4: Cwdn 1M 105
Butts Rd. SS3: Shoe 5N 139
SS17: Stan H 4L 147
Butts Way CM2: Chelm 7N 71
Buxey Cl. CO5: W Mer 2B 228
Buxton Av. SS9: Lgh S 3N 135
Buxton Cl. IG8: Wfd G 3K 107
SS9: Lgh S 3N 135
Buxton Ct. E11: Lon 2F 122
Buxton Dr. E11: Lon 8E 106
Buxton Ho. E11: Lon 8E 106
Buxton Link SS15: Lain 9G 115 (3J 41)
Buxton Rd. CM16: They B 6D 78
CO2: Colc 3A 174
CO6: Cogg 3K 197
DA8: Eri 5B 152
E4: Lon 6D 90
E15: Lon 7E 122
EN9: Wal A 2G 77
IG2: Ilf 1D 124
RM16: Grays 9A 146
Buxton Sq. SS9: Lgh S 3N 135
Buyl Av. SS8: Can I 9H 135
Buzzard Creek Ind. Est. IG11: Bark 5F 140
Byfield SS9: Lgh S 8E 120
Byfield Ct. CM13: W H'dn 1M 129
Byfletts SS16: Van 2G 132
Byford Cl. E15: Lon 9E 122
SS6: Ray 4L 119
Bylam La. IP9: Holb 1E 18
Byng Cl. CO16: T Sok 5M 179
Byng Ct. CO2: Colc 5A 174
Byng Cres. CO16: T Sok 5M 179
Byng Gdns. CM7: Brain 4L 193
Bynghams CM19: H'low 5M 53
By-Pass Rd. CO16: St O 8M 183 (3B 28)
SS17: Horn H 3J 147
Byrd Ct. SS15: Lain 7L 115
Byrd Mead CM15: Ston M 3D 82
Byrd's Farm La. CB10: Saf W 2D 218
(not continuous)
Byrd Way SS17: Stan H 2L 147
Byrne Dr. SS2: Sth S 1K 137
By Rd. CO10: Pos 1B 8
Byron Av. CO3: Colc 8G 164
E12: Lon 8L 123
E18: Lon 7F 106
SS2: Sth S 4N 137
Byron Cl. CM7: Brain 8J 193
SE28: Lon 8H 141
SS8: Can I 1J 151
Byron Ct. *E11: Lon* *8H 107*
(off Makepeace Rd.)
SS15: Lain 8K 115
Byron Dr. CM8: W Bis 2K 229
Byron Gdns. RM18: Til 6E 156
Byron Mans. RM14: Upm 5N 127
Byron Rd. CM2: Chelm 9M 59
CM13: Hut 6N 97
DA1: Dart 9M 153
E10: Lon 3B 122
E17: Lon 7A 106
Byron Way RM3: Romf 5G 110
Byron Works SS11: W'fd 9N 101
Bysouth Cl. IG5: Ilf 5A 108
Bywater Rd. CM3: S Fer 2J 103
Byway E11: Lon 9J 107

C

Cabbage Hall La. CO2: Colc 6B 174
Cabborns Cres. SS17: Stan H 5M 147
Cabinet Way SS9: Lgh S 9B 120
Cables Cl. DA17: Eri 1A 152
Cable St. E1: Lon 7C 38
Cadenhouse M. CO3: S'way 8F 164
Cadiz Ct. RM10: Dag 9B 126
Cadiz Rd. RM10: Dag 9A 126
Cadmore La. EN8: Chesh, Turn 3C 30
Cadogan Av. CM13: W H'dn 1N 129
Cadogan Gdns. E18: Lon 7H 107
Cadogan Ho. IG8: Ilf 4A 108
Cadogan Ter. E9: Lon 5D 38
SS13: Pits 8K 117
Caernarvon Cl. RM11: Horn 3L 127
SS5: Hock 1C 120
Caernarvon Dr. IG5: Ilf 5N 107
Cage End CM22: Hat O 8D 206 (3C 22)
Cage End Cl. CM22: Hat O 8D 206
Cagefield Rd. SS4: Stam 2A 44
Cage La. CO4: Boxt 3B 160 (2F 17)
Cairns Av. IG8: Wfd G 3L 107
Cairns Rd. CO2: Colc 4A 174
Cairo Rd. E17: Lon 8A 106
Caister Dr. SS13: Pits 9J 117
Caladonia La. SS12: W'fd 2M 117
Calamint Rd. CM8: Wthm 4A 230
Calbourne Av. RM12: Horn 7F 126
Calcott Cl. CM14: Brtwd 7E 96
Calcutta Rd. RM18: Til 7B 156 (2G 47)
Caldbeck EN9: Wal A 4D 76
(not continuous)
Caldbeck Way CM77: Gt N 2C 204
Calder RM18: E Til 2L 157
Calderon Rd. E11: Lon 6C 122
Caldwell Rd. SS17: Stan H 4K 147
Caledonia Ct. *IG11: Bark* *2H 141*
(off Keel Cl.)
Caledonian Cl. IG3: Ilf 3G 124
Caledonian Rd. N1: Lon 6A 38
N7: Lon 5A 38
Caledonian Road & Barnsbury Station (Rail)
5A 38
Caledonian Road Station (Tube) 5A 38
Caledon Rd. E6: Lon 9M 123
CALFORD GREEN 3A 8
California Cl. CO4: Colc 3B 166
California Rd. CO11: Mist 4M 163
Callan Gro. RM15: S Ock 7E 144
Callenders Cotts. DA17: Eri 9B 142
Callis St. CO10: Clare 3D 8
Callowood Cft. CM3: Pur 8K 215
Calmore Cl. RM12: Horn 7G 127
Calmpatch CM0: Bur C 4E 196
Calne Av. IG5: Ilf 5A 108
Calshot Av. RM16: Chaf H 9J 145
Calthorpe St. WC1: Lon 6A 38
Calverley Cres. RM10: Dag 4M 125
Calvert Dr. SS13: Bas 6K 117
Calves La. CO11: L Bro 2G 169
Calvinia Cl. SS15: Bas 5A 116
Camberton Rd. CM7: Brain 2G 193
Cambeys Rd. RM10: Dag 7N 125
Camborne Av. RM3: Romf 4J 111
Camborne Cl. CM1: Chelm 7N 59
Camborne Way RM3: Romf 4J 111
Cambrai Rd. CO2: Colc 2L 173
Cambria Cl. CO11: Mist 5N 163
SS8: Can I 2C 150
Cambria Ho. *DA8: Eri* *5C 152*
(off Larner Rd.)
Cambrian Av. IG2: Ilf 9D 108
Cambrian Rd. E10: Lon 2A 122
Cambridge Av. CO9: Sib H 7K 219
RM2: Romf 7G 111
Cambridge Cl. CM4: Stock 7M 85
SS16: Lang H 1H 131
Cambridge Ct. CO15: Clac S 9J 185
SS1: Sth S 7L 137
Cambridge Gdns.
RM16: Grays 2C 156
SS4: R'fd 2H 121
Cambridge Heath Rd. E2: Lon 6C 38
E1: Lon 6C 38
Cambridge Heath Station (Rail) 6C 38
Cambridge Pk. E11: Lon 2G 122 (4F 39)
Cambridge Rd. CB1: Abgtn 1B 6
CB2: Saws 1J 5
CB11: L'bry 1B 218 (6A 6)
CB11: Newp 1L 215 (1B 12)
CB11: Quen 4C 216 (4A 12)
CM20: H'low 6H 51 (5J 21)
CM21: Saw 1K 51 (4K 21)
CM22: Ugley 4C 216
CM24: Stan M 2D 220 (6A 12)
CO3: Colc 1K 173
CO13: Frin S 9K 181
CO15: Clac S 9J 185
E4: Lon 7D 90
E11: Lon 1F 122
IG3: Ilf 3D 124
IG11: Bark 9B 124
SG8: B'wy, Bar 7E 4
(not continuous)
SG8: Fow, Foxt, New, Thri 2G 5
SG8: Mel 3E 4
SG8: Orw, Wimp 1B 4
SG11: Puck 7E 10
SS0: Sth S, Wclf S 7K 137 (5J 43)
SS1: Wclf S 7K 137
SS8: Can I 2F 150
CAMBRIDGE TOWN 8H 139
Cambridge Wlk. CO3: Colc 1L 173
Cambridge Way CO8: Bures 8L 195
Camden Cl. RM16: Grays 2D 156
Camden High St. NW1: Lon 6A 38
Camden Pk. Rd. NW1: Lon 5A 38
Camden Rd. E11: Lon 1H 123
NW1: Lon 5A 38
RM16: Chaf H 1H 155
Camden Road Station (Rail) 5A 38
Camden St. NW1: Lon 6A 38
CAMDEN TOWN 6A 38
Camden Town Station (Tube) 5A 38
Camelford Ho. *RM3: Romf* *1J 111*
(off Chudleigh Rd.)
Camellia Av. CO16: Clac S 9G 184
Camellia Cl. CM1: Chelm 5A 60
RM3: H Wood 5J 111
Camellia Ct. CO4: Colc 7D 166
Camellia Cres. CO16: Clac S 8G 184
Camelot Cl. CM1: Chelm 6H 59
SE28: Lon 9C 140
Camelot Gdns. SS13: Bas 7K 117
CAMER 7H 47
Cameron Cl. CM4: Ing 6D 84
CM7: Brain 9H 191
CM14: War 1G 112
SS9: Lgh S 4B 136
SS17: Stan H 8A 132
Cameron Pl. SS12: W'fd 2M 117
Cameron Rd. IG3: Ilf 3D 124 (4H 39)
Camer Pk. Rd. DA13: Meop 7H 47
Camer Rd.
DA13: Meop, Sole S 7H 47
Cam Grn. RM15: S Ock 6E 144
Camoise Cl. CO9: Top 7B 8
Camomile Dr. SS11: W'fd 8M 101
Camomile Rd. RM7: Rush G 4B 126
Camomile Way CO4: Colc 5K 165
Campbell Av. IG6: Ilf 8A 108
Campbell Cl. CM2: Chelm 3B 72
CM17: H'low 5G 55
RM1: Romf 3C 110
SS12: W'fd 2L 117
Campbell Ct. CO3: Colc 9L 165
Campbell Dr. CO4: Colc 5E 166
Campbell Rd. CM8: Wthm 2C 230
E15: Lon 6F 122
E3: Lon 6D 38
Campden Cres. RM8: Dag 6G 125
Camperdown Rd. SS8: Can I 9J 135
(not continuous)
Camper M. SS1: Sth S 8B 138
Campernell Cl. CO7: B'sea 5E 182
Camper Rd. SS1: Sth S 8B 138
Campfield Rd. SS3: Shoe 8J 139 (5B 44)
Camp Folley Nth. CO2: Colc 9N 165
Camp Folley Sth. CO2: Colc 1A 174
Campion Cl. RM7: Rush G 4B 126
Campion Ct. RM17: Grays 4N 155
Campion Gdns. IG8: Wfd G 2G 107
Campion La. CO6: Nay 1C 16
Campion Pl. SE28: Lon 8F 140
Campion Rd. CO2: Colc 1A 174
Campions IG10: Lou 8N 77
Campions Hill CO6: Nay 1C 16
Campions, The CM24: Stan M 1D 220
SS1: Sth S 6G 139
Campion Way CM8: Wthm 3B 230
Cample La. RM15: S Ock 7D 144
Camp Rd. CO7: Gt Bro 8E 168
CAMPS END 4F 7
Campsey Gdns. RM9: Dag 9G 125
Campsey Rd. RM9: Dag 9G 124
Camps Rd. CB1: Bart 3E 6
CB9: Cas C, Hel B 4H 7
Camsix Chase CM3: Har E 3K 23
Camulodunum Way CO2: Colc 5K 173
Camulus Cl. CM7: Brain 6J 193
CO2: Colc, King 4H 173
Cam Way CM8: Wthm 5A 230
Canada Farm Rd. DA2: Dart 6E 46
DA3: Fawk 6E 46
DA4: S Dar 6E 46
Canada Rd. DA8: Eri 5F 152
Canada Water Station (Tube) 7C 38
Canal Rd. DA12: Grav 3H 47
ME3: High 4K 47

Canalside SE28: Lon 7J **141**
Canary Wharf Station (DLR, Tube) 7D 38
Canberra Cl. CM1: Chelm 6G 58
CO2: Colc 5A 174
RM10: Dag 1B 142
RM12: Horn 6G 127
Canberra Cres. RM10: Dag 9B 126
Canberra Sq. RM18: Til 7C 156
Can Bri. Way CM2: Chelm 1D 72
Cander Way RM15: S Ock 7E 144
Candlemakers, The SS2: Temp I 1M 137
Candlet Rd. IP11: T Mary 1K 19
Candover Rd. RM12: Horn 3F 126
Candy Ter. *SS1: Sth S* *7A 138*
(off Prospect Cl.)
Candytuft Rd. CM1: Chelm 5A 60
Cane Hill RM3: H Wood 6H 111
Caneland Ct. EN9: Wal A 4F 76
Canes La. CM17: H'wd, Thorn 9J 55 (1K 31)
Canesmill Ct. CM7: Brain 3J 193
CANEWDON 1N 105 (7K 35)
Canewdon Cl. SS11: W'fd 6L 101
Canewdon Gdns. SS11: W'fd 6L 101
Canewdon Hall Cl. SS4: Cwdn 1M 105
Canewdon Rd. SS0: Wclf S 6J 137
SS4: Cwdn, R'fd 8H 105 (1J 43)
Canewdon Vw. Rd. SS4: R'fd 1J 121
(not continuous)
Canfield Rd.
CM6: Gt Can, High R 3E 22
IG8: Wfd G 4L 107
RM13: Rain 1D 142
Canford Av. SS12: W'fd 8G 101
Canford Cl. CM2: Gt Bad 3F 72
Canhams Rd. CO10: Gt Cor 5K 9
Canna Gdns. SS12: W'fd 2N 117
Canney Rd. CM0: Stpl 2B 36
CANN HALL 6E 122 (4E 38)
Cann Hall Rd. E11: Lon 6E 122 (5E 38)
Canning St. CO12: Har 2M 209
Cannington Rd. RM9: Dag 8H 125
CANNING TOWN 7F 39
CANNING TOWN 7E 38
Canning Town Station (Rail, DLR & Tube) 7E 38
Cannon Circ. CM7: Weth 2A 14
Cannon Cl. SS17: Stan H 3A 148
Cannon Hill N14: Lon 1A 38
Cannon Leys CM2: Gall 7D 72
Cannon M. EN9: Wal A 3B 76
Cannon Retail Pk. SE28: Lon 7F 140
Cannon Rd. CO1: Colc 9B 166
Cannons Cl. CO2: Colc 2L 173
CANNON'S GREEN 1C 68 (1D 32)
Cannons Grn. CM5: Fy'd 1B 68
Cannons La. CM5: Fy'd 1B 68 (1D 32)
CM22: Hat O 8D 206 (3C 22)
Cannons Mead CM15: Ston M 3D 82
CM24: Stan M 2C 220
Cannons, The CO2: Colc 2K 173
Cannon St. CO1: Colc 9B 166
EC4: Lon 7B 38
Cannon St. Rd. E1: Lon 7C 38
Cannon Street Station (Rail & Tube) 7B 38
Cannons Vs. CM22: Hat O 8D 206
Canon Av. RM6: Chad H 9H 109
CANONBURY 5B 38
Canonbury Pk. Nth. N1: Lon 5B 38
Canonbury Rd. N1: Lon 5A 38
Canonbury Station (Rail) 5B 38
Canon Ct. SS13: Bas 5H 117
Canonium M. CO5: K'dn 3K 211
Canons Brook CM19: H'low 3N 53
Canons Cl. CM3: Bick 9E 74
Canons Ct. E15: Lon 6E 122
Canons Ga. CM20: H'low 2N 53
Canonsleigh Cres. SS9: Lgh S 5D 136
Canonsleigh Rd. RM9: Dag 9G 125
Canons Rdbt. CM19: H'low 3M 53
Canopy La. CM17: H'low 2H 55
Cansey La. CO11: Brad 4B 18
Canterbury Av. IG1: Ilf 2L 123
RM14: Upm 3C 128
SS2: Sth S 3B 138
Canterbury Cl. IG7: Chig 9E 92
SS6: Ray 2J 119
SS14: Bas 7G 116
Canterbury Ct. CM15: Pil H 4C 96
Canterbury Grange CM7: Brain 9H 191
Canterbury Ho. DA8: Eri 5D 152
IG11: Bark *9F 124*
(off Margaret Bondfield Av.)
Canterbury Pde. RM15: S Ock 3F 144
Canterbury Pl. RM17: Grays 3N 155
Canterbury Rd. CO2: Colc 1A 174
CO15: Hol S 8B 186
E10: Lon 2C 122
Canterbury Way CM1: Chelm 7G 59
CM13: Gt War 3F 112
RM19: W Thur 5B 154
RM20: W Thur 5B 154
Canters Mdw. Ct. CO15: Clac S 8L 185
Canters, The SS7: Thund 1H 135
Cantley Gdns. IG2: Ilf 1B 124
Cant Way CM7: Brain 7L 193
Canuden Rd. CM1: Chelm 1N 71
Canute Av. CM7: Weth 2A 14
Canute Cl. SS4: Cwdn 1N 105
CANVEY ISLAND 2E 150 (6E 42)
Canvey Island F.C. (Park Lane) 3M 151
Canvey Rd. SS8: Can I 1D 150 (6D 42)
SS9: Lgh S 5A 136
SS13: Pits 9N 117
CANVEY VILLAGE 2C 150 (6E 42)
Canvey Wlk. CM1: Chelm 5N 59
Canvey Way SS7: Ben, Can I, Pits 3A 134
SS8: Can I 4A 134 (4D 42)
SS13: Ben 3A 134 (4D 42)
Canvey Way SS16: Pits 4A 134 (4D 42)
Canwick Gro. CO2: Colc 2C 174
Capadocia St. SS1: Sth S 8C 138
Cape Cl. CO3: Colc 1G 173
IG11: Bark 9A 124
Capel Cl. CM1: Chelm 4K 59
CM77: Rayne 6B 192
SS17: Stan H 3N 147
Capel Gdns. IG3: Bark, Ilf 6E 124
Capel Pk. CO13: Walt 7H 181
Capel Rd. CM77: Rayne 6B 192
(not continuous)
CO3: Colc 1K 173
E7: Lon 6H 123 (5F 39)
E12: Lon 6H 123 (5F 39)
IP9: B'ley 1A 18
Capelston SS15: Lain 9A 116
Capel Ter. SS1: Sth S 7M 137 (5K 43)
Caper La. CO2: B'ch 8C 172 (2B 26)
(not continuous)
Capital Pl. *CM19: H'low* *4N 53*
(off Lovet Rd.)
Capitol Ind. Cen. SS11: W'fd 2A 118
Capon Cl. CM14: Brtwd 7E 96
Capons La. CM3: Dan 4G 74 (2E 34)
Cappell La. SG12: Stan A 5E 20
Cap Pillar Cl. CO7: W'hoe 4H 175
Capricorn Cen. RM8: Dag 2L 125
SS14: Bas 6G 116
Capstan Cen. Ind. Est. RM18: Til 5N 155
Capstan Cl. RM6: Chad H 1G 125
Capstan Ct. DA2: Dart 9N 153
Capstan Pl. CO4: Colc 1D 174
Captains Rd. CO5: W Mer 3B 228
Captains Wood Rd.
CM9: Gt Tot, Mal, W Bis 4M 229 (6H 25)
Capworth St. E10: Lon 3A 122 (4D 38)
Caracalla Way CO4: Colc 1A 166
Caradon Cl. E11: Lon 3E 122
Caravel Cl. RM16: Chaf H 1J 155
Carbis Cl. E4: Lon 7D 90
Carbone Hill EN6: N'thaw 3A 30
Carbury Cl. RM12: Horn 8G 127
Cardigan Av. SS0: Wclf S 3H 137
Cardigan Gdns. IG3: Ilf 4F 124
Cardigan Ho. *RM3: Romf* *2H 111*
(off Bridgwater Wlk.)
Cardinal Cl. CO4: Colc 8F 166
Cardinal Dr. IG6: Ilf 3B 108
Cardinal Rd. RM16: Chaf H 1H 155
CARDINAL'S GREEN 2F 7
Cardinal Way RM13: Rain 2H 143
Card's Rd. CM2: S'don 4K 73
Carew Cl. RM16: Chaf H 1H 155
Carey Rd. RM9: Dag 6K 125
Carfax Rd. RM12: Horn 6D 126
Carisbrook Cl. CM16: Epp 1F 78
Carisbrooke Av. CO15: Clac S 5L 185
Carisbrooke Cl. RM11: Horn 3L 127
SS13: Pits 9J 117
Carisbrooke Dr. CM3: S Fer 1J 103
SS17: Corr 1B 148
Carisbrooke Rd. CM15: Pil H 5E 96
SS0: Wclf S 5K 137
Carleton Ct. CO5: Rhdge 6E 174
Carlina Gdns. IG8: Wfd G 2H 107
Carlingford Dr. SS0: Wclf S 3H 137
Carlisle Cl. CO1: Colc 7A 166
Carlisle Gdns. IG1: Ilf 1L 123
Carlisle Rd. E10: Lon 3A 122
RM1: Romf 9E 110
Carlisle Way SS13: Pits 9J 117
Carlton Av. SS0: Wclf S 2G 137 (4J 43)
Carlton Cl. CO9: Gt Yel 2D 206
RM14: Upm 4M 127
Carlton Ct. IG6: Ilf 7C 108
Carlton Dr. IG6: Ilf 7C 108
SS7: Had 2J 135
SS9: Lgh S 5E 136
Carlton Ho. IG10: Lou 4K 91
Carlton Rd. CO15: Clac S 9M 185
DA8: Eri 4A 152 (2A 46)
E11: Lon 3F 122
E12: Lon 6K 123
RM2: Romf 9D 110
RM16: Grays 9B 146
SS11: W'fd 6K 101
SS13: Pits 7M 117
Carlton Ter. E11: 9H 107
(not continuous)
Carlton Ter. St. E7: Lon 9J 123
Carlyle Gdns. CM12: Bill 3H 99
SS12: W'fd 2M 117
Carlyle Rd. E12: Lon 6L 123
SE28: Lon 7G 141 (7J 39)
Carmania Cl. SS3: Shoe 5K 139
Carmelite Way CM9: Mal 6C 214
Carmel St. CB10: Gt Che 8D 202 (4A 6)
Carmen St. CB10: Gt Che 7D 202 (4A 6)
Carnach Grn. RM15: S Ock 7D 144
Carnanton Rd. E17: Lon 5D 106
Carnarvon Rd.
CO15: Clac S 1K 189 (4D 28)
E10: Lon 9C 106
E15: Lon 8F 122
E18: Lon 5F 106
SS2: Sth S 5L 137
Carnation Cl. CM1: Chelm 6A 60
RM7: Rush G 4C 126
Carnation Dr. CB10: Saf W 3E 218
Carnegie Cl. EN3: Enf 8B 76
CARNELES GREEN 1C 30
Carne Rasch Ct. *SS14: Bas* *1G 132*
(off Ash Tree Wlk.)
Carnforth Gdns. RM12: Horn 7D 126
Carnival Cl. SS14: Bas 6C 116
Carnival Gdns. SS9: Lgh S 2C 136
Carnoustie Cl. SE28: Lon 6J 141
Carol Cl. SS15: Lain 8M 115
Carol Ct. SS15: Lain 8M 115
Carolina Cl. E15: Lon 7E 122
Carolina Way CO5: Tip 5D 226
Caroline Cl. CO7: W'hoe 3J 175
Caroline Ct. CO2: Colc 3H 173
Caroline's Cl. SS2: Sth S 1K 137
Carolyn Ct. CO2: Colc 2C 174
Caro Rd. SS8: Can I 2J 151
Carousel Steps *SS1: Sth S* *7A 138*
(off Hawtree Cl.)
Carpenter Cl. CM12: Bill 5H 99
Carpenter Path CM13: Hut 4N 97
Carpenters Arms La. CM16: Thorn 4G 65
Carpenters Bus. Pk. E15: Lon 9B 122
Carpenters Cl. SS3: Lit W 3B 44
Carpenters Dr. CM77: Gt N 1B 204
Carpenter's Rd. E15: Lon 8A 122 (5D 38)
Carrack Ho. *DA8: Eri* *3C 152*
(off Saltford Cl.)
Carraways CM8: Wthm 7E 230
Carriage Dr. CM1: Chelm 4N 59
Carriage M. IG1: Ilf 4B 124
Carrick Dr. IG6: Ilf 5B 108
Carriers Cl. CO5: W Mer 2A 228
Carrington Cl. CO5: W Mer 2D 228
Carrington Gdns. E7: Lon 6G 123
Carrington Ho. CO5: W Mer 2D 228
Carringtons Rd. CO7: Gt Bro 4A 168 (5J 17)
Carrington Way CM7: Brain 9H 191
Carroll Cl. E15: Lon 7F 122
Carroll Gdns. SS12: W'fd 2L 117
Carroll Hill IG10: Lou 2M 91
Carron Mead CM3: S Fer 2M 103
Carrow Rd. RM9: Dag 9G 125
Carr Rd. E17: Lon 6A 106
IP11: Felix 2K 19
Carrs Rd. CO15: Clac S 1H 189
Carruthers Cl. SS11: W'fd 7L 101
Carruthers Dr. SS11: W'fd 7L 101
Carsey Cl. CM11: Rams H 4D 100
Carsey Hill CB1: Shudy C 3F 7
Carshalton End CO3: S'way 2G 173
Carson Rd. CM11: Bill 4M 99
Carstone Pl. CM1: Chelm 5F 58
Carswell Cl. CM13: Hut 5N 97
IG4: Ilf 8K 107
Carswell Gdns. SS12: W'fd 2L 117
Cartbridge Cl. CO14: Walt 6L 181
Cartel Cl. RM19: Purf 2A 154
Carte Pl. SS16: Lang H 1J 131
Carter Cl. RM5: Col R 4M 109
Carter Dr. RM5: Col R 2N 109
Carterhatch La. EN1: Enf 6B 30
Carterhatch Rd. EN3: Enf 6C 30
Carters Cl. CO16: Clac S 1F 188
Carters Cft. CB10: A'dn 7D 190
Cartersfield Rd. EN9: Wal A 4C 76
CARTER'S GREEN 6A 22
Carters Hill CM23: Man 5K 11
CO4: Boxt 2A 160 (2F 17)
Carters La. CM8: L Brax, W Bis 1L 229 (5H 25)
CM16: E Grn 3A 64
CM22: Hen 8D 210
Carters Mead CM17: H'low 5H 55
Carter's Vineyards 3M 159
Carthagena Est. EN10: Brox 8C 52
Cart La. E4: Lon 7E 90
Cartlodge Av. SS11: W'fd 8M 101
Cartt La. RM17: Grays 3L 155
Cart Track CO9: Gt Map, Hals 1H 207
Cartwright Rd. RM9: Dag 9L 125
SS7: Thund 8D 118
Cartwright Wlk. CM2: Chelm 9A 60
CARVER BARRACKS 1D 12
Carvers Wood CM11: Bill 9L 99
Cary Rd. E11: Lon 6E 122
Cascade Cl. IG9: Buck H 8K 91
Cascade Rd. IG9: Buck H 8K 91
Cascades *SS1: Sth S* *7A 138*
(off Prospect Cl.)
Casey La. CM0: T'ham 2K 225
Cashiobury Ter. SS1: Sth S 7L 137
Cashmere Way SS16: Van 4E 132
Cassel Av. SS8: Can I 9J 135
Cassino Rd. CM1: Chelm 5G 59
CO2: Colc 3K 173
Cassis Ct. IG10: Lou 3B 92
Cassland Rd. E9: Lon 5C 38
Castalia Ct. DA1: Dart 8K 153
Castellan Av. RM2: Romf 7F 110
Castell Rd. IG10: Lou 9B 78
Castile Ct. EN8: Wal X 4A 76
Castle Av. E4: Lon 2D 106
RM13: Rain 9C 126
SS7: Had 5K 135
Castle Bailey CO1: Colc 8N 165
CASTLE CAMPS 4G 7
Castle Cl. CM3: Gt L 8K 203
CO9: Cas H 3K 219
EN11: Rye P 2C 52
RM3: Romf 9G 95
SS3: Shoe 6L 139
SS6: Ray 6J 119
Castle Ct. CB10: Saf W 3C 218
CO15: Clac S 1J 189
SS6: Ray 6J 119
SS7: Had 4L 135
Castle Cross CB10: Saf W 2D 218
Castledon Rd. CM11: D'ham 4H 101 (7B 34)
SS12: W'fd 7H 101 (7B 34)
Castle Dr. IG4: Ilf 1L 123
SS6: Ray 4J 119
SS9: Lgh S 6A 136
Castle Folley CO1: Colc 7N 165
Castlegate St. CO12: Har 1N 209
CASTLE HEDINGHAM 3L 219 (1E 14)
Castle Hill CB10: Saf W 3C 218 (6B 6)
CO7: Ded 3M 161 (2H 17)
DA3: Fawk, Hley 7E 46
Castle Hill Pk. CO16: Clac S 6J 185
Castle House 3N 161
Castle La. CO9: Cas H 3L 219
DA12: Grav 4J 47
SS7: Had 5K 135
Castle Mdw. CO9: Sib H 5J 219
Castle Mus. 8N 165 (6E 16)
Castle Point Transport Mus. 2L 151 (6F 43)
Castle Rd. CO1: Colc 7A 166
CO15: Clac S 1J 189
EN11: Rye P 2C 52
RM9: Dag 1G 140
RM17: Grays 4J 155
SS6: Ray 6J 119 (2F 43)
SS7: Had 4K 135
Castle St. CB10: Saf W 3C 218 (6B 6)
CM5: Chip 8L 67
Castle Ter. SS6: Ray 5J 119
Castleton Av. DA7: Bexh 6B 152
Castleton Rd. E17: Lon 6D 106
IG3: Ilf 3F 124
SS2: Sth S 5C 138
Castleview Gdns. IG1: Ilf 1L 123
Castle Vw. Rd. SS8: Can I 8G 135
Castle Wlk. CM24: Stan M 3D 220
SS8: Can I 9G 135
SS13: Pits 9K 117
Castleward Cl. CO7: W'hoe 6J 175
Castle Way CO16: St O 9M 183
Caswell Cl. SS17: Corr 1B 148
Caswell M. CM2: Chelm 9A 60
Catalina Av. RM16: Chaf H 9J 145
Catalin Ct. *EN9: Wal A* *3D 76*
(off Howard Cl.)
Catchpole La. CM9: Gt Tot 3M 229 (6H 25)
Catchpool Rd. CO1: Colc 6N 165
Caterham Av. IG5: Ilf 6M 107
Caterham Cl. CO16: Clac S 7G 184
Caterham Ct. EN9: Wal A 4F 76
Cater Mus. 6J 99 (7J 33)
Cater Wood CM12: Bill 5K 99
Cates Cnr. CB10: Saf W 4C 218
Cathall Leisure Cen. 4E 122
Cathall Rd. E11: Lon 4D 122 (4E 38)
Catharine Cl. RM16: Chaf H 9J 145
Cathedral Dr. SS15: Lain 8L 115
Cathedral Wlk. CM1: Chelm 8K 59
Catherine Cl. CM3: E Han 3B 88
CM15: Pil H 4D 96
CO15: Clac S 8L 185
IG10: Lou 5M 91
Catherine Ct. IG2: Ilf 9B 108
Catherine Hunt Way CO2: Colc 4J 173
Catherine Lodge SS2: Sth S 5L 137
Catherine Rd. RM2: Romf 9F 110
SS7: Ben 2D 134
Catherines Cl. CM3: Gt L 8L 203
CATLEY CROSS 1G 15
CATMERE END 6K 5
Catons La. CB10: Saf W 1C 218
(not continuous)
CATTAWADE 1H 163 (2A 18)
Cattawade End SS14: Bas 8E 116
Cattawade Link SS14: Bas 8E 116
Cattawade St. CO11: Law 1H 163
Cattermole Cl. CO16: Clac S 1F 188
CATTLEGATE 4A 30
Cattlegate Rd. EN6: N'thaw 4A 30
Catt's La. CM22: Else 2M 199
Caulfield Rd. E6: Lon 9M 123
SS3: Shoe 7G 138 (5B 44)
Causeway CB2: Pam 2K 5
CAUSEWAY END 9K 199 (2J 23)
Causeway End CO11: Law 3G 163
Causeway End Rd. CM6: Fels 9K 199 (2K 23)
Causeway Reach CO15: Clac S 6J 185
Causeway, The CB11: Deb 2C 12
CM1: Writ 4F 70 (2H 33)
CM2: Gt Bad 3G 73
CM6: Gt D 1L 203 (7G 13)
CM7: Brain 4H 193
CM7: F'fld 3D 200 (2K 13)
CM9: Mal 4C 214 (1H 35)
CM9: Ult, Wdhm W 7F 25
CM23: Bis S 1K 21
CO4: Colc 6C 166
CO6: Gt Hork 5J 159 (3D 16)
CO9: Bay E, Ridg 6A 216 (5B 8)
CO9: Hals 5K 207
CO9: Top 7B 8
SG8: Bass 3B 4
SG8: Ther 7B 4
SG9: Bre P 3G 11
SG9: Bunt 4D 10
SG9: Fur P 5G 11
SG11: Abry, Fur P 5G 11
Causton Rd. CO1: Colc 7M 165
Causton Sq. RM10: Dag 9M 125
Caustonway SS6: Ray 3K 119
Cautherly La. SG12: Gt Amw 5D 20
Cavalier Cl. RM6: Chad H 8J 109
Cavell Cres. DA1: Dart 9L 153
RM3: H Wood 6J 111
Cavell Rd. CM11: Bill 7L 99

CAVENDISH 2F 9
Cavendish Av. CO2: Colc 2C 174
DA8: Eri 4A 152
IG8: Wfd G 5H 107
RM12: Horn 8F 126
Cavendish Ct. *CB11: Saf W 3E 218*
(off Radwinter Rd.)
Cavendish Cres. RM12: Horn 8F 126
Cavendish Dr. CO11: Law 5G 162
CO16: Clac S 9E 184
E11: Lon 3D 122
Cavendish Gdns. CM2: Chelm 8N 59
CM7: Brain 3L 193
IG1: Ilf 3N 123
IG11: Bark 7D 124
RM6: Chad H 9K 109
SS0: Wclf S 4G 136 (4H 43)
Cavendish La.
CO10: Caven, Glem 2F 9
Cavendish Manor Vineyard 2F 9
Cavendish Rd. CO10: Clare, Pos 3D 8
E4: Lon 3C 106
SS4: Hock 7E 104
Cavendish Way SS15: Lain 6M 115
Cavenham Gdns. IG1: Ilf 5C 124
RM11: Horn 9G 110
Caversham Av. SS3: Shoe 4J 139
Caversham Pk. Av. SS6: Ray 3J 119
(Deepdene Av.)
SS6: Ray 2J 119
(Manns Way)
Cawdor Av. RM15: S Ock 7D 144
Cawdor Ho. CM14: War 1G 112
Cawkell Cl. CM24: Stan M 2C 220
Cawkwell Cl. CM2: Chelm 7B 60
Cawley Hatch CM19: H'low 3M 53
Caxton Cl. CO5: Tip 7D 226
Caxton Pl. IG1: Ilf 5N 123
Caxton Rd. EN11: Hod 1B 52
Caxton Way RM1: Romf 8C 110
Cazenove Rd. E17: Lon 5A 106
N16: Lon 4B 38
Cecil Av. IG11: Bark 9C 124
RM11: Horn 7J 111
RM16: Chaf H 9J 145
Cecil Ct. CM18: H'low 6B 54
SS2: Sth S 3K 137
Cecil Ho. E17: Lon 5A 106
Cecil Rd. E11: Lon 5F 122
E17: Lon 5A 106
EN2: Enf 6B 30
EN11: Rye P 3C 52
IG1: Ilf 6A 124
RM6: Chad H 2J 125
Cecil Way SS6: Ray 5M 119
Cedar Av. CM1: Chelm 8J 59
CO5: Tip 4C 226
CO7: B'sea 6D 182
RM6: Chad H 9K 109
RM14: Upm 6L 127
SS12: W'fd 2K 117
Cedar Av. W. CM1: Chelm 8J 59
Cedar Chase CM9: Mal 3E 214
Cedar Cl. CM6: Gt D 2J 203
CM13: Hut 6N 97
CM21: Saw 3K 51
CO14: Walt 7K 181
IG9: Buck H 8K 91
RM7: Romf 8A 110
SS2: Sth S 4M 137
SS6: Ray 6M 119
Cedar Ct. CM16: Epp 1F 78
CO6: W Ber 2E 164
IG8: Wfd G 5G 106
Cedar Cres. CO11: Law 5H 163
Cedar Dr. CM8: Wthm 2D 230
DA4: S at H 6C 46
SS5: Hull 6L 103
Cedar Gdns. RM14: Upm 5N 127
Cedar Grn. EN11: Hod 6A 52
Cedar Gro. CM0: Bur C 2D 196
Cedar Hall Gdns. SS7: Thund 9G 118
Cedar M. SS5: Hock 1B 120
Cedar Pk. Cl. SS7: Thund 9G 119
Cedar Pk. Gdns. RM6: Chad H 2J 125
Cedar Ri. RM15: S Ock 4F 144
Cedar Rd. CM13: Hut 5N 97
DA8: Eri 6E 152
EN2: Enf 5A 30
RM7: Romf 8A 110
RM12: Horn 5G 126
RM16: Grays 1C 156
SS7: Thund 9G 119
SS8: Can I 1F 150
Cedars SS17: Stan H 3N 147
Cedars Av. E17: Lon 9A 106
Cedars Ho. E17: Lon 7B 106
Cedars Rd. CO2: Colc 9N 165
E15: Lon 8E 122
Cedars, The CM3: S Fer 9K 89
E15: Lon 9F 122
EN9: Wal A 5J 77
(off Woodbine Cl.)
IG9: Buck H 7G 91
SS3: Gt W 2M 139
Cedar Wlk. EN9: Wal A 4D 76
SS4: Cwdn 2M 105
Cedar Way CO7: Gt Ben 6K 177
Ceder Dr. IG10: Lou 2A 92
Cedric Av. RM1: Romf 7C 110
Celandine Cl. CM12: Bill 4H 99
RM15: S Ock 4F 144
Celandine Ct. CO4: Colc 5K 165
E4: Lon 9B 90
Celandine Dr. SE28: Lon 8G 140
Celedon Cl. RM16: Chaf H 1H 155
Celia Wlk. *CO4: Colc 8F 166*
(off Hamlet Dr.)
Cement Block Cotts. RM17: Grays 3M 155
Cemetery La. EN9: Naze 4F 62
Cemetery Rd. CM23: Bis S 1K 21
E7: Lon 7F 122
Centaur Way CM9: Mal 8C 214
Centaury Cl. CO3: S'way 8D 164
Centenary Way
CO16: Clac S, L Cla 4H 185 (2D 28)
Central Arc. CB10: Saf W 4C 218
Central Av. CM3: Alth 3B 190
CM12: Bill 3L 99
CM20: H'low 2C 54 (6H 21)
CO13: Frin S 8K 181
E11: Lon 4D 122
E12: Lon 5K 123
RM15: Ave 9N 143
RM18: Til 6C 156
RM20: W Thur 3C 154
SS2: Sth S 5N 137 (4K 43)
SS4: R'fd 2H 121
SS5: Hull 8M 103
SS7: Had 1L 135
SS8: Can I 1F 150
SS16: Lang H 2G 130
SS17: Corr 1B 148
SS17: Stan H 9N 131
Central Cl. SS7: Had 2L 135
Central Dr. RM12: Horn 5J 127
Central Gallery *IG1: Ilf 4A 124*
(in Exchange, The)
Central Maltings, The CO11: Mist 4J 163
Central Pde. E17: Lon 8A 106
IG2: Ilf 1C 124
Central Pk. Av. RM10: Dag 5N 125
Central Pk. Rd. E6: Lon 6F 39
Central Pk. Swimming Pool 2J 111
Central Rd. CM20: H'low 8F 50
DA1: Dart 9J 153
IP11: Felix 1J 19
SS17: Stan H 4M 147
Central Sq. CM1: Chelm 9K 59
Central St. EC1: Lon 6A 38
Central Wall SS8: Can I 8F 134
(not continuous)
Central Wall Cotts. SS8: Can I 9H 135
Central Wall Rd. SS8: Can I 9H 135 (5E 42)
Central Way SE28: Lon 8F 140 (7J 39)
Centre Av. CM16: Epp 2E 78
Centre Cl. CM16: Epp 2E 78
Centre Dr. CM16: Epp 2E 78
E7: Lon 6J 123
Centre Grn. CM16: Epp 2E 78
Centre Pl. *SS1: Sth S 7A 138*
(off Prospect Cl.)
Centre Rd. E7: Lon 4G 123 (4F 39)
E11: Lon 4G 123 (4F 39)
RM10: Dag 2N 141
Centre, The CO4: Colc 1C 166
(Crescent, The)
CO4: Colc 7E 166
(Hawthorn Av.)
CO5: Tip 6D 226
CO9: Hals 4K 207
Centre Way E17: Lon 4C 106
EN3: Enf 7A 76
IG1: Ilf 4B 124
Centurion Cl. SS3: Shoe 6K 139
Centurion Way CO2: Colc 4H 173
RM19: Purf 2K 153
Centuryan Pl. DA1: Cray 9F 152
Century Dr. CM7: Brain 6K 193
Century Rd. EN11: Hod 4A 52
Ceylon Rd. SS0: Wclf S 6J 137
Chadacre Av. IG5: Ilf 7M 107
Chadacre Rd. SS1: Sth S 5F 138
Chadfields RM18: Til 5C 156
Chadview Ct. RM6: Chad H 2J 125
Chadville Gdns. RM6: Chad H 9J 109
Chadway RM8: Dag 3H 125
Chadwell Av. RM6: Chad H 2G 125
Chadwell By-Pass RM16: Grays 3B 156 (1G 47)
CHADWELL HEATH 2J 125 (3J 39)
Chadwell Heath Ind. Pk. RM8: Dag 3K 125
Chadwell Heath La.
RM6: Chad H 8G 109 (3J 39)
Chadwell Heath Station (Rail) 2J 125 (4J 39)
Chadwell Hill RM16: Grays 3D 156
Chadwell Rd. RM17: Grays 2M 155 (1G 47)
CHADWELL ST MARY 1D 156 (1H 47)
Chadwick Av. E4: Lon 1D 106
Chadwick Ct. SS0: Wclf S 6H 137
Chadwick Dr. RM3: H Wood 6H 111
Chadwick Rd. CM3: S Fer 8L 89
E11: Lon 1E 122
IG1: Ilf 5A 124
SS0: Wclf S 6H 137
Chadwick Way SE28: Lon 7J 141
Chaffinch Cl. SS3: Shoe 6J 139
Chaffinch Cres. CM11: Bill 7L 99
Chaffinch Dr. CO12: Har 6G 209
Chaffinch Gdns. CO4: Colc 7F 166
Chaffinch Way CO9: Hals 5M 207
Chaffix CM6: Fels 7K 199
Chaffix Cl. CM6: Fels 7K 199
Chafford CM14: Brtwd 7E 96
Chafford Gdns. CM13: W H'dn 1N 129
CHAFFORD HUNDRED 1J 155 (1E 46)
Chafford Hundred Station (Rail) 2E 154 (1E 46)
Chafford Sports Complex 5G 142
Chafford Wlk. RM13: Rain 2G 142
Chafford Way RM6: Chad H 8H 109
RM16: Grays 8K 145
Chaingate Av. SS2: Sth S 4C 138
Chale Ct. SS17: Stan H 5L 147
Chalfont Cl. SS9: Lgh S 2C 136
Chalfont Rd. CO4: Colc 5C 166
Chalforde Gdns. RM2: Romf 8F 110
Chalford Wlk. IG8: Wfd G 5K 107
Chalgrove Cres. IG5: Ilf 6L 107
Chalice Cl. SS14: Bas 9F 116
CHALK 4J 47
Chalk Ct. *RM17: Grays 4K 155*
(off Jetty Wlk.)
CHALK END 6G 23
Chalk End SS13: Pits 9H 117
Chalk Farm La. CB11: Newp 3L 215
Chalk Hill CM1: Hghwd 7C 70
Chalklands CB10: Saf W 2D 218
CM2: S'don 7L 73
Chalk La. CM17: H'low 8N 51
CM17: H'low 9M 51 (6K 21)
Chalkney Wood Nature Reserve 9F 198
Chalk Rd. DA12: Grav 4J 47
ME3: High 4K 47
SS8: Can I 8G 134
Chalks Av. CM21: Saw 1J 51
Chalk's Rd. CM8: Wthm 4C 230
Chalkstone Way CB9: H'hll 2J 7
Chalk St. CM3: Ret C 9N 87 (6C 34)
Chalk Vs. CM6: Lea R 4C 212
CHALKWELL 6G 136 (5H 43)
Chalkwell Av. SS0: Wclf S 7G 137 (5H 43)
Chalkwell Bay *SS9: Lgh S 6F 136*
(off Undercliff Gdns.)
Chalkwell Esplanade
SS0: Can I, Wclf S 6F 136 (5H 43)
Chalkwell Lodge SS0: Wclf S 5H 137
Chalkwell Pk. Dr. SS9: Lgh S 5E 136
Chalkwell Station (Rail) 6F 136 (5H 43)
Chalky La. SG8: Chris 6H 5
Challacombe SS1: Sth S 5G 139
Challacombe Cl. CM13: Hut 7L 97
Challenge Way CO1: Colc 9B 166
Challinor CM17: H'low 3K 55
Challis Grn. CB2: Barr, Foxt 1E 4
Challis La. CM7: Brain 7H 193 (1D 24)
Challock Lees SS13: Pits 1K 133
Chalmers Ho. E17: Lon 9B 106
CHALVEDON 9K 117 (3B 42)
Chalvedon Av. SS13: Pits 8J 117
Chalvedon Sq. SS13: Pits 9H 117
Chamberlain Av. CO14: Walt 7L 181
SS8: Can I 1J 151
SS17: Corr 9B 132
Chamberlain Cl. CM17: H'low 3H 55
Chamberlains Ride CM3: S Fer 2K 103
Chamomile Ct. *E17: Lon 1A 122*
(off Yunus Khan Cl.)
Champion Cl. SS12: W'fd 1L 117
SS17: Stan H 2N 147
Champion Rd. RM14: Upm 4M 127
Champions Grn. EN11: Hod 2A 52
Champions Way CM3: S Fer 9J 89
EN11: Hod 2A 52
Champlain Av. SS8: Can I 9F 134
Champness Rd. IG11: Bark 8E 124
Chance Cl. RM16: Chaf H 1J 155
Chancel Cl. CM0: T'ham 2K 225
SS7: Thund 9C 118
(not continuous)
SS15: Lain 8L 115
Chancellor Av. CM2: Chelm 7C 60
Chancellor Rd. SS1: Sth S 7N 137 (5K 43)
Chancery Gro. CO2: Colc 6A 174
Chancery La. WC2: Lon 7A 38
Chancery Lane Station (Tube) 7A 38
Chancery Pl. CM1: Writ 1K 71
Chandler Rd. IG10: Lou 9A 78
Chandlers CM0: Bur C 2C 196
Chandlers Cl. CO16: Clac S 1F 188
CHANDLERS CORNER 3G 142 (6B 40)
Chandlers Cnr. RM13: Rain 3G 142
Chandlers Dr. DA8: Eri 2B 152
Chandlers Quay CM9: Mal 5C 214
Chandlers Row CO1: Colc 1C 174
Chandlers Wlk. CM15: Kel H 7B 82
Chandlers Way CM3: S Fer 1L 103
RM1: Romf 9C 110
SS2: Sth S, Temp I 1L 137
Chandos Av. E17: Lon 6A 106
Chandos Cl. IG9: Buck H 8H 91
Chandos Pde. SS7: Had 3M 135
Chandos Rd. E15: Lon 7D 122
Chaney Rd. CO7: W'hoe 4G 175
Chanlock Path RM15: S Ock 7E 144
Channing Cl. RM11: Horn 2K 127
Channocks CM20: Gil 5C 50
Chant Ct. CO4: Colc 4D 166
Chanterelle CO4: Colc 4B 166
Chanton Cl. SS9: Lgh S 8C 120
Chantress Cl. RM10: Dag 1A 142
Chantreywood CM13: Brtwd 9K 97
Chantry Chase CM11: Bill 6K 99
Chantry Cl. CO16: Clac S 6J 185
Chantry Cres. SS17: Stan H 4L 147
Chantry Dr. CM4: Ing 6D 84
CO6: Wmgfd 8L 229
Chantry Ho. RM13: Rain 2B 142
Chantry La. SS15: Lain 8L 115
Chantry, The CM20: H'low 1F 54
CO3: Colc 8K 165
E4: Lon 7C 90
Chantry Vw. CM8: Wthm 8D 230
Chantry Way CM11: Bill 6K 99
RM13: Rain 2B 142
Chant Sq. E15: Lon 9D 122
Chant St. E15: Lon 9D 122
Chapel Av. E12: Lon 5K 123
Chapel Cl. RM20: W Thur 4E 154
Chapel Ct. CM12: Bill 6K 99
Chapel Cft. CM4: Ing 5D 84
CO7: A'lgh 9L 161
Chapel Cut CO11: Mist 4M 163
Chapel Dr. CM3: L Walt 6K 57
CHAPEL END 5B 106
Chapel End CM6: Broxt 6D 12
CO9: Stamb 6A 8
EN11: Hod 6A 52
Chapel End Way CO9: Stamb 6A 8
Chapel Flds. CM17: H'low 5H 55
Chapelfields CO13: Frin S, Walt 8H 181
CHAPEL GREEN 1C 10
Chapel High *CM14: Brtwd 8F 96*
(off High St.)
Chapel High Shop. Cen. CM14: Brtwd 8F 96
Chapel Hill CM7: Brain 6K 193 (7D 14)
CM24: Stan M 2D 220 (6A 12)
CO9: Hals 4J 207 (3F 15)
CO10: Bel W 5F 9
Chapel La. CB11: Newp 3L 215
CM0: T'ham 2K 225
CM1: Cook G 1B 70
CM3: L Bad 8J 61 (1D 34)
CM3: Pur 9K 215
CM9: Hey B 9F 214
CM17: H'low 5H 55
CO4: Boxt 5A 160
CO6: W Ber 3F 164 (5D 16)
CO7: A'lgh 5H 167 (5G 17)
CO7: Elms 9N 167
CO7: Gt Bro 9G 168
CO7: Thorr 9F 176
CO10: L Cor 6K 9
CO13: Walt 8D 180
CO16: St O 9M 183
CO16: Ten 6C 18
IG7: Chig 9E 92
RM6: Chad H 2J 125
SG11: L Had 1G 21
SS3: Gt W 2M 139
SS7: Had 4J 135 (4F 43)
Chapel Lodge RM13: Rain 3E 142
Chapel M. IG8: Ilf 3N 107
Chapelmount Rd. IG8: Wfd G 3M 107
Chapel Path *E11: Lon 1H 123*
(off Woodbine Pl.)
Chapel Rd. CM0: Bur C 4E 196
CM9: Gt Tot 8J 205 (5J 25)
CM9: Tol D 2L 227 (5B 26)
CM16: Epp 9E 64
CO3: S'way 9D 164 (6C 16)
CO4: Boxt 5A 160 (3F 17)
CO4: L'ham 4C 160 (3F 17)
CO5: Fing 9F 174 (1G 27)
CO5: Tip 7D 226 (4A 26)
CO6: W Ber 4E 164 (5C 16)
CO7: B'sea 7F 182 (3K 27)
CO7: W'hoe 6H 175
CO9: Ridg 7D 216 (5B 8)
CO16: T Sok 6D 18
IG1: Ilf 5N 123 (4G 39)
SS3: Shoe 8K 139
Chapel St. CB2: Dux 2J 5
CB9: Stpl B 2L 223 (5K 7)
CM12: Bill 6J 99 (7J 33)
CO5: Rhdge 6F 174
CO9: Hals 4K 207
CO10: Stoke C 4B 8
Chapel St. Nth. CO2: Colc 9M 165
Chapel St. Sth. CO2: Colc 9M 165
Chapel Ter. IG10: Lou 3L 91
Chapel Wood Rd. TN15: Ash 7F 47
Chaplaincy Gdns. RM11: Horn 3J 127
Chaplin Cl. CM2: Gall 8C 72
SS15: Bas 6N 115
Chaplin Dr. CO4: Colc 6D 166
Chaplin Rd. RM9: Dag 9K 125
Chaplins CO13: Frin S 7J 181
Chapman Ct. *SS8: Can I 3L 151*
(off Seaview Rd.)
Chapman Rd. CO15: Clac S 1K 189
E9: Lon 5D 38
SS8: Can I 2N 151
Chapmans Cl. SS9: Lgh S 5A 136
Chapmans La. CO5: W Mer 1F 228 (4G 27)
Chapmans Wlk. SS9: Lgh S 5A 136
CHAPMORE END 3B 20
CHAPPEL 7C 196 (4K 15)
Chappel and Wakes Colne Station (Rail)
6C 196 (4K 15)
Chappel Cnr. CO6: Chap 7C 196
Chappel Hill CO6: Chap 7B 196 (4K 15)
Chappel Rd. CO6: For 4B 16
CO6: Gt Tey 1E 170 (5K 15)
CO8: Wak C 3A 16
Charfleets Cl. SS8: Can I 2D 150
Charfleets Farm Ind. Est.
SS8: Can I 2D 150
Charfleets Farm Way SS8: Can I 2D 150
Charfleets Ind. Est. SS8: Can I 2C 150
Charfleets Rd. SS8: Can I 2C 150
Charfleets Service Rd.
SS8: Can I 2D 150
Charing Cross Rd. W1: Lon 7A 38
Charing Cross Station (Rail, Tube) 7A 38
Charity Farm Chase CM12: Bill 5H 99
Charity La. CM3: Pur 1L 89
Charlbury Cl. RM3: Romf 3G 110
Charlbury Cres. RM3: Romf 3G 110
Charlbury Gdns. IG3: Ilf 4E 124
Charlecote Rd. CM77: Gt N 1C 204
RM8: Dag 5K 125

Charles Cl. SS0: Wclf S 1F 136
Charles Ct. CO3: S'way 9E 164
CO7: W'hoe 3J 175
DA8: Eri 4C 152
Charles Ho. CO1: Colc 7N 165
Charles Pell Rd. CO4: Colc 9E 166
Charles Pl. CO1: Colc 9C 166
Charles Rd. CO7: B'sea 7E 182
E7: Lon 9J 123
RM6: Chad H 1J 125
RM10: Dag 8B 126
Charles Smith Ho. CO2: Colc 3A 174
(off Ladbrook Dr.)
Charles St. CM16: Epp 2F 78
CO1: Colc 9A 166
RM17: Grays 4L 155
Charleston Av. SS13: Bas 6K 117
Charleston Ct. CO5: W Mer 3E 228
SS13: Bas 6K 117
CHARLIE BROWN'S RDBT. 6J 107 (2F 39)
Charlieville Rd. DA8: Eri 5A 152
Charlotte Av. SS12: W'fd 8K 101
Charlotte Cl. IG6: Ilf 5B 108
Charlotte Ct. CM3: S Fer 2K 103
IG2: Ilf 1N 123
Charlotte Dr. CO13: Walt 8H 181
Charlotte Gdns. RM5: Col R 3N 109
Charlotte M. SS2: Sth S 5L 137
Charlotte Pl. RM20: W Thur 4E 154
Charlotte Rd. RM10: Dag 8N 125
Charlotte Way CM8: Wthm 5E 230
Charlton Cl. EN11: Hod 5A 52
SS13: Pits 8K 117
Charlton Cres. IG11: Bark 2E 140
Charlton Mead La. EN11: Rye P 6D 52
Charlton St. RM20: Grays 4G 155
Charlton Way EN11: Hod 5A 52 (7D 20)
Charnock Cl. CO13: Frin S 8J 181
Charnwood Av. CM1: Chelm 1N 71
Charnwood Dr. E18: Lon 7H 107
Charnwood Wlk. SS7: Had 2L 135
Charter Av. IG2: Ilf 3C 124
Charter Ct. CO4: Colc 1C 166
Charter Ho. CM9: Mal 6C 214
Charterhouse SS16: Van 1D 132
Charterhouse St. EC1: Lon 7A 38
Charteris Rd. IG8: Wfd G 4H 107 (2F 39)
Charter Rd., The IG8: Wfd G 3E 106 (2E 38)
Charters Cross CM18: H'low 6C 54
Charters, The CM6: Gt D 1L 203
Charter Way CM7: Tye G 7L 193
CO4: Colc 3N 165
Chartfield Dr. CO13: Kir S 6G 181
Chart Hills Cl. SE28: Lon 6K 141
Chartwell Cl. CM7: Brain 1G 193
EN9: Wal A 3E 76
Chartwell Ct. IG8: Wfd G 4F 106
Chartwell Nth. SS2: Sth S 6M 137
(in Victoria Plaza Shop. Cen.)
Chartwell Sq. SS2: Sth S 6M 137
(off Victoria Plaza Shop. Cen.)
Chartwell W. SS2: Sth S 6M 137
(in Victoria Plaza Shop. Cen.)
Chase Cl. SS7: Thund 1F 134
Chase Ct. CO4: Colc 8E 166
Chase Ct. Gdns. SS1: Sth S 6A 138
(off Chase Rd.)
CHASE CROSS 4B 110 (2A 40)
Chase Cross Rd. RM5: Col R 4A 110 (2A 40)
Chase Dr. CM3: S Fer 9J 89
Chase End SS6: Ray 5M 119
Chase Gdns. E4: Lon 1A 106
SS0: Wclf S 3J 137
Chase Ho. Gdns. RM11: Horn 9K 111
Chase La. CO12: Har 5G 209
IG2: Ilf 9C 108
IG6: Ilf 9C 108
(not continuous)
IG7: Chig 9E 92
Chase Nature Reserve, The 5D 126
Chase Rd. CM14: Brtwd 9F 96
N14: Lon 7A 30
SS1: Sth S 6A 138
SS17: Corr 2B 148
Chase Rd. E. CO7: Gt Bro 8G 168 (6K 17)
Chase Rd. W. CO7: Gt Bro 9F 168
CHASE SIDE 6B 30
Chase Side EN2: Enf 6B 30
Chaseside SS6: Ray 7L 119
Chaseside Cl. RM1: Romf 3C 110
Chase Sports & Fitness Cen. 3H 137
Chase, The CB9: Stpl B 2K 223
CM0: S'min 2D 222
CM2: Gt Bad 4G 73
CM3: Bore 3F 60
CM3: S Fer 9J 89
CM6: Barns 3M 191
CM7: Brain 1H 193
CM9: Tol 7K 225
CM11: Bill 6L 99
CM12: Bas, L Bur 5K 115
CM13: Ingve 2M 113
CM14: Brtwd 9G 97
CM14: War 1E 112
(Cromwell Rd.)
CM14: War 2G 113
(Woodman Rd.)
CM17: H'low 2H 55
(not continuous)
CM22: Hen 7D 210
CM77: Gt N 3C 204
CO1: Colc 8D 166
(Davey Cl.)
CO1: Colc 8B 166
(East St.)
Chase, The CO3: S'way 9F 164
CO4: Colc 8E 166
CO5: K'dn 3K 211
CO5: W Mer 3C 228
CO6: Aldh 6A 16
CO6: Gt Tey 2E 170
CO7: Ded 4N 161
CO7: Elms 9A 168
CO10: Fox 3G 9
CO11: Mist 5J 163
CO15: Hol S 8B 186
E12: Lon 6K 123
IG7: Chig 1B 108
IG10: Lou 6K 91
RM1: Romf 7C 110
RM6: Chad H 1K 125
RM7: Rush G 5B 126
(not continuous)
RM13: Rain 1F 142
RM14: Upm 5B 128
RM20: Grays 4G 154
SS3: Fou I 1G 45
SS4: R'fd 9G 105
(not continuous)
SS6: Ray 6M 119 (2F 43)
SS7: Thund 1F 134
SS12: W'fd 3M 117
(Crossway, The)
SS12: W'fd 9H 101
(London Rd.)
SS16: Bas 3N 131
Chaseville Pk. Rd. N14: Lon 7A 30
Chaseway CM8: Wthm 2C 230
SS16: Van 2G 133
Chaseway End SS16: Van 3G 133
Chaseways CM21: Saw 4H 51
Chaseways Vs. RM5: Col R 5L 109
Chaseway, The CM4: Stock 9B 86 (6A 34)
CM7: Brain 6L 193
Chase Way, The CO3: Colc 7H 165
Chaters Hill CB10: Saf W 3D 218 (6C 6)
Chatfield Way SS13: Pits 8K 117
CHATHAM GREEN 1L 57 (4A 24)
Chatham Hall La. CM3: Gt Walt 2J 57 (4A 24)
Chatham Pavement SS13: Pits 8K 117
Chatham Rd. E18: Lon 6F 106
Chatham Way CM14: Brtwd 8F 96
Chatley Rd. CM3: Gt L 7K 203
Chatsworth SS7: Thund 9F 118
Chatsworth Av. CM77: Gt N 1B 204
Chatsworth Gdns. CO15: Clac S 2H 189
SS5: Hock 1C 120
Chatsworth Rd. CO5: W Mer 2C 228
DA1: Dart 9G 153
E5: Lon 4C 38
E15: Lon 7F 122
CHATTER END 6J 11
Chatterford End SS14: Bas 8B 116
Chatteris Av. RM3: Romf 3G 111
Chatton Cl. SS12: W'fd 2M 117
Chaucer Cl. CM9: Mal 8C 214
CO15: Jay 3E 188
RM18: Til 7E 156
Chaucer Ct. EN11: Hod 1B 52
Chaucer Cres. CM7: Brain 8J 193
Chaucer Ho. SS2: Sth S 4N 137
Chaucer Rd. CM2: Chelm 1E 72
E7: Lon 8G 123
E11: Lon 1G 122
E17: Lon 6C 106
RM3: Romf 4F 110
Chaucer Wlk. SS12: W'fd 2L 117
Chaucer Way CO3: Colc, S'way 9G 164
DA1: Dart 9L 153
(not continuous)
EN11: Hod 1A 52
CHEAPSIDE 2F 11
Cheapside E. SS6: Ray 3J 119
Cheapside W. SS6: Ray 3G 119
Cheddar Av. SS0: Wclf S 1F 136
Chedington SS3: Shoe 5G 138
Cheelson Rd. RM15: S Ock 2F 144
Cheethams Rd. E12: Lon 5L 123
Cheldon Barton SS1: Sth S 5G 138
Chelmer Av. CM3: L Walt 7K 57
SS6: Ray 6J 119
Chelmer Cl. CM9: L Tot 6K 25
CO13: Walt 7H 181
Chelmer Cres. IG11: Bark 2G 140
Chelmer Dr. CM6: Gt D 3M 203
CM13: Hut 5A 98
RM15: S Ock 7F 144
Chelmer Ho. RM16: Grays 3C 156
(off River Vw.)
Chelmer Ind. Pk. CM1: Chelm 7L 59
Chelmer La. CM9: Mal 3C 214
Chelmer Lea CM2: Gt Bad 3F 72
Chelmer Pl. CM2: Chelm 8L 59
Chelmer Rd. CM2: Chelm 1E 72 (1A 34)
CM7: Brain 7L 193
CM8: Wthm 5B 230
RM14: Upm 1A 128
RM16: Grays 3C 156
Chelmer Ter. CM9: Mal 6D 214
Chelmerton Av. CM2: Gt Bad 3F 72
Chelmer Valley Rd.
CM1: Chelm 7K 59 (1A 34)
CHELMER VILLAGE 8B 60 (1B 34)
Chelmer Village Retail Pk.
CM2: Chelm 9N 59
Chelmer Village Way
CM2: Chelm 9N 59 (1B 34)
Chelmer Way CM0: Bur C 2C 196
SS3: Shoe 7H 139
CHELMSFORD 9K 59 (1A 34)
Chelmsford & Essex Mus. 2B 72 (2A 34)
Chelmsford Av. RM5: Col R 4B 110
SS2: Sth S 5L 137
Chelmsford Cathedral 9K 59 (1A 34)
Chelmsford Crematorium
CM1: Chelm 2A 72 (2K 33)
Chelmsford Dr. RM14: Upm 5K 127
Chelmsford Gdns. IG1: Ilf 2L 123
Chelmsford Hill CM1: Writ 6G 70
Chelmsford Ho. CM6: Gt D 4M 203
Chelmsford Rd.
CM1: Chelm, Writ 1L 71 (1K 33)
CM1: Good E, Mar R 5E 22
CM3: E Han, S'don 9A 74 (3D 34)
CM3: Gt Walt 5H 57 (5K 23)
CM3: Haz, Pur 6H 215 (3G 35)
CM4: B'more 1J 83 (3F 33)
CM5: B'more, H Ong, Nor H . . . 6N 67 (3D 32)
CM6: Barns, Gt D 1J 191 (1G 23)
(not continuous)
CM6: Fels 8J 199 (1J 23)
CM6: Lea R, Mar R 4C 212 (5E 22)
CM6: Whi R 2F 210 (4B 22)
CM9: Wdhm M 3J 75 (2F 35)
CM15: Shenf 5J 97 (7F 33)
(not continuous)
CM22: Hat H 2F 210 (4B 22)
CO15: Hol S 8N 185
E11: Lon 3D 122
E17: Lon 1A 122
E18: Lon 5F 106
SS11: Raw 7E 102 (7E 34)
Chelmsford Rd. Ind. Est.
CM6: Gt D 4M 203
Chelmsford Station (Rail) 8K 59 (1A 34)
Chelmwood SS8: Can I 8G 134
Chelsea Av. SS1: Sth S 8B 138
Chelsea Flds. EN11: Hod 1B 52
Chelsea Gdns. CM17: H'low 4K 55
Chelsea M. CM7: Brain 6H 193
(off Notley Rd.)
CM7: Brain 7H 193
(Telford Rd.)
RM11: Horn 3F 126
Chelsworth Cl. RM3: H Wood 4K 111
SS1: Sth S 6D 138
Chelsworth Cres. SS1: Sth S 6C 138
Chelsworth Dr. RM3: H Wood 5J 111
Cheltenham Dr. SS7: Thund 8H 119
SS9: Lgh S 4E 136
Cheltenham Gdns. E6: Lon 6G 39
IG10: Lou 5L 91
Cheltenham Ho. IG8: Ilf 3N 107
Cheltenham Rd. E10: Lon 1C 122
SS1: Sth S 6A 138
SS5: Hock 9E 104
Chelwater CM2: Gt Bad 2E 72
Chelwood Cl. E4: Lon 5B 90
Cheneys Rd. E11: Lon 5E 122
Chenies Dr. SS15: Lain 6K 115
Chenies St. W1: Lon 7A 38
Chepstow Av. RM12: Horn 5J 127
Chepstow Cl. CM11: Bill 3M 99
Chepstow Cres. IG3: Ilf 1D 124
Chepstow Ho. RM3: Romf 2L 111
(off Leamington Rd.)
Chequers IG9: Buck H 7H 91
Chequers La. CM6: Gt D 3L 203
CM9: Mal 6C 214
(not continuous)
RM9: Dag 5L 141 (6K 39)
Chequers Pde. RM9: Dag 1L 141
Chequers Rd. CM1: Writ 2H 71 (2J 33)
CM14: Romf 8J 95
CO11: L Bro, Mist 6H 163 (3A 18)
IG10: Lou 4N 91
RM3: Romf 8J 95 (1C 40)
Chequers, The CO7: Alr 7N 175
Chequers Wlk. EN9: Wal A 3F 76
Cherbury Cl. SE28: Lon 6J 141
Cheriton Av. IG5: Ilf 6M 107
Cheriton Rd. CM7: Brain 7L 193
Cherries, The SS8: Can I 3H 151
Cherry Av. CM13: Brtwd 9J 97
Cherry Blossom Cl. CM17: H'low 8H 51
Cherry Blossom La. CM3: Cold N 8K 197
Cherrybrook SS1: Sth S 5G 138
Cherry Chase CO5: Tip 7D 226
Cherry Cl. E17: Lon 9B 106
SS5: Hock 9D 104
SS8: Can I 1E 150
Cherry Ct. IG6: Ilf 7A 108
SS8: Can I 4H 151
Cherry Cres. CM6: Gt D 2J 203
Cherrydene Cl. SS5: Hull 6L 103
Cherrydown RM16: Grays 8N 145
SS6: Ray 3K 119
Cherrydown Av. E4: Lon 9A 90
Cherrydown Cl. E4: Lon 9A 90
Cherrydown E. SS16: Bas 1B 132 (3A 42)
Cherrydown Wlk. RM7: Maw 6N 109
Cherrydown W. SS16: Bas 1B 132
Cherry Gdn. La. CB11: Newp 3K 215
CM2: Chelm 2B 72
CM3: Dan 3G 75
Cherry Gdn. Rd. CM3: Gt Walt 5G 57
CM9: Mal 6A 214
Cherry Gdns. CM12: Bill 4G 98
CM77: Gt N 8F 192
RM9: Dag 7L 125
CHERRY GREEN
CM6 . . . . . 4D 12
SG9 . . . . . 5C 10
Cherry La. CO9: Gt Yel 4D 206
SS11: W'fd 9A 102
Cherrymeade SS7: Ben 2G 134
(not continuous)
Cherry Orchard CM0: S'min 2E 222
Cherry Orchard La. SS4: R'fd 6G 120 (2H 43)
(not continuous)
Cherry Orchard Way
SS2: Sth A, Sth S 6G 121 (3H 43)
SS4: R'fd 6G 121 (2H 43)
Cherry Row CO3: Colc 1G 172
Cherry St. CM6: Broxt, Gt Eas 5E 12
RM7: Romf 9B 110
Cherry Tree Av. CO15: Clac S 3G 189 (4D 28)
Cherrytree Chase SS3: Shoe 5N 139
Cherry Tree Cl. CO9: Hals 4M 207
CO12: L Oak 8D 208
RM13: Rain 2E 142
RM17: Grays 4N 155
Cherrytree Ct. CO3: S'way 1G 172
Cherry Tree Dr. RM15: S Ock 4G 145
Cherry Tree La.
CO2: B'hth, Colc 7A 174 (1E 26)
RM13: Rain 3C 142 (6A 40)
Cherrytree Ri. CM8: Wthm 2D 230
Cherry Tree Ri. IG9: Buck H 1J 107
Cherry Tree Rd. E15: Lon 7E 122
EN11: Hod 4A 52
Cherrytrees CM12: Bill 8H 99
Cherry Wlk. RM13: Rain 2E 142
RM16: Grays 1C 156
Cherrywood Dr. CO3: Colc 1G 172
Cherrywoods CO7: Gt Ben 6J 177
Cherston Gdns. IG10: Lou 3N 91
Cherston Rd. IG10: Lou 3N 91
Chertsey Cl. SS3: Shoe 5H 139
Chertsey Rd. E11: Lon 4D 122
IG1: Ilf 6C 124
Chervil Cl. CO5: Tip 7C 226
Chervil M. SE28: Lon 8G 140
Cherwell Dr. CM1: Chelm 6E 58
Cherwell Gro. RM15: S Ock 7D 144
Chesham Cl. RM7: Romf 8B 110
Chesham Dr. SS15: Lain 6K 115
Chesham Ho. RM3: Romf 3J 111
(off Leyburn Cres.)
Cheshire Cl. E17: Lon 5B 106
RM11: Horn 9L 111
Cheshire St. E2: Lon 6C 38
CHESHUNT 3C 30
Cheshunt Dr. SS6: Ray 1H 119
Cheshunt Rd. E7: Lon 8H 123
Cheshunts SS13: Pits 9H 117
Cheshunt Station (Rail) 3D 30
Cheshunt Wash EN8: Chesh 3C 30
Chessington Mans. E10: Lon 2A 122
E11: Lon 2E 122
Chess La. CM8: Wthm 5D 230
Chester Av. RM14: Upm 4B 128
SS1: Sth S 8B 138
Chester Cl. IG10: Lou 9B 78
RM16: Chaf H 9H 145
Chesterfield Av. SS7: Thund 9C 118
Chesterfield Cres. SS9: Lgh S 9C 120
Chesterfield Rd. E10: Lon 1C 122
Chesterford Gdns. SS14: Bas 7G 116
Chesterford Grn. SS14: Bas 7G 117
Chesterford Rd. E12: Lon 7M 123
Chester Grn. IG10: Lou 9B 78
Chester Hall La. SS14: Bas 6B 116 (2A 42)
Chester M. E17: Lon 6A 106
Chester Path IG10: Lou 9B 78
Chester Pl. CM1: Chelm 6J 59
Chester Rd. E7: Lon 9K 123
E11: Lon 1H 123
IG3: Ilf 3E 124
IG7: Chig 9N 91
IG10: Lou 1A 92 (6G 31)
Chester Ter. IG11: Bark 8C 124
Chesterton Way RM18: Til 7E 156
Chester Way SS14: Bas 7G 116
Chestnut Av. CB11: Lit Gr 6K 5
CM3: Hat P 3L 61
CM9: Mal 2E 214
CM12: Bill 6H 99
CM14: S Wea 6B 96
CM77: Gt N 1C 204
CO2: Colc 6A 174
CO9: Gosf 7L 201
CO13: Walt 8F 180
CO15: Clac S 1G 188
CO16: Clac S 2E 188
E7: Lon 6H 123
E12: Lon 4L 123
IG9: Buck H 9K 91
RM12: Horn 4D 126
RM16: Grays 9L 145
Chestnut Av. Nth. E17: Lon 8D 106
Chestnut Av. Sth. E17: Lon 9C 106
Chestnut Cl. CM0: Bur C 3C 196
IG9: Buck H 9K 91
RM12: Horn 6G 127
SS5: Hock 1E 120
Chestnut Ct. CB11: Newp 3L 215
SS16: Van 2H 133
Chestnut Dr. CM22: Hat H 1D 210
E11: Lon 1G 122
Chestnut Farm Dr. CM3: Alth 3B 190
Chestnut Glen RM12: Horn 4D 126
Chestnut Gro. CM7: Brain 6G 192
CM14: Brtwd 8F 96
IG6: Ilf 3D 108
SS2: Sth S 4M 137
SS7: Ben 2B 134
Chestnut Ho. SS11: W'fd 9M 101
Chestnut La. SG8: Bass, Meld, Whad 3C 4
Chestnut M. CM22: Tak 3B 224

Chestnut Path SS4: Cwdn 2M 105
Chestnut Rd. CO7: Alr. 6A 176
SS16: Van 2H 133
Chestnuts CM13: Hut 7L 97
Chestnuts, The CM0: S'min 2D 222
IG10: Lou 4K 91
RM4: Abr 2G 92
SS6: Ray 3M 119
Chestnut Vw. CM6: Gt D 2K 203
Chestnut Wlk. CM1: Chelm 6J 59
CM3: L Bad 1E 74
CM6: Fels 7K 199
CM8: Wthm 3E 230
CM16: E Grn 4A 64
IG8: Wfd G 2G 106
SS8: Can I 2E 150
SS17: Corr 2C 148
Chestnut Way CM22: Tak 3C 224
CO5: Tip 5C 226
CO7: B'sea 6D 182
Chestwood Cl. CM12: Bill 3K 99
Cheswick Cl. DA1: Cray 9D 152
Chesworth Cl. DA8: Eri 7C 152
Chetwynd Rd. NW5: Lon 4A 38
Cheveley Cl. RM3: H Wood 5J 111
Cheveling Rd. CO2: Colc 4D 174
Chevely Cl. CM16: Coop 8J 65
Chevening Gdns. SS5: Hock 1B 120
Chevers Pawen SS13: Pits 1H 133
Chevington Pl. RM12: Horn 7H 127
Chevington Way RM12: Horn 6H 127
Cheviot Cl. DA7: Bexh 7C 152
Cheviot Dr. CM1: Chelm 5F 58
Cheviot Ho. SS2: Sth S 5L 137
Cheviot Rd. RM11: Horn 2E 126
Cheviot Wlk. *SS2: Sth S* *6M 137*
(in Victoria Plaza Shop. Cen.)
Cheviot Way IG2: Ilf 8D 108
Chevron Ho. RM17: Grays 5L 155
Chevy Ct. CO12: R'sy 5E 208
Cheyne Av. E18: Lon 7F 106
Cheyne Ct. SS12: W'fd 3M 117
Cheyney St. SG8: Stpl M 4A 4
Chichester Cl. RM15: Ave 8N 143
SS8: Can I 3G 151
SS14: Bas 7G 117
Chichester Dr. CM1: Chelm 7L 59
Chichester Gdns. IG1: Ilf 2L 123
Chichester Ho. *CM14: Brtwd* *8F 96*
(off Sir Francis Way)
Chichester Rd. CB11: Saf W 5D 218
E11: Lon 5E 122
SS1: Sth S 6M 137
SS2: Sth S 6M 137 (5K 43)
Chichester Way CM9: Mal 8D 214
Chichester Wharf DA8: Eri 3C 152
CHICKNEY 5D 12
Chickney Rd. CM22: Hen 7E 210 (4C 12)
Chieftan Dr. RM19: Purf 2L 153
Chigborough Rd. CM9: H'bri, L Tot, Mal 7J 25
Chignal Hall Rd. CM1: Chig J 2A 58
Chignall Rd. CM1: Chelm 4F 58 (6K 23)
CM1: Chig J, Chig S 9B 56 (6J 23)
CHIGNALL ST JAMES 3B 58 (7J 23)
CHIGNALL SMEALY 8B 56 (6J 23)
Chignalls, The SS15: Lain 9J 115
CHIGWELL 9A 92 (1H 39)
Chigwell La. IG7: Chig 4B 92 (7H 31)
IG10: Chig, Lou 4B 92 (6H 31)
Chigwell Pk. IG7: Chig 1A 108
Chigwell Pk. Dr. IG7: Chig 1N 107
Chigwell Ri. IG7: Chig 8N 91 (1G 39)
Chigwell Rd. E18: Lon 7H 107 (3F 39)
IG8: Wfd G 3M 107 (2F 39)
CHIGWELL ROW 9G 92 (1J 39)
Chigwell Station (Tube) 9A 92 (1G 39)
Chigwell Vw. RM5: Col R 3M 109
Chilburn Rd. CO15: Clac S 6K 185
CHILDERDITCH 7K 113 (3F 41)
Childerditch Hall Dr. CM13: L War 6J 113
(not continuous)
Childerditch Ind. Pk. CM13: L War 7J 113
Childerditch La. CM13: Brtwd, L War,
W H'dn 4H 113 (2F 41)
Childerditch St. CM13: L War 6K 113
Childers, The IG8: Wfd G 2M 107
Childs Cl. RM11: Horn 1G 127
Childwell All. CO1: Colc 9A 166
(not continuous)
Chilford Ct. CM7: Brain 5F 192
Chilford Hall Vineyard 1D 6
Chilham Cl. SS13: Pits 1K 133
Chiltern *SS2: Sth S* *6N 137*
(off Coleman St.)
Chiltern App. SS8: Can I 1E 150
Chiltern Cl. CO1: Colc 6M 165
DA7: Bexh 6C 152
SS6: Ray 4K 119
Chiltern Gdns. RM12: Horn 5G 127
Chiltern Rd. IG2: Ilf 9D 108
Chilterns, The SS8: Can I 1F 150
Chiltern Way IG8: Wfd G 9G 90
Chilton Cl. CM2: Gt Bad 3E 72
CO6: Gt Hork 9J 159
Chilton Cotts. CO6: Wmgfd 8L 229
Chilton Rd. RM16: Grays 1C 156
Chiltons, The E18: Lon 6G 106
CHILTON STREET 2C 8
Chilton St. CO10: Clare 2C 8
Chimes, The SS7: Ben 2E 134
Chimney Pot La.
CM3: Cock C, Haz 7L 75 (3F 35)
CHIMNEY STREET 1B 8
Chimney St. CO10: Pos 1B 8
Chimswell Way CB9: H'hll 3H 7
China La. RM14: Bulp 5N 129
Chinchilla Rd. SS1: Sth S 6B 138
Chindits La. CM14: War 2F 112
Chinery Pl. CM1: Chelm 7M 59
Chingdale Rd. E4: Lon 9E 90
CHINGFORD 7C 90 (1E 38)
Chingford Av. CO15: Clac S 5K 185
E4: Lon 9A 90
CHINGFORD GREEN 7D 90 (7E 30)
CHINGFORD HATCH 1D 106 (1E 38)
Chingford La. IG8: Lon 1E 106 (1E 38)
CHINGFORD MOUNT 1A 106 (1D 38)
Chingford Mt. Rd. E4: Lon 1A 106 (1D 38)
Chingford Rd. E4: Lon 3A 106 (2D 38)
E17: Lon 5B 106
Chingford Station (Rail) 6E 90 (7E 30)
Chinnel La. CB11: Wen A 7J 227
Chinook CO4: Colc 3B 166
Chippenham Cl. RM3: Romf 2H 111
Chippenham Gdns. RM3: Romf 2H 111
Chippenham Rd. RM3: Romf 3H 111
Chippenham Wlk. RM3: Romf 3H 111
Chipperfield Cl. RM14: Upm 3B 128
CHIPPING 3C 10
Chippingdell CM8: Wthm 3C 230
Chippingfield CM17: H'low 9H 51
CHIPPING HILL 3B 230 (4F 25)
Chipping Hill CM8: Wthm 4C 230 (4F 25)
CO9: Hals 4L 207
CHIPPING ONGAR 8L 67 (3C 32)
Chipping Row CM3: S Fer 1L 103
Chipstead Rd. DA8: Eri 5C 152
Chipstead Wlk. CO16: Clac S 7G 185
Chishill Rd. SG8: Bar 6F 5
SG8: Gt Chi, Hey 6G 5
Chisholm Ct. SS12: W'fd 2M 117
Chislet Row CM2: Chelm 2D 72
Chiswell St. EC2: Lon 7B 38
CHISWICK END 3D 4
Chittenden Cl. EN11: Rye P 2B 52
Chittock Cl. CO16: Clac S 1F 188
Chittock Ga. SS14: Bas 9F 116
Chittock Mead SS14: Bas 9F 116
Chitts Hill CO3: S'way 5E 164 (5C 16)
CHITTS HILLS 7E 164
Chitty's La. RM8: Dag 4J 125
Chivers Rd. CB9: H'hll 3H 7
CM15: Ston M 6C 82 (4D 32)
E4: Lon 9B 90
Chivers Sq. CM5: H Ong 6C 68
Choats Mnr. Way
RM9: Dag 2K 141 (6K 39)
Choats Rd. IG11: Bark 2H 141 (6J 39)
RM9: Bark 2H 141 (6J 39)
Choats Wood CO3: S'way 6A 164
Chobham Rd. E15: Lon 7D 122 (5E 38)
Chopwell Cl. E15: Lon 9D 122
Chorley Cl. SS16: Lang H 1H 131
CHRISHALL 6H 5
Chrishall Rd. SG8: Fow, Hey 3G 5
Chrismund Way CO6: Gt Tey 1E 170
Chrisp St. E14: Lon 7D 38
(not continuous)
Christchurch Av. DA8: Eri 4B 152
RM13: Rain 2D 142
SS12: W'fd 8H 101
Christ Chu. Ct. CO3: Colc 1K 173
Christchurch Ct. SS1: Sth S 6A 138
Christchurch Rd. IG1: Ilf 3A 124
RM18: Til 6C 156
SS2: Sth S 5A 138
Christie Gdns. RM6: Chad H 1G 125
Christie Rd. EN9: Enf 5B 76
Christina Rd. CM8: Wthm 7A 230
Christine Chase CO3: Colc 1G 173
Christine Ct. RM13: Rain 5E 142
Christmas Fld. CO9: Sib H 5J 219
Christopher Cl. RM12: Horn 6H 127
Christopher Dr. CO16: L Cla 4H 185
Christopher Gdns. RM9: Dag 7J 125
Christopher Martin Rd.
SS14: Bas 5F 116
Christy Av. CM1: Chelm 7H 59
Christy Cl. SS15: Lain 8G 115
Christy Ct. SS15: Lain 8G 115
Christy Way SS15: Lain 8G 115
Chudleigh Cres. IG3: Ilf 6D 124
Chudleigh Rd. RM3: Romf 1J 111
Churchacre CM9: Tol 8K 225
Church Av. CM1: Broom 1J 59
E4: Lon 3D 106
(not continuous)
E12: Lon 5K 123
Churchbank *E17: Lon* *8A 106*
(off Teresa M.)
Church Chase CM3: Ret C 3C 102
Church Cl. CM8: W Bis 2J 229
CM14: Kel H 7A 82
CM15: Mount 9A 84
CO6: W Ber 3F 164
IG10: Lou 1M 91
SS3: Shoe 8H 139
SS8: Can I 2F 150
SS17: Horn H 2H 147
Church Cnr. SS7: Ben 5D 134
Church Cotts. SS11: Runw 7M 101
Church Ct. EN10: Brox 8A 52
Church Cres. CM15: Mount 9A 84
CM21: Saw 2L 51
CO15: Clac S 2K 189
E9: Lon 5C 38
RM15: S Ock 3F 144
Church Dr. CM23: Ber 4J 11
Church Elm La. RM10: Dag 8M 125 (5K 39)
CHURCHEND 1F 45
CHURCH END
CM3 8M 203 (3B 24)
CB10 8B 190 (5D 6)
CM7 5B 14
CM6 2E 22
(GREAT CANFIELD)
CM6 1L 203 (7G 13)
(GREAT DUNMOW)
SG11 7H 11
CM6 9D 222 (7J 13)
(STEBBING)
Church End CB10: A'dn 9C 190 (5E 6)
CB11: Clav 3J 11
CB11: Wick B 2K 11
CM6: Broxt 5D 12
CM6: Gt D 1L 203 (7G 13)
CM6: Lndsl 5H 13
CM7: Pan 1D 192 (6B 14)
CM19: H'low 5N 53
E17: Lon 8B 106
SG2: Walk 5A 10
SG8: Bar 6F 5
Church End Av. SS11: Runw 6M 101
Church End La. SS11: Runw 6L 101 (7C 34)
Church End Vs. CM6: Gt D 7G 13
Chu. Farm Way CO4: Colc 3M 165
Church Fld. CB10: A'dn 8B 190
CB11: Saf W 6D 218
CM16: Epp 8F 64
Churchfield CM20: H'low 1F 54
(not continuous)
Churchfield Rd. CO6: Cogg 2L 197
Church Fld. Rd. CO10: Sud 4K 9
Churchfield Rd. CO14: Walt 6M 181
Church Fld. Rd. IP9: Stut 1C 18
Churchfields CM24: Stan M 3E 220
CO3: S'way 2D 172
CO5: W Mer 3B 228
Church Flds. CO9: Gt Yel 2C 206
Churchfields E18: Lon 5G 106
EN10: Brox 8A 52
IG10: Lou 3L 91
SS3: Shoe 4J 139
Churchfields Dr. CB9: Stpl B 3K 223
Churchfields La. EN10: Brox 8A 52
Churchfields Wlk. CB9: Stpl B 3K 223
Church Gdns. CM6: Gt D 1L 203
CHURCHGATE 3C 30
Church Ga. CO10: Glem 1G 9
Churchgate EN7: Chesh 3C 30
SS0: Wclf S 5H 137
Churchgate Rd. EN7: Chesh 3C 30
CHURCHGATE STREET 8L 51 (6K 21)
Churchgate St. CM17: H'low 8K 51 (6K 21)
Church Grn. CM1: Broom 2K 59
CM1: Rox 3N 217
CM3: Terl 4D 24
CM8: W Bis 2J 229
CO6: Cogg 2L 197 (7H 15)
CO9: L Yel 6D 8
SS4: Cwdn 2M 105
Church Gro. CO6: Aldh 6B 16
Church Hill CB9: Hel B 5H 7
CB10: A'dn 8C 190 (5E 6)
CM3: L Walt 6L 57
CM3: Pur 8K 215 (3H 35)
CM7: F'fld 3D 200 (2K 13)
CM8: Whi N 2E 24
CM9: Wdhm W 1F 35
CM16: Epp 8F 64
CO5: K'dn 3J 211 (2H 25)
CO5: Rhdge 6F 174
CO6: E Col 8D 198 (4J 15)
CO11: Law 4E 162 (3K 17)
CO12: R'sy 6C 208 (3F 19)
DA1: Cray 9C 152
DA2: Dart 4C 46
E17: Lon 8A 106 (3D 38)
IG10: Lou 2L 91 (6G 31)
IP9: Holb 1D 18
N21: Lon 7A 30
SS9: Lgh S 6D 136
SS13: Pits 2J 133
SS15: Lain 8M 115 (3K 41)
SS17: Stan H 4L 147 (6K 41)
Church Hill Cnr. CM24: Stan M 4E 220
Church Hill Rd. E17: Lon 8B 106
Church Hollow RM19: Purf 3L 153
Churchill Av. CO9: Hals 3L 207
Churchill Cl. CM5: Chip 6L 67
CO7: B'sea 5E 182
Churchill Ct. CO12: Har 3J 209
Churchill Cres. SS17: Stan H 1N 147
Churchill Ri. CM1: Chelm 4N 59
Churchill Rd. CM7: Brain 2G 193
CO5: Tip 6F 226
RM17: Grays 4N 155
Churchill Sth. *SS2: Sth S* *6M 137*
(in Victoria Plaza Shop. Cen.)
Churchill Sq. *SS2: Sth S* *6M 137*
(in Victoria Plaza Shop. Cen.)
Churchill Ter. CM7: Brain 2G 193
E4: Lon 1A 106
Churchill Way CO2: Colc 2B 174
Churchill Wlk. *SS2: Sth S* *6M 137*
(in Victoria Plaza Shop. Cen.)
Church La. CB1: Abgtn 1B 6
CB1: Cas C 4G 7
CB2: Pam 1K 5
CB11: Deb 2C 12
CM1: Chelm 7M 59 (1A 34)
(Arbour La.)
CM1: Chelm 9K 59
(Duke St.)
CM1: Writ 1K 71
Church La. CM2: W Han 4H 87
CM3: Har E 3J 23
CM3: L L'gh 7H 203 (3A 24)
CM3: S Han 9K 87 (6C 34)
CM3: Stow M 5G 35
CM4: Ing, Marg 3G 84 (4J 33)
CM5: Chip 8H 67
(Greensted)
CM5: Chip 3L 67
(Shelley)
CM6: L Can 1E 22
CM6: Whi R 5D 22
CM7: Brain 1H 193 (6C 14)
CM9: L Tot 7J 25
CM11: Cray H 9C 100 (1A 42)
CM13: Gt War 1G 128
CM13: Hut 7A 98 (7G 33)
CM15: Dodd, Hook E 8D 82 (5E 32)
CM16: N Wea 6N 65
CM22: Else 4M 199 (6C 12)
CM22: Srng 4B 210 (5A 22)
CM22: Tak 3B 224
CM23: Thor 2J 21
CO3: Colc 1G 173 (6D 16)
CO3: S'way 1B 172 (6C 16)
(not continuous)
CO5: E Mer 4H 27
CO5: Gt Wig 4D 26
CO6: L Tey, M Tey 3E 170 (7K 15)
CO6: M Tey 2J 171 (7A 16)
CO9: Cas H 3K 219
CO9: Ridg 8D 216
CO9: Top 7B 8
CO10: Lav 1J 9
CO11: Bran 1A 18
CO11: Mist 4K 163
CO12: Har 1N 209
CO13: Gt Hol 2E 186 (2F 29)
CO16: T Sok 6E 18
CO16: Wee, Wee H 7E 178
DA12: Grav 4K 47
E11: Lon 3E 122
E17: Lon 8B 106
EN8: Chesh 3C 30
EN10: Brox, Wmly 1C 30
IG10: Lou 2M 91
IP9: Hark 1E 18
N8: Lon 3A 38
RM1: Romf 8C 110
RM4: Abr 1K 93 (6J 31)
RM4: Stap A 3A 94
RM10: Dag 9A 126
RM13: Wen 6H 143
RM14: Bulp 6B 130 (5G 41)
RM14: N Ock 7E 128
RM19: Purf 3L 153
SG8: Reed 7D 4
SG10: M Hud 2G 21
SG12: D End 1B 20
SG14: Stfrd 3A 20
SS13: Bas 5H 117
Church La. Cotts. CM5: Chip 3M 67
CHURCH LANGLEY 4J 55 (7J 21)
Church Langley Way CM17: H'low 3H 55 (7J 21)
Church Leys CM18: H'low 4E 54
Church Mnr. CM23: Bis S 9A 220
Church Manorway DA8: Eri 1B 152
Church Mead CM8: Whi N 2E 24
CM19: Roy 2H 53
Church Mdws. CM7: Brain 2H 193
Church M. SS15: Lain 8K 115
Chu. Mill Grange CM17: H'low 9K 51
Church Pde. SS8: Can I 1E 150
Church Pk. Rd. SS13: Pits 1J 133
Church Path CB10: Saf W 3C 218
CB11: Wen A 7K 227
E11: Lon 9G 107
E17: Lon 8B 106
RM1: Romf 9C 110
RM17: Grays 4K 155
SS13: Pits 2J 133
Churchponds CO9: Cas H 3K 219
Church Ri. CB9: Hel B 5H 7
Church Rd. BR8: Crock 7A 46
(Crockenhill)
BR8: Swan 6B 46
(Swanley Village)
CB1: Shudy C 3G 7
CB10: Hpstd 7G 7
CM0: Bur C 2D 196 (6C 36)
CM2: W Han 5G 86 (5B 34)
CM3: Bore, L Bad 3F 60 (7C 24)
CM3: Hat P 2K 61 (6E 24)
CM3: N Fam 1E 104
(not continuous)
CM3: Terl 4D 24
CM5: Chip 3G 81 (4B 32)
CM5: M'ton 1B 32
CM8: Riven, Sil E 2G 25
CM8: W Bis 2J 229 (5G 25)
CM9: Gt Tot 6J 25
CM9: Tol M 1L 201 (6A 26)
CM9: Ult 7F 25
CM11: Rams B 7E 100
CM11: Rams H 4D 100 (7A 34)
CM13: Dun 1E 130 (3H 41)
CM13: Ing, Mount 9A 84
CM14: Kel H 7N 81 (5D 32)
CM15: Mount 9A 84 (6G 33)
CM17: H'low 6H 55
CM22: Gt Hal, L Hall 2A 22
CM24:Bur E, Stan M 3D 220 (6A 12)
CM77: Bla N 2A 194 (1C 24)
CM77: Tye G 6H 217 (1E 24)
(Cressing)

Church Rd. CM77: Tye G 6F 15
(Pattiswick)
CM77: Tye G 7F 15
(Perry Green)
CO2: Lay H 2D 26
CO4: Boxt, Gt Hork 2L 159 (2E 16)
CO5: Fing 9G 174 (1G 27)
CO5: K'dn 3K 211
CO5: Pel 3E 26
CO5: Tip 5C 226 (3K 25)
CO5: W Mer 3B 228
CO6: Cop 4M 171 (7B 16)
CO6: For 2A 164 (4B 16)
CO6: Wmgfd 8L 229 (3B 16)
CO7: Alr 7A 176 (1J 27)
CO7: B'sea 3C 182 (2J 27)
CO7: Elms 9N 167 (6J 17)
(Clacton Rd.)
CO7: Elms, Frat 3C 176 (7J 17)
(Frating Hill)
CO7: Gt Ben, L Ben 7L 169 (6A 18)
CO7: Thorr 8F 176 (1K 27)
CO9: G'std G 8M 207 (4G 15)
CO9: Gosf 9K 201 (4D 14)
CO9: Gt Map, L Map 2F 15
CO9: Gt Yel 2C 206 (6C 8)
CO9: Stamb 6A 8
CO9: Wick P 7G 9
CO10: Bulm 1K 195 (5H 9)
CO10: T'std 7H 9
CO11: Gt Bro, L Bro 3F 168 (5K 17)
CO11: Wrab 3D 18
CO14: Walt 6M 181 (1H 29)
CO15: Clac S 2K 189
DA3: Hley 7F 47
DA4: S at H 5C 46
(not continuous)
DA8: Eri 3B 152
DA13: Cobh 6H 47
E10: Lon 3A 122 (4D 38)
E12: Lon 7L 123 (5G 39)
IG2: Ilf 1D 124
IG9: Buck H 7H 91 (7F 31)
IG10: H Bee, Lou 2G 90 (6F 31)
IG11: Bark 8B 124
IP9: Stut 1C 18
RM3: H Wood 5L 111
RM4: Nave 1H 95 (6B 32)
RM4: Noak H 7G 95 (7B 32)
RM14: Bulp 6B 130 (5G 41)
(not continuous)
RM18: Til 6B 156
RM18: W Til 4G 156 (2J 47)
SG8: Chris 6H 5
SG13: E Grn, L Berk 1A 30
SS1: Sth S 7M 137
SS3: Barl M 3B 44
SS3: Shoe 8G 138
SS4: R'fd 9H 105
SS5: Hock 7A 104 (1G 43)
SS5: Ray 5L 119
SS6: Van 1E 132 (3A 42)
SS7: Had 3L 135
SS7: Thund 9B 118 (3D 42)
SS11: Raw 9C 102 (1D 42)
SS13: Ben, Pits 1L 133 (3C 42)
SS14: Bas 7D 116 (3A 42)
(not continuous)
SS15: Lain 6N 115
(not continuous)
SS17: Corr 2C 148 (6A 42)
Church Rd. Almshouses E10: Lon 4B 122
(off Church Rd.)
Church Rd. Ind. Est. E10: Lon 3A 122
Church Rd. Res. Pk. SS17: Corr 2D 148
Church Sq. CO8: Bures 7L 195
CO16: St O 9M 183
CHURCH STREET 4E 8
Church St. CB9: Stpl B 2K 223 (5J 7)
CB9: Wthfld 2H 7
CB10: Gt Che 8D 202 (4A 6)
CB10: I'tn 6A 202 (4K 5)
CB10: Saf W 3C 218
CB11: Newp 2L 215
CM1: Chelm 9K 59
CM2: Gt Bad 4G 73 (2B 34)
CM4: B'more 1H 83
CM6: Gt D 1L 203 (7G 13)
CM7: Brain 9H 191 (6C 14)
CM8: Wthm 2C 230
CM9: Gold 2K 201 (7A 26)
CM9: Mal 6D 214
CM9: Tol 8K 225 (6C 26)
CM9: Tol D 3K 227 (6B 26)
CM11: Bill 2K 115 (1J 41)
CM21: Saw 2K 51
CM22: Hen 7C 210 (4C 12)
CO1: Colc 8M 165
CO4: Boxt 1N 159 (2E 16)
CO5: K'dn 3J 211 (2H 25)
CO5: Rhdge 6F 174
CO6: Cogg 3L 197 (7H 15)
CO6: Coln E 3E 198 (3H 15)
CO9: Gest 6F 9
CO9: Gt Map 1F 15
CO9: Sib H 6J 219 (1D 14)
CO10: Bel O, Bel P 4E 8
CO10: Clare 3D 8
CO10: Pos 1B 8
CO10: Sud 5J 9
CO12: Har 1M 209
E16: Lon 8A 140
EN2: Enf 6B 30
EN9: Wal A 3C 76
N9: Lon 7B 30
Church St. RM10: Dag 8N 125
RM17: Grays 4M 155
SG8: Lit 4A 4
SG8: Thri 2H 5
SG8: Whad 2C 4
SG9: Bunt 4D 10
SS6: Ray 5K 119
Church Ter. CO10: Wixoe 4A 8
RM4: Stap A 3A 94
Church Trad. Est. DA8: Eri 5D 152
Church Vw. CO5: Fee 9A 170
CO6: Coln E 3D 198
CO7: A'lgh 9L 161
RM14: Upm 4M 127
RM15: Ave 9N 143
Church Vw. Rd. SS7: Thund 9E 118
Church Wlk. CB9: Stur 7J 223
CB11: L'bry 1B 218
CM9: Mal 5B 214
(off Bull La.)
CM15: Brtwd 6E 96
CM21: Saw 2L 51
CO1: Colc 8M 165
IP9: S'ly 1G 19
SS4: R'fd 6K 121
SS14: Bas 9B 116
Church Way SS7: Had 4M 135
Churchwell Av. CO5: Ethpe 7J 171
Churchwood Gdns. IG8: Wfd G 1G 107
Churnwood Cl. CO4: Colc 6D 166
Churnwood Rd. CO4: Colc 6D 166
Chuzzlewit Dr. CM1: Chelm 4G 58
Cillocks Cl. EN11: Hod 4A 52
Cimarron Cl. CM3: S Fer 1K 103
Cineworld
Charter Way 8L 193
5A 124
(off Winston Way)
Cinque Port Rd. CO7: B'sea 6E 182
Circle, The RM18: Til 6C 156
Circular Rd. E. CO2: Colc 1N 173
Circular Rd. Nth. CO2: Colc 1M 173
Circular Rd. Sth. CO2: Colc 2M 173
(not continuous)
Circular Rd. W. CO2: Colc 1L 173
Cistern Yd. CO1: Colc 8M 165
CITY AIRPORT 7G 39
City Limits Bowling Alley 6L 109
CITY OF LONDON 7B 38
City of London Crematorium E12: Lon 5L 123
City Rd. CO5: W Mer 3A 228
EC1: Lon 6A 38
City Thameslink Station (Rail) 7A 38
Civic Sq. CM20: H'low 3C 54
RM18: Til 7C 156 (2H 47)
Civic Theatre & Cramphorn Theatre 8J 59
Civic Way IG6: Ilf 8B 108
Clachar Cl. CM2: Chelm 8B 60
Clacton Factory Shop. Village
CO15: Clac S 4L 185
Clacton Leisure Cen. 9K 185
CLACTON-ON-SEA 2K 189 (4D 28)
Clacton-on-Sea Airfield 3F 188 (4C 28)
Clacton Pier 3K 189
Clacton Rd. CO7: Elms 1H 175 (6G 17)
CO7: Elms 1N 175 (6J 17)
CO7: Gt Ben, Thorr 9E 176 (1K 27)
CO11: Hor X, Mist 5J 163 (3A 18)
CO11: Wix 4D 18
CO12: Gt Oak, L Oak 9D 208 (4F 19)
CO12: Sto G 5D 18
CO13: Gt Hol 7C 186 (3F 29)
CO15: Gt Hol, Hol S 7C 186 (3F 29)
CO16: St O 9M 183 (4B 28)
CO16: Wee, Wee H 7D 178 (1C 28)
E6: Lon 6F 39
Clacton Station (Rail) 1K 189 (4D 28)
Claire C'way. DA2: Dart 9B 154
Claire Cl. CM13: Brtwd 1J 113
Claire Rd. CO13: Walt 8E 180
Claire Rd. Ind. Est. CO13: Walt 8E 180
Clairmont Cl. CM7: Brain 6H 193
Clairmont Rd. CO3: S'way 1F 172
Clairvale RM11: Horn 2J 127
Clandon Rd. IG3: Ilf 4D 124
CLANVER END 7K 5
CLAPGATE
STONDON MASSEY 4B 82 (4D 32)
BISHOP'S STORTFORD 6G 11
Clapgate Dr. CO16: L Cla 3G 185
Clap La. RM10: Dag 4N 125
Claps Ga. La. E6: Lon 4A 140
Clapton Comn. E5: Lon 4B 38
Clapton Hall La. CM6: Gt D 1J 191
(Ongar Rd.)
CM6: Gt D 2H 191 (1G 23)
(Philpot End La.)
CLAPTON PARK 5C 38
Clapton Station (Rail) 4C 38
Clara James Cotts. SS8: Can I 2G 151
(off Kitkatts Rd.)
Clara Reeve Cl. CO3: S'way 2G 172
CLARE 3D 8
Clare Ancient House Mus. 3D 8
Clare Av. SS11: W'fd 6L 101
Clare Castle 3D 8
Clare Cl. CO9: Hals 7J 207
Clare Ct. CM6: Thax 7B 224
Clare Gdns. E7: Lon 6G 122
IG11: Bark 8E 124
Clare M. CM5: Chip 5L 67
Claremont Cl. RM16: Grays 1M 155
Claremont Ct. SS0: Wclf S 5K 137
Claremont Cres. DA1: Cray 9C 152
Claremont Dr. SS16: Van 2H 133
Claremont Gdns. IG3: Ilf 4D 124
RM14: Upm 3A 128
Claremont Gro. IG8: Wfd G 3J 107
Claremont Hgts. CO1: Colc 6M 165
Claremont Pl. IG7: Chig 9A 92
Claremont Rd. CO7: W'hoe 6J 175
E7: Lon 7H 123
E11: Lon 5D 122
RM11: Horn 1E 126
SS0: Wclf S 5J 137
SS15: Lain 7L 115
Claremont St. N18: Lon 2C 38
Clarence Av. IG2: Ilf 1N 123
RM14: Upm 4L 127
Clarence Cl. CM2: Chelm 7B 60
SS7: Ben 2D 134
Clarence Ct. RM17: Grays 4L 155
(off Clarence Rd.)
Clarence Ga. IG8: Ilf, Wfd G 3N 107
Clarence Rd. CM15: Pil H 5E 96
CM24: Stan M 2D 220
E7: Lon 6J 123
E12: Lon 6J 123
RM17: Grays 4K 155 (2F 47)
SS1: Sth S 7M 137
SS6: Ray 7M 119 (3G 43)
SS7: Ben 3D 134
SS13: Pits 8N 117
SS17: Corr 1D 148
Clarence Rd. Nth. SS7: Ben 2D 134
Clarence St. SS1: Sth S 7M 137
Clarendon Gdns. IG1: Ilf 2M 123
Clarendon Pk. CO15: Clac S 8M 185
Clarendon Rd. CM6: L Can 3E 224
E11: Lon 3D 122
E17: Lon 1B 122
E18: Lon 7G 106
SS5: Hock 7E 104
SS8: Can I 1J 151
SS13: Pits 8K 117
Clarendon Way CO1: Colc 6M 165
Clare Priory 3D 8
Clare Rd. CM7: Brain 6F 192
CO9: Til C 5D 8
CO10: Clare, Pos 2D 8
CO10: Pos 1C 8
E11: Lon 1D 122
SS7: Thund 9A 118
Clare Way CO16: Clac S 8F 184
Claridge Rd. RM8: Dag 3J 125
Clarissa Rd. RM6: Chad H 2J 125
Clark Cl. DA8: Eri 6E 152
Clarkebourne Dr. RM17: Grays 4N 155
Clarke Mans. IG11: Bark 9E 124
(off Upney La.)
Clarke Ri. CM3: Cold N 8K 197
Clarkesmead CO5: Tip 7C 226
Clarke's Rd. CO12: Har 4H 209
Clarkhill CM18: H'low 6D 54
Clarkia Wlk. CO4: Colc 8D 166
Clarks Farm Rd. CM3: Dan, L Bad 2F 74
Clarks La. CM16: Epp 1E 78
CO2: B'ch 9M 171
Clarksons, The IG11: Bark 2B 140
Clarks Rd. IG1: Ilf 4C 124
Clarks Wood Dr. CM7: Brain 5M 193
Clark Way CM1: Broom 2K 59
Claston Cl. DA1: Cray 9C 152
Claters Cl. SS2: Sth S 4D 138
Clatterbury La. CB11: Clav 2J 11
Clatterfield Gdns. SS0: Wclf S 4F 136
CLATTERFORD END
CHIPPING ONGAR 9E 66 (3B 32)
GOOD EASTER 5F 23
FYFIELD 9B 200 (1D 32)
Claude Oliver Cl. CO11: Law 6F 162
Claude Rd. E10: Lon 4C 122
Claudian Way RM16: Grays 1D 156
Claud Ince Av. CM77: Tye G 2D 194
Claudius Ho. Ct. CO1: Colc 7N 165
(off St Peter's St.)
Claudius Rd. CO2: Colc 1A 174
Claudius Way CM8: Wthm 7B 230
Claughton Way CM13: Hut 5N 97
CLAVERHAMBURY 6H 63 (3F 31)
Claverhambury Rd. EN9: Wal A 7G 62 (3F 31)
CLAVERING 3J 11
Clavering SS16: Van 2G 133
Clavering Ct. SS6: Ray 4G 119
Clavering Gdns. CM13: W H'dn 1N 129
Clavering Rd. CM7: Brain 2H 193
CM23: Ber, Man 5K 11
E12: Lon 3K 123
Clavering Way CM13: Hut 5M 97
Claybrick Av. SS5: Hock 2C 120
Clayburn Circ. SS14: Bas 9E 116
Clayburn End SS14: Bas 9E 116
Clayburn Gdns. RM15: S Ock 7E 144
Clayburn Side SS14: Bas 9E 116
Claybury B'way. IG5: Ilf 7L 107
Claybury Rd. IG8: Wfd G 4L 107
Clay Ct. E17: Lon 7D 106
Claydon Cres. SS14: Bas 8D 116
Claydons La. SS6: Had, Ray 7J 119
SS7: Had 8J 119
(Daws Heath Rd.)
SS7: Had, Ray 7J 119
(Rayleigh Rd.)
CLAY END 6A 10
Clay End SG2: Walk 6A 10
Claygate Cl. RM12: Horn 6E 126
Claygate La. EN9: Wal A 9E 62
CLAYHALL 7L 107 (2G 39)
Clayhall Av. IG5: Ilf 7L 107 (2G 39)
Clayhall Rd. CO15: Clac S 8L 185
CLAY HILL 5B 30
Clay Hill CO10: Gt Hen 7J 9
EN2: Enf 5A 30
Clay Hill La. SS16: Van 3C 132
Clay Hill Rd. SS16: Bas, Van 1C 132 (3A 42)
Clay Hills CO9: Peb 2H 15
Clay La. CM6: L Dun 6D 212
CM6: Steb 6C 222
(not continuous)
CO16: St O 8N 183 (3B 28)
Clay La. Gro. CO4: Colc 3D 166
Claypit Hill CM24: Bur E 4K 221 (6C 12)
EN9: H Bee, Lou, Wal A 6J 77 (5F 31)
Clay Pit Piece CB11: Saf W 7D 218
Clay Pits CM7: Brain 5M 193
Claypits Av. CO8: Bures 8M 195
Claypits La. CO10: Fox 3G 9
Claypits Rd. CM3: Bore 2G 60
Claypits Vs. CM6: Thax 8D 224
Clay Pits Way CM7: Brain 5M 193
Claypole Ct. E17: Lon 9A 106
(off Yunus Khan Cl.)
Clay Ride IG10: Lou 9K 77
(not continuous)
Clayshotts Dr. CM8: Wthm 7E 230
Clayside IG7: Chig 2B 108
Clays La. E15: Lon 7B 122
Clay's La. IG10: Lou 9N 77 (6G 31)
Clays La. Cl. E15: Lon 7B 122
Clays Mdw. CB11: L'bry 1A 218
Clayspring Cl. SS5: Hock 9C 104
Clays Rd. CO14: Walt 6K 181
Clayton Av. RM14: Upm 7M 127
Clayton Hall Country Pk. 2D 62
Clayton Rd. CO12: R'sy 5E 208
RM7: Rush G 3A 126
Claytonville Ter. DA17: Belv 9A 142
Clayton Way CM9: Mal 8C 214
Clay Tye Rd. RM14: Upm 4F 128 (4E 40)
Claywall Bri. CB9: Stpl B 2L 223
Claywall Cotts. CB9: Stpl B 2K 223
Cleall Av. EN9: Wal A 4C 76
Clear Bay Pk. CO16: P Bay 9E 182
Clearview Health & Racquet Club 9J 113
Clearwater CO2: Colc 2B 174
Cleeborn St. CM3: S Fer 2H 103
Cleland Path IG10: Lou 9A 78
Clematis Cl. RM3: Romf 4G 111
Clematis Gdns. IG8: Wfd G 2G 107
Clematis Tye CM1: Chelm 4N 59
Clematis Way CO4: Colc 8E 166
Clemence Rd. RM10: Dag 1A 142
Clementhorpe Rd. RM9: Dag 8H 125
Clements Cl. CM2: Chelm 8C 60
Clements Ct. IG1: Ilf 5A 124
Clements Gdns. SS5: Hock 1F 120
Clements Grn. La. CM3: S Fer 9K 89 (6F 35)
Clements Hall La. SS5: Hock 1F 120
Clements Hall Leisure Cen. 3F 120
Clements Hall Way SS5: Hock 3F 120
Clement's La. CB9: H'hll 3J 7
Clements La. IG1: Ilf 5A 124
Clements Pl. CM3: S Fer 9K 89
Clements Rd. E6: Lon 9L 123
IG1: Ilf 5A 124
Clement St. BR8: Swan 5B 46
Clement Way RM14: Upm 5K 127
CLERKENWELL 6A 38
Clerkenwell Rd. EC1: Lon 6A 38
Clerk's Piece IG10: Lou 2M 91
Clevedon Cl. CM77: Gt N 1C 204
Cleveland Cl. CO4: Colc 3C 166
Cleveland Dr. SS0: Wclf S 3J 137
Cleveland Pk. Av. E17: Lon 8A 106
Cleveland Pk. Cres. E17: Lon 8A 106
Cleveland Rd. E18: Lon 7G 107
IG1: Ilf 5A 124
SS8: Can I 3H 151
SS14: Bas 9D 116
Clevelands, The IG11: Bark 8B 124
Cleveland St. W1: Lon 6A 38
Cleves Av. CM14: Brtwd 7E 96
Cleves Cl. IG10: Lou 5L 91
Cleves Ct. CM3: Bore 2F 60
Cleves Rd. CB9: H'hll 3J 7
Cleves Wlk. IG6: Ilf 4B 108
Clevis Dr. CM3: S Fer 3M 103
Clewer Ct. E10: Lon 3A 122
(off Leyton Grange Est.)
Clewer Ho. SE2: Lon 9J 141
(off Wolvercote Rd.)
Clicket Hill CO8: Bures 8N 195 (2A 16)
Clickett End SS14: Bas 9D 116
Clickett Hill SS14: Bas 9D 116
Clickett Side SS14: Bas 9D 116
(not continuous)
Clieveden Rd. SS1: Sth S 8D 138
Cliff Av. SS0: Wclf S 5K 137
SS9: Lgh S 6F 136
Cliff Ct. CO12: Har 4M 209
CO13: Frin S 8L 181
Cliff Cres. CM7: Shalf 4B 14
Cliff Gdns. SS9: Lgh S 6F 136 (5H 43)
Cliffield CM7: Shalf 4B 14
Clifford Av. IG5: Ilf 5A 108
Clifford Cl. SS15: Lain 1M 131
Clifford Rd. E17: Lon 6C 106
RM16: Chaf H 1J 155
Cliff Pde. CO14: Walt 2M 181
SS9: Lgh S 6D 136 (5H 43)
Cliff Pl. RM15: S Ock 3G 144
Cliff Rd. CO12: Har 4L 209 (3H 19)
CO15: Hol S 8B 186
SS9: Lgh S 6F 136
Cliffsea Gro. SS9: Lgh S 5E 136

Cliffs Pavilion ... 7K 137
CLIFFTOWN ... 7L 137
Clifftown Pde. SS1: Sth S ... 7L **137** (5J **43**)
Clifftown Rd. SS1: Sth S ... 7M **137**
Cliff Way CO13: Frin S ... 9L **181**
Clifton Av. SS7: Ben ... 2B **134**
Clifton Cl. SS7: Ben ... 2D **134**
Clifton Ct. IG8: Wfd G ... 3G **107**
Clifton Dr. SS0: Wclf S ... 7J **137**
Clifton Hatch CM18: H'low ... 6F **54**
Clifton Ho. E11: Lon ... 4E **122**
Clifton Marine Pde. DA11: Grav, N'fleet ... 3G **47**
(not continuous)
Clifton M. SS1: Sth S ... 7M **137**
Clifton Rd. E7: Lon ... 8K **123**
IG2: Ilf ... 1C **124**
IG10: Lou ... 3L **91**
RM11: Horn ... 1E **126**
SS4: R'fd ... 9G **105**
SS8: Can I ... 2H **151**
SS13: Pits ... 8N **117**
Clifton Ter. CM4: Ing ... 5E **84**
CO7: W'hoe ... 6H **175**
SS1: Sth S ... 7M **137**
Clifton Wlk. SS7: Ben ... 2D **134**
Clifton Way CM13: Hut ... 7N **97**
SS7: Ben ... 2C **134**
Climmen Rd. SS8: Can I ... 9H **135**
Clinton Cl. CM3: E Han ... 2C **88**
Clinton Cres. IG6: Ilf ... 3D **108**
Clinton Rd. E7: Lon ... 6G **123**
SS8: Can I ... 2D **150**
Clipped Hedge CM22: Hat H ... 1E **210**
Clipper Blvd. DA2: Dart ... 9B **154**
Clipper Blvd. W. DA2: Dart ... 8A **154**
Clitheroe Rd. RM5: Col R ... 2A **110**
Cliveden Cl. CM1: Chelm ... 8G **58**
CM15: Shenf ... 6J **97**
Clivedon Rd. E4: Lon ... 2E **106**
Clive Rd. CM13: Gt War ... 4F **112** (2E **40**)
CO2: Colc ... 1N **173**
RM2: Romf ... 9F **110**
Clobbs Yd. CM1: Broom ... 3K **59**
Clock Ct. E11: Lon ... 8H **107**
Clockhall La. CO10: Pos ... 1B **8**
Clock Ho. *E17: Lon* ... *8D **106***
(off Wood St.)
SS15: Lain ... 9K **115**
Clockhouse Av. IG11: Bark ... 1B **140**
Clockhouse La.
RM4: Col R, Hav ... 1N **109**
(not continuous)
RM5: Col R ... 2A **110** (2K **39**)
RM16: Chaf H ... 8G **145** (1F **47**)
(not continuous)
Clock Ho. Pde. E11: Lon ... 1H **123**
Clock Ho. Rd. CM12: L Bur ... 2G **115** (1J **41**)
Clockhouse Way CM7: Brain ... 6K **193**
Clock Twr. CM18: H'low ... 4G **55**
Clock Twr. M. SE28: Lon ... 7G **140**
Clodmore Hill CB11: A'den ... 1J **11**
Cloes La. CO15: Clac S ... 8F **184**
CO16: Clac S ... 8F **184** (3C **28**)
Cloister Cl. RM13: Rain ... 4F **142**
Cloisters SS17: Stan H ... 3N **147**
Cloisters, The CM7: Brain ... 3J **193**
CO5: K'dn ... 4J **211**
SS15: Lain ... 9L **115**
Clopton Grn. SS14: Bas ... 8C **116**
Close, The CB11: Deb ... 2C **12**
CM6: Gt D ... 4M **203**
CM14: Brtwd ... 9G **96**
CM22: Hat H ... 1E **210**
CM77: Tye G ... 2E **194**
CO12: Har ... 4J **209**
CO13: Frin S ... 9H **181**
CO13: Gt Hol ... 1D **186**
CO15: Jay ... 5F **188**
E4: Lon ... 4C **106**
IG2: Ilf ... 1D **124**
RM6: Chad H ... 1K **125**
RM16: Grays ... 9M **145**
SS5: Hock ... 7B **104**
SS6: Thund ... 7H **119**
SS7: Ben ... 6D **134**
Cloudberry Rd. RM3: Romf ... 3H **111**
Clouded Yellow Cl. CM7: Gt N ... 8G **193**
Cloudesley Rd. DA8: Eri ... 6D **152**
Clough Ho. SS0: Wclf S ... 2H **137**
Clough Rd. CO4: Colc ... 1D **166**
Clova Rd. E7: Lon ... 8F **122**
SS9: Lgh S ... 4E **136**
Clovelly Ct. RM11: Horn ... 4L **127**
Clovelly Gdns. RM7: Maw ... 5N **109**
SS11: W'fd ... 7K **101**
Clover Cl. E11: Lon ... 4D **122**
SS16: Van ... 3F **132**
Clover Ct. CO3: S'way ... 1E **172**
RM17: Grays ... 4N **155**
Clover Dr. CO7: Thorr ... 9F **176**
Cloverfield CM18: H'low ... 6F **54**
Cloverlands CO4: Colc ... 5C **166**
Clover Leas CM16: Epp ... 8E **64**
Cloverley Rd. CM5: Chip ... 9L **67**
Cloverleys IG10: Lou ... 4K **91**
Clovers CO9: Hals ... 5J **207**
Clover Way CO7: A'lgh ... 2H **167**
SS16: Van ... 3F **132**
Cluff Ct. CM14: War ... 1F **112**
Clunas Gdns. RM2: Romf ... 7H **111**
Clune Ct. CM15: Shenf ... 6K **97**
Clunford Pl. CM1: Chelm ... 4A **60**
Cluny Sq. SS2: Sth S ... 3A **138**
Clusters, The SS2: Sth S ... 5L **137**
Clyde RM18: E Til ... 2L **157**
Clyde Cres. CM1: Chelm ... 7F **58**
RM14: Upm ... 1B **128**
SS6: Ray ... 6J **119**
Clyde Pl. E10: Lon ... 2B **122**
Clyde Rd. EN11: Hod ... 7D **52**
Clydesdale Ho. *DA18: Eri* ... *9K **141***
(off Kale Rd.)
Clydesdale Rd. CM7: Brain ... 6G **192**
RM11: Horn ... 2D **126**
Clyde Way RM1: Romf ... 4C **110**
Clydon Cl. DA8: Eri ... 4C **152**
Clynes Ho. *RM10: Dag* ... *5M **125***
(off Uvedale Rd.)
Coach Ho. Way CM8: Wthm ... 5D **230**
Coach La. CM9: Mal ... 5B **214**
Coachmans Mead CM7: F'fld ... 3C **200**
Coach M. CM11: Bill ... 3M **99**
Coach Rd. CB10: Hpstd ... 6G **7**
CO6: Gt Hork ... 8F **158** (4D **16**)
CO7: Alr ... 7A **176** (1J **27**)
Coal Ct. RM17: Grays ... 5K **155**
COALHILL ... 9N **87** (5C **34**)
Coalhouse Fort ... 6M **157** (2K **47**)
Coalport Cl. CM17: H'low ... 4H **55**
Coal Rd. RM18: E Til, W Til ... 2H **157**
Coan Av. CO15: Clac S ... 3H **189**
Coaster Steps *SS1: Sth S* ... *7A **138***
(off Kursaal Way)
Coast Rd. CO5: W Mer ... 2A **228** (5F **27**)
Coates Cl. CM9: H'bri ... 4D **214**
Coates Lodge CM2: Chelm ... 8B **60**
Coates Quay CM2: Chelm ... 9L **59**
Coats Hutton Rd. CO2: Colc ... 3J **173**
Cobbetts Av. IG4: Ilf ... 9K **107**
Cobbinsbank EN9: Wal A ... 3D **76**
Cobbins Chase CM0: Bur C ... 1B **196**
Cobbins Cl. CM0: Bur C ... 1B **196**
Cobbinsend Rd. EN9: Wal A ... 7K **63**
Cobbins Gro. CM0: Bur C ... 1B **196**
Cobbins, The CM0: Bur C ... 1B **196**
EN9: Wal A ... 3E **76**
Cobbins Way CM17: H'low ... 8K **51**
Cobble Row *CO3: S'way* ... *9E **164***
(off Hedgerows)
Cobbles, The CM15: Brtwd ... 8H **97**
RM14: Upm ... 2C **128**
Cobbold Rd. E11: Lon ... 5F **122**
IP11: Felix ... 1K **19**
COBBS FENN ... 8J **219** (2D **14**)
Cobbs La. CM22: Tak ... 7D **12**
Cobbs Pl. CM1: Chelm ... 8M **59**
Cobden Rd. E11: Lon ... 5E **122**
Cobdens IG7: Chig ... 3C **108**
Cobden Wlk. SS13: Pits ... 8K **117**
(not continuous)
COBHAM ... 6J **47**
Cobham RM16: Grays ... 9L **145**
Cobhambury Rd.
DA12: Cobh ... 6J **47**
DA13: Ludd ... 6J **47**
Cobham Hall ... 6K **47**
Cobham Ho. DA8: Eri ... 5D **152**
IG11: Bark ... 1B **140**
(not continuous)
Cobham Rd. E17: Lon ... 5C **106**
IG3: Ilf ... 4D **124**
SS0: Wclf S ... 7H **137**
Cobill Cl. RM11: Horn ... 8G **111**
COBLER'S GREEN ... 2K **23**
Coborn Rd. E3: Lon ... 6D **38**
Coburg Gdns. IG5: Ilf ... 6K **107**
Coburg La. SS16: Lang H ... 2H **131**
Coburg Pl. CM3: S Fer ... 1K **103**
Cochrane Ct. *E10: Lon* ... *3A **122***
(off Leyton Grange Est.)
Cockabourne Ct. *RM3: H Wood* ... *6L **111***
(off Archibald Rd.)
Cockaynes La. CO7: Alr ... 6N **175** (1J **27**)
COCK CLARKS ... 8M **75** (3F **35**)
Cockerell Cl. SS13: Bas ... 6J **117**
Cockethurst Cl. SS0: Wclf S ... 2F **136**
Cockett Wick La. CO16: St O ... 3A **188** (4B **28**)
COCK GREEN ... 9N **199** (2K **23**)
Cock Grn. CM19: H'low ... 5A **54**
Cock Hill CB9: Ked ... 2A **8**
Cock La. CB11: Clav ... 3H **11**
CM1: Hghwd ... 8B **70** (3G **33**)
(not continuous)
CO7: Gt Bro ... 6G **168**
EN11: Brox ... 1C **30**
Cockrell's Rd.
CO6: L Hork, Wmgfd ... 8N **229** (3C **16**)
Cockridden Farm Ind. Est.
CM13: Heron ... 6A **114**
Cock Rd. CO9: L Map ... 1G **15**
Cocksure La. DA14: Sidc ... 4A **46**
Codenham Grn. SS16: Bas ... 2C **132**
Codenham Straight SS16: Bas ... 2C **132**
Codham Hall La. CM13: Gt War ... 9E **112**
(not continuous)
Codham Pk. Cotts. CM7: Shalf ... 4B **14**
Codham Pk. Dr. CM7: Shalf ... 4B **14**
Coeur De Lion CO4: Colc ... 5N **165**
COGGESHALL ... 3L **197** (7H **15**)
Coggeshall Grange Barn ... 4K **197** (7H **15**)
COGGESHALL HAMLET ... 1H **25**
Coggeshall Heritage Cen. ... 3K **197**
Coggeshall Pieces CO9: Hals ... 4M **207**
Coggeshall Rd.
CM7: Brain, Tye G ... 5H **193** (7C **14**)
CM77: Tye G ... 5N **193**
CO5: Cogg, K'dn ... 1J **211** (1H **25**)
CO5: Fee ... 9A **170** (7J **15**)
CO6: Cogg ... 4A **170**
(Houchin's La.)
Coggeshall Rd.
CO6: Cogg, Gt Tey ... 2D **170** (6J **15**)
(Buckley's La.)
CO6: Cogg, M Tey ... 7J **15**
(Marks Tey)
CO6: E Col ... 9D **198** (6H **15**)
CO7: A'lgh, Ded ... 6M **161** (3H **17**)
Coggeshall Way CO9: Hals ... 4M **207**
Cogmore CB11: Wen L ... 7J **5**
Cohen Cl. CM77: Bla N ... 3B **194**
Cohort Dr. CO2: Colc ... 4H **173**
Cokefield Av. SS2: Sth S ... 3A **138**
Coker Rd. SS8: Can I ... 3D **150**
Cokers Cl. CM77: Bla N ... 3C **194**
Coke St. CO12: Har ... 2M **209**
Colam La. CM3: L Bad ... 7K **61** (1D **34**)
Colbert Av. SS1: Sth S ... 7D **138**
Colbourne Cl. SS17: Stan H ... 2A **148**
COLCHESTER ... 8N **165** (6E **16**)
Colchester & East Essex Cricket Club ... 7N **165**
Colchester Av. E12: Lon ... 6M **123**
Colchester Bus. Pk. CO4: Colc ... 1C **166**
Colchester By-Pass CO3: Colc ... 7J **165**
Colchester By-Pass Rd. CO1: Colc ... 6A **166**
CO4: Colc ... 9E **166**
Colchester Castle ... 8N **165** (6E **16**)
Colchester Cl. SS2: Sth S ... 4L **137**
Colchester Crematorium
CO2: Colc ... 3N **173** (7E **16**)
Colchester Garrison Athletics Stadium ... 1M **173**
Colchester Leisure World ... 6A **166**
Colchester Megabowl ... 6N **165**
Colchester Retail Pk. CO3: Colc ... 7M **165**
Colchester Rd. CM2: Chelm ... 6B **60** (7B **24**)
CM8: Wthm ... 5D **230** (4G **25**)
CM9: Gt Tot ... 9H **205** (5J **25**)
CM9: Gt Wig, Vir ... 4C **26**
CM9: Mal ... 3D **214** (7H **25**)
CM9: Tol D ... 1N **227** (5C **26**)
CM14: H Wood ... 5H **111**
CO5: Abb, L'hoe, Pel ... 8B **174** (2F **27**)
CO5: Mess, Tip ... 4D **226** (3K **25**)
CO5: Pel, W Mer ... 1D **228** (5F **27**)
CO6: Chap, Wak C ... 6B **196** (4K **15**)
CO6: Cogg ... 3M **197** (7H **15**)
CO6: W Ber ... 2F **164** (4D **16**)
(Bures Rd.)
CO6: W Ber, Wmgfd ... 7B **158** (3C **16**)
(Packards La.)
CO6: Whi C ... 7E **198** (4J **15**)
CO7: A'lgh ... 4F **166**
(Parson's Heath)
CO7: A'lgh ... 2J **167** (4J **17**)
(Harwich Rd.)
CO7: A'lgh, Gt Bro ... 4M **167** (5J **17**)
(Bromley Rd.)
CO7: Colc ... 4F **166** (5G **17**)
(Parson's Heath)
CO7: Colc, Elms, W'hoe ... 1G **175** (6G **17**)
(Andrew's Av.)
CO7: Ded ... 3L **161** (2H **17**)
CO7: Elms ... 9L **167** (6H **17**)
CO7: Frat, Gt Ben ... 3F **176** (7K **17**)
CO8: Bures, M Bur ... 8L **195** (2A **16**)
CO9: Hals ... 4L **207** (3F **15**)
CO11: Law ... 5G **163** (3K **17**)
CO11: Wix ... 5B **18**
CO12: Sto G ... 5C **18**
CO15: Hol S ... 8N **185**
CO16: Gt Ben, St O ... 5L **183** (3A **28**)
CO16: T Sok ... 4F **178** (7C **18**)
CO16: Ten, Wee ... 5B **178** (7B **18**)
E10: Lon ... 2C **122**
E17: Lon ... 1A **122**
RM3: H Wood, Romf ... 5H **111** (2B **40**)
SS2: Sth S ... 4L **137**
Colchester Station (Rail) ... 6M **165** (5E **16**)
Colchester Town Station (Rail) ... 9A **166** (6F **17**)
Colchester United F.C. (Layer Road)
... 2K **173** (7E **16**)
Colchester Zoo ... 6D **172** (1C **26**)
COLDBLOW ... 4A **46**
COLD CHRISTMAS ... 3D **20**
Cold Christmas La.
SG12: Thun, Ware ... 3C **20**
Cold Hall Chase CO7: Gt Bro ... 9D **168**
Coldhall La. CM1: Marg, Writ ... 6G **71**
CM4: Marg ... 6G **71**
Coldharbour La. RM13: Rain ... 6C **142**
RM19: Rain ... 2E **152**
Coldharbour Pinnacles Est.
CM19: H'low ... 4N **53**
Coldharbour Rd. CM19: H'low ... 4M **53**
DA11: N'fleet ... 4G **47**
Coldnailhurst Av. CM7: Brain ... 4G **193**
COLD NORTON ... 7J **197** (4H **35**)
Cold Norton Rd. CM3: Latch ... 8H **211** (4J **35**)
Cole Av. RM16: Grays ... 2E **156**
Colebeck St. DA8: Eri ... 4D **152**
Colebrooke Dr. E11: Lon ... 2J **123**
Colebrook Gdns. IG10: Lou ... 1A **92**
Colebrook La. IG10: Lou ... 1A **92**
Colebrook Path IG10: Lou ... 1A **92**
Cole Cl. SE28: Lon ... 8G **141**
Cole Ct. RM3: Romf ... 2J **111**
COLE END ... 7D **6**
Cole End Rd. CB10: Sew E ... 7D **6**
Coleford Ho. *RM3: Romf* ... *3J **111***
(off Kingsbridge Rd.)
Colegrave Rd. E15: Lon ... 7D **122**
COLE GREEN ... 3G **11**
Cole Grn. CO10: Bel P ... 4E **8**
Cole Grn. Bypass
SG14: Bir G, Col G, Hert, Pans ... 5A **20**
Cole Hill CM3: Gt L ... 9M **203** (3B **24**)
Colehills Cl. *CB11: Clav* ... *2J **11***
(off High St.)
Coleman Ct. CO15: Clac S ... 1K **189**
Coleman Rd. RM9: Dag ... 8K **125**
Coleman's Av. SS0: Wclf S ... 2J **137**
COLEMAN'S INTERCHANGE ... 3F **230** (4G **25**)
Colemans La. CM3: Dan ... 3D **74**
Coleman's La. EN9: Naze ... 5D **62**
Coleman St. SS2: Sth S ... 5M **137**
Colenso Rd. IG2: Ilf ... 3D **124**
Coleridge Av. E12: Lon ... 8L **123**
Coleridge Ct. CM1: Chelm ... 6H **59**
Coleridge Rd. CM9: Mal ... 7C **214**
DA1: Dart ... 9M **153**
RM3: Romf ... 4F **110**
RM18: Til ... 7E **156**
Coleridge Wlk. CM13: Hut ... 6M **97**
Coles Cl. CM5: Chip ... 5L **67**
Coles Grn. CO10: Bel P ... 4E **8**
IG10: Lou ... 9N **77**
Coles La. CO14: Walt ... 6K **181**
Coles Oak La. CO7: Ded ... 2H **161** (2G **17**)
Colet Rd. CM13: Hut ... 4M **97**
Colgate Pl. EN3: Enf ... 7A **76**
Colhurst Gdns. EN11: Rye P ... 3D **52**
Colinton Rd. IG3: Ilf ... 4G **125**
Collard Av. IG10: Lou ... 1B **92**
Collard Grn. IG10: Lou ... 1B **92**
Collards Almshouses *E17: Lon* ... *9C **106***
(off Maynard Rd.)
College Av. RM17: Grays ... 2L **155**
College Cl. RM17: Grays ... 2M **155**
College Ct. CO11: Law ... 4H **163**
College Gdns. E4: Lon ... 6B **90**
IG4: Ilf ... 9L **107**
College Pl. CM16: They B ... 6B **78**
E17: Lon ... 8E **106**
College Point E15: Lon ... 8F **122**
College Rd. BR8: Swan ... 6A **46**
CM7: Brain ... 5G **193**
CO15: Clac S ... 1L **189**
E17: Lon ... 9C **106**
EN7: Chesh ... 3C **30**
RM17: Grays ... 2M **155**
College Sq. CM20: H'low ... 3C **54**
College St. NW1: Lon ... 5A **38**
College Way SS1: Sth S ... 6M **137**
Coller Rd. CO12: Har ... 2H **209**
Colles Brook Rd. CO7: Gt Ben ... 1L **183** (2A **28**)
Colletts Chase CO6: Wmgfd ... 8M **229**
Colley Bri. La. CM4: Cook G, Rad G ... 2N **69**
Colley Rd. CM2: Gt Bad ... 4H **73**
Collier Cl. E6: Lon ... 7A **140**
COLLIER ROW ... 4N **109** (2K **39**)
Collier Row CB10: A'dn ... 7D **190**
Collier Row La. RM5: Col R ... 4N **109** (2K **39**)
Collier Row Rd. RM5: Col R ... 5M **109** (2K **39**)
COLLIERS END ... 1D **20**
COLLIERS HATCH ... 1N **79** (3A **32**)
Colliers, The CM9: Hey B ... 8F **214**
Collier St. CM22: Hat O ... 2C **22**
Collindale Cl. SS8: Can I ... 1K **151**
Collindale Gdns. CO15: Clac S ... 8N **185**
Collingwood SS7: Ben ... 2E **134**
Collingwood Cl. CM7: Brain ... 3L **193**
RM13: Rain ... 2D **142**
Collingwood Rd. CM3: S Fer ... 2M **103**
CM8: Wthm ... 4C **230** (4F **25**)
CO3: S'way ... 9F **164**
CO15: Clac S ... 3H **189**
E17: Lon ... 1A **122**
SS16: Van ... 2E **132**
Collingwood Ter. SS16: Van ... 2E **132**
Collingwood Wlk. SS16: Van ... 1E **132**
Collingwood Way SS3: Shoe ... 5J **139**
Collins Cl. CM7: Brain ... 6H **193**
SS17: Stan H ... 3N **147**
Collins Cross CM23: Bis S ... 8A **220**
Collins Ho. SS17: Corr ... 1A **148**
Collins La. CM8: Wthm ... 5D **230**
Collins Mdw. CM19: H'low ... 3A **54**
Collins Rd. CO9: L Map ... 1G **15**
Collins Way CM13: Hut ... 4B **98**
SS9: Lgh S ... 9F **120**
Collinwood Gdns. IG5: Ilf ... 9M **107**
Collops Rd. CM6: Steb ... 9F **222** (7J **13**)
Collops Vs. CM6: Steb ... 9F **222**
Colman Cl. SS17: Stan H ... 2M **147**
Colmore Rd. EN3: Enf ... 6C **30**
Colne RM18: E Til ... 1L **157**
Colne Bank Av. CO1: Colc ... 7L **165**
CO3: Colc ... 7L **165** (6E **16**)
Colne C'way. CO2: Colc ... 1D **174** (6F **17**)
Colne Chase CM8: Wthm ... 5B **230**
Colne Cl. CM3: S Fer ... 1L **103**
RM15: S Ock ... 7F **144**
Colne Ct. CM7: Brain ... 7L **193**
RM18: E Til ... 1L **157**
Colne Dr. RM3: Romf ... 3K **111**
SS3: Shoe ... 5J **139**
COLNE ENGAINE ... 3E **198** (3H **15**)
Colne Engaine Rd. CO6: Coln E ... 3J **15**
Colneford Hill CO6: Whi C ... 7E **198** (4J **15**)
Colne Ho. CM9: Mal ... 3D **214**
IG11: Bark ... 9A **124**
Colneis Rd. IP11: Felix ... 1K **19**
Colne Pk. Rd. CO6: Whi C ... 6E **198** (4J **15**)
Colne Pl. SS16: Bas ... 2D **132**
Colne Ri. CO5: Rhdge ... 6F **174**
Colne Rd. CO6: Cogg ... 1L **197** (6H **15**)
(not continuous)
CO6: Coln E ... 1D **198** (2H **15**)
CO7: B'sea ... 7D **182** (3K **27**)
CO8: Bures ... 9H **195** (2K **15**)
CO9: Hals ... 4L **207** (3G **15**)

Colne Rd. CO9: Sib H 7K 219
CO15: Clac S 2K 189
Colne Springs CO9: Ridg 8D 216
Colne Ter. CO7: W'hoe 6H 175
Colne Valley RM14: Upm 1B 128
Colne Valley Cl. CO9: Hals 4J 207
Colne Valley Railway & Mus. 2H 219 (7D 8)
Colne Vw. CO16: St O 4K 27
Colne Vw. Retail Pk. CO1: Colc 6A 166
Colne Wlk. CM7: Brain 7M 193
Colne Way CO16: P Bay 9D 182 (4K 27)
Colombo Rd. IG1: Ilf 3B 124
Colson Gdns. IG10: Lou 3A 92
Colson Grn. IG10: Lou 4A 92
Colson Path IG10: Lou 3N 91
Colson Rd. IG10: Lou 3N 91
Colston Rd. E7: Lon 8K 123
Colt Hatch CM20: H'low 1A 54
Colthorpe Rd. CO15: Clac S 5K 185
Coltishall Cl. SS11: W'fd 1B 118
Coltishall Rd. RM12: Horn 8G 126
Colt M. EN3: Enf 7A 76
Coltsfield CM24: Stan M 1D 220
Coltsfoot Ct. CO4: Colc 5K 165
RM17: Grays 4N 155
Coltsfoot Path RM3: Romf 4G 111
(not continuous)
Columbia Rd. E2: Lon 6B 38
Columbia Wharf Rd. RM17: Grays 4K 155
Columbine Cen., The 5N 181
Columbine Gdns. CO14: Walt 7L 181
Columbine M. CO3: S'way 8D 164
Columbine Way RM3: H Wood 5J 111
Columbus Ct. DA8: Eri 5D 152
Columbus Sq. DA8: Eri 4D 152
Colvers CM17: Mat G 6B 22
Colville Cl. CM77: Gt N 1C 204
SS17: Corr 9A 132
Colville M. CM12: Bill 3H 99
Colville Rd. E11: Lon 5C 122
Colvin Chase CM2: Gall 9C 72
Colvin Cl. CO3: Colc 8G 165
Colvin Gdns. E4: Lon 9C 90
E11: Lon 8H 107
IG6: Ilf 5B 108
Colvin Rd. E6: Lon 9L 123
Colwall Gdns. IG8: Wfd G 2G 107
Colworth Cl. SS7: Had 2K 135
Colworth Rd. E11: Lon 1E 122
Colyers Cl. DA8: Eri 6C 152
Colyers La. DA8: Eri 6A 152 (2A 46)
Colyers Reach CM2: Chelm 9B 60
Colyers Wlk. DA8: Eri 6C 152
Colyn Pl. CB10: Saf W 2D 218
Comely Bank Rd. E17: Lon 9C 106
Comet Cl. E12: Lon 6K 123
RM19: Purf 2L 153
Comet Way SS2: Sth S 9G 120
Comet Way Ind. Est. SS2: Sth S 9G 120
Comfrey Ct. RM17: Grays 4N 155
Comma Cl. CM7: Gt N 7G 193
Commerce Pk. CO2: Colc 2D 174
Commerce Way CO2: Colc 2D 174
CO11: Law 3H 163
Commercial Rd. E1: Lon 7C 38
E14: Lon 7C 38
SS0: Wclf S 2J 137
Commercial St. E1: Lon 6B 38
Commodore Ho. SS14: Bas 9F 116
Common App. SS7: Thund 9G 118
Commonfields CM20: H'low 2D 54
Commonhall La. SS7: Had 3K 135
Common Hill CB10: Saf W 3C 218 (6B 6)
Common La. CM3: L Bad 9M 61
(not continuous)
CM4: Stock 7N 85
CM6: Gt Eas, L Eas 6E 12
CM9: Wdhm W 1E 34
CO9: Ridg 9D 216
DA2: Dart 4B 46
SS7: Thund 8G 119
Common Rd. CM4: Stock 6N 85
CM13: Ingve 2M 113
EN9: Naze 9L 53 (1G 31)
SS3: Gt W 2M 139
Commonside Rd. CM18: H'low 7D 54 (1H 31)
Commons, The CO3: Colc 1G 173 (6D 16)
Common, The CM3: Dan 4E 74 (2E 34)
CM3: E Han 1B 88 (4D 34)
E15: Lon 8E 122
SS7: Thund 8G 118
Community Rd. E15: Lon 7D 122
Como St. RM7: Romf 9B 110
Compasses Rd. CM77: Tye G 6F 15
Compasses Row CM1: Chelm 7J 59
Compass Gdns. CM0: Bur C 2C 196
Compton Av. CM13: Hut 7M 97
RM2: Romf 7G 110
Compton Ct. SS8: Can I 3K 151
SS11: W'fd 9M 101
Compton Pl. DA8: Eri 4D 152
Compton Rd. CO4: Colc 7B 166
N21: Lon 7A 30
Compton Ter. SS11: W'fd 9M 101
Compton Wlk. SS15: Lain 8K 115
Comyns Cl. CO4: Colc 1A 166
Comyns Pl. CM1: Writ 1K 71
Comyns Rd. RM9: Dag 9M 125
Conan Doyle Cl. CM7: Brain 8J 193
Concorde Ho. *RM12: Horn 8F 126*
(off Astra Cl.)
Concord Rd. SS8: Can I 9F 134
Conder Way CO2: Colc 2C 174
Condor Wlk. RM12: Horn 9F 126
Conduct La. SG9: Gt Hor 3F 11
Conduit La. CM9: Wdhm M 4K 75 (2F 35)
EN11: Hod 5A 52 (7D 20)
N18: Lon 1C 38
Conduit La. E. EN11: Hod 5B 52
Conduit St. *CM2: Chelm 9K 59*
(off High St.)
W1: Lon 7A 38
CONEY ACRE 2B 216
Coney Burrows E4: Lon 8E 90
Coney Byes La. CO6: W Ber 9D 158 (4C 16)
Coney Grn. CM21: Saw 1J 51
Conference Cl. E4: Lon 8C 90
Congregational Ho. *CO9: Hals 4L 207*
(off Parsonage St.)
Congreve Rd. EN9: Wal A 3E 76
Conies Rd. CO9: Hals 6J 207
Conifer Av. RM5: Col R 2N 109
Conifer Cl. CO4: Colc 7D 166
CO7: Alr 7M 175
Conifer Dr. CM14: War 2G 112
Conifers SS7: Had 3L 135
Coningsby Gdns. E4: Lon 3B 106
Coniston SS2: Sth S 8F 120
Coniston Av. IG11: Bark 9D 124
RM14: Upm 6N 127
Coniston Cl. CM77: Gt N 2D 204
DA7: Bexh 6A 152
DA8: Eri 5C 152
IG11: Bark 9D 124
SS6: Ray 5L 119
Coniston Ct. CM16: Epp 1F 78
Coniston Gdns. IG4: Ilf 8L 107
Coniston Rd. DA7: Bexh 6A 152
SS7: Thund 8E 118
SS8: Can I 2G 150
Coniston Way RM12: Horn 7E 126
Connaught Av. CO13: Frin S 9J 181 (1G 29)
E4: Lon 6D 90
IG10: Lou 3K 91
RM16: Grays 9L 145
Connaught Bri. E16: Lon 7F 39
Connaught Cl. CO15: Clac S 1M 189
Connaught Ct. *E17: Lon 8B 106*
(off Orford Rd.)
Connaught Dr. CM3: S Fer 1J 103
Connaught Gdns. CM7: Brain 4K 193
N13: Lon 1A 38
SS3: Shoe 8G 139
Connaught Gdns. E. CO15: Clac S 9M 185
Connaught Gdns. W. CO15: Clac S 9M 185
Connaught Hill IG10: Lou 3K 91
Connaught Ho. CO4: Colc 9C 160
Connaught La. IG1: Ilf 4B 124
Connaught Rd. CO16: L Cla, Wee H 9G 178
E4: Lon 6E 90
E11: Lon 3D 122
E17: Lon 9A 106
IG1: Ilf 4C 124
RM12: Horn 5H 127
SS6: Ray 7N 119
(not continuous)
Connaught Wlk. SS6: Ray 7N 119
Connaught Way CM12: Bill 3J 99
Connington Cres. E4: Lon 9D 90
Connor Cl. E11: Lon 2E 122
IG6: Ilf 5B 108
Connor Rd. RM9: Dag 6L 125
Conqueror Ct. RM3: Romf 4H 111
Conquerors Cl. CM3: Hat P 3M 61
Conrad Cl. RM16: Grays 9L 145
Conrad Gdns. RM16: Grays 9K 145
Conrad Rd. CM8: Wthm 2B 230
SS17: Stan H 3N 147
Consort Cl. CM14: War 2F 112
Constable Av. CO16: Clac S 7F 184
Constable Cl. CO4: Colc 3M 165
CO5: W Mer 2D 228
CO11: Law 4G 162
Constable Ct. CO2: Colc 3J 173
Constable Ho. CM7: Brain 5G 192
Constable M. CO7: Ded 1M 161
RM8: Dag 6G 125
Constable Row CO7: Ded 2N 161
Constable Vw. CM1: Chelm 5A 60
Constable Way CM77: Bla N 3B 194
SS3: Shoe 6K 139
Constance Cl. CM1: Broom 9J 57
CM8: Wthm 7E 230
Constantine Rd. CM8: Wthm 7B 230
CO3: Colc 1L 173
Constitution Hill SS7: Ben 3D 134
Consul Av. RM9: Dag, Rain 3A 142
RM13: Rain 3B 142
Convent Cl. SS15: Lain 9L 115
Convent Hill CM7: Brain 3J 193 (6D 14)
Convent La. CM7: Brain 3J 193
Convent Rd. SS8: Can I 2H 151
Con Way SS7: Ben 3D 134
Conway Av. SS3: Gt W 3L 139
Conway Cl. CO7: W'hoe 6J 175
CO9: Hals 6J 207
RM13: Rain 9E 126
Conway Cres. RM6: Chad H 1H 125
Conway Gdns. RM17: Grays 5L 155
Conways Rd. RM16: Ors 1C 146 (6H 41)
Conybury Cl. EN9: Wal A 2G 77
Conyer Cl. CM9: Mal 8B 214
Conyers Cl. IG8: Wfd G 3E 106
Conyers, The CM20: H'low 1B 54
Conyers Way IG10: Lou 2A 92
Cook Cl. CO12: Har 6H 209
Cook Ct. DA8: Eri 5D 152
Cook Cres. CO4: Colc 8E 166
Cooke Cl. RM16: Chaf H 1H 155
Cookes Cl. E11: Lon 4F 122
Cookham Ct. SS3: Shoe 4J 139
Cookham Rd. BR5: Orp, Swan 6A 46
Cookhill Rd. SE2: Lon 9G 140
Cook Pl. CM2: Chelm 8A 60
Cook Rd. RM9: Dag 1K 141
Cooks Cl. CO9: Hals 6L 207
Cook's Cl. RM5: Col R 5A 110
COOK'S GREEN 2M 185 (2E 28)
Cooks Grn. SS13: Bas 6K 117
Cooks Hall Rd. CO6: W Ber 4D 164
Cooks Hill CM22: Tak 3A 224 (1C 22)
CO4: Boxt 1A 160 (2F 17)
Cook's La. CM7: Gt Bar, L Bar 3J 13
CO3: Colc, S'way 7E 164
(not continuous)
COOKSMILL GREEN 1C 70 (1G 33)
Cook Sq. DA8: Eri 5D 152
Cooks Spinney CM20: H'low 1F 54
(not continuous)
Coolgardie Av. E4: Lon 2D 106
IG7: Chig 9N 91
Coolyne Way CO15: Clac S 6M 185
Coombe Dr. SS16: Bas 5L 131
Coombe Ho. E4: Lon 3A 106
Coombe Ri. CM1: Chelm 4K 59
CM15: Shenf 7J 97
SS17: Stan H 3N 147
Coombe Rd. CM0: S'min 2D 222
RM3: H Wood 7K 111
SG8: R'ton 6A 4
Coombes Cl. CM12: Bill 4H 99
Coombes Cnr. SS9: Lgh S 2D 136
Coombes Gro. SS4: R'fd 5M 121
Coombes Rd. RM9: Dag 1L 141
Coombewood Dr. RM6: Chad H 1L 125
SS7: Thund 1E 134
Cooper Ct. E15: Lon 7B 122
Cooper Dr. CM7: Brain 4F 192
Cooper Pk. CM7: Brain 4F 192
Coopers CM3: Bore 3F 60
COOPERSALE 8J 65 (3J 31)
Coopersale Cl. IG8: Wfd G 4J 107
Coopersale Comn.
CM16: Coop, Epp, N Wea 7J 65 (3J 31)
Coopersale La.
CM16: They B, They G 7F 78 (5J 31)
Coopersales SS15: Lain 9J 115
COOPERSALE STREET 1H 79 (4J 31)
Coopersale St. CM16: Epp, Fid 2H 79 (4J 31)
Coopers Av. CM9: H'bri 3E 214
Coopers Beach Holiday Pk. CO5: E Mer 5H 27
Coopers Cl. IG7: Chig 8G 93
RM10: Dag 8N 125
Coopers Cres. CM77: Gt N 8E 192
CO6: W Ber 3G 165
Coopers Dr. CM11: Bill 1L 115
COOPERS END 6M 221
Coopers End Rd. CM24: Stan Apt 6M 221
Coopers End Rdbt. CM22: Stan Apt 6N 221
Coopers Hill CM5: Chip 8L 67 (3C 32)
Coopers La. CM3: Gt L 7K 203
(not continuous)
Cooper's La. CO7: Ded 3M 161
Coopers La. CO15: Clac S 1G 188
E10: Lon 3B 122
Coopers La. Rd. EN6: Enf 4A 30
Coopers M. CM5: Chip 8L 67
Cooper's Row CM1: Chelm 6J 59
Cooper's Shaw Rd.
RM18: W Til 5F 156 (2H 47)
Coopers Wlk. E15: Lon 7E 122
Coopers Way SS2: Temp I 1M 137
Cooper Wlk. CO4: Colc 7D 166
Coote Gdns. RM8: Dag 5L 125
Coote Rd. RM8: Dag 5L 125
Copdoek SS14: Bas 8D 116
Copeland Rd. E17: Lon 1B 122
Copelands SS4: R'fd 1J 121
Copeman Rd. CM13: Hut 6N 97
Copenhagen St. N1: Lon 6A 38
COPFORD 2M 171 (7B 16)
Copford Av. SS6: Ray 6M 119
Copford Cl. CM11: Bill 6L 99
IG8: Wfd G 3L 107
COPFORD GREEN 4M 171 (7B 16)
Copford Rd. CM11: Bill 6L 99
Copland Cl. CM1: Broom 2J 59
CM2: Gt Bad 2G 72
Copland Rd. SS17: Stan H 4M 147
Coploe Rd. CB10: Gt Che, I'tn 7A 202 (4K 5)
Copped Hall 2M 77 (4G 31)
Coppen Rd. RM8: Dag 2L 125
Coppens Grn. SS12: W'fd 1M 117
Copperas Rd. CO7: B'sea 8E 182
Copperas Wood Nature Reserve 3A 208
Copper Beech Cl. IG5: Ilf 5N 107
Copper Beech Ct. IG10: Lou 9N 77
Copper Beeches CO3: S'way 1E 172
SS7: Had 8H 119
Copper Beech Rd. RM15: S Ock 3F 144
Copper Ct. CM7: Gt N 7G 193
CM21: Saw 2K 51
Copperfield CM11: Bill 1M 115
IG7: Chig 2C 108
Copperfield Gdns. CM14: Brtwd 7E 96
Copperfield Rd. CM1: Chelm 4F 58 (7K 23)
SE28: Lon 6H 141
Copperfields CB11: Saf W 5B 218
SS15: Lain 8L 115
Copperfields Way RM3: H Wood 5H 111
Coppergate Ct. *EN9: Wal A 4G 77*
(off Farthingale La.)
Coppice Cl. CM6: Gt D 2L 203
Coppice End CO4: Colc 4B 166
Coppice Hatch CM18: H'low 5C 54
Coppice La. SS15: Bas 6A 116
Coppice Path IG7: Chig 1G 108
Coppice Rd. CO7: Alr 6A 176
Coppice Row CM16: They B 6B 78 (5G 31)
Coppice, The CM15: Kel H 6B 82
CO15: Clac S 3H 189
Coppice Vw. CM11: Bill 5L 99
Coppice Way E18: Lon 8F 106
Coppingford End CO6: Cop 1M 171
Coppings, The EN11: Hod 2A 52
Coppins Cl. CM2: Chelm 7N 59
Coppins Rd. CO15: Clac S 9G 184 (4D 28)
Copse Hill CM19: H'low 6A 54
Copse, The CM6: Fels 7N 199
CM12: Bill 4J 99
CM23: Bis S 9B 220
CO4: Colc 4N 165
E4: Lon 7F 90
Copshall Cl. CM18: H'low 7D 54
Coptfold Cl. SS1: Sth S 5D 138
Coptfold Hall Dr. CM4: Marg 8F 70
Coptfold Rd. CM14: Brtwd 8F 96
COPTHALL GREEN 3L 77 (4F 31)
Copthall La. CM6: Thax 7C 224 (3F 13)
Copt Hall La. DA13: Meop 6H 47
Copt Hall Rd. CO5: L Wig 4D 26
Copt Hill CM3: Dan 4E 74 (2E 34)
Copthorne Av. IG6: Ilf 3A 108
Copthorne Gdns. RM11: Horn 9L 111
Copy Hill CB9: Hel B 4J 7
Coral Cl. CM3: S Fer 9J 89
RM6: Chad H 8H 109
Coralin Wlk. CO3: S'way 9D 164
Coralline Wlk. SE2: Lon 9H 141
Coram Grn. CM13: Hut 5N 97
Corasway SS7: Thund 1J 135
Corbets Av. RM14: Upm 7M 127
CORBETS TEY 7N 127 (5D 40)
Corbets Tey Rd. RM14: Upm 6M 127 (4C 40)
Corbett Rd. E11: Lon 1J 123
E17: Lon 7C 106
Corbicum E11: Lon 2E 122
Corbridge M. RM1: Romf 9D 110
Corcorans CM15: Pil H 5E 96
Cordelia Cres. SS6: Ray 4J 119
Cordwainers, The SS2: Temp I 1M 137
Cordy's La. IP11: T Mary 1J 19
Corfe Cl. SS13: Pits 9J 117
Corhaven Ho. DA8: Eri 5C 152
Coriander Rd. CO5: Tip 7C 226
Cories Cl. RM8: Dag 4J 125
Corinda Ho. CO13: Frin S 1J 187
Corinthian Manorway DA8: Eri 2B 152
Corinthian Rd. DA8: Eri 2B 152
Coriolanus Cl. CO2: Colc 3H 173
Corkers Path IG1: Ilf 4B 124
Cormorant Rd. E7: Lon 7F 122
Cormorant Wlk. CM2: Chelm 5D 72
RM12: Horn 8F 126
Cornard Rd. CO10: Sud 5J 9
CORNARD TYE 5K 9
Cornec Av. SS9: Lgh S 9A 120
Cornec Chase SS9: Lgh S 9B 120
Cornel Cl. CM8: Wthm 3A 230
Cornelia Pl. DA8: Eri 4C 152
Cornelius Vale CM2: Chelm 7C 60
Cornells La. CB11: Widd 3C 12
Cornell Way RM5: Col R 2M 109 (1K 39)
Corner Mdw. CM18: H'low 7F 54
Corner Pk. CB10: Saf W 2D 218
Corner Rd. CM11: Cray H 2E 116
Cornerways CM15: Dodd 8G 82
Cornfields CM3: S Fer 9J 89
Cornflower Cl. CO3: S'way 8D 164
Cornflower Dr. CM1: Chelm 6A 60
Cornflower Gdns. CM12: Bill 4H 99
Cornflower Rd. CO15: Jay 5E 188
Cornflower Way RM3: H Wood 5J 111
Cornford Way CO11: Law 4G 163
Cornhill CM1: Chelm 9K 59
Cornhill Av. SS5: Hock 9D 104
Corniche, The CM7: Gt Bar 3B 202
Cornish Gro. CM3: S Fer 2L 103
CORNISH HALL END 7K 7
Cornish Hall End Rd.
CO9: Stamb 6K 7
Cornmill EN9: Wal A 3B 76
Corn Mill Ct. CB11: Saf W 5D 218
Cornshaw Rd. RM8: Dag 3J 125
Cornsland CM14: Brtwd 9G 96
Cornsland Ct. CM14: Brtwd 9F 96
Cornwall Cl. CO11: Law 5G 162
IG11: Bark 8E 124
RM11: Horn 8L 111
Cornwall Cres. CM1: Chelm 4J 59
Cornwall Gdns. CM7: Brain 4K 193
SS4: R'fd 2H 121
Cornwallis Cl. DA8: Eri 4D 152
Cornwallis Dr. CM3: S Fer 1M 103
Cornwallis Pl. CB10: Saf W 3D 218
Cornwallis Rd. RM9: Dag 6J 125
Cornwall Rd. CM15: Pil H 4E 96
DA1: Dart 8K 153
SS13: Pits 8N 117
Cornwalls Dr. CO6: M Tey 3G 171
Corn Way E11: Lon 5D 122
Cornwell Cres. E7: Lon 6J 123
SS17: Stan H 2N 147
Cornworthy SS3: Shoe 6G 139
Cornworthy Rd. RM8: Dag 7H 125
Corona Rd. SS8: Can I 9K 135
SS16: Lang H 3K 131
Coronation Av. CM7: Brain 6H 193
CO2: Colc 5A 174
RM18: E Til 2K 157

Coronation Cl. IG6: Ilf . . . 8B 108
SS3: Gt W . . . 2K 139
Coronation Ct. DA8: Eri . . . 5B 152
E15: Lon . . . 8F 122
RM18: E Til . . . 2L 157
(off Coronation Av.)
Coronation Dr. RM12: Horn . . . 7F 126 (5B 40)
Coronation Hill CM16: Epp . . . 9E 64
Coronation Rd. CM0: Bur C . . . 4D 196
CO15: Clac S . . . 1G 189
Coronation Way CM77: Tye G . . . 2D 194
Corporation Rd. CM1: Chelm . . . 7J 59 (7A 24)
Corran Way RM15: S Ock . . . 7E 144
Corriander Dr. CM22: Else . . . 2L 199
CORRINGHAM . . . 1C 148 (5A 42)
Corringham Leisure Cen. . . . 1A 148
Corringham Rd. SS17: Stan H . . . 4M 147 (6K 41)
(not continuous)
Corry Ct. CO4: Colc . . . 7D 166
Corsel Rd. SS8: Can I . . . 2L 151
Cortoncroft Cl. CO13: Walt . . . 7J 181
Corton Trad. Est. SS7: Thund . . . 8D 118
Corve La. RM15: S Ock . . . 7E 144
Cory Dr. CM13: Hut . . . 6L 97
CORYTON . . . 4K 149 (6C 42)
CORYTON WHARVES . . . 5N 149
Cosgrove Av. SS9: Lgh S . . . 3A 136
Cossington Rd. SS0: Wclf S . . . 6K 137
Costead Mnr. Rd. CM14: Brtwd . . . 7E 96
Cosway Cvn. Pk. CO5: E Mer . . . 4J 27
Coteford Cl. IG10: Lou . . . 1A 92
Cotelands SS16: Van . . . 3G 132
Cotesmore Gdns. RM8: Dag . . . 6H 125
Cotleigh Rd. RM7: Romf . . . 1B 126
Cotman Av. CO11: Law . . . 3G 162
Cotman Lodge CM1: Chelm . . . 5A 60
Cotman M. RM8: Dag . . . 7H 125
(off Highgrove Rd.)
Cotman Rd. CO3: Colc . . . 1H 173
CO16: Clac S . . . 7H 185
Coton St. E14: Lon . . . 7E 38
Cotswold Av. SS6: Ray . . . 4K 119
Cotswold Cl. DA7: Bexh . . . 7C 152
Cotswold Ct. CO4: Colc . . . 3C 166
Cotswold Cres. CM1: Chelm . . . 5F 58
Cotswold Gdns. CM13: Hut . . . 6A 98
IG2: Ilf . . . 2C 124
Cotswold Rd. CO15: Clac S . . . 8K 185
RM3: H Wood . . . 6K 111
SS0: Wclf S . . . 6J 137
Cottage Dr. CO2: Colc . . . 3C 174
Cottage Grn. CO16: Clac S . . . 7G 184
Cottage Gro. CO16: Clac S . . . 7G 184
Cottage M. RM11: Horn . . . 8G 111
Cottage Museum, The . . . 3B 202
Cottage Pl. CM1: Chelm . . . 8K 59
Cottages, The SS3: Shoe . . . 7K 139
Cottage, The SS16: Van . . . 3F 132
(off London Rd.)
Cottage Wlk. CO16: Clac S . . . 7G 184
COTTERED . . . 4A 10
Cottered Rd. SG9: Thro . . . 3B 10
COTTERED WARREN . . . 4B 10
Cottesmore Av. IG5: Ilf . . . 6N 107
Cottesmore Cl. SS8: Can I . . . 3H 151
Cottesmore Ct. SS9: Lgh S . . . 4N 135
Cottesmore Gdns. SS9: Lgh S . . . 5N 135
Cottey Ho. CM2: Gall . . . 8C 72
Cottis Cl. SS16: Lang H . . . 3J 131
Cottis La. CM16: Epp . . . 9E 64
Cotton Cl. RM9: Dag . . . 9H 125
Cotton La. DA2: Dart, Grnh . . . 3D 46
Cottons App. RM7: Romf . . . 9B 110
Cottons Ct. RM7: Romf . . . 9B 110
Cottonwood Cl. CO2: Colc . . . 4L 173
Couchmore Av. IG5: Ilf . . . 6M 107
Coulde Dennis CM3: E Han . . . 2B 88
Coulsdon Cl. CO16: Clac S . . . 7G 184
Coulson Cl. RM8: Dag . . . 3H 125
Coulter M. CM11: Bill . . . 5K 99
Council Bungs. CM7: Brain . . . 1H 193
(off Church La.)
COUNTESS CROSS . . . 3J 15
Counting Ho. La. CM6: Gt D . . . 2L 203
County Gdns. IG11: Bark . . . 2D 140
County Pl. CM2: Chelm . . . 1C 72
County Rd. E6: Lon . . . 5A 140
Coupals Rd. CB9: H'hll, Stur . . . 3K 7
Courage Cl. RM11: Horn . . . 1G 126
Courage Ct. CM13: Hut . . . 5M 97
Courage Wlk. CM13: Hut . . . 5N 97
Courier Rd. RM9: Dag . . . 4A 142
RM13: Dag . . . 5B 142
Court 1 CM8: Wthm . . . 2C 230
Court 2 CM8: Wthm . . . 2C 230
Court 3 CM8: Wthm . . . 2C 230
Court 4 CM8: Wthm . . . 2C 230
Court 5 CM8: Wthm . . . 2B 230
Court 6 CM8: Wthm . . . 2C 230
Court 7 CM8: Wthm . . . 2C 230
Court 8 CM8: Wthm . . . 2C 230
Court 9 CM8: Wthm . . . 2C 230
Court 10 CM8: Wthm . . . 2C 230
Court 11 CM8: Wthm . . . 2C 230
Court 12 CM8: Wthm . . . 2C 230
Court 13 CM8: Wthm . . . 2C 230
Court 14 CM8: Wthm . . . 2C 230
Court 15 CM8: Wthm . . . 2C 230
Court 16 CM8: Wthm . . . 2C 230
Court 17 CM8: Wthm . . . 2C 230
Court 18 CM8: Wthm . . . 2C 230
Court 19 CM8: Wthm . . . 2C 230
Court 20 CM8: Wthm . . . 1C 230
Courtauld Cl. CO9: Hals . . . 5L 207
SE28: Lon . . . 8F 140
Courtauld Homes of Rest CO9: Hals . . . 3K 207
Courtauld Rd. CM7: Brain . . . 4J 193 (7D 14)
SS13: Bas . . . 6H 117 (2B 42)
Court Av. RM3: H Wood . . . 4L 111
Courtenay Dr. RM16: Chaf H . . . 1J 155
Courtenay Gdns. RM14: Upm . . . 3N 127
Courtenay Rd. E11: Lon . . . 5F 122
Courtfield Cl. EN10: Brox . . . 8A 52
Court Gdns. RM3: H Wood . . . 3L 111
Court Ind. Est. CM2: Chelm . . . 9L 59
Courtland Av. E4: Lon . . . 8F 90
IG1: Ilf . . . 4M 123
Courtland Cl. IG8: Wfd G . . . 5J 107
Courtland Dr. IG7: Chig . . . 9A 92
Courtland Gro. SE28: Lon . . . 6J 141
Courtland M. CM9: Mal . . . 8B 214
Courtland Pl. CM9: Mal . . . 8B 214
Courtlands CM1: Chelm . . . 5J 59
CM12: Bill . . . 6G 99
CO9: Hals . . . 6J 207
(off Ramsey Rd.)
SS9: Lgh S . . . 8A 120
(off Musket Gro.)
Courtney Pk. Rd. SS16: Lang H . . . 1K 131
Courtney Rd. RM16: Grays . . . 9E 146
Court Rd. CM1: Broom, L Walt . . . 8J 57 (6A 24)
COURTSEND . . . 1G 45
Courts, The SS6: Ray . . . 4L 119
Court St. CO6: Nay . . . 1D 16
Court Vw. CM4: Ing . . . 8B 84
Court Way IG6: Ilf . . . 7B 108
IG8: Wfd G . . . 2J 107
RM3: H Wood . . . 6J 111
Courtyard, The CM11: Bill . . . 7L 99
CM15: Brtwd . . . 6E 96
Coval Av. CM1: Chelm . . . 8J 59
Coval La. CM1: Chelm . . . 9J 59
Coval Wells CM1: Chelm . . . 9J 59
Covelees Wall E6: Lon . . . 6A 140
Covenbrook CM13: Brtwd . . . 9L 97
Covent Garden Station (Tube) . . . 7A 38
Coventry Cl. CO1: Colc . . . 7A 166
SS5: Hull . . . 7M 103
Coventry Hill SS5: Hull . . . 7L 103 (7F 35)
Coventry Rd. IG1: Ilf . . . 4A 124
Coverdale CM8: Wthm . . . 3B 230
(off Pennyroyal Cres.)
Coverdales, The IG11: Bark . . . 2C 140
Coverley Cl. CM13: Gt War . . . 3F 112
Covert Rd. IG6: Ilf . . . 2E 108
Coverts, The CM1: Writ . . . 1K 71
CM13: Hut . . . 7K 97
CO5: W Mer . . . 3D 228
Cowbridge SG14: Hart . . . 5B 20
Cowbridge La. IG11: Bark . . . 9A 124
Cowdray Av. CO1: Colc . . . 6M 165 (5E 16)
Cowdray Cen., The CO1: Colc . . . 6N 165
Cowdray Cres. CO1: Colc . . . 8N 165
Cowdray Way RM12: Horn . . . 6E 126
Cowdrie Way CM2: Chelm . . . 7C 60
Cowell Av. CM1: Chelm . . . 6G 59
Cowels Farm La. CM6: Lndsl . . . 4G 13
COWEY GREEN . . . 7F 168 (6K 17)
Cow La. CB10: Gt Che . . . 7E 202 (4A 6)
CO12: Har . . . 1N 209
CO16: St O . . . 4A 28
Cowley La. E11: Lon . . . 5E 122
Cowley Rd. E11: Lon . . . 9H 107
IG1: Ilf . . . 2M 123
RM3: Romf . . . 4F 110
Cowlins CM17: H'low . . . 8J 51
Cowpar M. CM7: Brain . . . 8J 193
Cowper Av. E6: Lon . . . 9L 123
RM18: Til . . . 6D 156
Cowper Rd. RM13: Rain . . . 4E 142
Cowslip Ct. CO3: S'way . . . 8D 164
Cowslip Mead SS14: Bas . . . 9C 116
Cowslip Rd. E18: Lon . . . 6H 107
Cow Watering La. CM1: Writ . . . 9A 58 (1J 33)
Coxbridge Ct. CM12: Bill . . . 6J 99
Coxes Cl. SS17: Stan H . . . 2M 147
Coxes Farm Rd. CM11: Bill . . . 8N 99 (1K 41)
COX HILL . . . 6E 12
Cox Ley CM22: Hat H . . . 1E 210
Cox Rd. CO7: Alr . . . 6A 176
Coxs Cl. CM3: S Fer . . . 9L 89
Cox's Hill CO11: Law . . . 5F 162 (3K 17)
COXTIE GREEN . . . 3A 96 (7D 32)
Coxtie Grn. Rd.
CM14: N'side, Pil H, S Wea . . . 3L 95 (7C 32)
Crabb Cft. CM7: Brain . . . 5L 193
CRABBS GREEN . . . 4H 11
Crabbs Grn. CM22: Hat O . . . 7F 206 (3C 22)
Crabb's Hill CM3: Hat P . . . 4K 61 (6E 24)
Crabb's La. SG9: Stoc P . . . 4H 11
Crabtree CO13: Kir S . . . 6F 180
Crabtree Av. RM6: Chad H . . . 8J 109
Crabtree Ct. E15: Lon . . . 7B 122
CRABTREE HILL . . . 6L 93
Crabtree La.
CO6: L Hork, Wmgfd . . . 6D 158 (3C 16)
Crabtree Manorway Nth. DA17: Belv, Eri . . . 9A 142
Crabtree Manorway Sth. DA17: Belv . . . 1A 152
Cracknell Cl. CO7: W'hoe . . . 4H 175
CRADLE END . . . 1H 21
Crafton Grn. CM24: Stan M . . . 2D 220
Craftsmans Sq. SS2: Temp I . . . 1M 137
Craig Ct. CO2: Colc . . . 3J 173
(off Iceni Way)
Craigdale Rd. RM11: Romf . . . 1D 126
Craigfield Av. CO15: Clac S . . . 7K 185
Craig Gdns. E18: Lon . . . 6F 106
CRAIG'S END . . . 7A 8
Craig's Hill CO8: M Bur . . . 2K 15
Craigs La. CO8: M Bur . . . 2A 16
Craiston Way CM2: Gt Bad . . . 5G 72
Crammavill St. RM16: Grays . . . 7K 145 (7F 41)
Crammerville Wlk. RM13: Rain . . . 4F 142
Crammond Pk. CM19: H'low . . . 4N 53
Cramphorn Wlk. CM1: Chelm . . . 8H 59
Cranborne Cl. CO4: Colc . . . 5N 165
Cranborne Gdns. RM14: Upm . . . 4M 127
Cranborne Rd. EN11: Rye P . . . 4B 52
IG11: Bark . . . 1C 140
Cranbourne Av. E11: Lon . . . 8H 107
Cranbourne Dr. EN11: Hod . . . 1C 52
Cranbourne Gdns. IG6: Ilf . . . 7B 108
Cranbourne Ho. EN11: Rye P . . . 1C 52
Cranbourne Rd. E12: Lon . . . 7L 123
E15: Lon . . . 6C 122
CRANBROOK . . . 3M 123 (4G 39)
Cranbrook Av. SS7: Had . . . 2J 135
Cranbrook Dr. RM2: Romf . . . 8G 110
Cranbrook Ho. DA8: Eri . . . 5D 152
(off Boundary St.)
Cranbrook Ri. IG1: Ilf . . . 1M 123
Cranbrook Rd. IG1: Ilf . . . 2N 123
IG2: Ilf . . . 2N 123 (3G 39)
IG6: Ilf . . . 9N 107 (3G 39)
Crane Av. CO3: S'way . . . 2C 172
Crane Cl. RM10: Dag . . . 8M 125
Cranell Grn. RM15: S Ock . . . 8E 144
CRANES . . . 5G 116 (2B 42)
Cranes Cl. SS14: Bas . . . 5G 117
Cranes Ct. SS14: Bas . . . 7D 116
Cranes Farm Rd. SS14: Bas . . . 7A 116 (3K 41)
Crane's Ct. CO5: K'dn . . . 2H 25
Cranes La. SS14: Bas . . . 7D 116
Cranfield Ct. SS12: W'fd . . . 8K 101
Cranfield Pk. Av. SS12: N Ben . . . 5M 117
Cranfield Pk. Ct. SS12: W'fd . . . 2L 117
Cranfield Pk. Rd. SS12: W'fd . . . 3L 117 (2C 42)
Cranford Cl. CO13: Frin S . . . 9H 181
CRANHAM . . . 2B 128 (4D 40)
Cranham Gdns. RM14: Upm . . . 3B 128
Cranham Marsh (Nature Reserve) . . . 6B 128
Cranham Rd. CM3: L Walt . . . 6N 57 (5B 24)
CM6: Broxt . . . 5D 12
RM11: Horn . . . 1F 126
Cranleigh Cl. CO16: Clac S . . . 7F 184
Cranleigh Dr. SS9: Lgh S . . . 4D 136 (4H 43)
Cranleigh Gdns. IG10: Lou . . . 5M 91
IG11: Bark . . . 9C 124
SS5: Hull . . . 7K 103
Cranley Av. SS0: Wclf S . . . 5J 137
Cranley Dr. IG2: Ilf . . . 2B 124
Cranley Gdns. N10: Lon . . . 3A 38
SS3: Shoe . . . 8G 139
Cranley Rd. IG2: Ilf . . . 1B 124
SS0: Wclf S . . . 6J 137
Cranmer Cl. CM12: Bill . . . 2K 99
Cranmere Ct. CO1: Colc . . . 8A 166
Cranmer Gdns. RM10: Dag . . . 6A 126
Cranmer Ho. CM2: Chelm . . . 3A 72
Cranmer Rd. E7: Lon . . . 6H 123
Cranmore Cl. CM22: Else . . . 2K 199
Cranmoregreen La. CO10: L Mel . . . 2H 9
Cranston Av. SS0: Wclf S . . . 1J 137
Cranston Gdns. E4: Lon . . . 3B 106
Cranston Pk. Av. RM14: Upm . . . 6M 127
Cranwell Gdns. CM23: Bis S . . . 8B 220
Cranworth Cres. E4: Lon . . . 7D 90
Craven Av. SS8: Can I . . . 2G 150
Craven Cl. SS4: R'fd . . . 2J 121
Craven Ct. RM6: Chad H . . . 1K 125
Craven Dr. CO4: Colc . . . 4C 166
Craven Gdns. IG6: Ilf . . . 6C 108 (2H 39)
IG11: Bark . . . 2D 140
RM3: H Wood . . . 3N 111
RM5: Col R . . . 2M 109
Crawford Av. RM16: Grays . . . 8L 145
Crawford Chase SS12: W'fd . . . 2M 117
Crawford Cl. CM12: Bill . . . 3L 99
Crawford Compton Cl. RM12: Horn . . . 8G 127
Crawley Cl. SS17: Corr . . . 9B 132
CRAWLEY END . . . 6H 5
Crawley Rd. E10: Lon . . . 3B 122
Craxe's Cnr. CO2: B'ch . . . 2C 26
Craydene Rd. DA8: Eri . . . 6D 152
Crayfields CM6: Gt D . . . 2L 203
CRAYFORD . . . 3A 46
Crayford Cl. CM9: Mal . . . 8A 214
Crayford High St. DA1: Cray . . . 9C 152 (3A 46)
Crayford Rd. DA1: Cray . . . 3A 46
Crayford Station (Rail) . . . 3A 46
Crayford Way DA1: Cray . . . 9E 152 (3A 46)
Craylands SS14: Bas . . . 8G 116
(not continuous)
Craylands La. DA10: Grnh, Swans . . . 3E 46
Craymill Sq. DA1: Cray . . . 7D 152
Cray Rd. BR8: Crock . . . 7A 46
CRAYS HILL . . . 3E 116 (1A 42)
Crays Hill CM11: Bill, Cray H . . . 3C 116 (2A 42)
Crays Hill Rd. CM11: Cray H . . . 2D 116
Crayside Ind. Est. DA1: Cray . . . 9F 152
Crays Vw. CM12: Bill . . . 8K 99
Crealock Gro. IG8: Wfd G . . . 2F 106
Creance Ct. CM2: Chelm . . . 9J 59
Creasen Butt Cl. CM9: Mal . . . 4C 214
Creasey Cl. RM11: Horn . . . 4F 126
Creasy Ct. SS14: Bas . . . 9G 116
Credon Cl. CO15: Clac S . . . 6K 185
Credon Dr. CO15: Clac S . . . 6K 185
Credo Way RM20: W Thur . . . 4E 154
Creeds Cotts. CM16: Epp . . . 2D 78
Creekhurst Cl. CO7: B'sea . . . 7F 182
CREEKMOUTH . . . 4E 140 (6H 39)
Creekmouth Ind. Pk. IG11: Bark . . . 4E 140
Creek Rd. IG11: Bark . . . 3E 140
SS8: Can I . . . 1K 151
CREEKSEA . . . 3A 196 (6B 36)
Creeksea Ferry Rd. SS4: Cwdn, Stam . . . 1A 44
Creeksea La. CM0: Bur C . . . 2A 196 (6B 36)
Creekside RM13: Rain . . . 4C 142
Creek Vw. SS16: Van . . . 3F 132
Creek Vw. Av. SS5: Hull . . . 5J 103
Creekview Rd. CM3: S Fer . . . 1M 103 (6F 35)
Creek Way RM13: Rain . . . 5C 142
Creephedge La.
CM3: E Han, S Fer . . . 4C 88 (4D 34)
Cree Way RM1: Romf . . . 4C 110
Creffield Rd. CO3: Colc . . . 9L 165 (6E 16)
Creighton Rd. N17: Lon . . . 2B 38
Crepping Hall Rd. CO6: Wak C . . . 7F 196 (4A 16)
Crescent Av. RM12: Horn . . . 4D 126
RM17: Grays . . . 3N 155
(not continuous)
Crescent Cl. CM6: Gt D . . . 2K 203
CM12: Bill . . . 4H 99
Crescent Ct. CM9: Mal . . . 3B 214
RM17: Grays . . . 3N 155
SS9: Lgh S . . . 5A 136
Crescent Dr. CM15: Shenf . . . 7H 97
Crescent Gdns. CM12: Bill . . . 4H 99
Crescent Rd. CM2: Gt Bad . . . 3H 73
CM9: Mal . . . 2B 214
CM9: Tol . . . 8L 225
CM12: Bill . . . 4H 99
(not continuous)
CM14: War . . . 1E 112 (1E 40)
CO14: Walt . . . 6M 181
DA8: Eri . . . 4D 152
E4: Lon . . . 6E 90
E10: Lon . . . 4B 122
E18: Lon . . . 5J 107
IP11: Felix . . . 1K 19
RM10: Dag . . . 5N 125
RM15: Ave . . . 9N 143
SS7: Ben . . . 4D 134
SS8: Can I . . . 2K 151
SS9: Lgh S . . . 5A 136
Crescent, The CB9: Stpl B . . . 2K 223
CM3: Gt L . . . 9J 203 (3A 24)
CM16: Epp . . . 2E 78
CM17: H'low . . . 6H 51
CO4: Colc . . . 1B 166 (4F 17)
CO6: Gt Hork . . . 7J 159
CO6: M Tey . . . 3J 171
CO6: W Ber . . . 2F 164
CO9: Gest . . . 6F 9
CO13: Frin S . . . 9J 181
CO13: Gt Hol . . . 1D 186
CO15: Clac S . . . 6M 185
CO16: T Sok . . . 4K 179
IG2: Ilf . . . 1N 123
IG10: Lou . . . 4K 91
RM14: Upm . . . 2B 128
SS7: Had . . . 3M 135
Crescent Vw. IG10: Lou . . . 5K 91
Crescent Wlk. RM15: Ave . . . 9N 143
Crescent Way RM15: Ave . . . 8A 144
Cressages Cl. CM6: Fels . . . 7N 199
Cress Cft. CM7: Brain . . . 7M 193
Cressells SS15: Lain . . . 9A 116
CRESSING . . . 6H 217 (1E 24)
Cressing Rd. CM7: Brain . . . 5K 193 (7D 14)
CM8: Fau, Wthm . . . 1A 230 (3F 25)
CM77: Tye G . . . 5K 193
Cressing Road Stadium . . . 6L 193
Cressing Station (Rail) . . . 3D 194 (1D 24)
Cressing Temple Barn . . . 2F 25
Crest Av. RM17: Grays . . . 5L 155
SS13: Pits . . . 9K 117
Cresthill Av. RM17: Grays . . . 3L 155
Crestlands CO7: Alr . . . 7A 176
Crest, The CM21: Saw . . . 2J 51
SS9: Lgh S . . . 9C 120
Creswick Av. SS6: Ray . . . 4J 119
Creswick Ct. SS6: Ray . . . 4J 119
Crete Hall Rd. DA11: N'fleet . . . 3G 47
CREWS HILL . . . 5A 30
Crews Hill Station (Rail) . . . 4A 30
Crichett Ter. CM1: Chelm . . . 8J 59
(off Primrose Hill)
Cricketers Cl. CM1: Broom . . . 2L 59
DA8: Eri . . . 3C 152
Cricketers La. CM13: Heron . . . 3N 113
Cricketers Row CM13: Heron . . . 4N 113
Cricketers Way SS13: Bas . . . 5H 117
Cricketfield Gro. SS9: Lgh S . . . 4E 136
Cricketfield La. CM23: Bis S . . . 1J 21
Cricketfield Rd. E5: Lon . . . 5C 38
Crickhollow CM3: S Fer . . . 3J 103
Cricklade Av. RM3: Romf . . . 3H 111
Cringle Lock CM3: S Fer . . . 3L 103
CRIPPLE CORNER . . . 1H 15
CRIPPLEGATE . . . 1E 222
Cripplegate CM0: S'min . . . 1E 222 (4D 36)
Cripsey Av. CM5: Chip . . . 5K 67
Crispe Ho. IG11: Bark . . . 2C 140
Crispin Ct. CO1: Colc . . . 8M 165
Crispins SS1: Sth S . . . 6E 138
Criton Ind. Est. RM16: Ors . . . 6G 146
Crittall Cl. CM8: Sil E . . . 8M 217
Crittall Ct. CM7: Brain . . . 4F 192
Crittall Dr. CM7: Brain . . . 4F 192
Crittall Rd. CM8: Wthm . . . 4E 230
Crix Grn. CM6: Chelm, Fels . . . 1A 24
Croasdaile Cl. CM24: Stan M . . . 1D 220
Croasdaile Rd. CM24: Stan M . . . 1D 220
CROCKENHILL . . . 7A 46
Crockenhill La. BR8: Crock . . . 7B 46
Crockenhill Rd. BR8: Crock . . . 7A 46
Crocklands CO9: G'std G . . . 5G 15
CROCKLEFORD HEATH . . . 5H 167 (5H 17)

Crockleford Hill CO7: A'lgh. 6G 166
Crockleford Rd. CO7: Elms. 9M 167 (6H 17)
Crocus Cl. CO16: Clac S. 9G 185
Crocus Flds. CB10: Saf W 2D 218
Crocus Way CM1: Chelm 4N 59
Croft Cl. CM7: Brain 5J 193
SS7: Ben. 1C 134
SS9: Lgh S 2D 136
Croft Ct. CM1: Chelm 3N 59
Crofters CM21: Saw 1K 51
Crofters End CM21: Saw. 1K 51
Crofters Wlk. CM77: Gt N 8F 192
Croft Ho. E17: Lon 8B 106
Croft La. CM3: Ples. 1B 56
Croft Lodge Cl. IG8: Wfd G. 3H 107
Crofton Av. SS17: Corr 1A 148
Crofton Gro. E4: Lon. 1D 106
Crofton Rd. RM16: Grays 9A 146
Croft Rd. CO5: K'dn. 3J 211
CO15: Clac S. 9H 185
SS7: Ben. 1B 134
Croftside CO8: Bures. 7L 195
Crofts, The SS3: Lit W. 2J 139
Croft, The CM22: Else. 3K 199
CO6: E Col. 8B 198
CO8: Bures 7L 195
CO9: Gt Yel 2D 206
E4: Lon 8E 90
IG10: Lou 1N 91
SS6: Ray 7M 119
Croft Way CM8: Wthm 4D 230
Crombie Cl. IG4: Ilf 9M 107
Crome Cl. CO3: Colc. 1H 173
CROMER 4A 10
Cromer Av. SS15: Lain 7K 115
Cromer Cl. SS15: Lain 7K 115
Crome Rd. CO16: Clac S. 7H 185
Cromer Rd. E10: Lon 2D 122
IG8: Wfd G 1G 107
RM6: Chad H. 1K 125
RM7: Romf 1A 126
RM11: Horn 2H 127
SS1: Sth S 6N 137
Cromer Windmill 4A 10
Crompton Av. SS15: Lain. 7M 115
Crompton Cl. SS14: Bas. 7A 116
Crompton Pl. EN3: Enf 8A 76
Crompton St. CM1: Chelm 2A 72
(not continuous)
Cromwell Av. CM12: Bill 5J 99
EN7: Chesh 3C 30
Cromwell Cen. CM8: Wthm 5E 230
IG6: Ilf. 2G 109
IG11: Bark 3F 140
Cromwell Cen., The RM8: Dag. 2L 125
(off Whalebone La. Sth.)
Cromwell Cl. CM3: Bore. 3E 60
Cromwell Hill CM9: Mal 5B 214
Cromwell La. CM9: Mal 5B 214
Cromwell Pk. CM6: Fels 8J 199
Cromwell Rd. CB11: Saf W 6D 218
CM14: War 1E 112
CO2: Colc 9N 165
E7: Lon 9J 123
E17: Lon 9C 106
RM17: Grays. 2K 155
SS2: Sth S 3M 137
SS5: Hock. 1D 120
Cromwells Mere RM1: Col R 3B 110
Cromwell Trad. Cen. IG11: Bark 3D 140
Cromwell Way CM8: Wthm 5B 230
CRONDON 2N 85 (4K 33)
Crondon Pk. La. CM4: Stock. 4N 85 (5K 33)
CROOKED BILLET 4A 106 (2D 38)
Crooked Elms CO12: Har 4K 209
Crooked Mile EN9: Wal A. 8C 62 (3E 30)
Crooked Way EN9: Naze 1E 62
Cropenburg Wlk. SS8: Can I. 9H 135
Croppath Rd. RM10: Dag. 6M 125
Croquet Gdns. CO7: W'hoe 5J 175
Crosbie Ho. E17: Lon 7C 106
(off Prospect Hill)
Crosby Ct. IG7: Chig 9F 92
Crosby Ho. E7: Lon. 8G 122
Crosby Rd. E7: Lon. 8G 122
RM10: Dag 2N 141
SS0: Wclf S. 6G 137
Cross Av. SS12: W'fd 1K 117
Crossbow Ct. CM5: Chip. 8L 67
Crossbow Rd. IG7: Chig 2E 108
Crossbrook St. EN8: Chesh. 4C 30
Crossby Cl. CM15: Mount. 9A 84
Cross Cotts. CO4: Boxt 2B 160
Cross Ct. SE28: Lon 7G 141
(off Titmuss Av.)
CROSS END. 2H 15
Crossfell Rd. SS7: Thund 8F 118
Crossfield Rd. CO15: Clac S 1J 189
EN11: Rye P 3B 52
SS2: Sth S. 4B 138
Crossfields IG10: Lou. 4A 92
Cross Fld. Way CO4: Boxt 2B 160
Crossfield Way CO13: Walt. 8E 180
Cross Grn. SS16: Bas 1A 132
Crossharbour & London Arena Station (DLR)
. . . . . 7D 38
Cross Hill CB11: Elm. 6J 5
CO12: Gt Oak. 5E 18
Crossing House Garden. 2E 4
Crossing Rd. CM16: Epp. 2F 78
Cross La. CO5: W Mer. 2F 228
Cross La. E. DA11: Grav. 4H 47
Cross La. W. DA11: Grav 4H 47
Cross Lees CM5: M'ton 1C 32
Crossley Av. CO15: Jay. 5C 188
Crossness Footpath DA18: Eri 8L 141
Crossness La. SE28: Lon 7K 141
Crossness Rd. IG11: Bark. 3E 140
Cross Rd. CM8: Wthm 2C 230
CM9: Mal. 7C 214 (1H 35)
E4: Lon 7D 90
IG8: Wfd G 3M 107
RM6: Chad H 2H 125
RM7: Maw 8M 109
SS7: Ben. 3H 135
SS13: Pits. 8N 117
Cross Roads CO9: Gest. 6F 9
IG10: H Bee 1H 91 (6F 31)
Cross St. CB10: Saf W 4C 218
CO10: Sud. 5J 9
DA8: Eri. 4C 152
N1: Lon. 6A 38
Cross Ter. EN9: Wal A. 4E 76
(off Stonyshotts)
Cross, The CO7: W'hoe 4H 175
Crosstree Wlk. CO2: Colc. 3A 174
Crossway CM17: H'low. 2J 55
Cross Way CO5: W Mer. 2E 228
IG8: Wfd G. 1J 107
Crossway RM8: Dag 5H 125
SE28: Lon. 6G 141 (7J 39)
SS17: Stan H. 2A 148
Crossways CM2: Chelm 3D 72
CM15: Shenf. 5K 97
CO6: Coln E. 2D 198
CO15: Jay 4D 188 (5C 28)
DA2: Dart 9N 153
IG10: Lou 4N 91
RM2: Romf 7F 110
SS8: Can I 1E 150
Crossways Blvd. DA2: Dart. 9N 153 (3D 46)
DA9: Dart. 9B 154 (3D 46)
Crossways 25 Bus. Pk. DA2: Dart 9N 153
Crossways Hill CM3: L Bad. 1E 34
Crossways, The SS0: Wclf S. 6F 136
Crossway, The CM11: Bill 5M 99
SS12: W'fd. 4M 117
Crouch Av. IG11: Bark. 2G 140
SS5: Hull. 7L 103
Crouch Beck CM3: S Fer. 1K 103
Crouch Cvn. Pk. SS5: Hull 4L 103
Crouch Ct. CM7: Brain 7M 193
CM20: H'low. 1B 54
Crouch Dr. CM8: Wthm. 5B 230
SS11: W'fd 8L 101
CROUCH END. 3A 38
Crouch End Hill N8: Lon. 4A 38
Crouch Grn. CO9: Cas H 3J 219
Crouch Hill N4: Lon 3A 38
N8: Lon. 3A 38
Crouch Hill Station (Rail) 4A 38
Crouch La. EN7: Chesh, G Oak. 3B 30
Crouchman Cl. RM16: Grays. 9M 145
Crouchmans SS3: Shoe 5K 139
Crouchmans Av. SS3: Gt W 3L 139
Crouchman's Farm Rd. CM9: Ult 7F 25
Crouch Mdw. SS5: Hull. 4L 103
Crouch Rd. CM0: Bur C 3D 196
RM16: Grays. 3C 156
Crouch St. CO3: Colc 9M 165
SS15: Bas. 6N 115
Crouch Valley RM14: Upm. 2B 128
Crouchview Cl. SS11: W'fd 9B 102
Crouch Vw. Cotts. CM3: Ret C 3C 102
Crouch Vw. Cres. SS5: Hock. 8F 104
Crouch Vw. Gro. SS5: Hull 5K 103
Crouch Way SS3: Shoe. 7H 139
Crowborough Rd. SS2: Sth S 4L 137
Crowden Way SE28: Lon 7H 141
Crowfoot Cl. SE28: Lon 8D 140
CROW GREEN. 2C 96 (6D 32)
Crow Grn. La. CM15: Pil H. 4D 96
Crow Grn. Rd. CM15: Pil H 4C 96 (7E 32)
Crowhall La. CO11: Brad 3B 18
Crowhurst Ct. CO3: Colc 8M 165
Crowhurst Rd. CO3: Colc. 8M 165
Crowland Rd. CB9: H'hll 3J 7
CROWLANDS 2N 125 (3K 39)
Crowlands Av. RM7: Romf. 1N 125
Crow La. CO16: Ten, T Sok, Wee. . . 2E 178 (7C 18)
RM7: Dag, Rush G. 2L 125 (4K 39)
SG8: Reed. 7D 4
Crown Av. SS13: Pits 9K 117
Crown Bays Rd. CO4: Colc 7C 166
Crown Bldgs. E4: Lon. 7C 90
Crown Cl. CM22: Srng 4A 210
SS13: Pits. 9K 117
Crown Cotts. RM5: Col R. 5M 109
Crown Ct. CO4: Colc. 1D 166
RM18: Til 7C 156
Crowndale Rd. NW1: Lon. 6A 38
Crownfield EN10: Brox 9A 52
Crownfield Av. IG2: Ilf 1D 124
Crownfield Rd. E15: Lon. 6D 122 (5E 38)
Crown Gdns. SS6: Ray 5J 119
Crown Ga. CM20: H'low 3C 54
(not continuous)
CO4: Colc 1D 166
Crown Hill CB10: A'dn 7D 190
(off Rectory La.)
EN9: Wal A. 3L 77 (4G 31)
SS6: Ray. 5J 119 (2F 43)
Crownhill Rd. IG8: Wfd G 4L 107
CROWN INTERCHANGE 9D 160 (4F 17)
Crown La. CO12: Har. 3M 209
CO16: Ten 4B 178 (7B 18)
DA12: Shorne 5K 47
Crown La. Nth. CO7: A'lgh. 9E 160 (4G 17)
Crown La. Sth. CO7: A'lgh 3G 166
Crown Mdw. CM7: Brain 4M 193
Crownmead Way RM7: Maw 8N 109
Crown Rd. CM3: Cold N 8K 197
CM11: Bill 6K 99
CM14: Kel H. 9A 82 (6D 32)
(Dudbrook Rd.)
CM14: Kel H 7N 81 (5D 32)
(Kelvedon Hall La.)
CO15: Clac S. 3G 189
IG6: Ilf. 8C 108
RM17: Grays. 4K 155
SS5: Hock. 2A 120
Crown St. CM7: Gt Bar. 2C 202 (3J 13)
CM14: Brtwd 8F 96
CO7: Ded. 2M 161 (2H 17)
CO9: Cas H 3K 219
RM10: Dag 8A 126
(not continuous)
Crown Way CM0: S'min 2B 222
Crown Yd. CM12: Bill 7J 99
Crow Pond Rd. CM3: Terl. 4D 24
Crows Fld. Cotts. CM2: W Han. 5G 86
CROW'S GREEN 6K 13
Crow's Green CM7: Bar S. 6K 13
Crowsheath La. CM11: D'ham 3F 100 (6B 34)
Crowsheath Wood Nature Reserve 2F 100
Crows La. CM3: Stow M, Wdhm F . . . 3H 89 (4E 34)
Crows Rd. CM16: Epp. 9E 64
IG11: Bark. 8A 124
Crowstone Av. SS0: Wclf S. 7H 137
Crowstone Cl. SS0: Wclf S 5J 137
Crowstone Ct. SS0: Wclf S 7J 137
(off Holland Rd.)
Crowstone Rd. RM16: Grays 9M 145
SS0: Wclf S. 6H 137
Crow St. CM22: Hen 8D 210 (4C 12)
Croxall Ct. CM8: Wthm. 5C 230
Croxford Way RM7: Rush G 3B 126
Croxon Way CM0: Bur C. 1D 196
CROYDON 1A 4
Croydon Hill SG8: Croy. 1A 4
Croydon Rd. SG8: Arr. 1A 4
Crozier Ter. CM2: Chelm. 7C 60
Cruce Way CO16: P Bay 4K 27
(off New Way)
Crucible Cl. RM6: Chad H 1G 125
Cruick Av. RM15: S Ock 6F 144
Cruikshank Rd. E15: Lon 6E 122
Cruise Terminal 1H 209
(Harwich International)
Crummock Cl. CM77: Gt N 2C 204
Crunch Cft. CB9: Stur 6J 223
Crusader Bus. Pk. CO15: Clac S. 5L 185
Crusader Cl. RM19: Purf 2L 153
Crusader Way CM7: Brain 6M 193
Crushes Cl. CM13: Hut 5A 98
Crushton Pl. CM1: Chelm 5H 59
Crusoe Rd. DA8: Eri 3B 152
Crutches La. ME2: High 6K 47
Crystal Av. RM12: Horn 6J 127
Crystal Steps SS1: Sth S 7A 138
(off Beresford Rd.)
Crystal Way RM8: Dag 3H 125
CUCKINGSTOOL END. 3L 215
Cuckoo Cnr. SS2: Sth S 2K 137
Cuckoo Hill CO8: Bures 7L 195 (1A 16)
CO9: Sib H 2D 14
Cuckoo La. RM16: N Stif. 8J 145
(not continuous)
Cuckoos La. CM6: Gt Can 2E 22
CUCKOO TYE 3J 9
Cuckoo Way CM77: Gt N 2B 204 (1B 24)
CUFFLEY. 3A 30
Cuffley Hill EN6: Cuff 3A 30
Cuffley Station (Rail) 3A 30
Culford Rd. RM16: Grays. 9M 145
Cullen Sq. RM15: S Ock 8F 144
Cullings Ct. EN9: Wal A. 3F 76
Culmley Rd. CM5: Toot. 9C 66
Culpeper Cl. IG6: Ilf 3A 108
Culver Arc. CO1: Colc 8M 165
Culverdown SS14: Bas 9B 116
Culver Ri. CM3: S Fer 1L 103
Culver Shop. Cen. CO1: Colc. 8M 165
Culver Sq. CO1: Colc 8M 165
(off Culver Shop. Cen.)
Culver St. E. CO1: Colc. 8N 165
Culver St. W. CO1: Colc. 8M 165
Culvert Cl. CO6: Cogg. 4K 197
Culver Wlk. CO1: Colc 8N 165
Cumberland Av. CM9: Mal 7A 214
RM12: Horn. 5J 127
SS2: Sth S. 4A 138
SS7: Ben 3C 134
Cumberland Cl. CM7: Brain 4K 193
IG6: Ilf. 5B 108
RM12: Horn. 5J 127
Cumberland Ct. CO15: Clac S 8M 185
EN11: Rye P 4A 52
Cumberland Cres. CM1: Chelm 4J 59
Cumberland Dr. SS15: Lain. 9J 115
Cumberland Ho. SE28: Lon 9B 140
(off Erebus Dr.)
Cumberland Rd. E12: Lon 6K 123
RM16: Chaf H. 9H 145
CUMBERLOW GREEN 3A 10
Cumbrae M. SS12: W'fd. 2N 117
Cumbrian Av. DA7: Bexh. 7C 152
Cumming Rd. CM11: D'ham. 6H 101
Cummings Hall La. RM3: Romf. 9G 95
Cunningham Cl. CO2: Colc. 2A 174
(off Mulberry Av.)
RM6: Chad H 9H 109
Cunningham Cl. SS3: Shoe 5K 139
Cunningham Dr. SS12: W'fd 2M 117
Cunningham Ho. CM16: N Wea 6L 65
Cunningham Ri. CM16: N Wea. 4A 66
Cunnington Rd. CM7: Brain 5L 193
Cunobelin Way CO2: King. 4G 173 (7D 16)
Cupid's Chase SS3: Shoe. 4N 139
Cuppers Cl. CM8: Wthm. 6B 230
Curds Rd. CO6: E Col 9B 198 (4H 15)
Curfew Ho. IG11: Bark 1B 140
Curlew Av. CM3: May 8L 213
Curlew Cl. CM9: H'bri. 3E 214
CO5: K'dn 3L 211
CO15: Clac S. 7K 185
SE28: Lon 7J 141
Curlew Cres. SS16: Van. 3C 132
Curlew Cft. CO4: Colc 7F 166
Curlew Dr. SS7: Ben. 4C 134
Curling La. RM17: Grays 3J 155
Curling Tye SS14: Bas 8E 116
CURLING TYE GREEN 1G 35
Curling Tye La. CM9: Mal, Wdhm W 1F 35
Curling Wlk. SS14: Bas 8E 116
Currants Farm Rd. CM7: Brain. 3G 193
Currents La. CO12: Har 1M 209
Curtain Rd. EC2: Lon 6B 38
Curteys CM17: H'low. 7J 51
Curtis Cl. CO16: Clac S 1F 188
CURTISMILL GREEN 3D 94 (6A 32)
Curtis Mill La. RM4: Nave 3C 94
(not continuous)
Curtis Rd. RM11: Horn. 3K 127
Curtis Way SE28: Lon. 7G 141
Curtisway SS6: Ray. 3L 119
Curwen Av. E7: Lon 6H 123
Curzon Cres. IG11: Bark 2E 140
Curzon Dr. RM17: Grays. 5L 155
Curzon Way CM2: Chelm 9A 60
Cusak Rd. CM2: Chelm. 8A 60
Custerson Ct. CB11: Saf W. 4C 218
Custerson Dr. CM77: Bla N. 3B 194
CUSTOM HOUSE 7F 39
Custom Ho. CO12: Har 3L 209
Custom House for ExCel Station (Rail & DLR)
. . . . . 7F 39
Custom Ho. La. CO12: Har 1M 209
Cut-a-Thwart La. CM9: Bee, Mal 1G 35
Cutforth Rd. CM21: Saw. 1K 51
Cuthberga Cl. IG11: Bark 9B 124
Cuthbert Rd. E17: Lon 7C 106
Cut Hedge CM77: Gt N 2C 204
Cuthedge La. CO6: Cogg 1G 25
CUTLERS GREEN 3E 12
Cutlers Rd. CM3: S Fer. 9L 89
Cutmore Pl. CM2: Chelm 2A 72
Cuton Hall La. CM2: Chelm. 6B 60 (7B 24)
Cutter Ridge Rd. DA13: Ludd 7J 47
Cut, The CO5: Tip 6C 226
CO7: Gt Ben 6K 177
SE1: Lon 7A 38
Cut Throat La. CM8: Wthm 4D 230
(not continuous)
Cutting Dr. CO9: Hals 5K 207
CUXTON 7K 47
Cygnet Ct. CO9: Sib H. 6K 219
SS11: W'fd 8L 101
Cygnet Vw. RM20: W Thur. 2C 154
Cygnet Wlk. CO3: S'way. 2C 172
Cygnet Way CM19: Roy 2G 52
(off Swan Way)
Cymbeline Way CO3: Colc 8G 164 (6D 16)
Cypress Cl. CO15: Clac S 6J 185
EN9: Wal A 4D 76
Cypress Ct. CM6: Gt D 2J 203
Cypress Dr. CM2: Chelm 4D 72
Cypress Gro. CO4: Colc 7E 166
IG6: Ilf. 3D 108
Cypress M. CO5: W Mer. 2B 228
Cypress Path RM3: Romf. 4H 111
Cypress Rd. CM8: Wthm. 3D 230 (4G 25)
Cyprus Pl. E6: Lon 7G 39
Cyprus Station (DLR) 7G 39
Cyril Child Cl. CO4: Colc. 8E 166
Cyril Dowsett Ct. CM9: Mal 6A 214
Czarina Ri. SS15: Lain. 7N 115

D

Daarle Av. SS8: Can I. 2G 150
Dabbling Cl. DA8: Eri 4F 152
Dabchicks Sailing Club 2A 228
Dacre Av. IG5: Ilf 6N 107
RM15: Ave 8A 144
Dacre Cl. IG7: Chig. 1B 108
Dacre Cres. RM15: Ave 8A 144
Dacre Gdns. IG7: Chig 1B 108
Dacre Rd. E11: Lon. 3F 122
Dad's Wood CM20: H'low. 3B 54
Daen Ingas CM3: Dan. 3C 74
Daffodil Av. CM15: Pil H 4E 96
Daffodil Gdns. IG1: Ilf. 7A 124
Daffodil Way CM1: Chelm 4N 59
DAGENHAM 8M 125 (5K 39)
Dagenham & Redbridge F.C.
(Victoria Road Stadium) 7N 125 (5K 39)
Dagenham Av. RM9: Dag 1K 141 (6K 39)
(not continuous)
Dagenham Dock Station (Rail) . . . 2L 141 (6K 39)
Dagenham East Station (Tube) . . . 7A 126 (5A 40)
Dagenham Heathway Station (Tube)
. . . . . 8L 125 (5K 39)
Dagenham Leisure Pk. RM9: Dag 1K 141
Dagenham Rd. RM7: Rush G 2B 126 (4A 40)
RM10: Dag, Rush G. 6A 126 (5A 40)
RM13: Rain 9B 126 (5A 40)
Dagmar Rd. RM10: Dag 9A 126

Dagnam Pk. Cl. RM3: Romf 2L 111
Dagnam Pk. Dr. RM3: Romf 2J 111 (1C 40)
Dagnam Pk. Gdns. RM3: Romf 3L 111
(not continuous)
Dagnam Pk. Sq. RM3: Romf 3M 111
Dagnets La. CM77: Bla N 4C 204 (2C 24)
Dagwood La. CM15: Dodd 8E 82 (5E 32)
Dahlia Cl. CM1: Chelm 6A 60
CO16: Clac S 9G 184
Dahlia Gdns. IG1: Ilf 8A 124
Dahlia Wlk. CO4: Colc 8D 166
Daiglen Dr. RM15: S Ock 4E 144 (7E 40)
Daimler Av. CO15: Jay 5B 188
Daines Cl. E12: Lon 5M 123
RM15: S Ock 4D 144
SS1: Sth S 6F 138
Daines Rd. CM11: Bill 6L 99
Daines Way SS1: Sth S 5E 138
Dairy Farm La. CM4: B'more 3G 82
Dairy Farm Rd. CM3: May 5B 36
Dairyhouse La. CO11: Brad 4C 18
Dairy Rd. CM2: Chelm 7A 60
Daisley Rd. CM6: Lndsl 5H 13
Daisleys La. CM3: L Walt 4B 24
Daisy Ct. CM1: Chelm 5B 60
Daisy Rd. E18: Lon 6H 107
Dakyn Dr. CM4: Stock 7M 85
Dakyn Rd. CM4: Stock 6M 85
Dale Cl. CO3: S'way 8C 164
CO7: Elms 9N 167
RM15: S Ock 6D 144
Dale Ct. CM21: Saw 3J 51
Dalefield *IG9: Buck H 7J 91*
(off Roebuck La.)
Dale Gdns. IG8: Wfd G 1H 107
Dalen Av. SS8: Can I 2G 151
Dale Rd. DA13: S'fleet 5F 47
SS9: Lgh S 5A 136
Daleside Gdns. IG7: Chig 9B 92
Dales, The CO12: Har 6H 209
SS4: R'fd 4J 121
Dalestone M. RM3: Romf 3F 110
Dale, The CO7: W'hoe 6J 175
EN9: Wal A 4E 76
SS7: Ben 2G 134
Dale Vw. DA8: Eri 7D 152
Daleview Av. CO11: Wix 4D 18
Dale Vw. Av. E4: Lon 8C 90
Dale Vw. Cres. E4: Lon 8C 90
Dale Vw. Gdns. E4: Lon 9D 90
Dalewood Cl. RM11: Horn 2K 127
Dalkeith Rd. IG1: Ilf 5B 124
Dallwood Way CM7: Brain 5K 193
Dalmatia Rd. SS1: Sth S 5B 138
Dalmeny SS16: Lang H 2K 131
Dalroy Cl. RM15: S Ock 6D 144
Dalrymple Cl. CM1: Chelm 8M 59
DALSTON 5B 38
Dalston Kingsland Station (Rail) 5B 38
Dalston La. E8: Lon 5B 38
Daltes La. CO16: St O 1A 188 (4B 28)
Daltons Fen SS13: Pits 7K 117
Daltons Rd. BR6: Orp 7A 46
Dalwood SS3: Shoe 5H 139
Dalwood Gdns. SS7: Had 2L 135
Daly Ct. E15: Lon 7B 122
Dalys Rd. SS4: R'fd 5K 121 (2J 43)
Damant's Farm La.
CO16: Kir S, T Sok 6A 180 (1E 28)
Damases La. CM3: Bore 6D 24
Damask M. CM7: Brain 6J 193
Damask Rd. CO3: S'way 8D 164
Dame Elizabeth Ct. CM1: Broom 9J 57
Dames Rd. E7: Lon 5G 122 (4E 38)
Dammant Ct. CO4: Colc 7D 166
Dampier Rd. CO6: Cogg 2K 197
Danacre SS15: Lain 8K 115
DANBURY 3D 74 (2D 34)
Danbury Cl. CM15: Pil H 4C 96
CO6: M Tey 3H 171
RM6: Chad H 7J 109
SS9: Lgh S 2E 136
DANBURY COMMON 4D 74 (2E 34)
Danbury Common Nature Reserve 5E 74
Danbury Country Pk. 3B 74
Danbury Cres. RM15: S Ock 6E 144
Danbury Down SS14: Bas 7E 116
Danbury Mans. *IG11: Bark 9A 124*
(off Whiting Av.)
Danbury Rd. IG10: Lou 6L 91
RM13: Rain 1D 142
SS6: Ray 4H 119
Danbury Va. CM3: Dan 4G 74
Danbury Way IG8: Wfd G 3J 107
Dancing Dick's La. CM8: Terl 4E 24
Dandelion Cl. RM7: Rush G 4C 126
Dandies Chase SS9: Lgh S 8D 120
Dandies Cl. SS9: Lgh S 8C 120
Dandies Dr. SS9: Lgh S 8C 120
Danebridge Rd. SG10: M Hud 2G 21
DANE END
SG12 1B 20
SG8 1C 10
Dane End Rd. SG11: H Cro 2C 20
Daneholes Rdbt. RM16: Grays 1N 155
Danehurst Gdns. IG4: Ilf 9L 107
Danemead EN11: Hod 2A 52
Dane O'Coys Rd. CM23: Bis S 7J 11
(not continuous)
Dane Rd. CM1: Chelm 9G 59
IG1: Ilf 7B 124
Danes Av. SS3: Shoe 9K 139
Danescroft Cl. SS9: Lgh S 2D 136
Danescroft Dr. SS9: Lgh S 2C 136
Danesfield SS7: Ben 4B 134
Danesleigh Gdns. SS9: Lgh S 2C 136
Danes Rd. RM7: Rush G 2A 126
Dane St. CM23: Bis S 1K 21
(not continuous)
SS3: Shoe 8L 139
Danes Way CM15: Pil H 4D 96
Danette Gdns. RM10: Dag 4M 125
Dangan Rd. E11: Lon 1G 122
Daniel Cl. RM16: Chaf H 9H 145
RM16: Grays 1D 156
Daniel Cole Rd. CO2: Colc 2N 173
Daniell Cl. CO16: Clac S 7G 185
Daniell Dr. CO2: Colc 4J 173
Daniells Ho. CO6: W Ber 3G 165
Daniel Way CM8: Sil E 8M 217
Dannatts *CM3: Gt Walt 5H 57*
(off Bakers Mead)
Dansie Ct. CO4: Colc 7C 166
Danyon Cl. RM13: Rain 2G 142
Daphne Cl. CM77: Gt N 1C 204
Daphne Ct. CO4: Colc 7D 166
Daphne Gdns. E4: Lon 9C 90
Dapifer Dr. CM7: Brain 5M 193
Darby Dr. EN9: Wal A 3C 76
D'Arcy Av. CM9: Mal 7D 214
D'Arcy Cl. CM0: Bur C 2E 196
Darcy Cl. CM13: Hut 6L 97
CO13: Frin S 8J 181
Darcy Gdns. RM9: Dag 1L 141
D'Arcy Hgts. CO2: Colc 3C 174
Darcy Ri. CM3: L Bad 1E 74
D'Arcy Rd. CO2: Colc 3C 174
CO5: Tip 8F 226 (4A 26)
CO16: St O 8N 183
D'Arcy Way CM9: Tol D 3L 227
Darcy Way CO7: B'sea 6D 182
Dare Ct. E10: Lon 2C 122
Dare Gdns. RM8: Dag 5K 125
Darell Way CM11: Bill 7M 99
DARENTH 5D 46
Darenth Hill DA2: Dart 5C 46
DARENTH INTERCHANGE 4C 46
Darenth La. RM15: S Ock 6D 144
Darenth Rd. DA1: Dart 4C 46
SS9: Lgh S 5A 136
Darenth Wood Rd. DA2: Dart 4D 46
Darent Ind. Pk. DA8: Eri 4H 153
Darina Ct. CO3: S'way 8C 164
Darkhouse La. CO5: Rhdge 6G 174
Dark La. CM14: Gt War 3C 112 (1D 40)
EN7: Chesh 3C 30
SG9: S'don 1A 10
SS7: Thund 9G 118
Darlinghurst Gro. SS9: Lgh S 4F 136
Darlington Ct. CM15: Pil H 5D 96
Darlington Gdns. RM3: Romf 2H 111
Darlington Path RM3: Romf 2H 111
Darlton Cl. DA1: Cray 8D 152
Darnay Ri. CM1: Chelm 5F 58
Darnel Way CO3: S'way 8C 164
Darnet Rd. CM9: Tol 8L 225
Darnicle Hill EN7: Ches, G Oak, New S 2A 30
Darnley Rd. DA11: Grav 4H 47
E9: Lon 5C 38
IG8: Wfd G 5G 107
RM17: Grays 4L 155
Darrell Cl. CM1: Chelm 5K 59
Dart Cl. CM8: Wthm 5A 230
RM14: Upm 1A 128
Dartfields RM3: Romf 3H 111
DARTFORD 3C 46
Dartford Borough Mus. 4C 46
Dartford By-Pass DA1: Dart 4A 46
DA2: Bean, Dart 4B 46
Dartford Crossing RM20: Dart 7B 154 (2D 46)
Dartford Gdns. RM6: Chad H 9G 109
DARTFORD HEATH 4A 46
Dartford Rd. DA1: Dart 3B 46
DA4: F'ham 7C 46
(not continuous)
DA5: Bex 4A 46
Dartford Station (Rail) 3C 46
Dartford Tunnel DA1: Dart 8A 154 (2D 46)
Dartford Tunnel App. Rd. DA1: Dart 9M 153
Dart Grn. RM15: S Ock 5E 144
Dartmouth Cl. SS6: Ray 2K 119
Dartmouth Pk. Hill N6: Lon 4A 38
Dartmouth Rd. CM1: Chelm 5N 59
Dartview Cl. RM17: Grays 2A 156
Darwin Cl. CM7: Brain 7H 193
CO2: Colc 5B 174
Darwin Rd. RM18: Til 6B 156
Dashes, The CM20: H'low 2D 54
(not continuous)
Dashwood Rd. DA11: Grav 4H 47
DASSELS 5E 10
Datchet Dr. SS3: Shoe 4J 139
Daubeney Rd. E5: Lon 5D 38
Davall Cl. CO12: Har 6E 208
Davenants SS13: Bas 7J 117 (2B 42)
Davenport CM17: H'low 4K 55
Davenport Cen. IG11: Bark 1G 141
Daventry Av. E17: Lon 1A 122
Daventry Gdns. RM3: Romf 2G 110
Daventry Grn. RM3: Romf 2G 110
Daventry Rd. RM3: Romf 2G 110
Davey Cl. CO1: Colc 9C 166
Davey Rd. E9: Lon 9A 122
David Av. SS11: W'fd 6L 101
David Crompton Lodge, The RM3: Romf 2J 111
David Dr. RM3: H Wood 3L 111
David Lloyd Leisure
Ghyllgrove 6C 116
Loughton 7M 91
David Rd. RM8: Dag 4K 125
Davidson Gdns. SS12: W'fd 2M 117
Davidson Terraces *E7: Lon 7H 123*
(off Claremont Rd., not continuous)
Davidson Way RM7: Rush G 2C 126
David St. E15: Lon 8D 122
David's Wlk. CM11: Bill 6L 99
David's Way IG6: Ilf 4D 108
David Ter. RM3: H Wood 4L 111
Davies Cl. RM13: Rain 3G 142
Davies Ct. CM7: Brain 6J 193
Davies La. E11: Lon 4E 122
Davington Gdns. RM8: Dag 7G 125
Davington Rd. RM8: Dag 8G 125
Davinia Cl. IG8: Wfd G 3M 107
Davis Rd. RM15: Ave 8A 144
RM16: Chaf H 1J 155
Davy Down Vis. Cen. 9F 144
Davy Rd. CO15: Clac S 5N 185
Dawberry Pl. CM3: S Fer 3K 103
Dawes Av. RM12: Horn 5H 127
Dawes La. CO5: W Mer 1E 228 (4G 27)
Dawley Grn. RM15: S Ock 6D 144
Dawlish Cres. SS6: Ray 2K 119
Dawlish Dr. IG3: Ilf 6D 124
SS9: Lgh S 5D 136
Dawlish Rd. CO15: Clac S 4G 189
E10: Lon 3C 122
Dawlish Wlk. RM3: Romf 5G 111
Dawn Cl. CM9: Mal 8D 214
Dawnford Cl. CO3: S'way 8D 164
Dawnford Ct. *CO3: S'way 8D 164*
(off Dawnford Cl.)
Dawnings, The CM3: S Fer 9J 89
Daws Cl. CM1: Writ 1H 71
DAW'S CROSS 2K 15
DAWS HEATH 9L 119 (3F 43)
Daws Heath Rd. SS6: Ray 6K 119 (2F 43)
SS7: Had 9J 119 (3F 43)
Daws Hill E4: Lon 1C 90 (6E 30)
Dawson Av. IG11: Bark 9D 124
Dawson Cl. CB10: Saf W 3E 218
Dawson Dr. RM13: Rain 9F 126
Dawson Gdns. IG11: Bark 9E 124
Dawson M. CM11: Bill 5K 99
Daw St. CM7: F'fld 3K 13
CO9: Bird 5A 8
Daylop Dr. IG7: Chig 9G 92
Days Cl. CM1: Broom 3K 59
Days La. CM15: Dodd, Pil H 3D 96 (6E 32)
Dayton Dr. DA8: Eri 3H 153
Dazeley's La. CO7: E Ber 1E 162
Deacon Dr. SS15: Lain 8L 115
Deacon Way IG8: Wfd G 4M 107
Dead La. CO7: A'lgh 9J 161 (4H 17)
CO7: Gt Ben 4L 183 (2A 28)
CO11: Law, Mist 6G 162 (3K 17)
CO13: Gt Hol 9E 180
CO16: L Cla, Wee H 4F 184
(not continuous)
Deadman's La.
CM2: Gall, Gt Bad 6D 72 (3A 34)
Deal Cl. CM7: Brain 2G 193
CO15: Clac S 4G 189
Dealtree Cl. CM15: Hook E 5E 82
Deal Way CO7: B'sea 5D 182
Dean Ct. RM7: Romf 9B 110
Deanery Gdns. CM7: Brain 1H 193
Deanery Hill CM7: Brain 1G 193 (6C 14)
Deanery Rd. E15: Lon 8E 122
Deane's Cl. CO12: Har 5J 209
Deane's La. CO12: Har 6G 208
Dean Gdns. E17: Lon 8D 106
Deanhill Av. CO15: Clac S 8M 185
Dean Rd. CB1: Bart 3E 6
DA13: Ludd, Meop 7J 47
SE28: Lon 8F 140
Dean Rogers Pl. CM7: Brain 1H 193
Deans Rd. CM14: War 1E 112
Dean St. CO7: B'sea 6D 182
E7: Lon 7G 122
Deans Wlk. CM7: Brain 9H 191
Dean Wlk. CO4: Colc 9E 166
Dean Way CM1: Chelm 1N 71
Dearsley Ho. RM13: Rain 2B 142
DEBDEN
IG10 3B 92 (6H 31)
CB11 2D 12
Debden Cl. IG8: Wfd G 4K 107
Debden Dr. CB10: Wim 1D 12
DEBDEN GREEN
IG10 8A 78 (5G 31)
CB11 2D 12
Debden Grn. SS16: Lang H 2L 131
Debden Ho. IG10: Lou 8A 78
Debden La. IG10: Lou 8B 78 (5G 31)
Debden Rd. CB11: Deb, Saf W 7D 218 (7C 6)
CB11: Newp 3L 215 (2B 12)
CB11: Saf W 4C 218 (7B 6)
IG10: Lou 8A 78 (5G 31)
Debden Station (Tube) 3B 92 (6H 31)
Debden Wlk. CO16: Clac S 7G 185
RM12: Horn 8F 126
Debden Way CM0: Bur C 2C 196
De Beauvoir Chase
CM11: D'ham, Rams H 5E 100
De Beauvoir Rd. N1: Lon 6B 38
DE BEAUVOIR TOWN 6B 38
Deben RM18: E Til 1L 157
Deben Cl. CM8: Wthm 5B 230
Deben Ct. *CM7: Brain 7M 193*
(off Elmer Rd.)
Deben Rd. CO4: Colc 6E 166
De Bohun Ct. CB10: Saf W 3D 218
Deborah Ct. *E18: Lon 7H 107*
(off Victoria Rd.)
Debrabant Cl. DA8: Eri 4B 152
De Burgh Rd. CO3: S'way 9F 164
DEDHAM 1M 161 (2J 17)
Dedham Art & Craft Cen. & Toy Mus. 1M 161 (2H 17)
Dedham Av. CO16: Clac S 8F 184
Dedham Cl. CM11: Bill 6L 99
Dedham Ct. *CO2: Colc 2B 174*
(off Stalin Rd.)
DEDHAM HEATH 4M 161 (3H 17)
Dedham Meade CO7: Ded 5M 161
Dedham Mill CO7: Ded 1M 161
Dedham Rd. CM11: Bill 6L 99
CO4: Boxt 3B 160 (2F 17)
CO7: A'lgh 6K 161 (3H 17)
CO7: Ded, Strat M 1H 17
CO11: Law 4D 162 (3K 17)
Dedham Vale Family Farm 2J 17
Dee Cl. RM14: Upm 1B 128
Deepdale SS7: Thund 1F 134
Deepdale Rd. CO12: Har 3J 209
Deepdene CM4: Ing 6D 84
SS16: Bas 1C 132
Deepdene Av. SS6: Ray 2J 119
(not continuous)
Deepdene Cl. E11: Lon 8G 107
Deepdene Path IG10: Lou 3N 91
(not continuous)
Deepdene Rd. IG10: Lou 3N 91
Deeping SS1: Sth S 6M 137
Deeping Wlk. CO16: St O 8N 183
Deepwater Rd. SS8: Can I 2E 150
Deerbank Rd. CM11: Bill 5L 99
Deere Av. RM13: Rain 8E 126
Deerhurst SS7: Thund 8H 119
Deerhurst Chase CM3: Bick 9F 74
Deerhurst Cl. SS7: Thund 8H 119
Deerleap Gro. E4: Lon 4B 90
Deerleap Way CM7: Brain 4M 193
Deer Mead Ct. RM1: Romf 9D 110
Deer Pk. CM19: H'low 6N 53
Deer Pk. Cl. CO9: Cas H 4L 219
Deerpark Way EN9: Enf 6B 76
DEER'S GREEN 3H 11
Deeside Wlk. SS12: W'fd 2M 117
Dee Way RM1: Romf 4C 110
Defoe Cl. DA8: Eri 6C 152
Defoe Cres. CO4: Colc 2L 165 (5E 16)
Defoe Pde. RM16: Grays 1D 156
Defoe Way RM5: Col R 3M 109
Deford Rd. CM8: Wthm 7A 230
Deirdre Av. SS12: W'fd 1J 117
Deirdre Cl. SS12: W'fd 9J 101
Delafield Rd. RM17: Grays 3N 155
Delamare Rd. EN8: Chesh 3D 30
Delamere Rd. CM1: Chelm 1N 71
CO4: Colc 4D 166
Delancey St. NW1: Lon 6A 38
Delargy Cl. RM16: Grays 1D 156
Delaware Cres. SS3: Shoe 7H 139
Delaware Ho. SS3: Shoe 6G 138
Delaware Rd. SS3: Shoe 7G 138 (5B 44)
Delder Av. SS8: Can I 3K 151
Delderfield Ho. *RM1: Romf 6B 110*
(off Portnoi Cl.)
Delft Rd. SS8: Can I 1G 151
Delfzul Rd. SS8: Can I 1G 151
Delgada Rd. SS8: Can I 2K 151
Delhi Rd. SS13: Pits 9K 117
Delimands SS15: Lain 9A 116
Delisle Rd. SE28: Lon 9D 140
(not continuous)
Delius Wlk. CO4: Colc 9E 166
Delius Way SS17: Stan H 2L 147
Dell Cl. IG8: Wfd G 9H 91
Dell Ct. RM12: Horn 4J 127
Dellfield Ct. CM17: H'low 8H 51
Dell La. CM22: L Hall, Spel 2H 213 (3K 21)
Dellow Cl. IG2: Ilf 2C 124
Dellows La. CM22: Ugley, U Grn 2H 199
Dell Rd. RM17: Grays 2L 155
Dells Cl. E4: Lon 6B 90
Dell, The CM2: Gt Bad 4G 72
CM6: Gt D 2M 203
CM13: Gt War 3E 112
CO1: Colc 9A 166
EN9: Enf 6C 76
IG8: Wfd G 9H 91
SS11: W'fd 9M 101
SS16: Van 3C 132
Dellwood Gdns. IG5: Ilf 7N 107
Delmar Gdns. SS11: W'fd 6K 101
Delmores SS16: Lang H 3L 131
Delta Rd. CM13: Hut 5N 97
De Luci Rd. DA8: Eri 3A 152
Delvers Mead RM10: Dag 6A 126
Delview SS8: Can I 9F 134
DELVIN END 1C 14
Delvins SS13: Bas 7H 117
Delvyn's La. CO9: Gest 7F 9
De Mandeville Rd. CM22: Else 2K 199
De-Marci Ct. CM7: Brain 5M 193
Denbar Pde. RM7: Maw 8A 110
Denbigh Cl. RM11: Horn 8L 111
Denbigh Ho. *RM3: Romf 3J 111*
(off Kingsbridge Cir.)
Denbigh Rd. SS15: Lain 1K 131
Denby Grange CM17: H'low 3K 55
Dencourt Cres. SS14: Bas 1G 132
Dene Cl. SS6: Ray 3K 119
Dene Ct. CM1: Chelm 6F 58
Denecroft Gdns. RM17: Grays 1N 155
Dene Gdns. SS6: Ray 3K 119
Denehurst Gdns. IG8: Wfd G 1H 107
SS16: Lang H 2G 131

Dene Path RM15: S Ock. . . . 6D 144
Dene Rd. IG9: Buck H. . . . 7K 91
Denesmere SS7: Ben 2C 134
Deneway SS16: Van 4E 132
Dengayne SS14: Bas. . . . 9E 116
DENGIE. . . . 4J 225 (4E 36)
Dengie Cl. CM8: Wthm. . . . 7C 230
Dengie 100 Sports Cen. . . . 4D 196
Denham Cl. CO7: W'hoe 6J 175
Denham Dr. IG2: Ilf. . . . 1B 124
Denham Rd. SS8: Can I 1G 150
Denham Va. SS6: Ray 5G 118
Denham Way IG11: Bark 1D 140
Denholm Ct. CM8: Wthm 7C 230
Denholme Wlk. RM13: Rain. . . . 8D 126
Denmark Ho. *CM2: Chelm 2D 72*
(off Baddow Rd.)
Denmark St. E11: Lon. . . . 5E 122
Denner Rd. E4: Lon 8A 90
Dennises La. RM14: Upm. . . . 1B 144 (6D 40)
Dennison Point E15: Lon 9C 122
Dennis Rd. RM15: S Ock. . . . 9D 128 (6E 40)
Denny Av. EN9: Wal A. . . . 4D 76
Denny Ct. CM23: Bis S 7A 220
Denny Gdns. RM9: Dag 9G 125
Densham Rd. E15: Lon. . . . 6E 38
Dent Cl. RM15: S Ock. . . . 6D 144
DENTON 4J 47
Denton App. SS0: Wclf S 2H 137
Denton Av. SS0: Wclf S 1H 137
Denton Cl. SS0: Wclf S 1H 137
Denton Cres. CM77: Bla N 3B 194
Denton Rd. DA1: Dart. . . . 4A 46
Denton's Ter. CO7: W'hoe. . . . 6H 175
Denver Dr. SS13: Bas 6K 117
Denver Ind. Est. RM13: Rain 5D 142
Denys Dr. SS14: Bas. . . . 6G 116
Derby Av. RM7: Romf 1A 126
RM14: Upm. . . . 5K 127
Derby Cl. CM3: May 7K 213
CM11: Bill. . . . 3M 99
SS16: Lang H 2H 131
Derbydale SS4: R'fd 1H 121
Derby Rd. E7: Lon 9K 123
E18: Lon 5F 106
EN11: Hod. . . . 7D 52
RM17: Grays. . . . 3L 155 (2F 47)
Derby Rd. Bri. RM17: Grays 4L 155
Dereham Cl. CO2: Colc. . . . 3K 173
Dereham Pl. RM5: Col R 3N 109
Dereham Rd. IG11: Bark. . . . 7E 124
Derek Gdns. SS2: Sth S 1K 137
Deres Bridge Rdbt. CM3: Gt L 9J 203
Derham Gdns. RM14: Upm 5N 127
Deri Av. RM13: Rain 4F 142
Dering Cres. SS9: Lgh S 8C 120
Derry Av. RM15: S Ock. . . . 6D 144
Dersingham Av. E12: Lon 6M 123
Derventer Av. SS8: Can I 8G 134
Derwent Av. SS6: Ray. . . . 5K 119
Derwent Gdns. CO15: Hol S. . . . 7N 185
IG4: Ilf. . . . 8L 107
Derwent Pde. RM15: S Ock 6D 144
Derwent Rd. CO4: Colc. . . . 2C 166
Derwent Way CM1: Chelm 7F 58
CM77: Gt N. . . . 2C 204
RM12: Horn. . . . 7F 126
Dessons Ct. SS17: Corr 1A 148
De Staunton Cl. CO7: Alr 7A 176
Detling Cl. RM12: Horn 7G 126
Detling Rd. DA8: Eri 5B 152
Devas St. E3: Lon. . . . 6D 38
Devenay Rd. E15: Lon 9F 122
Devenish Rd. SE2: Lon 9F 140
Devereaux Cl. CO14: Walt. . . . 6J 181
De Vere Av. CM9: Mal 7D 214
De Vere Cl. CM3: Hat P. . . . 3M 61
CO7: W'hoe. . . . 6H 175
De Vere Est. CO7: Gt Ben 6J 177
De Vere Gdns. IG1: Ilf 4M 123
De Vere La. CO7: W'hoe. . . . 5H 175
De Vere Rd. CO3: Colc 1H 173
CO6: E Col. . . . 7A 198
De Veres Rd. CO9: Hals 5J 207
Devereux Path SS13: Bas 6J 117
Devereux Pl. CO4: Colc 4K 165
Devereux Rd. RM16: Chaf H. . . . 1J 155
SS1: Sth S 7M 137
Devereux Way CM12: Bill 3J 99
De Vere Way CO12: Har 5H 209
Deverill Cl. CM1: Broom 1K 59
Deveron Gdns. RM15: S Ock 6C 144
Deveron Way RM1: Romf 5C 110
De Vigier Av. CB10: Saf W 3F 218
Devizes Ho. *RM3: Romf. . . . 2H 111*
(off Montgomery Cres.)
Devon Cl. IG9: Buck H 8H 91
Devon Gdns. SS4: R'fd. . . . 2H 121
Devonport Gdns. IG1: Ilf 1M 123
Devon Rd. CO2: Colc. . . . 3J 173
DA4: S Dar, S at H. . . . 6C 46
IG11: Bark. . . . 1D 140
Devonshire Cl. E15: Lon. . . . 6E 122
SS15: Lain. . . . 7J 115
Devonshire Gdns. CM7: Brain 4K 193
SS17: Linf 1J 157
Devonshire Ho. IG8: Ilf. . . . 4A 108
Devonshire Rd. CM0: Bur C 3D 196
CM0: S'min. . . . 2C 222
E17: Lon 1A 122
IG2: Ilf. . . . 2C 124
Devonshire Rd. RM12: Horn 4G 126
RM16: Chaf H, Grays 2H 155 (1F 47)
SS15: Lain. . . . 7J 115
Devons Rd. E3: Lon 7D 38
Devons Road Station (DLR). . . . 6D 38
Devon Way CO12: Har. . . . 5F 208
CO15: Hol S 6B 186
SS8: Can I 9H 135
Dewberry Cl. CO4: Colc 8D 166
DEWES GREEN. . . . 3H 11
Dewes Grn. Rd. CM23: Ber 3H 11
Dewey Path RM12: Horn 8G 127
Dewey Rd. RM10: Dag. . . . 8N 125
Dewlands CM77: Bla N. . . . 2B 194
SS14: Bas. . . . 8B 116
Dewlands Est. CM77: Bla N 2B 194
Dewsbury Cl. RM3: Romf 3J 111
Dewsbury Gdns. RM3: Romf 3H 111
Dewsbury Rd. RM3: Romf 3H 111
Dewsgreen SS16: Van. . . . 2F 132
Dewyk Rd. SS8: Can I 9J 135
Dexter Cl. RM17: Grays 1K 155
Deyncourt Gdns. RM14: Upm. . . . 4N 127
Deynecourt Gdns. E11: Lon 8J 107
Deynes Rd. CB11: Deb. . . . 2C 12
Dial Rd. CO7: Gt Ben. . . . 2K 183 (2A 28)
Diamond Cl. RM8: Dag 3H 125
RM16: Chaf H 1J 155
Diamond Ct. RM11: Horn 3E 126
Diana Cl. E18: Lon 5H 107
RM16: Chaf H 1J 155
Diana Ct. DA8: Eri. . . . 4C 152
Diana Way CO15: Clac S 2G 189
Diban Av. RM12: Horn 6F 126
Diban Ct. *RM12: Horn. . . . 6F 126*
(off Diban Av.)
Dickens Av. DA1: Dart. . . . 9L 153
RM18: Til 6D 156
Dickens Cl. CM7: Brain. . . . 8J 193
SS2: Sth S 4N 137
Dickens Ct. *E11: Lon 8G 107*
(off Makepeace Rd.)
SS15: Lain 8M 115
Dickens Dr. SS15: Lain. . . . 8L 115
Dickens Pl. CM1: Chelm 4F 58
Dickens Ri. IG7: Chig 9A 92
Dickens Way RM1: Romf 8C 110
Dickett's Hill CO9: Gt Yel 7D 8
Dicky Moors CM3: Gt Walt 5H 57
Digby Gdns. RM10: Dag 1M 141
Digby M. CO5: W Mer. . . . 3C 228
Digby Rd. IG11: Bark 9E 124
SS17: Corr 9C 132
Digby Wlk. RM12: Horn 8G 126
Diggens Ct. IG10: Lou 2L 91
Dilbridge Rd. E. CO4: Colc. . . . 7C 166
Dilbridge Rd. W. CO4: Colc 7B 166
Dillestone Ct. CB9: Stur 6J 223
Dilston CM3: Dan 4G 75
Dimond Cl. E7: Lon 6G 123
Dinant Av. SS8: Can I 9E 134
Dinant Link Rd. EN11: Hod. . . . 4A 52
Dinants Cres. CO6: M Tey 3G 170
Dinsdale Cl. CO4: Colc 7C 166
Discovery Cen., The 1A 204 (1B 24)
Disney Cl. CM4: Ing 5D 84
Disraeli Cl. SE28: Lon 8H 141
Disraeli Rd. E7: Lon. . . . 8G 123
SS6: Lgh S, Ray 6A 120
Distillery La. CO2: Colc 2C 174
Ditches Ride, The CM16: Lou, They B. . . . 8N 77
IG10: Lou, They B. . . . 8N 77
Ditchfield Rd. EN11: Rye P. . . . 2A 52
Ditton Ct. Rd. SS0: Wclf S 6J 137
Divisional Rd. E12: Lon 4K 123
Dixon Av. CM1: Chelm 7H 59
CO16: Clac S. . . . 7G 185
Dixon Cl. CO11: Law 4G 162
Dixon Ct. SS13: Pits 9J 117
Dixon Way CO7: W'hoe. . . . 3G 175
(not continuous)
Dobbies La. CO6: M Tey 3H 171 (7A 16)
DOBBS WEIR 6D 52 (7E 20)
Dobb's Weir Rd. CM19: Roy. . . . 6C 52
EN11: Hod, Roy 6C 52 (7E 20)
Dobsons Cl. SS6: Ray. . . . 6L 119
Dock App. Rd. RM16: Grays. . . . 4A 156
RM17: Grays. . . . 4A 156
Docker Ct. *CO2: Colc 2B 174*
(off Stalin Rd.)
Dockfield Av. CO12: Har. . . . 4H 209
DOCKLANDS 7G 39
Docklands Av. CM4: Ing 5E 84
Dock La. CO12: Gt Oak. . . . 7F 204 (5F 19)
Dock Rd. CM3: May 7M 213
IP11: Felix. . . . 2K 19
RM17: Grays 4N 155 (2G 47)
(Broadway)
RM17: Grays 4A 156 (2G 47)
(Dock App. Rd.)
RM18: Til. . . . 6A 156 (2G 47)
Dock St. E1: Lon. . . . 7C 38
Dockwra La. CM3: Dan 3F 74
Doctors La. CM0: Bur C 4E 196
Doctor's La. CO10: Ashen. . . . 4C 8
Docwra Rd. CO5: K'dn 3K 211
Docwra's Manor Gardens 1E 4
Doddenhill Cl. CB10: Saf W. . . . 2D 218
DODDINGHURST 6F 82 (5E 32)
Doddinghurst Rd.
CM15: Brtwd, Dodd, Pil H 7F 82 (5E 32)
Dodding's La. CO6: M Tey 6G 171
Doddington Lodge CM15: Dodd 6E 82
Doesgate La. RM14: Bulp. . . . 5C 130 (4H 41)
Doeshill Dr. SS12: W'fd. . . . 9M 101
Dog Chase CM7: Weth 8C 228
Dogden La. CM23: Man 5K 11
Doggetts Chase SS4: Cwdn, R'fd 1L 121
Doggetts Cl. SS4: R'fd 4L 121
Doggett's Cnr. RM11: Horn. . . . 4K 127
Doggetts La. CO6: M Tey 4H 171
Doghouse Rd. CM77: Tye G 6F 15
Dog Kennel La. CM4: Ing, Mill G 2D 84
Dolby Ri. CM2: Chelm 9A 60
Dollant Av. SS8: Can I 2G 151
Dolphin App. RM1: Romf. . . . 8D 110
Dolphin Cl. SE28: Lon. . . . 6J 141
Dolphin Ct. CO13: Frin S. . . . 8L 181
IG7: Chig. . . . 9A 92
Dolphin Gdns. CM12: Bill. . . . 3H 99
Dolphin Pk. Ind. Est. RM19: W Thur 3B 154
Dolphins SS0: Wclf S 1J 137
Dolphin Way RM19: W Thur. . . . 2B 154
Dombey Cl. CM1: Chelm 4H 59
Dome Village, The SS5: Hock 7B 104
Dominic Ct. EN9: Wal A 3B 76
Dominion Dr. RM5: Col R. . . . 3N 109
Dominion Way RM13: Rain. . . . 3E 142
Domitian Cl. CO4: Colc. . . . 2B 166
Domsey Bank CO6: M Tey 3G 171
Domsey Chase CO5: Fee 6D 170
Domsey La. CM3: L Walt. . . . 9N 57 (6B 24)
Doms La. CM3: Terl 4D 24
Donald Dr. RM6: Chad H 9H 109
Donald Hunter Ho. *E7: Lon 7H 123*
(off Post Office App., not continuous)
Donald Thorn Cl. SS12: W'fd 1L 117
Donald Way CM2: Chelm 3D 72
Donard Dr. CO6: W Ber. . . . 3E 164
Doncaster Way RM14: Upm 5K 127
Doncel Ct. E4: Lon 6D 90
Doncella Cl. RM16: Chaf H 1G 155
Don Ct. CM8: Wthm 5A 230
Donington Av. IG2: Ilf. . . . 9B 108
Donkey La. DA4: F'ham 7C 46
Donne Dr. CO15: Jay. . . . 4E 188
Donne Rd. RM8: Dag 4H 125
Donovan's Gdn. CM13: Heron 4N 113
Donside Wlk. SS12: W'fd. . . . 2L 117
Don Way RM1: Romf 4C 110
Donyland Way CO5: Rhdge. . . . 7F 174
Dooley Rd. CO9: Hals 5J 207
Doran Wlk. E15: Lon 9C 122
Dorchester Av. EN11: Rye P 3A 52
Dorchester Ct. *E18: Lon 5F 106*
(off Buckingham Rd.)
Dorchester End CO2: Colc 3B 174
Dorchester Gdns. E4: Lon 1A 106
Dorchester Rd. CM12: Bill. . . . 3J 99
Dordells SS15: Lain 9N 115
Dore Av. E12: Lon 7N 123
Doreen Capstan Ho. *E11: Lon 5E 122*
(off Apollo Pl.)
Dorewards Av. CM7: Brain 9H 191
Dorian Rd. RM12: Horn 3E 126
Doric Av. SS4: R'fd 2J 121
Doris Av. DA8: Eri 6A 152
Doris Rd. E7: Lon. . . . 9G 123
Dorking Cres. CO16: Clac S 7G 185
Dorking Gdns. RM3: Romf. . . . 2H 111
Dorking Ri. RM3: Romf 1H 111
Dorking Rd. RM3: Romf. . . . 2H 111
DORKING TYE 1A 16
Dorking Wlk. CM2: Gt Bad 3F 72
RM3: Romf 1H 111
Dorkins Way RM14: Upm 2B 128
Dormer Cl. E15: Lon. . . . 8F 122
Dorothy Curtice Ct. CO6: Cop. . . . 1N 171
Dorothy Farm Rd. SS6: Ray. . . . 6N 119
Dorothy Gdns. RM8: Dag 6G 125
SS7: Thund 1F 134
Dorothy L Sayers Cen. . . . 5D 230 (4G 25)
Dorothy Sayers Dr. CM8: Wthm 2C 230
Dorrington Gdns. RM12: Horn 3H 127
Dorset Av. CM2: Gt Bad 3E 72
RM1: Romf 8B 110
Dorset Cl. CM2: Gt Bad. . . . 4F 72
CO9: Hals 5K 207
CO15: Hol S 7B 186
Dorset Gdns. SS4: R'fd 2H 121
SS17: Linf 9J 147
Dorset Pl. E15: Lon 8D 122
Dorset Rd. CM0: Bur C 4E 196
CM9: Mal. . . . 8B 214
E7: Lon 9J 123
Dorset Way CM12: Bill 3J 99
SS8: Can I. . . . 9G 135
(off Hilton Rd.)
Dorvis La. CB10: A'dn. . . . 6C 190
Doubleday Cnr. *CO6: Cogg. . . . 3K 197*
(off Market Hill)
Doubleday Dr. CM9: Mal. . . . 3B 214
Doubleday Gdns. CM7: Brain 3K 193
Doubleday Rd. IG10: Lou 2B 92
Doublegate La. SS11: Raw 2B 118
Doublet M. CM11: Bill 3M 99
Douglas Av. E17: Lon 5A 106
RM3: H Wood 6J 111
Douglas Cl. CM2: Gall. . . . 7E 72
IG6: Ilf. . . . 4A 108
RM16: Chaf H. . . . 1H 155
Douglas Dr. SS12: W'fd 2L 117
Douglas Gro. CM8: Wthm 5A 230
Douglas Rd. CO12: Har 4K 209
CO15: Clac S. . . . 9G 184
E4: Lon 6E 90
IG3: Ilf 2F 124
RM11: Horn 1D 126
SS7: Had 3M 135
Douglas Wlk. CM2: Chelm 2B 72
Doug Siddons Ct. RM17: Grays. . . . 4M 155
Doulton Cl. CM17: H'low 4K 55
Doulton Way SS4: R'fd 1H 121
Dounsell Ct. CM15: Pil H 5D 96
Dove Cl. CM24: Stan M 2D 220
RM16: Chaf H 1H 155
Dovecote SS3: Shoe 5J 139
Dove Cres. CO12: Har 6F 208
Dovedale SS8: Can I. . . . 9K 135
Dovedale Av. IG5: Ilf 6N 107
Dovedale Cl. CM11: Rams H 4D 100
SS16: Lang H 2J 131
Dovedale Gdns. CO15: Clac S, Hol S 7N 185
Dovedale Sports Cen. . . . 2B 72
Dove Dr. SS7: Ben 4B 134
Dovehouse Cft. CM20: H'low 1F 54
Dove Ho. Gdns. E4: Lon. . . . 8A 90
Dovehouse Mead IG11: Bark 2C 140
Dove La. CM2: Chelm. . . . 4B 72
Dovercliff Rd. SS8: Can I 2L 151
Dover Cl. CM7: Brain 2G 193
CO15: Clac S. . . . 4H 189
RM5: Col R 6A 110
DOVERCOURT. . . . 4K 209 (3H 19)
Dovercourt By-Pass CO12: Har 3J 209 (3H 19)
Dovercourt Haven Cvn. Pk. CO12: Har. . . . 7J 209
Dovercourt Roller Skating Rink. . . . 5L 209
Dovercourt Station (Rail). . . . 3M 209 (3H 19)
Dovercourt Swimming Pool 6K 209
Dover Rd. CO7: B'sea 5E 182
(not continuous)
DA11: N'fleet. . . . 4G 47
E12: Lon 4J 123
RM6: Chad H. . . . 1K 125
Dover Rd. E. DA11: Grav 4G 47
DOVERS CORNER 3E 142 (6B 40)
Dovers Cnr. RM13: Rain 3E 142
Dovers Cnr. Ind. Est. RM13: Rain 3D 142
Dovervelt Rd. SS8: Can I 9H 135 (5E 42)
Dover Way SS13: Pits 1J 133
Doves Cotts. IG7: Chig 9F 92
Dovesgate SS7: Ben 2B 134
Doves La. CM6: Gt D 2F 23
Doves M. SS15: Lain. . . . 6M 115
Dovetree Ct. *RM3: Romf 1H 111*
(off N. Hill Dr.)
Dove Wlk. RM12: Horn. . . . 8F 126
Dowches Dr. CO5: K'dn 2K 211
Dowches Gdns. CO5: K'dn 2K 211
Dow Ct. CM0: S'min 2C 222
Dowding Cl. CO2: Colc. . . . 2A 174
Dowding Way RM12: Horn 9F 126
Dowland Cl. SS17: Stan H 2L 147
Dowland Wlk. SS15: Lain. . . . 8L 115
Dowling Rd. CO8: M Bur 3A 16
Dowmans Chase CO9: Peb. . . . 1H 15
Downbank Av. DA7: Bexh 6B 152
Downer Rd. SS7: Ben. . . . 2D 134
Downer Rd. Nth. SS7: Thund 1E 134
Downesway SS7: Ben. . . . 3D 134
Downey Cl. SS14: Bas 8D 116
Downfield Rd.
SG13: Hert H, Rush G. . . . 6C 20
Downhall Cl. SS6: Ray. . . . 3K 119
Downhall Cotts. CM0: Brad S. . . . 6C 194
Downhall Pk. Way SS6: Ray. . . . 1J 119
Downhall Rd. CM0: Brad S 6C 194 (7F 27)
CM17: Hat H, Mat G 5B 22
CM17: Mat G, Mat T 5B 22
Down Hall Rd. SS6: Ray 4J 119 (2F 43)
DOWNHAM. . . . 4F 100 (7B 34)
Downham Cl. RM5: Col R 4M 109
Downham Rd.
CM4: D'ham, Stock 5B 86 (5A 34)
CM11: D'ham. . . . 5B 86 (5A 34)
(Dowsett La.)
CM11: D'ham, Rams H 4D 100 (6A 34)
(Church Rd.)
N1: Lon. . . . 6B 38
SS8: Can I. . . . 2G 151
SS11: W'fd 6K 101
Downhills Pk. Rd. N17: Lon. . . . 3B 38
Downing Rd. RM9: Dag 9L 125
Downland Ct. E11: Lon. . . . 4E 122
Downlands EN9: Wal A 4E 76
Downleaze CM3: S Fer. . . . 9L 89
Downs Cres. CM6: Gt D 2K 203
Downsell Rd. E15: Lon. . . . 6C 122
Downs Footpath CM9: Mal 5C 214
Downs Gro. SS16: Van 3E 132
Downshall Av. IG3: Ilf. . . . 1D 124
Downshills Way N17: Lon 2B 38
Downsland Dr. CM14: Brtwd. . . . 9F 96
Downs Rd. CM9: Mal 5C 214
DA13: N'flt G. . . . 5G 47
EN1: Enf 6B 30
Downs Ter. CM6: Steb 7C 222
Downs, The CM6: Gt D 2L 203 (7G 13)
CM6: Steb 7C 222 (6H 13)
CM9: Mal. . . . 5C 214
CM20: H'low 3D 54
Downsway CM1: Chelm. . . . 5M 59
Downton Wlk. CO5: Tip 5D 226
Dowsett La. CM11: Rams H 9C 86 (6A 34)
Dowsett Rd. N17: Lon 2C 38
Doyle Cl. DA8: Eri. . . . 6C 152
Doyle Way RM18: Til 7E 156
Dragon Cl. CM0: Bur C. . . . 3C 196
Dragons Grn. CB10: Sew E. . . . 6D 6
Drake Av. CM3: May 8L 213
Drake Cl. CM14: War 2H 113
SS7: Thund 2J 135
Drake Ct. *DA8: Eri 5D 152*
(off Frobisher Rd.)
SS14: Bas. . . . 1G 132
(off Beech Rd.)
Drake Cres. SE28: Lon. . . . 6H 141
Drake Gdns. CM7: Brain 4L 193
Drake M. RM12: Rain. . . . 8E 126

Drake Rd. RM16: Chaf H ... 1H 155 (1E 46)
SS0: Wclf S ... 6H 137
SS15: Lain ... 9M 115
Drakes App. CO15: Jay ... 3E 188
Drake's Cnr. CO5: Gt Wig ... 4D 26
Drakes La. CM3: L Walt ... 5B 24
Drakes Mdw. CM17: H'low ... 8K 51
Drakes, The SS3: Shoe ... 6J 139
Drakes Way SS6: Ray ... 3L 119
Drapers Chase CM9: H'bri ... 4F 214
CM77: Rayne ... 1A 24
Drapers Ct. RM12: Horn ... 4J 127
DRAPERS GREEN ... 4H 7
Draper's La. CB9: Hel B ... 4H 7
Drapers Rd. CM3: S Fer ... 9L 89
E15: Lon ... 6D 122
EN2: Enf ... 6A 30
Draycot Rd. E11: Lon ... 1H 123
Dray Ct. CO6: W Ber ... 3G 165
Draymans Gro. CM77: Gt N ... 8E 192
Drayson Cl. EN9: Wal A ... 2E 76
Drayton Av. IG10: Lou ... 6M 91
Drayton Cl. CM9: Mal ... 7C 214
IG1: Ilf ... 3C 124
Drayton Ho. E11: Lon ... 3D 122
Drayton Pk. N5: Lon ... 5A 38
Drayton Park Station (Rail) ... 5A 38
Drayton Rd. E11: Lon ... 3D 122
Drewsteignton SS3: Shoe ... 6H 139
Dreys, The CB10: Sew E ... 7D 6
Driberg Way CM7: Brain ... 7J 193
Driffield Cl. CO5: Fee ... 1L 211
Drift, The CO7: Ded ... 1M 161
IP9: Stut ... 1D 18
Driftway SG8: Reed ... 1D 10
SS16: Van ... 3G 133
Drive, The CM1: Chelm ... 5J 59
CM3: May ... 7K 213 (3A 36)
CM3: S Fer ... 9H 89
(Ferrers Rd.)
CM3: S Fer ... 2H 103
(Treebeard Copse)
CM6: Thax ... 7B 224
CM8: Riven ... 3H 25
CM13: Gt War ... 2F 112 (2E 40)
CM20: H'low ... 2D 54
CM21: Saw ... 2K 51
CO12: Har ... 5K 209 (3H 19)
CO15: Clac S ... 6M 185
E4: Lon ... 6D 90
E17: Lon ... 7B 106
E18: Lon ... 8G 106
EN11: Rye P ... 3A 52
IG1: Ilf ... 1L 123 (3G 39)
IG9: Buck H ... 6J 91
IG10: Lou ... 2L 91
(not continuous)
IG11: Bark ... 9E 124
RM3: H Wood ... 5J 111
RM4: Stap A ... 6A 94
RM5: Col R ... 4B 110
SS0: Wclf S ... 5G 136
SS4: R'fd ... 5L 121
SS5: Hull ... 5K 103
SS6: Lgh S, Ray ... 7A 120
(not continuous)
Driveway, The *E17: Lon* ... *1B 122*
(off Hoe St.)
SS8: Can I ... 3H 151
Droitwich Av. SS2: Sth S ... 5B 138
Dronfield Gdns. RM8: Dag ... 7H 125
Drood Cl. CM1: Chelm ... 4H 59
Drovers Mead CM14: War ... 1E 112
Drovers Way CM2: Chelm ... 4C 60
Droveway IG10: Lou ... 1A 92
Druce, The CB11: Clav ... 3J 11
Druid St. SE1: Lon ... 7B 38
Drummond Av. RM7: Romf ... 8B 110
Drummond Cl. DA8: Eri ... 6C 152
Drummond Ct. CM15: Brtwd ... 6F 96
Drummond Pl. SS12: W'fd ... 2M 117
Drummond Rd. E11: Lon ... 1J 123
RM7: Romf ... 8B 110
Drummonds, The CM16: Epp ... 9F 64
IG9: Buck H ... 8H 91
Drury La. CM6: Ayt R ... 1B 212
CM7: Brain ... 5H 193
CO9: Ridg ... 8C 216 (5B 8)
WC2: Lon ... 7A 38
Drury Rd. CO2: Colc ... 1K 173 (6E 16)
Dryden Av. SS2: Sth S ... 4N 137
Dryden Cl. CM9: Mal ... 8C 214
IG6: Ilf ... 3E 108
Dryden Pl. RM18: Til ... 6D 156
Dry Dock CO7: W'hoe ... 6H 175
Drysdale Av. E4: Lon ... 6B 90
DRY STREET ... 5N 131 (4K 41)
Dry St. SS16: Bas, Lang H, Van ... 4L 131 (4K 41)
Drywoods CM3: S Fer ... 3K 103
Duarte Pl. RM16: Chaf H ... 1J 155
Dubarry Cl. SS7: Thund ... 1F 134
Du Cane Pl. CM8: Wthm ... 5D 230
Duchess Gro. IG9: Buck H ... 8H 91
DUCK END
CM7 ... 2D 200 (2K 13)
CM23 ... 8D 220 (7A 12)
CM6 ... 5H 13
Duckend Farm La. CM6: Lndsl ... 4G 13
DUCKEND GREEN ... 5A 192 (7B 14)
Ducketts Mead CM19: Roy ... 2H 53
SS4: Cwdn ... 1M 105
Ducking Stool Ct. RM1: Romf ... 8C 110
Duck La. CM16: Thorn ... 5H 65 (2J 31)
CO7: Ded ... 5M 161
Duckling La. CM21: Saw ... 2K 51
Duck St. CB11: Wen A ... 8K 227 (7A 6)
CM6: L Eas ... 6F 13
SG9: Fur P ... 4G 11
Duck Wood Community Nature Reserve ... 2M 111
Dudbrook Rd. CM14: Kel C, Nave ... 8J 81 (5C 32)
DUDDENHOE END ... 7H 5
Duddenhoe End Rd. CB11: A'den, Dun E ... 7H 5
Duddery Hill CB9: H'hll ... 3J 7
Dudley Cl. CM3: Bore ... 2F 60
CO2: Colc ... 2A 174
RM16: Chaf H ... 9H 145
Dudley Gdns. RM3: Romf ... 3H 111
Dudley Rd. CO5: Fing ... 2G 27
CO6: E Col ... 7A 198
CO15: Clac S ... 1H 189
E17: Lon ... 6A 106
IG1: Ilf ... 6A 124
RM3: Romf ... 3H 111
Duffield Cl. RM16: Chaf H ... 1J 155
Duffield Dr. CO4: Colc ... 8E 166
Duffield Rd. CM2: Gt Bad ... 4E 72
Duffries Cl. CM3: Gt Walt ... 5G 57
Duffs Hill CO10: Glem ... 1G 9
Dugard Av. CO3: S'way ... 2F 172 (7D 16)
Duggers La. CM7: Brain ... 7J 193
Dugmore Av. CO13: Kir S ... 6F 180
Duke Gdns. IG6: Ilf ... 8C 108
Duke Pl. SS15: Lain ... 7N 115
Duke Rd. IG6: Ilf ... 8C 108
Dukes Av. CM0: S'min ... 3D 222
CM16: They B ... 5D 78
Duke's Av. N10: Lon ... 3A 38
Dukes Av. RM17: Grays ... 1K 155
Dukes Cl. CM16: N Wea ... 6N 65
Dukes Farm Cl. CM12: Bill ... 3L 99
Dukes Farm Rd. CM12: Bill ... 4K 99
Dukes La. CM2: Chelm ... 7A 60
CM5: Will ... 7E 22
Dukes Orchard CM1: Writ ... 2K 71
CM22: Hat O ... 7D 206
Dukes Pk. CM2: Chelm ... 6B 60
Dukes Pk. Ind. Est. CM2: Chelm ... 6B 60
(not continuous)
Duke's Pas. E17: Lon ... 8C 106
Duke's Pl. CM15: Brtwd ... 7F 96
Dukes Rd. CM7: Brain ... 3G 193
CM11: Bill ... 4L 99
Duke St. CM1: Chelm ... 8J 59 (1A 34)
CO7: B'sea ... 7D 182
EN11: Rye P ... 4A 52 (7D 20)
Dulverton Av. SS0: Wclf S ... 2F 136
Dulverton Cl. SS0: Wclf S ... 1F 136
Dulverton Rd. RM3: Romf ... 3H 111
Dulwich Rd. CO15: Hol S ... 9N 185
Dumney La. CM3: Gt L ... 6J 203 (2B 24)
Dumont Av. CO16: St O ... 4K 27
Dunbar Av. RM10: Dag ... 5M 125
Dunbar Gdns. RM10: Dag ... 7M 125
Dunbar Pl. SS12: W'fd ... 2M 117
Dunbar Rd. E7: Lon ... 8G 123
N22: Lon ... 2A 38
Dunbridge St. E2: Lon ... 6C 38
Duncan Cl. SS12: W'fd ... 2N 117
Duncan Ri. CO9: Gt Yel ... 2C 206
Duncan Rd. CO2: Colc ... 2J 173
Dundas M. EN3: Enf ... 7A 76
Dundee Av. SS9: Lgh S ... 4A 136
Dundee Cl. SS9: Lgh S ... 4B 136
Dundonald Dr. SS9: Lgh S ... 5E 136
Dunedin Rd. E10: Lon ... 5B 122
IG1: Ilf ... 3B 124
RM13: Rain ... 3D 142
Dunfane CM11: Bill ... 3L 99
Dungannon Chase SS1: Sth S ... 8F 138
Dungannon Dr. SS1: Sth S ... 8F 138
Dunkeld Rd. RM8: Dag ... 4G 125
Dunkellin Gro. RM15: S Ock ... 6D 144
Dunkellin Way RM15: S Ock ... 6D 144
Dunkin Rd. DA1: Dart ... 9L 153
Dunkirk Rd. CM0: Bur C ... 4E 196
Dunlin Cl. CM3: S Fer ... 8K 89
CM9: Mal ... 2E 214
Dunlin Ct. CO5: K'dn ... 3K 211
Dunlop Cl. DA1: Dart ... 8J 153
Dunlop Rd. RM18: Til ... 6B 156
Dunmore Rd. CM2: Chelm ... 8B 60
Dunmow Cl. IG10: Lou ... 5L 91
RM6: Chad H ... 9H 109
Dunmow Dr. RM13: Rain ... 1D 142
Dunmow Gdns. CM13: W H'dn ... 1N 129
Dunmow Ho. RM9: Dag ... 1G 141
Dunmow La. CM3: Gt Walt ... 1E 56
Dunmow Rd.
CM5: Beau R, Fy'd ... 8D 200 (1D 32)
CM6: Ayt R, Lea R ... 1C 212 (4E 22)
CM6: Fels, Steb ... 7K 13
CM6: Gt Eas ... 6F 13
CM6: Har E, N End ... 3J 23
CM6: L Can ... 3B 224 (1D 22)
CM6: Steb ... 7A 222 (6H 13)
CM6: Thax ... 8C 224 (3F 13)
CM7: Gt Bar, L Bar ... 4A 202 (4J 13)
CM22: Hat H ... 1F 210 (4B 22)
CM22: Hat O ... 7D 206 (3C 22)
CM22: Tak ... 3B 224 (1C 22)
CM23: Bis S ... 9B 220 (1K 21)
E15: Lon ... 6D 122
Dunning Cl. CO11: Brad ... 4B 18
RM15: S Ock ... 6D 144
Dunningford Cl. RM12: Horn ... 7D 126
Dunnings La.
CM13: Bulp, W H'dn ... 2L 129 (4F 41)
RM14: Bulp ... 2L 129 (5F 41)
Dunnock Way CO4: Colc ... 8F 166
Dunoon Cl. CM7: Brain ... 4M 193
Dunsmure Rd. N16: Lon ... 4B 38
Dunspring La. IG5: Ilf ... 6A 108
Dunstable Cl. RM3: Romf ... 3H 111
Dunstable Rd. RM3: Romf ... 3H 111
SS17: Stan H ... 2L 147
Dunstalls CM19: H'low ... 7M 53
Dunstan Vw. CM13: Dun ... 1G 130
Dunster Av. SS0: Wclf S ... 1F 136
Dunster Cl. RM5: Col R ... 6A 110
Dunster Cres. RM11: Horn ... 4L 127
Dunthorne Rd. CO4: Colc ... 5E 166
Dunthorpe Rd. CO16: Clac S ... 7H 185
Dunton Pk. Cvn. Site CM13: Dun ... 9G 114
Dunton Rd. CM12: Dun, Lain ... 6F 114 (2H 41)
CM13: Dun, Heron ... 5C 114 (2H 41)
E10: Lon ... 2B 122
RM1: Romf ... 8C 110
SS15: Lain ... 6J 115 (2J 41)
Dunwich Ct. CO2: Colc ... 2N 173
Dupont Cl. CO16: Clac S ... 7H 185
Dupre Cl. RM16: Chaf H ... 1H 155
Durand La. CM6: Fels ... 9E 212
Durants Rd. EN3: Enf ... 6C 30
Durants Wlk. SS12: W'fd ... 1L 117
Durban Ct. E7: Lon ... 9K 123
Durban Gdns. RM10: Dag ... 9A 126
Durban La. SS15: Bas ... 5A 116
Durban Rd. IG2: Ilf ... 3D 124
Durdans, The SS16: Lang H ... 2K 131
Durell Gdns. RM9: Dag ... 7J 125
Durell Rd. RM9: Dag ... 7J 125
Durham Av. IG8: Buck H, Wfd G ... 2K 107
RM2: Romf ... 8G 110
Durham Cl. CM7: Gt Bar ... 3B 202
CM21: Saw ... 3H 51
Durham Ho. *IG11: Bark* ... *9F 124*
(off Margaret Bondfield Av.)
RM10: Dag ... 7A 126
Durham Pl. IG1: Ilf ... 6B 124
Durham Rd. E12: Lon ... 6K 123
RM10: Dag ... 7A 126
SS2: Sth S ... 4B 138
SS4: R'fd ... 2G 120
SS15: Lain ... 9H 115 (3J 41)
Durham Sq. CO1: Colc ... 8A 166
Durham Way SS6: Ray ... 2K 119
Duriun Way DA8: Eri ... 5F 152
Durley Av. SS12: W'fd ... 8G 100
Durley Cl. SS7: Ben ... 2E 134
Durnell Way IG10: Lou ... 2N 91
Durninge Wlk. RM16: Grays ... 7L 145
Durnsford Rd. N11: Lon ... 2A 38
Durrant Ct. CM1: Chelm ... 7L 59
Durrants Cl. RM13: Rain ... 2G 143
Durrington Cl. SS16: Bas ... 1D 132
Dury Falls Cl. RM11: Horn ... 3L 127
Dury Falls Cl. RM5: Col R ... 6A 110
Dutch Cottage ... 5J 119 (2F 43)
Dutch Cottage Mus. ... 1C 150 (6D 42)
DUTCH QUARTER ... 8M 165
DUTCH VILLAGE ... 1D 150 (6E 42)
DUTON HILL ... 5F 13
DUXFORD ... 2J 5
Duxford SS11: W'fd ... 1A 118
Duxford Airfield ... 3J 5
Duxford Cl. RM12: Horn ... 8G 126
Duxford Ho. *SE2: Lon* ... *9J 141*
(off Wolvercote Rd.)
Duxford Rd. CB2: Whitt ... 1J 5
CB10: Dux, Hxtn ... 3K 5
(Hinxton)
CB10: Dux, I'tn ... 3K 5
(Ickleton)
DYER'S END ... 6B 8
DYER'S GREEN ... 3C 4
Dyers Hall Rd. E11: Lon ... 3E 122
Dyers Hill Rd. E11: Lon ... 4D 122
Dyers Rd. CM9: Mal ... 6C 214
Dyer's Rd. CO3: S'way ... 3D 172 (7C 16)
Dyers Way RM3: Romf ... 4F 110
Dyke Cres. SS8: Can I ... 1D 150
Dykes Chase CM9: Mal ... 5A 214
Dymchurch Cl. IG5: Ilf ... 6N 107
Dymoke Rd. RM11: Horn ... 2D 126
Dymokes Way EN11: Hod ... 2A 52
Dyne's Hall Rd. CO9: Gt Map ... 1J 207 (2F 15)
Dynevor Gdns. SS9: Lgh S ... 5A 136
Dyson Rd. E11: Lon ... 1E 122
E15: Lon ... 8F 122
Dytchleys La. CM14: N'side ... 3L 95 (6C 32)
Dytchleys Rd. CM14: N'side ... 3K 95 (6C 32)

E

Eagle Av. CO14: Walt ... 5N 181
RM6: Chad H ... 1K 125
Eagle Cl. EN9: Wal A ... 4G 76
RM12: Horn ... 8F 126
Eagle Ct. E11: Lon ... 8G 107
Eagle Ga. CO1: Colc ... 8A 166
Eagle La. CM7: Brain ... 2H 193
CM15: Kel H ... 7B 82
E11: Lon ... 8G 106
Eagles Rd. DA9: Grnh ... 9D 154
Eagle Ter. IG8: Wfd G ... 4H 107
Eagle Way CM13: Gt War ... 3E 112 (2E 40)
SS3: Shoe ... 5J 139
Eagle Wharf Rd. N1: Lon ... 6B 38
Eardemont Cl. DA1: Cray ... 9D 152
Earles Colne Rd. CO6: Gt Tey ... 1D 170 (5J 15)
Earleswood SS7: Ben ... 2D 134
Earlham Ct. E11: Lon ... 2F 122
Earlham Gro. E7: Lon ... 7F 122
Earlhams Cl. CO12: Har ... 6H 209
Earl Mountbatten Dr. CM12: Bill ... 4H 99
Earl Rd. DA11: N'fleet ... 4G 47
EARLS COLNE ... 8C 198 (4H 15)
Earls Colne Airfield ... 5G 15
Earls Colne Ind. Pk. CO6: E Col ... 5H 15
Earlsdown Ho. IG11: Bark ... 2C 140
Earlsfield Dr. CM2: Chelm ... 8A 60
Earls Hall Av. SS2: Sth S ... 3J 137
Earls Hall Dr. CO16: Clac S ... 9C 184
Earls Hall Pde. SS2: Sth S ... 2K 137
Earls Mead CM8: Wthm ... 4C 230
Earl's Path IG10: Lou ... 1J 91 (6F 31)
Earl's Wlk. RM8: Dag ... 6G 124
Earlswood SS7: Ben ... 2D 134
Earlswood Gdns. IG5: Ilf ... 7N 107
Earlswood Way CO2: Colc ... 4L 173
Easebourne Rd. RM8: Dag ... 7H 125
Easedale Dr. RM12: Horn ... 7E 126
Easington Way RM15: S Ock ... 5D 144
East Anglian Railway Mus. ... 6C 196
East Av. CM3: Alth ... 3B 190
E12: Lon ... 9L 123 (5G 39)
E17: Lon ... 8B 106
East Bay CO1: Colc ... 8B 166
E. Beach Cvn. Pk. SS3: Shoe ... 7L 139
EAST BERGHOLT ... 1J 17
E. Boundary Rd. E12: Lon ... 5M 123
Eastbourne Gro. SS0: Wclf S ... 3H 137
East Bri. Rd. CM3: S Fer ... 9K 89
Eastbrook Av. RM10: Dag ... 6A 126
Eastbrook Dr. RM7: Rush G ... 5C 126
Eastbrookend Country Pk.
Chase, The ... 6C 126
Dagenham Rd. ... 5B 126
Eastbrook Rd. EN9: Wal A ... 3E 76
Eastbrooks SS13: Pits ... 8J 117
Eastbrooks M. SS13: Pits ... 8J 117
Eastbrooks Pl. SS13: Pits ... 8J 117
Eastbury Av. IG11: Bark ... 1D 140
SS4: R'fd ... 3J 121
Eastbury Ct. IG11: Bark ... 1D 140
Eastbury Manor House ... 1E 140
Eastbury Rd. RM7: Romf ... 1B 126
Eastbury Sq. IG11: Bark ... 1E 140
Eastby Cl. CB11: Saf W ... 5E 218
Eastcheap SS6: Ray ... 3J 119
Eastcliff Av. CO15: Clac S ... 9M 185
East Cl. RM13: Rain ... 4F 142
Eastcote Gro. SS2: Sth S ... 3B 138
East Cres. SS8: Can I ... 1F 150
E. Cross Cen. E15: Lon ... 8A 122
E. Cross Route E9: Lon ... 7A 122
E15: Lon ... 7A 122
E. Dene Dr. RM3: Romf ... 2H 111
E. Dock Rd. CO12: Har ... 1H 209
East Dr. CM21: Saw ... 3K 51
EAST END
CM0 ... 7D 194 (1F 37)
CO7 ... 1A 18
SG9 ... 5H 11
EASTEND ... 2L 53 (7F 21)
Eastend La. CM22: Else ... 1N 221
Eastend Rd. CM0: Brad S ... 8C 194 (1F 37)
E. End Rd. CO7: B'ley, E Ber ... 1A 18
Easten Greene CO6: Wmgfd ... 8L 229
East Entrance RM10: Dag ... 2N 141
Easterford Rd. CO5: K'dn ... 3K 211
Easterford Watermill ... 2L 211 (2J 25)
Easterling Cl. CO12: Har ... 3J 209
Eastern App. CM2: Chelm ... 6A 60
Eastern Av. E11: Lon ... 1H 123 (3F 39)
IG2: Ilf ... 1N 123 (3G 39)
IG4: Ilf ... 1L 123 (3G 39)
RM6: Chad H ... 1A 124 (3J 39)
RM15: Ave ... 8N 143
RM20: W Thur ... 3C 154 (2D 46)
SS2: Sth S ... 3M 137 (4K 43)
SS7: Ben ... 1C 134
Eastern Av. E. RM1: Romf ... 7B 110 (2A 40)
RM2: Romf ... 7B 110
RM3: Romf ... 7B 110
Eastern Av. W. RM6: Chad H ... 8K 109 (3K 39)
RM7: Maw, Romf ... 8K 109 (3K 39)
Eastern Cl. SS2: Sth S ... 3M 137
Eastern Cres. CM1: Chelm ... 6H 59
Eastern Esplanade
SS1: Shoe, Sth S ... 8A 138 (5K 43)
SS8: Can I ... 4J 151 (6F 43)
Eastern Ind. Est. DA18: Eri ... 9M 141
Eastern Path RM12: Horn ... 1H 143
RM13: Horn, Rain ... 1G 142
Eastern Prom. *CO16: P Bay* ... *4K 27*
(off New Way)
Eastern Rd. CM0: Bur C ... 2E 196
CO7: B'sea ... 7D 182
E17: Lon ... 9C 106
RM1: Romf ... 9C 110
RM17: Grays ... 2N 155
SS6: Ray ... 7H 119
Easternville Gdns. IG2: Ilf ... 1B 124
Eastern Way RM17: Grays ... 4K 155 (2F 47)
SE28: Lon ... 9F 140 (7J 39)
East Essex Aviation & Forties Mus. ... 9D 182 (4K 27)
Eastferry Rd. E14: Lon ... 7D 38
Eastfield Gdns. RM10: Dag ... 6M 125
Eastfield Rd. CM14: Brtwd ... 8G 96
E17: Lon ... 8A 106
EN3: Enf ... 5C 30
Eastfield Rd. RM9: Dag ... 6L 125
RM10: Dag ... 6L 125
SS8: Can I ... 9K 135
SS15: Bas ... 5A 116

East Ga. CB10: Gt Che 8D 202
CM20: H'low 2C 54
(not continuous)
Eastgate SS14: Bas. 9C 116
Eastgate Cen. SS14: Bas 1C 132
Eastgate Cl. SE28: Lon 6J 141
Eastgates CO1: Colc 8B 166
Eastgate St. CO12: Har 1M 209
EAST GORES 2C 170 (6K 15)
E. Gores Rd. CO6: Cogg. 1B 170 (6J 15)
E. Hall La. RM13: Wen 6H 143 (7B 40)
E. Hall Rd. BR5: Orp. 7A 46
EAST HAM 6G 39
E. Ham & Barking By-Pass IG11: Bark. 2D 140
Eastham Cres. CM13: Brtwd 1K 113
East Ham Station (Tube). 9L 123 (5G 39)
EAST HANNINGFIELD. 3C 88 (4D 34)
E. Hanningfield Rd. CM2: S'don 7L 73 (3C 34)
CM3: E Han, Ret C. 8A 88 (5D 34)
EAST HATLEY 1A 4
East Haven CO15: Clac S. 8J 185
East Hill CO1: Colc 8A 166 (6F 17)
DA1: Dart 4C 46
DA4: S Dar 6D 46
East Holme DA8: Eri 6B 152
EAST HORNDON 8A 114
EASTHORPE 7J 171 (1A 26)
Easthorpe Rd. CO5: Ethpe, Fee 7D 170 (1K 25)
(Easthorpe)
CO5: Ethpe, Mess 9H 171 (2A 26)
(Messing)
CO6: Cop. 7D 170
E. India Dock Rd. E14: Lon 7D 38
East India Station (DLR) 7E 38
East La. CO7: Ded 3N 161 (2J 17)
Eastleigh Rd. DA7: Bexh 8A 152
SS7: Ben 5E 134
Eastley SS16: Bas. 2A 132
E. Lodge La. EN2: Enf 5A 30
East Mall *RM17: Grays* *4L 155*
(in Mall, The)
East Mayne SS13: Bas. 8G 117 (3B 42)
EAST MERSEA 4J 27
E. Mersea Rd. CO5: Pel, W Mer 4F 27
East Mill CO9: Hals 4L 207
E. Milton Rd. DA12: Grav. 4H 47
Easton End SS15: Lain 9J 115
Easton Rd. CM8: Wthm 4D 230
Easton Way CO13: Frin S 8L 181
East Pk. CM17: H'low. 9H 51
CM21: Saw 3K 51
E. Park Cl. RM6: Chad H. 9J 109
E. Ridgeway EN6: Cuff 3A 30
East Rd. CM1: Chelm 8J 59
CM20: H'low. 8G 50
CO5: E Mer 4H 27
CO5: W Mer 2D 228 (5F 27)
EC1: Lon. 6B 38
RM6: Chad H. 9K 109
RM7: Rush G 2B 126
East Row E11: Lon 1G 122
East Side CO4: Boxt 4A 160
East Smithfield E1: Lon 7B 38
East Sq. SS14: Bas. 9C 116
E. Stockwell St. CO1: Colc. 8N 165
East St. CB10: Saf W. 4D 218 (6C 6)
CM7: Brain. 5J 193
CM9: Tol. 8K 225 (6C 26)
CO1: Colc 8B 166 (6F 17)
CO6: Cogg 3L 197 (7H 15)
CO7: W'hoe. 7H 175
CO10: Sud 5J 9
CO12: Har. 3M 209
IG11: Bark. 1B 140
RM17: Grays 4M 155
RM20: Grays. 4H 155
SS2: Sth S 4L 137 (4J 43)
SS4: R'fd 5L 121 (2J 43)
SS9: Lgh S. 6D 136
East Ter. CO14: Walt. 5N 181
E. Thamesmead Bus. Pk. DA18: Eri. 9L 141
East Thorpe SS14: Bas 9D 116
E. Thurrock Rd. RM17: Grays. 4M 155 (2G 47)
EAST TILBURY 2L 157 (1K 47)
E. Tilbury Rd. SS17: Linf 9J 147 (1J 47)
East Tilbury Station (Rail). 2K 157 (1K 47)
East Vw. CM1: Writ 1H 71 (1J 33)
CM22: Tak. 2C 224
E4: Lon 2C 106
E. View Cl. CB10: R'ter. 7F 7
Eastview Dr. SS6: Ray 2K 119
East Wlk. CM20: H'low. 2C 54
SS14: Bas 9C 116
E. Ward M. CO1: Colc. 8C 166
Eastway E9: Lon 5D 38
East Way E11: Lon 9H 107
Eastway Cycle Circuit 7B 122
Eastways CM8: Wthm. 4D 230
SS8: Can I 9F 134
EASTWICK 8A 50 (6G 21)
Eastwick Hall La. CM20: E'wck, Gil 5G 21
Eastwick Rd. CM20: E'wck, H'low. . . 8A 50 (6G 21)
CM20: Gil, Saw 7C 50 (6H 21)
SG12: Hun, Stan A 5F 21
EASTWOOD 9E 120 (3H 43)
Eastwood Blvd. SS0: Wclf S 3F 136 (4H 43)
EASTWOODBURY. 9K 121 (3J 43)
Eastwoodbury Cl. SS2: Sth S 9J 121
Eastwoodbury Cotts. SS2: Sth S 9H 121
Eastwoodbury Cres. SS2: Sth S. . . . 9K 121 (3J 43)
Eastwoodbury La. SS2: Sth A. 9G 120 (3H 43)
Eastwood Cl. E18: Lon 6G 107
Eastwood Dr. CO4: Colc 3B 166
RM13: Rain 6F 142
Eastwood Ind. Est. SS9: Lgh S. 9B 120
Eastwood La. Sth. SS0: Wclf S 4G 136
Eastwood Old Rd. SS9: Lgh S, Ray. 8M 119
Eastwood Pk. Cl. SS9: Lgh S 9D 120
Eastwood Pk. Dr. SS9: Lgh S. 8D 120
Eastwood Ri. SS9: Lgh S 8A 120
Eastwood Rd. E18: Lon 6G 107
IG3: Ilf 3F 124
SS6: Ray. 5K 119 (2F 43)
SS9: Lgh S. 4C 136 (4G 43)
Eastwood Rd. Nth. SS9: Lgh S 2B 136 (4G 43)
Eatington Rd. E10: Lon 9D 106
Eaton Cl. CM12: Bill 3J 99
Eaton Dr. RM5: Col R 4N 109
Eaton Gdns. RM9: Dag 9K 125
Eaton Ho. *CM23: Bis S* *9A 220*
(off Stortford Hall Rd.)
Eaton M. CO2: Colc. 3B 174
Eaton Ri. E11: Lon 9J 107
Eaton Rd. EN1: Enf 6B 30
RM14: Upm. 4A 128
SS9: Lgh S 4B 136
Eatons Mead E4: Lon 8A 90
Eaton Way CM9: Gt Tot. 7K 205
Ebbsfleet Station (Rail) 3F 47
Ebenezer Cl. CM8: Wthm 2B 230
Ebony Cl. CO2: Colc 4L 173
Eccleston Cres. RM6: Chad H 2G 124
Eccleston Gdns. CM12: Bill. 3J 99
Echo Hgts. E4: Lon 7B 90
Eckersley Rd. CM1: Chelm 8L 59
Eckersley Rd. Ind. Est. CM1: Chelm. 8L 59
Eddy Cl. RM7: Romf 1N 125
Eden Cl. CM8: Wthm 4B 230
EN3: Enf 8A 76
Edendale Rd. DA7: Bexh 6B 152
Eden Grn. RM15: S Ock 5E 144
Eden Gro. E17: Lon. 9B 106
Edenhall Cl. RM3: Romf 2G 111
Edenhall Glen RM3: Romf 2G 111
Edenhall Rd. RM3: Romf 2G 111
Eden Rd. E17: Lon 9B 106
Edenside CO13: Frin S, Walt. 7H 181
Eden Way CM1: Chelm 6E 58
Edgar Ho. E11: Lon 2G 123
Edgar Rd. RM6: Chad H 2J 125
Edgecotts SS16: Bas. 2N 131
Edgefield Av. CO11: Law 5G 162
IG11: Bark 9E 124
Edgefield Ct. *IG11: Bark* *9E 124*
(off Edgefield Av.)
Edgehill Gdns. RM10: Dag 6M 125
Edgware Rd. CO16: Clac S. 8H 185
Edinburgh Av. SS9: Lgh S. 4A 136
SS17: Corr 1A 148
Edinburgh Cl. CM8: Wthm 7D 230
SS6: Ray. 2H 119
Edinburgh Ct. DA8: Eri 5B 152
Edinburgh Dr. RM7: Romf 8A 110
Edinburgh Gdns. CM7: Brain 4K 193
Edinburgh Ga. CM20: H'low 9C 50
Edinburgh Ho. RM2: Romf. 7G 111
Edinburgh M. RM18: Til 7D 156
Edinburgh Pl. CM20: H'low. 8F 50
Edinburgh Rd. E17: Lon 9A 106
(not continuous)
Edinburgh Way CM20: H'low. 9C 50 (6H 21)
SS13: Pits 9J 117
Edison Av. RM12: Horn 3D 126
Edison Cl. CM7: Brain 7H 193
E17: Lon 9A 106
RM12: Horn 3C 126
Edison Gdns. CO4: Colc 6C 166
Edison Rd. CO15: Hol S 7B 186
Edison's Pk. DA2: Dart 8A 154
Edith Cavell Way CB9: Stpl B 3K 223
Edith Cl. SS8: Can I 2E 150
Edith Rd. CO13: Kir S 6G 181
CO15: Clac S 2J 189
E6: Lon. 9K 123
E15: Lon 7D 122
RM6: Chad H. 2J 125
SS2: Sth S. 4L 137
SS8: Can I. 2D 150
Edith Way SS17: Corr. 9B 132
EDMONTON 1C 38
Edmonton Green Station (Rail). 1C 38
Edmund Grn. CO9: Gosf 8L 201
Edmund Hurst Dr. E6: Lon 5A 140
Edmund Rd. CM8: Wthm 7B 230
RM13: Rain. 2C 142
RM16: Chaf H. 9G 144
Edmund's Twr. CM19: H'low 3B 54
EDNEY COMMON 5E 70 (2H 33)
Edridge Cl. RM12: Horn 7H 127
Edward Av. CO7: B'sea 6E 182
E4: Lon. 3B 106
Edward Bawden Ct. *CB10: Saf W* *4C 218*
(off High St.)
Edward Bright Cl. CM9: Mal 6C 214
Edward Cl. CM12: Bill. 3H 99
CO16: L Cla 9J 179
RM2: Romf 7G 110
RM16: Chaf H 9G 145
SS4: R'fd. 1H 121
Edward Ct. EN9: Wal A 3F 76
Edward Gdns. SS11: W'fd. 8L 101
Edwardian Club, The. 5J 99
Edward Mans. *IG11: Bark* *9E 124*
(off Upney La.)
Edward Marke Dr. CO5: L'hoe. 8B 174
Edward Rd. CO16: T Sok 7K 179
RM6: Chad H. 1K 125
Edwards Cl. CM13: Hut 5A 98
Edward St. CO12: Har. 2G 209
Edwards Wlk. CM9: Mal 5B 214
Edwards Way CM13: Hut 5A 98
Edward Temme Av. E15: Lon 9F 122
Edward Ter. CO16: L Cla 9J 179
Edwina Gdns. IG4: Ilf 9L 107
Edwin Cl. RM13: Rain 3D 142
Edwin Hall Vw. CM3: S Fer. 8J 89
Edwin's Hall Rd. CM3: Wdhm F. 6J 89 (5F 35)
Egbert Gdns. SS11: W'fd 7L 101
Egerton Ct. E11: Lon 2D 122
Egerton Dr. SS16: Lang H. 1G 131
Egerton Gdns. IG3: Ilf 5E 124
Egerton Grn. Rd. CO2: Colc 3H 173
Egg Hall CM16: Epp 8F 64
Eggshell La. CM7: Bird, Corn H, Stamb 6K 7
Eglantine La. DA4: F'ham. 7C 46
Eglington Rd. E4: Lon 6D 90
Eglinton Dr. CM2: Chelm 7C 60
Egremont St. CO10: Glem 2G 9
Egremont Way CO3: S'way. 2D 172
Egret Cres. CO4: A'lgh, Colc. 7G 166
Ehringshausen Way CB9: H'hll 3J 7
Eider Cl. E7: Lon 7F 122
Eight Acre La. CO2: Colc 4K 173
EIGHT ASH GREEN. 7B 164 (5C 16)
EIGHT ASH GREEN INTERCHANGE
. . . . . 9B 164 (6C 16)
Eighth Av. E12: Lon 6M 123
Eisenhower Rd. SS15: Lain 9J 115
Elan Rd. RM15: S Ock 5D 144
Elbourne Trad. Est. DA17: Belv 1A 152
Elbert Cl. SS2: Sth S 4C 138
Eldeland SS15: Lain 8N 115
Eldenwall Ind. Est. RM8: Dag 3K 125
Elder Av. SS12: W'fd 1J 117
Elderberry Cl. IG6: Ilf 4A 108
SS16: Lang H 1K 131
Elderberry Gdns. CM8: Wthm. 3E 230
Elderfield CM17: H'low 8J 51
Elder Fld. CM77: Gt N 3B 204
Elderfield Wlk. E11: Lon 9H 107
Elderflower Way E15: Lon 9E 122
Elderstep Av. SS8: Can I. 2L 151
ELDER STREET 1D 12
Elderton Rd. SS0: Wclf S 6J 137
Elder Tree Rd. SS8: Can I. 1J 151 (6F 43)
Elder Way RM13: Rain 3H 143
SS12: W'fd 1K 117
Elderwick Path SS8: Can I 1J 151
Eld La. CO1: Colc 8N 165
Eldon Cl. CO4: Colc. 6E 166
Eldon Rd. EN11: Hod 7D 52
Eldon Way SS5: Hock. 1C 120
Eldon Way Ind. Est. SS5: Hock 1D 120
Eldred Av. CO2: Colc. 3J 173
Eldred Gdns. RM14: Upm. 2B 128
Eldred Rd. IG11: Bark. 1D 140
Eleanor Chase SS12: W'fd 9K 101
Eleanor Cl. CO5: Tip. 5D 226
Eleanor Cross Rd. EN8: Wal X 4A 76 (4D 30)
Eleanor Gdns. RM8: Dag 4L 125
Eleanor Rd. E15: Lon 8F 122
Eleanor Wlk. CO5: Tip 5D 226
Eleanor Way CM14: War 2G 113
Electric Av. SS0: Wclf S 5H 137
Electric Palace Cinema *1N 209*
(off Kings Quay St.)
Electric Pde. *E18: Lon* *6G 106*
(off George La.)
IG3: Ilf. 4D 124
Elephant Grn. CB11: Newp 2L 215
Eleven Acre Ri. IG10: Lou 2M 91
Eleventh Av. CM24: Stan M 7G 221
Elfreda Ho. *CO2: Colc* *3J 173*
(off Iceni Way)
Elgar Cl. IG9: Buck H 8K 91
SS7: Thund 9B 118
SS15: Lain 7M 115
Elgar Dr. CM8: Wthm 8C 230
Elgar Gdns. RM18: Til. 6C 156
Elgin Av. CM1: Chelm 9J 59
RM3: H Wood 4M 111
Elgin Ho. CM14: War 1G 112
Elgin Rd. IG3: Ilf. 3D 124
Elham Dr. SS13: Pits 1K 133
Elianore Rd. CO3: Colc. 8J 165
Eliot Cl. SS12: W'fd 2K 117
Eliot M. SS2: Sth S. 4N 137
Eliot Rd. RM9: Dag 6J 125
Eliot Way CM9: Mal 7C 214
Elizabeth Av. CM8: Wthm. 7D 230
IG1: Ilf. 4C 124
SS6: Ray 6J 119
Elizabeth Cl. CB10: Saf W 3E 218
CO4: Colc 3C 166
EN9: Naze 2D 62
RM7: Maw 5N 109
RM18: Til 7D 156
SS5: Hock. 3D 120
Elizabeth Ct. CO12: Har 4J 209
CO14: Walt. 1M 181
IG8: Wfd G. 4J 107
Elizabeth Dr. CM16: They B 6D 78
SS12: W'fd 8J 101
Elizabeth Ho. RM2: Romf. 8G 111
RM16: Grays. 8L 145
SS7: Ben 3J 135
Elizabeth Rd. CM15: Pil H 5E 96
CO12: Har 4J 209
E6: Lon. 9K 123
Elizabeth Rd. RM13: Rain. 5F 142
RM16: Chaf H. 9J 145 (1F 47)
SS1: Sth S. 8B 138
Elizabeth Twr. *SS2: Sth S* *5L 137*
(off Baxter Av.)
Elizabeth Vs. CO5: Tip 9F 226
Elizabeth Way CB10: Saf W. 3E 218 (6C 6)
CM3: Hat P 2L 61
CM9: Mal. 3C 214
CM19: H'low. 4M 53 (7G 21)
CM20: H'low. 4M 53 (6G 21)
CO7: B'sea. 7E 182
CO7: W'hoe 3J 175
CO9: Hals 4K 207
SS7: Had 2J 135
SS15: Lain 1M 131
ELKIN'S GREEN. 1J 83 (4F 33)
Elkins, The RM1: Romf 6C 110
Ellenbrook Cl. SS9: Lgh S 3D 136
Ellen Ct. *E4: Lon* *7C 90*
(off Ridgeway, The)
Ellen Way CM77: Gt N 1C 204
Ellen Wilkinson Ho. RM10: Dag 5M 125
Ellerman Rd. RM18: Til 6B 156
Ellerton Gdns. RM9: Dag 9H 125
Ellerton Rd. RM9: Dag. 9H 125
Ellesmere Cl. E11: Lon. 9F 106
Ellesmere Gdns. IG4: Ilf. 9L 107
Ellesmere Rd. SS4: R'fd 7H 105
SS8: Can I 2E 150
Ellie Cl. SS17: Stan H. 3L 147
Ellingham Rd. E15: Lon. 6D 122
Elliot Cl. CM3: S Fer 2M 103
E15: Lon 9E 122
Elliot Dr. CM7: Brain. 5E 192
Elliot Pl. CM7: Brain. 5L 193
Elliots Dr. CO14: Walt. 6L 181
Elliott Gdns. RM3: Romf. 5F 110
Ellis Av. RM13: Rain. 5E 142
Ellis Cl. RM16: Ors 6F 146
Ellis Rd. CO4: Boxt 4N 159 (3E 16)
CO11: Brad 4B 18
CO15: Clac S 3J 189
Ellmore Cl. RM3: Romf. 5F 110
Ellswood SS15: Lain 6M 115
Elm Av. CM9: Mal. 3D 214
RM14: Upm 5M 127
Elm Bank Pl. SS17: Horn H 1H 147
Elmbridge CM17: H'low 9L 51
Elmbridge Hall CM5: Fy'd 1N 67
Elmbridge Rd. IG6: Ilf 3F 108 (2J 39)
Elm Bungs. CM7: Brain. 4F 192
Elm Cl. CM1: Broom. 3J 59
CM2: Gt Bad 4F 72
CM16: E Grn. 3A 64
CM22: Else 2K 199
CM22: Tak. 3C 224
CO5: Tip 4C 226
CO7: Alr. 6A 176
CO7: Gt Ben 6K 177
CO9: Sib H. 5J 219
E11: Lon. 1H 123
EN9: Wal A 4D 76
IG9: Buck H. 8K 91
RM7: Maw 5N 109
SS3: Shoe 7J 139
SS6: Ray. 4K 119
Elm Cl. Extension CM22: Tak. 3C 224
Elm Cotts. CM11: Bill 9N 99
SS0: Wclf S *4L 137*
(off Howards Chase)
Elm Ct. CB9: Stur 6J 223
CB11: Elm 6J 5
Elm Ct. Pk. CM4: B'more 9J 69
Elm Cres. CO4: Colc. 8D 166
Elmcroft CO7: Elms. 9N 167
Elmcroft Av. E11: Lon. 9H 107
Elmcroft Cl. E11: Lon. 8H 107
Elmdale Dr. CO11: Mist 5J 163
Elmden Ct. CO15: Clac S. 8J 185
Elmdene Av. RM11: Horn. 9K 111
ELMDON 6J 5
Elmdon Rd. RM15: S Ock. 5D 144
Elm Dr. CO7: B'sea 6C 182
CO9: Hals 5L 207
CO12: Har 4L 209
SS6: Ray. 4K 119
Elmer App. SS1: Sth S. 6M 137
Elmer Av. RM4: Hav 9C 94
SS1: Sth S 6M 137
Elmer Cl. RM13: Rain. 9E 126
Elmer Gdns. RM13: Rain 9E 126
Elmfield Cl. CO15: Hol S 6B 186
Elmfield Rd. E4: Lon 8C 90
Elm Gdns. CM16: N Wea 5N 65
Elm Grn. CM11: Bill 6N 99
SS13: Pits 1H 133
Elm Grn. La. CM3: Dan. 2C 74 (2D 34)
Elm Gro. CB10: Saf W 4C 218
CO7: W'hoe. 5H 175
CO13: Walt 8F 180
CO15: Clac S. 7K 185
CO16: Clac S 2E 188
DA8: Eri. 5B 152
IG8: Wfd G. 2F 106
RM11: Horn. 1J 127
SS1: Sth S. 6E 138
SS5: Hull. 6K 103
Elmgrove Ho. CB10: Saf W. 4C 218
Elm Hall Gdns. E11: Lon 9H 107
(not continuous)
Elm Hatch CM18: H'low 4E 54
Elmhurst Av. SS7: Ben 2B 134
Elmhurst Dr. E18: Lon 6G 107
RM11: Horn 3G 126
Elmhurst Rd. CO12: Har 4L 209
E7: Lon 9H 123
Elmhurst Way IG10: Lou 6M 91
Elm La. CM1: Rox 1J 217 (7G 23)
CO5: Fee. 6C 170 (1K 25)

Elm La. CO6: M Tey 6C **170** (7K **15**)
Elmore Rd. E11: Lon 5C **122**
Elmores IG10: Lou 3N **91**
Elm Pde. RM12: Horn 6F **126**
ELM PARK 6F 126 (5B 40)
Elm Pk. Av. RM12: Horn 6E **126** (5A **40**)
Elm Park Station (Tube) 6F 126 (5B 40)
Elm Ri. CM8: Wthm 2C **230**
Elm Rd. CM2: Chelm 2B **72** (2A **34**)
CM3: S Fer 9J **89**
CM6: Gt D 1J **203**
CO7: E Ber 1J **17**
CO16: L Cla 2G **184** (2D **28**)
DA8: Eri 6E **152**
E7: Lon 8F **122**
E11: Lon 4D **122**
E17: Lon 9C **106**
RM7: Maw 6N **109**
RM15: Ave 8A **144**
RM17: Grays 4M **155**
SS3: Shoe 7J **139** (5B **44**)
SS7: Had 4K **135**
SS8: Can I 2J **151**
SS9: Lgh S 5D **136** (5H **43**)
(not continuous)
SS11: W'fd 8L **101**
SS13: Pits 6M **117**
Elms Dr. CM1: Chelm 7J **59**
Elms Farm Rd. RM12: Horn 7G **126**
Elms Gdns. RM9: Dag 6L **125**
Elms Hall Rd. CO6: Coln E 4B **198** (4G **15**)
Elms Ind. Est. RM3: H Wood 4M **111**
Elmsleigh Dr. SS9: Lgh S 3D **136** (4H **43**)
Elmslie Cl. IG8: Wfd G 3M **107**
Elms Rd. CM1: Rox 2K **217** (7G **23**)
ELMSTEAD 6N 167 (6H 17)
Elmstead Cl. SS17: Corr 9C **132**
ELMSTEAD HEATH 3N 175 (7J 17)
ELMSTEAD MARKET 9N 167 (6H 17)
Elmstead Rd. CO4: Colc 9D **166** (6F **17**)
CO7: Elms, W'hoe 3J **175** (7H **17**)
DA8: Eri 6C **152**
IG3: Ilf 4D **124**
Elms, The CB10: Gt Che 7E **202**
CM5: Chip 9L **67**
E12: Lon 8K **123**
EN9: Wal A 5J 77
(off Woodbine Cl.)
IG10: Lou 1F **90**
Elmswood IG7: Chig 3C **108**
Elm Ter. RM20: W Thur 4E **154**
Elmtree Av. CM15: Kel H 7C **82**
Elm Tree Av. CO13: Frin S, Walt 8J **181** (1G **29**)
CO14: Walt 8J **181** (1G **29**)
Elmtree Cl. CO13: Frin S 8J **181**
Elmtree Rd. SS16: Van 2G **133**
Elm Vw. Rd. SS7: Ben 3B **134**
Elm Wlk. CM77: Rayne 6B **192**
RM2: Romf 7E **110**
Elm Way CM3: Bore 2F **60**
CM14: Brtwd 1D **112**
Elmway RM16: Grays 7M **145**
Elmwood CM21: Saw 3L **51**
Elmwood Av. CO2: Colc 4K **173**
SS5: Hock 3D **120**
Elmwood Ct. *E10: Lon 3A 122*
(off Goldsmith Rd.)
Elmwood Dr. CO5: W Mer 3D **228**
Elounda Ct. SS7: Ben 2D **134**
Elrick Cl. DA8: Eri 4C **152**
Elrington Rd. IG8: Wfd G 2G **107**
Elronds Rest CM3: S Fer 2J **103**
Elsdale St. E9: Lon 5C **38**
Elsden Chase CM0: S'min 2D **222**
ELSENHAM 3K 199 (5B 12)
Elsenham Ct. SS6: Ray 4H **119**
Elsenham Cres. SS14: Bas 9G **117**
ELSENHAM CROSS 3L 199
Elsenham M. SS14: Bas 9G **117**
Elsenham Rd. CM24: Stan M 4H **199** (6A **12**)
E12: Lon 7N **123**
Elsenham Station (Rail) 2K 199 (5B 12)
Elsham Dr. CM77: Gt N 2B **204**
Elsham Rd. E11: Lon 5E **122**
Elsinor Av. SS8: Can I 8F **134**
Elstow Gdns. RM9: Dag 1K **141**
Elstow Rd. RM9: Dag 9K **125**
Elstree Gdns. IG1: Ilf 7B **124**
Elthorne Pk. CO16: Clac S 9H **185**
Eltisley Rd. IG1: Ilf 6A **124**
Elton Wlk. CO5: Tip 5D **226**
Elverston Cl. SS15: Lain 7M **115**
Elvet Av. RM2: Romf 8G **111**
Elwes Cl. CO4: Colc 6D **166**
Elwick Ct. DA1: Cray 9E **152**
Elwick Rd. RM15: S Ock 6F **144**
Elwin Rd. CO5: Tip 6D **226**
Elwood CM17: H'low 4K **55**
Ely Cl. CM0: S'min 2D **222**
DA8: Eri 7D **152**
Ely Gdns. IG1: Ilf 2L **123**
RM10: Dag 5A **126**
Ely Pl. IG8: Wfd G 3N **107**
Ely Rd. E10: Lon 1C **122**
SS2: Sth S 4N **137**
Elysian Gdns. CM9: Tol 8J **225**
Ely Way SS6: Ray 3J **119**
SS14: Bas 8F **116**
Emanuel Rd. SS16: Lang H 2K **131**
Embankment Station (Tube) 7A 38
Embankment, The SS5: Hock 7C **104**
Embassy Ct. CM9: Mal 6C **214**
Emberson Ct. CM2: Chelm 7A **60**
Emberson Way CM16: N Wea 5A **66**
Ember Way CM0: Bur C 2C **196**
Emblems CM6: Gt D 1K **203**
Embroidery Bus. Cen. *IG8: Wfd G 6K 107*
(off Southend Rd.)
Emerald Gdns. RM8: Dag 3M **125**
Emerson Dr. RM11: Horn 2H **127**
EMERSON PARK 2J 127 (3C 40)
Emerson Pk. Ct. RM11: Horn 2H **127**
Emerson Park Station (Rail) 2J 127 (4C 40)
Emerson Rd. IG1: Ilf 2N **123**
Emes Rd. DA8: Eri 5A **152**
Emily May Ct. CO12: Har 4H **209**
Emily White Ct. SS11: W'fd 8N **101**
Emmanuel Ct. E10: Lon 2B **122**
Emmaus Way IG7: Chig 2N **107**
Emmott Av. IG6: Ilf 9B **108**
Empire Cinema 4J 207
Empire Rd. CO12: Har 4M **209**
Empire Wlk. *CM2: Chelm 9L 59*
(off Springfield Rd.)
Empress Av. CO5: W Mer 2D **228**
E4: Lon 4B **106**
E12: Lon 4J **123**
IG1: Ilf 4M **123**
IG8: Wfd G 4F **106**
Empress Dr. CO5: W Mer 3D **228**
Empress Pde. E4: Lon 4A **106**
Emson Cl. CB10: Saf W 3C **218**
Emsworth Rd. IG6: Ilf 6A **108**
Enborne Grn. RM15: S Ock 5D **144**
Endean Ct. CO7: W'hoe 4G **175**
Endeavour Cl. CM9: Tol 7K **225**
Endeavour Dr. SS14: Bas 6C **116**
Endeavour Way IG11: Bark 2F **140**
Endell St. WC2: Lon 7A **38**
Endlebury Rd. E4: Lon 8C **90** (1E **38**)
Endsleigh Ct. CO3: Colc 8K **165**
Endsleigh Gdns. IG1: Ilf 4M **123**
Endway SS7: Had 4K **135**
Endway, The CB9: Stpl B 1L **223** (5K **7**)
CM3: Alth, May 3E **190** (5B **36**)
CM6: Gt Eas 6F **13**
Endymion Rd. N4: Lon 4A **38**
ENFIELD 6B 30
Enfield Chase Station (Rail) 6B 30
ENFIELD HIGHWAY 6C 30
Enfield Ho. *RM3: Romf 4J 111*
(off Leyburn Cres.)
ENFIELD ISLAND VILLAGE 7A 76
ENFIELD LOCK 5D 30
Enfield Lock Station (Rail) 5D 30
Enfield Rd. EN2: Enf 6A **30**
SS11: W'fd 9C **102**
ENFIELD TOWN 6B 30
Enfield Town Station (Rail) 6B 30
ENFIELD WASH 5C 30
Engayne Gdns. RM14: Upm 3M **127**
Englands La. IG10: Lou 1N **91** (6G **31**)
Englefield Cl. SS5: Hock 3F **120**
Englefield Rd. N1: Lon 5B **38**
Englefields CM0: T'ham 3K **225**
Engleric SG8: Chris 6H **5**
Enid Way CO4: Colc 5L **165**
Ennerdale Av. CM77: Gt N 2C **204**
RM12: Horn 7E **126**
Ennerdale Ct. *E11: Lon 2G 122*
(off Cambridge Rd.)
Ennismore Gdns. SS2: Sth S 3M **137**
Enoch Ho. CO4: Colc 7E **166**
Ensign Ct. SS9: Lgh S 5F **136**
Enterprise Cen., The SS14: Bas 5F **116**
Enterprise Ct. CM7: Brain 6K **193**
CM8: Wthm 4D **230**
Enterprise Ho. E4: Lon 6C **90**
IG11: Bark 3E **140**
Enterprise Trad. Est. CM77: Rayne 6B **192**
Enterprise Way SS11: W'fd 1N **117**
Enville Way CO4: Colc 3B **166**
EPPING 9F 64 (3J 31)
Epping Cl. CM1: Chelm 1N **71**
CO15: Clac S 5K **185**
RM7: Maw 7N **109**
SS9: Lgh S 8D **120**
Epping Forest District Mus. 3C 76 (4E 30)
Epping Forest Nature Reserve 8J 77
Epping Glade E4: Lon 5C **90**
EPPING GREEN
CM16 3A 64 (2G 31)
SG13 1A 30
Epping La. RM4: Abr, Stap T 1G **92** (6J **31**)
Epping New Rd.
IG9: Buck H 8H **91** (1F **39**)
IG10: H Bee, Lou 9J **77** (7F **31**)
Epping Rd. CM5: Chip, N Wea 3C **66** (2B **32**)
CM5: They M, Toot 9A **66** (3A **32**)
CM16: Chip, N Wea 3C **66** (2A **32**)
(High Rd.)
CM16: Epp, E Grn, Epp Up, Naze 7L **53**
(Eureka Gdns)
CM16: Epp, N Wea 7H **65** (3J **31**)
(Woodyard, The)
CM16: Epp, They B 6M **77** (5G **31**)
(Goldings Hill)
CM16: They M 9A **66**
CM19: Roy 3H **53** (7F **21**)
EN9: Naze, Roy 7L **53**
Epping Sports Cen. 1E 78
Epping Station (Tube) 1F 78 (4J 31)
EPPING UPLAND 4C 64 (2H 31)
Epping Way CM8: Wthm 7B **230**
E4: Lon 5B **90**
Epsom Cl. CM11: Bill 3M **99**
CO16: Clac S 7G **185**
Epsom Ho. *RM3: Romf 2J 111*
(off Dagnam Pk. Dr.)
Epsom M. CM0: S'min 2E **222**
Epsom Rd. E10: Lon 1C **122**
IG3: Ilf 1E **124**
Epsom Way RM12: Horn 6K **127**
Epstein Rd. SE28: Lon 8F **140**
Erebus Dr. SE28: Lon 9B **140**
Erica Wlk. CO4: Colc 8D **166**
Eric Clarke La. IG11: Bark 4A **140**
Eric Cl. E7: Lon 6G **122**
Erick Av. CM1: Chelm 4K **59**
Eric Rd. E7: Lon 6G **122**
RM6: Chad H 2J **125**
SS13: Pits 9N **117**
Eridge Cl. CM1: Chelm 4M **59**
Erin Cl. IG3: Ilf 1F **124**
ERITH 3D 152 (1A 46)
Erith Ct. RM19: Purf 2L **153**
Erith Cres. RM5: Col R 5A **110**
Erith High St. DA8: Eri 3C **152** (2A **46**)
Erith Mus. 1A 46
Erith Playhouse 3D 152
Erith Rd. DA7: Bexh, Eri 3A **46**
DA8: Bexh 6A **152**
DA8: Eri 3A **152**
DA17: Belv, Eri 3A **152** (1A **46**)
Erith Small Bus. Cen. *DA8: Eri 4D 152*
(off Erith High St.)
Erith Sports Cen. 5C 152
Erith Stadium 5C 152
Erith Station (Rail) 3C 152 (1A 46)
Erith Swimming Baths 3C 152
Erle Havard Rd. CO6: W Ber 3F **164**
Ermine St. SG12: Thun 3C **20**
Ermine Way SG8: Arr 1B **4**
Ernalds Cl. CO6: E Col 7C **198**
Ernan Cl. RM15: S Ock 5D **144**
Ernan Rd. RM15: S Ock 5D **144**
Ernest Rd. CO7: W'hoe 5H **175**
RM11: Horn 1J **127**
Ernulph Wlk. CO1: Colc 8A **166**
Erriff Dr. RM15: S Ock 5C **144** (7E **40**)
Errington Cl. RM16: Grays 1D **156**
Errington Rd. CO3: Colc 1L **173**
Erroll Rd. RM1: Romf 8D **110**
Erskine Pl. SS12: W'fd 1M **117**
Erskine Rd. CO11: Mist 4J **163**
ERWARTON 1F 19
Erwarton Wlk. IP9: Anw 1G **19**
Esdaile Gdns. RM14: Upm 2A **128**
Esdaile La. EN11: Hod 6A **52**
Esher Av. RM7: Romf 1A **126**
Esher Rd. IG3: Ilf 5D **124**
Eskley Gdns. RM15: S Ock 5E **144**
(not continuous)
Esk Way RM1: Romf 4B **110**
Esmond Cl. RM13: Rain 9F **126**
Esplanade CO13: Frin S 2J **187** (2G **29**)
Esplanade Ct. SS1: Shoe 8C **138**
Esplanade Gdns. SS0: Wclf S 6G **136**
Esplanade, The CM3: May, Mun 7H **213**
CO15: Hol S 7C **186**
SS5: Hull 5J **103**
Esporta Health & Fitness Club
Chelmsford 9J 59
Woodford Bridge 4N 107
Romford 1C 126
Essex Av. CM1: Chelm 4J **59**
CO15: Jay 6C **188**
Essex Cl. RM7: Maw 8N **109**
SS6: Ray 6M **119**
SS8: Can I 3G **150**
SS15: Lain 9K **115**
Essex County Cricket Ground 9K 59 (1A 34)
Essex Gdns. RM11: Horn 9L **111**
SS9: Lgh S 2D **136**
SS17: Linf 9J **147**
Essex Hall Rd. CO1: Colc 6M **165**
Essex Hill CB11: Elm, Wen L 6J **5**
Essex Horse & Pony Protection Society 3J 133
Essex Mans. E11: Lon 2D **122**
Essex Regiment Way
CM1: Broom 1M **59** (6A **24**)
CM3: Gt Walt, Har E, L Walt 1H **57** (4K **23**)
Essex Rd. CM0: Bur C 3E **196**
CM7: Brain 4K **193**
CM9: Mal 7B **214**
E4: Lon 7E **90**
E10: Lon 1C **122** (3E **38**)
E12: Lon 7L **123**
E18: Lon 6H **107**
EN11: Hod, Rye P 4B **52** (7D **20**)
(not continuous)
IG11: Bark 9C **124**
N1: Lon 6A **38**
RM6: Chad H 2H **125**
RM7: Maw 8N **109**
RM10: Dag 7A **126**
RM20: W Thur 4D **154**
SS8: Can I 1J **151**
Essex Rd. Sth. E11: Lon 2D **122** (4E **38**)
Essex Road Station (Rail) 5A 38
Essex Showground 2B 24
Essex St. CO2: Colc 9M **165**
E7: Lon 7G **122**
SS2: Sth S 6M **137**
Essex Way CM13: Gt War 3F **112**
CM77: Tye G 4F **194**
CO4: L'ham 1D **160**
CO7: Ded 1K **161**
Essex Way SS7: Ben 5D **134** (4E **42**)
Essex Yacht Club 7D 136
Essex Yeomanry Way
CO3: S'way 9C **164** (6C **16**)
Estate Rd. SS7: Had 3M **135**
Estate Way E10: Lon 3A **122**
Estate Yd., The CM3: Terl 4D **24**
Estella Mead CM1: Chelm 4G **58**
Estfeld Cl. EN11: Rye P 2B **52**
Esther Rd. E11: Lon 2E **122**
Estuary Cl. CO4: Colc 3M **165**
IG11: Bark 3G **141**
Estuary Ct. *CM9: Tol 7K 225*
(off Hunts Farm Cl.)
Estuary Cres. CO15: Clac S 1H **189**
Estuary Gdns. SS3: Gt W 4N **139**
Estuary Lodge SS1: Sth S 8D **138**
Estuary M. CM9: Tol 7K **225**
SS3: Shoe 8J **139**
Estuary Pk. Rd. CO5: W Mer 3E **228**
Etchingham Rd. E15: Lon 6C **122**
Ethelbert Gdns. IG2: Ilf 9M **107**
Ethelbert Rd. DA8: Eri 5A **152**
SS4: R'fd 7H **105**
Ethelburga Rd. RM3: H Wood 5K **111**
Etheldore Av. SS5: Hock 8D **104**
Ethelred Gdns. SS11: W'fd 7L **101**
Ethel Rd. SS6: Ray 7A **120**
Etheridge Grn. IG10: Lou 2B **92**
Etheridge Rd. IG10: Lou 1A **92**
Etloe Ho. E10: Lon 3A **122**
Etloe Rd. E10: Lon 4A **122**
Eton Cl. SS8: Can I 9H **135**
Eton Mnr. Ct. *E10: Lon 4A 122*
(off Leyton Grange Est.)
Eton Rd. CO13: Frin S 9K **181**
CO15: Clac S 9K **185**
IG1: Ilf 6B **124**
Eton Wlk. SS3: Shoe 4J **139**
Eton Way DA1: Dart 9G **152**
Etton Cl. RM12: Horn 4J **127**
Euclid Way RM20: W Thur 2C **154**
Eudo Rd. CO2: Colc 2K **173**
Eugene Cl. RM2: Romf 8G **110**
Eureka Gdns. CM16: E Grn 9N **53**
Europa Ct. CM8: Wthm 4D **230**
Europa Trad. Cen. RM20: Grays 3F **154**
Europa Trad. Est. DA8: Eri 3B **152**
Europa Way CO12: Har 3H **209**
Eustace Rd. RM6: Chad H 2J **125**
Euston Rd. NW1: Lon 6A **38**
Euston Square Station (Tube) 6A 38
Euston Station (Rail, Tube) 6A 38
EUSTON UNDERPASS 6A **38**
Evansdale RM13: Rain 3D **142**
Evanston Av. E4: Lon 4C **106**
Evanston Gdns. IG4: Ilf 1L **123**
Eva Rd. RM6: Chad H 2H **125**
Evelyn Pl. CM1: Chelm 2A **72**
Evelyn Rd. CM3: Will G 2A **24**
E17: Lon 8C **106**
SS5: Hock 2D **120**
Evelyn Sharp Cl. RM2: Romf 7H **111**
Evelyn Sharp Ho. RM2: Romf 7H **111**
Evelyn Wlk. CM13: Gt War 3F **112**
Evelyn Wood Rd. CM77: Tye G 2E **194**
Evenlode Ho. *SE2: Lon 9H 141*
(off Coralline Wlk.)
Everard Rd. SS14: Bas 7H **117**
Everest SS6: Ray 2K **119**
Everest Ri. CM12: Bill 7H **99**
Everest Way CM9: Mal 3D **214**
Evergreen Ct. SS12: W'fd 1K **117**
Evergreen Dr. CO4: Colc 3D **166**
Evering Rd. N16: Lon 4B **38**
Everitt Rd. CB10: Saf W 3E **218**
Everitt Way CO9: Sib H 5K **219**
Eve Rd. E11: Lon 6E **122**
Eversholt St. NW1: Lon 6A **38**
Eversleigh Gdns. RM14: Upm 3A **128**
EVERSLEY 9L 117 (3C 42)
Eversley Av. DA7: Bexh 7B **152**
Eversley Cl. IG10: Lou 2B **92**
Eversley Ct. SS7: Thund 8C **118**
Eversley Cross DA7: Bexh 7C **152**
Eversley Leisure Cen. 9L 117
Eversley Lodge EN11: Hod 5A **52**
Eversley Pk. Rd. N21: Lon 7A **30**
Eversley Rd. SS7: Thund 8B **118**
SS13: Pits 1L **133**
EVES CORNER 1A 196
Eves Cnr. CM3: Dan 3E **74**
Eves Ct. CO12: Har 6F **208**
Eves Cres. CM1: Chelm 6J **59**
Evesham Av. E17: Lon 6A **106**
Evesham Rd. E15: Lon 9F **122**
Evesham Way IG5: Ilf 7N **107**
Eves Orchard CO8: Bures 7L **195**
Ewan Cl. CO3: S'way 9D **164**
SS9: Lgh S 3N **135**
Ewanrigg Ter. IG8: Wfd G 2J **107**
Ewan Rd. RM3: H Wood 6H **111**
Ewan Way CO3: S'way 9D **164**
SS7: Lgh S 3N **135**
Ewell Hall Chase CO5: K'dn 4K **211**
Ewellhurst Rd. IG5: Ilf 6L **107**
ExCeL 7F 39
Exchange St. RM1: Romf 5C **110**
Exchange, The IG1: Ilf 4A **124**
Exchange Way CM1: Chelm 9K **59**
Exeter Cl. CM7: Brain 3K **193**
CO6: Gt Hork 9J **159**
SS3: Shoe 5K **139**
SS14: Bas 8G **116**
Exeter Dr. CO1: Colc 8A **166**
Exeter Gdns. IG1: Ilf 3L **123**
Exeter Ho. *IG11: Bark 9F 124*
(off Margaret Bondfield Av.)
SS3: Shoe 5K **139**
Exeter Rd. CM1: Chelm 6N **59**
E17: Lon 9A **106**
RM10: Dag 8N **125**

Exford Av. SS0: Wclf S 2F 136
Exhibition La. SS3: Gt W 3K 139
Exley Cl. CM4: Ing 5D 84
Exmoor Cl. CM1: Chelm 1M 71
IG6: Ilf 5B 108
Exmouth Dr. SS6: Ray 2K 119
Exmouth Rd. RM17: Grays 4L 155
Express Dr. IG3: Ilf 3G 124
Exton Gdns. RM8: Dag 7H 125
Eyhurst Av. RM12: Horn 5E 126
EYNSFORD 7C 46
Eynsford Castle 7C 46
Eynsford Rd. BR8: Crock 7A 46
DA4: Eyns, F'ham 7C 46
IG3: Ilf 4D 124
Eynsham Dr. SE2: Lon 9G 141 (7J 39)
Eynsham Way SS13: Bas 6H 117
Eyre Cl. RM2: Romf 8F 110

F

Faber Rd. CM8: Wthm 7B 230
Fabians Cl. CO6: Cogg 2L 197
Factory Hill CO5: Tip 7D 226 (4A 26)
Factory La. CO11: Bran, Law 1H 163
Factory La. E. CO9: Hals 4K 207
Factory La. W. CO9: Hals 5K 207
Factory Rd. E16: Lon 7G 39
Factory Ter. CO9: Hals 4K 207
Fagbury Rd. IP11: Felix 1J 19
Faggoters La. CM5: H Lav 7B 22
CM17: Mat T 6A 22
Faggot Yd. CM7: Brain 3H 193
Fagus Av. RM13: Rain 3H 143
Fairbank Cl. CM5: Chip 8K 67
Fairbrother Ct. CO4: Colc 7D 166
Fairburn Cl. SS1: Sth S 6A 138
Fair Cl. CO7: B'sea 7F 182
Fairclough Av. CO16: Clac S 1F 188
FAIR CROSS 7D 124 (5H 39)
Faircross Av. IG11: Bark 8B 124
RM5: Col R 4B 110
Faircross Pde. IG11: Bark 7D 124
Fairfax Av. SS13: Bas 7K 117
Fairfax Dr. SS0: Wclf S 4G 137 (4J 43)
Fairfax Mead CM2: Chelm 9A 60
Fairfax Rd. CO2: Colc 9N 165
RM17: Grays 3L 155
RM18: Til 6B 156
Fairfield CM4: Ing 5E 84
SS3: Gt W 3L 139
Fairfield Av. RM14: Upm 5N 127
RM16: Grays 8M 145
Fairfield Chase CM9: Mal 6B 214
Fairfield Cl. CO7: Gt Bro 8F 168
RM12: Horn 3E 126
Fairfield Cres. SS9: Lgh S 8E 120
Fairfield Gdns. CO4: Colc 7C 166
SS9: Lgh S 9E 120
Fairfield Ho. CM9: Mal 6B 214
Fairfield Ri. CM12: Bill 8H 99
(not continuous)
Fairfield Rd. CM1: Chelm 9J 59
CM5: Chip 8K 67
CM7: Brain 6H 193 (7C 14)
CM14: Brtwd 9F 96
CM16: Epp 8G 64
CO15: Clac S 9J 185
E3: Lon 6D 38
EN11: Rye P 3A 52
IG1: Ilf 8A 124
IG8: Wfd G 3G 106
SS9: Lgh S 8D 120
Fairfields CM3: Pur 9K 215
Fairfield Way CO9: Hals 5L 207
Fairford Av. DA7: Bexh 6B 152
Fairford Cl. RM3: Romf 3M 111
Fairford Way RM3: Romf 3M 111
Fairham Av. RM15: S Ock 7D 144
Fairhaven Av. CO5: W Mer 2E 228
Fairhaven Ct. CO5: W Mer 4E 228
Fairhead Rd. Nth. CO4: Colc 7C 166
Fairhead Rd. Sth. CO4: Colc 7C 166
Fairholme Av. RM2: Romf 9E 110
Fairholme Gdns. RM14: Upm 2C 128
Fairholme Rd. IG1: Ilf 2M 123
Fairhouse Ct. SS14: Bas 9E 116
Fairkytes Av. RM11: Horn 3H 127
Fairland Cl. SS6: Ray 2L 119
Fairland Rd. E15: Lon 8F 122
Fairlands Av. IG9: Buck H 8G 91
Fairlawn Dr. IG8: Wfd G 4G 107
Fairlawn Gdns. SS2: Sth S 1K 137
Fairlawns CM14: Brtwd 9D 96
CM16: Epp 8G 64
SS1: Sth S 7D 138
Fairlawns Cl. RM11: Horn 2K 127
Fairleads CM3: Dan 2F 74
Fair Leas CB10: Saf W 2D 218
Fairleigh Av. SS13: Pits 1L 133
Fairleigh Dr. SS9: Lgh S 5C 136
Fairleigh Rd. SS13: Pits 1L 133
Fairlight Av. E4: Lon 8D 90
IG8: Wfd G 3G 107
Fairlight Cl. E4: Lon 8D 90
Fairlight Rd. SS7: Had 3J 135
FAIRLOP 5D 108 (2H 39)
Fairlop Av. SS8: Can I 1G 151
Fairlop Cl. CO15: Clac S 5K 185
RM12: Horn 8F 126
Fairlop Ct. E11: Lon 3D 122
Fairlop Gdns. IG6: Ilf 4B 108
SS14: Bas 9E 116
Fairlop Rd. E11: Lon 2D 122 (4E 38)
IG6: Ilf 6B 108
Fairlop Sailing Cen. 5E 108
Fairlop Station (Tube) 5C 108 (2H 39)
Fairlop Waters Country Pk. Nature Reserve 6E 108
Fairmead SS6: Ray 3H 119
Fair Mead SS14: Bas 7D 116
Fairmead Av. SS0: Wclf S 5H 137
SS7: Had 1L 135
Fairmead Gdns. IG4: Ilf 9L 107
Fairmead Rd. IG10: H Bee, Lou 4H 91 (6F 31)
Fairmeads IG10: Lou 1A 92
Fairmeadside IG10: Lou 4J 91
Fairoak Gdns. RM1: Romf 6C 110
Fair Oak Pl. IG6: Ilf 6B 108
FAIRSTEAD 3D 24
Fairstead Hall Rd. CM3: F'std, Terl 3C 24
Fairstead Rd. CM3: F'std, Terl 3D 24
Fairsted SS14: Bas 9B 116
Fair Vw. CM6: Gt D 3L 203
Fairview CM12: Bill 7J 99
DA8: Eri 5D 152
SS8: Can I 9F 134
Fairview Av. CM13: Hut 6A 98
RM13: Rain 2H 143
SS17: Stan H 4L 147
Fairview Chase SS17: Stan H 5L 147
Fairview Cl. IG7: Chig 1D 108
SS7: Thund 8C 118
Fairview Cres. SS7: Thund 8C 118
Fairview Dr. IG7: Chig 1D 108
SS0: Wclf S 2H 137
Fairview Est. EN11: Rye P 4C 52
Fairview Gdns. IG8: Wfd G 5H 107
SS9: Lgh S 4B 136
Fairview Ind. Pk. RM13: Rain 5B 142
Fair Vw. Lodge SS9: Lgh S 4B 136
Fairview Rd. IG7: Chig 1D 108
SS14: Bas 9E 116
(Church Rd.)
SS14: Bas 1F 132
(Timberlog La.)
Fairview Vs. E4: Lon 4B 106
Fairview Wlk. SS7: Thund 8C 118
Fairville M. SS0: Wclf S 4H 137
Fairway CM2: Gt Bad 3E 72
CM21: Saw 2K 51
Fair Way IG8: Wfd G 2J 107
Fairway RM16: Grays 8L 145 (7F 41)
SS12: W'fd 4M 117
Fairway Dr. CM0: Bur C 3D 196
SE28: Lon 6J 141
Fairway Gdns. IG1: Ilf 7B 124
SS9: Lgh S 1B 136
Fairway Gdns. Cl. SS9: Lgh S 1B 136
Fairways CO4: Colc 4J 165
E17: Lon 8C 106
EN9: Wal A 4E 76
SS1: Sth S 6D 138
Fairways, The CM3: Cold N 8K 197
Fairway, The CM18: H'low 5E 54
RM14: Upm 2N 127
SS7: Thund 8C 118
SS9: Lgh S 1B 136 (3G 43)
SS16: Bas 4L 131
Fairycroft Rd. CB10: Saf W 4D 218 (6B 6)
Fairyhall La. CM7: Weth 6F 228
Fairy Hall La. CM77: Rayne 8B 192
(not continuous)
Falbro Cres. SS7: Had 2K 135
Falcon Av. RM17: Grays 5L 155
Falcon Cl. CM21: Saw 3H 51
EN9: Wal A 4G 76
SS6: Ray 4H 119
SS9: Lgh S 1D 136
Falcon Ct. E18: Lon 7H 107
(off Albert Rd.)
Falcon Cres. CO1: Colc 1B 174
Falconer Rd. IG6: Ilf 2G 109
Falconers Pk. CM21: Saw 3J 51
Falcon Flds. CM9: Mal 8B 214
Falcon M. CM9: Mal 8B 214
Falcon Pk. SS14: Bas 7A 116
Falcon Rd. CM0: S'min 2C 222
Falcon Sq. CO9: Cas H 3L 219
(off Luces La.)
Falcon Way CM2: Chelm 4B 72
CO15: Clac S 7K 185
E11: Lon 8G 107
RM12: Rain 9E 126
SS3: Shoe 5J 139
SS16: Bas 2D 132
Falcon Yd. CO7: W'hoe 6H 175
Fal Dr. CM8: Wthm 5B 230
Falkenham End SS14: Bas 8D 116
Falkenham Path SS14: Bas 8D 116
Falkenham Ri. SS14: Bas 8D 116
Falkenham Row SS14: Bas 8D 116
Falkirk Cl. RM11: Horn 3L 127
Falkland Cl. CM3: Bore 3F 60
Falkland Ct. CM7: Brain 4K 193
Falkland Grn. CM9: Wdhm M 4L 75
Falklands Dr. CO11: Mist 4J 163
Falklands Rd. CM0: Bur C 3D 196
Falkner Cl. CM4: Stock 6A 86
Fallaize Av. IG1: Ilf 6A 124
Fallow Cl. IG7: Chig 2E 108
Fallowden La. CB10: A'dn 8B 190 (5D 6)
Fallowfield SS3: Shoe 5H 139
Fallowfield Cl. CO12: Har 4H 209
Fallowfield Rd. CO2: Colc 4K 173
Fallow Flds. IG10: Lou 5J 91
Fallows, The SS8: Can I 8F 134
Falmer Rd. E17: Lon 7B 106
Falmouth Av. E4: Lon 2D 106 (1E 38)
Falmouth Gdns. IG4: Ilf 8K 107
Falmouth Rd. CM1: Chelm 6N 59
Falmouth St. E15: Lon 7D 122
Falstones SS15: Lain 9M 115
Fambridge Chase CM8: Whi N 2E 24
Fambridge Cl. CM9: Mal 7C 214
Fambridge Ct. RM7: Romf 9B 110
(off Marks Rd.)
Fambridge Dr. SS12: W'fd 1M 117
Fambridge Rd. CM3: Alth, Latch 3A 190
CM3: Cold N, Latch 6M 197 (5J 35)
CM3: N Fam 1G 104
CM9: Cold N, Latch, Mun 6M 197
CM9: Mal 6B 214 (1H 35)
(Friars La.)
CM9: Mal 9B 214 (2H 35)
(Limebrook Way)
CM9: Mun 6N 215
RM8: Dag 3M 125
SS4: R'fd 4F 104 (7H 35)
Fambridge Station (Rail) 6H 35
Fane Rd. SS7: Thund 7D 118
(not continuous)
Fanhams Hall Rd. SG12: Ware 4D 20
FANNER'S GREEN 7E 56 (5J 23)
Fanns Ri. RM19: Purf 2L 153
Fanny's La. CO16: Gt Ben, Wee H 3B 184
Fanshawe Av. IG11: Bark 8B 124 (5H 39)
Fanshawe Cres. RM9: Dag 7K 125
RM11: Horn 1H 127
Fanshawe Rd. RM16: Grays 1C 156
Fantasia Ct. CM14: War 2E 112
Fanton Av. SS12: W'fd 4N 117
Fanton Chase SS11: W'fd 1A 118
Fanton Gdns. SS11: W'fd 1B 118
Fanton Hall Cotts. SS12: N Ben 5A 118
Fanton Wlk. SS11: W'fd 9B 102
Faraday Cl. CM7: Brain 7H 193
CO15: Clac S 5L 185
Faraday Rd. E15: Lon 8F 122
SS9: Lgh S 9B 120
Faringdon Av. RM3: Romf 5G 111 (2B 40)
Faringford Rd. E15: Lon 9E 122
Farley Dr. IG3: Ilf 3D 124
Farmadine CB11: Saf W 4D 218
Farmadine Ct. CB11: Saf W 4D 218
Farmadine Gro. CB11: Saf W 4D 218
Farmadine Ho. CB11: Saf W 4D 218
FARMBRIDGE END 6G 23
Farm Cl. CM13: Hut 6M 97
CM19: Roy 2H 53
IG9: Buck H 9J 91
RM10: Dag 9A 126
SG8: Chris 6H 5
Farm Cres. SS11: Bat 4E 102
Farm Dr. RM16: Grays 7M 145
Farm End E4: Lon 4E 90
Farmer Rd. E10: Lon 3B 122
Farmers Ct. EN9: Wal A 3G 76
Farmers Way CO16: Clac S 1F 188
Farmfield Rd. CO6: Gt Tey 1D 170
Farm Hill Rd. EN9: Wal A 3D 76 (4E 30)
Farmilo Rd. E17: Lon 2A 122
Farm La. EN11: Rye P 3C 52
SG8: Thri 2G 5
Farmleigh Av. CO15: Clac S 5K 185
Farm Pl. DA1: Cray 9E 152
Farm Rd. CO12: Gt Oak 7C 204 (5E 18)
E12: Lon 4L 123
N21: Lon 7B 30
RM13: Rain 3G 142
RM16: Ors 9B 146
RM18: E Til 2L 157
SS8: Can I 9H 135
Farm Vw. SS6: Ray 2K 119
Farm Wlk. CO7: B'sea 5D 182
Farm Way IG9: Buck H 1J 107 (1F 39)
Farmway RM8: Dag 5H 125
Farm Way RM12: Horn 6G 126
SS7: Thund 9H 119
Farnaby Way SS17: Stan H 2L 147
Farnan Av. E17: Lon 6A 106
Farne Dr. SS12: W'fd 2N 117
Farnes Av. SS12: W'fd 1K 117
Farnes Dr. RM2: Romf 6G 111
FARNHAM 6J 11
Farnham Cl. CM21: Saw 3H 51
FARNHAM GREEN 6J 11
Farnham Rd. IG3: Ilf 2E 124
RM3: Romf 2H 111
FARNINGHAM 7C 46
Farningham Road Station (Rail) 6C 46
Farnley Rd. E4: Lon 6E 90
Farnol Rd. DA1: Dart 9L 153
Farrance Rd. RM6: Chad H 1K 125
Farr Av. IG11: Bark 2F 140
Farriers Chase CO5: W Mer 3D 228
Farriers Dr. CM12: Bill 3J 99
Farriers End CO3: S'way 1E 172
Farriers Way CM77: Gt N 1B 204
SS2: Temp I 1L 137
Farringdon Rd. WC1: Lon 6A 38
Farringdon Service Rd. SS1: Sth S 6M 137
Farringdon Station (Rail, Tube) 7A 38
Farrington Cl. CO1: Colc 9C 166
Farrow Gdns. RM16: Grays 8L 145
Farrow Rd. CM1: Chelm 3N 71
FARTHER HOWEGREEN 6J 197 (4H 35)
Farthingale Ct. EN9: Wal A 4G 76
Farthingale La. EN9: Wal A 4G 76
(not continuous)
Farthingale Wlk. E15: Lon 9D 122
Farthing Cl. CM7: Brain 4M 193
DA1: Dart 9K 153
Farthings Chase CO5: W Mer 3E 228
Farthings Cl. E4: Lon 9E 90
FAR THORPE GREEN 4G 178
Fastnet SS2: Sth S 8F 120
Faulds Wlk. CO2: Colc 3A 174
FAULKBOURNE 3E 24
Faulkbourne Rd.
CM8: Fau, Wthm 3A 230 (3F 25)
Faulkner Cl. RM8: Dag 2J 125
Fauna Cl. RM6: Chad H 1H 125
Fauners SS16: Bas 1B 132
Faversham Av. E4: Lon 7E 90
Faversham Cl. IG7: Chig 8G 93
Faversham Lodge SS1: Sth S 8C 138
(off Eastern Esplanade)
Fawcett Dr. SS15: Lain 6N 115
FAWKHAM 7E 46
FAWKHAM GREEN 7E 46
Fawkham Grn. Rd. DA3: Fawk 7E 46
Fawkham Rd. DA3: Fawk, Long 6E 46
Fawkner Cl. CM2: Chelm 9A 60
Fawkon Wlk. EN11: Hod 5A 52
Fawn Rd. IG7: Chig 2E 108
Fawters Cl. CM13: Hut 5N 97
Faymore Gdns. RM15: S Ock 6D 144
Fearns Mead CM14: War 2F 112
Fears Grn. SG8: S'don 1B 10
SG9: S'don 1B 10
Featherbed La. RM4: Abr 3J 93
(not continuous)
Featherby Way SS4: R'fd 6M 121
Feathers Hill CM22: Hat O 7C 206 (3C 22)
Feeches Rd. SS2: Sth S 1H 137
Feedhams Cl. CO7: W'hoe 3J 175
Feenan Highway RM18: Til 5C 156 (2H 47)
FEERING 9A 170 (1J 25)
Feering & Kelvedon Local History Mus. 4J 211 (2H 25)
Feeringbury Manor Garden 1H 25
Feering Dr. SS14: Bas 1G 133
Feering Gdns. SS14: Bas 1G 133
Feering Hill CO5: Fee 2L 211 (2J 25)
Feering Rd. CM11: Bill 6L 99
CO6: Cogg 3M 197 (7H 15)
Feering Row SS14: Bas 1G 132
Felbrigg Cl. CM77: Gt N 1B 204
Felbrigge Rd. IG3: Ilf 4E 124
Felhurst Cres. RM10: Dag 6N 125
Felicia Way RM16: Grays 2D 156
Felipe Rd. RM16: Chaf H 1F 154
Felix Ct. E17: Lon 9B 106
FELIXSTOWE 1K 19
Felixstowe Cl. CO16: Clac S 9E 184
Felixstowe Ct. E16: Lon 8A 140
Felixstowe Station (Rail) 1K 19
Fell Christy CM1: Chelm 6K 59
Fellcroft SS13: Pits 9K 117
Fellowes Cl. CO4: Colc 5N 165
Fell Rd. CO9: Bird, New E 4A 8
Felmongers CM20: H'low 1G 54
FELMORE 7J 117 (3B 42)
Felmore Ct. SS13: Bas 7J 117
(off Felmores End)
Felmores SS13: Bas 7H 117 (3B 42)
Felmores End SS13: Bas 7J 117
Fels Cl. RM10: Dag 5N 125
Fels Farm Av. RM10: Dag 5A 126
Felstead Av. IG5: Ilf 5N 107
Felstead Cl. CM13: Hut 5M 97
CO2: Colc 6A 174
SS7: Ben 2D 134
Felstead Rd. CM3: Gt L, L L'gh 6H 203 (2A 24)
E11: Lon 2G 123
IG10: Lou 6L 91
RM5: Col R 4A 110
SS7: Ben 2D 134
FELSTED 8J 199 (1J 23)
Felsted Rd. CM11: Bill 6L 99
Felsted Vineyard 1A 24
Felton Gdns. IG11: Bark 1D 140
Felton Rd. IG11: Bark 2D 140
Fencepiece Rd. IG6: Ilf 2B 108 (2H 39)
IG7: Chig 2B 108 (1H 39)
Fen Chase CO7: Elms 1L 175
Fenchurch Street Station (Rail) 7B 38
Fen Cl. CM15: Shenf 3M 97
RM14: Bulp 6B 130
Fengates CM3: S Fer 9J 89
Fen La. CO5: E Mer 4H 27
CO7: A'lgh 7K 161 (3H 17)
RM14: Bulp 7M 129 (5G 41)
RM14: N Ock 7F 128 (5E 40)
RM16: Ors 3B 146 (7G 41)
Fenman Ct. CM22: Else 2K 199
Fenman Gdns. IG3: Ilf 3G 124
Fenn Cl. CM3: S Fer 9J 89
CO7: Frat 3F 176
Fennel Cl. CO5: Tip 6C 226
Fennells CM19: H'low 8B 54
Fenner Rd. RM16: Chaf H 2F 154 (1E 46)
Fenners Way SS13: Bas 5H 117
Fennes Rd. CM7: Brain 8H 191 (5C 14)
Fennfields Rd. CM3: S Fer 9H 89
Fennings Chase CO1: Colc 8A 166
Fenno Cl. CO3: S'way 2F 172
Fenn Rd. CO9: Hals 4M 207 (3G 15)
Fenny La. SG8: Meld 2D 4
Fen Rd. SG8: Bass 3A 4
FENSTEAD END 1F 9
Fentiman Way RM11: Horn 3J 127
Fenton Grange CM17: H'low 3H 55
Fenton Rd. RM16: Chaf H 1H 155
Fenton Way SS15: Lain 8H 115 (3J 41)
Fenwick Way SS8: Can I 8G 135
Ferdinand Wlk. CO4: Colc 8F 166

Ferguson Av. RM2: Romf 6G 111
Ferguson Cl. CB11: Saf W 4F 218
Ferguson Ct. RM2: Romf 6H 111
Ferme Pk. Rd. N4: Lon 3A 38
N8: Lon 3A 38
Fermoy Rd. SS1: Sth S 7E 138
Fernbank CM12: Bill 7H 99
IG9: Buck H 7H 91
Fernbank Av. RM12: Horn 6G 126
Fernbrook Av. SS1: Sth S 6B 138
Fern Cl. CM12: Bill 4K 99
DA8: Eri 6F 152
Fern Ct. SS17: Stan H 2M 147
Ferndale Av. E17: Lon 9D 106
Ferndale Cl. CO15: Clac S 6K 185
SS15: Lain 9K 115
Ferndale Cres. SS8: Can I 3H 151
Ferndale Rd. CO12: Har 2M 209
E7: Lon 9H 123
E11: Lon 4E 122
RM5: Col R 6A 110
SS2: Sth S 4A 138
SS6: Ray 1K 119
Ferndale St. E6: Lon 7A 140
Fernden Way RM7: Romf 1N 125
Ferndown RM11: Horn 1K 127
Ferndown Cl. SS1: Sth S 6A 138
Ferndown Rd. CO13: Frin S 9H 181
Ferndown Way CM3: Hat P 2M 61
Fernhall Dr. IG4: Ilf 9K 107
Fernhall La. EN9: Wal A 1K 77 (4F 31)
FERN HILL 1G 9
Fernhill CM18: H'low 7D 54
Fern Hill CO10: Glem 1G 9
SS16: Lang H 2L 131
Fernhill Ct. E17: Lon 6D 106
Fern Hill La. CM18: H'low 7E 54
Fernie Cl. IG7: Chig 2F 108
Fernie Rd. CM7: Brain 6F 192
Fernie Way IG7: Chig 2F 108
Fernlea CO4: Colc 5K 165
Fernlea Rd. CM0: Bur C 3D 196
CO12: Har 3M 209
SS7: Ben 3E 134
Fernleigh Ct. RM7: Romf 9A 110
Fernleigh Dr. SS9: Lgh S 5F 136
Fernside IG9: Buck H 7H 91
Fernside Cl. SS17: Corr 9C 132
Ferns Rd. E15: Lon 8F 122
Fern Wlk. SS8: Can I 2F 150
SS16: Lang H 2G 131
Fern Way CO15: Jay 5D 188
Fernways IG1: Ilf 6A 124
Fernwood SS7: Had 2L 135
Fernwood Av. CO15: Hol S 8C 186
Ferrers Rd. CM3: S Fer 9H 89
Ferriers La. CO8: Bures 8H 195
Ferris Av. CM3: Cold N 8K 197
Ferris Steps SS1: Sth S 7A 138
(off Prospect Cl.)
Ferro Rd. RM13: Rain 4E 142
Ferry La. N17: Lon 3C 38
RM13: Rain 7C 142 (7A 40)
Ferry La. Ind. Est. RM13: Rain 5D 142
Ferrymead SS8: Can I 9F 134
Ferry Passenger Terminal 1H 209
(Harwich International)
Ferry Rd. CM0: Bur C 4A 196 (7B 36)
CM3: N Fam 1F 104 (6H 35)
CO5: Fing 8H 175 (1G 27)
IP11: Felix 1K 19
RM18: Til 8C 156 (3G 47)
SS5: Hull 7K 103 (7F 35)
SS7: Ben 6D 134 (5D 42)
Feryby Rd. RM16: Grays 1D 156
Feryings Cl. CM17: H'low 8J 51
Fesants Cft. CM20: H'low 9G 51
Festival Cl. DA8: Eri 5D 152
Festival Gdns. CM9: Tol D 3K 227
Festival Leisure Pk. SS14: Bas 6C 116
Festival Link SS14: Bas 7C 116
Festival Way SS14: Bas 6C 116
Fetherston Rd. SS17: Stan H 3M 147
Fetter La. EC4: Lon 7A 38
Feverills Rd. CO16: L Cla 1G 185
Fiat Av. CO15: Jay 6B 188
Fiddler's Cl. DA9: Grnh 9E 154
Fiddlers Folly CO3: S'way 5B 16
FIDDLERS HAMLET 2H 79 (4J 31)
Fiddlers Hill CO3: S'way 6A 164 (5B 16)
Fiddlers La. CO7: E Ber 1J 17
Field Cl. E4: Lon 3B 106
IG9: Buck H 9J 91
RM4: Abr 2G 92
Field Ct. CO4: Colc 7E 166
Fielders, The SS8: Can I 3G 150
Fieldfare CM11: Bill 8L 99
Fieldfare Rd. SE28: Lon 7H 141
Fieldgate Dock CO7: B'sea 8D 182
Fld. Gate La. CM22: U Grn 1H 199
Fieldhouse Cl. E18: Lon 5H 107
Fielding Av. RM18: Til 6D 156
Fielding Way CM13: Hut 5M 97
Field Point E7: Lon 6G 122
Field Rd. E7: Lon 6F 122
RM15: Ave 8N 143
Fields Cl. CO16: Wee 8D 178
Fields Farm Rd. CO2: Lay H 2D 26
Fieldside CB11: Saf W 6D 218
Flds. Park Cres. RM6: Chad H 9J 109
Field Vw. Cl. CO4: Colc 3N 165
Field Vw. Dr. CM9: L Tot 5K 25
Field Wlk. CO14: Walt 6K 181
Field Way CO7: W'hoe 4J 175
EN11: Hod 1C 52
Fieldway RM8: Dag 5H 125
RM16: Grays 8K 145
SS12: W'fd 4L 117
SS13: Pits 2K 133
Fiennes Cl. RM8: Dag 3H 125
Fifth Av. CM1: Chelm 5J 59
CM20: H'low 8B 50 (6H 21)
(Eastwick Rd.)
CM20: H'low 1C 54
(Allendale Av., not continuous)
CM24: Stan Apt, Stan M 7G 221
CO9: Hals 5N 207
CO13: Frin S 9H 181
E12: Lon 6M 123
RM20: W Thur 4D 154
SS7: Thund 9G 119
SS8: Can I 1E 150
SS11: W'fd 1A 118
Filey Rd. CM0: S'min 4A 222
Fillebrook Av. SS9: Lgh S 4F 136
Fillebrook Rd. E11: Lon 3D 122
Fillioll Cl. CM3: E Han 3B 88
Filston Rd. DA8: Eri 3A 152
Finch Ct. CM5: Chip 5L 67
Finchdale CO15: Clac S 7K 185
Finch Dr. CM7: Brain 3F 192
CO7: Gt Ben 5J 177
Finches Cl. SS17: Corr 9D 132
Finches, The SS7: Thund 8G 119
Finchfield SS6: Ray 6K 119
Finch Gdns. E4: Lon 2A 106
Finch Hill CO10: Bulm 5H 9
FINCHINGFIELD 3C 200 (2J 13)
Finchingfield Av. IG8: Wfd G 4J 107
Finchingfield Guildhall 3D 200
Finchingfield Rd. CB9: Stpl B 3L 223 (5K 7)
CB10: Gt Sam, L Sam 3L 205 (1H 13)
CB10: Hpstd 6H 7
CM7: F'fld, Stamb 1A 14
Finchingfields, The CM15: Kel H 7B 82
Finchingfield Way CO2: Colc 6A 174
SS12: W'fd 2K 117
Finchingfield Windmill 3D 200
Finchland Vw. CM3: S Fer 2K 103
Finch La. CO7: Elms 1A 176
Finchley Av. CM2: Chelm 2B 72
Finchley Rd. RM17: Grays 4L 155
SS0: Wclf S 6J 137
Finchmoor CM18: H'low 6C 54
Finch's CM8: W Bis 1L 229
Finden Rd. E7: Lon 7J 123
Findon Gdns. RM13: Rain 5E 142
Finer Cl. CO16: Clac S 6G 185
FINGRINGHOE 9F 174 (1G 27)
Fingringhoe Rd. CO2: Colc 4D 174 (7F 17)
CO5: Colc, Fing, Rhdge 6E 174
CO5: L'hoe 8B 174 (2F 27)
Fingrith Hall La.
CM4: B'more, Nor H 5H 69 (3F 33)
(not continuous)
Finham Cl. CO4: Colc 8F 166
FINKLE GREEN 6A 8
Finnymore Rd. RM9: Dag 9K 125
FINSBURY 6A 38
FINSBURY PARK 4A 38
Finsbury Park Station (Rail, Tube) 4A 38
Finsbury Pl. CO9: Hals 4L 207
Finucane Gdns. RM13: Rain 8E 126
Firbank Rd. RM5: Col R 2N 109 (1K 39)
Firecrest Rd. CM2: Chelm 5D 72
Firfield Rd. SS7: Had 9H 119
Firham Pk. Av. RM3: H Wood 4L 111
Firle, The SS16: Lang H 3L 131
Firlie Wlk. CO2: Colc 4A 174
Firmans SS16: Lang H 3K 131
Firmins Ct. CO6: W Ber 3E 164
Fir Pk. CM19: H'low 6A 54
Firs Cvn. Pk. CO16: L Cla 3H 185
Firs Chase CO5: W Mer 2A 228 (5F 27)
Firs Chase Cvn. Pk. CO5: W Mer 2A 228
Firs Dr. CM1: Writ 1K 71
IG10: Lou 9N 77
Firsgrove Cres. CM14: War 1E 112
Firsgrove Rd. CM14: War 1E 112
Firs Hamlet CO5: W Mer 3A 228
Firs La. N13: Lon 1B 38
N21: Lon 7B 30
Firs Rd. CO5: Tip 7D 226
CO5: W Mer 3B 228 (5F 27)
First Av. CM1: Chelm 6J 59
CM12: Bill 9G 99
CM15: Hook E 4F 82
CM20: H'low 2C 54 (6H 21)
(not continuous)
CM24: Stan Apt, Stan M 7G 220
CO9: Hals 5N 207
CO12: Har 4L 209
CO13: Frin S 1H 187
CO14: Walt 3N 181
CO15: Clac S 9M 185
CO16: Wee 5D 178
E12: Lon 6L 123
E17: Lon 9A 106
EN1: Enf 7B 30
EN9: Wal A 8H 63
RM6: Chad H 9H 109
RM10: Dag 2N 141
RM20: W Thur 4D 154
First Av. SS0: Wclf S 6G 137 (5H 43)
SS5: Hull 7M 103
SS7: Thund 9G 119
SS8: Can I 1D 150
SS11: W'fd 1A 118
SS16: Bulp 2F 130
SS17: Stan H 2M 147 (6K 41)
Firs, The CM15: Pil H 5D 96
CO2: Lay H 8H 173
E6: Lon 9L 123
EN9: Wal A 5J 77
(off Woodbine Cl.)
IG8: Wfd G 4J 107
RM16: Grays 8M 145
SS8: Can I 9F 134
Firstore Dr. CO3: S'way 8F 164
Firs Wlk. IG8: Wfd G 2G 106
Fir Tree Cl. CO4: Colc 3B 166
RM1: Romf 7B 110
RM17: Grays 4N 155
Fir Tree La. CM3: L Bad 1E 74
Fir Tree Ri. CM2: Chelm 4B 72
Fir Trees CM16: Epp 8G 64
RM4: Abr 2G 93
Fir Tree Wlk. CM9: Mal 3E 214
RM10: Dag 5A 126
Fir Wlk. SS8: Can I 9F 134
Fir Way CO15: Jay 6E 188
Firwood's Rd. CO9: Hals 6K 207
Fisher Cl. EN3: Enf 7B 76
Fishermans Wlk. SE28: Lon 9D 140
Fisherman's Way EN11: Rye P 3D 52
Fishers Cl. EN8: Wal X 4A 76
FISHERS GREEN 8B 62 (3D 30)
Fishers Grn. La. EN9: Wal A 8B 62
Fishers Hatch CM20: H'low 2D 54
(off St Michaels Cl.)
Fishers La. CM16: Epp 2D 78
Fisher's La. SG8: Orw 1C 4
Fishers Way DA17: Belv 8A 142
Fisher Way CM7: Brain 4L 193
Fishguard Way E16: Lon 8A 140
(not continuous)
Fishmarket St. CM6: Thax 8C 224
Fishpits La. CO8: Bures 2J 15
Fishponds Hill
CO6: Gt Hork, L Hork 3F 158 (2D 16)
Fishponds La. IP9: Holb 1D 18
Fish St. CM9: Gold 3K 201 (7A 26)
Fisin Wlk. CO3: S'way 3F 172
Fiske Ct. IG11: Bark 2C 140
Fitch's Cres. CM9: Mal 7D 214
Fitch's M. CM9: Mal 7D 214
Fitzgerald Cl. CO11: Law 4G 163
Fitzgerald Ct. E10: Lon 3B 122
(off Leyton Grange Est.)
Fitzgerald Rd. E11: Lon 9G 107
Fitzgilbert Rd. CO2: Colc 2K 173
Fitzilian Av. RM3: H Wood 5K 111
Fitzpiers CB10: Saf W 3D 218
Fitzroy Cl. CM12: Bill 4J 99
Fitzstephen Rd. RM8: Dag 7G 124
Fitzwalter La. CM3: Dan 4D 74
Fitzwalter Pl. CM1: Chelm 8G 59
CM6: Gt D 3L 203
Fitzwalter Rd. CM3: Bore 3G 60
CM6: Fels 8E 212
CO3: Colc 9J 165
Fitzwarren SS3: Shoe 5H 139
Fitzwilliam Ct. CM17: H'low 8L 51
Fitzwilliam Rd. CO3: Colc 8J 165
SS7: Had 4J 135
Five Acres CM3: Dan 7F 74
CM18: H'low 6D 54
CM24: Stan M 1D 220
CO14: Walt 6L 181
Fiveash La. CM77: Tye G 7F 15
Five Elms Rd. RM9: Dag 5L 125
Fivefields CO4: Colc 8E 166
(off Centre, The)
Five Oaks SS7: Ben 2H 135
Five Oaks La. IG7: Chig 3K 109
Five Ways CO3: S'way 2E 172
Fiveways Retail Pk. CO3: S'way 2E 172
Flack Ct. E10: Lon 2B 122
FLACK'S GREEN 4D 24
Fladgate Rd. E11: Lon 1E 122
Flag Hill CO7: Gt Ben 4L 183 (2A 28)
Flagstaff Cl. EN9: Wal A 3B 76
Flagstaff Rd. CO2: Colc 9N 165
EN9: Wal A 3B 76
Flail Cl. CO7: Elms 9M 167
Flambird's Chase CM3: Pur 3M 89
Flamboro Cl. SS9: Lgh S 9C 120
Flamboro Wlk. SS9: Lgh S 9C 120
Flamingo Wlk. RM12: Rain 8E 126
FLAMSTEAD END 3C 30
Flamstead End Rd. EN7: Chesh 3C 30
Flamstead Gdns. RM9: Dag 9H 125
Flamstead Rd. RM9: Dag 9H 125
Flanders Cl. CM7: Brain 3G 192
Flanders Fld. CO2: Colc 3B 174
FLANDERS GREEN 4B 10
Flandrian Cl. EN3: Lon 8B 76
Flatford CO7: E Ber 1C 162 (2J 17)
Flatford Dr. CO16: Clac S 9F 184
Flatford Mill 2J 17
Flatford Rd. CO7: E Ber 1J 17
Flaxen Cl. E4: Lon 9B 90
Flaxen Rd. E4: Lon 9B 90
Flax La. CO10: Glem 2G 9
Flecks La. SG8: Shin W 2A 4
Fleece Yd. CO9: Hals 4K 207
Fleet Av. RM14: Upm 1A 128
Fleet Cl. RM14: Upm 1A 128
FLEET DOWNS 4D 46
Fleethall Gro. RM16: Grays 8K 145
Fleethall Rd. SS4: R'fd 7M 121
Fleet Rd. SS7: Ben 4D 134
Fleet St. EC4: Lon 7A 38
Fleetway SS16: Van 2G 132
Fleetwood SS8: Can I 3L 151
Fleetwood Av. CO15: Hol S 6A 186
SS0: Wclf S 5H 137
Fleetwood Cl. CO15: Hol S 6B 186
Fleming Cl. CM7: Brain 7H 193
Fleming Gdns. RM3: H Wood 6H 111
RM18: Til 6E 156
Fleming Rd. RM16: Chaf H 2F 154 (1E 46)
Flemings CM13: Gt War 3F 112
Flemings Farm Rd. SS9: Lgh S 7C 120
Fleming Way SE28: Lon 7J 141
Flemish Ct. CO1: Colc 8N 165
(off Northgate St.)
Flemming Av. SS9: Lgh S 3C 136
Flemming Cres. SS9: Lgh S 3C 136
Flemming Rd. EN9: Enf 5B 76
Fletcher Cl. E6: Lon 6A 140
Fletcher Ct. CM11: Bill 6M 99
Fletcher Dr. SS12: W'fd 1M 117
Fletcher La. E10: Lon 2C 122
Fletcher Rd. IG7: Chig 2E 108
Fletchers SS16: Bas 3N 131
Fletchers Sq. SS2: Temp I 1M 137
Flex Mdw. CM19: H'low 4L 53 (7G 21)
Flicks Cinema 1J 189
Flights Leisure Cen. 8H 121
Flint Cl. SS16: Lang H 1H 131
FLINT CROSS 4F 5
Flint St. RM20: W Thur 4E 154
Flintwich Mnr. CM1: Chelm 4G 58
Flitch Ind. Est., The CM6: Gt D 4L 203
Flitch La. CM6: Gt D 4M 203
Flitch Way CM6: Gt D 3J 203
CM6: L Can 3E 224
CM22: Tak 3E 224
CM77: Brain, Gt N 6C 192
Flitch Way Vis. Cen. 7B 192
Flixton Cl. CO16: Clac S 9E 184
Floathaven Cl. SE28: Lon 8F 140
Flood La. CO4: Colc 1B 166
Flora Gdns. RM6: Chad H 1H 125
Flora Rd. CM8: Wthm 3A 230 (4F 25)
Florence Cl. CM17: H'low 5H 55
RM12: Horn 4J 127
RM20: Grays 4H 155
SS7: Had 3K 135
Florence Ct. E11: Lon 8H 107
Florence Elson Cl. E12: Lon 6N 123
Florence Gdns. SS7: Had 3J 135
Florence Neale Ho. SS8: Can I 2G 151
(off Kitkatts Rd.)
Florence Rd. CO14: Walt 4N 181
SS8: Can I 1J 151
Florence Way SS16: Lang H 1K 131
Florie's Rd. CO6: Gt Tey 6J 15
Flowers Way CO15: Jay 5E 188
Flux's La. CM16: Epp 3F 78
FOBBING 9E 132 (5A 42)
Fobbing Farm Cl. SS16: Bas 3B 132
Fobbing Rd. SS17: Corr 1C 148 (6A 42)
Focal Point Gallery 5M 137
Fodderwick SS14: Bas 1B 132
Fogerty Cl. EN3: Enf 7B 76
Foksville Rd. SS8: Can I 2J 151 (6F 43)
Fold Croft CM20: H'low 2N 53
Fold, The SS14: Bas 9C 116
Folkards La. CO7: B'sea 5E 182
Folkes La. RM14: Upm 9C 112 (3D 40)
Folkestone Rd. E6: Lon 3A 140
E17: Lon 8B 106
Folley, The CO2: Lay H 8H 173 (1D 26)
CO3: S'way 1E 172
Folly Chase SS5: Hock 1A 120
FOLLY GREEN 6F 15
Folly Green CM77: Tye G 6F 15
Folly La. SS5: Hock 1A 120 (1G 43)
Folly Mill La. CM6: Thax 4F 13
Folly Rd. CO10: Clare, Pos 1C 8
CO10: Gt Wal 4K 9
Folly, The CO5: Tip 8F 226
CO7: W'hoe 7H 175
Fontayne Av. IG7: Chig 1B 108
RM1: Romf 6C 110
RM13: Rain 9C 126
Font Cl. SS15: Lain 9L 115
Fonteyn Cl. SS15: Lain 7L 115
Fonteyne Gdns. IG8: Wfd G 6K 107
Fonthill Rd. N4: Lon 4A 38
Fontwell Pk. Gdns.
RM12: Horn 6J 127
Forbes Cl. RM11: Horn 3F 126
Ford Cl. RM13: Rain 9D 126
SS15: Lain 9J 115
FORD END
CB11 3H 11
CM3 3J 23
Ford End CB11: Clav 3H 11
IG8: Wfd G 3H 107
Ford End Rd. CM3: Ples 2C 56 (4J 23)
FORDHAM 2A 164 (4B 16)
Fordham Cl. RM11: Horn 2L 127
FORDHAM HEATH 5A 164 (5B 16)
Fordham Rd.
CO6: For, W Ber 9C 158 (4C 16)
CO6: Wak C 3A 16
CO6: Wmgfd 9K 229 (3B 16)
Fordhams Row RM16: Ors 5D 146
Ford Hill SG11: L Had 1G 21
Ford Ind. Pk. RM9: Dag 4N 141
Ford La. CO4: Colc 3K 165
CO7: Alr, B'sea 3A 182 (2J 27)
RM13: Rain 9D 126 (5A 40)
Ford Pl. RM15: S Ock 7G 144
Ford Rd. CO15: Clac S 1H 189
RM9: Dag 9L 125
Ford Rd. Ind. Est. CO15: Clac S 1H 189

Fords Gro. N21: Lon . . . 7B 30
Fordson Rd. CM2: Chelm . . . 5C 60
FORD STREET . . . 5B 16
Ford St. CO6: Aldh . . . 5B 16
SG11: Brau . . . 6E 10
Fordstreet Hill CO6: Aldh . . . 5B 16
Fordview Ind. Est.
RM13: Rain . . . 3B 142
Fordwater Cl. CO9: New E . . . 8M 223
Fordwich Rd. CO7: B'sea . . . 4D 182
Fordyce Cl. RM11: Horn . . . 2K 127
Fordyke Rd. RM8: Dag . . . 4L 125
Forebury Av. CM21: Saw . . . 2L 51
Forebury Cres. CM21: Saw . . . 2L 51
Forebury, The CM21: Saw . . . 2L 51
(Forebury Cres.)
CM21: Saw . . . 2K 51
(Knight St.)
Fore Fld. CM7: Brain . . . 5M 193
Forefield Grn. CM1: Chelm . . . 4A 60
Forelands Pl. CM21: Saw . . . 2K 51
Foremark Cl. IG6: Ilf . . . 2E 108
Foresight Rd. CO2: Colc . . . 4D 174
Forest App. E4: Lon . . . 6E 90
IG8: Wfd G . . . 4G 106
Forest Av. E4: Lon . . . 6E 90
IG7: Chig . . . 2N 107
SS1: Sth S . . . 7N 137
Forest Cl. E11: Lon . . . 9G 106
EN9: Wal A . . . 7H 77
IG8: Wfd G . . . 9H 91
Forest Ct. E4: Lon . . . 7F 90
E11: Lon . . . 8E 106
Forest Dr. CM1: Chelm . . . 1N 71
CM5: Fy'd . . . 1N 67
CM16: They B . . . 6D 78
E12: Lon . . . 5K 123 (4F 39)
IG8: Wfd G . . . 4D 106
Forest Dr. E. E11: Lon . . . 2D 122
Forest Dr. W. E11: Lon . . . 2C 122
Forest Edge IG9: Buck H . . . 1J 107 (1F 39)
Forester Ct. CM12: Bill . . . 5H 99
Forester's Ct. CO7: W'hoe . . . 5H 175
Foresters Dr. E17: Lon . . . 8D 106
FOREST GATE . . . 7G 122 (5E 38)
Forest Gate Station (Rail) . . . 7G 123 (5F 39)
Forest Glade CM16: N Wea . . . 6K 65
E4: Lon . . . 1E 106
E11: Lon . . . 1E 122
SS16: Lang H . . . 2H 131
Forest Glade Ct. SS7: Ben . . . 1B 134
Foresthall Rd.
CM24: Bchgr, Stan M . . . 5C 220 (7A 12)
Forest Hgts. IG9: Buck H . . . 8G 91
Forest Ind. Pk. IG6: Ilf . . . 5D 108
Forest La. E7: Lon . . . 7F 122 (5E 38)
E15: Lon . . . 7E 122 (5E 38)
IG7: Chig . . . 2N 107 (1G 39)
Forest Mt. Rd. IG8: Wfd G . . . 4D 106
Forest Pk. Av. CO15: Clac S . . . 6J 185
Forest Point *E7: Lon* . . . *7H 123*
(off Windsor Rd.)
Fore St. CM17: H'low . . . 8H 51
N9: Lon . . . 1C 38
N18: Lon . . . 2C 38
SS15: Bas . . . 5N 115
Forest Ri. E17: Lon . . . 7D 106
(not continuous)
Forest Rd. CM8: Wthm . . . 1D 230 (3G 25)
CO4: Colc . . . 8D 166
DA8: Eri . . . 6E 152
E7: Lon . . . 6G 123
E11: Lon . . . 2D 122
E17: Lon . . . 3C 38
EN9: Epp, Wal A . . . 6L 77
IG6: Chig, Ilf . . . 6C 108 (2H 39)
IG8: Wfd G . . . 9G 90
IG10: Lou . . . 2K 91 (6F 31)
N17: Lon . . . 7A 106
RM7: Maw . . . 7N 109
Forest Side CM16: Epp . . . 3C 78
E4: Lon . . . 6F 90 (7E 30)
E7: Lon . . . 6H 123
EN9: Wal A . . . 6J 77 (5F 31)
IG9: Buck H . . . 7J 91
Forest St. E7: Lon . . . 7G 122
Forest Ter. IG7: Chig . . . 2N 107
Forest, The E11: Lon . . . 8E 106
Forest Vw. E4: Lon . . . 6D 90
E11: Lon . . . 2F 122
Forest Vw. Av. E10: Lon . . . 9D 106
Forest Vw. Dr. SS9: Lgh S . . . 3N 135
Forest Vw. Rd. E12: Lon . . . 6L 123
E17: Lon . . . 5C 106
IG10: Lou . . . 3K 91
Forest Way CM16: Epp Up . . . 5L 63
(not continuous)
IG8: Wfd G . . . 1H 107
IG10: Lou . . . 2L 91
Forfar Cl. SS9: Lgh S . . . 4A 136
Forfields Way CM77: Tye G . . . 2E 194
Forge Cres. CM77: Tye G . . . 7F 15
Forge La. DA4: Hort K . . . 6D 46
DA12: Shorne . . . 5K 47
ME3: High . . . 5K 47
Forge Mus. . . . 2G 21
Forges Rd. E12: Lon . . . 4K 123
Forge St. CO7: Ded . . . 2M 161
Formation, The *E16: Lon* . . . *9A 140*
(off Woolwich Mnr. Way)
Formby Rd. ME2: Hall . . . 7K 47
Forres CO13: Frin S . . . 1J 187
Forres Cl. EN11: Rye P . . . 3A 52
Forres Ho. CM14: War . . . 1F 112
Forrest Cl. CM3: S Fer . . . 1J 103
FORREY'S GREEN . . . 2C 14
Forster Cl. E4: Lon . . . 4D 106
Forsters Cl. RM6: Chad H . . . 1L 125
Forsyth Dr. CM7: Brain . . . 8J 193
Forsythia Cl. CM1: Chelm . . . 4N 59
IG1: Ilf . . . 7A 124
Forterie Gdns. IG3: Bark, Ilf . . . 5F 124
Fortescue Chase SS1: Sth S . . . 5D 138
Fortess Rd. NW5: Lon . . . 5A 38
Forth Rd. RM14: Upm . . . 1A 128
Fortinbras Way CM2: Chelm . . . 3C 72
Fortin Cl. RM15: S Ock . . . 7D 144
Fortin Path RM15: S Ock . . . 7D 144
Fortin Way RM15: S Ock . . . 7D 144
Fortress Distribution Pk. RM18: Til . . . 9C 156
Fort Rd. RM18: Til, W Til . . . 9D 156 (3H 47)
Fortune Cl. CM3: Gt L . . . 7L 203
Fortune Ct. IG11: Bark . . . 2H 141
Fortune Steps *SS1: Sth S* . . . *7A 138*
(off Kursaal Way)
Fortunes, The CM18: H'low . . . 5E 54
Fort William Rd. SS16: Van . . . 4C 132
Forty Hall & Mus. . . . 5B 30
FORTY HILL . . . 5B 30
Forty Hill EN2: Enf . . . 5B 30
Fosset Lodge DA7: Bexh . . . 6A 152
Fossetts La. CO6: For . . . 2A 164 (5B 16)
Fossetts Way SS2: Sth S . . . 2A 138
Fossway RM8: Dag . . . 4H 125
Fostal Cl. SS9: Lgh S . . . 3D 136
Foster Ct. CM8: Wthm . . . 5D 230
Foster Rd. CM9: Gt Tot . . . 3M 229
CO12: Har . . . 2G 209
SS8: Can I . . . 1J 151
Fosters Cl. CM1: Writ . . . 1H 71
E18: Lon . . . 5H 107
FOSTER STREET . . . 5L 55 (7K 21)
Foster St. CM17: H'low . . . 5K 55 (7K 21)
Foulgar Cl. CM3: S Fer . . . 9L 89
Founder Cl. E6: Lon . . . 6A 140
Founders Rd. EN11: Rye P . . . 2B 52
Foundry Ct. CO11: Law . . . 4H 163
Foundry La. CM0: Bur C . . . 3C 196
CO6: Cop . . . *2M 171*
(off Westbury Cl.)
CO6: Cop . . . 1M 171
(Queensbury Av.)
CO6: E Col . . . 8C 198 (4H 15)
Founes Dr. RM16: Chaf H . . . 1H 155
Fountain Ct. CO5: W Mer . . . 2D 228
Fountain Farm CM18: H'low . . . 5E 54
Fountain La. CO6: Cop, S'way . . . 6N 171 (1B 26)
SS5: Hock . . . 2A 120 (1G 43)
Fountain Pl. EN9: Wal A . . . 4C 76
Fountains, The IG10: Lou . . . 6K 91
Four Acres CB10: Gt Che . . . 7D 202
CB11: Saf W . . . 4D 218
Four Acres, The CM21: Saw . . . 3L 51
Four Ash Hill CO9: Bay E, Bird . . . 6A 216 (5B 8)
Four Oaks CM15: Brtwd . . . 9H 97
FOUR SISTERS . . . 1J 17
Four Sisters Cl. SS9: Sth S . . . 1E 136
FOUR SISTERS INTERCHANGE . . . 1J 17
Four Sisters Way SS9: Sth S . . . 9E 120
Fourth Av. CM1: Chelm . . . 6J 59
CM19: H'low . . . 3M 53 (7G 21)
CM20: H'low . . . 3A 54 (7G 21)
CM24: Stan M . . . 7G 221
CO9: Hals . . . 5N 207
CO13: Frin S . . . 9J 181 (1G 29)
CO15: Clac S . . . 9N 185
E12: Lon . . . 6M 123 (5G 39)
RM7: Rush G . . . 3B 126
RM20: W Thur . . . 4D 154
SS5: Hull . . . 8M 103
SS7: Thund . . . 9G 119
SS11: W'fd . . . 1A 118
SS16: Lang H . . . 3G 130
SS17: Stan H . . . 9N 131
Fourth Wlk. SS8: Can I . . . 1E 150
FOUR WANTZ . . . 6F 23
Four Wantz, The CM5: Chip . . . 6L 67
Fourways CM22: Else . . . 3K 199
Fourways Ct. EN11: Hod . . . 4A 52
Four Wents, The E4: Lon . . . 8D 90
Fowes La. CO10: Bel O . . . 5E 8
Fowey Av. IG4: Ilf . . . 9K 107
Fowler Cl. SS1: Sth S . . . 6A 138
Fowler Ct. CM2: Chelm . . . 6B 72
Fowler Rd. E7: Lon . . . 6G 122
IG6: Ilf . . . 3G 109
Fowley Mead Pk. EN8: Wal X . . . 4A 76
FOWLMERE . . . 3F 5
Fowlmere Aerodrome . . . 3F 5
Fowlmere Rd. CB2: Fow, Foxt, Thri . . . 1F 5
SG8: Gt Chi, Hey . . . 5G 5
(not continuous)
SG8: Mel . . . 2E 4
SG8: Shepr . . . 2E 4
SG8: Thri . . . 2G 5
FOXASH ESTATE . . . 7B 162 (3J 17)
Foxborough Chase CM4: Stock . . . 4B 86
Fox Burrow Rd. IG7: Chig . . . 7M 193
Fox Burrows La. CM1: Writ . . . 9D 58
Fox Cl. RM5: Col R . . . 2N 109
SS7: Thund . . . 9F 118
Fox Cres. CM1: Chelm . . . 7H 59
Foxendale Folly CO3: S'way . . . 8D 164
FOXENDOWN . . . 7H 47
Foxendown La. DA13: Meop . . . 7H 47
Foxes Grn. RM16: Ors . . . 9C 146
Foxes Gro. CM13: Hut . . . 6D 98
Foxes La. CO10: Ashen . . . 6F 216 (4C 8)
Foxes Pde. *EN9: Wal A* . . . *4C 76*
(off Rue de St Lawrence)
Foxfield Cl. SS5: Hock . . . 1F 120
Foxfield Dr. SS17: Stan H . . . 9N 131
Foxglove Cl. CM8: Wthm . . . 4A 230
CO15: Clac S . . . 6K 185
EN11: Rye P . . . 2C 52
Foxglove Gdns. E11: Lon . . . 8J 107
Foxglove Rd. RM7: Rush G . . . 4C 126
RM15: S Ock . . . 5F 144
Foxgloves, The CM12: Bill . . . 4H 99
Foxglove Wlk. CO4: Colc . . . 8E 166
Foxglove Way CM1: Chelm . . . 5A 60
Foxgrove La. IP11: Felix . . . 1K 19
Foxhall Rd. CM0: May . . . 4B 36
RM14: Upm . . . 7N 127
FOX HATCH . . . 7C 82 (5D 32)
Fox Hatch CM15: Kel H . . . 8B 82
Foxhatch SS12: W'fd . . . 1M 117
Fox Hatch Ho. CM15: Kel H . . . 7B 82
Fox Hills Rd. RM16: Grays . . . 8N 145
Foxholes Rd. CM2: Gt Bad . . . 4G 72
Foxhounds La. DA13: S'fleet . . . 4F 47
Foxhunter Wlk. CM11: Bill . . . 2M 99
Foxlands Cres. RM10: Dag . . . 7A 126
Foxlands La. RM10: Dag . . . 7B 126
Foxlands Rd. RM10: Dag . . . 7A 126
Fox La. N13: Lon . . . 1A 38
Foxleigh CM12: Bill . . . 8J 99
Foxleigh Cl. CM12: Bill . . . 8J 99
Foxley Cl. IG10: Lou . . . 1A 92
Foxley Dr. CM23: Bis S . . . 9A 220
Fox Mnr. Way RM20: W Thur . . . 4E 154
Fox Mead CM8: Riven . . . 3G 25
Fox Mdws. SS7: Thund . . . 9F 118
Fox Rd. CM1: Mash . . . 5H 23
FOX STREET . . . 3G 166 (5G 17)
FOXTON . . . 1F 5
Foxton Rd. EN11: Hod . . . 5A 52
RM20: Grays . . . 4G 155
Foxton Station (Rail) . . . 1F 5
Foxwood Chase EN9: Enf . . . 5C 76
Foxwood Cl. CO11: Law . . . 6A 162
Foxwood Ct. SS9: Lgh S . . . 4B 136
Foxwood Pl. SS9: Lgh S . . . 4C 136
Fox Yd. CO9: Wick P . . . 7G 9
Foyle Dr. RM15: S Ock . . . 5D 144 (7E 40)
Foys Wlk. CM11: Bill . . . 9L 99
Frambury La. CB11: Newp . . . 3K 215
Frame, The SS15: Lain . . . 8M 115
Framlingham Ct. SS6: Ray . . . 6J 119
Framlingham Way CM77: Gt N . . . 2C 204
Frampton Rd. CM16: Epp . . . 7F 64
SS14: Bas . . . 6H 117
Frances Av. RM16: Chaf H . . . 2F 154
Frances Cl. CO7: W'hoe . . . 4H 175
Frances Cottee Lodge SS6: Ray . . . 7N 119
Frances Ct. E17: Lon . . . 1A 122
Frances Gdns. RM15: S Ock . . . 6C 144
Frances Grn. CM1: Chelm . . . 4B 60
Frances Rd. E4: Lon . . . 3A 106
Francis Av. IG1: Ilf . . . 4C 124
Francis Cl. CO5: Tip . . . 7C 226
SS17: Horn H . . . 2H 147
Francisco Cl. RM16: Chaf H . . . 1F 154
Francis Ct. CM8: Sil E . . . 7K 217
CM20: H'low . . . 1A 54
SS14: Bas . . . 1G 132
Francis Greene Ho. *EN9: Wal A* . . . *3B 76*
(off Grove Ct.)
Francis M. CM9: Mal . . . 8D 214
Francis Rd. CM7: Brain . . . 6F 192
E10: Lon . . . 3C 122 (4E 38)
IG1: Ilf . . . 4C 124
Francis St. CO7: B'sea . . . 8E 182
E15: Lon . . . 7E 122
IG1: Ilf . . . 4C 124
Francis Wlk. SS6: Ray . . . 5K 119
Francis Way CM8: Sil E . . . 7K 217
CO4: Colc . . . 6D 166
Francombe Gdns. RM1: Romf . . . 9E 110
Frank Bailey Wlk. E12: Lon . . . 7N 123
Frank Bretton Ho. CM5: Chip . . . 7L 67
Frank Clater Cl. CO4: Colc . . . 7C 166
Frank Foster Ho. CM16: They B . . . 7D 78
Frankland Cl. IG8: Wfd G . . . 2J 107
Frankland Rd. E4: Lon . . . 2A 106
Franklin Rd. CM3: N Fam . . . 6H 35
RM12: Horn . . . 8G 127
Franklins Way SS11: W'fd . . . 8M 101
Franklyn Gdns. IG6: Ilf . . . 3C 108
Frank Naylor Ct. *CO1: Colc* . . . *8N 165*
(off E. Stockwell St.)
Franks Cotts. RM14: Upm . . . 3D 128
Franks La. DA4: Hort K . . . 7C 46
Franmil Rd. RM12: Horn . . . 3E 126
Fraser Cl. CM2: Chelm . . . 2D 72
SS3: Shoe . . . 5K 139
SS15: Lain . . . 9H 115
Fraser Rd. DA8: Eri . . . 3B 152 (1A 46)
E17: Lon . . . 9B 106
FRATING . . . 5D 176 (7K 17)
Frating Abbey Farm Rd.
CO7: Frat, Gt Ben, Thorr . . . 7G 177 (1K 27)
Frating Ct. CM7: Brain . . . 7M 193
Frating Cres. IG8: Wfd G . . . 3H 107
FRATING GREEN . . . 3F 176 (7K 17)
Frating Hill CO7: Elms, Frat . . . 3C 176 (7J 17)
Frating Pk. Cvn. Site
CO7: Frat . . . 3E 176
Frating Rd. CO7: A'gh . . . 1M 167 (4H 17)
CO7: Frat, Gt Bro . . . 9E 168 (6K 17)
(Parsons Hill)
CO7: Frat, Thorr . . . 6F 176 (1K 27)
(Station Rd.)
Frayes Chase CM5: Beau R . . . 6E 22
Frazer Cl. RM1: Romf . . . 2D 126
Frederica Rd. E4: Lon . . . 6D 90
Frederick Andrews Ct. RM17: Grays . . . 4N 155
Frederick Rd. RM13: Rain . . . 2B 142
Fred Leach Ho. SS8: Can I . . . 2G 151
Freeborne Gdns. RM13: Rain . . . 8E 126
Freebournes Ct. CM8: Wthm . . . 5D 230
Freebournes Rd. CM8: Wthm . . . 4E 230 (4G 25)
Freebournes Rd. Ind. Est. CM8: Wthm . . . 4E 230
Freeland Rd. CO15: Clac S . . . 3J 189
Freelands CO7: B'sea . . . 7G 183 (3K 27)
Freeland Way DA8: Eri . . . 6E 152
Freeman Ct. SS17: Stan H . . . 2A 148
Freeman Way RM11: Horn . . . 1K 127
Freemasons Rd. E16: Lon . . . 7F 39
Freewood La. CB11: Elm . . . 6J 5
Freezes Barns CB9: Stpl B . . . 2K 223
FREEZY WATER . . . 5D 30
Freightmaster Est. RM13: Rain . . . 6C 142
Fremantle SS3: Shoe . . . 9H 139
Fremantle Cl. CM3: S Fer . . . 8K 89
Fremantle Ho. RM18: Til . . . 6B 156
Fremantle Rd. CO2: Colc . . . 5B 174
IG6: Ilf . . . 6A 108 (2G 39)
Fremnells, The SS14: Bas . . . 8E 116 (3A 42)
FRENCHES GREEN . . . 1A 24
French Rd. CM3: N Fam . . . 5H 35
French's Sq. *CM2: Chelm* . . . *9L 59*
(off Meadows Shop. Cen., The)
French's Wlk. *CM2: Chelm* . . . *9L 59*
(off Meadows Shop. Cen., The)
Frensham Cl. CO3: S'way . . . 8E 164
Frere Way CO5: Fing . . . 8H 175
Frerichs Cl. SS12: W'fd . . . 2L 117
Freshfields CO12: Har . . . 6H 209
Freshfields Av. RM14: Upm . . . 7M 127
Freshwater Cres. CM9: H'bri . . . 4D 214
Freshwater Dr. SS16: Van . . . 3G 133
Freshwater La. CO15: Clac S . . . 5K 185
Freshwater Rd. RM8: Dag . . . 3J 125
Freshwaters CM20: H'low . . . 2D 54
Freshwell Av. RM6: Chad H . . . 8G 109
Freshwell Gdns. CB10: Saf W . . . 3B 218
CM13: W H'dn . . . 1N 129
Freshwell St. CB10: Saf W . . . 4B 218
Fresh Wharf Rd. IG11: Bark . . . 1A 140
Fresian Cl. CM7: Brain . . . 6E 192
Frettons SS14: Bas . . . 1F 132
Friars Av. CM15: Shenf . . . 7K 97 (7F 33)
Friar's Cl. CM15: Shenf . . . 6K 97
Friars Cl. CO4: Colc . . . 5C 166
CO7: W'hoe . . . 6J 175
CO9: Sib H . . . 5H 219
CO15: Clac S . . . 7J 185
E4: Lon . . . 9C 90
SS15: Lain . . . 9L 115
Friars Ct. CO2: Colc . . . 3C 174
Friarscroft EN10: Brox . . . 8A 52
Friars Ga. Cl. IG8: Wfd G . . . 1G 107
Friars La. CM7: Brain . . . 4H 193
CM9: Mal . . . 6B 214
CM22: Hat H . . . 3F 210 (4B 22)
Friars Mead CB9: Stur . . . 7K 223
Friars Rd. SG11: Brau . . . 6E 10
Friars St. CO10: Sud . . . 5J 9
SS3: Shoe . . . 7K 139
Friars, The CM19: H'low . . . 5N 53
IG7: Chig . . . 1D 108
Friars Wlk. CM2: Chelm . . . 9K 59
Friars Wood CM23: Bis S . . . 9B 220
Friary Flds. CM9: Mal . . . 6C 214
Friary La. IG8: Wfd G . . . 1G 106
FRIDAY HILL . . . 8E 90 (1E 38)
Friday Hill E4: Lon . . . 8E 90 (1E 38)
Friday Hill E. E4: Lon . . . 9E 90
(not continuous)
Friday Hill W. E4: Lon . . . 8E 90
Friday Rd. DA8: Eri . . . 3B 152
Friday Wood Grn. CO2: Colc . . . 6N 173
Friedberg Av. CM23: Bis S . . . 1J 21
Friends Fld. CO8: Bures . . . 7L 195
Friends Wlk. CB11: Saf W . . . 5C 218
Friern Gdns. SS12: W'fd . . . 9J 101
Friern Pl. SS12: W'fd . . . 1J 117
Friern Wlk. SS12: W'fd . . . 9J 101
Frietuna Rd. CO13: Frin S, Walt . . . 8H 181
Frimley Av. RM11: Horn . . . 3L 127
Frimley Rd. IG3: Ilf . . . 5D 124
Frinsted Rd. DA8: Eri . . . 5B 152
Frinton & Walton Swimming Pool . . . 5N 181
Frinton Ct. CO13: Frin S . . . 2J 187
Frinton Dr. IG8: Wfd G . . . 4D 106
Frinton M. IG2: Ilf . . . 1N 123
FRINTON-ON-SEA . . . 1J 187 (2G 29)
Frinton-on-Sea Station (Rail) . . . 9J 181 (1G 29)
Frinton Rd.
CO13: Frin S, Walt . . . 8E 180 (1F 29)
CO15: Hol S . . . 8A 186 (3E 28)
CO16: T Sok . . . 5M 179 (7E 18)
RM5: Col R . . . 4L 109
Friston Path IG7: Chig . . . 2D 108
Frith Rd. E11: Lon . . . 6C 122
Frithwood Cl. CM12: Bill . . . 9H 99
Frithwood La. CM12: Bill . . . 8H 99
Frizlands La. RM10: Dag . . . 4N 125 (4K 39)
Frobisher Cl. CM9: Mal . . . 8C 214
SS15: Lain . . . 9M 115
Frobisher Dr. CO15: Jay . . . 3D 188
Frobisher Gdns. E10: Lon . . . 2B 122
Frobisher Rd. CO12: Har . . . 6H 209
DA8: Eri . . . 5D 152
Frobisher Way CM7: Brain . . . 4L 193
DA9: Grnh . . . 9E 154
SS3: Shoe . . . 5J 139
Froden Brook CM11: Bill . . . 9L 99
Froden Cl. CM11: Bill . . . 9L 99

Froden Ct. CM11: Bill 1L 115
Frog End SG8: Shepr. 2E 4
Frogge St. CB10: I'tn 6A 202 (4K 5)
Frog Hall Cl. CO5: Fing 8J 175
Froghall La. IG7: Chig 1C 108
Frog La. RM13: Rain 6B 142
Frogmore Ind. Pk. RM20: W Thur 3D 154
Frog St. CM15: Dodd, Kel H 9B 82 (6D 32)
Frome RM18: E Til 2L 157
Fronk's Av. CO12: Har 5L 209
Fronk's Rd. CO12: Har 4J 209 (3H 19)
Front La. RM14: Upm 4B 128 (4D 40)
Frowick La. CO16: Gt Ben, St O, Wee H 4M 183 (2B 28)
Fry Art Gallery, The 6B 6
Fryatt Av. CO12: Har 3J 209
Fry Cl. RM5: Col R 2M 109
FRYERNING 4C 84 (4H 33)
Fryerning La. CM4: Fry, Ing 4C 84 (4G 33)
FRYERNS 7F 116 (3B 42)
Fry Ho. E7: Lon 9J 123
Fry Rd. E6: Lon 9K 123
Fryth, The SS14: Bas 7F 116
Fuchsia Cl. RM7: Rush G 4C 126
Fuchsia Ct. CO4: Colc 7D 166
Fuchsia Way CO16: Clac S 8G 184
Fulbourne Rd. E17: Lon 5C 106 (2E 38)
Fulbrook La. RM15: S Ock 7C 144
Fulcher Av. CM2: Chelm 8A 60
Fulfen Way CB11: Saf W 6C 218
Fulford Dr. SS9: Lgh S 9F 120
Fullarton Cres. RM15: S Ock 6C 144
Fullbridge CM9: Mal 5C 214 (1H 35)
Fuller Rd. RM8: Dag 5G 125
Fullers Almshouses *CM24: Stan M 3D 220*
(off Church Rd.)
Fullers Av. IG8: Wfd G 4F 106
Fuller's Cl. CO5: K'dn 3J 211
Fullers Cl. EN9: Wal A 3G 76
RM5: Col R 4A 110
Fullers Ct. CM22: Else 3L 199
FULLER'S END 4K 199 (6B 12)
Fullers Ga. CO5: K'dn 3J 211
Fullers La. RM5: Col R 4A 110
Fullers Mead CM17: H'low 4H 55
Fuller's Rd. CO2: Colc 4D 174
Fullers Rd. E18: Lon 4F 106
FULLER STREET 4C 24
Fullwell Av. IG5: Ilf 5M 107 (2G 39)
IG6: Ilf 5M 107 (2G 39)
FULLWELL CROSS 5B 108 (2H 39)
Fullwell Cross IG6: Ilf 6C 108 (2H 39)
Fullwell Pde. IG5: Ilf 5N 107
Fulmar Cl. CO4: Colc 7G 166
Fulmar Rd. RM12: Horn 9E 126
Fulmar Way SS11: W'fd 2A 118
Fulready Rd. E10: Lon 9D 106
Fulton Cres. CM23: Bis S 9B 220
Fulton Rd. SS7: Thund 8D 118
Fulwell Cross Swimming Pool & Recreation Cen. 6C 108
Furlongs SS16: Van 2E 132
Furlongs, The CM4: Ing 5C 84
Furneaux La. CO5: Fing 9F 174 (1G 27)
Furner Cl. DA1: Cray 8D 152
Furness Cl. RM16: Grays 3D 156
(not continuous)
Furness Way RM12: Horn 7E 126
FURNEUX PELHAM 4G 11
Furrow Cl. CO3: S'way 1F 172
Furrowfelde SS16: Bas 3B 132
FURTHER FORD END 2H 11
Further Mdw. CM1: Writ 2J 71
Furtherwick Rd. SS8: Can I 1H 151 (6E 42)
Furze Cres. CO7: Alr 7N 175
Furze Farm Cl. RM6: Chad H 6K 109
Furze Glade SS16: Lang H 2J 131
FURZE HILL INTERCHANGE 1H 85 (3J 33)
Furze La. CM4: Stock 9B 86 (6A 34)
CO7: Gt Bro 1F 176
Fusedale Way RM15: S Ock 7C 144
FYFIELD 9C 200 (1D 32)
Fyfield Av. SS12: W'fd 2K 117
Fyfield Cl. CM13: W H'dn 1N 129
Fyfield Ct. E7: Lon 8G 123
Fyfield Dr. RM15: S Ock 7C 144
Fyfield Path SS6: Ray 4G 119
Fyfield Rd. CM5: Chip 5L 67 (2C 32)
CM5: Fy'd 1E 32
CM5: M'ton 1C 32
E17: Lon 7D 106
IG8: Wfd G 4J 107
RM13: Rain 1D 142
Fyfields SS13: Pits 8K 117

G

Gabion Av. RM19: Purf 2A 154
Gablefields CM2: S'don 4K 73
Gables, The CB9: Stur 6K 223
CM21: Saw 2K 51
CM22: Else 3K 199
CO12: Har 4M 209
IG11: Bark 8B 124
RM17: Grays 2J 155
SS9: Lgh S 9N 119
Gables, The SS13: Bas 7J 117
Gabriel Cl. RM5: Col R 4A 110
RM16: Chaf H 1F 154
Gabrielspring Rd. DA3: Fawk 7D 46
Gabrielspring Rd. E. DA3: Fawk 7D 46
Gaces Acre CB11: Newp 2L 215
Gadsden Cl. RM14: Upm 1B 128
GADSHILL 5K 47
Gadwall Reach CO5: K'dn 3L 211
Gadwall Way SE28: Lon 9C 140
Gafzelle Dr. SS8: Can I 2L 151
Gager Dr. CO5: Tip 6E 226
Gage's Grn. CO10: Bel P 5E 8
Gaiger Cl. CM1: Chelm 4M 59
Gainsborough Av. *E12: Lon 8N 123*
(off Barrington Rd.)
E12: Lon 7N 123
(Church Rd.)
RM18: Til 6C 156
SS8: Can I 2L 151
Gainsborough Cl. CM11: Bill 7K 99
CO5: W Mer 3D 228
CO16: Clac S 7F 184
Gainsborough Ct. *CM14: War 1F 112*
(off Gt. Eastern Rd.)
Gainsborough Cres. CM2: Chelm 8N 59
Gainsborough Dr. CO11: Law 4G 163
SS0: Wclf S 3K 137
Gainsborough Ho. *RM8: Dag 6G 124*
(off Earl's Wlk.)
Gainsborough Pl. CM13: Hut 7N 97
IG7: Chig 9E 92
Gainsborough Rd. CM77: Bla N 3A 194
CO3: Colc 1H 173
CO10: Sud 5J 9
E11: Lon 2E 122 (4E 38)
IG8: Wfd G 3L 107
RM8: Dag 6G 124
RM13: Rain 1E 142
Gainsborough's House 5J 9
Gainsborough St. CO10: Sud 5J 9
Gains Cl. SS8: Can I 1K 151
Gainsfield Ct. E11: Lon 5E 122
Gainsford Av. CO15: Clac S 9M 185
GAINSFORD END 1B 14
Gainsford End Rd. CO9: Top 7B 8
Gainsthorpe Rd. CM5: Chip 2G 67 (2B 32)
Gaitskell Ho. E17: Lon 7B 106
RM16: Grays 8L 145
(off Crammavill St.)
Gala Club Bingo 2D 154
Galadriel Spring CM3: S Fer 2J 103
Galahad Cl. CM0: Bur C 3D 196
Galeborough Av. IG8: Wfd G 4D 106
Gale St. RM9: Dag 7H 125 (5J 39)
Gales Way IG8: Wfd G 4L 107
Galey Grn. RM15: S Ock 5E 144
Gall End La. CM24: Stan M 2E 220
Galleon Blvd. DA2: Dart 9A 154
Galleon Cl. DA8: Eri 2B 152
Galleon Rd. RM16: Chaf H 2F 154
Galleons Dr. IG11: Bark 3F 140
Galleydene SS7: Had 3J 135
Galleydene Av. CM2: Gall 7D 72
GALLEYEND 7E 72 (3A 34)
Galley Grn. SG13: Hail 1A 52
Galley Hill Rd. DA10: N'fleet 3F 47
DA11: N'fleet 3F 47
Galleyhill Rd. EN9: Wal A 3E 76 (4E 30)
(not continuous)
Galley Rdbt. CM77: Tye G 7M 193
GALLEYWOOD 7C 72 (3A 34)
Galleywood Cres. RM5: Col R 3B 110
Galleywood Rd. CM2: Chelm 4B 72 (2A 34)
CM2: Gt Bad 6E 72 (2A 34)
GALLEYWOOD/STOCK INTERCHANGE 1C 86
Galliard Rd. N9: Lon 7C 30
Galliford Rd. CM9: Mal 4C 214
Galliford Rd. Ind. Est. CM9: Mal 3C 214
Gallions Cl. IG11: Bark 3F 140
Gallions Entrance E16: Lon 8B 140
Gallions Reach Shop. Pk. E6: Lon 5B 140
Gallions Reach Station (DLR) 7A 140 (7H 39)
Gallions Rdbt. E16: Lon 7A 140
Gallions Vw. Rd. SE28: Lon 9D 140
Gallops, The SS16: Lang H 1K 131
Galloway Dr. CO16: L Cla 2G 185
GALLOWS CORNER 6G 110
GALLOWS CORNER 5G 111 (2B 40)
GALLOWS GREEN
CM6 5G 13
CO6 5B 16
Gallows Grn. Rd. CM6: Dut H, Lndsl 5G 13
Gallows Hill CB11: Saf W 6B 218
Galsworthy Av. RM6: Chad H 2G 124
Galsworthy Cl. SE28: Lon 8G 140
Galsworthy Rd. RM18: Til 6E 156
Galt Cl. SS12: W'fd 3L 117
Galton Rd. SS0: Wclf S 6G 137
GAMBLE'S GREEN 4D 24
Gambleside SS16: Van 3F 132
Gamuel Cl. E17: Lon 1A 122
Gandalfs Ride CM3: S Fer 2J 103
Gandhi Cl. E17: Lon 1A 122
Gandish Rd. CO7: E Ber 1J 17
Ganels Cl. CM11: Bill 9L 99
Ganels Rd. CM11: Bill 9L 99
Gangies Hill CM21: H Wych 1E 50 (4H 21)
Ganley Cl. CM11: Bill 6K 99
Gant Ct. EN9: Wal A 4F 76
GANTS HILL 1N 123 (3G 39)
GANTS HILL 1N 123 (3G 39)
Gantshill Cres. IG2: Ilf 9N 107
Gants Hill Cross IG2: Ilf 1N 123 (3G 39)
Gants Hill Station (Tube) 1N 123 (3G 39)
Gap, The CB11: A'den 1K 11
CO15: Hol S 7D 186
Garbutt Rd. RM14: Upm 4N 127
Garden Cl. CM0: Stpl 3B 36
CM3: Alth 1C 190
E4: Lon 2A 106
Garden Ct. CO13: Frin S 2J 187
Garden Dr. CO3: S'way 9F 164
Garden End CM4: Stock 7A 86
Gardeners CM2: Gt Bad 5E 72
Gardeners La. SS4: Cwdn 2N 105 (7A 36)
Gardeners Rd. CO9: Hals 5L 207
Gardeners Row CO6: Cogg 3L 197
Garden Farm CO5: W Mer 2D 228
Garden Fld. CM3: Hat P 3K 61
Garden Flds. CM0: Stpl 3B 36
CM5: Chip 4J 81
CM6: Steb 7C 222
CO6: Gt Tey 2E 170
Garden Ho's., The CM21: Saw 1N 51
Gardenia Pl. CO16: Clac S 9F 184
Gardenia Wlk. CO4: Colc 8E 166
Gardenia Way IG8: Wfd G 3G 107
Garden Rd. CO14: Walt 7K 181
CO15: Jay 5E 188
Gardens, The CM15: Dodd 6E 82
SS9: Lgh S 6D 136
Gardens Way E12: Lon 5L 123
Garden Ter. CO9: Hals 4L 207
Garden Ter. Rd. CM17: H'low 8H 51
Garden Vw. E7: Lon 6J 123
Garden Way IG10: Lou 8N 77
Gardiner Cl. RM8: Dag 6J 125
Gardiners Cl. SS14: Bas 6E 116
Gardiners La. Nth. CM11: Cray H 1E 116 (1A 42)
Gardiners La. Sth. SS14: Bas 5F 116 (2B 42)
Gardiners Link SS14: Bas 5D 116
Gardiners, The CM17: H'low 4G 55
Gardiners Way SS14: Bas 5E 116
Gardner Av. SS17: Corr 9A 132
Gardner Cl. E11: Lon 1H 123
Garenne Ct. E4: Lon 7C 90
Garfield Rd. E4: Lon 7D 90
Garganey Wlk. SE28: Lon 7H 141
Garland Rd. CO12: Har 2H 209
Garlands Rd. CO2: B'ch, Lay H 9E 172 (2C 26)
Garland Way RM11: Horn 8J 111
Garling Wlk. CO6: W Ber 4F 164
Garner Cl. RM8: Dag 3J 125
Garner Rd. E17: Lon 5C 106
Garners, The SS4: R'fd 5L 121
Garnet St. E1: Lon 7C 38
Garnetts CM22: Tak 2B 224
Garnetts La. CM6: Fels 7K 199 (1K 23)
Garnetts Vs. CM6: Fels 8K 199
Garnon Mead CM16: Coop 7J 65
Garnons Chase CO6: Wmgfd 8M 229
Garon Pk. SS2: Sth S 3B 138
Garret Pl. CO6: W Ber 3G 164
Garrettlands CM2: S'don 4N 73
Garretts La. CM7: Shalf 5A 14
Garrison La. IP11: Felix 1K 19
Garrison Pde. RM19: Purf 2L 153
Garrod Ct. CO2: Colc 7B 174
Garron La. RM15: S Ock 6C 144
Garry Cl. RM1: Romf 4C 110
Garry Way RM1: Romf 4C 110
Garth Rd. RM15: S Ock 4F 144
Garthwood Cl. CO6: W Ber 3F 164
Gartmore Rd. IG3: Ilf 4E 124
Garton La. RM15: S Ock 6C 144
Gascoigne Gdns. IG8: Wfd G 4E 106
Gascoigne Rd. CO4: Colc 7C 166
IG11: Bark 1B 140 (6H 39)
Gascoigne Way CM11: Bill 6M 99
Gascoyne Cl. RM3: Romf 4H 111
Gascoyne Dr. DA1: Cray 8D 152
Gascoyne Rd. E9: Lon 5C 38
Gascoyne Way SG14: Hart 5B 20
Gasfield *CO11: Mist 4J 163*
(off Malthouse Rd.)
GASTON GREEN 3K 213 (3K 21)
Gaston Hill CM22: L Hall 3K 213 (3K 21)
Gaston St. CO7: E Ber 1J 17
Gatacre Ct. CO2: Colc 3J 173
Gatefield Cl. CO14: Walt 7J 181
Gatehope Dr. RM15: S Ock 6C 144
Gatehouse M. CM4: Ing 6D 84
Gatehouse Vs. CM6: Gt D 4M 203
Gatekeeper Cl. CM7: Gt N 7H 193
Gate Lodge Sq. SS15: Bas 5A 116
Gate Lodge Way SS15: Bas 5A 116
Gate St. CM9: Mal 5B 214
Gate St. M. CM9: Mal 5B 214
Gateway SS14: Bas 9C 116
Gateway Ho. IG11: Bark 1B 140
Gateway Retail Pk. E6: Lon 4A 140
Gateway Rd. E10: Lon 5B 122
Gatewoods La. CM77: Rayne 7A 192
GATLEY END 5A 4
Gatscombe Cl. SS5: Hock 1C 120
Gattens, The SS6: Ray 3M 119
Gatwick Cl. CM23: Bis S 8A 220
Gatwick Vw. CM12: Bill 8K 99
Gatwick Way RM12: Horn 5K 127
Gauden Rd. CM7: Brain 1H 193
GAUNT'S END 2M 221 (6C 12)
Gavenney Path RM15: S Ock 6C 144
Gavin Way CO4: Colc 1B 166
Gawsworth Cl. E15: Lon 7F 122
GAY BOWERS 5G 74 (2E 34)
Gay Bowers SS5: Hock 1A 120
SS14: Bas 8E 116
Gay Bowers La. CM3: Dan 3F 74 (2E 34)
Gay Bowers Rd. CM3: Dan 6E 74 (3E 34)
Gay Bowers Way CM8: Wthm 8D 230
Gayfere Rd. IG5: Ilf 7M 107
Gay Gdns. RM10: Dag 6A 126
Gayleighs SS6: Ray 3K 119
Gay Links SS14: Bas 8C 116
Gaylor Rd. RM18: Til 6B 156
Gaynes Ct. RM14: Upm 6M 127
Gaynesford SS16: Bas 2N 131
Gaynes Hill Rd. IG8: Wfd G 3L 107
Gaynes Pk. Est. CM16: Coop 1K 79
Gaynes Pk. Rd. RM14: Upm 6L 127 (5C 40)
Gaynes Rd. RM14: Upm 4M 127
Gaysham Av. IG2: Ilf 9N 107
Gaysham Hall IG5: Ilf 7A 108
Gays La. SS4: Cwdn 1N 105
Gayton Rd. SS2: Sth S 4M 137
Gaywood SS15: Lain 8J 115
Gaywood Rd. E17: Lon 7A 106
Gazelle Ct. CO4: Colc 3B 166
Gean Ct. E11: Lon 6D 122
Geariesville Gdns. IG6: Ilf 8A 108
Geary Ct. CM14: Brtwd 7F 96
Geary Dr. CM14: Brtwd 7F 96
Geddings Rd. EN11: Hod 5B 52
Geddington Ct. EN8: Wal X 3A 76
Geddy Ct. RM2: Romf 7F 110
Geerings, The SS17: Stan H 2B 148
Geesh Rd. SS8: Can I 9J 135
Geisthorp Ct. EN9: Wal A 3G 77
Gelsthorpe Rd. RM5: Col R 4N 109
Generals La. CM3: Bore 1C 60
Genesta Cl. CM9: Tol 7K 225
Genesta Rd. SS0: Wclf S 6H 137 (5J 43)
Geneva Gdns. RM6: Chad H 9K 109
Genever Cl. E4: Lon 2A 106
Genk Cl. SS8: Can I 9H 135
Gennep Rd. SS8: Can I 9H 135
Gennep Rd. Sth. SS8: Can I 9H 135
Gentian Ct. CO4: Colc 5K 165
Gentry Cl. SS17: Stan H 3L 147
Geoffrey Av. RM3: H Wood 3L 111
Geoffrey Bower Sports Cen. 6M 107
Geoff Seaden Cl. CO1: Colc 9C 166
George Av. CO7: B'sea 6E 182
George Avey Cft. CM16: N Wea 5N 65
George Cardnell Way CM3: May 7J 213
George Cl. CO15: Clac S 2G 189
SS8: Can I 8F 134
George Comberton Wlk. E12: Lon 7N 123
George Crooks Ho. *RM17: Grays 4L 155*
(off New Rd.)
George Cut CO7: B'sea 7E 182
George Davies Lodge *IG2: Ilf 9B 108*
(off Veronique Gdns.)
George Gent Cl. CB9: Stpl B 3K 223
George Grn. *CM22: L Hall 1K 213*
(off Lower Rd.)
George Grn. Bungs. CM22: L Hall 2K 213
George Grn. Vs. CM22: L Hall 2K 213
George La. E18: Lon 6G 106 (2F 39)
(not continuous)
George Lovell Dr. EN3: Enf 7A 76
George Rd. CM7: Brain 5F 192
E4: Lon 3A 106
Georges Dr. CM15: Pil H 4C 96
George St. CB10: Saf W 4C 218
CM2: Chelm 1C 72
CO1: Colc 8N 165
CO12: Har 1M 209
IG11: Bark 9B 124
RM1: Romf 1D 126
RM17: Grays 4K 155
SS3: Shoe 8L 139
George Tilbury Ho. RM16: Grays 9D 146
Georgeville Gdns. IG6: Ilf 8A 108
George Williams Way CO1: Colc 9A 166
George Yd. CM7: Brain 5H 193
George Yd. Shop. Cen. *CM7: Brain 5H 193*
(off George Yd.)
Gepp Pl. CM2: Chelm 7C 60
Gepps Cl. CM1: High E 4G 23
Gerald Rd. RM8: Dag 4L 125
Geranium Cl. CO16: Clac S 9G 184
Geranium Wlk. CO4: Colc 8D 166
Gerard Gdns. RM13: Rain 2C 142
Gerard Rd. CO16: Clac S 7G 184
Gernon Bushes Nature Reserve 8K 65
Gernon Cl. CM1: Broom 9K 57
RM13: Rain 2H 143
Gernon Rd. CO7: A'lgh 9L 161
Gernons SS16: Bas 2A 132
Gerpins La. RM14: Upm 2K 143 (6C 40)
Gerrard Cres. CM14: Brtwd 9F 96
Gerry Raffles Sq. E15: Lon 9D 122
Gershwin Av. CM8: Wthm 8C 230
Gershwin Blvd. CM8: Wthm 8C 230
GESTINGTHORPE 6F 9
Gestingthorpe Rd. CO9: Gt Map 1F 15
CO9: L Map 1G 15
CO10: Bel W 5F 9
Geylen Rd. SS8: Can I 1K 151
GHYLLGROVE 8C 116 (3A 42)
Ghyllgrove SS14: Bas 8C 116 (3A 42)
Ghyllgrove Cl. SS14: Bas 7C 116
Gibb Cft. CM18: H'low 7D 54
(not continuous)
Gibberd Garden 6L 51
Gibbfield Cl. RM6: Chad H 7K 109
Gibbins Rd. E15: Lon 9C 122
Gibbons Ct. CM6: Gt D 2L 203
Gibcracks SS14: Bas 9F 116
Gibraltar Cl. CM13: Gt War 3F 112
Gibraltar Wlk. SS12: W'fd 9L 101
Gibson Cl. CB10: Saf W 4C 218
CM16: N Wea 4A 66
Gibson Ct. RM1: Romf 1C 126
Gibson Gdns. CB10: Saf W 4C 218
Gibson Rd. CO9: Sib H 7J 219
RM8: Dag 3H 125
Gibson Va. CM1: Broom 3K 59
Gibson Way CB10: Saf W 4C 218
Gidea Av. RM2: Romf 7E 110

Gidea Cl. RM2: Romf 7E 110
RM15: S Ock 3F 144
(off Benyon Path)
GIDEA PARK 7F 110 (3B 40)
Gidea Park Station (Rail) 8F 110 (3B 40)
Gideons Way SS17: Stan H 2M 147
Giffins Cl. CM7: Brain 7G 193
Gifford Grn. SS13: Pits 1J 133
Gifford Pl. CM14: War 2G 112
Gifford Rd. SS7: Ben 1D 134
Giffords Cross Av. SS17: Corr 1B 148
Giffords Cross Rd. SS17: Corr 2B 148 (6A 42)
Giffordside RM16: Grays 3D 156
Gifford's La. SG11: Haul 7B 10
Gifhorn Rd. SS8: Can I 2L 151
Gilberd Ct. CO4: Colc 1C 166
Gilberd Rd. CO2: Colc 1B 174
Gilbert Cl. SS6: Ray 5M 119
Gilbert Dr. SS16: Lang H 1J 131
Gilbert Ho. E17: Lon 7B 106
Gilbert Rd. RM1: Romf 8D 110
RM16: Chaf H 1F 154
Gilbert St. E15: Lon 6E 122
Gilbert Way CM7: Brain 3L 193
Gilbey Cotts. CM22: Else 3K 199
Gilbey Cres. CM24: Stan M 1D 220
Gilbey Grn. CB11: Newp 2K 215
Gilchrist Way CM7: Brain 4G 193
Gilda Ter. CM77: Gt N 6D 192
Gildborne Cl. SS17: Fob 9E 132
Gilden Cl. CM17: H'low 8K 51
Gildenhill Rd. BR8: Swan 5B 46
Gilden Way CM17: H'low 9H 51 (6J 21)
Gilderdale Cl. CO4: Colc 4D 166
Gilders CM21: Saw 2J 51
Gilders Way CO16: Clac S 8G 185
Giles Cl. RM13: Rain 2H 143
Gillam Way RM13: Rain 8E 126
Gillards M. E17: Lon 8A 106
Gillards Way E17: Lon 8A 106
Gill Cl. CM9: Mal 2B 214
Gillespie Rd. N5: Lon 4A 38
Gillian Cres. RM2: Romf 6G 111
Gilliflower Ho. EN11: Hod 6A 52
Gillingham Ho. *RM3: Romf 2J 111*
(off Lindfield Rd.)
Gills Av. SS8: Can I 1J 151
Gills Rd. DA2: Dart 6D 46
DA4: S Dar 6D 46
Gill, The SS7: Had 1K 135
Gilmore Way CM2: Gt Bad 3J 73
Gilmour Ri. CM12: Bill 7H 99
Gilpin Way CM77: Gt N 1C 204
Gilroy Cl. RM13: Rain 8D 126
Gilsland EN9: Wal A 5E 76
Gilson Cl. CM2: Chelm 9A 60
Gilstead Ho. IG11: Bark 2G 141
GILSTON 7C 50 (5H 21)
Gilston Pk. CM20: Gil 5B 50
Giltspur St. EC4: Lon 7A 38
Gilwell Cl. E4: Lon 3B 90
Gilwell La. E4: Lon 3B 90
(not continuous)
GILWELL PARK 3D 90
Gilwell Pk. E4: Lon 2D 90
Gilwell Pk. Cl. CO3: Colc 2H 173
Gimli Watch CM3: S Fer 2K 103
Gimson Cl. CM8: Wthm 5C 230
Ginns Rd. SG9: Fur P, Stoc P 4H 11
Gippeswyck SS14: Bas 8D 116
Gipsey La. CM24: Stan M 6A 12
Gipson Pk. Cl. SS9: Lgh S 9C 120
Gipsy La.
CM23: Bis S, Farnh, Stan M 5A 220 (7A 12)
CO12: Har 6F 208
RM17: Grays 4M 155
Girling St. CO10: Sud 5J 9
Girona Cl. RM16: Chaf H 1F 154
Gisborne Gdns. RM13: Rain 3D 142
Gladden Ct. CM18: H'low 7D 54
Gladden Flds. CM3: S Fer 2J 103
Gladding Rd. E12: Lon 6K 123
Glade Bus. Cen., The RM20: W Thur 3C 154
Glade Ct. IG5: Ilf 5M 107
Glade Rd. E12: Lon 5M 123
Glade, The CM13: Hut 7K 97
CO4: Colc 5E 166
IG5: Ilf 5M 107
IG8: Wfd G 9H 91
RM14: Upm 7N 127
SS16: Van 2D 132
Glade Vw. CO15: Clac S 6K 185
Gladeway, The EN9: Wal A 3D 76
Gladfen Hall Rd. CO9: G'std G 9J 207 (4F 15)
Gladiator Way CO2: Colc 4G 173
Gladstone Av. E12: Lon 9L 123
Gladstone Ct. CM2: Chelm 1C 72
Gladstone Gdns. SS6: Ray 6J 119
Gladstone Rd. CO1: Colc 1B 174
CO5: Tip 7D 226
EN11: Rye P 4B 52
IG9: Buck H 7J 91
SS5: Hock 2D 120
Gladwin Rd. CO2: Colc 2K 173
Gladwyns SS15: Lain 8N 115
Gladwyns Cotts. CM22: Hat H 1D 210
Gladys Dimson Ho. E7: Lon 7F 122
Glamis Dr. RM11: Horn 3J 127
Glan Avon M. CM17: H'low 4H 55
Glanmead CM15: Shenf 7H 97
Glanmire CM11: Bill 2M 99
Glanthams Cl. CM15: Shenf 8J 97
Glanthams Rd. CM15: Shenf 8J 97
Glanville Dr. RM11: Horn 3K 127
Glasier Ct. E15: Lon 9E 122
Glasseys La. SS6: Ray 7J 119
Glastonbury Av. IG8: Wfd G 4K 107
Glastonbury Chase SS0: Wclf S 1G 136
Glazenwood Rd. CM77: Tye G 7F 15
Glebe Av. CM7: Brain 1H 193
IG8: Wfd G 3G 106
Glebe Cl. CO7: Elms 9N 167
CO11: Wix 4D 18
SS1: Sth S 6C 138
SS6: Ray 4J 119
Glebe Ct. CM23: Bis S 9A 220
Glebe Cres. CM1: Broom 2K 59
CM8: Wthm 3B 230
Glebe Dr. SS6: Ray 4J 119
Glebe End CM22: Else 3L 199
Glebe Fld. SS14: Bas 7D 116
Glebefield Rd. CM3: Hat P 2M 61
Glebe Gdns. CM13: Heron 4A 114
CO5: Fee 9A 170
Glebe Ho. CM1: Chelm 8J 59
Glebelands CM20: H'low 9E 50
CO6: Gt Hork 7J 159
DA1: Cray 9D 152
E10: Lon 4B 122
IG7: Chig 9G 92
SS7: Thund 8B 118
Glebelands Av. E18: Lon 6G 106
IG2: Ilf 2C 124
Glebe La. CM0: Deng 3E 36
CM6: L Eas 6F 13
Glebe Mdw. CM3: Gt Walt 5G 57
Glebe Rd. CM1: Chelm 8K 59
CM5: Chip 8K 67
CM9: Mal 3E 214
CM11: Rams B 8F 100
CO2: Colc 4K 173
CO5: K'dn 3J 211
CO5: Tip 6C 226
RM10: Dag 8N 125
RM13: Rain 3G 142
SS11: W'fd 9M 101
Glebe, The CB11: Saf W 6D 218
CM3: Pur 8K 215 (4G 35)
CM20: H'low 1D 54
CM22: Else 3K 199
CO5: Pel 3E 26
Glebe Vw. CM2: Gall 7C 72
Glebe Way CM0: Bur C 2D 196
CO13: Frin S 9J 181
CO15: Jay 5E 188
DA8: Eri 4C 152
IG8: Wfd G 2J 107
RM11: Horn 2J 127
SS7: Had 3M 135
GLEMSFORD 2G 9
Glen Av. CO3: Colc 8J 165 (6D 16)
Glenavon Rd. E15: Lon 9E 122
Glenbervie Dr. SS9: Lgh S 4E 136
Glencoe Av. IG2: Ilf 2C 124
Glencoe Dr. RM10: Dag 6M 125
SS11: W'fd 8A 102
Glen Ct. SS7: Ben 2H 135
Glencree CM11: Bill 2M 99
Glen Cres. IG8: Wfd G 3H 107
Glencrofts SS5: Hock 1E 120
Glendale CM3: S Fer 8L 89
Glendale Av. RM6: Chad H 2H 125
Glendale Cl. CM15: Shenf 7H 97
Glendale Gdns. SS9: Lgh S 5C 136
Glendale Gro. CO4: Colc 4C 166
Glendale Rd. CM0: Bur C 2E 196
DA8: Eri 2A 152
Glendale Way SE28: Lon 7H 141
Glendower Rd. E4: Lon 7D 90
Gleneagles SS7: Ben 1B 134
Gleneagles Cl. RM3: H Wood 4K 111
Gleneagles Rd. SS9: Lgh S 1B 136
Gleneagles Way CM3: Hat P 2M 61
Glenester Cl. EN11: Hod 2A 52
GLEN FABA 4E 52
Glen Faba Rd. CM19: Roy 5E 52 (7E 20)
Glenfield Rd. SS17: Corr 9C 132
Glengall Rd. IG8: Wfd G 3G 107
Glenham Dr. IG2: Ilf 9A 108
Glen Hazel CM15: Hook E 5G 83
Glenhurst Mans. SS1: Sth S 6N 137
Glenhurst Rd. SS2: Sth S 4M 137
Glenmead IG9: Buck H 7J 91
Glenmere SS16: Van 4E 132
Glenmere Pk. Av. SS7: Ben 3H 135
Glenmore St. SS2: Sth S 5B 138
Glenmore Way IG11: Bark 2F 140
Glenny Rd. IG11: Bark 8B 124
Glenparke Rd. E7: Lon 8H 123
Glenridding SS7: Ben 1D 134
Glen Ri. IG8: Wfd G 3H 107
Glen Rd. SS7: Ben 1E 134
SS9: Lgh S 6F 136
SS16: Van 1G 132
Glenside CM11: Bill 6M 99
IG7: Chig 3A 108
Glen, The RM13: Rain 4G 142
SS5: Hull 4L 103
SS6: Ray 7L 119
SS16: Van 2H 133
SS17: Stan H 2A 148
Glenthorne Gdns. IG5: Ilf 7N 107
Glenton Cl. RM1: Romf 4C 110
Glenton Way RM1: Romf 4C 110
Glentress Cl. CO4: Colc 4D 166
Glenway Cl. CO6: Gt Hork 7J 159
Glenwood SS8: Can I 9F 134
Glenwood Av. RM13: Rain 4E 142
SS0: Wclf S 4J 137
SS5: Hock 2E 120
Glenwood Av. SS9: Lgh S 8A 120
Glenwood Ct. E18: Lon 7G 106
Glenwood Dr. RM2: Romf 9E 110
Glenwood Gdns. IG2: Ilf 9N 107
SS16: Lang H 2G 131
Gleten Rd. SS8: Can I 1K 151
Glisson Sq. CO2: Colc 2J 173
Globe Cl. CO5: Tip 5D 226
Globe Cres. CM23: Farnh 6J 11
Globe Ind. Est. RM17: Grays 3M 155
Globe Rd. E2: Lon 6C 38
(not continuous)
E1: Lon 6C 38
E15: Lon 7F 122
IG8: Wfd G 3J 107
RM11: Horn 1E 126
GLOBE TOWN 6C 38
Globe Wlk. CO5: Tip 5D 226
Glossop Ho. *RM3: Romf 2J 111*
(off Lindfield Rd.)
Gloucester Av. CM2: Chelm 3B 72 (2A 34)
CM9: Mal 7B 214
CO2: Colc 3K 173
RM11: Horn 8L 111
RM16: Grays 9M 145
RM18: E Til 3L 157
SS6: Ray 7N 119
Gloucester Ct. RM18: Til 7B 156
Gloucester Cres. CM1: Chelm 6J 59
Gloucester Gdns. CM7: Brain 4K 193
IG1: Ilf 2L 123
Gloucester M. E10: Lon 2A 122
Gloucester Park Swimming Pool 9B 116
Gloucester Pl. CM12: Bill 3J 99
Gloucester Rd. CM15: Pil H 4E 96
E10: Lon 2A 122
E11: Lon 9H 107
E12: Lon 5M 123
RM1: Romf 1C 126
Gloucester Ter. SS1: Sth S 8D 138
Glovers Fld. CM15: Kel H 7C 82
Glovershotts CM1: Broom 1K 59
Glovers La. CM17: H'wd 8K 55
Glyders SS7: Ben 5E 134
Glynde Way SS2: Sth S 5D 138
Glynn Rd. CM0: Bur C 3D 196
Goat Hall La. CM2: Chelm 8A 72 (3K 33)
Goat Ho. La. CM3: Haz 7L 75 (3F 35)
Goat Lodge Rd. CM9: Gt Tot 1M 229 (5H 25)
Goatsmoor La. CM4: Stock 2A 100 (6K 33)
CM11: Bill 3N 99 (6K 33)
Goatswood La.
RM4: N'side, Noak H 6F 94 (7B 32)
Gobions SS16: Bas 2B 132
Gobions Av. RM5: Col R 4B 110
Goda Cl. CM8: Wthm 7A 230
Goddard Rd. RM16: Grays 8K 145
Goddards Way IG1: Ilf 3C 124
Goddard Way CB10: Saf W 2D 218
CM2: Chelm 9A 60
Goddarts Ho. E17: Lon 7A 106
Godden Lodge SS7: Thund 9F 118
Godfrey's M. CM2: Chelm 1C 72
Godfrey Way CM6: Gt D 1K 203
Godlings Way CM7: Brain 6G 193 (7C 14)
Godman Rd. RM16: Grays 1C 156
Godmans La. CO6: M Tey 3F 170
Godric Pl. CM7: Brain 5G 193
Godric Rd. CM8: Wthm 7B 230
Godsafe CM17: H'low 9K 51
Godstow Rd. SE2: Lon 9G 141
Godwin Cl. CO9: Hals 5J 207
E4: Lon 8C 76
Godwin Rd. E7: Lon 6H 123
Godwit Ct. CO5: K'dn 3L 211
Goff's La. CO16: T Sok 6D 18
EN7: Chesh, G Oak 3B 30
GOFFS OAK 3B 30
Goings La. CO5: W Mer 3C 228
Goings Wharf Ind. Est. CM9: Mal 3D 214
Goirle Av. SS8: Can I 1J 151
Goldace RM17: Grays 4J 155
Gold Berry Mead CM3: S Fer 2J 103
Gold Cl. CM22: Else 1J 199
Goldcrest Cl. CO4: A'lgh, Colc 7F 166
SE28: Lon 7H 141
Goldcrest Dr. CM11: Bill 7L 99
Goldenacres CM1: Chelm 3A 60
Goldencross M. SS4: R'fd 2J 121
Golden Cross Pde. *SS4: R'fd 2J 121*
(off Ashingdon Rd.)
Golden Cross Rd. SS4: R'fd 1J 121
Golden Dawn Way CO4: Colc 5M 165
Golden La. CB10: R'ter 6F 7
CO16: T Sok 4J 179 (7D 18)
EC1: Lon 6B 38
Golden Lion La. CO12: Har 2N 209
Golden Mnr. Dr. SS7: Thund 1F 134
Golden Noble Hill CO1: Colc 9A 166
Golden Pde. *E17: Lon 7C 106*
(off Wood St.)
Golden Sq. CO6: Wak C 3A 16
Goldfinch Cl. CO4: Colc 8F 166
Goldfinch La. SS7: Thund 8G 118
Goldfinch Rd. SE28: Lon 9C 140
GOLDHANGER 2K 201 (7A 26)
Goldhanger Cl. SS6: Ray 4G 119
Goldhanger Ct. CM7: Brain 8M 193
Goldhanger Cross SS14: Bas 8F 116
Goldhanger Rd. CM9: H'bri, Mal 3E 214 (1J 35)
Goldhaze Ct. IG8: Wfd G 4J 107
Golding Ct. IG1: Ilf 5N 123
Golding Cres. SS17: Stan H 2N 147
Goldingham Av. IG10: Lou 1B 92
Goldingham Dr. CM7: Brain 8J 193
Goldings CM23: Bis S 9A 220
Goldings Cres. SS16: Van 3F 132
Goldings Hill IG10: Lou 6M 77 (5G 31)
Goldings Ri. IG10: Lou 9N 77
Goldings Rd. IG10: Lou 9N 77
Golding Thoroughfare CM2: Chelm 7A 60
Goldington Cres. CM12: Bill 3H 99
Golding Way CO16: St O 8M 183
Goldlay Av. CM2: Chelm 2D 72
Goldlay Gdns. CM2: Chelm 1D 72
Goldlay Rd. CM2: Chelm 1D 72
Goldmer Cl. SS3: Shoe 6G 138
Goldsands Rd. CM0: S'min 4E 222
CM9: S'min 5D 36
Goldsborough Cres. E4: Lon 8B 90
Goldsel Rd. BR8: Crock 7A 46
Goldsmere Ct. RM11: Horn 3J 127
Goldsmith Av. E12: Lon 8L 123
RM7: Rush G 2M 125
Goldsmith Dr. SS6: Ray 9J 103
(not continuous)
Goldsmith Rd. E10: Lon 3A 122
Goldsmiths CM18: H'low 5D 54
RM17: Grays 4J 155
SS16: Lang H 5J 131
Goldsmiths Av. SS17: Corr, Stan H 2A 148
Goldsmith's Row E2: Lon 6C 38
Goldsmiths Wharf RM17: Grays 5K 155
Golds Nursery Bus. Pk. CM22: Else 1K 199
Gold St. CB10: Saf W 4C 218
DA12: Ludd, Sole S 7H 47
Goldsworthy Dr. SS3: Gt W 4N 139
Golfe Rd. IG1: Ilf 5C 124
Golf Grn. Rd. CO15: Jay 4E 188 (5C 28)
Golf Ride SS7: Ben 3D 134
Goodall Rd. E11: Lon 5C 122
Goodchild Way CO9: Gt Yel 2D 206
GOOD EASTER 5G 23
Gooderham Ho. RM16: Grays 9D 146
Goodey Cl. CO1: Colc 1A 174
Goodey Rd. IG11: Bark 9E 124
Goodfellows Chase CM6: Tilty 6F 13
Goodge St. W1: Lon 7A 38
Goodge Street Station (Tube) 7A 38
Goodlake Cl. CO12: Har 5H 209
Goodliffe Pk. CM23: Bchgr 7A 220
Goodman Rd. E10: Lon 2C 122
Goodmans SS3: Gt W 3M 139
Goodmans La. CM3: Gt L 9K 203 (3B 24)
GOODMAYES 3F 124 (4J 39)
Goodmayes Av. IG3: Ilf 3F 124
Goodmayes La. IG3: Ilf 6F 124 (4J 39)
Goodmayes Retail Pk. RM6: Chad H 3G 125
Goodmayes Rd. IG3: Ilf 3F 124 (4J 39)
Goodmayes Station (Rail) 3F 124 (4J 39)
Goodmayes Wlk. SS12: W'fd 1L 117
Goods Way NW1: Lon 6A 38
Goodview Rd. SS14: Bas 5B 116
Goodwins Cl. CB11: L'bry 2A 218
Goodwood Av. CM13: Hut 5B 98
RM12: Horn 6J 127
Goodwood Cl. EN11: Hod 4A 52
SS7: Thund 8G 119
Goojerat Rd. CO2: Colc 1L 173
Goor Av. SS8: Can I 1K 151
GOOSEBERRY GREEN 5H 99 (7J 33)
Gooseberry Grn. CM12: Bill 5H 99
Goose Cotts. SS11: Raw 7E 102
GOOSE GREEN
CO11 5B 18
CO16 6C 18
SG13 7C 20
Goose La.
CM22: Gt Hal, L Hall 3M 213 (3A 22)
Gooseley La. E6: Lon 4A 140
(Claps Ga. La.)
E6: Lon 3A 140
(Vicarage La.)
Gooshays Dr. RM3: Romf 2J 111 (1C 40)
Gooshays Gdns. RM3: Romf 3J 111
Gordon Av. E4: Lon 3E 106
RM12: Horn 4D 126
Gordon Cl. CM12: Bill 5H 99
E17: Lon 1A 122
RM18: E Til 5M 157
Gordon Dr. CO4: Colc 2C 166
Gordon Hill EN2: Enf 6B 30
Gordon Hill Station (Rail) 6A 30
Gordon Pl. SS1: Sth S 6L 137
Gordon Rd. CM2: Chelm 4B 72
CM15: Shenf 7K 97
CO12: Har 5K 209
DA17: Belv 2A 152
E4: Lon 6E 90
E11: Lon 1G 122
E15: Lon 6C 122
E18: Lon 5H 107
EN9: Wal A 4A 76
IG1: Ilf 5C 124
IG11: Bark 1D 140
RM6: Chad H 1L 125
RM16: Grays 9A 146
SS1: Sth S 6L 137
SS9: Lgh S 4A 136
SS14: Bas 1E 132
SS17: Corr, Stan H 1A 148 (6K 41)
SS17: Horn H 2H 147
Gordons SS13: Pits 1H 133
Gordon Sq. WC1: Lon 6A 38
Gordon Way CO12: Har 5K 209
Gorefield CM22: Tak 3C 224
Gorefield Rd. CM22: Tak 5N 221
Gorefield Rdbt. CM22: Tak 5N 221
Gore La. SG11: H Cro 2E 20
GORE PIT 1M 211 (2J 25)

Gore Rd. CM77: Rayne 6C 192 (7B 14)
DA2: Dart 4D 46
GORESBROOK INTERCHANGE 2L 141 (6K 39)
Goresbrook Leisure Cen. 1J 141
Goresbrook Rd. RM9: Dag 1G 141 (6J 39)
Gore, The CM77: Rayne 6C 192
SS14: Bas 9B 116
Goring Cl. RM5: Col R 5A 110
Goring Gdns. RM8: Dag 6H 125
Goring Rd. CO4: Colc 6C 166
RM10: Dag 8B 126
Gorse Hill DA4: F'ham, Fawk 7C 46
Gorse La. CO5: Tip 7D 226
CO15: Clac S 5L 185 (3E 28)
Gorse La. Ind. Est. CO15: Clac S 5M 185
Gorse Rd. BR5: Orp 7A 46
Gorse Wlk. CO4: Colc 8D 166
(not continuous)
Gorse Way CO3: S'way 2E 172
CO15: Jay 5D 188
Gorseway RM7: Rush G 3C 126
Gosbecks Rd. CO2: Colc 3H 173 (7D 16)
Gosbeck's Vw. CO2: Colc, King 4H 173
GOSFIELD 8L 201 (4E 14)
Gosfield Cl. SS6: Ray 4G 118
Gosfield Hall 8K 201
Gosfield Lake Resort CO9: Gosf 9K 201
Gosfield Rd. CM7: Brain 6M 191 (5D 14)
CM7: Weth 3B 14
CO2: Colc 6A 174
RM8: Dag 4M 125
Gosford Gdns. IG4: Ilf 9M 107
Goshawk Dr. CM2: Chelm 5C 72
GOSLAND GREEN 1D 8
Goslings CM8: Sil E 7K 217
Goslings, The SS3: Shoe 7L 139
Gosport Dr. RM12: Horn 8G 126
Gosport Rd. E17: Lon 3D 38
Gosset St. E2: Lon 6C 38
Gossetts, The CM6: Mar R 6F 23
Goss Hill BR8: Swan 5B 46
Goswell Rd. EC1: Lon 6A 38
Gough Rd. E15: Lon 6F 122
Gould Cl. CM5: M'ton 1B 32
Gouldings Av. CO14: Walt 6L 181
Goulds Cotts. RM4: Abr 2G 92
Goulds Rd. CO8: Alph 1J 15
Goul La. CB10: Saf W 4C 218
Goulton Rd. CM1: Broom 2J 59
Gourney Gro. RM16: Grays 7L 145
Government Row EN3: Enf 8A 76
Govier Cl. E15: Lon 9E 122
Gowan Brae SS7: Ben 1B 134
Gowan Cl. SS7: Ben 1B 134
Gowan Ct. SS7: Ben 1B 134
Gower Ho. E17: Lon 7B 106
Gower Rd. E7: Lon 8G 123
Gowers Av. CM2: Gt Bad 4F 72
Gowers La. RM16: Ors 9B 146
Gowers, The CM20: H'low 1F 54
Gower St. NW1: Lon 6A 38
Goya Ri. SS3: Shoe 6L 139
Grace Cl. IG6: Ilf 3E 108
Graces Cl. CM8: Wthm 8D 230
Graces La. CM3: L Bad 1B 74 (1D 34)
Grace's Wlk. CM3: L Bad, S'don 9F 60
Graces Wlk. CO13: Frin S 8K 181
Graften Pl. CM2: Chelm 7B 60
Grafton Gdns. RM8: Dag 4K 125
Grafton Rd. CO12: Har 3M 209
RM8: Dag 4K 125
SS8: Can I 3J 151
Graham Cl. CM12: Bill 3K 99
CM13: Hut 4M 97
SS5: Hock 9D 104
SS17: Stan H 1N 147
Grahame Ct. SS12: W'fd 2L 117
Grahame Ho. SS2: Sth S 3A 138
Graham Mans. *IG11: Bark 9F 124*
(off Lansbury Av.)
Graham Rd. E8: Lon 5C 38
Grainger Cl. SS2: Sth S 5M 137
Grainger Rd. SS2: Sth S 5M 137
Grainger Rd. Ind. Est. SS2: Sth S 5M 137
Gramer Cl. E11: Lon 4D 122
Grampian SS0: Wclf S 5K 137
Grampian Gro. CM1: Chelm 5F 58
Granaries, The EN9: Wal A 4E 76
Granary Cl. CM3: Latch 8M 211
Granary Ct. CM6: Gt D 3L 203
CM21: Saw 2K 51
Granary Mans. *SE28: Lon 9B 140*
(off Erebus Dr.)
Granary Mdw. CM15: Wy G 6H 83
Granary, The CM19: Roy 2H 53
Granchester Ct. *CO4: Colc 3C 166*
(off Bignell Cft.)
Grand Ct. W. *SS9: Lgh S 6E 136*
(off Grand Dr.)
Grand Dr. SS9: Lgh S 6E 136 (5H 43)
Grand Pde. N4: Lon 3A 38
SS9: Lgh S 6E 136 (5H 43)
Grandview Rd. SS7: Thund 8F 118
Grange Av. CM3: May 9M 213 (4A 36)
IG8: Wfd G 3G 106
SS7: Had 1N 135
SS12: W'fd 1J 117
Grange Cl. CM13: Ingve 2M 113
CO9: Hals 7K 207
CO14: Walt 7K 181
IG8: Wfd G 4G 106
SS9: Lgh S 3D 136
Grange Ct. CM2: Chelm 3A 72
CO16: Clac S 9E 184
EN9: Wal A 4C 76
Grange Ct. IG10: Lou 4K 91
Grange Cres. IG7: Chig 2C 108
SE28: Lon 6H 141
Grange Farm CO2: Colc 2D 174
Grange Farm Av.
IP11: Felix 1K 19
Grange Farm Rd. CO2: Colc 2D 174
Grange Gdns. SS1: Sth S 6N 137
SS6: Ray 4H 119
Grange Grn. CM6: Tilty 5E 12
GRANGE HILL 3C 108 (2H 39)
Grange Hill CO6: Cogg 4K 197 (7H 15)
CO9: G'std G 5G 15
Grange Hill Station (Tube) 1C 108 (1H 39)
Grange Ho. DA8: Eri 7E 152
Grange La. CM6: L Dun 8B 212 (1H 23)
CM11: D'ham 4H 101
CM19: Roy 3J 53
DA3: Hley 7F 47
Grange Pde. CM11: Bill 9L 99
GRANGE PARK 7A 30
Grange Pk. Dr. SS9: Lgh S 4E 136
Grange Pk. Rd. E10: Lon 3B 122
Grange Park Station (Rail) 7A 30
Granger Av. CM9: Mal 7B 214
Grange Rd. CB2: Dux, Hey 4H 5
CB10: I'tn 5J 5
CM0: T'ham 3K 225 (3E 36)
CM3: Ples 2A 56 (4J 23)
CM8: W Bis 3J 229 (6G 25)
CM11: Bill 9L 99 (1K 41)
CO5: Gt Br, Tip 6A 226 (4J 25)
CO6: Gt Hork 9J 159
CO11: A'lgh, Law, L Bro 1C 168 (4J 17)
CO12: Har 5J 209
E10: Lon 3A 122
E13: Lon 6E 38
IG1: Ilf 6A 124
IP11: Felix 1K 19
RM3: Romf 3F 110
RM15: Ave 8N 143
RM17: Grays 4L 155
SE1: Lon 7B 38
SS7: Thund 7E 118
(not continuous)
SS9: Lgh S 5C 136
SS11: W'fd 6K 101
SS13: Pits 7M 117
Granger Row CM1: Chelm 5H 59
Granger Way RM1: Romf 1E 126
Grange, The EN11: Hod 6A 52
Grange Way CO2: Colc 2D 174
DA8: Eri 5F 152
IG8: Wfd G 1J 107
Grangeway SS7: Thund 9G 119
Grange Way Bus. Pk. CO2: Colc 3D 174
Grangeway Gdns. IG4: Ilf 9L 107
Grangewood SS7: Ben 1D 134
Grangewood Av. RM13: Rain 4G 142
RM16: Grays 1A 156
Grangewood Cl. CM13: Brtwd 9J 97
Granites Chase CM11: Bill 1A 116
Granleigh Rd. E11: Lon 4E 122
GRANSMORE GREEN 7K 13
Granta Cl. CB10: Gt Che 9D 202
Grant Cl. SS12: W'fd 2M 117
Grant Ct. *E4: Lon 7C 90*
(off Ridgeway, The)
Grantham Av. CM77: Gt N 1B 204
Grantham Ct. CO1: Colc 8A 166
RM6: Chad H 2L 125
Grantham Gdns. RM6: Chad H 1L 125
Grantham Rd. CO6: Gt Hork 9J 159
E12: Lon 6N 123
Grantham Way RM16: Grays 8K 145
Grantley Cl. CO6: Cop 1M 171
Grantock Rd. E17: Lon 5D 106
Granton Av. RM14: Upm 5K 127
Granton Rd. IG3: Ilf 3F 124
Granville Cl. CM12: Bill 3H 99
CO6: W Ber 4F 164
SS7: Ben 2E 134
Granville Gdns. EN11: Hod 1A 52
Granville Rd. CM16: Epp 8G 64
CO1: Colc 1B 174
CO15: Clac S 1K 189
E17: Lon 1B 122
E18: Lon 6H 107
IG1: Ilf 3A 124
SS5: Hock 6E 104
Granville Ter. CM0: Bur C 4E 196
Granville Way CO7: B'sea 6F 182
Grapnells SS16: Van 2G 133
Grasby Cl. CO7: W'hoe 4H 175
Grasmead Av. SS9: Lgh S 4E 136
Grasmere Av. SS5: Hull 5J 103
Grasmere Cl. CM77: Gt N 2C 204
IG10: Lou 1M 91
Grasmere Gdns. CO13: Walt 7J 181
IG4: Ilf 9M 107
Grasmere Ho. *SS6: Ray 5L 119*
(off Derwent Av.)
Grasmere Rd. DA7: Bexh 7A 152
SS7: Thund 9E 118
SS8: Can I 2E 150
Grassfields CO13: Walt 8H 181
GRASS GREEN 6B 8
Grasshaven Way SE28: Lon 8E 140
(not continuous)
Grassmere CO4: Colc 2B 166
Grassmere Rd. RM11: Horn 8K 111
Grass Rd. CO9: Hals 8J 207
(Oak Rd.)
RM18: E Til 4K 157
Gratmore Grn. SS16: Van 3F 132
Gravel Cl. IG7: Chig 8F 92
Gravel Hill CO6: Nay 1D 16
DA6: Bexh 3A 46
IG10: H Bee 8G 77 (5F 31)
Gravel Hill Way CO12: Har 6G 209
Gravel La. IG7: Chig 4E 92 (7J 31)
Gravelly La. SG11: Brau 6E 10
Gravel Pit Hill SG8: Thri 3H 5
Gravel Rd. SS9: Lgh S 7A 120
Gravel, The CO6: Cogg 3K 197 (7H 15)
GRAVESEND
DA12 3H 47
SG11 6G 11
Gravesend & Northfleet F.C. 3F 47
Gravesend Rd. DA12: Shorne 5K 47
ME3: High 5K 47
Gravesend Station (Rail) 4H 47
Graves Hall Rd.
CO9: Cas H, Sib H 4H 219 (1D 14)
Gray Av. RM8: Dag 3L 125
Gray Gdns. RM13: Rain 8E 126
Graylands CM16: They B 7C 78
RM17: Grays 4H 155
Grayling Cl. CM7: Gt N 7G 193
Grayling Dr. CO4: Colc 6F 166
Gray Rd. CO3: Colc 9L 165
GRAYS 4K 155 (1F 47)
Grays Athletic F.C. 4L 155
Grays Av. SS16: Bas 5L 131
Grays Brewery Yd. CM2: Chelm 9L 59
Grays Cl. CO5: W Mer 3C 228
Grays Cotts. CO1: Colc 8B 166
Grays Ct. RM10: Dag 9N 125
Gray's End Cl. RM17: Grays 1K 155
Gray's Inn Rd. WC1: Lon 6A 38
Gray's La. CM7: Weth 6E 228 (2B 14)
Grays Mead CO9: Sib H 5J 219
Graysons Cl. SS6: Ray 5L 119
Grays Shop. Cen. RM17: Grays 4K 155
Grays Station (Rail) 4K 155 (2F 47)
Grays Wlk. CM13: Hut 6N 97
GREAT ABINGTON 1B 6
GREAT AMWELL 5D 20
Gt. Augur St. CM17: H'low 2J 55
GREAT BADDOW 3G 73 (2B 34)
GREAT BARDFIELD 2C 202 (3K 13)
GREAT BENTLEY 6K 177 (1A 28)
Gt. Bentley Rd. CO7: Frat, Thorr 3F 176 (1K 27)
Great Bentley Station (Rail) 7K 177 (1A 28)
GREAT BERRY 1H 131 (3J 41)
Gt. Berry Farm Chase SS16: Lang H 2J 131
Gt. Berry La. SS16: Lang H 2J 131
(not continuous)
Gt. Blunts Cotts. CM4: Stock 2L 99
GREAT BRAXTED 4J 25
Great Brays CM18: H'low 4F 54
GREAT BROMLEY 6D 168 (5K 17)
Gt. Burches Rd. SS7: Thund 8G 118
GREAT BURSTEAD 2L 115 (1K 41)
GREAT CAMBRIDGE JUNCTION 1B 38
Gt. Cambridge Rd. N9: Lon 1B 38
N17: Lon 2B 38
N18: Lon 2B 38
GREAT CANFIELD 2E 22
Gt. Canfield Rd. CM6: Tak 1D 22
CM22: Tak 3D 224 (1D 22)
GREAT CHESTERFORD 8D 202 (4A 6)
Gt. Chesterford Ct. CB10: Gt Che 8C 202
Great Chesterford Station (Rail) 9C 202 (4A 6)
GREAT CHISHILL 6G 5
Great Chishill Postmill 6F 5
GREAT CLACTON 9J 185 (3D 28)
Great Cob CM1: Chelm 6N 59
GREAT CORNARD 5K 9
Great Cullings RM7: Rush G 4C 126
Gt. Dover St. SE1: Lon 7B 38
GREAT DUNMOW 3L 203 (7F 13)
Great Dunmow Mus., The 2L 203
Gt. Eastern Av. SS2: Sth S 5M 137
Gt. Eastern Ct. CO14: Walt 7M 181
Gt. Eastern Rd. CM14: War 1F 112
E15: Lon 9D 122 (5E 38)
SS5: Hock 2D 120
Gt. Eastern St. EC2: Lon 6B 38
GREAT EASTON 6F 13
Greate Ho. Farm Rd. CO2: Lay H 9H 173
Greatfields Rd. IG11: Bark 1C 140
Gt. Fleete Way IG11: Bark 2H 141
Gt. Fox Mdw. CM15: Kel H 8C 82
Gt. Galley Cl. IG11: Bark 3G 141
Gt. Gardens Rd. RM11: Horn 1F 126
Gt. Gibcracks Chase CM2: S'don 8A 74
Gt. Godfreys CM1: Writ 1H 71
Gt. Gregorie SS16: Bas 2N 131
Gt. Gregories La. CM16: Epp 3D 78
Gt. Hadham Rd. CM23: Bis S, Thor 2H 21
SG10: M Hud, Thor 2H 21
GREAT HALLINGBURY 2A 22
Great Harrods CO14: Walt 7K 181
Gt. Hays SS9: Lgh S 1B 136
GREAT HENNY 7J 9
GREAT HOLLAND 1D 186 (2F 29)
GREAT HOLLAND COMMON 3A 186 (2F 29)
Gt. Holland Comn. Rd.
CO15: Clac S 3A 186 (2E 28)
Great Holland Pits Nature Reserve 2B 186
GREAT HORKESLEY 9J 159 (3D 16)
GREAT HORMEAD 4F 11
Greathouse Chase SS17: Fob 8D 132
Gt. Knightleys SS15: Lain 9M 115 (3K 41)
Great Lawn CM5: Chip 6L 67
GREAT LEIGHS 7K 203 (3B 24)
Great Leighs By-Pass
CM3: Gt L, Gt N 9J 203 (3B 24)
CM77: Gt N 4B 204
Gt. Leighs Way SS13: Bas 6K 117
Great Leylands CM18: H'low 4F 54
GREAT MAPLESTEAD 1F 15
Gt. Maplestead Rd. CO9: Gest 7F 9
Gt. Marlborough St. W1: Lon 7A 38
Great Mead SS3: Shoe 5J 139
Great Mdw. EN10: Brox 1A 62
Gt. Mistley SS16: Van 1D 132
GREAT MUNDEN 7C 10
Gt. Nelmes Chase RM11: Horn 9K 111
GREAT NOTLEY 1C 204 (1C 24)
Gt. Notley Av. CM77: Gt N 3B 204 (1C 24)
Great Notley Country Pk. 1A 204
Gt. Notley Rdbt. CM77: Bla N 4C 204
Gt. Oak Ct. CO9: Gt Yel 3D 206
GREAT OAKLEY 7C 204 (5E 18)
Great Oaks CM13: Hut 5L 97
IG7: Chig 1B 108
SS14: Bas 9B 116
Gt. Owl Rd. IG7: Chig 9N 91
Gt. Oxcroft SS15: Lain 9K 115
GREAT OXNEY GREEN 1H 71 (1J 33)
GREAT PARNDON 5A 54 (7G 21)
Great Plumtree CM20: H'low 1E 54
Gt. Portland St. W1: Lon 7A 38
Great Portland Street Station (Tube) 6A 38
Gt. Prestons La. CM4: Stock 8C 86 (5A 34)
Gt. Queen St. WC2: Lon 7A 38
Gt. Ranton SS13: Pits 7K 117
Gt. Ropers La. CM14: Gt War 3D 112 (2E 40)
GREAT SALING 6A 14
Gt. Saling SS11: W'fd 1A 118
GREAT SAMPFORD 3K 205 (1G 13)
Gt. Smials CM3: S Fer 2J 103
Great Spenders SS14: Bas 7E 116
Great Sq. CM7: Brain 5H 193
GREAT STAMBRIDGE 2K 43
Great Stony Arts & Education Cen. 6L 67
Gt. Stony Pk. CM5: Chip 6L 67
GREAT TEY 2E 170 (5K 15)
Gt. Tey Rd. CO6: Gt Tey, L Tey 2F 170 (6K 15)
GREAT THURLOW 1J 7
GREAT TOTHAM 6J 25
GREAT TOTHAM NORTH 7J 205 (5J 25)
Gt. Totham Rd. CM8: W Bis 2L 229 (5H 25)
GREAT TOTHAM SOUTH 3N 229
GREAT WAKERING 2L 139 (4C 44)
Great Wakering Sports Cen. 2K 139
GREAT WALDINGFIELD 4K 9
GREAT WALTHAM 5H 57 (5K 23)
Great Waltham Guildhall 4H 57 (5K 23)
GREAT WARLEY 5D 112 (2E 40)
Gt. Warley St. CM13: Gt War 5D 112 (2E 40)
Gt. Wheatley Rd. SS6: Ray 5G 118 (2E 42)
(not continuous)
GREAT WIGBOROUGH 4D 26
GREAT WRATTING 1K 7
Great Yd. CO9: Hals 6K 207
GREAT YELDHAM 3D 206 (6D 8)
Gt. Yeldham Rd. CO9: Gt Yel, Top 7C 8
Greaves Cl. IG11: Bark 9C 124
Grebe Cl. CM3: May 8L 213
E7: Lon 7F 122
IG11: Bark 4F 140
Grebe Crest RM20: W Thur 2D 154
Greding Wlk. CM13: Hut 8L 97
Greenacre Gdns. E17: Lon 8C 106
Greenacre La. CM4: Stock 9N 85
Greenacre M. SS9: Lgh S 4D 136
Greenacres CM16: Epp 8E 64
CO4: Colc 4M 165
Green Acres CO6: Cogg 4K 197
Greenacres CO15: Clac S 8L 185
SS7: Had 3L 135
Greenacres Cl. RM13: Rain 3J 143
Grn. Acres Rd. CO2: Lay H 9G 173
Green Av. SS8: Can I 2E 150
Greenaway Cvn. Pk. *CM24: Stan M 5F 220*
(off Old Burylodge La.)
Grn. Bank Cl. E4: Lon 8C 90
Greenbank Cl. RM3: Romf 9H 95
Green Banks RM14: Upm 4B 128
Greenbanks SS9: Lgh S 4F 136
Green Cl. CM1: Chelm 7M 59
CM1: Writ 1K 71
CM3: Hat P 3N 61
CM16: E Grn 3A 64
Green Ct. Rd. BR8: Crock 7A 46
Green Dragon La. N21: Lon 7A 30
Greendyke SS8: Can I 9F 134
GREEN END
SG12 7B 10
SG9 2B 10
Grn. End La. CO13: Gt Hol 9D 180
Greene Vw. CM7: Brain 8K 193
Green Farm La. DA12: Shorne 4K 47
Green Farm Rd. CO6: Coln E 2E 198 (3H 15)
Greenfield CM8: Wthm 6D 230
Greenfield Dr. CO6: Gt Tey 2D 170
Greenfield Gdns. RM9: Dag 1J 141
Greenfield Ho's. CO2: B'ch 8D 172
Greenfield Rd. RM9: Dag 9H 125
Greenfields CM12: Bill 8J 99
CM24: Stan M 2D 220
CO9: Gosf 9L 201
Gibson Cl. CO13: Walt 7J 181
IG10: Lou 3N 91
Greenfields Cl. CM12: Bill 8J 99
CM13: Gt War 3F 112
IG10: Lou 3N 91
Greenfield St. EN9: Wal A 4C 76
Greenfields Way CB9: H'hll 3J 7
Greenfinch End CO4: Colc 7F 166
Greenford Rd. CO15: Clac S 1G 189
Greengate Pde. IG2: Ilf 1C 124

Greengates Home Pk. CO16: L Cla 1G **184**
Greengate St. E13: Lon. 6F **39**
Green Glade CM16: They B 7D **78**
Green Glades RM11: Horn 1K **127**
Greenhaven Dr. SE28: Lon. 6G **140**
Greenheys Dr. E18: Lon 7F **106**
Greenhill IG9: Buck H 7J **91**
Greenhill Gro. E12: Lon 6L **123**
Greenhills CM20: H'low 3D **54**
GREENHITHE. 9E 154 (3E 46)
Greenhithe for Bluewater Station (Rail). . . . 3E 46
Greenhurst Rd. CO7: B'sea 7F **182**
Greenlands SS4: R'fd 3J **121**
Green La. CM0: Bur C 1C **196** (6B **36**)
CM0: S'min 4C **36**
CM1: Rox 4M **217** (1H **33**)
(not continuous)
CM3: Alth 4A **36**
CM3: Gt Walt 7E **56** (5K **23**)
CM3: S Fer 9K **89**
CM4: B'more. 1G **83**
CM6: Gt D 2K **203**
CM8: Whi N. 2C **24**
CM9: L Tot 6K **25**
CM12: Bill, L Bur. 3E **114**
(Botney Hill Rd.)
CM12: L Bur 5J **115**
(New Rd.)
CM13: Dun 3E **114**
CM14: Brtwd. 7D **96**
CM14: Gt War. 4D **112**
CM14: Kel H 1N **95** (6D **32**)
(not continuous)
CM15: Pil H. 4F **96**
CM17: H'low 4M **55** (7K **21**)
CO4: Boxt. 3L **159** (2E **16**)
CO4: Colc 4E **166**
CO5: Tip 5D **226**
CO6: Aldh 6A **16**
CO6: Gt Hork. 1K **165**
CO7: A'lgh 6H **167** (5H **17**)
(Chapel La.)
CO7: A'lgh 9K **161**
(Colchester Rd.)
CO7: High 1H **17**
CO9: Ridg 7E **216**
CO11: Mist. 5J **163**
CO14: Walt 4N **181**
CO16: Wee H. 8E **178**
DA13: Meop 7H **47**
E4: Lon 9E **76**
EN9: Wal A 4J **77**
EN10: Brox 2B **62**
IG1: Ilf 4C **124** (4H **39**)
IG3: Ilf. 3G **124**
IG7: Chig 7B **92**
RM8: Dag. 3G **124** (4J **39**)
RM14: Ave, Upm. 1A **144**
RM16: N Stif, Ors 5L **145**
(not continuous)
SS8: Can I 2F **150**
SS9: Lgh S 8C **120**
SS16: Bas 2N **131**
Green Lanes N4: Lon 3A **38**
N8: Lon 3A **38**
N13: Lon 2A **38**
N16: Lon. 4A **38**
N21: Lon 2A **38**
Greenlawns CO16: L Cla. 3G **185**
Greenleafe Dr. IG6: Ilf 7A **108**
Greenleaf Rd. E17: Lon 7A **106**
Greenleas EN9: Wal A. 4E **76**
SS7: Thund 9H **119**
Green Man La. CM8: L Brax. 5H **25**
Grn. Manor Way DA11: N'fleet 9J **155**
GREEN MAN RDBT. 2F **122** (3E **38**)
Green Mead CM3: S Fer 1J **103**
Green Mdws. CM3: Dan 4G **75**
Green Oaks Cl. SS7: Ben 3E **134**
Greenock Way RM1: Romf 4C **110**
Green Pk. 7A 38
Green Park Station (Tube) 7A 38
Green Point E15: Lon 8E **122**
Green Ride CM16: Epp 5A **78**
IG10: Lou. 3J **91**
(not continuous)
Green Rd. CB11: Quen, Rick G 3C **216** (4A **12**)
DA2: Dart. 5E **46**
SS7: Ben. 5D **134**
Greens Cl., The IG10: Lou 1N **91**
Greens Farm La. CM11: Bill 6L **99** (7K **33**)
Greenshaw CM14: Brtwd 7E **96**
Greens Health & Fitness 1C 106
Green Side RM8: Dag. 3H **125**
Greenslade Rd. IG11: Bark. 9C **124**
Greensleeves Dr. CM14: Gt War. 2E **112**
Greensmill CO11: Law 3G **163**
GREENSTEAD 7E 166 (6F 17)
Greenstead CM21: Saw 3K **51**
Greenstead Av. IG8: Wfd G. 4J **107**
Greenstead Cl. CM13: Hut 6A **98**
IG8: Wfd G. 3J **107**
Greenstead Ct. CO1: Colc. 9D **166**
Greenstead Gdns. IG8: Wfd G. 3J **107**
GREENSTEAD GREEN 9M 207 (4F 15)
Greenstead Grn. Rd. CM77: Tye G 6F **15**
Greenstead Rd. CO1: Colc. 8C **166** (6F **17**)
CO2: Colc 9D **166**
Greenstead Rdbt. CO4: Colc 9D **166**
GREENSTED. 8H 67 (3B 32)
Greensted Cl. SS14: Bas 1G **133**
GREENSTED GREEN. 7F 66 (3B 32)
Greensted Rd. CM5: Chip, G'sted . . . 7E **66** (3B **32**)
IG10: Lou 6L **91**
Greensted Saxon Wooden Church. . .8H 67 (3B 32)
Greensted, The SS14: Bas 1G **132**
Greenstone M. E11: Lon 1G **122**
GREEN STREET
CM4 . . . . 4M 83 (4G 33)
SG11. . . . . 7H 11
Green St. CM4: Fry, Ing 3M **83** (4G **33**)
CM6: Gt Can 2D **22**
CM17: H'low 2H **55**
CM22: Else. 2M **221**
DA1: Dart 4C **46**
DA2: Dart 4C **46**
E7: Lon. 8H **123** (5F **39**)
E13: Lon. 8H **123** (5F **39**)
EN3: Enf 6C **30**
GREEN STREET GREEN 5E 46
Greensward La. SS5: Hock. 1D **120** (1H **43**)
Green's Yd. CO1: Colc 8M **165**
GREEN, THE. 4C 194 (2D 24)
Green, The CB10: Saf W. 2C **218**
CB11: Rick G 3B **216** (4A **12**)
CM1: Chelm 7H **59**
CM1: Chig J 3B **58**
CM1: Writ. 1K **71** (1J **33**)
CM3: Hat P 3N **61**
CM4: B'more 1H **83** (4F **33**)
CM7: Weth 8C 228
(off High St.)
CM16: They B 6D **78** (5H **31**)
(not continuous)
CO5: Fee 9A **170**
CO9: Wick P 7G **9**
CO10: Bor 4G **9**
CO10: T'std 7H **9**
CO11: Mist 4L **163**
CO12: Har 5G **209**
CO16: Clac S 2F **188**
E4: Lon. 7C **90** (7E **30**)
E11: Lon 1H **123**
E15: Lon 8E **122**
EN9: Wal A 4C **76**
IG8: Wfd G 2G **107**
IG9: Buck H. 7H **91**
N9: Lon 1C **38**
N14: Lon. 1A **38**
(not continuous)
N21: Lon. 7A **30**
RM3: Romf 8G **95**
RM4: Hav 9C **94**
RM13: Wen 7J **143**
RM15: S Ock. 3G **144**
RM16: Ors. 5C **146**
RM18: W Til 4G **156** (2H **47**)
SS9: Lgh S 8D **120**
SS17: Stan H 4M **147**
Green Trees CM16: Epp 1F **78**
Grn. Trees Av. CM3: Cold N 8K **197**
GREEN TYE 2H 21
Greenview *SS8: Can I. 9F 134*
(off Helmsdale)
Grn. View Pk. CO15: Clac S 7L **185**
Green Wlk. CM5: Chip 9K **67**
DA1: Cray 9D **152**
IG8: Wfd G. 3L **107** (2G **39**)
IG10: Lou 6L **91**
Green Wlk., The E4: Lon 7D **90**
Greenway CM11: Bill 7M **99**
CM13: Hut. 6K **97**
CM19: H'low 3L **53**
CO6: Coln E. 2E **198**
CO13: Frin S 9J **181**
Green Way IG8: Wfd G 2J **107**
Greenway RM3: H Wood 3M **111**
RM8: Dag 4H **125**
Greenway Av. E17: Lon 8D **106**
Greenway Cl. CO15: Clac S 6M **185**
Greenway Ct. IG1: Ilf 3N **123**
Greenway Gdns. CM77: Gt N 1D **204**
Greenways CB11: Saf W. 6D **218**
CM1: Chelm 5K **59**
CM9: Mal. 6B **214**
CO5: Fee 2L **211**
CO9: Gosf 9L **201**
SS1: Sth S. 7C **138**
SS4: R'fd. 5L **121**
SS7: Ben. 4C **134**
SS8: Can I 9F **134**
Greenways Ct. RM11: Horn 1H **127**
Greenways, The CO6: Cogg 2L **197**
Greenway, The CO15: Clac S. 6M **185**
SS11: Runw 5K **101**
Greenwich Way EN9: Enf 6C **76**
Greenwood Av. RM10: Dag 6N **125**
SS7: Ben 5E **134**
Greenwood Dr. E4: Lon 2D **106**
Greenwood Gdns. IG6: Ilf 4B **108**
Greenwood Gro. CO4: Colc. 4C **166**
Greenwood Mans. *IG11: Bark. 9F 124*
(off Lansbury Av.)
Greenwood Rd. IG7: Chig. 1G **108**
Greenyard EN9: Wal A 3C **76**
Greg Cl. E10: Lon 1C **122**
Gregory Cl. SS5: Hock. 3E **120**
Gregory M. EN9: Wal A. 2B **76**
Gregory Rd. RM6: Chad H 8J **109**
Gregory St. CO10: Sud 5J **9**
Gregson's Ride IG10: Lou 8N **77**
Grendel Way CO15: Hol S. 7C **186**
Grenfell Av. CO15: Hol S 6B **186**
RM12: Horn 3D **126**
Grenfell Cl. CO4: Colc 6C **166**
Grenfell Gdns. IG3: Ilf. 9E **108**
Grennan Cl. CM13: Ingve 3N **113**
Grenville Gdns. IG8: Wfd G 5J **107**
Grenville Rd. CM7: Brain 5G **193**
RM16: Chaf H 2E **154**
Gresham Cl. CM14: Brtwd 9F **96**
Gresham Ct. CM14: Brtwd 9F **96**
Gresham Dr. RM6: Chad H 9G **108**
Gresham Lodge E17: Lon 9B **106**
Gresham Rd. CM14: Brtwd 9F **96**
Gresley Cl. CO4: Colc. 5N **165**
Gresley Dr. CM7: Brain 6J **193**
Grested Ct. SS4: R'fd 5L **121**
Grevatt Lodge SS13: Pits 1J **133**
Greville Cl. CO14: Walt 2M **181**
Greville Rd. E17: Lon 8C **106**
Greyfriars CM13: Hut 6L **97**
Greygoose Pk. CM19: H'low. 6N **53**
Greyhound Hill CO4: L'ham 4E **160** (3G **17**)
Greyhound La. RM16: Ors 9C **146**
Greyhound Retail Pk. SS2: Sth S 5M **137**
Greyhound Way SS2: Sth S. 5M **137**
Grey Ladys CM2: Gall 8C **72**
Grey M. CM11: Bill 5K **99**
Greys Hollow CB11: Rick G 3B **216**
Grey's La. CB9: B'dstn 1A **8**
Greystone Gdns. IG6: Ilf 6B **108**
Greystone Path *E11: Lon 2F 122*
(off Mornington Rd.)
Greystones Cl. CO3: Colc. 3H **173**
Grey Towers Av. RM11: Horn. 2H **127**
Grey Towers Gdns. RM11: Horn. 2G **127**
Gridiron Pl. RM14: Upm 5M **127**
Grieves Ct. CO3: S'way 2D **172**
Griffin Av. RM14: Upm 1B **128**
SS8: Can I 9J **135**
Griffins, The RM16: Grays 9L **145**
Griffin's Wood Cotts.
CM16: Epp 2C **78**
Griffith Cl. RM8: Dag 2H **125**
Grifon Rd. RM16: Chaf H 2F **154**
Griggs App. IG1: Ilf 4B **124** (4H **39**)
Griggs Gdns. RM12: Horn 7G **127**
Griggs La. CM3: Terl. 4D **24**
Griggs Rd. E10: Lon 1C **122**
Grimsby Gro. E16: Lon. 9A **140**
Grimshaw Way RM1: Romf 9D **110**
Grimstone Cl. RM5: Col R 3N **109**
Grimston Rd. CO2: Colc 2A **174**
SS14: Bas 7G **117**
Grimston Way CO14: Walt 7L **181**
Grinstead La. CM22: L Hall 4L **213** (3A **22**)
Grip, The CB1: Lin 2C **6**
Groome Ct. CO4: Colc 8D **166**
Groom Ho. CO15: Clac S. 9J **185**
Groom Pk. CO15: Clac S 9J **185**
Groom Side CM7: Brain 6J **193**
Grooms La. CM8: Sil E. 8M **217**
Grosvenor Av. N5: Lon 5B **38**
Grosvenor Cl. CM2: Gt Bad. 3E **72**
CO5: Tip 6D **226**
IG10: Lou 9A **78**
Grosvenor Ct. E10: Lon 3B **122**
SS0: Wclf S 7H **137**
SS2: Sth S. 4L **137**
Grosvenor Dr. IG10: Lou. 1A **92**
RM11: Horn 3G **126**
Grosvenor Gdns. CM12: Bill 4J **99**
IG8: Wfd G 3G **107**
RM14: Upm. 3A **128**
Grosvenor Ho. CM23: Bis S 9A **220**
Grosvenor Mans. *SS0: Wclf S 6H 137*
(off Grosvenor Rd.)
Grosvenor M. SS0: Wclf S 7H **137**
Grosvenor Pk. Rd. E17: Lon. 9A **106**
Grosvenor Path IG10: Lou 9A **78**
Grosvenor Ri. E. E17: Lon 9B **106**
Grosvenor Rd. E7: Lon. 8H **123**
E10: Lon 3C **122**
E11: Lon 9H **107**
IG1: Ilf. 5B **124**
N10: Lon. 2A **38**
RM7: Rush G 2B **126**
RM8: Dag 3L **125**
RM16: Ors. 6F **146**
SS0: Wclf S. 7H **137**
SS6: Ray. 2G **119**
SS7: Ben 6E **134**
Grove Av. CO5: W Mer 4C **228**
CO14: Walt 6L **181**
N10: Lon. 2A **38**
SS16: Lang H 3K **131**
Grovebury Cl. DA8: Eri 4B **152**
Grovebury Rd. SE2: Lon. 9G **141**
Grove Cen., The CM8: Wthm 6D **230**
Grove Cl. SS6: Ray 5M **119**
Grove Cotts. CO6: Cop. 4M **171**
Grove Ct. CM6: Gt D 4M **203**
EN9: Wal A 3B **76**
RM14: Upm. 6L **127**
SS0: Wclf S. 3G **137**
SS6: Ray. 6N **119**
Grove Cres. E18: Lon 6F **106**
Grove Cres. Rd. E15: Lon. 8D **122**
Grove End E18: Lon. 6F **106**
Grove Farm Rd. CM9: Tip, Tol M 4K **25**
Gro. Farm Rd. CM9: Tip, Tol M 6M **205**
Grove Fld. CM7: Brain 8L **191**
Grove Flats, The CO14: Walt 6L **181**
Grove Gdns. RM10: Dag. 5A **126**
Grove Grn. Rd. E10: Lon 5C **122** (4E **38**)
Groveherst Rd. DA1: Dart. 8K **153**
Grove Hill CM24: Stan M 2E **220** (6A **12**)
CO4: L'ham. 4F **160** (3G **17**)
CO7: Ded. 4K **161**
E18: Lon 6F **106**
SS9: Lgh S 8A **120**
Grove Ho. CM14: War. 1E **112**
Grovelands Rd. SS12: W'fd 1L **117**
Grovelands Way RM17: Grays 3J **155**
Grove La. CM16: Epp 9F **64**
IG7: Chig 9E **92**
IP9: Hark 1F **19**
Grove Orchard CM7: Brain 8L **191**
Grove Pk. E11: Lon. 1H **123**
Gro. Park Av. E4: Lon 4B **106**
Gro. Park Rd. RM13: Rain 1E **142**
Grove Pl. IG11: Bark. 9B **124**
Grove Rd. CM2: Chelm. 1C **72**
CM12: Bill 6H **99**
CO5: Tip. 6D **226** (3K **25**)
CO16: L Cla. 9H **179**
DA7: Bexh 9A **152**
E4: Lon 1C **106**
E9: Lon 6C **38**
E11: Lon 2F **122**
E17: Lon 1B **122** (3D **38**)
E18: Lon 6F **106**
IP9: B'ley. 1A **18**
IP11: Felix. 1K **19**
RM6: Chad H 2G **125** (4J **39**)
RM17: Grays. 4L **155**
SS6: Lgh S, Ray 5M **119** (2F **43**)
(not continuous)
SS7: Ben. 4D **134**
SS8: Can I 1J **151**
SS17: Stan H 5M **147**
Grover St. SS1: Sth S. 6M **137** (5K **43**)
Grover Wlk. SS17: Corr 2A **148**
Groves Cl. RM15: S Ock. 7C **144**
Groveside Rd. E4: Lon 8E **90**
Grove, The CM3: Bick. 9F **74**
CM8: Wthm 5D **230** (4G **25**)
CM11: Bill 4L **99**
CM14: Brtwd 1C **112**
CM22: Gt Hal. 1B **22**
CO6: E Col. 8C **198**
CO15: Clac S. 2K **189**
E15: Lon. 8E **122** (5E **38**)
RM14: Upm 6M **127**
SS2: Sth S 4N **137**
SS17: Stan H 5M **147**
Grove Vs. CM7: Gt Sal 6A **14**
Grove Wlk. SS3: Shoe. 7J **139**
Groveway RM8: Dag 6J **125**
Grovewood Av. SS9: Lgh S. 8A **120**
Grovewood Cl. SS9: Lgh S. 8A **120**
Grovewood Pl. IG8: Wfd G 3M **107**
GRUBB STREET 5E 46
Grymes Dyke Ct. CO3: S'way 9F **164**
Gryme's Dyke Way CO3: S'way 3E **172**
Guardian Bus. Cen.
RM3: Romf 4H **111**
Guardian Cl. RM11: Horn. 4F **126**
Guardsman Cl. CM14: War 2G **113**
Gubbins La. RM3: H Wood 4K **111** (2C **40**)
GUBBION'S GREEN 6M 203 (3C 24)
Guelph's La. CM6: Thax. 7C **224**
Guernsey Ct. CM9: Mal. 6B **214**
Guernsey Gdns. SS11: W'fd 7L **101**
Guernsey Rd. E11: Lon 3D **122**
Guernsey Way CM7: Brain 6E **192**
Guildford Gdns. RM3: Romf 3J **111**
Guildford Rd. CO1: Colc 7A **166**
E17: Lon 5C **106**
IG3: Ilf. 4D **124**
RM3: Romf 3J **111**
SS2: Sth S 5M **137**
Guildhall Way CB10: A'dn 8B **190**
(not continuous)
Guild Rd. DA8: Eri 5D **152**
Guild Way CM3: S Fer. 1L **103**
Guilfords CM17: H'low 7J **51**
Guilford St. WC1: Lon 6A **38**
Guinea Cl. CM7: Brain. 4M **193**
Guithavon Ri. CM8: Wthm 5C **230**
Guithavon Rd. CM8: Wthm 6C **230** (4F **25**)
Guithavon St. CM8: Wthm 5C **230**
Guithavon Valley CM8: Wthm 5C **230** (4F **25**)
Gulls Cft. CM7: Brain 5L **193**
Gull's La. CO7: Ded 5N **161**
Gull Wlk. RM12: Horn. 9F **126**
Gulpher Rd. IP11: Felix. 1K **19**
Gumley Rd. RM20: Grays. 4G **155**
Gunfleet SS3: Shoe 7G **139**
Gunfleet Cl. CO5: W Mer 2B **228**
Gunfleet Ct. CO15: Clac S 9N **185**
Gun Hill CO7: Ded, L'ham 1H **161** (2G **17**)
RM18: W Til 4F **156** (2H **47**)
Gun Hill Pl. SS16: Bas 1D **132**
Gunner Dr. EN3: Enf 7A **76**
Gunners Gro. E4: Lon. 9C **90**
Gunners Rd. SS3: Shoe 7L **139**
Gunning Rd. RM17: Grays 3N **155**
Gunson Ga. CM2: Chelm. 3E **72**
Gurdon Rd. CO2: Colc 3N **173**
Gurney Benham Cl. CO2: Colc 2J **173**
Gurney Cl. E15: Lon 7E **122**
IG11: Bark. 8A **124**
Gurney Rd. E15: Lon. 7E **122**
Gurton Rd. CO6: Cogg 2L **197**
Gustedhall La. SS5: Hock. 5D **120** (2H **43**)
Gutteridge Hall La.
CO16: Wee. 7B **178** (1C **28**)
Gutteridge La. RM4: Stap A 5A **94**
Gutters La.
CM1: Broom, Chelm 4K **59**
Guys Farm Rd. CM3: S Fer. 1K **103**
Guysfield Cl. RM13: Rain 1E **142**
Guysfield Dr. RM13: Rain. 1E **142**
Guys Retreat IG9: Buck H. 6J **91**
Gwendalen Av. SS8: Can I 1K **151**
Gwyn Cl. CM3: Bore 2F **60**
Gwynne Pk. Av. IG8: Wfd G. 3M **107**
Gwynne Rd. CO12: Har 3M **209**

Gyllyngdune Gdns. IG3: Ilf . . . 4E 124
Gypsy La. CO5: Fee . . . 8E 170
SG12: Gt Amw . . . 6D 20

H

Haarlem Rd. SS8: Can I . . . 1D 150
Haarle Rd. SS8: Can I . . . 3K 151
Haase Cl. SS8: Can I . . . 8G 135
Habgood Rd. IG10: Lou . . . 2L 91
Hackamore SS7: Thund . . . 1H 135
Hackmans La.
CM3: Cock C, Haz, Pur . . . 7L 75 (3F 35)
Hackman's La. CM3: Pur . . . 8H 197
HACKNEY . . . 5C 38
Hackney Central Station (Rail) . . . 5C 38
Hackney Downs Station (Rail) . . . 5C 38
Hackney Rd. E2: Lon . . . 6B 38
HACKNEY WICK . . . 5D 38
HACKNEY WICK . . . 5D 38
Hackney Wick Station (Rail) . . . 8A 122 (5D 38)
Hacks Dr. SS7: Thund . . . 8H 119
HACTON . . . 7K 127 (5C 40)
Hacton Dr. RM12: Horn . . . 6H 127
Hacton La. RM12: Horn, Upm . . . 4K 127 (4C 40)
RM14: Upm . . . 5K 127 (5C 40)
Hacton Pde. RM12: Horn . . . 5K 127
Haddon Cl. SS6: Ray . . . 3G 118
Haddon Mead CM3: S Fer . . . 3K 103
Haddon Pk. CO1: Colc . . . 9C 166
Hadfelda Sq. CM3: Hat P . . . 2L 61
Hadfield Dr. CM77: Bla N . . . 3B 194
Hadfield Rd. SS17: Stan H . . . 4M 147
HADHAM CROSS . . . 2G 21
HADHAM FORD . . . 7G 11
Hadham Rd. CM23: Bis S, Thor . . . 1J 21
SG11: Stdn . . . 7E 10
HADLEIGH . . . 3L 135 (4F 43)
Hadleigh Castle . . . 5K 135 (4F 43)
Hadleigh Castle Country Pk. . . . 6G 134
Hadleigh Ct. *CB10: Saf W . . . 3E 218*
(off Carnation Dr.)
CM14: Brtwd . . . 9D 96
CO15: Clac S . . . 1L 189
E4: Lon . . . 6E 90
Hadleigh Hall Ct. *SS9: Lgh S . . . 5B 136*
(off Hadleigh Rd.)
Hadleigh Pk. Av. SS7: Ben . . . 3J 135
Hadleigh Rd. CO7: E Ber . . . 1J 17
CO7: High . . . 1G 17
CO7: Strat M . . . 1J 17
CO13: Frin S . . . 9J 181
CO16: Clac S . . . 9F 184
SS0: Wclf S . . . 7K 137
SS9: Lgh S . . . 5B 136 (4G 43)
Hadley Cl. CM7: Brain . . . 8K 191
Hadley Grange CM17: H'low . . . 3H 55
Hadley Rd. EN2: Barn, Enf . . . 5A 30
Hadley Way N21: Lon . . . 7A 30
Hadrian Cl. CO4: Colc . . . 1B 166
Hadrians Cl. CM8: Wthm . . . 7B 230
Hadrians Way CM9: Mal . . . 4C 214
HADSTOCK . . . 3D 6
HADSTOCK COMMON . . . 4C 6
Haggars La. CO7: Frat . . . 3E 176
Hagger Ct. E17: Lon . . . 7D 106
Haggers Cl. CB10: Gt Che . . . 8D 202
HAGGERSTON . . . 6B 38
Haig Ct. CM2: Chelm . . . 1B 72
Haig Rd. RM16: Grays . . . 1C 156
Haigville Gdns. IG6: Ilf . . . 8A 108
Hailes Wood CM22: Else . . . 2L 199
Hailes Wood Cl. CM22: Else . . . 3L 199
HAILEY . . . 6D 20
Hailey Av. EN11: Hod . . . 1A 52
Hailey La. SG13: Hail, Hert H, Hod . . . 6C 20
Hailey Rd. DA18: Eri . . . 9M 141
Hailey Rd. Bus. Pk. DA18: Eri . . . 9M 141
Hailmores EN10: Brox . . . 7A 52
Hailsham Cl. RM3: Romf . . . 2G 111
Hailsham Gdns. RM3: Romf . . . 2G 110
Hailsham Rd. RM3: Romf . . . 2G 110
HAINAULT . . . 2E 108 (2J 39)
Hainault Av. SS0: Wclf S . . . 4J 137
SS4: R'fd . . . 3H 121
Hainault Bus. Pk. IG6: Ilf . . . 2H 109
Hainault Cl. SS7: Had . . . 2L 135
Hainault Ct. E17: Lon . . . 8D 106
Hainault Forest Country Pk. . . . 9J 93
Hainault Forest Country Pk. Vis. Cen. . . . 1J 109
Hainault Gore RM6: Chad H . . . 9K 109
Hainault Gro. CM1: Chelm . . . 1N 71
IG7: Chig . . . 1B 108
Hainault Ind. Est. IG6: Ilf . . . 2H 109
Hainault Rd. CM3: N Fam . . . 5H 35
E11: Lon . . . 3C 122 (4E 38)
IG7: Chig . . . 9A 92 (1G 39)
RM5: Col R, Romf . . . 6A 110
RM6: Chad H . . . 1L 125
(High Rd.)
RM6: Chad H . . . 4G 108 (2J 39)
(Forest Rd.)
Hainault Station (Tube) . . . 4D 108 (2H 39)
Hainault St. IG1: Ilf . . . 4B 124
Halbutt Gdns. RM9: Dag . . . 5L 125
Halbutt St. RM9: Dag . . . 6L 125
Halcyon Cvn. Pk. SS5: Hull . . . 4M 103
Halcyon Way RM11: Horn . . . 3K 127
Haldane Cl. EN3: Enf . . . 8B 76
Haldane Rd. SE28: Lon . . . 7J 141
Haldan Rd. E4: Lon . . . 3C 106
Haldon Cl. IG7: Chig . . . 2D 108
Hale Cl. E4: Lon . . . 9C 90
HALE END . . . 3E 106 (2E 38)
Hale End RM3: Romf . . . 3F 110
Hale End Rd. E4: Lon . . . 3D 106 (2E 38)
E17: Lon . . . 5C 106 (2E 38)
IG8: Wfd G . . . 4D 106 (2E 38)
Hale Ho. *RM11: Horn . . . 1E 126*
(off Benjamin Cl.)
Hale Rd. N17: Lon . . . 3C 38
SG13: Hart . . . 5B 20
Halesworth Cl. RM3: Romf . . . 4J 111
Halesworth Rd. RM3: Romf . . . 3J 111
Hale, The E4: Lon . . . 4D 106
Halfacre La. CO12: Har . . . 5J 209
Halfacres CM8: Wthm . . . 8D 230
Halfhide La. EN8: Chesh, Turn . . . 3C 30
Halfhides EN9: Wal A . . . 3D 76
Half Moon CM16: Epp . . . 1E 78
Halford Rd. E10: Lon . . . 9D 106
Halfpence La. DA12: Cobh . . . 6J 47
Halfway Ct. RM19: Purf . . . 2L 153
Halidon Ri. RM3: H Wood . . . 3M 111
Halifax Ho. *RM3: Romf . . . 2J 111*
(off Lindfield Rd.)
Hallam Cl. CM15: Dodd . . . 6E 82
Hallam Ct. CM12: Bill . . . 4H 99
Hall Av. RM15: Ave . . . 8N 143
Hall Barn CO5: W Mer . . . 3B 228
Hall Barns, The CM16: Epp . . . 1M 77
Hall Bri. Ri. CM9: H'bri . . . 4D 214
Hall Chase CO6: M Tey . . . 3K 171
Hall Cl. CM2: Gt Bad . . . 4H 73
CM22: Hen . . . 8D 210
SS17: Stan H . . . 1N 147
Hall Cotts., The CO6: Cop . . . 4N 171
Hall Cres. CO15: Hol S . . . 7C 186
RM15: Ave . . . 9N 143
SS7: Had . . . 3K 135
Hallcroft Chase CO4: Colc . . . 3C 166
Hall Cut CO7: B'sea . . . 7E 182
Hall Dr. CO9: Gosf . . . 8K 201
Hall Est. CM9: Gold . . . 2K 201
Hallet Rd. SS8: Can I . . . 2L 151
Hallett Rd. CM6: Fels . . . 9E 212
Halley Rd. E7: Lon . . . 8J 123
E12: Lon . . . 8J 123
EN9: Enf . . . 6B 76
Hall Farm Cl. CO5: Fee . . . 1L 211
SS7: Ben . . . 5D 134
Hall Farm Rd. SS7: Ben . . . 4D 134
HALL GREEN . . . 6E 8
Hall Grn. CM22: L Hall . . . 3A 22
Hall Grn. La. CM13: Hut . . . 6M 97 (7G 33)
Halliford St. N1: Lon . . . 5B 38
Hallingbury Cl. CM22: L Hall . . . 1K 213
Hallingbury Ct. E17: Lon . . . 7B 106
Hallingbury Rd. CM21: Saw . . . 1M 51 (4K 21)
CM22: Bis S . . . 1K 21
CM23: Bis S . . . 1K 21
HALLINGBURY STREET . . . 2B 22
Halling Hill CM20: H'low . . . 1E 54
(not continuous)
HALL LANE . . . 1C 38
Hall La. CM2: S'don . . . 5L 73
(Sandon Hall Bridleway)
CM2: S'don . . . 4K 73
(Woodhill Rd.)
CM2: W Han . . . 4D 86
CM4: Ing . . . 7D 84 (5H 33)
CM15: Pil H, Shenf . . . 2H 97 (6F 33)
CO9: Ridg . . . 8D 216
CO12: Har . . . 5J 209 (3H 19)
CO14: Walt . . . 2M 181
(First Av.)
CO14: Walt . . . 4N 181 (7H 19)
(Naze Pk. Rd.)
CO16: T Sok . . . 6M 179
E4: Lon . . . 1A 106 (1D 38)
RM14: Upm . . . 6N 111 (4D 40)
RM15: S Ock . . . 2G 144
Hallowell Down CM3: S Fer . . . 2L 103
Hall Pk. Av. SS0: Wclf S . . . 6G 137
Hall Pk. Rd. RM14: Upm . . . 7N 127
Hall Pk. Way SS0: Wclf S . . . 6G 136
Hall Place . . . 3A 46
Hall Ri. CM8: Wthm . . . 7C 230
Hall Rd. CB9: B'dstn . . . 1A 8
CM0: Ashel . . . 4D 36
CM0: S'min . . . 2E 222 (5D 36)
CM7: Pan . . . 1B 192 (6B 14)
CM9: Gt Tot . . . 3N 229 (6H 25)
CM9: H'bri, Mal . . . 4D 214
CM9: Tol . . . 8K 225
CM22: Else . . . 3L 199 (5B 12)
CO5: Tip . . . 7C 226 (4K 25)
CO6: Cop . . . 3N 171
CO6: For . . . 2A 164
CO6: W Ber . . . 2D 164 (4C 16)
CO7: Gt Bro . . . 4A 168 (5J 17)
CO8: M Bur . . . 3A 16
CO10: Bel W . . . 5G 9
CO10: Bor . . . 4H 9
CO10: Pos . . . 1C 8
DA1: Dart . . . 9K 153
DA11: N'fleet, S'fleet . . . 4G 47
E15: Lon . . . 6D 122 (5E 38)
RM2: Romf . . . 7F 110
RM6: Chad H . . . 1H 125
RM15: Ave . . . 9N 143 (1D 46)
SS4: R'fd . . . 4F 120 (2H 43)
Hall Rd. SS5: Hock . . . 4F 120 (2H 43)
Hall Rd. Cotts. CO6: W Ber . . . 1E 164
Hall Rd. Ind. Est. CM0: S'min . . . 3E 222
Hallsford Bri. Ind. Est.
CM5: Chip . . . 1N 81
HALLS GREEN . . . 6J 53 (7F 21)
Hall St. CM2: Chelm . . . 1C 72
CO10: L Mel . . . 3J 9
Hall Ter. RM3: H Wood . . . 4L 111
RM15: Ave . . . 9A 144
Hall Vw. Rd. CO7: Gt Ben . . . 7K 177
Hall Vs. CM7: Gt Bar . . . 3C 202
Hallwood Cres. CM15: Shenf . . . 6H 97
Halsham Cres. IG11: Bark . . . 7E 124
HALSTEAD . . . 4K 207 (4F 15)
Halstead Ct. SS12: W'fd . . . 2K 117
Halstead Hill EN7: G Oak . . . 3B 30
Halstead Ho. *RM3: Romf . . . 3H 111*
(off Dartfields)
Halstead Leisure Pool . . . 5L 207
Halstead Rd. CM7: Brain, Gosf . . . 6M 191 (5E 14)
CO3: S'way . . . 8C 164 (6C 16)
CO6: Aldh, Eig G . . . 6A 164 (5B 16)
CO6: E Col . . . 7A 198 (4H 15)
CO6: For . . . 8F 196 (5A 16)
CO9: Gosf, Hals . . . 7L 201 (3E 14)
CO9: Sib H . . . 9L 219 (2E 14)
CO13: Kir S, Walt . . . 8E 180 (1F 29)
DA8: Eri . . . 6C 152
E11: Lon . . . 9G 107
N21: Lon . . . 7B 30
Halstead Sports Cen. . . . 4M 207
Halstead Way CM13: Hut . . . 5M 97
Halston Ct. SS17: Corr . . . 1C 148
Halston Pl. CM9: Mal . . . 8B 214
Halstow Way SS13: Pits . . . 1K 133
Halt Dr. SS17: Linf . . . 2J 157
Halton Rd. RM16: Grays . . . 1D 156
Halt Robin Rd. DA17: Belv . . . 2A 152
Haltwhistle Rd. CM3: S Fer . . . 9J 89
Halyard Reach CM3: S Fer . . . 3L 103
Hamberts Rd. CM3: S Fer . . . 8K 89
Hamble Cl. CM8: Wthm . . . 5B 230
Hamble La. RM15: S Ock . . . 5C 144
Hamble Way CM0: Bur C . . . 2C 196
Hamboro Gdns. SS9: Lgh S . . . 5A 136
Hambro Av. SS6: Ray . . . 3K 119
Hambro Cl. SS6: Ray . . . 3L 119
Hambro Hill SS6: Ray . . . 2K 119 (1F 43)
Hamden Cres. RM10: Dag . . . 5N 125
Hamels La. SG9: W'mll . . . 6D 10
Hamel Way CB11: Widd . . . 3B 12
Hamford Cl. CO14: Walt . . . 3N 181
Hamford Dr. CO12: Gt Oak . . . 8C 204
Hamfrith Rd. E15: Lon . . . 8F 122
Hamilton Av. EN11: Rye P . . . 3A 52
IG6: Ilf . . . 8A 108
RM1: Romf . . . 6B 110
Hamilton Cl. SS9: Lgh S . . . 4N 135
Hamilton Ct. CM1: Chelm . . . 5F 58
CM3: S Fer . . . 2L 103
DA8: Eri . . . 5D 152
(off Frobisher Rd.)
Hamilton Cres. CM14: War . . . 1F 112
Hamilton Dr. RM3: H Wood . . . 6J 111
Hamilton Gdns. SS5: Hock . . . 9D 104
Hamilton M. CB10: Saf W . . . 3E 218
SS6: Ray . . . 4M 119
Hamilton Rd. CM6: L Can . . . 2F 224
CO3: Colc . . . 1L 173
CO7: W'hoe . . . 6H 175
CO13: Gt Hol . . . 9D 180
IG1: Ilf . . . 6A 124
IP11: Felix . . . 1K 19
RM2: Romf . . . 9F 110
Hamilton St. CO12: Har . . . 2H 209
Hamilton Wlk. DA8: Eri . . . 5D 152
Hamlet Cl. RM5: Col R . . . 4M 109
Hamlet Ct. CO8: Bures . . . 8K 195
Hamlet Ct. M. SS0: Wclf S . . . 5K 137
Hamlet Ct. Rd. SS0: Wclf S . . . 6J 137 (5J 43)
Hamlet Dr. CO4: Colc . . . 8F 166
Hamlet Hill CM19: Roy . . . 7G 52 (1F 31)
Hamlet Ho. DA8: Eri . . . 5C 152
Hamlet Ind. Est. E9: Lon . . . 9A 122
Hamlet Intl. Trad. Est. DA8: Eri . . . 3B 152
Hamlet Rd. CB9: H'hll . . . 3J 7
CM2: Chelm . . . 1C 72
RM5: Col R . . . 4M 109
SS1: Sth S . . . 7L 137
Hamley Cl. SS7: Thund . . . 9B 118
Hammarskjold Rd. CM20: H'low . . . 1B 54
Hammond Ct. CO13: Frin S . . . 9J 181
E10: Lon . . . 4B 122
(off Crescent Rd.)
Hammonds Cl. RM8: Dag . . . 5H 125
Hammonds La. CM11: Bill . . . 9L 99
CM13: Gt War . . . 3E 112
Hammonds Rd. CM2: L Bad, S'don . . . 1L 73
CM3: L Bad, S'don . . . 1L 73 (2C 34)
CM22: Hat O . . . 7E 206 (3C 22)
HAMMOND STREET . . . 2B 30
Hammondstreet Rd. EN7: Chesh . . . 2A 30
Hammond Way SE28: Lon . . . 7G 140
Ham Pk. Rd. E7: Lon . . . 9F 122
E15: Lon . . . 9F 122
Hampden Cl. CM16: N Wea . . . 6M 65
Hampden Cres. CM14: War . . . 1F 112
Hampden Rd. RM5: Col R . . . 4N 109
RM17: Grays . . . 3L 155
Hampden Way N14: Lon . . . 1A 38
HAMPERDEN END . . . 3D 12
Hampit Rd. CB11: A'den . . . 1J 11
Hampshire Gdns. SS17: Linf . . . 9J 147
Hampshire Rd. RM11: Horn . . . 8L 111
Hampstead Av. CO16: Clac S . . . 8G 185
IG8: Wfd G . . . 4N 107
Hampstead Cl. SE28: Lon . . . 8G 140
Hampstead Gdns. RM6: Chad H . . . 9G 108
SS5: Hock . . . 9E 104
Hampstead Rd. NW1: Lon . . . 6A 38
Hampton Cl. SS2: Sth S . . . 2K 137
Hampton Ct. SS5: Hock . . . 1B 120
Hampton Gdns. CM21: Saw . . . 5G 51
SS2: Sth S . . . 2K 137
Hampton Ho. CM2: Gt Bad . . . 4E 72
Hampton Mead IG10: Lou . . . 2A 92
Hampton Rd. CM2: Gt Bad . . . 4F 72
E4: Lon . . . 2A 106
E7: Lon . . . 7H 123
E11: Lon . . . 3D 122
IG1: Ilf . . . 6B 124
Hamstel M. SS2: Sth S . . . 5B 138
Hamstel Rd. CM20: H'low . . . 2A 54
SS2: Sth S . . . 3B 138 (4K 43)
Hamsters Cl. CO9: Peb . . . 2H 15
Hanbury Dr. E11: Lon . . . 2F 122
Hanbury Gdns. CO4: Colc . . . 2B 166
Hanbury Manor Golf Course . . . 3C 20
Hanbury Rd. CM1: Chelm . . . 2N 71
Hance La. CM77: Rayne . . . 6B 192
Hanchetts Orchard CM6: Thax . . . 7C 224
HANCHETT VILLAGE . . . 2H 7
Handel Cres. RM18: Til . . . 5C 156
Handel Rd. SS8: Can I . . . 3K 151
Handel Wlk. CO4: Colc . . . 9E 166
Handforth Rd. IG1: Ilf . . . 5A 124
Hand La. CM21: Saw . . . 3H 51
HANDLEY GREEN . . . 1F 84 (4H 33)
Handley Grn. SS15: Lain . . . 1L 131
Handleys Chase SS15: Bas . . . 5A 116
Handleys Ct. SS15: Bas . . . 5A 116
Handley's La. CM8: W Bis . . . 2L 229
Handsworth Av. E4: Lon . . . 3D 106
Handtrough Way IG11: Bark . . . 2A 140
Handy Fisher Ct. CO3: Colc . . . 2J 173
Hanford Rd. RM15: Ave . . . 8N 143
Hangboy Slade IG10: Lou . . . 7N 77
Hanging Hill La.
CM13: Brtwd, Hut . . . 9L 97 (1F 41)
Hangings, The CO12: Har . . . 3K 209
Hankin Av. CO12: Har . . . 6E 208
Hanlee Brook CM2: Gt Bad . . . 5G 72
Hanley Rd. N19: Lon . . . 4A 38
Hannah Cl. SS8: Can I . . . 8G 135
Hannards Way IG6: Ilf . . . 2G 108
Hannett Rd. SS8: Can I . . . 2L 151
Hanningfield Cl. SS6: Ray . . . 4G 118
Hanningfield Reserve Bird Sanctuary . . . 9E 86
Hanningfield Reservoir Vis. Cen.
. . . 9J 87 (6B 34)
Hanningfield Way CO4: Colc . . . 2B 166
Hanover Cl. SS14: Bas . . . 1F 132
Hanover Ct. CM8: Wthm . . . 6D 230
CO12: Har . . . 4L 209
CO14: Walt . . . 6K 181
EN9: Wal A . . . 3C 76
(off Quakers La.)
EN11: Hod . . . 5A 52
Hanover Dr. SS14: Bas . . . 9F 116
Hanover Gdns. IG6: Ilf . . . 4B 108
Hanover M. SS5: Hock . . . 1C 120
Hanover Pl. CB10: Saf W . . . 4B 218
CM14: Gt War . . . 2E 112
Hanover Sq. CO5: Fee . . . 8B 170
Hansells Mead CM19: Roy . . . 3H 53
Hanson Cl. IG10: Lou . . . 1B 92
Hanson Ct. E17: Lon . . . 1B 122
Hanson Dr. IG10: Lou . . . 1B 92
Hanson Grn. IG10: Lou . . . 1B 92
Hanwell Cl. CO16: Clac S . . . 8H 185
Harberts Rd. CM19: H'low . . . 3A 54 (7G 21)
Harberts Way SS6: Ray . . . 2J 119
Harbet Rd. N18: Lon . . . 2C 38
Harborough Hall La. CO5: Mess . . . 1E 226 (2K 25)
Harborough Hall Rd. CO5: Mess . . . 1D 226
Harbour Cres. CO12: Har . . . 2N 209
Harbourer Cl. IG6: Ilf . . . 2G 108
Harbourer Rd. IG6: Ilf . . . 2G 108
Harcamlow Way CB10: Saf W . . . 2E 218
CB11: Deb, Newp . . . 2N 215
(Bromley La.)
CB11: Newp . . . 3M 215
CM6: Thax . . . 9B 224
Harcourt Av. CO12: Har . . . 3J 209
E12: Lon . . . 6M 123
SS2: Sth S . . . 5L 137
Harcourt Ho. SS2: Sth S . . . 5L 137
Harcourt M. RM2: Romf . . . 9D 110
Hardie Rd. RM10: Dag . . . 5A 126
SS17: Stan H . . . 3M 147
Harding Rd. RM16: Grays . . . 1C 156
Hardings Cl. CO6: Aldh . . . 5A 16
Hardings Elms Rd.
CM11: Cray H . . . 3C 116 (2A 42)
Harding's La. CM4: Ing . . . 2B 84
Hardings Reach CM0: Bur C . . . 4E 196
Hardley Cres. RM11: Horn . . . 8H 111
Hardwick Cl. CM77: Gt N . . . 1B 204
SS6: Ray . . . 6K 119
Hardwick Ct. DA8: Eri . . . 4B 152
SS0: Sth S . . . 3K 137
Hardwicke St. IG11: Bark . . . 1B 140
Hardy SS3: Shoe . . . 9H 139
Hardy Cl. CM7: Brain . . . 8J 193
CO11: Bran . . . 1H 163
Hardy Ct. DA8: Eri . . . 5D 152
Hardy Gro. DA1: Dart . . . 9L 153
HARDY'S GREEN . . . 8N 171 (1B 26)
Hardy's Way SS8: Can I . . . 8G 134
Harebell Cl. CM12: Bill . . . 4H 99
CO4: Colc . . . 4B 166
Harebell Dr. CM8: Wthm . . . 4B 230
Harebell Way RM3: Romf . . . 4H 111
Harefield CM20: H'low . . . 2F 54
HARE GREEN . . . 9F 168 (6K 17)

Harehall La. RM2: Romf 8F 110
Hares Chase CM12: Bill 5H 99
Haresfield Rd. RM10: Dag 8M 125
Haresland Cl. SS7: Had 9M 119
HARE STREET
CHIPPING ONGAR 4J 81 (4C 32)
HARLOW 3A 54 (7G 21)
BUNTINGFORD 4E 10
COTTERED 4A 10
Hare St. CM19: H'low 3A 54
Hare St. Rd. SG9: Bunt, Hare S 4D 10
Hare St. Springs CM19: H'low 3B 54
Hare Ter. RM20: Grays 3G 155
Harewood Av. SS4: R'fd 2H 121
Harewood Dr. IG5: Ilf 6M 107
Harewood Hill CM16: They B 5D 78
Harewood Rd. CM1: Chelm 1N 71
CM15: Pil H 5E 96
Harford Cl. E4: Lon 6B 90
Harford Rd. E4: Lon 6B 90
Harfred Av. CM9: Hey B 8F 214
Hargrave Cl. CM24: Stan M 1D 220
Harkilees Way CM7: Brain 3H 193
Harkness Cl. RM3: Romf 2K 111
HARKNETT'S GATE 9L 53 (1G 31)
HARKSTEAD 1E 18
Harkstead Rd. IP9: Holb 1D 18
Harlech Cl. SS13: Pits 1J 133
Harlequin Steps *SS1: Sth S* *7A 138*
(off Hawtree Cl.)
Harlesden Cl. RM3: Romf 3K 111
Harlesden Rd. RM3: Romf 3K 111
Harlesden Wlk. RM3: Romf 4K 111
Harley Ct. E11: Lon 2G 123
Harley Ho. E11: Lon 2D 122
Harley St. SS9: Lgh S 5B 136
Harlings Gro. CM1: Chelm 8K 59
HARLOW 2C 54 (7H 21)
Harlow (Blackwater) Sailing Club 6J 213
Harlow Bus. Pk. CM19: H'low 3L 53
Harlow Comn. CM17: H'low 6H 55 (7J 21)
Harlow Gdns. RM5: Col R 3A 110
Harlow Greyhound Stadium 2L 53
Harlow Mans. *IG11: Bark* *9A 124*
(off Whiting Av.)
Harlow Mill Station (Rail) 7H 51 (5J 21)
Harlow Mus. 4B 54 (7H 21)
Harlow Outdoor Cen. for Outdoor Learning 9B 50
Harlow Pool & Fitness Cen. 1D 54
Harlow Rd. CM5: M'ton 7B 22
CM17: H'low, Srng 6A 22
CM19: Roy 3J 53 (7F 21)
CM22: H'low, Srng 5N 51 (5K 21)
RM13: Rain 1D 142
Harlow Seedbed Cen. *CM19: H'low* *4N 53*
(off Lovet Rd.)
Harlow Ski Cen. 1B 54
Harlow Sports Cen. 1B 54
Harlow Study & Vis. Cen. 4E 54
Harlow Town Station (Rail) 9C 50 (6H 21)
HARLOW TYE 9N 51 (6A 22)
Harlton Ct. EN9: Wal A 4F 76
Harman Av. IG8: Wfd G 3F 106
Harman Cl. E4: Lon 1D 106
Harman Wlk. CO16: Clac S 8G 185
Harmer St. DA12: Grav 3H 47
Harness Cl. CM1: Chelm 4N 59
Harness Rd. SE28: Lon 9F 140
Harnham Dr. CM77: Gt N 1C 204
Harold Cl. CM19: H'low 4M 53
CO9: Hals 5L 207
Harold Ct. RM3: H Wood 4M 111
Harold Ct. Rd. RM3: H Wood 3M 111
Harold Cres. EN9: Wal A 2C 76
Harold Gdns. SS11: W'fd 7L 101
Harold Gro. CO13: Frin S 1J 187
HAROLD HILL 3K 111 (1C 40)
Harold Hill Ind. Est. RM3: Romf 4H 111
HAROLD PARK 3M 111 (2C 40)
Harold Ri. CM9: Mal 3B 214
Harold Rd. CM7: Brain 5G 192
CO13: Frin S 1J 187
CO15: Clac S 1K 189
E4: Lon 1C 106
E11: Lon 3E 122
IG8: Wfd G 5G 107
Harold's Bridge 3C 76
Harold Sims Ho. *CO6: E Col* *7C 198*
(off Sims Cl.)
Harolds Rd. CM19: H'low 4M 53
Harold Vw. RM3: H Wood 6K 111
Harold Way CO13: Frin S 1J 187
Harold Wilson Ho. SE28: Lon 8G 141
HAROLD WOOD 5K 111 (2C 40)
Harold Wood Hall *RM3: Romf* *5H 111*
(off Widecombe Cl.)
Harold Wood Station (Rail) 5K 111 (2C 40)
Haron Cl. SS8: Can I 2H 151
Harpenden Rd. E12: Lon 4J 123
Harper Cl. RM16: Chaf H 3F 154
Harper Rd. SE1: Lon 7B 38
Harper's Hill CO6: Nay 1D 16
Harpers La. CM15: Dodd 7G 82
Harper Way SS6: Ray 4J 119
Harp Mdw. La. CO2: Colc 2L 173
Harpour Rd. IG11: Bark 8B 124
Harrap Chase RM17: Grays 3J 155
Harridge Cl. SS9: Lgh S 3D 136
Harridge Rd. SS9: Lgh S 3D 136
Harrier Av. E11: Lon 1H 123
Harrier Cl. RM12: Horn 8F 126
SS3: Shoe 5J 139
Harrier M. SE28: Lon 9C 140
Harrier Way EN9: Wal A 4G 76
Harriescourt EN9: Wal A 2G 76
HARRINGAY 3B 38
Harringay Green Lanes Station (Rail) 3A 38
Harringay Station (Rail) 3A 38
Harrington Cl. CO5: Tip 6B 226
Harrington Rd. E11: Lon 3E 122
Harris Cl. RM3: Romf 4J 111
SS12: W'fd 2N 117
SS17: Corr 1C 148
Harris Ct. SS5: Hock 2D 120
Harris Grn. CM6: Gt D 4M 203
Harrison Cl. CM13: Hut 4N 97
Harrison Ct. CO5: W Mer 3C 228
Harrison Dr. CM7: Brain 7J 193
CM16: N Wea 5N 65
Harrison Gdns. SS5: Hull 6K 103
Harrison Rd. CO2: Colc 3N 173
EN9: Enf 5C 76
RM10: Dag 8N 125
Harrisons CM23: Bchgr 7C 220
Harrisons Wharf RM19: Purf 3L 153
Harris Rd. RM9: Dag 7L 125
Harrods Ct. CM11: Bill 6M 99
Harrogate Dr. SS5: Hock 8E 104
Harrogate Rd. SS5: Hock 9E 104
Harrold Rd. RM8: Dag 7G 125
Harrowbond St. CM17: H'low 2H 55
Harrow Cl. RM11: Horn 3F 126
SS5: Hock 2F 120
Harrow Cres. RM3: Romf 4F 110
HARROWCROSS 8H 219 (2D 14)
Harrow Dr. RM11: Horn 1F 126
Harrow Gdns. SS5: Hock 2F 120
Harrow Grn. E11: Lon 5E 122
Harrow Hill CO9: Top 7B 8
Harrow La. RM14: Bulp 7M 129
Harrow Mnr. Way SE2: Lon 8H 141 (7J 39)
SE28: Lon 7H 141
(not continuous)
Harrow Rd. CO15: Clac S 9K 185
E11: Lon 5E 122 (4E 38)
IG1: Ilf 6B 124
IG11: Bark 1D 140
SS8: Can I 9H 135
SS12: N Ben 5N 117 (2C 42)
Harrow Way CM2: Gt Bad 4H 73
Harsnett Rd. CO1: Colc 1B 174
HARSTON 1G 5
Harston Dr. EN3: Enf 8A 76
Harston Rd. CB2: Hars, New 1G 5
Hart Cl. SS7: Thund 9G 118
Hart Ct. E6: Lon 9N 123
Hart Cres. IG7: Chig 2E 108
Hartford Cl. SS6: Ray 3G 119
HARTFORD END 3K 23
Hartford End SS13: Pits 1H 133
Hartington Pl. SS1: Sth S 7N 137
Hartington Rd. SS1: Sth S 7N 137
Hartland Cl. SS9: Lgh S 8C 120
Hartland Rd. CM16: Epp 1F 78
E15: Lon 9F 122
RM12: Horn 4E 126
Hartlepool Ct. E16: Lon 8A 140
HARTLEY 6F 47
Hartley Bottom Rd. DA3: Hley 7F 47
Hartley Cl. CM2: Chelm 7B 60
HARTLEY GREEN 7F 47
HARTLEY HILL 7F 47
Hartley Hill DA3: Hley 7F 47
Hartley Ho. CM7: Brain 6L 193
Hartley Rd. DA3: Long 6F 47
E11: Lon 3F 122
Hartmann Rd. E16: Lon 7G 39
Hart Rd. CM17: H'low 7H 51
SS7: Thund 9F 118 (3E 42)
Harts Gro. IG8: Wfd G 2G 107
Hart's La. CO7: A'lgh 7F 160 (3G 17)
Harts La. IG11: Bark 8A 124
Hartslock Dr. SE2: Lon 9J 141
Hart St. CM2: Chelm 1B 72
CM14: Brtwd 8F 96
Hartswood Cl. CM14: War 1H 113
Hartswood Rd. CM13: Gt War 1H 113
CM14: War 1H 113 (1E 40)
Hart Ter. RM20: Grays 3G 154
Hartwell Dr. E4: Lon 3C 106
Harty Cl. RM16: Grays 8L 145
Harvard Ct. CO4: Colc 3B 166
SS6: Ray 3H 119
Harvard Wlk. RM12: Horn 6E 126
Harvest Cl. CM3: S Fer 1K 103
CO6: M Tey 2K 171
Harvest Ct. CO5: Fee 1M 211
CO6: Gt Hork 7J 159
Harvest End CO3: S'way 1E 172
Harvesters CM9: Tol D 3K 227
Harvesters Way CO6: Gt Tey 2D 170
Harvest La. IG10: Lou 6K 91
Harvest Rd. SS8: Can I 9H 135
Harvest Way CM9: Mal 3B 214
CO7: Elms 9M 167
Harvey RM16: Grays 9L 145
Harvey Cen. App. CM20: H'low 3C 54
Harvey Cen. (Shop. Cen.) CM20: H'low 3B 54
Harvey Cl. CO11: Law 4G 163
SS13: Bas 6J 117
Harvey Ct. E17: Lon 9A 106
Harvey Cres. CO3: S'way 2D 172
Harveyfields EN9: Wal A 4C 76
Harvey Gdns. E11: Lon 3F 122
IG10: Lou 2A 92
Harvey Ho. RM6: Chad H 8J 109
Harvey Rd. CM9: Gt Tot 3M 229
CO2: Colc 4J 173
CO7: W'hoe 5H 175
Harvey Rd. E11: Lon 3E 122
IG1: Ilf 7A 124
SS13: Bas 5J 117
Harveys La. RM7: Rush G 4B 126
Harvey St. CO9: Hals 4L 207
Harvey Way CB10: Hpstd 6G 7
CB10: Saf W 3E 218
Harwater Dr. IG10: Lou 1M 91
Harwell Cl. CM7: Brain 4M 193
HARWICH 1N 209 (2J 19)
Harwich High Lighthouse 2N 209 (2J 19)
Harwich Ind. Est. CO12: Har 2H 209
Harwich International Station (Rail) 1H 209 (2G 19)
Harwich Low Lighthouse & Maritime Mus. 2N 209 (2J 19)
Harwich Redoubt 2N 209 (2J 19)
Harwich Rd. CO1: Colc 8C 166
CO4: Colc 7C 166 (6F 17)
CO7: A'lgh 3H 167 (4G 17)
(Springvalley La.)
CO7: A'lgh, Law 8M 161 (4H 17)
(Colchester Rd.)
CO7: Gt Bro, L Ben 9C 168 (6J 17)
CO7: Hor X, L Ben, L Bro 5L 169
CO11: Brad 3C 18
(Bradfield)
CO11: Brad, Mist 5M 163 (3B 18)
(Mistley)
CO11: Wix 4D 18
CO11: Wrab 3D 18
CO12: Gt Oak 7D 204 (5E 18)
CO12: L Oak 7E 208 (4F 19)
CO16: Gt Oak, T Sok 1M 179 (6D 18)
CO16: L Cla, T Sok 1G 185 (1D 28)
Harwich Town Station (Rail) 2M 209 (2J 19)
Harwich Treadmill Crane, The (Re-erected) 1N 209
Harwood Av. RM11: Horn 7J 111
Harwood Cl. CO2: Colc 2A 174
Harwood Hall La. RM14: Upm 8M 127 (5C 40)
Haselbury Rd. N9: Lon 1B 38
N18: Lon 1B 38
Haselfoot Rd. CM3: Bore 3G 60
Haskard Rd. RM9: Dag 6J 125
Haskell M. CM7: Brain 7G 193
Haskins SS17: Stan H 2A 148
Haslemere Est., The EN11: Rye P 5D 52
Haslemere Gdns. CO13: Frin S 7J 181
Haslemere Rd. IG3: Ilf 4E 124
SS11: W'fd 6K 101
Hasler Cl. SE28: Lon 7G 141
Hasler Pl. CM6: Gt D 3L 203
Hasler Rd. CM9: Tol 7K 225
Haslers Ct. CM4: Ing 5E 84
Haslers La. CM6: Gt D 3L 203
Haslewood Av. EN11: Hod 5A 52
Haslingden Ho. *RM3: Romf* *2J 111*
(off Dagnam Pk. Dr.)
Haslingfield Rd. CB2: Barr 1E 4
Hassell Rd. SS8: Can I 2K 151
Hassenbrook Rd. SS17: Stan H 3N 147
Hastings Av. CO15: Clac S 4G 189
IG6: Ilf 8B 108
Hastings Cl. RM17: Grays 4H 155
Hastings Pl. CO7: B'sea 5E 182
Hastings Rd. CO3: Colc 2H 173
RM2: Romf 9F 110
SS1: Sth S 6N 137
Hastings, The SS11: W'fd 7L 101
HASTINGWOOD 7K 55 (1K 31)
Hastingwood Ct. CM5: Chip 5K 67
E17: Lon 9B 106
Hastingwood Rd. CM5: Mag L 8J 55 (7K 21)
CM17: H'low, H'wd, Mag L 8J 55 (1K 31)
Hatchcroft Gdns. CO7: Elms 9N 167
Hatcher Cres. CO2: Colc 1C 174
Hatches Farm Rd. CM12: L Bur 2F 114 (1H 41)
Hatchfields CM3: Gt Walt 5H 57
Hatch Grn. CM22: L Hall 2K 213
Hatch Gro. RM6: Chad H 8K 109
Hatch La. E4: Lon 1D 106 (1E 38)
(not continuous)
Hatch Rd. CM15: Pil H 4D 96 (7E 32)
Hatch Side IG7: Chig 2N 107
Hatchwood Cl. IG8: Wfd G 1F 106
HATFIELD BROAD OAK 7D 206 (3C 22)
Hatfield Broad Oak Rd.
CM22: Tak 4C 224 (1D 22)
Hatfield Cl. CM13: Hut 6N 97
IG6: Ilf 7A 108
RM12: Horn 7H 127
Hatfield Dr. CM11: Bill 6M 99
Hatfield Gro. CM1: Chelm 1M 71
(not continuous)
HATFIELD HEATH 1E 210 (4B 22)
Hatfield Heath Rd.
CM21: Hat H, Saw 1A 210 (4K 21)
HATFIELD PEVEREL 2L 61 (6E 24)
HATFIELD PEVEREL INTERCHANGE NTH. 1L 61 (5E 24)
HATFIELD PEVEREL INTERCHANGE STH. 2K 61 (6E 24)
Hatfield Peverel Station (Rail) 1K 61 (5E 24)
Hatfield Rd. CM3: Hat P, L Bad 7D 24
CM3: Terl 4D 24
CM8: W Bis 6F 25
CM8: Wthm 9A 230 (5F 25)
CM9: L'frd, Ult 7G 25
Hatfield Rd. E15: Lon 7E 122
RM9: Dag 8K 125
RM16: Chaf H 3G 154
SS6: Ray 4H 119 (2E 42)
Hatfields IG10: Lou 2A 92
Hathaway Cres. E12: Lon 8M 123
Hathaway Gdns. RM6: Chad H 9J 109
RM17: Grays 1K 155
Hathaway Rd. RM17: Grays 1L 155 (1F 47)
Hatherleigh Way RM3: Romf 5H 111
Hatherley Ct. CB11: Saf W 3D 218
Hatherley Gdns. E6: Lon 6F 39
Hatherley Ho. E17: Lon 8A 106
Hatherley M. E17: Lon 8A 106
Hatherley Rd. E17: Lon 8A 106
Hatherley, The SS14: Bas 8E 116
Hatley Av. IG6: Ilf 8B 108
Hatley Gdns. SS7: Ben 1B 134
Hatterill SS15: Bas, Lain 9L 115 (3K 41)
Hatton Cl. RM16: Chaf H 1G 154
Hatton Gdn. EC1: Lon 7A 38
Haubourdin Ct. CO9: Hals 4M 207
HAULTWICK 7B 10
Havana Cl. RM1: Romf 9C 110
RM3: Romf *2J 111*
(off Gooshays Dr.)
Havana Dr. SS6: Ray 9H 103
Havant Ho. *RM3: Romf* *4J 111*
(off Kingsbridge Cir.)
Havant Rd. E17: Lon 7C 106
Havelock Rd. N17: Lon 2C 38
Havelock St. IG1: Ilf 4A 124
Havelon Cl. SS14: Bas 8E 116
Haven Av. CO15: Hol S 7D 186
Haven Cl. SS8: Can I 2E 150
SS16: Van 3F 132
Havencourt CM1: Chelm 8K 59
Haven Ct. CM3: Hat P 2K 61
Havencroft Ct. CO14: Walt 6M 181
Havengore CM1: Chelm 6N 59
SS13: Pits 7K 117
Havengore Cl. SS3: Gt W 3N 139
Havengore Ho. SS9: Lgh S 5D 136
Haven Pl. RM16: Grays 9M 145
Haven Ri. CM11: Bill 1M 115
Haven Rd. CO2: Colc 1D 174 (6F 17)
SS8: Can I 4C 150 (6D 42)
Havenside SS3: Lit W 1J 139
Haven, The CO12: Har 4H 209
RM16: Grays 3C 156
Havenvale Ct. CO15: Clac S 9J 185
Haven Village 7D 182
Havenwood Cl. CM13: Gt War 3F 112
HAVERHILL 3J 7
Haverhill & District Local History Mus. 3J 7
Haverhill By-Pass CB9: H'hll 2H 7
Haverhill Rd. CB1: Cas C 4G 7
CB1: H'hth 2F 7
CB9: H'hll, L Wra 2J 7
(Haverhill)
CB9: H'hll, Stpl B 1K 223 (4J 7)
(Bumpstead Rd.)
CB9: Hel B 5H 7
E4: Lon 7C 90
HAVERING-ATTE-BOWER 9C 94 (1A 40)
Havering Cl. CO4: Colc 6B 166
CO15: Clac S 6J 185
SS3: Gt W 2M 139
Havering Country Pk. 1A 110
Havering Dr. RM1: Romf 8C 110
Havering Gdns. RM6: Chad H 9H 109
HAVERING PARK 2N 109
Havering Rd. RM1: Hav, Romf 2B 110 (2A 40)
HAVERING'S GROVE 6D 98 (7H 33)
Havering Way IG11: Bark 3G 140
Havers La. CM23: Bis S 1K 21
Havisham Way CM1: Chelm 4G 58
Havis Rd. SS17: Stan H 1N 147
Hawbridge Rd. E11: Lon 3D 122
HAWBUSH GREEN 3F 194 (1E 24)
Hawbush Grn. CM77: Tye G 3F 194 (1E 24)
SS13: Bas 6J 117
Hawes La. E4: Enf 8C 76
Hawfinch Rd. CO2: Lay H 9H 173
Hawfinch Wlk. CM2: Chelm 5C 72
Hawk Cl. EN9: Wal A 4G 76
Hawk Cnr. RM20: Chaf H 3G 154
Hawkdene E4: Lon 5B 90
Hawkenbury CM19: H'low 5A 54
Hawkendon Rd. CO16: Clac S 9E 184
Hawkesbury Bush La. SS16: Van 4B 132
Hawkesbury Cl. SS8: Can I 3F 150
Hawkesbury Rd. SS8: Can I 2E 150
Hawkes Cl. RM17: Grays 4L 155
Hawkes Rd. CO6: Cogg 2K 197
Hawkes Way CO15: Clac S 7K 185
Hawk Hill SS11: Bat 5C 102 (7D 34)
Hawkhurst Cl. CM1: Chelm 9G 58
Hawkhurst Gdns. RM5: Col R 3B 110
Hawkinge Way RM12: Horn 8G 126
Hawkins SS3: Shoe 8H 139
Hawkins Cl. CM3: Cock C 8L 75
SS11: W'fd 9N 101
Hawkins Dr. RM16: Chaf H 9G 145
HAWKINS HILL 2J 13
Hawkins Rd. CO2: Colc 9D 166
CO7: Alr 6A 176
Hawkins Way CM7: Brain 4L 193
Hawk La. SS11: Bat 6D 102
Hawkridge SS3: Shoe 6G 139
Hawkridge Cl. RM6: Chad H 1H 125
Hawkridge Dr. RM17: Grays 3N 155
Hawks Cl. CM3: Dan 5G 74
Hawks Hill CM16: N Wea 6M 65
Hawks La. SS5: Hock 2D 120
Hawksmoor Grn. CM13: Hut 4N 97
(not continuous)
Hawksmouth E4: Lon 6C 90
HAWKSPUR GREEN 2H 13
Hawkspur Green CM7: L Bar 3H 13
Hawksway SS16: Bas 2C 132

Hawkswood Rd. CM11: D'ham 9D 86 (6A 34)
Hawk Ter. RM20: Grays 3G 154
HAWKWELL 2E 120 (2H 43)
Hawkwell Chase SS5: Hock 2D 120
Hawkwell Ct. E4: Lon 9C 90
Hawkwell Ho. RM8: Dag 3M 125
Hawkwell Pk. Dr. SS5: Hock 2E 120
Hawkwell Rd. SS5: Hock 1D 120
Hawkwood Cl. CM3: S Fer 8L 89
Hawkwood Cres. E4: Lon 5B 90
Hawkwood Rd. CO9: Sib H 7J 219
HAWLEY 5C 46
Hawley Rd. DA1: Dart 4C 46
Hawlmark End CO6: M Tey 3G 171
Hawsted IG9: Buck H 6H 91
Hawthorn Av. CM13: Brtwd 9J 97
CO4: Colc 7E 166 (6G 17)
RM13: Rain 4F 142
Hawthorn Cl. CM2: Chelm 4D 72
CM22: Tak 3C 224
CO9: Hals 3M 207
SS5: Hock 2E 120
Hawthorne Gdns. SS5: Hock 1A 120
Hawthorne Rd. E17: Lon 7A 106
SS17: Corr 1A 148
Hawthornes CM3: Pur 8K 215
Hawthorn Pl. DA8: Eri 3A 152
Hawthorn Ri. CM8: Wthm 2D 230
Hawthorn Rd. CM3: Hat P 1L 61
CO15: Clac S 6J 185
EN11: Rye P 3B 52
IG9: Buck H 1K 107
SS8: Can I 2J 151
Hawthorns CM18: H'low 7E 54
CO9: Sib H 5J 219
CO13: Walt 7J 181
IG8: Wfd G 9G 90
SS7: Ben 2C 134
SS9: Lgh S 2D 136
Hawthorns, The CM0: Bur C 1C 196
CM3: Dan 3G 75
IG10: Lou 3N 91
SS17: Corr 1D 148
Hawthorn Wlk. CM3: S Fer 8L 89
Hawthorn Way SS6: Ray 7M 119
Hawtree Cl. SS1: Sth S 7A 138
Hayburn Way RM12: Horn 3D 126
Hay Cl. E15: Lon 9E 122
Hayden Rd. EN9: Enf 5C 76
Haydens CM6: Steb 7H 13
Haydens Rd. CM20: H'low 3B 54 (7H 21)
Hayden Way RM5: Col R 6A 110
Haydock Cl. RM12: Horn 6K 127
Haydocks La. CO5: W Mer 4G 27
Haydon Cl. RM3: Romf 4F 110
Haydon Rd. RM8: Dag 4H 125
Haye La. CO5: Fing 1F 27
Hayes Barton SS1: Sth S 6G 138
Hayes Chase SS11: Bat 3F 102
(not continuous)
Hayes Cl. CM2: Chelm 1C 72
RM20: Grays 4F 154
Hayes Dr. RM13: Rain 9F 126
Hayes Farm Cvn. Pk.
SS11: Bat 4G 103
Hayes Hill Farm 7C 62 (3E 30)
Hayes La. SS8: Can I 2F 150
Hayes Rd. CO15: Clac S 2J 189
HAY GREEN 4H 83 (4F 33)
Hay Green CM3: Dan 2F 74
Hay Grn. La. CM4: B'more 4J 83
CM15: Hook E 5G 82 (5E 32)
Hayhouse Rd. CO6: E Col 9B 198 (4H 15)
Hay La. CM7: Brain 5L 193
Hayle RM18: E Til 1L 157
Hayley Cl. RM16: Chaf H 1F 154
Hayling Gro. SS12: W'fd 2A 118
Hayllar Ct. EN11: Hod 5A 52
Haymarket SW1: Lon 7A 38
Haymeads Ct. CM9: Mal 3C 214
Haynes Grn. Rd. CO5: Lay M 2F 226 (2A 26)
Haynes Rd. RM11: Horn 8H 111
Hayrick Cl. SS16: Lang H 2J 131
Haysoms Cl. RM1: Romf 8C 110
HAY STREET 5E 10
Hayter Ct. E11: Lon 4H 123
Haytor Cl. CM7: Brain 6L 193
Haywain, The CO3: S'way 1E 172
Hayward Ct. CO1: Colc 8C 166
Hayward Rd. EN11: Rye P 3C 52
Haywards Cl. CM13: Hut 5A 98
RM6: Chad H 9G 109
Haywood Ct. EN9: Wal A 4F 76
Haywood La. SG8: Ther 7C 4
Haywood Pl. RM16: Grays 9E 146
Hazelbrouck Gdns. IG6: Ilf 4C 108
Hazel Cl. CM6: Gt D 2K 203
CM8: Wthm 3D 230
CO7: Thorr 9F 176
RM12: Horn 5F 126
SS7: Had 4M 135
SS9: Lgh S 4B 136
SS15: Bas 5A 116
Hazel Ct. IG10: Lou 2M 91
Hazel Cres. RM5: Col R 5N 109
Hazeldene SS6: Ray 3K 119
Hazeldene Rd. IG3: Ilf 4G 125
Hazeldon Cl. CM3: L Walt 6L 57
Hazel Dr. DA8: Eri 6E 152
RM15: S Ock 3G 144
HAZELEIGH 6M 75 (3G 35)
Hazeleigh CM13: Brtwd 9L 97
Hazeleigh Gdns. IG8: Wfd G 2L 107
Hazeleigh Hall La. CM9: Wdhm M 2G 35
HAZEL END 4A 220 (6K 11)
Hazelend Rd.
CM23: Bis S, Farnh 4A 220 (6K 11)
Hazel Gdns. CM21: Saw 3L 51
RM16: Grays 1A 156
Hazel Gro. CM7: Brain 7G 192
RM6: Chad H 7K 109
Hazel La. IG6: Ilf 3A 108
Hazell Av. CO2: Colc 3H 173
Hazellville Rd. N19: Lon 4A 38
Hazelmere SS13: Pits 2H 133
Hazelmere Gdns. RM11: Horn 9G 110
Hazel M. CO7: B'sea 6D 182
Hazel Ri. RM11: Horn 1G 126
Hazel Rd. DA8: Eri 6E 152
E15: Lon 7E 122
Hazel Shrub IP9: B'ley 1A 18
HAZEL STUB 3H 7
Hazelton Rd. CO4: Colc 6D 166
Hazelville Cl. CO12: Har 6G 209
Hazelwood IG10: Lou 4K 91
SS5: Hock 3E 120
SS7: Thund 8B 118
SS17: Linf 2J 157
Hazelwood Ct. CM9: Mal 2D 214
Hazelwood Cres. CO16: L Cla 4G 185
Hazelwood Gdns. CM15: Pil H 5D 96
Hazelwood Gro. SS9: Lgh S 1D 136
Hazelwood La. N13: Lon 1A 38
Hazelwood Pk. Cl. IG7: Chig 2D 108
Hazle Ceramics Workshop 9E 112
Hazlemere Rd. CO15: Hol S 9N 185
SS7: Thund 1D 134
Headcorn Cl. SS13: Pits 1K 133
Headgate CO3: Colc 9M 165 (6E 16)
Headingley Cl. IG6: Ilf 3E 108
SS13: Bas 5H 117
Head La. CO10: Gt Cor 5K 9
Headley App. IG2: Ilf 9A 108
Headley Chase CM14: War 1F 112
Headley Dr. IG2: Ilf 1A 124
Headley Rd. CM11: Bill 4L 99
Head St. CM9: Gold 3K 201 (7A 26)
CO1: Colc 8M 165 (6E 16)
CO5: Rhdge 6G 174 (1G 27)
CO9: Hals 4L 207 (3F 15)
Heard's La. CM7: Corn H 7K 7
Heards La. CM15: Shenf 2J 97
Hearn Rd. RM1: Romf 1D 126
Hearsall Av. CM1: Chelm 4K 59
SS17: Stan H 3N 147
Heath Cl. CM12: Bill 7H 99
RM2: Romf 7E 110
Heathclose Rd. DA1: Dart 4B 46
Heathcote Av. IG5: Ilf 6M 107
Heathcote Ct. IG5: Ilf 5M 107
(Glade Ct.)
IG5: Ilf 6M 107
(Heathcote Av.)
Heathcote Gdns. CM17: H'low 3K 55
Heathcote Gro. E4: Lon 9C 90
Heathcroft Gdns. E17: Lon 5D 106
Heath Dr. CM2: Chelm 4C 72
CM16: They B 6D 78
RM2: Romf 5E 110
Heather Av. RM1: Romf 6B 110
Heather Bank CM11: Bill 6L 99
Heather Cl. CM15: Pil H 4E 96
CO2: Lay H 9G 173
CO15: Clac S 6M 185
E6: Lon 6A 140
RM1: Romf 5B 110
SS8: Can I 3F 150
Heather Ct. CM1: Chelm 6A 60
Heathercroft Rd. SS11: W'fd 1A 118
Heather Dr. CO3: Colc 1G 173
RM1: Romf 6B 110
SS7: Had 4N 135
Heather Gdns. EN9: Enf 6C 76
RM1: Romf 6B 110
Heather Glen RM1: Romf 6B 110
Heatherley Dr. IG5: Ilf 7L 107
Heather Way RM1: Romf 6B 110
Heatherwood Cl. E12: Lon 4J 123
HEATHFIELD 2H 5
Heathfield E4: Lon 9C 90
SS6: Ray 6K 119
SS7: Had 9J 119
Heathfield Ho. *SS1: Wclf S* *7L 137*
(off Westcliff Pde.)
Heathfield Pk. Dr. RM6: Chad H 9G 108
Heathfield Rd. CM1: Chelm 3K 59
Heathfields CO6: Eig G 7B 164
Heathfields Ho. CO2: Colc 3C 174
Heathgate CM8: W Bis 1J 229
Heathlands CO7: Thorr 9F 176
Heath La. CM8: L Brax 1M 229 (5H 25)
DA1: Dart 4B 46
Heathleigh Dr. SS16: Lang H 2K 131
HEATH PARK 1E 126 (3B 40)
Heath Pk. Ct. RM2: Romf 9E 110
Heath Pk. Rd. RM1: Romf 9E 110
RM2: Romf 9E 110 (3B 40)
Heath Rd. CM4: Nor H 5H 69
CM11: Rams H 4N 99 (7K 33)
CO3: Colc, S'way 1G 172 (6D 16)
CO3: S'way 2E 172
(Peartree Rd.)
Heath Rd. CO3: S'way 6A 164 (5B 16)
(Wood La.)
CO5: Rhdge 6F 174
CO7: Alr 6A 176
CO7: W'hoe 4H 175
CO11: Brad 4B 18
CO11: Mist 6N 163 (3B 18)
CO16: Hor X, Ten 4M 169 (5B 18)
Heath Rd. CO16: Wee H 4B 184 (2B 28)
RM6: Chad H 2J 125
RM16: Grays, Ors 8B 146 (7G 41)
Heath Row CM23: Bis S 8A 220
Heathside CO6: W Ber 3F 164
Heathside Cl. IG2: Ilf 9C 108
HEATH, THE
CM22 2E 210 (4B 22)
IP9 1B 18
Heath, The CM22: Hat H 1E 210 (4B 22)
CO2: Lay H 8H 173
CO7: Ded 4N 161 (3J 17)
CO10: Gt Wal 4K 9
IP9: B'ley 1B 18
Heath Vw. Gdns. RM16: Grays 1M 155
Heath Vw. Rd. RM16: Grays 9M 145
HEATHWAY 1M 141 (6K 39)
Heath Way DA8: Eri 6A 152
IG8: Wfd G 2J 107
Heathway RM9: Dag 5L 125 (5K 39)
RM10: Dag 6M 125 (5K 39)
Heathway Ind. Est. RM10: Dag 6N 125
Heatley Way CO4: Colc 7F 166
Heaton Av. RM3: Romf 4F 110
Heaton Cl. E4: Lon 9C 90
RM3: Romf 4G 110
Heaton Grange Rd. RM2: Romf 6D 110
Heaton Way CO5: Tip 5D 226
RM3: Romf 4G 110
HEBING END 7A 10
HECKFORDBRIDGE 6B 172 (1C 26)
Heckfords Rd. CO7: Gt Ben 6K 177 (7A 18)
Heckworth Cl. CO4: Colc 1C 166
Hedge Dr. CO2: Colc 3J 173
Hedgehope Av. SS6: Ray 3K 119
Hedgelands CO6: Cop 1M 171
Hedge La. N13: Lon 1A 38
SS7: Had 2K 135
Hedgemans Rd. RM9: Dag 9J 125 (5J 39)
Hedgemans Way RM9: Dag 8K 125
Hedge Pl. Rd. DA9: Grnh 3D 46
Hedgerow Ct. SS15: Bas 5A 116
Hedgerows CM21: Saw 2L 51
CO3: S'way 9E 164
Hedgerows Bus. Pk. CM2: Chelm 5B 60
Hedgerow, The SS16: Van 2E 132
Hedgers Cl. IG10: Lou 3N 91
Hedgewood Gdns. IG5: Ilf 9N 107
Hedgley IG4: Ilf 8M 107
Hedingham Castle 3L 219 (1E 14)
Hedingham Dr. SS12: W'fd 1N 117
Hedingham Ho. SS6: Ray 6J 119
Hedingham Pl. *CO9: Sib H* *6K 219*
(off Summerfields)
SS4: R'fd 3J 121
Hedingham Rd.
CO9: Gosf, Sib H 6L 201 (3E 14)
CO9: Hals 1J 207 (3F 15)
CO9: Wick P 7G 9
CO10: Bulm, Wick P 7G 9
RM8: Dag 7G 124
RM11: Horn 3L 127
RM16: Chaf H 3F 154
Hedley Av. RM20: Grays 5F 154
Hedley St. RM1: Romf 9C 110
Heenan Cl. IG11: Bark 8B 124
Heeswyk Rd. SS8: Can I 9K 135
Heideburg Rd. SS8: Can I 9K 135
Heideck Gdns. CM13: Hut 8L 97
Heigham Rd. E6: Lon 9L 123
Heighams CM19: H'low 6M 53
Heights, The CM3: Dan 3C 74
EN9: Naze 4H 63
IG10: Lou 1M 91
Heilsburg Rd. SS8: Can I 9K 135
Helden Av. SS8: Can I 9H 135
Helena Cl. SS5: Hock 2E 120
Helena Ct. CM3: S Fer 2K 103
Helena Rd. E17: Lon 9A 106
SS6: Ray 5L 119
Helen How CM3: Gt L 7L 203
Helen Rd. RM11: Horn 7H 111
Helford Ct. CM8: Wthm 5A 230
RM15: S Ock 7E 144
Helford Way RM14: Upm 1A 128
HELHAM GREEN 3F 21
Helham Green SG12: W'side 4F 21
HELIONS BUMPSTEAD 5H 7
Helions Bumpstead Rd. CB9: H'hll 4J 7
Helions Rd. CB9: Stpl B 3J 223 (5J 7)
CM19: H'low 3A 54
Helleborine RM17: Grays 3J 155
Hellendoorn Rd. SS8: Can I 3K 151
HELLMAN'S CROSS 2E 22
Helm Cl. CO6: Gt Hork 9K 159
Helmons La. CM2: W Han 5H 87
Helmore Ct. SS15: Lain 9H 115
Helmore Rd. IG11: Bark 9E 124
Helmores SS15: Lain 9H 115
Helmsdale SS8: Can I 9F 134
Helmsdale Cl. RM1: Romf 4C 110
Helmsdale Rd. RM1: Romf 4C 110
Helmsley Ho. *RM3: Romf* *4J 111*
(off Leyburn Cres.)
Helpeston SS14: Bas 9E 116
Helston Rd. CM1: Chelm 5N 59
Helwys Ct. E4: Lon 3B 106
Hemingway Rd. CM8: Wthm 2C 230
Hemley Rd. RM16: Ors 6F 146
Hemlock Cl. CM8: Wthm 3D 230
Hemmells SS15: Lain 7K 115
Hemmings Ct. CM9: Mal 8A 214
Hemnall St. CM16: Epp 1E 78
HEMP'S GREEN 4A 16
Hempstalls SS15: Lain 1A 132
HEMPSTEAD 6G 7
Hempstead Cl. IG9: Buck H 8G 90
Hempstead Rd.
CB9: Hpstd, Stpl B 4H 223 (6G 7)
CB10: R'ter 7F 7
E17: Lon 7D 106
Hemsted Rd. DA8: Eri 5C 152
Henbane Path RM3: Romf 4H 111
Henderson Cl. RM11: Horn 4F 126
Henderson Dr. DA1: Dart 9K 153 (3C 46)
Henderson Gdns. SS12: W'fd 2M 117
Henderson Ho. *RM10: Dag* *5M 125*
(off Kershaw Rd.)
Henderson Rd. E7: Lon 8J 123
Hendon Cl. CO16: Clac S 8H 185
SS12: W'fd 1L 117
Hendon Gdns. RM5: Col R 3A 110
Hengist Gdns. SS11: W'fd 7L 101
Hengist Rd. DA8: Eri 5A 152
HENHAM 8D 210 (4C 12)
Henham Cl. CM11: Bill 6M 99
Henham Ct. RM5: Col R 5A 110
Henham Rd. CB11: Deb G 3D 12
CM22: Else, Hen 3L 199 (5C 12)
HENHURST 6J 47
Henhurst Rd. DA13: Cobh 6H 47
Henley Ct. CO3: Colc 9G 164
Henley Cres. SS0: Wclf S 2J 137
Henley Gdns. RM6: Chad H 9K 109
Henley Rd. IG1: Ilf 6B 124
HENLEY STREET 7J 47
Henley St. DA13: Ludd 7J 47
Henney Cl. CM3: Cold N 7K 197
Henniker Gdns. E6: Lon 6F 39
Henniker Ga. CM2: Chelm 7B 60
Henniker Point *E15: Lon* *7E 122*
(off Leytonstone Rd.)
Henniker Rd. E15: Lon 7D 122
Henny Back Rd. CO8: Alph 1J 15
Henny Rd. CO8: Lmsh 7K 9
HENNY STREET 6J 9
Henrietta Cl. CO7: W'hoe 3J 175
Henrietta St. E15: Lon 7C 122
Henry Addlington Cl. E6: Lon 5A 140
Henry Cl. CO15: Clac S 2G 189
Henry De Grey Cl. RM17: Grays 2J 155
Henry Dixon Rd. CM8: Riven 3G 25
Henry Dr. SS9: Lgh S 4N 135
Henry Rd. CM1: Chelm 7K 59
Henrys Av. IG8: Wfd G 2F 106 (2E 38)
Henry's Ter. CM15: Ston M 4E 82
Henry St. RM17: Grays 4M 155
Henry's Wlk. IG6: Ilf 4C 108
Henshawe Rd. RM8: Dag 5J 125
Henson Av. SS8: Can I 2L 151
Henwood Side IG8: Wfd G 3M 107
Hepscott Rd. E9: Lon 8A 122
Hepworth Gdns. IG11: Bark 7F 124
Heralds Way CM3: S Fer 1L 103
Herbage Pk. Rd. CM9: Wdhm W 1J 75 (1F 35)
Herbert Gdns. RM6: Chad H 2J 125
Herbert Gro. SS1: Sth S 7N 137
Herbert Rd. CO15: Clac S 1J 189
E12: Lon 6L 123
IG3: Ilf 4D 124
RM11: Horn 2J 127
SS3: Shoe 8G 139
SS8: Can I 1J 151
Herd La. SS17: Corr 1D 148
Hereford Ct. CM2: Gt Bad 5H 73
CO15: Hol S 8B 186
Hereford Dr. CM7: Brain 3M 193
Hereford Gdns. IG1: Ilf 2L 123
Hereford Rd. CO1: Colc 8A 166
CO15: Hol S 8B 186
E11: Lon 9H 107
Hereford Wlk. SS14: Bas 8G 116
Herent Dr. IG5: Ilf 8L 107
Hereward Cl. CO7: W'hoe 3J 175
EN9: Wal A 2D 76
Hereward Gdns. SS11: W'fd 7L 101
Hereward Grn. IG10: Lou 9B 78
Hereward Way CM7: Weth 8C 228
Herga Hyll RM16: Ors 5C 146
Herington Gro. CM13: Hut 6K 97
Heriot Av. E4: Lon 8A 90
Heriot Way CM9: Gt Tot 3N 229
Heritage Way CM3: Latch 8M 211
SS4: R'fd 5K 121
Hermes Dr. CM0: Bur C 3D 196
Hermes Way SS3: Shoe 6E 138
Hermitage Av. SS7: Ben 2G 135
Hermitage Cl. E18: Lon 8F 106
SS7: Ben 2G 135
Hermitage Ct. E18: Lon 8G 106
Hermitage Dr. SS15: Lain 9L 115
Hermitage Ho. *CM24: Stan M* *2C 220*
(off Bentfield Rd.)
Hermitage Rd. N4: Lon 4A 38
N15: Lon 4B 38
SS0: Wclf S 6K 137
Hermitage Wlk. E18: Lon 8F 106
Hermit Rd. E16: Lon 6E 38
Hermon Hill E11: Lon 9G 107 (3F 39)
E18: Lon 9G 107
Hernen Rd. SS8: Can I 9J 135
Hernshaw CM13: Heron 4N 113
Heron Av. SS11: W'fd 1N 117
Heron Chase CM13: Heron 4A 114
Heron Cl. CM21: Saw 3J 51
IG9: Buck H 7G 91
SS6: Ray 5H 119
Heron Ct. CM5: Chip 5L 67
CM13: Heron 5A 114
Heron Dale SS14: Bas 9E 116

Heron Flight Av. RM12: Horn 9E 126
Heron Gdns. SS6: Ray 4H 119
HERONGATE 4A 114 (2G 41)
Herongate SS3: Shoe 6J 139
SS7: Ben 2B 134
Herongate Rd. E12: Lon 4J 123
Heron Glade CO15: Clac S 6K 185
Heron Hill DA17: Belv 1A 46
Heron Ho. E6: Lon 9L 123
Heron Mead EN3: Enf 8A 76
Heron M. IG1: Ilf 4A 124
Heron Quays Station (DLR) 7D 38
Heron Rd. CO5: K'dn 3L 211
Heronsgate CO13: Frin S 8J 181
Heronsgate Trad. Est. SS14: Bas 5H 117
Herons La. CM5: Fy'd 1N 67 (1D 32)
Herons, The E11: Lon 1F 122
RM12: Horn 3H 127
Herons Wood CM20: H'low 1A 54
Heronswood EN9: Wal A 4E 76
Heron Way CM3: May 8L 213
CM9: H'bri 3E 214
Heronway CM13: Hut 7L 97
Heron Way CM19: Roy 2G 52
CO13: Frin S 8H 181
IG8: Wfd G 1J 107
RM14: Upm 3B 128
RM20: W Thur 3E 154 (1E 46)
Herrick Pl. CO3: Colc 9H 165
Herringham Grn. CM2: Chelm 7B 60
Herring's Way CO6: For 1A 164
HERRINGWORTH HALL 7C 10
Herschell Rd. SS9: Lgh S 4B 136
HERTFORD 5B 20
Hertford Dr. SS17: Fob 5D 132
Hertford East Station (Rail) 5B 20
HERTFORD HEATH 6C 20
Hertford La. SG8: Chris 5H 5
Hertford Mus. 5B 20
Hertford North Station (Rail) 5A 20
Hertford Rd. EN3: Enf, Wal X 6C 30
IG2: Ilf 1D 124
IG11: Bark 9N 123
N9: Lon 1C 38
SG12: Ware 5C 20
SG13: Hert H 6C 20
SS8: Can I 2F 150
HERTINGFORDBURY 6A 20
Hertingfordbury Rd. SG14: Hert 6A 20
(not continuous)
Hervilly Way CO14: Walt 7L 181
Heseltine Ct. CO15: Clac S 1M 189
Hesketh Rd. E7: Lon 5G 122
Hesper Rd. CO2: Colc 1C 174
Hesselyn Dr. RM13: Rain 9F 126
Hester Ho. CM20: H'low 1B 54
Hester Pl. CM0: Bur C 3E 196
Hetherington Cl. CO2: Colc 6A 174
Hetzand Rd. SS8: Can I 2M 151
Hever Cl. SS5: Hock 1C 120
Hever Ct. Rd. DA11: Grav 5H 47
Hewes Cl. CO4: Colc 8F 166
Hewett Rd. RM8: Dag 7J 125
Hewins Cl. EN9: Wal A 2E 76
Hewitt Rd. CO12: Har, R'sy 6E 208
Hewitt Wlk. CM8: Wthm 5D 230
Hexagon Ho. RM1: Romf 9D 110
(off Mercury Gdns.)
HEXTABLE 5B 46
HEYBRIDGE
CM4 8B 84 (5H 33)
CM9 4D 214 (7H 25)
Heybridge App. CM9: L'frd, Mal 2B 214 (7H 25)
HEYBRIDGE BASIN 8F 214 (1J 35)
Heybridge Ct. CO15: Clac S 1M 189
(off Connaught Gdns. E.)
Heybridge Dr. IG6: Ilf 6C 108
SS12: W'fd 9M 101
Heybridge Ho. Ind. Est.
CM9: Mal 4D 214
Heybridge Rd. CM4: Ing 8B 84
Heybridge St. CM9: Mal 3D 214 (7H 25)
Heycroft Dr. CM77: Tye G 2D 194
Heycroft Rd. SS5: Hock 2E 120
SS9: Lgh S 9E 120
Heycroft Way CM2: Gt Bad 5G 73
CO5: Tip 5D 226
Heydon SG8: Hey 5G 5
Heydon La. CB11: Elm 6H 5
SG8: Hey 5G 5
Heydon Rd. SG8: Gt Chi 6G 5
Heygate Av. SS1: Sth S 7M 137 (5K 43)
Heynes Rd. RM8: Dag 6H 125
Heythrop, The CM2: Chelm 7M 59
CM4: Ing 6C 84
Heywood Ct. CM9: Mal 2D 214
Heywood La. CM6: Gt D 4L 203
Heywood Way CM9: Mal 3D 214
Heyworth Rd. E15: Lon 7F 122
Hibernia Point SE2: Lon 9J 141
(off Wolvercote Rd.)
Hickbush CO10: Gt Hen 7J 9
HICKFORD HILL 3D 8
Hickford Hill
CO10: Bel P, Clare, Pent 3D 8
Hickling Cl. SS9: Lgh S 9A 120
Hickling Rd. IG1: Ilf 7A 124
Hickman Av. E4: Lon 3C 106
Hickman Rd. RM6: Chad H 2H 125
Hickory Av. CO4: Colc 7D 166
Hicks Ct. RM10: Dag 5N 125
Hickstars La. CM12: Bill 9L 99 (1K 41)
Hicks Way CB9: Stur 6J 223
Hidcote Way CM77: Gt N 1B 204
Hides, The CM20: H'low 2C 54
HIGHAM
STRATFORD ST MARY 1G 17
HIGHAM UPSHIRE 5K 47
HIGHAM HILL 2D 38
Higham Hill Rd. E17: Lon 2D 38
Higham Marsh CO6: Stok 1G 17
Higham Rd. CO7: High 1G 17
IG8: Wfd G 3G 106
Highams Chase CM9: Gold 1L 201
Highams Ct. E4: Lon 9D 90
HIGHAMS PARK 3D 106 (1E 38)
Highams Pk. Ind. Est. E4: Lon 3C 106
Highams Park Station (Rail) 3D 106 (2E 38)
Highams Rd. SS5: Hock 2D 120
Higham Sta. Av. E4: Lon 3A 106
Highams, The E17: Lon 5C 106
Higham Vw. CM16: N Wea 5N 65
High Ash Cl. SS17: Linf 1J 157
Highbank SS5: Hull 4L 103
High Bank SS16: Lang H 2H 131
Highbank Cl. SS9: Lgh S 1E 136
High Barrets SS14: Bas 1H 133
HIGH BEECH 8H 77 (5F 31)
High Beeches SS7: Ben 3B 134
High Beech Rd. IG10: Lou 3K 91
Highbirch Rd.
CO16: Gt Ben, Wee H 9B 178 (2B 28)
Highbridge Retail Pk. EN9: Wal A 4B 76
High Bri. Rd. CM1: Chelm 1A 34
CM2: Chelm 1D 72
Highbridge Rd. IG11: Bark 1A 140
Highbridge St. EN9: Wal A 3B 76 (4D 30)
(not continuous)
HIGHBURY 5A 38
Highbury & Islington Station (Rail, Tube) 5A 38
Highbury Av. EN11: Rye P 3A 52
HIGHBURY CORNER 5A 38
Highbury Gdns. IG3: Ilf 4D 124
Highbury Gro. N5: Lon 5A 38
Highbury Pk. N5: Lon 5A 38
Highbury Stadium 5A 38
Highbury Ter. CO9: Hals 4L 207
High Chelmer CM1: Chelm 9K 59
High Chelmer Shop. Cen. CM1: Chelm 9K 59
(off Market Rd.)
Highclere Rd. CM77: Gt N 2B 204
CO4: Colc 3B 166
Highcliff Cres. SS4: R'fd 9H 105
High Cliff Dr. SS9: Lgh S 6E 136
Highcliffe Cl. SS11: W'fd 8N 101
Highcliffe Dr. SS12: W'fd 8G 100
Highcliffe Gdns. IG4: Ilf 9L 107
Highcliffe Rd. SS11: W'fd 9N 101
Highcliffe Way SS11: W'fd 9N 101
Highcliff Rd. SS7: Ben 5E 134
High Cloister CM11: Bill 6K 99
High Cft. CO6: Coln E 2E 198
HIGH CROSS 2C 20
Highcross La. CM6: L Can 2E 22
Highcross Rd. DA2: S'fleet 5E 46
HIGH EASTER 4G 23
High Easter Rd. CM6: Barns 4K 191 (2G 23)
CM6: Lea R 4D 212 (5E 22)
High Elms IG7: Chig 1D 108
IG8: Wfd G 2G 106
RM14: Upm 3B 128
High Elms La. SG14: B'tn 1A 20
High Elms Rd. SS5: Hull 7L 103
Highfield CM18: H'low 4F 54
CM21: Saw 1K 51
SS5: Hull 5L 103
Highfield App. CM11: Bill 8M 99
Highfield Av. CO12: Har 4K 209 (3H 19)
DA8: Eri 4A 152
SS7: Ben 2H 135
Highfield Cloisters SS9: Lgh S 5B 136
(off Hadleigh Rd.)
Highfield Cl. CM3: Dan 4D 74
CM7: Brain 2J 193
RM5: Col R 3A 110
SS0: Wclf S 4J 137
Highfield Cres. RM12: Horn 4K 127
SS0: Wclf S 4J 137 (4J 43)
SS6: Ray 5K 119
Highfield Dr. CO3: Colc 9K 165
SS0: Wclf S 3J 137
Highfield Gdns. RM16: Grays 9N 145
SS0: Wclf S 3J 137 (4J 43)
Highfield Grn. CM16: Epp 1D 78
Highfield Gro. SS0: Wclf S 3J 137
Highfield Link RM5: Col R 3A 110
Highfield Pl. CM16: Epp 1D 78
Highfield Ri. CM3: Alth 2D 190
Highfield Rd. CM1: Chelm 7F 58
CM11: Bill 9M 99
DA1: Dart 4B 46
IG8: Wfd G 4L 107
IP11: Felix 1K 19
RM5: Col R 4A 110
RM12: Horn 4K 127
Highfields CB10: Saf W 3D 218
CB11: Deb 2C 12
High Flds. CM6: Gt D 3K 203
Highfields CM8: Wthm 5B 230 (4F 25)
CM22: Hen 7D 210
CO9: Gt Yel 2D 206
CO9: Hals 6K 207
Highfields La. CO5: K'dn 3J 25
Highfields Mead CM3: E Han 1B 88
Highfields Rd. CM8: Wthm 4B 230
Highfield Stile Rd. CM7: Brain 2J 193
Highfield Towers RM5: Col R 2B 110
Highfield Way RM12: Horn 4K 127
SS0: Wclf S 3J 137
High Gables IG10: Lou 4K 91
HIGH GARRETT 7L 191 (5D 14)
High Garrett CM7: Brain 8L 191 (5D 14)
Highgate Gro. CM21: Saw 2J 51
Highgate Hill N6: Lon 4A 38
Highgate Rd. NW5: Lon 5A 38
Highgrove CM15: Pil H 5E 96
Highgrove Ho. CM14: Brtwd 8F 96
(off Regency Ct.)
Highgrove M. RM17: Grays 3M 155
Highgrove Rd. RM8: Dag 7H 125
High Holborn WC2: Lon 7A 38
High Ho. Est. CM17: H'low 8L 51
High Ho. La. RM18: W Til 1F 156 (1H 47)
Highland Av. CM15: Brtwd 7F 96
IG10: Lou 5L 91
RM10: Dag 5A 126
(not continuous)
Highland Ct. E18: Lon 5H 107
Highland Gro. CM11: Bill 6K 99
Highland Rd. EN9: Naze 1E 62
SS16: Van 4C 132
(not continuous)
Highlands CO9: Gosf 7L 201
Highlands Av. SS16: Van 2E 132
(not continuous)
Highlands Blvd. SS9: Lgh S 3N 135
Highlands Chalet Pk. CO15: Clac S 6L 185
Highlands Ct. SS9: Lgh S 4A 136
Highlands Cres. SS13: Pits 9N 117
Highlands Dr. CM9: Mal 6A 214
Highlands Gdns. IG1: Ilf 3M 123
Highlands Hill BR8: Swan 6B 46
CM3: May 4B 36
Highlands Rd. SS11: Raw 6H 103
SS13: Pits 9N 117
High La. CM22: Mat T, Srng 5A 22
CM24: Stan M 1E 220 (6A 12)
HIGH LAVER 7B 22
High Laver Rd. CM17: Mat G 6B 22
High Leigh CM15: Dodd 6E 82
High Lighthouse 2N 209
Highmead CM24: Stan M 1D 220
High Mead IG7: Chig 8B 92
SS5: Hock 2D 120
Highmead SS6: Ray 5H 119
Highmead Ct. CM15: Brtwd 7G 96
SS6: Ray 5H 119
High Mdw. CM6: Gt D 3K 203
CM11: Bill 6L 99
High Mdws. IG7: Chig 2C 108
High Oak Rd. SG12: Ware 4C 20
High Oaks CO12: Har 5D 208
SS16: Lang H 3K 131
HIGH ONGAR 6A 68 (3D 32)
High Ongar Rd.
CM5: Chip, H Ong 6L 67 (3C 32)
HIGH PARK CORNER 8H 175 (1G 27)
High Pasture CM3: L Bad 8L 61
High Pastures CM22: Srng 4B 210
High Pavement SS14: Bas 9B 116
High Ridge CM8: Gt Br 6H 205
High Rd. CM16: Epp 3A 78 (4G 31)
(Epping Rd.)
CM16: Epp, Thorn 2G 65 (2J 31)
(London Rd.)
CM16: N Wea 5N 65 (3K 31)
CO2: Lay H 9G 173 (1D 26)
CO6: Ass 1C 16
DA2: Dart 4B 46
E18: Lon 5G 106 (2E 38)
EN10: Brox, Turn, Wmly 2D 30
IG1: Ilf 5A 124 (4H 39)
(not continuous)
IG3: Chad H, Ilf 3E 124 (4H 39)
IG7: Chig 2N 107 (1G 39)
IG9: Buck H, Lou 8H 91 (1F 39)
IP11: T Mary 1J 19
N15: Lon 3B 38
N17: Lon 3B 38
N22: Lon 2A 38
RM6: Chad H 2J 125
RM16: N Stif 8G 145 (7E 40)
RM16: Ors 6A 146 (7G 41)
SG8: Croy 2A 4
SG11: H Cro 2D 20
SG14: Hart, Stfrd, W'frd 3A 20
SS5: Hock, Ray 3N 119 (2G 43)
SS6: Ray 7J 119 (2F 43)
SS7: Ben 1B 134 (3D 42)
SS13: Pits 1J 133
SS16: Lang H 5K 131 (4J 41)
(not continuous)
SS16: Pits, Van 2G 132 (4B 42)
SS17: Corr, Stan H 4A 148 (6K 41)
SS17: Fob 5D 132 (5A 42)
SS17: Horn H 1H 147 (6J 41)
High Rd. E. IP11: Felix 1K 19
High Rd. Leyton E10: Lon 1B 122 (4E 38)
E15: Lon 4B 122 (5E 38)
High Rd. Leytonstone E11: Lon 6E 122 (5E 38)
High Rd. Nth. SS15: Lain 6L 115 (2K 41)
High Rd. Turnford EN10: Turn 2D 30
High Rd. W. IP11: Felix 1K 19
High Rd. Woodford Grn. IG8: Wfd G 3F 106 (2E 38)
HIGH RODING 3F 23
High Silver IG10: Lou 3K 91
Highstead Cres. DA8: Eri 6C 152
High Stile CM6: Gt D 3K 203
Highstone Av. E11: Lon 1G 122
Highstone Ct. E11: Lon 1F 122
(off New Wanstead)
High St. BR8: Swan 6A 46
CB1: B'shm 1E 6
CB1: Cas C 4G 7
CB1: Gt Ab 1B 6
High St. CB1: Lin 2C 6
CB1: W W'ck 1F 7
CB2: Bab 1A 6
CB2: Barr 1E 4
CB2: Foxt 1F 5
CB2: Pam 1K 5
CB2: Saws 1K 5
CB2: Whitt 1J 5
CB9: H'hll 3J 7
CB10: Gt Che 8D 202 (4A 6)
CB10: Gt Sam 2K 205 (1H 13)
CB10: Hpstd 7G 7
CB10: Hxtn 3K 5
CB10: L Ches 5A 6
CB10: Saf W 3C 218 (6B 6)
CB11: Clav 3J 11
CB11: Deb 2C 12
CB11: Elm 6J 5
CB11: L'bry 1B 218 (6A 6)
CB11: Newp 3L 215 (1B 12)
CB11: Widd 3B 12
CM0: Brad S 7C 194 (1F 37)
CM0: Bur C 4D 196 (7C 36)
CM0: S'min 2D 222 (5C 36)
CM1: Chelm 9K 59
CM2: Gt Bad 3G 73 (2B 34)
CM4: Ing 7C 84 (5H 33)
CM4: Stock 7N 85 (5K 33)
CM5: Chip 6L 67 (3C 32)
CM6: Gt D 3L 203 (1G 23)
CM6: Steb 8D 222 (6H 13)
CM7: Brain 6G 193 (7C 14)
CM7: Gt Bar 3B 202 (3J 13)
CM7: Weth 8C 228 (3A 14)
CM9: Mal 5B 214 (1H 35)
CM9: Tol 8J 225 (6C 26)
CM12: Bill 7J 99 (7J 33)
CM14: Brtwd 8F 96 (1E 40)
CM16: Epp 1E 78 (4H 31)
CM17: H'low 8H 51 (6J 21)
(not continuous)
CM19: Roy 2H 53 (6F 21)
CM22: Else 3K 199 (5B 12)
CM22: Hat O 7D 206 (3C 22)
CM22: Hen 8D 210 (4C 12)
CM23: Bis S 1K 21
CO1: Colc 8N 165 (6E 16)
CO4: L'ham 4C 160 (3F 17)
CO5: K'dn 4J 211 (2J 25)
CO5: Rhdge 6G 174
CO5: W Mer 3B 228 (5F 27)
CO6: E Col 8C 198 (4H 15)
CO6: Nay 1D 16
CO7: B'sea 7E 182 (3K 27)
CO7: Ded 2L 161 (2H 17)
CO7: W'hoe 6H 175 (1G 27)
CO8: Bures 7L 195 (1A 16)
CO9: Gt Yel 3D 206 (6D 8)
CO9: Hals 4K 207 (3F 15)
CO10: Act 3K 9
CO10: Caven 2F 9
CO10: Clare 3D 8
CO10: L Mel 2J 9
CO11: Mist 4J 163 (3A 18)
(Manningtree, not continuous)
CO12: Gt Oak 7C 204 (5E 18)
CO12: Har 3M 209 (3H 19)
CO14: Walt 6M 181 (1H 29)
CO15: Clac S 2K 189 (4D 28)
CO16: T Sok 4K 179 (7D 18)
DA1: Dart 4C 46
DA2: Bean 4E 46
DA4: Eyns 7C 46
DA4: F'ham 7C 46
DA9: Grnh 9E 154 (3E 46)
DA10: Swans 3F 47
DA11: N'fleet 3F 47
E11: Lon 9G 106 (3F 39)
E13: Lon 6F 39
E15: Lon 9D 122 (6E 38)
E17: Lon 8A 106
EN3: Enf 7C 30
EN8: Chesh 3C 30
EN8: Wal X 4C 30
(not continuous)
EN11: Brox, Hod 7A 52 (1D 30)
IG6: Ilf 7B 108 (3H 39)
IP11: Felix 1K 19
N14: Lon 1A 38
RM7: Romf 9C 110
RM11: Horn 3H 127 (4B 40)
RM12: Horn 3H 127 (4B 40)
RM15: Ave 8N 143 (7D 40)
RM17: Grays 4K 155
(not continuous)
RM19: Purf 3L 153
SE18: Lon 7G 39
SG2: Walk 6A 10
SG8: Ab P 3A 4
SG8: B'wy 1E 10
SG8: Bar 6E 4
SG8: Bass 4B 4
SG8: Chris 6H 5
SG8: Croy 1A 4
SG8: Fow 2F 5
SG8: Hey 5G 5
SG8: Mel 3E 4
SG8: Meld 2D 4
SG8: Orw 1D 4
SG8: Reed 7D 4
SG9: Bunt 4D 10
SG10: M Hud 2G 21
SG11: Puck 7E 10
SG11: Stdn 7E 10
SG12: Hun 4F 21

High St. SG12: Stan A 6E 20
SG12: Ware 4C 20
SG12: Wid 4G 21
SG14: Wat S 2A 20
SS1: Sth S 6M 137
(not continuous)
SS2: Sth S 5K 43
SS3: Gt W 2K 139 (4B 44)
SS3: Shoe 8K 139 (5C 44)
SS4: Cwdn 1M 105 (7K 35)
SS6: Ray 5J 119 (2F 43)
SS7: Ben 5D 134 (4D 42)
SS7: Had 3K 135 (4F 43)
SS8: Can I 1J 151 (6F 43)
SS9: Lgh S 6B 136
SS12: W'fd 9L 101 (1C 42)
SS17: Stan H 4L 147 (6K 41)
HIGHSTREET GREEN 1D 14
High St. Hornsey N8: Lon 3A 38
High St. Nth. CO5: W Mer 3C 228 (5F 27)
E6: Lon 7L 123
E12: Lon 7L 123 (5G 39)
High St. Nth E6: Lon 9L 123 (5G 39)
High St. Sth. E6: Lon 6G 39
HIGH, THE 3C 54 (7H 21)
High Tor Vw. SE28: Lon 8D 140
High Tree La. CO14: Walt 4N 181
High Trees CM4: Stock 7M 85
Hightrees Ct. CM14: War 1F 112
High Vw. *CM0: St La* *2C 36*
(off Mountview Cres.)
CM23: Bchgr 6B 220
High Vw. Av. CO15: Clac S 7J 185
RM17: Grays 3M 155
Highview Av. SS16: Lang H 1H 131
High Vw. Cl. CO15: Clac S 7J 185
IG10: Lou 4J 91
Highview Ct. *IG10: Lou* *4K 91*
(off High Rd.)
Highview Cres. CM13: Hut 5M 97
Highview Gdns. RM14: Upm 4M 127
High Vw. Gdns. RM17: Grays 3M 155
Highview Ho. RM6: Chad H 8K 109
High Vw. Pde. IG4: Ilf 9M 107
High Vw. Ri. CM11: Cray H 2D 116
High Vw. Rd. E18: Lon 6F 106
Highview Rd. SS7: Thund 8G 118
Highway, The E1: Lon 7C 38
HIGHWOOD 5C 70 (2H 33)
Highwood Cl. CM14: Brtwd 6E 96
SS9: Lgh S 2E 136
Highwood Gdns. IG5: Ilf 9M 107
Highwood La. IG10: Lou 4N 91
Highwood Rd. CM1: Ed C, Hghwd 6A 70 (3G 33)
CM1: Writ 3G 70 (2J 33)
HIGHWOODS 3B 166 (5F 17)
HIGH WOODS 8B 70 (3G 33)
Highwoods App. CO4: Colc 3B 166 (5F 17)
High Woods Country Pk. 4A 166
Highwoods Sq. CO4: Colc 3B 166
HIGH WYCH 3F 50 (4J 21)
High Wych La.
CM21: H Wych, Saw 3F 50 (4J 21)
High Wych Rd.
CM21: Gil, H Wych, Saw 6D 50 (5H 21)
Hilary Cl. DA8: Eri 6A 152
RM12: Horn 7H 127
SS4: R'fd 2K 121
Hilary Cres. SS6: Ray 5L 119
Hilary Dennis Ct. E11: Lon 8G 107
Hilbery Rd. SS8: Can I 2J 151
Hilda Rd. E6: Lon 9K 123
Hildaville Dr. SS0: Wclf S 5H 137
Hilden Dr. DA8: Eri 5F 152
HILDERSHAM 1C 6
Hildersham Rd. CB1: Abgtn, Hdshm 1B 6
Hillary Cl. CM1: Chelm 7M 59
CM9: Mal 3D 214
CM77: Tye G 7F 15
Hillary Mt. CM12: Bill 7H 99
Hill Av. SS11: W'fd 9N 101
Hillboro Ct. E11: Lon 2D 122
Hillborough Mans. SS0: Wclf S 3J 137
Hillborough Rd. SS0: Wclf S 3J 137
Hill Cl. SS7: Ben 2E 134
Hill Ct. RM1: Romf 8D 110
Hill Cres. CM2: Chelm 9M 59
RM11: Horn 1G 127
Hillcrest CM3: May 7L 213
CO13: Kir S 6G 180
CO15: Clac S 7L 185
Hillcrest Av. RM20: W Thur 4D 154
SS5: Hull 7L 103
SS16: Lang H 2G 131
Hillcrest Cl. SS17: Horn H 1H 147
Hillcrest Cotts. CO4: L'ham 2E 160
Hillcrest Ct. CO12: Har 4L 209
RM5: Col R 5B 110
SS17: Horn H *2H 147*
(off Hillcrest Rd.)
Hillcrest Rd. CM3: S Fer 1J 103
CM5: Toot 9C 66
E17: Lon 6D 106
E18: Lon 6F 106
IG10: Lou 5K 91
RM11: Horn 2E 126
SS1: Sth S 6N 137
Hillcrest Rd. SS5: Hock 2D 120
SS17: Horn H 2G 147
Hillcrest Vw. SS16: Van 3E 132
Hillcrest Way CM16: Epp 1F 78
Hillcroft IG10: Lou 1N 91
Hillcroft Rd. E6: Lon 5A 140
Hilldene Av. RM3: Romf 3G 110 (2B 40)
Hilldene Cl. RM3: Romf 2H 111
HILLEND 1H 199
Hill Farm Cotts. CM11: Cray H 1E 116
Hill Farm Ind. Est. CO4: Boxt 2A 160
Hill Farm Rd. CB2: Whitt 2J 5
Hillfield CO5: Fee 1L 211
Hillfoot Av. RM5: Col R 5A 110
Hillfoot Rd. RM5: Col R 5A 110
HILL GREEN 2K 11
Hill Gro. RM1: Romf 7C 110
Hillgrove Bus. Pk. EN9: Naze 1C 62
Hillhouse EN9: Wal A 3F 76
Hillhouse Cl. CM12: Bill 4K 99
Hillhouse Ct. CM12: Bill 4K 99
Hill Ho. Ct. CO7: B'sea 6F 182
Hillhouse Dr. CM12: Bill 4K 99
RM16: Grays 3D 156
Hillhouse La. CO16: Ten, T Sok 3E 178 (7C 18)
Hill Ho. Pk. CM9: Mal 5B 214
Hilliards Rd. CO7: Gt Bro 5G 168 (5K 17)
Hillie Bunnies CO6: E Col 7C 198
Hillingdon Rd. DA7: Bexh 7A 152
Hillington Gdns. IG8: Wfd G 6K 107
Hill La. CB9: Stur 8K 223 (4K 7)
SS5: Hock 2E 120
Hillman Av. CO15: Jay 6C 188
Hillman Cl. RM11: Horn 7H 111
Hillmarton Rd. N7: Lon 5A 38
Hillridge CO4: Colc 4B 166
Hill Ri. RM14: Upm 4L 127
Hillrise Rd. RM5: Col R 3A 110
Hill Rd. CB10: Gt Sam 3K 205 (1H 13)
CB10: Hpstd 7G 7
CM2: Chelm 9M 59
CM14: Brtwd 9D 96
CM16: They B 8D 78
CO6: Cogg 3M 197
CO12: Har 3L 209
CO15: Clac S 7J 185
SS2: Sth S 1L 137
SS7: Ben 3E 134
Hill Rd. Sth. CM2: Chelm 9M 59
Hill's Chace CM14: War 1F 112
Hills Cl. CM7: Brain 4H 193
Hills Cres. CO3: Colc 1H 173
HILLSIDE 2A 152
Hillside CB2: Saws 1K 5
CM9: Mal 5C 214
CM17: H'low 5H 55
CO13: Frin S 1H 187
DA8: Eri 2A 152
RM3: Romf 1H 111
RM17: Grays 1N 155
Hillside Av. IG8: Wfd G 3J 107 (2F 39)
SS5: Hock 2E 120
Hillside Cl. CM11: Bill 7K 99
IG8: Wfd G 2J 107
Hillside Cotts. CM23: Bchgr 6B 220
SS11: Runw 6A 102
Hillside Cres. CO15: Hol S 7N 185
SS9: Lgh S 6F 136
Hillside End CM23: Bchgr 6B 220
Hillside Gdns. CM7: Brain 7H 193
E17: Lon 7D 106
Hillside Gro. CM2: Chelm 4B 72
Hillside Ho. CM7: Brain 7H 193
Hillside M. CM2: Chelm 3B 72
Hillside Rd. CM0: Bur C 3D 196
CM0: S'min 2C 222
CM11: Bill 7K 99 (7J 33)
SS5: Hock 2A 120
SS7: Ben 5D 134
SS9: Lgh S 2D 136
(Leigh Hill)
SS9: Lgh S 7B 120
(Eastwood Rise)
Hillside Wlk. CM14: Brtwd 9C 96
Hills Rd. CO9: Sib H 7J 219
IG9: Buck H 7H 91
Hillston Cl. CO2: Colc 4B 174
Hill St. CB10: Saf W 4C 218 (6B 6)
Hill Ter. SS17: Corr 1D 148
Hill, The CM17: H'low 8H 51
DA11: N'fleet 3G 47
Hilltop E17: Lon 7B 106
Hill Top IG10: Lou 1N 91
Hilltop Av. SS5: Hull 7L 103
Hill Top Av. SS7: Ben 4H 135
Hilltop Cl. CO2: Colc 2D 174
Hill Top Cl. IG10: Lou 2N 91
Hilltop Cl. SS6: Ray 6J 119
Hill Top Cl. IG8: Wfd G 3M 107
Hilltop Cres. CO16: Wee 5D 178
Hill Top La. CB11: Saf W 6D 218
Hill Top Pl. IG10: Lou 2N 91
Hilltop Ri. CO16: Wee 5C 178
Hill Top Ri. SS16: Lang H 2H 131
Hilltop Rd. RM20: W Thur 4E 154
SS15: Lain 8M 115
Hill Top Vw. IG8: Wfd G 3M 107
Hill Tree Cl. CM21: Saw 3J 51
Hillview CM3: Bick 9F 74
Hill Vw. SG9: Bkld 2C 10
Hillview Av. RM11: Horn 1G 127
Hillview Cl. CO5: Rhdge 6F 174
Hill Vw. Cres. IG1: Ilf 1M 123
Hill Vw. Dr. SE28: Lon 8D 140
Hillview Gdns. SS17: Stan H 9A 132
Hill Vw. Rd. CM1: Chelm 7L 59
Hillview Rd. SS6: Ray 4J 119
Hillway CM11: Bill 6M 99 (7K 33)
SS0: Wclf S 6F 136
Hillway, The CM4: Mount 9A 84
(not continuous)
Hillwood Cl. CM13: Hut 7L 97
Hillwood Gro. CM13: Hut 7L 97
Hillwood Gro. SS11: W'fd 9M 101
Hillybroom Gdns. CO5: W Mer 3D 228
Hilly Fld. CM18: H'low 7E 54
Hillyfields IG10: Lou 1N 91 (6G 31)
Hilly Rd. SS15: Lain 8M 115
Hilton Cl. CO11: Mist 4J 163
Hilton Rd. SS8: Can I 9G 134
Hilton Wlk. CO9: Sib H 7K 219
SS8: Can I 9G 135
Hilton Way CO9: Sib H 7K 219
Hilversum Way SS8: Can I 9H 135
Hind Cl. IG7: Chig 2E 108
Hind Cres. DA8: Eri 4B 152
Hindles Rd. SS8: Can I 1K 151
Hindmans Way RM9: Dag 4L 141 (6K 39)
Hind Ter. RM20: Grays 4G 154
Hines Cl. CO6: Aldh 6A 16
Hinguar St. SS3: Shoe 8K 139
Hinksey Path SE2: Lon 9J 141
Hinton Ct. *E10: Lon* *4B 122*
(off Leyton Grange Est.)
Hintons CM19: H'low 7N 53
HINXTON 3K 5
Hinxton Rd. CB2: Dux 3K 5
Hinxton Watermill 3K 5
Hispano M. EN3: Enf 7A 76
Hitcham M. CM7: Brain 8K 193
Hitcham Rd. CO6: Cogg 2K 197
Hitchcock's Meadows Nature Reserve 4F 74
Hitch Comn. Rd. CB11: Newp 3K 215
Hitchin Cl. RM3: Romf 1G 110
Hither Blakers CM3: S Fer 9K 89
Hitherfield Rd. RM8: Dag 4K 125
Hitherwood Cl. RM12: Horn 6H 127
Hitherwood Rd. CO2: Colc 4K 173
Hive Cl. CM14: Brtwd 8D 96
Hobart Cl. CM1: Chelm 6G 58
Hobart Rd. IG6: Ilf 6B 108
RM9: Dag 6J 125
RM18: Til 6C 156
Hobbiton Hill CM3: S Fer 2J 103
HOBBS CROSS
HARLOW 2N 55 (6K 21)
THEYDON GARNON 6J 79 (5J 31)
Hobbs Cross Open Farm 6J 79
Hobbs Cross Rd.
CM16: Abr, Epp, Fid, They G 4H 79
CM17: H'low 2M 55 (6K 21)
Hobbs Dr. CO4: Boxt 3A 160
Hobbs La. CO10: Glem 2G 9
Hobbs M. IG3: Ilf 4E 124
Hobhouse Rd. SS17: Stan H 1M 147
Hobleythick La. SS0: Wclf S 3J 137 (4J 43)
Hoblongs Ind. Est. CM6: Gt D 1J 191
Hobtoe Rd. CM20: H'low 2N 53
HOCKENDEN 6A 46
Hockenden La. BR8: Swan 6A 46
HOCKERILL 1K 21
Hockerill St. CM23: Bis S 1K 21
HOCKLEY 1C 120 (1H 43)
Hockley Cl. CM0: Brad S 8E 194
SS14: Bas 9E 116
Hockley Ct. E18: Lon 5G 106
Hockley Dr. RM2: Romf 6F 110
Hockley Grn. SS14: Bas 9F 116
Hockley La. CM0: Brad S 7E 194 (1F 37)
Hockley M. IG11: Bark 3D 140
Hockley Mobile Homes SS5: Hock 6B 104
Hockley Ri. SS5: Hock 2D 120
Hockley Rd. SS6: Ray 5K 119 (2F 43)
SS14: Bas 9E 116
Hockley Station (Rail) 1D 120 (1H 43)
HODDESDON 5A 52 (7D 20)
Hoddesdon Bus. Cen. EN11: Hod 5A 52
Hoddesdon Open Air Swimming Pool 7A 52
Hoddesdon Rd.
SG12: Hod, Stan A 1B 52 (6E 20)
Hoddeson Ind. Cen. EN11: Rye P 4C 52
Hodges Cl. RM16: Chaf H 3G 154
Hodges Holt *CM8: Wthm* *8D 230*
(off Maldon Rd.)
Hodgkin Cl. SE28: Lon 7J 141
Hodgson Ct. SS11: W'fd 2A 118
Hodgson Way SS11: W'fd 1N 117 (1C 42)
Hodings Rd. CM20: H'low 2A 54
Hodson Pl. EN3: Enf 8A 76
Hoecroft EN9: Naze 1F 62
Hoe Dr. CO3: Colc 1H 173
Hoe La. CM3: Gt Walt 6G 56
CM3: Ret C 2N 101 (6D 34)
CO10: Pent 3F 9
EN1: Enf 5C 30
EN3: Enf 5C 30
EN9: Naze 1F 62 (1E 30)
RM4: Abr 2G 92 (6J 31)
SG12: Ware 5C 20
Hoe Mill Rd. CM9: Wdhm W 1F 35
Hoestock Rd. CM21: Saw 2J 51
Hoe St. CM1: Rox 1H 33
E17: Lon 8A 106 (3D 38)
Hoe, The CM12: Bill 3K 115
Hoffmans Way CM1: Chelm 7K 59
Hogarth Av. CM15: Brtwd 9H 97
Hogarth Cl. CO5: W Mer 3E 228
Hogarth Ct. *CM1: Chelm* *5N 59*
(off Rembrandt Gro.)
Hogarth Dr. SS3: Shoe 6L 139
Hogarth End CO13: Walt 7H 181
Hogarth Reach IG10: Lou 4M 91
Hogarth Rd. RM8: Dag 7G 125
RM16: Grays 8K 145
Hogarth Way SS4: R'fd 1H 121
Hogges Cl. EN11: Hod 5A 52
Hogg La. RM16: Grays 1K 155 (1F 47)
RM17: Grays 1K 155 (1F 47)
Hogg La. RM17: Grays 9K 145
Hog Hill Rd. RM5: Col R 4L 109 (2K 39)
Hog's La. CO7: E Ber 1D 162
SG8: Chris 6H 5
Hogwell Chase CM3: Stow M 5G 35
Hogwell Sidings CM3: Stow M 6G 35
Holbech Rd. SS14: Bas 7G 117
Holbeck La. EN7: Chesh 2B 30
Holbein Ter. *RM8: Dag* *6H 125*
(off Marlborough Rd.)
Holbek Rd. SS8: Can I 2L 151
HOLBORN 7A 38
Holborn WC1: Lon 7A 38
Holborn Station (Tube) 7A 38
Holborn Viaduct EC1: Lon 7A 38
Holborough Cl. CO4: Colc 8F 166
HOLBROOK 1D 18
Holbrook Cl. CM3: S Fer 1K 103
CM11: Bill 6M 99
CO16: Clac S 9F 184
Holbrooke Wlk. *CO5: Tip* *6E 226*
(off Wilkin Dr.)
Holbrook Rd. IP9: Holb 1E 18
IP9: Stut 1C 18
Holcombe Rd. IG1: Ilf 2N 123
HOLDBROOK 4D 30
Holdbrook Way RM3: H Wood 6K 111
Holden Cl. CM7: Brain 6J 193
RM8: Dag 5G 124
HOLDEN END 6C 190
Holden Gdns. CM14: War 2G 113
SS14: Bas 6G 116
Holden Rd. CO4: Colc 5N 165
SS14: Bas 6G 116
Holden Wlk. SS14: Bas 6G 116
Holden Way RM14: Upm 3A 128
HOLDER'S GREEN 4G 13
Holecroft EN9: Wal A 4E 76
Hole Farm La. CM13: Gt War 7E 112
Holford Rd. RM16: Ors 8H 147
SS17: Ors, W Til 8H 147
(not continuous)
Holgate SS13: Pits 7K 117
Holgate Ct. *RM1: Romf* *9C 110*
(off Western Rd.)
Holgate Gdns. RM10: Dag 8M 125
Holgate Rd. RM10: Dag 7M 125
Holiday Hill CM2: W Han 5F 86 (5B 34)
Holkham Av. CM3: S Fer 3K 103
Holland Av. SS8: Can I 9D 134
Holland Cl. RM7: Romf 9A 110
Holland Ct. *E17: Lon* *8C 106*
(off Evelyn Rd.)
Holland Haven Country Pk. 5E 186
Holland Ho. E4: Lon 1D 106
HOLLAND-ON-SEA 7A 186 (3F 29)
Holland Pk. CO15: Clac S 9L 185
Holland Pk. Av. IG3: Ilf 1D 124
Holland Rd. CO13: Frin S 2H 187
CO13: Walt 8E 180 (1F 29)
CO15: Clac S, Hol S 2K 189 (4E 28)
(not continuous)
CO16: Clac S, L Cla 3H 185 (2D 28)
E6: Lon 9N 123
SS0: Wclf S 7J 137
Hollands Rd. CB9: H'hll 3J 7
Holland Wlk. SS16: Van 4E 132
Holledge Cres. CO13: Walt 8H 181
Holley Gdns. CM11: Bill 5K 99
Hollidge Way RM10: Dag 9N 125
Hollies Rd. CM77: Tye G 7F 15
Hollies, The *E11: Lon* *9G 106*
(off New Wanstead)
EN9: Wal A *5J 77*
(off Woodbine Cl.)
SS17: Stan H 4L 147
Holliland Cft. CO6: Gt Tey 2E 170
Hollingtons Gro. CO2: B'ch 8D 172
Hollis Lock CM2: Chelm 8B 60
Hollis Pl. RM17: Grays 2K 155
Holliwell Cl. CO3: S'way 9E 164
HOLLOWAY 4A 38
Holloway Cl. CM6: Lea R 4C 212
Holloway Cres. CM6: Lea R 3C 212
Holloway Rd. CM9: Mal 2B 214 (7H 25)
E11: Lon 5D 122
N19: Lon 4A 38
Holloway Road Station (Tube) 5A 38
Hollow Cotts. RM19: Purf 3L 153
Hollowfield Av.
RM17: Grays 2N 155
Hollow La.
CM1: Broom, Chelm, Chig S 4F 58 (7K 23)
CO8: Bures 1A 16
Hollow Rd. CB11: Elm 6J 5
CB11: Widd 3B 12
CM6: Fels 2A 24
CO5: K'dn 3H 211 (2H 25)
CO10: Ashen, Clare 4C 8
SG8: Chris 6H 5
Hollow, The IG8: Wfd G 1F 106
Hollybank CM8: Wthm 6C 230
Holly Bank SS16: Lang H 2H 131
Hollybush Cl. E11: Lon 9G 106
Hollybush Hill CO7: Gt Ben 2K 183 (2A 28)
E11: Lon 1F 122 (3E 38)
Holly Cl. CM0: Bur C 3D 196
CO2: Colc 4K 173
IG9: Buck H 9K 91
Holly Ct. CM12: Bill 6J 99
CO15: Clac S 9J 185
Holly Cres. IG8: Wfd G 4D 106
Hollycroft CM2: Gt Bad 4J 73
Hollycross Rd. SG12: Stan A 5D 20
Hollydown Way E11: Lon 5D 122 (4E 38)

Holly Dr. E4: Lon 6B **90**
RM15: S Ock 4G **145**
Hollyfield CM19: H'low 6A **54**
Hollyford CM11: Bill 3M **99**
(not continuous)
Holly Gdns. DA7: Bexh 9A **152**
Holly Gro. SS16: Lang H 1H **131**
Holly Gro. Rd. SG14: B'fld 4A **20**
Holly Hill Rd. DA8: Eri 3A **152**
Hollyhock Rd. CB10: Saf W 3D **218**
Holly Ho. CM15: Brtwd 7G **97**
Holly La. CO6: Boxt, Gt Hork 4K **159** (3E **16**)
Hollymead SS17: Corr 1N **147**
Hollymead Cl. CO4: Colc 4N **165**
Holly Oaks CO6: Wmgfd 8L **229**
Holly Rd. CO3: S'way 1D **172**
E11: Lon 2F **122**
Hollytree Ct. CO2: Colc 3K **173**
Hollytree Gdns. SS6: Ray 7H **119**
Hollytrees Mus. 8N 165
Holly Vw. Cl. CO16: Ten 1D **178**
Holly Wlk. CM8: Wthm 2E **230**
(not continuous)
SS8: Can I 1F **150**
Holly Way CM2: Chelm 3E **72**
CM22: Tak 3B **224**
Hollyway CO5: Tip 6C **226**
Holly Way CO7: Elms 9M **167**
Hollywood Bowl Pipps Hill 6C 116
Hollywood Bowl Barking 3B 140
Hollywood Cl. CM2: Gt Bad 4F **72**
Hollywood Way DA8: Eri 5F **152**
IG8: Wfd G 4D **106**
Holman Cres. CO3: Colc 2H **173**
Holman Rd. CO9: Hals 6K **207**
Holmans CM3: Bore 3F **60**
Holmbrook Way CO13: Frin S 9H **181**
Holmcroft Ho. E17: Lon 8B **106**
Holmer Ct. CO2: Colc 9M **165**
Holme Rd. RM11: Horn 3L **127**
Holmes Cl. SS17: Horn H 2H **147**
Holmes Ct. *SS8: Can I* *1K* ***151***
(off High St.)
Holmesdale Hill DA4: S Dar 6D **46**
Holmesdale Rd. DA4: S Dar 6D **46**
Holmes Mdw. CM19: H'low 9A **54**
Holmes Rd. CO9: Hals 6K **207**
Holme Wlk. SS12: W'fd 2N **117**
Holm Oak CO2: Colc 3A **174**
Holmsdale Cl. SS0: Wclf S 3H **137**
Holmsdale Gro. DA7: Bexh 7C **152**
Holmswood SS8: Can I 9L **135**
Holmwood Av. CM15: Shenf 5K **97**
Holmwood Cl. CO16: Clac S 7F **184**
Holmwood Rd. IG3: Ilf 4D **124**
Holness Rd. E15: Lon 8F **122**
Holst Av. CM8: Wthm 8C **230**
SS15: Lain 7L **115**
Holst Cl. SS17: Stan H 2L **147**
Holstock Rd. IG1: Ilf 4B **124**
Holsworthy SS3: Shoe 6H **139**
Holsworthy Ho. RM3: Romf 5H **111**
Holt Cl. IG7: Chig 2E **108**
SE28: Lon 7G **141**
Holt Ct. E15: Lon 7C **122**
Holt Dr. CM8: W Bis 2K **229**
CO2: Colc 7A **174**
Holt Farm Way SS4: R'fd 3J **121**
Holton Rd. SS6: Ray 6N **119**
SS8: Can I 2M **151**
HOLTON ST MARY 1H 17
Holt Rd. RM3: Romf 4J **111**
Holt's Rd. CO6: L Hork 5C **158** (3C **16**)
Holt, The IG6: Ilf 3B **108**
Holt Way IG7: Chig 2E **108**
Holtwhite's Hill EN2: Enf 6A **30**
Holtynge SS7: Ben 2C **134**
Holy Acre CM19: Roy 2G **52**
Holybread La. CM3: L Bad 7K **61** (1D **34**)
Holy Cross Hill EN10: Brox, Chesh, Wmly 2C **30**
HOLYFIELD 8D **62** (3E **30**)
Holyfield Hall Farm 5C 62 (2E 30)
Holyfield Rd. EN9: Wal A 8C **62** (3E **30**)
Holyoak La. SS5: Hock 3D **120**
Holyrood CO12: Har 5H **209**
Holyrood Dr. SS0: Wclf S 4G **136**
Holyrood Gdns. RM16: Grays 2E **156**
Homebridge CB10: Gt Sam 3K **205**
Homebush Ho. E4: Lon 6B **90**
Home Cl. CB9: Stpl B 2L **223**
CM20: H'low 3E **54**
Homecove Ho. *SS0: Wclf S* *7J* ***137***
(off Holland Rd.)
Homecroft Gdns. IG10: Lou 3A **92**
Home Farm Cl. SS3: Gt W 2M **139**
Home Farm La.
CO7: A'lgh 7N **161** (4J **17**)
Home Farm Rd.
CM13: Brtwd, L War 5H **113** (2F **41**)
Homefield CM0: S'min 1E **222**
EN9: Wal A 2G **76**
Homefield Av. IG2: Ilf 9D **108**
Homefield Cl. CM1: Chelm 6F **58**
CM11: Bill 1M **115**
CM16: Epp 9F **64**
Homefield Rd. CB9: H'hll 3J **7**
CM8: Wthm 3D **230**
CO2: Colc 5K **173**
Homefields Av. SS7: Ben 1B **134**
Homefield Way CM77: Tye G 2D **194**
CO6: E Col 7C **198**
Home Gdns. DA1: Dart 3C **46**
RM10: Dag 5A **126**
Homeheather Ho. IG4: Ilf 9M **107**
Homehurst Ho. CM15: Brtwd 7G **97**
Homelands Ct. CO14: Walt 7K **181**
Homelands Gro. CM11: Rams H 4D **100**
Homelye Chase CM6: Gt D, L Dun 6B **212**
Home Mead CM1: Writ 1J **71**
CM2: Gall 8D **72**
SS15: Lain 7K **115**
Home Mdws. CM12: Bill 6J **99**
Home Pastures CM22: Hat H 1E **210**
Homer Cl. DA7: Bexh 6A **152**
Homeregal Ho. *SS6: Ray* *5K* ***119***
(off Bellingham La.)
HOMERTON 5C 38
Homerton Cl. CO15: Clac S 5K **185**
Homerton High St. E9: Lon 5C **38**
Homerton Rd. E9: Lon 6A **122** (5D **38**)
Homerton Station (Rail) 5C 38
Homesdale Cl. E11: Lon 9G **106**
Homestead CM1: Chelm 4K **59**
Homestead Ct. SS7: Had 3K **135**
Homestead Dr. SS16: Bas 4L **131**
Homestead Gdns. CO15: Clac S 7J **185**
SS7: Had 4K **135**
Homestead Rd.
CM11: Rams B 8E **100**
RM8: Dag 4L **125**
SS7: Had 4K **135**
SS13: Pits 9M **117**
Homestead Way SS7: Had 4K **135**
Homeway RM3: H Wood 3M **111**
Homing Rd. CO16: L Cla 1G **184**
Honey Brook EN9: Wal A 3E **76**
Honey Cl. CM2: Gt Bad 4D **72**
CM15: Hook E 5G **82**
RM10: Dag 8N **125**
Honeycroft CO11: Law 5G **163**
IG10: Lou 3A **92**
Honey La. CB11: Clav 3H **11**
EN9: Wal A 3E **76** (4E **30**)
Honey La. Ho. EN9: Wal A 4G **76**
Honeymeade CM21: Saw 5H **51**
(not continuous)
Honey Pot Hall CO15: Clac S 1L **189**
Honeypot La. CM1: Mash 5A **56**
Honey Pot La. CM3: Pur 9H **197** (5G **35**)
Honeypot La. CM4: Stock 8L **85** (5K **33**)
CM9: Tol K 4A **26**
CM14: Brtwd 9D **96** (1E **40**)
CO7: Gt Bro 7H **169** (5A **18**)
CO11: Wix 5C **18**
CO16: Wee H 1E **184**
EN9: Wal A 4J **77**
SS14: Bas 8C **116**
(not continuous)
Honeypots CM2: Gt Bad 4D **72**
Honeysuckle Cl. CM15: Pil H 4E **96**
RM3: Romf 3G **111**
Honeysuckle Ct. E12: Ilf 8A **124**
Honeysuckle Path CM1: Chelm 5A **60**
Honeysuckle Way CM8: Wthm 3A **230**
CO4: Colc 7E **166**
CO7: Thorr 9F **176**
Honeytree Ct. IG10: Lou 1A **92**
HONEY TYE 1C 16
Honeywood Av. CO6: Cogg 2L **197**
Honeywood Rd. CO9: Hals 3M **207**
Honiley Av. SS12: W'fd 4M **117**
Honington Cl. SS11: W'fd 1B **118**
Honiton Rd. RM7: Romf 1B **126**
SS1: Sth S 6A **138**
Honorius Dr. CO4: Colc 1B **166**
Honor Link CM1: Chelm 4B **60**
Honor St. CM17: H'low 2H **55**
Honywood Cl. CO6: M Tey 3G **170**
Honywood Rd. CO3: Colc 9L **165**
SS14: Bas 5G **116**
Honywood Way CO13: Walt 7J **181**
Hood Cl. SS12: W'fd 1M **117**
Hood Gdns. CM7: Brain 4L **193**
Hood Rd. RM13: Rain 2C **142**
Hood Wlk. RM7: Maw 5N **109**
HOOK END 5G **82** (5E **32**)
Hook End La. CM15: Hook E 5F **82** (4E **32**)
Hook End Rd. CM15: Hook E 5E **82** (5E **32**)
Hook Fld. CM18: H'low 5D **54**
HOOK GREEN
MEOPHAM 7H **47**
SOUTHFLEET 5F **47**
Hook Grn. La. DA2: Dart 4A **46**
Hook Grn. Rd. DA13: S'fleet 5F **47**
Hook La. RM4: Abr, Stap A 5L **93** (7K **31**)
Hookshall Dr. RM10: Dag 5A **126**
Hookstone Way IG8: Wfd G 4K **107**
Hooley Dr. SS6: Ray 1J **119**
Hoo, The CM17: H'low 7H **51**
Hoover Dr. SS15: Lain 9H **115**
Hope Av. SS17: Stan H 9N **131**
Hope Cl. CM15: Mount 9A **84**
IG8: Wfd G 3J **107**
RM6: Chad H 8J **109**
HOPE END GREEN 4E **224** (1D **22**)
Hope Rd. CM11: Cray H 2D **116**
SS7: Ben 5D **134**
SS8: Can I 2K **151**
SS17: Stan H 5M **147**
HOPE'S GREEN 4C **134** (4D **42**)
Hopes La. CM4: Marg 1L **85**
Hope Ter. RM20: Grays 3G **155**
Hopewell Cl. RM16: Chaf H 3G **154**
Hop Gdns. La. CM9: Wdhm W 1F **35**
Hopgrounds, The CM7: F'fld 3D **200**
Hopkins Cl. CO13: Frin S 8J **181**
RM2: Romf 7G **110**
Hopkins Mead CM2: Chelm 9A **60**
Hopkirk Cl. CM3: Dan 2F **74**
Hoppers Rd. N13: Lon 1A **38**
Hopper Wlk. CO4: Colc 9D **166**
(not continuous)
Hoppet, The CM4: Ing 5E **84**
Hoppett Rd. E4: Lon 8E **90**
Hopping Jacks La. CM3: Dan 3F **74** (2E **34**)
Hoppit Mead CM7: Brain 7H **193**
Hoppitt, The CM5: M'ton 1B **32**
Horace Av. RM7: Rush G 3A **126**
Horace Rd. CM11: Bill 4L **99**
E7: Lon 6H **123**
IG6: Ilf 7B **108**
SS1: Sth S 7N **137**
Hordle Pl. CO12: Har 3M **209**
Hordle St. CO12: Har 3M **209**
Horkesley Hill CO6: Gt Hork, Nay 1H **159** (2D **16**)
Horkesley Rd. CO4: Boxt 8L **159** (4E **16**)
Horkesley Way SS12: W'fd 1M **117**
Horksley Gdns. CM13: Hut 5M **97**
Horley Cl. CO16: Clac S 7G **185**
Horn & Horseshoe La. CM17: H'low 5K **55**
Hornbeam Av. RM14: Upm 6L **127**
Hornbeam Chase RM15: S Ock 3G **145**
Hornbeam Cl. CM2: Chelm 4B **72**
CM13: Brtwd 9L **97**
CM16: They B 7C **78**
CO2: Colc 4L **173**
IG1: Ilf 7C **124**
IG9: Buck H 9K **91**
IG11: Bark 3F **140**
Hornbeam Gro. E4: Lon 9E **90**
Hornbeam Ho. IG9: Buck H 9K **91**
Hornbeam La. DA7: Bexh 7A **152**
E4: Lon 4E **90**
Hornbeam Rd. CM16: They B 7C **78**
IG9: Buck H 9K **91**
Hornbeams SS7: Thund 7B **118**
Hornbeams, The CM20: H'low 1B **54**
CO12: L Oak 8D **208**
Hornbeam Wlk. CM8: Wthm 3D **230**
Hornbeam Way SS15: Lain 6M **115**
Horn Book CB11: Saf W 4E **218**
Hornby Av. SS0: Wclf S 1H **137**
Hornby Cl. SS0: Wclf S 1J **137**
HORNCHURCH 4J **127** (4B **40**)
Hornchurch Cl. SS11: W'fd 1A **118**
Hornchurch Country Pk. 9G 126
Hornchurch Rd. RM11: Horn 3E **126** (4B **40**)
RM12: Horn 3E **126** (4A **40**)
Hornchurch Sports Cen. 4G 126
Hornchurch Station (Tube) 5H 127 (4B 40)
Horndon Cl. RM5: Col R 5A **110**
Horndon Grn. RM5: Col R 5A **110**
Horndon Ind. Pk. CM13: W H'dn 1M **129**
HORNDON ON THE HILL 2H **147** (6J **41**)
Horndon Rd. RM5: Col R 5A **110**
SS17: Horn H 4J **147** (6J **41**)
HORNELLS CORNER 2A **24**
Hornells Cnr. CM3: L L'gh 2A **24**
HORNE ROW 5D **74** (2D **34**)
Horne Row CM3: Dan 4D **74**
Horner Pl. CM8: Wthm 5D **230**
HORNE'S GREEN 2K **15**
HORNESTREET 3D **160** (2G **17**)
Hornet Way CM0: Bur C 3D **196**
Hornford Way RM7: Rush G 2C **126**
Horn Hill CO9: Sib H 9H **219** (2D **14**)
Horn La. CO6: Cogg 3L **197**
IG8: Wfd G 3G **107**
Hornminster Glen RM11: Horn 4L **127**
Hornsby La. RM16: Ors 9C **146**
Hornsby Sq. SS15: Lain 8G **115**
(not continuous)
Hornsby Way SS15: Lain 8H **115** (3J **41**)
HORNS CROSS 3D **46**
Hornsea Vs. CM6: Steb 6C **222**
HORNSEY 3A **38**
Hornsey La. N19: Lon 4A **38**
Hornsey Pk. Rd. N8: Lon 3A **38**
Hornsey Ri. N19: Lon 4A **38**
Hornsey Rd. N19: Lon 4A **38**
Hornsey Station (Rail) 3A 38
HORNSEY VALE 3A **38**
Hornsland Rd. SS8: Can I 2L **151**
Horns Mill Rd. SG13: Hart 6B **20**
(not continuous)
Horns Rd. IG2: Ilf 8C **108** (3H **39**)
IG6: Ilf 8C **108**
Horrocks Cl. CO2: Colc 2A **174**
Horsa Rd. DA8: Eri 5A **152**
Horse & Groom La.
CM2: Chelm, Gall 8B **72**
Horsebridge Cl. RM9: Dag 1K **141**
Horsecroft Pl. CM19: H'low 4L **53**
Horsecroft Rd. CM19: H'low 3L **53**
HORSEHEATH 2F **7**
Horseheath Rd. CB1: Lin 2D **6**
CB9: Wthfld 2H **7**
Horseman Ct. CM15: Kel H 7B **82**
HORSEMAN SIDE 3J **95** (6C **32**)
Horseman Side CM14: N'side 6F **94** (7B **32**)
Horse Ride CM16: Epp, They B 5A **78**
Horseshoe Barracks SS3: Shoe 8K **139**
Horseshoe Cl. CB11: Elm 6J **5**
CM12: Bill 3J **99**
EN9: Wal A 4G **77**
Horseshoe Cres. SS3: Shoe 8K **139**
Horseshoe Hill EN9: Wal A 3J **77** (4F **31**)
SG9: Gt Hor 4F **11**
Horseshoe La. SG9: L Hor 4E **10**
Horseshoe Lawns SS5: Hull 4L **103**
Horsey Rd. CO13: Kir S 6F **180**
Horshams CM19: H'low 3B **54**
HORSLEY CROSS 4M **169** (5B **18**)
Horsley Cross SS14: Bas 8C **116**
HORSLEYCROSS STREET 1M **169** (4B **18**)
Horsley Rd. E4: Lon 8C **90**
HORTON KIRBY 6D **46**
Horton Rd. DA4: Hort K, S Dar 6D **46**
Hortus Rd. E4: Lon 8C **90**
Hospital App. CM1: Broom 9K **57** (6A **24**)
Hospital Cres. RM3: H Wood 5K **111**
Hospital Fld. CM77: Bla N 3B **194**
Hospital La. CO3: Colc 9L **165**
Hospital Rd. CO3: Colc 9L **165**
SS3: Shoe 8K **139**
Houblon Dr. CM2: Gall 8D **72**
Houblons Hill CM16: Coop 1H **79** (4J **31**)
Houchin Dr. CM5: Fy'd 9C **200**
Houchin's La. CO6: Cogg 3A **170** (7J **15**)
Houndsden Rd. N21: Lon 7A **30**
HOUNSLOW GREEN 2H **23**
House on the Hill Toy Mus. 2E 220 (6A 12)
HOUSHAM TYE 6A **22**
Hove Cl. CM13: Hut 8M **97**
RM17: Grays 4K **155**
Hovefields Av. SS12: W'fd 4L **117**
SS13: Bas 5L **117**
Hovefields Caravan Site SS13: Bas 5K **117**
Hovefields Ct. Ind. Est. SS13: Bas 5L **117**
Hovefields Dr. SS12: W'fd 4L **117**
Hoveton Rd. SE28: Lon 6H **141**
Hoveton Way IG6: Ilf 4A **108**
Howard Av. CO12: Har 5H **209**
Howard Bus. Pk. EN9: Wal A 4D **76**
Howard Chase SS14: Bas 7A **116**
Howard Cl. CM7: Brain 5K **193**
EN9: Wal A 3D **76**
IG10: Lou 5L **91**
Howard Ct. IG11: Bark 1C **140**
Howard Cres. SS13: Pits 1K **133**
Howard Dr. CM2: Chelm 9B **60**
Howard Lodge Rd. CM14: Kel C 7N **81** (5C **32**)
Howard Pl. SS8: Can I 3H **151**
Howard Rd. CB10: Saf W 3D **218**
CO15: Hol S 9N **185**
E11: Lon 5E **122**
E17: Lon 7A **106**
IG1: Ilf 6A **124**
IG11: Bark 1C **140**
RM14: Upm 4N **127**
RM16: Chaf H 1F **154**
Howards Chase SS0: Wclf S 4K **137**
Howards Cl. CM3: Bore 3F **60**
Howards Ct. SS0: Wclf S 6K **137**
Howards Cft. CO4: Colc 2L **165**
Howard Vyse Ct. CO15: Clac S 8J **185**
Howard Way CM20: H'low 9E **50** (6H **21**)
Howarth Ct. *E15: Lon* *7C* ***122***
(off Clays La.)
Howbridge Hall Rd. CM8: Wthm 7C **230**
(not continuous)
Howbridge Rd. CM8: Wthm 7C **230** (5F **25**)
Howbury La. DA8: Eri 7E **152** (2A **46**)
Howden Cl. SE28: Lon 7J **141**
Howe Chase CO9: Hals 2K **207**
Howe Cl. CB11: Stret 6K **5**
CO4: Colc 8D **166**
RM7: Maw 5M **109**
HOWE GREEN
CM22 2A **22**
CM2 8L **73** (3C **34**)
HOWEGREEN 9K **215** (4G **35**)
Howe Green CM22: Gt Hal 2A **22**
HOWE GREEN INTERCHANGE 6J **73** (3C **34**)
Howe Grn. Rd. CM3: Pur 6H **197** (4G **35**)
Howe La. CB10: Gt Sam, Hpstd 1K **205** (7H **7**)
Howell Cl. RM6: Chad H 9J **109**
Howell Ct. E10: Lon 2B **122**
Howell Rd. SS17: Corr, Stan H 8A **132**
HOWE STREET
CM3 2H **57** (4K **23**)
CM7 1K **13**
Howfield Grn. EN11: Hod 2A **52**
HOWLETT END 1E **12**
Howse Rd. EN9: Enf 5B **76**
Hows Mead CM16: N Wea 3B **66**
HOXTON 6B **38**
Hoxton Cl. CO16: Clac S 8H **185**
Hoylake Gdns. RM3: H Wood 4L **111**
Hoynors CM3: Dan 3G **74**
Hoy Ter. RM20: Grays 3G **155**
Hubbards Chase CO14: Walt 6L **181**
RM11: Horn 9L **111**
Hubbards Cl. RM11: Horn 9L **111**
Hubert Rd. CM14: Brtwd 9E **96**
CO3: Colc 7J **165**
RM13: Rain 3D **142**
Hucklesbury Av. CO15: Hol S 6B **186**
Hucknall Cl. RM3: Romf 3K **111**
Huddlestone Rd. E7: Lon 6F **122**
Hudson Cl. CO12: Har 6J **209**
CO16: Clac S 8G **184**
Hudson Ct. *SS9: Lgh S* *9D* ***120***
(off Hudson Cres.)
Hudson Cres. SS9: Lgh S 9D **120**
Hudson La. CB9: B'dstn 1A **8**
Hudson Rd. SS9: Lgh S 9C **120**
Hudsons Cl. SS17: Stan H 2M **147**
Hudson's Hill CM7: Weth 8D **228** (3A **14**)
Hudsons La. CO6: Stok 1F **17**
Hudson Way SS8: Can I 8G **135**
Hughan Rd. E15: Lon 7D **122**
Hugh Dickson Rd. CO4: Colc 5M **165**
Hughendon Ter. E15: Lon 6C **122**
Hughes Rd. RM16: Grays 1C **156**
Hughes Stanton Way
CO11: Law 4G **162**
Hugh's Twr. CM20: H'low 2C **54**
Hugo Gdns. RM13: Rain 8E **126**
HULLBRIDGE 6K **103** (7F **35**)

Hullbridge Rd. CM3: S Fer 8J **89** (6F **35**)
(not continuous)
SS6: Ray 7K **103** (1F **43**)
Hullett's La. CM15: Pil H 2B **96**
Hull Grn. CM17: Mat G 6B **22**
Hull Gro. CM19: H'low 8N **53**
Hull La. CM3: Terl 4D **24**
Hull Pl. E16: Lon 8B **140**
Hull's La. CM2: S'don 4M **73** (2C **34**)
Hulse Av. IG11: Bark 8C **124**
RM7: Maw 5N **109**
Hulton Cl. CM3: Bore 3F **60**
Humber Av. CO15: Jay 6C **188**
RM15: S Ock 6C **144**
Humber Cl. SS6: Ray 6J **119**
Humber Dr. RM14: Upm 1A **128**
Humber Rd. CM1: Chelm 6L **59**
CM8: Wthm 5A **230**
Hume Av. RM18: Til 8C **156** (3H **47**)
Hume Cl. RM18: Til 8C **156**
Humphrey Cl. IG5: Ilf 5M **107**
Humphrey Lodge CM6: Thax 7C **224**
Humphrey's Farm La.
CM3: Gt Walt 5E **56** (5K **23**)
Humphries Cl. RM9: Dag 6L **125**
HUNDON 1B **8**
Hundon Rd. CB9: Ked, Pos 2A **8**
Hundred Acres EN8: Wal X 4A **76**
Hundred La. CO4: Boxt, L'ham 4B **160**
Hungerdown E4: Lon 7C **90**
Hungerdown La. CO7: A'lgh, Law 9B **162** (4J **17**)
CO11: Law 9B **162** (4J **17**)
Hunnable Rd. CM7: Brain 5G **192**
HUNSDON 4F **21**
HUNSDONBURY 5F **21**
Hunsdon Cl. RM9: Dag 8K **125**
Hunsdon Rd. SG12: Hun, Stan A 6E **20**
SG12: Wid 4F **21**
Hunt Av. CM9: Mal 3D **214**
Hunt Cl. CO5: Fee 1L **211**
Hunt Dr. CO16: Clac S 8H **185**
Hunter Av. CM15: Shenf 5K **97**
Hunter Dr. CM7: Brain 6L **193**
CO11: Law 5G **162**
RM12: Horn 6G **127**
SS12: W'fd 2M **117**
Hunter Rd. IG1: Ilf 7A **124**
Hunters Av. CM12: Bill 9K **99**
Hunters Chase CM5: Chip 9L **67**
CM13: Hut 7E **98**
Hunter's Chase CO7: A'lgh 6K **161** (3H **17**)
Hunters Cnr. CO3: Colc 1G **172**
Hunters Ct. CM22: Else 2K **199**
Hunters Gro. RM5: Col R 2N **109**
Hunters Hall Rd. RM10: Dag 6M **125**
Hunters Ridge CO4: Colc 3B **166**
Hunters Sq. RM10: Dag 6M **125**
Hunters Way CB11: Saf W 6C **218**
CM1: Chelm 4A **60**
Hunters Yd. CB11: Saf W 4C **218**
Huntingdon Rd. SS1: Sth S 6B **138**
Huntingdon Way CO15: Clac S 7J **185**
Hunting Ga. CO1: Colc 8C **166**
Huntings Farm IG1: Ilf 4D **124**
Huntings Rd. RM10: Dag 8M **125**
Huntland Cl. RM13: Rain 5F **142**
Hunt Rd. CO6: E Col 8B **198**
Hunt's Cl. CM1: Writ 2K **71**
Hunt's Dr. CM1: Writ 2K **71**
Hunts Farm Cl. CM9: Tol 7K **225**
Hunts Hill CO10: Glem 2G **9**
Huntsman La. CO10: Fox 3G **9**
Huntsman Rd. IG6: Ilf 2G **109**
Huntsmans Dr. RM14: Upm 7N **127**
Hunts Mead CM12: Bill 7H **99**
Hunts Rd. CB2: Dux 3J **5**
Hunt Way CO13: Walt 8H **181**
Hunwicke Rd. CO4: Colc 8E **166**
Hurdleditch Rd. SG8: Orw 1C **4**
Hurlock Rd. CM11: Bill 6K **99**
Hurnard Dr. CO3: Colc 8H **165**
Hurrell Down CM3: Bore 2G **60**
CO4: Colc 3A **166**
Hurrells La. CM3: L Bad 8F **60** (1C **34**)
Hurricane Cl. SS11: W'fd 2B **118**
Hurricane Ho. *SS11: W'fd* *2A* ***118***
(off Hurricane Way)
Hurricane Way CM16: N Wea 6M **65**
SS11: W'fd 2A **118**
Hurry Cl. E15: Lon 9E **122**
Hursley Rd. IG7: Chig 2E **108**
Hurst Av. E4: Lon 1A **106**
Hurstbourne Gdns. IG11: Bark 8D **124**
Hurst Cl. CO7: B'sea 7F **182**
E4: Lon 9A **90**
Hurstcombe IG9: Buck H 8G **91**
HURST GREEN 7F **182** (3K **27**)
Hurst Ho. SS7: Thund 8H **119**
Hurstlands Cl. RM11: Horn 2G **126**
Hurstleigh Gdns. IG5: Ilf 5M **107**
Hurst Pk. Av. RM12: Horn 6J **127**
Hurst Rd. DA5: Bex 4A **46**
DA8: Eri 6A **152**
E17: Lon 7B **106**
IG9: Buck H 7K **91**
Hurst Way CM2: Chelm 9A **60**
SS9: Lgh S 2E **136**
Hurstwood Av. CM15: Pil H 6E **96**
DA8: Eri 6C **152**
E18: Lon 8H **107**
Hurstwood Ct. RM14: Upm 3N **127**
Huskards RM14: Upm 4M **127**
Hutchins Cl. E15: Lon 9C **122**
RM12: Horn 5J **127**
Hutchinson Cl. CO5: Tip 7D **226**
Hutchinson Ct. RM6: Chad H 8J **109**
Hutchins Rd. SE28: Lon 7F **140**
Hutson Ter. RM19: Purf 4A **154**
HUTTON 4M **97** (7G **33**)
Hutton Cl. IG8: Wfd G 3H **107**
Hutton Ct. CM13: Hut 6B **98**
Hutton Dr. CM13: Hut 6M **97**
Hutton Ga. CM13: Hut 6L **97**
HUTTON MOUNT 7L **97** (7F **33**)
Hutton Pl. CM13: Hut 5N **97**
(Cedar Rd.)
CM13: Hut 5L **97**
(Reubens Rd.)
Hutton Rd. CM15: Shenf 6J **97** (7F **33**)
Hutton Village CM13: Hut 6A **98** (7G **33**)
Huxley Dr. RM6: Chad H 2G **124**
Huxley Rd. E10: Lon 4C **122**
Huxtables La. CO3: S'way 6B **164**
Hyacinth Cl. CM9: Tol 8L **225**
CO16: Clac S 9G **184**
IG1: Ilf 8A **124**
Hyacinth Ct. CM1: Chelm 4N **59**
Hyams Way CO2: Colc 9N **165**
Hycliffe Gdns. IG7: Chig 1B **108**
Hydaway Ho. CM15: Kel H 7A **82**
Hyde Chase CM9: Wdhm M 6K **75**
Hyde Cl. RM16: Chaf H 1G **154**
Hyde Farm Chase CM3: Dan 6H **75**
Hyde Grn. CM3: Dan 3H **75**
Hyde Hall 5E **88**
Hyde Hall La.
CM3: Gt Walt, L Walt 2J **57** (4A **24**)
Hyde Hall Rd. CM3: Ret C 5D **88**
Hyde La. CM3: Dan 3G **75** (2E **34**)
CM7: Gt Sal 5A **14**
Hyde Mead EN9: Naze 2E **62**
Hyde Mead Ho. EN9: Naze 2E **62**
Hyderabad Way E15: Lon 9E **122**
Hyde Rd. N1: Lon 6B **38**
Hyder Rd. RM16: Grays 1E **156**
Hyde, The CB11: Clav 3J **11**
SS16: Lang H 2L **131**
Hydeway SS7: Thund 1F **134**
Hyde Way SS12: W'fd 1L **117**
Hyde Wood La. SS4: Cwdn 8L **105** (1J **43**)
Hydewood Rd. CO9: L Yel 1E **206** (6D **8**)
Hyland Cl. RM11: Horn 2F **126**
Hyland Ga. CM11: Bill 1M **115**
Hylands Cl. CM6: Barns 3L **191**
Hylands House 5L **71**
Hylands Pde. CM2: Chelm 4B **72**
Hylands Pk. 5M **71** (2K **33**)
Hylands Pk. Gardens 5L **71** (2K **33**)
Hylands Rd. E17: Lon 6D **106**
Hylands, The SS5: Hock 2C **120**
Hyland Way RM11: Horn 2F **126**
Hyll Cl. CB10: Gt Che 7D **202**
Hyndman Ho. *RM10: Dag* *5M* ***125***
(off Kershaw Rd.)
Hynton Rd. RM8: Dag 4H **125**
Hythe Cl. CM7: Brain 2G **193**
CO15: Clac S 4H **189**
Hythe Gro. CO7: B'sea 4D **182**
Hythe Hill CO1: Colc 9C **166** (6F **17**)
Hythe Quay CO2: Colc 9D **166** (6F **17**)
Hythe Station (Rail) 9D **166** (6F **17**)
Hythe Sta. Rd. CO2: Colc 9C **166** (6F **17**)
HYTHE, THE 9C **166** (6F **17**)
Hythe, The CM9: Mal 6D **214**

I

Ian Rd. CM12: Bill 4H **99**
Ibbetson Path IG10: Lou 2A **92**
Ibrox Ct. IG9: Buck H 8J **91**
Ibscott Cl. RM10: Dag 8A **126**
Iceni Ct. IG9: Buck H 7H **91**
Iceni Way CO2: Colc 3J **173**
ICKLETON 6A **202** (3K **5**)
Ickleton Rd. CB2: Dux 3J **5**
CB10: Dux, Hxtn 3K **5**
CB10: Gt Che 8C **202** (4A **6**)
CB11: Elm 6J **5**
Icknield Cl. CB10: I'tn 7A **202**
Icknield Dr. IG2: Ilf 9A **108**
Ickworth Cl. CM77: Gt N 1C **204**
Idleigh Ct. Rd. DA13: Meop 7F **47**
Idmiston Rd. E15: Lon 6F **122**
Ilchester Rd. RM8: Dag 7G **124**
Ilex Cl. CO2: Colc 4L **173**
ILFORD 5A **124** (5G **39**)
Ilford Hill IG1: Ilf 5N **123** (4G **39**)
Ilford La. IG1: Bark, Ilf 5A **124** (5G **39**)
Ilford Pools 4D **124**
Ilford Station (Rail) 5N **123** (4G **39**)
Ilford Trad. Est. SS14: Bas 5F **116**
Ilfracombe Av. SS1: Sth S 6B **138**
SS13: Pits 1L **133**
Ilfracombe Cres. RM12: Horn 6G **127**
Ilfracombe Gdns. RM6: Chad H 2G **124**
Ilfracombe Rd. SS2: Sth S 5A **138**
Ilgars Rd. SS11: W'fd 7M **101**
Ilmington Dr. SS13: Bas 6H **117**
Imogen Cl. CO4: Colc 8F **166**
Imperial Av. CM3: May 7H **213** (3A **36**)
SS0: Wclf S 5G **137**
Imperial Ct. *SS0: Wclf S* *7K* ***137***
(off Westcliff Pde.)
Imperial Lodge SS0: Wclf S 5H **137**
Imperial Pk. SS6: Ray 1J **119**
Imperial Trad. Est. RM13: Rain 4H **143**
Imperial War Mus 2J **5**
Imphal Cl. CO2: Colc 5K **173**
Impressa Pk. EN11: Rye P 4C **52**
Imprimo Pk. IG10: Lou 3C **92**
Inchbonnie Rd. CM3: S Fer 2J **103** (6F **35**)
Indikart Racing Club 2D **174**
Ingarfield Rd. CO15: Hol S 7B **186**
INGATESTONE 6D **84** (5H **33**)
Ingatestone By-Pass
CM4: Ing, Marg 7B **84** (5G **33**)
Ingatestone Hall 7E **84** (5H **33**)
Ingatestone Rd. CM1: Hghwd 6A **70** (3G **33**)
CM4: B'more, Fry 2J **83** (4F **33**)
CM4: Ing, Stock 7G **85** (5J **33**)
E12: Lon 3J **123**
IG8: Wfd G 4H **107**
Ingatestone Station (Rail) 6E **84** (5H **33**)
Ingaway SS16: Bas 1A **132**
Ingelrica Av. CM3: Hat P 3M **61**
Ingels Mead CM16: Epp 8E **64**
Ingess Pk. Av. DA9: Grnh 9E **154**
Ingestre Rd. E7: Lon 6G **122**
Ingestre St. CO12: Har 3M **209**
Ingleby Gdns. IG7: Chig 9G **92**
Ingleby Rd. IG1: Ilf 3A **124**
RM10: Dag 8N **125**
RM16: Grays 1D **156**
Inglefield Rd. SS17: Fob 7D **132**
Ingleglen RM11: Horn 2L **127**
Inglehurst Gdns. IG4: Ilf 9M **107**
Inglenook CO15: Clac S 6L **185**
Ingleside Ct. CB10: Saf W 4C **218**
Inglewood Cl. IG6: Ilf 3E **108**
RM12: Horn 6H **127**
Inglewood Rd. DA7: Bexh 9B **152**
Inglis Rd. CO3: Colc 9L **165**
Ingram M. CM7: Brain 8K **193**
Ingram Rd. RM17: Grays 2M **155**
Ingrams Piece CO7: A'lgh 8L **161**
Ingram's Well Rd. CO10: Sud 5J **9**
INGRAVE 2M **113** (2G **41**)
Ingrave Cl. SS12: W'fd 1M **117**
INGRAVE COMMON 1K **113** (1F **41**)
Ingrave Ho. RM9: Dag 1G **141**
Ingrave Rd. CM13: Brtwd 8G **97** (1F **41**)
CM15: Brtwd 8G **96** (1E **40**)
RM1: Romf 8C **110**
Ingrebourne Ct. E4: Lon 9B **90**
Ingrebourne Gdns. RM14: Upm 3N **127**
Ingrebourne Rd. RM13: Rain 4F **142** (6B **40**)
Ingress Abbey 9F **154**
INGRESS PARK 9F **154**
Ingreway RM3: H Wood 3M **111**
Inkerpole Pl. CM2: Chelm 7A **60**
Inks Grn. E4: Lon 2C **106**
Inmans Row IG8: Wfd G 1G **107**
Innes Cl. SS12: W'fd 2L **117**
Innham Hill CO9: Sib H 9H **219** (2D **14**)
Innova Way EN3: Enf 6A **76**
Inskip Cl. E10: Lon 4B **122**
Inskip Dr. RM11: Horn 3J **127**
Inskip Rd. RM8: Dag 3J **125**
Institute Rd. CM16: Coop 8J **65**
Instone Rd. DA1: Dart 3C **46**
Integer Gdns. E11: Lon 2D **122**
International Bus. Pk. SS8: Can I 2D **150**
Inverclyde Gdns. RM6: Chad H 8H **109**
(not continuous)
Inverness Av. SS0: Wclf S 4J **137**
Inverness Cl. CO1: Colc 7A **166**
Inverness Dr. IG6: Ilf 3D **108**
Inverness M. E16: Lon 8B **140**
Invicta Cen., The IG11: Bark 1F **140**
Invicta Ct. CM12: Bill 5G **99**
INWORTH 4N **211** (3J **25**)
Inworth La. CO6: Wak C 3K **15**
Inworth Rd. CO5: Fee 1M **211** (2J **25**)
Inworth Wlk. CO2: Colc 5A **174**
SS11: W'fd 8A **102**
Iona Way SS12: W'fd 1N **117**
Ipswich M. SS16: Lang H 1H **131**
Ipswich Rd. CO1: Colc 8B **166**
CO4: Colc, Ded 7B **166** (6F **17**)
CO4: Ded 8E **160**
CO7: Colc, Ded 8E **160** (6F **17**)
CO7: Ded 3H **161**
(Blackbrook Hill)
CO7: Ded, L'ham 1H **161** (2G **17**)
(Gun Hill)
CO11: Bran 1A **18**
CO11: Law 3G **162** (2K **17**)
CO15: Hol S 7A **186**
IP9: Hark, Holb 1E **18**
(Harkstead)
IP9: Holb 1D **18**
(Holbrook)
Ireton Pl. RM17: Grays 2K **155**
Ireton Rd. CO3: Colc 1L **173**
Iris Cl. CM1: Chelm 6A **60**
CM15: Pil H 4E **96**
Iris Path RM3: Romf 4G **111**
Iron Latch La. CO3: Eig G, S'way 7D **164**
Iron Latch Meadow Nature Reserve 7C **164**
Iron Mill La. DA1: Cray 9C **152** (3A **46**)
Iron Mill Pl. DA1: Cray 9D **152**
Irons Way RM5: Col R 4A **110**
Ironwell La. SS4: R'fd 4F **120**
SS5: Hock, R'fd 4F **120** (2H **43**)
(not continuous)
Irvine Gdns. RM15: S Ock 6C **144**
Irvine Pl. SS12: W'fd 2N **117**
Irvine Rd. CO3: Colc 1K **173**
Irvine Way CM12: Bill 7J **99**
Irving Cl. SS5: Hock 2D **120**
Irvington Cl. SS9: Lgh S 2C **136**
Irvon Hill Rd. SS12: W'fd 9K **101**
Isaac Sq. CM2: Gt Bad 4J **73**
Isabel Evans Ct. SS17: Stan H 9A **132**
Isbell Gdns. RM1: Romf 4C **110**
Isbourne Rd. CO4: Colc 8F **166**
Ishams Chase CM8: Wthm 8F **230**
Isis Dr. RM14: Upm 1B **128**
Island Cen. Way EN3: Enf 7A **76**
Island La. CO13: Kir S, Walt 6H **181**
Island Rd. CO13: T Sok, Walt 2H **181**
Isledon Rd. N7: Lon 4A **38**
ISLINGTON 5A **38**
Islington Pk. St. N1: Lon 5A **38**
Ismailia Rd. E7: Lon 9H **123**
ISTEAD RISE 5G **47**
Italstyle Bldg., The CM21: H'low 6H **51**
Ive Farm Cl. E10: Lon 4A **122**
Ive Farm La. E10: Lon 4A **122**
Iver Rd. CM15: Pil H 5E **96**
Ives Gdns. RM1: Romf 8D **110**
Ivinghoe Rd. RM8: Dag 7G **124**
Ivor Brown Ct. CO4: Colc 3B **166**
Ivy Barn La. CM4: Marg, Mill G 1C **84** (3H **33**)
Ivybridge EN10: Brox 7A **52**
IVY CHIMNEYS 3F **78** (4H **31**)
Ivy Chimneys Rd. CM16: Epp 2D **78** (4H **31**)
Ivyhouse Rd. RM9: Dag 8J **125**
Ivy La. CO5: E Mer 4J **27**
Ivy Lodge La. RM3: H Wood 5M **111**
Ivy Lodge Rd.
CO6: Boxt, Gt Hork 8K **159** (4E **16**)
Ivy Path SS14: Bas 9F **116**
Ivy Rd. E17: Lon 1A **122**
SS7: Thund 9A **118**
Ivy Ter. EN11: Rye P 3C **52**
Ivy Todd Hill CB11: Deb 2C **12**
Ivy Wlk. RM9: Dag 8K **125**
SS8: Can I 1F **150**

J

Jacaranda Cl. CM1: Chelm 5A **60**
Jack Andrews Dr. CO4: Colc 2C **166**
Jack Cook Ho. IG11: Bark 9A **124**
Jack Cornwell St. E12: Lon 6N **123**
Jackdaw Cl. CM11: Bill 8L **99**
SS3: Shoe 6J **139**
Jack Evans Ct. RM15: S Ock 6D **144**
Jack Hatch Way CO7: W'hoe 3G **175**
Jacklin Grn. IG8: Wfd G 1G **106**
Jacks Cl. SS11: W'fd 9N **101**
JACK'S GREEN 2E **224**
JACK'S HATCH 9N **53** (1G **31**)
Jack's La. CM22: Tak 3D **224**
Jackson Cl. RM11: Horn 8K **111**
Jackson Ct. E7: Lon 8H **123**
Jackson Ho. *CO4: Colc* *1B* ***166***
(off Honorius Dr.)
Jackson Pl. CM2: Gt Bad 4E **72**
Jackson Rd. CO15: Clac S 2J **189**
IG11: Bark 1C **140**
Jacksons Cl. CM5: Chip 8K **67**
Jacksons Hill CM20: H'low 1D **54**
Jackson's La. CB10: Gt Che 8D **202** (4A **6**)
Jacksons La. CM11: Bill 5K **99** (7J **33**)
Jackson's La. SG8: Reed 7D **4**
Jacksons M. CM11: Bill 6L **99**
Jackson's Sq. CB10: Gt Che 7D **202**
Jackson Wlk. CO2: Colc 2B **174**
Jack Stevens Cl. CM17: H'low 5H **55**
Jacob Ho. *DA18: Eri* *9J* ***141***
(off Kale Rd.)
Jacobs Av. RM3: H Wood 6J **111**
Jacobs Cl. RM10: Dag 6N **125**
Jacquard Way CM7: Brain 6J **193**
Jacqueline Ct. *CO3: Colc* *8H* ***165***
(off Lexden Rd.)
Jacqueline Gdns. CM12: Bill 4K **99**
Jacqueline Vs. *E17: Lon* *9C* ***106***
(off Shernhall St.)
Jade Cl. RM8: Dag 3H **125**
Jade Ho. RM13: Rain 4E **142**
Jaffe Rd. IG1: Ilf 3C **124**
Jaggard's Rd. CO6: Cogg 2K **197**
Jakapeni Rare Breeds Farm 8M **103** (1F **43**)
Jamaica Rd. SE1: Lon 7B **38**
SE16: Lon 7B **38**
James Av. RM8: Dag 3L **125**
James Carter Rd. CO3: S'way 3F **172**
James Cl. CO7: W'hoe 3J **175**
RM2: Romf 9E **110**
James Cft. CM2: Gall 8C **72**
James Gdns. CO16: St O 8N **183**
James La. E10: Lon 2C **122** (3E **38**)
E11: Lon 1D **122** (3E **38**)
James Lee Sq. EN3: Enf 8A **76**
Jameson Rd. CO15: Clac S 1G **189**
James Rd. CO15: Clac S 2G **189**
James Sq. CM11: Bill 6N **99**
James St. CM16: Epp 7F **64**
CO1: Colc 9A **166**
CO7: B'sea 7E **182**
IG11: Bark 9B **124**
James Watt Way DA8: Eri 4D **152**
James Yd. E4: Lon 3D **106**
Janette Av. SS8: Can I 2E **150**
Janice M. IG1: Ilf 4A **124**
JANKE'S GREEN 4A **16**
Janmead CM8: Wthm 4D **230**
CM13: Hut 6L **97**
Janson Cl. E15: Lon 7E **122**
Janson Rd. E15: Lon 7E **122**
Japan Rd. RM6: Chad H 1J **125**
Japonica Ct. CO15: Clac S 9N **185**
Jardine Rd. SS13: Pits 7K **117**

Jarmin Rd. CO1: Colc. 7N 165
Jarndyce CM1: Chelm. 5H 59
Jarrah Cotts. RM19: Purf 4A 154
Jarrow Rd. RM6: Chad H 1H 125
Jarvis Cl. IG11: Bark. 1C 140
Jarvis Fld. CM3: L Bad 6L 61
Jarvis Rd. SS7: Ben 2E 134
SS8: Can I. 8G 135
Jarvis Way RM3: H Wood 6J 111
Jasmine Cl. CM1: Chelm 4N 59
CO4: Colc 7D 166
IG1: Ilf. 7A 124
SS8: Can I. 3F 150
SS16: Lang H 2H 131
Jasmine Rd. RM7: Rush G 4C 126
Jasmine Ter. CM15: Pil H. 4C 96
Jasmine Way CO15: Jay 5E 188
Jason Cl. CM14: Brtwd 1C 112
RM16: Ors 6G 146
SS8: Can I. 9H 135
JASPER'S GREEN 5B 14
Jasper's Green CM7: Shalf 5B 14
Jay Cl. CM77: Gt N 8F 192
Jay Ct. CM20: H'low 2D 54
Jays La. CO6: M Tey 3H 171
Jays, The CO4: Colc 4B 166
JAYWICK 4E 188 (5C 28)
Jaywick La. CO15: Clac S, Jay. 1E 188 (4C 28)
CO16: Clac S 1E 18 (4C 28)
Jeffcut Rd. CM2: Chelm 9N 59
Jefferson Av. SS15: Lain 9J 115
Jefferson Cl. CO3: S'way 1F 172
IG2: Ilf. 9A 108
Jeffery Rd. CM2: Gt Bad. 3H 73
Jeffrey Cl. CO3: Colc 1G 173
Jeffrey's Rd. CM77: Tye G 2D 194
Jeffries Way SS17: Stan H 2A 148
Jekylls La. CM7: Corn H. 1K 13
Jellicoe Way CM7: Brain. 4L 193
Jena Cl. SS3: Shoe 7J 139
Jenkins Dr. CM22: Else. 1K 199
Jenkin's Hill CO11: Brad. 3B 18
Jenkins La. IG11: Bark 2B 140
Jenner Cl. CM7: Brain 7H 193
Jenner Mead CM2: Chelm 8B 60
Jenningham Dr. RM16: Grays 8K 145
Jennings Cl. CO1: Colc. 9C 166
Jennings Pl. CM4: Marg 1J 85
Jenningtree Rd. DA8: Eri 5F 152
Jenningtree Way DA17: Belv 9A 142
Jenny Hammond Cl. E11: Lon 5F 122
Jenny Path RM3: Romf 4H 111
Jephson Rd. E7: Lon. 9J 123
Jericho Pl. CM4: B'more 1H 83
Jermayns SS15: Lain 9N 115
Jermyn St. SW1: Lon 7A 38
Jerningham Av. IG5: Ilf. 6A 108
Jerounds CM19: H'low 5A 54
Jersey Cl. EN11: Hod 4A 52
Jersey Gdns. SS11: W'fd 8L 101
Jersey Rd. CM9: Mal 7D 214
E11: Lon 3D 122
IG1: Ilf. 6A 124
RM13: Rain 9E 126
Jersey Way CM7: Brain 6F 192
Jervis Ct. RM10: Dag 8N 125
Jeskyns Rd. DA13: Cobh, Sole S 6H 47
Jesmond Dene CM16: They B. 6C 78
Jesmond Rd. RM16: Grays. 8N 145
SS8: Can I. 3H 151
Jessel Dr. IG10: Lou. 9B 78
Jesse Rd. E10: Lon. 3C 122
Jessett Cl. DA8: Eri. 2B 152
Jessica Cl. CO4: Colc 8F 166
Jessop Ct. EN9: Wal A. 4F 76
Jessops Cl. CO15: Clac S 5L 185
Jetty Wlk. RM17: Grays 4K 155
Jewel Rd. E17: Lon 7A 106
Jim Desormeaux Bungs. CM20: H'low. 1D 54
Joan Gdns. RM8: Dag. 4K 125
Joan Rd. RM8: Dag 4K 125
Jocelyns CM17: H'low 8H 51
Jodrell Rd. E3: Lon 5D 38
Jodrell Way RM20: W Thur 3C 154
Joes Rd. CO10: Corn T. 5K 9
John Ball Wlk. CO1: Colc. 8N 165
John Barnes Wlk. E15: Lon. 8F 122
John Belcher Wlk. CO4: Colc 9E 166
John Burns Dr. IG11: Bark 9D 124
John Childs Way SS6: Ray 5L 119
John Clay Gdns. RM16: Grays 7L 145
John Ct. EN11: Hod 2A 52
John Dane Player Ct.
CB10: Saf W 4D 218
John Drinkwater Cl. E11: Lon. 2F 122
John Eliot Cl. EN9: Naze 9E 52
John English Av. CM7: Brain 4G 192
John Harper St. CO1: Colc. 7M 165
John Kent Av. CO2: Colc 4J 173
John King Ct. CO7: B'sea 7E 182
John Parker Cl. RM10: Dag 9N 125
John Raven Ct. CO5: Fee 2L 211
John Ray Gdns. CM77: Bla N 3B 194
John Ray St. CM7: Brain. 5K 193
Johnson Cl. CM7: Brain 9J 193
SS4: R'fd. 2J 121
SS12: W'fd 2L 117
Johnson Ct. SS4: R'fd. 5L 121
Johnson Rd. CM2: Gt Bad 5H 73
CO16: St O 9N 183
Johnsons Ct. CB10: Saf W 3C 218
Johnson's Dr. CO7: Elms 9N 167
Johnsons Yd. CB10: Saf W 3C 218
John's Ter. RM3: H Wood 3M 111
Johns, The CM5: Chip. 6L 67
Johnston Cl. CO9: Hals 6L 207
CO15: Hol S 8B 186
Johnstone Rd. SS1: Sth S 7E 138
Johnston Rd. IG8: Wfd G 3G 106
Johnston Way CM9: Mal. 8N 214
John St. CO7: B'sea. 7E 182
RM17: Grays 4M 155
SS3: Shoe 8L 139
John Strype Ct. E10: Lon 3B 122
John Tibauld Ct. CB9: Stpl B 3K 223
John Warner Sports Cen., The 2C 52
Joint, The SG8: B'wy, Reed 7C 4
Jollyboys La. Nth. CM6: Fels 7K 199
(not continuous)
Jollyboys La. Sth. CM6: Fels 9K 199
Jonathans RM11: Horn 3J 127
(off High St.)
Jones Cl. SS2: Sth S 3K 137
Jones Cnr. SS9: Lgh S 8C 120
Jones Rd. EN7: G Oak. 3A 30
Jonquil Way CO4: Colc 5K 165
Jordan Cl. RM10: Dag 6N 125
Jordans, The SS2: Sth S 4M 137
Jordans Way RM13: Rain. 2H 143
Jordan Way SS14: Bas 8G 117
Joseph Gdns. CM8: Sil E 8M 217
Joseph Lister Ct. E7: Lon. 9G 123
Joseph Ray Rd. E11: Lon 4E 122
Joshua Wlk. EN8: Wal X. 4A 76
Josling Cl. RM17: Grays 4J 155
Joslin Rd. RM19: Purf 3N 153
Joslyn Cl. EN3: Enf. 8A 76
Josselin Cl. CO6: E Col. 8C 198
Josselin Ct. SS13: Bas 5K 117
Josselin Rd. SS13: Bas 5N 53
Jotmans La. SS13: Pits 4N 133
Journeymans Way SS2: Temp I 1L 137
Jovian Way CO4: Colc. 1B 166
Joyce Brooks Ho. CO3: Colc. 9L 165
(off Oxford Rd.)
Joyce Ct. EN9: Wal A 4D 76
Joyce Dawson Way SE28: Lon 7F 140
JOYCE GREEN 9K 153 (3C 46)
Joyce Grn. La. DA1: Dart 9K 153
Joyce Grn. Wlk. DA1: Dart 9K 153
Joyce's Chase CM9: Gold 1M 201 (7A 26)
JOYDENS WOOD 5A 46
Joydon Dr. RM6: Chad H 1G 125
Joyes Cl. RM3: Romf. 1H 111
Joyners Cl. RM9: Dag. 6L 125
Joyners Fld. CM18: H'low 7B 54
Jubilee Av. CM1: Broom 1J 59
CO16: Clac S 6J 185
E4: Lon 3C 106
RM7: Romf. 9N 109
Jubilee Cl. CO12: Har. 5G 209
RM7: Romf. 9N 109
SS5: Hock. 2D 120
Jubilee Ct. CM6: Gt D. 2K 203
CO9: Sib H 7K 219
EN9: Wal A 3F 76
Jubilee Dr. SS11: W'fd. 8K 101
Jubilee End CO11: Law 3H 163
Jubilee La. CO7: A'lgh 4J 167 (5H 17)
Jubilee Mkt. IG8: Wfd G 3J 107
Jubilee Pde. IG8: Wfd G 3J 107
Jubilee Ri. CM3: Dan. 4G 74
Jubilee Rd. CM11: Cray H 3D 116
RM20: W Thur. 4E 154
SS6: Ray. 5L 119 (2F 43)
Jubilee St. E1: Lon. 7C 38
Jubilee Ter. CM1: Chelm. 6J 59
Jubilee Way CO13: Frin S. 8J 181
Judd St. WC1: Lon 6A 38
Judge Rd. CM2: Chelm. 7C 60
Judith Anne Ct. RM14: Upm. 4B 128
Judith Av. RM5: Col R 3N 109
Julia Ct. E17: Lon. 9B 106
Julia Gdns. IG11: Bark 2J 141
Julian Av. CO4: Colc. 1B 166
Julian Cl. CM1: Broom. 2K 59
Julie Ho. EN11: Rye P 3C 52
Julien Ct. Rd. CM7: Brain. 4J 193
Juliers Cl. SS8: Can I 2K 151
Juliers Rd. SS8: Can I 2K 151
Juliette Way RM15: Ave 9K 143
Jumbo Water Tower 8M 165
Junction Rd. CM3: Cold N. 7L 197
CM14: War 1F 112
NW5: Lon 4A 38
RM1: Romf. 8D 110
SS16: Pits 2J 133
Junction Rd. E. RM6: Chad H. 2K 125
Junction Rd. W.
RM6: Chad H. 2K 125
Juniper Cl. CM11: Bill. 4L 99
CO9: Hals 6K 207
Juniper Ct. CM6: Gt D. 2J 203
CM13: Brtwd 9J 97
(off Beech Av.)
RM6: Chad H 1G 125
Juniper Cres. CM8: Wthm 3D 230
Juniper Dr. CM2: Chelm 4C 72
RM15: S Ock. 3H 145
Juniper Rd. CM3: Bore 3F 60
CO3: S'way 1D 172
IG1: Ilf. 5N 123
SS9: Lgh S 2E 136
Juniper Way CO4: Colc. 7D 166
RM3: H Wood 5J 111
Juno M. CO2: Colc 5K 173
Jupe's Hill CO6: Wak C. 3K 15
Jupes Hill CO7: Ded. 3B 162 (2J 17)
Jupp Rd. E15: Lon 9D 122
Jurgens Rd. RM19: Purf. 4A 154
Jutsums Av. RM7: Romf. 1N 125
Jutsums Ct. RM7: Romf. 1N 125
Jutsums La.
RM7: Romf, Rush G 1N 125 (3K 39)
Juvina Cl. CM8: Wthm 8C 230

K

Kale Cft. CO3: S'way 1E 172
Kale Rd. DA18: Eri 9J 141
SS7: Ben 2E 134
Kamerwyk Av. SS8: Can I 1J 151
Kandlewood CM13: Hut 6L 97
Kane M. CO1: Colc. 7M 165
(off Northgate St.)
Kangles, The CB11: Lang U 1H 11
Karen Cl. CM15: Brtwd 6F 96
RM13: Rain. 2C 142
SS7: Ben. 6D 134
SS12: W'fd 1K 117
SS17: Stan H. 3L 147
Karen Ter. E11: Lon. 4F 122
Karina Cl. IG7: Chig 2D 108
Kate Daniels Ho. CO16: Wee 5D 178
Katella Trad. Est. IG11: Bark 3D 140
Kate's La. CB10: A'dn 8D 190 (5E 6)
Katherine Cl. SS6: Ray. 6N 119
Katherine Gdns. IG6: Ilf 4B 108
Katherine Rd. E6: Lon 7J 123 (5F 39)
E7: Lon. 7J 123 (5F 39)
SS13: Pits 8M 117
KATHERINES 6M 53 (7G 21)
Katherines Hatch CM19: H'low 5N 53
(off Brookside)
Katherines Ho. CM19: H'low 5N 53
(off Brookside)
Katherine's Way CM19: H'low. 6N 53 (7G 21)
Kathleen Cl. SS17: Stan H. 1M 147
Kathleen Dr. SS9: Lgh S 4E 136
Kathleen Ferrier Cres. SS15: Lain 7L 115
Kathryn Ct. SS3: Shoe. 8J 139
(off Avon Way)
Katonia Av. CM3: May 7K 213
Kavanaghs Rd. CM14: Brtwd. 9D 96 (1E 40)
Kavanaghs Ter. CM14: Brtwd 9E 96
Kay Cl. CM3: Gt L 7L 203
Kay St. E15: Lon. 9D 122
Kay Ter. E18: Lon 5F 106
Keable Rd. CO6: M Tey 3G 171
Keating Cl. CO11: Law 4G 163
Keatings, The CM15: Kel H 7B 82
Keats Av. CM7: Brain 8H 193
RM3: Romf 4F 110
Keats Cl. CM9: Mal. 8C 214
E11: Lon 9H 107
IG7: Chig 3B 108
Keats Gdns. RM18: Til 7D 156
Keats Ho. SS2: Sth S 4N 137
Keats Rd. CO3: Colc 9G 164
DA17: Belv 1A 152
Keats Sq. CM3: S Fer 2L 103
Keats Wlk. CM13: Hut 6N 97
SS6: Ray. 5N 119
Keats Way SS12: W'fd 9K 101
Kebbell Ter. E7: Lon. 7H 123
(off Claremont Rd.)
Keble Cl. CO3: Colc 9L 165
Keddington Hill CO10: L Cor 6K 9
KEDINGTON 2A 8
Keeble Cl. CO5: Tip. 6E 226
Keeble Ct. CO7: Gt Ben 7K 177
Keeble Pk. CM9: Mal 8B 214
Keeble Way CM7: Brain 5J 193
Keefield CM19: H'low. 8A 54
Keegan Pl. SS8: Can I. 1J 151
Keelars La. CO7: W'hoe 5K 175 (7H 17)
Keel Cl. IG11: Bark. 2H 141
Keelers Way CO6: Gt Hork 9J 159
Keelings La. CM0: Deng 4E 36
Keelings Rd. CM0: Deng 4E 36
Keene Memorial Homes
CM1: Chelm. 7J 59
Keene Way CM2: Gall 7C 72
Keepers Cotts. CM11: Bill 3N 99
Keepers Grn. CO4: Colc 4J 165
Keer Av. SS8: Can I. 3K 151
KEERES GREEN 2C 212 (4E 22)
Keevil Cl. CM23: Bis S 8B 220
Keighley M. SS3: Shoe 4H 139
Keighley Rd. RM3: Romf 4J 111
Keir Hardie Way IG11: Bark 9F 124
Keith Av. SS11: W'fd. 7L 101
Keith Cl. CO15: Clac S 5M 185
Keith Rd. IG11: Bark. 2C 140
Keith Way RM11: Horn 2J 127
SS2: Sth S. 1K 137
Kelburn Way RM13: Rain 3E 142
Keller Cres. E12: Lon 6K 123
Kellington Rd. SS8: Can I 9J 135
(not continuous)
Kelly Rd. SS13: Pits 9M 117
Kelly Way RM6: Chad H 9K 109
Kelsall St. SG8: Kel 7B 4
KELSHALL 7B 4
Kelsie Way IG6: Ilf 3D 108
Kelso Cl. CO6: Gt Hork 1K 165
Kelston Rd. IG6: Ilf. 6A 108
KELVEDON 2K 211 (2J 25)
Kelvedon Cl. CM1: Chelm. 5J 59
CM11: Bill 6L 99
CM13: Hut. 5A 98
SS6: Ray. 4G 119
KELVEDON COMMON 9A 82 (5D 32)
Kelvedon Grn. CM15: Kel H 7B 82
Kelvedon Hall La. CM14: Kel H 6M 81 (5C 32)
KELVEDON HATCH 7B 82 (5D 32)
KELVEDON NTH. INTERCHANGE
9B 170 (1K 25)
Kelvedon Rd. CM8: Gt Br. 4H 25
(Rivenhall End)
CM8: Gt Br, L Brax, W Bis 1L 229 (5H 25)
CM9: Tol D 1J 227 (5A 26)
CM11: Bill 6L 99
CO5: Inw, Mess, Tip. 1B 226 (2J 25)
(not continuous)
CO5: K'dn 4H 25
CO6: Cogg. 1H 25
KELVEDON SOUTH INTERCHANGE 3H 25
Kelvedon Station (Rail) 2K 211 (2J 25)
Kelvedon Wlk. RM13: Rain 1D 142
Kelvedon Way IG8: Wfd G 3M 107
Kelvin Ct. CO13: Frin S 2J 187
Kelvin Rd. RM18: Til 7C 156
SS7: Thund. 8D 118
Kelvinside SS17: Stan H 1N 147
Kembles SS6: Ray 2L 119
Kempe Rd. CM7: F'fld 3D 200
Kemp Ho. E6: Lon 8N 123
Kempley Ct. RM17: Grays 4N 155
Kemp Rd. RM8: Dag. 3J 125
Kempton Av. RM12: Horn. 6K 127
Kempton Cl. DA8: Eri 4A 152
SS7: Thund. 8H 119
Kempton Pk.
CO16: L Cla, Wee H. 1F 184
Kemsley Rd. CO6: E Col 8B 198
Ken Cooke Ct. CO1: Colc 8N 165
Kencot Way DA18: Eri. 9L 141
Kendal Av. CM16: Epp 9F 64
IG11: Bark. 1D 140
Kendal Cl. IG8: Wfd G. 8F 90
SS5: Hull 7L 103
SS6: Ray 5L 119
Kendal Ct. SS11: W'fd 2A 118
Kendal Cft. RM12: Horn 7E 126
Kendale RM16: Grays. 1D 156
Kendall Lodge CM16: Epp 9F 64
Kendall Rd. CO1: Colc 9A 166
Kendall Rd. Folley CO1: Colc. 9A 166
Kendall Ter. CO1: Colc 9A 166
Kendal Rd. EN9: Enf. 5C 76
Kendal Way SS9: Lgh S 8D 120
Kendon Cl. E11: Lon. 9H 107
Kenholme SS9: Lgh S 2D 136
Kenilworth Av. E17: Lon. 6A 106
RM3: Romf. 3M 111
Kenilworth Cl. CM12: Bill. 6G 99
Kenilworth Gdns. IG3: Ilf 4E 124
IG10: Lou. 5M 91
RM12: Horn 5G 127
SS0: Wclf S 3F 136 (4H 43)
SS6: Ray. 4H 119
Kenilworth Gro. CO16: T Sok 4L 179
Kenilworth Pl. SS15: Bas. 6N 115
Kenilworth Rd. CO15: Hol S 7B 186
Kenley Cl. SS11: W'fd 1B 118
Kenley Gdns. RM12: Horn 4K 127
Kenmore Cl. SS8: Can I 3L 151
Kennard Rd. E15: Lon 9D 122
Kennedy Av. SS15: Lain. 9H 115
Kennedy Cl. SS6: Ray 7N 119
SS7: Thund. 8B 118
Kennedy Rd. IG11: Bark. 1D 140
Kennedy Way CO15: Clac S 8L 185
Kennel La. CM11: Bill. 9L 99
CM12: Bill. 9K 99 (1J 41)
CM15: Kel H 9B 82
Kennet Cl. RM14: Upm. 1B 128
Kennet Grn. RM15: S Ock. 7E 144
Kenneth Av. IG1: Ilf. 6A 124
Kenneth Gdns. SS17: Stan H 9A 132
Kenneth More Rd. IG1: Ilf 5A 124
Kenneth More Theatre. 5A 124
Kenneth Rd. RM6: Chad H 2J 125
SS7: Thund. 9F 118 (3E 42)
SS13: Pits. 8K 117
Kennet Rd. DA1: Cray. 8E 152
Kennet Way CM1: Chelm 6F 58
SS14: Bas. 8G 116
KENNINGHALL 2C 38
Kenninghall Rd. E5: Lon 4C 38
Kenning Rd. EN11: Rye P. 3A 52
Kennington Av. SS7: Thund 1C 134
Kennington Rd. SE1: Lon. 7A 38
Kennylands Rd. IG6: Ilf. 4F 108
Kensington Av. E12: Lon. 8L 123
Kensington Ct. RM17: Grays 4M 155
Kensington Dr. IG8: Wfd G 6K 107
Kensington Gdns. CM12: Bill 4J 99
IG1: Ilf 3M 123
RM18: E Til. 2L 157
(off Princess Av.)
Kensington Ho. IG8: Ilf. 4N 107
Kensington Rd. CM15: Pil H. 5D 96
RM7: Romf. 1A 126
SS1: Sth S. 6B 138
Kensington Way SS5: Hock 1B 120
Kent Av. RM9: Dag. 4M 141
SS8: Can I. 9H 135
SS9: Lgh S 4E 136
Kent Cl. CO7: B'sea. 6E 182
SS15: Lain. 9K 115
Kent Dr. RM12: Horn 6H 127
Kent Elms Cl. SS2: Sth S 1E 136
Kent Gdns. CM7: Brain. 4K 193
Kent Grn. Cl. SS5: Hock 2E 120
Kentings, The CM7: Brain 6G 193
Kentish Town Rd. NW1: Lon 5A 38

Kentish Town Station (Rail, Tube) 5A 38
Kentlea Rd. SE28: Lon 9D 140
Kentmere CO4: Colc 4E 166
Kenton Rd. E9: Lon 5C 38
Kenton Way SS16: Lang H 1H 131
Kent Rd. RM10: Dag 7N 125
RM17: Grays 4M 155
Kent's Av. CO15: Hol S 7B 186
Kents Farm La. CM2: W Han 5E 86 (5A 34)
Kents Grass CM9: Tol 7K 225
Kents Hill Rd. SS7: Ben 3D 134 (4D 42)
Kents Hill Rd. Nth. SS7: Thund 1D 134
Kents La. CM16: N Wea 1A 32
Kent's La. SG11: Stdn 7E 10
Kents Yd. CB11: L'bry 1B 218
Kent Vw. RM13: Wen 7H 143
RM15: Ave 9N 143
Kent Vw. Av. SS9: Lgh S 6F 136
Kent Vw. Ct. SS8: Can I 4H 151
Kent Vw. Gdns. IG3: Ilf 4D 124
Kent Vw. Rd. SS16: Van 1G 132
Kent Way SS6: Ray 7N 119
Kentwell Ct. SS7: Ben 3C 134
Kentwell Hall 2J 9
Kent Wood Chase CM3: Pur 7N 75
Kenway RM5: Col R 6A 110
RM13: Rain 3H 143
SS2: Sth S 4M 137
Kenway Cl. RM13: Rain 3G 143
Kenway Wlk. RM13: Rain 3H 143
Kenwood Gdns. E18: Lon 7H 107
IG2: Ilf 9N 107
IG5: Ilf 8N 107
Kenwood Rd. SS17: Corr 1C 148
Kenworthy Rd. CM7: Brain 6G 193
E9: Lon 5D 38
Keogh Rd. E15: Lon 8E 122
Keppel Rd. E6: Lon 9M 123
RM9: Dag 6K 125
Kerby Ri. CM2: Chelm 9A 60
Kernow Cl. RM12: Horn 4J 127
Kerridge's Cut CO11: Mist 4M 163
Kerril Cft. CM20: H'low 2N 53
Kerry Av. RM15: Ave 1L 153
Kerry Cl. RM14: Upm 2C 128
Kerry Ct. CO1: Colc 8C 166
Kerry Dr. RM14: Upm 2C 128
Kerry Rd. RM16: Grays 8N 145
Kersbrooke Way SS17: Corr 9C 132
Kersey Ct. CO2: Colc 3K 173
Kersey Dr. CO16: Clac S 8F 184
Kersey Gdns. RM3: H Wood 4J 111
Kershaw Cl. RM11: Horn 2J 127
RM16: Chaf H 2F 154
Kershaw Rd. RM10: Dag 5M 125
Kershaws Cl. SS12: W'fd 1K 117
Kesteven Cl. IG6: Ilf 3E 108
Kestrel Cl. IG6: Ilf 1G 109
RM12: Horn 9F 126
Kestrel Gro. SS6: Ray 4H 119
Kestrel M. CM9: Mal 8D 214
Kestrel Pk. CM13: Hut 4A 98
Kestrel Ri. CO9: Hals 5L 207
Kestrel Rd. EN9: Wal A 4G 76
Kestrel Wlk. CM2: Gall 6C 72
Kestrel Way CO15: Clac S 7K 185
Keswick Av. CO15: Hol S 7N 185
RM11: Horn 3H 127
SS5: Hull 6L 103
Keswick Cl. CO13: Frin S 7J 181
SS6: Ray 5L 119
Keswick Gdns. IG4: Ilf 8L 107
Keswick Ho. *RM3: Romf 3H 111*
(off Dartfields)
Keswick Rd. SS7: Thund 9E 118
Ketley Cl. CO5: Tip 5E 226
Ketleys CM2: Gall 7D 72
Ketleys Vw. CM7: Pan 1C 192
Kettering Rd. RM3: Romf 4J 111
Kettlebury Way CM5: Chip 9K 67
KETTLE GREEN 2F 21
Kettle Grn. Rd. SG10: M Hud 2G 21
Kevan Ct. E17: Lon 8A 106
Kevin Cl. CM11: Bill 9M 99
Kew La. CO13: Gt Hol 1D 186
Keyes Cl. SS3: Shoe 5J 139
Keyes Rd. DA1: Dart 9K 153
Keyes Way CM7: Brain 4L 193
Keymer Way CO3: S'way 2G 172
Keynes Ct. *SE28: Lon 7G 141*
(off Attlee Rd.)
Keynes Way CO12: Har 6H 209
Keynsham Av. IG8: Wfd G 1E 106
Key Rd. CO15: Clac S 1J 189
KEYSERS ESTATE 1A 62 (1D 30)
Keysers Rd. EN10: Brox 1A 62
Keysland SS7: Thund 9H 119
Khartoum Rd. IG1: Ilf 7A 124
Kibcaps SS16: Bas 2A 132
Kidder Rd. CM77: Rayne 7B 192
Kidman Cl. RM2: Romf 7G 111
Kielder Cl. IG6: Ilf 3E 108
Kier Hardie Ho. RM16: Grays 8A 146
Kilbarry Wlk. CM11: Bill 2M 99
Kilburn Gdns. CO16: Clac S 8H 185
Kildermorie Cl. CO4: Colc 4D 166
Kildowan Rd. IG3: Ilf 3F 124
KILLEMS GREEN 1G 11
Kilmaine Rd. CO12: Har 5H 209
Kilmarnock Gdns. RM8: Dag 5H 125
Kilmartin Rd. IG3: Ilf 4F 124
Kilmartin Way RM12: Horn 7F 126
Kilmington Cl. CM13: Hut 8L 97
Kiln Barn Av. CO15: Clac S 6K 185
Kiln Cotts. CO7: Ded 2M 161
Kilnfield CM5: Chip 8K 67
Kiln Fld. CM15: Wy G 5G 82
Kiln La. CM17: H'low 4H 55 (7J 21)
CO11: Mist 4J 163
Kiln Rd. CM16: N Wea 6M 65
SS7: Ben, Thund 2F 134 (4E 42)
Kiln Shaw SS16: Lang H 2L 131
Kilns Hill CO6: Cogg 6H 15
Kiln Way RM17: Grays 3J 155
Kilnwood Av. SS5: Hock 2C 120
Kiln Wood La. RM5: Hav 2B 110
Kilowan Cl. SS16: Lang H 2H 131
Kilsby Wlk. RM9: Dag 8G 124
Kiltie Rd. CO5: Tip 6E 226
Kilworth Av. CM15: Shenf 5K 97
SS1: Sth S 6N 137
Kimberley Av. IG2: Ilf 2C 124
RM7: Romf 1A 126
Kimberley Ct. SS7: Ben 3C 134
Kimberley Dr. SS15: Bas 5A 116
Kimberley Rd. CO1: Colc 1B 174
E4: Lon 7E 90
E11: Lon 4D 122
SS3: Lit W 3B 44
SS7: Ben 3C 134
Kimberley Way E4: Lon 7E 90
Kimpton Av. CM15: Brtwd 6E 96
Kimpton's Cl. CM5: Chip 5K 67
Kincaid Rd. CO16: St O 9M 183
Kinder Cl. SE28: Lon 7J 141
Kinfauns Av. RM11: Horn 1G 126
Kinfauns Rd. IG3: Ilf 3F 124
Kingaby Gdns. RM13: Rain 9E 126
King Alfred Rd. RM3: H Wood 6K 111
King Charles Rd. CO5: W Mer 3D 228
King Coel Rd. CO3: S'way 8E 164 (6C 16)
King Ct. E10: Lon 2B 122
King Edward Av. CM0: Bur C 2D 196
RM13: Rain 2H 143
King Edward Ct. CM1: Chelm 8J 59
King Edward Dr. RM16: Grays 9A 146 (1G 47)
King Edward Quay CO2: Colc 1D 174
King Edward Rd. CM14: Brtwd 9F 96
E10: Lon 3C 122
RM1: Romf 1D 126
SS15: Lain 7K 115
King Edward's Rd. CM3: S Fer 9J 89
King Edwards Rd. IG11: Bark 1C 140 (6H 39)
King Edward's Rd. SG12: Ware 4D 20
SS17: Stan H 5M 147
King Edward Ter. SS15: Lain 8K 115
King Edward VI's Almhouses
CB10: Saf W 4C 218
King Edward Way CM8: Wthm 7B 230
Kingfisher Av. E11: Lon 1H 123
Kingfisher Cl. CM9: H'bri 3E 214
CM13: Hut 6K 97
CO4: Colc 7F 166
SE28: Lon 7H 141
SS3: Shoe 5J 139
Kingfisher Cres. SS6: Ray 4H 119
Kingfisher Dr. CO12: Har 6G 209
SS7: Ben 4C 134
Kingfisher Ga. CM7: Brain 3J 193
Kingfisher Lodge CM2: Gt Bad 3G 72
Kingfisher Mdws. CO9: Hals 5L 207
Kingfisher Rd. RM14: Upm 3C 128
Kingfishers CM4: Ing 5E 84
CO15: Clac S 7K 185
SS16: Bas 2D 132
Kingfishers, The SS11: W'fd 2A 118
Kingfisher Way *CM19: Roy 2G 52*
(off Heron Way)
CO5: K'dn 3K 211
King George Av. IG2: Ilf 9C 108
King George VI Av. RM18: E Til 2K 157
King George Cl. RM7: Maw 7A 110
King George Rd. CO2: Colc 2N 173
EN9: Wal A 4C 76
King George's Av. CO12: Har 3K 209
King George's Cl. SS6: Ray 5K 119
King George's Pl. *CM9: Mal 6C 214*
(off High St.)
King Georges Rd. CM15: Pil H 5E 96
King Harold Ct. *EN9: Wal A 3C 76*
(off Sun St.)
King Harold Rd. CO3: Colc 2H 173
King Henrys Ct. EN9: Enf 6C 76
King Henry's Dr. SS4: R'fd 8L 121
King Henry's M. *EN3: Enf 7A 76*
(off Mollison Av.)
Kingley Cl. SS12: W'fd 9J 101
Kingley Dr. SS12: W'fd 9J 101
Kings Acre CO6: Cogg 3K 197
Kings Arms Yd. RM1: Romf 9C 110
Kings Av. CO15: Hol S 8N 185 (3E 28)
King's Av. IG8: Wfd G 3H 107 (2F 39)
IG9: Buck H 8K 91
(Queen's Rd.)
IG9: Buck H 3H 107
(Station Way)
Kings Av. RM6: Chad H 1L 125
Kingsbridge Cir. RM3: Romf 3J 111
Kingsbridge Cl. CM7: Brain 9H 191
RM3: Romf 3J 111
Kingsbridge Rd. IG11: Bark 2C 140
RM3: Romf 3J 111
Kingsbridge Wharf
IG11: Bark 3D 140
Kingsbury Cl. CO6: M Tey 5H 171
Kings Chase CM8: Wthm 6D 230
CM14: Brtwd 9F 96
Kings Cl. CO11: Law 4H 163
King's Cl. CO16: St O 4B 28
DA1: Cray 9C 152
Kings Cl. E10: Lon 2B 122
SS6: Ray 5L 119
SS8: Can I 2C 150
Kings Ct. CM0: Bur C 4D 196
CM6: Gt D 2L 203
CO5: Tip 4C 226
CO12: Har 4K 209
CO15: Hol S 8A 186
IG9: Buck H 8K 91
Kings Cres. SS15: Lain 6K 115
Kings Cft. CM0: S'min 2D 222
KING'S CROSS 6A 38
KING'S CROSS 6A 38
King's Cross Rd. WC1: Lon 6A 38
King's Cross St Pancras Station (Tube) 6A 38
King's Cross Station (Rail) 6A 38
King's Cross Thameslink Station (Rail) 6A 38
Kingsdale Ct. *EN9: Wal A 4G 77*
(off Lamplighters Cl.)
Kingsdale Ind. Est. CM1: Chelm 8L 59
Kingsdon La. CM17: H'low 4H 55
Kingsdown Cl. SS13: Pits 9K 117
Kingsdown Rd. E11: Lon 5E 122
Kingsdown Wlk. SS8: Can I 9G 134
KINGS FARM 4H 47
Kings Farm E17: Lon 5B 106
SS6: Ray 2L 119
Kingsfield EN11: Rye P 3A 52
Kings Ford Ct. CO2: Colc 3J 173
Kingsford Dr. CM2: Chelm 8B 60
Kings Gdns. IG1: Ilf 3C 124
RM14: Upm 2B 128
Kings Grn. IG10: Lou 2L 91
Kings Gro. RM1: Romf 9E 110
Kingshawes SS7: Thund 9H 119
Kings Head Ct. CM21: Saw 2K 51
CO1: Colc 7N 165
Kings Head Hill E4: Lon 6B 90 (7D 30)
King's Head St. CO12: Har 1M 209
Kings Head Wlk. *CM2: Chelm 9L 59*
(off Can Bri. Way)
Kings Hill CB9: Ked 2A 8
CO10: Gt Cor 5K 9
King's Hill IG10: Lou 1L 91
Kingshill Av. RM5: Col R 3A 110
KINGSLAND 5B 38
Kingsland CM18: H'low 5B 54
Kingsland Beach CO5: W Mer 4C 228
Kingsland Cl. CO5: W Mer 4C 228
Kingsland Hgts. CO5: W Mer 3C 228
Kingsland High St. E8: Lon 5B 38
Kingsland Rd. CO5: W Mer 4C 228 (5F 27)
E2: Lon 6B 38
E8: Lon 6B 38
King's La. CB11: Elm 6J 5
Kings La. CM77: Tye G 4N 193 (7E 14)
Kingsleigh Pk. Homes
SS7: Thund 9H 119
Kingsley Cl. RM10: Dag 6N 125
Kingsley Ct. RM2: Horn 1F 126
Kingsley Cres. SS6: Ray 7H 119
Kingsley Gdns. E4: Lon 2A 106
RM11: Horn 8H 111
Kingsley La. SS7: Thund 7H 119
Kingsley Mdws. SS12: W'fd 2L 117
Kingsley Rd. CM13: Hut 6N 97
E7: Lon 9G 123
E17: Lon 6C 106
IG6: Ilf 5B 108
IG10: Lou 2C 92
Kingsley Wlk. RM16: Grays 2C 156
Kings Lodge SS7: Had 3J 135
Kings Lynn Cl. RM3: Romf 3H 111
Kings Lynn Dr. RM3: Romf 3H 111
Kings Lynn Path RM3: Romf 3H 111
Kingsman Dr. CO16: Clac S 8G 184
RM16: N Stif 7L 145
Kingsman Rd. SS17: Stan H 4K 147
Kingsmans Farm Rd. SS5: Hull 4M 103 (7F 35)
Kingsmead CM21: Saw 3K 51
Kings Mead CO9: Peb 2H 15
Kingsmead Av. RM1: Romf 1C 126
Kingsmead Cvn. Pk.
CM7: Brain 4L 193
Kingsmead Cl. CM19: Roy 4H 53
KINGSMEAD HILL 4H 53
Kingsmead Mans. *RM1: Romf 1D 126*
(off Kingsmead Av.)
Kings Mdw. Ct. CO5: K'dn 2K 211
EN9: Wal A 4G 77
(off Horseshoe Cl.)
Kings Mdw. Rd. CO1: Colc 7N 165
Kingsmead Pk. CM7: Brain 4L 193
Kingsmere SS7: Thund 1H 135
Kingsmere Cl. CO5: W Mer 3D 228
Kings M. CO7: W'hoe 2J 175
IG7: Chig 8B 92
Kings Mill CB10: Gt Che 8C 202
Kingsmill Gdns. RM9: Dag 7L 125
Kingsmill Rd. RM9: Dag 7L 125
KINGSMOOR 7B 54 (1H 31)
Kingsmoor Rd. CM19: H'low 5A 54 (7G 21)
Kings Oak RM7: Maw 7M 109
Kings Pde. CO15: Clac S 3J 189
CO15: Hol S 9N 185 (4E 28)
SS17: Stan H 4L 147
(off King St.)
Kings Pk. SS7: Thund 1F 134
SS8: Can I 1L 151
Kingspark Ct. E18: Lon 7G 106
Kings Pas. E11: Lon 2E 122
Kings Pl. IG9: Buck H 8J 91
IG10: Lou 6K 91
Kings Quay St. CO12: Har 1N 209
(not continuous)
Kings Rd. CM0: Bur C 4D 196
CM0: S'min 3D 222 (5C 36)
CM1: Chelm 7H 59 (1K 33)
King's Rd. CM7: Brain 3G 193
Kings Rd. CM9: Gt Tot 7J 205
CM14: Brtwd 1E 40
King's Rd. CM14: Brtwd 8F 96
Kings Rd. CO9: Hals 5K 207 (3F 15)
King's Rd. CO12: Har 4K 209
CO15: Clac S 3H 189
Kings Rd. E4: Lon 7D 90 (7E 30)
E11: Lon 2E 122
IG11: Bark 9B 124
King's Rd. RM1: Romf 9E 110
SS0: Wclf S 5F 136 (4H 43)
Kings Rd. SS6: Ray 5L 119
King's Rd. SS7: Ben 4E 134
Kings Rd. SS8: Can I 2C 150
SS15: Lain 6K 115
Kingsteignton SS3: Shoe 5G 139
King Stephen Rd. CO1: Colc 9B 166
Kingston Av. CM2: Chelm 8N 59
SS3: Shoe 4J 139
Kingston Chase CM9: Mal 3B 214
Kingston Cl. RM6: Chad H 7K 109
(not continuous)
Kingston Cres. CM2: Chelm 8N 59
Kingston Hill SS16: Bas 4M 131
Kingston Hill Av. RM6: Chad H 7K 109
Kingston Ridge SS16: Bas 4M 131
Kingston Rd. IG1: Ilf 6A 124
RM1: Romf 8D 110
Kingston Way SS7: Thund 9F 118
SS16: Bas 3N 131
KING STREET 7E 68 (3E 32)
King St. CB10: Saf W 4C 218
CM5: Chip, H Ong, Nine A 6C 68 (3E 32)
CM9: Mal 7C 214
CO9: Cas H 3L 219
CO10: Sud 5J 9
CO11: Brad 4B 18
SS17: Stan H 4L 147 (6K 41)
Kingsview Ct. SS11: W'fd 1N 117
Kings Wlk. CM9: Tol 8L 225
RM17: Grays 4K 155
Kings Way CM3: S Fer 8J 89
CM11: Bill 1M 115
Kingsway CO5: Tip 5C 226
CO12: Har 3M 209 (3H 19)
Kings Way IG8: Wfd G 2J 107
Kingsway SG12: Ware 4C 20
SS0: Wclf S 4F 136
SS5: Hull 7K 103
WC2: Lon 7A 38
Kingsway M. SS0: Wclf S 4G 136
KINGSWOOD 2C 132 (4A 42)
Kingswood Chase SS9: Lgh S 3C 136
Kingswood Cl. CM11: Bill 6L 99
Kingswood Ct. CM0: Brad S 7D 194
E4: Lon 2A 106
SS16: Van 1F 132
Kingswood Cres. SS6: Ray 6H 119
Kingswood Rd. CO4: Colc 3N 165
E11: Lon 2E 122
IG3: Ilf 3F 124
SS16: Bas 1D 132
Kings Yd. E9: Lon 8A 122
E15: Lon 8A 122
Kingwell Av. CO15: Clac S 8J 185
King Williams Ct. *EN9: Enf 5C 76*
(off Deerpark Way)
Kinlett Cl. CO4: Colc 3B 166
Kinloch Chase CM8: Wthm 8C 230
Kinnaird Way IG8: Wfd G 3M 107
Kino Rd. CO14: Walt 6N 181
Kipling Av. RM18: Til 6D 156
Kipling Cl. CM1: Chelm 6J 59
CM14: War 2E 112
Kipling M. SS2: Sth S 4M 137
Kipling Way CM7: Brain 2B 192
Kirby Av. RM15: Ave 9K 143
Kirby Cl. IG6: Ilf 3D 108
IG10: Lou 6L 91
RM3: Romf 2L 111
KIRBY CROSS 8E 180 (1G 29)
Kirby Cross Station (Rail) 8E 180 (1F 29)
Kirby Hall Rd. CO9: Cas H 1J 219 (7D 8)
KIRBY-LE-SOKEN 6G 180 (7G 19)
Kirby Rd. CO13: Gt Hol, Walt 1D 186 (2F 29)
CO14: Walt 6J 181 (1G 29)
SS14: Bas 9F 116
Kirkbaye CO13: Walt 8H 181
Kirkdale Rd. E11: Lon 3E 122
Kirkham Av. SS17: Horn H 7H 131
Kirkham Ho. *RM3: Romf 2H 111*
(off Montgomery Cres.)
Kirkham Rd. SS17: Horn H 7H 131
Kirkham Shaw SS17: Horn H 6H 131
Kirkhurst Cl. CO7: B'sea 7F 182
Kirkland Av. IG5: Ilf 6N 107
Kirklees CM1: Chelm 7H 59
Kirklees Rd. RM8: Dag 7H 125
Kirkmans Rd. CM2: Gall 7E 72
Kirk Pl. CM2: Chelm 8A 60
Kirton Cl. RM12: Horn 8G 127
Kitchener Rd. CM3: N Fam 5H 35
E7: Lon 8H 123
E17: Lon 5B 106
RM10: Dag 8N 125
Kitchen Fld. CM7: Brain 5M 193
Kitchen Hill CO10: Bulm, Sud 5H 9
Kitkatts Rd. SS8: Can I 2G 151
(not continuous)
Kit's La. SG7: Wall 2A 10
Kitson Way CM20: H'low 2B 54

Kittiwake Dr. CM9: Mal 3E 214
Knapton Cl. CM1: Chelm 4M 59
Knares, The SS16: Bas 2N 131 (4K 41)
Knebworth Av. E17: Lon 5A 106
KNEESWORTH 3B 4
Kneesworth St. SG8: R'ton 5C 4
Knightbridge Wlk. CM12: Bill 5J 99
Knight Cl. RM8: Dag 4H 125
Knight Ct. E4: Lon 7C 90
(off Ridgeway, The)
Knighton Cl. IG8: Wfd G 1H 107
RM7: Romf 1B 126
Knighton Dr. IG8: Wfd G 1H 107
Knighton Grn. IG9: Buck H 8H 91
Knighton La. IG9: Buck H 8H 91
Knighton Rd. E7: Lon 5G 123
RM7: Romf 1A 126
Knights SS15: Lain 8M 115
Knightsbridge Cl. CO2: Colc 3K 173
Knightsbridge Ct. CO15: Clac S 1M 189
(off Connaught Gdns. E.)
Knightsbridge Gdns. RM7: Romf 9B 110
Knights Cl. CO5: Tip 8F 226
CO11: Law 4H 163
Knights Ct. CM21: Saw 2K 51
SS14: Bas 7G 117
Knights Farm 8B 196
Knights Rd. CM7: Brain 7M 193
CO6: Cogg 3K 197
Knight St. CM3: S Fer 1L 103
CM21: Saw 2K 51
(Bell St.)
CM21: Saw 2K 51 (4K 21)
(Duckling La.)
Knights Wlk. RM4: Abr 2G 93
Knights Way CM6: Gt D 2L 203
CM13: Brtwd 9K 97
IG6: Ilf 3B 108
Knightswick Cen. SS8: Can I 1J 151
Knightswick Rd. SS8: Can I 1H 151 (6E 42)
Knightswood Ct. CM0: S'min 1B 222
Knightswood Rd. RM13: Rain 2E 142
Knivet Cl. SS6: Ray 6L 119
KNOCKHALL 3E 46
Knockhall Rd. DA9: Grnh 3E 46
Knole Cl. CM3: S Fer 3K 103
Knole La. CB11: Wen L 7J 5
Knollcroft SS3: Shoe 9H 139
Knoll, The CM12: Bill 4K 99
SS6: Ray 5K 119
Knotts Grn. M. E10: Lon 1B 122
Knotts Grn. Rd. E10: Lon 1B 122
Knowles Cl. CO9: Hals 5K 207
Knowle, The EN11: Hod 6A 52
SS16: Van 2D 132
KNOWL GREEN 5E 8
Knowlton Cotts. RM15: S Ock 5F 144
Knox Cl. CM9: Mal 8C 214
Knox Ct. CO15: Clac S 8J 185
SS12: W'fd 2N 117
KNOX END 6C 190
Knox Gdns. CO15: Clac S 8J 185
Knox Rd. CO15: Clac S 8J 185
E7: Lon 8F 122
Kohima Rd. CO2: Colc 5J 173
Kolburg Rd. SS8: Can I 3K 151
Kollum Rd. SS8: Can I 2M 151
Koln Cl. SS8: Can I 2C 150
Komberg Cres. SS8: Can I 9J 135
Konnybrook SS7: Thund 2G 134
Korndyk Av. SS8: Can I 1J 151
Kreswell Gro. CO12: Har 5K 209
Kubrick Bus. Est. E7: Lon 6H 123
(off Station App.)
Kuhn Way E7: Lon 7G 123
Kursaal SS1: Sth S 7A 138
Kursaal Bowl 7A 138
Kursaal Pavement SS1: Sth S 7A 138
Kursaal Way SS1: Sth S 7A 138
Kyme Rd. RM11: Horn 1D 126
Kynance Cl. RM3: Romf 1G 111
Kynaston Pl. CM8: Wthm 5E 230
Kynaston Rd. CM7: Pan 1C 192 (6B 14)
Kynoch Ct. SS17: Stan H 4N 147

L

Laars Av. SS8: Can I 1J 151
Laburnham Cl. RM14: Upm 2D 128
Laburnham Gdns. RM14: Upm 2C 128
Laburnum Av. RM12: Horn 4E 126
SS12: W'fd 1K 117
Laburnum Cl. CM22: Srng 4A 210
CO7: Gt Ben 6K 177
CO15: Clac S 1G 188
SS5: Hock 1B 120
SS12: W'fd 1K 117
Laburnum Cres. CO13: Walt 8G 180
Laburnum Dr. CM2: Chelm 4C 72
SS17: Corr 1C 148
Laburnum Gro. CO4: Colc 7E 166
RM15: S Ock 3F 144
SS5: Hock 1A 120
SS8: Can I 2D 150
Laburnum Rd. CM16: Coop 8H 65
EN11: Rye P 3B 52
Laburnum Wlk. RM12: Horn 7G 126
Laburnum Way CM3: Hat P 3L 61
CM8: Wthm 2D 230
SS6: Ray 1H 119
Labworth La. SS8: Can I 3J 151
(not continuous)
Labworth Rd. SS8: Can I 3J 151
Lacy Dr. RM8: Dag 5H 125
Ladbrook Dr. CO2: Colc 3A 174
Ladbroke Rd. CO16: Clac S 7H 185
Ladell Cl. CO3: S'way 3F 172
Ladram Cl. SS1: Sth S 6G 138
Ladram Rd. SS1: Sth S 6F 138
Ladram Way SS1: Sth S 6F 138
Ladyfields IG10: Lou 3B 92
Ladyfields Cl. IG10: Lou 3B 92
Ladygate Cen. SS12: W'fd 9L 101
Lady Hamilton Ct. SS1: Sth S 6F 138
Lady La. CM2: Chelm 2C 72
Lady Pl. CM11: Bill 5K 99
Ladyshot CM20: H'low 2G 54
Ladysmith Av. CO7: B'sea 6D 182 (3K 27)
IG2: Ilf 2C 124
Ladysmith Way SS15: Bas 5A 116
Ladywell La. CM2: Gt Bad 5J 73
Ladywell Prospect CM21: Saw 3M 51
Lagonda Av. IG6: Ilf 3E 108
Lagonda Way DA1: Dart 9G 152
LAINDON 8L 115 (3K 41)
Laindon Cen. SS15: Lain 9L 115
Laindon Comn. Rd.
CM12: L Bur 2H 115 (1J 41)
Laindon Link SS15: Lain 9L 115 (3K 41)
Laindon Rd. CM12: Bill 7J 99 (1J 41)
SS17: Lang H 8H 131
Laindon Station (Rail) 1L 131 (3K 41)
Laing Cl. IG6: Ilf 3C 108
Laing Rd. CO4: Colc 9E 166
Laird Av. RM16: Grays 9N 145
Lake Av. CM12: Bill 5J 99
CO15: Clac S 1G 188
RM13: Rain 2H 143
Lake Cl. RM8: Dag 5J 125
Lake Dr. SS7: Thund 1E 134
Lakefields Cl. RM13: Rain 2H 143
Lake Footpath SE2: Lon 9J 141
Lake Gdns. RM10: Dag 7M 125
Lake Ho. Rd. E11: Lon 5G 122 (4E 38)
Lakeland Cl. IG7: Chig 1G 109
Lake Mdws. Office Village CM12: Bill 5H 99
Lakenham Ho. SS2: Sth S 1K 137
(off Manners Way)
Lake Ri. RM1: Romf 6D 110
RM20: W Thur 2D 154
Lake Rd. EN9: Naze 9E 52
RM6: Chad H 8J 109
RM9: Dag 4N 141
Lakeside CM12: Bill 4J 99
RM13: Rain 2J 143
SS6: Ray 3K 119
Lakeside Av. IG4: Ilf 8K 107
SE28: Lon 8F 140
Lakeside Cl. IG7: Chig 1E 108
Lakeside Cres. CM14: Brtwd 9G 96
SS8: Can I 9K 135
Lakeside Karting Cen. 9E 144
Lakeside Leisure Pk. RM20: W Thur 2D 154
Lakeside Path SS8: Can I 9G 134
Lakeside Retail Pk. RM20: W Thur 2D 154
Lakeside Wlk. CO3: S'way 2D 172
Lakes Ind. Pk. CM7: Brain 6K 193
Lakes Mdw. CO6: Cogg 3L 197
Lakes Rd. CM7: Brain 6K 193 (7D 14)
Lake Vw. CM5: M'ton 1B 32
Lakeview SS8: Can I 9G 134
Lake Vw. SS16: Lang H 2H 131
Lakeview Pk. RM4: Hav 9G 94
Lake Wlk. CO15: Clac S 1G 188
Lake Way CO15: Jay 6D 188
Lakin Cl. CM2: Chelm 8B 60
LAMARSH 1K 15
Lamarsh Hill CO8: Bures 7K 195 (1K 15)
CO8: Lmsh 7K 9
Lamarsh Hill Bungs.
CO8: Bures 8K 195
Lamarsh Rd. CO8: Alph 1K 15
Lamb Cl. RM18: Til 7E 156
LAMB CORNER 4K 161 (3H 17)
Lamberhurst Rd. RM8: Dag 3L 125
Lambert Ct. DA8: Eri 4A 152
(off Park Cres.)
Lambert Cross CB10: Saf W 2D 218
Lambert's Rd. CO6: E Col 5J 15
LAMBETH 7A 38
Lambeth M. SS4: R'fd 6L 121
(off Millview Mdws.)
SS5: Hock 1B 120
(off Mey Wlk.)
Lambeth North Station (Tube) 7A 38
Lambeth Pal. Rd. SE1: Lon 7A 38
Lambeth Rd. SS7: Thund 9C 118
SS9: Lgh S 9D 120
Lambeth Wlk. CO15: Clac S 8J 185
Lamb La. CO9: Sib H 8H 219 (2D 14)
Lambley Rd. RM9: Dag 8G 125
Lambourn Cl. SS3: Shoe 4J 139
LAMBOURNE 3J 93 (6J 31)
Lambourne RM18: E Til 2L 157
SS8: Can I 3G 150
Lambourne Cl. CO3: S'way 2E 172
CO15: Clac S 5K 185
IG7: Chig 9G 93
Lambourne Ct. IG8: Wfd G 4J 107
Lambourne Cres. IG7: Chig 8G 93
SS14: Bas 1G 132
Lambourne Dr. CM13: Hut 6A 98
LAMBOURNE END 6K 93 (7K 31)
Lambourne Gdns. E4: Lon 8A 90
IG11: Bark 9E 124
RM12: Horn 4H 127
Lambourne Gro. CM9: Mal 8B 214
Lambourne Hall Rd. SS4: Cwdn 1N 105 (7A 36)
Lambourne Rd. E11: Lon 2C 122
IG3: Ilf 4D 124
IG7: Chig 1E 108 (1H 39)
IG11: Bark 9D 124
Lambourne Sq. RM4: Abr 7H 93
Lambs La. Ind. Est. RM13: Rain 4G 143
Lamb's La. Nth. RM13: Rain 4H 143
Lamb's La. Sth. RM13: Rain 5F 142
Lambs Mdw. IG8: Wfd G 6K 107
Lamerton Rd. IG6: Ilf 6A 108
Lammas Dr. CM7: Brain 5M 193
Lammas Way CO7: W'hoe 4J 175
Lamont Dr. SS12: W'fd 2M 117
Lamorna Cl. E17: Lon 6C 106
Lampern Cl. CM12: Bill 2K 99
Lampern Cres. CM12: Bill 2K 99
Lampern M. CM12: Bill 2K 99
Lampeter Ho. RM3: Romf 4J 111
(off Kingsbridge Cir.)
Lampetsdowne SS17: Corr 1C 148
Lampits EN11: Hod 5B 52
Lampits Hill SS17: Corr 8B 132 (5A 42)
Lampits Hill Av. SS17: Corr 9B 132
Lampits La. SS17: Corr 9B 132
Lamplighters Cl. EN9: Wal A 4G 77
Lamson Rd. RM13: Rain 4D 142
Lancaster Av. E18: Lon 8H 107
IG11: Bark 9D 124
Lancaster Cl. CM15: Pil H 4D 96
Lancaster Cres. SS1: Sth S 6N 137
(off Hastings Rd.)
Lancaster Dr. IG10: Lou 5L 91
RM12: Horn 7F 126
SS16: Lang H 1H 131
Lancaster Gdns. SS1: Sth S 6N 137
SS6: Ray 7N 119
Lancaster Gdns. E. CO15: Clac S 9L 185
Lancaster Gdns. W. CO15: Clac S 9L 185
Lancaster Pl. IG1: Ilf 7B 124
WC2: Lon 7A 38
Lancaster Rd. CM16: N Wea, Thorn 5M 65
(not continuous)
E7: Lon 9G 123
E11: Lon 4E 122
EN2: Enf 6B 30
RM16: Chaf H 3G 154
SS6: Ray 7N 119
(not continuous)
Lancaster Way CM7: Brain 4G 192
CO6: E Col 5H 15
Lancelot Rd. IG6: Ilf 3D 108
Lancer Way CM12: Bill 5H 99
Lanchester Av. CO15: Jay 6B 188
Lancia Av. CO15: Jay 6C 188
Lancing Rd. IG2: Ilf 1C 124
RM3: Romf 4J 111
Landau Way DA8: Eri 3H 153
Land Cl. CO16: Clac S 8G 184
LANDERMERE 2N 179
Landermere SS14: Bas 8C 116
Landermere Rd. CO16: T Sok 5L 179 (7E 18)
Lander Rd. RM17: Grays 3N 155
Landers Ct. CM1: Chelm 6G 59
Landguard Fort and Mus. 2K 19
Landisdale CM3: Dan 3G 75
Land La. CO1: Colc 8A 166
Landsburg Rd. SS8: Can I 9K 135
Landscape Rd. IG8: Wfd G 4H 107
Landscape Vw. CB11: Saf W 7C 218 (7B 6)
Landseer Av. E12: Lon 7N 123
Landseer Cl. RM11: Horn 3F 126
Landseer Ct. CO15: Clac S 2K 189
Landseer Rd. CO3: Colc 1J 173
Landview Gdns. CM5: Chip 9K 67
Landwick La. CM0: Deng 4E 36
LANE END
FRINTON-ON-SEA 5D 180
DARTFORD 5D 46
Lane End CM17: H'low 4K 55 (7K 21)
Lane M. E12: Lon 5M 123
Lane Rd. CO6: Wak C 6A 196 (4K 15)
Laneside Av. RM8: Dag 2L 125
Lane, The CO5: W Mer 2A 228
CO11: Mist 4L 163
CO15: Clac S 1G 188
Langdale CM77: Gt N 1C 204
Langdale Cl. RM8: Dag 3H 125
Langdale Dr. CO4: Colc 3B 166
Langdale Gdns. CM2: Chelm 2D 72
RM12: Horn 7E 126
Langdale St. CM17: H'low 2H 55
LANGDON HILLS 2J 131 (4J 41)
Langdon Hills Country Pk. 4N 131
Langdon M. CM11: Bill 5K 99
Langdon Rd. SS6: Ray 4H 119
Langdon Way SS17: Corr 9C 132
Langemore Way CM11: Bill 7K 99
LANGENHOE 9B 174 (2F 27)
Langenhoe SS12: W'fd 1M 117
Langenhoe Hall La. CO5: L'hoe 3F 27
Langenhoe Pk. CO5: L'hoe 9B 174
Langer Rd. IP11: Felix 2K 19
Langfield Cl. EN9: Naze 1E 62
LANGFORD 7G 25
Langford Cres. SS7: Thund 9F 118
Langford Grn. CM13: Hut 4M 97
Langford Gro. SS13: Bas 7K 117
Langford Rd. CM8: Mal, W Bis 4H 229 (6G 25)
CM9: L'frd, Mal 2A 214 (7H 25)
CM9: Ult 7F 25
IG8: Wfd G 3J 107
Langfords IG9: Buck H 8K 91
LANGHAM 4F 160 (3G 17)
Langham Ct. RM11: Horn 2H 127
Langham Cres. CM12: Bill 8K 99
Langham Dr. CO16: Clac S 9F 184
RM6: Chad H 1G 124
SS6: Ray 4G 118
Langham La. CO4: Boxt, L'ham 8A 160 (4F 17)
Langham Lodge La. CO4: L'ham 8E 160
LANGHAM MOOR 4D 160 (3F 17)
Langham Pl. CO4: Colc 4B 166
Langham Rd. CO4: Boxt 7N 159 (3E 16)
LANGHAM WICK 4F 160 (3G 17)
Langhorne Rd. RM10: Dag 9M 125
Langland Cl. SS17: Corr 1A 148
LANGLEY 1H 11
Langley Av. CM7: Weth 2A 14
Langley Cl. CO12: Har 4L 209
RM3: Romf 4H 111
SS1: Sth S 6A 138
SS9: Lgh S 8A 120
Langley Cres. E11: Lon 2J 123
RM9: Dag 9H 125
Langley Dr. CM14: Brtwd 9D 96
E11: Lon 2H 123 (4F 39)
Langley Gdns. RM9: Dag 9J 125
LANGLEY GREEN 6B 170 (1J 25)
Langley Grn. EN9: Naze 1D 62
Langley Mdw. IG10: Lou 1C 92
Langley Pl. CM12: Bill 5G 99
Langleys CO6: Gt Tey 1E 170
SS16: Bas 2C 132
Langport Dr. SS0: Wclf S 2F 136
Langport Ho. RM3: Romf 4J 111
(off Leyburn Rd.)
Langside Cl. SS15: Lain 7K 115
Langston Rd. IG10: Lou 4B 92
Langthorne Cres.
RM17: Grays 2M 155
Langthorne Rd. E11: Lon 5C 122 (5E 38)
Langthorns CM12: Bill 6K 99
Langton Av. CM1: Chelm 6G 59
Langton Way RM16: Grays 2E 156
Langwood CO5: W Mer 2C 228
Lanham Farm Rd. CM77: Tye G 1E 24
LANHAM GREEN 1E 24
Lanham Green CM77: Tye G 1E 24
Lanham Grn. Rd. CM77: Tye G 1E 24
Lanham Pl. SS13: Bas 7J 117
Lanhams SS13: Pits 7J 117 (3B 42)
Lanhams Ct. SS13: Pits 7J 117
Lansbury Av. IG11: Bark 9F 124
RM6: Chad H 9K 109
Lansbury Ct. SE28: Lon 7G 140
(off Saunders Way)
Lansbury Gdns. RM18: Til 6C 156
Lansdown Av. SS7: Had 9M 119
Lansdowne Av. SS9: Lgh S 5F 136
Lansdowne Cl. CO5: Tip 5C 226
Lansdowne Ct. EN10: Brox 7A 52
IG5: Ilf 7L 107
Lansdowne Dr. E8: Lon 5C 38
SS6: Ray 4H 119
Lansdowne Rd. E4: Lon 8A 90
E11: Lon 4F 122
E17: Lon 1A 122
E18: Lon 7G 107
IG3: Ilf 3E 124
N17: Lon 2C 38
RM18: Til 7B 156
Lansdown Rd. E7: Lon 9J 123
Lantern Ter. SS1: Sth S 7A 138
(off Kursaal Way)
Lanvalley Rd. CO3: S'way 9F 164
La Plata Gro. CM14: Brtwd 9E 96
Lappmark Rd. SS8: Can I 2K 151
Lapwater Cl. SS9: Lgh S 4B 136
Lapwater Ct. SS9: Lgh S 4B 136
(off London Rd.)
Lapwing Cl. DA8: Eri 5F 152
Lapwing Dr. CM9: H'bri 3E 214
CO5: K'dn 3L 211
Lapwing Rd. SS11: W'fd 6K 101
Larch Cl. CO4: Colc 7D 166
SS15: Lain 6L 115
Larches, The CM3: Bore 3F 60
SS7: Thund 7C 118
Larch Gro. CM2: Chelm 4D 72
CM8: Wthm 2D 230
Larch Rd. E10: Lon 4A 122
Larch Wlk. CM3: Hat P 2L 61
(off Woodland Clo.)
CM9: H'bri, Mal 2E 214
Larch Way CM6: Gt D 2J 203
Larchwood Av. RM5: Col R 3N 109
Larchwood Cl. RM5: Col R 3A 110
SS9: Lgh S 9A 120
Larchwood Gdns. CM15: Pil H 5D 96
Largo Wlk. DA8: Eri 6C 152
Lark Cl. CM14: War 1E 112
Larke Ri. SS0: Sth S 2J 137
Larkfield SS17: Corr 9C 132
Larkfield Cl. SS4: R'fd 3J 121
Larkfield Rd. CO7: Gt Ben 5J 177
Lark Hill Rd.
SS4: Cwdn, R'fd 7L 105 (7J 35)
Larkin Cl. CM13: Hut 6M 97
Larkins Rd. SG8: Croy 1A 4
Larksfield Cres. CO12: Har 3K 209
Larks Gro. IG11: Bark 9D 124
Larkshall Ct. RM7: Maw 6A 110
Larkshall Cres. E4: Lon 1C 106
Larkshall Rd. E4: Lon 2C 106 (2E 38)
Lark's La. CM3: Gt Walt 7G 57 (5K 23)
Larkspur Cl. CM8: Wthm 3B 230
RM15: S Ock 3F 144
Larkspur Ct. CM1: Chelm 5A 60
Larks Ri. CO9: Hals 5M 207
Larkswood CM17: H'low 5H 55

Larkswood Cl. DA8: Eri 6E 152
Larkswood Ct. E4: Lon 2D 106
Larkswood Leisure Cen. 1C 106
Larkswood Rd. E4: Lon 1A 106
SS17: Corr 9C 132
Larkswood Wlk. SS12: W'fd 1L 117
Lark Way CO13: Walt 7H 181
SS14: Bas 8G 116
Larner Rd. DA8: Eri 5C 152
Larneys, The CO13: Walt 7H 181
Larsen Dr. EN9: Wal A 4D 76
Larup Av. SS8: Can I 1J 151
Larup Gdns. SS8: Can I 1J 151
Lascelles Cl. CM15: Pil H 4D 96
E11: Lon 4D 122
Lascelles Gdns. SS4: R'fd 2H 121
Latchett Rd. E18: Lon 5H 107
Latchetts Shaw SS16: Bas 2C 132
LATCHFORD 1E 20
Latchford Pl. IG7: Chig 1G 108
Latching Cl. RM3: Romf 1H 111
LATCHINGDON 8M 211 (4K 35)
Latchingdon Cl. SS6: Ray 4G 119
Latchingdon Gdns. IG8: Wfd G 3L 107
Latchingdon Rd. CM3: Cold N 8J 197 (4H 35)
LATCHMORE BANK 2K 21
Latchmore Bank CM22: L Hall 1K 213 (2K 21)
LATCHMORE COMMON 1K 213 (2K 21)
Lathcoates Cres. CM2: Gt Bad 2F 72
Lathom Rd. E6: Lon 9L 123
Latimer Dr. RM12: Horn 5H 127
SS15: Lain 6K 115
Latimer Ho. CM1: Chelm 8M 59
Latimer Rd. E7: Lon 6H 123
LATTINFORD HILL 1J 17
LATTON BUSH 6F 54 (1H 31)
Latton Bush Cen. CM18: H'low 6D 54
Latton Comn. Rd. CM18: H'low 6F 54
Latton Grn. CM18: H'low 7E 54
Latton Hall Cl. CM20: H'low 2F 54
Latton Ho. CM18: H'low 6G 54
Latton St. CM17: H'low 6H 55
CM18: H'low 4G 55
CM20: H'low 2F 54
(not continuous)
Launceston Cl. CO2: Colc 5B 174
RM3: Romf 5G 111
Launder's La. RM13: Rain 3K 143 (6C 40)
Laundry La. CM6: L Eas 7F 13
CM15: Mount 9N 83
EN9: Naze 3E 62 (2E 30)
Launds Farm La. CO10: Ashen 4C 8
Laura Cl. E11: Lon 9J 107
Laurel Av. CO12: Har 5H 209 (3G 19)
SS12: W'fd 9K 101
Laurel Cl. CM13: Hut 4L 97
CO15: Clac S 6M 185
IG6: Ilf 3B 108
SS9: Lgh S 6C 136
Laurel Ct. CM13: Hut 5M 97
(off Spinney, The)
CO4: Colc 7E 166
(off Magnolia Dr.)
Laurel Cres. RM7: Rush G 3C 126
Laurel Dr. CM6: Gt D 2J 203
RM15: S Ock 4G 144
Laurel Gdns. E4: Lon 6B 90
Laurel Gro. CM2: Chelm 2B 72
Laurel La. RM12: Horn 4J 127
Laurels, The CM3: S Fer 9K 89
CM7: Brain 5J 193
IG9: Buck H 7J 91
SS6: Ray 7M 119
Laurel Way E18: Lon 8F 106
Laurence Av. CM8: Wthm 7D 230 (5G 25)
Laurence Cl. CO7: Elms 9M 167
Laurence Ct. E10: Lon 2B 122
Laurence Cft. CM1: Writ 1K 71
Laurence Ind. Est. SS2: Sth S 9G 121
Laurie Wlk. RM1: Romf 9C 110
Lauriston Farm Chase CM9: Gold 2N 201
Lauriston Rd. E9: Lon 5C 38
Lavender Av. CM15: Pil H 4E 96
Lavender Cl. CM8: Wthm 3B 230
CM20: H'low 2D 54
CO5: Tip 7C 226
RM3: Romf 4H 111
RM15: S Ock 4H 145
Lavender Ct. CM1: Chelm 6A 60
Lavender Dr. CM0: S'min 3C 222
Lavender Fld. CB10: Saf W 3E 218
Lavender Gdns. EN2: Enf 6A 30
Lavender Gro. SS0: Wclf S 3J 137
Lavender Hill EN2: Enf 6A 30
Lavender M. SS0: Wclf S 3J 137
SS8: Can I 3F 150
Lavender Pl. IG1: Ilf 7A 124
Lavender Sq. E11: Lon 5D 122
Lavender St. E15: Lon 8E 122
Lavender Wlk. CO15: Jay 5E 188
Lavender Way CO4: Colc 5K 165
SS12: W'fd 9K 101
Lavenha Ct. CM15: Brtwd 7G 96
LAVENHAM 1K 9
Lavenham Cl. CO16: Clac S 9F 184
Lavenham Ct. CO2: Colc. 4K 173
(off Layer Rd.)
Lavers, The SS6: Ray 4L 119
LAWFORD 5G 163 (3K 17)
Lawford Cl. RM12: Horn 6G 127
Lawford La. CM1: Writ 1K 71
(not continuous)
Law Ho. IG11: Bark 2F 140
Lawling Av. CM9: H'bri 3E 214
Lawlinge Rd. CM3: Latch 8M 211
Lawn Av. SS2: Sth S 4N 137
Lawn Chase CM8: Wthm 6C 230
Lawn Dr. E7: Lon 6K 123
Lawn Farm Gro. RM6: Chad H 8K 109
Lawn Hall Chase CM6: N End 3H 23
Lawn La. CM1: Chelm 4M 59 (7A 24)
Lawns Cl. CO5: W Mer 2C 228
Lawnscourt SS7: Thund 8B 118
Lawns Cres. RM17: Grays 4N 155
Lawns Pl. RM17: Grays 4N 155
Lawns, The CM1: Chelm 6M 59
CM14: War 2H 113
(off Uplands Rd.)
E4: Lon 2A 106
SS7: Thund 8C 118
Lawns Way RM5: Col R 4A 110
Lawn, The CM20: H'low 9G 50
Lawrence Av. CM21: Saw 1L 51
E12: Lon 6N 123
Lawrence Cres. RM10: Dag 5N 125
Lawrence Gdns. RM18: Til 5D 156
Lawrence Hill E4: Lon 8A 90
Lawrence Ho. CM21: Saw 5K 51
Lawrence Moorings CM21: Saw 3L 51
Lawrence Rd. N15: Lon 3B 38
RM2: Romf 9F 110
SS13: Pits 7N 117
Laws Cl. CB11: Saf W 6C 218
Lawshall's Hill CO6: Coln E 6E 198 (4J 15)
Lawson Gdns. DA1: Dart 9H 153
Lawson Rd. DA1: Dart 9H 153
Lawton Rd. E10: Lon 3C 122
IG10: Lou 1A 92
Laxton Ct. CO3: Colc 2H 173
Laxton Gro. CO13: Gt Hol 1D 186
Laxton Rd. CO7: Alr 6A 176
Laxtons SS17: Stan H 2M 147
Laxtons, The SS4: R'fd 2J 121
Layborne Av. RM3: Noak H 8G 95
Laybrook Lodge E18: Lon 8F 106
LAYER BRETON 2C 26
Layer Breton Hill CO2: Lay B 2C 26
Layer Ct. CO2: Colc 2L 173
Layer Cross CO2: Lay H 9G 173
LAYER-DE-LA-HAYE 9G 173 (2D 26)
LAYER MARNEY 3B 26
Layer Marney Tower 3B 26
Layer Road Stadium 2K 173
Layer Rd.
CO2: Colc, King, Lay H 8J 173 (1D 26)
CO5: Abb 2E 26
(Abberton)
CO5: Abb 8A 174 (2F 27)
(Oxley Hill)
CO5: Gt Wig 4C 26
Leabank Sq. E9: Lon 8A 122
LEA BRIDGE 4C 38
Lea Bri. Rd. E5: Lon 4C 38
Lea Bridge Rd. E10: Lon 2A 122
Lea Bri. Rd. E10: Lon 4C 38
Lea Bridge Rd. E17: Lon 9D 106 (3E 38)
Leach Cl. CM2: Gt Bad 3J 73
Lea Cl. CM7: Brain 7M 193
CM23: Bis S 8A 220
Lea Ct. E4: Lon 8C 90
Leadale Av. E4: Lon 8A 90
Leaden Cl. CM6: Lea R 3C 212
LEADEN RODING 4C 212 (5E 22)
Leader Av. E12: Lon 7N 123
Leafy Way CM13: Hut 7N 97
Lea Gro. CM3: Ult 6F 25
CM23: Bis S 8A 220
Lea Hall Gdns. E10: Lon 3A 122
Lea Hall Rd. E10: Lon 3A 122
LEA INTERCHANGE 7A 122 (5D 38)
Lea La. CM8: Gt Br, L Brax 4H 25
Lea Manning Cen. CM20: H'low 1C 54
Leam Cl. CO4: Colc 8F 166
Leamington Av. E17: Lon 9A 106
Leamington Cl. E12: Lon 7L 123
RM3: Romf 3L 111
Leamington Gdns. IG3: Ilf 4E 124
Leamington Rd. RM3: Romf 2L 111 (1C 40)
SS1: Sth S 6A 138
SS5: Hock 9E 104
Leander Dr. DA12: Grav 5J 47
Leapingwell Cl. CM2: Chelm 8B 60
Lea Rd. EN9: Wal A 4A 76
EN11: Rye P 3C 52
RM16: Grays 3C 156
SS7: Ben 1C 134
Lea Rd. Ind. Pk. EN8: Wal A 4A 76
Lea Rd. Trad. Est. EN9: Wal A 4A 76
Leas Cl. SS0: Wclf S 6G 136
Leas Gdns. SS0: Wclf S 6G 136
Lea Side CO5: W Mer 3D 228
Leaside SS7: Thund 9B 118
Leas La. CO2: B'ch 8E 172
Leasowes Rd. E10: Lon 3A 122
Leas Rd. CO2: Colc 5K 173
CO15: Clac S 3G 189 (4D 28)
Leas, The CM0: Bur C 2E 196
CM4: Ing 7C 84
CO13: Frin S 8L 181
RM14: Upm 2A 128
SS0: Wclf S 7H 137 (5J 43)
Leasway CM14: Brtwd 9G 96
RM14: Upm 6N 127
RM16: Grays 8M 145
SS0: Wclf S 6G 136
SS6: Ray 5J 119
SS12: W'fd 1J 117
Leat Cl. CM21: Saw 1L 51
Leathart Cl. RM12: Horn 9F 126
Leatherbottle Hill CM4: Stock 7B 86
Leather La. CM7: Brain 5H 193
(off Great Sq.)
CO9: Gt Yel 3D 206 (6D 8)
RM11: Horn 3H 127
SS1: Sth S 6M 137
Lea Va. DA1: Cray 9B 152
Lea Valley Rd. E4: Lon 5A 90
EN3: Enf 7D 30
Lea Valley Viaduct E4: Lon 1C 38
N18: Lon 1C 38
LEAVENHEATH 1C 16
Lea Vw. EN9: Wal A 3B 76
Leaway CM12: Bill 8K 99
Le Cateau Rd. CO2: Colc 9M 165
Lechmere App. IG8: Wfd G 6J 107
Lechmere Av. IG7: Chig 1B 108
IG8: Wfd G 6K 107
Leconfield Wlk. RM12: Horn 8G 126
Lede Rd. SS8: Can I 1H 151
Lee Av. RM6: Chad H 1K 125
Lee Chapel La. SS16: Bas 3L 131
LEE CHAPEL NORTH 9N 115 (3K 41)
LEE CHAPEL SOUTH 2A 132 (4K 41)
Leech's La. CO4: Colc 3L 165
Leecon Way SS4: R'fd 4J 121
Lee Ct. CM2: Gt Bad 3F 72
Leeds Rd. IG1: Ilf 3C 124
Leeford CM1: Chelm 5H 59
Lee Gdns. Av. RM11: Horn 3L 127
Lee Gro. IG7: Chig 8A 92
Lee Lotts SS3: Gt W 2L 139
LEE-OVER-SANDS 5A 28
Lee Rd. CO12: Har 4L 209
SS13: Pits 9N 117
Leeside Rd. N17: Lon 2C 38
Lee Valley Cvn. Pk. EN11: Hod 7C 52
Lee Valley Leisure Pool 9A 52
Lee Valley Pk. Info. Cen. 3C 76
Lee Valley Regional Pk. 1A 76
Lee Wlk. SS16: Bas 1N 131
Leeward Rd. CM3: S Fer 3L 103
Leeway, The CM3: Dan 3F 74
Lee Wick La. CO16: St O 4A 28
Lee Woottens La. SS16: Bas 1B 132 (4A 42)
(not continuous)
Leez La. CM3: Har E 2K 23
Legg St. CM1: Chelm 8K 59
Legon Av. RM7: Rush G 3A 126
Leicester Av. SS4: R'fd 7L 121
Leicester Cl. CO1: Colc 7A 166
CO15: Jay 3D 188
Leicester Ct. CM8: Sil E 9L 217
Leicester Gdns. IG3: Ilf 2D 124
Leicester Rd. E11: Lon 9H 107
RM18: Til 6B 156
Leicester Square Station (Tube) 7A 38
Leige Av. SS8: Can I 8G 135
Leigham Ct. Dr. SS9: Lgh S 5E 136
Leighams Rd. CM3: Bick, E Han 4E 88 (4E 34)
Leigh Av. IG4: Ilf 8K 107
LEIGH BECK 2L 151 (6F 43)
Leigh Beck La. SS8: Can I 3L 151
Leigh Beck Rd. SS8: Can I 2M 151
Leigh Cliff Rd. SS9: Lgh S 6E 136
Leighcroft Gdns. SS9: Lgh S 2C 136
Leigh Dr. CM8: W Bis 2J 229
CM22: Else 3K 199
RM3: Romf 1H 111
Leigh Flds. SS13: Pits 9K 117
Leighfields SS7: Thund 9H 119
Leighfields Av. SS9: Lgh S 9C 120
Leighfields Rd. SS9: Lgh S 9C 120
Leigh Gdns. SS9: Lgh S 5B 136
Leigh Hall Rd. SS9: Lgh S 5D 136
Leigh Heath Ct. SS9: Lgh S 4N 135
Leigh Hgts. SS7: Had 3M 135
Leigh Heritage Cen. & Mus. 6C 136 (5G 43)
Leigh Hill SS9: Lgh S 6D 136 (5H 43)
Leigh Hill Cl. SS9: Lgh S 6D 136
Leigh Ho. SS9: Lgh S 6D 136
Leighlands Rd. CM3: S Fer 1K 103
Leigh National Nature Reserve 7A 136
LEIGH-ON-SEA 5D 136 (4G 43)
Leigh-on-Sea Station (Rail) 6B 136 (5G 43)
Leigh Pk. Cl. SS9: Lgh S 5B 136
Leigh Pk. Rd. SS9: Lgh S 6C 136
Leigh Rd. E6: Lon 8N 123
E10: Lon 2C 122
SS8: Can I 3H 151
SS9: Lgh S 5E 136 (4H 43)
Leighs Rifleman CM12: Bill 5G 99
Leighs Rd. CM3: L Walt 6N 57 (5B 24)
Leighton Av. E12: Lon 7N 123
SS9: Lgh S 5E 136
Leighton Gdns. RM18: Til 5C 156
Leighton Rd. NW5: Lon 5A 38
SS7: Thund 8C 118
Leigh Vw. Dr. SS9: Lgh S 2D 136
Leighville Gro. SS9: Lgh S 5C 136
Leighwood Av. SS9: Lgh S 1C 136
Leinster Rd. SS15: Lain 8L 115 (3K 41)
Leitrim Av. SS3: Shoe 8G 138
Lekoe Rd. SS8: Can I 8F 134
Leman St. E1: Lon 7C 38
Lemna Rd. E11: Lon 2F 122
Lena Kennedy Cl. E4: Lon 3C 106
Lenham Way SS13: Pits 9K 117
Lenmore Av. RM17: Grays 1M 155
Lennard Row RM15: Ave 8A 144
Lennox Cl. RM1: Romf 1D 126
RM16: Chaf H 2F 154
Lennox Dr. SS12: W'fd 2N 117
Lennox Gdns. IG1: Ilf 3M 123
Lennox Rd. DA11: Grav 4G 47
E17: Lon 1A 122
Lens Rd. E7: Lon 9J 123
Lenthall Av. RM17: Grays 9K 145
Lenthall Rd. IG10: Lou 3C 92
Leonard Av. RM7: Rush G 3B 126
Leonard Davis Ho. CM16: N Wea 6M 65
Leonard Dr. SS6: Ray 3G 119
Leonard M. CM7: Brain 8K 193
Leonard Rd. E4: Lon 3A 106
E7: Lon 6G 122
SS0: Wclf S 6J 137
SS16: Van 4C 132
Leonard Robbins Path SE28: Lon 7G 140
(off Tawney Rd.)
Leonard Way CM14: Brtwd 1B 112
Leon Dr. SS16: Van 3E 132
Leopold Rd. E17: Lon 9A 106
IP11: Felix 1K 19
Les Bois CO2: Lay H 9H 173
Leslie Cl. SS9: Lgh S 9C 120
Leslie Dr. SS9: Lgh S 9C 120
Leslie Gdns. SS6: Ray 6M 119
Leslie Newnham Ct. CM9: Mal 7C 214
Leslie Pk. CM0: Bur C 4E 196
Leslie Rd. E11: Lon 6C 122
SS6: Ray 6L 119
Lesney Farm Est. DA8: Eri 5B 152
Lesney Gdns. SS4: R'fd 4J 121
Lesney Pk. DA8: Eri 4B 152
Lesney Pk. Rd. DA8: Eri 4B 152
Lessingham Av. IG5: Ilf 7N 107
Lessington Av. RM7: Romf 1A 126
LESSNESS HEATH 2A 46
Leston Cl. RM13: Rain 3F 142
Letfield La. CM3: Gt Walt 4B 56
Lethe Gro. CO2: Colc 6N 173
Lettons Chase CM3: S Fer 2K 103
Lett Rd. E15: Lon 9D 122
LETTY GREEN 6A 20
Letzen Rd. SS8: Can I 1G 151
Leveller Row CM12: Bill 5H 99
LEVEL'S GREEN 6J 11
LEVENS GREEN 7C 10
Levens Way CM77: Gt N 2C 204
Lever La. SS4: R'fd 6L 121
Lever Sq. RM16: Grays 2B 156
Lever St. EC1: Lon 6A 38
Leverton Way EN9: Wal A 3C 76 (4E 30)
Leveson Rd. RM16: Grays 1D 156
Levett Gdns. IG3: Ilf 6E 124
Levett Rd. IG11: Bark 8D 124
SS17: Stan H 3N 147
Levine Gdns. IG11: Bark 2J 141
Lewes Cl. RM17: Grays 4K 155
Lewes Rd. RM3: Romf 1H 111
SS2: Sth S 3A 138
Lewes Way SS7: Thund 8H 119
Lewin Pl. CM3: Bore 3F 60
Lewis Av. E17: Lon 5A 106
Lewis Cl. CM15: Shenf 6J 97
Lewis Ct. CM6: Gt D 2L 203
Lewis Dr. CM2: Chelm 4C 72
Lewis Rd. DA13: Ist R 6G 47
RM11: Horn 1G 127
Lewis Way RM10: Dag 8N 125
LEXDEN 1H 173 (6D 16)
Lexden Ct. CO3: Colc 8K 165
Lexden Dr. RM6: Chad H 1G 124
Lexden Earthworks 9F 164
Lexden Gathering Grounds Nature Reserve 8G 164
Lexden Gro. CO3: Colc 8G 165
Lexden M. CO3: Colc 8G 165
Lexden Pl. CO3: S'way 8F 164
Lexden Rd. CO3: Colc 8G 165 (6D 16)
CO6: W Ber 4E 164 (5C 16)
Lexden Springs Local Nature Reserve 8H 165
Lexden Ter. EN9: Wal A 4C 76
(off Sewardstone Rd.)
Lexham Ho. IG11: Bark 1C 140
(off St Margarets)
Lexington Way RM14: Upm 1C 128
Leybourne Dr. CM1: Chelm 4M 59
Leybourne Rd. E11: Lon 3F 122
Leyburn Cl. E17: Lon 8B 106
Leyburn Cres. RM3: Romf 4J 111
Leyburn Rd. RM3: Romf 4J 111
Leycroft Cl. IG10: Lou 4N 91
Leycroft Gdns. DA8: Eri 6F 152
Leydenhatch La. BR8: Swan 6A 46
Leyd Rd. SS8: Can I 1H 151
Ley Fld. CM22: Tak 3C 224
Leyfield CM77: Tye G 9M 193
Ley Fld. CO6: M Tey 3G 170
Leyfields CM77: Rayne 7B 192
Leyland Ct. SS2: Sth S 6N 137
Leyland Gdns. IG8: Wfd G 2J 107
Leys Av. RM10: Dag 1A 142
Leysdown Av. DA7: Bexh 9A 152
Leys Dr. CO16: L Cla 4G 185
Leyside CM77: Rayne 6B 192
Leysings SS16: Bas 2N 131
Leyspring Rd. E11: Lon 3F 122
Leys Rd. CO7: W'hoe 3J 175
Leys, The CB10: Wim 1E 12
CM2: Chelm 6A 60
SS16: Van 2D 132
Ley St. IG1: Ilf 4A 124 (4H 39)
IG2: Ilf 4B 124 (4H 39)
Leyswood Dr. IG2: Ilf 9D 108
Ley, The CM7: Brain 7M 193
LEYTON 4C 122 (4D 38)

Leyton Bus. Cen. E10: Lon . . . 4A 122
Leyton Ct. CO15: Clac S . . . 5K 185
Leyton Cross Rd. DA2: Dart . . . 4A 46
Leyton Grange Est. E10: Lon . . . 4A 122
Leyton Grn. Rd. E10: Lon . . . 1C 122 (3E 38)
Leyton Grn. Twr. E10: Lon . . . 1C 122
(off Leyton Grn. Rd.)
Leyton Leisure Lagoon . . . 2C 122
Leyton Midland Road Station (Rail) . . . 3C 122 (4E 38)
Leyton Orient F.C. (Matchroom Stadium) . . . 4B 122 (4D 38)
Leyton Pk. Rd. E10: Lon . . . 5C 122
Leyton Rd. E15: Lon . . . 7C 122 (5E 38)
Leyton Station (Tube) . . . 5C 122 (4E 38)
LEYTONSTONE . . . 5E 122 (4E 38)
Leytonstone High Road Station (Rail) . . . 4E 122 (4E 38)
Leytonstone Ho. E11: Lon . . . 2F 122
(off Hanbury Dr.)
Leytonstone Rd. E15: Lon . . . 6E 122 (5E 38)
Leytonstone Station (Tube) . . . 3E 122 (4E 38)
Leyton Way E11: Lon . . . 2E 122
Leywood Cl. CM7: Brain . . . 6M 193
Liberty 2 Cen. (Shop. Cen.)
RM1: Romf . . . 8D 110
Liberty Ct. IG11: Bark . . . 2G 141
Liberty, The RM1: Romf . . . 9C 110
Library Hill CM14: Brtwd . . . 8F 96
Libro Ct. E4: Lon . . . 1A 106
Lichfield Cl. CM1: Chelm . . . 7G 59
CO1: Colc . . . 7A 166
Lichfield Rd. IG8: Wfd G . . . 1E 106
RM8: Dag . . . 6G 125
Lichfields, The SS14: Bas . . . 8G 116
Lichfield Ter. RM14: Upm . . . 4B 128
Lie Field Cl. CM7: Brain . . . 5M 193
Lifchild Cl. CM8: Wthm . . . 8D 230
Lifeboat Mus. . . . 1N 209
Lifstan Way SS1: Sth S . . . 6C 138 (5A 44)
Lilac Av. SS8: Can I . . . 9J 135
SS12: W'fd . . . 1K 117
Lilac Cl. CM2: Chelm . . . 4D 72
CM15: Pil H . . . 4E 96
Lilac Ct. CO7: W'hoe . . . 4G 175
Lilac Gdns. RM7: Rush G . . . 3C 126
Lilac Rd. EN11: Rye P . . . 3B 52
Lilac Tree Ct. CO4: Colc . . . 7E 166
Lilford Rd. CM11: Bill . . . 4L 99
Lilian Cres. CM13: Hut . . . 8M 97
Lilian Gdns. IG8: Wfd G . . . 5H 107
Lilian Impey Way CO4: Colc . . . 2B 166
Lilian Pl. SS6: Ray . . . 7N 119
Lilian Rd. CM0: Bur C . . . 3D 196
Lillechurch Rd. RM8: Dag . . . 8G 125
Lilley Cl. CM14: Brtwd . . . 1C 112
Lilley's La. CO7: Gt Bro . . . 3B 168 (5J 17)
Lilliard Cl. EN11: Hod . . . 2B 52
Lillies, The CM7: Brain . . . 8K 191
Lilliput Rd. RM7: Rush G . . . 2B 126
Lily Cl. CM1: Chelm . . . 5A 60
Lily Rd. E17: Lon . . . 1A 122
Lilystone Cl. CM4: Stock . . . 8M 85
Lilyville Wlk. SS6: Ray . . . 6N 119
Limbourne Av. RM8: Dag . . . 2L 125
Limbourne Dr. CM9: H'bri . . . 3F 214
Limburg Rd. SS8: Can I . . . 1D 150
Lime Av. CM13: Brtwd . . . 9J 97
CO4: Colc . . . 7D 166
CO12: Har . . . 4K 209
RM14: Upm . . . 6L 127
SS9: Lgh S . . . 4B 136
Limebrook Way CM9: Mal . . . 8A 214 (2H 35)
Lime Cl. CM8: Wthm . . . 2D 230
CO15: Clac S . . . 1G 188
IG9: Buck H . . . 8K 91
RM7: Romf . . . 8A 110
RM15: S Ock . . . 3F 144
Lime Ct. CO12: Har . . . 4K 209
E11: Lon . . . 4E 122
(off Trinity Cl.)
E17: Lon . . . 9C 106
SS5: Hock . . . 1D 120
Limefields CB10: Saf W . . . 1C 218
Lime Gro. CM15: Dodd . . . 7F 82
IG6: Ilf . . . 3E 108
Limeharbour E14: Lon . . . 7D 38
LIMEHOUSE . . . 7D 38
Limehouse Station (Rail & DLR) . . . 7D 38
Limekiln La. CM24: Stan M . . . 3B 220 (6A 12)
Lime Lodge SS9: Lgh S . . . 4B 136
Lime Mdw. CB10: Sew E . . . 6D 6
Lime Pl. SS15: Lain . . . 6L 115
Limerick Gdns. RM14: Upm . . . 2C 128
Lime Rd. SS7: Ben . . . 2E 134
(not continuous)
Limes Av. E11: Lon . . . 8H 107
E12: Lon . . . 5L 123
IG7: Chig . . . 2B 108
(not continuous)
Limes Ct. CM15: Brtwd . . . 7G 97
EN11: Hod . . . 5A 52
Limeslade Cl. SS17: Corr . . . 1B 148
Limes, The CM2: Gall . . . 8C 72
CM4: Ing . . . 6E 84
CM13: Brtwd . . . 9J 97
CO7: A'lgh . . . 9M 161
CO9: Gosf . . . 9L 201
RM11: Horn . . . 7H 111
RM19: Purf . . . 3L 153
SS6: Ray . . . 7M 119
Limestone Wlk. DA18: Eri . . . 9J 141
Lime St. CO7: B'sea . . . 8E 182
Limetree Av. SS7: Ben . . . 2B 134
Lime Tree Cotts. CM6: Gt D . . . 1L 203
Lime Tree Ct. CB10: Saf W . . . 3C 218
(off Church St.)
Lime Tree Hill CM6: Gt D . . . 1L 203
Limetree Rd. SS8: Can I . . . 1K 151
Lime Wlk. CM2: Chelm . . . 4C 72
Lime Way CM0: Bur C . . . 2C 196
Limewood Ct. IG4: Ilf . . . 9M 107
Limewood Rd. DA8: Eri . . . 5A 152
Lincefield SS16: Lang H . . . 3K 131
Lincewood Pk. Dr. SS16: Lang H . . . 2J 131
Lincoln Av. CO15: Jay . . . 6B 188
RM7: Rush G . . . 4B 126
Lincoln Chase SS2: Sth S . . . 3C 138
Lincoln Cl. DA8: Eri . . . 7D 152
RM11: Horn . . . 9L 111
Lincoln Gdns. IG1: Ilf . . . 2L 123
Lincoln La. CO6: Gt Hork . . . 7K 159
Lincoln Rd. DA8: Eri . . . 7D 152
(not continuous)
E7: Lon . . . 8K 123
E18: Lon . . . 5G 106
EN2: Enf . . . 6B 30
(not continuous)
EN3: Enf . . . 7C 30
SS4: R'fd . . . 1G 121
SS14: Bas . . . 8G 116
Lincolns Fld. CM16: Epp . . . 9E 64
Lincolns La.
CM14: Pil H, S Wea . . . 4N 95 (7D 32)
Lincoln St. E11: Lon . . . 4E 122
Lincoln Way CO1: Colc . . . 8A 166
SS6: Ray . . . 2J 119
SS8: Can I . . . 1E 150
Linda Gdns. CM12: Bill . . . 4G 98
Linden Cl. CM2: Chelm . . . 3D 72
CO4: Colc . . . 6E 166
CO11: Law . . . 5G 162
RM19: Purf . . . 4N 153
SS6: Ray . . . 6M 119
SS7: Thund . . . 9C 118
Linden Ct. SS9: Lgh S . . . 4F 136
(off London Rd.)
Linden Cres. IG8: Wfd G . . . 3H 107
Linden Dr. CO15: Clac S . . . 6J 185
Linden Leas SS7: Thund . . . 9C 118
Linden Ri. CM14: War . . . 2G 112
Linden Rd. SS7: Thund . . . 1C 134
Lindens, The CM4: Stock . . . 7A 86
CM7: Brain . . . 7J 193
CO9: Hals . . . 6L 207
E17: Lon . . . 8B 106
(off Prospect Hill)
EN9: Wal A . . . 5J 77
(off Woodbine Cl.)
IG10: Lou . . . 4M 91
SS16: Lang H . . . 1J 131
Linden St. RM7: Romf . . . 8B 110
Linden Way SS8: Can I . . . 1F 150
Linde Rd. SS8: Can I . . . 1H 151
Lindfield Rd. RM3: Romf . . . 2J 111
Lindhurst Dr. CM11: Rams H . . . 4D 100
Lindisfarne Av. SS9: Lgh S . . . 4F 136
Lindisfarne Ct. CM9: Mal . . . 8A 214
SS12: W'fd . . . 2A 118
Lindisfarne Rd. RM8: Dag . . . 5H 125
Lindley Rd. E10: Lon . . . 4C 122
Lindon Rd. SS11: W'fd . . . 5K 101
LINDSELL . . . 5H 13
Lindsell Grn. SS14: Bas . . . 1F 132
Lindsell La. CM6: Lndsl, Steb . . . 5H 13
SS14: Bas . . . 1F 132
Lindsey Cl. CM14: Brtwd . . . 1D 112
Lindsey Ct. SS6: Ray . . . 4G 118
SS12: W'fd . . . 2M 117
Lindsey Rd. CM23: Bis S . . . 7K 11
RM8: Dag . . . 6H 125
SS3: Gt W . . . 2M 139
Lindsey St. CM16: Epp . . . 7C 64 (3H 31)
Lindsey Way RM11: Horn . . . 9G 111
Linfold Cl. CM7: Brain . . . 4M 193
LINFORD . . . 9J 147 (1J 47)
Linford Cl. CM19: H'low . . . 5A 54
Linford Dr. SS14: Bas . . . 9F 116
Linford End CM19: H'low . . . 5B 54
Linford M. CM9: Mal . . . 8A 214
Linford Rd. E17: Lon . . . 7C 106
RM16: Grays, W Til . . . 2D 156 (1H 47)
Lingcroft SS16: Bas . . . 2B 132
Lingfield Av. RM14: Upm . . . 5K 127
Lingfield Dr. SS4: R'fd . . . 5M 121
Lingmere Cl. IG7: Chig . . . 8B 92
Ling Rd. DA8: Eri . . . 4A 152
Lingrove Gdns. IG9: Buck H . . . 8H 91
Ling's La. IP9: Holb . . . 1E 18
Lingwood Cl. CM3: Dan . . . 3E 74
Lingwood Common Nature Reserve . . . 2D 74
Link Cl. CO4: Colc . . . 3M 165
Linkdale CM12: Bill . . . 8K 99
Link Pl. IG6: Ilf . . . 3E 108
Link Rd. CM23: Bis S . . . 1K 21
CO7: B'sea . . . 7F 182
CO9: Hals . . . 6J 207
CO15: Clac S . . . 2H 189
E12: Lon . . . 4L 123
RM9: Dag . . . 2N 141
SS6: Ray . . . 4K 119
SS8: Can I . . . 2E 150 (6E 42)
SS17: Stan H . . . 2M 147
Links Av. RM2: Romf . . . 6F 110
Links Ct. SS1: Sth S . . . 7C 138
(not continuous)
Links Dr. CM2: Chelm . . . 3A 72
Links Ho. CM15: Hook E . . . 5E 82
Linkside CO13: Frin S . . . 2H 187
IG7: Chig . . . 2B 108
Links Rd. CM77: Tye G . . . 1F 25
IG8: Wfd G . . . 2G 106
Links, The CM12: Bill . . . 4G 98
Links Way SS7: Had . . . 3M 135
Linksway SS9: Lgh S . . . 2B 136
Linkway CM20: H'low . . . 3B 54
(off Kitson Way)
RM8: Dag . . . 6H 125
Link Way RM11: Horn . . . 3J 127
Linkway SS14: Bas . . . 9C 116
Linkway Rd. CM14: Brtwd . . . 9C 96
Linley Cl. RM18: E Til . . . 5M 157
Linley Cres. RM7: Maw . . . 7N 109
Linley Gdns. CO15: Clac S . . . 2H 189
Linne Rd. SS8: Can I . . . 9J 135
Linnet Cl. SE28: Lon . . . 7H 141
SS3: Shoe . . . 6J 139
Linnet Dr. CM2: Chelm . . . 5B 72
SS7: Ben . . . 4C 134
Linnets CO15: Clac S . . . 7K 185
SS16: Bas . . . 3B 132
Linnett Cl. E4: Lon . . . 1C 106
Linnetts La. CB9: Stur . . . 7L 223
Linnet Way CO7: Gt Ben . . . 6J 177
RM19: Purf . . . 3M 153
Linroping Av. SS8: Can I . . . 2M 151
Linsdell Rd. IG11: Bark . . . 1B 140
Linsey Ct. E10: Lon . . . 3A 122
(off Grange Rd.)
Linstead Cl. CO16: Clac S . . . 9E 184
LINTON . . . 2D 6
Linton Cl. CB11: Saf W . . . 5E 218
Linton Ct. RM1: Romf . . . 6C 110
Linton Rd. CB1: B'shm . . . 1D 6
CB1: Gt Ab . . . 1B 6
CB1: H'hth . . . 2F 7
CB1: Hads, Lin . . . 3C 6
IG11: Bark . . . 9B 124
SS3: Shoe . . . 8J 139
Lintons, The CM2: S'don . . . 4L 73
IG11: Bark . . . 9B 124
Linton Zoo . . . 2C 6
Linwood CM21: Saw . . . 2K 51
Lion & Lamb Ct. CM14: Brtwd . . . 8F 96
(off High St.)
Lionel Oxley Ho. RM17: Grays . . . 4L 155
(off New Rd.)
Lionel Rd. SS8: Can I . . . 2G 151
Lionfield Ter. CM1: Chelm . . . 8M 59
Lion Hill SS17: Fob . . . 1E 148 (6A 42)
Lion La. CM12: Bill . . . 6J 99
Lion Mdw. CB9: Stpl B . . . 2K 223
Lion Rd. CO10: Glem . . . 1G 9
Lion Wlk. CO1: Colc . . . 8N 165
Lion Wlk. Shop. Cen. CO1: Colc . . . 8N 165
Liphook Cl. RM12: Horn . . . 6D 126
Lippits Hill SS16: Lang H . . . 3L 131
Lippitts Hill IG10: Lou . . . 9E 76 (6E 30)
Lipton Cl. SE28: Lon . . . 7H 141
Lisa Cl. CM12: Bill . . . 2K 99
Lisle Pl. RM17: Grays . . . 1K 155
Lisle Rd. CO2: Colc . . . 1A 174
Lister Av. RM3: H Wood . . . 6H 111
Lister Rd. CM7: Brain . . . 8H 193
E11: Lon . . . 3E 122
RM18: Til . . . 7C 156
Lister Tye CM2: Chelm . . . 3D 72
Lister Wlk. SE28: Lon . . . 7J 141
LISTON . . . 3H 9
LISTON GARDEN . . . 3H 9
Liston La. CO10: Lis . . . 3H 9
Liston Way IG8: Wfd G . . . 4J 107
Listowel Rd. RM10: Dag . . . 5M 125
Litchborough Pk. CM3: L Bad . . . 2F 74
Litchfield CO12: Har . . . 5G 209
Litchfield Av. E15: Lon . . . 8E 122
Litchfield Cl. CO15: Clac S . . . 8J 185
Litchfield Ct. E17: Lon . . . 1A 122
LITLINGTON . . . 4A 4
Litlington Rd. SG8: Lit, Stpl M . . . 4A 4
Littell Tweed CM2: Chelm . . . 8B 60
LITTLE ABINGTON . . . 1B 6
Lit. and Gt. Sir Hughes La.
CM2: Gt Bad . . . 8H 73
Lit. Aston Rd. RM3: H Wood . . . 4L 111
LITTLE BADDOW . . . 7L 61 (1E 34)
Lit. Baddow Rd. CM3: Dan . . . 3E 74 (2E 34)
CM9: L Bad, Wdhm W . . . 1E 34
Little Bakers CO14: Walt . . . 7K 181
LITTLE BARDFIELD . . . 3H 13
Lit. Belhus Cl. RM15: S Ock . . . 4D 144
LITTLE BENTLEY . . . 7L 169 (6B 18)
Little Bentley SS14: Bas . . . 8C 116
Lit. Bentley Rd. CO7: L Ben, Ten . . . 6N 169 (5B 18)
LITTLE BERKHAMSTED . . . 1A 30
Lit. Berry La. SS16: Lang H . . . 2J 131
LITTLE BRAXTED . . . 5F 230 (4G 25)
Lit. Braxted La.
CM8: L Brax, Riven . . . 4F 230 (4G 25)
Little Brays CM18: H'low . . . 4F 54
LITTLE BROMLEY . . . 1G 168 (4K 17)
Lit. Bromley Rd.
CO7: A'lgh, L Bro . . . 9M 161 (4J 17)
CO7: Gt Bro, L Bro . . . 4D 168 (5K 17)
CO7: L Ben . . . 6K 169 (5A 18)
Littlebrook Bus. Cen. DA1: Dart . . . 7M 153
LITTLEBROOK INTERCHANGE . . . 9M 153 (3C 46)
Littlebrook Mnr. Way DA1: Dart . . . 9M 153 (3C 46)
Lit. Brook Rd. CM19: Roy . . . 3J 53
LITTLE BURSTEAD . . . 3H 115 (1J 41)
LITTLEBURY . . . 1B 218 (6A 6)
Marden Ash . . . 2L 81 (4C 32)
Littlebury Ct. CM15: Kel H . . . 7C 82
SS13: Bas . . . 7H 117
Littlebury Gdns. CO2: Colc . . . 2C 174
LITTLEBURY GREEN . . . 6K 5
Littlebury Grn. SS13: Bas . . . 7H 117
Littlebury Grn. Rd.
CB11: A End, L'bry . . . 2A 218 (6K 5)
LITTLE CAMBRIDGE . . . 5G 13
LITTLE CANFIELD . . . 1D 22
Little Cattins CM19: H'low . . . 7M 53
Little Charlton SS13: Pits . . . 9K 117
LITTLE CHESTERFORD . . . 4A 6
LITTLE CHISHILL . . . 7G 5
Lit. Chishill Rd. SG8: Bar, Lit C . . . 7F 5
Little Chittock SS14: Bas . . . 9F 116
Lit. Church St. CO12: Har . . . 1M 209
(off West St.)
LITTLE CLACTON . . . 3H 185 (2D 28)
Lit. Clacton By-Pass CO15: Clac S . . . 1E 184
CO16: Clac S, L Cla . . . 1E 184
CO16: Ten, Wee, Wee H . . . 5B 178 (7B 18)
Lit. Clacton Rd.
CO13: Clac S, Gt Hol . . . 3A 186 (2E 28)
CO16: Clac S, L Cla, Wee H . . . 6F 184 (3C 28)
LITTLE COMMON . . . 8B 192
LITTLE CORNARD . . . 6K 9
Littlecotes CO4: Colc . . . 3L 165
Littlecroft CM3: S Fer . . . 2K 103
Little Docklands CM2: Chelm . . . 9L 59
(off Provident Sq.)
Little Dodden SS16: Bas . . . 2A 132
Little Dorrit CM1: Chelm . . . 4G 59
Little Dragons IG10: Lou . . . 3K 91
LITTLE DUNMOW . . . 8D 212 (1H 23)
LITTLE EASTON . . . 7F 13
LITTLE END . . . 4J 81 (4C 32)
Littlefield CO7: W'hoe . . . 5J 175
Littlefield Cl. CO2: Colc . . . 4K 173
Littlefield Rd. CO2: Colc . . . 4K 173
Little Flds. CM3: Dan . . . 3G 74
Little Fretches SS9: Lgh S . . . 2D 136
Lit. Friday Rd. E4: Lon . . . 8E 90
Little Gth. SS13: Pits . . . 1H 133
Lit. Gaynes Gdns. RM14: Upm . . . 6M 127
Lit. Gaynes La. RM14: Upm . . . 6K 127 (5C 40)
Little Gearies IG6: Ilf . . . 8A 108
Lit. Gerpins La. RM14: Upm . . . 1K 143 (6C 40)
Lit. Goldings Est. IG10: Lou . . . 9N 77
Lit. Gregories La. CM16: They B . . . 5C 78
Lit. Grove Fld. CM19: H'low . . . 3B 54
Lit. Gypps Cl. SS8: Can I . . . 1F 150
Lit. Gypps Ct. SS8: Can I . . . 1F 150
Lit. Gypps Rd. SS8: Can I . . . 2F 150
LITTLE HADHAM . . . 7H 11
LITTLE HALLINGBURY . . . 2K 213 (3A 22)
Little Harrods CO14: Walt . . . 7K 181
Little Haven Nature Reserve . . . 8L 119
Lit. Hayes Chase CM3: Stow M . . . 5G 35
Little Hays SS9: Lgh S . . . 9A 120
LITTLE HEATH . . . 8G 108 (3J 39)
Little Heath CM22: Hat H . . . 1D 210
RM6: Chad H . . . 8G 109
Lit. Heath Rd. DA7: Bexh . . . 2A 46
LITTLE HENHAM . . . 4B 12
LITTLE HENNY . . . 7H 9
Little Holt E11: Lon . . . 9G 106
LITTLE HORKESLEY . . . 3F 158 (2C 16)
Lit. Horkesley Rd. CO6: Wmgfd . . . 8M 229 (3C 16)
LITTLE HORMEAD . . . 4F 11
Littlehurst La. SS15: Bas . . . 5A 116
Lit. Hyde Cl. CO9: Gt Yel . . . 2D 206
Lit. Hyde La. CM4: Fry, Ing . . . 3D 84 (4H 33)
Lit. Hyde Rd. CM4: Ing . . . 3F 84
CO9: Gt Yel . . . 2D 206
LITTLE ILFORD . . . 7M 123 (5G 39)
Lit. Ilford La. E12: Lon . . . 6M 123 (5G 39)
Little Kingston SS16: Bas . . . 4M 131
Little Larchmount CB11: Saf W . . . 5C 218
LITTLE LAVER . . . 7C 22
Lit. Laver Rd. CM5: Lit L, M'ton . . . 1C 32
CM17: Mat G . . . 6C 22
LITTLE LEIGHS . . . 9J 203 (3A 24)
LITTLE LONDON . . . 1M 211
Clavering . . . 4J 11
Finchingfield . . . 1K 13
Lit. London Hill CM7: F'fld . . . 1D 200 (2K 13)
Lit. London La. CM9: Ult, Wdhm W . . . 1F 35
Little Lullaway SS15: Lain . . . 8N 115
Lit. Malgraves Ind. Est. SS16: Lang H . . . 5H 131
LITTLE MAPLESTEAD . . . 2G 15
Lit. Maplestead Rd. CO9: Gest . . . 7F 9
Little Mdw. CM1: Writ . . . 1J 71
Little Mdws. CM9: Wdhm M . . . 4L 75
Littlemoor Rd. IG1: Ilf . . . 5C 124
Littlemore Rd. SE2: Lon . . . 9F 140
Little Nell CM1: Chelm . . . 4G 59
Lit. Norsey Rd. CM11: Bill . . . 4L 99
LITTLE OAKLEY . . . 8D 208 (4G 19)
Little Oaks SS14: Bas . . . 9B 116
Little Oxcroft SS15: Lain . . . 9K 115
LITTLE OXNEY GREEN . . . 2G 70 (2J 33)
Lit. Paddocks CM77: Rayne . . . 7B 192
LITTLE PARNDON . . . 2A 54 (6G 21)
Lit. Pastures CM14: Brtwd . . . 1C 112
Lit. Pluckett's Way IG9: Buck H . . . 7K 91
Littlepound CM15: Dodd . . . 6F 82
Little Pynchons CM18: H'low . . . 6F 54
Little Russets CM13: Hut . . . 6A 98
Little St Mary's CO10: L Mel . . . 3J 9
LITTLE SAMPFORD . . . 2H 13
Little Searles SS13: Pits . . . 8J 117
Little Spenders SS14: Bas . . . 7E 116
Little Sq. CM7: Brain . . . 5H 193
(off Great Sq.)

Lit. Stambridge Hall La.
SS4: R'fd … 5N 121 (2K 43)
Little Stile CM1: Writ … 2J 71
Lit. Stone Ct. CO15: Clac S … 4G 189
Little St. EN9: Enf … 6C 76
LITTLE TEY … 7K 15
Lit. Tey Rd. CO5: Fee … 7B 170 (1J 25)
Little Thorpe SS1: Sth S … 5E 138
SS16: Van … 2G 132
LITTLE THURLOW … 1J 7
LITTLE THURROCK … 2N 155 (1G 47)
Littleton Av. E4: Lon … 7F 90
LITTLE TOTHAM … 9N 205 (6K 25)
Lit. Totham Rd.
CM9: Gold, L Tot … 1H 201 (6K 25)
LITTLE WAKERING … 1J 139 (3B 44)
Lit. Wakering Hall La. SS3: Gt W … 1L 139
Lit. Wakering Rd. SS3: Barl M … 1J 139 (3B 44)
LITTLE WALDEN … 5C 6
Lit. Walden Rd.
CB10: L Wal, Saf W … 3C 218 (6B 6)
Little Wlk. CM20: H'low … 2C 54
LITTLE WALTHAM … 6K 57 (5A 24)
Lit. Waltham Rd.
CM1: Broom, Chelm … 2M 59 (6A 24)
LITTLE WARLEY … 6H 113 (2F 41)
Lit. Warley Hall La.
CM13: L War … 6H 113 (2F 41)
Lit. Wheatley Chase
SS6: Ray … 4G 118 (2E 42)
LITTLE WIGBOROUGH … 4E 26
Little Wood CO13: Frin S, Walt … 8H 181
LITTLE WRATTING … 2K 7
LITTLE YELDHAM … 6E 8
Lit. Yeldham Rd.
CO9: Gt Yel, L Yel … 2E 206 (6D 8)
LITTLEY GREEN … 3K 23
Liverpool Rd. E10: Lon … 1C 122
N7: Lon … 5A 38
Liverpool Street Station (Rail, Tube) … 7B 38
Livesey Cl. SE28: Lon … 9B 140
Livingstone Cl. CM5: Chip … 8L 67
Livingstone Ct. E10: Lon … 1C 122
Livingstone Rd. E17: Lon … 1B 122
Livingstone Ter. RM13: Rain … 1C 142
Llewellyn Cl. CM1: Chelm … 8M 59
Lloyd M. EN3: Enf … 8A 76
Lloyd Pk. Ho. E17: Lon … 7A 106
Lloyd Rd. RM9: Dag … 8L 125
Lloyd Wise Cl. SS2: Sth S … 3B 138
Loamy Hill Rd. CM9: Tip, Tol M … 6M 205
CO5: Tip … 4J 25
Loates Pasture CM24: Stan M … 1C 220
Lobelia Cl. CM1: Chelm … 5B 60
Locarno Av. SS11: Runw … 7M 101
Locke Cl. RM13: Rain … 8D 126
SS17: Stan H … 2L 147
Lockhart Av. CO3: Colc … 8K 165
Lock Hill CM9: Hey B … 9F 214
Lockram La. CM8: Wthm … 5C 230
(Guithavon Valley)
CM8: Wthm … 5D 230
(Newlands Dr.)
Lock Rd. CO9: Hals … 6K 207
Locks Hill SS4: R'fd … 6L 121
Locksley Cl. SS2: Sth S … 4D 138
Lock Vw. CM21: Saw … 2L 51
Lockwood Wlk. RM1: Romf … 9C 110
Lockyer M. EN3: Enf … 8B 76
Lockyer Rd. RM19: Purf … 4N 153
Lodge Av. CM2: Gt Bad … 3G 72
RM2: Romf … 8E 110
RM9: Dag … 1F 140 (6J 39)
Lodge Cl. CM13: Hut … 6A 98
CO12: L Oak … 7D 208
CO15: Clac S … 9J 185
IG7: Chig … 9F 92
SS6: Ray … 6L 119
SS7: Thund … 1G 134
Lodge Ct. CO6: W Ber … 3G 164
RM12: Horn … 4J 127
Lodge Cres. CM3: Bore … 4F 60
Lodge Farm Cl. SS9: Lgh S … 1C 136
Lodge Farm La. CO16: St O … 9B 184 (4B 28)
Lodge Gardens … 1J 17
Lodge Hall CM18: H'low … 7D 54
Lodge Hill IG4: Ilf … 8L 107
Lodgelands Cl. SS6: Ray … 6M 119
Lodge La. CM3: Pur … 8H 215 (3G 35)
CO4: L'ham … 8C 160 (4F 17)
CO5: L'hoe … 9C 174 (2F 27)
CO5: Pel … 3E 26
CO7: A'lgh … 1J 167
(Colchester Rd.)
CO7: A'lgh … 1G 166 (4G 17)
(Crown La. Nth.)
CO7: B'sea … 6C 182
CO16: Ten … 6C 18
EN9: Wal A … 5D 76
RM5: Col R … 4M 109 (2K 39)
RM16: Grays … 9K 145 (1F 47)
RM17: Grays … 9K 145
Lodge Rd. CM1: Writ … 2H 71 (2J 33)
CM3: Bick … 3E 88 (4E 34)
CM3: Haz … 6N 75 (3G 35)
CM7: Brain … 7H 193
CM9: Mal … 5B 214
CM9: Wdhm M … 6N 75 (2G 35)
CM16: Epp, Wal A … 4N 77
CO5: Mess … 2K 25
CO7: B'sea … 5D 182
CO12: L Oak … 7E 208
CO16: L Cla … 8K 179 (2E 28)
SG8: Thri … 2G 5
Lodge Vs. IG8: Wfd G … 3F 106
Lodwick SS3: Shoe … 9G 138
Loewen Rd. RM16: Grays … 1C 156
Loftin Way CM2: Gt Bad … 3E 72 (2A 34)
Logan Ct. RM1: Romf … 9C 110
Logan Link SS12: W'fd … 2N 117
Logan M. RM1: Romf … 9C 110
Loman Path RM15: S Ock … 6C 144
Lombard Av. IG3: Ilf … 3D 124
Lombard Ct. *RM7: Romf … 8A 110*
(off Poplar St.)
Lombards Chase CM13: W H'dn … 1N 129
Lombards, The RM11: Horn … 2K 127
Lombard St. CM7: F'fld … 7A 228 (3A 14)
DA4: Hort K … 7D 46
Lombardy Cl. IG6: Ilf … 4A 108
SS13: Pits … 9K 117
Lombardy Pl. CM1: Chelm … 8K 59
Lonbarn Hill CO11: Brad … 3C 18
London Arena … 7D 38
London Bri. SE1: Lon … 7B 38
London Bridge Station (Rail, Tube) … 7B 38
LONDON CITY AIRPORT … 7G 39
Londonderry Pde. DA8: Eri … 5B 152
London Eye … 7A 38
London Fields Station (Rail) … 5C 38
London Hill SS6: Ray … 4K 119 (2F 43)
London Ind. Pk., The E6: Lon … 5A 140
London Intl. Cruise Terminal RM18: Til … 9C 156
London Knights Ice Hockey (London Arena)
… 7D 38
London Land Cotts. CO6: Wmgfd … 8L 229
London Leopards Basketball (London Arena)
… 7D 38
London Master Bakers Almshouses
E10: Lon … 1B 122
London Rd. BR8: Swan … 6A 46
(not continuous)
CB2: Saws … 1K 5
CB10: Gt Che, L Ches … 8C 202 (4A 6)
CB11: A End, L'bry … 2B 218 (6A 6)
(Littlebury)
CB11: A End, Newp, Wen A … 6L 227 (7A 6)
(Wendens Ambo, not continuous)
CB11: Newp, Widd … 3L 215 (2B 12)
CB11: Saf W … 5C 218 (7B 6)
CM2: Chelm … 4N 71 (2K 33)
CM3: Bore, Hat P … 3J 61 (6D 24)
CM5: Chip … 7E 80 (5B 32)
CM7: Brain, Gt N … 8G 192
(not continuous)
CM8: K'dn, Riven … 3F 230 (3G 25)
CM9: Mal … 5A 214 (1G 35)
CM11: Cray H, Rams B … 1E 116 (1A 42)
CM14: Brtwd … 1C 112 (1D 40)
CM17: H'low … 7H 55 (1J 31)
(Hastingwood)
CM17: H'low … 9H 51 (6J 21)
(Old Harlow)
CM17: H'low … 6H 55 (7J 21)
(Potter Street)
CM17: H'low, Thorn … 1G 65 (2J 31)
CM18: H'low … 7H 55 (1J 31)
CM21: Saw … 3J 51 (4K 21)
CM23: Bis S … 1K 21
CM23: Thor … 2K 21
(not continuous)
CM77: Bla N, Gt N … 4B 204 (2B 24)
CO3: Colc, S'way … 9D 164 (7B 16)
CO5: Fee … 1M 211 (2J 25)
CO5: K'dn … 4J 211 (2H 25)
CO6: Cop, M Tey … 2L 171 (7B 16)
CO6: Fee, M Tey … 5G 170
CO6: Gt Hork … 4G 159 (4D 16)
CO15: Clac S … 7J 185 (3D 28)
CO16: Clac S, L Cla … 3H 185 (2D 28)
DA1: Cray … 3A 46
DA2: Dart, Grnh, Swans … 3D 46
DA4: F'ham … 7B 46
DA10: Swans … 3E 46
DA11: N'fleet … 3G 47
EN2: Lon … 7B 30
IG11: Bark … 9A 124
IG11: Bark … 6F 98 (7H 33)
RM4: Abr … 3E 92 (6J 31)
RM4: Chip, Stap T … 9A 80 (5A 32)
RM7: Chad H, Romf … 1M 125 (3K 39)
RM15: Ave, Purf … 8K 143 (1C 46)
RM17: Grays … 4F 154
RM18: Til … 7D 156 (2H 47)
RM19: Purf … 1L 153 (1C 46)
RM19: Purf, W Thur … 3L 153 (1C 46)
(not continuous)
RM20: W Thur … 4B 154 (2D 46)
SE1: Lon … 7A 38
SG8: B'wy … 1E 10
SG8: Bar … 6E 4
SG8: Fow, Hey … 4F 5
SG8: R'ton … 5C 4
SG9: Bunt … 4D 10
SG12: Gt Amw … 5D 20
SG13: Hart … 5B 20
SS0: Wclf S … 5G 136 (4H 43)
SS1: Sth S … 4A 136
SS6: Ray … 2D 118 (2E 42)
SS7: Ben, Thund … 1B 134 (3D 42)
SS7: Had, Lgh S … 3J 135 (4F 43)
SS9: Lgh S, Sth S, Wclf S … 4L 135 (4G 43)
SS11: Raw … 9B 102 (1D 42)
(Oak Av.)
SS11: Raw … 2D 118 (1D 42)
(Old London Rd.)
SS12: W'fd … 1E 116 (1B 42)
SS13: Pits … 1K 133 (3C 42)
London Rd. SS16: Van … 4D 132 (4A 42)
SS17: Stan H … 4K 147 (6J 41)
Londons Cl. RM14: Upm … 7N 127
LONDON-SOUTHEND AIRPORT … 8J 121 (3J 43)
LONDON STANSTED AIRPORT … 7H 221 (7B 12)
London Wall EC2: Lon … 7B 38
Londs La. CO6: Stok … 1F 17
Lones La. CM7: Shalf … 4B 14
Longacre CM1: Chelm … 2M 71
CM17: H'low … 8G 51
CO4: Colc … 5M 165
SS14: Bas … 9D 116
Long Acre WC2: Lon … 7A 38
Longacre Rd. CM77: Tye G … 2E 194
E17: Lon … 5D 106
Long Acres CM7: Brain … 7J 193
CO5: Fee … 8B 170
Longaford Way CM13: Hut … 7M 97
Long Banks CM18: H'low … 7C 54
Long Border Rd.
CM24: Bis S, Stan Apt … 9G 220 (1B 22)
Longborough Cl. SS13: Bas … 6H 117
Longbow SS2: Sth S … 4C 138
Long Brandocks CM1: Writ … 1H 71
Longbridge Ho. *RM8: Dag … 6G 124*
(off Gainsborough Rd.)
Longbridge Rd. IG11: Bark … 8C 124 (5H 39)
RM8: Dag … 6F 124 (5J 39)
Long Cl. SG8: Fow … 3G 5
Long Comn. CM9: Mal … 3B 214
Long Ct. RM19: Purf … 2L 153
Longcroft CB10: Hpstd … 7G 7
CM22: Tak … 3C 224
Long Cft. CM24: Stan M … 1C 220
Long Cft. Dr. EN8: Wal X … 4A 76
Longcroft Ri. IG10: Lou … 4N 91
Longcroft Rd. CO4: Colc … 7C 166
Longcrofts EN9: Wal A … 4E 76
Long Deacon Rd. E4: Lon … 7E 90
Longdon Ct. RM1: Romf … 9D 110
Longdryve CO2: Colc … 2K 173
(not continuous)
Longfellow Dr. CM13: Hut … 6M 97
Longfellow Rd. CM9: Mal … 7C 214
LONGFIELD … 6F 47
Longfield CM8: Wthm … 2B 230
CM9: Mal … 7C 214
CM18: H'low … 5F 54
IG10: Lou … 4K 91
Longfield Av. RM11: Horn … 2D 126
Longfield Cl. SS11: W'fd … 9A 102
LONGFIELD HILL … 6G 47
Longfield La. EN7: Chesh … 3C 30
Longfield Rd. CM2: Gt Bad … 3F 72
CM3: S Fer … 9K 89
DA3: Long, Meop … 7G 47
SS11: W'fd … 9A 102
Long Flds. CM5: Chip … 8L 67
Longfields CM9: Mal … 6C 214
CO16: St O … 9N 183
Longfield Station (Rail) … 6F 47
Long Gages SS14: Bas … 8C 116
(not continuous)
LONG GARDENS … 7H 9
Long Grn. CM77: Tye G … 8N 193 (1E 24)
CO6: M Tey … 3G 171
IG7: Chig … 1D 108
Long Grn. La. CM7: Bar S … 5K 13
Long Gro. RM3: H Wood … 6J 111
Longhams Dr. CM3: S Fer … 9K 89
Longhayes Av. RM6: Chad H … 8J 109
Longhayes Ct. RM6: Chad H … 8J 109
Longhedges CB11: Saf W … 4D 218
Long Horse Cft. CB11: Saf W … 6D 218
Long Ho. *CM18: H'low … 5E 54*
(off Bush Fair)
Longhouse Rd. RM16: Grays … 1D 156
Long La. CB11: A'den … 1K 11
CM77: Rayne … 8B 192
CO13: Gt Hol … 2F 186
CO16: Ten … 1C 178
DA7: Bexh … 2A 46
RM16: Grays … 9K 145 (7F 41)
(not continuous)
SE1: Lon … 7B 38
SS5: Hull … 7M 103 (7F 35)
(not continuous)
Longleaf Dr. CM7: Brain … 8H 193
Longleat Cl. CM1: Chelm … 4H 59
Long Ley CM20: H'low … 3E 54
(not continuous)
Long Leys E4: Lon … 3B 106
Long Lynderswood SS15: Lain … 9A 116
Longmans *SS3: Shoe … 8L 139*
(off Rampart St.)
Longmarsh La. SE28: Lon … 8D 140
Longmead SS13: Pits … 7K 117
Longmead Av. CM2: Gt Bad … 2G 72
Longmead Cl. CM15: Shenf … 7H 97
Long Mdw. CM12: Bill … 4J 99
(not continuous)
CM13: Hut … 8M 97
CM77: Gt N … 3B 204
RM3: Romf … 8G 95
Long Mdw. Dr. SS11: W'fd … 8M 101
Long Mdws. CO12: Har … 5G 209
Longmeads CM8: W Bis … 2K 229
Longmeads Cl. CM1: Writ … 1J 71
LONG MELFORD … 3J 9
Long Melford By-Pass CO10: L Mel … 4J 9
Longmore Av. CM2: Gt Bad … 2F 72
Longport Cl. IG6: Ilf … 3F 108
Longreach Ct. IG11: Bark … 2C 140
Longreach Rd. DA8: Eri … 5F 152
Long Reach Rd. IG11: Bark … 4E 140
Longridge CO4: Colc … 7F 166 (6G 17)
Longridge Rd. IG11: Bark … 9B 124
Long Riding SS14: Bas … 9C 116
(not continuous)
Long Ridings Av. CM13: Hut … 4L 97 (7F 33)
Longrise CM12: Bill … 8K 99
Long Rd. CO11: Law, Mist … 6G 162 (3K 17)
SS8: Can I … 2E 150 (6E 42)
Long Rd. E. CO7: Ded … 5N 161 (3J 17)
Long Rd. W. CO7: Ded … 5K 161 (3H 17)
Longsands SS3: Shoe … 7H 139
Longshaw Rd. E4: Lon … 9D 90
Longship Way CM9: Mal … 8A 214
Longshots Cl. CM1: Broom … 2J 59
Longs La. CM3: L Walt … 4B 24
Longstomps Av. CM2: Chelm … 4B 72 (2A 34)
Longstraw Cl. CO3: S'way … 9E 164
Long St. EN9: Wal A … 9K 63 (3G 31)
Longtail CM11: Bill … 3L 99
Longtown Cl. RM3: Romf … 2G 110
Longtown Rd. RM3: Romf … 2G 110
Long Vw. SS8: Can I … 1F 150
Longview Vs. RM5: Col R … 5L 109
Longview Way RM5: Col R … 5B 110
Long Wlk. EN9: Wal A … 9A 62
Longwick SS16: Lang H … 2L 131
Long Wood CM18: H'low … 8C 54
Longwood Cl. RM14: Upm … 7N 127
Longwood Ct. *RM14: Upm … 7N 127*
(off Corbets Tey Rd.)
Longwood Gdns. IG5: Ilf … 8M 107 (3G 39)
IG6: Ilf … 8M 107
Longworth Cl. SE28: Lon … 6J 141
Long Wyre St. CO1: Colc … 8N 165
Lonsdale Av. CM13: Hut … 5N 97
E6: Lon … 6F 39
RM7: Romf … 1A 126
Lonsdale Cres. IG2: Ilf … 1A 124
Lonsdale Rd. CO16: T Sok … 4L 179
E11: Lon … 1F 122
SS2: Sth S … 4B 138
Looe Gdns. IG6: Ilf … 7A 108 (3G 39)
Loompits Way CB11: Saf W … 6C 218
Loopys Hill CM24: Stan M … 3D 220
Lord Av. IG5: Ilf … 8M 107
Lord Butler Leisure Cen. … 6E 218
Lord Ct. IG5: Ilf … 8M 107
Lord Gdns. IG5: Ilf … 8M 107
Lord Holland Rd. CO2: Colc … 3N 173
Lord Roberts Av. SS9: Lgh S … 5E 136
Lords Cl. CB10: Sew E … 6D 6
Lord's Cft. La. CB9: H'hll … 3J 7
Lordship Cl. CM13: Hut … 6N 97
Lordship Gardens … 7A 10
Lordship La. N17: Lon … 2A 38
N22: Lon … 2A 38
Lordship Pk. N4: Lon … 4B 38
Lordship Rd. CM1: Writ … 9D 58 (1J 33)
N16: Lon … 4B 38
Lordsland La. CM7: Tye G … 5F 15
Lord St. EN11: Hod … 7C 20
Lords Way SS13: Bas … 5J 117
Lordswood Rd. CO2: Colc … 4K 173
Lordswood Vw. CM6: Lea R … 4D 212
Lorien Gdns. CM3: S Fer … 2J 103
Lorimar Bus. Cen. RM13: Rain … 5C 142
Lorkin's La. CO9: T'std … 1H 15
Lorkin Way CO6: W Ber … 3G 165
Lorne Gdns. E11: Lon … 8J 107
Lorne Rd. CM14: War … 1F 112
E7: Lon … 6H 123
E17: Lon … 9A 106
Lornes Cl. SS2: Sth S … 3B 138
Lorraine Cl. CM11: Bill … 1M 115
Lorrimore Cl. CM12: Bill … 3H 99
Loten Rd. SS7: Ben … 4B 134
Lottem Rd. SS8: Can I … 3K 151
Lott's La. CO16: L Cla … 1F 184
Lotts Yd. CO1: Colc … 9B 166
Lotus Way CO15: Jay … 5C 188
Loudoun Av. IG6: Ilf … 9A 108
LOUGHTON … 3L 91 (7G 31)
Loughton Ct. EN9: Wal A … 3H 77
Loughton La. CM16: They B … 8C 78 (5H 31)
Loughton Leisure Cen. … 3L 91
Loughton Seedbed Cen. IG10: Lou … 4C 92
Loughton Station (Tube) … 4L 91 (7G 31)
Loughton Way IG9: Buck H … 7K 91 (7F 31)
IG10: Lou … 7K 91 (7G 31)
Louisa Av. SS7: Thund … 9B 118
Louis Cl. SS6: Ray … 4G 119
Louis Dr. SS6: Ray … 3G 118
Louis Dr. E. SS6: Ray … 4H 119
Louis Dr. W. SS6: Ray … 3G 118
Louise Cl. CO14: Walt … 1M 181
Louise Gdns. RM13: Rain … 3C 142
Louise Rd. E15: Lon … 8E 122
SS6: Ray … 5L 119
Lousehall La. EN9: Naze … 5D 62
Louse La. CO7: Ded … 5L 161
Louvain Dr. CM1: Chelm … 4A 60
Louvaine Av. SS12: W'fd … 8J 101
Louvain Rd. CO12: Har … 6J 209
Loveday Cl. SG8: Chris … 6H 5
Lovelace Av. SS1: Sth S … 6B 138
Lovelace Gdns. IG11: Bark … 6F 124
SS2: Sth S … 5B 138
Loveland Mans. *IG11: Bark … 9E 124*
(off Upney La.)
Love La. CM5: Chip … 7L 67
CO7: B'sea … 5D 182
IG8: Wfd G … 3M 107
RM15: Ave … 9N 143 (1D 46)

Love La. RM18: E Til 4K 157 (2K 47)
SS6: Ray 5J 119
Lovell Ri. SS9: Lgh S 9F 120
Lovell Wlk. RM13: Rain 8E 126
Lovens Cl. SS8: Can I 3J 151
Lover's La. CO7: Gt Ben 7M 177 (1B 28)
Lovers La. DA9: Grnh 9F 154
Lovers Wlk. RM5: Hav 2B 110
LOVES GREEN 5C 70 (2H 33)
Loves Wlk. CM1: Writ 2K 71
CM2: Gt Bad 3F 72
Lovet Rd. CM19: H'low 4N 53
Love Way CO16: Clac S 7G 185
Lovibond Pl. CM2: Chelm 7A 60
Lowbrook Rd. IG1: Ilf 6A 124
Lowe Chase CO14: Walt 6L 181
Lowe Cl. IG7: Chig 2F 108
Lowefields CO6: E Col 9E 198
Lowen Rd. RM13: Rain 2B 142
Lwr. Alderton Hall La. IG10: Lou 4N 91
Lwr. Anchor St. CM2: Chelm 1B 72
Lower Av. SS13: Pits 7M 117
Lwr. Bedfords Rd.
RM1: Hav, Romf 3C 110 (2A 40)
LOWER BOBBINGWORTH GREEN
3F 66 (2B 32)
Lwr. Bovinger Grn. CM5: Chip 3F 66 (2B 32)
Lwr. Broad St. RM10: Dag 1M 141
Lwr. Burnham Rd.
CM3: Cold N, Latch, N Fam,
Pur, Stow M 8N 89 (5G 35)
Lwr. Bury La. CM16: Epp 1D 78 (4H 31)
LOWER BUSH 7K 47
Lwr. Chapel Hill CM7: Brain 6K 193
Lwr. Chase CM3: Alth 1C 190
Lwr. Church Rd. SS7: Thund 9B 118
LOWER CLAPTON 5C 38
Lwr. Clapton Rd. E5: Lon 5C 38
Lower. Cloister CM11: Bill 6K 99
Lower Cres. SS17: Linf 1J 157
Lwr. Dunton Rd. CM13: Dun 7F 114 (3H 41)
RM14: Bulp 2F 130 (3H 41)
(Stack Av.)
RM14: Bulp, Horn H 5G 131
(Old Chu. Hill)
SS17: Horn H 3H 41
SS17: Horn H 5G 131
LOWER EDMONTON 7C 30
Lwr. Farm Rd. CO4: Boxt 2F 17
LOWER GREEN 1G 11
Anstey 2G 11
Great Sampford 1F 13
Langley 1G 11
Sandon 4K 73 (2C 34)
Wethersfield 3C 14
Lower Grn. CB11: Lang L 1G 11
CM2: Gall 9C 72 (3A 34)
(not continuous)
CO6: Wak C 3K 15
CO8: Lmsh 1J 15
Lwr. Green Gdns. CO7: B'sea 7E 182
Lwr. Green Rd. CM7: Bla E 3B 14
CM7: F'fld 2D 200 (2K 13)
Lwr. Hall La. E4: Lon 1D 38
(not continuous)
Lwr. Hatfield Rd.
SG13: Bayf, Hart, Howe G 7A 20
LOWER HIGHAM 4K 47
Lwr. Higham Rd.
DA12: Grav, Shorne 4J 47
LOWER HOLBROOK 1D 18
LOWER HOLLOWAY 5A 38
Lwr. Holt St. CO6: E Col 8E 198 (4J 15)
Lower Ho's. CO10: Bulm 2H 195 (6G 9)
Lwr. Howe St. CM7: F'fld 1E 200 (2K 13)
Lower King CM7: Brain 7M 193
Lwr. Lambricks SS6: Ray 3K 119
Lower Langley CO6: Gt Tey 1E 170
Lwr. Lea Crossing E14: Lon 7E 38
E16: Lon 7E 38
LOWER LUDDESDOWN 7J 47
Lwr. Mardyke Av. RM13: Rain 2A 142
Lwr. Marine Pde. CO12: Har 5K 209 (3H 19)
Lower Mdw. CM18: H'low 7D 54
Lwr. Mill Fld. CM6: Gt D 4M 203
LOWER NAZEING 1E 62 (2E 30)
Lwr. Noke Cl. CM14: Romf, S Wea 8J 95
Lwr. Park Rd.
CO7: B'sea 7D 182 (3K 27)
IG10: Lou 4K 91
SS12: W'fd 3K 117
Lwr. Pond St. CB11: Dun E 7H 5
Lwr. Queen's Rd. IG9: Buck H 8K 91
Lower Rd. BR8: Swan 5A 46
CM13: Mount 2N 97
CM15: Mount 1N 97 (6G 33)
CM22: L Hall 2K 213 (3K 21)
CO2: B'ch 9A 172 (1C 26)
CO2: Lay M 3C 26
CO5: Pel 3E 26
CO8: M Bur, Wmgfd 6H 229 (2A 16)
CO10: Bor 4H 9
CO10: Glem 2G 9
CO10: Pos 1B 8
DA8: Eri 1A 46
DA11: N'fleet 9H 155
(not continuous)
DA12: Shorne 4K 47
DA17: Belv 1A 152 (1A 46)
IG10: Lou 9N 77 (6G 31)
SE16: Lon 7C 38
(not continuous)
SG8: Arr, Croy 1A 4
SG12: Gt Amw 5D 20
Lower Rd. SS5: Hock, Hull 7K 103 (7F 35)
(Watery La., not continuous)
SS5: Hock, Hull 7M 103 (7H 35)
(Long La.)
LOWER SHEERING 2M 51 (4K 21)
LOWER SHORNE 4K 47
Lwr. Southend Rd. SS11: W'fd 8L 101
Lower Sq. CB10: Saf W 3C 218
Lwr. Stock Rd. CM2: W Han 6B 86 (5A 34)
CM4: Stock, W Han 6B 86 (5A 34)
Lower St. CM24: Stan M 3D 220 (6A 12)
CO7: Ded 1J 161 (2H 17)
CO10: Caven 2F 9
CO10: S'std 1G 9
IP9: Stut 1C 18
SG8: Thri 2G 5
SS15: Bas 6N 115
Lower Swaines CM16: Epp 9D 64
Lwr. Thames St. EC3: Lon 7B 38
Lowestoft M. E16: Lon 9A 140
Lowe, The IG7: Chig 1F 108
Lowewood Mus. 6A 52 (7D 20)
Lowfield CM21: Saw 3J 51
Lowfield Ct. EN11: Hod 5A 52
Lowfield La. EN11: Hod 5A 52
Lowfield St. DA1: Dart 4C 46
Lowgate La. SG12: Sac 2C 20
(not continuous)
Low Hall Cl. E4: Lon 6B 90
Low Hill Rd. CM19: Roy 5F 52 (7E 20)
Lowlands Gdns. RM7: Romf 1N 125
Lowlands Rd. RM15: Ave 8N 143
Lowleys La. CM3: Gt L 4B 24
Low Rd. CO12: Har 6G 208 (3H 19)
SS3: Shoe 9J 139
Lowry Cl. DA8: Eri 2B 152
SS3: Shoe 5K 139
Lowry Rd. RM8: Dag 7G 125
Lowshoe La. RM5: Col R 5M 109
LOW STREET 4H 157
Low St. CO10: Glem 1G 9
Low St. La. RM18: W Til 2H 157 (1J 47)
LOXFORD 7B 124 (5H 39)
Loxford SS13: Bas 7H 117
Loxford La. IG1: Ilf 7B 124 (5H 39)
IG3: Ilf 6D 124
Loxford Rd. IG11: Bark 8A 124
Loxford Ter. IG11: Ilf 8B 124
Loxham Rd. E4: Lon 4B 106
LOYTER'S GREEN 7A 22
Luard Way CM8: Wthm 6C 230
CO2: B'ch 8D 172
Lubbards Cl. SS6: Ray 2K 119
Lubberhedges La. CM6: Steb 5H 13
Lucam Lodge *SS4: R'fd 6L 121*
(off Garners, The)
Lucas Av. CM2: Chelm 4D 72
CO6: For 2A 164
Lucas Ct. EN9: Wal A 3F 76
LUCAS END 3B 30
Lucas Rd. CO2: Colc 9N 165
RM17: Grays 1K 155
Lucas's La. CM5: Will 2J 69
CO16: T Sok 6D 18
Lucerne Dr. SS11: W'fd 9A 102
Lucerne Gro. E17: Lon 8D 106
Lucerne Rd. CO7: Elms 9N 167
Lucerne Wlk. SS11: W'fd 9A 102
Lucerne Way CM1: Writ 2K 71
RM3: Romf 3H 111
Luces La. CO9: Cas H 3L 219
Lucius Cres. CO4: Colc 1B 166
Lucking St. CO9: Gt Map 1F 15
Lucksfield Way CM2: Gt Bad 5G 73
Luck's La. CM3: Gt Walt 2H 57 (4K 23)
Luckyn La. SS14: Bas 7A 116 (3K 41)
Lucton M. IG10: Lou 3A 92
Luctons Av. IG9: Buck H 7J 91
Lucy Cl. CO3: S'way 9D 164
Lucy Gdns. RM8: Dag 5K 125
Lucy La. Nth. CO3: S'way 8C 164
Lucy La. Sth. CO3: S'way 8D 164
Lucy Rd. SS1: Sth S 7N 137
LUDDESDOWN 7J 47
Luddesdown Rd. DA13: Ludd 7J 47
Ludgate Hill EC4: Lon 7A 38
Ludgores La. CM3: Dan 5D 74
Ludgrove CM3: Latch 7L 211
Ludham Cl. IG6: Ilf 5B 108
SE28: Lon 6H 141
Ludham Hall La. CM77: Bla N 1D 204
Ludlow M. SS13: Pits 9J 117
Ludlow Pl. RM17: Grays 1L 155
LUFFENHALL 4A 10
Luff Way CO14: Frin S, Walt 7J 181
Lufkin Rd. CO4: Colc 4N 165
Lugar Cl. CO4: Colc 9E 166
Lugg App. E12: Lon 5N 123
Luker Rd. SS1: Sth S 6M 137
Lukes Cl. SS15: Lain 9L 115
Lukin Cres. E4: Lon 9D 90
Lukin's Dr. CM6: Gt D 4L 203
Lukintone Cl. IG10: Lou 5L 91
Lullingstone La. DA4: Eyns 7B 46
Lullingstone Roman Villa 7B 46
Lullington Rd. RM9: Dag 9K 125
Lulworth Cl. CO15: Clac S 4G 189
SS17: Stan H 5K 147
Lulworth Dr. RM5: Col R 2N 109
Lumber Leys CO14: Walt 7K 181
Lumiere Bldg., The *E7: Lon 7K 123*
(off Romford Rd.)
Luncies Rd. SS14: Bas 1F 132
Lundy Cl. SS2: Sth S 8G 120
Lunnish Hill CO12: R'sy 5B 208 (3F 19)
Lupin Cl. RM7: Rush G 4B 126
Lupin Cres. IG1: Ilf 8A 124
Lupin Dr. CM1: Chelm 5A 60
Lupin M. CM1: Chelm 5A 60
Lupin Way CO16: Clac S 9G 185
Luppits Cl. CM13: Hut 7K 97
Lushes Ct. IG10: Lou 4A 92
Lushes Rd. IG10: Lou 4A 92
Lushington Av. CO13: Walt 8G 181
Lushington Rd. CO11: Law 4H 163
Lutea Cl. SS15: Lain 6M 115
Luther Dr. CO5: Tip 6E 226
Luther King Rd. CM20: H'low 3C 54
Luthers Cl. CM15: Kel H 7B 82
Luton Ho. *RM3: Romf 2J 111*
(off Lindfield Rd.)
Luxborough La. IG7: Chig 9L 91
Luxford Pl. CM21: Saw 3L 51
Lych Ga. SS15: Lain 9L 115
Lychgate Ind. Est. SS6: Ray 6E 118
Lydeard Rd. E6: Lon 9M 123
Lydford Rd. SS0: Wclf S 7K 137
Lydgate Cl. CO11: Law 4G 163
Lydia Dr. CO16: St O 4K 27
Lydia Rd. DA8: Eri 4D 152
Lylt Rd. SS8: Can I 2G 151
Lyme Rd. SS2: Sth S 5A 138
Lymington Av. CO15: Clac S 5K 185
SS9: Lgh S 4D 136
Lymington Rd. RM8: Dag 3J 125
Lympstone Cl. SS0: Wclf S 1F 136
Lynbrook Cl. RM13: Rain 2B 142
Lynceley Grange CM16: Epp 8F 64
LYNCH, THE 7D 20
Lyndale CM15: Kel H 7C 82
Lyndale Av. SS2: Sth S 3N 137
Lyndale Est. RM20: W Thur 4E 154
Lyndbourne Ct. SS7: Thund 9C 118
Lyndene SS7: Thund 9B 118
Lynders Wood La. CM3: Bla N, Gt L 2B 24
Lynderwood La. CM3: Gt L 6M 203
Lyndhurst Ct. E18: Lon 5G 107
Lyndhurst Dr. CM3: Bick 9F 74
E10: Lon 2C 122
RM11: Horn 3G 126
Lyndhurst Gdns. IG2: Ilf 1C 124
IG11: Bark 8D 124
Lyndhurst Ri. IG7: Chig 1N 107
Lyndhurst Rd. CO15: Hol S 9N 185
DA7: Bexh 8A 152
E4: Lon 4C 106
SS4: R'fd 7H 105
(not continuous)
SS17: Corr 1A 148
Lyndhurst Way CM13: Hut 6M 97
Lynford Gdns. IG3: Ilf 4E 124
Lynfords Av. SS11: Runw 5N 101
Lynfords Dr. SS11: Runw 5N 101
(Runwell Chase)
SS11: Runw 6N 101
(Runwell Rd.)
Lynmouth Av. CM2: Chelm 2D 72
Lynmouth Gdns. CM2: Chelm 1D 72
Lynmouth Ho. *RM3: Romf 2J 111*
(off Dagnam Pk. Dr.)
Lynne Cl. CO13: Walt 8H 181
Lynnett Rd. RM8: Dag 4J 125
Lynn M. E11: Lon 4E 122
Lynn Rd. E11: Lon 4E 122
IG2: Ilf 2C 124
Lynn Vw. Cl. SS7: Ben 1C 134
Lynross Cl. RM3: H Wood 6K 111
Lynstede SS14: Bas 1H 133
Lynton Av. RM7: Maw 5M 109
Lynton Cl. CO12: Har 3K 209
Lynton Cres. IG2: Ilf 1A 124
Lynton Dr. CM1: Chelm 6N 59
Lynton Ho. IG1: Ilf 4B 124
Lynton Rd. E4: Lon 2B 106
SS1: Sth S 8D 138
SS7: Had 3J 135
Lynwood Cl. E18: Lon 5J 107
RM5: Col R 3N 109
Lynwood Dr. RM5: Col R 3N 109
Lynwood Grn. SS6: Ray 7N 119
Lyon Bus. Pk. IG11: Bark 2D 140
Lyon Cl. CM2: Gall 7C 72
CO15: Clac S 9L 185
Lyon Rd. RM1: Romf 2D 126
Lyons Ct. CM1: Chelm 6N 59
Lyons Hall Rd.
CM7: Brain, Tye G 8L 191 (6D 14)
Lyster Av. CM2: Gt Bad 3H 73
Lytham Cl. SE28: Lon 6K 141
Lyttelton Rd. E10: Lon 5B 122
Lytton Cl. IG10: Lou 2C 92
Lytton Rd. E11: Lon 2E 122
RM2: Romf 9F 110
RM16: Grays 2C 156
Lytton Strachey Path SE28: Lon 7G 141
Lyttons Way EN11: Hod 2A 52

M

Mabbitt Way CO4: Colc 2B 166
Maberly Ct. CB10: Saf W 3D 218
Mabey's Wlk. CM21: H Wych 3G 50
Mabledon Pl. NW1: Lon 6A 38
Mablin Lodge IG9: Buck H 7J 91
McAdam Cl. EN11: Rye P 3A 52
Macarthur Cl. E7: Lon 8G 123
Macaulay Av. SS16: Lang H 1J 131
Macaulay Rd. SS16: Lang H 1J 131
Macaulay Way SE28: Lon 8G 141
Macbeth Cl. CO4: Colc 8F 166
McCalmont Dr. SS6: Ray 9J 103
Macclesfield Ho. *RM3: Romf 2J 111*
(off Dagnam Pk. Dr.)
McClintock Pl. EN3: Enf 8B 76
McCudden Rd. DA1: Dart 8K 153
McDivitt Wlk. SS9: Lgh S 9F 120
Macdonald Av. RM10: Dag 5N 125
RM11: Horn 7J 111
SS0: Wclf S 4K 137
Macdonald Rd. E7: Lon 6G 122
E17: Lon 6C 106
Macdonald Way RM11: Horn 8J 111
Mace Ct. RM17: Grays 4A 156
Mace Wlk. CM1: Chelm 8H 59
McGrail Ct. *SS8: Can I 2M 151*
(off Aalten Av.)
McGrath Rd. E15: Lon 7F 122
Macgregor Dr. SS12: W'fd 2M 117
McIntosh Cl. RM1: Romf 7C 110
McIntosh Rd. RM1: Romf 7C 110
Macintyres Wlk. SS4: R'fd 1H 121
Mackay Ct. CO2: Colc 5B 174
Mackenzie Cl. SS12: W'fd 1M 117
McKenzie Rd. EN10: Brox 8A 52
MacKenzie Rd. N7: Lon 5A 38
Mackley Dr. SS17: Corr 9A 132
Maclarens CM8: W Bis 1M 229
Maclaren Way SS12: W'fd 2M 117
Maclennan Av. RM13: Rain 3H 143
Macleod Cl. RM17: Grays 2N 155
Macmillan Ct. *CM2: Chelm 1C 72*
(off Godfreys M.)
Macmillan Gdns. DA1: Dart 9L 153
Macmurdo Cl. SS9: Lgh S 8C 120
Macmurdo Rd. SS9: Lgh S 8C 120
Macon Way RM14: Upm 2B 128
Macs Ho. E17: Lon 7B 106
Maddox Rd. CM20: H'low 2D 54 (6H 21)
Madeira Av. SS9: Lgh S 4D 136
Madeira Gro. IG8: Wfd G 3J 107
Madeira Rd. CO15: Hol S 9N 185
E11: Lon 3D 122
Madeira Wlk. CM15: Brtwd 9H 97
Madeleine Cl. RM6: Chad H 1H 125
Madeline Gro. IG1: Ilf 7C 124
Madeline Pl. CM1: Chelm 5G 58
Madells CM16: Epp 1E 78
Madgements Rd. CM77: Tye G 6E 14
Madles La. CM4: Stock 8A 86 (5K 33)
Madras Rd. IG1: Ilf 6A 124
Madrid Av. SS6: Ray 9G 103
Maeldune Heritage Cen. (Mus.)
5C 214 (1H 35)
Mafeking Av. IG2: Ilf 2C 124
Magazine Farm Way CO3: Colc 9H 165
Magazine Rd. SS3: Shoe 8J 139
Magdalen Cl. CO15: Clac S 9J 185
Magdalene Cres. CM8: Sil E 9L 217
Magdalen Gdns. CM13: Hut 5A 98
Magdalen Grn. CM6: Thax 8C 224
CO1: Colc 9B 166
MAGDALEN LAVER 7A 22
Magdalen Rd. CO15: Clac S 9J 185
Magdalen St. CO1: Colc 9A 166 (6F 17)
Magenta Cl. CM12: Bill 5G 99
MAGGOTS END 5J 11
Magna Mead SS3: Barl M 3B 44
Magnet Rd. RM20: Grays 4F 154
Magnet Ter. SS17: Stan H 1N 147
Magnolia Cl. CM2: Chelm 4C 72
CM8: Wthm 2D 230
E10: Lon 4A 122
RM15: S Ock 4H 145
SS8: Can I 3G 150
Magnolia Dr. CO4: Colc 7E 166
Magnolia Gdns. E10: Lon 4A 122
Magnolia La. SS15: Lain 6L 115
Magnolia Lodge E4: Lon 9B 90
Magnolia Pl. SS17: Stan H 1N 147
Magnolia Rd. SS4: Hock, R'fd 1F 120
Magnolias CM11: Bill 1L 115
Magnolia Way CM15: Pil H 4E 96
SS4: R'fd 7M 121
Magnum Cl. RM13: Rain 4F 142
Magnus Dr. CO4: Colc 1B 166
Magpie Cl. CO12: Har 6G 209
E7: Lon 7F 122
Magpie La. CM13: L War 6G 112 (2E 40)
Magpies, The CM16: E Grn 3N 63
Magwitch Cl. CM1: Chelm 4H 59
Mahonia Dr. SS16: Lang H 2H 131
Maida Av. E4: Lon 6B 90
Maida Way E4: Lon 6B 90
Maidenburgh St. CO1: Colc 8N 165
(not continuous)
Maiden La. DA1: Cray 8E 152
Maiden Rd. E15: Lon 9E 122
Maidment Cres. CM8: Wthm 7C 230
Maidstone Av. RM5: Col R 6A 110
Maidstone Rd. BR8: Swan 6A 46
DA14: Swan 5A 46
IP11: Felix 1K 19
RM17: Grays 4K 155
Mailers La. CM23: Man 5K 11
Main Av. EN1: Enf 7C 30
Main Dr. CM13: Dun 1G 130
Maine Cres. SS6: Ray 3H 119
Main Ho., The CM21: Saw 1N 51
Main Rd. BR8: Crock 7A 46
BR8: Swan 5A 46

Main Rd. CM0: St La 2C 36
CM1: Broom, Chelm 6K 57 (5A 24)
CM2: Dan 3N 73
CM3: Bick, S Fer, Wdhm F 9F 74 (3E 34)
CM3: Bore 4D 60 (7C 24)
CM3: Broom, Chelm, L Walt . . . 6K 57 (5A 24)
CM3: Dan. . . . 3D 74 (2D 34)
CM3: E Han. . . . 1B 88
(Common, The)
CM3: E Han. . . . 3C 88
(Rettendon Rd.)
CM3: Gt L. . . . 9K 203 (3B 24)
(not continuous)
CM3: Gt Walt. . . . 4K 23
CM3: Ret C, Runw 7A 88 (5D 34)
CM3: Will G. . . . 2B 24
CM4: Marg 1H 85
CO6: Wmgfd 8K 229 (3B 16)
CO7: Frat 3D 176 (7K 17)
CO12: Har 3M 209 (3H 19)
(High St.)
CO12: Har 5G 208 (3G 19)
(Oakley Rd.)
CO12: R'sy 6C 208 (3F 19)
CO13: Gt Hol 1D 186 (2F 29)
DA3: Long, Long H 6E 46
DA4: S at H. . . . 5C 46
IP9: S'ly 1G 19
RM1: Romf 8D 110 (3A 40)
RM2: Romf 8D 110 (3A 40)
SG14: B'fld, Stfrd 4A 20
SS5: Hock 2B 120 (1G 43)
(Aldermans Hill)
SS5: Hock 2D 120 (1H 43)
(Southend Rd.)
SS5: Hull. . . . 4L 103
SS7: Thund. . . . 9H 119
Main St. CB1: Shudy C 3F 7
SS5: Hock. . . . 7B 104
Maitland Pl. SS3: Shoe. . . . 5J 139
Maitland Rd.
CM24: Stan M. . . . 3D 220
E15: Lon 8F 122
SS12: W'fd. . . . 2M 117
Maitlands IG10: Lou 2M 91
Maizey Ct. CM15: Pil H 4D 96
Major Rd. E15: Lon. . . . 7D 122 (5E 38)
Makemores CM77: Rayne. . . . 6B 192
Makepeace Rd. E11: Lon. . . . 8G 107
Makinen Ho. IG9: Buck H 7J 91
Makins Rd. CO12: Har 2H 209
Malan Sq. RM13: Rain 8F 126
Malcolm Ct. E7: Lon 8F 122
Malcolm Way E11: Lon 9G 106
MALDON 5B 214 (1H 35)
Maldon & District Agricultural & Domestic Mus. 2K 201
Maldon Cl. E15: Lon. . . . 7E 122
Maldon Ct. CO3: Colc 9M 165
Maldon District Mus. 6D 214 (1H 35)
Maldon Embroidery 5C 214
Maldon Moot Hall. . . . 5B 214
Maldon Rd. CM0: Brad S. . . . 9A 194 (2D 36)
CM0: Bur C 2C 196 (6B 36)
CM0: May, Stpl 8N 213 (4B 36)
CM2: Dan, Gt Bad, S'don. . . . 3H 73 (2B 34)
CM2: Gt Bad 3G 72 (2B 34)
CM3: Dan. . . . 3E 74 (2E 34)
(Lit. Baddow Rd.)
CM3: Dan. . . . 6H 75 (2E 34)
(Southwood Chase)
CM3: Hat P, Ult. . . . 2L 61 (6E 24)
CM3: Latch, Mun 6J 211 (4J 35)
CM4: Marg 1J 85 (4J 33)
CM8: Tip. . . . 7J 205 (5J 25)
CM8: W Bis, Wthm 6D 230 (5F 25)
(not continuous)
CM9: Gold, Tol D, Tol M 4J 227 (7K 25)
CM9: Gt Tot. . . . 4N 229 (6H 25)
(Broad St. Grn. Rd.)
CM9: Gt Tot. . . . 7J 205 (5J 25)
(Mill Rd.)
CM9: L'frd 2A 214 (7G 25)
CM9: Mal, Wdhm M. . . . 4K 75 (2F 35)
CO2: B'ch, S'way 9A 172 (2B 26)
CO3: Colc. . . . 1K 173 (6E 16)
CO3: S'way 5C 172
CO5: Gt Wig 4C 26
CO5: K'dn 4J 211 (2J 25)
CO5: Tip. . . . 9A 226 (5J 25)
RM7: Rush G 2A 126
SS2: Sth S 5M 137
Maldon Wlk. IG8: Wfd G. . . . 3J 107
Maldon Way CO16: Clac S 9F 184
Maldon Yacht Club 6D 214
Malford Ct. E18: Lon 6G 106
Malford Gro. E18: Lon 8F 106
Malgraves SS13: Pits 8J 117
Malgraves Pl. SS13: Pits 8J 117
Malkin Dr. CM17: H'low 4K 55
Mallard Cl. CM9: Tol. . . . 7K 225
CM77: Gt N. . . . 3C 204
CO2: Lay H 9H 173
CO5: K'dn 2K 211
RM14: Upm. . . . 2C 128
Mallard Ct. E17: Lon 7D 106
SS1: Sth S. *6A 138*
(off Windermere Rd.)
Mallard Rd. CM2: Chelm 5B 72
Mallards CM3: May. . . . 8L 213
E11: Lon *2G 123*
(off Blake Hall Rd.)
SS3: Shoe 5J 139
Mallards Ri. CM17: H'low. . . . 3J 55
Mallards Rd. IG8: Wfd G 4H 107
IG11: Bark 3F 140
Mallard Way CM13: Hut 6L 97
CM19: Roy *2G 52*
(off Swan Way)
Mallinson Cl. RM12: Horn 7G 127
Mallion Ct. EN9: Wal A 3F 76
Mallory Way CM12: Bill 7J 99
Mallow Ct. RM17: Grays 4N 155
Mallow Gdns. CM12: Bill 3H 99
Mallows Fld. CO9: Hals 4L 207 (3F 15)
MALLOWS GREEN. . . . 5J 11
Mallows Grn. CM19: H'low 8N 53
CM23: Man 5J 11
Mallows Grn. Rd. CM23: Man 5J 11
Mallows La. CO9: Top 1B 14
Mallows, The CM9: Mal 8C 214
Mall, The E15: Lon. . . . 9D 122
RM10: Dag. . . . 8M 125
RM11: Horn. . . . 3F 126
Malmesbury Rd. E18: Lon 5F 106
Malmsmead SS3: Shoe 6G 139
Malpas Rd. RM9: Dag. . . . 8J 125
RM16: Grays. . . . 1E 156
Malta Rd. E10: Lon. . . . 3A 122
RM18: Til 7B 156
Maltbeggar's La. CO6: Cogg 2A 170
Maltese Rd. CM1: Chelm 8J 59
Malt Ho. Pl. RM1: Romf. . . . 9C 110
Malthouse Rd. CO11: Mist 4J 163
Malthus Path SE28: Lon. . . . 8H 141
Malting Cotts. CB9: Stur. . . . 7K 223
Malting Farm La. CO7: A'lgh 6J 161 (3H 17)
MALTING GREEN. . . . 9J 173
Malting Grn. Rd. CO2: Lay H 9G 173 (1D 26)
Malting La. CO13: Kir S 4F 180
RM16: Ors. . . . 4C 146
SG10: M Hud 2G 21
SG11: Brau 6E 10
Malting Rd. CO2: Colc 5K 173
CO5: Pel 3E 26
Maltings Chase CM4: Ing. . . . 6D 84
Maltings Cl. CO8: Bures. . . . 7K 195
Maltings Ct. CM8: Wthm 7C 230
Maltings Dr. CM16: Epp 8F 64
Maltings Hill CM5: M'ton 1B 32
Maltings Ind. Est., The CM0: S'min. . . . 2E 222
Maltings La. CB9: Stpl B. . . . 1N 223 (5K 7)
CM8: Wthm 7B 230 (5F 25)
CM16: Epp 8F 64 (3J 31)
Maltings Pk. Rd. CO6: W Ber. . . . 3G 165
Maltings Rd. CM2: Gt Bad 5H 73
CO7: B'sea. . . . 5D 182
SS11: Bat. . . . 6D 102 (7D 34)
Maltings, The *CB10: Saf W* *4C 218*
(off Gold St.)
CB11: Newp. . . . 3L 215
CM0: S'min. . . . 2E 222
CM6: Gt D 2L 203
CM6: Thax. . . . 8C 224
CM21: Saw 2L 51
CM77: Rayne. . . . 6C 192
CO12: R'sy 7A 208 (4F 19)
RM1: Romf 2D 126
Maltings Vw. CM7: Brain 5J 193
Maltings Wharf CO11: Mist. . . . 4J 163
Malting Vs. Rd. SS4: R'fd. . . . 5L 121
Malting Yd. CO7: W'hoe. . . . 6H 175
Malton La. SG8: Meld, Orw 1D 4
Malton Rd. SG8: Orw. . . . 1D 4
Malvern *SS2: Sth S* *5N 137*
(off Coleman St.)
Malvern Av. E4: Lon 4D 106
SS8: Can I. . . . 2D 150
Malvern Cl. CM1: Chelm. . . . 5F 58
SS6: Ray 4K 119
Malvern Dr. IG3: Bark, Ilf 6E 124
IG8: Wfd G. . . . 2J 107
Malvern Gdns. IG10: Lou 5M 91
Malvern Rd. E11: Lon. . . . 4E 122
RM11: Horn. . . . 1E 126
RM17: Grays. . . . 2A 156
SS5: Hock 8E 104
Malvern Way CO6: Gt Hork. . . . 9J 159
Malwood Dr. SS7: Ben 1B 134
Malwood Rd. SS7: Ben. . . . 1B 134
Malyon Ct. Cl. SS7: Ben. . . . 2H 135
Malyon Rd. CM8: Wthm. . . . 7C 230
Malyons SS13: Bas 7J 117
Malyons Cl. SS13: Bas 7J 117
Malyons Grn. SS13: Bas. . . . 7J 117
Malyons La. SS5: Hull 6K 103
Malyons M. SS13: Bas 7J 117
Malyons Pl. SS13: Bas 7J 117
Malyons, The SS7: Ben 2H 135
Manbey Gro. E15: Lon 8E 122
Manbey Pk. Rd. E15: Lon. . . . 8E 122
Manbey Rd. E15: Lon. . . . 8E 122
Manbey St. E15: Lon 8E 122
Manchester Dr. SS9: Lgh S. . . . 4C 136 (4H 43)
(not continuous)
Manchester Rd. CO15: Hol S 7B 186
E14: Lon 7E 38
Manchester Way RM10: Dag 6N 125
Mandela Av. CM20: H'low 1D 54
(not continuous)
Mandeville Cl. CM17: H'low 5H 55
Mandeville Rd. CB11: Saf W 5C 218
CO6: M Tey. . . . 3G 170
Mandeville St. E5: Lon. . . . 4C 38
Mandeville Wlk. CM6: Fels. . . . 9E 212
CM13: Hut. . . . 6A 98
Mandeville Way CM1: Broom. . . . 9K 57
CO13: Frin S 7J 181
Mandeville Way SS7: Thund 8C 118
SS15: Bas, Lain, Lang H 9G 115 (3J 41)
Mandrake Way E15: Lon. . . . 9E 122
Manfield CO9: Hals 4L 207
Manfield Gdns. CO16: St O 8N 183
Manford Cl. IG7: Chig 1F 108
Manford Ct. *IG7: Chig.* *2E 108*
(off Manford Way)
Manford Cross IG7: Chig. . . . 2F 108
Manford Ind. Est. DA8: Eri 4F 152
Manford Way IG7: Chig. . . . 2D 108 (1H 39)
Mangapp Chase CM0: Bur C 1A 196
Mangapps Farm Railway Mus. . . . 1A 196 (5C 36)
Mangrove La. SG13: Hart. . . . 6B 20
Mangrove Rd. SG13: Hart 5B 20
Manilla Rd. SS1: Sth S 7A 138
Mannering Gdns. SS0: Wclf S 3F 136
Manners Cnr. SS2: Sth S 1K 137
Manners Way SS2: Sth S. . . . 9K 121 (3J 43)
Manning Ct. *SE28: Lon* *8G 141*
(off Titmuss Av.)
Manning Gro. SS16: Lang H. . . . 2L 131
Manning Rd. RM10: Dag. . . . 8M 125
Mannings Cl. CB11: Saf W. . . . 6D 218
Manning St. RM15: Ave 8N 143
MANNINGTREE 4J 163 (3A 18)
Manningtree Mus. 4J 163 (3A 18)
Manningtree Rd. CO7: Ded 2N 161 (2J 17)
CO7: E Ber. . . . 1K 17
CO7: L Ben 7K 169
IP9: Stut 1C 18
Manningtree Sports Cen. 4H 163
Manningtree Station (Rail) 3F 162 (2K 17)
Mannin Rd. RM6: Chad H. . . . 2G 124
Mannock Dr. IG10: Lou. . . . 1B 92
Mannock Rd. DA1: Dart 8K 153
Manns Way SS6: Ray. . . . 2J 119
Manns Yd. CM5: Will 1E 32
Manor Av. E7: Lon. . . . 6J 123
RM11: Horn 9G 110
SS13: Pits 8K 117
Manor Cl. CM11: Rams H. . . . 5D 100
CO6: Gt Hork. . . . 9K 159
DA1: Cray 9B 152
RM1: Romf 9E 110
RM10: Dag 8B 126
RM15: Ave 8N 143
SE28: Lon 7H 141
SS6: Ray 7K 119
Manor Cl. Sth. RM15: Ave 8N 143
Manor Ct. E4: Lon. . . . 7E 90
E10: Lon 3B 122
IG11: Bark 9E 124
SS1: Sth S. . . . 7A 138
SS7: Thund. . . . 8D 118
Manor Cres. CM3: L Walt 7K 57
RM11: Horn 9G 111
Manor Dene SE28: Lon 6H 141
Manordene Rd. SE28: Lon. . . . 6H 141
Manor Dr. CM2: Gt Bad 3G 73
Mnr. Farm Dr. E4: Lon 9E 90
Manor Gdns. CO3: Colc 8L 165
Manorhall Gdns. E10: Lon 3A 122
Manor Hatch CM18: H'low 4F 54
Mnr. Hatch Cl. CM18: H'low. . . . 4G 54
MANOR HOUSE 4B 38
Mnr. House Gdn. E11: 1H 123
Manor House Station (Tube) 4B 38
Manor Ho. Way CO7: B'sea 6D 182
Manor La. CB10: Gt Che. . . . 8D 202
CO12: Har 5J 209
(not continuous)
DA3: Fawk. . . . 7E 46
TN15: Fawk. . . . 7E 46
Manor Links CM23: Bis S. . . . 9C 220
MANOR PARK 6K 123 (5F 39)
Manor Pk. DA8: Eri 4E 152
Manor Park Crematorium E7: Lon 6J 123
Mnr. Park Rd. E12: Lon 6K 123
(not continuous)
Manor Park Station (Rail). . . . 6K 123 (5F 39)
Manor Rd. CB9: H'hll 3J 7
CM0: Deng 4J 225 (3E 36)
CM2: Chelm 1C 72
CM3: Hat P. . . . 5N 61
CM3: S Fer. . . . 9J 89
CM6: L Eas 6F 13
CM8: Wthm. . . . 3D 230
CM9: Mal, Wdhm W 7F 25
CM17: H'low 7H 51
CM24: Stan M. . . . 4D 220
CO3: Colc 8L 165
CO6: W Ber 2F 164
CO7: W'hoe 5J 175
CO12: Har 4J 209
CO13: Gt Hol 2D 186 (2F 29)
DA1: Cray. . . . 9C 152 (3A 46)
DA3: Long. . . . 7G 47
DA8: Eri 4D 152 (2A 46)
DA10: Swans. . . . 4E 46
E10: Lon 2A 122
E15: Lon 6E 38
E16: Lon 6E 38
EN9: Wal A 3D 76
EN11: Rye P 4A 52
IG7: Chig. . . . 2B 108
IG8: Wfd G 3M 107 (2G 39)
IG10: H Bee 9H 77 (5F 31)
IG10: Lou. . . . 5H 91 (7F 31)
IG11: Bark. . . . 8E 124
N16: Lon. . . . 4B 38
RM1: Romf 9E 110
RM4: Abr, Stap A 8H 93 (7J 31)
RM6: Chad H. . . . 1J 125
Manor Rd. RM10: Dag 8A 126
RM17: Grays 4M 155
RM18: Til 7C 156
RM20: W Thur. . . . 4F 154
SS0: Wclf S 7J 137
SS5: Hock. . . . 1B 120
SS7: Thund. . . . 9C 118
SS15: Lain. . . . 8K 115
SS17: Stan H 3M 147
Manor Row CB11: Elm 6J 5
Manor Sq. RM8: Dag 4H 125
Manors, The CM8: Sil E 8L 217
Manor St. CM7: Brain 5H 193 (7C 14)
Manors Way CM8: Sil E 8K 217
Manor Trad. Est. SS7: Thund. . . . 8D 118
Manor Way CM14: Brtwd. . . . 9D 96
CO15: Hol S 7D 186
DA7: Bexh 8B 152
DA10: Swans 9G 155
DA11: N'fleet. . . . 9K 155
E4: Lon. . . . 1D 106
IG8: Wfd G. . . . 2J 107
RM13: Rain 4C 142 (6A 40)
RM17: Grays 5L 155
SS16: Pits 5L 133
SS17: Stan H. . . . 3B 148
Manor Way Bus. Cen. RM13: Rain. . . . 5B 142
Manorway, The
SS17: Corr, Stan H. . . . 3L 147 (6K 41)
Manpreet Ct. E12: Lon. . . . 7M 123
Mansard Cl. RM12: Horn 4E 126
MAN'S CROSS 1B 206 (6C 8)
Manse Chase CM9: Mal 7C 214
Mansel Cl. SS9: Lgh S. . . . 9D 120
Mansel Gro. E17: Lon. . . . 5A 106
Mansell St. EC3: Lon 7B 38
Manser Rd. RM13: Rain. . . . 3C 142
Mansfield CM21: H Wych 3F 50
Mansfield Gdns. RM12: Horn 4H 127
Mansfield Hill E4: Lon 6B 90 (7D 30)
Mansfield Outdoor Cen. 6K 93
Mansfield Rd. E11: Lon 1H 123
IG1: Ilf. . . . 4N 123
Mansfields CM1: Writ. . . . 1H 71
Mansion House Station (Tube) 7B 38
Manstead Gdns. RM13: Rain 6F 142
Mansted Cl. CM13: Dun. . . . 1G 130
Mansted Gdns. RM6: Chad H 2H 125
SS4: R'fd 2J 121
Manston Dr. CM23: Bis S 8A 220
Manston Rd. CM20: H'low 3D 54 (7H 21)
Manston Way RM12: Horn 8F 126
Mantle Way E15: Lon 9E 122
Manton Rd. EN3: Enf 7A 76
Manton Way EN3: Enf. . . . 8B 76
MANUDEN. . . . 5K 11
MANWOOD GREEN. . . . 5C 22
Maple Av. CM7: Brain 6F 192
CM9: Mal. . . . 2E 214
RM14: Upm 5M 127
SS9: Lgh S 6E 136
Maple Cl. CM13: Brtwd. . . . 9J 97
CM16: They B 7C 78
CO9: Hals. . . . 4M 207
CO12: Har 4L 209
CO15: Clac S 1F 188
IG6: Ilf. . . . 2D 108
IG9: Buck H. . . . 9K 91
RM12: Horn. . . . 5F 126
Maplecroft La. EN9: Naze. . . . 9E 52
Mapledene Av. SS5: Hull 6L 103
Maple Dr. CM2: Chelm 4C 72
CM8: Wthm. . . . 2D 230
CO13: Walt 8G 181
RM15: S Ock. . . . 4G 144
SS6: Ray 9J 103
MAPLE END. . . . 7E 6
Mapleford Sweep SS16: Van 2E 132
Maple Ga. IG10: Lou 1N 91
Maple Ho. E17: Lon 7B 106
Maple La. CB10: R'ter, Wim. . . . 1E 12
Maple Leaf CO5: Tip. . . . 4C 226
Mapleleaf Cl. SS5: Hock. . . . 9F 104
Mapleleafe Gdns. IG6: Ilf. . . . 7A 108
Mapleleaf Gdns. SS12: W'fd 1J 117
Maple Mead CM12: Bill 8K 99
Maple Rd. E11: Lon 1E 122
RM17: Grays 4M 155
Maples SS17: Stan H 3N 147
Maplescombe La. DA4: F'ham 7C 46
Maplesfield SS7: Had. . . . 2K 135
Maple Springs EN9: Wal A. . . . 3G 77
Maple Sq. SS2: Sth S. . . . 4N 137
Maplestead SS14: Bas. . . . 7E 116
Maplestead Rd. CO9: Gest. . . . 1G 15
RM9: Dag 1G 140
Maples, The CM19: H'low 8A 54
EN9: Wal A 5J 77
SS12: W'fd 2K 117
Maple St. RM7: Romf. . . . 8A 110
Mapleton Rd. E4: Lon. . . . 9C 90
Mapletree La. CM4: Fry, Mill G 2L 83
Maple Tree La. SS16: Lang H 1H 131
Maple Way CM0: Bur C 2C 196
CO2: Colc 2A 174
EN9: Wal A 8H 63
SS8: Can I 2E 150 (6E 42)
Maplin Cl. SS7: Thund 8C 118
Maplin Ct. CO15: Hol S 9A 186
SS3: Shoe *8L 139*
(off Rampart Ter.)
Maplin Gdns. SS14: Bas. . . . 1F 132
Maplin Ho. *SE2: Lon.* *9J 141*
(off Wolvercote Rd.)

Maplin M. SS3: Shoe 8J 139
Maplin Way SS1: Shoe, Sth S 7G 138 (5B 44)
Maplin Way Nth. SS1: Sth S 6G 138 (5B 44)
Mapperley Cl. E11: Lon 1F 122
Mapperley Dr. IG8: Wfd G 4E 106
Maran Way DA18: Eri 9J 141
Marasca End CO2: Colc 7A 174
Maraschino Cres. CO2: Colc 7A 174
Marathon Way SE28: Lon 9E 140
Marchant Rd. E11: Lon 4D 122
Marchmant Cl. RM12: Horn 5G 127
Marconi Athletic & Social Club 4F 72
Marconi Bungs. CM16: N Wea 3B 66
Marconi Gdns. CM15: Pil H 4F 96
Marconi Rd. CM1: Chelm 8K 59
E10: Lon 3A 122
Marcos Rd. SS8: Can I 2K 151
Marcus Av. SS1: Sth S 8F 138
Marcus Chase SS1: Sth S 7F 138
Marcus Cl. CO4: Colc 1B 166
Marcus Gdns. SS1: Sth S 7F 138
MARDEN ASH 9L 67 (3C 32)
Marden Ash SS15: Lain 9J 115
Marden Cl. IG7: Chig 8G 92
Marden Rd. RM1: Romf 1C 126
Mardyke Cl. RM13: Rain 2A 142
Mardyke Ho. RM13: Rain 2B 142
Mardyke Rd. CM20: H'low 1F 54
Mardyke Vw. RM19: Purf 1B 154
Mardyke Wlk. RM16: Grays 8K 145
Mare Hill CO10: Pos 1B 8
Marennes Cres. CO7: B'sea 6D 182
Maresby Ho. E4: Lon 8B 90
Mare St. E8: Lon 6C 38
Mareth Rd. CO2: Colc 4K 173
Margaret Av. CM15: Shenf 6J 97
E4: Lon 5B 90
Margaret Bondfield Av. IG11: Bark 9F 124
Margaret Cl. CM16: Epp 8E 64
CO7: B'sea 7F 182
EN9: Wal A 3D 76
RM2: Romf 9F 110
Margaret Dr. RM11: Horn 3K 127
Margaret Rd. CM16: Epp 8F 64
CO1: Colc 7M 165
RM2: Romf 9F 110
MARGARET RODING 5F 23
Margaret's Ho. CO5: K'dn 3K 211
Margaret St. CM6: Thax 7C 224
MARGARETTING 1J 85 (4J 33)
Margaretting Rd. CM1: Writ 6J 71 (3J 33)
CM2: Chelm, Gall 9A 72 (3K 33)
E12: Lon 3J 123
MARGARETTING TYE 2L 85 (4K 33)
Margaret Way CB10: Saf W 4C 218
IG4: Ilf 1L 123
Margarite Way SS12: W'fd 8J 101
Margery Allingham Pl. CM9: Tol D 3K 227
Margery Pk. Rd. E7: Lon 8G 122
Margery Rd. RM8: Dag 5J 125
Margery St. WC1: Lon 6A 38
Margeth Rd. CM12: Bill 4L 115
Margeth Works CM12: Bill 6F 98
Margherita Pl. EN9: Wal A 4F 76
Margherita Rd. EN9: Wal A 4G 76
Margraten Av. SS8: Can I 3K 151
Marguerite Dr. SS9: Lgh S 5E 136
Maria Ct. CO2: Colc 1C 174
(off Hesper Rd.)
Mariam Gdns. RM12: Horn 4K 127
Marian Cl. RM16: N Stif 8H 145
Maria St. CO12: Har 2M 209
Marie Cl. SS17: Fob 6B 132
Marigold Av. CO16: Clac S 8G 185
Marigold Cl. CM1: Chelm 5A 60
CO4: Colc 7E 166
Marigold La. CM4: Stock 9N 85 (5K 33)
Marigold Pl. CM17: H'low 8G 51
Marina Av. SS6: Ray 4J 119
Marina Cl. SS2: Sth S 2K 137
Marina Gdns. CO15: Clac S 8N 185
RM7: Romf 9N 109
Marina M. CO14: Walt 6M 181
Marina Point CO15: Clac S 3H 189
Marina Rd. CM3: Hat P 2L 61
Marine App. SS8: Can I 3H 151
Marine Av. SS0: Wclf S 7K 137 (5J 43)
SS8: Can I 3L 151
SS9: Lgh S 5C 136
Marine Cl. SS9: Lgh S 5N 135
Marine Ct. CO13: Frin S 1J 187
DA8: Eri 5D 152
RM19: Purf 2K 153
Marine Dr. IG11: Bark 4F 140
Marine Pde. CM3: May 7J 213 (3A 36)
CO12: Har 4L 209 (3H 19)
SS1: Sth S 7N 137 (5K 43)
SS8: Can I 3M 151
SS9: Lgh S 5N 135 (4G 43)
Marine Pde. E. CO15: Clac S 2K 189 (4D 28)
Marine Pde. W. CO15: Clac S 3H 189 (4D 28)
Mariner Rd. E12: Lon 6N 123
Mariners Ct. DA9: Grnh 9E 154
(off High St.)
SS3: Gt W 3N 139
Mariners Wlk. DA8: Eri 4D 152
Mariners Way CM9: Mal 8C 214
Marion Av. CO15: Clac S 7J 185
Marion Cl. IG6: Ilf 4C 108
Marionette Steps SS1: Sth S 7A 138
(off Kursaal Way)
Marion Gro. IG8: Wfd G 2E 106
Marisco Cl. RM16: Grays 2D 156
Mariskals SS13: Pits 1H 133
Maritime Av. CM9: Hey B 8F 214
Marjorams Av. IG10: Lou 1N 91
Mark Av. E4: Lon 5B 90
Market Av. SS12: W'fd 8K 101
Market Cl. CO1: Colc 7M 165
Market End CO6: Cogg 3K 197 (7H 15)
Market Gro. CO9: Gt Yel 3D 206
Market Hill CB10: Saf W 3C 218
CM9: Mal 5C 214 (1H 35)
CO6: Cogg 3K 197
CO9: Hals 4K 207
CO10: Clare 3D 8
CO10: Sud 5J 9
SG8: R'ton 5C 4
Market Ho. CM20: H'low 2C 54
(off Post Office Rd.)
Market Link RM1: Romf 8C 110
Market Pde. E10: Lon 1C 122
(off High Rd.)
Market Pavement SS14: Bas 9B 116
Market Pav. E10: Lon 5A 122
Market Pl. CB10: Saf W 3C 218
(off Market St.)
CM4: Ing 5D 84
CM6: Gt D 2L 203 (7G 13)
CM7: Brain 5H 193
RM1: Romf 9C 110
RM4: Abr 2G 92 (6J 31)
RM18: Til 7C 156
SS1: Sth S 7M 137
Market Rd. CM1: Chelm 9K 59 (1A 34)
N7: Lon 5A 38
SS12: W'fd 9K 101
Market Row CB10: Saf W 4C 218
Market Sq. CM3: S Fer 1L 103
EN9: Wal A 3C 76
SS4: R'fd 5L 121
SS14: Bas 1B 132
Market St. CB10: Saf W 3C 218
CM7: Brain 5H 193
CM17: H'low 8H 51
CO12: Har 1N 209
DA1: Dart 4C 46
Market Wlk. CB10: Saf W 4C 218
(off Market Row)
Markfield Gdns. E4: Lon 6B 90
Mark Hall Cycle Mus. 9G 50 (6J 21)
Mark Hall Gardens 1F 54
Mark Hall Moors CM20: H'low 9G 50
MARK HALL NORTH 9F 50 (6J 21)
MARK HALL SOUTH 2F 54 (6J 21)
Markham Ho. RM10: Dag 5M 125
(off Uvedale Rd.)
Markhams SS17: Stan H 2A 148
Markhams Chase SS15: Lain 8M 115 (3K 41)
Markhams Chase Leisure Cen. 9M 115
Markhouse Rd. E17: Lon 3D 38
Markings Fld. CB10: Saf W 3D 218
Markland Cl. CM2: Gall 7D 72
Markland Dr. CM9: Mal 7A 214
Marklay Dr. CM3: S Fer 1J 103
Mark Rd. CM0: T'ham 2E 36
Mark's Av. CM5: Chip 6K 67
Marks Cl. CM4: Ing 8B 84
CM12: Bill 4G 99
Marks Ct. SS1: Sth S 7A 138
Marks Gdns. CM7: Brain 5L 193
MARKS GATE 5K 109 (2K 39)
Marks Hall Estate 6G 15
Marks Hall La. CM6: Mar R 6F 23
CM22: Hat O 4C 22
Marks Hall Rd. CO6: Cogg 6H 15
(not continuous)
Marks Hill Nature Reserve 2L 131
Marks La. CM3: Ret C 9N 87
Marks Lodge RM7: Romf 9B 110
Marks Rd. RM7: Romf 9A 110
(not continuous)
Marks Rdbt. CM7: Brain, Tye G 5N 193
MARKS TEY 3G 171 (7A 16)
MARKS TEY INTERCHANGE 2K 171 (7A 16)
Marks Tey Rdbt. CO6: M Tey 2J 171
Marks Tey Station (Rail) 2K 171 (7A 16)
Mark St. E15: Lon 9E 122
Mark Wade Cl. E12: Lon 3K 123
Markwells CM22: Else 2K 199
Markwell Wood CM19: H'low 9A 54
Markyate Rd. RM8: Dag 7G 125
Marlands Rd. IG5: Ilf 7L 107
Marlborough Av. CM0: T'ham 3K 225
Marlborough Cl. CO15: Clac S 1G 189
RM14: Upm 3B 128
RM16: Grays 9M 145
SS7: Thund 8D 118
Marlborough Ct. IG9: Buck H 8J 91
Marlborough Dr. IG5: Ilf 7L 107
Marlborough Gdns. RM14: Upm 3A 128
Marlborough Rd. CM2: Chelm 2B 72
CM7: Brain 4J 193
CM15: Pil H 5D 96
E4: Lon 3B 106
E7: Lon 9J 123
E15: Lon 6E 122
E18: 6G 107
N19: Lon 4A 38
RM7: Maw 8M 109
RM8: Dag 6G 124
SS1: Sth S 6B 138
Marlborough Ter. CM2: Chelm 1B 72
Marlborough Wlk. SS5: Hock 1B 120
Marlborough Way CM12: Bill 3J 99
Marle Gdns. EN9: Wal A 2C 76
Marler Ho. DA8: Eri 7D 152
Marlescroft Way IG10: Lou 4A 92
Marlin Cl. SS7: Had 9L 119
Marlow Av. RM19: Purf 2L 153
Marlowe Cl. CM9: Mal 8C 214
CM12: Bill 3K 99
IG6: Ilf 5B 108
Marlowe Gdns. RM3: Romf 5G 111
Marlowe Ho. IG8: Wfd G 4N 107
Marlowe Rd. CO15: Jay 3E 188
E17: Lon 8C 106
Marlowes, The DA1: Cray 9B 152
Marlowe Way CO3: Colc 9G 165
Marlow Gdns. SS2: Sth S 2K 137
Marlpits Rd. CM3: Haz 5K 75
CM9: Wdhm M 5K 75 (2F 35)
Marlyon Rd. IG6: Ilf 2G 109
Marmion App. E4: Lon 1A 106
Marmion Av. E4: Lon 1A 106
Marmion Cl. E4: Lon 1A 106
Marne Rd. CO2: Colc 2M 173
Marney Cl. CM2: Gt Bad 2F 72
Marney Dr. SS14: Bas 1G 132
Marney Way CO13: Frin S 8L 181
Marquis Ct. IG11: Bark 7D 124
Marram Cl. CO3: S'way 9C 164
Marram Ct. RM17: Grays 4A 156
Marriots, The CM17: H'low 7H 51
Mar Rd. RM15: S Ock 4F 144
Marsden Ct. CO3: S'way 2F 172
Marshall Cl. CO5: Fee 1L 211
SS9: Lgh S 3N 135
Marshall Path SE28: Lon 7G 140
Marshall Rd. E10: Lon 5B 122
Marshalls SS4: R'fd 3J 121
Marshalls Cl. SS6: Ray 5M 119
Marshalls Dr. CM7: Brain 7G 192
RM1: Romf 7C 110
Marshall's La. SG12: D End, H Cro, Sac 2C 20
Marshalls Piece CM6: Steb 7C 222
Marshalls Rd. CM7: Brain 7G 193
RM7: Romf 8B 110
Marshall Way E10: Lon 5B 122
Marsham St. SW1: Lon 7A 38
Marsh Cres. CO5: Rhdge 6G 174 (1G 27)
Marsh Farm Country Pk. 3M 103
Marsh Farm La. CO7: Alr 7L 175
CO7: Gt Ben, Thorr 3J 183
Marsh Farm Rd. CM3: S Fer 4K 103 (7F 35)
Marshfoot Rd. RM16: Grays 3B 156
RM17: Grays 3A 156 (1G 47)
Marshgate CM20: H'low 9D 50
Marshgate La. E15: Lon 9B 122 (5D 38)
Marshgate Trad. Est. E15: Lon 9B 122
Marsh Grn. Rd. RM10: Dag 1M 141
Marsh Hill E9: Lon 5D 38
EN9: Naze, Wal A 6E 62 (3E 30)
Marsh La. CM6: Gt Can 3E 22
CM13: Mount 1C 98
CM17: H'low 6K 51
CO12: Har 7H 209
E10: Lon 4A 122
SS17: Fob 8E 132
Marsh Rd. CM0: Bur C 2D 196 (6C 36)
CM0: S'min 2E 222
CM0: T'ham 2K 225 (3E 36)
SS3: Shoe 9J 139
Marsh St. DA1: Dart 7L 153
(not continuous)
Marsh Vw. Ct. SS16: Van 3F 132
Marsh Wall E14: Lon 7D 38
Marsh Way CO7: B'sea 7D 182
RM13: Dag, Rain 3B 142
(not continuous)
Marston Av. RM10: Dag 4M 125
Marston Beck CM2: Chelm 9B 60
Marston Cl. RM10: Dag 5M 125
Marston Ho. RM17: Grays 4K 155
Marston Rd. EN11: Hod 4B 52
IG5: Ilf 5L 107
Martello Cvn. Pk. CO14: Walt 5M 181
Martello Holiday Pk. CO14: Walt 6M 181
Martello Rd. CO14: Walt 6M 181
Martello Tower 6B 188
Walton-on-the-Naze 5M 181
Martello Twr. Est. CO16: P Bay 9D 182
Martello Tower No.1 9D 182 (4K 27)
Martello Tower No. 3 5G 188
Martello Tower No. 2 4H 189
Marten Rd. E17: Lon 6A 106
Martens Av. DA7: Bexh 9A 152
Martens Cl. DA7: Bexh 9A 152
Martens Mdw. CM7: Brain 5M 193
Martham Cl. IG6: Ilf 5A 108
SE28: Lon 7J 141
Martha Rd. E15: Lon 8E 122
Martha Ter. IG7: Chig 2D 108
Martin Cl. CM11: Bill 7K 99
Martindale Av. SS15: Bas 5M 115
Martin Dr. RM13: Rain 4F 142
Martin End CO2: Lay H 9H 173
Martingale SS7: Thund 1H 135
Martingale Cl. CM11: Bill 3M 99
Martingale Dr. CM1: Chelm 4A 60
Martingale Rd. CM11: Bill 3M 99
Martin Gdns. RM8: Dag 6H 125
Martini Dr. EN3: Enf 7A 76
Martin Pl. SE28: Lon 8D 140
(off Martin St.)
Martin Rd. RM8: Dag 6H 125
RM15: Ave 8A 144
Martins Cl. SS17: Stan H 2M 147
Martin's Ct. SS2: Sth S 4M 137
Martinsdale CO15: Clac S 7K 185
Martinsfield Cl. IG7: Chig 1D 108
Martin's La. CM3: Stow M 6M 89
Martins M. SS7: Ben 2C 134
Martin's Rd. CO9: Hals 5K 207
Martinstown Cl. RM11: Horn 1L 127
Martin St. SE28: Lon 8D 140
Martin Wlk. SE28: Lon 8D 140
(off Martin St.)
SS5: Hock 3E 120
Martlesham Cl. RM12: Horn 7G 126
Martley Dr. IG2: Ilf 9A 108
Martock Av. SS0: Wclf S 1F 136
Martyns Gro. SS0: Wclf S 4G 136
Marvens CM2: Gall 7E 72
Marwell Cl. RM1: Romf 9E 110
Maryborough Gro. CO2: Colc 4B 174
Maryland Ct. CO2: Colc 5A 174
Maryland Ind. Est. E15: Lon 7E 122
(off Maryland Rd.)
Maryland Pk. E15: Lon 7E 122
Maryland Point E15: Lon 8E 122
(off Grove, The)
Maryland Rd. E15: Lon 7D 122
Marylands Av. SS5: Hock 9C 104
MARYLANDS INTERCHANGE 2M 97 (6G 33)
Maryland Sq. E15: Lon 7E 122
Maryland Station (Rail) 8E 122 (5E 38)
Maryland St. E15: Lon 7D 122
Mary La. CO10: Pos 1B 8
Mary La. Nth. CO7: Gt Bro 7E 168 (6K 17)
Mary La. Sth. CO7: Gt Bro 8G 168
MARYLEBONE 6A 38
Mary Macarthur Ho. RM10: Dag 5M 125
(off Wythenshawe Rd.)
Mary McArthur Pl. CM24: Stan M 1D 220
Mary Rose Cl. RM16: Chaf H 2F 154
Mary Ruck Way CM77: Bla N 3A 194
Mary Warner Rd. CO7: A'lgh 9L 161
Mascalls Gdns. CM14: Brtwd 1C 112
Mascalls La. CM13: Gt War 1C 112
CM14: Brtwd, Gt War 1C 112 (1D 40)
Mascalls, The CM2: Gt Bad 2F 72
Mascalls Way CM2: Gt Bad 2F 72
Mascot Sq. CO4: Colc 1D 174
Masefield Cl. DA8: Eri 6D 152
RM3: Romf 5F 110
Masefield Ct. CM14: War 1F 112
Masefield Cres. RM3: Romf 5G 110
Masefield Dr. CO3: Colc 9G 165
RM14: Upm 2N 127
Masefield Rd. CM7: Brain 8H 193 (1C 24)
CM9: Mal 8C 214
RM16: Grays 9A 146
Masham Ho. DA18: Eri 9J 141
(off Kale Rd.)
MASHBURY 6H 23
Mashbury Rd. CM1: Chig J 3B 58 (7J 23)
CM1: Good E, Mash, Ples 5H 23
CM1: Gt Walt, Mash 5A 56 (5J 23)
CM3: Gt Walt 5A 56 (5J 23)
Mashey Rd. CO9: Bel P, L Yel 5D 8
Mashiters Hill RM1: Romf 5B 110
Mashiters Wlk. RM1: Romf 7C 110
Mason Cl. CO2: Colc 3J 173
Mason Dr. RM3: H Wood 6J 111
Mason Rd. CO1: Colc 6N 165
CO16: Clac S 1F 188
IG8: Wfd G 1E 106
Mason Way EN9: Wal A 3E 76
Masthead Cl. DA2: Dart 9N 153
Matcham Rd. E11: Lon 5E 122
MATCHING 6B 22
Matching Fld. CM15: Kel H 7C 82
MATCHING GREEN 6C 22
Matching Grn. SS14: Bas 7E 116
Matching La. CM6: Ab R 6D 22
Matching Rd.
CM17: H'low, Mat T 8N 51 (6K 21)
CM22: Hat H 2F 210 (4B 22)
MATCHING TYE 6A 22
Matchroom Stadium 4B 122 (4D 38)
Matfield Cl. CM1: Chelm 4M 59
Mathews Cl. CO9: Hals 3M 207
Mathews Pk. Av. E15: Lon 8F 122
Matlock Gdns. RM12: Horn 5J 127
Matlock Rd. E10: Lon 1C 122
SS8: Can I 2F 150
Matson Ct. IG8: Wfd G 4E 106
Matthew Ct. E17: Lon 7C 106
Matthews Cl. RM3: H Wood 5K 111
Matthews Ct. E17: Lon 5A 106
(off Chingford Rd.)
Matthias Rd. N16: Lon 5B 38
Maud Gdns. IG11: Bark 2E 140
Maudlyn Rd. CO1: Colc 9C 166 (6F 17)
Maud Rd. E10: Lon 5C 122
Maugham Cl. SS12: W'fd 2L 117
Maunder Cl. RM16: Chaf H 2G 155
Maund's Hatch CM18: H'low 7C 54
Maurice Ct. SS8: Can I 3K 151
(off Maurice Rd.)
Maurice Rd. SS8: Can I 3K 151
Maury Rd. N16: Lon 4C 38
Mavis Gro. RM12: Horn 4J 127
MAWNEY 8A 110 (3K 39)
Mawney Cl. RM7: Maw 6N 109
Mawney Rd. RM7: Maw 6N 109 (3K 39)
Maxey Gdns. RM9: Dag 6K 125
Maxey Rd. RM9: Dag 7K 125
Maximfeldt Rd. DA8: Eri 3C 152
Maxim Rd. DA8: Eri 2C 152
Maximus Dr. CO4: Colc 1B 166
Maxwell Ct. IG7: Chig 9G 93
Maya Angelou Ct. E4: Lon 1C 106
Maya Cl. SS3: Shoe 7J 139
Mayall Cl. EN3: Lon 8A 76

May Av. SS8: Can I 1J 151
(not continuous)
Maybank Av. E18: Lon 6H 107
RM12: Horn 7F 126
Maybank Lodge RM12: Horn 7G 127
Maybank Rd. E18: Lon 5H 107
Maybells Commercial Est.
IG11: Bark 2J 141
Mayberry Wlk. CO2: Colc 3A 174
Maybrick Rd. RM11: Horn 1G 126
Maybury Cl. CO6: M Tey 3H 171
IG10: Lou 3A 92
Maybury Rd. IG11: Bark 2E 140
Maybush Rd. RM11: Horn 2J 127
May Ct. RM17: Grays 4A 156
Maycroft Av. RM17: Grays 3N 155
Maycroft Gdns. RM17: Grays 3N 155
Mayda Cl. CO9: Hals 5J 207
Maydells SS13: Pits 1J 133
Maydells Ct. SS13: Pits 1J 133
Maydene CM3: S Fer 1K 103
Mayer Rd. EN9: Enf 6B 76
Mayesbrook Pk. 7F 124
Mayesbrook Pk. Arena 7F 124
Mayesbrook Rd. IG3: Ilf 5F 124
IG11: Bark 1E 140
RM8: Dag 5F 124
Mayesford Rd. RM6: Chad H 2H 125
Mayes La. CM2: S'don 4M 73 (2C 34)
CM3: Dan 4E 74 (2E 34)
CO12: R'sy 6D 208 (3F 19)
Mayes Pl. CM6: Thax 4F 13
Mayes Rd. N22: Lon 2A 38
Mayfair Av. IG1: Ilf 4M 123
RM6: Chad H 1J 125
SS13: Pits 7K 117
Mayfair Ct. CO2: Colc 2C 174
Mayfair Gdns. IG8: Wfd G 4G 107
Mayfair Ind. Area CM3: Latch 7K 211
Mayfield EN9: Wal A 4D 76
Mayfield Av. IG8: Wfd G 3G 106
SS2: Sth S 2K 137
SS5: Hull 6L 103
Mayfield Cen. CM0: Bur C 3C 196
CO15: Clac S 1K 189
Mayfield Cl. CM17: H'low 8L 51
CO4: Colc 6C 166
Mayfield Ct. EN9: Wal A 4G 77
(off Lamplighters Cl.)
Mayfield Gdns. CM14: Brtwd 7E 96
Mayfield Rd. CM1: Writ 1J 71
DA17: Belv 2A 152
E4: Lon 8C 90
RM8: Dag 3H 125 (4J 39)
Mayfields RM16: Grays 9M 145
Mayflower Av. CO12: Har 2N 209
Mayflower Cl. CO3: S'way 9E 164
EN9: Naze 2E 62
RM15: S Ock 4F 144
SS2: Sth S 9G 120
Mayflower Ct. CM5: Chip 6L 67
CM19: H'low 7N 53
SS8: Can I 3J 151
Mayflower Dr. CM9: Mal 8C 214
Mayflower Ho. CM13: Gt War 3F 112
IG11: Bark 1C 140
(off Westbury Rd.)
Mayflower Path CM13: Gt War 3F 112
Mayflower Retail Pk. SS14: Bas 5E 116
Mayflower Rd. CM11: Bill 6K 99
RM16: Chaf H 3F 154
Mayflowers SS7: Thund 8B 118
Mayflower Way CM5: Chip 6L 67
Mayford Way CO16: Clac S 7F 184
Maygreen Cres. RM11: Horn 2E 126
Mayhew Cl. E4: Lon 9A 90
MAYLAND 8L 213 (4B 36)
Mayland Av. SS8: Can I 3F 150
Mayland Cl. CM3: May 9L 213
CM9: H'bri 4E 214
Mayland Grn. CM3: May 8L 213
Mayland Grn. Ind. Est.
CM3: May 8M 213
Mayland Hill CM3: May 4B 36
Mayland Ho. CM8: Wthm 5D 230
Mayland Mans. IG11: Bark 9A 124
(off Whiting Av.)
Mayland Rd. CM8: Wthm 5D 230
Maylands Av. RM12: Horn 6F 126
Maylands Dr. CM77: Gt N 8F 192
MAYLANDSEA 7J 213 (3A 36)
Maylandsea Bay Sailing Club 7J 213
Maylands Way RM3: H Wood 3N 111
Maylins Dr. CM21: Saw 2J 51
Maynard Cl. CM6: Gt D 2L 203
DA8: Eri 5D 152
Maynard Ct. EN9: Wal A 4F 76
Maynard Path E17: Lon 9C 106
Maynard Rd. E17: Lon 9C 106
Maynards RM11: Horn 2J 127
Maynards La. CB10: L Sam 2N 205 (1H 13)
Mayne Crest CM1: Chelm 4N 59
Mayor's Wlk. CO1: Colc 8N 165
Mayplace Av. DA1: Cray 9E 152
Mayplace Rd. E. DA1: Cray 9C 152 (3A 46)
DA7: Bexh 8A 152 (3A 46)
Mayplace Rd. W. DA6: Bexh 3A 46
Maypole Cl. CB11: Saf W 6B 218
Maypole Cres. DA8: Eri 4H 153
IG6: Ilf 4C 108
Maypole Dr. CO16: St O 9M 183
IG7: Chig 9F 92
MAYPOLE GREEN 5K 173 (7E 16)
Maypole Grn. Rd. CO2: Colc 5K 173
Maypole Rd. CM8: Mal, W Bis 2L 229 (6H 25)
CM9: Mal, W Bis 1B 214 (7H 25)
CO5: Tip 5C 226 (3K 25)
Maypole St. CM17: H'low 2H 55
Maypole, The CM6: Thax 7B 224
May Rd. E4: Lon 3A 106
Maysent Av. CM7: Brain 3H 193
May's La. CO7: Ded 5L 161
May St. SG8: Gt Chi 6G 5
Mayswood Gdns. RM10: Dag 8A 126
Maytree Cl. RM13: Rain 2C 142
Maytree Gdns. CM22: Else 1K 199
Maytree Wlk. SS7: Thund 9C 118
Mayville Rd. E11: Lon 4E 122
IG1: Ilf 7A 124
May Wlk. CM2: Chelm 3D 72
CM24: Stan M 3H 199
Maywin Dr. RM11: Horn 3K 127
Mazers Ct. CM7: Brain 6H 193
Maze, The SS9: Lgh S 8C 120
Mead Cl. IG10: Lou 1A 92
RM2: Romf 6E 110
RM16: Grays 9L 145
Mead Ct. CM24: Stan M 2C 220
EN9: Wal A 4B 76
Mead Cres. E4: Lon 1C 106
Meade Cl. CM11: Bill 3M 99
Meade Rd. CM11: Bill 3M 99
Meades, The CM2: Chelm 1B 72
Meadgate SS13: Bas 7K 117
Meadgate Av. CM2: Gt Bad 2E 72
IG8: Wfd G 2L 107
Meadgate Rd. EN9: Brox, Naze 8D 52
EN10: Brox 8C 52
Meadgate Ter. CM2: Gt Bad 2E 72
Mead Gro. RM6: Chad H 7J 109
Mdw. Brook Ct. CO1: Colc 8B 166
Mdw. Brown Ct. CM7: Gt N 7G 193
Meadow Cl. CM7: Pan 1C 192
CO7: Elms 9M 167
CO7: Gt Bro 9F 168
CO9: Hals 6L 207
CO15: Clac S 6M 185
E4: Lon 7B 90
RM3: Romf 9G 95
SS7: Thund 9H 119
SS17: Linf 1J 157
Meadow Ct. CM11: Bill 6L 99
CM18: H'low 7D 54
SS8: Can I 8F 134
SS11: W'fd 8M 101
Meadowcroft CM24: Stan M 2D 220
Meadowcroft Ct. SS17: Horn H 2H 147
(off Gordon Rd.)
Meadowcroft Way CO13: Frin S 7J 181
Meadowcross EN9: Wal A 4E 76
Meadow Dr. SS1: Sth S 6C 138
SS16: Lang H 6K 131
MEADOWEND 9E 216 (5C 8)
Meadowend CO9: Ridg 9F 216 (6C 8)
Meadowford CB11: Newp 2K 215
Meadowford Cl. SE28: Lon 7F 140
Meadow Ga. CM4: Stock 7A 86
Mdw. Grass Cl. CO3: S'way 9C 164
Meadowland Rd. SS11: W'fd 1A 118
Meadowlands RM11: Horn 2J 127
Meadow La. CO5: W Mer 4C 228
SS11: Runw 6M 101
(not continuous)
Meadow M. CM3: S Fer 9H 89
Meadow Ri. CM4: B'more 1H 83
(not continuous)
CM11: Bill 6L 99 (7K 33)
Meadow Rd. CB10: Gt Che 7D 202
CM3: Ret C 3C 102
CM16: Epp 8E 64
CO2: Colc 5L 173
IG10: Lou 4L 91
IG11: Bark 9E 124
RM7: Rush G 3A 126
RM9: Dag 8L 125
RM16: Grays 8M 145
SS5: Hull 6L 103
SS7: Had 4L 135
Meadows Cl. CM13: Ingve 3M 113
E10: Lon 4A 122
Meadowside CM1: Chelm 7K 59
CM2: Chelm 8L 59
CM7: Brain 3G 193
SS6: Ray 5K 119
SS7: Ben 3B 134
Meadowside Rd. RM14: Upm 7N 127
Meadows Shop. Cen., The CM2: Chelm 9L 59
Meadows, The CM2: Chelm 9L 59
(off High St.)
CM13: Ingve 3M 113
CM21: Saw 2M 51
Meadow Vw. CM3: Bick 9E 74
CM16: Epp 8F 64
CO5: Tip 6B 226
SS16: Lang H 2G 131
Meadow Vw. Cl. CO3: S'way 1F 172
Meadow Vw. Wlk. SS8: Can I 1E 150
Meadow Wlk. CM2: Chelm 9L 59
E18: Lon 8G 106
RM9: Dag 8L 125
Meadow Way CM0: Bur C 1C 196
CM3: Latch 7L 211
CM21: Saw 3M 51
CM77: Bla N 3C 194
CO5: Abb, L'hoe 9B 174
CO15: Jay 4E 188 (5C 28)
IG7: Chig 9B 92
RM14: Upm 5N 127
Meadow Way SS5: Hock 2D 120
SS12: W'fd 4L 117
Meadow Way, The CM11: Bill 6L 99
Mead Pk. Ind. Est. CM20: H'low 8E 50
Mead Pastures CM9: Wdhm W 1F 35
Mead Path CM2: Chelm 2A 72
Meads Cl. CM4: Ing 5D 84
Meads Ct. E15: Lon 8F 122
Meadside CM7: Weth 8B 228
Meads La. IG3: Ilf 2D 124
Meads, The CB11: Wick B 2K 11
CM4: Ing 5D 84
CM24: Stan M 3E 220
RM14: Upm 4B 128
SS16: Van 2H 133
Meadsway CM13: Gt War 3E 112
Mead, The CM6: Gt D 1K 203
CM6: Thax 7C 224
CO7: B'sea 5E 182
EN10: Brox 9B 52
SS15: Lain 7K 115
Mead Wlk. CM5: Chip 9K 67
Meadway CM9: Mal 7D 214
CO9: Gosf 8L 201
CO11: Law 5F 162
EN11: Hod 7A 52
IG3: Bark, Ilf 6D 124
Mead Way IG8: Wfd G 2J 107
Meadway RM2: Romf 6E 110
RM17: Grays 2N 155
SS6: Ray 6M 119
SS7: Thund 8C 118
SS8: Can I 3J 151
Meadway Ct. RM8: Dag 4L 125
Meadway, The IG9: Buck H 7K 91
IG10: Lou 5M 91
(not continuous)
SS0: Wclf S 6G 136
Meakins Cl. SS9: Lgh S 8E 120
Meanley Rd. E12: Lon 6L 123
Mearns Pl. CM2: Chelm 7A 60
Meath Rd. IG1: Ilf 5B 124
Mecca Bingo 1K 141
Grays 3K 155
Medcalf Hill SG12: Wid 3G 21
Medebridge Rd. RM16: N Stif, S Ock 7J 145
Mede Way CO7: W'hoe 3J 175
Median Rd. E5: Lon 5C 38
Medick Ct. RM17: Grays 4A 156
Medina Ho. DA8: Eri 5C 152
Medina Rd. RM17: Grays 3N 155
Medlar Cl. CM8: Wthm 3D 230
Medlar Dr. RM15: S Ock 4H 145
Medlar Rd. RM17: Grays 4N 155
Medlars Mead CM22: Hat O 8D 206
Medley Rd. CM77: Rayne 6B 192
Medoc Cl. SS13: Pits 7K 117
Medora Rd. RM7: Romf 8B 110
Medway CM0: Bur C 2C 196
(off Maple Way)
Medway Av. CM8: Wthm 5A 230
Medway Cl. CM1: Chelm 7F 58
IG1: Ilf 7B 124
Medway Cres. SS9: Lgh S 5A 136
Medway Rd. DA1: Cray 8E 152
Meers, The CO13: Walt 8H 181
MEESDEN 2G 11
Meeson Mdws. CM9: Mal 8A 214
Meeson Rd. E15: Lon 9F 122
Meesons La. RM17: Grays 2J 155
Meesons Mead SS4: R'fd 4J 121
Meeting La. CO5: E Mer 4H 27
CO9: Ridg 7D 216
SG8: Lit 4A 4
Megabowl 3N 71
Dagenham 1N 141
Meggison Way SS7: Ben 3C 134
Megs Way CM7: Brain 6K 193
Meister Cl. IG1: Ilf 3C 124
Melba Ct. CM1: Writ 1L 71
Melba Gdns. RM18: Til 5C 156
MELBOURN 3E 4
Melbourne Av. CM1: Chelm 6F 58 (7K 23)
Melbourne Chase CO2: Colc 5B 174
Melbourne Ct. CM1: Chelm 6G 59
Melbourne Gdns. RM6: Chad H 9K 109
Melbourne Pde. CM1: Chelm 6G 59
Melbourne Pk. Athletics Cen. 5G 59
Melbourne Rd. CO15: Clac S 9H 185
E10: Lon 2B 122
IG1: Ilf 3A 124
RM18: Til 6A 156
Melbourn Rd. SG8: R'ton 5C 4
Melbourn St. SG8: R'ton 5C 4
Melcombe Rd. SS7: Ben 3C 134
MELDRETH 2D 4
Meldreth Rd. SG8: Meld 2E 4
SG8: Whad 2C 4
Meldreth Station (Rail) 3D 4
Meldrum Rd. IG3: Ilf 4F 124
Melford Av. IG11: Bark 8D 124
Melford Gro. CM77: Gt N 1B 204
Melford Hall 2J 9
Melford Pl. CM15: Brtwd 7F 96
Melford Rd. CO10: Act 2K 9
CO10: Caven 2F 9
CO10: Sud 4J 9
E11: Lon 4E 122
IG1: Ilf 4C 124
Melksham Cl. RM3: Romf 4K 111
Melksham Dr. RM3: Romf 4K 111
Melksham Gdns. RM3: Romf 4J 111
Melksham Grn. RM3: Romf 4K 111
Melliker La. DA3: Meop 7G 47
Mellish Cl. IG11: Bark 1E 140
Mellish Flats E10: Lon 2A 122
Mellish Gdns. IG8: Wfd G 2G 107
Mellish Way RM11: Horn 9G 111
Mellor Chase CO3: S'way 8F 164
Mellor Cl. CM4: Ing 5D 84
Mellow Mead SS15: Lain 7K 115
Mellow Purgess SS15: Lain 9L 115
Mellow Purgess Cl. SS15: Lain 9L 115
Mellow Purgess End SS15: Lain 9L 115
Mellows Rd. IG5: Ilf 7M 107
Mell Rd. CM9: Tol 8L 225 (6D 26)
Melon Rd. E11: Lon 5E 122
Melrose Gdns. CO15: Clac S 8N 185
Melrose Rd. CO5: W Mer 3C 228
Melstock Av. RM14: Upm 6N 127
Melton Cl. CO16: Clac S 9E 184
Melton Gdns. RM1: Romf 2D 126
Melton St. NW1: Lon 6A 38
Melville Ct. RM3: Romf 4J 111
Melville Dr. SS12: W'fd 3L 117
Melville Gdns. N13: Lon 2A 38
Melville Heath CM3: S Fer 2L 103
Melville Rd. RM5: Col R 4N 109
RM13: Rain 4E 142
Memorial Av. E12: Lon 4L 123
Memory Cl. CM9: Mal 9C 214
Mendip Cl. SS6: Ray 4L 119
SS11: W'fd 9M 101
Mendip Cres. SS0: Wclf S 1F 136
Mendip Rd. CM1: Chelm 5F 58
DA7: Eri 6C 152
IG2: Ilf 9D 108
RM11: Horn 2E 126
SS0: Wclf S 2F 136
Mendlesham Cl. CO16: Clac S 9F 184
Mendoza Cl. RM11: Horn 9J 111
Menin Rd. CO2: Colc 2L 173
Menish Way CM2: Chelm 8B 60
Menthone Pl. RM11: Horn 2H 127
Mentley La. SG11: Nasty, Old G 7C 10
Mentley La. W. SG11: Nasty, Old G 7D 10
Mentmore SS16: Lang H 2K 131
Menzies Av. SS15: Lain 9H 115
Meon Cl. CM1: Chelm 5L 59
MEOPHAM 7G 47
Meopham Ct. CO2: Colc 2B 174
(off Stalin Rd.)
MEOPHAM GREEN 7H 47
MEOPHAM STATION 7H 47
Meopham Station (Rail) 7G 47
Meopham Windmill 7G 47
Meppel Av. SS8: Can I 8G 135
Merbury Rd. SE28: Lon 9D 140 (7H 39)
Mercer Av. SS3: Gt W 2L 139
Mercer Rd. CM11: Bill 3M 99
Mercers CM19: H'low 6N 53
Mercers Row CB10: Saf W 3C 218
(off King St.)
Mercers Way CO1: Colc 7M 165
Merchants Lodge E17: Lon 8A 106
(off Westbury Rd.)
Merchant St. CM3: S Fer 1L 103
Mercia Cl. CM2: Gt Bad 5H 73
Mercury Cl. CO2: Colc 3H 173
SS11: W'fd 8N 101
Mercury Ct. RM1: Romf 9D 110
Mercury Gdns. RM1: Romf 8C 110 (3A 40)
Mercury Pl. CM9: Mal 3B 214
Mercury Theatre 8M 165
Merdle Sq. CM1: Chelm 5H 59
Meredene SS14: Bas 1G 133
Meredith Rd. CO15: Clac S 1J 189
RM16: Grays 2C 156
Merediths Cl. CO7: W'hoe 6H 175
Merefield CM21: Saw 3K 51
Meres Cl. CM8: Wthm 6C 230
Merewood Rd. DA7: Bexh 7A 152
Meriadoc Dr. CM3: S Fer 2K 103
Meriden Cl. IG6: Ilf 5B 108
Meriden Ct. CO15: Clac S 7L 185
MERIDIAN PARK 6C 76
Meridian Sq. E15: Lon 9D 122
Meridian Way N9: Lon 1C 38
N18: Lon 1C 38
Merilies Cl. SS0: Wclf S 3G 136
Merilies Gdns. SS0: Wclf S 3G 136
Merino Cl. E11: Lon 8J 107
Merivale Cl. CO11: Law 5G 163
Merivale Rd. CO11: Law 5G 163
Merks Hill CM6: Gt D 1N 203
Merlin Cl. EN9: Wal A 4G 76
IG6: Ilf 2H 109
RM5: Col R 3B 110
RM16: Chaf H 1H 155
Merlin Ct. SS8: Can I 1H 151
Merlin End CO4: Colc 6F 166
Merlin Gdns. RM5: Col R 3B 110
Merlin Gro. IG6: Ilf 4A 108
Merlin Pl. CM1: Chelm 6H 59
Merlin Rd. E12: Lon 4K 123
RM5: Col R 3B 110
Merlin Way
CM16: N Wea, Thorn 5M 65 (2K 31)
SS11: W'fd 7L 101
Mermagen Dr. RM13: Rain 9F 126
Mermaid Way CM9: Mal 8D 214
Merriam Cl. E4: Lon 2C 106
Merricks La. SS16: Van 4F 132
Merrielands Cres. RM9: Dag 2L 141 (6K 39)
Merrielands Retail Pk. RM9: Dag 1L 141
Merrilees Cres. CO15: Hol S 7A 186
Merritt Ho. RM1: Romf 2D 126
(off Frazer Cl.)

Merrivale N14: Lon. . . . 7A 30
SS7: Ben . . . 4C 134
Merrivale Av. IG4: Ilf . . . 8K 107
Merriwigs La. SS16: Pits . . . 4F 132
Merrydown SS15: Lain . . . 8J 115
Merryfield SS9: Lgh S . . . 2D 136
Merryfield App. SS9: Lgh S . . . 3D 136
Merryfields Av. SS5: Hock . . . 9C 104
Merryhill Cl. E4: Lon . . . 6B 90
Merrylands SS15: Lain . . . 8J 115
Merrylands Chase CM13: Dun . . . 8F 114
Merrymeade Chase CM15: Brtwd . . . 7G 97
Merrymount Gdns. CO15: Clac S . . . 8M 185
Mersea Av. CO5: W Mer . . . 3B 228
Mersea Ct. CO5: W Mer . . . 2B 228
Mersea Cres. SS12: W'fd . . . 1N 117 (1C 42)
Mersea Fleet Way CM7: Brain . . . 7L 193
Mersea Ho. IG11: Bark . . . 8A 124
Mersea Island Mus. . . . 3B 228 (5F 27)
Mersea Rd.
CO2: Abb, B'hth, Colc, Fing . . . 6B 174 (1F 27)
CO2: Colc . . . 9N 165 (6E 16)
CO5: Abb, Fing, L'hoe . . . 8B 174 (1F 27)
CO5: Pel . . . 3E 26
Mersey Av. RM14: Upm . . . 1A 128
Mersey Rd. CM8: Wthm . . . 5B 230
Mersey Way CM1: Chelm . . . 6E 58
Merstham Dr. CO16: Clac S . . . 7G 184
Merten Rd. RM6: Chad H . . . 2K 125
Merton Ct. CO2: Colc . . . 7A 174
IG1: Ilf . . . 1L 123
Merton Pl. CB11: L'bry . . . 1A 218 (5A 6)
CM3: S Fer . . . 2M 103
RM16: Grays . . . 2C 156
Merton Rd. E17: Lon . . . 9C 106
IG3: Ilf . . . 2E 124
IG11: Bark . . . 9E 124
SS5: Hock . . . 8N 103
SS7: Ben . . . 2C 134
Messant Cl. RM3: H Wood . . . 6H 111
Messines Rd. CO2: Colc . . . 2L 173
MESSING . . . 1D 226 (2A 26)
Messing Grn. CO5: Mess . . . 1D 226
Messing Rd. CO5: Tip . . . 4C 226 (3K 25)
Mess Rd. SS3: Shoe . . . 9K 139
Meteor Rd. SS0: Wclf S . . . 6J 137
Meteor Way CM1: Chelm . . . 9H 59
Metford Cres. EN3: Enf . . . 8A 76
Methersgate SS14: Bas . . . 8D 116
Metsons La. CM1: Hghwd . . . 8N 69
(not continuous)
Metz Av. SS8: Can I . . . 1G 151
Mews Ct. CM2: Chelm . . . 1C 72
Mews Pl. IG8: Wfd G . . . 1G 107
Mews, The CM18: H'low . . . 7D 54
CM21: Saw . . . 1K 51
CM24: Stan M . . . 2E 220
CO12: Har . . . 4L 209
CO13: Frin S . . . 1J 187
(Old Rd.)
CO13: Frin S . . . 9K 181
(Pole Barn La.)
IG4: Ilf . . . 9K 107
RM1: Romf . . . 8C 110
RM17: Grays . . . 2M 155
SS5: Hock . . . 1B 120
Meyel Av. SS8: Can I . . . 9J 135
Meyer Rd. DA8: Eri . . . 4B 152
Meynell Av. SS8: Can I . . . 3J 151
Meynell Rd. RM3: Romf . . . 4F 110
Meyrick Cres. CO2: Colc . . . 1N 173
Mey Wlk. SS5: Hock . . . 1B 120
Micawber Way CM1: Chelm . . . 4F 58
Michael Gdns. RM11: Horn . . . 8H 111
Michael Rd. E11: Lon . . . 3F 122
Michael's Cotts. SS3: Shoe . . . 8H 139
Michaels La. DA3: Fawk . . . 7E 46
Michaels Rd. CM23: Bis S . . . 7A 220 (7K 11)
Michaelstowe Cl. CO12: Har . . . 5E 208
Michaelstowe Dr. CO12: Har . . . 5E 208
Michen Rd. CM20: H'low . . . 1E 54
Michigan Av. E12: Lon . . . 6M 123
Midas Bus. Cen. RM10: Dag . . . 6N 125
Mid Colne SS16: Van . . . 2E 132
Middleborough CO1: Colc . . . 7M 165 (6E 16)
(not continuous)
Middle Boy RM4: Abr . . . 2H 93
Middle Cloister CM11: Bill . . . 6K 99
Middle Crockerford SS16: Van . . . 2F 132
Middle Dr. SS17: Fob . . . 5C 132
Middlefield CO9: Hals . . . 5L 207
Middlefield Av. EN11: Rye P . . . 3A 52
Middlefield Cl. EN11: Rye P . . . 3A 52
Middlefield Gdns. IG2: Ilf . . . 1A 124
Middlefield Rd. CO11: Mist . . . 5M 163
EN11: Rye P . . . 3A 52 (7D 20)
Middle Grn. CM15: Dodd . . . 7F 82
CO6: Wak C . . . 3K 15
Middle King CM7: Brain . . . 7M 193
Middle La. N8: Lon . . . 3A 38
Middlemead CM2: S Han, W Han . . . 5G 87 (5B 34)
CM3: Ret C, S Han, W Han . . . 5G 87 (5B 34)
Middle Mead SS4: R'fd . . . 5L 121
SS11: W'fd . . . 8N 101
Middlemead Cl. CM2: W Han . . . 5G 87
Middlemill Rd. CO1: Colc . . . 7N 165
Middlemoor Rd. CB2: Whitt . . . 1J 5
Middle Rd. CM13: Ingve . . . 2M 113
Middlesborough Ho. *RM3: Romf . . . 4J 111*
(off Kingsbridge Cir.)
Middlesburg Rd. SS8: Can I . . . 9E 134
Middlesex Av. SS9: Lgh S, Wclf S . . . 3E 136
Middleside Cvn. Pk. *CM24: Stan M . . . 5F 220*
(off Old Burylodge La.)
Middle St. CB11: Clav . . . 3J 11
EN9: Naze . . . 1E 62 (1E 30)
SG8: Thri . . . 2G 5
MIDDLETON . . . 6J 9
Middleton Av. E4: Lon . . . 9A 90
Middleton Cl. CO16: Clac S . . . 7H 185
Middleton Gdns. IG2: Ilf . . . 1A 124
Middleton Hall La.
CM15: Shenf . . . 8H 97 (1E 40)
Middleton Rd. CM15: Shenf . . . 7H 97
CO10: Mdltn, Sud . . . 5J 9
Middleton Row CM3: S Fer . . . 2L 103
Middlewick Cl. CO2: Colc . . . 5A 174
Midfield Av. DA7: Bexh . . . 8A 152
Midfield Pde. DA7: Bexh . . . 8A 152
Midguard Way CM9: Mal . . . 8B 214
Midhurst Av. SS0: Wclf S . . . 2J 137
Midhurst Cl. RM12: Horn . . . 6E 126
Midland Cl. CO2: Colc . . . 2N 173
Midland Rd. E10: Lon . . . 2C 122
NW1: Lon . . . 6A 38
Midsummer Mdw. SS3: Shoe . . . 5J 139
Midway CO15: Jay . . . 6B 188
Midway Rd. CO2: Colc . . . 4K 173
Mighell Av. IG4: Ilf . . . 9K 107
Milbanke Cl. SS3: Shoe . . . 5J 139
Milbourn Ct. SS4: R'fd . . . 5L 121
Milburn Cres. CM1: Chelm . . . 1M 71
MILCH HILL . . . 1B 24
Mildenhall Ho. *RM3: Romf . . . 2L 111*
(off Redcar Rd.)
Mildmay Cl. CM6: Fels . . . 8E 212
Mildmayes SS16: Lang H . . . 2L 131
Mildmay Gro. N1: Lon . . . 5B 38
Mildmay Ind. Est. CM0: Bur C . . . 3D 196
Mildmay Pk. N1: Lon . . . 5B 38
Mildmay Rd. CM0: Bur C . . . 3E 196
CM2: Chelm . . . 2C 72
IG1: Ilf . . . 5A 124
RM7: Romf . . . 9A 110
Mildmays CM3: Dan . . . 2C 74
Mildred Rd. DA8: Eri . . . 3C 152
Mile Cl. EN9: Wal A . . . 3C 76
MILE END . . . 3M 165 (5E 16)
Stepney . . . 6D 38
Mile End Rd. CO4: Colc . . . 3L 165 (5E 16)
E1: Lon . . . 7C 38
E3: Lon . . . 7C 38
Mile End Station (Tube) . . . 6D 38
Milehams Ind. Est. RM19: Purf . . . 1L 153
Miles Cl. CM19: H'low . . . 4A 54
CO3: S'way . . . 9D 164
Miles Dr. SE28: Lon . . . 8D 140
Miles Gray Rd. SS14: Bas . . . 6N 115 (2K 41)
Milestone Rd. CM17: H'low . . . 1H 55
Milford Cl. CO7: W'hoe . . . 5J 175
Milford Rd. RM16: Grays . . . 8N 145
Military Rd. CO1: Colc . . . 9A 166 (6F 17)
Military Way CO12: Har . . . 5E 208
Milk St. E16: Lon . . . 8A 140
Milkwell Gdns. IG8: Wfd G . . . 4H 107
Millais Av. E12: Lon . . . 7N 123
Millais Pl. RM18: Til . . . 5C 156
Millais Rd. E11: Lon . . . 6C 122
Millard Ter. RM10: Dag . . . 8M 125
Millars Cl. CM3: S Fer . . . 9L 89
Millar, The CM1: Broom . . . 9J 57
Millbank CM2: Chelm . . . 7C 60
Millbank Av. CM5: Chip . . . 8K 67
Mill Bri. CO9: Hals . . . 5K 207
SG14: Hart . . . 5B 20
Millbridge Rd. CM8: Wthm . . . 5C 230
Millbrook Gdns. RM2: Romf . . . 6C 110
RM6: Chad H . . . 1L 125
Mill C'way. SG8: Chris . . . 5H 5
Mill Chase CB9: Stpl B . . . 4L 223
CO9: Hals . . . 4K 207
Mill Cl. CM0: T'ham . . . 2K 225
CM1: Rox . . . 3M 217
CM7: Gt Bar . . . 2C 202
CM22: Else . . . 3K 199
CO5: Tip . . . 5C 226
CO12: Har . . . 3L 209
Mill Cotts. SS11: Raw . . . 6D 102
SS17: Fob . . . 8E 132
Mill Ct. CM6: Gt D . . . 3L 203
CM6: L Can . . . 1E 22
CM7: Brain . . . 6K 193
E10: Lon . . . 5C 122
SE28: Lon . . . 7G 141
(off Titmuss Av.)
MILL END . . . 6N 221 (7C 12)
Bradwell on Sea . . . 2E 36
Cumberlow Green . . . 3A 10
Great Dunmow . . . 7F 13
Sandon . . . 2B 10
Takeley . . . 7C 12
Mill End CB11: Clav . . . 2J 11
CM0: Brad S . . . 2E 36
CM6: Thax . . . 8C 224 (3F 13)
MILL END GREEN . . . 5F 13
Millennium Cen., The . . . 6B 126
Millennium Dome . . . 7E 38
Millennium Gardens . . . 5C 214
Millennium Wlk. *CM14: Brtwd . . . 8G 96*
(off High St.)
Millennium Way
CM7: Brain, Tye G . . . 7L 193 (7D 14)
SE10: Lon . . . 7E 38
Miller Av. EN3: Enf . . . 8A 76
Miller's Barn Rd. CO15: Jay . . . 3E 188
Miller's Cl. CM6: Barns . . . 3L 191
Millers Cl. CM7: Brain . . . 9J 191
CO3: S'way . . . 9D 164
Millers Cl. CO6: Gt Hork . . . 9J 159
IG7: Chig . . . 8G 93
Millers Cft. CM2: Gt Bad . . . 4G 73
CM6: Gt D . . . 2M 203
Millersdale CM19: H'low . . . 7A 54
Millers Dr. CM77: Gt N . . . 1C 204
Millers Gdns. CO5: K'dn . . . 3J 211
MILLER'S GREEN . . . 1E 32
Miller's Grn. Rd. CM5: Will . . . 1E 32
Millers La. CO3: S'way . . . 9E 164
Miller's La. IG7: Chig . . . 7G 92 (7J 31)
Millers Mead CO5: Fee . . . 1M 211
Millers M. CM4: Ing . . . 5E 84
Millers Reach CO11: Mist . . . 4L 163
Millers Row CM7: Corn H . . . 7K 7
Millfield CM0: Bur C . . . 4D 196
CM5: H Ong . . . 7N 67
Mill Fld. CM6: Barns . . . 3L 191
CM17: H'low . . . 8H 51
Millfield Cl. SS6: Ray . . . 4L 119
Millfield La. SG11: L Had . . . 1H 21
Millfields CM0: Bur C . . . 4D 196
CM1: Writ . . . 1J 71
CM3: Dan . . . 4G 75
CM21: Saw . . . 1K 51
CM24: Stan M . . . 3D 220
CO2: Lay H . . . 9K 173
CO5: Tip . . . 5C 226
Millfields Cvn. Site
CM0: Bur C . . . 4C 196
Millfields Rd. E5: Lon . . . 5C 38
Millfields Way CB9: H'hll . . . 3J 7
Mill Grange CM0: Bur C . . . 1D 196
MILL GREEN . . . 2B 84 (4H 33)
Haverhill . . . 3G 7
Mill Grn. CB1: H'hth . . . 2F 7
CM0: Bur C . . . 4D 196
SS13: Pits . . . 9H 117
Mill Grn. Ct. SS13: Pits . . . 8J 117
Mill Grn. Pl. SS13: Pits . . . 8J 117
Mill Grn. Rd. CM4: Fry, Mill G . . . 2B 84 (4G 33)
Mill Gro. CM5: H Ong . . . 6A 68
Mill Hatch CM20: H'low . . . 8F 50
Millhaven Cl. RM6: Chad H . . . 1G 125
Millhead Way SS4: R'fd . . . 6N 121
Mill Hill CB11: Clav . . . 2J 11
CM2: Gall . . . 8A 72 (3K 33)
CM3: Pur . . . 9J 215 (3G 35)
CM7: Brain . . . 6K 193 (7D 14)
(not continuous)
CM15: Shenf . . . 6H 97
CM23: Bis S, Farnh . . . 6J 11
CM24: Stan M . . . 3D 220
CO6: Wmgfd . . . 6L 229 (2B 16)
CO10: Sud . . . 5J 9
CO11: Law . . . 4C 162 (3J 17)
(Long Rd. E.)
CO11: Law, Mist . . . 4H 163 (3A 18)
(Colchester Rd.)
SS7: Ben . . . 6E 134
Mill Hill Dr. CM12: Bill . . . 3K 99
Mill Hill La. DA12: Shorne . . . 5K 47
Millhoo Ct. EN9: Wal A . . . 4F 76
Mill Ho. IG8: Wfd G . . . 2F 106
Millhurst M. CM17: H'low . . . 8K 51
Milligans Chase CM2: Gall . . . 9C 72
Milliners Ct. IG10: Lou . . . 1N 91
Mill La. CB1: Lin . . . 2D 6
CB2: Saws . . . 1J 5
CB9: Ked, L Wra . . . 2K 7
CB10: I'tn . . . 6B 202
CB10: Saf W . . . 3D 218
CB11: Clav . . . 2J 11
CB11: L'bry . . . 2B 218 (6A 6)
CM1: Broom, Chelm . . . 2K 59 (6A 24)
(not continuous)
CM3: Dan . . . 3F 74 (2E 34)
CM3: Gt L . . . 7M 203 (3B 24)
CM3: Har E . . . 3K 23
CM3: L Bad . . . 8M 61 (1E 34)
CM3: Pur . . . 8J 215
CM3: Terl . . . 4D 24
CM4: Mill G . . . 3C 84 (4H 33)
CM4: Stock . . . 7A 86 (5K 33)
CM5: Chip, H Ong . . . 9N 67 (3D 32)
CM5: M'ton . . . 7B 22
CM5: Toot . . . 8C 66 (3A 32)
CM6: Gt D . . . 3L 203
CM6: Steb . . . 8C 222
CM7: F'fld . . . 1K 13
CM8: Wthm . . . 6C 230 (4F 25)
CM9: Mal . . . 5B 214
CM9: Tol M . . . 6A 26
CM9: Vir . . . 5C 26
CM11: Rams H . . . 2C 100
(not continuous)
CM15: Hook E . . . 5G 82 (5E 32)
CM15: Kel H . . . 7B 82
CM17: H'low . . . 8K 51
CM21: Saw . . . 1L 51
CM22: Hat H . . . 1D 210
(not continuous)
CM22: L Hall . . . 4K 213
CM77: Rayne . . . 8A 192 (1A 24)
CM77: Tye G . . . 9M 193 (1D 24)
CO2: B'ch . . . 8C 172
CO2: Lay H . . . 9J 173
CO5: Fee . . . 5A 170 (7J 15)
CO6: Coln E . . . 3E 198 (3H 15)
CO7: A'lgh, Gt Bro . . . 3A 168 (5J 17)
CO7: Ded . . . 1M 161 (2H 17)
CO9: Gt Map . . . 2F 15
CO9: L Yel . . . 1D 206
CO10: Caven . . . 3E 8
Mill La. CO11: Brad . . . 3B 18
CO11: Law, Mist . . . 4J 163
CO12: Har . . . 3M 209
CO13: Gt Hol . . . 2B 186
CO14: Walt . . . 5M 181
CO16: T Sok . . . 5K 179
CO16: Wee, Wee H . . . 8D 178 (1C 28)
E4: Lon . . . 2B 90
EN10: Brox . . . 1D 30
IG8: Wfd G . . . 2F 106
IP11: Felix . . . 1K 19
RM4: Nave . . . 8F 80 (6B 32)
RM6: Chad H . . . 1K 125 (3J 39)
RM16: Chaf H . . . 2G 154
(not continuous)
RM16: Ors . . . 5C 146
SG8: Arr, Croy, Shin W . . . 1A 4
SG8: Ther . . . 7B 4
SG9: Mee . . . 2G 11
SG14: Wat S . . . 2A 20
SS4: R'fd . . . 6N 121 (2K 43)
SS17: Fob . . . 8D 132
SS17: Horn H . . . 1H 147
Mill La. Cl. CO16: Wee H . . . 8E 178
Mill La. Nth. SS17: Fob . . . 6C 132
MILL MEADS . . . 6E 38
Mill Pk. Av. RM12: Horn . . . 4J 127
Mill Pk. Dr. CM7: Brain . . . 7K 193
Mill Pl. DA1: Cray . . . 9E 152
Mill Pond Rd. DA1: Dart . . . 3C 46
Mill Rd. CB9: Hel B . . . 5H 7
CB9: Ked . . . 2A 8
CB10: Wim . . . 1E 12
CB11: Deb . . . 2C 12
CB11: Wen A . . . 7L 227
CM0: Bur C . . . 1D 196 (6C 36)
CM0: T'ham . . . 2K 225
CM1: Good E . . . 5G 23
CM3: May . . . 7M 213
CM4: Stock . . . 7N 85 (5K 33)
CM6: N End . . . 9H 199 (2J 23)
CM7: F'fld . . . 4D 200 (2K 13)
CM7: Gt Bar . . . 2C 202 (3J 13)
CM9: Gt Tot . . . 7J 205 (5J 25)
CM9: Mal . . . 6D 214 (1H 35)
CM11: Bill . . . 1M 115 (1K 41)
CM22: Else, Hen . . . 1M 199 (5C 12)
CO4: Boxt . . . 4N 159 (3E 16)
CO4: Colc . . . 3M 165 (5E 16)
CO5: W Mer . . . 2C 228 (5F 27)
CO6: For . . . 2A 164 (5B 16)
CO6: M Tey . . . 2L 171
CO7: E Ber . . . 1K 17
CO9: Bay E . . . 4B 8
CO9: Ridg . . . 8D 216 (5B 8)
CO9: Stamb . . . 6A 8
CO10: Fox . . . 3G 9
CO10: Pos . . . 1B 8
DA8: Eri . . . 5A 152
IG1: Ilf . . . 5N 123
RM15: Ave . . . 7N 143 (7D 40)
RM19: Purf . . . 4M 153
SG8: Fow, Shepr . . . 2F 5
SG8: R'ton . . . 5C 4
Mill Row CM6: Thax . . . 8B 224
Mills Ho. E17: Lon . . . 7D 106
Mill Side CM24: Stan M . . . 3C 220
Millside Ind. Est. DA1: Dart . . . 9H 153
Mills La. CO10: L Mel . . . 4J 9
Millsmead Way IG10: Lou . . . 1M 91
Millson Bank CM2: Chelm . . . 7B 60
Mill St. CM17: H'low . . . 5K 55 (7K 21)
CO1: Colc . . . 9A 166
CO6: Nay . . . 1D 16
CO7: B'sea . . . 7F 182 (3K 27)
CO16: St O . . . 9L 183 (4A 28)
Mills Way CM13: Hut . . . 7M 97
Mill Ter. RM20: Chaf H, Grays . . . 3G 154
Mill Va. Lodge *CM8: Wthm . . . 5C 230*
(off Guithavon St.)
Mill Vw. CB10: Gt Che . . . 8C 202
Mill Vw. Ct. SS4: R'fd . . . 6L 121
Millview Mdws. SS4: R'fd . . . 6L 121
Mill Vue Rd. CM2: Chelm . . . 9A 60
Mill Wlk. CO5: Tip . . . 5C 226
MILLWALL . . . 7D 38
Millways CM9: Gt Tot . . . 3N 229
Millwell Cres. IG7: Chig . . . 2C 108
Millwrights CO5: Tip . . . 5C 226
Milne Ct. E18: Lon . . . 5G 106
Milner Pl. CM12: Bill . . . 3H 99
Milner Rd. CO10: Sud . . . 5K 9
RM8: Dag . . . 4H 125
MILTON . . . 3H 47
Milton Av. CM7: Brain . . . 8J 193
E6: Lon . . . 9K 123
RM12: Horn . . . 4D 126
SS0: Wclf S . . . 7K 137
SS16: Lang H . . . 2H 131
Milton Cl. CO3: Colc . . . 9G 165
SS2: Sth S . . . 5M 137
SS6: Ray . . . 5N 119
(not continuous)
Milton Ct. E17: Lon . . . 8A 106
EN9: Wal A . . . 4C 76
RM6: Chad H . . . 2H 125
SS0: Wclf S . . . 7K 137
Milton Cres. CM5: Chip . . . 5K 67
IG2: Ilf . . . 2A 124
Milton Gdns. RM18: Til . . . 6D 156
Milton Hall Cl. SS3: Gt W . . . 3L 139
Milton Ho. E17: Lon . . . 8A 106
Milton Pl. CM1: Chelm . . . 6H 59
SS1: Sth S . . . 7L 137

Milton Rd. CM8: Wthm 2C 230
CM9: Mal 8C 214
CM14: War 1F 112
CO11: Law 6G 162
CO12: Har 3M 209
DA10: Swans 3F 47
DA12: Grav 3H 47
E17: Lon 8A 106
RM1: Romf 1E 126
RM17: Grays 2L 155
SS0: Wclf S 7K 137 (5J 43)
SS17: Corr, Stan H 8A 132
Milton St. DA10: Swans 3E 46
EN9: Wal A 4C 76
SS2: Sth S 5M 137
Miltsin Av. SS8: Can I 9J 135
Milverton Gdns. IG3: Ilf 4E 124
Milwards CM19: H'low 7A 54
Mimosa Cl. CM1: Chelm 5A 60
CM15: Pil H 4E 96
RM3: Romf 4G 111
SS16: Lang H 2H 131
Mimosa Ct. CO4: Colc 7E 166
Minehead Ho. *RM3: Romf* *2J 111*
(off Dagnam Pk. Dr.)
Minerva Cl. CO12: Har 6H 209
Minerva End CO2: Colc 5K 173
Minerva Rd. E4: Lon 4B 106
MINNOW END 5J 57 (5K 23)
Minories EC3: Lon 7B 38
Minories Art Gallery, The 8A 166
Minsmere Dr. CO16: Clac S 7G 184
Minster Cl. SS6: Ray 6N 119
Minster Ct. RM11: Horn 4L 127
Minster Rd. SS15: Lain 9L 115
Minster Way CM9: Mal 8A 214
RM11: Horn 3K 127
Minton Hgts. SS4: R'fd 1H 121
Minton La. CM17: H'low 3H 55
Miramar Av. SS8: Can I 2E 150
Miramar Way RM12: Horn 7H 127
Miranda Wlk. CO4: Colc 8E 166
Mirosa Dr. CM9: Mal 7D 214
Mirosa Reach CM9: Mal 8C 214
Mirravale Trad. Est. RM8: Dag 2K 125
Mirror Steps *SS1: Sth S* *7A 138*
(off Kursaal Way)
MISTLEY 4L 163 (3A 18)
Mistley End SS16: Van 1D 132
MISTLEY HEATH 6N 163 (3B 18)
Mistley Path SS16: Van 1D 132
(not continuous)
Mistley Place Pk. Environmental & Animal Rescue Cen. 4K 163
Mistley Rd. CM20: H'low 1F 54
Mistley Side SS16: Van 1D 132
(not continuous)
Mistley Station (Rail) 4L 163 (3A 18)
Mistley Towers 3L 163 (2A 18)
Mitcham Rd. IG3: Ilf 2E 124
Mitchell Av. CO9: Hals 6K 207
Mitchell Circ. CM7: Weth 2A 14
Mitchell Cl. DA17: Belv 1A 152
RM13: Rain 2G 143
Mitchells Av. SS8: Can I 1K 151 (6F 43)
Mitchells Wlk. SS8: Can I 1K 151
Mitchell Way CM3: S Fer 9K 89
Mitre Av. E17: Lon 7A 106
Mitton Va. CM2: Chelm 9A 60
Moat Cl. CM11: Rams H 5D 100
CM15: Dodd 6F 82
Moat Edge Gdns. CM12: Bill 4J 99
Moat End SS1: Sth S 5F 138
Moat Farm CO9: Bird 5A 8
Moat Farm Chase CM8: Wthm 4C 230
Moat Fld. SS14: Bas 7D 116
Moatfields CO6: For 1A 164
Moat La. CO8: Alph 1J 15
DA8: Eri 6E 152
Moat Ri. SS6: Ray 6K 119
Moat Rd. CM7: Tye G 5F 15
CO6: For 1A 164 (4B 16)
CO9: Bird 5A 8
Moat St. CO9: Gest 7F 9
Moat, The CM5: Toot 8D 66
MOBY DICK 8K 109 (3K 39)
Modlen Rd. CO14: Walt 7K 181
Mohmmad Khan Rd. E11: Lon 3F 122
Mole Hall Wildlife Pk. 3C 12
MOLEHILL GREEN 6D 12
Broxted 6D 12
Felsted 2A 24
Mole Hill Grn. Rd. CM6: Fels 1A 24
Molesworth EN11: Hod 1A 52
Molineaux Ct. CM12: Bill 5J 99
Mollands SS16: Van 2G 132
Mollands Ct. RM15: S Ock 4H 145
Mollands La. RM15: S Ock 4F 144
Mollison Av.
EN3: Enf, Wal A, Wal X 7A 76 (5D 30)
Mollys Dr. SS16: Lang H 3J 131
Molrams La. CM2: Gt Bad 4J 73 (2B 34)
Momples Rd. CM20: H'low 3F 54 (7J 21)
Monach Cl. RM13: Rain 2E 142
Monarch Cl. RM18: Til 7D 156
Monarch M. E17: Lon 1B 122
Monarch Pl. IG9: Buck H 8J 91
Monarchs Way EN8: Wal X 4D 30
Monastery Rd. SS15: Lain 9L 115
Monega Rd. E7: Lon 8J 123
E12: Lon 8J 123
Monier Rd. E3: Lon 9A 122
Monkchester Cl. IG10: Lou 9M 77
Monkdowns Rd. CO6: Cogg 2M 197
Monk Gdns. SS17: Stan H 2N 147
Monkhams EN9: Wal A 9C 62
Monkham's Av. IG8: Wfd G 2H 107
Monkham's Dr. IG8: Wfd G 2H 107
Monkham's La. IG8: Wfd G 2G 107 (1F 39)
IG9: Buck H 9H 91
Monklands Ct. CO9: Hals 5J 207
Monksbury CM18: H'low 6F 54
Monks Chase CM13: Ingve 2M 113
Monks Cl. EN10: Brox 8A 52
Monks Cnr. CB10: Gt Sam 2L 205
Monks Ct. CM8: Wthm 4B 230
Monksford Dr. SS5: Hull 7K 103
Monksgrove IG10: Lou 4N 91
Monks Haven SS17: Stan H 2N 147
Monks Hill CB11: Saf W 5E 218
Monkside SS14: Bas 8E 116
Monk's La. CO7: Ded 4K 161 (3H 17)
(not continuous)
Monks Lodge Rd. CO9: Gt Map 1F 15
Monks Mead CM3: Bick 8F 74
Monks Rd. CO6: E Col 7C 198
MONK STREET 4F 13
Monks Wlk. CM9: Tol 9L 225
Monkswick Rd. CM20: H'low 1E 54
Monkswood Av. EN9: Wal A 3D 76
Monkswood Gdns. IG5: Ilf 7N 107
Monkwick Av. CO2: Colc 4N 173
Monkwick Sports Cen. 4N 173
Monkwood Cl. RM1: Romf 9E 110
Monmouth Av. E18: Lon 7H 107
Monmouth M. SS16: Lang H 1H 131
Monmouth Rd. N9: Lon 1C 38
RM9: Dag 7L 125
Monmouth St. WC2: Lon 7A 38
Monnow Grn. RM15: Ave 7N 143
Monnow Rd. RM15: Ave 7N 143
Monoux Almshouses E17: Lon 8B 106
Monoux Cl. CM11: Bill 7M 99
Monoux Gro. E17: Lon 5A 106
Mons Av. CM11: Bill 6M 99
Mons Rd. CO2: Colc 2L 173
Montague Av. SS9: Lgh S 4A 136
Montague Bldgs. SS1: Sth S 6N 137
Montague Pl. SS8: Can I 2E 150
WC1: Lon 7A 38
Montague Rd. E11: Lon 4F 122
Montague Way CM12: Bill 4J 99
Montagu Gdns. CM1: Chelm 4A 60
Montagu Rd. N9: Lon 1C 38
N18: Lon 1C 38
Montalt Rd. IG8: Wfd G 1F 106
Montbretia Cl. CO3: S'way 9E 164
Montbretia Ct. CO16: Clac S 9G 184
Monteagle Av. IG11: Bark 8B 124
Montefiore Av. SS6: Ray 8J 103
Montfort Av. SS17: Corr 1B 148
Montfort Gdns. IG6: Ilf 3B 108
Montgomery Cl. CM1: Chelm 4N 59
CO2: Colc 2B 174
RM16: Grays 9M 145
Montgomery Ct. SS3: Shoe 5J 139
Montgomery Cres. RM3: Romf 2G 111
Montpelier Cl. CM12: Bill 3J 99
Montpelier Gdns. RM6: Chad H 2H 125
Montpellier Ho. IG7: Chig 2B 108
Montreal Rd. IG1: Ilf 2B 124
RM18: Til 8C 156
Montrose Av. RM2: Romf 6G 111
Montrose Cl. IG8: Wfd G 1G 106
Montrose Rd. CM2: Chelm 7A 60
MONTSALE 6F 37
Montsale SS13: Pits 7K 117
Montserrat Av. IG8: Wfd G 4D 106
Monument Station (Tube) 7B 38
Monument Way N17: Lon 3B 38
Moon Hall Way CB9: H'hll 3J 7
Moons Cl. SS4: R'fd 9J 105
Moorcroft SS4: R'fd 1J 121
Moorcroft Av. SS7: Had 9L 119
Moore Av. RM18: Til 7D 156
RM20: Grays 3H 155
Moore Cl. CM11: Bill 3M 99
Moore Cres. RM9: Dag 1G 140
Moore Ho. *RM11: Horn* *1E 126*
(off Globe Rd.)
Moor End
CB10: Gt Sam, Hpstd 1H 205 (7G 7)
Moores Av. SS17: Fob 5D 132
Moorescroft CM15: Kel H 7B 82
Moores Pl. CM14: Brtwd 8G 96
Moore Wlk. E7: Lon 6G 123
Moorfield Ct. CM8: Wthm 6C 230
Moorfield Rd. CB2: Dux 2J 5
Moorfields CM18: H'low 8B 54
Moorgate EC2: Lon 7B 38
Moorgate Station (Rail, Tube) 7B 38
MOOR GREEN 5B 10
Moor Hall La.
CM3: Bick, Dan, E Han 9E 74 (3E 34)
CM23: Bis S, Thor 2J 21
Moor Hall Rd. CM17: H'low 8L 51 (6K 21)
Moorhen Av. CM0: St La 2C 36
Moorhen Cl. DA8: Eri 5F 152
Moorhen Way *CM19: Roy* *2G 52*
(off Holy Acre)
Moorhouse Grn. CO7: A'lgh 8L 161
Moorland Cl. RM5: Col R 4N 109
Moorlands Reach CM21: Saw 3L 51
Moor La. RM14: Upm 3B 128
Moor Pk. Cl. SS9: Lgh S 1B 136
Moor Pk. Gdns. SS9: Lgh S 1B 136
Moor Rd. CO4: L'ham 5D 160 (3F 17)
CO6: Aldh, Gt Tey 2E 170 (6K 15)
Moors Cl. CO5: Fee 9A 170
CO7: Gt Ben 5K 177
Moors Cft. CM7: Brain 5M 193
Moors Farm Chase CM9: L Tot 6K 25
Moorside CO1: Colc 8B 166
Moor's La. CO7: Gt Ben 5K 177
Mope La. CM8: W Bis 1J 229 (5G 25)
Mopsies Rd. SS14: Bas 9F 116
Moran Av. CM1: Chelm 4K 59
Morant Gdns. RM5: Col R 2N 109
Morant Rd. CO1: Colc 1B 174
RM16: Grays 1D 156
Moray Cl. RM1: Romf 4C 110
Moray Way RM1: Romf 4B 110
Mordaunt Gdns. RM9: Dag 9K 125
MORDEN GREEN 4A 4
Morden Rd. RM6: Chad H 2K 125
Mordon Rd. IG3: Ilf 2E 124
Morebarn Rd. CO7: Gt Bro 5D 168 (5K 17)
Morecambe Cl. RM12: Horn 7F 126
Morecambe Ho. *RM3: Romf* *2J 111*
(off Chudleigh Rd.)
Moreland Av. RM16: Grays 9M 145
SS7: Thund 9C 118
Moreland Cl. SS3: Gt W 2L 139
SS7: Thund 9C 118
Moreland Rd. SS11: W'fd 6K 101
Moreland St. EC1: Lon 6A 38
Moreland Way E4: Lon 9B 90
Morella Cl. CO7: Gt Ben 7K 177
Morello Ct. CO2: Colc 7A 174
Moremead EN9: Wal A 3D 76
Mores La. CM14: Pil H 3N 95 (7D 32)
MORETON 1B 32
Moreton Bay Ind. Est.
RM2: Romf 6H 111
Moreton Bri. CM5: Chip, M'ton 1H 67 (1B 32)
Moreton Ct. DA1: Cray 8D 152
Moreton Gdns. IG8: Wfd G 2L 107
Moreton Ga. CM5: M'ton 1B 32
MORETON MILL 7B 22
Moreton Rd. CM5: Chip 1H 67 (1B 32)
(Bobbingworth)
CM5: Chip, M'ton 3E 66 (2B 32)
(Bovinger)
CM5: Fy'd 8A 200 (1C 32)
Moretons CM2: Gall 8C 72
SS13: Pits 9H 117
Moretons Ct. SS13: Pits 9H 117
Moretons M. SS13: Pits 9H 117
Moretons Pl. SS13: Pits 9H 117
Morgan Av. E17: Lon 8D 106
Morgan Cl. RM10: Dag 9M 125
Morgan Cres. CM16: They B 6C 78
Morgan Way IG8: Wfd G 3L 107
RM13: Rain 3G 143
Morland Ct. CO6: Gt Hork 7J 159
Morland Rd. IG1: Ilf 4A 124
RM10: Dag 9M 125
Morlands Ind. Est. CM3: Ret C 8M 87
Morley Av. E4: Lon 4D 106
Morley Gro. CM20: H'low 1B 54
Morley Hill SS17: Stan H 8A 132 (5K 41)
Morley Link SS17: Corr, Stan H 9A 132
Morley Rd. CO5: Tip 7D 226
CO9: Hals 4L 207
E10: Lon 3C 122
IG11: Bark 1C 140
RM6: Chad H 9K 109
Morley Sq. RM16: Grays 2C 156
Morleys Rd. CO6: E Col 8B 198
Morning La. E9: Lon 5C 38
Mornington Av. IG1: Ilf 2N 123
SS4: R'fd 5M 121
Mornington Cl. IG8: Wfd G 1G 106
Mornington Cres. SS7: Had 3M 135
SS8: Can I 1J 151
Mornington Crescent Station (Tube) 6A 38
Mornington Ho. SS0: Wclf S 6H 137
Mornington Rd. E4: Lon 6D 90
E11: Lon 2F 122
(not continuous)
IG8: Wfd G 1F 106
IG10: Lou 2B 92
SS8: Can I 9H 135
Morningtons CM19: H'low 7B 54
Morrab Gdns. IG3: Ilf 5E 124
Morrells SS16: Bas 2A 132
Morris Av. CM11: Bill 7M 99
CO15: Jay 6C 188
E12: Lon 7M 123
Morris Ct. E4: Lon 9B 90
EN9: Wal A 4F 76
SS15: Lain 8K 115
MORRIS GREEN 2C 14
Morris Harp CB10: Saf W 2D 218
Morrison Av. E4: Lon 3A 106
Morrison Ho. RM16: Grays 9N 145
Morrison Rd. IG11: Bark, Dag 2K 141
Morris Rd. CM2: Chelm 9M 59
E14: Lon 7D 38
E15: Lon 6E 122
RM3: Romf 4F 110
RM8: Dag 4L 125
Morrow La. CO7: A'lgh 1N 167 (4J 17)
Morses La. CO7: B'sea 5E 182
Morten Rd. CO1: Colc 7M 165
Mortimer Rd. CM3: Hat P 2L 61
DA8: Eri 4B 152
SS6: Ray 2K 119
Mortimer St. W1: Lon 7A 38
Mortlake Rd. IG1: Ilf 6B 124
Mortlock Ct. E7: Lon 6K 123
Mortlock St. SG8: Mel 3E 4
Morton Rd. CM9: Gt Tot 3M 229
E15: Lon 9F 122
Morton Way CO9: Hals 3M 207
N14: Lon 1A 38
Mosbach Gdns. CM13: Hut 8L 97
Moseley St. SS2: Sth S 5B 138
Moss Bank RM17: Grays 3J 155
(not continuous)
Moss Cl. SS16: Van 3F 132
Moss Dr. SS16: Van 3F 132
Mosses La. CM3: S Fer, Wdhm F 7H 89
Mossfield Cl. CO3: Colc 9K 165
Mossford Ct. IG6: Ilf 6A 108
Mossford Grn. IG6: Ilf 7A 108
Mossford La. IG6: Ilf 6A 108
Moss La. CM17: H'low 2H 55
RM1: Romf 1D 126
Moss Path CM2: Gall 7D 72
Moss Rd. CM8: Wthm 4E 230
CO3: S'way 2F 172
RM10: Dag 9M 125
RM15: S Ock 5F 144
Moss Wlk. CM2: Chelm 4C 72
Moss Way CO6: W Ber 4F 164
Motehill SS16: Lang H 2L 131
Motherwell Way RM20: W Thur 3D 154 (2E 46)
Motts Cl. CM7: Brain 4G 192
MOTT'S GREEN 4M 213 (3A 22)
Motts La. CM8: Wthm 3D 230
(not continuous)
Mott's La. CO6: M Tey 2F 170
Mott St. E4: Lon, Lou 8D 76 (5E 30)
IG10: H Bee, Lou 9E 76
Motts Yd. CM6: Steb 8D 222
Moules La. CB1: Hads 3D 6
MOULSHAM 1C 72 (2A 34)
Moulsham Chase CM2: Chelm 2D 72
Moulsham Dr. CM2: Chelm 2C 72
Moulsham Hall La. CM3: Will G 2B 24
Moulsham St. CM2: Chelm 2B 72 (2A 34)
(not continuous)
Moulsham Thrift CM2: Chelm 4B 72
Moultrie Way RM14: Upm 1B 128
Mountain Ash Av. SS9: Lgh S 9A 120
Mountain Ash Cl. CO4: Colc 5C 166
SS9: Lgh S 9A 120
Mountains Farm Rd. CM6: Gt D 2G 23
Mountains Rd. CM9: Gt Tot 7H 205 (5H 25)
Mount Av. CM13: Hut 5K 97
E4: Lon 9A 90
RM3: H Wood 3N 111
SS0: Lgh S 5F 136
SS5: Hock 1C 120
SS6: Ray 4J 119
Mountbatten Ct. IG9: Buck H 8K 91
Mountbatten Dr. CO2: Colc 3B 174
SS3: Shoe 5J 139
Mountbatten Ho. RM2: Romf 8G 111
Mountbatten Rd. CM7: Brain 4K 193
Mountbatten Way CM1: Chelm 4M 59
Mt. Bovers La. SS5: Hock 4D 120
MOUNT BURES 2A 16
Mt. Bures Rd. CO6: Wak C 6F 196 (3A 16)
Mount Cl. SS6: Ray 5J 119
SS11: W'fd 8M 101
Mount Cres. CM14: War 1G 112
SS5: Hock 9C 104
SS7: Ben 2E 134
Mountdale Gdns. SS9: Lgh S 2D 136 (4H 43)
Mount Dr. CM24: Stan M 4D 220
Mt. Echo Av. E4: Lon 8B 90
Mt. Echo Dr. E4: Lon 7B 90
MOUNT END 2L 79 (4K 31)
Mountfield Cl. SS17: Stan H 2N 147
Mountfields SS13: Pits 2J 133
Mountfitchet Castle & Norman Village 3E 220 (6A 12)
Mountfitchet Rd. CM24: Stan M 4D 220
Mountgrove Rd. N5: Lon 4B 38
Mount Hill CO9: Hals 6H 207 (4F 15)
Mounthill Av. CM2: Chelm 8M 59
Mountjoy Cl. SE2: Lon 9G 141
Mt. Liell Ct. SS0: Wclf S 7H 137
Mt. Lodge Chase CM9: Gt Tot 8J 205
MOUNTNESSING 9A 84 (6G 33)
Mountnessing SS7: Had 4K 135
Mountnessing By-Pass
CM15: Mount, Shenf 2N 97 (6G 33)
Mountnessing La. CM15: Dodd 8G 83 (5E 32)
Mountnessing Post Mill 8N 83 (5G 33)
Mountnessing Rd.
CM4: B'more, Mount, Wy G 3J 83 (4F 33)
CM12: Bill 2F 98 (6H 33)
CM15: Mount, Wy G 3J 83
Mountney Cl. CM4: Ing 8B 84
MOUNT PLEASANT 2B 8
Mt. Pleasant CM9: Mal 6B 214
CO9: Hals 5K 207
CO10: Pos 2B 8
CO16: Wee 5D 178
IG1: Ilf 7B 124
Mt. Pleasant Av. CM13: Hut 5A 98
Mt. Pleasant Cotts. CB11: Saf W 5C 218
Mt. Pleasant Est. CM9: Gt Tot 8K 205
Mt. Pleasant Rd. CB11: Saf W 5C 218 (7B 6)
CM3: S Fer 1K 103
IG7: Chig 1C 108
N17: Lon 2B 38
RM5: Col R 3B 110
Mount Ri. CO9: Hals 5J 207
Mount Rd. CB9: H'hll 3J 7
CM7: Brain 5J 193
CM16: Fid, Stap T, They M 2J 79 (4J 31)
CO6: Cogg 3M 197

Mount Rd. RM4: Stap T 4L 79
RM8: Dag 3L 125
SS7: Ben 3F 134
(not continuous)
SS11: W'fd 8M 101
Mounts Rd. DA9: Grnh 3E 46
Mount, The CM9: Tol 8K 225
CM11: Bill 5N 99
CO3: Colc 9G 165
RM3: Romf 9G 95
SS17: Stan H 2A 148
Mount Vw. CM11: Bill 6N 99
Mountview Cl. SS16: Van 3F 132
Mountview Cres. CM0: St La 2C 36
Mountview Rd. CO15: Clac S 8L 185
Mount Vw. Rd. E4: Lon 6D 90
Mount Way SS11: W'fd 8M 101
Moverons La. CO7: B'sea 3B 182 (2J 27)
MOVERS LANE 2D 140 (6H 39)
Movers La. IG11: Bark 1C 140 (6H 39)
Mowbray Rd. CM20: H'low 1E 54
Mowbrays Cl. RM5: Col R 5A 110
Mowbrays Rd. RM5: Col R 6A 110
Mowbrey Gdns. IG10: Lou 9B 78
MOWDEN 6D 24
Mowden Hall La. CM3: Hat P 5J 61 (6D 24)
Moyers Rd. E10: Lon 2C 122
Moyn's Pk. 3N 223 (5K 7)
Moy Rd. CO2: Colc 5A 174
MUCH HADHAM 2G 21
MUCKING 6M 147 (7K 41)
MUCKINGFORD 1J 157 (1J 47)
Muckingford Rd. RM18: W Til 2F 156 (1H 47)
SS17: W Til 2F 156 (1J 47)
Mucking Hall Rd. SS3: Barl M 3A 44
Mucking Wharf Rd.
SS17: Stan H 6L 147 (7K 41)
Mudlands Ind. Est. RM13: Rain 3C 142
Muggeridge Rd. RM10: Dag 6N 125
Muir Pl. SS12: W'fd 2L 117
Muirway SS7: Thund 8B 118
Mulberries, The CM7: Brain 6J 193
(off South St.)
Mulberry Av. CO2: Colc 2A 174
Mulberry Cl. E4: Lon 8A 90
RM2: Romf 8G 110
Mulberry Ct. E11: Lon 6D 122
(off Langthorne Rd.)
IG11: Bark 8E 124
Mulberry Dr. RM19: Purf 2K 153
Mulberry Gdns. CM8: Wthm 3D 230
SS16: Lang H 1K 131
Mulberry Grn. CM17: H'low 8J 51 (6J 21)
Mulberry Harbour Way CO7: W'hoe 6H 175
Mulberry Hill CM15: Shenf 6J 97
Mulberry La. CO11: L Bro 3H 169
Mulberry Rd. SS8: Can I 2C 150
Mulberrys, The SS2: Sth S 3M 137
Mulberry Ter. CM17: H'low 8G 51
(off Broadway Av.)
Mulberry Way CM1: Chelm 6M 59
DA17: Belv 9A 142
E18: Lon 6H 107 (2F 39)
IG6: Ilf 8B 108
Mullein Ct. RM17: Grays 4N 155
Mullins Rd. CM7: Brain 2H 193
Mullions, The CM12: Bill 5H 99
Multon Lea CM1: Chelm 4B 60
Mumford Cl. CO6: W Ber 3F 164
Mumford Rd. CO6: W Ber 4E 164
Mumfords La. CO13: Kir S, Walt 7D 180
Munden Rd. SG12: D End 1B 20
MUNDON 3J 35
Mundon Gdns. IG1: Ilf 3C 124
Mundon Rd. CM7: Brain 7M 193
CM9: Mal, Mun 7C 214 (1H 35)
Mungo Pk. Rd. RM13: Rain 8E 126 (5B 40)
Munnings Dr. CO16: Clac S 7H 185
Munnings Rd. CO3: Colc 1H 173
Munnings Way CO11: Law 3G 163
Munro Ct. SS12: W'fd 2M 117
Munro Rd. CM8: Wthm 2C 230
Munsons All. CM0: S'min 2D 222
Munsons Ct. CM0: S'min 2D 222
Munsterburg Rd. SS8: Can I 9K 135
Munster Ct. CM12: Bill 3H 99
Murchison Cl. CM1: Chelm 6G 58
Murchison Rd. E10: Lon 4C 122
EN11: Rye P 2B 52
Murfitt Way RM14: Upm 6L 127
Muriel Ct. E10: Lon 2B 122
Murray Cl. CM7: Brain 2H 193
Murray Way SS12: W'fd 2L 117
Murrell Lock CM2: Chelm 7B 60
Murrels La. SS5: Hock 9N 103
Murthering La.
RM4: Nave, Stap A 6D 94 (7A 32)
Murtwell Dr. IG7: Chig 3B 108
Muscade Cl. CO5: Tip 5D 226
Muscovy Ho. DA18: Eri 9K 141
(off Kale Rd.)
Mus. of Power 7G 25
Museum St. CB10: Saf W 3C 218
CO1: Colc 8N 165
Musgrave Cl. CO12: Har 6H 209
Musk Cl. CO3: S'way 8E 164
Musket Gro. SS9: Lgh S 8A 120
Muskham Rd. CM20: H'low 9F 50
Mussenden La. DA3: Fawk 7D 46
DA4: Hort K 7D 46
MUSWELL HILL 2A 38
Muswell Hill N10: Lon 3A 38
Muswell Wlk. CO16: Clac S 8H 185
Mutlow Cl. CB11: Wen A 7L 227
Mutlow Hill CB11: Wen A 7L 227 (7A 6)
Mutton Row CM5: Chip 8G 66 (3B 32)
Myddelton Av. EN1: Enf 5B 30
Myddelton House Gardens 5C 30
Myddleton Rd. N22: Lon 2A 38
Myddylton Pl. CB10: Saf W 3C 218
Mygrove Cl. RM13: Rain 2H 143
Mygrove Gdns. RM13: Rain 2H 143
Mygrove Rd. RM13: Rain 2H 143
Myland Hall Chase CO4: Colc 4C 166
Mylne Ct. EN11: Rye P 2A 52
Myln Mdw. CM4: Stock 7A 86
Mynchens SS15: Lain 9N 115
Myneer Pk. CO6: Cogg 3M 197
Mynott Ct. CO5: Tip 7D 226
Myrtle Cl. DA8: Eri 6C 152
Myrtle Gro. CO2: Colc 1B 174
RM15: Ave 9N 143
Myrtle Rd. CM14: War 1F 112
IG1: Ilf 4A 124
RM3: Romf 3G 110
Mytchett Cl. CO16: Clac S 7F 184

N

Nabbott Rd. CM1: Chelm 9G 58
Nafferton Ri. IG10: Lou 4K 91
Nagle Cl. E17: Lon 6D 106
NAG'S HEAD 4A 38
Nags Head La. CM14: Brtwd 6N 111 (2D 40)
RM14: Upm 6N 111 (2D 40)
Nags Head Rd. EN3: Enf 6C 30
Nairn Ct. RM18: Til 7B 156
Nalla Gdns. CM1: Chelm 5J 59
Namur Rd. SS8: Can I 1J 151
Nancy Smith Cl. CO2: Colc 1N 173
Nansen Av. SS4: R'fd 1J 121
Nansen Rd. CO15: Hol S 7A 186
Nantwich Ho. RM3: Romf 2J 111
(off Lindfield Rd.)
Napier Av. CO15: Jay 6B 188
SS1: Sth S 6L 137
Napier Cl. RM11: Horn 3F 126
SS14: Bas 9E 116
Napier Ct. CM1: Chelm 6G 58
Napier Ct. W. SS1: Sth S 6L 137
(off Gordon Pl.)
Napier Cres. SS12: W'fd 2M 117
Napier Gdns. SS7: Had 9J 119
Napier Ho. RM13: Rain 3D 142
(off Dunedin Rd.)
Napier Rd. CO2: Colc 9N 165
E11: Lon 6E 122
SS6: Ray 4M 119
Narboro Ct. RM1: Romf 9E 110
Nare Rd. RM15: Ave 7N 143
Narrow Boat Cl. SE28: Lon 9C 140
Narvik Cl. CM9: Mal 8A 214
Naseby Rd. IG5: Ilf 5M 107
RM10: Dag 5M 125
Nash Bank DA13: Ist R, Meop 6G 47
Nash Cl. CO3: Colc 1J 173
CO11: Law 3G 162
Nash Dr. CM1: Broom 9J 57
Nash Ho. E17: Lon 7B 106
Nash Rd. RM6: Chad H 8J 109
NASH STREET 6H 47
Nassau Path SE28: Lon 8H 141
Nassau Rd. CO16: St O 9N 183
NASTY 6C 10
Natal Rd. IG1: Ilf 6A 124
Natasha Ct. RM3: Romf 4G 111
Nathan Cl. RM14: Upm 3B 128
Nathan Ct. CO2: Colc 6B 174
Nathan's La. CM1: Ed C, Writ 5E 70 (2H 33)
Nathan Way SE28: Lon 9F 140 (7H 39)
National Motorboat Mus. 4J 133 (4B 42)
National Vintage Wireless &
Television Mus., The 2N 209 (2J 19)
Nation Way E4: Lon 7C 90
Nats La. CB11: Wen A 6K 227
Natural History Mus. 8N 165
Naunton Way RM12: Horn 5H 127
Navarre Gdns. RM5: Col R 2N 109
NAVESTOCK 1H 95 (6B 32)
Navestock Cl. E4: Lon 9C 90
SS6: Ray 4G 118
Navestock Cres. IG8: Wfd G 4J 107
Navestock Gdns. SS1: Sth S 5D 138
Navestock Ho. IG11: Bark 2G 141
NAVESTOCK SIDE 1N 95 (6D 32)
Navestockside
CM14: Kel C, N'side 1N 95 (6C 32)
Navigation Dr. EN3: Enf 8A 76
Navigation Pl. CM9: Mal 4D 214
Navigation Rd. CM2: Chelm 9L 59
NAYLAND 1D 16
Nayland Airfield 1C 16
Nayland Cl. SS12: W'fd 9M 101
Nayland Dr. CO16: Clac S 9F 184
Nayland Ho. SS2: Sth S 1K 137
(off Manners Way)
Nayland Rd. CO4: Colc 1K 165
CO6: Gt Hork 9K 159 (4E 16)
(Causeway, The)
CO6: Gt Hork 2H 159 (2D 16)
(Horkesley Hill)
CO6: Gt Hork, W Ber 1E 164 (4C 16)
(White Hart La.)
CO8: Bures 8L 195 (2A 16)
Nayling Rd. CM7: Brain 6E 192
Nazareth Ho. SS2: Sth S 6L 137
Naze Ct. CO14: Walt 1M 181
NAZEING 1J 63 (1F 31)
Nazeingbury Cl. EN9: Naze 1D 62
Nazeingbury Pde. EN9: Naze 1D 62
(off Nazeing Rd.)
Nazeing Comn. EN9: Naze 3H 63 (2F 31)
NAZEING GATE 3J 63 (2F 31)
Nazeing Glass Works 1E 30
NAZEING LONG GREEN 4G 63 (2F 31)
NAZEING MARSH 2B 62
NAZEING MEAD 7C 52
Nazeing New Rd. EN10: Brox 9A 52 (1D 30)
Nazeing Rd. EN9: Brox, Naze 1C 62 (1E 30)
Nazeing, The SS14: Bas 9F 116
Nazeing Wlk. RM13: Rain 9D 126
Naze Pk. Rd. CO14: Walt 4N 181 (7H 19)
NAZE, THE 4N 181
Naze Tower, The 1N 181
Neal Ct. EN9: Wal A 3F 76
Neale Rd. CO9: Hals 5K 207
Neasden Av. CO16: Clac S 8H 185
Neasham Rd. RM8: Dag 7G 124
Neave Cres. RM3: Romf 5G 111
Needham Cl. CM11: Bill 5K 99
NEEDHAM GREEN 9F 206 (4C 22)
Neil Armstrong Way SS9: Lgh S 8F 120
(not continuous)
Nelmes Cl. RM11: Horn 9K 111
Nelmes Cres. RM11: Horn 9J 111
Nelmes Rd. RM11: Horn 2J 127
Nelmes Way RM11: Horn 8H 111
Nelson Cl. CM14: War 2G 113
RM7: Maw 5N 109
SS6: Ray 3M 119
Nelson Ct. CM0: Bur C 4E 196
DA8: Eri 5D 152
(off Frobisher Rd.)
Nelson Cres. CM9: Mal 8D 214
Nelson Dr. SS9: Lgh S 5E 136
Nelson Gdns. CM7: Brain 4L 193
SS6: Ray 3M 119
Nelson Gro. CM1: Chelm 8H 59
Nelson Ho. RM3: Romf 2J 111
(off Lindfield Rd.)
Nelson M. SS1: Sth S 7M 137
Nelson Pl. CM3: S Fer 2L 103
Nelson Rd. CO3: S'way 8F 164
CO12: Har 3L 209
CO15: Clac S 3J 189
E4: Lon 3B 106 (2D 38)
E11: Lon 8G 107
RM13: Rain 2D 142
RM15: S Ock 2F 144
RM16: Ors 6F 146
SS4: R'fd 1J 121
SS6: Ray 4M 119
SS9: Lgh S 4F 136
SS14: Bas 9F 116
Nelson St. CO7: B'sea 8D 182
SS1: Sth S 7M 137
Nelwyn Av. RM11: Horn 9K 111
N. End Rd. CB10: Hxtn 3K 5
CO9: Bel W, Gest, L Yel 6E 8
SG8: Arr 1B 4
Neptune Cl. RM13: Rain 2D 142
Neptune Ct. CO1: Colc 9C 166
(off Maudlyn Rd.)
DA8: Eri 5D 152
(off Frobisher Rd.)
Neptune Wlk. DA8: Eri 2B 152
Ness Rd. DA8: Eri 4H 153
SS3: Shoe 7H 139 (5B 44)
Ness Wlk. CM8: Wthm 5A 230
Nesta Rd. IG8: Wfd G 3E 106
Nestuda Ho. SS9: Lgh S 8A 120
Nestuda Way SS2: Sth S 9G 121 (3H 43)
Nethan Dr. RM15: Ave 7N 143
Nether Ct. CO9: Hals 5M 207
Netherfield SS7: Ben 2G 134
Netherfield Gdns. IG11: Bark 8C 124
Netherfield La. SG12: Stan A 1E 52
Nethergate St. CO10: Clare 3D 8
Nether Hall (remains of) 6F 52
(Netherhall Rd.)
Nether Hall 2E 8
(Peacocks Rd.)
Netherhall Rd. CM19: Roy 5F 52
Nether Hill CO10: Bel W, Gest 6F 9
Nether Mayne SS16: Bas, Van 1B 132 (3A 42)
Netherpark Dr. RM2: Romf 6D 110
Nether Priors CO9: Hals 5L 207
(off Colchester Rd.)
SS14: Bas 9D 116
NETHER STREET 5E 22
Nether St. CM5: Ab R 6E 22
SG12: Wid 3G 21
Netley Rd. IG2: Ilf 9C 108
NETTESWELL 2D 54 (6H 21)
Netteswell Dr. CM20: H'low 2C 54
Netteswell Orchard CM20: H'low 2C 54
Netteswell Rd. CM20: H'low 9D 50
Netteswell Twr. CM20: H'low 2C 54
Nevada Rd. SS8: Can I 9J 135
Nevell Rd. RM16: Grays 1D 156
NEVENDON 3J 117 (2C 42)
Nevendon Grange SS12: W'fd 1K 117
Nevendon M. SS13: Bas 5H 117
Nevendon Rd. SS12: Bas 5H 117 (2B 42)
(not continuous)
SS12: W'fd 4H 117 (2B 42)
Nevendon Rd. By-Pass
SS12: W'fd 2L 117 (1C 42)
Nevern Cl. SS6: Ray 7M 119
Nevern Rd. SS6: Ray 7L 119
Neville Cl. E11: Lon 5F 122
Neville Gdns. RM8: Dag 5J 125
Neville Rd. CB10: Saf W 3D 218
E7: Lon 9G 123
IG6: Ilf 5B 108
RM8: Dag 4J 125
Neville Shaw SS14: Bas 9C 116
Nevill Way IG10: Lou 5L 91
Nevin Dr. E4: Lon 7B 90
Nevis Cl. RM1: Romf 3C 110
Nevyll Ct. SS1: Sth S 6F 138
New Acres Rd. SE28: Lon 9D 140
(not continuous)
Newark Knok E6: Lon 5A 140
Newarks Rd. CM1: Good E 6H 23
NEW ASH GREEN 7F 47
New Av. SS16: Lang H 2J 131
NEW BARN 6G 47
Longfield 6G 47
New Barn La.
CM22: Gt Hal, L Hall 1K 213 (2A 22)
New Barn Rd. BR8: Swan 6A 46
Newbarn Rd. CO6: Gt Tey 1D 170 (5K 15)
New Barn Rd. DA3: Long 6G 47
New Barns La. SG10: M Hud 2F 21
New Barn St. E13: Lon 6F 39
New Barns Way IG7: Chig 9A 92
Newberry Side SS15: Lain 9L 115
Newbery Rd. DA8: Eri 6D 152
Newbiggen St. CM6: Thax 7B 224 (3F 13)
New Bond St. W1: Lon 7A 38
New Bowers Way CM1: Chelm 5A 60 (7B 24)
Newbridge Hill CO3: S'way 5E 164 (5C 16)
CO6: W Ber 5E 164 (5C 16)
Newbridge Rd. CO5: Lay M, Tip 6E 226 (3A 26)
New Bri. St. EC4: Lon 7A 38
Newburgh Rd. RM17: Grays 3N 155
Newbury Av. EN3: Enf 5D 30
Newbury Cl. RM3: Romf 3G 111
Newbury Gdns. RM3: Romf 3H 111
RM14: Upm 5K 127
New Bury Mdw. CM22: Hat O 8D 206
NEWBURY PARK 9C 108 (3H 39)
Newbury Park Station (Tube) 1C 124 (3H 39)
Newbury Rd. E4: Lon 3C 106
IG2: Ilf 1D 124
RM3: Romf 2H 111
Newbury Wlk. RM3: Romf 2H 111
New Captains Rd. CO5: W Mer 3B 228
Newcastle Av. CO3: S'way 2F 172
IG6: Ilf 3F 108
New Century Rd. SS15: Lain 9J 115
New Chu. Rd. CO6: W Ber 3E 164 (5D 16)
New City Rd. E13: Lon 6F 39
New College of Cobham 6J 47
Newcomen Rd. E11: Lon 5F 122
Newcomen Way CO4: Colc 1B 166
New Common CM22: Hat H 4A 22
New Cotts. RM13: Wen 6G 143
SS13: Pits 1L 133
Newcourt Bus. Pk. CM18: H'low 7B 54
Newcourt Rd. CM2: Chelm 8M 59
Newcroft CB10: Saf W 4D 218
New Cut CO2: Lay H 9G 172 (1D 26)
CO7: Gt Ben 6K 177
CO8: Bures 8K 195
New Dukes Way CM2: Chelm 7A 60
Newell Av. SS3: Shoe 6L 139
Newell La. SG2: Clot 4A 10
New Empire Theatre 7M 137
NEW ENGLAND 9M 223 (4A 8)
New England Cl. CM3: Bick 9F 74
New England Cres. SS3: Gt W 4N 139
New England Ind. Est. IG11: Bark 2B 140
New Farm Cotts. SS3: Shoe 6H 139
New Farm Dr. RM4: Abr 2H 93 (6J 31)
New Farm Rd. CO3: S'way 9E 164 (6C 16)
New Ford Rd. EN8: Wal X 5A 76
New Forest La. IG7: Chig 3N 107
New Frontiers Science Pk. Nth.
CM19: H'low 3M 53
New Frontiers Science Pk. Sth.
CM19: H'low 4M 53
Newgate St Village EN6: New S 2A 30
NEWGATE STREET
Hertford 2A 30
Newgate St. CO14: Walt 6M 181
E4: Lon 9E 90
(not continuous)
SG13: New S 2A 30
Newgatestreet Rd. EN7: G Oak 2A 30
New Grn. CM7: Bar S 5K 13
Newhall SS4: R'fd 1H 121
Newhall Ct. EN9: Wal A 3F 76
New Hall Dr. RM3: H Wood 5J 111
New Hall La. CM9: Mun 3J 35
New Hall Rd. SS5: Hock 7F 104
New Hall Vineyards 7K 215
Newham College of Futher Education
(Stratford Campus) 9E 122
Newham Pl. RM16: Grays 2C 156
Newham Way E6: Lon 3A 140 (7F 39)
E16: Lon 7E 38
Newhaven La. CO12: Har 1M 209
(off West St.)
NEWHOUSE 7C 22
NEW HOUSE 4G 47
Northfleet 4G 47
Newhouse Av. RM6: Chad H 7J 109
SS12: W'fd 9G 101
New Ho. La. CB10: A'dn 6E 6
Newhouse La. CM5: Chip 1G 67
New Ho. La. CM16: N Wea 4A 66
DA11: N'fleet 4G 47

Newhouse Rd. CO6: E Col 9A 198 (5H 15)
Newhythe CO3: S'way 8F 164
NEWINGTON 7B 38
Newington Av. SS2: Sth S 4B 138
Newington Cl. SS2: Sth S 4D 138
Newington Gdns. CO15: Clac S 5K 185
SS2: Sth S. 4C 138
Newington Grn. N1: Lon 5B 38
Newington Grn. Rd. N1: Lon 5B 38
New Jubilee Ct. IG8: Wfd G 4G 106
New Kiln Rd. CO3: Colc 8K 165
Newland Av. CM7: Gt Bar. 3C 202
Newland End La. CB11: A'den 1J 11
Newland Grove Nature Reserve 1L 59
Newland Pl. CM8: Wthm 6D 230
Newland Pct. CM8: Wthm 5D 230
(off Newland St.)
Newlands Cl. CM12: Bill. 4K 99
CM13: Hut. 6N 97
Newlands Dr. CM8: Wthm 5D 230
Newlands End SS15: Lain. 7K 115
Newlands Rd. CM12: Bill 4K 99
IG8: Wfd G. 8F 90
SS8: Can I 9K 135
(not continuous)
SS12: W'fd 3L 117
Newlands Shopping Cen., The
CM8: Wthm. 5D 230
Newland St. CM8: Wthm 6C 230 (4G 25)
New La. CO5: Fee. 9B 170 (1J 25)
IP9: Holb. 1D 18
New Lodge Stadium 7G 99
New Lodge Chase CM3: L Bad 8J 61 (1D 34)
New London Rd. CM2: Chelm 2B 72 (2A 34)
(not continuous)
New Maltings RM15: Ave 8A 144
Newman Cl. RM11: Horn 9J 111
Newman Dr. CO4: Boxt. 4A 160
Newmans Cl. IG10: Lou 2N 91
Newmans Dr. CM13: Hut 6M 97
NEWMAN'S END. 5A 22
NEWMAN'S GREEN. 4K 9
Newmans La. IG10: Lou. 2N 91
Newmarket Ho. RM3: Romf 2J 111
(off Lindfield Rd.)
Newmarket Rd. CB10: Gt Che 7C 202 (4A 6)
SG8: R'ton 5D 4
Newmarket Way RM12: Horn 6J 127
Newmarsh Rd. SE28: Lon. 8E 140
NEW MISTLEY 4N 163 (3B 18)
New Moor Cl. CM0: S'min 2E 222
New Moor Cres. CM0: S'min 2E 222
New Mt. St. E15: Lon. 9D 122
New Nabbotts Way CM1: Chelm 4N 59 (7B 24)
NEWNEY GREEN 1H 33
Newnham Cl. CM7: Brain. 6G 192
IG10: Lou 5K 91
Newnham Grn. CM9: Mal 5A 214
Newnham Ho. IG10: Lou 5K 91
New Nth. Rd. IG6: Ilf. 4C 108 (2H 39)
N1: Lon. 5B 38
New Orleans Flats CO5: W Mer 4B 228
New Oxford St. W1: Lon. 7A 38
New Pk. CO9: Cas H 4L 219
New Pk. Rd. SS5: Hock. 8F 104
SS7: Ben 1C 134
New Pk. St. CO1: Colc 9B 166
New Parsonage La. CM7: Gt Sal 6K 13
Newpasture La. CM6: Steb. 7J 13
Newpiece IG10: Lou 2A 92
New Pier St. CO14: Walt 6M 181
New Pl. Gdns. RM14: Upm 4A 128
New Plaistow Rd. E15: Lon 6E 38
New Plymouth Ho. RM13: Rain 3D 142
(off Dunedin Rd.)
New Pond La. CB10: Saf W 4B 218
Newpond St. CM17: H'low 2J 55
NEWPORT 2L 215 (1B 12)
Newport Av. CM3: Cold N, Latch 8M 197
Newport Cl. CM2: Gt Bad 4J 73
CO12: Har 6J 209
Newport Ct. SS6: Ray. 3H 119
Newport Dr. CB11: Quen. 3A 12
CO15: Clac S 6L 185
NEWPORT POND. 4L 215
Newport Rd. CB11: A End, Saf W . . . 7N 227 (7B 6)
CB11: Widd. 2C 12
E10: Lon 4C 122
Newports CM21: Saw 3H 51
Newport Station (Rail) 3L 215 (2B 12)
Newport Way CO13: Frin S. 8K 181
Newpots Cl. CO5: Pel 3E 26
Newpots La. CO5: Pel 3E 26
New River Cl. EN11: Rye P. 4B 52
New Rd. CB1: H'hth, Shudy C. 3F 7
CB2: Saws. 1K 5
CB10: Hxtn 3K 5
CB10: Saf W 4D 218
CM0: Bur C 3E 196
CM1: Broom 2K 59
CM2: Gt Bad 4G 73
CM3: Hat P 2L 61
CM3: Terl 4D 24
CM4: Ing 4E 84
CM9: Tol 7K 225
CM12: L Bur 5J 115
CM14: Brtwd. 8G 96
CM17: H'low 8J 51
CM22: Else. 2K 199 (5B 12)
CM77: Rayne 7B 192 (7B 14)
CO3: S'way 9E 164
CO5: K'dn 3J 211
CO5: Mess 1C 226 (2K 25)
CO5: Tip. 6D 226 (3K 25)
New Rd. CO6: Aldh 5A 16
CO9: Gosf 4E 14
CO11: Mist. 5J 163 (3A 18)
E4: Lon 1B 106 (1D 38)
E1: Lon 7C 38
E12: Lon 4L 123
EN10: Brox 7A 52
IG3: Ilf. 4D 124
RM4: Abr 5J 93 (7J 31)
RM9: Dag 2M 141 (6K 39)
RM10: Dag 2M 141 (6K 39)
RM13: Ave, Rain, Wen 3E 142 (6A 40)
(not continuous)
RM17: Grays 4K 155
(not continuous)
SG8: Gt Chi, Hey 4F 5
SG8: Hey, Mel 3E 4
SG8: Stpl M. 3A 4
SG11: L Had 1G 21
SG12: Ware. 4C 20
SS3: Gt W 3M 139 (4C 44)
SS7: Had 3K 135 (4F 43)
SS8: Can I 2E 150
SS9: Lgh S. 6C 136 (5G 43)
New Row CM22: Srng. 4A 210
NEWSELLS 7E 4
New Spitalfields Mkt. E10: Lon 5B 122
New Sq. SS5: Hock. 7B 104
Newstead Ho. RM3: Romf 1H 111
(off Troopers Dr.)
Newstead Rd. SS3: Gt W. 2M 139
New St. CM1: Chelm 9K 59 (1A 34)
CM6: Gt D 3L 203
CM7: Brain 5H 193
(not continuous)
CM9: Mal. 6B 214
CM21: Saw 1K 51
CO7: B'sea 8E 182 (3K 27)
CO9: Hals. 5J 207
CO10: Glem. 1G 9
New St. Flds. CM6: Gt D. 3L 203
New St. Pas. CM6: Gt D. 3L 203
New St. Rd. DA13: Meop 7G 47
Newsum Gdns. SS6: Ray 4G 118
Newteswell Dr. EN9: Wal A 2D 76
New Thorpe Av. CO16: T Sok 4L 179
NEW THUNDERSLEY 9D 118 (3D 42)
NEWTON. 1G 5
Newton Cl. CM7: Brain. 7H 193
EN11: Hod. 1B 52
SS17: Corr 1B 148
Newton Dr. CM21: Saw 3J 51
Newton Grn. CM6: Gt D 2K 203
Newton Gro. CM6: Gt D 2J 203
Newton Hall Chase CM6: Gt D 1J 203
Newton Hall Gdns. SS4: R'fd 1J 121
Newton Ho. E17: Lon 7B 106
(off Prospect Hill)
Newton Ind. Est. RM6: Chad H. 8J 109
Newton Pk. Rd. SS7: Thund. 8H 119
Newton Rd. CB2: Hars 1G 5
CB2: Whitt. 1H 5
CO10: Gt Cor, Sud. 5J 9
CO12: Har 4J 209
E15: Lon 7D 122
IG7: Chig, Ilf 2G 108
RM18: Til 8C 156
Newtons Cl. RM13: Rain 9D 126
Newtons Ct. DA2: Dart 9A 154
Newton Way CO16: St O 8M 183
NEWTOWN. 1K 211
NEW TOWN
Dartford 3C 46
Newtown Rd. CM23: Bis S 1K 21
New Town Rd. CO1: Colc 9A 166
CO16: T Sok 4K 179
(not continuous)
New Village CO11: Law 1H 163
New Wanstead E11: Lon 1F 122 (3F 39)
New Waverley Rd. SS15: Bas 6N 115
NEW WAY 7A 22
New Way CO16: P Bay 4K 27
New Way La. CM17: H'low, Mat T. . . 4N 55 (7A 22)
NEW WIMPOLE 1C 4
New Writtle St. CM2: Chelm 1B 72
New Zealand Way RM13: Rain. 3D 142
Nicholas Cl. CM1: Writ. 1K 71
RM15: S Ock. 3F 144
Nicholas Ct. CM1: Chelm 5F 58
CM8: Wthm. 5C 230
Nicholas Rd. RM8: Dag 4L 125
Nicholas Wlk. RM16: Grays 9D 146
Nicholl Rd. CM16: Epp 1E 78
SS15: Lain. 8L 115
Nicholls Fld. CM18: H'low 4F 54
Nichols Cl. CO11: Law 5G 163
Nichols Gro. CM7: Brain. 5K 193
Nicholson Ct. EN11: Hod 5B 52
Nicholson Cres. SS7: Ben 3H 135
Nicholson Gro. SS12: W'fd 2M 117
Nicholson Ho. SS2: Sth S 6N 137
Nicholson Pl. CM3: E Han 2B 88
Nicholson Rd. SS7: Ben. 3H 135
Nicholsons Gro. CO1: Colc. 9A 166
Nickelby Cl. SE28: Lon. 6H 141
Nickleby Rd. CM1: Chelm 4F 58
Nicola M. IG6: Ilf 3A 108
Nien-Oord CO16: Clac S 9G 184
Nigel M. IG1: Ilf 6A 124
Nigel Rd. E7: Lon 7J 123
Nightingale Av. E4: Lon 2E 106
RM14: Upm. 3C 128
Nightingale Cl. CM8: Wthm 7B 230
CO4: Colc 7G 166
Nightingale Cl. CO12: Har 6H 209
CO15: Clac S. 8K 185
E4: Lon 1D 106
SS2: Sth S. 9K 121
SS6: Ray. 4H 119
Nightingale Cnr. CM9: Mal. 7C 214
Nightingale Gro. DA1: Dart. 9L 153
Nightingale Hall Rd. CO6: E Col 4G 15
Nightingale Ho. CO4: L'ham 2F 160 (2G 17)
Nightingale La. CM13: Dun 7E 114
CM13: W H'dn. 9B 114
E11: Lon 8H 107
Nightingale M. CB10: Saf W. 3E 218
E11: Lon 9G 107
Nightingale Pl. CO3: S'way 2D 172
Nightingale Rd. N9: Lon. 7C 30
SS8: Can I 2J 151
Nightingales CM17: H'low 5H 55
EN9: Wal A 4E 76
SS16: Lang H 1H 131
Nightingale Way CO15: Clac S 8K 185
Nineacres CM7: Brain 7J 193
Nine Acres Cl. E12: Lon 7L 123
NINE ASHES 8F 68 (3E 32)
Nine Ashes Rd.
CM4: B'more, Nine A 1E 82 (3E 32)
CM15: Hook E, Ston M. 3E 82 (4E 32)
Ninefields EN9: Wal A 3F 76
Ninth Av. CM24: Stan M 7G 221
Nipsells Chase CM3: May 6K 213
Nita Rd. CM14: War 2F 112
Niton Ct. SS17: Stan H 5L 147
Niven Cl. SS12: W'fd 2M 117
NOAK BRIDGE. 6N 115 (2K 41)
Noakes Av. CM2: Gt Bad 5F 72
Noakes La. CM3: L Walt. 5C 24
NOAK HILL 4L 115 (2K 41)
Harold Hill 8J 95 (1C 40)
Noak Hill Cl. CM12: Bill 3K 115
Noak Hill Rd. CM12: Bill. 1J 115 (1J 41)
RM3: Romf. 2F 110 (1B 40)
SS15: Bas. 1J 115 (2K 41)
SS15: Lain. 6M 115 (2K 41)
Nobel Sq. SS13: Bas 5K 117
Nobel Vs. EN9: Wal A. 4D 76
NOBLAND GREEN 3F 21
NOBLESGREEN 8D 120 (3H 43)
Nobles Grn. Cl. SS9: Lgh S 8D 120
Nobles Grn. Rd. SS9: Lgh S. 8D 120
NOEL PARK 2A 38
Noel Sq. RM8: Dag. 6H 125
Nonsuch Cl. IG6: Ilf 3A 108
Nook, The CO7: W'hoe 6J 175
Norbury Cl. CO6: M Tey 3H 171
Norbury Gdns. RM6: Chad H. 9J 109
Norbury Rd. E4: Lon. 2A 106
Nordenfeldt Rd. DA8: Eri 3B 152
Nordland Rd. SS8: Can I 1K 151
Nordmann Pl. RM15: S Ock. 4G 144
Noredale SS3: Shoe 8H 139
Nore Rd. SS9: Lgh S 7B 120
(not continuous)
Nore Vw. SS16: Lang H 3H 131
Norfolk Av. CO5: W Mer 2D 228
CO15: Hol S 7B 186
SS9: Lgh S 3E 136
Norfolk Cl. CM9: Mal 7A 214
SS8: Can I. 9G 135
SS15: Lain. 9J 115
Norfolk Ct. SS4: R'fd 2J 121
Norfolk Cres. CO4: Colc 6B 166
Norfolk Dr. CM1: Chelm 4J 59
Norfolk Gdns. CM7: Brain. 4K 193
Norfolk Pl. RM16: Chaf H 3F 154
Norfolk Rd. CM9: Mal 7A 214
DA12: Grav 3H 47
(not continuous)
IG3: Ilf. 3D 124
IG11: Bark. 9D 124
RM7: Romf 1A 126
RM10: Dag 7N 125
RM14: Upm. 5L 127
Norfolk St. E7: Lon. 7G 123
Norfolk Way SS8: Can I. 9F 134
Norlington Rd. E10: Lon. 3C 122
E11: Lon 3C 122
Norman Booth Leisure Cen. 9J 51
Norman Cl. CO6: M Tey 3G 170
CO16: St O 9M 183
EN9: Wal A 3D 76
RM5: Col R. 5N 109
Norman Ct. CM24: Stan M 2D 220
IG2: Ilf. 2C 124
Norman Cres. CM13: Brtwd 9K 97
SS6: Ray 2L 119
Normandie Way CO8: Bures. 8K 195
Normandy Av. CM0: Bur C 3E 196
CO2: Colc 3A 174
Normandy Way DA8: Eri. 6C 152
EN11: Rye P 4C 52
Norman Harris Ho. SS1: Sth S. 7N 137
Norman Hill. CM3: Terl. 4D 24
Normanhurst CM13: Hut 5M 97
Norman Pl. SS9: Lgh S 6D 136
(off Church Hill)
Norman Rd. CO11: Mist 4J 163
CO15: Hol S 6A 186
DA17: Belv 9N 141
(not continuous)
E11: Lon. 4D 122
IG1: Ilf. 7A 124
RM11: Horn. 2E 126
Normansfield CM6: Gt D 4M 203
Normanshire Dr. E4: Lon 1A 106
Normans Rd. SS8: Can I. 1K 151
Norman's Way CM24: Stan M 2D 220
Norman Ter. SS9: Lgh S. 6D 136
(off Leigh Hill)
Normanton Pk. E4: Lon. 8E 90
Norman Way CO3: Colc. 1J 173
(Commons, The)
CO3: Colc. 9J 165
(Park Rd.)
CO16: P Bay 4K 27
(off New Way)
Norpar Flowers 8H 81
Norris Cl. CM7: Brain 3L 193
Norris La. EN11: Hod 4A 52
Norris Rd. EN11: Hod. 5A 52
Norris Way DA1: Cray. 8D 152
Norseman Cl. IG3: Ilf 3G 125
Norsey Cl. CM11: Bill 5K 99
Norsey Ct. CM11: Bill 5K 99
Norsey Dr. CM11: Bill 5L 99
Norsey Rd. CM11: Bill 6K 99 (7J 33)
Norsey Vw. Dr. CM12: Bill 2K 99
Norsey Wood Nature Reserve 4M 99
Northallerton Way RM3: Romf. 2H 111
Northall Rd. DA7: Bexh 7A 152 (2A 46)
Northampton Cl. CM7: Brain 3M 193
Northampton Gro. SS16: Lang H 2H 131
Northampton Ho. RM3: Romf. 1J 111
(off Broseley Rd.)
Northampton Mdw. CM7: Gt Bar 2B 202
Nth. Ash Rd. DA3: New Ash 7F 47
North Av. CM1: Chelm 6H 59 (7K 23)
SS2: Sth S 5N 137 (4K 43)
SS8: Can I 1F 150
Northaw Rd. EN6: N'thaw 4A 30
Northaw Rd. E. EN6: N'thaw. 4A 30
Northbank Rd. E17: Lon 6C 106
North Barn EN10: Brox 9B 52
NORTH BENFLEET 7N 117 (3C 42)
Nth. Benfleet Hall Rd. SS12: N Ben 6N 117
Nth. Birkbeck Rd. E11: Lon 5D 122 (4E 38)
Nth. Boundary Rd. E12: Lon. 5K 123
Northbourne Rd. CO15: Clac S 1K 189
NORTH BROOK END 3A 4
Nth. Brook End SG8: Stpl M 4A 4
Northbrook Rd. IG1: Ilf 4N 123 (4G 39)
Northbrooks CM19: H'low 4B 54
Nth. Circular Rd. E4: Lon 4A 106
E18: Lon 6J 107
IG1: Ilf 4M 123
IG11: Bark. 9N 123
N13: Lon. 1A 38
North Cl. IG7: Chig 2F 108
RM10: Dag. 1M 141
Nth. Colchester Rd. CO5: W Mer 2C 228
North Colne SS16: Van 2E 132
North Ct. CM4: Ing 5E 84
(off Summerfields)
Nth. Cray Rd. DA5: Bex 4A 46
DA14: Sidc 4A 46
North Cres. CB9: Stpl B 2K 223
SS2: Sth S 1H 137
SS12: W'fd 9L 101
North Crockerford SS16: Van 2F 132
Nth. Cross Rd. IG6: Ilf 8B 108
North Dell CM1: Chelm 4M 59
Northdene IG7: Chig 2C 108
Northdown Gdns. IG2: Ilf 9D 108
Northdown Rd. RM11: Horn 2F 126
North Dr. CM2: Gt Bad 3G 72
CM3: May 6K 213
CM13: Hut. 5D 98
RM2: Romf 7G 110
NORTHEND 6B 6
NORTH END 6D 152 (2A 46)
Erith 2A 46
Felsted. 2J 23
Great Yeldham 6E 8
North End CM0: S'min 1E 222 (4D 36)
CM14: War 2F 112
IG9: Buck H 6J 91
RM3: Noak H 8G 94
SG8: Bass. 3B 4
SG8: Meld. 2D 4
Northend Rd. DA8: Eri. 5D 152 (2A 46)
Northend Trad. Est. DA8: Eri 6C 152
Northern Av. SS7: Ben 1C 134
Northern Pct. RM20: W Thur 2C 154
Northern Rd. CO10: Sud. 4K 9
Northfalls Rd. SS8: Can I 2M 151
NORTH FAMBRIDGE. 1F 104 (6H 35)
Northfield CM7: Gt Bar. 1C 202
IG10: Lou 3K 91
Northfield Cl. CM11: Bill. 6L 99
Northfield Cres. SS3: Gt W. 2L 139
Northfield Gdns. CO4: Colc 3A 166
RM9: Dag 6L 125
Northfield Ho. SS2: Sth S. 5L 137
Northfield Path RM9: Dag. 6L 125
Northfield Rd. CB11: Saf W 5D 218
E6: Lon. 9M 123
RM9: Dag 6L 125
Northfields RM17: Grays 2M 155
NORTHFLEET. 3G 47
NORTHFLEET GREEN 5G 47
Northfleet Grn. Rd. DA13: N'flt G. 5G 47
Northfleet Ind. Est. DA11: N'fleet 9J 155
Northfleet Station (Rail) 3F 47
North Ga. CM20: H'low. 2B 54
Northgate End CM23: Bis S 1K 21
Northgate Ind. Pk. RM5: Col R. 5L 109
Northgate St. CO1: Colc. 8M 165
North Greenwich Station (Tube) 7E 38
North Gro. CM18: H'low 4F 54

North Gunnels SS14: Bas 9C 116
NORTH HALLING 7K 47
Nth. Hall Rd. CB11: Quen 1E 216
CB11: Widd 3B 12
CM22: Hen, Ugley 6A 210
North Hill CM3: L Bad 6L 61 (7D 24)
CO1: Colc 8M 165 (6E 16)
SS17: Horn H 8H 131 (5J 41)
Nth. Hill Dr. RM3: Romf 9H 95 (1B 40)
Nth. Hill Grn. RM3: Romf 1H 111
North Ho. *CM18: H'low* 5E 54
(off Bush Fair)
Northlands App. SS16: Bas 5L 131
Northlands Cl. SS17: Stan H 9N 131
Northlands Pavement SS13: Pits 1J 133
North La. CO6: M Tey 1K 171 (6A 16)
North Mall *RM17: Grays* 4L 155
(in Mall, The)
Nth. Mill Pl. CO9: Hals 3K 207
NORTH OCKENDON 8E 128 (5E 40)
Northolme Cl. RM16: Grays 1M 155
Northolt Av. CM23: Bis S 8A 220
Northolt Way RM12: Horn 8G 126
North Pl. CM20: H'low 7G 50
EN9: Wal A 3B 76
North Rd. CB2: Whitt 1J 5
CM9: Tol 7J 225 (6C 26)
CM11: Cray H 2E 116
CM14: Brtwd 7F 96
CM22: Tak 2C 224
CO7: B'sea 6E 182
CO9: Gt Yel 2C 206 (6D 8)
CO10: Bel W 5F 9
CO15: Clac S 7J 185 (3D 28)
DA17: Belv 9N 141
EN11: Hod 4A 52
IG3: Ilf 4D 124
N7: Lon 5A 38
RM4: Hav 9C 94 (1A 40)
RM6: Chad H 9K 109
RM15: S Ock 9F 128 (6E 40)
RM19: Purf 2N 153
(not continuous)
SG14: Hart 5A 20
SS0: Wclf S 4K 137
North Rd. Av. CM14: Brtwd 7F 96
North Rd. Ind. Area SS0: Wclf S 5K 137
Nth. Sea Vw. CO12: Har 5H 209
Nth. Service Rd. CM14: Brtwd 8F 96
NORTH SHOEBURY 5H 139 (4B 44)
Nth. Shoebury Rd. SS3: Shoe 5H 139 (4B 44)
North Side EN9: Wal A 9H 63
Nth. Station Rd. CO1: Colc 6M 165 (5E 16)
NORTH STIFFORD 8H 145 (7F 41)
North St. CB9: Stpl B 2K 223 (5J 7)
CM0: S'min 2D 222 (5C 36)
CM0: T'ham 2K 225 (3E 36)
CM6: Gt D 2L 203 (7G 13)
CM9: Mal 6D 214
CM9: Tol D 2L 227 (5B 26)
CM23: Bis S 1K 21
CO11: Mist 4J 163
CO14: Walt 5M 181
EN9: Naze 1E 62 (1E 30)
IG11: Bark 8A 124
RM1: Romf 7B 110 (3A 40)
(not continuous)
RM11: Horn 2H 127 (4B 40)
SS3: Gt W 2M 139
SS4: R'fd 5L 121 (2J 43)
SS9: Lgh S 6D 136
Northumberland Av. E12: Lon 3J 123
RM11: Horn 9G 111
SS1: Sth S 7A 138
SS15: Lain 1L 131
WC2: Lon 7A 38
Northumberland Cl. CM7: Brain 4K 193
DA8: Eri 5A 152
Northumberland Ct. CM2: Chelm 7A 60
Northumberland Cres. SS1: Sth S 7B 138
NORTHUMBERLAND HEATH 6B 152 (2A 46)
Northumberland Ho. IG8: Wfd G 4N 107
Northumberland Pk. DA8: Eri 5A 152
N17: Lon 2C 38
Northumberland Park Station (Rail) 2C 38
Northumberland Rd. E17: Lon 2A 122
SS17: Linf 9H 147
Northumberland Way DA8: Eri 6A 152
Nth. View Av. RM18: Til 6C 156
Nth. View Cotts. CO6: Gt Hork 9J 159
Nth. View Dr. IG8: Wfd G 6K 107
Northview Dr. SS0: Wclf S 5H 137
Northville Dr. SS0: Wclf S 2N 137
North Weald Airfield 4K 65 (2K 31)
North Weald Airfield Mus. 6M 65 (3K 31)
NORTH WEALD BASSETT 6N 65 (2A 32)
Nth. Weald Cl. SS11: W'fd 1B 118
NORTHWICK 5D 42
Northwick Rd. SS8: Can I 1N 149 (6C 42)
Northwold Rd. N16: Lon 4B 38
Northwood RM16: Grays 9D 146
Northwood Av. RM12: Horn 6E 126
Northwood Gdns. IG5: Ilf 8N 107
NORTH WOOLWICH 7G 39
North Woolwich Station (Rail) 7G 39
Norton Av. SS8: Can I 2L 151
Norton Cl. E4: Lon 2A 106
SS17: Corr 1B 148
NORTON END 8K 227 (1A 12)
NORTON HEATH 5G 69 (2E 32)
Norton Heath Rd. CM5: Will 2G 69 (2E 32)
Norton La. CM4: Nor H 4D 68
CM5: H Ong, Nor H 4D 68 (2E 32)
NORTON MANDEVILLE 4C 68 (2D 32)
Norton Rd. CM1: Chelm 8J 59
CM4: Ing 5D 84
RM10: Dag 8B 126
Norvic Ho. DA8: Eri 5D 152
Norway Cres. CO12: Har 4H 209
Norway Ho. CM16: N Wea 6L 65
Norway Wlk. RM13: Rain 4G 142
Norwich Av. SS2: Sth S 3A 138
Norwich Cl. CO1: Colc 7A 166
CO16: Clac S 7H 185
SS2: Sth S 4A 138
Norwich Cres. SS6: Ray 2J 119
Norwich M. IG3: Ilf 3F 124
Norwich Rd. E7: Lon 7G 122
RM9: Dag 2M 141
Norwich Wlk. SS14: Bas 8G 116
Norwood Av. CO15: Clac S 8M 185
RM7: Rush G 2C 126
Norwood Dr. SS7: Ben 5E 134
NORWOOD END 6C 200 (7D 22)
Norwood End CM5: Fy'd 6C 200 (7D 22)
SS14: Bas 8E 116
Norwood La. DA13: Meop 7H 47
Norwood Way CO14: Walt 7K 181
Nosterfield End
CB1: Cas C, Shudy C 3G 7
Notley Grn. CM77: Gt N 2B 204 (1B 24)
Notley Rd. CM7: Brain 9H 193 (7C 14)
Notley Sports Cen. 8H 193
Nottage Cl. CO7: W'hoe 6J 175
SS17: Corr 1A 148
Nottingham Rd. CO15: Hol S 7B 186
E10: Lon 1C 122
Nottingham Way SS15: Lang H 1H 131
NOUNSLEY 5M 61 (6F 25)
Nounsley Rd. CM3: Hat P 5M 61 (6E 24)
No. 10 Bowling Alley 1C 126
Number Ten Bowling Alley 8L 193
Nuneaton Rd. RM9: Dag 9K 125
Nunnery St. CO9: Cas H 3J 219 (1D 14)
Nunns Cl. CO6: Cogg 3L 197
Nunn's Rd. CO1: Colc 8M 165
Nunns Way RM17: Grays 2N 155
Nun's Mdw. CO9: Gosf 8L 201
Nuns Wlk. CO9: Gt Yel 3C 206
Nunty's La. CM77: G'std G, Tye G 6F 15
NUPER'S HATCH 6C 94 (7A 32)
Nursery Cl. CO3: S'way 1D 172
IG8: Wfd G 2H 107
RM6: Chad H 1J 125
RM15: S Ock 4F 144
SS6: Ray 6K 119
Nursery Dr. CM7: Brain 3J 193
Nursery Flds. CM21: Saw 2J 51
Nursery Gdns. SS15: Lain 7L 115
Nursery La. CM3: Dan 2F 74 (2E 34)
E7: Lon 8G 123
Nursery Ri. CM6: Gt D 4L 203
Nursery Rd. CM2: Chelm 2C 72
CM15: Hook E 4F 82
E12: Lon 4L 123
EN9: Naze 1D 62
EN9: Wal A 1C 76
EN11: Hod 2B 52
IG10: H Bee 9J 77 (6F 31)
IG10: Lou 4J 91
SS17: Stan H 2N 147
Nursery, The DA8: Eri 5D 152
Nursery Wlk. RM7: Rush G 2B 126
Nurstead Chu. La.
DA13: Meop, Sole S 6G 47
Nurstead La. DA3: Long H 6G 47
Nutberry Av. RM16: Grays 9K 145
Nutberry Cl. RM16: Grays 9K 145
Nutbrowne Rd. RM9: Dag 1L 141
Nutcombe Cres. SS4: R'fd 3J 121
Nutfield Gdns. IG3: Ilf 4E 124
Nutfield Rd. E15: Lon 6C 122
NUTHAMPSTEAD 1F 11
Nuthampstead Airfield 1F 11
Nuthampstead Rd. SG8: B'wy, Nuth 1E 10
Nuthatch Cl. CM11: Bill 8L 99
Nuthatch Gdns. SE28: Lon 9C 140
(not continuous)
Nutter La. E11: Lon 1J 123
Nuxley Rd. DA17: Belv 2A 46
N. Woolwich Rd. E16: Lon 7F 39
Nyall Ct. RM2: Romf 7G 111
Nyssa Cl. IG8: Wfd G 3M 107
Nyth Cl. RM14: Upm 1A 128

O

Oakapple Cl. CO2: Colc 5L 173
Oak Av. CM11: Cray H 3D 116
(not continuous)
CO16: Clac S 2E 188
RM14: Upm 5M 127
SS11: Raw, W'fd 9C 102
Oakbank CM13: Hut 4A 98
Oak Bungs. CM7: Brain 5G 192
Oak Chase SS12: W'fd 9H 101
Oak Cl. CM9: Mal 8D 214
CO6: W Ber 3F 164
CO16: T Sok 5L 179
DA1: Cray 9D 152
EN9: Wal A 4D 76
Oak Cotts. CM3: Bore 3F 60
Oak Ct. RM15: S Ock 2F 144
SS7: Had 4L 135
Oakdale Ct. E4: Lon 2C 106
Oakdale Gdns. E4: Lon 2C 106
Oakdale Rd. E7: Lon 9H 123
E11: Lon 4D 122
E18: Lon 6H 107
Oakdene RM3: H Wood 6K 111
Oakdene Av. DA8: Eri 4A 152
Oakdene Cl. RM11: Horn 1F 126
Oakdene Rd. SS13: Pits 7K 117
Oak Dr. CM21: Saw 4H 51
Oak End CM18: H'low 5E 54
Oakenden Rd. DA13: Ludd, Meop 7H 47
Oaken Grange Dr. SS2: Sth S 1K 137
Oakenholt Ho. SE2: Lon 8J 141
Oaker Hill CO9: Gt Yel, Ridg 6C 8
Oak Fall CM8: Wthm 2D 230
Oak Farm Rd. CM9: Wdhm W 1L 75 (1F 35)
Oakfield E4: Lon 2B 106
Oakfield Cl. SS7: Ben 3C 134
Oakfield Dr. CO4: Boxt 3A 160
Oakfield La. CM3: Terl 4D 24
DA1: Bex 4A 46
DA2: Dart 4B 46
Oakfield Lodge *IG1: Ilf* 5A 124
(off Albert Rd.)
Oakfield Rd. IG1: Ilf 5A 124
SS5: Hock 8F 104
SS7: Ben 3C 134
Oakfields IG10: Lou 4N 91
Oak Glade CM16: Coop 8J 65
Oak Glen RM11: Horn 7J 111
Oak Grn. CM11: Bill 7M 99
Oakhall Ct. E11: Lon 1H 123
Oak Hall Rd. E11: Lon 1H 123
Oakham Cl. SS16: Lang H 1H 131
Oakham Ct. SS9: Lgh S 4D 136
Oak Haven CO12: Har 6H 209
Oak Hill CM7: Bla E 4B 14
IG8: Wfd G 4D 106 (2E 38)
Oak Hill Cl. IG8: Wfd G 4D 106
Oak Hill Ct. IG8: Wfd G 4D 106
Oak Hill Cres. IG8: Wfd G 4D 106
Oak Hill Gdns. IG8: Wfd G 5E 106
Oak Hill Rd. RM4: Stap A 6B 94 (7A 32)
Oakhill Rd. RM19: Purf 3M 153
Oakhurst Cl. E17: Lon 8E 106
IG6: Ilf 5A 108
SS12: W'fd 1K 117
Oakhurst Ct. *E17: Lon* 8E 106
(off Woodford New Rd.)
Oakhurst Dr. SS12: W'fd 1J 117
Oakhurst Gdns. E4: Lon 7F 90
E17: Lon 8E 106
Oakhurst Rd. SS2: Sth S 4M 137
SS6: Ray 7M 119
Oak Ind. Pk. CM6: Gt D 4N 203
Oakland Gdns. CM13: Hut 4M 97
Oakland Pl. IG9: Buck H 8G 91
Oakland Rd. CO12: Har 4L 209
E15: Lon 6D 122
Oaklands Av. CO3: S'way 1F 172
RM1: Romf 7C 110
Oaklands Cl. CM23: Bis S 7A 220
CM77: Gt N 8F 192
Oaklands Cres. CM2: Chelm 2C 72
Oaklands Dr. CM17: H'low 4H 55
CM23: Bis S 7A 220
RM15: S Ock 5F 144
Oaklands Farm Ind. Est. CM4: Stock 2A 100
Oaklands M. SS4: R'fd 3H 121
Oaklands Pk. CM23: Bis S 7A 220
Oaklands Pk. Av. IG1: Ilf 4B 124
Oaklands Way CM3: L Bad 9M 61
Oak La. CM11: Cray H 4D 116
(not continuous)
IG8: Wfd G 1F 106
Oaklea Av. CM2: Chelm 7N 59
Oakleafe Gdns. IG6: Ilf 7A 108
Oaklea Lodge IG3: Ilf 5F 124
Oakleigh Av. SS1: Sth S 6B 138
SS5: Hull 6L 103
Oakleigh Pk. Dr. SS9: Lgh S 5D 136
Oakleigh Ri. CM16: Epp 2F 78
Oakleigh Rd. CO15: Clac S 5K 185
Oakleighs SS7: Ben 2C 134
Oakley Av. IG11: Bark 9E 124
SS6: Ray 4F 118
Oakley Cl. E4: Lon 9C 90
RM20: Grays 4F 154
Oakley Ct. IG10: Lou 1N 91
Oakley Dr. CM12: Bill 3H 99
RM3: Romf 2L 111
Oakley Rd. CM7: Brain 1H 193
CO11: Gt Oak, Wix 6A 204 (4D 18)
CO12: Har, L Oak, R'sy 5G 208 (3G 19)
Oakley Sq. NW1: Lon 6A 38
Oak Lodge E11: Lon 1G 122
Oak Lodge Av. IG7: Chig 2C 108
Oak Lodge Tye CM1: Chelm 5B 60
Oakmead Rd. CO16: St O 4K 27
Oakmoor Way IG7: Chig 2D 108
Oak Piece CM16: N Wea 4A 66
Oak Ridge CO12: L Oak 8D 208
Oak Ri. IG9: Buck H 9K 91
Oak Rd. CM8: Riven 1F 230 (3G 25)
CM9: Mal 2D 214
CM11: Cray H 4C 116 (2A 42)
CM11: D'ham 3E 100
CM16: Epp 9E 64
CO5: Tip 4B 226 (3K 25)
CO6: Chap, E Col 9A 196 (5K 15)
CO9: Hals 6J 207 (4F 15)
CO9: L Map 2G 15
CO9: Peb 1H 15
DA8: Eri 5A 152
(Mill Rd.)
Oak Rd. DA8: Eri 6E 152
(Moat La.)
RM3: H Wood 5K 111
RM17: Grays 4M 155
SS4: R'fd 5K 121
SS8: Can I 2J 151
Oak Rd. Nth. SS7: Had 4L 135
Oak Rd. Sth. SS7: Had 4L 135
Oakroyd Av. CM6: Gt D 3M 203
Oakroyd Ho. CM6: Gt D 3M 203
Oaks Av. RM5: Col R 6A 110
Oaks Dr. CO3: Colc 8L 165
Oaks End *CO2: Lay H* 9H 173
(off High St.)
Oaks Gro. E4: Lon 8E 90
Oaks La. IG2: Ilf 9D 108
Oaks Pl. CO4: Colc 4M 165
Oaks Retail Pk., The CM20: H'low 9E 50
Oaks, The CM11: Bill 1L 115
CO13: Frin S 8J 181
EN9: Wal A 5J 77
(off Woodbine Cl.)
IG8: Wfd G 4E 106
Oak St. RM7: Romf 9A 110
Oakthorpe Rd. N13: Lon 1A 38
Oaktree Cl. CM13: Brtwd 9J 97
Oak Tree Cl. IG10: Lou 9B 78
Oaktree Gro. IG1: Ilf 7C 124
Oak Tree Rd. CO7: Alr 6A 176
Oaktrees CM9: L Tot 9N 205
Oakview CO12: Har 6H 209
Oak Wlk. CM21: Saw 4J 51
CO9: Sib H 5J 219
SS5: Hock 9D 104
SS7: Thund 7B 118
(not continuous)
SS9: Lgh S 2C 136
Oakway RM16: Grays 8L 145
OAKWOOD 7A 30
Southgate 7A 30
Oakwood EN9: Wal A 5E 76
Oakwood Av. CM13: Hut 5A 98
CO5: W Mer 1D 228
CO15: Hol S 7B 186
SS9: Lgh S 2D 136
Oakwood Bus. Pk. CO15: Clac S 4L 185
Oakwood Chase RM11: Horn 1K 127
Oakwood Cl. CO13: Frin S, Walt 8H 181
IG8: Wfd G 3L 107
SS7: Ben 1B 134
Oakwood Ct. CM3: Alth 2D 190
SS9: Lgh S 1D 136
Oakwood Dr. CM12: Bill 3L 99
CO5: W Mer 2D 228
DA7: Bexh 9A 152
Oakwood Est. CM20: H'low 8G 50
Oakwood Gdns. CO5: W Mer 2D 228
IG3: Ilf 4E 124
Oakwood Gro. SS13: Pits 9J 117
Oakwood Hill IG10: Lou 5M 91 (7G 31)
Oakwood Hill Ind. Est. IG10: Lou 4B 92
Oakwood House Art Gallery 6B 214
(off High St.)
Oakwood Rd. SS6: Ray 3J 119
SS17: Corr 1C 148
Oakwood Station (Tube) 7A 30
Oak Yd. CO9: Hals 4K 207
Oasis Ct. CM2: Chelm 6A 60
Oasthouse Ct. CB10: Saf W 4C 218
Oast Ho. Spinney CM7: Brain 2H 193
Oast Way SS4: R'fd 5L 121
Oates Rd. RM5: Col R 2N 109
Oatfield Cl. CO3: S'way 9E 164
Oatlands CO7: Elms 9M 167
Oban Ct. SS11: W'fd 2A 118
Oban Ho. IG11: Bark 2C 140
Oban Rd. SS2: Sth S 5A 138
Oberon Cl. CO4: Colc 8F 166
Obrey Way CM23: Bis S, Thor 2K 21
Observer Way CO5: K'dn 1K 211
Occupation La. CM19: Roy 3H 53
Ockelford Av. CM1: Chelm 6H 59
Ockenden Leisure Cen. 5D 144
Ockendon Rd.
RM14: N Ock, Upm 7N 127 (5D 40)
Ockendon Station (Rail) 3E 144 (6E 40)
Ockendon Way CO14: Walt 6K 181
Octavia Dr. CM8: Wthm 7B 230
Octavia Way SE28: Lon 7G 141
Oddcroft CO6: Coln E 3D 198
Oddmark Rd. IG11: Bark 2C 140
Odell Cl. IG11: Bark 9E 124
Odeon Cinema 7C 166
(off St Andrew's Av.)
Chelmsford 9L 59
Colchester 9M 165
Harlow 2B 54
Southend 6M 137
South Woodford 6G 106
Odeon, The IG11: Bark 9C 124
Odessa Rd. E7: Lon 5F 122 (4E 38)
SS8: Can I 2J 151
O'Donaghue Ho's. SS17: Stan H 3N 147
ODSEY 6A 4
Office La. CM9: L Tot 9M 205 (5K 25)
Offord Rd. N1: Lon 5A 38
Ogard Rd. EN11: Rye P 3C 52
Ogilvie Ct. SS12: W'fd 2M 117
Oglethorpe Rd. RM10: Dag 5L 125
O'Grady Ho. E17: Lon 7B 106
Okehampton Rd. RM3: Romf 3G 110
Okehampton Sq. RM3: Romf 3G 110
Old Barn La. CM3: Ret C 8N 87
(not continuous)

Old Barn Rd. CO8: M Bur 2A **16**
Old Barns La. CM1: B'more 5L **69**
CM4: B'more, Rad G 5L **69**
Old Barn Way DA7: Bexh 8B **152**
Old Bell Cl. CM24: Stan M 3C **220**
Old Bell La. CM3: Ret C 8B **88**
Old Bethnal Grn. Rd. E2: Lon 6C **38**
OLD BEXLEY 4A 46
Old Bexley La. DA5: Bex, Dart 4A **46**
(not continuous)
Oldbury Av. CM2: Gt Bad 3G **72**
Old Burylodge La. CM24: Stan M 5F **220**
Old Chapel Rd. BR8: Crock 7A **46**
Oldchurch Gdns. RM7: Rush G 2B **126**
Old Chu. Hill SS16: Lang H 5G **131** (4J **41**)
Old Chu. La. CM13: Mount 3A **98** (6G **33**)
CO6: W Ber 1E **164**
CO10: Bulm 3L **195**
(not continuous)
SG12: Thun 3D **20**
Oldchurch Ri. RM7: Rush G 2C **126**
Old Chu. Rd. CM3: E Han 3B **88** (4D **34**)
CM13: Bill, Mount 1B **98** (6H **33**)
E4: Lon 1A **106** (1D **38**)
Oldchurch Rd. RM7: Rush G 2B **126** (3A **40**)
Old Chu. Rd. SS13: Pits 1N **133**
Old Chu. Rd., The SG14: Bir G, Hert 6A **20**
Old Coach Rd. CO1: Colc 8B **166**
Old Ct. CM1: Chelm 8M **59**
Old Ct. Rd. CM2: Chelm 8M **59**
Old Cft. Cl. CM1: Good E 5G **23**
Old Crown La. CM14: Kel H 9A **82**
Olde Forge CO7: B'sea 4D **182**
Oldegate Ho. E6: Lon 9K **123**
Old Farm Ct. CM12: Bill 4J **99**
Old Farm Yd., The CM22: Srng 4A **210**
Old Ferry Rd. CO7: W'hoe 6H **175**
Oldfields CM14: War 1F **112**
OLD FORD 6D 38
OLD FORD 6D **38**
Old Ford Rd. E2: Lon 6C **38**
E3: Lon 6C **38**
Old Forge Ct. *EN9: Wal A* *4G 77*
(off Lamplighters Cl.)
Old Forge Rd. CM3: Bore 3F **60**
CO2: Lay H 9G **173**
Old Fortune Cotts. SS15: Lain 6L **115**
Old Hall Cl. CB9: Stpl B 2L **223**
Old Hall Ct. SS3: Gt W 2L **139**
OLD HALL GREEN 7D 10
Old Hall La. CM9: Tol D 6C **26**
CO14: Walt 1M **181**
Old Hall Ri. CM17: H'low 3K **55** (7K **21**)
Old Hall Rd. CB9: Stpl B 4M **223** (5J **11**)
IP9: S'ly 1G **19**
OLD HARLOW 9H 51 (6J 21)
OLD HEATH 3C 174 (7F 17)
Old Heath Rd. CM0: May, S'min 3A **222** (5B **36**)
CO1: Colc 1B **174** (6F **17**)
CO2: Colc 1B **174** (6F **17**)
Old Highway EN11: Rye P 2B **52** (6D **20**)
Old Hill Av. SS16: Lang H 6K **131**
Oldhouse Cft. CM20: H'low 1D **54**
Old Ho. La. CM19: Roy 6K **53** (7F **21**)
CO4: Boxt 6N **159**
EN9: Naze 2F **62**
Old Ho. Rd. CO6: Gt Hork 8G **159** (4D **16**)
Old Ho., The (Council Offices)
SS4: R'fd 6L **121** (2J **43**)
Oldhouse Vs. CM22: Tak 2C **224**
Old Ipswich Rd. CO7: A'lgh 9E **160** (4G **17**)
Old Jenkins Cl. SS17: Stan H 4K **147**
Old La. CM77: Tye G 6F **15**
Old Leigh Rd. SS9: Lgh S, Wclf S 5F **136**
Old London Rd. CM9: Wdhm W 2J **75** (1F **35**)
CM17: H'low 9H **51** (7J **21**)
(not continuous)
SS11: Raw 1D **118** (1D **42**)
Old Macdonalds Educational Farm Pk.
7K 95 (7C 32)
Old Mnr. Way DA7: Bexh 7B **152**
Old Market Retail Pk. SS13: Pits 1J **133**
OLD MEAD 9A 210 (5B 12)
Old Mead SS2: Sth S 8F **120**
Oldmead Ho. RM10: Dag 8N **125**
Old Mead La. CM22: Hen 9A **210**
Old Mead Rd. CM22: Else, Hen 1K **199** (4B **12**)
Old Mill Chase CM7: Weth 8C **228**
Old Mill Cl. CM9: Mal 5C **214**
E18: Lon 7J **107**
Old Mill Pde. RM1: Romf 9D **110**
Old Mill Pl. RM7: Romf 1B **126**
Old Mill Rd. CB11: Saf W 5D **218**
CO4: Boxt, L'ham 3C **160** (2F **17**)
Old Nazeing Rd. EN9: Naze 1C **62**
EN10: Brox 9A **52** (1D **30**)
Old Nth. Rd. SG8: Bass 3C **4**
SG8: R'ton 5C **4**
Old Oaks EN9: Wal A 2E **76**
Old Orchard CM18: H'low 5C **54**
Old Pk. Av. N21: Lon 7B **30**
Old Pk. Ridings N21: Lon 7A **30**
Old Parsonage Way CO13: Frin S 9J **181**
Old Pier St. CO14: Walt 6M **181**
Old Rectory Ct. CO6: M Tey 2J **171**
SS2: Sth S 5C **138**
Old Rectory La.
CM8: Riven, Wthm 1D **230** (3G **25**)
Old Rectory Rd. CM5: Chip 4F **80** (4B **32**)
Old Rd. CM14: Nave, N'side 1H **95**
CM17: H'low 6H **51** (5J **21**)
CM77: Tye G 6F **15**
CO5: Cogg, Fee 4A **170** (7J **15**)
CO6: Cogg 7J **15**
Old Rd. CO9: Wick P 7G **9**
CO13: Frin S 1J **187**
CO15: Clac S 1J **189** (4D **28**)
DA1: Cray 9B **152** (3A **46**)
RM4: Nave 1H **95** (6B **32**)
(not continuous)
Old Rd. E. DA11: Grav 4H **47**
Old Rd. W. DA11: Grav 4G **47**
Old Rose Gdn. CO4: Colc 4L **165**
Old Roxwell Rd. CM1: Writ 7B **58** (1J **33**)
Old School Ct. CM3: Hat P 2M **61**
CO7: B'sea 7D **182**
Old School Cres. E7: Lon 8G **122**
Old School Fld. CM1: Chelm 7N **59**
Old School La. CO7: Elms 9N **167**
Old School Mdw. SS3: Gt W 2J **139**
Old School Yd. CB11: Saf W 4C **218**
Old Ship La. SS4: R'fd 5L **121**
Old Shire La. EN9: Wal A 5G **77**
Old Southend Rd. CM2: Howe G 9L **73** (3C **34**)
SS1: Sth S 7N **137**
Old Sta. Rd. IG10: Lou 4L **91** (7G **31**)
OLD STREET **6B 38**
Old St. EC1: Lon 6B **38**
Old St. Hill CM22: Hat O, Hat H 8A **206** (4B **22**)
Old Street Station (Rail, Tube) 6B 38
Old Sungate Cotts. RM5: Col R 5L **109**
Old Vicarage Cl. CM1: High E 4G **23**
Old Vicarage Rd. CO12: Har 4K **209**
Old Watling St. ME2: Roch 6K **47**
Old Way CO13: Frin S 1J **187**
Old Wickford Rd. CM3: S Fer 9H **89**
Old Wimpole Rd. SG8: Arr 1C **4**
Oldwyk SS16: Van 2F **132**
Olive Av. SS9: Lgh S 4N **135**
Olive Gro. CO2: Colc 4L **173**
Oliver Cl. EN11: Rye P 3B **52**
RM20: W Thur 5C **154**
Oliver Pl. CM8: Wthm 5E **230**
Oliver Rd. CM15: Shenf 4K **97**
E10: Lon 4B **122** (4D **38**)
E17: Lon 9C **106**
RM13: Rain 1D **142**
RM20: W Thur 6C **154** (2E **46**)
(not continuous)
Olivers Cl. CO15: Clac S 9J **185**
Olivers Ct. CO15: Clac S 9J **185**
Olivers Cres. SS3: Gt W 2M **139**
Olivers Dr. CM8: Wthm 8C **230**
Olivers La. CO2: King 7G **172** (1D **26**)
Olivers Rd. CO15: Clac S 9J **185** (4D **28**)
Oliver Way CM1: Chelm 5G **59** (7K **23**)
Olive St. RM7: Romf 9B **110**
Oliveswood Rd. CM6: Gt D 4L **203**
Olivia Dr. SS9: Lgh S 4E **136**
Ollard's Ct. IG10: Lou 4K **91**
Ollard's Gro. IG10: Lou 3K **91**
Olley Wlk. CO5: Tip 5E **226**
OLMSTEAD GREEN 5G 7
Olympic Bus. Cen. SS14: Bas 5G **116**
Omnibus Way E17: Lon 6A **106**
One Tree Hill
SS17: Bas, Fob, Van 4A **132** (4K **41**)
One Tree Hill Country Pk. 6N 131
Ongar Castle 7L 67 (3C 32)
Ongar Cl. CO16: Clac S 9F **184**
RM6: Chad H 9H **109**
Ongar Ent. Cen. CM5: Chip 5L **67**
Ongar Leisure Cen. 5L 67
Ongar Pl. CM14: Brtwd 8G **96**
Ongar Rd. CM1: Cook G, Writ 4K **69** (1J **33**)
(Bassett's La.)
CM1: Cook G, Writ 2G **71** (2H **33**)
(Highwood Rd.)
CM4: Cook G, Rad G, Writ 4K **69** (2G **33**)
(not continuous)
CM5: Chip, Fy'd 9C **200** (2C **32**)
(Fyfield)
CM5: Chip, Ston M 9N **67** (4D **32**)
(Marden Ash)
CM6: Gt D 4M **203** (1G **23**)
CM6: Mar R 6E **22**
CM15: Brtwd, Kel H, Pil H 2M **81** (4C **32**)
CM15: Ston M 9N **67** (4D **32**)
RM4: Abr, Stap T 2G **92** (6J **31**)
Ongar Rd. Trad. Est. CM6: Gt D 4M **203**
Ongar Way RM13: Rain 1C **142**
Onra Rd. E17: Lon 2A **122**
Onslow Cl. E4: Lon 8C **90**
Onslow Cres. CO2: Colc 6A **174**
Onslow Gdns. CM5: Chip 6L **67**
E18: Lon 7H **107**
Opal M. IG1: Ilf 4A **124**
Ophir Rd. CO7: B'sea 8E **182**
Optima Bus. Pk. EN11: Rye P 4C **52**
Optima Pk. DA1: Cray 7E **152**
Orange Gro. E11: Lon 5E **122**
(not continuous)
IG7: Chig 3B **108**
Orange Rd. SS8: Can I 1K **151**
(Wamburg Rd.)
SS8: Can I 2K **151**
(Westerland Av.)
Orange St. CM6: Thax 8C **224**
Orange Tree Cl. CM2: Chelm 4D **72**
Orange Tree Hill RM4: Hav 2B **110** (1A **40**)
Orbital Cen., The IG8: Wfd G 6K **107**
Orchard Av. CM11: Rams B 6E **100**
CM12: Bill 3L **99** (6K **33**)
CM13: Brtwd 9J **97**
CO9: Hals 4J **207**
RM13: Rain 4G **142**
SS5: Hock 9D **104**
SS6: Ray 7J **119**
Orchard Cl. CB11: Newp 3K **215**
CB11: Saf W 6C **218**
CM0: S'min 2D **222**
CM1: Writ 1K **71**
CM2: Gt Bad 5D **72**
CM3: Hat P 2L **61**
CM6: Thax 7C **224**
CM9: Mal 6B **214**
CM9: Tol 8L **225**
CM22: Srng 4A **210**
CO6: Cop 4M **171**
CO7: Elms 9N **167**
CO9: Ridg 8D **216**
CO12: Gt Oak 8C **204**
CO12: R'sy 5C **208**
CO16: Clac S 8G **184**
E4: Lon 1A **106**
E11: Lon 8H **107**
RM15: S Ock 4F **144**
SS3: Gt W 2M **139**
SS5: Hock 9E **104**
Orchard Cotts. CM3: Bore 1H **61**
CO4: L'ham 4F **160**
Orchard Ct. CM12: Bill 4H **99**
CO3: Colc 8K **165**
E10: Lon 3B **122**
Orchard Cft. CM20: H'low 1F **54**
Orchard Dr. CM3: May 7L **213**
CM7: Brain 7J **193**
CM16: They B 6D **78**
CM19: Roy 4H **53**
CO13: Gt Hol 1D **186**
RM17: Grays 9K **145**
Orchard End CM5: Chip 5K **67**
Orchard Gdns. CO4: Colc 7B **166**
EN9: Wal A 4C **76**
Orchard Gro. SS9: Lgh S 9E **120**
Orchard Ho. DA8: Eri 6D **152**
Orchard La. CM15: Pil H 4C **96**
IG8: Wfd G 1J **107**
Orchard Lea CM21: Saw 3H **51**
Orchard Lodge *CO5: Tip* *7D 226*
(off Station Rd.)
Orchard Mead SS9: Lgh S 1D **136**
Orchard M. CO5: Tip 7C **226**
Orchard Piece CM4: B'more 9H **69**
Orchard Pightle CB1: Hads 3D **6**
Orchard Rd. CM0: Bur C 4E **196** (7C **36**)
CM0: S'min 2D **222**
CM9: Mal 6B **214**
CM23: Bis S 8A **220**
CO1: Colc 7M **165**
CO5: K'dn 2K **211**
CO7: Alr 6A **176**
RM7: Maw 5N **109**
RM10: Dag 1M **141**
RM15: S Ock 4F **144**
SS7: Thund 8B **118**
Orchards CM8: Wthm 6C **230**
Orchard Side SS9: Lgh S 9E **120**
Orchards, The CM16: Epp 2F **78**
CM21: Saw 1K **51**
Orchard St. CM2: Chelm 1C **72**
Orchard, The CM6: Fels 8K **199**
EN10: Brox 8A **52**
SS12: W'fd 9J **101**
Orchard Vw. CM13: Dun 1G **130**
Orchard Way IG7: Chig 9F **92**
Orchid Av. CM8: Wthm 3B **230**
Orchid Cl. RM4: Abr 2G **93**
Orchid Fld. Ct. CO5: W Mer 3E **228**
Orchid Pl. CM3: S Fer 9K **89**
Orchill Dr. SS7: Had 2L **135**
Orchis Gro. RM17: Grays 3J **155**
Orchis Way RM3: Romf 3K **111**
Ordnance Cres. SE10: Lon 7E **38**
Ordnance Rd. EN3: Enf 5C **30**
Oregon Av. E12: Lon 6M **123**
Oreston Rd. RM13: Rain 3H **143**
Orford Cres. CM1: Chelm 6L **59**
Orford Rd. E17: Lon 9A **106**
E18: Lon 7H **107**
Organ La. E4: Lon 8C **90**
(not continuous)
Oriel Gdns. IG5: Ilf 7M **107**
Orient Ind. Pk. E10: Lon 4A **122**
Orient Way E10: Lon 4A **122**
Oriole Way CM23: Bis S 1J **21**
SE28: Lon 7G **140**
Orion Ct. SS14: Bas 6G **117**
Orion Way CM7: Brain 4K **193**
Orkney Gdns. SS12: W'fd 2N **117**
Orlando Ct. CO14: Walt 6M **181**
Orlando Dr. SS13: Bas 6K **117**
Ormesby Chine CM3: S Fer 3J **103**
Ormesby Cl. SE28: Lon 7J **141**
Ormond Cl. RM3: H Wood 6H **111**
Ormonde Av. SS4: R'fd 4K **121**
SS7: Had 4N **135**
Ormonde Cl. CO6: W Ber 3F **164**
Ormonde Ct. *RM11: Horn* *2D 126*
(off Clydesdale Rd.)
Ormonde Gdns. SS9: Lgh S 4N **135**
Ormonde Ri. IG9: Buck H 7J **91**
Ormonds Cres. CM3: Wdhm F 5H **89**
Ormsby Rd. SS8: Can I 3D **150**
Orpen Cl. CO6: W Ber 3E **164**
Orpen's Hill CO2: B'ch 9B **172** (1C **26**)
Orrmo Rd. SS8: Can I 2M **151**
ORSETT 5C 146 (6H 41)
Orsett Av. SS9: Lgh S 1B **136**
Orsett End SS14: Bas 8D **116**
ORSETT HEATH 9C 146 (1H 47)
Orsett Heath Cres. RM16: Grays 1C **156**
Orsett Rd. RM16: Horn H, Ors 4E **146** (6H **41**)
RM17: Grays 3K **155** (1F **47**)
SS17: Horn H 4E **146** (6H **41**)
Orsett Smockmill 6A 146
Orsett Ter. IG8: Wfd G 4J **107**
Orsino Wlk. CO4: Colc 8F **166**
Orton Cl. CM4: Marg 1J **85**
Orton Ho. *RM3: Romf* *4J 111*
(off Leyburn Rd.)
Orvis La. CO7: E Ber 1K **17**
ORWELL 1D 4
Orwell RM18: E Til 2L **157**
Orwell Cl. CO4: Colc 6E **166**
RM13: Rain 5B **142**
Orwell Ct. SS11: W'fd 2B **118**
Orwell Rd. CB2: Barr 1E **4**
CO12: Har 3M **209**
CO15: Clac S 2K **189**
IP11: Felix 1K **19**
Orwell Wlk. CM8: Wthm 4B **230**
Orwell Way CM0: Bur C 2C **196**
CO16: Clac S 8G **184**
Osbert Rd. CM8: Wthm 7B **230**
Osborne Av. SS5: Hock 1B **120**
Osborne Cl. CO15: Clac S 6L **185**
RM11: Horn 1F **126**
Osborne Cotts. CO5: Mess 1D **226**
Osborne Ct. E10: Lon 2B **122**
Osborne Rd. CM15: Pil H 5D **96**
CO5: W Mer 3E **228**
E7: Lon 7H **123**
E10: Lon 4B **122**
EN10: Brox 7A **52**
IG9: Buck H 7H **91**
RM9: Dag 7L **125**
RM11: Horn 1F **126**
SS0: Wclf S 5K **137**
SS13: Pits 7M **117**
SS16: Van 1D **132**
Osbornes Ct. CO7: B'sea 7E **182**
Osborne Sq. RM9: Dag 6L **125**
Osborne St. CO2: Colc 9N **165** (6E **16**)
Osbourne Hgts. CM14: War 1E **112**
Osbourne Ho. IG8: Wfd G 4N **107**
Osea Rd. CM9: Gold 1K **35**
Osea Way CM1: Chelm 6A **60**
OSIDGE 7A 30
Osidge La. N14: Lon 7A **30**
Osier Ct. RM7: Romf 1B **126**
Osier Dr. SS15: Lain 6L **115**
Osier Way E10: Lon 5B **122**
Osmond Cl. CM77: Bla N 3B **194**
Osney Ho. SE2: Lon 9J **141**
Osprey Cl. E11: Lon 8G **107**
E18: Lon 8G **107**
SS3: Shoe 5J **139**
Osprey Ct. CM14: Brtwd 9E **96**
EN9: Wal A 4E **76**
Osprey Rd. EN9: Wal A 4G **76**
Ospreys CO15: Clac S 7K **185**
Ospreys, The *SS9: Lgh S* *5E 136*
(off Leigh Rd.)
Osprey Way CM2: Chelm 5B **72**
Ostell Cres. EN3: Enf 8A **76**
OSTEND 6B 36
Osterberg Rd. DA1: Dart 9K **153**
Osterley Dr. SS16: Lang H 1H **131**
Osterley Pl. CM3: S Fer 3K **103**
Othello Cl. CO4: Colc 7F **166**
Otley App. IG2: Ilf 1A **124**
Otley Dr. IG2: Ilf 9A **108**
Ottawa Gdns. RM10: Dag 9B **126**
Ottawa Rd. RM18: Til 7C **156**
Otten Rd. CO10: Bel O 4E **8**
Otterbourne Rd. E4: Lon 9D **90**
Ottershaw Way CO16: Clac S 7F **184**
Oudle La. SG10: M Hud 2G **21**
Ouida Rd. SS8: Can I 2K **151**
Oulton Av. SS8: Can I 9F **134**
Oulton Cl. CO12: Har 4H **209**
SE28: Lon 6H **141**
Oulton Cres. IG11: Bark 7E **124**
Oulton Hall CO15: Clac S 1L **189**
Oundle Ho. *RM3: Romf* *2H 111*
(off Montgomery Cres.)
Ouse Chase CM8: Wthm 5A **230**
Outing Cl. SS1: Sth S 7A **138**
Outing's La. CM15: Dodd, Hook E 5E **82** (5E **32**)
Outpart Eastward CO12: Har 1N **209**
Outwood Comn. Rd. CM11: Bill 4N **99** (1K **41**)
(Norsey Rd.)
CM11: Bill 9L **99** (1K **41**)
(Southend Rd.)
Outwood Farm Cl. CM11: Bill 6N **99**
Outwood Farm Rd. CM11: Bill 6N **99** (7K **33**)
Oval Gdns. RM17: Grays 1M **155**
Oval Rd. Nth. RM10: Dag 1N **141** (6K **39**)
Oval Rd. Sth. RM10: Dag 2N **141**
Overcliff SS0: Wclf S 7J **137**
Overcliffe DA11: Grav 3G **47**
Overcliff Rd. RM17: Grays 3N **155**
(not continuous)
Overhall Hill CO6: Coln E 3J **15**
Over Hall La. CB10: A'dn 6F **190** (4E **6**)
Overmead Dr. CM3: S Fer 9L **89**
Overstrand Ho. RM12: Horn 4F **126**
Overton Cl. SS7: Thund 9C **118**
Overton Ct. E11: Lon 2G **123**
Overton Dr. E11: Lon 2G **123** (4F **39**)
RM6: Chad H 2H **125**
SS7: Thund 9C **118**
Overton Rd. SS7: Thund 9B **118**
Overton Way SS7: Thund 9B **118**
Overy St. DA1: Dart 3C **46**

OVINGTON 4D 8
Ovington Gdns. CM12: Bill 3J 99
Owen Cl. RM5: Col R 3N 109
SE28: Lon 8H 141
Owen Gdns. IG8: Wfd G 3L 107
Owen Ward Cl. CO2: Colc 3H 173
Owl Cvn. Site, The IG10: Lou 2F 90
Owles La. SG9: Bunt 4D 10
Owlets Hall Cl. RM11: H Wood 7K 111
Owletts 6J 47
Owl's Hill CM3: Terl 4D 24
Owls Retreat CO4: Colc 7F 166
Oxborrow Cl. CO13: Walt 8D 180
Oxcroft Ct. SS15: Lain 9K 115
Oxenden Dr. EN11: Hod 6A 52
OXEN END 4J 13
Oxen End CM7: L Bar 4J 13
Oxenford Cl. CO12: Har 6H 209
Oxford Av. RM11: Horn 8L 111
RM16: Grays 2C 156
Oxford Circus Station (Tube) 7A 38
Oxford Cl. SS16: Lang H 1H 131
Oxford Ct. CM2: Chelm 7N 59
CM14: War 1G 112
CO3: Colc 9L 165
CO6: E Col 8C 198
Oxford Cres. CO15: Clac S 9J 185
Oxford La. CO9: Sib H 5H 219
Oxford Mdw. CO9: Sib H 5J 219
Oxford Pl. CO6: E Col 8C 198
Oxford Rd. CO3: Colc 9L **165** (6E **16**)
CO9: Hals 5J 207
CO11: Mist 4J 163
CO13: Frin S 9K 181
CO15: Clac S 1K **189** (4D **28**)
E15: Lon 8D 122
(not continuous)
IG1: Ilf 7B 124
IG8: Wfd G 2K 107
RM3: Romf 3K 111
SS4: R'fd 3J 121
SS8: Can I 1J 151
SS17: Horn H 1G 147
SS17: Stan H 4K 147
Oxford St. W1: Lon 7A 38
Oxleas E6: Lon 6A 140
Oxley Cl. RM2: Romf 6G 111
Oxley Gdns. SS17: Stan H 9M 131
OXLEY GREEN 4A 26
Oxley Hill CM9: Tol D 4A 26
CO5: Abb 8A **174** (2E **26**)
Oxley Ho. CM77: Bla N 2B 194
Oxley Parker Dr. CO4: Colc 1A 166
Oxleys Rd. EN9: Wal A 2G 77
Oxleys, The CM17: H'low 8K 51
Oxlip Rd. CM8: Wthm 3B 230
Oxlow La. RM9: Dag 6L **125** (5K **39**)
RM10: Dag 6M 125
RM10: Dag 6M **125** (5K **39**)
Oxney Ho. CM1: Writ 1H 71
Oxney Mead CM1: Writ 2H 71
Oxney Vs. CM6: Fels 7L 199
Oxted Ho. *RM3: Romf 2K 111*
(off Redcar Rd.)
Oxwich Cl. SS17: Corr 1B 148
Ox Yard CO9: Gosf 9M 201
Oyster Bus. Cen. CM9: Tol 7L 225
Oyster Cl. CO5: W Mer 2C 228
Oyster Pk. CO1: Colc 9D 166
Oyster Pl. CM2: Chelm 7A 60
Oyster Tank Rd. CO7: B'sea 8D 182
Ozier Ct. CB11: Saf W 6D 218
Oziers CM22: Else 2K 199
Ozonia Av. SS12: W'fd 2K 117
Ozonia Cl. SS12: W'fd 2J 117
Ozonia Wlk. SS12: W'fd 2K 117
Ozonia Way SS12: W'fd 2K 117

P

Paarl Rd. SS8: Can I 1G 151
Pace Heath Cl. RM5: Col R 3B 110
Packards La. CO6: Wmgfd 7A **158** (3B **16**)
Packe Cl. CO5: Fee 1L 211
Paddock Cl. CM11: Bill 9L 99
CO12: Har 3L 209
RM16: Ors 5C 146
SS9: Lgh S 8D 120
Paddock Dr. CM1: Chelm 4N 59
Paddock Mead CM18: H'low 8B 54
Paddocks, The CM4: Ing 6D 84
CM6: High R 3F 23
CM8: Wthm 5D 230
CM9: Gt Tot 3M 229
CO5: Abb 9A 174
CO5: W Mer 3D 228
CO7: Gt Ben 9L 177
CO8: Bures 8K 195
CO10: Ashen 5C 8
RM4: Stap A 5D 94
RM16: Ors 5C 146
SS6: Ray 5M 119
Paddock, The CM4: Stock 6N 85
EN10: Brox 8A 52
Paddock Way CO7: W'hoe 3J 175
Padgets, The EN9: Wal A 4E 76
Padgetts Way SS5: Hull 5K 103
PADHAM'S GREEN 9D **84** (6H **33**)
Padham's Grn. Rd. CM4: Ing 9D **84** (6H **33**)
Padnall Ct. RM6: Chad H 7J 109
Padnall Rd. RM6: Chad H 7J 109
Paeony Chase CO5: W Mer 1C 228
Pageant Cl. RM18: Til 6E 156
Page Cl. CM8: Wthm 7A 230
RM9: Dag 7K 125
Page Cres. DA8: Eri 5D 152
Page Rd. CO15: Clac S 1J 189
SS13: Pits 8N 117
Pages La. CM9: Tol D 7B 26
RM3: H Wood 6M 111
Paget Ct. CM22: Else 3K 199
Paget Dr. CM12: Bill 3J 99
Paget Rd. CO5: Rhdge 6F 174
CO7: W'hoe 6J 175
(not continuous)
IG1: Ilf 6A 124
Pagette Way RM17: Grays 3K 155
Pagles Fld. CM13: Hut 5M 97
PAGLESHAM CHURCHEND 1B 44
PAGLESHAM EASTEND 1C 44
Paglesham Rd. SS4: Stam 1A 44
Paignton Av. CM1: Chelm 6M 59
Paignton Cl. SS6: Ray 2K 119
Paines Brook Rd. RM3: Romf 3K 111
Paines Brook Way RM3: Romf 3K 111
Painswick Av. SS17: Stan H 9A 132
Painters Rd. IG2: Ilf 7E **108** (3J **39**)
Pakes Way CM16: They B 7D 78
Palace Ct. SS1: Sth S 7M 137
Palace Gdns. IG9: Buck H 7K 91
Palace Gates Rd. N22: Lon 2A 38
Palace Gro. SS15: Lain 7N 115
Palace Theatre 5J 137
Palace Vw. Rd. E4: Lon 2B 106
Palamos Rd. E10: Lon 3A 122
Palatine Pk. SS15: Lain 9H 115
PALE GREEN 4H 7
Paley Gdns. IG10: Lou 2A 92
Palins Way RM16: Grays 8K 145
Palliser Dr. RM13: Rain 5E 142
Pallister Rd. CO15: Clac S 2K 189
Pall Mall SS9: Lgh S 5D 136
SW1: Lon 7A 38
Palm Cl. CM2: Chelm 4D 72
CM8: Wthm 2D 230
E10: Lon 5B 122
Palmeira Arches SS0: Wclf S 7J 137
Palmeira Av. SS0: Wclf S 7J 137
Palmeira Ct. SS0: Wclf S 7J 137
Palmeira Pde. *SS0: Wclf S 7J 137*
(off Station Rd.)
Palmer Cl. SS15: Lain 9M 115
Palmer Rd. RM8: Dag 3J 125
Palmers SS17: Stan H 2A 148
Palmers Av. RM17: Grays 3M **155** (1G **47**)
Palmers Cft. CM2: Chelm 9B 60
Palmers Dr. RM17: Grays 2M 155
PALMERS GREEN 1A 38
Palmers Green Station (Rail) 1A 38
Palmers Gro. EN9: Naze 1F 62
Palmers Hill CM16: Epp 8F **64** (3J **31**)
Palmers La. SG8: Chris 6H 5
Palmerston Ct. IG9: Buck H 7J 91
Palmerstone Rd. SS8: Can I 2D 150
Palmerston Gdns. RM20: Grays 3G 155
Palmerston Lodge CM2: Gt Bad 3G 72
Palmerston Rd. CO16: T Sok 4L 179
E7: Lon 8H 123
E17: Lon 3D 38
IG9: Buck H 8H **91** (7F **31**)
N22: Lon 2A 38
RM13: Rain 2G 142
RM20: Grays 4G 155
SS0: Wclf S 7J 137
Palm M. SS15: Lain 6M 115
Palm Rd. RM7: Romf 9A 110
Pampas Cl. CO4: Colc 3A 166
PAMPISFORD 1K 5
Pampisford Rd. CB1: Abgtn 1B 6
Pamplins SS15: Lain 9A 116
Panadown SS15: Lain 9A 116
Pancras Rd. NW1: Lon 6A 38
Pancroft RM4: Abr 2G 93
PANFIELD 1C **192** (6B **14**)
Panfield La. CM7: Brain 4G **192** (6C **14**)
Panfield M. IG2: Ilf 1N 123
Panfield Rd. CM7: Brain, Pan 1F **192** (6C **14**)
SE2: Lon 9G 140
Panfields SS15: Lain 9J 115
Pan La. CM3: E Han, Ret C 4M **87** (4C **34**)
Pannells Ash CO10: Ashen 4C 8
PANNEL'S ASH 4C 8
Pantile Av. SS2: Sth S 3A 138
Pantile Cl. CM8: Wthm 8D 230
Pantile Cotts. RM14: Upm 9A 112
Pantile Hill CM0: S'min 2C **222** (5C **36**)
Pantile Ho. SS2: Sth S 3A 138
Pantiles, The CM12: Bill 4J 99
Panton Cres. CO4: Colc 8E 166
Panton M. CM7: Brain 8J 193
Pan Wlk. CM1: Chelm 6F 58
Papenburg Rd. SS8: Can I 8G 134
Papillon Ho. *CO1: Colc 8M 165*
(off Balkerne Gdns)
Papillon Rd. CO3: Colc 8L 165
Paprills SS16: Bas 2N 131
Parade Dr. CO12: Har 6E 208
Parade, The CM1: Chelm 5J 59
CM14: Brtwd 9F 96
CO2: Colc 5A 174
CO14: Walt 7M **181** (1H **29**)
RM3: H Wood 3M 111
SS13: Pits 1J 133
Paradise Centre Gardens 7J 9
Paradise Rd. CM1: Writ 2K 71
EN9: Wal A 4C 76
Paradise Wildlife Pk. 1B 30
Parent Shopping Mall *E18: Lon 6G 107*
(off Marlborough Rd.)
Pargat Dr. SS9: Lgh S 8B 120
Pargeters Hyam SS5: Hock 1E 120
Pargeters Sq. SS2: Temp I 1M 137
Parham Dr. IG2: Ilf 1A 124
Paringdon Rd. CM18: H'low 7A 54
CM19: H'low 7A **54** (1G **31**)
Parish Cl. RM11: Horn 4F 126
Parish Way SS15: Lain 8L 115
Parkanaur Av. SS1: Sth S 8E 138
Park and Ride
North Station 6M 165
Park Av. CM1: Chelm 8H **59** (1K **33**)
CM13: Hut 7M 97
CM17: H'low 6H 55
E15: Lon 8E 122
EN1: Enf 7B 30
IG1: Ilf 3N 123
IG8: Wfd G 2H 107
IG11: Bark 8B 124
N22: Lon 2A 38
RM14: Upm 2B 128
RM20: W Thur 4D 154
SS8: Can I 2M 151
SS9: Lgh S 9D 120
Park Blvd. CO15: Hol S 7B 186
RM2: Romf 5D 110
Park Bungs. CM22: L Hall 3N 213
Park Chase CO16: St O 8A 184
SS7: Had 4L 135
Park Cl. CM16: N Wea 6M 65
SS12: W'fd 1K 117
Pk. Corner Rd. DA2: S'fleet 5F 47
Park Ct. CM20: H'low 1C 54
CO9: Sib H 6J 219
E4: Lon 8C 90
E17: Lon 9B 106
Park Cres. DA8: Eri 4A 152
RM11: Horn 2E 126
SS0: Wclf S 6L 137
Park Cres. Rd. DA8: Eri 4B 152
Parkdale CM3: Dan 3C 74
Park Dr. CM4: Ing 5E 84
CM7: Brain 8J 193
CM9: Mal 6D **214** (1H **35**)
CM22: Hat H 2F 210
CO7: B'sea 6D 182
CO9: Hals 5K 207
RM1: Romf 8B 110
RM10: Dag 5A 126
RM14: Upm 6M 127
SS12: W'fd 1K 117
Park Drive Fitness & Squash Club 7D 214
Park Dr. Pde. CO7: B'sea 6D 182
Pk. End Rd. RM1: Romf 8C 110
Parker Av. IP11: T Mary 1J 19
RM18: Til 6E 156
Parker Rd. CM2: Chelm 1D 72
RM17: Grays 3J 155
Parker's Farm Rd.
RM16: Bulp, Ors 7B **130** (5G **41**)
Parker Way CO9: Hals 6K 207
Parkes Rd. IG7: Chig 2D 108
PARKESTON 2H **209** (2G **19**)
Parkeston Rd. CO12: Har 3H **209** (3H **19**)
(Dovercourt By-Pass)
CO12: Har 2H 209
(Garland Rd.)
Park Farm Industries CM77: Bla N 9J 193
Pk. Farm Rd. RM14: Upm 7K **127** (5C **40**)
Park Flds. CM19: Roy 3G 53
Parkfields CO9: Sib H 6J 219
SS7: Had, Thund 2H 135
Parkfield St. CO5: Rhdge 7F 174
Park Gdns. DA8: Eri 2B 152
E10: Lon 3A 122
SS5: Hock 2E 120
(not continuous)
Parkgate SS0: Wclf S 6L 137
Parkgate Rd. CM8: K'dn, Riven, Sil E 2G 25
Park Ga. Rd. SS17: Fob 6B 132
Park Grange IG7: Chig 2C 108
PARK GREEN 4J 11
Park Gro. DA7: Bexh 9A 152
Park Gro. Rd. E11: Lon 4E 122
Parkhall Rd. CM7: Gosf, Shalf 4C 14
CO9: Gosf 9H 201
Park Hill CM17: H'low 8G 51
DA3: Long 6G 47
IG10: Lou 4K 91
Parkhill Cl. RM12: Horn 4G 126
Parkhill Rd. DA5: Bex 4A 46
E4: Lon 7C 90
Park Ho's. SS17: Corr 1A 148
Parkhurst Dr. SS6: Ray 1J 119
Parkhurst Grn. La. CO6: Whi C 3K 15
Parkhurst Rd. E12: Lon 6N 123
N7: Lon 5A 38
SS13: Pits 1J 133
Parkinson Dr. CM1: Chelm 2A 72
Parkland Av. RM1: Romf 7C 110
RM14: Upm 7M 127
Parkland Cl. EN11: Hod 2B 52
Parkland Ct. CO1: Colc 1C 174
E15: Lon 7E 122
(off Maryland Pk.)
Parkland Rd. IG8: Wfd G 4H 107
Parklands CM7: Brain 8J 193
CM11: Bill 5K 99
CM16: Coop 8J 65
(not continuous)
CO6: Cogg 3L 197
Parklands EN9: Wal A 3C **76** (4E **30**)
IG7: Chig 9B 92
SS4: R'fd 3J 121
SS8: Can I 9G 135
Parklands Av. SS6: Ray 5L 119
Parklands Cl. IG2: Ilf 2B 124
IG7: Chig 9B 92
Parklands Ct. CO16: Clac S 1F 188
Parklands Dr. CM1: Chelm 8L 59
Parklands Way CM2: Gall 8D 72
Parkland Way CM5: Chip 9K 67
Park Lane 3M 151
Park La. CB1: Cas C 4G 7
CB10: Saf W 4B 218
(not continuous)
CB11: Lang L, Lit C 1G 11
CM9: Tol K 4A 26
CM11: Rams H 4D **100** (7A **34**)
CM13: Heron 4N 113
CM20: H'low 1C 54
CO4: L'ham 5D **160** (3F **17**)
CO5: Tip 6F 226
CO6: E Col 8C **198** (4H **15**)
CO9: Gosf 9M 201
CO9: Top 7B 8
CO10: Bulm 4L 195
CO10: Glem 1G 9
EN7: Chesh 2B 30
EN10: Brox, Hod 1D 30
RM6: Chad H 1J 125
RM11: Horn 1D **126** (3A **40**)
RM12: Horn 8F 126
RM15: Ave 8A 144
(not continuous)
SG8: Lit C 7G 5
SS0: Wclf S 6L 137
SS1: Sth S 6A 138
SS8: Can I 2M 151
Pk. Lane Cl. CO6: E Col 8C 198
Park La. Paradise EN7: Brox 2C 30
EN7: Chesh 2C 30
Park Lodge CM12: Bill 4J 99
Park Mead CM20: H'low 2A 54
Parkmead IG10: Lou 4N 91
Park Mdw. CM15: Dodd 8G 83
Park M. RM13: Rain 8E 126
RM15: Ave 8A 144
Parkmill Cl. SS17: Corr 1B 148
Parkmore Cl. IG8: Wfd G 1G 106
Park Rd. CB9: H'hll 2H 7
CB10: Gt Che, Hxtn 6D **202** (4A **6**)
CM0: Bur C 4D 196
CM1: Chelm 9J 59
CM3: Ples 1A **56** (4J **23**)
CM6: L Eas 7F 13
CM8: Riven, Sil E 2G 25
CM9: Mal 6B 214
CM14: Brtwd 7E 96
CM22: Else 2L 199
CM24: Stan M 3D 220
(not continuous)
CO3: Colc 9K 165
CO6: Boxt, Nay 1K **159** (2D **16**)
CO6: Stok 1E 16
CO7: A'lgh 4M **167** (5H **17**)
CO7: Colc 2G 174
CO7: E Ber 1K 17
CO7: Gt Bro 7H **169** (6A **18**)
CO7: W'hoe 6H 175
CO9: Wick P 7G 9
CO12: Har 3M 209
CO15: Clac S 2H 189
DA1: Dart 4C 46
E10: Lon 3A 122
E12: Lon 3H 123
EN11: Hod 5A 52
IG1: Ilf 5C 124
N8: Lon 3A 38
N18: Lon 1C 38
RM17: Grays 3L 155
SS0: Sth S 7L 137
SS7: Thund 9F 118
SS8: Can I 2M 151
SS9: Lgh S 5A 136
SS17: Corr 2B 148
SS17: Stan H 4K 147
Parkside CB10: Saf W 4B 218
CM6: Steb 7D 222
Park Side CM11: Bill 6L 99
Parkside IG9: Buck H 8H 91
RM16: Grays 1N 155
Park Side SS0: Wclf S 5F 136
SS13: Pits 8H 117
Parkside Av. DA7: Bexh 7B **152** (2A **46**)
RM1: Romf 7B 110
RM18: Til 7D 156
(not continuous)
Parkside Cen. SS2: Temp I 1L 137
Parkside Ct. *E11: Lon 1G 122*
(off Wanstead Pl.)
Parkside Cross DA7: Bexh 7C 152
Parkside Ho. RM10: Dag 5A 126
Parkside Lodge DA17: Belv 3A 152
Parkside Pde. *DA1: Cray 7D 152*
(off Northend Rd.)
Parkside Quarter CO1: Colc 7N 165
Parkside Rd. DA17: Belv 2A 152
Park Sq. RM4: Abr 5J 93
Park Sq. E. CO15: Jay 3D 188
Park Sq. W. CO15: Jay 3D 188
Parkstone Av. RM11: Horn 1J 127
SS7: Ben 2H 135
SS12: W'fd 8G 101
Parkstone Dr. SS2: Sth S 3K 137

Parkstone Rd. E17: Lon 7C 106
Park St. CM6: Thax 8C 224 (3F 13)
CO6: Stok 1E 16
SS0: Wclf S 6L 137
Park Ter. CO12: Har 3M 209
SS0: Wclf S 6L 137
Park, The CO11: Mist 4J 163
Pk. Vale Cl. CO9: Cas H 3K 219
Pk. Vale Ct. CM14: Brtwd 7F 96
Park Vw. EN11: Hod 5A 52 (7D 20)
RM6: Chad H 1J 125
RM15: Ave 8A 144
Parkview Ct. IG2: Ilf 1D 124
Park Vw. Ct. SS9: Lgh S 9D 120
Park Vw. Cres. CM2: Gt Bad 5G 73
Park Vw. Dr. SS9: Lgh S 1A 136
Pk. View Gdns. IG4: Ilf 8M 107
IG11: Bark 2D 140
RM17: Grays 3L 155
Pk. View Ho. E4: Lon 2A 106
Parkview Ho. RM12: Horn 4F 126
Pk. View Rd. N17: Lon 3C 38
Park Vs. RM6: Chad H 1J 125
Park Wlk. *IG1: Ilf 4A 124*
(in Exchange, The)
Parkway CM1: Chelm 8J 59 (1A 34)
CM2: Chelm 8J 59 (1A 34)
Park Way CM15: Shenf 7J 97
Parkway CM19: H'low 3L 53 (7G 21)
CM21: Saw 3K 51
Park Way CO15: Clac S 3H 189
Parkway IG3: Ilf 5E 124
Park Way IG8: Wfd G 2J 107
Parkway RM2: Romf 6D 110
RM13: Rain 4E 142
RM16: Ors 5C 146
SS6: Ray 7M 119
SS17: Corr 9D 132
Parkway Cl. SS9: Lgh S 8E 120
Parkway, The SS8: Can I 3H 151
Parkwood CM15: Dodd 8G 83
Parkwood Av. CO7: W'hoe 5H 175
Pk. Wood La. CM9: L Tot 6K 25
Parnall Rd. CM18: H'low 6C 54 (7H 21)
Parndon Ho. IG10: Lou 6L 91
Parndon Mill La. CM20: H'low 9A 50
Parndon Wood Crematorium
CM19: H'low 9B 54 (1H 31)
Parndon Wood Nature Reserve 9C 54
Parndon Wood Rd. CM19: H'low 8B 54 (1H 31)
Parnell Cl. CO2: Colc 5A 174
RM16: Chaf H 3F 154
Parnell Rd. E3: Lon 6D 38
(not continuous)
PARNEY HEATH 4H 161 (3H 17)
Parr Cl. CM7: Brain 4M 193
RM16: Chaf H 2F 154
Parr Dr. CO3: S'way 2F 172
Parrington Way CO11: Law 5F 162
Parrock Rd. DA12: Grav 4H 47
Parrock St. DA11: Grav 4H 47
Parrotts Fld. EN11: Hod 4B 52
Parry Cl. SS17: Stan H 2M 147
Parry Dr. CO16: Clac S 8G 184
Parsley Ho. *CO1: Colc 8M 165*
(off Balkerne Gdns.)
Parsloe Rd. CM16: E Grn 9N 53 (1G 31)
CM19: H'low 9A 54 (1G 31)
Parsloes Av. RM9: Dag 6J 125 (5J 39)
Parsonage Chase CM9: Mun 4J 35
Parsonage Cl. CM1: Broom 2J 59
Parsonage Ct. *IG10: Lou 2B 92*
(off Rectory La.)
PARSONAGE DOWNS 7F 13
Parsonage Downs CM6: L Eas 7G 13
Parsonage Farm La.
CB10: Gt Sam 2L 205 (1H 13)
Parsonage Farm Trad. Est.
CM24: Stan M 6D 220
Parsonage Fld. CM15: Dodd 7G 82
PARSONAGE GREEN 3H 59 (6K 23)
Parsonage Gro. CO8: Bures 8K 195
Parsonage Hill CO8: Bures 8K 195
Parsonage La. CM3: Gt Walt 2H 57 (4K 23)
CM3: L Bad 9L 61
CM4: Marg 2J 85 (4J 33)
CM6: Barns 3M 191 (2H 23)
CM21: Saw 3J 21
CM23: Bis S 9A 220 (1K 21)
CM24: Stan M 6D 220
CO16: Ten 6C 18
DA14: Sidc 5A 46
EN2: Enf 6B 30
SS15: Lain 9L 115
Parsonage Leys CM20: H'low 3E 54
Parsonage Manorway DA7: Belv 2A 46
Parsonage Rd. CM22: Tak 1B 224 (7C 12)
CO4: Boxt 1N 159 (2F 17)
RM13: Rain 2G 142
RM20: Grays 4F 154
Parsonage St. CO9: Hals 5L 207 (3F 15)
CO9: Hals 4L 207
Parsonon Wlk. CO4: Colc 8E 166
Parsons Cnr. SS3: Shoe 4H 139
Parsons Ct. *CO9: Hals 4L 207*
(off Parsonage St.)
Parson's Fld. CO7: Ded 2M 161
PARSON'S HEATH 6E 166 (5F 17)
Parson's Heath CO4: Colc 6E 166 (5G 17)
Parson's Hill CO3: Colc 9H 165
Parsons Hill CO7: Gt Bro 7D 168 (6K 17)
Parsons La. CO1: Colc 9C 166
(not continuous)
DA2: Dart 4B 46
Parsons Lawn SS3: Shoe 5H 139
Parsons Rd. SS7: Thund 8D 118
Partridge Av. CM1: Chelm 6H 59 (7K 23)
Partridge Cl. CO12: Gt Oak 7D 204
Partridge Ct. CM18: H'low 5D 54
Partridge Dr. CO6: For 2A 164
PARTRIDGE GREEN 8G 57 (6K 23)
Partridge Grn. SS13: Pits 1H 133
Partridge Rd. CM18: H'low 5C 54 (7H 21)
Partridge Way CO3: S'way 2D 172
PARVILLES 5B 22
Parvills EN9: Wal A 2D 76
Paschal Way CM2: Gt Bad 2F 72
Pasfield Cl. EN9: Wal A 3D 76
Paslowes SS16: Van 2G 132
PASLOW WOOD COMMON 1E 82 (3E 32)
Passfield Path SE28: Lon 7G 141
PASSINGFORD BRIDGE 1A 94 (6A 32)
Passingham Av. CM11: Bill 1L 115
Passingham Cl. CM11: Bill 1L 115
PASSMORES 5C 54 (7H 21)
Pasteur Dr. RM3: H Wood 6H 111
Paston Cl. CM3: S Fer 8L 89
Pastoral Way CM14: War 2E 112
Pasture Rd. CM8: Wthm 6E 230 (4G 25)
RM9: Dag 6L 125
Patching Hall La.
CM1: Broom, Chelm 3H 59 (7K 23)
Paternoster Cl. EN9: Wal A 3F 76
Paternoster Hill EN9: Wal A 2F 76 (4E 30)
Paternoster Row CO14: Walt 6M 181
RM4: Noak H 7G 95
Pathfields Rd. CO15: Clac S 9H 185
Path, The CO7: Gt Ben 6K 177
Pathways SS16: Bas 1F 132
Pathway, The CO13: Walt 8H 181
PATIENT END 5G 11
Patmore End CM22: Ugley 4A 12
Patmore Flds. CM22: Ugley 4A 12
PATMORE HEATH 5H 11
Patmore Rd. CO4: Colc 6D 166
EN9: Wal A 4E 76
Patmore Way RM5: Col R 2N 109
Patricia Dr. RM11: Horn 3J 127
SS17: Fob 8D 132
Patricia Gdns. CM11: Bill 9M 99
Patrick Gro. EN9: Wal A 3B 76
Patten Cl. CO6: M Tey 3H 171
Patterdale SS7: Thund 8B 118
Pattison Cl. CM8: Wthm 7D 230
PATTISWICK 7F 15
Pattiswick Cnr. SS14: Bas 8F 116
Pattiswick Sq. SS14: Bas 8F 116
Pattocks SS14: Bas 9E 116
Pattock's La. CO6: Chap 5K 15
Pattrick's La. CO12: Har 3L 209
Paul Ct. RM7: Romf 9A 110
Pauline Cl. CO15: Clac S 7M 185
Pauline Gdns. CM12: Bill 4H 99
Pauls Ct. EN11: Hod 5A 52
SS8: Can I 8G 135
Paul's Cres. CO7: Elms 1M 175
Pauls La. EN11: Hod 5A 52
Paul Spendlove Ct. CO4: Colc 6E 166
Paul's Rd. SS15: Lain 7L 115
Paul St. E15: Lon 9E 122
EC1: Lon 6B 38
Pauls Way CO15: Jay 3E 188
Pavement M. RM6: Chad H 2J 125
Pavement, The *E11: Lon 3C 122*
(off Hainault Rd.)
Pavet Cl. RM10: Dag 8N 125
Pavilion Cl. SS2: Sth S 5C 138
Pavilion Dr. SS9: Lgh S 4E 136
Pavilion Pl. CM12: Bill 4H 99
Pavilion Rd. IG1: Ilf 2M 123
Pavilions, The CM5: Chip 6L 67
CM16: N Wea 4A 66
SS1: Wclf S 7K 137
Pavilion Ter. IG2: Ilf 9D 108
Pavitt Mdw. CM2: Gall 8D 72
Pawle Cl. CM2: Gt Bad 3H 73
Paxfords SS15: Lain 9H 115
Paxman Av. CO2: Colc 3H 173
Paxton Rd. CO15: Clac S 5M 185
Paycocke Cl. SS14: Bas 5G 116
Paycocke M. SS14: Bas 5F 116
Paycocke Rd. SS14: Bas 5F 116
Paycocke's 4K 197 (7H 15)
Paycocke Way CO6: Cogg 2L 197
Paycock Rd. CM19: H'low 5N 53
Payne Cl. IG11: Bark 9D 124
Payne End SG9: S'don 1A 10
Payne Pl. CM3: E Han 3B 88
Paynes La. CM3: Bore 3D 60
Payne's La. CO11: Gt Bro, L Bro 4H 169 (5A 18)
Paynes La. EN9: Naze, Wal A 4C 62
Paynters Mead SS16: Van 3F 132
Paynters Ter. CO9: Hals 4L 207
Payzes Gdns. IG8: Wfd G 3F 106
Peacehaven CO13: Frin S 9K 181
Peace Rd. CO3: S'way 9D 164
Peach Av. SS5: Hock 8D 104
Peach Gro. E11: Lon 5D 122
Peacock Cl. CM7: Gt N 7H 193
RM8: Dag 3H 125
RM11: Horn 8J 111
Peacocks CM19: H'low 5M 53
Peacocks Rd. CO10: Caven 2F 9
Peake Av. CO13: Walt 8D 180
Peakes Cl. CO5: Tip 7B 226
Peakes La. EN7: Chesh 3B 30
Peakes Way EN7: Chesh 3B 30
Peaketon Av. IG4: Ilf 8K 107
Pea La. RM14: Upm 8D 128 (5E 40)
Peal Rd. CB11: Saf W 6E 218
Pearce Mnr. CM2: Chelm 2A 72
Pearcroft Rd. E11: Lon 4D 122
Pearcy Cl. RM3: Romf 4J 111
Peareswood Rd. DA8: Eri 6D 152
Pearl Rd. E17: Lon 7A 106
Pearmain Cl. SS11: W'fd 7L 101
Pearmain Way CO3: S'way 2D 172
Pear Rd. E11: Lon 5D 122
Pearsons SS17: Stan H 2A 148
Pearsons Av. SS6: Ray 3H 119
Peartree Bus. Cen. CO3: S'way 2F 172
Peartree Cl. CM7: Brain 7J 193
CM9: Gold 3K 201
CM15: Dodd 8G 83
Pear Tree Cl. CO9: Hals 3M 207
Peartree Cl. DA8: Eri 6B 152
RM15: S Ock 2F 144
SS2: Sth S 3A 138
Pear Tree Cl. SS15: Lain 6L 115
Pear Tree Ct. E18: Lon 5H 107
Peartree Gdns. RM7: Maw 6N 109
RM8: Dag 6G 125
PEARTREE GREEN 7F 82 (5E 32)
Peartree Hill CO8: M Bur 7H 229 (3A 16)
(not continuous)
Peartree La. CM3: Dan 7F 74 (3E 34)
CM15: Dodd 7F 82
DA12: Shorne 5K 47
RM14: Bulp 5B 130
Pear Tree Mead CM18: H'low 6F 54
Peartree Rd. CO3: S'way 2E 172 (7C 16)
Pear Trees CM13: Ingve 3M 113
SS7: Ben 2F 134
Pear Tree Wlk. CM12: Bill 4J 99
Peartree Way CO16: L Cla 3G 185
Pease Cl. RM12: Horn 9F 126
Pease Pl. CM3: E Han 3B 88
Peaslands Rd. CB11: Saf W 5D 218 (7C 6)
Peas Mead Ter. E4: Lon 1C 106
Peawood La. CO7: A'lgh 8L 161
PEBMARSH 2H 15
Pebmarsh Cl. CO2: Colc 6A 174
Pebmarsh Dr. SS12: W'fd 1M 117
Pebmarsh Rd. CO6: Coln E 2D 198 (3H 15)
CO9: L Map 2G 15
CO9: Peb 2J 15
CO10: T'std 1H 15
Peck's Hill EN9: Naze 9E 52 (1E 30)
Pedder's Cl. CO3: Colc 3G 173
Pedlars Cl. CM3: Dan 4G 74
PEDLARS END 1B 32
Pedlars La. SG8: Ther 7B 4
Pedlars Path CM3: Dan 4G 74
Pedley Rd. RM8: Dag 3H 125
Peel Av. SS3: Shoe 6L 139
Peel Cl. E4: Lon 8B 90
Peel Cres. CM7: Brain 5G 192
Peel Dr. IG5: Ilf 7L 107
Peel Pl. IG5: Ilf 6L 107
Peel Rd. CM2: Chelm 7N 59
E18: Lon 5F 106
Peel Way RM3: H Wood 6K 111
Peerage Way RM11: Horn 2K 127
Peers Sq. CM2: Chelm 7B 60
Peerswood Rd. CO2: Colc 4L 173
Pegasus Ct. *IG9: Buck H 8K 91*
(off Victoria Rd.)
Pegasus Way CM7: Brain 3G 192
CO4: Colc 6C 166
Pegelm Gdns. RM11: Horn 2K 127
Peggotty Cl. CM1: Chelm 5H 59
Peggy's Wlk. CB11: L'bry 1A 218
Peg Millar's La. CM3: Terl 3D 24
Pegrams Ct. CM18: H'low 6B 54
Pegrams Rd. CM18: H'low 6B 54
Pegs La. SG12: Wid 3F 21
SG13: Hart 5B 20
PELDON 3E 26
Peldon Pavement SS14: Bas 7E 116
Peldon Rd. CM19: H'low 3N 53
(not continuous)
CO5: Abb, Pel 9A 174 (3E 26)
CO5: Gt Wig 4D 26
Pelham Av. IG11: Bark 1E 140
Pelham Cl. CO12: Har 5H 209
Pelham Pl. SS17: Stan H 1N 147
Pelham Rd. CB11: Clav 3J 11
DA11: Grav 4G 47
E18: Lon 7H 107
IG1: Ilf 4C 124
SG11: Brau 6E 10
SS2: Sth S 5C 138
Pelham Rd. Sth.
DA11: Grav, N'fleet 4G 47
Pelhams La. CO1: Colc 8N 165
Pelly Av. CM8: Wthm 7D 230
Pelly Ct. CM16: Epp 1E 78
Pemberry Hall SS14: Bas 9E 116
Pemberton Av. CM4: Ing 5D 84
RM2: Romf 7F 110
Pemberton Ct. CM4: Ing 5D 84
Pemberton Fld. SS4: Cwdn 4G 104
Pemberton Gdns. RM6: Chad H 9K 109
Pembrey Way RM12: Horn 8G 126
Pembridge La. EN10: Brick, Brox 1B 30
Pembroke Av. CM9: Mal 7B 214
SS17: Corr 1B 148
Pembroke Bus. Cen. SS14: Bas 5F 116
Pembroke Cl. CM12: Bill 3K 99
CO2: Colc 3C 174
RM11: Horn 8K 111
Pembroke Ct. SS13: Pits 1J 133
Pembroke Gdns. CO15: Hol S 7B 186
RM10: Dag 5N 125
Pembroke Ho. SS4: R'fd 8L 121
Pembroke M. SS13: Pits 7K 117
Pembroke Pde. DA8: Eri 3A 152
Pembroke Pl. CM1: Chelm 4K 59
(not continuous)
Pembroke Rd. DA8: Eri 3A 152 (1A 46)
E17: Lon 9B 106
IG3: Ilf 3E 124
Pembury Rd. E5: Lon 5C 38
SS0: Wclf S 7H 137
Pendine Cl. SS17: Corr 1B 148
Pendle Cl. SS14: Bas 6H 117
Pendle Dr. SS14: Bas 7G 117
Pendlestone SS7: Thund 2J 135
Pendlestone Rd. E17: Lon 9B 106
Penerley Rd. RM13: Rain 5F 142
Penfold Rd. CO15: Clac S 2J 189
Penhaligon Ct. *CM8: Wthm 5D 230*
(off Newlands Dr.)
Penhurst Av. SS2: Sth S 4L 137
Penhurst Rd. IG6: Ilf 4A 108
Penistone Wlk. RM3: Romf 3G 111
Penlan Hall La. CO6: For 8F 196 (5A 16)
Penlow Rd. CM18: H'low 6C 54
Penn Cl. RM16: Ors 4D 146
Penn Gdns. RM5: Col R 4M 109
Pennial Rd. SS8: Can I 1G 151
Pennine *SS2: Sth S 5M 137*
(off Coleman St.)
Pennine Rd. CM1: Chelm 5F 58
Pennine Way DA7: Bexh 6C 152
DA7: Bexh 6C 152
Pennington Cl. RM5: Col R 2M 109
Pennington La.
CM24: Stan M, Ugley 1C 220 (6A 12)
Penn M. CM7: Brain 8J 193
Penn St. N1: Lon 6B 38
Pennsylvania La. CO5: Tip 5A 226
(not continuous)
Penny Cl. RM13: Rain 3F 142
Pennyfields CM14: War 1F 112
Penny La. SS17: Stan H 1N 147
Pennymead CM20: H'low 2F 54
Pennypot CO7: Ded 2M 161
Pennypot Cnr. CO9: Hals 4E 14
Pennyroyal Cres. CM8: Wthm 3B 230
Penny Royal Rd. CM3: Dan 4D 74 (2D 34)
Penny's La. CM4: Marg 1H 85
Penny Steps *SS1: Sth S 7A 138*
(off Hawtree Cl.)
Pennystone Rd. CB11: Saf W 5D 218
Penrhyn Av. E17: Lon 5A 106
Penrhyn Cres. E17: Lon 5A 106
Penrhyn Gro. E17: Lon 5A 106
Penrice Cl. CO4: Colc 9E 166
Penrith Cres. RM13: Rain 7E 126
Penrith Rd. IG6: Ilf 3E 108
RM3: Romf 3L 111
Penrose Mead CM1: Writ 2K 71
Penshurst CM17: H'low 9G 51
Penshurst Dr. CM3: S Fer 3K 103
Penshurst Pl. CM77: Gt N 2B 204
Penson's La. CM5: Chip 7F 66
(not continuous)
Penticton Rd. CM7: Brain 6F 192
Pentire Cl. RM14: Upm 1B 128
Pentire Rd. E17: Lon 5D 106
Pentland Av. CM1: Chelm 5J 59
SS3: Shoe 8G 139
PENTLOW 3F 9
Pentlow La. CO10: Caven 2F 9
Pentlow St. CO10: Bel W 5F 9
CO10: Caven, Pent 2F 9
Pentlow Way IG9: Buck H 6L 91
Pentney Rd. E4: Lon 7D 90
Penton Ho. SE2: Lon 8J 141
Penton St. N1: Lon 6A 38
Pentonville Rd. N1: Lon 6A 38
Penventon Ct. *RM18: Til 7C 156*
(off Dock Rd.)
Penwood Cl. CM11: Bill 2M 99
Penzance Cl. CM1: Chelm 6N 59
CO15: Clac S 4G 189
Penzance Gdns. RM3: Romf 3L 111
(not continuous)
Penzance Rd. RM3: Romf 3L 111
Peony Cl. CM15: Pil H 5E 96
Peony Ct. IG8: Wfd G 4E 106
Pepper All. IG10: Lou 1F 90
Peppercorn Cl. CO4: Colc 5N 165
Pepper Ct. *CB10: Gt Che 8D 202*
(off School St.)
Pepper Hill SG12: Gt Amw 5D 20
Peppermint Pl. E11: Lon 5E 122
PEPPER'S GREEN 6G 23
Pepper's Rd. CO4: Boxt 7M 159
Pepples La. CB10: Wim 1E 12
Pepys Cl. DA1: Dart 9L 153
RM18: Til 6E 156
Pepys St. CO12: Har 2M 209
Percival Gdns. RM6: Chad H 1H 125
Percival Rd. CO13: Kir S 5G 180
CO14: Walt 4N 181
RM11: Horn 1G 127
Percival St. EC1: Lon 6A 38
Percy Cottis Rd. SS4: R'fd 4K 121
Percy Rd. E11: Lon 2E 122
IG3: Ilf 2F 124
N21: Lon 7B 30
RM7: Maw 7N 109
SS9: Lgh S 4C 136
Percy St. RM17: Grays 4M 155

Peregrine Cl. CO15: Clac S 6K 185
SS3: Shoe 5J 139
SS16: Bas 2C 132
Peregrine Ct. CO4: Colc 7F 166
Peregrine Dr. CM2: Chelm 5B 72
SS7: Ben 4C 134
Peregrine Gdns. SS6: Ray 4H 119
Peregrine Ho. CM16: Epp 9E 64
Peregrine Rd. EN9: Wal A 4G 76
IG6: Ilf 2G 109
Peregrine Wlk. RM12: Horn 8F 126
Perkins Rd. IG2: Ilf 9C 108
Perriclose CM1: Chelm 4M 59
Perrin Pl. CM2: Chelm 1B 72
Perry Cl. RM13: Rain 2B 142
Perryfield CM17: Mat G 6B 22
Perryfield La. CM5: Fy'd 6C 200
PERRY GREEN 3G 21
Bradwell 7F 15
Perry Green CM77: Tye G 7F 15
Perry Grn. SS14: Bas 7C 116
Perry Gro. DA1: Dart 9L 153
Perry Hill CM1: Chelm 8M 59
EN9: Naze 2F 62
Perry Ho. RM13: Rain 2B 142
Perry La. CO4: L'ham 4F 160
Perry Lodge E12: Lon 3K 123
Perrymans Farm Rd. IG2: Ilf 1C 124
Perry Rd. CM8: Wthm 7E 230
CM18: H'low 7B 54
CO5: Tip 6B 226
RM9: Dag 5L 141
SS7: Ben 3B 134
Perry Spring CM17: H'low 5H 55
SS16: Van 1E 132
PERRY STREET 4G 47
Perry St. CM12: Bill 5H 99 (7J 33)
DA1: Cray 9C 152 (3A 46)
DA11: N'fleet 4G 47
Perry Way CM8: Wthm 6E 230
RM15: Ave 7N 143
Perrywood La. SG14: Wat S 2A 20
Persardi Ct. CO2: Colc 7A 174
Pershore Cl. IG2: Ilf 9A 108
Pershore End CO3: S'way 1F 172
Perth Cl. CO2: Colc 5A 174
Perth Ho. RM18: Til 7C 156
Perth Rd. IG2: Ilf 1N 123 (3G 39)
IG11: Bark 2C 140
N22: Lon 2A 38
Perth Ter. IG2: Ilf 2B 124
Pertwee Cl. CO7: B'sea 5D 182
Pertwee Dr. CM2: Gt Bad 4G 72
CM3: S Fer 1J 103
Pertwees Ct. CO1: Colc 9C 166
Pertwee Way CO5: L'hoe 9B 174
Pesthouse La. CO12: Gt Oak 8C 204 (5E 18)
Petands Ct. *RM12: Horn 5H 127*
(off Randall Dr.)
Petches Bri. CM7: Gt Bar 9A 228
Peterborough Av. RM14: Upm 3B 128
Peterborough Gdns. IG1: Ilf 2L 123
Peterborough Rd. E10: Lon 9C 106
Peterborough Way SS14: Bas 7G 117
Peter Bruff Av. CO16: Clac S 8G 185
Peterfield's La. CO9: Gosf 4E 14
Peter May Cen., The 4C 106
Peters Cl. RM8: Dag 3J 125
Peters Ct. SS15: Lain 9K 115
Petersfield CM1: Chelm 5K 59
Petersfield Av. RM3: Romf 3J 111 (2C 40)
Petersfield Cl. RM3: Romf 3L 111
Peterson Ct. IG10: Lou 1N 91
Peterstone Rd. SE2: Lon 9G 141
Peter St. CM4: Stock 8A 86
Peterswood CM18: H'low 7C 54
(not continuous)
Petherton Rd. N5: Lon 5B 38
Petit Way CM77: Tye G 8H 217 (2E 24)
Petlands. CB10: L Wal 5C 6
Peto Av. CO4: Colc 5N 165
Petrebrook CM2: Chelm 8B 60
Petre Cl. CM4: Ing 7C 84
CM13: W H'dn 1M 129
Petrel Way CM2: Chelm 4D 72
Petresfield Way CM13: W H'dn 1M 129
Petrolea Cl. CO4: Colc 6M 165 (5E 16)
Petronius Way CO4: Colc 2B 166
Pett Cl. RM11: Horn 4F 126
Pettits Blvd. RM1: Romf 5C 110
Pettits Cl. RM1: Romf 6C 110
Pettits La. CM15: Wy G 7H 83 (5F 33)
RM1: Romf 6C 110 (2A 40)
Pettits La. Nth.
RM1: Romf 5B 110 (2A 40)
Pettits Pl. RM10: Dag 7M 125
Pettits Rd. RM10: Dag 7M 125
Pettley Gdns. RM7: Romf 9B 110
Petts La. CB10: L Wal 5C 6
Petunia Cres. CM1: Chelm 5A 60
Petworth Cl. CM77: Gt N 1B 204
CO7: W'hoe 6J 175
Petworth Gdns. SS2: Sth S 4D 138
Petworth Way RM12: Horn 6D 126
Pevensey Cl. SS13: Pits 9J 117
Pevensey Dr. CO15: Clac S 4G 189
Pevensey Gdns. SS5: Hull 7M 103
Pevensey Rd. E7: Lon 6F 122
Peverel Av. CM3: Hat P 5N 61
Peverel Ho. RM10: Dag 4M 125
Peverells CB10: Wim 1D 12
Pewsey Cl. E4: Lon 2A 106
PHARISEE GREEN 1F 23
Pharisee Grn. CM6: Gt D 1F 23
Pharos La. CO5: W Mer 3C 228
Pheasanthouse Wood Nature Reserve 1F 74
Phelips Rd. CM19: H'low 8N 53
Philan Way RM5: Col R 3B 110
Philbrick Cres. SS6: Ray 4J 119
(not continuous)
Philip Av. RM7: Rush G 3B 126
Philip Cl. CM15: Pil H 5E 96
CO14: Walt 6K 181
RM7: Rush G 3B 126
Philip La. N15: Lon 3B 38
Philippa Way RM16: Grays 2D 156
Philip Rd. CM8: Wthm 7B 230
RM13: Rain 3C 142
Philips Cl. CM77: Rayne 6B 192
Philips Rd. CM77: Rayne 6B 192
Philip Sydney Rd. RM16: Chaf H 3G 154
Phillida Rd. RM3: H Wood 6L 111
Phillip Rd. CO7: W'hoe 6H 175
Phillips Chase CM7: Brain 3J 193
Philmead Rd. SS7: Ben 4B 134
PHILPOT END 2F 23
Philpot End La. CM6: Gt D 2F 23
Philpot Path IG1: Ilf 5B 124
Philpott Av. SS2: Sth S 4B 138
Phipps Hatch La. EN2: Enf 5B 30
Phoenix Ct. CO2: Colc 1D 174
E4: Lon 9B 90
Phoenix Gro. CM2: Chelm 2B 72
Phoenix Way SS7: Had, Ray 8J 119
Picardy Manorway DA17: Belv 9N 141 (7K 39)
Picardy Rd. DA17: Belv 1A 46
Picasso Way SS3: Shoe 6L 139
Piccadilly W1: Lon 7A 38
Piccadilly Circus Station (Tube) 7A 38
Piccotts La. CM7: Gt Sal 6A 14
Pickers Way CO15: Hol S 6B 186
Picketts SS8: Can I 1D 150
Picketts Av. SS9: Lgh S 2D 136
Picketts Cl. SS9: Lgh S 2D 136
Picketts Lock La. N9: Lon 1C 38
Pickford Wlk. CO4: Colc 8F 166
Pick Hill EN9: Wal A 2F 76
Picknage Rd. SG8: Bar 6F 5
Pickpocket La. CM77: Bla N 2D 204
(not continuous)
Pickwick Av. CM1: Chelm 5F 58
Pickwick Cl. SS15: Lain 8M 115
Picton Cl. SS6: Ray 6L 119
Picton Gdns. SS6: Ray 6L 119
Pier App. SS1: Sth S 7M 137
Pier Av. CO15: Clac S 1J 189 (4D 28)
Pierce Glade CO5: Tip 6C 226
Piercing Hill CM16: They B 5C 78 (5H 31)
Piercys SS13: Pits 1J 133
Pier Gap CO15: Clac S 2K 189
Pier Hill SS1: Sth S 7M 137
Pier Mus. 8M 137
Pierrefitte Way CM7: Brain 5G 193 (7C 14)
Pier Rd. DA8: Eri 4C 152
(not continuous)
DA9: Grnh 9E 154
E16: Lon 7G 39
Pierrot Steps *SS1: Sth S 7A 138*
(off Kursaal Way)
Pier Way SE28: Lon 9B 140
Pier Wharf RM17: Grays 5K 155
Piggs Cnr. RM17: Grays 1M 155
Pightle, The CB9: H'hill 3J 7
CM7: F'fld 3D 200
Pightle Way CO14: Walt 7K 181
Pig La. CM22: Bis S 2K 21
CM23: Bis S, Thor 2K 21
PIG STREET 8K 179
PIGSTYE GREEN 1J 69 (1F 33)
Pigstye Grn. Rd. CM5: Will 2J 69 (2F 33)
Pike La. RM14: Upm 7C 128 (4D 40)
Pike Way CM16: N Wea 6L 65
Pilborough Way CO3: S'way 3F 172
Pilcox Hall La. CO16: Ten 6B 18
Pilgrim Cl. CM7: Brain 3H 193
Pilgrims Cl. CB10: Gt Che 8D 202
CM11: Bill 6K 99
SS2: Sth S 5C 138
Pilgrim's Cl. CM15: Pil H 4C 96
PILGRIMS HATCH 5E 96 (7E 32)
Pilgrims La RM16: Chaf H 1G 154
Pilgrims La. CM14: Pil H 3A 96
RM16: N Stif 8F 144 (7E 40)
Pilgrims Rd. DA10: N'fleet, Swans 9H 155
Pilgrims Rdbt. RM16: Chaf H, N Stif 9F 144
Pilgrims Wlk. CM11: Bill 6K 99
Pilgrims Way ME2: Hall 7K 47
SS7: Had 3M 135
Pilgrim Way SS15: Lain 9L 115
Pilkingtons CM17: H'low 3J 55
Pilot Cl. SS11: W'fd 2B 118
Pimblett Row CM22: Hen 8D 210
Pimpernel Way RM3: Romf 3H 111
Pinceybrook Rd. CM18: H'low 7B 54
Pincey Mead SS13: Pits 1H 133
Pincey Rd. CM24: Stan Apt 6L 221
Pincey Rdbt. CM24: Stan Apt 6M 221
Pinchpools Rd. CM23: Man 5K 11
Pindar Rd. EN11: Rye P 4C 52
Pine Av. CM6: Gt D 2J 203
E15: Lon 7D 122
Pine Cl. CM4: Ing 5E 84
CO7: Gt Ben 6L 177
E10: Lon 4B 122
SS8: Can I 2E 150
SS9: Lgh S 1A 136
SS12: W'fd 2K 117
Pinecourt RM14: Upm 6M 127
Pine Cres. CM13: Hut 3N 97
Pinecroft CM13: Hut 6L 97
RM2: Romf 8G 110
Pinecroft Gdns. CO4: Colc 4B 166
Pine Dr. CM4: Ing 5E 84
Pine Gro. CM8: Wthm 2D 230
CO5: W Mer 2B 228
Pine Rd. SS7: Had 4K 135
Pines Hill CM24: Stan M 4C 220 (6A 12)
Pines Rd. CM1: Chelm 6F 58
Pines, The CM3: Hat P 1L 61
IG8: Wfd G 9G 90
RM16: Grays 8L 145
SS15: Lain 6L 115
Pine Tree Ct. CO4: Colc 6E 166
Pinetrees SS7: Ben 3J 135
Pineview Ct. E4: Lon 7C 90
Pine Vw. Mnr. CM16: Epp 9F 64
Pinewood Av. RM13: Rain 4F 142
SS9: Lgh S 9C 120
Pinewood Cl. CM17: H'low 4H 55
CO13: Walt 8G 181
CO15: Clac S 6J 185
SS5: Hull 6L 103
SS17: Linf 1K 157
Pinewood Rd. RM4: Hav 1A 110
(not continuous)
Pinewood Way CM13: Hut 4N 97
Pinkeneys SG8: Chris 5H 5
Pinkham Dr. CM8: Wthm 7C 230
Pinkham Way N11: Lon 2A 38
Pinkney Cl. CB10: Wim 1D 12
Pinkuah La. CO10: Pent 3F 9
Pinley Gdns. RM9: Dag 1G 140
Pinmill SS14: Bas 9C 116
PINNACLES 4M 53 (7G 21)
Pinnacles EN9: Wal A 4E 76
Pinners Cl. CM0: Bur C 6B 36
Pintail Cres. CM77: Gt N 2C 204
Pintail Rd. IG8: Wfd G 4H 107
Pintails SS13: Pits 9K 117
Pintolls CM3: S Fer 2K 103
Pioneer Mkt. *IG1: Ilf 5A 124*
(off Winston Way)
Pioneer Pl. CO1: Colc 9A 166
Pipchin Rd. CM1: Chelm 5H 59
Piper Rd. CO3: Colc 8J 165
Piper's Tye CM2: Gall 7E 72
Pippin Ct. SS11: W'fd 8N 101
Pippins Rd. CM0: Bur C 2E 196
Pippins, The CO9: Hals 4J 207
PIPPS HILL 7A 116 (3K 41)
Pipps Hill Ind. Est. SS14: Bas 6A 116
Pipps Hill Retail Pk. SS14: Bas 7N 115
Pipps Hill Rd. Nth.
CM11: Cray H 4C 116 (2A 42)
Pirie Rd. CO6: W Ber 3F 164
Pishiobury Dr. CM21: Saw 4H 51
Pishiobury M. CM21: Saw 5J 51
Pitcairn Cl. RM7: Maw 8M 109
Pitchford St. E15: Lon 9D 122
Pitchway CM17: H'low 2J 55
Pitfield CM2: Gt Bad 2E 72
Pitfield Cres. SE28: Lon 8F 140
Pitfield Grn. CO10: L Hen 6H 9
Pitfield St. EC1: Lon 6B 38
Pit La. CO5: Tip 5C 226
Pitmans Cl. SS1: Sth S 6M 137
Pitmire La. CO8: Lmsh 7K 9
PITSEA 2H 133 (4C 42)
Pitsea Hall La. SS16: Pits 5J 133 (4B 42)
Pitsea Leisure Cen. 1J 133
Pitsea Rd. SS13: Pits 9H 117 (3B 42)
Pitsea Station (Rail) 2J 133 (4B 42)
Pitsea Swimming Pool 1J 133
Pitsea Vw. Rd. CM11: Cray H 3E 116
Pitseaville Gro. SS16: Van 2F 132
Pitt Av. CM8: Wthm 7D 230
Pitt Chase CM2: Gt Bad 4F 72
Pittfields SS16: Lang H 1J 131
Pitt Grn. CM8: Wthm 7D 230
Pittman Cl. CM13: Ingve 2M 113
Pittman Gdns. IG1: Ilf 7B 124
Pittman's Fld. CM20: H'low 2E 54
Pittwood CM15: Shenf 7K 97
Place Farm Ct. CO2: Colc 4D 174
Place Farm La.
CM15: Dodd, Kel H 7D 82 (5E 32)
Pladda M. SS12: W'fd 2N 117
Plains Farm Cl. CO7: A'lgh, Colc 1D 166
Plains Fld. CM7: Brain 7M 193
Plains Rd.
CM9: Gt Tot, L Tot, Tol M 8K 205 (5J 25)
Plain, The CM16: Epp 8G 64 (3J 31)
PLAISTOW 6E 38
Plaistow Cl. SS17: Stan H 3M 147
PLAISTOW GREEN 9J 207 (4F 15)
Plaistow Grn. Rd. CO9: Hals 9H 207 (4F 15)
Plaistow Rd. E15: Lon 6E 38
Plaistow Station (Tube) 6E 38
Plaiters Way CM7: Brain 5M 193
Plane Tree Cl. CM0: Bur C 2D 196
CM2: Chelm 4C 72
Plane Vw. Cl. CO16: Clac S 2F 188
Plantaganet Pl. EN9: Wal A 3B 76
Plantagenet Gdns. RM6: Chad H 2J 125
Plantagenet Pl. RM6: Chad H 2J 125
Plantain Gdns. *E11: Lon 5D 122*
(off Hollydown Way, not continuous)
Plantation Cl. CB11: Saf W 7D 218
Plantation Rd. CM3: Bore 3G 61 (7C 24)
DA8: Eri 6E 152
Planton Way CO7: B'sea 6C 182
PLASHET 8L 123 (5G 39)
Plashet Cl. SS17: Stan H 3M 147
Plashet Gdns. CM13: Brtwd 1K 113
Plashet Gro. E6: Lon 9K 123 (6F 39)
Plashet Rd. E13: Lon 9J 123 (6F 39)
Plashets, The CM22: Srng 3A 210
Plashetts SS14: Bas 8E 116
Plas Newydd SS1: Sth S 8C 138
Plas Newydd Cl. SS1: Sth S 8C 138
Platford Grn. RM11: Horn 8J 111
Plaw Hatch Cl. CM23: Bis S 9A 220
Plaxton Ct. E11: Lon 5F 122
Players Ct. CM6: Fels 7K 199
Playfield Av. RM5: Col R 5A 110
Playhouse Sq. CM20: H'low 3B 54
Playle Chase CM9: Gt Tot 3M 229
Plaza Way SS1: Sth S 6B 138
Pleasant Dr. CM12: Bill 4G 99
Pleasant M. SS1: Sth S 7N 137
Pleasant Rd. SS1: Sth S 7N 137
Pleasants M. CO5: W Mer 3C 228
Pleasant Ter. *SS9: Lgh S 6D 136*
(off Church Hill)
Pleasant Valley CB11: Saf W 6C 218 (7B 6)
Pleasant Vw. DA8: Eri 3C 152
PLEDGDON GREEN 5C 12
PLESHEY 2A 56 (4H 23)
Pleshey Castle 3B 56 (4J 23)
Pleshey Cl. SS1: Sth S 6D 138
SS12: W'fd 1M 117
Pleshey Rd. CM3: Gt Walt, Ples 2C 56
(Pleshey)
CM3: Gt Walt, Ples 4J 23
(Rolphy Green)
CM3: Har E, Ples 4J 23
Plevna Rd. N9: Lon 1C 38
Plough Dr. CO3: Colc 1H 173
Plough Hill EN6: Cuff 3A 30
Plough La. CO6: L'hth 1C 16
Ploughman's Headland CO3: S'way 1E 172
Ploughmans La. CM77: Gt N 8E 192
Plough Ri. RM14: Upm 2B 128
Plough Rd. CO7: Gt Ben 6K 177 (1A 28)
Plover Cl. CO13: Frin S 8H 181
Plover Gdns. RM14: Upm 3C 128
Plovers Barron CM15: Wy G 6G 82
Plovers Mead CM15: Wy G 6G 83
Plovers, The CM0: St La 2C 36
Plover Wlk. CM2: Chelm 5C 72
Plowmans SS6: Ray 3L 119
Plowman Way RM8: Dag 3H 125
Plowright Ho. *CO1: Colc 7M 165*
(off St Peter's St.)
Ployters Rd. CM18: H'low 8B 54 (1H 31)
Plumberow SS15: Lain 9N 115
Plumberow Av. SS5: Hock 6D 104
(not continuous)
Plumberow Mt. Av. SS5: Hock 8D 104
Plume Av. CM9: Mal 7B 214
CO3: Colc 2H 173
Plumleys SS13: Pits 8J 117
Plummers Rd. CO6: For 4B 16
Plumpton Av. RM12: Horn 6J 127
Plumpton Rd. EN11: Rye P 3C 52
Plumptre La. CM3: Dan 5D 74
Plums La. CM7: Bar S 5K 13
Plum St. CO10: Glem 1F 9
Plumtree Av. CM2: Gt Bad 4G 72
Plumtree Cl. RM10: Dag 8N 125
Plumtree Mead IG10: Lou 2N 91
Plymouth Ho. *IG11: Bark 9F 124*
(off Keir Hardie Way)
Plymouth Rd. CM1: Chelm 6N 59
CO15: Clac S 4H 189
RM16: Chaf H 2F 154
Plymtree SS1: Sth S 5G 138
Pochard Way CM77: Gt N 3C 204
Pocklington Cl. CM2: Chelm 7B 60
Pods Brook Rd.
CM7: Brain, Gt N 6F 192 (7C 14)
Pods La. CM77: Rayne 6A 192 (7A 14)
POINT CLEAR 9D 182 (4K 27)
Point Clear Rd. CO16: St O 4K 27
Point Cl. SS8: Can I 2M 151
Pointer Cl. SE28: Lon 6J 141
Point Rd. SS8: Can I 2L 151 (6F 43)
Point Ter. *E7: Lon 7H 123*
(off Claremont Rd.)
Pointwell La. CO6: Cogg 1H 25
Pole Barn La. CO13: Frin S 9J 181 (1G 29)
Polecat Rd. CM77: Tye G 6H 217 (1E 24)
Pole Hill Rd. E4: Lon 6C 90
Pole La. CM8: Whi N 2D 24
Polesworth Rd. RM9: Dag 9J 125
Poley Rd. SS17: Stan H 4L 147
Police Row SG8: Ther 7B 4
Pollard Cl. IG7: Chig 2F 108
Pollard Hatch CM19: H'low 6A 54
Pollards Cl. IG10: Lou 4J 91
SS4: R'fd 5K 121
Pollards Ct. SS4: R'fd 5K 121
Pollards Grn. CM2: Chelm 8A 60
Pollards Vs. CM7: Bar S 5K 13
Pollard Wlk. CO16: Clac S 8G 185
Polley Cl. CO13: Walt 7H 181
Polstead Cl. SS6: Ray 5G 118
Polsteads SS16: Van 3F 132
Polstead St. CO6: Stok 1E 16
Polstead Way CO16: Clac S 9F 184
Polsten M. EN3: Enf 7A 76
Pomfret Mead SS14: Bas 9B 116
Pompadour Cl. CM14: War 2F 112
Pond Chase CO3: Colc 2H 173
Pond Cl. SS5: Hull 5L 103
Pond Cross Farm CB11: Newp 3L 215

Pond Cross Way CB11: Newp 3L 215
PONDERS END 7C 30
Ponders End Station (Rail) 7C 30
Ponders Rd. CO6: For 2A 164 (5B 16)
Pondfield CM6: Gt D 2L 203
Pond Fld. End IG10: Lou 6K 91
Pondfield La. CM13: Brtwd 1K 113 (1F 41)
Pondfield Rd. CO4: Colc 6D 166
RM10: Dag 7N 125
Pondholton Dr. CM8: Wthm 8C 230
Pond Ho. La. CO15: Clac S 5A 186
Pond La. CM22: Hat H 1E 210 (4B 22)
Pond Lees Cl. RM10: Dag 9B 126
Ponds Rd. CM2: Gall 8C 72 (3A 34)
POND STREET 7J 5
Pondtail Ct. CO13: Walt 8F 180
Pond Wlk. RM14: Upm 4B 128
Poney Chase CM8: W Bis 2L 229
Pontypool Wlk. RM3: Romf 3G 111
Poole Ho. RM16: Grays 9E 146
Poole Rd. RM11: Horn 2K 127
Pooles La. SS5: Hull 5L 103 (7F 35)
Poole St. CO9: Gt Yel 4D 206 (7D 8)
CO10: Caven 2F 9
Poolhurst Wlk. *SS5: Hull* *4L 103*
(off Crouch Mdw.)
Pool's La. CM1: Hghwd 6B 70
POOL STREET 7D 8
Poore St. CB11: A'den, Wick B 2K 11
Poors La. SS7: Had 2L 135
Poors La. Nth. SS7: Had 1M 135 (3G 43)
Poor's Piece Nature Reserve 1F 74
Poperinghe Rd. CO2: Colc 2N 173
Popes Ct. CB9: Stur 6J 223
Popes Cres. SS13: Pits 1J 133
Pope's La. CO3: Colc 8M 165
Popes La. CO6: Chap 8B 196
Popes Wlk. SS6: Ray 5N 119
POPLAR 7D 38
Poplar Av. CO16: Clac S 2E 188
Poplar Cl. CM2: Chelm 4D 72
CM3: S Fer 9J 89
CM4: B'more 1H 83
CM4: Ing 7C 84
CM8: Wthm 2D 230
CO9: Gt Yel 3D 206
CO9: Hals 6L 207
CO15: Clac S 2F 188
RM15: S Ock 4G 145
Poplar Ct. SS5: Hock 1D 120
Poplar Dr. CM13: Hut 5M 97
Poplar Gdns. SE28: Lon 7H 141
Poplar Gro. CM0: Bur C 3D 196
Poplar Hall Cl. CO1: Colc 6M 165
Poplar High St. E14: Lon 7D 38
Poplar Mt. DA17: Belv 2A 142
Poplar Pl. SE28: Lon 7H 141
Poplar Rd. E12: Lon 4L 123
SS6: Ray 7M 119
SS8: Can I 2J 151
Poplar Row CM16: They B 7D 78 (5H 31)
Poplars Av. SS5: Hock 3D 120
Poplars Cl. CO7: Alr 7A 176
Poplar Shaw EN9: Wal A 3F 76
Poplars Rd. E17: Lon 1B 122
Poplar Station (DLR) 7D 38
Poplars, The CM6: Gt D 1K 203
EN9: Wal A 5J 77
RM4: Abr 2G 92
SS13: Pits 9K 117
Poplar St. RM7: Romf 8A 110
Poplar Way CO13: Walt 8G 181
IG6: Ilf 8B 108
Poppleton Rd. E11: Lon 1E 122
Poppy Cl. CM15: Pil H 4E 96
DA17: Belv 9N 141
Poppyfield Cl. SS9: Lgh S 9C 120
Poppy Gdns. CO2: Colc 3C 174
Poppy Grn. CM1: Chelm 5B 60
Porchester Cl. RM11: Horn 1J 127
Porchester Rd. CM12: Bill 3J 99
Pork La.
CO13: Gt Hol, T Sok, Walt 7B 180 (1F 29)
Porlock Av. SS0: Wclf S 2F 136
Portal Pct. CO1: Colc 8N 165
Portchester Ct. *SS9: Lgh S* *5E 136*
(off Chalkwell Pk. Dr.)
Porter Cl. RM20: Grays 4F 154
Porters SS13: Bas 7K 117
Porters Av. RM8: Dag 8G 124 (5J 39)
RM9: Dag 8G 124 (5J 39)
Porters Brook Wlk. CO4: Colc 5C 166
Porters Cl. CM14: Brtwd 7D 96
CO3: S'way 5A 164
Porters Cotts. CO3: S'way 5A 164
PORTERS GREEN 8K 171 (1B 26)
Porters Hall Rd. CM6: Steb 7J 13
Porter's La. CO3: S'way 5A 164
Porters Pk. CM3: Bore 1H 61
Porter Way CO16: Clac S 9F 184
Port Hill SG14: Hart 5B 20
(not continuous)
Portia Ct. IG11: Bark 9F 124
Portland Av. CO12: Har 4L 209
SS1: Sth S 6N 137
Portland Cl. CM7: Brain 5K 193
RM6: Chad H 9K 109
Portland Commercial Est. IG11: Bark 2H 141
Portland Cres. CO12: Har 4L 209
Portland Gdns. RM6: Chad H 9J 109
Portland Pl. W1: Lon 7A 38
Portland Rd. CO2: Colc 9N 165
Port La. CM22: L Hall 2K 21
CO1: Colc 9B 166
Portlight Cl. CO11: Mist 4M 163
Portmadoc Ho. *RM3: Romf* *1J 111*
(off Broseley Rd.)
Portman Dr. CM12: Bill 3K 99
IG8: Wfd G 6K 107
Portmeadow Wlk. SE2: Lon 9J 141
Portmore Gdns. RM5: Col R 2M 109
Portnoi Cl. RM1: Romf 6B 110
Portobello Rd. CO14: Walt 6M 181
Port of Felixstowe Rd.
IP11: Felix, T Mary 1K 19
PORT OF FELIXSTOWE, THE 2K 19
Portreath Pl. CM1: Chelm 4J 59
Portsea Rd. RM18: Til 8E 156
Portsmouth Rd. CO15: Clac S 4H 189
Portway CM2: Chelm 7C 60
E15: Lon 6E 38
RM13: Rain 1E 142
Portway Ct. CO9: Hals 3L 207
Posford Ct. CO4: Colc 2N 165
POSLINGFORD 1D 8
Postman's La. CM3: L Bad 8M 61
(not continuous)
Post Mdw. CM11: Bill 1M 115
Post Office App. E7: Lon 7H 123
Post Office La. CM9: L Tot 6K 25
Post Office Rd. CM1: Broom 3K 59
CM4: Ing 6D 84
CM9: Wdhm M 5L 75 (2F 35)
CM20: H'low 2C 54
Post Office Row CM8: Fau 3E 24
Post Office Wlk. *CM20: H'low* *2C 54*
(off Post Office Rd.)
Postway M. IG1: Ilf 5A 124
(not continuous)
Potash Rd. CM11: Bill 2M 99 (6K 33)
CM17: Mat G 6B 22
Potiphar Pl. CM14: War 1E 112
Pot Kiln Chase CO9: Gest 6F 9
Pot Kiln Rd. CO10: Gt Cor 5K 9
Potters Cl. CM3: Dan 4G 74
IG10: Lou 1L 91
Potters Fld. CM17: H'low 5J 55
POTTER'S GREEN 1C 20
Potters La. CM3: Ret C 7D 88
POTTER STREET 5H 55 (7J 21)
Potter St. CM17: H'low 4H 55 (7J 21)
CM23: Bis S 1K 21
CO9: Sib H 8K 219 (2E 14)
Potters Way SS2: Temp I 1L 137
Pottery La. CM1: Chelm 6J 59
CO9: Cas H 4L 219
Potton Dr. SS12: W'fd 2N 117
Poulk Hall La. CM3: Gt L 9L 203 (4B 24)
Poulteney Rd. CM24: Stan M 1D 220
Poulton Cl. CM9: Mal 8C 214
Pound Cl. EN9: Naze 2E 62
Pound Farm Dr. CO12: Har 4H 209
Poundfield Cl. CO7: Alr 7A 176
Poundfield Rd. IG10: Lou 4N 91
Pound Flds. CM1: Writ 2K 71
Poundgate CM6: Steb 7C 222
Pound Hill CM6: L Dun 7D 212 (1H 23)
Pound La. RM16: Ors 4C 146
SS12: N Ben 7N 117 (3C 42)
SS13: Pits 9N 117 (3C 42)
SS15: Lain 7M 115
Pound La. Central SS15: Lain 6M 115
Pound La. Nth. SS15: Lain 6M 115
Pound Wlk. CB10: Saf W 3C 218
Pound Wood Nature Reserve 9M 119
Powdermill La. EN9: Wal A 3B 76
Powdermill M. *EN9: Wal A* *3B 76*
(off Powdermill La.)
Powell Cl. CO5: Tip 6E 226
Powell Ct. E17: Lon 7B 106
SS4: R'fd 6L 121
Powell Gdns. RM10: Dag 6M 125
Powell Rd. IG9: Buck H 6J 91
SS15: Lain 8K 115
Powerleague Soccer Cen. 4E 108
Barking 3B 140
Powerscroft Rd. E5: Lon 5C 38
POWERS HALL END 4B 230 (4F 25)
Powers Hall End CM8: Wthm 4A 230 (4F 25)
Power Works DA8: Eri 6E 152
Pownall Cres. CO2: Colc 2N 173 (7E 16)
Pownsett Ter. IG1: Ilf 7B 124
Powys La. N13: Lon 1A 38
Poynder Rd. RM18: Til 6D 156
Poynings Av. SS2: Sth S 5B 138
Poynings Way RM3: H Wood 5J 111
Poyntens SS6: Ray 6J 119
Poynter Pl. CO13: Walt 7H 181
Poynter's Chase SS3: Shoe 5N 139
Poynters La. SS3: Shoe 4H 139 (4B 44)
Prail Ct. CO6: Cogg 3K 197
Pratts Farm La. CM3: L Walt 8L 57 (6A 24)
(not continuous)
Pratt St. NW1: Lon 6A 38
Prayors Hill CO9: Sib H 5H 219 (1D 14)
Prebend St. N1: Lon 6B 38
Precinct, The SS17: Stan H 4M 147
Premier Av. RM16: Grays 9M 145
Prentice Cl. SS4: R'fd 5L 121
Prentice Hall La. CM9: Tol 9H 225 (7C 26)
Prentice Pl. CM17: H'low 5H 55
Prescott SS16: Lang H 3L 131
Prescott Grn. IG10: Lou 2B 92
President Rd. CO3: S'way 1F 172
Presidents Ct. SS15: Lain 9H 115
Prestbury Rd. E7: Lon 9J 123
Preston Av. E4: Lon 3D 106
Preston Dr. E11: Lon 9J 107
Preston Gdns. IG1: Ilf 1L 123
SS6: Ray 3K 119
Preston Ho. *RM10: Dag* *5M 125*
(off Uvedale Rd.)
Preston Rd. CO15: Hol S 8A 186
E11: Lon 1E 122
RM3: Romf 1H 111
SS0: Wclf S 6J 137
Preston's Rd. E14: Lon 7E 38
Prestwick Dr. CM23: Bis S 8A 220
Prestwood Cl. SS7: Thund 9F 118
Prestwood Dr. RM5: Col R 2A 110
SS7: Thund 9G 118
Pretoria Av. SS15: Bas 6A 116
Pretoria Cl. SS15: Bas 6A 116
Pretoria Cres. E4: Lon 7C 90
Pretoria Ho. DA8: Eri 5C 152
Pretoria Rd. CO9: Hals 4L 207 (3F 15)
E4: Lon 7C 90
E11: Lon 3D 122
IG1: Ilf 7A 124
N17: Lon 2B 38
RM7: Romf 8A 110
Pretoria Rd. Nth. N18: Lon 2B 38
Prettygate Rd. CO3: Colc 1H 173
(not continuous)
Priestley Ct. RM17: Grays 2M 155
Priestley Gdns. RM6: Chad H 1G 124
Priests Av. RM1: Romf 6B 110
Priest's Fld. CM13: Ingve 2M 113
Priests La. CM15: Brtwd, Shenf 6J 97 (1F 41)
Prime's Cl. CB10: Saf W 4C 218
Primley La. CM22: Srng 3A 210
Primrose Av. RM6: Chad H 2G 124
Primrose Cl. SS8: Can I 8G 134
SS16: Lang H 2K 131
Primrose Ct. CM14: Brtwd 9F 96
Primrose Fld. CM18: H'low 5E 54
Primrose Glen RM11: Horn 8J 111
Primrose Hill CM1: Chelm 8H 59
CM14: Brtwd 9F 96
CO11: Wrab 3E 18
Primrose La. CO5: Tip 5C 226
CO12: R'sy 3E 18
Primrose Pl. CM8: Wthm 3B 230
Primrose Rd. CO15: Hol S 7B 186
E10: Lon 3B 122
E18: Lon 6H 107
Primrose Wlk. CM0: S'min 3C 222
CM9: Mal 7D 214
CO4: Colc 7E 166
Primula Cl. CO16: Clac S 9G 184
Primula Way CM1: Chelm 5B 60
Prince Albert Rd. CO5: W Mer 3D 228 (5F 27)
Prince Av. SS0: Sth S, Wclf S 1E 136 (3H 43)
SS2: Sth S 2H 137 (4J 43)
Prince Av. Nth. SS0: Wclf S 1G 136 (3H 43)
Prince Charles Av. RM16: Ors 4D 146 (6H 41)
Prince Charles Cl. CO15: Clac S 3G 189
Prince Charles Rd. CO2: Colc 4A 174
Prince Cl. SS0: Wclf S 1H 137
Prince Edward Rd. CM11: Bill 6L 99
Prince George Av. N14: Lon 7A 30
Princel La. CO7: Ded 1M 161
Princel M. CO7: Ded 1M 161
Prince of Wales Rd.
CM9: Gt Tot, W Bis 3M 229 (6H 25)
Prince of Wales Rdbt. CO6: M Tey 2K 171
Prince Philip Av. CO15: Clac S 3G 189
RM16: Grays 8K 145
Prince Philip Rd. CO2: Colc 5N 173
Prince Regent La. E13: Lon 6F 39
Prince Regent Station (DLR) 7F 39
Princes Av. CM0: S'min 2D 222
CM3: May 8L 213
IG8: Wfd G 1H 107
SS7: Thund 1F 134
SS17: Corr 2B 148
Princes Cl. CM12: Bill 2L 99
CM16: N Wea 4A 66
SS15: Lain 7N 115
Princes Ct. CM12: Bill 2L 99
SS2: Sth S 4M 137
Prince's Esplanade CO14: Walt 6N 181 (1H 29)
Princesfield Rd. EN9: Wal A 3H 77
Princes Ga. CM0: S'min 2D 222
CM20: H'low 9D 50
Princes Mall *SS1: Sth S* *7M 137*
(in Royals Shop. Cen., The)
Princes M. CM12: Bill 2L 99
Princes Pk. RM13: Rain 9E 126
Princes Rd. CM0: Bur C 2D 196
CM2: Chelm 3B 72 (2A 34)
CM9: Mal 6C 214
Prince's Rd. CM14: Kel C, N'side 9J 81 (6C 32)
Princes Rd. CO12: Har 4K 209
CO15: Hol S 7A 186
DA1: Dart 3B 46
(not continuous)
IG6: Ilf 8C 108
IG9: Buck H 8J 91
Prince's Rd. RM1: Romf 9E 110
Princes Rd. SS8: Can I 2F 150
PRINCES ROAD INTERCHANGE 4C 46
Princess Alice Way SE28: Lon 9C 140
Princess Anne Cl. CO15: Clac S 3G 189
Princess Av. RM18: E Til 2L 157
Princess Cl. SE28: Lon 6J 141
Princess Ct. SS11: W'fd 8A 102
Princess Dr. CO4: Colc 2C 166
Princess Gdns. SS4: R'fd 2H 121
Princess Margaret Rd.
RM18: E Til 1K 157 (1J 47)
SS17: E Til, Linf 1K 157 (1J 47)
Princess Pde. RM10: Dag 2M 141
Princess Rd. SS6: Ray 4M 119
Princess St. CO12: Har 2H 209
Princes St. CM9: Mal 5B 214
SS1: Sth S 6L 137
Princes Way CM13: Hut 8K 97
IG9: Buck H 8J 91
Princes Well CB10: R'ter 7F 7
Princeton M. CO4: Colc 3B 166
Prince William Av. SS8: Can I 8F 134
Printers Way CM20: H'low 7F 50
Prior Chase RM17: Grays 2J 155
Prior Cl. CO9: Hals 6J 207
Priories, The SS5: Hull 7K 103
Prior Rd. IG1: Ilf 5N 123
Priors Cl. SS14: Bas 9D 116
Priors Ct. CM0: S'min 2E 222
CM21: Saw 2M 51
Priors E. SS14: Bas 9D 116
Priors Hall Barn 3B 12
Priors Pk. RM12: Horn 5G 126
Priors Way CM0: S'min 2E 222
CO6: Cogg 2L 197
Priors Wood Ct. CM22: Tak 3C 224
Priors Wood Rd. CM22: Tak 2C 224
Prior Way CO4: Colc 5L 165
Priory Av. CM17: H'low 7H 51 (5J 21)
E4: Lon 9A 90
E17: Lon 9A 106
SS2: Sth S 3L 137
Priory Cl. CB10: I'tn 7A 202
CM1: Chelm 9G 59
CM3: Hat P 5M 61
CM15: Pil H 4D 96
E18: Lon 5G 106
EN11: Hod 6A 52
Priory Ct. CM3: Hat P 2L 61
CM18: H'low 6G 55
Priory Cres. SS2: Sth S 2K 137 (4J 43)
Priory Cres. Ind. Area SS2: Sth S 3L 137
Priory Dr. CM24: Stan M 4D 220
Priory Farm Rd. CM3: Hat P 4M 61
Priory Gro. RM3: Romf 9J 95
Priory Ho. SS0: Wclf S 3K 137
Priory Ind. Pk. SS2: Sth S 2M 137
Priory La. CM3: Bick 8F 74
CM77: Gt N 8E 192
CO4: L'ham 3G 160
Priory Mead CM15: Dodd 6F 82
Priory M. CM3: Hat P 4N 61
RM12: Horn 3F 126
Priory Pk. CO16: St O 9M 183
Priory Path RM3: Romf 9J 95
Priory Place Vineyard 8C 212
Priory Rd. CM3: Bick 9E 74 (3E 34)
CO5: Tip 4J 25
CO6: Chap, E Col 9A 196
CO15: Clac S 1J 189
IG10: Lou 3L 91
IG11: Bark 9C 124
N8: Lon 3A 38
RM3: Romf 9J 95
SS17: Stan H 3N 147
Priory Rd. Nth. DA1: Dart 9H 153
Priory Rd. Sth. DA1: Dart 3B 46
Priory St. CO1: Colc 8N 165 (6F 17)
CO6: E Col 7C 198
Priory, The CM1: Writ 1K 71
CM12: Bill 3L 99
Priory Vw. Rd. SS9: Lgh S 1D 136
Priory Wlk. CO1: Colc 8N 165
Priory Wood CO9: Cas H 3K 219
Priory Wood Cres. SS9: Lgh S 1D 136
Priorywood Dr. SS9: Lgh S 1D 136
Priory Wood Rdbt. CM22: Bis S 9F 220
Pritchard's Rd. E2: Lon 6C 38
Pritchett Cl. EN3: Enf 7A 76
Prittle Cl. SS7: Had 1J 135
PRITTLEWELL 4J 137 (4J 43)
Prittlewell Chase SS0: Wclf S 3G 137 (4J 43)
Prittlewell Path SS2: Sth S 4M 137
Prittlewell Priory 3L 137
Prittlewell Priory Mus. 3L 137 (4J 43)
Prittlewell Sq. SS1: Sth S 7L 137
Prittlewell Station (Rail) 3M 137 (4K 43)
Prittlewell St. SS2: Sth S 5M 137
Private Rd. CM2: Chelm 6M 71
Proctor Cl. CO5: L'hoe 9C 174
Proctor Way CO6: M Tey 3G 171
Professional Pl. SS11: W'fd 2A 118
Progress Ct. CM7: Brain 5G 193
Progress Rd. SS9: Lgh S 9B 120 (3G 43)
Progress Way CO16: L Cla 4G 185 (2D 28)
Promenade CM3: May 6K 213
CO12: Har 6K 209
CO15: Clac S, Jay 5F 188
CO15: Hol S 9A 186
CO16: St O 6A 188
Promenade, The CM0: Bur C 4C 196
SS3: Shoe 9G 138
SS5: Hull 5K 103
Promenade Way CO7: B'sea 8C 182
Prospect Av. SS17: Stan H 5K 147
Prospect Bus. Pk. IG10: Lou 3C 92
Prospect Cl. CM3: Hat P 3L 61
SS1: Sth S 7A 138
Prospect Hill E17: Lon 8B 106 (3D 38)
Prospect Ho. *E17: Lon* *7C 106*
(off Prospect Hill)
Prospect Pk. CO13: Gt Hol 9D 180
Prospect Pl. CB11: Saf W 4E 218
CO9: Hals 5K 207
RM5: Col R 6A 110
RM17: Grays 4L 155

Prospect Rd. IG8: Wfd G 3J 107
RM11: Horn 7K 111
Prospect Way CM13: Hut 3A 98
Prospero Cl. CO4: Colc 8F 166
Protea Way SS8: Can I 1H 151
Prout Ind. Est. SS8: Can I 2M 151
Provence Cl. CO3: S'way 8D 164
Providence CM0: Bur C 4E 196
Providence Pl. CO1: Colc 9B 166
RM5: Col R 5L 109
Provident Sq. CM2: Chelm 9L 59
Prower Cl. CM11: Bill 7K 99
Prunus Ct. CO2: Colc 7A 174
Prykes Dr. CM1: Chelm 9H 59
Pryor Cl. CM8: Wthm 6D 230
Pryors Rd. CM2: Gall 8D 72
PUCKERIDGE 7E 10
Puck La. EN9: Wal A 8E 62
SS16: Bas 1D 132
Puckleside SS16: Lang H 2L 131
Pudding La. CO2: B'ch 2C 26
IG7: Chig 5D 92 (7H 31)
Pudding Mill Lane Station (DLR) 6D 38
Puddings Wood Lane CM1: Broom 9J 57
Puddledock La. DA2: Dart 5A 46
Pudsey Hall La. SS4: Cwdn 6M 105
Puffin Cl. IG11: Bark 3G 140
SS12: W'fd 2N 117
Puffin Pl. SS3: Shoe 5J 139
Puffinsdale CO15: Clac S 8K 185
Pugh Pl. SS17: Stan H 1M 147
Pulborough Ho. *RM3: Romf* *4J 111*
(off Kingsbridge Cir.)
Pulford Pl. CM6: Steb 6C 222
Pullman Ct. SS11: W'fd 8L 101
Pulpitfield Cl. CO14: Walt 6K 181
Pulpits Cl. SS5: Hock 9E 104
Pulteney Gdns. E18: Lon 7H 107
Pulteney Rd. E18: Lon 7H 107
Pump Hill CM2: Gt Bad 4G 73
CO16: St O 9A 184 (3B 28)
IG10: Lou 1M 91
Pumphill SG9: Bre P 3G 11
Pump La. CM1: Chelm 3N 59 (7B 24)
CM3: Dan 5D 74
CM3: Ples 3A 56
CM3: Pur 8K 215
CM16: E Grn 3A 64
Pump Mead Cl. CM0: S'min 2D 222
Pump Rd. CO2: Colc 3G 35
Pump St. SS17: Horn H 3J 147 (6J 41)
Punchard Cres. EN3: Enf 8B 76
Punders Fld. CM7: Brain 7M 193
Purbeck Ct. CM2: Gt Bad 4F 72
CO1: Colc *8D 166*
(off Tabor Rd.)
Purbeck Rd. RM11: Horn 2E 126
Purcell Cl. CO4: Colc 9E 166
SS15: Lain 7M 115
SS17: Stan H 2L 147
Purcell Cole CM1: Writ 1J 71
Purcell Rd. CM8: Wthm 8B 230
Purcell Way SS17: Stan H 2L 147
Purdeys Ind. Est. SS4: R'fd 7M 121
Purdeys Way SS4: R'fd 7M 121
PURFLEET 2L 153 (1C 46)
Purfleet By-Pass RM19: Purf 2M 153 (1C 46)
Purfleet F.C. 1B 154
Purfleet Ind. Pk. RM15: Ave 8K 143
(Centre Pl.)
RM15: Ave 9K 143
(Kirby Av.)
Purfleet Rd. RM15: Ave 9L 143 (1C 46)
Purfleet Station (Rail) 3L 153 (1C 46)
Purfleet Thames Terminal RM19: Purf 5N 153
Purford Grn. CM18: H'low 4F 54
Purland Cl. RM8: Dag 3L 125
Purland Rd. SE28: Lon 9E 140
PURLEIGH 8K 215 (3G 35)
Purleigh Av. IG8: Wfd G 3L 107
Purleigh Cl. SS13: Bas 6K 117
Purleigh Gro. CM3: Cold N 8L 197
Purleigh Rd. SS6: Ray 4H 119
Purleigh St. CM3: Mun 8N 215 (3H 35)
Purley Cl. IG5: Ilf 6N 107
Purley Way CO16: Clac S 7F 184
SS0: Wclf S 1H 137
Purlieu Way CM16: They B 5D 78
PURTON END 1C 12
Purvis Way CO4: Colc 2B 166
Putney Gdns. RM6: Chad H 9G 109
Putticks La. CO7: Strat M 1J 17
PUTTOCK END 5F 9
PUTTOCK'S END 2D 22
PYE CORNER 5H 21
Pye Cnr. CM20: Gil 7C 50
CO9: Cas H 3K 219
Pyefleet Cl. CO5: Fing 8J 175
CO7: B'sea 6D 182
Pyefleet Ho. *CO5: W Mer* *2D 228*
(off Carrington Ct.)
Pyefleet Vw. CO5: L'hoe 8B 174
Pyenest Rd. CM19: H'low 6A 54 (7G 21)
Pyesand CO13: Kir S 6F 180
Pyes Bridge CM6: Fels 1A 24
Pygot Pl. CM7: Brain 4G 192
Pym Pl. RM17: Grays 2K 155
Pyms Rd. CM2: Gall 7C 72
Pynchon M. CM1: Chelm 8M 59
Pynchon Paddocks CM22: L Hall 3M 213
Pyne Ga. CM2: Gall 9C 72
Pynest Grn. La. EN9: Lou, Wal A 8G 76 (5F 31)
Pypers Hatch CM20: H'low 3E 54
Pyrles Grn. IG10: Lou 9A 78
Pyrles La. IG10: Lou 1A 92 (6G 31)
Pytt Fld. CM17: H'low 4G 55

Q

'Q' Tower 1K 19
Quadrangle, The E15: Lon 8E 122
Quadrant Arc. RM1: Romf 9C 110
Quadrant, The RM19: Purf 2N 153
Quaker La. EN9: Wal A 4C 76 (4E 30)
Quakers All. CO1: Colc 8N 165
Quakers Pl. E7: Lon 7K 123
Quale Rd. CM2: Chelm 7C 60
Quantock *SS2: Sth S* *6M 137*
(off Chichester Rd.)
Quantock Rd. DA7: Bexh 7C 152
Quarles Cl. RM5: Col R 4M 109
Quarry Hill RM17: Grays 3K 155
Quarry M. RM19: Purf 2L 153
Quarry Spring CM20: H'low 3F 54
Quarter Ga. CM3: S Fer 3L 103
Quarter Mile La. E10: Lon 6B 122
Quatre Ports E4: Lon 2D 106
Quatro Pk. SS14: Bas 5G 117
Quay Courtyard CO11: Mist 4J 163
Quay La. CO13: Kir S 5G 180
CO16: T Sok 2M 179 (7E 18)
DA9: Grnh 9E 154
Quayside Ind. Est. CM9: Mal 4D 214
Quay St. CO7: W'hoe 6H 175
CO11: Mist 4J 163
Quay, The CM0: Bur C 4E 196
CO7: W'hoe 7H 175
CO12: Har 1M 209 (2H 19)
CO16: St O 9L 183
Quebec Av. SS1: Sth S 6M 137
(not continuous)
Quebec Gdns. CM3: S Fer 2K 103
Quebec Rd. IG1: Ilf 2A 124
IG2: Ilf 2B 124
RM18: Til 7C 156
Queen Anne Dr. CO5: W Mer 3D 228
Queen Anne Gdns. CO5: W Mer 2D 228
Queen Anne Rd. CO5: W Mer 3D 228
(not continuous)
Queen Anne's Cl. SS0: Wclf S 2H 137
Queen Anne's Dr. SS0: Wclf S 2H 137
Queen Anne's M. SS0: Wclf S 2H 137
Queen Ann's Gro. SS5: Hull 8K 103
Queenborough Gdns. IG2: Ilf 8N 107
Queenborough La. CM77: Gt N 8E 192 (1C 24)
CM77: Rayne 7C 192 (7B 14)
Queenborough Rd. CM0: S'min 5C 36
CM0: S'min 2D 222
Queenbridge Ind. Pk. RM20: W Thur 4D 154
Queenbury Cl. CO5: W Mer 3E 228
Queen Edith Dr. CB9: Stpl B 3K 223
Queen Elizabeth Av. CO15: Clac S 3G 189
RM18: Til 2K 157
Queen Elizabeth II Bri. DA1: Dart 8A 154
RM20: Dart, W Thur 8A 154 (2D 46)
Queen Elizabeth Chase SS4: R'fd 8L 121
Queen Elizabeth Ct. *EN9: Enf* *6C 76*
(off Greenwich Way)
Queen Elizabeth Distribution Pk.
RM19: Purf 3A 154
Queen Elizabeth Dr. SS17: Corr 9A 132
Queen Elizabeth's Hunting Lodge
6F 90 (7E 30)
Queen Elizabeth II Sq. CM3: S Fer 1L 103
Queen Elizabeth Way CO2: Colc 5A 174
Queen Mary Av. CO2: Colc 2N 173
RM18: E Til 2L 157
Queen Mary Cl. RM1: Romf 1D 126
Queen Mary Ct. RM18: E Til 2L 157
Queen Marys Ct. *EN9: Enf* *5C 76*
(off Harrison Ct.)
Queens All. CM16: Epp 1E 78
Queen's Av. CM9: Mal 7C 214
IG8: Wfd G 2H 107
Queens Av. SS5: Hull 4L 103
SS9: Lgh S 5D 136
Queensberry Pl. E12: Lon 7K 123
Queensborough La. CM77: Gt N 1D 204
Queensbridge Rd. E8: Lon 5B 38
Queensbury Av. CO6: Cop 2M 171
Queens Cl. CM24: Stan M 1D 220
Queens Cnr. CO5: W Mer 2D 228
Queens Ct. CM0: Bur C 4D 196
CO5: W Mer *2D 228*
(off East Rd.)
Queen's Ct. CO15: Hol S 9A 186
Queens Ct. IG9: Buck H 8K 91
Queen's Ct. SS9: Lgh S 6E 136
Queens Ct. SS9: Lgh S 5D 136
Queens Dr. E10: Lon 2A 122
Queen's Dr. EN8: Wal X 4A 76
Queens Farm Rd. DA12: Grav, Shorne 4K 47
Queen's Gdns. CM7: Pan 1C 192
RM13: Rain 2B 142
Queens Gdns. RM14: Upm 1C 128
Queensgate Cen. CM20: H'low 8D 50
Queens Ga. Cen. RM17: Grays 3K 155
Queens Ga. M. CM12: Bill 4L 99
Queens Gro. Rd. E4: Lon 7D 90
Queen's Head Rd. CO4: Boxt 6L 159 (3E 16)
Queens Head Yd. CM22: Srng 3C 210
Queen's Ho. CO13: Frin S 1J 187
Queensland Av. SS4: R'fd 8L 121
Queensland Cres. CM1: Chelm 6F 58
Queensland Dr. CO2: Colc 5A 174
Queens Lodge SS7: Had 3J 135
Queens Mall *SS1: Sth S* *7M 137*
(in Royals Shop. Cen., The)
Queensmere SS7: Thund 2H 135
Queens M. CO5: W Mer 3B 228
QUEEN'S PARK 3K 99 (6J 33)
Queens Pk. Av. CM12: Bill 4J 99 (6J 33)
Queen's Pk. Country Pk. 2K 99
Queens Pk. Ct. CM12: Bill 3H 99
Queen's Pk. Rd. RM3: H Wood 5L 111
Queens Rd. CM0: Bur C 3D 196
Queen's Rd. CM2: Chelm 9M 59
Queens Rd. CM7: Brain 3H 193
CM11: Cray H 3C 116
CM14: Brtwd 9F 96 (1E 40)
CM16: N Wea 5N 65
Queen's Rd. CO3: Colc 9K 165
CO6: E Col 8C 198
CO6: W Ber 4E 164
CO7: W'hoe 6H 175
CO12: Har 5J 209
CO13: Frin S 1J 187
CO15: Clac S 3H 189
DA8: Eri 4C 152 (2A 46)
Queens Rd. E11: Lon 2D 122
E17: Lon 3D 38
Queen's Rd. E17: Lon 1A 122
IG9: Buck H 8H 91 (1F 39)
IG10: Lou 2L 91
Queens Rd. IG11: Bark 8B 124
SG8: R'ton 5C 4
Queen's Rd. SS1: Sth S, Wclf S 6L 137
Queens Rd. SS6: Ray 6K 119
Queen's Rd. SS7: Ben 4D 134
Queens Rd. SS9: Lgh S 6E 136
SS15: Lain 6L 115
Queens Theatre 2H 127
Queenstown Gdns. RM13: Rain 3D 142
Queen St. CB9: Wthfld 2H 7
CM0: S'min 2B 222 (5C 36)
CM2: Chelm 1B 72
CM5: Fy'd 9D 200 (1D 32)
CM9: Mal 6C 214
CM14: War 2F 112
CO1: Colc 8N 165 (6E 16)
CO6: Cogg 3L 197
CO7: B'sea 7E 182 (3K 27)
CO9: Cas H 4K 219 (1E 14)
CO9: Sib H 8L 219 (2E 14)
CO12: Gt Oak 7C 204
DA8: Eri 4C 152
RM7: Romf 1B 126
Queens Wlk. E4: Lon 7D 90
Queensway CM5: Chip 5K 67
CO5: Tip 5C 226
CO11: Law 4H 163
CO15: Hol S 8A 186
SS1: Sth S 6L 137 (5K 43)
Queenswood Av. CM13: Hut 3N 97
E17: Lon 5C 106
Queenswood Gdns. E11: Lon 3H 123
Queenswood Ho. *CM14: Brtwd* *8G 96*
(off Eastfield Rd.)
Queen Victoria St. EC4: Lon 7A 38
QUENDON 2C 216 (3A 12)
Quendon Dr. EN9: Wal A 3D 76
Quendon Rd. SS14: Bas 7F 116
Quendon Way CO13: Frin S 8K 181
Quennell Way CM13: Hut 6M 97
Quickset Rd. CB11: Elm 5J 5
Quicksie Hill CB11: A'den 1K 11
Quilp Dr. CM1: Chelm 4H 59
Quilters Cl. CO15: Hol S 7C 186
SS14: Bas 7E 116
Quilters Dr. CM12: Bill 8J 99
QUILTERS GREEN 1A 164
Quilters Straight SS14: Bas 7E 116
Quince Tree Cl. RM15: S Ock 4F 144
Quinion Cl. CM1: Chelm 4F 58
Quintons Cnr. CO7: E Ber 1J 17
Quorn Gdns. SS9: Lgh S 5N 135
Quorn, The CM4: Ing 7C 84

R

Rabbits Rd. DA4: S Dar 6D 46
E12: Lon 6L 123
Rachael Clarke Cl. SS17: Corr 1N 147
Rachael Ct. *CM2: Chelm* *1C 72*
(off Hall St.)
Rachael Gdns. CM8: Sil E 8M 217
Rachel Cl. IG6: Ilf 7C 108
Rackenford SS3: Shoe 6H 139
Radbourne Cres. E17: Lon 6D 106
Radburn Cl. CM18: H'low 7F 54
Radford Bus. Cen. CM12: Bill 5H 99
Radford Ct. CM12: Bill 5K 99
Radford Cres. CM12: Bill 5J 99
Radford Ho. CM12: Bill 5K 99
Radford Way CM12: Bill 5H 99 (7J 33)
IG11: Bark 3E 140
Radlett Cl. E7: Lon 8F 122
Radley Av. IG3: Bark, Ilf 6F 124
RADLEY GREEN 3M 69 (2G 33)
Radley Grn. Rd. CM4: Rad G 4L 69
Radley Green Rd. CM5: Rad G, Will 3L 69
Radley Grn. Rd. CM5: Will 2F 33
Radley Ho. *SE2: Lon* *9J 141*
(off Wolvercote Rd.)
RADLEY'S END 5F 13
Radley's La. E18: Lon 6G 106
Radleys Mead RM10: Dag 8N 125
Radlix Rd. E10: Lon 3A 122
Radnor Cres. IG4: Ilf 9M 107
Radnor Rd. SS4: R'fd 7H 105
Radstock Ho. *RM3: Romf* *2H 111*
(off Darlington Gdns.)
Radstocks CM12: Bill 5K 99
RADWINTER 7F 7
Radwinter Av. SS12: W'fd 9L 101 (1C 42)
RADWINTER END 6G 7
Radwinter Rd. CB10: A'dn 7D 190 (5E 6)
CB10: Saf W 4D 218 (6C 6)
CB10: Sew E 6D 6
CB11: Saf W 4D 218 (6C 6)
Raeburn Cl. CO13: Walt 7J 181
Raeburn Ct. CM1: Chelm 5N 59
Ragey Cl. CM77: Gt N 2B 204
Raglan M. CO15: Clac S 1G 188
Raglan Rd. CO13: Frin S 9K 181
E17: Lon 9C 106
Rags La. EN7: Chesh, G Oak 3B 30
Rahn Rd. CM16: Epp 1F 78
Raider Cl. RM7: Maw 5M 109
Railey Rd. CB11: Saf W 6D 218
Railway App. SS15: Lain 8J 115
(not continuous)
Railway Arches *E7: Lon* *6G 122*
(off Winchelsea Rd.)
E10: Lon *2B 122*
(off Capworth St.)
E11: Lon *3D 122*
(off Sidings, The)
E11: Lon *4E 122*
(off Leytonstone High Rd.)
E17: Lon *9A 106*
(off Yunus Khan Cl.)
Railway Cotts. CB11: Wen A 6L 227
Railway Pde. *CM15: Shenf* *6K 97*
(off Hutton Rd.)
Railway Sq. CM1: Chelm 8J 59
CM14: Brtwd 9F 96
Railway St. CM1: Chelm 8J 59
CM7: Brain 5J 193 (7D 14)
CO11: Mist 4J 163
RM6: Chad H 2H 125
Railway Ter. CO15: Clac S 1K 189
E17: Lon 5C 106
SS2: Sth S 3M 137
Rainbow Av. SS8: Can I 1J 151
Rainbow La. RM18: W Til 2F 156
SS17: Stan H 3A 148 (6K 41)
Rainbow Mead CM3: Hat P 1L 61
Rainbow M. CM9: Mal 3B 214
Rainbow Rd. CM17: Mat T 6A 22
CO5: W Mer 3D 228
RM16: Chaf H 2F 154 (1E 46)
SS8: Can I 1J 151
Rainbow Way CO6: Coln E 3D 198
RAINHAM 4E 142 (6B 40)
Rainham Hall 4E 142 (6B 40)
Rainham Rd. RM12: Horn, Rain 7D 126 (5B 40)
RM13: Rain 7E 126 (5A 40)
Rainham Rd. Nth. RM10: Dag 4M 125 (4K 39)
Rainham Rd. Sth. RM10: Dag 6N 125 (5A 40)
Rainham Station (Rail) 4E 142 (6B 40)
Rainham Trad. Est. RM13: Rain 4D 142
Rainham Way CO13: Frin S 8L 181
Rainsborowe Rd. CO2: Colc 2K 173
Rainsford Av. CM1: Chelm 7H 59
Rainsford La. CM1: Chelm 9H 59 (1K 33)
Rainsford Rd. CM1: Chelm 8H 59 (1K 33)
CM24: Stan M 1C 220
Rainsford Way RM12: Horn 3E 126
Raleigh Cl. DA8: Eri 4D 152
Raleigh Ct. DA8: Eri 5D 152
Raleigh Dr. SS15: Lain 1M 131
Rambler Cl. CO3: S'way 8E 164
Ramblers La. CM17: H'low 2J 55
Ramblers Way CM0: Bur C 4F 196
Ram Gorse CM20: H'low 1A 54
Ram Kuteer Dr. CO6: Gt Hork 1J 165
Ramparts Cl. CO6: Gt Hork 9J 159
Ramparts Cotts. CO6: Gt Hork 9J 159
Ramparts Ct. CO4: Colc 4J 165
Ramparts, The SS6: Ray 5M 119
Rampart St. SS3: Shoe 8K 139
Rampart Ter. SS3: Shoe 8L 139
Ramplings Av. CO15: Clac S 8J 185
Rampton Cl. E4: Lon 9A 90
Ramsay Dr. SS16: Van 3F 132
Ramsay Gdns. RM3: Romf 5G 110
Ramsay Rd. E7: Lon 6E 122
RAMSDEN BELLHOUSE 8F 100 (1A 42)
Ramsden Cl. CO15: Clac S 8L 185
Ramsden Dr. RM5: Col R 4M 109
RAMSDEN HEATH 4D 100 (7A 34)
Ramsden Pk. Rd.
CM11: Rams B 7D 100 (7A 34)
Ramsden Rd. DA8: Eri 5B 152
Ramsden Vw. Rd. SS12: W'fd 1G 116
RAMSEY 6C 208 (3F 19)
Ramsey Chase CM3: Latch 7L 211
SS12: W'fd 1N 117
Ramsey Cl. CM9: H'bri 4F 214
Ramsey Ct. SS0: Wclf S 3G 136
RAMSEY ISLAND 2C 36
Ramsey M. CO2: Colc 2A 174
Ramsey Rd. CO9: Hals 5J 207
CO12: Har, R'sy 6D 208 (3F 19)
Rams Farm Rd. CO6: For 1B 164 (4B 16)
Ramsgill App. IG2: Ilf 8E 108
Ramsgill Dr. IG2: Ilf 9E 108
Rams Gro. RM6: Chad H 8K 109
Ramshaw Dr. CM2: Chelm 8A 60
Ramuz Dr. SS0: Wclf S 5J 137
Rana Ct. CM7: Brain 4H 193

Rana Dr. CM7: Brain 4H 193
Rancliffe Rd. E6: Lon 6G 39
Randall Cl. CM6: Gt D 2L 203
DA8: Eri 4A 152
Randall Ct. RM13: Rain 4F 142
Randall Dr. RM12: Horn 6G 127
Randalls Dr. CM13: Hut 5A 98
Randolph Av. CM7: Weth 2A 14
Randolph Cl. CM9: Mal 8B 214
DA7: Bexh 8A 152
SS9: Lgh S 3D 136
Randolph Gro. RM6: Chad H 9H 109
Randolph Rd. E17: Lon 9B 106
Rands Rd. CM6: High R 3F 23
Randulph Ter. CM1: Chelm 8M 59
Randway SS6: Ray 6K 119
Ranelagh Gdns. E11: Lon 9J 107
IG1: Ilf 3M 123
Ranelagh Rd. E11: Lon 6E 122
Ranger's Rd. E4: Lon 6E 90 (7E 30)
IG10: Lou 6G 91
Ranger Wlk. CO2: Colc 3B 174
Rangoon Cl. CO2: Colc 5J 173
RANK'S GREEN 2C 24
Rank's Grn. Rd.
CM3: F'std, Gt L 6N 203 (2C 24)
Ransomes Way CM1: Chelm 7K 59
Ransom Rd. CO5: Tip 6C 226
Rantree Fold SS16: Bas 2A 132
Ranulf Cl. CM17: H'low 6H 51
Ranulph Way CM3: Hat P 3M 61
Ranworth Av. EN11: Hod 1B 52
Ranworth Cl. DA8: Eri 7C 152
Raphael Av. RM1: Romf 7D 110
RM18: Til 5C 156
Raphael Dr. CM1: Chelm 4A 60
SS3: Shoe 6K 139
Raphaels SS15: Lain 1N 131
Rapier Cl. RM19: Purf 2K 153
Ratcliff Ct. CO5: K'dn 3J 211
Ratcliffe Rd. CO3: S'way 9F 164
Ratcliff Rd. E7: Lon 7J 123
Rat Hill IP9: Anw, Hark 1F 19
Rat La. SS6: Ray 7J 119
Ratsborough Chase CM0: S'min 4C 222
Rats La. IG10: H Bee, Lou 8H 77
Rattwick Dr. SS8: Can I 2M 151
Ratty's La. EN11: Rye P 5D 52
Ravel Av. CM8: Wthm 8C 230
Ravel Gdns. RM15: Ave 6N 143
Ravel Rd. RM15: Ave 6N 143
Raven Cl. CM12: Bill 4H 99
Raven Cres. CM12: Bill 4H 99
Ravencroft RM16: Grays 9D 146
Ravendale Way SS3: Shoe 4H 139
Raven Dr. SS7: Ben 4B 134
Ravenings Pde. IG3: Ilf 3F 124
Raven La. CM12: Bill 4H 99
Ravenoak Way IG7: Chig 2D 108
Raven Rd. E18: Lon 6J 107
Raven's Av. CO9: Hals 5L 207
Ravensbourne Cres. RM3: H Wood 7K 111
Ravensbourne Dr. CM1: Chelm 1N 71
Ravensbourne Gdns. IG5: Ilf 5N 107
Ravensbourne Rd. DA1: Cray 8E 152
Ravenscourt CM15: Brtwd 6F 96
Ravens Ct. SS1: Sth S 7L 137
Ravenscourt Cl. RM12: Horn 5J 127
Ravenscourt Dr. RM12: Horn 5J 127
SS16: Van 1F 132
Ravenscourt Gro. RM12: Horn 4J 127 (4C 40)
Ravens Cres. CM6: Fels 6M 199
Ravensdale CO15: Clac S 7K 185
SS16: Bas, Van 2C 132
Ravensfield SS14: Bas 9G 117
Ravensfield Cl. RM9: Dag 6J 125
Ravensfield La. CO8: Bures 2K 15
RAVENS GREEN 2J 177 (6A 18)
RAVEN'S GREEN 9H 169 (6A 18)
Ravensmere CM16: Epp 1F 78
Ravenstock La. CB10: L Wal 4C 6
Ravenswood Chase
SS4: R'fd 8L 121
Ravenswood Cl. RM5: Col R 2N 109
Ravenswood Ind. Est.
E17: Lon 8C 106
Ravenswood Rd. E17: Lon 8C 106
Raven Way CO4: Colc 3M 165
Rawden Cl. CO12: Har 3K 209
Rawdon Dr. EN11: Hod 6A 52
Rawlings Cres. CO4: Colc 2B 166
Rawlyn Cl. RM16: Chaf H 3F 154
RAWRETH 9E 102 (1E 42)
Rawreth Gdns. SS11: Raw 7E 102
Rawreth Ind. Est. SS6: Ray 2G 119
Rawreth La. SS6: Ray 9F 102
SS11: Raw, Ray 9F 102 (1E 42)
RAWRETH SHOT 9C 102 (1D 42)
Rawstorn Rd. CO3: Colc 8M 165
Ray Av. CO12: Har 3J 209
Rayburne Ct. IG9: Buck H 7J 91
Rayburn Rd. RM11: Horn 2L 127
Raycliffe Av. CO15: Clac S 7J 185
Ray Cl. SS8: Can I 3G 150
SS9: Lgh S 5A 136
Raydons Gdns. RM9: Dag 6K 125
Raydons Rd. RM9: Dag 7K 125
Raydon Way CO10: Gt Cor 5K 9
Rayfield CM16: Epp 9F 64
Rayfield Cl. CM6: Barns 3L 191
Ray Gdns. IG11: Bark 2F 140
Rayhaven CO12: R'sy 5E 208
Ray Ho. *CO5: W Mer 2D 228*
(off Carrington Ct.)
Ray Lamb Way DA8: Eri 4F 152
Ray La. CO12: Har, R'sy 4B 208
RAYLEIGH 5K 119 (2F 43)
Rayleigh Av. SS0: Wclf S 5K 137
SS9: Lgh S 7A 120
Rayleigh Castle (Motte & Bailey) 5J 119 (2F 43)
Rayleigh Cl. CM7: Brain 4L 193
CM13: Hut 5M 97
CO4: Colc 6B 166
Rayleigh Downs Rd. SS6: Ray 8N 119
Rayleigh Dr. SS9: Lgh S 3C 136
Rayleigh Indoor Karting Stadium 7J 119
Rayleigh Mans. CO2: Colc 1K 173
Rayleigh Rd. CM13: Hut 5L 97 (7F 33)
IG8: Wfd G 3J 107
SS7: Had, Thund 8H 119 (3E 42)
SS9: Lgh S, Sth S 8A 120 (3G 43)
SS17: Stan H 4K 147
Rayleigh Station (Rail) 4J 119 (2F 43)
Rayleigh Tower Mill 4K 119
Rayles La. CM16: N Wea, Thorn 3M 65
Rayley La. CM16: N Wea, Thorn 3M 65 (2K 31)
Ray Lodge Rd. IG8: Wfd G 3J 107
Ray Mead CM3: Gt Walt 5H 57
Rayment Av. SS8: Can I 2K 151
Raymond Av. E18: Lon 7F 106
Raymond Gdns. IG7: Chig 9G 92
Raymond Postage Ct. SE28: Lon 7G 141
Raymond Rd. IG2: Ilf 2C 124
Raymonds Cl. CM3: S Fer 1J 103
Raymonds Dr. SS7: Thund 9F 118
Raymouth Ho. CO2: Colc 4M 173
RAYNE 6B 192 (7B 14)
Rayne Ct. E18: Lon 8F 106
Rayne Hall 5C 192
Rayne Hatch CM7: Brain 5E 14
Rayne Rd. CM7: Brain 5F 192 (7C 14)
CM77: Gt N, Rayne 6C 192 (7B 14)
Rayner Rd. CO2: Colc 3J 173
Rayner Towers *E10: Lon 2A 122*
(off Albany Rd.)
Rayner Way CO9: Hals 5K 207
Raynes Av. E11: Lon 2J 123
Rayne Station Cen. 7B 192
Raynham Cl. CM23: Bis S 9B 220
Raynham Rd. CM23: Bis S 9A 220
Raynhams *CB10: Saf W 3C 218*
(off High St.)
Ray Rd. RM5: Col R 2N 109
Rays Hill DA4: Hort K 6C 46
Rayside SS14: Bas 9D 116
(not continuous)
Ray, The CM1: Chelm 6N 59
Ray Wlk. SS9: Lgh S 5A 136
Read Cl. SS5: Hock 3F 120
Read Ct. E17: Lon 1A 122
EN9: Wal A 3G 77
Readers Ct. CM2: Gt Bad 5K 71
Reading Cl. SS16: Lang H 1H 131
Readings, The CM18: H'low 6E 54
Reads Cl. IG1: Ilf 5A 124
Reaper Rd. CO3: Colc 2H 173
Rebecca Gdns. CM8: Sil E 8M 217
Rebecca Meade CM6: Gt Eas 6F 13
Rebel Air Mus. 5H 15
Rebels La. SS3: Gt W, Sth S 3C 138 (4A 44)
(not continuous)
Rebow Rd. CO7: W'hoe 6H 175
CO12: Har 5J 209
Rebow St. CO1: Colc 9B 166
Reckitts Cl. CO15: Clac S 9M 185
Recreation Av. RM3: H Wood 6K 111
RM7: Romf 9A 110
SS9: Lgh S 4E 136
SS16: Lang H 3J 131
SS17: Corr 9D 132
Recreation Ground CM24: Stan M 3D 220
Recreation Rd. CO1: Colc 1B 174
CO9: Sib H 7J 219
CO15: Clac S 1K 189
Recreation Wlk. CM11: Rams H 3D 100
Recreation Way CO7: B'sea 6E 182
Rectory Av. SS4: R'fd 9G 105
Rectory Chase CM2: S'don 4K 73
CM13: L War 8G 113
CM15: Dodd 7F 82
Rectory Cl. CB11: L'bry 1B 218
CM3: L Walt 6L 57
CM4: Ing 5D 84
CM4: Stock 7M 85
CO4: Colc 5M 165
DA1: Cray 9D 152
E4: Lon 9A 90
SS7: Had 3L 135
Rectory Cotts. SS16: Van 4D 132
Rectory Ct. E18: Lon 5F 106
SS13: Pits 8K 117
Rectory Cres. E11: Lon 1J 123
(not continuous)
Rectory Dr. CM23: Farnh 6J 11
Rectory Fld. CM19: H'low 5A 54
Rectory Gdns. RM14: Upm 4A 128
SS13: Pits 9K 117
Rectory Gth. SS6: Ray 4K 119
Rectory Gro. SS9: Lgh S 6C 136 (5G 43)
SS11: W'fd 9N 101
Rectory Hill CO6: Stok 1E 16
CO7: E Ber 1J 17
CO7: W'hoe 5J 175 (7H 17)
Rectory La. CB10: A'dn 7C 190 (4D 6)
CM1: Chelm 7K 59 (1A 34)
CM3: Gt L, L L'gh 6H 203 (3B 24)
CM3: Latch 9M 211 (5K 35)
Rectory La. CM9: Wdhm M 3M 75 (2F 35)
CM13: Heron 4A 114
CM19: H'low 5A 54
CM23: Farnh 6J 11
CO5: Abb 8A 174 (2E 26)
CO9: Wick P 7G 9
CO12: L Oak, R'sy 6C 208
(not continuous)
IG10: Lou 1N 91 (6G 31)
SS11: Bat 2E 102
Rectory Mdw. CM77: Tye G 7F 15
Rectory Mdws. CO9: Sib H 6J 219
Rectory Pk. Dr. SS13: Pits 1J 133
Rectory Rd. CB9: Ked 2A 8
CM1: Writ 2K 71
CM3: N Fam 6H 35
(not continuous)
CM9: Tol K 4A 26
CM9: Wdhm W 1F 35
CM12: L Bur 3H 115 (2J 41)
CM77: Tye G 6E 14
CO4: L'ham 2F 160 (2G 17)
CO5: Rhdge 6E 174 (1G 27)
CO5: Tip 6C 226
CO6: Aldh 6A 16
CO6: Cop 5L 171 (1B 26)
CO7: Frat 5D 176 (7K 17)
CO7: L Ben 7K 169 (6A 18)
CO7: W'hoe 4J 175 (7H 17)
CO9: Sib H 6J 219 (1D 14)
CO10: Gt Wal 4K 9
CO10: Mdltn 6J 9
CO11: Wrab 3E 18
CO12: Gt Oak, L Oak 8A 208 (4F 19)
CO13: Gt Hol 2D 186 (2F 29)
CO16: Wee H 3D 184 (2C 28)
E12: Lon 7M 123
E17: Lon 8B 106
IP9: Hark 1E 18
N16: Lon 4B 38
RM10: Dag 8N 125
RM16: Ors 4C 146 (7H 41)
RM17: Grays 1N 155 (1G 47)
RM18: W Til 4F 156 (1H 47)
SS4: R'fd 4E 120 (2J 43)
SS5: Hock, R'fd 3H 121 (2H 43)
SS7: Had 3L 135 (4F 43)
SS13: Pits 1K 133 (3C 42)
(not continuous)
SS17: Stan H 4L 147
Rectory Road Station (Rail) 4B 38
Rectory Ter. SS5: Hock 3F 120
SS17: Stan H 4L 147
Rectory Wood CM20: H'low 2B 54
Red Barn La. CO12: Gt Oak 8B 204 (5E 18)
Red Barn Rd. CO7: B'sea 5E 182 (3K 27)
Redbond Lodge CM6: Gt D 3L 203
Redbourne Dr. SE28: Lon 6J 141
Redbrick Row CM22: L Hall 2K 213
REDBRIDGE 1L 123 (3G 39)
Redbridge Ent. Cen. IG1: Ilf 4B 124
Redbridge Foyer *IG1: Ilf 4B 124*
(off Sylvan Rd.)
Redbridge La. E. IG4: Ilf 1K 123 (3G 39)
Redbridge La. W. E11: Lon 1H 123 (3F 39)
Redbridge Rd. CO15: Clac S 5K 185
REDBRIDGE RDBT. 1K 123 (3F 39)
Redbridge Sports Cen. 5C 108
Redbridge Station (Tube) 1K 123 (3G 39)
Redbrooke Ct. SS17: Linf 1J 157
Redbury Cl. RM13: Rain 4G 142
Redcar Rd. RM3: Romf 2K 111
Redcliff Dr. SS9: Lgh S 6E 136
Redcliffe Gdns. IG1: Ilf 3N 123
Redcliffe Rd. CM2: Chelm 1B 72
Redden Ct. RM3: H Wood 6K 111
Redden Ct. Rd. RM3: H Wood 7J 111
Reddings Cl. CB11: Saf W 6D 218
Reddings La.
CM0: Ashel, T'ham 3H 225 (3E 36)
Reddy Rd. DA8: Eri 4D 152
Redfern Gdns. RM2: Romf 6H 111
Redgate Cl. SS11: W'fd 8A 102
Redgates La. CB10: Saf W 6D 6
Redgates Pl. CM2: Chelm 7M 59
Redgrave Rd. SS16: Van 2F 132
REDHILL 2A 10
Redhill Rd. TN15: Ash 7F 47
Redhills Rd. CM3: S Fer 9L 89
Redhouse La. CO4: Boxt 6M 159
Redif Ho. RM10: Dag 6N 125
Redinge, The CM11: Bill 9M 99
Redlie Cl. SS17: Stan H 1M 147
Red Lion Cres. CM17: H'low 5H 55
Red Lion La. CM17: H'low 5H 55
Red Lion St. WC1: Lon 7A 38
Red Lion Yd. CO1: Colc 8N 165
Redmayne Dr. CM2: Chelm 2A 72
Redmill CO3: Colc 3H 173
Redoaks Hill CB10: A'dn 6F 7
Red Oaks Mead CM16: They B 7C 78
Redo Ho. *E12: Lon 7N 123*
(off Dore Av.)
Red Post Ho. E6: Lon 9K 123
Redricks La. CM21: Saw 6D 50 (5H 21)
Redriff Rd. RM7: Maw 6N 109
SE16: Lon 7C 38
Red Rd. CM14: War 1E 112
Redrose La. CM4: B'more 9H 69 (3F 33)
Redrose Wlk. CO16: Clac S 9G 185
Redruth Cl. CM1: Chelm 6N 59
Redruth Gdns. RM3: Romf 2K 111
Redruth Rd. RM3: Romf 2K 111
Redruth Wlk. RM3: Romf 2K 111
Redshank Cres. CM3: S Fer 8K 89
Redshank Dr. CM9: H'bri, Mal 3E 214
Redstock Rd. SS2: Sth S 4M 137
Red St. DA13: S'fleet 5F 47
Red Willow CM19: H'low 6M 53
Redwing Ct. RM3: Romf 5H 111
Redwing Dr. CM11: Bill 8L 99
Redwing Path SE28: Lon 9C 140
Redwood CM15: Dodd 6F 82
Redwood Chase RM15: S Ock 4F 144
Redwood Cl. CM8: Wthm 2D 230
CO4: Colc 6E 166
IG9: Buck H 8H 91
Redwood Ct. CO4: Colc 7E 166
Redwood Dr. CM1: Writ 1H 71
SS15: Lain 6M 115
Redwood Gdns. E4: Lon 5B 90
IG7: Chig 2F 108
Redwoods, The SS8: Can I 2E 150
REED 7D 4
Reed Cl. CO16: Clac S 8G 185
Reede Gdns. RM10: Dag 7N 125
REED END 7C 4
Reede Rd. RM10: Dag 8M 125 (5K 39)
Reede Way RM10: Dag 8N 125
Reed Hall Av. CO2: Colc 3K 173
(not continuous)
Reed Pond Wlk. RM2: Romf 6D 110
SS16: Lang H 2K 131
Reeds Way SS12: W'fd 8K 101
Reesland Cl. E12: Lon 8N 123
Reeves Cl. CM15: Ston M 4E 82
SS16: Lang H 2H 131
Reeves La. CM19: Roy 7J 53 (1F 31)
Reeves Way CM3: S Fer 1L 103
Refinery Rd. CO12: Har 2F 208
Reflection, The *E16: Lon 9A 140*
(off Woolwich Mnr. Way)
Regal Cl. CM2: Chelm 2E 72
Regan Cl. SS17: Stan H 1N 147
Regarder Rd. IG7: Chig, Ilf 2F 108
Regarth Av. RM1: Romf 1C 126
Regatta Ct. SS9: Lgh S 6E 136
Regency Cl. CM2: Chelm 8M 59
IG7: Chig 2B 108
SS4: R'fd 5K 121
SS11: W'fd 6L 101
Regency Ct. CM9: Mal 3C 214
CM14: Brtwd 8F 96
CM18: H'low 6F 54
CO2: Colc 2C 174
SS5: Hock 1D 120
Regency Gdns. RM11: Horn 2G 127
Regency Grn. CO3: Colc 2G 173
SS2: Sth S 3L 137
Regency Lodge CO15: Clac S 8J 185
IG9: Buck H 8K 91
Regent Cl. CO7: B'sea 5E 182
RM16: Grays 9M 145
SS6: Ray 3H 119
Regent Ct. RM15: Ave 8A 144
SS15: Lain 7N 115
Regent Dr. CM12: Bill 3H 99
Regent Gdns. IG3: Ilf 2F 124
Regent Ho. CM14: Brtwd 9E 96
Regent Rd. CM16: Epp 9E 64
CO7: B'sea 6E 182 (3K 27)
Regents Cl. CM0: S'min 2D 222
CO4: Colc 2C 166
Regents Ct. CM0: Bur C 4D 196
Regents Dr. IG8: Wfd G 3N 107
Regents Pl. IG10: Lou 6K 91
Regent St. CO5: Rhdge 6F 174
CO11: Mist 4J 163
W1: Lon 7A 38
Regimental Way CO12: Har 6E 208
Reginald M. *CM17: H'low 2H 55*
(off Green St.)
Reginald Rd. E7: Lon 9G 122
RM3: H Wood 5L 111
Reginald Sorenson Ho. E11: Lon 2D 122
Regina Rd. CM1: Chelm 8L 59
Reigate Av. CO16: Clac S 7H 185
Reigate Rd. IG3: Ilf 4E 124
Rembrandt Cl. SS3: Shoe 6L 139
SS8: Can I 2G 150
Rembrandt Gro. CM1: Chelm 5N 59
Rembrandt Way CO3: Colc 1J 173
Remembrance Av. CM0: Bur C 4D 196
CM3: Hat P 3L 61
Remembrance Rd. E7: Lon 6K 123
Remercie Rd. CO11: Mist 4M 163
Remus Cl. CO4: Colc 2N 165
Remus Rd. E3: Lon 9A 122
Renacres SS16: Bas 2A 132
Rennie Pl. CM2: Chelm 8C 60
Renoir Pl. CM1: Chelm 4A 60
Renovation, The *E16: Lon 9A 140*
(off Woolwich Mnr. Way)
Renown Cl. RM7: Maw 5M 109
Renown Shop. Cen., The SS3: Shoe 6K 139
Renwick Ind. Est. IG11: Bark 2G 141
Renwick Rd. IG11: Bark 4G 141 (6J 39)
Repton Av. RM2: Romf 7E 110
Repton Cl. SS13: Bas 6H 117
Repton Ct. IG5: Ilf 5M 107
SS13: Bas 6H 117
Repton Dr. RM2: Romf 8E 110
Repton Gdns. RM2: Romf 7E 110
Repton Gro. IG5: Ilf 5M 107
SS2: Sth S 8F 120
Repulse Cl. RM5: Col R 5M 109
Reservoir Rd. IG10: H Bee 9H 77 (6F 31)
Retford Cl. RM3: Romf 3L 111

Retford Path RM3: Romf . . . 3L 111
Retford Rd. RM3: Romf . . . 3K 111
Retingham Way E4: Lon . . . 8B 90
Retreat Rd. SS0: Wclf S . . . 7K 137
SS5: Hock . . . 1D 120
Retreat, The CM8: Wthm . . . 6D 230
CM13: Hut . . . 5L 97
CM14: Brtwd . . . 7E 96
CO6: W Ber . . . 4E 164
RM17: Grays . . . 4L 155
Retreat Way IG7: Chig . . . 9G 92
RETTENDON . . . 8A 88 (5D 34)
Rettendon Cl. SS6: Ray . . . 4G 119
Rettendon Gdns. SS11: W'fd . . . 7M 101
Rettendon Rd. CM3: E Han . . . 4C 88 (4D 34)
Rettendon Vw. SS11: W'fd . . . 8N 101
Reubens Rd. CM13: Hut . . . 5L 97
Reverdy Ho. CO2: Colc . . . 4M 173
Review Rd. RM10: Dag . . . 1N 141
Rewsalls La. CO5: E Mer . . . 4G 27
Rex Cl. RM5: Col R . . . 4N 109
Reydon Av. E11: Lon . . . 9J 107
Reymead Cl. CO5: W Mer . . . 3C 228
Reynards Cl. CO13: Walt . . . 8G 181
Reynards Copse CO4: Colc . . . 4A 166
Reynards Ct. CM2: Gt Bad . . . 4G 73
Reynolds Av. CO3: Colc . . . 1J 173
E12: Lon . . . 7N 123
RM6: Chad H . . . 2H 125
Reynolds Ct. CB11: Newp . . . 2L 215
RM6: Chad H . . . 7J 109
Reynolds Ga. CM3: S Fer . . . 2L 103
Rhapsody Cres. CM14: War . . . 1E 112
Rhoda Rd. SS7: Ben . . . 2D 134
Rhoda Rd. Nth. SS7: Thund . . . 1E 134
Rhodesia Rd. E11: Lon . . . 4D 122
Rhodeswell Rd. E14: Lon . . . 7D 38
R.H.S. Garden (Hyde Hall) . . . 5E 88 (5E 34)
Rhubarb M. *CM17: H'low* . . . *2J 55*
(off Chase, The)
Rhum M. SS12: W'fd . . . 2A 118
Ribble Cl. IG8: Wfd G . . . 3J 107
Ricardo Path SE28: Lon . . . 8H 141
Rice Bri. Ind. Est. CO16: T Sok . . . 7L 179
Richard Av. CO7: B'sea . . . 7E 182
CO7: W'hoe . . . 3J 175
Richard Blackburn Ho. RM7: Rush G . . . 4C 126
Richard Burton Ct. *IG9: Buck H* . . . *8J 91*
(off Palmerston Rd.)
Richard Fell Ho. *E12: Lon* . . . *6N 123*
(off Walton Rd.)
Richards Av. RM7: Romf . . . 1A 126
Richardson Gdns. RM10: Dag . . . 8N 125
Richardson Pl. CM1: Chelm . . . 8H 59
Richardson Wlk. *CM8: Wthm* . . . *5E 230*
(off Oliver Pl.)
CO3: Colc . . . 1G 173
Richards Pl. E17: Lon . . . 7A 106
Richards Wlk. CO15: Clac S . . . 7J 185
Rich Cl. CM3: Gt L . . . 7K 203
Riche Cl. CM6: Fels . . . 8J 199
Riches Rd. IG1: Ilf . . . 4B 124
Richmer Rd. DA8: Eri . . . 5E 152
Richmond Av. E4: Lon . . . 2D 106
SS0: Wclf S . . . 6K 137
SS1: Sth S . . . *7M 137*
(off High St.)
SS3: Shoe . . . 7H 139
SS7: Ben . . . 4C 134
Richmond Ct. *IG10: Lou* . . . *4K 91*
(off High Rd.)
Richmond Cres. CO12: Har . . . 5K 209
E4: Lon . . . 2D 106
Richmond Dr. CO15: Jay . . . 3E 188
IG8: Ilf . . . 4N 107
SS0: Wclf S . . . 2H 137
SS6: Ray . . . 7K 119
Richmond Pk. IG10: Lou . . . 6K 91
Richmond Rd. CM2: Chelm . . . 7B 60
CO5: W Mer . . . 3D 228
E4: Lon . . . 7D 90
E7: Lon . . . 7H 123
E8: Lon . . . 5B 38
E11: Lon . . . 4D 122
IG1: Ilf . . . 5B 124
RM1: Romf . . . 1D 126
RM17: Grays . . . 4M 155
SS11: W'fd . . . 6K 101
RICHMOND'S GREEN . . . 4G 13
Richmond St. SS2: Sth S . . . 5B 138
Richmond Way E11: Lon . . . 4G 122
Ricketts Dr. CM12: Bill . . . 5H 99
RICKLING . . . 3A 12
Rickling SS16: Van . . . 2G 132
RICKLING GREEN . . . 3B 216 (4A 12)
Rickling Hall . . . 2A 216 (3A 12)
Rickling Rd. CB11: R'lng, Wick B . . . 2K 11
Rickstones Rd.
CM8: Riven, Wthm . . . 3C 230 (3F 25)
Riddiford Dr. CM1: Chelm . . . 7H 59
Riddings La. CM18: H'low . . . 7E 54
(not continuous)
Riddles Dr. CO4: Colc . . . 5N 165
Ridge Av. N21: Lon . . . 7B 30
Ridge Cl. SE28: Lon . . . 9C 140
RIDGEMARSH . . . 7G 37
Ridgemont Pl. RM11: Horn . . . 1H 127
Ridgemount SS7: Ben . . . 2E 134
Ridge Rd. N21: Lon . . . 7B 30
Ridge, The CM3: L Bad . . . 8M 61 (1E 34)
CO14: Walt . . . 6L 181
Ridgeway CM4: Ing . . . 8C 84
CM9: Mal . . . 8C 214
CM12: Bill . . . 8J 99
Ridgeway CM13: Hut . . . 7L 97
CO4: Colc . . . 3A 166
Ridge Way IG8: Wfd G . . . 1J 107
Ridgeway RM17: Grays . . . 2A 156
SS5: Hull . . . 4L 103
SS6: Ray . . . 6J 119
Ridgeway Gdns. IG4: Ilf . . . 9L 107
SS0: Wclf S . . . 6G 136
Ridgeways CM17: H'low . . . 3K 55
Ridgeway, The CM7: Brain . . . 7J 193
CO12: Har . . . 4J 209
DA12: Shorne . . . 5K 47
E4: Lon . . . 8B 90 (1D 38)
EN2: Enf . . . 5A 30
EN6: Cuff, N'thaw . . . 3A 30
RM2: Romf . . . 8E 110
RM3: H Wood . . . 5K 111
SS0: Wclf S . . . 6F 136 (5H 43)
RIDGEWELL . . . 8D 216 (5C 8)
Ridgewell Airfield . . . 5C 8
Ridgewell Av. CM1: Chelm . . . 7H 59
RM16: Ors . . . 4C 146
Ridgewell Cl. RM10: Dag . . . 1N 141
Ridgewell Rd. CO9: Bay E . . . 4B 8
CO9: Gt Yel . . . 1A 206 (6C 8)
CO10: Ashen . . . 4C 8
Ridgewell Way CO2: Colc . . . 5N 173
Ridings Av. CM77: Gt N . . . 1B 204
Ridings, The CM2: Gt Bad . . . 3E 72
E11: Lon . . . 9G 106
IG7: Chig . . . 1G 108
SS4: R'fd . . . 6L 121
SS8: Can I . . . 9G 134
Ridlands Cl. CM77: Tye G . . . 2E 194
Ridley Cl. IG11: Bark . . . 9E 124
RM3: Romf . . . 5F 110
Ridley Gdns. CM22: Else . . . 2K 199
Ridley Rd. CM1: Broom . . . 3K 59
E7: Lon . . . 6J 123
SS13: Bas . . . 6K 117
Riffams Ct. SS13: Bas . . . 7K 117
Riffams Dr. SS13: Bas . . . 7K 117
Riffhams CM13: Brtwd . . . 9L 97
Riffhams Chase CM3: L Bad . . . 1C 74 (1D 34)
Riffhams Dr. CM2: Gt Bad . . . 3H 73
Riffhams La. CM3: Dan . . . 2C 74 (2D 34)
Rifle Hill CM7: Brain . . . 7H 193
Rigby Av. CO11: Mist . . . 5M 163
Rigby Gdns. RM16: Grays . . . 2D 156
Rigby M. IG1: Ilf . . . 4N 123
Rigby Pl. EN3: Enf . . . 7A 76
Rigby Rd. CO11: Mist . . . 4M 163
Rigdon's La. CO14: Walt . . . 5J 181
Rignals La. CM2: Gall . . . 8D 72 (3A 34)
Riley Av. CO15: Jay . . . 6C 188
Rimini Cl. CO2: Colc . . . 3K 173
RINGTAIL GREEN . . . 3J 23
Ringwood Av. RM12: Horn . . . 4H 127
Ringwood Dr. SS9: Lgh S . . . 8A 120
Rio Cinema . . . 4D 196
Ripley Cl. CO16: Clac S . . . 7F 184
Ripley Ct. IG7: Chig . . . 8B 92
Ripley M. E11: Lon . . . 1E 122
Ripley Rd. IG3: Ilf . . . 4E 124
Ripley Vw. IG10: Lou . . . 8A 78
Ripon Gdns. IG1: Ilf . . . 1L 123
Ripon Ho. *RM3: Romf* . . . *3H 111*
(off Dartfields)
Rippers Ct. CO9: Sib H . . . 5K 219
Ripple Rd. IG11: Bark . . . 9B 124 (6H 39)
RM9: Bark, Dag . . . 1G 140
RIPPLE ROAD JUNCTION . . . 1F 140 (6J 39)
RIPPLESIDE . . . 1G 140
Rippleside SS14: Bas . . . 1G 133
Rippleside Commercial Est.
IG11: Bark . . . 2H 141
Ripple Way CO4: Colc . . . 6B 166
Risby Cl. CO16: Clac S . . . 9E 184
Risdens CM18: H'low . . . 6B 54
Risebridge Chase RM1: Romf . . . 4D 110
Risebridge Rd. RM2: Romf . . . 6D 110
Risedale Rd. DA7: Bexh . . . 8A 152
RISE PARK . . . 6C 110 (2A 40)
Rise Pk. SS15: Lain . . . 9A 116
Rise Pk. Blvd. RM1: Romf . . . 5D 110
Rise Pk. Pde. RM1: Romf . . . 6C 110
Rise, The CO6: Eig G . . . 7B 164
DA1: Cray . . . 9D 152
E11: Lon . . . 9G 106
EN9: Wal A . . . 9H 63
IG9: Buck H . . . 6K 91
Riseway CM15: Brtwd . . . 9H 97
Risings Ter. *RM11: Horn* . . . *7K 111*
(off Prospect Rd.)
Risings, The E17: Lon . . . 8D 106
Rising, The CM11: Bill . . . 7M 99
Rivendell Va. CM3: S Fer . . . 2J 103
RIVENHALL . . . 3G 25
Rivenhall SS6: Ray . . . 7H 119
SS11: W'fd . . . 1A 118
RIVENHALL END . . . 3H 25
Rivenhall Gdns. E18: Lon . . . 8F 106
River Av. EN11: Rye P . . . 4B 52
River Blackwater Chalet Site
CM9: H'bri . . . 4D 214
River Cl. CO9: Hals . . . 5L 207
E11: Lon . . . 1J 123
EN8: Wal X . . . 4A 76
RM13: Rain . . . 5F 142
River Cotts. CM3: Bore . . . 3G 61
River Ct. CM21: Saw . . . 1L 51
RM19: Purf . . . 2K 153
Riverdale SS9: Lgh S . . . 8C 120
Riverdale Rd. DA8: Eri . . . 3A 152
Riverdene Rd. IG1: Ilf . . . 5N 123
River Dr. RM14: Upm . . . 1N 127
Riverfield La. CM21: Saw . . . 1K 51
River Lee Country Pk. . . . 8A 62
River Mead CM7: Brain . . . 4J 193
Rivermead Ind. Est. CM1: Chelm . . . 7K 59
Rivermill CM20: H'low . . . 1B 54
River Rd. CM14: Brtwd . . . 1C 112
IG9: Buck H . . . 7L 91
IG11: Bark . . . 2D 140 (6H 39)
River Rd. Bus. Pk. IG11: Bark . . . 3E 140
Riversdale Rd. RM5: Col R . . . 4N 109
Riverside CM2: Chelm . . . 8L 59
CM6: Gt D . . . 2M 203
CM23: Bis S . . . 1K 21
CM77: Tye G . . . 7F 15
DA4: Eyns . . . 7B 46
Riverside Av. EN10: Brox . . . 1A 62
Riverside Av. E. CO11: Law . . . 3H 163
Riverside Av. W. CO11: Law . . . 3H 163
Riverside Bus. Pk. CM24: Stan M . . . 3D 220
Riverside Cen., The CM7: Brain . . . 6J 193
Riverside Cotts. IG11: Bark . . . 2C 140
Riverside Ct. CM20: H'low . . . 6H 51
Riverside Ho. *SS11: W'fd* . . . *8L 101*
(off Lwr. Southend Rd.)
Riverside Ice & Leisure Cen. . . . 9L 59
Riverside Ind. Est. CM9: Mal . . . 5B 214
DA1: Dart . . . 9J 153
IG11: Bark . . . 3F 140
SS4: R'fd . . . 6L 121
Riverside Maltings CO6: Cogg . . . 4L 197
Riverside Rail Freight Terminal
RM18: Til . . . 9C 156
Riverside Retail Pk. CM1: Chelm . . . 8L 59
Riverside Rd. CM0: Bur C . . . 4E 196
EN10: Hod . . . 7C 52
Riverside Swimming Cen. . . . 6J 141
Riverside Wlk. CO1: Colc . . . 7M 165
SS12: W'fd . . . 8J 101
Riverside Way CO5: K'dn . . . 4K 211
Riverside Works IG11: Bark . . . 9A 124
Riversmead EN11: Hod . . . 6A 52
Riverton Dr. CM0: Stpl . . . 1C 36
Rivertons SS16: Van . . . 2G 133
River Vw. CM7: Brain . . . 7G 193
(not continuous)
CM8: Wthm . . . 7D 230
Riverview CO11: Law . . . 4H 163
DA1: Dart . . . *9M 153*
(off Henderson Dr.)
River Vw. *EN9: Wal A* . . . *3B 76*
(off Powdermill La.)
RM16: Grays . . . 2B 156 (1H 47)
Riverview SS5: Hull . . . 4L 103
SS16: Van . . . 2H 133
River Vw. Cl. SS15: Lain . . . 6L 115
Riverview Ct. SS16: Van . . . 2F 132
Riverview Flats RM19: Purf . . . 3M 153
Riverview Gdns. SS5: Hull . . . 5J 103
RIVERVIEW PARK . . . 5J 47
Riverview Rd. SS7: Ben . . . 4D 134
River Vw. Ter. CM3: Alth . . . 3B 190
River Way CM20: H'low . . . 7F 50
IG10: Lou . . . 5M 91
River Wharf Bus. Pk. DA17: Belv . . . 8B 142
Riviera Dr. SS1: Sth S . . . 6A 138
Rivington Av. IG8: Wfd G . . . 6K 107
Rixsen Rd. E12: Lon . . . 7L 123
Roach RM18: E Til . . . 2L 157
Roach Av. SS6: Ray . . . 6J 119
Roach Rd. E3: Lon . . . 9A 122
Roach Va. CO4: Colc . . . 6E 166
SS9: Lgh S . . . 8E 120
ROAST GREEN . . . 2H 11
Robert Cl. CM2: Chelm . . . 7A 60
CM12: Bill . . . 6H 99
IG7: Chig . . . 2E 108
Robert Daniels Ct. CM16: They B . . . 7D 78
Robert Leonard Ind. Est. SS2: Sth A . . . 8H 121
Robert Leonard Ind. Pk. SS2: Sth S . . . 1L 137
Roberts Cl. RM3: Romf . . . 5F 110
Roberts Ct. CM2: Gt Bad . . . 3G 72
Robert's Hill CO8: M Bur . . . 3A 16
Robertson Ct. *RM17: Grays* . . . *2L 155*
(off Hathaway Rd.)
Robertson Dr. SS12: W'fd . . . 2M 117
Roberts Rd. CM3: N Fam . . . 1F 104
CO2: Colc . . . 1A 174
E17: Lon . . . 5B 106
SS15: Lain . . . 8K 115
Robert St. E16: Lon . . . 8A 140
NW1: Lon . . . 6A 38
Robert Suckling Ct. CB9: Stpl B . . . 3K 223
Robert Way CO7: W'hoe . . . 3J 175
SS11: W'fd . . . 1N 117 (1C 42)
Robin Cl. CM12: Bill . . . 2L 99
CO7: Gt Ben . . . 6J 177
RM5: Col R . . . 4B 110
Robin Cres. CO3: S'way . . . 2C 172
ROBINHOOD END . . . 7A 8
Robin Hood Rd. CM15: Brtwd . . . 6E 96
CM22: Else . . . 3K 199 (5B 12)
Robinia Cl. IG6: Ilf . . . 2D 108
SS15: Lain . . . 6M 115
Robinia Ct. *CO4: Colc* . . . *8E 166*
(off Blackthorn Av.)
Robinia Cres. E10: Lon . . . 4B 122
Robinsbridge Rd. CO6: Cogg . . . 3K 197
Robinsdale CO15: Clac S . . . 7K 185
Robin's La. CM16: They B . . . 6B 78
Robins Nest Hill SG13: Howe G, L Berk . . . 7A 20
Robinson Cl. E11: Lon . . . 5E 122
RM12: Horn . . . 9F 126
Robinson Rd. CO7: B'sea . . . 6F 182 (3K 27)
RM10: Dag . . . 6M 125
SS17: Horn H . . . 1F 146
Robinsons Cl. CM0: S'min . . . 3C 222
Robins, The CM15: Hook E . . . 5G 82
Robins Way EN9: Wal A . . . 4E 76
Robin Way CM2: Chelm . . . 5B 72
Robjohns Rd. CM1: Chelm . . . 3N 71
Robletts Way CO6: Wmgfd . . . 8L 229
Roborough Wlk. RM12: Horn . . . 8G 126
Rochdale Rd. E17: Lon . . . 2A 122
Rochdale Way CO4: Colc . . . 9E 166
Roche Av. SS4: R'fd . . . 5K 121
Rochefort Dr. SS4: R'fd . . . 7L 121
Rochehall Way SS4: R'fd . . . 7M 121
Rochelle Cl. CM6: Thax . . . 7C 224
Rochester Cl. CM7: Brain . . . 4M 193
Rochester Ct. CB10: Saf W . . . 3E 218
Rochester Dr. SS0: Wclf S . . . 2H 137
Rochester Gdns. IG1: Ilf . . . 2M 123
Rochester M. SS0: Wclf S . . . 2H 137
Rochester Rd. DA12: Grav . . . 4J 47
ME2: Hall . . . 7K 47
(not continuous)
Rochester Way DA1: Dart . . . 4A 46
DA5: Bex . . . 3A 46
SS14: Bas . . . 8G 117
Rocheway SS4: R'fd . . . 5L 121 (2J 43)
ROCHFORD . . . 5L 121 (2J 43)
Rochford Av. CM15: Shenf . . . 4K 97
EN9: Wal A . . . 4D 76
IG10: Lou . . . 2B 92
RM6: Chad H . . . 9H 109
SS0: Wclf S . . . 5K 137
Rochford Cl. CM24: Stan M . . . 4D 220
RM12: Horn . . . 8F 126
SS11: W'fd . . . 1N 117
Rochford Gdn. Way SS4: R'fd . . . 4K 121
Rochford Grn. IG10: Lou . . . 2B 92
Rochford Hall Cl. SS4: R'fd . . . 6L 121
Rochford Hall Cotts. SS4: R'fd . . . 6J 121
Rochford Rd. CM2: Chelm . . . 1D 72
(not continuous)
CM23: Bis S . . . 8A 220
CO16: St O . . . 9N 183
SS2: Sth S . . . 2J 137 (3J 43)
SS8: Can I . . . 2K 151
Rochford Station (Rail) . . . 6K 121 (2J 43)
Rochford Way CO13: Frin S . . . 7J 181
CO14: Walt . . . 6K 181
Rockall SS2: Sth S . . . 8F 120
Rockchase Gdns. RM11: Horn . . . 1J 127
Rock Gdns. RM10: Dag . . . 7N 125
Rockhampton Wlk. CO2: Colc . . . 5A 174
Rockingham Av. RM11: Horn . . . 1F 126
Rockingham Cl. CO4: Colc . . . 4D 166
Rock La. CB10: A'dn . . . 9D 190
Rockleigh Av. SS9: Lgh S . . . 5F 136
Rockleigh Ct. CM15: Shenf . . . 6K 97
Rockwell Rd. RM10: Dag . . . 7N 125
RODBRIDGE CORNER . . . 3J 9
Rodbridge Dr. SS1: Sth S . . . 6D 138
Rodbridge Hill CO10: L Mel . . . 4H 9
Roddam Cl. CO3: Colc . . . 9K 165
Roden Cl. CM17: H'low . . . 8L 51
Roden St. IG1: Ilf . . . 5N 123
Roden Way *IG1: Ilf* . . . *5N 123*
(off Roden St.)
Rodeo Cl. DA8: Eri . . . 6F 152
Roding CM14: Brtwd . . . 7E 96
Roding Av. IG8: Wfd G . . . 3L 107
Roding Cl. CM5: Fy'd . . . 9C 200
SS3: Gt W . . . 2M 139
Roding Ct. CM7: Brain . . . 7M 193
Roding Dr. CM15: Kel H . . . 7C 82
Roding Gdns. IG10: Lou . . . 5L 91
Roding La. IG7: Chig . . . 7L 91 (7G 31)
IG9: Buck H . . . 7L 91 (7G 31)
Roding La. Nth. IG8: Wfd G . . . 3L 107 (2G 39)
Roding La. Sth. IG4: Ilf . . . 8K 107 (3F 39)
IG8: Wfd G . . . 7K 107 (3F 39)
Roding Leigh CM3: S Fer . . . 1L 103
Roding Rd. E6: Lon . . . 5A 140
IG10: Lou . . . 4L 91 (7G 31)
Rodings Av. SS17: Stan H . . . 1M 147
Rodings, The IG8: Wfd G . . . 3J 107
RM14: Upm . . . 1A 128
SS9: Lgh S . . . 8C 120
Roding Trad. Est. IG11: Bark . . . 9A 124
Roding Valley Meadows Nature Reserve . . . 6N 91
Roding Valley Nature Reserve . . . 7N 91
Roding Valley Station (Tube) . . . 1K 107 (1F 39)
Roding Vw. CM5: Chip . . . 6M 67
IG9: Buck H . . . 7K 91
Roding Way RM13: Rain . . . 2H 143
SS12: W'fd . . . 1M 117
Rodney Cres. EN11: Rye P . . . 3A 52
Rodney Gdns. CM7: Brain . . . 4L 193
Rodney Rd. CM5: Chip . . . 8K 67
E11: Lon . . . 8H 107
Rodney Way CM1: Chelm . . . 3N 71
RM7: Maw . . . 5N 109
Roebuck La. IG9: Buck H . . . 6J 91
Roebuck Rd. IG6: Ilf . . . 2G 109
Roebuck Rd. Trad. Est. IG6: Ilf . . . 3G 109
Roedean Cl. SS2: Sth S . . . 5D 138
Roedean Dr. RM1: Romf . . . 8C 110
Roedean Gdns. SS2: Sth S . . . 4D 138
ROE GREEN . . . 2A 10
Rogation Cl. CO3: S'way . . . 1E 172
Roger Reede's Almshouses RM1: Romf . . . 8C 110
ROGERS END . . . 7D 190
Rogers Gdns. RM10: Dag . . . 7D 125
Roger's Ho. RM10: Dag . . . 5M 125

Rogers Rd. RM10: Dag 7M 125
RM17: Grays 2M 155
Roggel Rd. SS8: Can I 3K 151
Rohan Ct. CM3: S Fer 2K 103
Rokeby Gdns. IG8: Wfd G 5G 107
Rokells SS14: Bas 8B 116
Rokell Way CO13: Frin S, Walt 8H 181
Rokescroft SS13: Pits 1H 133
Rokesly Av. N8: Lon 3A 38
Roland La. SS8: Can I 1H 151
Roland Rd. E17: Lon 8D 106
Rolands Cl. CM1: Chelm 4K 59
Roles Gro. RM6: Chad H 8J 109
Rollerworld 8B 166
Rollesby Way SE28: Lon 6H 141
Rollestons CM1: Writ 2H 71
Rolley La. CO5: K'dn 3K 211
Roll Gdns. IG2: Ilf 9N 107
Rolls Pk. Av. E4: Lon 2A 106
Rolls Pk. Rd. E4: Lon 2B 106
Rolph Cl. CO16: T Sok 4L 179
ROLPHY GREEN 4J 23
Romagne Cl. SS17: Horn H 2H 147
Romainville Way SS8: Can I 2C 150
Roman RM18: E Til 2L 157
Roman Cl. CM9: Mal 4B 214
CM15: Mount 9A 84
RM13: Rain 2B 142
Roman Ct. CB11: Saf W 6D 218
CM7: Brain 7L 193
SS11: W'fd 2A 118
Roman Hill CO2: B'hth 7B 174 (1F 27)
Roman Ho. RM13: Rain 2B 142
Romanhurst CM9: Mal 4C 214
Roman La. CM24: Stan Apt, Stan M 8G 220
Roman M. EN11: Hod 4A 52
Roman Ri. CM21: Saw 2J 51
Roman River Valley 8G 172
Roman Rd. CB11: L'bry 1B 218
CM2: Chelm 1C 72
CM3: L Walt 7K 57
CM4: Ing 7B 84 (5H 33)
CM4: Marg 3G 84 (4J 33)
CM4: Mount 2M 97
CM15: Mount, Shenf 2M 97 (6G 33)
CO1: Colc 7A 166
E2: Lon 6C 38
E3: Lon 6C 38
IG1: Ilf 8A 124
Roman Rdbt. CM20: H'low 8F 50
Romans Farm Chase CM0: Bur C 1E 196
Romans Pl. CM1: Writ 1K 71
Roman Sq. SE28: Lon 8F 140
Roman St. EN11: Hod 4A 52
Romans Way CM1: Writ 1K 71
Roman Va. CM17: H'low 7H 51
Roman Villa Rd. DA2: Dart 5D 46
DA4: S Dar, S at H 5D 46
Roman Way CM0: Bur C 1B 196
CM12: Bill 8J 99
CO2: Colc 5M 173
CO16: P Bay 4K 27
EN9: Enf 5B 76
Romany Steps *SS1: Sth S 7A 138*
(off Beresford Rd.)
Rom Cres. RM7: Rush G 2D 126
Romeland EN9: Wal A 3C 76
ROMFORD 9D 110 (3A 40)
Romford Cl. CO4: Colc 6B 166
Romford Greyhound Stadium 1A 126
Romford Ice Rink 2C 126
Romford Rd. CM5: Chip 3J 81 (4C 32)
E7: Lon 8E 122 (5E 38)
E12: Lon 7J 123 (5F 39)
E15: Lon 8E 122 (5E 38)
IG7: Chad H, Chig 9G 92 (1J 39)
RM5: Col R 4K 109 (2K 39)
RM15: Ave 7N 143 (7C 40)
Romford Station (Rail) 1C 126 (3A 40)
Romney Chase RM11: Horn 1K 127
Romney Cl. CM7: Brain 2G 193
CO7: B'sea 4D 182
CO13: Walt 7H 181
CO16: Clac S 8H 185
Romney Ho. SS4: R'fd 5L 121
Romney Rd. CM12: Bill 7H 99
Romsey Cl. SS5: Hock 1C 120
SS7: Ben 1B 134
SS17: Stan H 4K 147
Romsey Cres. SS7: Ben 1B 134
Romsey Dr. SS7: Ben 1B 134
Romsey Gdns. RM9: Dag 1J 141
Romsey Rd. RM9: Dag 1J 141
SS7: Ben 1A 134
Romsey Way SS7: Ben 1B 134
Romulus Cl. CO4: Colc 2N 165
Rom Valley Way
RM7: Rush G 2C 126 (4A 40)
Ronald Dr. SS6: Ray 3G 119
Ronald Hill Gro. SS9: Lgh S 5C 136
Ronald Pk. Av. SS0: Wclf S 5H 137
Ronald Rd. CO9: Hals 6K 207
RM3: H Wood 5L 111
Roneo Cnr. RM12: Romf 3D 126
Roneo Link RM12: Horn 3D 126
Ron Green Ct. DA8: Eri 4B 152
Ron Leighton Way E6: Lon 6G 39
Ronnie La. E12: Lon 6N 123
Roodegate SS14: Bas 9B 116
Rook Cl. RM12: Rain 9E 126
ROOK END 2C 12
Rook End La. CB11: Deb 2C 12
Rookeries, The CO6: M Tey 2L 171
Rookery Chase CO7: A'lgh 6K 161
Rookery Cl. CB10: Gt Che 7D 202
CM3: Hat P 2L 61
SS6: Ray 5J 119
SS17: Stan H 4K 147
Rookery Ct. RM20: W Thur 4D 154
Rookery Cres. RM10: Dag 9N 125
Rookery Hill SS17: Corr 2C 148 (6A 42)
Rookery La. CB11: Wen A 8K 227 (1A 12)
CM9: Gt Tot 7J 205
CO5: Tip 4C 226
RM17: Grays 3N 155
Rookery Rd. CM4: B'more 8F 68 (3E 32)
Rookery, The CM24: Stan M 1D 220
CO11: Law 4H 163
RM20: W Thur 4D 154
Rookery Vw. RM17: Grays 3N 155
Rookes CB10: Saf W 1C 218
Rookes Cres. CM1: Chelm 1A 72
Rooks Nest La. SG8: Ther 7C 4
Rookwood Av. IG10: Lou 2B 92
Rookwood Cl. CO15: Clac S 6H 185
RM17: Grays 2L 155
Rookwood Gdns. E4: Lon 8F 90
IG10: Lou 2B 92
Rookwood Ho. IG11: Bark 2C 140
Rookwood Way CB9: H'hil 3J 7
Rookyards SS16: Van 1F 132
Roosevel Av. SS8: Can I 1G 151
Roosevelt Rd. SS15: Lain 9J 115
Roosevelt Way CO2: Colc 2B 174
RM10: Dag 8B 126
Roos Hill CB11: Deb 8D 218
ROOST END 7L 223 (4A 8)
Roothings, The CM9: Mal 3D 214
Roots Hall Stadium 4K 137
Roots Hall Av. SS2: Sth S 4L 137
Roots Hall Dr. SS2: Sth S 4K 137
Roots La. CM8: W Bis 2K 229 (5H 25)
Ropers Av. E4: Lon 2B 106
Roper's Chase CM1: Writ 3H 71
Rope Wlk. CM9: Mal 7C 214
CO7: B'sea 7F 182
Rosabelle Av. CO7: W'hoe 5H 175
Rosabell Rd. CM17: H'low 2H 55
Rosalind Cl. CO4: Colc 8F 166
Rosalind Ct. *IG11: Bark 9F 124*
(off Meadow Rd.)
Rosary Gdns. SS0: Wclf S 2G 137
Rosbach Rd. SS8: Can I 2K 151
Rosberg Rd. SS8: Can I 2L 151
Roscommon Way SS8: Can I 1B 150 (6D 42)
Rose Acre SS14: Bas 9G 117
Roseacre Cl. RM11: Horn 2K 127
Roseacres CM21: Saw 1J 51
CM22: Tak 3C 224
Rose & Crown M. CM0: S'min 2D 222
Rose & Crown Wlk. CB10: Saf W 3C 218
Rose Av. CO3: S'way 2D 172
E18: Lon 6H 107
Rose Bank CM14: Brtwd 9G 96
Rosebank CO12: Har 4J 209
EN9: Wal A 3E 76
Rosebank Av. RM12: Horn 7G 126
Rosebank Rd. CO5: W Mer 3B 228
E17: Lon 1B 122
Rosebank Vs. E17: Lon 8A 106
Rosebay Av. CM12: Bill 3H 99 (6J 33)
Rosebay Cl. CM8: Wthm 4A 230
Roseberry Av. SS7: Thund 9C 118
SS16: Lang H 2K 131
Roseberry Cl. RM14: Upm 1C 128
Roseberry Ct. SS7: Thund 8C 118
Roseberry Gdns. RM14: Upm 1B 128
Roseberry Wlk. SS7: Thund 8C 118
Rosebery Av. CO1: Colc 8A 166
E12: Lon 8L 123
EC1: Lon 6A 38
Rosebery Rd. CM2: Chelm 2C 72
RM17: Grays 4H 155
Rosebury Ct. CM13: Hut 5N 97
Rosebury Sq. IG8: Ilf 4N 107
Rose Cl. SS12: W'fd 2M 117
Rose Ct. CO2: Colc 6B 174
Rose Cres. CO4: Colc 5L 165
Rosecroft Cl. CO15: Clac S 7J 185
SS16: Lang H 2J 131
ROSEDALE 3C 30
Rosedale Cotts. CO3: S'way 1A 172
Rosedale Gdns. RM9: Dag 9G 124
Rosedale Rd. E7: Lon 7J 123
RM1: Col R 6A 110
RM9: Dag 9G 124
RM17: Grays 3N 155
Rosedale Way EN7: Chesh 3C 30
Rosedene Gdns. IG2: Ilf 8N 107
Rosedene Ter. E10: Lon 4B 122
Rose Dr. CM0: S'min 3D 222
Rose Gdns. CM7: Brain 6J 193
Rose Glen CM2: Chelm 3D 72
RM7: Rush G 3C 126
ROSE GREEN 7D 196 (4K 15)
Rose Hatch Av. RM6: Chad H 7J 109
Rose Hill CB9: Wthfld 1J 7
CM7: Brain 6J 193 (7D 14)
Roselaine SS14: Bas 8C 116
Rose La. CB10: Gt Che 8E 202
CM9: Salc 5C 26
CM12: Bill 6J 99
CO7: W'hoe 7H 175
RM6: Chad H 7J 109 (3J 39)
Roselawn Flds. CM1: Broom 3K 59
Roseley Cotts. CM20: E'wck 8A 50
Rosemary Almshouses
CO3: S'way 1A 172
Rosemary Av. CM7: Brain 4G 193
RM1: Romf 7D 110
Rosemary Cl. CM6: Gt D 2K 203
CM17: H'low 8H 51
CO5: Tip 6C 226
RM15: S Ock 3F 144
Rosemary Ct. CO4: Colc 7E 166
CO9: Hals 4K 207
(off Rosemary La.)
Rosemary Cres. CM6: Gt D 2K 203
CO5: Tip 6C 226
CO15: Clac S 2K 189
Rosemary Dr. IG4: Ilf 9K 107
Rosemary Gdns. RM8: Dag 3L 125
Rosemary La. CM6: Gt D 2K 203 (7G 13)
CM6: Steb 6B 222
CO7: Thorr 9G 176
CO9: Cas H 2M 219 (7E 8)
CO9: Hals 4K 207
Rosemary Rd. CO15: Clac S 2J 189 (4D 28)
Rosemary Rd. W. CO15: Clac S 2J 189
Rosemary Way CO15: Jay 5E 188
Rosemead SS7: Thund 8C 118
Rosemead Gdns. CM13: Hut 3N 97
Rosemount CM19: H'low 5A 54
Rosemount Cl. IG8: Wfd G 3M 107
Rosepark Ct. IG5: Ilf 6M 107
Roserna Rd. SS8: Can I 2K 151
Rose Rd. SS8: Can I 2G 151
Rosery M. CO13: Gt Hol 1D 186
Roses, The IG8: Wfd G 4F 106
Rose Tree M. IG8: Wfd G 3L 107
Rosetta Cl. CO7: W'hoe 4H 175
Rosetti Ter. *RM8: Dag 6G 125*
(off Marlborough Rd.)
Rose Va. EN11: Hod 5A 52 (7D 20)
Rose Valley CM14: Brtwd 9F 96
Rose Valley Cres. SS17: Stan H 1N 147
Rose Wlk. CM77: Bla N 3A 194
CO9: Ridg 8D 216
Rose Way SS4: R'fd 7M 121
Rosewood Av. RM12: Horn 7E 126
Rosewood Cl. CO4: Colc 3A 166
RM15: S Ock 3H 145
Rosewood Ct. E11: Lon 6D 122
RM6: Chad H 9H 109
Rosewood Dr. SS15: Lain 6M 115
Rosewood La. SS3: Shoe 7K 139
Rosher Cl. E15: Lon 9D 122
ROSHERVILLE 3G 47
Rosherville Way DA11: N'fleet 4G 47
Rosilian Dr. SS5: Hock 7B 104
Roslings Cl. CM1: Chelm 5F 58
Roslyn Gdns. RM2: Romf 6D 110
Rossall Cl. RM11: Horn 1E 126
Ross Av. RM8: Dag 4L 125
Ross Cl. CB11: Saf W 7D 218
Rossdene Gdns. CM6: Lea R 4D 212
Rossendale CM1: Chelm 1N 71
Rossendale Cl. CO4: Colc 4D 166
Rosshill Ind. Pk. SS2: Sth S 2M 137
Rossiter Rd. SS3: Shoe 6M 139
Rosslyn Av. E4: Lon 8F 90
RM3: H Wood 6J 111
RM8: Dag 2L 125
Rosslyn Cl. SS5: Hock 9D 104
Rosslyn Rd. CM12: Bill 6H 99
E17: Lon 8C 106
IG11: Bark 9C 124
SS5: Hock 9D 104
Ross Way SS16: Lang H 3K 131
Ross Wyld Lodge *E17: Lon 7A 106*
(off Forest Rd.)
Rothbury Av. RM13: Rain 5F 142
Rothbury Rd. CM1: Chelm 1M 71
E9: Lon 9A 122 (5D 38)
Roth Dr. CM13: Hut 8L 97
ROTHERHITHE 7C 38
Rotherhithe Station (Tube) 7C 38
Rotherhithe Tunnel E1: Lon 7C 38
Rothesay Av. CM2: Chelm 2B 72
Rothmans Av. CM2: Gt Bad 4F 72
Rothsay Rd. E7: Lon 9J 123
Rothwell Cl. SS9: Lgh S 9B 120
Rothwell Gdns. RM9: Dag 9H 125
Rothwell Rd. RM9: Dag 1H 141
ROTTEN END 4B 14
Rotten End CM7: Weth 4B 14
Rotunda, The *RM7: Romf 9B 110*
(off Yew Tree Gdns.)
Roughtallys CM16: N Wea 6L 65
Roughtons CM2: Gall 7D 72
Roundacre CO9: Hals 6K 207
SS15: Lain 9B 116 (3K 41)
Roundaway Rd. IG5: Ilf 5M 107
ROUNDBUSH 9N 215 (4H 35)
ROUNDBUSH GREEN 1C 212 (4E 22)
Roundbush Rd. CM9: Mun 8N 215 (4H 35)
CO5: Lay M 2B 26
Round Cl. CO3: Colc 8J 165
Round Coppice Rd.
CM24: Bis S, Stan Apt,
Stan M 7G 220 (1B 22)
Round Hill Rd. SS7: Ben 4G 135
Roundhills EN9: Wal A 4E 76
Round House, The 9D 94 (1A 40)
Roundmead Av. IG10: Lou 1N 91
Roundmead Cl. IG10: Lou 2N 91
ROUND STREET 6H 47
Round St. DA13: Sole S 6H 47
Roundway, The N17: Lon 2B 38
Roundwood Av. CM13: Hut 7K 97
Roundwood Gro. CM13: Hut 6L 97
Rounton Rd. EN9: Wal A 3E 76
Rous Chase CM2: Gall 9C 72
Rouses La. CO16: Clac S 9D 184
Rous Rd. IG9: Buck H 7L 91
Rover Av. CO15: Jay 5C 188
IG6: Ilf 3E 108
Rowallan Cl. CO3: Colc 3H 173
Rowallen La. CM12: Bill 2H 99
Rowallen Pde. RM8: Dag 3H 125
Rowan Chase CO5: Tip 5C 226
Rowan Cl. CO3: S'way 2E 172
CO7: Gt Ben 6L 177
CO12: Har 4K 209
CO15: Clac S 1G 188
IG1: Ilf 7C 124
SS6: Ray 1H 119
Rowan Dr. CM9: Mal 3E 214
Rowan Grn. E. CM13: Brtwd 1J 113
Rowan Grn. W. CM13: Brtwd 9J 97
Rowan Gro. RM15: Ave 7N 143
Rowan Pl. CO1: Colc 6M 165
Rowans, The CM11: Bill 8M 99
EN9: Wal A 5J 77
(off Woodbine Cl.)
RM15: Ave 8N 143
SS9: Lgh S 9A 120
Rowans Way IG10: Lou 3M 91
SS11: W'fd 8M 101
Rowan Wlk. CM21: Saw 2K 51
RM11: Horn 8H 111
SS9: Lgh S 9C 120
Rowan Way CM3: Hat P 3L 61
CM6: Gt D 2K 203
CM8: Wthm 2D 230
RM6: Chad H 7H 109
RM15: S Ock 4F 144
SS4: Cwdn 2N 105
Rowden Pk. Gdns. *E4: Lon 4A 106*
(off Chingford Rd.)
Rowden Rd. E4: Lon 3B 106
Rowdowns Rd. RM9: Dag 1L 141
Rowe Gdns. IG11: Bark 2E 140
Rowenhall SS15: Lain 9H 115
ROW GREEN 3D 204 (1C 24)
ROW HEATH 1E 184 (2C 28)
ROWHEDGE 6G 174 (1G 27)
Rowhedge CM13: Brtwd 9K 97
Rowhedge Cl. SS13: Bas 5K 117
Rowhedge Rd. CO2: Colc 4D 174 (7F 17)
CO5: Fing, Rhdge 4D 174 (7F 17)
Rowherns La. CO7: L Ben 2K 177
Rowland Cres. IG7: Chig 1D 108
Rowlands Rd. RM8: Dag 4L 125
Rowlands, The SS7: Ben 3E 134
Rowland's Yd. CO12: Har 5G 209
Rowland Wlk. RM4: Hav 9C 94
Rowley Ct. CB9: Stur 6J 223
Rowley Hill CB9: Stur 6H 223 (3K 7)
Rowley Mead CM16: Thorn 4H 65
Rowley Rd. RM16: Ors 5C 146 (7H 41)
Rowney Av. *CB10: Wim 1D 12*
(off Broad Oakes Clo.)
Rowney Gdns. CM21: Saw 4H 51
RM9: Dag 8H 125
Rowney La. SG12: D End, Sac 1C 20
Rowney Rd. RM9: Dag 8G 125
Rowney Wood CM21: Saw 3H 51
Rowntree Path SE28: Lon 8G 141
Rowntree Way CB11: Saf W 6C 218
Rows, The *CM20: H'low 2C 54*
(off Stone Cross)
Row, The CB1: Hads 3C 6
CM22: Hen 8D 210
CO7: Strat M 1H 17
Roxborough Cl. CO6: M Tey 3G 170
Roxburgh Av. RM14: Upm 5N 127
Roxburghe Rd. CO16: Wee 8D 178
ROXWELL 2N 217 (7H 23)
Roxwell Av. CM1: Chelm 8F 58
Roxwell Gdns. CM13: Hut 4M 97
Roxwell Ho. IG10: Lou 6L 91
Roxwell Rd.
CM1: Chelm, Rox, Writ 6A 58 (7J 23)
IG11: Bark 2F 140
Roxwell Way IG8: Wfd G 4J 107
Roxy Av. RM6: Chad H 2H 125
Royal Albert Station (DLR) 7F 39
Royal Albert Way E16: Lon 7A 140 (7F 39)
Royal Artillery Way SS2: Sth S 3B 138 (4A 44)
Royal Cl. IG3: Ilf 2F 124
SS4: R'fd 2J 121
Royal Ct. CM9: Mal 7C 214
CO4: Colc 6E 166
SS15: Lain 8K 115
Royal Docks Rd. E6: Bark 6A 140 (7G 39)
IG11: Bark 6A 140 (6H 39)
Royal Gunpowder Mills 2B 76
Royal Gunpowder Mills Vis. Cen. 2B 76 (4D 30)
Royal Jubilee Ct. RM2: Romf 7E 110
Royal M. SS1: Sth S 7M 137
(not continuous)
Royal Mint St. E1: Lon 7B 38
Royal Oak Chase SS15: Lain 7N 115
Royal Oak Dr. SS11: W'fd 8A 102
Royal Pde. *RM10: Dag 8N 125*
(off Church St.)
Royal Sq. CO7: Ded 1M 161
Royals Shop. Cen., The SS1: Sth S 7M 137
Royal Ter. SS1: Sth S 7M 137
Royal Victoria Station (DLR) 7F 39
Roycraft Av. IG11: Bark 2E 140
Roycroft Cl. E18: Lon 5H 107
ROYDON 2H 53 (6F 21)
Roydon Bri. SS14: Bas 7E 116
Roydonbury Ind. Est. CM19: H'low 3M 53

Roydon Cl. IG10: Lou 6L **91**
ROYDON HAMLET 8J **53** (1F 31)
Roydon Lodge Chalet Est. CM19: Roy 2J **53**
Roydon Rd. CM19: H'low 2L **53** (6G 21)
SG12: Stan A 6E **20**
Roydon Station (Rail) 2H **53** (6F 21)
Roydon Way CO13: Frin S 8J **181**
Royds La. CM14: Kel H 9N **81** (6D 32)
Royer Cl. SS5: Hock 3F **120**
Roy Gdns. IG2: Ilf 8D **108**
Royle Cl. RM2: Romf 9F **110**
ROYSTON 5D **4**
Royston and District Mus. 5C **4**
Royston Av. E4: Lon 2A **106**
SS2: Sth S 3M **137**
SS15: Lain 6M **115**
Royston Gdns. IG1: Ilf 1K **123**
Royston La. CB11: Elm 5J **5**
SG8: Hey, I'tn 4H **5**
Royston Pde. IG1: Ilf 1K **123**
Royston Rd. CB2: Foxt, Hars 1F **5**
CB2: Whitt 2J **5**
CB11: Lit Gr, Wen A 7H **227** (7K **5**)
RM3: H Wood 4L **111**
SG8: B'wy 7E **4**
SG8: Bar 6E **4**
SG8: Lit, R'ton 4A **4**
SG8: Mel 4D **4**
SG9: Bunt, Chipp 3C **10**
Royston Station (Rail) 5C **4**
Ruaton Dr. CO16: Clac S 9G **184**
Rubens Cl. SS3: Shoe 6L **139**
Rubens Ga. CM1: Chelm 4A **60**
Rubicon Av. SS11: W'fd 8N **101**
Rubin Pl. EN3: Enf 7A **76**
Ruby Ct. SS9: Lgh S 1D **136**
Ruby M. E17: Lon 7A **106**
Ruby Rd. E17: Lon 7A **106**
Ruckholt Cl. E10: Lon 5B **122**
Ruckholt Rd. E10: Lon 6A **122** (5D 38)
Rudd Ct. CO4: Colc 6F **166**
Rudkin Rd. CO4: Colc 2N **165**
Rudland Rd. DA7: Bexh 8A **152**
RUDLEY GREEN 6J **215** (3G 35)
Rudley Grn. La. CM3: Pur 6J **215**
Rudsdale Way CO3: Colc 1G **173**
Rue de Jeunes CM7: Brain 6H **193**
Rue de St Lawrence EN9: Wal A 4C **76**
Ruffels Pl. CM6: Steb 9D **222**
Ruffles Cl. SS6: Ray 4L **119**
Ruffles Yd. CO9: Cas H 3K **219**
Rugby Gdns. RM9: Dag 8H **125**
Rugby Rd. RM9: Dag 8G **124**
Rugged La. EN9: Wal A 3K **77**
Rugosa Cl. CO3: S'way 8D **164**
Rumbold Rd. EN11: Rye P 3C **52**
Rumbullion Dr. CM12: Bill 5H **99**
Rumford Shop. Hall *RM1: Romf* *8C 110*
(off Market Pl.)
Rumsey Flds. CM3: Dan 3F **74**
Runcorn Ho. *RM3: Romf* *3J 111*
(off Kingsbridge Cir.)
Rundells CM18: H'low 7F **54**
Rundells Wlk. SS14: Bas 8F **116**
Rundels Cotts. *SS7: Thund* *9G 119*
(off Rundels, The)
Rundels, The SS7: Thund 1G **135**
Runnacles St. CM8: Sil E 7K **217**
Running Mare La. CM2: Chelm, Gall 7B **72**
Running Waters CM13: Brtwd 1K **113** (1F **41**)
(not continuous)
Runnymede Chase SS7: Thund 2G **134**
Runnymede Ct. SS17: Stan H 4L **147**
Runnymede Rd. SS8: Can I 2H **151**
SS17: Stan H 4L **147**
Runnymede Swimming Pool 1G **135**
Runsell Cl. CM3: Dan 3F **74**
RUNSELL GREEN 3F **74** (2E 34)
Runsell La. CM3: Dan 2F **74** (2E **34**)
Runsell Vw. CM3: Dan 2G **74**
RUNWELL 7M **101** (7C 34)
Runwell Chase SS11: Runw 6A **102** (7D **34**)
Runwell Gdns. SS11: Runw 6L **101**
Runwell Rd. SS11: W'fd 8L **101** (7C **34**)
Runwell Ter. SS1: Sth S 7L **137**
Runwood Rd. SS8: Can I 2C **150**
Rupert Jarvis Ct. SS5: Hock 1C **120**
Rupert Rd. CM0: S'min 2C **222**
Rural Cl. RM11: Horn 3F **126**
Rurik Ct. CM9: Mal 8B **214**
Rushbottom La. SS7: Thund 8B **118** (3D **42**)
SS12: N Ben 6B **118**
Rush Cl. SS7: Thund 9B **118**
Rushcroft Rd. E4: Lon 4B **106**
RUSHDEN 3A **10**
Rushdene Rd. CM12: Bill 7H **99**
CM15: Brtwd 5F **96**
Rushden Gdns. IG5: Ilf 6N **107**
Rushden Rd. SG9: S'don 2A **10**
Rushdon Cl. RM1: Romf 9E **110**
RM17: Grays 1K **155**
Rush Dr. EN9: Enf 6C **76**
Rushes La. CM0: St La 3D **36**
Rushes Mead CM18: H'low 5D **54**
Rushfield CM21: Saw 2K **51**
RUSH GREEN 1F **188** (4C 28)
Romford 3B **126** (4A 40)
Rush Grn. Gdns. RM7: Rush G 3A **126**
Rush Grn. Rd. CO16: Clac S 2E **188** (4C **28**)
RM7: Rush G 3N **125** (4A **40**)
Rush La. CM22: Else 3K **199**
Rushley SS13: Bas, Pits 7L **117** (3C **42**)
Rushley Cl. RM16: Grays 8N **145**
SS3: Gt W 2L **139**
Rushleydale CM1: Chelm 6N **59**
RUSHLEY GREEN 1L **219** (7E 8)
Rushmere Av. RM14: Upm 5N **127**
Rushmere Cl. CO5: W Mer 3D **228**
Rushmoor Dr. CM7: Brain, Tye G 7K **193**
Rusholme Av. RM10: Dag 5M **125**
Rushton Gro. CM17: H'low 3J **55**
Ruskin Av. E12: Lon 8L **123**
EN9: Wal A 4E **76**
RM14: Upm 2N **127**
SS2: Sth S 4M **137**
Ruskin Cl. CO13: Walt 7H **181**
Ruskin Dene CM12: Bill 5J **99**
Ruskin Gdns. RM3: Romf 4F **110**
Ruskin Path SS12: W'fd 2L **117**
Ruskin Rd. CM2: Chelm 9N **59**
RM16: Grays 2C **156**
SS17: Stan H 4L **147**
Ruskins, The CM77: Rayne 7B **192**
Ruskoi Rd. SS8: Can I 9F **134**
Rusper Rd. RM9: Dag 8H **125**
Russell Cl. CM15: Brtwd 6E **96**
DA1: Cray 9E **152**
SS15: Lain 9K **115**
Russell Ct. *CO2: Colc* *2B 174*
(off Stalin Rd.)
E10: Lon 2B **122**
SS11: W'fd 9N **101**
Russell Gdns. CM2: Chelm 6B **72**
IG2: Ilf 2C **124**
SS11: W'fd 9M **101** (1C **42**)
RUSSELL GREEN 5C **24**
Russell Gro. SS4: R'fd 5M **121**
Russell Lodge E4: Lon 8C **90**
Russell Rd. CM3: N Fam 5H **35**
CO15: Clac S 1L **189**
E10: Lon 1B **122**
EN1: Enf 5B **30**
IG9: Buck H 7H **91**
RM17: Grays 2K **155**
RM18: Til 6A **156**
Russell Square Station (Tube) 6A **38**
Russell's Rd. CO9: Gosf, Hals 6H **207** (3E **14**)
Russell St. WC1: Lon 7A **38**
Russell Way CM1: Chelm 3N **71**
Russet Cl. CM7: Brain 7J **193**
SS17: Stan H 2M **147**
Russet Ho. RM17: Grays 5M **155**
Russets CM2: Gall 7E **72**
Russets Cl. E4: Lon 1D **106**
Russetts RM11: Horn 8J **111**
SS16: Lang H 1J **131**
Russetts, The SS4: R'fd 2J **121**
Russet Way CM0: Bur C 2E **196**
Rustic Cl. RM14: Upm 3B **128**
Rustle Ct. CM17: H'low 4H **55**
Rutherford Cl. CM12: Bill 3J **99**
SS9: Lgh S 9B **120**
Rutherfords CM1: Broom 2K **59**
Ruthven Cl. SS12: W'fd 2L **117**
Rutland App. RM11: Horn 9L **111**
Rutland Av. CO2: Colc 3J **173**
SS1: Sth S 6C **138**
Rutland Cl. SS15: Lain 9J **115**
Rutland Dr. RM11: Horn 9L **111**
SS6: Ray 9H **103**
Rutland Gdns. CM7: Brain 4J **193**
RM8: Dag 7H **125**
SS4: R'fd 2H **121**
Rutland Pl. CM7: Gt Bar 2C **202**
Rutland Rd. CM1: Chelm 5J **59**
CM3: N Fam 1F **104**
E7: Lon 9K **123**
E11: Lon 9H **107**
E17: Lon 1A **122**
IG1: Ilf 5A **124**
Rutley Cl. RM3: H Wood 6H **111**
Rydal Cl. SS5: Hull 5K **103**
SS6: Ray 5L **119**
Rydal Dr. CM9: Mal 8D **214**
Rydal Way CM77: Gt N 2C **204**
Ryde Av. CO15: Clac S 5L **185**
Ryde Cl. SS9: Lgh S 1A **136**
Ryde Dr. SS17: Stan H 5L **147**
Ryder Cl. E10: Lon 4B **122**
Ryder Gdns. RM13: Rain 8D **126**
Ryder Way SS13: Bas 5L **117**
Ryde, The SS9: Lgh S 1A **136**
Rye Cl. CM3: Hat P 3L **61**
CO3: S'way 1F **172**
CO7: B'sea 4D **182**
RM12: Horn 7G **127**
Ryecroft CM19: H'low 3A **54**
Ryecroft Av. IG5: Ilf 6A **108**
Ryedene SS16: Van 3F **132**
Ryedene Cl. SS16: Van 3F **132**
Ryedene Pl. SS16: Van 3F **132**
Ryefeld Cl. EN11: Hod 1C **52**
Rye Field, The CM3: L Bad 8L **61**
Ryegate Rd. CO1: Colc 7N **165**
Rye Grass Way CM7: Brain 7K **193**
RYE HILL 1D **64** (1H 31)
Rye Hill Rd.
CM18: H'low, Thorn 8C **54** (1H **31**)
Rye Hills CO9: Hals 6L **207**
Rye House Gatehouse 2D **52** (6E 20)
Rye House Nature Reserve 2C **52**
Rye House Station (Rail) 3C **52** (7E 20)
Rye Mead SS16: Lang H 2L **131**
Rye Mead Cotts. EN11: Rye P 3C **52**
RYE MEADS 2D **52**
Rye Meads Nature Reserve 1D **52**
Rye Mill La. CO5: Fee 1L **211**
RYE PARK 4B **52** (7D 20)
Rye Rd. EN11: Rye P 3B **52** (7D **20**)
SG12: Rye P, Stan A 3B **52** (7D **20**)
Ryes La. CM22: Hat O, Hat H 3B **22**
CO10: Bulm, L Hen 4M **195** (6H **9**)
Rye St. CM23: Bis S 7K **11**
Rye Wlk. CM4: Ing 7C **84**
Rykhill RM16: Grays 1D **156**
(not continuous)
Rylands Rd. SS2: Sth S 4A **138**
Ryle, The CM1: Writ 2J **71**
Rylstone Way CB11: Saf W 5E **218**
Rysley CM3: L Bad 7L **61**

S

Sabina Rd. RM16: Grays 2E **156**
SABINE'S GREEN 2J **95** (6C 32)
Sabine's Rd. CM14: Nave 1H **95**
RM4: Nave, N'side 1H **95** (6B **32**)
Sable Ct. SS15: Lain 8H **115**
Sable Way SS15: Lain 8H **115**
Sacketts Gro. Cvn. Pk. CO16: Jay 2D **188**
Sackville Cl. CM1: Chelm 8G **58**
Sackville Cres. RM3: H Wood 5J **111**
Sackville Gdns. IG1: Ilf 3M **123**
Sackville Rd. SS2: Sth S 5C **138**
Sackville Way CO6: W Ber 3E **164**
SACOMBE 2B **20**
SACOMBE GREEN 2C **20**
Sacombe Grn. Rd. SG12: Sac 2B **20**
Sacombe Pound SG12: Sac 2B **20**
Sacombe Rd.
SG14: Chap E, Hart, Stfrd, W'frd 4A **20**
Sacombs Ash La. CM21: A Grn 3H **21**
Saddle M. CO3: S'way 9E **164**
Saddle Ri. CM1: Chelm 3N **59**
Saddlers Cl. CM77: Gt N 1B **204**
Saddleworth Rd. RM3: Romf 3G **111**
Saddleworth Sq. RM3: Romf 3G **111**
Sadler Cl. CO2: Colc 2B **174**
Sadlers SS7: Thund 9B **118**
Sadlers Cl. CM11: Bill 3M **99**
CO13: Walt 8F **180**
Sadlers Mead CM18: H'low 4F **54**
Saffory Cl. SS9: Lgh S 8B **120**
Saffron Bus. Cen. CB10: Saf W 3E **218**
Saffron Cl. CM7: Weth 8C **228**
CM13: W H'dn 1N **129**
SS17: Horn H 2J **147**
Saffron Ct. CB11: Saf W 4C **218**
E15: Lon *7E 122*
(off Maryland Pk.)
SS15: Lain 9H **115**
Saffron Gdns. CM7: Weth 8B **228**
Saffron Rd. RM5: Col R 6B **110**
RM16: Chaf H 2F **154**
SAFFRON WALDEN 4C **218** (6B 6)
Saffron Walden Castle 3D **218** (6C 6)
Saffron Walden Hedge Maze 3C **218**
Saffron Walden Mus. 3C **218** (6B 6)
Saffron Walden Turf Maze 3D **218**
Saffron Wlk. CM7: Weth 8B **228**
CM11: Bill 6K **99**
Saffron Way CO5: Tip 7C **226**
Sage Rd. CO2: Colc 4A **174**
Sages CM22: Hen 8D **210**
Sages End Rd. CB9: Hel B 5H **7**
Sage Wlk. CO5: Tip 7C **226**
Sains SS15: Lain 8M **115**
St Agnes Dr. SS8: Can I 2D **150**
St Agnes Rd. CM12: Bill 4L **115**
St Aidans Ct. IG11: Bark 2G **141**
St Alban's Av. RM14: Upm 4B **128**
St Alban's Cres. IG8: Wfd G 4G **106**
St Alban's Rd. CM16: Coop 8J **65**
CO3: Colc 8L **165**
St Albans Rd. CO15: Clac S 1L **189**
IG3: Ilf 3E **124**
St Alban's Rd. IG8: Wfd G 4G **106**
St Andrew's Av.
CO4: Colc, Elms 1F **174** (6F **17**)
(Colchester By-Pass Rd.)
CO4: Colc, Elms 7C **166** (6F **17**)
(Ipswich Rd.)
RM12: Horn 7D **126**
St Andrews Cl. CM16: N Wea 3B **66**
CO7: Alr 7A **176**
SE28: Lon 6J **141**
SS8: Can I 1D **150**
St Andrews Dr. CM11: Bill 5K **99**
St Andrews Gdns. CO4: Colc 7C **166**
St Andrews Ho. *CM20: H'low* *1E 54*
(off Stow, The)
St Andrews La. SS15: Lain 8L **115**
St Andrews Mdw. CM18: H'low 4E **54**
St Andrew's Pl. CM15: Shenf 8J **97**
St Andrews Pl. CO7: B'sea 4D **182**
St Andrew's Ri. CO10: Bulm 1K **195**
St Andrews Rd. CM3: Bore 2G **60**
CO9: Hals 4L **207**
E12: Lon 4L **123**
SS4: R'fd 5K **121**
St Andrew's Rd. CM3: Hat P 2L **61**
CO15: Clac S 1J **189**
CO16: Wee 5D **178**
E11: Lon 1E **122**
IG1: Ilf 2M **123**
RM7: Romf 1B **126**
RM18: Til 6A **156** (2G **47**)
SS3: Shoe 8G **139**
St Andrew St. SG14: Hart 5B **20**
St Annes Cl. CO6: Cogg 3M **197**
RM16: Grays 8L **145**
SS15: Lain 8L **115**
St Anne's Ct. *CM2: Chelm* *8L 59*
(off St Ann's Pl.)
St Anne's Pk. EN10: Brox 8A **52**
St Anne's Pl. CM2: Chelm 8L **59**
St Anne's Rd.
CM15: Mount, Shenf 9M **83** (6G **33**)
E11: Lon 4D **122**
St Annes Rd. CO4: Colc 7C **166**
CO15: Clac S 9J **185**
SS8: Can I 2K **151**
St Annes Ter. IG6: Chig 2D **108**
St Ann's IG11: Bark 1B **140**
St Ann's Rd. IG11: Bark 1B **140**
N15: Lon 3A **38**
SS2: Sth S 5M **137**
St Anthony's Av. IG8: Wfd G 3J **107**
St Anthony's Dr. CM2: Chelm 4D **72**
St Antony's Rd. E7: Lon 9H **123**
St Augustine Cl. CM6: Fels 9F **212**
St Augustine M. CO1: Colc 8A **166**
St Augustine Rd. RM16: Grays 2D **156**
St Augustine's Av. SS1: Sth S 8F **138**
St Augustine's Rd. DA17: Belv 1A **46**
St Austell Rd. CO4: Colc 5D **166**
St Austin's La. CO12: Har 1M **209**
St Awdry's Rd. IG11: Bark 9C **124**
St Awdry's Wlk. IG11: Bark 9B **124**
St Barbara's Rd. CO2: Colc 2L **173**
St Barnabas Rd. E17: Lon 1A **122**
IG8: Wfd G 5H **107** (2F **39**)
St Bartholomew Cl. CO4: Colc 4C **166**
St Benet's Rd. SS2: Sth S 3L **137**
St Bernard Rd. CO4: Colc 5D **166**
St Botolph's Chu. Wlk. CO2: Colc 9N **165**
St Botolph's Cir. CO2: Colc 9N **165**
St Botolphs Priory 9N **165**
St Botolph's St. CO2: Colc 9N **165**
St Botolph's Ter. CO14: Walt 6M **181**
St Brelades Ct. CO15: Clac S 8M **185**
St Bride Ct. CO4: Colc 5D **166**
St Brides Cl. DA18: Eri 9J **141**
St Catherines Cl. CO2: Colc 5L **173**
SS11: W'fd 8N **101**
St Catherine's Rd. CM1: Chelm 9G **58**
E4: Lon 8A **90**
EN10: Brox 7A **52**
St Catherines Twr. E10: Lon 2B **122**
St Cecilia Rd. RM16: Grays 2D **156**
St Cedd's Ct. RM16: Grays 8L **145**
St Chads Cl. SS15: Lain 8L **115**
St Chad's Gdns. RM6: Chad H 2K **125**
St Chad's Rd. RM6: Chad H 2K **125**
St Chads Rd. RM16: Grays 7C **156** (2H **47**)
RM18: Grays, Til 7C **156** (2H **47**)
St Charles Dr. SS11: W'fd 9M **101**
St Charles Rd. CM14: Brtwd 7E **96**
St Christopher Rd. CO4: Colc 5D **166** (5F **17**)
St Christophers Cl. SS8: Can I 1D **150**
St Christophers Way CO15: Jay 5E **188**
St Clair Cl. CO15: Clac S 5K **185**
IG5: Ilf 6M **107**
St Clair's Dr. CO16: St O 8N **183**
St Clair's Rd. CO16: St O 8N **183**
St Clare Dr. CO3: Colc 8H **165**
St Clare Mdw. SS4: R'fd 4L **121**
St Clare Rd. CO3: Colc 9H **165**
St Clement Rd. CO4: Colc 5D **166**
St Clements CM6: Thax 8C **224**
St Clement's Av. RM20: W Thur 4D **154**
St Clements Av. SS9: Lgh S 4D **136**
St Clement's Cl. SS5: Hock 3F **120**
SS7: Ben 1C **134**
St Clements Ct. CO16: Clac S 8F **184**
RM17: Grays 4J **155**
RM19: Purf 2L **153**
SS9: Lgh S 6C **136**
St Clements Ct. E. *SS9: Lgh S* *6C 136*
(off Broadway W.)
St Clement's Cres. SS7: Ben 1D **134**
St Clements Dr. SS9: Lgh S 3D **136**
St Clement's Rd. RM20: Grays 5F **154**
SS7: Ben 1C **134**
St Clements Way DA9: Blue, Grnh 4E **46**
St Cleres Cres. SS11: W'fd 9N **101**
St Clere's Hall La. CO16: St O 4B **28**
St Cleres Way CM3: Dan 3D **74**
St Columbas Ho. E17: Lon 8B **106**
St Columb Ct. CO4: Colc 5C **166**
St Cross Ct. EN11: Hod 7A **52**
St Cuthbert's Rd. EN11: Rye P 2C **52**
St Cyrus Rd. CO4: Colc 5D **166**
St Davids Cl. CO4: Colc 8C **166**
St David's Ct. E17: Lon 7C **106**
St David's Dr. SS9: Lgh S 3N **135**
St Davids Dr. SS9: Lgh S 3N **135**
St Davids Rd. BR8: Swan 5A **46**
St David's Rd. SS16: Lang H 2K **131**
St David's Ter. SS9: Lgh S 3N **135**
St Davids Wlk. SS8: Can I 1D **150**
St David's Way SS11: W'fd 9M **101**
St Denis Cl. CO12: Har 6J **209**
St Dionis Rd. E12: Lon 5L **123**
St Dominic Rd. CO4: Colc 5D **166**
St Dunstan's Rd. E7: Lon 8H **123**
St Edith's Ct. CM12: Bill 7J **99**
SS9: Lgh S 6E **136**
St Edith's La. CM12: Bill 7J **99**
St Edmunds Cl. CO12: Har 6J **209**
DA18: Eri 9J **141**
St Edmund's Cl. SS2: Sth S 3A **138**
St Edmund's Ct. CO4: Colc 7C **166**

St Edmunds Cft. CM6: Gt D 2M 203
St Edmunds Flds. CM6: Gt D 1M 203
St Edmund's Hill CO10: Bures 7K 9
St Edmunds Ho. CO4: Colc 7E 166
(off Tamarisk Way)
St Edmunds La. CM6: Gt D 1M 203 (7G 13)
St Edmund's La. CO8: Bures 7L 195 (1A 16)
St Edmund's Rd. DA1: Dart 9L 153
IG1: Ilf 1M 123
St Edmund's Way CM17: H'low 8H 51
St Edwards Ct. E10: Lon 2B 122
St Edwards Way RM1: Romf 9B 110 (3A 40)
St Egberts Way E4: Lon 7C 90
St Elizabeth Ct. E10: Lon 2B 122
St Erkenwald M. IG11: Bark 1C 140
St Erkenwald Rd. IG11: Bark 1C 140
St Ethelburga Ct. RM3: H Wood 6L 111
St Fabian's Dr. CM1: Chelm 7G 58
St Faith Rd. CO4: Colc 5D 166
St Ferndale Rd. CO12: Har 2M 209
St Fidelis Rd. DA8: Eri 2B 152
St Fillan Rd. CO4: Colc 5D 166
St Francis Rd. DA8: Eri 2B 152
St Francis Way IG1: Ilf 6C 124
RM16: Grays 1E 156
St Gabriel's Cl. E11: Lon 4H 123
St Gabriels Ct. SS13: Pits 1J 133
St George's Av. CO12: Har 5L 209
E7: Lon 9H 123
RM11: Horn 2K 127
RM17: Grays 2M 155
St Georges Cl. CM9: Hey B 8F 214
CM15: Hook E 5E 82
CO7: Gt Bro 6D 168
SE28: Lon 6J 141
St George's Ct. CM14: Brtwd 6E 96
St Georges Ct. E17: Lon 9D 106
St George's Dr. SS0: Wclf S 3K 137
St George's La. SS3: Shoe 8K 139
St George's Pk. Av. SS0: Wclf S 5G 137
St George's Rd. E7: Lon 9H 123 (5F 39)
E10: Lon 5C 122
IG1: Ilf 2M 123
RM9: Dag 7K 125
SE1: Lon 7A 38
St George's Sq. E7: Lon 9H 123
St George's Wlk. SS7: Thund 9B 118
SS8: Can I 1D 150
St Giles Av. RM10: Dag 9N 125
St Giles Cl. CM9: Mal 6A 214
CO9: Gt Map 1F 15
RM10: Dag 9N 125
RM16: Ors 4C 146
St Giles Cres. CM9: Mal 6A 214
St Giles Leper Hospital (ruins) 6A 214 (1H 35)
St Guiberts Rd. SS8: Can I 9E 134
St Helena M. CO3: Colc 1L 173
St Helena Rd. CO3: Colc 1L 173
St Helens Av. CO15: Clac S 5L 185
St Helens Ct. CM16: Epp 9F 64
St Helen's Ct. RM13: Rain 4E 142
St Helen's Grn. CO12: Har 2N 209
St Helens La. CO1: Colc 8N 165
St Helen's Rd. DA18: Eri 9J 141
IG1: Ilf 1M 123
SS0: Wclf S 6K 137
St Helens Wlk. CM12: Bill 4H 99
St Helier Ct. CO15: Clac S 9M 185
St Helier's Rd. E10: Lon 1C 122
St Ives Cl. CO16: Clac S 1F 188
RM3: Romf 4K 111
St Ives Rd. CO5: Pel 3E 26
St Ivian's Dr. RM2: Romf 7E 110
St James' Av. CM5: Chip 9K 67
St James Av. SS1: Sth S 8F 138
St James Av. E. SS17: Stan H 2N 147
St James Av. W. SS17: Stan H 2N 147
St James Cen. CM20: H'low 8F 50
St James Cl. SS0: Wclf S 3F 136
SS8: Can I 1D 150
St James Ct. CB10: Saf W 3E 218 (6C 6)
(not continuous)
CO7: B'sea 7D 182
E12: Lon 4J 123
RM1: Romf 8D 110
SS8: Can I 4H 151
St James Gdns. IG2: Ilf 8G 108
SS0: Wclf S 3F 136
St James Ga. IG9: Buck H 7H 91
St James Ho. RM1: Romf 9D 110
(off Eastern Rd.)
St James La. DA2: Grnh 4D 46
St James M. CM12: Bill 6J 99
St James Pk. CM1: Chelm 7F 58
St James Rd. CM7: Brain 3H 193
St James' Rd. E15: Lon 7F 122
St James Rd. EN7: G Oak 3B 30
SS16: Van 1E 132
(not continuous)
ST JAMES'S 7A 38
St James's Park Station (Tube) 7A 38
St James's Rd. CM14: Brtwd 9F 96
St James's St. CO9: Cas H 3L 219 (1E 14)
W1: Lon 7A 38
St James St. E17: Lon 3D 38
St James Street,
Walthamstow Station (Rail) 3D 38
St James's Wlk. SS5: Hock 1B 120
(off Belvedere Av.)
St James Way CM23: Bis S, Thor 1J 21
St Jean Wlk. CO5: Tip 5D 226
St John Av. CM7: Brain 6H 193
St John's Abbey Gate 9N 165
St Johns Arts & Recreation Cen. 8H 51
St John's Av. CM2: Chelm 2C 72
CM14: War 1G 112
CM17: H'low 8H 51
CO2: Colc 9N 165
St Johns Cl. CB10: Gt Che 8D 202
CB11: Saf W 6C 218
SS15: Lain 8L 115
St John's Cl. CO4: Colc 3D 166
RM13: Rain 9E 126
SS3: Gt W 3M 139
St Johns Ct. CM3: May 8L 213
St John's Ct. CM9: Tol 8J 225
DA8: Eri 2B 152
IG9: Buck H 7H 91
SS0: Wclf S 7L 137
St John's Cres. CM24: Stan M 2D 220
St Johns Cres. SS8: Can I 1D 150
St Johns Dr. SS6: Ray 3F 118
St John's Gdns. CO15: Clac S 7J 185
St John's Grn. CM1: Writ 1K 71
CO2: Colc 9N 165
St John's Gro. N19: Lon 4A 38
St John's Jerusalem Garden 5C 46
St John's La. CM24: Stan M 2D 220
St John's M. SS17: Corr 1A 148
St Johns Pl. CM11: Rams H 4C 100
St John's Pl. CO2: Colc 9N 165
St John's Rd. CM1: Writ 1K 71
CM2: Chelm 1C 72
CM11: Bill 5K 99
CM16: Epp 9E 64
CM24: Stan M 2D 220
CO4: Colc 4D 166 (5F 17)
CO7: W'hoe 7J 175
CO15: Clac S 8J 185
CO16: Clac S, St O 9B 184 (4C 28)
DA8: Eri 3B 152
E4: Lon 1B 106
E17: Lon 6B 106
IG2: Ilf 2C 124
IG10: Lou 1M 91
IG11: Bark 1D 140
St Johns Rd. RM5: Col R 2A 110
RM16: Grays 3D 156
St John's Rd. SS0: Wclf S 6K 137
SS3: Gt W 3M 139
SS7: Had 3J 135
St Johns St. CB2: Dux 2J 5
St John's St. CM9: Tol 8J 225
CO2: Colc 9M 165 (6E 16)
St John's Ter. E7: Lon 8H 123
St John St. EC1: Lon 6A 38
St Johns Wlk. CM17: H'low 8H 51
St John's Wlk. CO2: Colc 9N 165
St John's Way N19: Lon 4A 38
SS17: Corr 1A 148
St John's Wynd CO1: Colc 9M 165
St Joseph Rd. CO4: Colc 4C 166
St Joseph's Ct. E4: Lon 6D 90
St Jude Cl. CO4: Colc 5D 166
St Jude Gdns. CO4: Colc 5D 166
St Julian Gro. CO1: Colc 9A 166
St Katharines Grn. CM7: L Bar 3H 13
St Katherines Ct. SS8: Can I 2E 150
St Katherine's Rd. DA18: Eri 9J 141
St Kathryn's Pl. RM14: Upm 4N 127
St Kilda's Rd. CM15: Brtwd 6E 96
ST LAWRENCE 2D 36
St Lawrence Ct. CM7: Brain 5H 193
SS9: Lgh S 9D 120
St Lawrence Dr. CM0: Stpl 2C 36
St Lawrence Gdns. CM4: B'more 1G 83
SS9: Lgh S 9D 120
St Lawrence Hill CM0: St La 2D 36
St Lawrence Rd.
CM0: St La, T'ham 1H 225 (2D 36)
CO4: Colc 5D 166
RM14: Upm 4N 127
St Leonard's Av. E4: Lon 3D 106
St Leonards Cl. CB11: Newp 1L 215
RM17: Grays 4J 155
St Leonard's Gdns. IG1: Ilf 7B 124
ST LEONARDS HAMLET 3F 126 (4B 40)
St Leonard's Rd. CO1: Colc 9C 166
SS1: Sth S 7N 137
St Leonards Rd. EN9: Naze, Wal A 2E 62 (2E 30)
(not continuous)
St Leonards Ter. CO1: Colc 9C 166
(off St Leonard's Rd)
St Leonards Way RM11: Horn 4F 126
St Luke's Av. IG1: Ilf 7A 124
St Luke's Chase CO5: Tip 7D 226
St Luke's Cl. CO4: Colc 5D 166
St Lukes Cl. SS8: Can I 1D 150
St Lukes Ct. E10: Lon 2B 122
(off Capworth St.)
St Luke's Path IG1: Ilf 7A 124
St Luke's Rd. SS2: Sth S 4N 137
ST MARGARETS 6E 20
Hoddesdon 6E 20
St Margaret's IG11: Bark 1C 140
St Margaret's Av. SS17: Stan H 5L 147
St Margaret's Cross CO4: L'ham 4F 160
St Margaret's Gro. E11: Lon 5F 122
St Margaret's Rd. CM2: Chelm 8N 59
E12: Lon 4J 123
SG12: Stan A 1A 52
St Margarets Rd. DA2: Dart 5D 46
DA4: S Dar 6D 46
St Margarets Station (Rail) 6E 20
St Margaret St. SW1: Lon 7A 38
St Mark Dr. CO4: Colc 5D 166
St Marks Ct. E10: Lon 2B 122
(off Capworth St.)
St Marks Fld. SS4: R'fd 4L 121
St Marks Rd. CO15: Clac S 9J 185
EN1: Enf 7B 30
SS8: Can I 1D 150
St Mark's Rd. SS7: Had 3J 135
St Martins Cl. CM6: Whi R 5C 22
CO15: Clac S 9J 185
St Martin's Cl. CM13: Hut 8M 97
DA18: Eri 9J 141
SS6: Ray 7J 119
SS7: Thund 8B 118
St Martins La. WC2: Lon 7A 38
St Martins M. CM5: Chip 8L 67
St Martins Sq. SS14: Bas 9B 116
St Mary Rd. E17: Lon 8A 106
St Mary's IG11: Bark 1C 140
St Mary's App. E12: Lon 7M 123
St Mary's Art Cen. 8M 165
St Mary's Av. CM12: Bill 6J 99
CM15: Shenf 4K 97
E11: Lon 2H 123
St Marys Cl. CM2: Gt Bad 4G 72
CM7: Pan 1D 192
CO7: Gt Ben 9L 177
RM17: Grays 4N 155
St Mary's Cl. SS3: Gt W 5H 139
SS7: Ben 5D 134
St Mary's Ct. CM7: Gt Bar 3C 202
CM9: Mal 6D 214
(off Mill Rd.)
CO15: Clac S 1J 189
SS2: Sth S 4K 137
St Mary's Cres. SS13: Pits 9K 117
St Mary's Dr. CM24: Stan M 3E 220
SS7: Ben 5D 134
St Mary's La. CM9: Mal 6D 214
CM13: W H'dn 2L 129
RM14: Upm 4L 127 (4D 40)
SG14: Hart, Hert 6A 20
St Mary's Mead CM1: Broom 2J 59
St Mary's M. CM9: Tol 7K 225
(off Station Rd.)
St Mary's Path SS13: Pits 8K 117
St Mary's Pl. CM6: L Dun 8D 212
St Mary's Rd. CM0: Bur C 2D 196
CM7: Brain 5K 193
CM8: Riven 3G 25
CO5: K'dn 3K 211
CO7: Gt Ben 9L 177 (1A 28)
CO13: Frin S 9K 181
CO15: Clac S 9J 185
E10: Lon 5C 122
IG1: Ilf 4B 124
RM16: Grays 1D 156
SS2: Sth S 4L 137
SS7: Ben 6D 134
St Marys Rd. SS12: W'fd 2J 117
St Mary's Sq. CO5: K'dn 4J 211
St Marys Vw. CB10: Saf W 1D 218
St Mary's Vs. CM7: Gt Bar 3C 202
St Marys Wlk. CB9: Stpl B 3K 223
St Mary's Way IG7: Chig 2N 107
St Matthew's Cl. RM13: Rain 9E 126
St Matthews Ct. E10: Lon 2B 122
St Mellion Cl. SE28: Lon 6J 141
St Michaels Av. SS13: Pits 2J 133
St Michael's Chase CO6: Cop 4M 171
St Michaels Cl. CM3: Latch 8L 211
CM20: H'low 2D 54
St Michael's Cl. DA18: Eri 9J 141
RM15: Ave 7N 143
St Michaels Ct. CO11: Mist 4J 163
St Michael's Dr. CM1: Rox 3M 217
St Michael's La. CM7: Brain 6H 193
St Michaels M. CM6: Lea R 4C 212
CM7: Brain 6H 193
St Michael's Rd. CM2: Chelm 2C 72
CM7: Brain 6H 193 (7C 14)
St Michaels Rd. CO2: Colc 5K 173
SS8: Can I 1D 150
St Michael's Rd. CO12: Har 5K 209
CO16: T Sok 4K 179
RM16: Grays 3D 156
SS7: Had, Ray 9M 119 (3F 43)
St Michael's Wlk. CM2: Gall 8D 72
St Mildreds Rd. CM2: Chelm 2C 72
St Monance Way CO4: Colc 5D 166
St Nazaire Rd. CM1: Chelm 5G 59 (7K 23)
St Neots Cl. CO4: Colc 5D 166
St Neot's Rd. RM3: Romf 4K 111
St Nicholas Av. RM12: Horn 5E 126
St Nicholas Cl. CM8: Wthm 3C 230
St Nicholas Fld. CM23: Ber 4J 11
St Nicholas Gdns. CM7: Brain 9H 191
St Nicholas Grn. CM17: H'low 2H 55
St Nicholas Gro. CM13: Ingve 2M 113
St Nicholas La. SS15: Lain 8L 115 (3K 41)
St Nicholas Pas. CO1: Colc 8N 165
St Nicholas Pl. IG10: Lou 3N 91
St Nicholas Rd. CM0: T'ham 1K 225
CM8: Wthm 3C 230
St Nicholas St. CO1: Colc 8N 165
St Nicholas Way CO6: Cogg 2L 197
St Omer Cl. SS12: W'fd 1M 117
ST OSYTH 9M 183 (4B 28)
St Osyth Beach Holiday Pk. CO16: St O 6A 188
ST OSYTH HEATH 3B 184 (2B 28)
St Osyth Priory 9M 183 (4B 28)
St Osyth Rd. CO7: Alr, Thorr 7B 176 (1J 27)
CO15: Clac S 1G 188 (4D 28)
CO16: L Cla, Wee H 5F 184 (3C 28)
St Osyth Rd. E. CO16: L Cla 4G 184
St Osyth Rd. W. CO16: L Cla 4F 184
ST PANCRAS 6A 38
St Pancras Station (Rail) 6A 38
St Pancras Way NW1: Lon 5A 38
St Patrick's Ct. IG8: Wfd G 4E 106
St Patrick's Pl. RM16: Grays 2D 156
St Paul's Cl. RM15: Ave 7N 143
St Pauls Ct. SS0: Wclf S 6K 137
(off Salisbury Av.)
St Paul's Dr. E15: Lon 7D 122
St Pauls Gdns. CM12: Bill 4J 99
St Pauls Pl. RM15: Ave 7N 143
St Paul's Rd. CO1: Colc 7M 165
CO15: Clac S 1L 189
DA8: Eri 5A 152
IG11: Bark 1B 140 (6H 39)
N1: Lon 5A 38
SS8: Can I 1D 150
St Paul's Station (Tube) 7B 38
St Pauls Twr. E10: Lon 2B 122
(off Beaumont Rd.)
St Paul's Way E3: Lon 7D 38
St Pauls Way EN9: Wal A 3D 76
St Peter's Av. CM5: Chip 5K 67
CM9: Mal 6B 214
E17: Lon 8E 106
St Peter's Cl. CM7: Brain 5H 193
IG2: Ilf 8D 108
St Peters Cl. CM9: Gold 3K 201
St Peter's Ct. CO1: Colc 7M 165
(off Middleborough)
SS0: Wclf S 2H 137
St Peters Fld. CM0: Bur C 1C 196
St Peter's in the Flds. CM7: Brain 4H 193
St Peter's Path E17: Lon 7E 106
St Peter's Pavement SS14: Bas 6G 117
St Peter's Rd. CM1: Chelm 9G 58
CM7: Brain 4H 193
CM14: War 1E 112
CO5: W Mer 3B 228
CO6: Cogg 2M 197 (7H 15)
RM16: Grays 2D 156
St Peters Rd. SS5: Hock 9A 104
SS8: Can I 1D 150
St Peter's St. CB2: Dux 3J 5
CO1: Colc 7M 165
St Peter's Ter. SS12: W'fd 9K 101
St Peter's Vw. CO9: Sib H 6J 219
St Peter's Wlk. CM7: Brain 5H 193
(off St Peters Rd.)
St Peters Wlk. CM12: Bill 4H 99
St Peter's Way CM3: Bick, E Han 2C 88
CM4: Marg 3K 85
St Ronan's Cres. IG8: Wfd G 4G 106
St Runwald St. CO1: Colc 8N 165
St Saviour Cl. CO4: Colc 5D 166
Saints Dr. E7: Lon 7K 123
St Stephen's Av. E17: Lon 9C 106
St Stephen's Cl. E17: Lon 9B 106
St Stephens Ct. CM3: May 8L 213
(off Mallards)
St Stephen's Cres. CM13: Brtwd 1K 113
St Stephen's La. CO5: Gt Wig 4D 26
St Stephens Pde. E7: Lon 9J 123
St Stephens Rd. CM3: Cold N 8K 197 (4H 35)
St Stephen's Rd. E6: Lon 9J 123
E17: Lon 9B 106
Saint's Wlk. RM16: Grays 2E 156
St Teresa's Cl. SS14: Bas 1G 133
St Teresa Wlk. RM16: Grays 2D 156
St Theresa Ct. E4: Lon 6D 90
St Thomas Cl. CO4: Colc 5E 166
St Thomas Ct. E10: Lon 2B 122
(off Beaumont Rd.)
St Thomas Gdns. IG1: Ilf 8B 124
St Thomas Pl. RM17: Grays 4L 155
St Thomas' Rd. CM14: Brtwd 8G 96
St Thomas Rd. DA17: Belv 9A 142
SS4: R'fd 4F 104
St Thomas's Cl. EN9: Wal A 3H 77
St Thomas St. SE1: Lon 7B 38
St Valery CM22: Tak 3C 224
St Vincent Chase CM7: Brain 3K 193
St Vincent Rd. CO15: Clac S 3H 189
St Vincents Av. DA1: Dart 3C 46
ST VINCENT'S HAMLET 7M 95 (7C 32)
St Vincents Rd. CM2: Chelm 2C 72
DA1: Dart 3C 46
SS0: Wclf S 7K 137
St Winefride's Av. E12: Lon 7M 123
St Winifred's Cl. IG7: Chig 2B 108
Sairard Cl. SS9: Lgh S 8C 120
Sairard Gdns. SS9: Lgh S 8C 120
Sakins Cft. CM18: H'low 6E 54
Saladin Dr. RM19: Purf 2L 153
Salamons Way RM13: Rain 6C 142
Salary Cl. CO4: Colc 6E 166
Salcombe Dr. RM6: Chad H 1L 125
Salcombe Pk. IG10: Lou 4K 91
Salcombe Rd. CM7: Brain 7L 193
SALCOTT 5C 26
Salcott Creek Ct. CM7: Brain 7M 193
Salcott Cres. SS12: W'fd 9L 101 (1C 42)
SALCOTT-CUM-VIRLEY 5C 26
Salcott M. SS12: W'fd 1N 117
Salcott St. CM9: Salc 5C 26
Salem Wlk. SS6: Ray 3H 119
Salerno Cres. CO2: Colc 4K 173
Salerno Way CM1: Chelm 5G 59
Salesbury Dr. CM11: Bill 6M 99
Salforal Cl. CM3: Ret C 8B 88
Salhouse Cl. SE28: Lon 6H 141
Saling Grn. SS15: Bas 5A 116
Saling Hall Garden 6K 13
Saling Rd. CM6: Steb 6K 13
CM7: Shalf 5A 14

Salisbury Av. CO3: Colc 9M 165
IG11: Bark 9C 124
SS0: Wclf S 5K 137
SS17: Stan H 4M 147
Salisbury Cl. RM14: Upm 4B 128
Salisbury Ct. CO15: Hol S 8N 185
SS9: Lgh S 5C 136
Salisbury Gdns. IG9: Buck H 8K 91
Salisbury Hall Gdns. E4: Lon 3A 106
Salisbury Rd. CO15: Hol S 8N 185
E4: Lon 9A 90
E7: Lon 8G 122
E10: Lon 4C 122
E12: Lon 7K 123
E17: Lon 9C 106
EN11: Rye P 3C 52
IG3: Ilf 4D 124
RM2: Romf 9F 110
RM10: Dag 8N 125
RM17: Grays 4M 155
SS9: Lgh S 5B 136
Salix Rd. RM17: Grays 4N 155
Sally Murray Cl. E12: Lon 6N 123
Salmon Cl. CO3: S'way 2G 172
Salmonds Gro. CM13: Ingve 2M 113
Salmon La. E14: Lon 7D 38
Salmon Rd. DA1: Dart 8K 153
Salmons Cl. CM6: Barns 2L 191
SALMON'S CORNER 3D 170 (7K 15)
Salmon's La. CO6: Cogg 2C 170 (7K 15)
Salmons La. CO7: Thorr 9G 176
Saltash Rd. IG6: Ilf 4C 108
Saltcoats CM3: S Fer 9K 89
Saltcote Maltings CM9: H'bri 7F 214
Salter Pl. CM2: Chelm 9A 60
Salter Rd. SE16: Lon 7C 38
Salters Mdw. CM9: Tol D 3K 227
Salters Rd. E17: Lon 8D 106
Saltford Cl. DA8: Eri 3C 152
Saltings, The SS7: Had 3K 135
Salvia Cl. CO16: Clac S 9G 185
Salway Cl. IG8: Wfd G 4G 106
Salway Pl. E15: Lon 8D 122
Salway Rd. E15: Lon 8D 122
Samantha M. RM4: Hav 9C 94
Samian Cl. CM9: Mal 3B 214
Sampford Rd. CB10: Hpstd, R'ter 7F 7
CM7: Corn H 7J 7
Samphire Cl. CM8: Wthm 4A 230
Samphire Ct. RM17: Grays 4A 156
Sampson's La. CO5: Pel 4E 26
Samson Ho. SS15: Lain 6K 115
Samsons Cl. CO7: B'sea 5D 182
Samson's Rd. CO7: B'sea 4D 182 (2K 27)
Samuel Mnr. CM2: Chelm 8A 60
Samuel Rd. SS16: Lang H 2K 131
SAMUEL'S CORNER 4C 44
Samuels Dr. SS1: Sth S 6F 138
Sanctuary Gdns. SS17: Stan H 3N 147
Sanctuary Rd. SS9: Lgh S 3N 135
Sandbanks SS7: Had 4K 135
Sandbanks Hill DA2: Bean, Dart 5E 46
Sandcliff Rd. DA8: Eri 2B 152
Sanderling Ct. SE28: Lon 7H 141
Sanderling Gdns. CM9: Mal 3E 214
Sanderlings SS7: Ben 4C 134
Sanders Cl. CM24: Stan M 3C 220
Sanders Dr. CO3: Colc 8J 165
Sanderson Cl. CM13: W H'dn 1M 129
Sanderson Ct. SS7: Ben 1C 134
Sanderson M. CO1: Colc 8N 165
CO5: Rhdge 6F 174
Sanders Rd. SS8: Can I 8G 134
Sandford Av. IG10: Lou 2B 92
Sandford Cl. CO7: W'hoe 6J 175
SANDFORDHALL GREEN 9L 171 (1B 26)
Sandford Mill Rd.
CM2: Chelm 9A 60 (1B 34)
(Dolby Ri.)
CM2: Chelm, Gt Bad 9B 60 (1B 34)
(Pollards Grn., not continuous)
Sandford Rd. CM2: Chelm 8M 59 (1A 34)
Sandgate Cl. RM7: Rush G 2A 126
Sandhill Rd. SS9: Lgh S 7B 120
Sandhurst SS8: Can I 2C 150
Sandhurst Cl. SS9: Lgh S 2E 136
Sandhurst Cres. SS9: Lgh S 2E 136
Sandhurst Dr. IG3: Bark, Ilf 6E 124
Sandhurst Rd. RM18: Til 7E 156
Sandleigh Rd. SS9: Lgh S 5F 136
Sandmartin Cres. CO3: S'way 2D 172
SANDON 4L 73 (2C 34)
Buntingford 1B 10
Sandon Brook Pl. CM2: S'don 2M 73
Sandon Cl. CO6: Gt Hork 9K 159
SS4: R'fd 4J 121
SS14: Bas 1G 133
Sandon Ct. SS14: Bas 1G 133
Sandon Green CM2: S'don 4K 73
Sandon Hall Bridleway
CM2: Howe G, S'don 7L 73
Sandon Hill CM3: Har E 3J 23
SANDON INTERCHANGE 3L 73 (2C 34)
Sandon La. SG9: Bunt, S'don 2B 10
Sandon Pl. CM5: Chip 9L 67
Sandon Rd. SS14: Bas 1G 133
Sandown Av. RM10: Dag 8A 126
RM12: Horn 4H 127
SS0: Wclf S 4G 136
Sandown Cl. CO15: Clac S 5L 185
SS11: W'fd 9N 101
Sandown Rd. RM16: Ors 5G 147
SS7: Thund 8H 119
SS11: W'fd 9A 102
Sandpiper Cl. CM9: H'bri 3E 214
CO4: Colc 7G 166
SS3: Shoe 6J 139
Sandpiper Dr. DA8: Eri 5F 152
Sandpipers SS3: Shoe 8L 139
(off Rampart Ter.)
Sandpiper Ter. IG5: Ilf 7A 108
Sandpiper Wlk. CM2: Chelm 4D 72
Sandpit La. CM0: Bur C 3E 196
CM7: Brain 5H 193
CM14: Pil H, S Wea 7C 96 (7D 32)
CM15: Pil H 7C 96
Sandpit Rd. DA1: Dart 9G 153
SS3: Shoe 6M 139
Sandpits La. CO7: Strat M 1H 17
Sandpits Nature Reserve 8M 201
Sandringham Av. CM19: H'low 3L 53
SS5: Hock 1B 120
Sandringham Cl. IG6: Ilf 7B 108
SS17: Stan H 2N 147
Sandringham Dr. CO2: Colc 2A 174
Sandringham Gdns. IG6: Ilf 7B 108
Sandringham Pl. CM2: Chelm 9L 59
Sandringham Rd. CM15: Pil H 5E 96
E7: Lon 7J 123
E8: Lon 5B 38
E10: Lon 1D 122
IG11: Bark 7E 124
SS1: Sth S 6B 138
SS15: Lain 7N 115
Sands Way IG8: Wfd G 3M 107
Sandwich Cl. CM7: Brain 2G 193
Sandwich Rd. CO7: B'sea 5E 182
CO15: Clac S 4G 189
Sandy Hill CO6: Wmgfd 7J 229 (2B 16)
Sandyhill Rd. IG1: Ilf 6A 124
Sandy La. CO10: Bulm, Sud 2K 195 (5H 9)
DA2: Bean 4E 46
(not continuous)
RM15: Ave, Wen 7K 143 (7C 40)
RM16: Grays 4D 156
(not continuous)
RM20: W Thur 3E 154
Sanity Cl. CO7: W'hoe 6J 175
San Juan Dr. RM16: Chaf H 2F 154
San Luis Dr. RM16: Chaf H 2F 154
San Marcos Dr. RM16: Chaf H 2F 154
San Remo Pde. SS0: Wclf S 7K 137
San Remo Rd. SS8: Can I 2K 151
Sansom Rd. E11: Lon 4F 122
Sans Souci SS9: Lgh S 6C 136
(off Leigh Pk. Rd.)
Santiago Way RM16: Chaf H 3G 154
Sappers Cl. CM21: Saw 2L 51
Sapphire Cl. RM8: Dag 3H 125
Sara Cres. DA9: Grnh 9E 154
Sara Ho. DA8: Eri 5C 152
Sarah's Wlk. CM22: Tak 3B 224
Saran Ct. CO7: W'hoe 4G 175
Sarbir Ind. Est. CM20: H'low 6H 51
Sarcel CM77: Tye G 6F 15
Sargeant Cl. CO2: Colc 3B 174
Sargents La. CB1: Hads 3C 6
Sark Gro. SS12: W'fd 2N 117
Sark Twr. SE28: Lon 9B 140
(off Erebus Dr.)
Sarre Av. RM12: Horn 8G 127
Sarre Way CO7: B'sea 5D 182
Sassoon Way CM9: Mal 7C 214
Satanita Rd. SS0: Wclf S 6H 137
Saul's Av. CM8: Wthm 7D 230
Sauls Bri. Cl. CM8: Wthm 7E 230
Sauls Grn. E11: Lon 5E 122
Saunders Av. CM7: Brain 5G 192
Saunders Cl. CM22: Else 3K 199
Saunders Way SE28: Lon 7G 140
Saunton Rd. RM12: Horn 4E 126
Savernake Rd. CM1: Chelm 1N 71
Saville Ct. CB11: Clav 3J 11
Saville Rd. RM6: Chad H 1L 125
Savilles CO10: Bel P 5E 8
Saville St. CO14: Walt 5M 181
Savill Ho. E16: Lon 8A 140
(off Robert St.)
Savill Rd. CO2: Colc 4C 174
Savill Row IG8: Wfd G 3F 106
Savoy Cl. SS16: Lang H 1J 131
Savoy Wood CM19: H'low 9A 54
SAWBRIDGEWORTH 2K 51 (4J 21)
Sawbridgeworth Rd.
CM22: Hat H 1C 210 (4A 22)
CM22: L Hall 3K 213 (3K 21)
(Gaston Hill)
CM22: L Hall 4K 213 (3K 21)
(Grinstead La.)
Sawbridgeworth Station (Rail)
1M 51 (4K 21)
Sawkins Av. CM2: Gt Bad 4E 72
Sawkins Cl. CM2: Gt Bad 4E 72
CO5: L'hoe 9B 174
Sawkins Gdns. CM2: Gt Bad 4E 72
Sawney Brook CM1: Writ 1J 71
Sawpit La. CM23: Ber 4J 11
SAWSTON 1K 5
Sawyers Chase RM4: Abr 2G 93
Sawyers Ct. RM10: Dag 8A 126
Sawyers Ct. CM15: Shenf 6J 97
Sawyers Gro. CM15: Brtwd 7G 96
Sawyers Hall La. CM15: Brtwd 6F 96
Sawyer's Rd. CM9: L Tot 5K 25
Saxham Rd. IG11: Bark 2D 140
Saxlingham Rd. E4: Lon 9D 90
Saxmundham Way CO16: Clac S 9E 184
Saxon Bank CM7: Brain 6K 193
Saxon Cl. CM13: Brtwd 9K 97
CO3: Colc 2G 173
CO9: Hals 4L 207
E17: Lon 2A 122
RM3: H Wood 6K 111
SS6: Ray 2L 119
SS11: W'fd 7M 101
Saxon Ct. CM9: Mal 5C 214
(off Bull La.)
SS7: Thund 1C 134
(not continuous)
Saxon Dr. CM8: Wthm 4B 230
Saxon Gdns. SS3: Shoe 7G 139
Saxon Pl. SS4: R'fd 5L 121
Saxon Rd. IG1: Ilf 8A 124
Saxonville SS7: Ben 2B 134
Saxon Way CB11: Saf W 4B 218
CM1: Broom 4K 59
CM9: Mal 7D 214
CO15: Hol S 7C 186
CO16: P Bay 4K 27
EN9: Wal A 3C 76
SS7: Ben 4C 134
Saxted Dr. CO16: Clac S 9E 184
Sayers SS7: Thund 9G 119
Sayesbury Av. CM21: Saw 1J 51
Sayesbury Rd. CM21: Saw 2K 51
Sayes Gdns. CM21: Saw 1L 51
Saywell Brook CM2: Chelm 9B 60
Scalby Rd. CM0: S'min 4A 222
Scaldhurst SS13: Pits 7K 117
Scarborough Dr. SS9: Lgh S 4D 136
Scarborough Rd. CM0: S'min 4A 222
E11: Lon 3D 122
Scarfe Way CO4: Colc 9E 166
Scarletts SS14: Bas 7D 116
Scarletts Chase CO6: Gt Hork, W Ber 1F 164
Scarletts Cl. CM8: Wthm 8D 230
Scarletts Rd. CO1: Colc 1C 174
Sceptre Cl. CM9: Tol 7K 225
Scheregate CO2: Colc 8N 165
Scholar's Hill SG12: W'side 4E 20
Scholars Rd. E4: Lon 7D 90
Scholars Wlk. CM3: S Fer 9L 89
School Chase CO9: Hals 6K 207
School Ct. CO12: Har 3M 209
School Cres. DA1: Cray 9D 152
School Farm La. CO10: Act 2K 9
School Fld. CO9: Bird 5A 8
Schoolfield Rd. RM20: W Thur 4D 154
SCHOOL GREEN 3B 14
School Green CM7: Bla E 3B 14
School Grn. La. CM16: N Wea 4A 66
School Hill CO2: B'ch 8B 172 (1C 26)
Schoolhouse Gdns. IG10: Lou 3A 92
School La. BR8: Swan 6B 46
CB11: Newp 2K 215 (1A 12)
CB11: Wen L 7J 5
CM1: Broom 3H 59 (7A 24)
CM1: High E 4F 23
CM3: Gt L 6J 203 (3B 24)
CM4: Stock 7M 85 (5K 33)
CM5: Ab R 6D 22
CM5: Beau R 6E 22
CM5: H Lav 7A 22
CM13: Ingve 3M 113
CM20: H'low 9D 50
CM22: Hen 8D 210
CM22: Tak 6D 12
CO2: B'ch 8C 172 (2B 26)
CO5: Gt Wig 3D 26
CO6: Gt Hork 6G 158 (3D 16)
CO6: L Hork 2E 158
CO6: W Ber 3F 164
CO7: Ded 1M 161
CO7: Frat 6F 176 (1K 27)
CO7: Strat M 1H 17
CO11: Bran 1A 18
CO11: Law 6F 162 (3K 17)
CO11: Mist 4L 163
DA2: Bean 5E 46
DA3: Fawk, S Dar 6D 46
DA4: Hort K 6D 46
IG7: Chig 1E 108
ME3: High 5K 47
RM16: Ors 5C 146 (7H 41)
SG8: Thri 2G 5
SS7: Ben 6D 134
SS12: N Ben 5A 118
School M. CO6: Cogg 3K 197
School Rd. CM1: Good E 5G 23
CM5: Chip, Toot 9D 66 (3A 32)
CM8: Sil E 9M 217
CM8: W Bis 2L 229 (5H 25)
CM9: Gt Tot 4N 229 (6H 25)
CM9: L Tot 6K 25
CM11: D'ham 3G 100 (6B 34)
CM12: Bill 8J 99
CM15: Dodd, Kel H 7B 82 (5D 32)
CM77: Rayne 9A 192 (1B 24)
CO2: Colc 4A 174
CO4: L'ham 4E 160 (3G 17)
CO5: Mess 2C 226 (2K 25)
CO6: Cop 2M 171 (7B 16)
CO6: L Hork 4D 158 (3C 16)
CO7: Alr, Elms 3M 175 (7H 17)
CO7: E Ber 1J 17
CO9: L Map 2G 15
CO9: L Yel 6D 8
CO9: Sib H 7H 219 (2D 14)
CO9: Wick P 7G 9
CO10: Pent 3F 9
CO12: Gt Oak 8C 204 (5E 18)
CO13: Frin S 9H 181
School Rd. CO16: Ten 1C 178 (6C 18)
E12: Lon 6M 123
RM10: Dag 1M 141
School Row CB11: Elm 6J 5
School St. CB10: Gt Che 8D 202 (4A 6)
CO10: Fox 3G 9
School Vw. CM7: Brain 6G 192
School Vw. Rd. CM1: Chelm 8H 59
School Vs. CM6: Broxt 5D 12
CM6: Lea R 4C 212
School Wlk. CM7: Brain 5H 193
School Way RM8: Dag 5H 125
(not continuous)
SS9: Lgh S 3E 136
Schooner Cl. IG11: Bark 3G 140
Schooner Ct. DA2: Dart 9N 153
Scilla Ct. RM17: Grays 4N 155
Scimitar Pk. SS13: Bas 5L 117
Scoter Cl. IG8: Wfd G 4H 107
Scotland Grn. Rd. EN3: Enf 7C 30
Scotland Rd. IG9: Buck H 7J 91
Scotneys La. CO9: Gt Yel 7C 8
Scotney Wlk. RM12: Horn 7G 127
Scott Av. CM7: Weth 2A 14
Scott Cl. CM7: Brain 8J 193
Scott Cres. DA8: Eri 6D 152
Scott Dr. CO3: Colc 9G 165
SS12: W'fd 2L 117
Scottes La. RM8: Dag 3J 125
Scott Ho. RM11: Horn 1E 126
(off Benjamin Cl.)
SS9: Lgh S 8F 120
Scott Rd. RM16: Grays 2C 156
Scotts Cl. RM12: Horn 7G 127
Scott's Grotto 5C 20
Scotts Hall Rd. SS4: Cwdn 2M 105 (1K 43)
Scotts Hill CM0: May 5B 36
CM0: S'min 2A 222
Scott's Rd. E10: Lon 3C 122
Scotts Wlk. CM1: Chelm 6F 58
SS6: Ray 5N 119
Scraley Rd. CM9: Mal 2E 214 (7J 25)
Scratchers La. DA3: Fawk 7D 46
Scratton Rd. SS1: Sth S 7L 137 (5J 43)
SS17: Stan H 3M 147
Scrattons Ter. IG11: Bark 2J 141
Scrip's Rd. CO6: Cogg 1H 25
Scrub La. SS7: Had 3L 135
Scrub Ri. CM12: Bill 8H 99
Scrubs Wood Nature Reserve 2F 74
Scudders Hill DA3: Fawk 7E 46
Sculpins La. CM7: Weth 6A 228 (2A 14)
Scurvy Hall La.
CM3: Gt Walt, L Walt 4K 57
Scylla Cl. CM9: Mal 2E 214
Scythe Way CO3: Colc 2G 173
Seaborough Rd. RM16: Grays 1E 156
Seabrink SS9: Lgh S 6E 136
Seabrooke Ri. RM17: Grays 4L 155
Seabrook Gdns. CM3: Bore 2G 60
RM7: Rush G 2M 125
Seabrook Rd. CM2: Gt Bad 4H 73
RM8: Dag 5J 125
Seaburn Cl. RM13: Rain 2C 142
Sea Cornflower Way CO15: Jay 5E 188
Seacourt Rd. SE2: Lon 9J 141
Sea Cres. CO15: Jay 6D 188
Seafield Av. CO11: Mist 4N 163
Seafield Rd. CO12: Har 5K 209
Seafields Gdns. CO15: Clac S 8N 185
Seafields Rd. CO15: Clac S, Hol S 8N 185
Sea Flowers Way CO15: Jay 5E 188
Seaford Rd. E17: Lon 7B 106
Seaforth Av. SS2: Sth S 4A 138
Seaforth Cl. RM1: Romf 4C 110
Seaforth Gdns. IG8: Wfd G 2J 107
Seaforth Gro. SS2: Sth S 4B 138
Seaforth Rd. SS0: Wclf S 7J 137
Seagers CM9: Gt Tot 3N 229
Sea Glebe Way CO15: Jay 5E 188
Seagry Rd. E11: Lon 2G 123
Seagull Cl. IG11: Bark 3F 140
Sea Holly Way CO15: Jay 6E 188
Sea King Cres. CO4: Colc 3B 166
Sea La. CO15: Clac S, Hol S 8N 185
Sea Lavender Way CO15: Jay 5E 188
Sea Life Cen. 8A 138 (5K 43)
Seally Rd. RM17: Grays 3K 155
Seamans La. CM4: Stock 7C 86
Seamer Rd. CM0: S'min 4A 222
Seamore Av. SS7: Thund 9C 118
Seamore Cl. SS7: Thund 9B 118
Seamore Wlk. SS7: Thund 8C 118
Sea Pink Way CO15: Jay 6E 188
Sea Reach SS9: Lgh S 6D 136
Searles Dr. E6: Lon 5A 140
Searle Way CO6: Eig G 6C 164
Sea Rd. IP11: Felix 2K 19
Sea Rosemary Way CO15: Jay 5E 188
Sea Shell Way CO15: Jay 6E 188
Sea Thistle Way CO15: Jay 5E 188
Seaton Av. IG3: Ilf 7E 124
Seaton Cl. CO11: Law 5G 162
Seaton Rd. IP11: Felix 1K 19
Seaview Av. CO5: W Mer 2E 228 (5G 27)
CO12: L Oak 8E 208
SS16: Van 3E 132
Seaview Cvn. Pk. CO5: W Mer 3F 228
Seaview Dr. SS3: Gt W 3N 139
Seaview Gdns. CO7: B'sea 6E 182
Seaview Hgts. CO14: Walt 7M 181
Sea Vw. Pde. CM0: St La 1C 36
(off Wick Farm Rd.)
CM3: May 6K 213

Sea Vw. Prom. CM0: St La. 1C 36
(off Spar Dri.)
Seaview Rd. CO7: B'sea 6E 182
CO16: St O 5B 28
SS3: Shoe 8H 139
SS8: Can I. 2L 151 (6F 43)
SS9: Lgh S 6D 136
Seaview Ter. CO16: P Bay 4K 27
SS7: Had 5K 135
Seaway CM0: St La 2C 36
Sea Way CO15: Jay 5D 188
Seaway SS1: Sth S 7N 137
SS8: Can I 3H 151
SEAWICK 5A 188 (5B 28)
Seawick Holiday Cen. CO16: St O 5A 188
Seawick Rd. CO16: St O 5B 28
Seax Ct. SS15: Lain 8H 115
Seax Way SS15: Lain 8H 115
Sebastian Av. CM15: Shenf 5K 97
Sebastian Cl. CO4: Colc 8E 166
Sebastian Ct. IG11: Bark 1E 140
Sebert Cl. CM11: Bill 9M 99
Sebert Rd. E7: Lon 7H 123
Second Av. CM1: Chelm 6J 59
CM12: Bill 9G 99
CM15: Hook E 4F 82
CM17: H'low 4G 55
CM18: H'low 7H 21
CM20: H'low 3D 54 (7H 21)
CM24: Stan Apt 7G 220
CO9: Hals 5N 207
CO12: Har 4L 209
CO13: Frin S 1H 187 (2G 29)
CO14: Walt 1M 181
CO15: Clac S 9M 185
CO16: Wee 6D 178
E12: Lon 6L 123
E17: Lon 9A 106
EN9: Wal A 9H 63
RM6: Chad H 9H 109
RM10: Dag 1N 141
RM20: W Thur 4D 154
SS0: Wclf S 7G 137
SS5: Hull 7M 103
SS7: Thund 9G 119
SS8: Can I 1D 150
(not continuous)
SS11: W'fd 1A 118
SS16: Lang H 2F 130
SS17: Stan H 2M 147
Secret Nuclear Bunker 6M 81
Seddons Wlk. SS5: Hock 1D 120
Seden Ct. CO15: Clac S 4M 185
Sedge Ct. RM17: Grays 5A 156
Sedgefield Cl. RM3: Romf 1K 111
Sedgefield Cres. RM3: Romf 2K 111
Sedgefield Way CM7: Brain 7K 193
Sedge Grn. CM19: Roy 8E 52 (1E 30)
EN9: Naze, Roy 8E 52 (1E 30)
Sedgemoor SS3: Shoe 5H 139
Sedgemoor Dr. RM10: Dag 6M 125
Sedgwick Rd. E10: Lon 4C 122
Sedley Ri. IG10: Lou 1M 91
Sedop Cl. CB11: Saf W 6C 218
Seedbed Cen. CO4: Colc 1C 166
Seedbed Cen., The RM7: Romf 2C 126
Seedfield, The CO5: W Mer 3B 228
Seeleys CM17: H'low 8B 51
Sejant Ho. RM17: Grays 4L 155
(off Bridge Rd.)
Selborne Av. E12: Lon 6N 123
Selborne Rd. E17: Lon 9A 106
IG1: Ilf 4N 123
Selborne Wlk. Shop. Cen. E17: Lon 8A 106
Selbourne Rd. SS2: Sth S 3N 137
SS5: Hock 1D 120
SS7: Thund 1D 134
Selby Cl. CO2: Colc 5L 173
Selby Rd. E11: Lon 5E 122
Seldon Cl. SS0: Wclf S 3G 136
Seldon Rd. CO5: Tip 6D 226
Selhurst Ct. CO14: Walt 7J 181
Selinas La. RM8: Dag 2K 125
Selkirk Dr. DA8: Eri 6C 152
Selsdon Cl. RM5: Col R 5A 110
Selsdon Rd. E11: Lon 2G 123
Selsey Av. CO15: Clac S 4G 189
Selwood Rd. CM14: Brtwd 9C 96
Selworthy Cl. CM11: Bill 9L 99
E11: Lon 9G 106
Selwyn Av. E4: Lon 3C 106 (2E 38)
IG3: Ilf 1E 124
Selwyn Ct. E17: Lon 9A 106
(off Yunus Khan Cl.)
Selwyn Rd. RM18: Til 7B 156
SS2: Sth S 4A 138
Semper Rd. RM16: Grays 9E 146
Semples SS17: Stan H 3A 148
Serbin Cl. E10: Lon 2C 122
Sergeantsgreen La. EN9: Wal A 3J 77
Serpentine Wlk. CO1: Colc 7M 165
Service La. CM4: B'more 1G 83
Seton Gdns. RM9: Dag 9H 125
Settle Rd. RM3: Romf 1L 111
Seven Acres SS11: W'fd 8M 101
Seven Arches Rd. CM14: Brtwd 9G 97 (1E 40)
Seven Ash Grn. CM1: Chelm 6L 59
Seven Devils La. CB11: Saf W 6B 218
(not continuous)
SEVEN KINGS 3D 124 (4H 39)
Seven Kings Rd. IG3: Ilf 3D 124 (4H 39)
Seven Kings Station (Rail) 3D 124 (4H 39)
Sevenoaks Cl. RM3: Romf 1G 111
SEVEN SISTERS 3B 38
Seven Sisters Rd. N7: Lon 4A 38
N15: Lon 4A 38
Seven Sisters Station (Rail, Tube) 3B 38
Sevens Sisters Rd. N4: Lon 4A 38
SEVEN STAR GREEN 8A 164 (6B 16)
Seventh Av. CM1: Chelm 5K 59
CM24: Stan Apt, Stan M 7G 221
E12: Lon 6M 123
SS8: Can I 1E 150
Severalls Ind Est. CO4: Colc 2C 166
Severalls La. CO4: Boxt, Colc 8A 160 (4F 17)
Severn RM18: E Til 1K 157
Severn Av. RM2: Romf 7F 110
Severn Dr. RM14: Upm 1A 128
Severn Rd. CO15: Clac S 8K 185
RM15: Ave 6N 143
Severns Fld. CM16: Epp 8F 64
SEWARDS END 6D 6
Sewards End SS12: W'fd 1M 117
SEWARDSTONE 9C 76 (6E 30)
SEWARDSTONEBURY 4E 90 (6F 31)
Sewardstone Gdns. E4: Lon 4B 90
Sewardstone Rd. E2: Lon 6C 38
E4: Lon 6B 90 (7D 30)
EN9: Enf, Wal A 4C 76 (4E 30)
Sewardstone St. EN9: Wal A 4C 76
Sewell Cl. RM16: Chaf H 3F 154
Sewell Harris Cl. CM20: H'low 2E 54
Sewell Rd. SE2: Lon 9F 140
Sewells La. CO10: Bel O 4E 8
Sexton Cl. CO2: Colc 6B 174
RM13: Rain 1D 142
Sexton Rd. RM18: Til 6B 156
Sextons La. CM8: Gt Br 4H 25
Seymer Rd. RM1: Romf 7B 110
Seymour Cl. IG10: Lou 5L 91
RM11: Horn 2H 127
SS15: Lain 9M 115
Seymour Ct. E4: Lon 8F 90
Seymour Gdns. CM12: Bill 3J 99
IG1: Ilf 3M 123
Seymour M. CM21: Saw 5K 51
Seymour Rd. CO15: Jay 3D 188
E4: Lon 7B 90
RM18: Til 6B 156
SS0: Wclf S 5H 137
SS7: Had 4M 135
Seymours CM19: H'low 6M 53
Seymours, The IG10: Lou 9N 77
Seymour St. CM2: Chelm 9J 59
S. Green Rd. CO5: Fing 2G 27
Shackleton Cl. CO12: Har 6H 209
SHACKLEWELL 5B 38
Shacklewell La. N16: Lon 5B 38
SHADWELL 7C 38
Shadwell Station (Tube) 7C 38
Shadwell Wood Nature Reserve 8A 190
SHAFTENHOE END 7F 5
Shaftenhoe End Rd. SG8: Bar 6F 5
Shafter Rd. RM10: Dag 8A 126
Shaftesbury IG10: Lou 2K 91
Shaftesbury Av. CO12: Har 3K 209
SS1: Sth S 8B 138
W1: Lon 7A 38
Shaftesbury Ct. SS13: Pits 7J 117
Shaftesbury La. DA1: Dart 9M 153
Shaftesbury Rd. CM16: Epp 8E 64
E4: Lon 7D 90
E7: Lon 9J 123
E10: Lon 3A 122
E17: Lon 1B 122
RM1: Romf 1D 126
Shaftesburys, The IG11: Bark 2B 140
Shaftsbury Ct. DA8: Eri 6D 152
(off Selkirk Dr.)
Shair La. CO16: Ten 4N 177 (7B 18)
Shakespeare Av. CM11: Bill 6L 99
RM18: Til 7D 156
SS0: Wclf S 4K 137
SS6: Ray 5N 119
SS16: Lang H 1J 131
Shakespeare Cl. CM7: Brain 9J 193
Shakespeare Ct. EN11: Hod 1B 52
Shakespeare Cres. E12: Lon 8M 123
Shakespeare Dr. CM9: Mal 8C 214
SS0: Wclf S 4K 137
Shakespeare Rd. CO3: Colc 9G 164
DA1: Dart 9L 153
RM1: Romf 1D 126
Shakespeare Sq. IG6: Ilf 3B 108
Shakeston Cl. CM1: Writ 2K 71
Shakletons CM5: Chip 7L 67
Shalfleet Ct. CO15: Clac S 5K 185
SHALFORD 4A 14
SHALFORD GREEN 5A 14
Shalford Lodge CM1: Chelm 3K 59
Shalford Rd. CM7: Gt Sal, Rayne 5A 14
CM11: Bill 6N 99
CM77: Rayne 5A 192 (7B 14)
Shamrock Cl. CM9: Tol 7K 225
Shamrock Ho. CO15: Clac S 4H 189
Shangrila W. Cvn. Pk. SS5: Hull 4M 103
Shanklin Av. CM12: Bill 6J 99
Shanklin Cl. CO15: Clac S 5L 185
Shanklin Dr. SS0: Wclf S 4G 136
Shannon Av. SS6: Ray 6J 119
Shannon Cl. SS9: Lgh S 2D 136
Shannon Sq. SS8: Can I 2D 150
Shannon Way RM15: Ave 7N 143
SS8: Can I 2D 150
Shardelow Av. CM1: Chelm 4A 60
Sharlands Cl. SS11: W'fd 8N 101
Sharnbrook SS3: Shoe 4H 139
Sharpecroft CM19: H'low 3B 54
Sharpington Cl. CM2: Gall 7D 72
Sharp Way DA1: Dart 8K 153
Shatters Rd. CO2: Lay B 2C 26
Shaw Av. IG11: Bark 2K 141
Shawbridge CM19: H'low 6B 54
Shaw Cl. CO13: Frin S 7J 181
RM11: Horn 3F 126
SE28: Lon 8G 141
SS12: W'fd 2L 117
Shaw Cres. CM13: Hut 3N 97
RM18: Til 6D 156
Shaw Dr. CM7: Weth 2A 14
Shaw Gdns. IG11: Bark 2K 141
SHAW GREEN 2A 10
Shawlands Av. CO10: Gt Cor 5K 9
Shaw Rd. CM8: Wthm 2C 230
Shaw, The CM22: Hat H 1E 210
Shearers Way CM3: Bore 2G 61
Shearing Pl. CO10: Bel P 3E 8
Shears Ct. CO5: W Mer 4D 228
Shears Cres. CO5: W Mer 4D 228
Shearwater Cl. IG11: Bark 3F 140
Shearwood Cres. DA1: Cray 8D 152
Sheds La. CB10: Saf W 3D 218
Sheene Gro. CM7: Brain 3M 193
Sheepcoates La. CM9: Gt Tot 6J 25
SHEEPCOTE GREEN 2H 11
Sheepcote La. BR5: Orp, Swan 6A 46
CM22: Hen 6C 210
CM23: Man 5K 11
Sheepcotes CM2: Chelm 5C 60
Sheepcotes La. CM0: S'min 1D 222
CM3: L Walt 6L 57
(not continuous)
CM8: Sil E 8M 217 (1F 25)
Sheepcotes Rd. RM6: Chad H 8K 109
Sheepcot Rd. CO9: Cas H 4K 219 (1E 14)
Sheepen Pl. CO3: Colc 7M 165
Sheepen Rd. CO3: Colc 7L 165 (6E 16)
SHEERING 4A 210 (5A 22)
Sheering Ct. SS6: Ray 4G 119
Sheering Dr. CM17: H'low 9K 51
Sheering Hall Dr. CM17: H'low 5M 51
Sheering Lwr. Rd. CM17: H'low 5L 51 (5K 21)
CM21: H'low, Saw 5L 51 (5K 21)
Sheering Mill La. CM21: Saw 2K 51 (4K 21)
Sheering Rd. CM17: H'low 8K 51 (6K 21)
CM22: Hat H 2D 210 (4A 22)
Sheering Wlk. CO2: Colc 4N 173
Sheerness M. E16: Lon 9A 140
Sheerwater Cl. CM0: Bur C 3D 196
Sheerwater M. CO4: A'lgh, Colc 7G 166
Sheffield Dr. RM3: Romf 2L 111
Sheffield Gdns. RM3: Romf 2L 111
Sheila Cl. RM5: Col R 4N 109
Sheila Rd. RM5: Col R 4N 109
Sheilings, The RM11: Horn 9K 111
Shelbourne Rd. N17: Lon 2C 38
Sheldon Av. IG5: Ilf 6A 108
Sheldon Cl. CM17: H'low 3K 55
SS17: Corr 9D 132
Sheldon Rd. RM9: Dag 9K 125
SS8: Can I 2L 151
Sheldrick Link CM2: Chelm 7C 60
Shelduck Cl. E7: Lon 7F 122
Shelduck Cres. CM77: Gt N 3C 204
Shelford Rd. CB2: L She, Whitt 1J 5
Shellards La. CO9: Wick P 7G 9
Shellbank La. DA2: Bean, Dart 5E 46
Shellbeach Rd. SS8: Can I 3K 151
Shellcroft CO6: Coln E 3D 198
SHELLEY 3L 67 (2C 32)
Shelley Av. CO5: Tip 6E 226
E12: Lon 8L 123
RM12: Horn 4D 126
SS16: Lang H 1J 131
Shelley Cl. CM5: Chip 5K 67
CM9: Mal 8C 214
Shelley Ct. E10: Lon 2B 122
(off Skelton's La.)
E11: Lon 8H 107
(off Makepeace Rd.)
EN9: Wal A 3F 76
(off Ninefields)
Shelley Gro. IG10: Lou 3M 91
Shelley La. CO16: L Cla 4K 185
Shelley Pl. RM18: Til 6D 156
SS6: Ray 4G 118
Shelley Rd. CM2: Chelm 9M 59
CM13: Hut 6N 97
CO3: Colc 9G 164
Shelleys La. CM77: Tye G 9N 193
Shelley Sq. SS2: Sth S 4N 137
Shelley Wlk. CM7: Brain 8J 193
(off Chaucer Cres.)
SHELL HAVEN 3H 149
SHELLOW BOWELLS 1F 33
Shellow Rd. CM5: Will 1F 33
Shelly Rd. CO16: Clac S 8E 184
Shelsley Dr. SS16: Lang H 3L 131
SHENFIELD 5K 97 (7F 33)
Shenfield Ct. CM18: H'low 6B 54
Shenfield Cres. CM15: Brtwd 8H 97
Shenfield Gdns. CM13: Hut 5L 97
Shenfield Grn. CM15: Shenf 6K 97
Shenfield Pl. CM15: Shenf 6H 97
Shenfield Rd.
CM15: Brtwd, Shenf 8G 97 (7E 32)
IG8: Wfd G 4H 107
Shenfield Station (Rail) 6K 97 (7F 33)
Shen Pl. Almshouses CM15: Brtwd 8G 97
Shenstone Cl. DA1: Cray 9B 152
Shenstone Gdns. RM3: Romf 5G 111
Shenval Ind. Est. CM20: H'low 8F 50
Shepard Cl. SS9: Lgh S 9F 120
Shepeshall SS15: Lain 1N 131
Shepherdess Wlk. N1: Lon 6B 38
Shepherds Cl. RM6: Chad H 9J 109
SS7: Had 2L 135
Shepherd's Cft. CO3: S'way 1E 172
Shepherd's Hill N6: Lon 3A 38
Shepherds Hill RM3: H Wood 6L 111 (2C 40)
RM14: H Wood 6L 111
Shepherds La. CO10: Glem 1G 9
Shepherd's La. DA1: Dart 4B 46
Shepherds Ley SE28: Lon 8D 140
Shepherd's Path CM14: S Wea 6B 96
Shepherds Wlk. SS7: Had 2L 135
Shepherds Way CB10: Saf W 3E 218
Shepley M. EN3: Enf 7A 76
Sheppard Cl. CO16: Clac S 7H 185
Sheppard Dr. CM2: Chelm 7B 60
Sheppards CM19: H'low 6M 53
Shepperton Rd. N1: Lon 6B 38
Sheppey Cl. DA8: Eri 5F 152
Sheppey Gdns. RM9: Dag 9H 125
Sheppey Rd. RM9: Dag 9G 124
SHEPRETH 1E 4
Shepreth Rd. CB2: Barr 1E 4
CB2: Foxt 2F 5
Shepreth Station (Rail) 1E 4
Sherards Orchard CM19: H'low 5A 54
Sherborne Cl. CO13: Frin S 7J 181
Sherborne Dr. SS13: Bas 6H 117
Sherborne Gdns. RM5: Col R 2M 109
Sherborne Rd. CM1: Chelm 6M 59
Sherbourne Gdns. SS2: Sth S 9L 121
Sherbourne Rd. CO4: Colc 8F 166
Sheredan Rd. E4: Lon 2D 106
Shere Rd. IG2: Ilf 9N 107
Sherfield Rd. RM17: Grays 4L 155 (2F 47)
Sheridan Av. SS7: Ben 3H 135
Sheridan Cl. RM3: Romf 4G 110
SS6: Ray 5M 119
Sheridan Ct. DA1: Dart 9L 153
Sheridan M. E11: 1H 123
Sheridan Rd. E7: Lon 5F 122
E12: Lon 7L 123
Sheridan Wlk. CO3: Colc 9G 164
Sheriffs Way CO15: Clac S 6J 185
Sheringham Av. E12: Lon 6M 123
RM7: Romf 1A 126
Sheringham Cl. SS17: Stan H 2N 147
Sheringham Dr. IG11: Bark 7E 124
Sheringham Way CM77: Gt N 1C 204
Sheriton Sq. SS6: Ray 3K 119
Shermanbury Pl. DA8: Eri 5D 152
Sherman Gdns. RM6: Chad H 1H 125
Shernbroke Rd. EN9: Wal A 4F 76
Shernhall St. E17: Lon 7C 106 (3E 38)
Sherrard Rd. E7: Lon 8J 123
E12: Lon 8J 123
Sherrin Rd. E10: Lon 6B 122
Sherry M. IG11: Bark 9C 124
Sherry Way SS7: Had 9L 119
Sherwood RM16: N Stif 8H 145
Sherwood Av. E18: Lon 7H 107
Sherwood Cl. CO4: Colc 8D 166
SS16: Lang H 2J 131
Sherwood Cres. SS7: Had 2L 135
Sherwood Dr. CM1: Chelm 1M 71
CO15: Clac S 7J 185
Sherwood Gdns. IG11: Bark 9C 124
Sherwood Ho. CM18: H'low 5E 54
Sherwood Rd. IG6: Ilf 8C 108
Sherwood Way CO5: Fee 1L 211
SS2: Sth S 3C 138
Shevon Way CM14: Brtwd 1C 112
Shewell Wlk. CO1: Colc 8N 165
Shields Ct. RM18: E Til 2L 157
(off Coronation Av.)
Shillibeer Wlk. IG7: Chig 9E 92
Shillingstone SS3: Shoe 5H 139
Shillito Cl. CO3: S'way 2G 172
SHINGAY 2A 4
Shingle Ct. EN9: Wal A 3G 76
Shingle Hall Rd. CM16: Epp Up 4C 64 (2H 31)
Ship Hill CO11: Brad 3C 18
Ship La. DA4: S at H 6C 46
RM15: Ave, Purf 8A 144 (7D 40)
RM19: Purf 1A 154 (1D 46)
Shipley Hills Rd. DA13: Meop 7G 47
Ship Rd. CM0: Bur C 4E 196
CM2: W Han 4C 86 (4A 34)
Shipton Cl. RM8: Dag 5J 125
Shipwrights Cl. SS7: Ben 4H 135
Shipwrights Dr. SS7: Ben 4H 135
Shipwrights, The CO7: W'hoe 6H 175
Shipyard Est. CO7: B'sea 8E 182
Shirebourn Va. CM3: S Fer 2K 103
Shire Cl. CM1: Chelm 4A 60
CM11: Bill 4M 99
Shirehall Rd. DA2: Dart 5B 46
Shirehill CB11: Saf W 4E 218
Shire Hill Ind. Est. CB11: Saf W 4E 218
Shire Hill La. CB10: Saf W 5F 218
CB11: Saf W 5E 218
Shire La. CO6: W Ber 3G 165
Shires Cl. CM77: Gt N 1B 204
SHIRES, THE 5E 218
Shirley Cl. DA1: Dart 9G 153
Shirley Ct. CO15: Jay 3E 188
IG10: Lou 1M 91
Shirley Gdns. IG11: Bark 8D 124
RM12: Horn 4G 127
SS13: Bas 7K 117
Shirley Rd. E15: Lon 9E 122
SS9: Lgh S 1D 136

Shirleys Cl. E17: Lon 9B 106
Shoebridge's Hill CO7: Ded 2L 161 (2H 17)
Shoebury Av. SS3: Shoe 7K 139
Shoebury Comn. Rd. SS3: Shoe 9G 138 (5B 44)
SHOEBURYNESS 8L 139 (5B 44)
Shoeburyness Leisure Cen. 7H 139
Shoeburyness Station (Rail) 7K 139 (5B 44)
Shoebury Rd. E6: Lon 9M 123
SS1: Sth S 5E 138
SS3: Gt W 3M 139 (4C 44)
Shoe La. CM17: H'low 4L 55
Shonks Mill Rd. RM4: Chip, Nave 7E 80 (5B 32)
Shooters Dr. EN9: Naze 1E 62
SHOP CORNER 1F 19
Shopland Rd. SS3: Gt W 1D 138 (3A 44)
SS4: Gt W, R'fd 8N 121 (3K 43)
Shop La. CO5: E Mer 4H 27
Shop Rd. CO11: L Bro 1G 168 (4K 17)
SHOREDITCH 6B 38
Shoreditch High St. E1: Lon 6B 38
Shoreditch Station (Tube) 6C 38
Shorefield Gdns. SS0: Wclf S 7K 137
Shorefield Rd. SS0: Wclf S 7J 137 (5J 43)
Shorefields SS7: Ben 3B 134
Shoreham Rd. CO15: Clac S 4G 189
Shore La. CO11: Brad 3C 18
Shore Rd. CM0: Bur C 4E 196
SHORNE 5K 47
Shorne Ifield Rd. DA12: Shorne 5J 47
SHORNE RIDGEWAY 5K 47
Shortacre SS14: Bas 9D 116
Short Cft. CM15: Kel H 7C 82
Shortcroft CM23: Bis S 9C 220
Shortcrofts Rd. RM9: Dag 8L 125
Short Cut Rd. CO1: Colc 8M 165
Shorter Av. CM15: Shenf 6J 97
Shortgrove CB11: Newp 8N 227
Shortlands SS14: Bas 9C 116
Shortlands Av. CM5: Chip 5K 67
Shortlands Rd. E10: Lon 2B 122
Short La. CM11: Rams H 5D 100 (7A 34)
CO13: Gt Hol 2F 186
Shortridge Ct. CM8: Wthm 7C 230
Short Rd. E11: Lon 4E 122
SS7: Had 4K 135
SS8: Can I 1H 151
Short St. SS1: Sth S 5M 137
SS2: Sth S 5M 137
Short Wyre St. CO1: Colc 8N 165
Shorwell Ct. RM19: Purf 3M 153
SHOTGATE 1A 118 (1D 42)
Shotgate Thickets Nature Reserve 7B 102
SHOTLEY 1G 19
Shotley Cl. CO16: Clac S 1E 188
SHOTLEY GATE 1G 19
Showcase Cinema 3C 140
Shrewsbury Cl. SS16: Lang H 1H 131
Shrewsbury Dr. SS7: Thund 8D 118
Shrewsbury Rd. E7: Lon 7K 123
Shropshire Cl. CM2: Gt Bad 5G 73
Shrubberies, The CM1: Writ 2H 71
E18: Lon 6G 107
IG7: Chig 2B 108
Shrubbery Cl. SS15: Lain 7M 115
Shrubbery Rd. DA4: S Dar 6D 46
Shrubbery, The E11: Lon 9H 107
RM14: Upm 5N 127
SHRUB END 3H 173 (7D 16)
Shrub End Rd. CO2: Colc 4G 173
CO3: Colc, S'way 4G 173 (7D 16)
Shrubland Ct. CO15: Clac S 8M 185
Shrubland Rd. CO2: Colc 9A 166
CO11: Mist 5L 163
E10: Lon 2A 122
E17: Lon 9A 106
Shrublands CB10: Saf W 2D 218
Shrublands Cl. CM2: Chelm 9L 59
IG7: Chig 3B 108
SHUDY CAMPS 3F 7
Shut La. CO6: E Col 8C 198
Shuttle Rd. DA1: Cray 8E 152
SIBLE HEDINGHAM 6K 219 (2D 14)
Sibley Gro. E12: Lon 9L 123
Sibley Row EN9: Naze 9L 53
SIBLEY'S GREEN 4F 13
Sibleys La. CM6: Thax 4F 13
Sibneys Grn. CM18: H'low 7D 54
Sickle Cnr. RM9: Dag 4N 141
Siddons Cl. SS17: Linf 1J 157
Sidings, The E11: Lon 3C 122
IG10: Lou 5L 91
Sidmouth Av. SS0: Wclf S 1J 137
Sidmouth Rd. CM1: Chelm 5N 59
E10: Lon 5C 122
Sidmouth St. WC1: Lon 6A 38
Sidney Pl. CM1: Chelm 4B 60
Sidney Rd. CM16: They B 6C 78
E7: Lon 5G 122
Sidney St. E1: Lon 7C 38
Sidwell Av. SS7: Ben 5E 134
Sidwell Chase SS7: Ben 5E 134
Sidwell La. SS7: Ben 5E 134
Sidwell Pk. SS7: Ben 5E 134
Siena M. CO2: Colc 2B 174
Sierra Dr. RM9: Dag 2N 141
Silchester Cnr. SS3: Gt W 3F 138
Silcock Cl. CO4: Colc 5C 166
Silcott St. CO7: B'sea 7D 182
Silks Ct. E11: Lon 3F 122
Silks Way CM7: Brain 6H 193
Sillett Cl. CO16: Clac S 7H 185
Silva Island Way SS12: W'fd 2N 117
Silvanus Cl. CO3: Colc 9L 165
Silver Birch Av. CM16: N Wea 6K 65
Silver Birch Cl. SE28: Lon 8F 140
Silver Birches CM13: Hut 7K 97
Silver Birch M. IG6: Ilf 3B 108
Silverdale SS6: Ray 7L 119
SS7: Thund 8F 118
SS17: Stan H 1M 147
Silverdale Av. IG3: Ilf 8L 109
SS0: Wclf S 4K 137
Silverdale Dr. RM12: Horn 7F 126
Silverdale E. SS17: Stan H 1M 147
Silverdale Rd. E4: Lon 3D 106
SILVER END 8L 217 (2F 25)
Silver End Rd. CM77: Tye G 1F 25
Silver La. CM5: Will 1F 33
Silverlocke Rd. RM17: Grays 4N 155
Silvermead E18: Lon 5G 107
Silvermere SS16: Lang H 1J 131
Silvermere Av. RM5: Col R 3N 109
Silverpoint Marine SS8: Can I 2N 151
Silver Rd. CM0: Bur C 4E 196 (7C 36)
Silvers *IG9: Buck H* *7J 91*
(off Palmerston Rd.)
Silversea Dr. SS0: Wclf S 4F 136
Silver St. CB9: Ked 2A 8
CB9: Wthfld 2G 7
CM7: Weth 8B 228 (3A 14)
CM8: Sil E 8L 217
CM9: Mal 5B 214
CM24: Stan M 3C 220 (6A 12)
EN2: Enf 6B 30
EN7: G Oak, Wal X 3A 30
EN9: Wal A 4C 76
N18: Lon 1B 38
RM4: Abr 2G 92
SG8: Lit 4A 4
Silver Street Station (Rail) 1B 38
Silverthorn SS8: Can I 2F 150
Silverthorn Cl. SS4: R'fd 3J 121
Silverthorne Cl. CO2: Colc 3A 174
Silverthorn Gdns. E4: Lon 8A 90
SILVERTOWN 7F 39
Silvertown & City Airport Station (Rail) 7F 39
Silvertown Av. SS17: Stan H 3M 147
Silvertown Station (Rail) 7F 39
Silvertown Way E16: Lon 7E 38
(not continuous)
Silvertree Cl. SS5: Hock 1A 120
Silver Way RM7: Maw 7N 109
SS11: W'fd 8K 101
Silverwood Cl. RM16: Grays 7K 145
Silvesters CM19: H'low 5M 53
Silvester Way CM2: Chelm 7C 60
Simmonds La. CM9: Mun 8N 215 (3H 35)
Simmonds Way CM3: Dan 2F 74
Simmons La. E4: Lon 8D 90 (1E 38)
Simmons Pl. RM16: Grays 8K 145
Simms La. CB9: Ked, Pos 2A 8
Simonds Rd. E10: Lon 4A 122
Simons La. CO1: Colc 9A 166
Simons Wlk. E15: Lon 7D 122
Simplicity La. CM17: H'low 2J 55
Simpson Rd. RM13: Rain 8D 126
Simpsons La. CO5: Tip 8A 226 (4K 25)
Sims Cl. CO6: E Col 7C 198
RM1: Romf 8D 110
Sinclair Cl. CO4: Colc 5N 165
Sinclair Rd. E4: Lon 2A 106
Sinclair Wlk. SS12: W'fd 2L 117
Singer Av. CO15: Jay 5C 188
Singleton Cl. RM12: Horn 6D 126
Singleton Rd. RM9: Dag 7L 125
SINGLEWELL 5H 47
Singlewell Rd. DA11: Grav 4H 47
Sinnington End CO4: Colc 3C 166
Sioux Cl. CO4: Colc 3C 166
Sippets Ct. IG1: Ilf 3C 124
Sir Alfred Munnings Art Mus. 3N 161 (2J 17)
Sirdar Rd. SS6: Ray 7K 119
Sir Francis Way CM14: Brtwd 8E 96
Sir Isaac's Wlk. CO1: Colc 8M 165
Sir Walter Raleigh Dr. SS6: Ray 3H 119
Siskin Cl. CO4: Colc 7F 166
Sisley Rd. IG11: Bark 1D 140
Sittang Cl. CO2: Colc 5K 173
Sitwell Cl. CO11: Law 4G 163
Siviter Way RM10: Dag 9N 125 (5K 39)
Siward Rd. CM8: Wthm 7A 230
Six Bells Ct. CM7: Brain 3H 193
Sixth Av. CM1: Chelm 5K 59
CM24: Bur E 6H 221
E12: Lon 6M 123
SS7: Thund 1G 135
SS8: Can I 1E 150
Skarnings Ct. EN9: Wal A 3G 76
Skates Hill CO10: Glem 2G 9
Skeet Hill BR5: Orp 7A 46
Skeins Way CB11: Clav 3J 11
Skelley Rd. E15: Lon 9F 122
Skelmersdale Rd. CO15: Clac S 1K 189 (4D 28)
Skelter Steps *SS1: Sth S* *7A 138*
(off Hawtree Cl.)
Skelton Cl. CO11: Law 4H 163
Skelton Rd. E7: Lon 8G 123
Skelton's La. E10: Lon 2B 122
Skerry Ri. CM1: Chelm 4K 59
Skibbs La. BR5: Orp 7A 46
Skiddaw Cl. CM77: Gt N 1D 204
Skinner's La. CM2: Gall 7C 72
Skinner St. EC1: Lon 6A 38
Skinney La. DA4: Hort K, S Dar 6D 46
Skiphatch La. CO11: Hor X, L Bro, Mist 1J 169
Skipper Ct. CM7: Gt N 8H 193
IG11: Bark 8N 123
Skipper's Island (Nature Reserve) 1E 180
Skippers La. CB9: Wthfld 1G 7
Skippers, The *CM9: Tol* *8K 225*
(off Station Rd.)
Skitts Hill CM7: Brain 7J 193 (7D 14)
Skitts Hill Ind. Est. CM7: Brain 7K 193
Skreens Ct. CM1: Chelm 7F 58
SKYE GREEN 5A 170 (7J 15)
Sky Hall Hill CO4: Boxt, L'ham 1C 160 (1F 17)
Skylark Cl. CM11: Bill 7L 99
Skylark Wlk. CM2: Chelm 5C 72
Sky Peals Rd. IG8: Wfd G 4D 106
Skyrmans Fee CO13: Walt 8H 181
Slacksbury Hatch CM19: H'low 3A 54
Sladbury's La.
CO15: Clac S, Hol S 3N 185 (2E 28)
Slade End CM16: They B 6D 78
Slade Gdns. DA8: Eri 6D 152
SLADE GREEN 7E 152 (2B 46)
Slade Grn. Rd. DA8: Eri 5F 152 (2B 46)
Slade Green Station (Rail) 6E 152 (2B 46)
Slade Rd. CO15: Hol S 7N 185
Slades Hill EN2: Enf 6A 30
Slade's La. CM2: Gall 7B 72 (3A 34)
Slades, The SS16: Van 3F 132
Slade Twr. *E10: Lon* *4A 122*
(off Leyton Grange Est.)
Slaney Rd. RM1: Romf 9C 110
Slaters Cl. CO13: Frin S, Walt 8J 181
Sleepers Farm Rd. RM16: Grays 9D 146
Slewins Cl. RM11: Horn 9G 111
Slewins La. RM2: Horn 3B 40
RM11: Horn 9G 110
Slipe La. EN10: Wmly 3A 62
Sloane M. CM12: Bill 3H 99
Slocum Cl. SE28: Lon 7H 141
Sloe Hill CO9: Hals 4H 207 (3F 15)
Slough Farm Rd. CO9: Hals 4J 207
Slough Ho. Cl. CM7: Brain 7M 193
Slough La. CM3: Dan, Haz 7K 75 (3F 35)
CM16: N Wea 3A 66
CO7: A'gh 4K 167 (5H 17)
CO7: Elms 9H 167 (6G 17)
CO10: Act 3K 9
Slough Rd. CM1: Ayt R, High E 4F 23
CM3: Dan 8H 75 (3E 34)
CM21: A Grn, H Wych 3H 21
CO7: Bran, E Ber 1A 18
Smallbridge Entry CO8: Bures 2B 16
Smallgains Av. SS8: Can I 1K 151
Smallgains La. CM4: Stock 9M 85 (6K 33)
Smallshoes Hill CM1: Good E 5H 23
Smallwood Rd. CO2: Colc 3J 173
Smart Cl. RM3: Romf 5F 110
Smart's La. IG10: Lou 3K 91
Smartt Av. SS8: Can I 1G 151
Smeaton Cl. CO4: Colc 1C 166
EN9: Wal A 2E 76
Smeaton Rd. EN3: Enf 7A 76 (5D 30)
IG8: Wfd G 2M 107
Smeed Rd. E3: Lon 9A 122
Smeetham Hall La. CO10: Bulm 1K 195 (5H 9)
Smilers Ind. Est. SS12: Pits 7N 117
Smithers Chase SS2: Sth S 1N 137
Smithers Dr. CM2: Gt Bad 4H 73
Smithies Ct. E15: Lon 7C 122
Smiths Av. CM3: May 8L 213
(not continuous)
SMITH'S END 7E 4
Smith's End La. SG8: Bar 6E 4
Smiths Fld. CM77: Rayne 6B 192
CO1: Colc 1C 174
SMITHS GREEN 2D 12
SMITH'S GREEN
Takeley 3D 224 (1D 22)
Smiths Grn. CM22: Tak 3D 224 (1D 22)
Smith St. SS3: Shoe 8K 139 (5B 44)
Smollett Pl. SS12: W'fd 3L 117
Smyatts Cl. CM0: S'min 3D 222
Smythe Cl. CM11: Bill 3M 99
CO16: Clac S 7G 185
Smythe Rd. CM11: Bill 3M 99
SMYTHE'S GREEN 2B 26
Smythies Av. CO1: Colc 8A 166
Snakes Hill CM14: N'side, Pil H 1N 95 (6D 32)
Snakes La.
CM22: Stan M, Ugley 2H 199 (5B 12)
SS2: Sth S 1E 136 (3H 43)
Snakes La. E.
IG8: Buck H, Wfd G 3J 107 (2F 39)
Snakes La. W. IG8: Wfd G 2G 106 (1F 39)
Snape Cl. CO16: Clac S 9E 184
Snape Way CO13: Frin S 7J 181
SNARESBROOK 9G 106 (3F 39)
Snaresbrook Hall E18: Lon 8G 106
Snaresbrook Rd. E11: Lon 8E 106 (3E 38)
Snaresbrook Station (Tube) 9G 106 (3F 39)
Sneating Hall La.
CO13: Kir S, Walt 6A 180 (1E 28)
Snelling Gro. CM2: Gt Bad 4G 72
Snipe Cl. DA8: Eri 5F 152
Sniveller's La. CO5: K'dn 2G 25
Snoreham Gdns. CM3: Latch 8L 211
Snowberry Cl. E11: Lon 6D 122
Snowberry Ct. CM7: Brain 4M 193
Snowberry Gro. CO2: Colc 3A 174
Snowdon Ct. RM2: Romf 8G 111
Snowdonia Cl. SS13: Pits 7K 117
Snowdrop Cl. CM1: Chelm 4N 59
CM8: Wthm 3B 230
Snowdrop Pl. RM3: Romf 4H 111
SNOW END 2F 11
Snow Hill CM6: Dut H, Gt Eas 5F 13
CO10: Clare 2D 8
Snowley Pde. *CM23: Bis S* *8A 220*
(off Manston Dr.)
Snowshill Rd. E12: Lon 7L 123
Soames Mead CM15: Ston M 3D 82
Soane St. SS13: Bas 6J 117
Soft Rd. CO10: Bel W 5F 9
Softwater La. SS7: Had 3K 135
SOHO 7A 38
Soils, The CO12: Gt Oak 6E 204 (4F 19)
Solby's La. SS7: Had 3L 135
SOLE STREET 7C 46
Meopham 7H 47
Sole St. DA13: Sole S 7H 47
Sole Street Station (Rail) 7H 47
Solid La. CM15: Dodd, Pil H 9C 82
(not continuous)
Solway RM18: E Til 1L 157
Solway Ct. CO4: Colc 7E 166
Somerby Cl. EN10: Brox 9A 52
Somerby Rd. IG11: Bark 9C 124
Somercotes SS15: Lain 1L 131
Somercotes Ct. SS15: Lain 1L 131
Somerdean *SS13: Pits* *9K 117*
(off Manor Av.)
Somerdene SS13: Pits 9K 117
Somersby Gdns. IG4: Ilf 9M 107
Somerset Av. SS0: Wclf S 2G 136
SS4: R'fd 4K 121
Somerset Cl. CO2: Colc 3J 173
IG8: Wfd G 5G 107
Somerset Ct. IG9: Buck H 8J 91
Somerset Cres. SS0: Wclf S 2G 136
Somerset Gdns. RM11: Horn 3L 127
SS13: Pits 9J 117
(not continuous)
Somerset Pl. CM1: Chelm 4J 59
Somerset Rd. E17: Lon 9A 106
EN3: Enf 8A 76
SS15: Lain 9K 115
SS17: Linf 9J 147
Somerset Way CO15: Jay 3D 188
Somers Rd. CO3: Colc 2H 173
Somerton Av. SS0: Wclf S 1G 136
Somerville Gdns. SS9: Lgh S 6E 136
Somerville Rd. RM6: Chad H 1H 125
Somme Rd. CO2: Colc 2L 173
Somnes Av. SS8: Can I 8E 134 (5E 42)
Songers Cotts. CO4: Boxt 3B 160
Sonnell Ct. CO7: W'hoe 4H 175
Sonning Way SS3: Shoe 5H 139
Sonters Down CM3: Ret C 3C 102
Soper M. EN3: Enf 8A 76
Soper Sq. CM17: H'low 2H 55
Sophia Rd. E10: Lon 3B 122
Sopwith Cres. SS11: W'fd 2B 118
Sorensen Ct. *E10: Lon* *4B 122*
(off Leyton Grange Est.)
Sorrel Cl. CO4: Colc 5K 165
SE28: Lon 8F 140
Sorrel Ct. RM17: Grays 4N 155
Sorrell Cl. CM3: L Walt 6K 57
CM9: Gold 2K 201
Sorrell Gro. CM77: Gt N 1B 204
Sorrells, The SS7: Thund 8D 118
SS17: Stan H 3A 148 (6K 41)
Sorrel Wlk. RM1: Romf 7D 110
Southall Ho. *RM3: Romf* *3J 111*
(off Kingsbridge Cir.)
Southall Way CM14: Brtwd 1C 112
Southampton Row WC1: Lon 7A 38
South Av. E4: Lon 6B 90
SS2: Sth S 5N 137
SS5: Hull 7L 103
SS16: Lang H 6K 131
Sth. Beech Av. SS11: W'fd 9L 101
SOUTH BENFLEET 3E 134 (4D 42)
Sth. Birkbeck Rd. E11: Lon 5D 122
Southborough Dr. SS0: Wclf S 4G 136
Southborough Rd. CM2: Chelm 2B 72
Sth. Boundary Rd. E12: Lon 5M 123
Southbourne Gdns. IG1: Ilf 7B 124
SS0: Wclf S 2G 136
Southbourne Gro. SS0: Wclf S 5G 137 (4H 43)
SS5: Hock 1F 120
SS12: W'fd 8H 101
Southbrook CM21: Saw 3K 51
Southbury Cl. RM12: Horn 7H 127
Southbury Rd. EN2: Enf 6B 30
EN2: Enf 6B 30
Southbury Station (Rail) 6C 30
Sth. Charlton Mead La. EN11: Rye P 6C 52
SOUTH CHINGFORD 1D 38
SOUTHCHURCH 5B 138 (4A 44)
Southchurch Av. SS1: Sth S 6N 137 (5K 43)
SS3: Shoe 7L 139
Southchurch Blvd. SS2: Sth S 5C 138 (4A 44)
Southchurch Hall & Mus. 5K 43
Southchurch Hall Cl. SS1: Sth S 6A 138
Southchurch Hall Mus. 7A 138
Southchurch Rectory Chase SS2: Sth S 5C 138
Southchurch Rd. SS1: Sth S 6N 137 (5K 43)
Southcliff CO14: Walt 7M 181
SS7: Ben 2C 134
Southcliff Ct. CO15: Clac S 9M 185
Southcliff Pk. CO15: Clac S 9L 185
Southcliff Prom. CO13: Walt 9L 181
CO14: Walt 8M 181
South Cl. CO9: Hals 6K 207
CO16: St O 9N 183
RM10: Dag 1M 141
Sth. Colne SS16: Van 2E 132
Southcote Cres. SS14: Bas 7F 116
Southcote Dr. CM8: Wthm 3C 230
Southcote Row SS14: Bas 7G 116

Southcote Sq. SS14: Bas 7F 116
South Ct. CM4: Ing 6E 84
South Cres. SS2: Sth S 1J 137
Sth. Crockerford SS16: Van 2F 132
Southcroft Cl. CO13: Walt 8F 180
Sth. Cross Rd. IG6: Ilf 9B 108
Southdale IG7: Chig 3C 108
SOUTH DARENTH 6D 46
Southdown Cres. IG2: Ilf 9D 108
Southdown Rd. RM11: Horn 2F 126
South Dr. CM14: War 1G 112
E12: Lon 5L 123
RM2: Romf 7G 110
SOUTH-END 3G 21
South End SG8: Bass 4B 4
Southend Airport Retail Pk.
SS2: Sth A 9K 121
Southend Arterial Rd.
CM13: W H'dn 8A 114 (3F 41)
RM2: H Wood, Horn 6H 111
RM3: H Wood 6H 111
RM11: Horn 6H 111 (3C 40)
RM14: Horn, Upm 9A 112 (3E 40)
SS6: Ray 7H 119 (2E 42)
SS9: Lgh S 7H 119 (3G 43)
SS12: W'fd 5A 118 (2B 42)
SS14: Bas 6A 116 (2K 41)
SS15: Bas, Lain 7G 114 (2J 41)
Southend Central Mus. 5M 137 (4K 43)
Southend Central Station (Rail)
6M 137 (5K 43)
Southend East Station (Rail) 6B 138 (5K 43)
Southend La. EN9: Wal A 4H 77
Southend Leisure & Tennis Cen., The 2B 138
SOUTHEND-ON-SEA 7M 137 (5K 43)
Southend-on-Sea Crematorium
SS2: Sth S 2N 137 (4K 43)
Southend Pier 8N 137 (5K 43)
Southend Planetarium 5M 137
Southend Rd.
CM2: E Han, Howe G, Ret C 7K 73 (3C 34)
CM3: Ret C 1L 87
CM9: Wdhm M 5J 75 (2F 35)
CM11: Bill 8K 99
CM12: Bill 7J 33
E4: Lon 2D 38
E6: Lon 9M 123
E17: Lon 5B 106 (2D 38)
E18: Lon 5G 107 (2F 39)
IG8: Wfd G 6J 107
RM17: Grays 2M 155 (1G 47)
SS3: Gt W 3F 138 (4A 44)
SS4: R'fd 9L 121 (3J 43)
SS5: Hock 2C 120 (1H 43)
SS11: W'fd 8M 101 (1C 42)
(not continuous)
SS17: Corr, Fob, Stan H 6B 132 (5A 42)
(Marie Cl.)
SS17: Corr, Stan H 3M 147 (6K 41)
(King St.)
Sth. End Rd. RM12: Horn 8F 126 (5B 40)
RM13: Horn, Rain 1E 142 (6A 40)
Southend United F.C. (Roots Hall)
4K 137 (4J 43)
Southend Victoria Station (Rail)
5M 137 (4K 43)
Souther Cross CM1: Good E 5G 23
Southern Dr. CM3: S Fer 1J 103
IG10: Lou 5M 91
SOUTHERN GREEN 3A 10
Southernhay IG10: Lou 3K 91
SS9: Lgh S 1C 136
SS14: Bas 1B 132 (3A 42)
(not continuous)
Southern Lodge CM19: H'low 6B 54
Southern Ter. EN11: Hod 2B 52
Southern Way CM18: H'low 6C 54 (7H 21)
CM19: H'low 6N 53 (7G 21)
RM7: Romf 1M 125
Sth. Esk Rd. E7: Lon 8J 123
South Essex Crematorium
RM14: Upm 7A 128 (5D 40)
Southey Cl. CM9: H'bri 4E 214
SOUTHEY GREEN 2D 14
Southey Wlk. RM18: Til 6D 156
Southfalls Rd. SS8: Can I 2M 151
SOUTH FAMBRIDGE 4F 104 (7H 35)
Southfield CB10: I'tn 7A 202
Southfield Chase CM12: Lain 6G 115
Southfield Cl. SS7: Had 1L 135
Southfield Ct. E11: Lon 5F 122
Southfield Dr. SS7: Had 1L 135
Southfield Rd. CM0: S'min 5C 36
EN11: Rye P 4A 52
SOUTHFIELDS 9H 115 (3J 41)
Southfields CO7: Ded 2M 161
Southfields Ind. Pk. SS15: Lain 8H 115
Southfield Way CM0: S'min 2B 222
SOUTHFLEET 5F 47
Southfleet Rd. DA2: Bean 5E 46
DA10: Swans 4F 47
SOUTHGATE 1A 38
South Ga. CM20: H'low 3C 54
Southgate RM19: Purf 2N 153
Southgate Cres. CO5: Tip 6E 226
Sth. Gate Rd. E12: Lon 5K 123
Southgate Rd. N1: Lon 6B 38
Southgates Ind. Pk. CB11: Saf W 6E 218
Southgate Station (Tube) 7A 30
Southgate St. CO10: L Mel 3J 9
SOUTH GREEN 9L 99 (1K 41)
Fingringhoe 2G 27
South Grn. CB11: Widd 3B 12
Southgreen Gdns. CO16: Clac S 9G 184
South Gro. E17: Lon 3D 38
Sth. Gunnels SS14: Bas 9C 116
SOUTH HACKNEY 5C 38
Sth. Hall Dr. RM13: Rain 5F 142
SOUTH HANNINGFIELD 9K 87 (6C 34)
Sth. Hanningfield Rd.
CM3: Runw 2H 101 (6B 34)
SS11: Ret C, Runw, S Han 2H 101
Sth. Hanningfield Way SS11: Runw 5L 101
(not continuous)
SOUTH HEATH 2L 183 (2B 28)
Sth. Heath Rd. CO7: Gt Ben 1L 183 (2A 28)
South Hill SS16: Horn H, Lang H 8J 131 (5J 41)
SS17: Horn H 2J 147 (6J 41)
(Square, The)
SS17: Horn H, Lang H 8J 131 (5J 41)
(North Hill)
Sth. Hill Cl. CM3: Dan 4D 74
Sth. Hill Cres. SS17: Horn H 2J 147
SOUTH HORNCHURCH 2D 142 (6A 40)
South Ho. Chase CM9: Mal 9E 214
Southland Cl. CO4: Colc 6C 166
Southlands Chase CM2: S'don 8M 73
Southlands Cotts. SS11: Runw 6A 102
Southlands Rd. CM11: Cray H 1E 116
South Mall *RM17: Grays 4K 155*
(in Mall, The)
Sth. Mayne SS13: Bas, Pits 9H 117 (3B 42)
Southmill Rd. CM23: Bis S 1K 21
SOUTHMINSTER 2D 222 (5D 36)
Southminster Rd. CM0: Ashel, St La 2D 36
CM0: Bur C 1B 196 (6C 36)
CM0: S'min 1E 222 (4D 36)
(Asheldham)
CM0: S'min 4B 222 (6C 36)
(Stoneyhills)
CM3: Alth, May 1C 190 (5A 36)
Southminster Station (Rail) 2E 222 (5D 36)
SOUTH OCKENDON 6D 144 (7E 40)
Sth. Ordnance Rd. EN3: Enf 8A 76
South Pde. SS8: Can I 3L 151
Sth. Park Cres. IG1: Ilf 5C 124
Sth. Park Dr. IG3: Ilf 4D 124 (4H 39)
IG11: Bark 7D 124 (5H 39)
Sth. Park Rd. IG1: Ilf 5C 124
Sth. Park Ter. IG1: Ilf 5D 124
Sth. Park Vs. IG3: Ilf 6D 124
South Pl. CM20: H'low 8F 50
EN9: Wal A 3C 76
Sth. Primrose Hill CM1: Chelm 8H 59
South Quay Station (DLR) 7D 38
Sth. Ridge CM11: Bill 7L 99
Sth. Riding SS14: Bas 9F 116
South Rd. CB11: Saf W 4D 218
CM11: Cray H 2E 116
CM20: H'low 9F 50
CM22: Tak 2C 224
CM23: Bis S 1K 21
DA8: Eri 5D 152
RM6: Chad H 9H 109
(Chadwell Heath La.)
RM6: Chad H 1K 125
(West Rd.)
RM15: S Ock 5F 144 (7E 40)
(not continuous)
SG11: Puck, Stdn 7E 10
SS17: Fob 5D 132
Southsea Av. SS9: Lgh S 4C 136
Southsea Ho. *RM3: Romf 2H 111*
(off Darlington Gdns.)
South Side EN9: Wal A 9H 63
SOUTH STIFFORD 4G 155 (1F 47)
South Strand CO11: Law 3H 163
South St. CB10: Gt Che 8D 202 (4A 6)
CM0: Brad S 8C 194 (1F 37)
CM0: T'ham 2K 225 (3E 36)
CM3: Gt Walt 5G 57 (5K 23)
CM7: Brain 6H 193 (7C 14)
CM9: Tol D 3K 227 (6B 26)
CM14: Brtwd 8F 96
CM23: Bis S 1K 21
CO2: Colc 9M 165
CO11: Mist 4J 163
EN3: Enf 7C 30
RM1: Romf 9C 110 (3A 40)
(not continuous)
RM13: Rain 2A 142
SG8: Lit 4A 4
SS4: R'fd 6L 121 (2J 43)
SOUTH TOTTENHAM 3B 38
South Tottenham Station (Rail) 3B 38
South Vw. CM6: Gt D 3K 203
CO7: Ded 2N 161
RM16: Ors 5D 146
Sth. View Av. RM18: Til 6C 156
Southview Cl. CM3: S Fer 9K 89
South Vw. Cl. SS6: Ray 7M 119
Southview Cres. IG2: Ilf 1A 124
Southview Dr. CO14: Walt 7M 181
CO15: Hol S 7C 186
Sth. View Dr. E18: Lon 7H 107
RM14: Upm 5L 127
Southview Dr. SS0: Wclf S 5H 137
SS13: Pits 7L 117
Sth. View Hgts. RM20: Grays 4F 154
Southview Pde. RM13: Rain 3B 142
Southview Rd. CM3: Dan 4D 74
South Vw. Rd. CM3: Ret C 3C 102
Sth. View Rd. IG10: Lou 5M 91
RM20: Grays 4F 154
Southview Rd. SS5: Hock 9E 104
South Vw. Rd. SS7: Ben 3C 134
Southview Rd. SS16: Van 1F 132
South Wlk. SS14: Bas 1B 132
Southwalters SS8: Can I 1F 150
SOUTHWARK 7A 38
Southwark Bri. SE1: Lon 7B 38
Southwark Bri. Rd. SE1: Lon 7A 38
Southwark Pk. Rd. SE16: Lon 7C 38
Southwark Path SS14: Bas 8G 116
Southwark Station (Tube) 7A 38
Southwark St. SE1: Lon 7A 38
Sth. Wash Rd. SS15: Bas 6N 115
Southway CO2: Colc 9M 165 (6E 16)
CO3: Colc 9M 165
CO7: B'sea 6E 182
South Way EN9: Enf 6C 76
RM19: Purf 1B 154
Southway SS16: Bas 5N 131
Southways Pde. IG2: Ilf 9N 107
SOUTH WEALD 8B 96 (7D 32)
Sth. Weald Dr. EN9: Wal A 3D 76
Sth. Weald Rd. CM14: Brtwd 9D 96
Southwell Gro. Rd. E11: Lon 4E 122
Southwell Rd. RM16: Chaf H 3F 154
SS7: Ben 2E 134
Southwest Rd. E11: Lon 3D 122
Southwick Gdns. SS8: Can I 2F 150
Southwick Rd. SS8: Can I 2F 150
Southwold Cres. SS7: Ben 1C 134
Southwold Dr. IG11: Bark 7F 124
Southwold Way CO16: Clac S 8E 184
Southwood Chase CM3: Dan 6G 75
Southwood Ct. SS14: Bas 6E 116
SOUTH WOODFORD 6G 107 (3E 38)
South Woodford Station (Tube) 6H 107 (2F 39)
Sth. Woodford to Barking Relief Rd.
E6: Lon 6N 123 (5G 39)
E11: Lon 8J 107 (3F 39)
E12: Lon 6N 123 (4G 39)
IG1: Ilf 1K 123 (3F 39)
IG4: Ilf 8J 107 (3F 39)
IG11: Bark 6N 123 (5G 39)
Southwood Gdns. IG2: Ilf 8A 108
SS9: Lgh S 7A 120
SOUTH WOODHAM FERRERS 1L 103 (5F 35)
Southwood Rd. SE28: Lon 8G 140
Sovereign Cl. CM7: Brain 4M 193
SS4: R'fd 5K 121
Sovereign Ct. CM19: H'low 6A 54
Sovereign Cres. CO3: Colc 9K 165
Sovereign Park Ind. Est. SS14: Bas 6F 116
Sovereign Rd. IG11: Bark 3H 141
Sowerberry Cl. CM1: Chelm 4H 59
SOWLEY GREEN 1A 8
Sowley Grn. CB9: B'dstn 1K 7
Sowrey Av. RM13: Rain 8D 126
Spa Cl. SS5: Hock 1D 120
Spa Ct. SS5: Hock 1D 120
Spa Dr. CM0: St La 1C 36
Spains Hall Garden 1J 13
Spains Hall Pl. SS16: Bas 1D 132
Spains Hall Rd. CM5: Will 1J 69 (1F 33)
CM7: Corn H, F'fld 1B 200 (1J 13)
Spalding Av. CM1: Chelm 6G 59
Spalding Cl. CM7: Brain 4G 193
Spalding Ct. CM1: Chelm 8J 59
Spalding Way CM2: Gt Bad 2G 72
Spalt Cl. CM13: Hut 8L 97
Spanbeek Rd. SS8: Can I 9H 135
Spanbrook IG7: Chig 9A 92
Spansey Ct. CO9: Hals 5J 207
Spareleaze Hill IG10: Lou 3M 91
Sparepenny La. DA4: Eyns, F'ham 7B 46
Sparepenny La. Nth. CB10: Gt Sam 2K 205
(not continuous)
Sparepenny La. Sth. CB10: Gt Sam 2L 205
Sparkbridge SS15: Lain 9J 115
Sparkey Cl. CM8: Wthm 8D 230
Sparks Cl. RM8: Dag 4J 125
Sparks La. CO9: Ridg 8C 216 (5B 8)
Spar La. CM3: Pur 6J 215
Sparling Cl. CO2: Colc 4K 173
Sparlings, The CO13: Kir S 6F 180
Spa Rd. CM8: Wthm 4B 230 (4F 25)
CO5: Fee 2M 211
SS5: Hock 1C 120 (1H 43)
Sparrow Cl. CO9: Sib H 7J 219
Sparrow Grn. RM10: Dag 5N 125
Sparrows Cl. CM1: Hghwd 5C 70
Sparrows Corner CO12: Gt Oak 6E 204
SPARROWS END 7M 227 (7B 6)
Sparrowsend Hill
CB11: Newp, Wen A 8M 227 (1B 12)
Sparrows Herne CO15: Clac S 7K 185
SS16: Bas 3B 132 (4A 42)
Sparrows La. CM22: Mat G 5C 22
Sparsholt Cl. *IG11: Bark 1D 140*
(off St John's Rd.)
Sparsholt Rd. IG11: Bark 1D 140
Sparpoint Gdns. IG2: Ilf 9E 108
Speckled Wood Ct. CM7: Gt N 8G 193
Spectrum Twr. *IG1: Ilf 4B 124*
(off Hainault St.)
Speedgate Hill DA3: Fawk 7E 46
Speedwell Cl. CM8: Wthm 3A 230
Speedwell Ct. RM17: Grays 5A 156
Speedwell Rd. CO2: Colc 4D 174
SPELLBROOK 2H 213 (3K 21)
Spellbrook Cl. SS12: W'fd 1N 117
Spellbrook La. E.
CM23: Spel 2H 213 (3K 21)
Spellbrook La. W.
CM21: Saw, Spel, Trimms 3H 213 (3J 21)
Spells Cl. CM0: S'min 2D 222
Spencer Cl. CM9: Mal 8C 214
CM12: Bill 3H 99
Spencer Cl. CM16: Epp 8G 65
CM22: Else 1K 199
CM24: Stan M 3C 220
IG8: Wfd G 2J 107
Spencer Ct. CM3: S Fer 1L 103
Spencer Gdns. SS4: R'fd 2K 121
Spencer Ho. SS9: Lgh S 5F 136
(Ensign Cl.)
SS9: Lgh S 3D 136
(Windsor Cl.)
Spencer Rd. CB10: Gt Che 7D 202
CO16: T Sok 4L 179
E17: Lon 6C 106
IG3: Ilf 3E 124
RM13: Rain 3B 142
SS7: Thund 1D 134
Spencers SS5: Hock 3E 120
Spencers Ct. SS12: W'fd 9K 101
Spencers Cft. CM18: H'low 5G 54
Spencers Piece CO4: L'ham 4E 160
Spencer Sq. CM7: Brain 9H 191
Spencer St. EC1: Lon 6A 38
Spencer Wlk. RM18: Til 7C 156
Spendells Cl. CO14: Walt 4N 181
Spenders Cl. SS14: Bas 7E 116
Spenlow Dr. CM1: Chelm 4F 58
Spennells, The CO16: T Sok 4L 179
Spenser Cres. RM14: Upm 2N 127
Spenser Way CO15: Jay 3D 188
Speyside Wlk. SS12: W'fd 2M 117
Spey Way RM1: Romf 4C 110
Spicers La. CM17: H'low 8H 51
Spielman Rd. DA1: Dart 9K 153
Spike, The CB11: Saf W 3F 218
Spillbutters CM15: Dodd 6E 82
Spilsby Rd. RM3: Romf 4H 111
Spindle Beams SS4: R'fd 6L 121
Spindles RM18: Til 5C 156
Spindle Wood CO4: Colc 3A 166
Spingate Cl. RM12: Horn 7G 127
Spinks La. CM8: Wthm 6B 230 (4F 25)
Spinnaker Cl. CO15: Clac S 4H 189
IG11: Bark 3G 140
Spinnaker Dr. CM9: Hey B 8F 214
Spinnakers, The SS7: Ben 2B 134
Spinnaker, The CM3: S Fer 3L 103
Spinnel's Hill CO11: Brad 3C 18
Spinnel's La. CO11: Wix 3D 18
Spinney Cl. RM13: Rain 2C 142
SS11: W'fd 9N 101
Spinney Ct. CM21: Saw 1K 51
Spinneyfields CO5: Tip 5D 226
Spinney Gdns. RM9: Dag 7K 125
Spinneys, The SS5: Hock 2C 120
SS6: Ray 6N 119
SS9: Lgh S 8D 120
Spinney, The CB11: Newp 4L 215
CM3: Hat P 3M 61
CM5: Chip 9K 67
CM7: Brain 7L 193
CM12: Bill 4K 99
CM13: Hut 5M 97
CM24: Stan M 4D 220
CO6: E Col 8B 198
(off Halstead Rd.)
IG10: Lou 3A 92
RM16: Ors 4C 146
Spinneywood SS15: Lain 7J 115
Spinning Wheel Mead CM18: H'low 6F 54
Spire Grn. Cen. CM19: H'low 4L 53
Spire Rd. SS15: Lain 8L 115
Spires, The CM2: Gt Bad 4G 73
SPITALBROOK 7A 52 (7D 20)
SPITALFIELDS 6C 38
Spital La. CM14: Brtwd 9C 96
Spital Rd. CM9: Mal 2G 35
(Maldon Rd.)
CM9: Mal 7A 214 (1H 35)
(W. Station Yd.)
Sporehams La. CM2: Dan, S'don 6N 73
CM3: Dan 6N 73 (3C 34)
Sporhams SS16: Bas 2N 131
Sportsmans La. CM3: Hat P 4L 61 (6E 24)
Sportsway CO1: Colc 7N 165
Spots Wlk. CM2: Gall 7E 72
Spout La. CO10: L Cor 7K 9
Spratt Hall Rd. E11: Lon 1G 122
Spratts La.
CO11: Gt Bro, L Bro 3F 168 (5K 17)
Spread Eagle Pl. CM4: Ing 5E 84
Spriggs Ct. *CM16: Epp 8F 64*
(off Palmers Hill)
Spriggs La. CM4: B'more 7J 69 (3F 33)
Spriggs Oak *CM16: Epp 8F 64*
(off Palmers Hill)
Springbank Av. CO11: Law 5G 162
RM12: Horn 7G 127
Springbok Ho. CM2: Gt Bad 5G 72
Spring Chase CO7: B'sea 6D 182 (3K 27)
CO7: W'hoe 4H 175
Spring Cl. CM3: L Bad 6L 61
CO4: Colc 4C 166
CO16: Clac S 8G 184
RM8: Dag 3J 125
Spring Elms La. CM3: L Bad 8M 61 (1E 34)
Springfarm Cl. RM13: Rain 3H 143
SPRINGFIELD 4A 60 (7A 24)
Springfield CM16: Epp 2E 78
SS7: Had 2K 135
Springfield Av. CM13: Hut 6A 98
Springfield Basin *CM2: Chelm 9L 59*
(off Wharf Rd.)
Springfield Cl. CM5: Chip 5K 67
Springfield Cotts. CM9: Mal 3C 214

Springfield Ct. IG1: Ilf ... 7A 124
RM14: Upm ... 5M 127
SS6: Ray ... 3G 119
Springfield Dr. IG2: Ilf ... 9B 108
SS0: Wclf S ... 3J 137
Springfield Gdns. IG8: Wfd G ... 4J 107
RM14: Upm ... 5M 127
Springfield Grn. CM1: Chelm ... 7M 59 (7B 24)
Springfield Hall La. CM1: Chelm ... 5L 59
(not continuous)
Springfield Ind. Est. CM0: Bur C ... 3C 196
Springfield Lyons App. CM2: Chelm ... 5B 60
Springfield Nursery Est. CM0: Bur C ... 2C 196
Springfield Pk. Av. CM2: Chelm ... 9M 59
Springfield Pk. Hill CM2: Chelm ... 9M 59
Springfield Pk. La. CM2: Chelm ... 8N 59
Springfield Pk. Pde. CM2: Chelm ... 9M 59
Springfield Pk. Rd. CM2: Chelm ... 9M 59
Springfield Pl. CM1: Chelm ... 6M 59
Springfield Rd. CM0: Bur C ... 2C 196
CM2: Chelm ... 9L 59 (1A 34)
(not continuous)
CM12: Bill ... 3K 99
E4: Lon ... 7E 90
E6: Lon ... 9M 123
RM16: Grays ... 9N 145
SS8: Can I ... 2M 151
SS11: W'fd ... 8N 101
Springfields CM6: Gt D ... 3K 203
CM77: Gt N ... 6E 192
CO7: B'sea ... 7E 182
EN9: Wal A ... 4E 76
SS16: Van ... 3G 133
Springfields Dr. CO2: Colc ... 3H 173
Spring Gdns. IG8: Wfd G ... 4J 107
RM7: Romf ... 9A 110
RM12: Horn ... 6F 126
SS6: Ray ... 5J 119
Spring Gdns. Rd.
CO6: Chap, Wak C ... 6C 196 (4K 15)
Spring Gro. IG10: Lou ... 5K 91
Springhall Ct. *CM21: Saw* ... 2K 51
(off London Rd.)
Springhall La. CM21: Saw ... 3K 51
(not continuous)
Springhall Rd. CM21: Saw ... 2K 51
Springhead Rd. DA8: Eri ... 4D 152
DA11: N'fleet ... 4G 47
Spring Health Leisure Club ... 4F 112
Spring Hill CB11: A End ... 6B 6
Springhill CB11: Widd ... 2B 12
Springhill Cl. CO7: Gt Bro ... 6D 168
Springhill Rd. CB11: Saf W ... 5C 218
Spring Hills CM20: H'low ... 2N 53
Springhouse La. SS17: Corr ... 2B 148 (6A 42)
Springhouse Rd. SS17: Corr ... 1N 147 (6K 41)
Springlands Way CO10: Sud ... 4J 9
Spring La. CM8: Hat P, W Bis ... 6F 25
CM9: Gt Tot ... 7J 205
CM9: Mal ... 4D 214
CO3: Colc ... 7H 165 (6D 16)
CO3: S'way ... 7B 164 (5C 16)
CO5: Fing ... 8H 175
CO6: Eig G ... 7B 164 (6C 16)
CO6: W Ber ... 3F 164
CO7: W'hoe ... 4H 175
(off Avenue, The)
CO7: W'hoe ... 4H 175
(Broome Gro., not continuous)
SG8: Bass ... 4B 4
SPRING LANE INTERCHANGE ... 7F 164 (6D 16)
Spring La. Rdbt. CO3: Colc ... 8H 165
Springleigh Pl. SS0: Wclf S ... 4J 137
Springmead CM77: Gt N ... 1D 204
Spring M. CM21: Saw ... 2K 51
Springpond Cl. CM2: Gt Bad ... 2F 72
Spring Pond Mdw. CM15: Hook E ... 5F 82
Springpond Rd. RM9: Dag ... 7K 125
Spring Ri. CM2: Gall ... 8D 72
Spring Rd. CO5: Tip ... 7C 226 (4K 25)
CO7: B'sea ... 6E 182
CO16: St O ... 9M 183 (4B 28)
Spring Sedge Cl. CO3: S'way ... 8D 164
Springvalley La. CO7: A'lgh ... 3H 167 (5G 17)
Spring Wlk. EN10: Brox ... 1C 30
Springwater Cl. SS9: Lgh S ... 8B 120
Springwater Gro. SS9: Lgh S ... 8B 120
Springwater Rd. SS9: Lgh S ... 7A 120
Spring Way CO9: Sib H ... 6K 219
SPRINGWELL ... 5B 6
Springwell Rd. CB10: L Ches ... 5B 6
Springwood Ct. CM7: Brain ... 5F 192
Springwood Dr. CM7: Brain ... 4E 192 (7C 14)
Springwood Ind. Est.
CM7: Brain ... 5E 192
Springwood Way RM1: Romf ... 9E 110
Sprowston M. E7: Lon ... 8G 122
Sprowston Rd. E7: Lon ... 7G 123
Spruce Av. CM6: Gt D ... 2J 203
CO4: Colc ... 7D 166
Spruce Cl. CM8: Wthm ... 3D 230
CO5: W Mer ... 2B 228
SS15: Lain ... 6L 115
Spruce Hill CM18: H'low ... 8D 54
Spruce Hills Rd. E17: Lon ... 6C 106
Sprundel Av. SS8: Can I ... 3K 151
Spur Cl. RM4: Abr ... 2G 93
Spurgate CM13: Hut ... 8K 97
Spurgeon Cl. CO9: Sib H ... 6K 219
Spurgeon Pl. CO5: K'dn ... 3K 211
Spurgeon St. CO1: Colc ... 9C 166
(not continuous)
Spurling Rd. RM9: Dag ... 8L 125
Spur, The SS5: Hock ... 7B 104
Spurway Pde. *IG2: Ilf* ... 9M 107
(off Woodford Av.)
Squadrons App. RM12: Horn ... 8G 127
Square St. CM17: H'low ... 2H 55
Square, The CM0: T'ham ... 2K 225
CM4: Marg ... 1J 85
CM4: Stock ... 7N 85 (5K 33)
CM9: Mal ... 3C 214
CM14: Brtwd ... 8F 96
CM21: Saw ... 2K 51 (4K 21)
CM77: Gt N ... 2B 204
CO2: Colc ... 3J 173
CO5: W Mer ... 3B 228
E10: Lon ... 5C 122
IG1: Ilf ... 2N 123
IG8: Wfd G ... 2G 106
SS17: Horn H ... 2H 147
Squat La. CO12: Har ... 5J 209
Squires Ct. CO6: E Col ... 8C 198
EN11: Hod ... 6A 52
Squires Mead CM7: Gt Bar ... 3C 202
Squires, The RM7: Romf ... 1A 126
Squire St. CM3: S Fer ... 1L 103
Squirrells Ct. CM1: Chelm ... 6H 59
Squirrels SS16: Lang H ... 3K 131
Squirrels Chase RM16: Ors ... 9C 146
Squirrels Fld. CO4: Colc ... 2N 165
SQUIRREL'S HEATH ... 7H 111 (3B 40)
Squirrels Heath Av. RM2: Romf ... 7F 110
Squirrels Heath La.
RM2: Horn, Romf ... 8G 110 (3B 40)
RM11: Horn ... 8G 110
Squirrels Heath Rd.
RM3: H Wood ... 7J 111 (2C 40)
Squirrel's La. IG9: Buck H ... 9K 91
Stable Cl. CO3: S'way ... 9F 164
CO5: W Mer ... 2E 228
Stablecroft CM1: Chelm ... 3N 59
Stablefield Rd. CO14: Walt ... 7K 181
Stable M. CO5: W Mer ... 1E 228
Stables, The CM20: Gil ... 6B 50
CM21: Saw ... 1N 51
IG9: Buck H ... 6J 91
Stacey Cl. E10: Lon ... 9D 106
Stacey Dr. SS16: Bas ... 4L 131
Stacey's Mt. CM11: Cray H ... 2D 116
Stack Av. SS16: Lang H ... 2F 130
Stackfield CM20: H'low ... 9F 50
Stack La. DA4: Hort K ... 6D 46
Stackyard, The CB10: I'tn ... 7A 202
Staddles CM22: L Hall ... 2K 213
Stadium Rd. SS2: Sth S ... 5M 137
Stadium Trad. Est. SS7: Had ... 8K 119
Stadium Way CM19: H'low ... 2M 53
SS7: Had ... 8J 119
Staffa Cl. SS12: W'fd ... 2N 117
Stafford Av. RM11: Horn ... 7H 111
Stafford Cl. CO13: Walt ... 8H 181
RM16: Chaf H ... 2F 154
SS9: Lgh S ... 9F 120
SS17: Linf ... 1J 157
Stafford Ct. EN10: Brox ... 8A 52
Stafford Cres. CM7: Brain ... 4M 193
Stafford Dr. EN10: Brox ... 8A 52
Stafford Grn. SS16: Lang H ... 2H 131
Stafford Ho. EN10: Brox ... 8A 52
Stafford Ind. Est. RM11: Horn ... 7H 111
Stafford Rd. E7: Lon ... 9J 123
Staffords CM17: H'low ... 8K 51
STAFFORD'S CORNER ... 3C 26
Stafford Wlk. SS8: Can I ... 9G 135
STAGDEN CROSS ... 4G 23
Stagden Cross SS14: Bas ... 1G 133
Stagden Cross Vs. CM1: High E ... 4G 23
Staggart Grn. IG7: Chig, Ilf ... 2E 108
Stag La. IG9: Buck H ... 8H 91
Stainer Cl. CM8: Wthm ... 8C 230
STAINES GREEN ... 6A 20
Staines Rd. IG1: Ilf ... 7B 124
Stainforth Rd. E17: Lon ... 8A 106
IG2: Ilf ... 2C 124
Stairs Rd. SS3: Gt W, Shoe ... 4D 44
Stalham Way IG6: Ilf ... 5A 108
Stalin Rd. CO2: Colc ... 2A 174
Stallards Cres. CO13: Frin S, Walt ... 8H 181
STAMBOURNE ... 6A 8
STAMBOURNE GREEN ... 6A 8
Stambourne Rd.
CB10: Gt Sam, L Sam ... 3L 205 (1H 13)
CM7: Bla E ... 3B 14
CO9: Gt Yel ... 1A 206 (6B 8)
CO9: Ridg, Stamb ... 9B 216 (6B 8)
CO9: Top ... 7B 8
Stambridge Rd. CO15: Clac S ... 9G 185
SS4: R'fd, Stam ... 5L 121 (2K 43)
Stamford Gdns. RM9: Dag ... 9H 125
STAMFORD HILL ... 3B 38
Stamford Hill N16: Lon ... 4B 38
Stamford Hill Station (Rail) ... 3B 38
Stamford Rd. N1: Lon ... 5B 38
RM9: Dag ... 1G 140
Stamford St. SE1: Lon ... 7A 38
Stammers Ct. CM0: S'min ... 2D 222
Stammers Rd. CO4: Colc ... 3N 165
STANBOOK ... 4F 13
Stanbrook Rd. CM6: Thax ... 9B 224 (4F 13)
SE2: Lon ... 9G 140
Standard Av. CO15: Jay ... 5B 188
Standard Rd. CO1: Colc ... 9C 166
Standen Av. CM3: S Fer ... 3J 103
RM12: Horn ... 5J 127
Standfield Gdns. RM10: Dag ... 8M 125
Standfield Rd. RM10: Dag ... 7M 125
Standingford CM19: H'low ... 8A 54
Standley Rd. CO14: Walt ... 5N 181
STANDON ... 7E 10
STANDON GREEN END ... 1D 20
Standon Hill SG11: Puck, Stdn ... 7E 10
Standon Rd. SG11: Abry, L Had ... 7G 11
Standrums CM6: Gt D ... 3L 203
Stane Fld. CO6: M Tey ... 3F 170
Stanes Rd. CM7: Brain ... 2H 193
Staneway SS16: Bas ... 3L 131 (4K 41)
Stanfield Cl. CO3: S'way ... 3F 172
Stanfield Rd. SS2: Sth S ... 5M 137
Stanford Cl. IG8: Wfd G ... 2L 107
RM7: Romf ... 1N 125
Stanford Ct. EN9: Wal A ... 3G 76
Stanford Gdns. RM15: Ave ... 8B 144
Stanford Hall SS17: Corr ... 2A 148
Stanford Ho. IG11: Bark ... 2G 141
STANFORD-LE-HOPE ... 4M 147 (6K 41)
Stanford-le-Hope By-Pass
SS17: Horn H, Lang H, Stan H, Van ... 9N 131
Stanford-le-Hope Station (Rail) ... 4L 147 (6K 41)
STANFORD RIVERS ... 3H 81 (4B 32)
Stanford Rivers Rd. CM5: Chip ... 1L 81 (4C 32)
Stanford Rd.
RM16: Grays, Horn H, Ors ... 1N 155 (1G 47)
SS8: Can I ... 2G 150
SS17: Horn H ... 6F 146 (7J 41)
Stanford Warren Nature Reserve ... 6M 147
Stanham Pl. DA1: Cray ... 9E 152
Stanhope Gdns. IG1: Ilf ... 3M 123
RM8: Dag ... 5L 125
Stanhope Ind. Pk. SS17: Stan H ... 6A 148
Stanhope Rd. DA10: Swans ... 3F 47
E17: Lon ... 9B 106
RM8: Dag ... 4L 125
RM13: Rain ... 2E 142
Stanier Cl. SS1: Sth S ... 6A 138
Stanley Av. CO7: B'sea ... 6F 182
IG11: Bark ... 2E 140
RM2: Romf ... 8E 110
RM8: Dag ... 3L 125
Stanley Cl. RM2: Romf ... 8E 110
RM12: Horn ... 4G 127
Stanley Pl. CM5: Chip ... 8L 67
Stanley Ri. CM2: Chelm ... 8A 60
Stanley Rd. CB10: Gt Che ... 7E 202
CO7: W'hoe ... 5J 175
CO9: Hals ... 4J 207
CO15: Clac S ... 2F 188
E4: Lon ... 7D 90
E10: Lon ... 1B 122
E12: Lon ... 7L 123
E18: Lon ... 5F 106
IG1: Ilf ... 4C 124
RM12: Horn ... 4G 127
RM14: Bulp ... 6B 130
RM17: Grays ... 3L 155 (1F 47)
SS1: Sth S ... 7N 137
SS4: R'fd ... 9G 105
SS7: Thund ... 1D 134
SS8: Can I ... 1K 151
Stanley Rd. Nth. RM13: Rain ... 1C 142
Stanley Rd. Sth. RM13: Rain ... 2D 142
Stanleys Farm Rd. CB11: Saf W ... 5E 218
Stanley Ter. CM12: Bill ... 7J 99
Stanley Wooster Way CO4: Colc ... 8E 166
Stanmore Cl. CO16: Clac S ... 8H 185
Stanmore Rd. DA17: Belv ... 2A 152
E11: Lon ... 3F 122
SS11: W'fd ... 1B 118
Stanmore Way CO16: St O ... 9N 183
IG10: Lou ... 9N 77
Stannard Way CO10: Gt Cor ... 5K 9
Stannetts SS15: Lain ... 7K 115
(not continuous)
Stansfeld Rd. E6: Lon ... 7F 39
Stansfield Ct. *SS7: Thund* ... 8B 118
(off Stansfield Rd.)
Stansfield Rd. SS7: Thund ... 8B 118
Stansgate Rd. CM0: Stpl ... 2B 36
RM10: Dag ... 4M 125
STANSTEAD ... 1H 9
STANSTEAD ABBOTS ... 6E 20
Stanstead Dr. EN11: Rye P ... 3B 52
Stanstead Pl. *CO9: Hals* ... 6L 207
(off Stanstead Rd.)
Stanstead Rd. CO9: Hals ... 6L 207
E11: Lon ... 9H 107
EN11: Rye P ... 4B 52 (7D 20)
SG13: Hart ... 5C 20
STANSTED AIRPORT ... 7J 221 (7B 12)
Stansted Airport Station (Rail) ... 5N 221 (7C 12)
Stansted Cl. CM1: Chelm ... 1N 71
CM11: Bill ... 6M 99
RM12: Horn ... 8F 126
Stansted Hill SG10: M Hud ... 2G 21
STANSTED MOUNTFITCHET ... 3D 220 (6A 12)
Stansted Mountfitchet Station (Rail)
... 3D 220 (6A 12)
Stansted Mountfitchet Windmill
... 3C 220 (6A 12)
Stansted Rd.
CM22: Else, Stan M ... 4J 199 (6B 12)
CM23: Bchgr, Bis S ... 8A 220 (1K 21)
CO2: Colc ... 5A 174
Stansted Way CO13: Frin S ... 8K 181
Stantons CM20: H'low ... 2A 54
STANWAY ... 1A 172 (6C 16)
Stanway Cl. IG7: Chig ... 2D 108
STANWAY GREEN ... 2D 172
Stanway Rd. EN9: Wal A ... 3G 77
SS7: Ben ... 1C 134
Stanwell St. CO2: Colc ... 9N 165 (6E 16)
Stanwyck Dr. IG7: Chig ... 2B 108
Stanwyck Gdns. RM3: Romf ... 2F 110
Stanwyn Av. CO15: Clac S ... 1J 189
STAPLEFORD ... 3A 20
STAPLEFORD ABBOTTS ... 4A 94 (7A 32)
Stapleford Av. IG2: Ilf ... 9D 108
Stapleford Cl. CM2: Chelm ... 1B 72
E4: Lon ... 9C 90
Stapleford End SS11: W'fd ... 2B 118
Stapleford Gdns. RM5: Col R ... 3M 109
Stapleford Rd.
RM4: Stap A, Stap T ... 2A 94 (7K 31)
STAPLEFORD TAWNEY ... 6A 80 (5K 31)
Stapleford Tawney Aerodrome ... 1M 93 (6K 31)
Stapleford Way IG11: Bark ... 3G 141
Staplegrove SS3: Shoe ... 6H 139
Staplers Cl. CM9: Gt Tot ... 3N 229
Staplers Heath CM9: Gt Tot ... 3N 229
Staplers Wlk. CM9: Gt Tot ... 3N 229
Staple's Rd. IG10: Lou ... 2K 91
(not continuous)
Stapleton Cres. RM13: Rain ... 8E 126
Stapleton Hall Rd. N4: Lon ... 4A 38
Staple Tye CM18: H'low ... 6B 54
Staple Tye M. CM18: H'low ... 6B 54
Starboard Vw. CM3: S Fer ... 3L 103
Star Bus. Cen. RM13: Rain ... 5B 142
Starch Ho. La. IG6: Ilf ... 6C 108
Star La. BR5: Orp ... 6A 46
CM4: Ing ... 5E 84
CM6: Gt D ... 2L 203
CM16: Epp ... 9F 64
E16: Lon ... 6E 38
SS3: Gt W ... 3J 139 (4B 44)
Star La. Ind. Est. SS3: Gt W ... 3K 139
Starling Cl. IG9: Buck H ... 7G 91
STARLING'S GREEN ... 3H 11
Starling's Hill CO9: Sib H ... 3E 14
Starmans Cl. RM9: Dag ... 1K 141
Star Mead CM6: Thax ... 8C 224
Starr Rd. CM22: Hen ... 8D 210
Star St. SG12: Ware ... 4D 20
START HILL ... 7A 12
Station App. CM0: Bur C ... 3D 196
CM3: N Fam ... 6H 35
CM3: S Fer ... 9J 89
CM7: Brain ... 6H 193
CM13: W H'dn ... 2M 129
CM16: They B ... 6D 78 (5H 31)
CM20: H'low ... 7H 51
CO12: Har ... 2N 209
CO13: Frin S ... 9J 181
DA7: Bexh ... 7A 152
E4: Lon ... 3D 106
E7: Lon ... 6H 123
E11: Lon ... 9G 106
E17: Lon ... 9A 106
(not continuous)
E18: Lon ... 6H 107
IG9: Buck H ... 1K 107
IG10: Lou ... 4L 91
(Old Sta. Rd.)
IG10: Lou ... 3B 92
(Rectory La.)
RM14: Upm ... 4N 127
RM15: S Ock ... 3F 144
RM17: Grays ... 4K 155
SS1: Sth S ... 6M 137
SS2: Sth S ... 4L 137
SS5: Hock ... 1D 120
SS8: Can I ... 8F 134
SS11: W'fd ... 8L 101
SS15: Lain ... 1L 131
SS16: Pits ... 2J 133
Station Av. SS2: Sth S ... 3M 137
SS6: Ray ... 4H 119
SS11: W'fd ... 7K 101
Station Cotts. EN10: Brox ... 8A 52
Station Ct. SS11: W'fd ... 8L 101
Station Cres. CM3: Cold N ... 8K 197
SS6: Ray ... 4J 119
Station Est. E18: Lon ... 6H 107
Station Ga. SS15: Lain ... 1L 131
Station Hill CO8: Bures ... 8K 195 (2A 16)
Station Ind. Est. CM0: Bur C ... 3C 196
Station La. CM4: Ing ... 6D 84 (5H 33)
CO12: Har ... 3L 209
RM12: Horn ... 5H 127 (4C 40)
SS13: Pits ... 1J 133
Station Pde. DA8: Eri ... 3C 152
E11: Lon ... 9G 106
IG9: Buck H ... 1K 107
IG11: Bark ... 9B 124
RM1: Romf ... 1C 126
RM9: Dag ... 8M 125
RM12: Horn ... 6F 126
Station Pas. E18: Lon ... 6H 107
Station Rd. CB2: Abgtn, Pam ... 1A 6
CB2: Hars ... 1G 5
CB11: Newp ... 3L 215
CB11: Saf W ... 5C 218
CB11: Wen A ... 7L 227 (7A 6)
CM0: Bur C ... 3D 196 (6C 36)
CM0: S'min ... 2D 222 (5E 36)
CM3: Alth ... 4C 190 (5A 36)
CM3: Cold N ... 8L 197
CM3: Hat P ... 1K 61 (5E 24)
CM6: Fels ... 8H 199 (1J 23)
CM6: Gt D ... 3M 203
CM7: Brain ... 6H 193
CM8: W Bis ... 3H 229 (6F 25)
CM8: Whi N ... 2E 24
CM8: Wthm ... 4D 230
CM9: Mal ... 5C 214

Station Rd. CM9: Tol 7K 225 (6C 26)
CM9: Tol D 2L 227 (5B 26)
CM12: Bill 6H 99
CM13: W H'dn 1M 129 (3G 41)
CM16: Epp 1E 78 (4J 31)
CM16: N Wea 6N 65
CM17: H'low 8H 51 (6J 21)
CM21: Saw 1K 51 (4K 21)
CM22: Else 2K 199 (5B 12)
CM22: Tak 3C 224 (1D 22)
CM23: Bis S 1K 21
CM24: Stan M 3D 220
CM77: Rayne 7B 192
CO5: K'dn 2K 211 (2J 25)
CO5: Tip 7C 226 (4K 25)
CO6: Coln E, E Col 4D 198 (3H 15)
CO6: M Tey 2J 171 (7A 16)
CO6: Wak C 6C 196 (4K 15)
CO6: Whi C 7F 198 (4J 15)
CO7: A'lgh 9L 161 (4H 17)
CO7: Alr 6A 176 (1J 27)
CO7: B'sea 7D 182 (3K 27)
CO7: Frat, Thorr 6F 176 (1K 27)
CO7: Gt Ben 6K 177
CO7: Thorr 9E 176 (1K 27)
CO7: W'hoe 6H 175 (1G 27)
CO9: Bird 5A 8
CO9: Sib H 5J 219 (1D 14)
CO10: L Mel 3J 9
CO11: Brad 3C 18
CO11: Law 3G 162 (2K 17)
CO11: Wrab 3D 18
CO12: Har 2H 209 (2G 19)
(Coller Rd.)
CO12: Har 2M 209
(Main Rd.)
CO12: Har 3M 209
(Station La.)
CO13: Walt 8E 180
CO15: Clac S 2K 189 (4D 28)
CO16: T Sok 6K 179 (1D 28)
DA1: Cray 3A 46
DA3: Long 6F 47
DA4: Eyns 7B 46
DA4: S Dar 6C 46
DA9: Grnh 9D 154 (3E 46)
(not continuous)
DA13: S'fleet 5F 47
E4: Lon 7D 90 (7E 30)
E7: Lon 6G 122
E12: Lon 6L 123
EN6: Cuff 3A 30
EN9: Wal A, Wal X 4A 76 (4D 30)
EN10: Brox 1D 30
IG1: Ilf 5A 124
IG6: Ilf 7C 108
IG7: Chig 9A 92
IG10: Lou 3L 91 (7G 31)
IP9: B'ley 1A 18
IP11: T Mary 1K 19
ME2: Cux 7K 47
N11: Lon 1A 38
N21: Lon 7A 30
N22: Lon 2A 38
RM2: Romf 8F 110 (3B 40)
RM3: H Wood 5K 111
RM6: Chad H 2J 125 (4J 39)
RM14: Upm 4N 127 (4C 40)
RM18: E Til, W Til 4H 157 (2J 47)
SG7: Odsey, Stpl M 5A 4
SG8: Barr, Shepr 1E 4
SG8: Meld 3D 4
SG9: Bunt 4D 10
SG11: Puck, Stdn 7E 10
SG12: Stan A 6E 20
SG14: Wat S 2A 20
SS0: Wclf S 6H 137 (5J 43)
SS1: Sth S 6F 138 (5A 44)
SS5: Hock 1D 120
SS6: Ray 4J 119 (2F 43)
SS7: Ben 6D 134
SS8: Can I 2L 151
SS9: Lgh S 3D 136 (4H 43)
(not continuous)
SS11: W'fd 6K 101
Station Rd. Ind. Est. CM6: Gt D 3M 203
CM9: Tol D 2L 227
Station Sq. RM2: Romf 8F 110
Station St. CB11: Saf W 4C 218
CO14: Walt 6M 181
E16: Lon 8A 140
Station Ter. RM19: Purf 3M 153
Station Wlk. IG1: Ilf 4A 124
(in Exchange, The)
Station Way IG9: Buck H 1J 107 (1F 39)
SS16: Bas 1B 132
Staton Ct. E10: Lon 2B 122
(off Kings Cl.)
Staveley Ct. E11: Lon 9G 107
Staverton Rd. RM11: Horn 1H 127
Steadman Ho. RM10: Dag 5M 125
(off Uvedale Rd.)
Steamer Ter. CM1: Chelm 8J 59
Steam Mill Rd.
CO11: Brad, Mist 8M 163 (4B 18)
STEBBING 8D 222 (6J 13)
STEBBING GREEN 7K 13
Stebbing Rd. CM6: Bar S 6K 13
CM6: Fels 6J 199 (1J 23)
CM7: Bar S, Gt Sal 6K 13
Stebbings SS16: Lang H 2L 131
Stebbing Way IG11: Bark 2F 140
Steed Cl. RM11: Horn 4F 126
Steeds Way IG10: Lou 2L 91
Steele Cl. CO6: M Tey 3H 171
Steele Rd. E11: Lon 6E 122
Steen Cl. CM4: Ing 5D 84
STEEPLE 3B 36
STEEPLE BUMPSTEAD 2L 223 (5J 7)
Steeple Bumpstead Rd.
CB9: Hel B, Stpl B 2H 223 (5H 7)
Steeplechase CO10: Pos 1B 8
Steeple Cl. CM9: H'bri 3F 214
SS4: R'fd 4J 121
Steeplefield SS9: Lgh S 9C 120
Steeplehall SS13: Pits 1J 133
Steeple Hgts. SS7: Thund 9A 118
Steeple Mdws. CM0: S'min 2B 222
STEEPLE MORDEN 4A 4
Steeple Rd. CM0: S'min 1B 222 (4C 36)
CM0: Stpl 3C 36
CM3: Latch, May 9H 213 (4K 35)
STEEPLE VIEW 6L 115 (2J 41)
Steeple Way CM15: Dodd 6E 82
Steerforth Cl. CM1: Chelm 4F 58
Steli Av. SS8: Can I 8F 134
Stella Maris Cl. SS8: Can I 2M 151
Stelling Rd. DA8: Eri 5B 152
Sten Cl. EN3: Enf 7A 76
Stenning Av. SS17: Linf 2J 157
Stepfield CM8: Wthm 5E 230
Stephen Av. RM13: Rain 8E 126
Stephen Cranfield Cl. CO5: Rhdge 7G 174
Stephen Marshall Av. CM7: F'fld 3C 200
Stephen Neville Ct. CB11: Saf W 5C 218
(off Debden Rd.)
Stephen Rd. DA7: Bexh 8A 152
Stephens Cl. RM3: Romf 2G 111
Stephens Cres. SS17: Horn H 2H 147
Stephenson Av. RM18: Til 6C 156
Stephenson Rd. CM3: N Fam 6H 35
CM7: Brain 7J 193
CO4: Colc 1D 166
CO15: Clac S 5M 185 (3E 28)
SS9: Lgh S 9B 120
Stephenson Rd. W.
CO15: Clac S 4L 185 (2E 28)
Stephenson St. E16: Lon 6E 38
STEPNEY 7C 38
Stepney Grn. E1: Lon 7C 38
Stepney Green Station (Tube) 6C 38
Stepney Way E1: Lon 7C 38
Ster Century Cinema 1C 126
Sterling Cl. CO3: S'way 1F 172
Sterling Ind. Est. RM10: Dag 6N 125
Sterling Way N18: Lon 1B 38
Stern Cl. IG11: Bark 2H 141
Sterry Cres. RM10: Dag 7M 125
Sterry Gdns. RM10: Dag 8M 125
Sterry Rd. IG11: Bark 1E 140
RM10: Dag 6M 125
Stevenage Rd. E6: Lon 8N 123
Stevens Cl. SS8: Can I 1K 151
Stevens La. CM6: Fels 7N 199
Stevenson Cl. DA8: Eri 5F 152
Stevenson Way SS12: W'fd 2K 117
Stevens Rd. CM8: Wthm 6B 230
RM8: Dag 5G 125
Stevens Wlk. CO4: Colc 8F 166
Stevens Way IG7: Chig 1D 108
STEVENTON END 6F 190 (4E 6)
STEWARDS 7C 54 (1H 31)
Stewards Cl. CM16: Epp 2F 78
CO13: Frin S 7J 181
Stewards Elm Farm La. SS4: Stam 1K 43
STEWARD'S GREEN 2G 79 (4J 31)
Stewards Grn. La. CM16: Epp 2G 79
Stewards Grn. Rd.
CM16: Epp, Fid 3F 78 (4J 31)
Stewards Wlk. RM1: Romf 9C 110
Stewart Av. RM14: Upm 5M 127
Stewart Ct. SS9: Lgh S 4A 136
Stewart Pl. SS12: W'fd 2N 117
Stewart Rainbird Ho. E12: Lon 7N 123
(off Parkhurst Rd.)
Stewart Rd. CM2: Chelm 4B 72
E15: Lon 6D 122
Stewarts Way CM23: Man 5K 11
Steyning Av. SS2: Sth S 4C 138
STICKING HILL 2E 146
STICKLING GREEN 2J 11
Stifford Clays Rd.
RM16: Grays, N Stif, Ors 8J 145 (7F 41)
(not continuous)
Stifford Hill RM15: N Stif, S Ock 7F 144 (7E 40)
RM16: N Stif 8G 144 (7E 40)
Stifford Rd. RM15: Ave, S Ock 8B 144 (7D 40)
Stile Cft. CM18: H'low 5F 54
Stile La. SS6: Ray 5K 119
Stilemans SS11: W'fd 8L 101
Stilemans Wood CM77: Tye G 7M 193
Stiles, The CM9: Hey B 8F 214
Stillwells SS4: R'fd 5M 121
Stirling Av. SS9: Lgh S 4A 136
Stirling Cl. RM13: Rain 3F 142
SS6: Ray 2H 119
Stirling Pl. SS13: Bas 7J 117
Stirrup Cl. CM1: Chelm 4N 59
Stirrup M. CO3: S'way 9E 164
Stivvy's Rd. CM9: Wdhm W 1F 35
(not continuous)
STOCK 7N 85 (5K 33)
Stock Chase CM9: Mal 3D 214
Stock Cl. SS2: Sth S 2L 137
Stockdale Rd. RM8: Dag 4L 125
Stocker Gdns. RM9: Dag 9H 125
Stock Farm La. CM77: Rayne 7C 192
Stockfield Av. EN11: Rye P 3A 52
Stock Hill CM4: Stock 8M 85
Stockhouse Cl. CM9: Tol K 4A 26
Stockhouse Rd. CO5: Lay M 3A 26
Stock Ind. Pk. SS2: Sth S 2L 137
STOCKING GREEN 6E 6
STOCKING PELHAM 4H 11
STOCK INTERCHANGE 4A 34
Stockland Rd. RM7: Romf 1B 126
Stock La. CM4: Ing 5E 84 (5H 33)
Stock Pk. Ct. SS9: Lgh S 9D 120
Stock Rd.
CM2: Gall, Stock, W Han 7B 72 (3A 34)
(not continuous)
CM4: Stock 1L 99 (6K 33)
CM4: W Han 6N 85 (5K 33)
CM12: Bill 5K 99 (7J 33)
SS2: Sth S 1L 137
Stocksfield CM15: Kel H 7C 82
Stocksfield Rd. E17: Lon 7C 106
STOCKS GREEN 7B 170
Stocks La. CM15: Kel H 7C 82 (5D 32)
STOCKSTREET 7G 15
Stock Ter. CM9: Mal 3D 214
Stockton Rd. N18: Lon 2C 38
Stock Towermill 7A 86 (5K 33)
Stockwell CO1: Colc 8N 165
Stockwell Cl. CM11: Bill 9M 99
Stockwood SS7: Thund 8H 119
Stoke Ash Cl. CO16: Clac S 1E 188
Stoke Av. IG6: Ilf 3F 108
STOKE BY CLARE 4C 8
STOKE-BY-NAYLAND 1E 16
Stokefelde SS13: Pits 8J 117
STOKE NEWINGTON 4B 38
Stoke Newington Chu. St. N16: Lon 4B 38
Stoke Newington High St. N16: Lon 4B 38
Stoke Newington Rd. N16: Lon 5B 38
Stoke Newington Station (Rail) 4B 38
Stoke Rd. CO6: Nay 1D 16
CO10: Clare 3C 8
RM13: Rain 2H 143
Stokes Cotts. IG6: Ilf 5B 108
Stokes, The CO14: Walt 5L 181
Stonard Rd. N13: Lon 1A 38
RM8: Dag 7G 125
Stonards Hill CM16: Coop, Epp 8F 64 (3J 31)
IG10: Lou 5M 91
STONDON MASSEY 3D 82 (4E 32)
Stondon Rd. CM4: Nine A 2E 82
CM5: Chip 9M 67 (3C 32)
STONE 3D 46
STONEBRIDGE 1E 138 (3A 44)
Stonebridge Hill CO6: E Col 4G 15
Stonebridge Rd. DA11: N'fleet 3F 47
Stonebridge Wlk. CM2: Chelm 9K 59
Stonechat Rd. CM11: Bill 8L 99
Stone Cl. CM7: Brain 6H 193
RM8: Dag 4L 125
Stone Ct. DA8: Eri 3D 152
Stonecroft Rd. DA8: Eri 5A 152
Stonecrop CO4: Colc 5K 165
Stone Cross CM20: H'low 2C 54
Stone Crossing Station (Rail) 3D 46
Stonehall Av. IG1: Ilf 1L 123
Stone Hall Dr. CO16: L Cla 4H 185
Stonehall La. CO12: Sto G 5C 18
Stoneham St. CO6: Cogg 3K 197 (7H 15)
Stonehill Cl. SS9: Lgh S 2E 136
Stonehill Ct. E4: Lon 6B 90
Stonehill Rd. CM1: Rox 4L 217 (1G 33)
SS9: Lgh S 2D 136
Stonehill Way CO5: W Mer 3A 228
Stonehouse La. RM19: Purf 4B 154 (1D 46)
Stone La. CO5: Tip 9A 226
CO11: Wrab 2D 18
Stoneleigh CM21: Saw 1J 51
Stoneleigh Ct. IG5: Ilf 7L 107
Stoneleigh Dr. EN11: Hod 2B 52
Stoneleigh Pk. CO3: Colc, S'way 3G 173
Stoneleigh Rd. IG5: Ilf 7L 107
Stoneleighs SS7: Thund 9F 118
Stoneness Rd. RM20: W Thur 4E 154 (2E 46)
Stone Path Dr. CM3: Hat P 2K 61
Stone Pl. Rd. DA9: Grnh 3D 46
Stone Rd. CO7: Gt Bro 7F 168 (5K 17)
Stones Cross Rd. BR8: Crock 7A 46
STONES GREEN 5D 18
Stone's Grn. Rd. CO12: Gt Oak 8A 204
Stones Grn. Rd.
CO12: Gt Oak, Sto G 5D 18
Stonewood Rd. DA8: Eri 3C 152
Stoney Bridge Dr. EN9: Wal A 4G 77
Stoney Comn. CM24: Stan M 4D 220
Stoney Comn. Rd. CM24: Stan M 4C 220
Stoneycroft Rd. IG8: Wfd G 3L 107
Stoneyfield Dr. CM24: Stan M 3D 220
STONEYHILLS 6C 36
Stoney Hills CM0: Bur C 6C 36
CM11: Rams H 3C 100
SG12: Chap E 3B 20
Stoney La. CO7: B'sea 5F 182
Stoney Pl. CM24: Stan M 4D 220
Stonham Av. CO16: Clac S 9E 184
Stony Cnr. DA3: Long 6G 47
Stony La. CM5: Chip 2F 66 (2B 32)
CM6: Thax 8C 224
Stony Path IG10: Lou 9M 77
(not continuous)
Stonyshotts EN9: Wal A 4E 76
Stony Wood CM18: H'low 4C 54
Stopford Rd. E13: Lon 6F 39
Stores La. CO5: Tip 5C 226
Store St. E15: Lon 7D 122
Stork Rd. E7: Lon 8F 122
Stormonts Way SS16: Bas 4M 131
Stornoway Rd. SS2: Sth S 5A 138
Storr Gdns. CM13: Hut 4N 97
Stortford Hall Pk. CM23: Bis S 9A 220
Stortford Hall Rd. CM23: Bis S 9A 220
Stortford Rd. CB11: Clav 3J 11
CM6: Gt D 3H 203 (1G 23)
CM6: L Can 3F 224 (1E 22)
CM6: Lea R, Whi R 4B 212 (5D 22)
CM22: Hat H 1D 210 (4A 22)
EN11: Rye P 4B 52
SG11: L Had 7H 11
SG11: Stdn 7E 10
Stort Mill CM20: H'low 6G 51
Stort Twr. CM20: H'low 1E 54
Stort Valley Ind. Pk. CM23: Bis S 7A 220
Stour Cl. CO12: Har, R'sy 5F 208
SS3: Shoe 8J 139
Stour Ct. CM7: Brain 7M 193
(off Elmer Rd.)
Stourdale Cl. CO11: Law 5F 162
Stour Rd. CO12: Har 2M 209
DA1: Cray 8E 152
E3: Lon 9A 122
RM10: Dag 4M 125
RM16: Grays 3C 156
Stour St. CO10: Caven 3E 8
CO10: Sud 5J 9
CO11: Mist 4J 163
Stourton Rd. CM8: Wthm 4B 230
Stour Valley Path CO6: L Hork, Wmgfd 2C 158
CO7: E Ber 1C 162
Stour Vw. CO7: Ded 1M 161
Stour Vw. Av. CO11: Mist 4M 163
Stourview Cl. CO11: Mist 4N 163
Stour Vw. Ct. CO12: Har 2M 209
Stour Wlk. CO4: Colc 5E 166
Stour Way RM14: Upm 1B 128
Stow Ct. CO4: Colc 2N 165
Stowe's La. CM0: T'ham 2H 225
STOW MARIES 9H 197 (5G 35)
Stow Rd. CM3: Pur 9H 197 (4G 35)
Stow, The CM20: H'low 1E 54
Stracey Rd. E7: Lon 6G 123
Stradbroke Dr. IG7: Chig 3N 107
Stradbroke Gro. IG5: Ilf 7L 107
IG9: Buck H 7K 91
Stradbroke Pk. IG7: Chig 3A 108
Stradishall Rd. CO10: Pos 1C 8
Strafford Av. IG5: Ilf 6N 107
Straight Rd. CO3: S'way 9F 164 (6D 16)
CO4: Boxt 8M 159 (4E 16)
CO7: E Ber 1K 17
CO7: Gt Ben 2L 183 (2B 28)
CO11: Brad, Mist 3B 18
RM3: Romf 2F 110 (1B 40)
Straight Way CO2: B'ch 9D 172
Strand WC2: Lon 7A 38
Strangman Av. SS7: Ben 3H 135
Strasbourg Rd. SS8: Can I 9K 135
STRATFORD 9D 122 (5E 38)
Stratford Cen., The E15: Lon 9D 122
Stratford Circus (Performing Arts Cen.)
8D 122
Stratford Cl. IG11: Bark 9F 124
RM10: Dag 9A 126
Stratford Gdns. SS17: Stan H 2M 147
Stratford Ho. RM3: Romf 3H 111
(off Dartfields)
Stratford (Low Level) Station
(Rail, Tube & DLR) 9D 122 (5E 38)
STRATFORD MARSH 9B 122 (5D 38)
STRATFORD NEW TOWN 7C 122 (5E 38)
Stratford Office Village, The E15: Lon 9E 122
(off Romford Rd.)
Stratford Picture House 8D 122
Stratford Pl. CO14: Walt 6M 181
Stratford Rd. CO7: Ded 1J 161 (2H 17)
CO15: Hol S 7A 186
STRATFORD ST MARY 1G 17
STRATFORD ST MARY INTERCHANGE 1H 17
Stratford Shop. Cen. E15: Lon 9D 122
(off Stratford Cen., The)
Stratford Station (Rail) 8D 122 (5E 38)
Strathfield Gdns. IG11: Bark 8C 124
Strathmore RM18: E Til 2L 157
Strathmore Gdns. RM12: Horn 3D 126
Stratton Dr. IG11: Bark 7D 124
Stratton Rd. RM3: Romf 2L 111
Stratton Wlk. RM3: Romf 2L 111
Strawberry Cl. CM7: Brain 7J 193
Strawberry La. CO5: Tip 8E 226 (4A 26)
Strawbrook Hill
CM3: Gt L, L Walt 9J 203 (3A 24)
(not continuous)
Street Farm Ct. CM77: Rayne 6B 192
Street Ind. Est., The CM9: Mal 3D 214
STREETLY END 2F 7
Streetly End CB1: W W'ck 1F 7
Street, The CB9: B'dstn, Gt Wra 1K 7
CB9: Stur 6J 223 (3K 7)
CB9: Thurl 1J 7
CM0: Stpl 3B 36
CM1: High E 4G 23
CM1: Rox 2M 217 (7H 23)
CM2: Gall 8C 72
CM3: Hat P 3J 61 (6E 24)
CM3: L Walt 6K 57 (5A 24)
CM3: Latch 8K 211 (4K 35)
CM3: Mun, Pur 9L 215 (4H 35)
CM3: Ples 2A 56 (4J 23)
CM3: Pur, Stow M 9H 197 (5G 35)

Street, The CM3: Terl 4D 24
CM3: Wdhm F. 5H 89
CM5: H Ong. 6N 67 (3D 32)
CM6: High R 3F 23
CM6: L Dun. 7D 212 (1H 23)
CM7: Gt Sal. 6A 14
CM8: W Bis 2K 229 (5H 25)
CM8: Whi N. 2E 24
CM9: L Tot. 9N 205 (5K 25)
CM9: Salc 5C 26
CM9: Wdhm W 1F 35
CM22: Gt Hal. 1B 22
CM22: Srng 4A 210 (5K 21)
CM23: Ber 4J 11
CM23: Man 5K 11
CM77: Bla N 3B 194
CM77: Rayne 7A 192 (7B 14)
CM77: Tye G 7F 15
(Bradwell)
CM77: Tye G 6H 217 (1E 24)
(Cressing)
CM77: Tye G 6E 14
(Stisted)
CO5: Fee. 9A 170 (1J 25)
CO5: Mess 1D 226 (2K 25)
CO6: Chap 7B 196 (4K 15)
CO6: Gt Tey 2D 170 (6K 15)
CO7: A'lgh 8L 161 (4H 17)
CO7: E Ber. 1J 17
CO9: Bird. 5A 8
CO9: Gosf. 8L 201 (4E 14)
CO9: Peb. 2H 15
CO9: Top 7B 8
CO10: Ashen 4C 8
CO10: Bel O. 5E 8
CO10: Bulm 1K 195 (5H 9)
CO10: Fox. 3G 9
CO10: Gt Wal 4K 9
CO10: Mdltn 6J 9
CO10: Pos. 1D 8
CO10: Stoke C. 4B 8
CO11: Brad 3C 18
CO11: Bran. 1B 18
CO12: R'sy 6C 208 (3F 19)
CO13: Kir S. 5E 180 (7F 19)
CO16: L Cla. 1G 185 (2D 28)
CO16: Ten 1C 178 (6C 18)
CO16: Wee. 6D 178 (7C 18)
DA4: Hort K. 6C 46
DA12: Cobh. 6J 47
DA12: Shorne 5K 47
DA13: Meop 7H 47
IP9: Anw 1F 19
IP9: Hark. 1E 18
IP9: Holb. 1D 18
IP9: S'ly 1G 19
SG7: Wall 2A 10
SG9: Fur P 4G 11
SG11: Brau 6E 10
SG11: Haul 7B 10
Stretford Ct. CM8: Sil E. 9L 217
STRETHALL 6K 5
Strethall Rd. CB11: L'bry. 1A 218 (5K 5)
Strickland Av. DA1: Dart. 8K 153
(not continuous)
Strode Rd. E7: Lon. 6G 123
Stroma Av. SS8: Can I. 8F 134
Stroma Gdns. SS3: Shoe 8H 139
Stromburg Rd. SS8: Can I 9E 134
Stromness Pl. SS2: Sth S. 6A 138
Stromness Rd. SS2: Sth S 5A 138
Strone Rd. E7: Lon. 8J 123
E12: Lon 8J 123
Strood Av. RM7: Rush G. 3B 126
Strood Cl. CO5: W Mer 2B 228
Strood, The CO5: Pel. 4F 27
STROUD GREEN 5G 120 (2H 43)
Harringay. 4A 38
Stroud Grn. Rd. N4: Lon. 4A 38
Stroud Ho. *RM3: Romf. 2H 111*
(off Montgomery Cres.)
Stroud's Cl. RM6: Chad H 9G 109
Struan Av. SS17: Stan H. 9N 131
Strudwick Cl. CM7: Brain. 6H 193
Strutt Cl. CM3: Hat P 2L 61
Stuart Cl. CM2: Gt Bad 4J 73
CM15: Pil H. 4E 96
SS2: Sth S 4M 137
SS3: Gt W. 2K 139
SS8: Can I. 1H 151
Stuart Ho. CO1: Colc 7N 165
Stuart Mantle Way DA8: Eri 5C 152
Stuart Pawsey Ct. CO7: W'hoe 5J 175
Stuart Rd. DA11: Grav 3H 47
IG11: Bark. 9E 124
RM17: Grays. 3L 155
SS2: Sth S 4M 137
Stuarts *RM11: Horn 3K 127*
(off High St.)
Stuarts Way CM7: Brain 6K 193
Stuart Way CM11: Bill. 7N 99
Stubbers Adventure Cen. 8B 128
Stubbers La. RM14: Upm 8A 128 (5D 40)
Stubbings Hall La. EN9: Wal A. 7C 62
Stubbs Cl. CO11: Law. 4G 162
CO13: Walt 7H 181
Stubbs La. CM7: Brain 6L 193
Stubbs M. *RM8: Dag 6G 125*
(off Marlborough Rd.)
Stublands SS14: Bas 9G 117
Studd's La. CO4: Colc. 3L 165
Studland Av. SS12: W'fd 8G 100
Studley Av. E4: Lon 4D 106
Studley Dr. IG4: Ilf 1K 123
Studley Rd. E7: Lon 8H 123
RM9: Dag 9J 125
Stukeley Rd. E7: Lon 9H 123
STUMP CROSS 3A 6
Stump La. CM1: Chelm. 7M 59 (1A 34)
Stump Rd. CM16: Thorn. 6H 65
Sturge Av. E17: Lon 6B 106
STURMER. 7J 223 (4K 7)
Sturmer Ct. *CO2: Colc 5A 174*
(off Queen Elizabeth Way)
Sturmer Rd. CB9: H'hll 3J 7
CB9: Ked. 2A 8
CB9: Stpl B 1M 223 (5K 7)
CO9: New E. 8M 223 (4A 8)
Sturrick La. CO7: Gt Ben. 5J 177
Sturrocks SS16: Van 3F 132
STUTTON 1C 18
Stutton Grn. IP9: Stut. 1D 18
Stutton La. IP9: B'ley 1B 18
Stutton Rd. CO11: Bran, Stut 1B 18
Styles CM7: L Bar. 3H 13
Sucklings Yd. CB9: Stpl B. 2L 223
SUCKSTED GREEN 4E 12
Sudbourne Av. CO16: Clac S. 9E 184
Sudbrook Cl. SS12: W'fd 1L 117
SUDBURY 5J 9
Sudbury Airfield
Belchamp Water. 5F 9
Sudbury Cl. SS5: Hock 3E 120
Sudbury Rd. CM11: D'ham 3G 101 (6B 34)
CO6: Stok 1E 16
CO8: Bures. 7L 195 (1A 16)
CO9: Bulm, Gest 6F 9
CO9: Cas H. 3L 219 (1E 14)
CO9: Hals, L Map 3L 207 (3F 15)
CO9: L Map. 1G 15
CO10: Act 3K 9
CO10: Bulm 1L 195 (5H 9)
CO10: L Mel 4H 9
IG11: Bark. 7E 124
SS8: Can I 8E 134
Sudburys Farm Rd. CM12: L Bur. 1D 114
Sudbury Station (Rail, Tube) 5J 9
Sudeley Gdns. SS5: Hock. 1C 120
Sudicamps Ct. EN9: Wal A. 3G 76
Sue Ryder Foundation Mus. 2F 9
SUFFIELD HATCH 1C 106
Suffield Rd. E4: Lon. 9B 90
Suffolk Av. CO5: W Mer 2D 228
SS9: Lgh S 3E 136
Suffolk Cl. CO4: Colc 6B 166
CO15: Hol S 6B 186
Suffolk Ct. E10: Lon 2A 122
IG3: Ilf. 1D 124
SS4: R'fd. 5K 121
Suffolk Dr. CM2: Chelm 7B 60
SS15: Lain. 9K 115
Suffolk Rd. CM9: Mal 7A 214
IG3: Ilf. 1D 124
IG11: Bark. 9C 124
RM10: Dag 7A 126
Suffolk St. CO14: Walt. 6M 181
E7: Lon. 6G 122
Suffolk Wlk. SS8: Can I. 1E 150
Suffolk Way RM11: Horn 8L 111
SS8: Can I 1E 150
Sugar La. CO9: Sib H 2C 14
Sugden Av. SS12: W'fd. 9H 101
Sugden Way IG11: Bark 2E 140
Sullivan Cl. CO4: Colc 9E 166
Sullivan Rd. RM18: Til 6C 156
Sullivan Way SS16: Lang H 1J 131
Sultan Rd. E11: Lon. 8H 107
Summercourt Rd. SS0: Wclf S. 6K 137
Summerdale CM3: Alth 2D 190
CM12: Bill 6J 99
Summerfield Rd. IG10: Lou. 5K 91
Summer Flds. CM4: Ing 6E 84
Summerfields CO9: Sib H. 6K 219
Summerhill CM3: Alth 2C 190
Summerhill Rd. CB11: Saf W. 5C 218
Summerhouse Dr. DA2: Dart 5A 46
DA5: Bex. 4A 46
Summerlands SS8: Can I 9F 134
Summerleaze Ct. CM77: Gt N 1D 204
Summerton Way SE28: Lon 6J 141
Summerwood Cl. SS7: Ben. 3J 135
Summit Dr. IG8: Wfd G. 6K 107
Summit Rd. E17: Lon. 8B 106
Summit, The IG10: Lou 9M 77
SUMNERS 7N 53 (1G 31)
Sumners Farm Cl.
CM19: H'low. 8A 54
Sumners Leisure Cen 7N 53
Sumpners Link SS15: Lain. 9G 115
Sumpters Way SS2: Temp I 2H 137
Sunbank CM6: Gt D 3M 203
Sunbeam Av. CO15: Jay 6C 188
Sunbeam Cl. CO5: Rhdge. 6G 174
Sunbury Ct. SS3: Shoe 4J 139
Sunbury Way CM9: Mal 8B 214
Sun Ct. DA8: Eri 7D 152
Sundale Cl. CO15: Hol S 7C 186
Sunderland Way E12: Lon 4K 123
Sundew Ct. RM17: Grays 4N 155
Sunflower Cl. CM1: Chelm 5A 60
Sunflower Way RM3: H Wood 5H 111
Sungate Cotts. RM5: Col R. 5L 109
Sun Hill DA3: Fawk 7E 46
SUNKEN MARSH. 1J 151
Sun Lido Sq. Gdns. CM77: Gt N. 6E 192
Sunnedon SS16: Van. 1E 132
Sunnedon Ct. SS16: Van. 1E 132
Sunningdale SS8: Can I 1J 151
Sunningdale Av. IG11: Bark 1C 140
RM13: Rain. 4F 142
SS9: Lgh S 5F 136
Sunningdale Cl. SE28: Lon 6K 141
Sunningdale Ct. *SS1: Sth S. 6M 137*
(off Gordon Pl.)
Sunningdale Fall CM3: Hat P 2M 61
Sunningdale Rd. CM1: Chelm 7G 58
CM3: Alth 3B 190
RM13: Rain. 9E 126
Sunningdale Way CO13: Walt 7H 181
Sunnings La. RM14: Upm. 7N 127 (5D 40)
Sunnybank Cl. SS9: Lgh S 9E 120
Sunny Cft. CM18: H'low 6E 54
Sunnycroft Gdns. RM14: Upm 2C 128
Sunnydene Av. E4: Lon. 2D 106
Sunnydene Cl. RM3: H Wood. 4K 111
Sunnyfield Gdns. SS5: Hock 1A 120
Sunnyfields Rd. CM7: Brain 7M 191 (5D 14)
Sunnymead Flats CM0: Bur C. 4E 196
SUNNYMEDE 7N 99 (7K 33)
Sunnymede IG7: Chig. 9G 93
Sunnymede Cl. SS7: Thund 9G 118
Sunnymede Dr. IG2: Ilf. 9A 108
IG6: Ilf. 9A 108
Sunny M. RM5: Col R. 4A 110
Sunny Point CO14: Walt. 1M 181
Sunny Rd. SS5: Hock. 2D 120
Sunnyside CM7: Brain 5G 193
CM24: Stan M. 3D 220
EN9: Naze 1F 62
SS16: Lang H 2H 131
Sunnyside Av. SS13: Pits 2K 133
Sunnyside Dr. E4: Lon 6C 90
Sunnyside Gdns. RM14: Upm 5N 127
Sunnyside Rd. CM16: Epp 3E 78
CO6: For 2A 164
E10: Lon 3A 122
IG1: Ilf. 5B 124
Sunnyside Way CO16: L Cla. 4G 185
Sunnyway CM0: St La. 2C 36
CM3: Dan 7E 74
Sun Ray Av. CM13: Hut 5A 98
Sunrise Av. CM1: Chelm 6J 59
RM12: Horn 5G 126
Sunset Av. E4: Lon 7B 90
IG8: Wfd G. 1F 106
Sunset Cl. DA8: Eri 5F 152
Sunset Ct. IG8: Wfd G. 4J 107
Sunset Dr. RM4: Hav. 2F 110
Sunset Rd. SE28: Lon. 8F 140
Sunshine Cl. SS5: Hull 5L 103
Sun St. CM12: Bill 7J 99
CM21: Saw 3L 51
EC2: Lon. 7B 38
EN9: Wal A 3C 76
Sun St. Ind. Units CM21: Saw 3L 51
Surbiton Av. SS1: Sth S 6B 138
Surbiton Rd. SS2: Sth S. 5B 138
Surig Rd. SS8: Can I 1G 150
Surlingham Cl. SE28: Lon 7J 141
Surman Cres. CM13: Hut. 6M 97
Surmans Cl. RM9: Dag. 1H 141
SURREX 4A 170 (7J 15)
Surrey Av. SS9: Lgh S. 3E 136
Surrey Dr. RM11: Horn. 8L 111
Surrey La. CO5: Tip 7C 226
Surrey Quays Rd. SE16: Lon 7C 38
Surrey Rd. IG11: Bark. 9D 124
RM10: Dag 7N 125
Surrey Way SS15: Lain. 9K 115
Surridge Cl. RM13: Rain 3G 142
Susan Cl. RM7: Maw 7A 110
Susan Fielder Cotts. *SS8: Can I. 2G 151*
(off Kitkatts Rd.)
Susan Lawrence Ho. *E12: Lon. 6N 123*
(off Walton Rd.)
Sussex Av. RM3: H Wood. 4K 111
Sussex Cl. CM3: Bore. 3G 60
EN11: Hod. 4A 52
IG4: Ilf 9M 107
SS8: Can I. 9G 135
SS15: Lain. 9K 115
Sussex Ct. CM12: Bill 2K 99
Sussex Gdns. CO15: Hol S. 7B 186
Sussex Rd. CM14: War. 1E 112
CO3: Colc 8K 165
Sussex Way CM12: Bill. 2K 99
SS8: Can I. 9G 135
Sutcliffe Cl. SS12: W'fd 1L 117
Sutherland Blvd. SS9: Lgh S 4A 136
Sutherland Ho. CM1: Chelm 7J 59
IG8: Wfd G 4N 107
Sutherland Pl. SS12: W'fd 2L 117
Sutor Cl. CM8: Wthm 6B 230
Sutton Acres CM22: L Hall. 3M 213
SUTTON AT HONE. 5C 46
Sutton Cl. IG10: Lou. 6L 91
Sutton Ct. SS2: Sth S 4A 138
Sutton Ct. Dr. SS4: R'fd 8L 121
Sutton Gdns. IG11: Bark. 1D 140
Sutton Grn. *IG11: Bark 1D 140*
(off Felton Gdns.)
Sutton Mead CM2: Chelm. 7B 60
Sutton Pk. Av. CO3: Colc 3H 173
Sutton Rd. IG11: Bark. 2D 140
SS2: Sth S, Temp I. 3M 137
SS4: R'fd, Sth S, Temp I. 7L 121 (3J 43)
Suttons Av. RM12: Horn 5G 126 (4B 40)
Suttons Bus. Pk. RM13: Rain. 3B 142
Suttons Gdns. RM12: Horn 5H 127
Suttons La. RM12: Horn 7H 127 (5B 40)
Suttons Rd. SS3: Gt W. 4N 139
SS3: Shoe 7M 139
Swains Ind. Est. SS4: R'fd 4J 121
Swale Cl. RM15: Ave. 6N 143
Swale Rd. DA1: Cray 9E 152
SS7: Thund. 1H 135
Swallowcliffe SS3: Shoe 5H 139
Swallow Cl. CO2: Lay H. 9H 173
CO12: Har. 6G 209
DA8: Eri. 6C 152
RM16: Chaf H 2F 154
SS6: Ray. 4H 119
Swallow Ct. IG2: Ilf. 9A 108
Swallowdale CO2: Colc 3C 174
CO15: Clac S. 6K 185
Swallow Dale SS16: Bas, Van 2C 132
Swallow Dr. SS7: Ben. 4B 134
Swallow Fld. CO6: E Col. 8C 198
Swallow Path CM2: Chelm. 6C 72
Swallow Rd. SS11: W'fd 6K 101
Swallows CM17: H'low. 8H 51
SWALLOWS CROSS. 7K 83 (5F 33)
Swallows Cross Rd.
CM15: Mount 7K 83 (5F 33)
Swallow's Row CO7: Gt Ben 6N 177 (1B 28)
Swallows, The CM11: Bill. 8L 99
Swallow Wlk. CO9: Hals. 5L 207
RM12: Horn. 8F 126
Swanage Rd. E4: Lon. 4C 106
SS2: Sth S 5N 137
Swan & Pike Rd. EN3: Enf. 8A 76
Swan Av. RM14: Upm. 3C 128
Swanbourne Dr. RM12: Horn. 7G 127
Swan Bus. Pk. DA1: Dart. 9H 153
Swan Chase CO9: Sib H 7K 219
Swan Cl. CM3: Hat P 2K 61
CO4: Colc 9E 166
SS15: Lain 9N 115
Swan Ct. CM9: H'bri. 4D 214
CO9: Sib H 7K 219
CO11: Mist. 5M 163
(off High St.)
SS7: Thund. 1B 134
Swandale CO15: Clac S 6K 185
Swanfield Cotts. CO3: S'way. 1N 171
Swan Gro. CO6: Chap. 7B 196
Swan La. CM4: Marg, Stock 3L 85 (4K 33)
CM15: Kel H 7B 82
DA1: Dart 4A 46
IG10: Lou. 6J 91
SS11: W'fd. 6L 101 (7C 34)
SWANLEY 6A 46
Swanley By-Pass DA14: Swan 6A 46
SWANLEY INTERCHANGE 7B 46
Swanley La. BR8: Swan. 6A 46
Swanley Station (Rail) 6A 46
SWANLEY VILLAGE 6B 46
Swanley Village Rd. BR8: Swan 6B 46
Swan Mead SS16: Van 2E 132
Swan Paddock CM14: Brtwd. 8F 96
Swan Pas. CO1: Colc 8N 165
Swan Rd. CO16: T Sok 1G 179 (6D 18)
SWANSCOMBE. 3F 47
Swanscombe Station (Rail) 3F 47
Swanscombe St. DA10: Swans. 3F 47
Swanscomb Rd. CO6: E Col 5J 15
Swansea Ct. E16: Lon 8A 140
Swans Grn. Cl. SS7: Thund 9G 118
Swanshope IG10: Lou. 1A 92
Swan Side CM7: Brain 5H 193
Swans Pasture CM1: Chelm 5M 59
Swanstead SS16: Van. 2F 132
SWAN STREET 9B 196 (5K 15)
Swan St. CO5: K'dn. 2L 211
CO6: Chap 9B 196 (5K 15)
CO9: Sib H 5J 219 (1E 14)
Swan Wlk. RM1: Romf. 9C 110
Swan Way CM19: Roy 2G 52
Swan Yd. CO6: Cogg. 3L 197
Swatchways SS1: Shoe 8B 138
Sweden Cl. CO12: Har 3H 209
Sweet Briar Av. SS7: Ben. 4D 134
Sweet Briar Dr. SS15: Lain 6M 115
Sweetbriar Lodge *SS8: Can I 1E 150*
(off Link Rd.)
Sweet Briar Rd. CO3: S'way. 8D 164
Sweetland Ct. RM8: Dag 8G 124
Sweet Mead CB10: Saf W 2D 218
Swell Ct. E17: Lon 1A 122
Sweyne Av. SS2: Sth S 5L 137
SS5: Hock 3F 120
Sweyne Cl. SS6: Ray 3H 119
Sweyne Ct. SS6: Ray 5K 119
Sweyns, The CM17: H'low 5H 55
Swift Av. CO3: S'way 2D 172
CO15: Jay 6D 188
Swift Cl. CM7: Brain 8J 193
RM14: Upm. 3B 128
Swiftsure Rd. RM16: Chaf H 2F 154
Swinborne Ct. SS13: Bas 5J 117
Swinborne Rd. SS13: Bas 6K 117
Swinbourne Dr. CM7: Brain 5F 192
Swinburne Gdns. RM18: Til 7D 156
Swinburns Cft. CO6: Cogg 4J 197
Swindon Cl. IG3: Ilf 4D 124
RM3: Romf. 2K 111
Swindon Gdns. RM3: Romf 2K 111
Swindon La. RM3: Romf 2K 111
Swingboat Ter. *SS1: Sth S. 7A 138*
(off Outing Cl.)
Swiss Av. CM1: Chelm 7H 59
Sycamore Av. RM14: Upm 5L 127
Sycamore Cl. CM8: Wthm 2D 230
CM22: Tak. 3C 224
IG10: Lou 1A 92
RM18: Til 7C 156

Sycamore Cl. SS6: Ray 1H 119
SS8: Can I 2F 150
Sycamore Ct. *DA8: Eri 3B 152*
(off Sandcliff Rd.)
E7: Lon 8G 122
SS11: W'fd 9L 101
Sycamore Dr. CM14: Brtwd 7F 96
Sycamore Fld. CM19: H'low 7M 53
Sycamore Gro. CM7: Brain 6F 192
SS2: Sth S 4N 137
Sycamore Ho. IG9: Buck H 8K 91
Sycamore M. *DA8: Eri 3B 152*
(off St John's Rd.)
Sycamore Pl. CO7: Gt Ben 6K 177
Sycamore Rd. CM9: Mal 2D 214
CO4: Colc 7D 166
Sycamores, The CM5: Chip 9L 67
EN9: Wal A 5J 77
RM15: Ave 8A 144
SS13: Pits 9K 117
Sycamore Wlk. IG6: Ilf 8B 108
Sycamore Way CM2: Chelm 4D 72
CO13: Walt 8G 180
CO15: Clac S 1G 188
RM15: S Ock 4G 144
SS4: Cwdn 2M 105
Sydenham Cl. RM1: Romf 7D 110
Sydervelt Rd. SS8: Can I 1G 150
Sydner Cl. CM2: Gt Bad 5H 73
Sydney Rd. E11: Lon 1H 123
EN2: Enf 6B 30
(not continuous)
IG6: Ilf 6B 108
IG8: Wfd G 1G 106
RM18: Til 7C 156
SS7: Ben 2C 134
SS9: Lgh S 4A 136
Sydney St. CO2: Colc 5B 174
CO7: B'sea 8E 182
Syers Fld. CM7: Bla E 3B 14
Sykes Mead SS6: Ray 6K 119
Sylvan Av. RM6: Chad H 1L 125
RM11: Horn 1J 127 (3C 40)
Sylvan Cl. CM2: Chelm 4C 72
RM16: Chaf H 2H 155
SS8: Can I 3H 151
SS15: Lain 9K 115
Sylvan Ct. SS15: Lain 8H 115
Sylvan Rd. E7: Lon 8H 123
E11: Lon 9G 106
E17: Lon 9A 106
IG1: Ilf 4B 124
Sylvan Tryst CM12: Bill 4K 99
Sylvan Way IG7: Chig 9G 93
RM8: Dag 6G 124
SS9: Lgh S 2N 135
SS15: Lain 8H 115
Sylvester Gdns. IG6: Ilf 2G 109
Sylvia Av. CM13: Hut 8M 97
Sylvia Pankhurst Ho. *RM10: Dag 5M 125*
(off Wythenshawe Rd.)
Symmons Cl. CM77: Rayne 7B 192
Symonds Ct. CO9: Hals 4L 207
Symonds La. CB1: Lin 2C 6
Symons Av. SS9: Lgh S 8D 120
Syracuse Av. RM13: Rain 3J 143
Syringa Ct. *CO4: Colc 8E 166*
(off Blackthorn Av.)
RM17: Grays 5N 155

T

Taber Pl. CM8: Wthm 4E 230
Tabora Av. SS8: Can I 9F 134
Tabor Av. CM7: Brain 5G 192
Tabor Cl. CO7: B'sea 5E 182
Tabor Rd. CO1: Colc 8C 166
Tabors Av. CM2: Gt Bad 2G 72
Tabors Ct. CM15: Shenf 6K 97
Tabor's Hill CM2: Gt Bad 3G 72
Tabrum's La. SS11: Bat 2G 102
Tabrums, The CM3: S Fer 8J 89
Tabrums Way RM14: Upm 2B 128
Tadlows Cl. RM14: Upm 7M 127
Tadworth Pde. RM12: Horn 6F 126
Taffrail Gdns. CM3: S Fer 3L 103
Tailors Cl. CM77: Gt N 1C 204
Tailors Ct. SS2: Temp I 1L 137
Tait M. CM9: Mal 6C 214
Taits SS17: Stan H 2A 148
TAKELEY 3C 224 (1D 22)
Takeley Bus. Cen. CM22: Tak 3C 224
Takeley Cl. EN9: Wal A 3D 76
RM5: Col R 6B 110
TAKELEY STREET 1C 22
Takely End SS16: Bas 1B 132
Takely Ride SS16: Bas 1B 132
Talbot Av. CO15: Jay 6D 188
SS6: Ray 4J 119
Talbot Gdns. IG3: Ilf 4F 124
Talbot Rd. CO16: L Cla 1F 184
E7: Lon 6G 122
RM9: Dag 8L 125
Talbot St. CO12: Har 2M 209
Talbrook CM14: Brtwd 9C 96
Talcott Rd. CO2: Colc 4A 174
Talgarth Ho. *RM3: Romf 3J 111*
(off Kingsbridge Cir.)
Talisman Cl. CO5: Tip 5D 226
IG3: Ilf 3G 125
Talisman Wlk. CM11: Bill 2M 99
CO5: Tip 5D 226
Tallis Cl. SS17: Stan H 2L 147
Tallis Rd. SS15: Lain 7M 115
Tallis Way CM14: Gt War 2E 112
Tallon Rd. CM13: Hut 4A 98
Tallow Ga. CM3: S Fer 2L 103
Tall Trees CO4: Colc 4M 165
Tall Trees Cvn. Pk. *CM24: Stan M 5F 220*
(off Old Burylodge La.)
Tall Trees Cl. RM11: Horn 1H 127
Tally-Ho Dr. CM13: Hut 7D 98
Tally Ho. CO4: Colc 3B 166
Talus Cl. RM19: Purf 2A 154
Talza Way *SS2: Sth S 6M 137*
(in Victoria Plaza Shop. Cen.)
Tamage Rd. CO10: Act 3K 9
Tamar Av. CM8: Wthm 5B 230
Tamar Cl. RM14: Upm 1B 128
Tamar Dr. RM15: Ave 6N 143
Tamarisk SS7: Ben 2C 134
Tamarisk Rd. RM15: S Ock 3F 144
Tamarisk Way CO4: Colc 7E 166
CO15: Jay 6D 188 (5C 28)
Tamar Ri. CM1: Chelm 5L 59
Tamar Sq. IG8: Wfd G 3H 107
Tambour Cl. CO6: Gt Tey 2E 170
Tamdown Way CM7: Brain 4E 192
Tamworth Av. IG8: Wfd G 3E 106
Tamworth Chase CO2: Colc 4A 174
Tanfield Dr. CM12: Bill 6J 99
Tangent Link RM3: Romf 5H 111
Tangerine Cl. CO4: Colc 9D 166
Tangham Wlk. SS14: Bas 8C 116
Tangmere Cl. SS11: W'fd 1B 118
Tangmere Cres. RM12: Horn 8F 126
Tan Ho. La. CM14: N'side 3K 95 (6C 32)
Tankerville Dr. SS9: Lgh S 3C 136
Tank Hill Rd. RM19: Ave, Purf 2L 153 (1C 46)
Tank La. RM19: Purf 2L 153
Tan La. CO16: L Cla 9J 179 (1D 28)
Tanner Cl. CO16: Clac S 1F 188
Tanners La. IG6: Ilf 7B 108 (3H 39)
Tanners Mdw. CM7: Brain 6M 193
Tanner St. IG11: Bark 8B 124
SE1: Lon 7B 38
Tanners Way CB10: Saf W 4D 218
CM3: S Fer 9J 89
Tannery Cl. RM10: Dag 5N 125
Tanswell Av. SS13: Pits 9J 117
Tanswell Cl. SS13: Pits 9J 117
Tanswell Ct. SS13: Pits 8J 117
Tansy Cl. RM3: Romf 3J 111
Tantelen Rd. SS8: Can I 9F 134
Tantony Gro. RM6: Chad H 7J 109
Tanyard Hill DA12: Shorne 5K 47
Tanyard, The CM6: Thax 8C 224 (3F 13)
Tany's Dell CM20: H'low 9F 50
Tapestry Ct. CO6: E Col 8C 198
Tapestry Wlk. CM7: Brain 6M 193
Tapley Rd. CM1: Chelm 4H 59
Tapsworth Cl. CO16: Clac S 8G 185
Tapwoods CO3: Colc 8H 165
Tara Cl. CO4: Colc 6D 166
Taranto Rd. SS8: Can I 2K 151
Tarlings CM20: H'low 9E 50
Tarnworth Rd. RM3: Romf 2L 111
TARPOTS 1B 134 (3D 42)
Tarragona M. CO2: Colc 2B 174
Tarragon Cl. CO5: Tip 6C 226
Tasker Ho. IG11: Bark 2C 140
Tasker Rd. RM16: Grays 1D 156
Tasman Cl. SS17: Corr 1A 148
Tasman Ct. CM1: Chelm 6G 58
Tatsfield Av. EN9: Naze 2D 62
Tattenham Rd. SS15: Lain 8K 115
(not continuous)
Tattersall Gdns. SS9: Lgh S 5N 135 (4G 43)
Tattersalls Chase CM0: S'min 2E 222
Tattersall Way CM1: Chelm 3N 71
Tattle Hill SG14: B'fld 4A 20
Tatton St. CM17: H'low 2H 55
Taunton Cl. DA7: Bexh 7B 152
IG6: Ilf 3E 108
Taunton Dr. SS0: Wclf S 2G 136
Taunton Ho. *RM3: Romf 2K 111*
(off Redcar Rd.)
Taunton Rd. CM1: Chelm 6N 59
RM3: Romf 1G 111
Taveners Grn. Cl. SS12: W'fd 1M 117
TAVERNERS GREEN 3D 22
Taverners Wlk. CM8: Wthm 3C 230
Taverners Way E4: Lon 7E 90
EN11: Hod 5A 52 (7D 20)
Tavistock Cl. RM3: Romf 5H 111
Tavistock Dr. CM12: Bill 3H 99
Tavistock Gdns. IG3: Ilf 6D 124
Tavistock Ho. IG8: Wfd G 3N 107
Tavistock Pl. WC1: Lon 6A 38
Tavistock Rd. CM1: Chelm 6N 59
E7: Lon 6F 122
E15: Lon 8F 122
E18: Lon 7G 106
SS15: Lain 7L 115
Tavistock Sq. NW1: Lon 6A 38
Tavy Bri. SE2: Lon 9H 141
Tawell M. CO5: Tip 6D 226
TAWNEY COMMON 1N 79 (4K 31)
Tawney Comn. CM16: They M 9N 65 (4K 31)
Tawney Rd. SE28: Lon 7G 140
Tawney's Ride CO8: Bures 7M 195
Tawneys Rd. CM18: H'low 5D 54 (7H 21)
Tawny Av. RM14: Upm 7M 127
Taylifers CM19: H'low 8N 53
Taylor Av. CM1: Chelm 6G 59
Taylor Cl. RM5: Col R 4M 109
Taylor Ct. CM24: Stan Apt 8L 221
CO1: Colc 8N 165
E15: Lon 7C 122
Taylor Dr. CO11: Law 4H 163
Taylor Row RM3: Noak H 8G 95
Taylors IG7: Chig 6F 92
Taylors Av. EN11: Hod 6A 52
Taylors End Rd. CM24: Stan Apt 8K 221
Taylor's La. ME3: High 5K 47
Taylor's Rd. CO5: Rhdge 6F 174
Tayside Wlk. SS12: W'fd 2L 117
Tayspill Ct. *CO2: Colc 3J 173*
(off Coats Hutton Rd.)
Tay Way RM1: Romf 5D 110
Teagles SS15: Lain 9N 115
Teak Wlk. CM8: Wthm 3D 230
Teal Av. CM3: May 8L 213
Teal Cl. CM77: Gt N 3B 204
CO4: A'lgh 7G 166
Teal Way CO5: K'dn 3L 211
Teasel Cres. SE28: Lon 8D 140
Tedder Cl. CO2: Colc 2A 174
Ted Hennem Ho. RM10: Dag 5N 125
Tees Cl. CM8: Wthm 5B 230
RM14: Upm 1A 128
Teesdale Rd. E11: Lon 1F 122
Tees Dr. RM3: Romf 9H 95 (1B 40)
Tees Rd. CM1: Chelm 5L 59
Teign Dr. CM8: Wthm 5A 230
Teigngrace SS3: Shoe 6H 139
Teignmouth Dr. SS6: Ray 2K 119
Telegraph Hill ME3: High 5K 47
Telegraph M. IG3: Ilf 3F 124
Telese Av. SS8: Can I 2K 151
Telford Pl. CM1: Chelm 7M 59
Telford Rd. CM7: Brain 7J 193
CO15: Clac S 5M 185 (3E 28)
N11: Lon 1A 38
Telford Way CO4: Colc 1D 166
Temperance Yd. CO6: E Col 8C 198
Tempest Mead CM16: N Wea 6N 65
Tempest Way RM13: Rain 8E 126
Templar Dr. SE28: Lon 6J 141
Templar Ho. RM13: Rain 2B 142
Templar Rd. CM7: Brain 6M 193
Templars Cl. CM8: Wthm 3C 230
Templars Ho. E15: Lon 7B 122
Temple Av. RM8: Dag 3M 125
Temple Bank CM20: H'low 6G 51
Temple Cl. CM12: Bill 3H 99
CO13: Frin S 8K 181
E11: Lon 2E 122
SS7: Had 3M 135
SS15: Lain 8L 115
Temple Ct. CO4: Colc 5D 166
SS2: Sth S 3A 138
TEMPLE END
Ballingdon 4G 9
Great Thurlow 1H 7
Temple End CB9: Thurl 1J 7
Temple Farm Ind. Est. SS2: Temp I 1M 137
Temple Farm Trad. Est.
CM2: W Han 2C 86
TEMPLE FIELDS 8F 50 (5J 21)
Templefields Ent. Cen. CM20: H'low 9F 50
Temple Gdns. RM8: Dag 5J 125
Temple Gro. Cvn. Pk. CM2: W Han 2D 86
Temple Hall Ct. E4: Lon 8D 90
TEMPLE HILL 3C 46
Temple Hill DA1: Dart 3C 46
Temple Hill Sq. DA1: Dart 3C 46
Temple La. CM8: Sil E, Tye G 9J 217 (2F 25)
Templemead CM8: Wthm 4C 230
Temple Mead CM19: Roy 3H 53
Temple Mill La. E10: Lon 6B 122
(not continuous)
E15: Lon 6C 122 (5E 38)
TEMPLE MILLS 6B 122 (5D 38)
Temple Mills E10: Lon 5C 122
Temple Pattle CO11: Bran 1H 163
Templer Av. RM16: Grays 2C 156
Temple Rd. CO2: King 4H 173
Temple Station (Tube) 7A 38
Templeton Av. E4: Lon 1A 106
Templeton Pk. CM2: W Han 2C 86
Temple Way CM9: Mal 3B 214
Templewood Ct. SS7: Had 3K 135
Templewood Rd. CO4: Colc 6E 166
SS7: Had 3K 135
Temptin Av. SS8: Can I 2L 151
Ten Acre App. CM9: Mal 3B 214
Tenbury Cl. E7: Lon 7K 123
Tenby Cl. RM6: Chad H 1K 125
Tenby Rd. RM6: Chad H 1K 125
TENDRING 1C 178 (6C 18)
Tendring Av. SS6: Ray 4G 119
Tendring Ct. CM13: Hut 4N 97
TENDRING GREEN 5B 18
Tendring Rd. CM18: H'low 5B 54 (7H 21)
(not continuous)
CO7: L Ben 7L 169 (6A 18)
CO16: T Sok 2G 179 (7D 18)
CO16: Ten 5B 18
Tendring Way RM6: Chad H 9H 109
Tennants Row RM18: Til 7A 156
Tenny Ho. RM17: Grays 5L 155
Tennyson Av. E11: Lon 2G 123
E12: Lon 9L 123
EN9: Wal A 4E 76
RM17: Grays 1L 155
SS2: Sth S 4N 137
Tennyson Cl. CM7: Brain 8H 193
SS9: Lgh S 4N 135
Tennyson Dr. SS13: Pits 1J 133
Tennyson Rd. CM1: Chelm 6H 59
CM9: Mal 8C 214
CM13: Hut 6M 97
E10: Lon 3B 122
E15: Lon 9E 122
RM3: Romf 4G 110
Tennyson Wlk. RM18: Til 7D 156
Tennyson Way RM12: Horn 4D 126
Tenpenny Hill CO7: Alr, Thorr 8C 176 (1K 27)
Tensing Gdns. CM12: Bill 7J 99
Tenter Cl. CM7: Brain 3H 193
Tenterden Rd. RM8: Dag 4L 125
Tenterfield Rd. CM9: Mal 6C 214
Tenterfields CB11: Newp 2K 215
CM6: Gt D 3M 203
SS13: Bas 7K 117
Tenth Av. CM24: Stan Apt, Stan M 7G 221
Tentree Rd. CO10: Act, Gt Wal 3K 9
Teramo Rd. SS8: Can I 2K 151
Tercel Path IG7: Chig 1G 109
Terence Messenger Twr. *E10: Lon 4B 122*
(off Alpine Rd.)
Terence Webster Rd. SS12: W'fd 1M 117
Teresa M. E17: Lon 8A 106
TERLING 4D 24
Terling SS16: Bas 1C 132
Terling Cl. CO2: Colc 5A 174
E11: Lon 5F 122
Terling Hall Rd. CM3: Hat P, Terl 5D 24
Terling Rd. CM3: Hat P 1K 61 (5E 24)
CM8: Wthm 4A 230 (4E 24)
RM8: Dag 4M 125
Terlings, The CM14: Brtwd 9D 96
Terminal Cl. SS3: Shoe 7K 139
Terminal Cl. Ind. Est. SS3: Shoe 7K 139
Terminal Rd. Nth.
CM22: Stan Apt, Tak 6N 221 (7C 12)
Terminal Rd. Sth.
CM22: Stan Apt, Tak 6N 221 (7C 12)
Terminus Dr. SS16: Pits 2J 133
Terminus St. CM20: H'low 2C 54
Terms Av. SS8: Can I 9G 135
Tern Cl. CM3: May 8L 213
CO5: K'dn 2L 211
Terndale CO15: Clac S 7K 185
Tern Gdns. RM14: Upm 3B 128
Terni Rd. SS8: Can I 2K 151
Tern M. CO7: W'hoe 6H 175
Tern Way CM14: Brtwd 1B 112
Ter. Hall Chase CO6: Gt Hork 1K 165
Terrace, The CM3: Hat P 1M 61
DA11: Grav 3H 47
(not continuous)
E4: Wfd G 9E 90
(off Newgate St.)
IG8: Wfd G 3G 106 (2F 39)
SS3: Shoe 8K 139
SS7: Ben 6D 134
SS9: Lgh S 6D 136
Terrace Wlk. RM9: Dag 7K 125
Teviot Av. RM15: Ave 6N 143
Tew Cl. CO5: Tip 6D 226
Tewkesbury Cl. IG10: Lou 5L 91
Tewkesbury Rd. CO15: Clac S 9J 185
Tewkes Rd. SS8: Can I 9K 135
Tey Gdns. CO6: M Tey 3E 170
Tey Rd. CO6: Aldh 5K 15
CO6: Cogg 2M 197 (7J 15)
CO6: E Col 8E 198 (4J 15)
Tey Rd. Cl. CO6: E Col 8E 198
Thackeray Av. RM18: Til 6D 156
Thackeray Cl. CM7: Brain 8J 193
Thackeray Dr. RM6: Chad H 2F 124
Thackeray Row SS12: W'fd 2L 117
Thal Massing Cl. CM13: Hut 8L 97
Thames Av. CM1: Chelm 6E 58
RM9: Dag 4N 141
Thamesbank Pl. SE28: Lon 6H 141
Thames Barrier Vis. Cen. 7F 39
Thames Cl. CM7: Brain 7M 193
RM13: Rain 6F 142
SS6: Ray 6J 119
SS9: Lgh S 5A 136
SS17: Corr 2B 148
Thames Cres. SS17: Corr 9C 132
Thames Dr. RM16: Grays 3C 156
SS9: Lgh S 5N 135 (4G 43)
Thames Flood Barrier, The 7F 39
Thames Gateway RM9: Dag 2L 141
RM13: Ave, Rain, Wen 2L 141
RM15: Ave, Purf 8K 143
THAMES HAVEN 5K 149 (7B 42)
Thames Haven Rd. SS17: Corr 2C 148
Thameshill Av. RM5: Col R 6A 110
Thameside Aviation Mus. 6M 157 (2K 47)
Thameside Community Nature Reserve 4F 140
Thameside Cres. SS8: Can I 2F 150
Thameside Ind. Est. DA8: Eri 4H 153
Thameside Pk. City Farm 3F 140
Thameside Theatre 3L 155
Thameside Wlk. SE28: Lon 6H 141
SE28: Lon 6F 140
Thames Ind. Pk. RM18: E Til 3K 157
THAMESMEAD 8F 140 (7J 39)
THAMESMEAD CENTRAL 8E 140 (7J 39)
THAMESMEAD EAST 9M 141
THAMESMEAD NORTH 6J 141
THAMESMEAD SOUTH 9J 141 (7J 39)
THAMESMEAD SOUTH WEST 9E 140 (7H 39)
THAMESMEAD WEST 7H 39
Thamesmere Dr. SE28: Lon 7F 140
Thamesmere Leisure Cen. 7F 140
Thames Rd. DA1: Cray 7D 152 (2A 46)
IG11: Bark 3E 140 (6H 39)

Thames Rd. RM17: Grays . . . 5L 155
SS8: Can I . . . 3F 150
Thames Vw. RM16: Grays . . . 3C 156
SS16: Bas . . . 5L 131
Thamesview Ct. SS7: Had . . . 4M 135
Thames Way CM0: Bur C . . . 2C 196
DA11: Grav, N'fleet . . . 4G 47
Thamley RM19: Purf . . . 2L 153
Thanet Grange SS2: Sth S . . . 1H 137
Thanet Rd. DA8: Eri . . . 5C 152
Thanet Wlk. *CO5: Rhdge* . . . *6G 174*
(off High St.)
Thant Cl. E10: Lon . . . 5B 122
Thatchers Cl. IG10: Lou . . . 1B 92
Thatchers Cft. CM3: Latch . . . 7J 211
Thatchers Dr. CO7: Elms . . . 9M 167
Thatchers Way CM77: Gt N . . . 8E 192
Thatches Gro. RM6: Chad H . . . 8K 109
THAXTED . . . 7C 224 (3F 13)
Thaxted Bold CM13: Hut . . . 4N 97
Thaxted Grn. CM13: Hut . . . 4M 97
Thaxted Guildhall . . . 8C 224 (3F 13)
Thaxted Ho. RM10: Dag . . . 9N 125
Thaxted "John Webb's" Towermill
. . . 8B 224 (3F 13)
Thaxted Rd.
CB10: Gt Sam, L Sam . . . 4J 205 (2G 13)
CB10: Saf W, Wim . . . 4D 218 (7C 6)
CB11: Deb . . . 2C 12
CB11: Saf W . . . 4D 218 (6C 6)
IG9: Buck H . . . 6L 91
Thaxted Wlk. CO2: Colc . . . 6A 174
RM13: Rain . . . 9C 126
Thaxted Way EN9: Wal A . . . 3D 76
Thear Cl. SS0: Wclf S . . . 2H 137
Theatre Royal . . . 9D 122
Theatre Sq. E15: Lon . . . 8D 122
Theberton St. N1: Lon . . . 6A 38
Theleway Cl. EN11: Rye P . . . 2B 52
Thelma Av. SS8: Can I . . . 1G 151
Thelsford Wlk. CO4: Colc . . . 8F 166
Theobald Rd. E17: Lon . . . 2A 122
Theobalds Av. RM17: Grays . . . 3M 155
Theobald's Ct. SS9: Lgh S . . . 5B 136
Theobalds Grove Station (Rail) . . . 4C 30
Theobalds La. EN8: Chesh, Wal X . . . 4C 30
(not continuous)
Theobalds Pk. Rd. EN2: Enf . . . 5A 30
Theobald's Rd. SS9: Lgh S . . . 5B 136
Theobalds Rd. WC1: Lon . . . 7A 38
THERFIELD . . . 7B 4
Thetford Ct. CM1: Chelm . . . 1N 71
Thetford Gdns. RM9: Dag . . . 9K 125
Thetford Pl. SS15: Lain . . . 6M 115
Thetford Rd. RM9: Dag . . . 9J 125
THEYDON BOIS . . . 6D 78 (5H 31)
Theydon Bois Station (Tube) . . . 6E 78 (5H 31)
Theydon Bold CM13: Hut . . . 4A 98
Theydon Bower CM16: Epp . . . 1F 78
Theydon Ct. EN9: Wal A . . . 3G 77
Theydon Cres. SS14: Bas . . . 6G 116
Theydon Gdns. RM13: Rain . . . 9C 126
THEYDON GARNON . . . 5H 79 (5J 31)
Theydon Gro. CM16: Epp . . . 9F 64
IG8: Wfd G . . . 3J 107
THEYDON MOUNT . . . 6M 79 (5K 31)
Theydon Pk. Rd. CM16: They B . . . 7D 78 (5H 31)
Theydon Pl. CM16: Epp . . . 1E 78
Theydon Rd. CM16: Epp . . . 2C 78 (5H 31)
Thicket Gro. RM9: Dag . . . 8H 125
Thielen Rd. SS8: Can I . . . 1G 150
Thieves La. SG14: Pans . . . 5A 20
Third Av. CM1: Chelm . . . 6J 59
CM18: H'low . . . 4A 54 (7H 21)
CM19: H'low . . . 4M 53 (7G 21)
CM24: Stan Apt . . . 7G 221
CO9: Hals . . . 5N 207
CO12: Har . . . 4L 209
CO13: Frin S . . . 1H 187
CO14: Walt . . . 1M 181
CO15: Clac S . . . 9N 185
E12: Lon . . . 6L 123
E17: Lon . . . 9A 106
EN9: Wal A . . . 9H 63
RM6: Chad H . . . 1H 125
RM10: Dag . . . 1N 141
RM20: W Thur . . . 4D 154
SS7: Thund . . . 9G 119
SS8: Can I . . . 1E 150
SS11: W'fd . . . 1A 118
SS16: Lang H . . . 3G 130
SS17: Stan H . . . 1N 147
Third Wlk. SS8: Can I . . . 1E 150
Thirlmere Cl. CM77: Gt N . . . 1D 204
Thirlmere Rd. DA7: Bexh . . . 7A 152
SS7: Thund . . . 8E 118
Thirslet Dr. CM9: H'bri . . . 4E 214
Thirtle Cl. CO16: Clac S . . . 7H 185
Thisselt Rd. SS8: Can I . . . 9G 134
Thistle Cl. SS15: Bas . . . 6A 116
Thistledene Av. RM5: Col R . . . 2N 109
Thistledown CM7: Pan . . . 1C 192
CO4: Colc . . . 4B 166
SS14: Bas . . . 9D 116
Thistledown Ct. SS14: Bas . . . 9D 116
Thistle Mead IG10: Lou . . . 2N 91
Thistley Cl. CM9: Gold . . . 3K 201
SS9: Lgh S . . . 2E 136
Thistley Cres. CB11: Rick G . . . 2C 216
THISTLEY GREEN . . . 1K 193 (6D 14)
Felsted . . . 2K 23
Thistley Grn. Rd. CM7: Brain . . . 1K 193
(not continuous)
Thistly Rd. CM9: Tol . . . 9K 225
Thoby La. CM15: Mount . . . 8M 83 (5G 33)
Thomas Bata Av. RM18: E Til . . . 2K 157
Thomas Bell Rd. CO6: E Col . . . 8B 198
Thomas Cl. CM2: Chelm . . . 8A 60
CM15: Brtwd . . . 8H 97
Thomas Ct. CO1: Colc . . . 8B 166
Thomas Dr. SS8: Can I . . . 9E 134
Thomas England Ho. *RM7: Romf* . . . *1B 126*
(off Waterloo Gdns.)
Thomasin Rd. SS13: Bas . . . 6K 117
Thomas Lodge E17: Lon . . . 9B 106
Thomas More St. E1: Lon . . . 7C 38
Thomas Rd. CO15: Clac S . . . 9H 185
SS13: Pits . . . 8M 117
Thomas Sims Ct. RM12: Rain . . . 8F 126
Thomas St. CO7: B'sea . . . 7E 182
Thomas Wakley Cl. CO4: Colc . . . 2N 165
Thompson Av. CO3: Colc . . . 9G 165
SS8: Can I . . . 2M 151
Thompson Cl. IG1: Ilf . . . 4B 124
Thompson Rd. RM9: Dag . . . 5L 125
Thompson's La. IG10: Lou . . . 8G 76
THONG . . . 5J 47
Thong La. DA12: Grav, Shorne . . . 5J 47
Thorington Av. SS7: Had . . . 9K 119
Thorington Cl. CM77: Gt N . . . 2C 204
Thorington Rd. SS6: Ray . . . 6N 119
THORINGTON STREET . . . 1F 17
Thorins Ga. CM3: S Fer . . . 2J 103
THORLEY . . . 2J 21
Thorley Hill CM23: Bis S . . . 1K 21
Thorley La. CM23: Thor . . . 2J 21
(Thorley)
CM23: Thor . . . 1J 21
(Thorley Houses)
Thorley Rd. RM16: Grays . . . 8K 145
THORLEY STREET . . . 2K 21
Thornberry Av. CO16: Wee . . . 5D 178
Thornborough Av. CM3: S Fer . . . 1L 103
Thornbridge SS7: Ben . . . 2B 134
Thornbrook CM16: N Wea . . . 4B 66
Thornbury Cl. EN11: Hod . . . 1B 52
Thornbury Ho. *RM3: Romf* . . . *2H 111*
(off Bridgwater Wlk.)
Thornbury Rd. CO15: Clac S . . . 9K 185
Thornbush SS15: Lain . . . 9N 115
Thorncroft CB10: Saf W . . . 3E 218
RM11: Horn . . . 1F 126
Thorndale SS7: Thund . . . 8H 119
Thorndales CM14: War . . . 1G 112
Thorndene SE28: Lon . . . 7G 141
Thorndon App. CM13: Heron . . . 4M 113
Thorndon Av. CM13: W H'dn . . . 8M 113 (3G 41)
Thorndon Cl. CO16: Clac S . . . 9E 184
Thorndon Country Pk. . . . 3K 113
Thorndon Country Pk. Vis. Cen. . . . 3K 113
Thorndon Ga. CM13: Ingve . . . 2M 113
Thorndon Pk. Cl. SS9: Lgh S . . . 1B 136
Thorndon Pk. Cres. SS9: Lgh S . . . 1A 136
Thorndon Pk. Dr. SS9: Lgh S . . . 1A 136
Thorne Cl. E11: Lon . . . 6D 122
Thorne Rd. CO5: K'dn . . . 3J 211
Thorney Bay Pk. SS8: Can I . . . 3F 150
Thorney Bay Rd. SS8: Can I . . . 2F 150 (6E 42)
Thorneycroft Dr. EN3: Enf . . . 7A 76
Thornford Gdns. SS2: Sth S . . . 1L 137
Thornham Gro. E15: Lon . . . 7D 122
Thornhill CM3: Pur . . . 8K 215
CM16: N Wea . . . 5A 66
SS9: Lgh S . . . 2D 136
Thornhill Cl. CO13: Walt . . . 7J 181
Thornhill Gdns. E10: Lon . . . 4B 122
IG11: Bark . . . 9D 124
Thornhill Rd. E10: Lon . . . 4B 122
N1: Lon . . . 5A 38
Thorn La. RM13: Rain . . . 2H 143
Thornridge CM14: Brtwd . . . 7E 96
Thorns, The CM15: Kel H . . . 9B 82
Thorns Way CO14: Walt . . . 6K 181
Thornton Dr. CO4: Colc . . . 5N 165
Thornton Pl. CM4: Stock . . . 7N 85
Thornton Rd. CM6: L Can . . . 2F 224
E11: Lon . . . 4D 122
IG1: Ilf . . . 6A 124
Thorntons CM13: Ingve . . . 3M 113
Thornton's Farm Av. RM7: Rush G . . . 3A 126
Thornton Way SS15: Lain . . . 9J 115
THORNWOOD . . . 2G 65
Thornwood CO4: Colc . . . 3N 165
Thornwood Cl. CO5: W Mer . . . 3D 228
E18: Lon . . . 6H 107
THORNWOOD COMMON . . . 4H 65 (2J 31)
Thornwood Ct. SS9: Lgh S . . . 9C 120
Thornwood Ho. IG9: Buck H . . . 6L 91
Thornwood Rd.
CM16: Epp, Thorn . . . 8G 64 (3J 31)
Thorogood Gdns. E15: Lon . . . 7E 122
Thorogood Way RM13: Rain . . . 1C 142
Thorold Rd. IG1: Ilf . . . 4A 124
Thorolds SS16: Van . . . 3F 132
Thoroughgood Rd. CO15: Clac S . . . 1K 189
THORPE BAY . . . 6F 138 (5A 44)
Thorpe Bay Gdns. SS1: Sth S . . . 8E 138
Thorpe Bay Station (Rail) . . . 6F 138 (5A 44)
Thorpe Bold CM13: Hut . . . 4A 98
Thorpe Cl. SS5: Hock . . . 3E 120
SS12: W'fd . . . 1N 117
THORPE CROSS . . . 6A 180 (1F 29)
Thorpedale Gdns. IG2: Ilf . . . 8N 107
IG6: Ilf . . . 8A 108
Thorpedene Av. SS5: Hull . . . 6L 103
Thorpedene Gdns. SS3: Shoe . . . 7H 139
Thorpe Esplanade
SS1: Shoe, Sth S . . . 8D 138 (5A 44)
Thorpe Gdns. SS5: Hock . . . 3E 120
THORPE GREEN . . . 3J 179 (7D 18)
Shoeburyness . . . 7K 139
Thorpe Hall Av. SS1: Sth S . . . 5E 138 (4A 44)
Thorpe Hall Cl. SS1: Sth S . . . 6E 138
Thorpe Hall Rd. E17: Lon . . . 5C 106
THORPE-LE-SOKEN . . . 5L 179 (7E 18)
Thorpe-le-Soken Station (Rail) . . . 7K 179 (1D 28)
Thorpe Lodge RM11: Horn . . . 1J 127
Thorpe Pk. La. CO16: T Sok . . . 7L 179 (1E 28)
(not continuous)
Thorpe Rd. CO13: Walt . . . 6A 180 (1E 28)
CO15: Clac S . . . 7K 185 (3D 28)
CO16: Clac S, L Cla . . . 4L 185 (3D 28)
CO16: T Sok, Wee . . . 5D 178 (7C 18)
CO16: Ten, T Sok . . . 1D 178 (6C 18)
E7: Lon . . . 6F 122
E17: Lon . . . 6C 106
IG11: Bark . . . 9C 124
SS5: Hock . . . 3E 120
Thorpe Wlk. CO4: Colc . . . 8F 166
Thorp Leas SS8: Can I . . . 3H 151
THORRINGTON . . . 9F 176 (1K 27)
Thorrington Bold CM13: Hut . . . 4N 97
Thorrington Cross SS14: Bas . . . 9D 116
Thorrington Rd.
CO7: Frat, Gt Ben . . . 7G 177 (1K 27)
CO16: L Cla . . . 2G 184
Thorrington Tide Mill . . . 2D 182 (2K 27)
Thors Oak SS17: Stan H . . . 3N 147
Thracian Cl. CO2: Colc . . . 4H 173
Thrapston Ho. *RM3: Romf* . . . *2J 111*
(off Dagnam Pk. Dr.)
Threadneedle St. CM1: Chelm . . . 9K 59
CO7: Ded . . . 1L 161
Three Acres CO16: St O . . . 9M 183
Three Colts La. E2: Lon . . . 6C 38
Three Crowns Rd. CO4: Colc . . . 5M 165
Three Gates Cl. CO9: Hals . . . 6J 207
Three Gates Rd. DA3: Fawk . . . 7D 46
Three Horseshoes Rd. CM19: H'low . . . 5A 54
Three Mile Hill CM2: Chelm . . . 8K 71 (3K 33)
CM4: Chelm, Marg, Writ . . . 8K 71 (3J 33)
Thremhall Av.
CM22: Bis S, Stan Apt . . . 9E 220 (1A 22)
CM22: Stan Apt, Tak . . . 7M 221 (7C 12)
CM24: Stan Apt . . . 9E 220 (1B 22)
Threshelford SS16: Bas . . . 2A 132
Threshelfords Bus. Pk. CO5: Fee . . . 1M 211
Thresher Ri. CM77: Gt N . . . 8E 192
THRESHERS BUSH . . . 4N 55 (7A 22)
Threshers End CO3: S'way . . . 1E 172
Thrift Grn. CM13: Brtwd . . . 9K 97
Thrifts Hall Farm M. CM16: They B . . . 7E 78
Thrifts Mead CM16: They B . . . 7D 78
THRIFT, THE . . . 6A 4
Thrift Wood CM3: Bick . . . 9E 74
Thrimley La. CM23: Farnh . . . 6J 11
THRIPLOW . . . 2G 5
Thriplow Rd. SG8: Fow, Thri . . . 2G 5
THROCKING . . . 3B 10
Throcking La. SG9: Thro . . . 3C 10
Throwley Cl. SS13: Pits . . . 1K 133
Throws Cnr. CM6: Steb . . . 6D 212 (7H 13)
Thrushdale CO15: Clac S . . . 7K 185
THUNDERSLEY . . . 9F 118 (3E 42)
Thundersley Chu. Rd. SS7: Ben . . . 1D 134
(not continuous)
Thundersley Gro. SS7: Thund . . . 1F 134
Thundersley Oaks Nature Pk. . . . 8E 118
Thundersley Pk. Rd. SS7: Ben . . . 4D 134
THUNDRIDGE . . . 3C 20
Thurgood Rd. EN11: Rye P . . . 3A 52
Thurlby Cl. IG8: Wfd G . . . 2M 107
Thurlestone Av. IG3: Bark, Ilf . . . 6E 124
Thurloe Gdns. RM1: Romf . . . 1D 126 (3A 40)
Thurloe Wlk. RM17: Grays . . . 1K 155
Thurlow Cl. E4: Lon . . . 3C 106
Thurlow Dr. SS1: Sth S . . . 6D 138
Thurlow Gdns. IG6: Ilf . . . 3C 108
Thurlow Rd. CB9: Gt Wra . . . 1K 7
CB9: Wthfld . . . 1H 7
Thurlston Cl. CO4: Colc . . . 6D 166
Thurlstone SS7: Thund . . . 1J 135
Thurrock Bus. Cen. RM20: W Thur . . . 4C 154
Thurrock Commercial Cen.
RM15: Ave . . . 9K 143
Thurrock Ent. Cen. RM17: Grays . . . 4K 155
THURROCK LAKESIDE . . . 1D 154 (1E 46)
Thurrock Lakeside Shop. Cen.
RM20: W Thur . . . 1E 154
Thurrock Mus. . . . 3L 155 (1F 47)
Thurrock Pk. Way RM18: Til . . . 5N 155
Thurrock Yacht Club . . . 5L 155
Thurso Cl. RM3: H Wood . . . 3M 111
Thurstable Cl. CM9: Tol . . . 7L 225
Thurstable Rd. CM9: Tol . . . 7K 225
Thurstable Way CM9: Tol . . . 7L 225
Thurstans CM19: H'low . . . 8A 54
Thurston Av. SS2: Sth S . . . 5C 138
Thwaite Cl. DA8: Eri . . . 4A 152
Thyme M. CM8: Wthm . . . 4B 230
Thyme Rd. CO5: Tip . . . 6C 226
Thynne Rd. CM11: Bill . . . 6L 99
Tiberius Cl. CO4: Colc . . . 2B 166
Tiberius Gdns. CM8: Wthm . . . 7B 230
Tickenhall Dr. CM17: H'low . . . 4J 55
Tickfield Av. SS2: Sth S . . . 4L 137
Tickford Cl. SE2: Lon . . . 9H 141
Tidelea Twr. *SE28: Lon* . . . *9B 140*
(off Erebus Dr.)
Tideswell Cl. CM7: Brain . . . 4M 193
Tideway CM9: Mal . . . 8D 214
Tidings Hill CO9: Hals . . . 7K 207 (4F 15)
Tidlock Ho. *SE28: Lon* . . . *9C 140*
(off Erebus Dr.)
Tidworth Av. SS11: Runw . . . 6M 101
Tidy's La. CM16: Epp . . . 8G 64
Tiffin Dr. CO5: Tip . . . 6E 226
Tighfield Wlk. CM3: S Fer . . . 3J 103
Tilburg Rd. SS8: Can I . . . 1G 150
(not continuous)
TILBURY . . . 7B 156 (2H 47)
Tilbury Fort . . . 9E 156 (3H 47)
Tilbury Go-Karting Track . . . 6B 156
TILBURY GREEN . . . 8F 216 (5C 8)
Tilbury Hall Chase CO9: Til C . . . 6C 8
TILBURY JUXTA CLARE . . . 5D 8
Tilbury Leisure Cen. . . . 7D 156
Tilbury Mead CM18: H'low . . . 5F 54
Tilbury Rd. CM13: W H'dn . . . 8A 114 (3G 41)
CO9: Gt Yel . . . 2D 206 (6D 8)
CO9: Ridg . . . 7D 216 (5C 8)
CO9: Til C . . . 5D 8
E10: Lon . . . 2C 122
Tilbury Town Station (Rail) . . . 7B 156 (2G 47)
Tildesley Cl. CO13: Walt . . . 8D 180
Tile Barn La. CO11: Law . . . 6B 162 (3J 17)
TILEGATE GREEN . . . 7A 22
Tilegate Rd. CM18: H'low . . . 5E 54
Tile Ho. Rd. CO6: Gt Hork . . . 8J 159
Tilehurst Point SE2: Lon . . . 9J 141
(Blewbury Ho.)
SE2: Lon . . . 9H 141
(Tavy Bri.)
TILEKILN GREEN . . . 1B 22
Tile Kiln La. DA5: Bex . . . 4A 46
(not continuous)
Tile Works La. CM3: Ret C . . . 9M 87
TILKEY . . . 2K 197 (7H 15)
Tilkey Rd. CO6: Cogg . . . 1K 197 (7H 15)
Tillet Pl. RM18: Til . . . 6D 156
TILLINGHAM . . . 2K 225 (3E 36)
Tillingham Bold CM13: Hut . . . 4N 97
Tillingham Ct. EN9: Wal A . . . 3G 76
Tillingham Grn. SS15: Lain . . . 9J 115
Tillingham Rd.
CM0: Ashel, Deng, T'ham . . . 4H 225 (4D 36)
Tillingham Way SS6: Ray . . . 4G 119
Tillotson Rd. IG1: Ilf . . . 2N 123
Tillwicks Cl. CO6: E Col . . . 7B 198
Tillwicks Rd. CM18: H'low . . . 4E 54 (7H 21)
Tilney Ct. IG9: Buck H . . . 8G 91
Tilney Dr. IG9: Buck H . . . 8G 91
Tilney Rd. RM9: Dag . . . 8L 125
(not continuous)
Tilney Turn SS16: Van . . . 2F 132
(not continuous)
Tilston Cl. E11: Lon . . . 5F 122
TILTY . . . 5E 12
Tilty Chu. Rd. CM6: Tilty . . . 5F 13
Timber Ct. RM17: Grays . . . 4K 155
Timberdene Av. IG6: Ilf . . . 5B 108
Timber Hill CO1: Colc . . . 9C 166
Timberlog Cl. SS14: Bas . . . 9F 116
Timberlog La. SS14: Bas . . . 9F 116 (3B 42)
Timbermans Vw. SS16: Van . . . 2G 132
Timbers Cl. CM77: Gt N . . . 1B 204
Time Sq. SS14: Bas . . . 1B 132
Timothy Ho. *DA18: Eri* . . . *9K 141*
(off Kale Rd.)
Timsons La. CM2: Chelm . . . 7N 59
Tindall Cl. RM3: H Wood . . . 6K 111
Tindal Sq. CM1: Chelm . . . 9K 59
Tindal St. CM1: Chelm . . . 9K 59
TINDON END . . . 1F 13
Tindon End Rd.
CB10: Gt Sam, L Sam . . . 3H 205 (1F 13)
Tine Rd. IG7: Chig . . . 2D 108
(not continuous)
Tinker Av. CM7: Weth . . . 2A 14
Tinkers La. CM19: Roy . . . 8J 53
Tinker's La. SS4: R'fd . . . 7L 121
Tinker St. CO12: R'sy . . . 7A 208 (4E 18)
Tinkler Side SS14: Bas . . . 9C 116
Tinnocks La. CM0: St La . . . 1C 36
Tintagel Ct. RM11: Horn . . . 3L 127
Tintagel Way CM9: Mal . . . 8A 214
Tintern Av. SS0: Wclf S . . . 5H 137
Tiplers Bri. CM11: Rams H . . . 3C 100
Tippersfield SS7: Ben . . . 2E 134
Tippett Cl. CO4: Colc . . . 9E 166
Tipps Cross La. CM15: Hook E . . . 4E 82 (4E 32)
Tipps Cross Mead CM15: Hook E . . . 5E 82
TIP'S CROSS . . . 4E 82 (4E 32)
TIPTREE . . . 6D 226 (3K 25)
Tiptree Cl. E4: Lon . . . 9C 90
RM11: Horn . . . 3L 127
SS9: Lgh S . . . 2E 136
Tiptree Ct. CM13: Hut . . . 4N 97
Tiptree Cres. IG5: Ilf . . . 6N 107
Tiptree Gro. SS12: W'fd . . . 9L 101
Tiptree Hall La. CO5: Tip . . . 8B 226
TIPTREE HEATH . . . 8A 226 (4K 25)
Tiptree Heath Nature Reserve . . . 9A 226
Tiptree Rd. CM8: Gt Br . . . 6H 205 (4J 25)
CM8: W Bis . . . 2L 229 (5H 25)
Tiptree (Tolleshunt Knights) Towermill
. . . 5A 226 (3K 25)
Tiree Chase SS12: W'fd . . . 2N 117
Titania Cl. CO4: Colc . . . 8F 166
Titan Ind. Est. RM17: Grays . . . 2K 155
Titan Rd. RM17: Grays . . . 3K 155
Titan Way RM17: Grays . . . 3K 155
Tithe Cl. CM8: Wthm . . . 4B 230
Tithelands CM19: H'low . . . 6M 53
Tithe, The SS12: W'fd . . . 1J 117
Titley Cl. E4: Lon . . . 2A 106

Titmuss Av. SE28: Lon 7G **141**
Titus Way CO4: Colc 1B **166**
Tiverton Av. IG5: Ilf 7N **107**
Tiverton Gro. RM3: Romf 2L **111**
Tobruk Rd. CM1: Chelm 5H **59**
CO2: Colc 3L **173**
Toddbrook CM19: H'low 4A **54**
Todd Cl. RM13: Rain 4H **143**
Toft Av. RM17: Grays 2N **155**
Tofts Chase CM3: L Bad 6L **61** (7E **24**)
Tofts Wlk. CM7: Brain 5H **193**
Toga Cl. CO2: King 4H **173**
Tog La. CO6: Gt Hork 5G **159** (3D **16**)
Tokely Rd. CO7: Frat 3F **176**
Tolbut Ct. RM1: Romf 1D **126**
Toldish Hall Rd. CO9: Gt Map 2F **15**
Toledo Cl. SS1: Sth S 6N **137**
Toledo Rd. SS1: Sth S 6N **137**
TOLLESBURY 8K 225 (6C 26)
Tollesbury Cl. SS12: W'fd 1M **117**
Tollesbury Ct. CM13: Hut 4N **97**
Tollesbury Gdns. IG6: Ilf 7C **108**
Tollesbury Rd. CM9: Tol, Tol D 8H **225** (6B **26**)
TOLLESHUNT D'ARCY 3K 227 (6B 26)
Tolleshunt D'arcy Rd. CM9: Tol M 6A **26**
TOLLESHUNT KNIGHTS 8F 226 (4A 26)
TOLLESHUNT MAJOR 6A 26
Tollgate SS7: Had 9J **119**
Tollgate Cen., The CO3: S'way 1D **172**
Tollgate Ct. CO3: S'way 9D **164**
Tollgate Dr. CO3: S'way 9C **164**
Tollgate E. CO3: S'way 9D **164**
Tollgate Rd. CO3: S'way 9D **164** (6C **16**)
E16: Lon 7F **39**
Tollgate Rdbt. CO3: S'way 9C **164**
Tollgate W. CO3: S'way 1C **172** (6C **16**)
Tollhouse Way N19: Lon 4A **38**
Tolliday Cl. CO7: W'hoe 4G **175**
Tollington Pk. N19: Lon 4A **38**
Tollington Rd. N7: Lon 5A **38**
Tollington Way N7: Lon 4A **38**
Tolworth Gdns. RM6: Chad H 9J **109**
Tolworth Pde. RM6: Chad H 9K **109**
Tom Allen Arts Cen. 8D 122
Tom Groves Cl. E15: Lon 7D **122**
Tom Hood Cl. E15: Lon 7D **122**
Tomkins Cl. SS17: Stan H 2L **147**
Tomkyns La. RM14: Upm 6A **112** (2D **40**)
Tomlins Orchard IG11: Bark 1B **140**
Tomlyns Cl. CM13: Hut 5A **98**
Tom Mann Cl. IG11: Bark 1D **140**
Tom Oakman Cen. E4: Lon 8D **90**
Tom's La. CM7: F'fld 3A **200**
Tomswood Ct. IG6: Ilf 5B **108**
Tomswood Hill IG6: Ilf 3A **108** (2G **39**)
Tomswood Rd. IG7: Chig 3N **107** (2G **39**)
Tom Tit La.
CM9: Wdhm M, Wdhm W 2L **75** (2F **35**)
Tonbridge Rd. RM3: Romf 4H **111**
SS5: Hock 8E **104**
Tongres Rd. SS8: Can I 1G **150**
TONWELL 3B 20
Tony Webb Cl. CO4: Colc 3C **166**
Took Dr. CM3: S Fer 2J **103**
Tooley St. SE1: Lon 7B **38**
TOOT HILL 8D 66 (3A 32)
Toot Hill Rd.
CM5: Chip, G'sted, Toot 8D **66** (3A **32**)
Top Dartford Rd. BR8: Swan 5A **46**
DA2: Dart 5B **46**
Top Ho. Ri. E4: Lon 6C **90**
Toplands Av. RM15: Ave 8M **143**
TOPPESFIELD 7B 8
Toppesfield Av. SS12: W'fd 2K **117**
Toppesfield Rd.
CM7: F'fld, Top 3F **200** (2K **13**)
CO9: Gt Yel 4C **206** (7C **8**)
Top Rd. CB10: Wim 1E **12**
CM9: Tol K 4A **26**
CM9: Wdhm W 1F **35**
Tora Ct. IG9: Buck H 8J **91**
Torbitt Way IG2: Ilf 9E **108**
Tor Bryan CM4: Ing 7C **84**
Tor Gro. SE28: Lon 8D **140**
Torney Cl. SS16: Lang H 2H **131**
Toronto Av. E12: Lon 6M **123**
Toronto Rd. IG1: Ilf 3A **124**
RM18: Til 7C **156**
Torquay Cl. SS6: Ray 2K **119**
Torquay Dr. SS9: Lgh S 5D **136**
Torquay Gdns. IG4: Ilf 8K **107**
Torquay Rd. CM1: Chelm 6M **59**
Torrance Cl. RM11: Horn 3F **126**
Torrens Rd. E15: Lon 8F **122**
Torrens Sq. E15: Lon 8F **122**
Torriano Av. NW5: Lon 5A **38**
Torridge RM18: E Til 2L **157**
Torrington SS3: Shoe 6H **139**
Torrington Cl. CM1: Chelm 6N **59**
Torrington Dr. IG10: Lou 3B **92**
Torrington Gdns. IG10: Lou 3B **92**
Torrington Pl. W1: Lon 7A **38**
Torrington Rd. E18: Lon 7G **107**
RM8: Dag 3L **125**
Torsi Rd. SS8: Can I 2K **151**
Tortoiseshell Way CM7: Gt N 7G **192**
Tortosa Cl. CO2: Colc 2B **174**
Torver Cl. CM77: Gt N 2C **204**
TOTHAM HILL 8K 205 (5J 25)
Totham Hill Grn. CM9: Gt Tot 8K **205** (5J **25**)
Totlands Dr. CO15: Clac S 6K **185**
Tot La. CM23: Bchgr, Stan M 6C **220** (7A **12**)
Totman Cl. SS6: Ray 7K **119**
Totman Cres. SS6: Ray 7K **119**
Totnes Wlk. CM1: Chelm 5N **59**
TOTTENHAM 2B 38
Tottenham Ct. Rd. W1: Lon 6A **38**
Tottenham Court Road Station (Tube) 7A 38
TOTTENHAM HALE 3C 38
TOTTENHAM HALE GYRATORY 3B **38**
Tottenham Hale Station (Rail, Tube) 3C 38
Tottenham Hotspur F.C. (White Hart Lane) 2C 38
Tottenham La. N8: Lon 3A **38**
Totteridge Cl. CO16: Clac S 8H **185**
Totts La. SG2: Walk 5A **10**
Toucan Cl. SS3: Shoe 5J **139**
Toucan Way CO15: Clac S 7K **185**
SS16: Bas 3B **132**
Toulmin Rd. CM3: Hat P 2L **61**
Tourist Info. Cen.
Bexley 3A 46
Bexleyheath 3A 46
Bishop's Stortford 1A 22
(Birchanger Green Services)
Bishop's Stortford 1K 21
(Windhill)
Braintree 5H 193 (7C 14)
Brentwood 8G 96 (1E 40)
Chelmsford 9K 59 (1A 34)
Clacton-on-Sea 2K 189 (4D 28)
Colchester 8A 166 (6F 17)
Dedham 1M 161
Felixstowe 1K 19
Gravesend 3H 47
Great Dunmow 3L 203
Hertford 5B 20
Ilford 5A 124
Maldon 5B 214 (1H 35)
Parkeston 3J 209 (2H 19)
Redbridge 4A 124 (4G 39)
Saffron Walden 3C 218 (6B 6)
Southend-on-Sea 7M 137 (5K 43)
Sudbury 5J 9
Thurrock Services 1C 154 (1E 46)
Waltham Abbey 3C 76
Tovey Av. EN11: Rye P 3A **52**
Tovey Cl. EN9: Naze 2F **62**
Tower Av. CM1: Chelm 7H **59**
SS15: Lain 8L **115**
Tower Bri. SE1: Lon 7B **38**
Tower Bri. Rd. SE1: Lon 7B **38**
Tower Cvn. Pk. SS5: Hull 5L **103**
Tower Cen., The EN11: Hod 5A **52**
Tower Cl. CM16: N Wea 3B **66**
IG6: Ilf 3A **108**
Tower Ct. CM5: Chip 8L **67**
CM14: Brtwd 8F **96**
SS0: Wclf S 7K **137**
Tower Ct. M. SS0: Sth S, Wclf S 7K **137**
Tower Cut CO7: B'sea 7E **182**
Tower Est. CO16: P Bay 9D **182**
Towerfield Cl. SS3: Shoe 7J **139**
Towerfield Rd. SS3: Shoe 7J **139**
Towerfield Rd. Ind. Est. SS3: Shoe 7J **139**
Tower Gateway Station (DLR) 7B 38
Twr. Hamlets Rd. E7: Lon 6F **122**
E17: Lon 7A **106**
TOWER HILL 7B **38**
Tower Hill CM14: Brtwd 8F **96**
SG10: M Hud 2G **21**
Tower Hill Station (Tube) 7B 38
Tower M. E17: Lon 8A **106**
Tower Rd. CM1: Writ 1H **71**
CM16: Epp 9D **64**
CO7: W'hoe 4H **175**
CO15: Clac S 3J **189**
DA17: Belv 2A **152**
Tower Side SS5: Hull 4L **103**
Towers Rd. CM9: Mal 3E **214**
RM17: Grays 3M **155**
Towers, The CO15: Clac S 1L **189**
Tower St. CO7: B'sea 8E **182**
Town Cft. CM1: Chelm 6J **59**
Towneley Cotts. RM4: Stap A 7C **94**
Town End Fld. CM8: Wthm 7B **230**
Townfield CM6: Thax 8D **224**
Townfield Rd. SS4: R'fd 5L **121**
Townfield St. CM1: Chelm 8K **59**
Townfield Wlk. SS3: Gt W 2J **139**
Towngate Theatre 9B 116
Town Grn. Rd. SG8: Orw 1C **4**
Town Hall & Princes Theatre 1K 189
Town La. CB2: Pam 1K **5**
SG2: B'tn 7A **10**
Townley Ct. E15: Lon 8F **122**
Townley Rd. DA6: Bexh 3A **46**
Townmead Rd. EN9: Wal A 4C **76**
Town Quay IG11: Bark 1A **140**
Town Quay Wharf IG11: Bark 1A **140**
Town Rd. N9: Lon 1C **38**
Townsend Rd. CO5: Tip 4C **226** (3K **25**)
Town Sq. DA8: Eri 4C **152**
SS14: Bas 9B **116**
Town St. CB2: New 1G **5**
CM6: Thax 8C **224** (3F **13**)
Town, The EN2: Enf 6B **30**
Towse Cl. CO16: Clac S 8G **184**
Tracyes Rd. CM18: H'low 5G **54**
Traddles Ct. CM1: Chelm 5H **59**
Trader Rd. E6: Lon 6A **140**
Trafalgar Bus. Cen. IG11: Bark 4E **140**
Trafalgar Ct. CM7: Brain 4K **193**
DA8: Eri *5D* ***152***
(off Frobisher Rd.)
Trafalgar Pl. E11: Lon 8G **107**
Trafalgar Rd. CO3: S'way 8F **164**
CO15: Clac S 3J **189**
Trafalgar Rd. RM13: Rain 2D **142**
SS3: Shoe 7H **139**
Trafalgar Sq. SW1: Lon 7A **38**
Trafalgar Way CM7: Brain 4K **193**
CM12: Bill 3K **99**
Trafford Cl. E15: Lon 7B **122**
IG6: Ilf 3E **108**
Trafford Ho. SS9: Lgh S 4E **136**
Trajan Cl. CO4: Colc 1B **166**
Tramway Av. E15: Lon 9E **122**
Tranquil Ri. DA8: Eri 3C **152**
Trap's Hill IG10: Lou 2M **91** (6G **31**)
Traps Hill Cen. 3M 91
Travers Way SS13: Pits 9H **117**
Treacle Mine Rdbt. RM16: Grays, N Stif 9J **145**
Tredegar Rd. E3: Lon 6D **38**
Treebeard Copse CM3: S Fer 2H **103**
Tree Cl. CO15: Clac S 6K **185**
Treecot Dr. SS9: Lgh S 2E **136**
Treelawn Dr. SS9: Lgh S 2E **136**
Treelawn Gdns. SS9: Lgh S 2E **136**
Tree Top M. RM10: Dag 8B **126**
Tree Tops CM15: Brtwd 7F **96**
Treetops CO4: Colc 4B **166**
Treetops Ct. CO4: Colc 2N **165**
Treetops Vw. IG10: Lou 6K **91**
Trefgarne Rd. RM10: Dag 4M **125**
Trefoil Ho. *DA18: Eri* *9K* ***141***
(off Kale Rd.)
RM17: Grays 5L **155**
Tregelles Rd. EN11: Rye P 2A **52**
Trego Rd. E9: Lon 9A **122**
Trehearn Rd. IG6: Ilf 4C **108**
Trelawney Rd. IG6: Ilf 4C **108**
Trelawn Rd. E10: Lon 5C **122**
Trelawny Cl. E17: Lon 8B **106**
Trenance Gdns. IG3: Ilf 5F **124**
Trenchard Cres. CM1: Chelm 4M **59**
Trenchard Lodge CM1: Chelm 4M **59**
Trenders Av. SS6: Ray 1H **119**
Trenham Av. SS13: Pits 8K **117**
Trent RM18: E Til 2L **157**
Trent Av. RM14: Upm 1A **128**
Trentbridge Cl. IG6: Ilf 3E **108**
Trent Cl. CM0: Bur C 2C **196**
SS12: W'fd 1L **117**
Trent Pk. (Country Pk.) 6A 30
Trent Rd. CM1: Chelm 6E **58**
CM8: Wthm 5B **230**
IG9: Buck H 7H **91**
Trescoe Gdns. RM5: Col R 2A **110**
Tresco Gdns. IG3: Ilf 4F **124**
Tresco Way SS12: W'fd 2N **117**
Tresham Rd. IG11: Bark 9E **124**
Treswell Rd. RM9: Dag 1K **141**
Trevelyan Av. E12: Lon 6M **123**
Trevelyan Cl. DA1: Dart 9K **153**
Trevelyan Rd. E15: Lon 6F **122**
Trevera Ct. EN11: Hod 4A **52**
Treviria Av. SS8: Can I 1J **151**
Trevithick Dr. DA1: Dart 9K **153** (3C **46**)
Trevor Cl. CM12: Bill 9H **99**
Trevor Rd. IG8: Wfd G 4G **107**
Trevose Rd. E17: Lon 5D **106**
Trewsbury Ho. SE2: Lon 8J **141**
Trews Gdns. CO5: K'dn 2K **211**
Triangle Shop. Cen. CO13: Frin S 7J **181**
Triangle, The IG11: Bark 8B **124**
SS16: Lang H *2K* ***131***
(off High Rd.)
Trianon Ct. SS13: Pits 9K **117**
Trident Ind. Est. EN11: Rye P 5C **52**
Trillo Ct. IG2: Ilf 2D **124**
Trimble Cl. CM4: Ing 5D **84**
Trimley Cl. CO16: Clac S 9F **184**
SS14: Bas 8D **116**
TRIMLEY LOWER STREET 1J 19
TRIMLEY ST MARY 1J 19
Trimley Station (Rail) 1K 19
TRIMS GREEN 3J 21
Trindehay SS15: Lain 1N **131**
Trinder Way SS12: W'fd 1J **117**
Tring Cl. IG2: Ilf 9C **108**
RM3: Romf 1K **111**
Tring Gdns. RM3: Romf 1J **111**
Tring Grn. RM3: Romf 1J **111**
Tring Wlk. RM3: Romf 1J **111**
Trinidad Gdns. RM10: Dag 9B **126**
Trinity Av. IP11: Felix 1K **19**
SS0: Wclf S 7K **137**
Trinity Cl. CM2: Chelm 8M **59**
CM11: Bill 1L **115**
CO5: W Mer 2C **228**
CO7: W'hoe 5J **175**
CO11: Mist 5J **163**
E11: Lon 4E **122**
SS6: Ray 6L **119**
SS15: Lain 9L **115**
Trinity Ct. CO9: Hals 5K **207**
Trinity Ho. *CO9: Hals* *4J* ***207***
(off Trinity St.)
Trinity M. CO5: W Mer 2C **228**
Trinity Rd. CM2: Chelm 9M **59**
CM11: Bill 1L **115**
CO9: Hals 5J **207**
CO11: Mist 5J **163** (3A **18**)
IG6: Ilf 7B **108**
SS2: Sth S 5A **138**
SS6: Ray 6L **119** (2F **43**)
Trinity Sq. CM3: S Fer 1L **103**
CO1: Colc 8N **165**
Trinity St. CO1: Colc 8N **165**
CO9: Hals 5J **207** (3F **15**)
Trinity Wood Rd. SS5: Hock 8F **104**
Trinovantian Way CM7: Brain 6J **193**
Tripat Cl. SS17: Fob 9E **132**
Trippier Ho. *CO4: Colc* *8E* ***166***
(off Blackthorn Av.)
Tripton Rd. CM18: H'low 4D **54** (7H **21**)
Tristram Cl. E17: Lon 7D **106**
Triton Way SS7: Thund 9G **119**
Triumph Av. CO15: Jay 5C **188**
Triumph Cl. CO4: Colc 1E **174**
RM16: Chaf H 2F **154**
Triumph Ho. IG11: Bark 3F **140**
Trojan Ter. CM21: Saw 1K **51**
Troon Cl. SE28: Lon 6J **141**
Troopers Dr. RM3: Romf 1H **111**
Trotters Fld. CM7: Brain 5K **193**
Trotters Rd. CM18: H'low 6F **54** (7J **21**)
Trot Wood IG7: Chig 3C **108**
Trotwood Cl. CM1: Chelm 4G **58**
CM15: Shenf 7H **97**
Troubridge Cl. CM3: S Fer 1M **103**
Trowbridge Rd. RM3: Romf 3H **111**
Troys Chase CM3: F'std 3D **24**
Troys La. CM8: Fau 3E **24**
TRUELOVES INTERCHANGE 7B **84** (5G **33**)
Trueloves La. CM4: Ing 6A **84** (5G **33**)
Truman Bldg., The CO6: W Ber 3G **165**
Truman Cl. SS15: Lain 9J **115**
Trumpeter Ct. CM12: Bill 5H **99**
Trumpington Rd. E7: Lon 6F **122**
Trunette Rd. CO15: Clac S 1G **189**
Trunnions, The SS4: R'fd 6L **121**
Truro Cres. SS6: Ray 2J **119**
Truro Gdns. IG1: Ilf 2L **123**
Truro Rd. N22: Lon 2A **38**
Truro Wlk. RM3: Romf 3G **111**
Trusses Rd. CM0: Brad S 7B **194** (1E **36**)
Truston's Gdns. RM11: Horn 2E **126**
Tryfan Cl. IG4: Ilf 9K **107**
Tryon Ct. CO9: Hals 5J **207**
Tucker Dr. CM8: Wthm 7C **230**
Tuck Rd. RM13: Rain 8E **126**
Tudor Av. CM1: Chelm 8J **59**
RM2: Romf 7E **110**
SS17: Stan H 1N **147**
Tudor Chambers SS13: Pits 1J **133**
Tudor Cl. CM4: Ing 7C **84**
CM8: Wthm 7C **230**
CM15: Shenf 5K **97**
CO7: B'sea 5D **182**
CO14: Walt 4N **181**
CO15: Jay 3E **188**
IG7: Chig 1N **107**
IG8: Wfd G 2H **107**
SS6: Ray 5M **119**
SS7: Thund 1F **134**
SS9: Lgh S 8B **120**
Tudor Ct. CM21: Saw 1K **51**
CO5: W Mer 2C **228**
RM3: H Wood 3M **111**
SS15: Bas 5A **116**
Tudor Cres. IG6: Ilf 3A **108**
Tudor Dr. RM2: Romf 8E **110**
Tudor Gdns. RM2: Romf 8E **110**
RM14: Upm 4N **127**
SS3: Shoe 7H **139**
SS9: Lgh S 3C **136**
Tudor Grn. CO15: Jay 3D **188**
Tudor Mans. SS13: Pits 1J **133**
Tudor M. RM1: Romf 9D **110**
SS9: Lgh S 7B **120**
Tudor Pde. CO15: Jay 3E **188**
RM6: Chad H 2J **125**
Tudor Pl. CM3: May 8L **213**
Tudor Rd. E4: Lon 3B **106**
IG11: Bark 1E **140**
SS0: Wclf S 4K **137**
SS8: Can I 2D **150**
SS9: Lgh S 8B **120**
Tudor Rose Cl. CO3: S'way 8D **164**
Tudor Wlk. SS12: W'fd 9H **101**
Tudor Way EN9: Wal A 3D **76**
SS5: Hock 3E **120**
SS12: W'fd 9H **101**
Tudwick Rd. CM9: Tol M 5A **26**
CO5: Tip 8E **226**
TUFNELL PARK 5A 38
Tufnell Park Station (Tube) 5A 38
Tufnell Way CO4: Colc 5K **165**
Tufted Cl. CM77: Gt N 3C **204**
Tufter Rd. IG7: Chig 2E **108**
Tufton Rd. E4: Lon 1A **106**
Tugboat St. SE28: Lon 9D **140**
Tugby Pl. CM1: Chelm 5G **59**
Tukes Way CB11: Saf W 6E **218**
Tulip Cl. CM1: Chelm 4N **59**
CM15: Pil H 4E **96**
RM3: Romf 3G **111**
Tulip Gdns. E4: Lon 9D **90**
IG1: Ilf 8A **124**
Tulip Wlk. CO4: Colc 8D **166**
Tulip Way CO16: Clac S 9G **184**
Tumbler Rd. CM18: H'low 4F **54**
TUMBLER'S GREEN 6F 15
Tumulus Way CO2: Colc 4G **173**
Tunbridge Av. SS2: Sth S 4M **137**
Tunbridge Rd. SS2: Sth S 4L **137**
Tunfield Rd. EN11: Hod 2B **52**
Tunnel App. SE16: Lon 7C **38**
Tunnel Est. RM20: W Thur 2C **154**
Tunnmeade CM20: H'low 2F **54**
Tunstall Av. IG6: Ilf 3F **108**
Tunstall Cl. CO16: St O 8N **183**
SS13: Pits 1K **133**
Tupelo Rd. E10: Lon 4B **122**

Tupman Cl. CM1: Chelm 5F 58
Tuppy St. SE28: Lon 9B 140
Turkey Cock La.
CO3: Eig G, S'way 1N 171 (6B 16)
CO6: Eig G 8A 164 (6B 16)
Turkey Oaks CM1: Chelm 8L 59
Turkey St. EN1: Enf 5C 30
EN3: Enf 5C 30
Turkey Street Station (Rail) 5C 30
Turnage Rd. RM8: Dag 3K 125
Turnbury Cl. SE28: Lon 6J 141
Turner Av. CO11: Law 3G 163
Turner Cl. CM77: Bla N 4B 194
CO7: W'hoe 5J 175
SS3: Shoe 6K 139
Turner Rd. CO4: Colc 3N 165 (5E 16)
E17: Lon 7C 106
Turners Cl. CM5: Chip 8K 67
Turners Ct. RM4: Abr 2G 93
Turner's Hill EN8: Chesh 3C 30
TURNFORD 2D 30
Turnip Lodge La. CO7: Elms 8J 167 (6H 17)
Turnors CM19: H'low 3B 54
Turnpike Cl. CO4: A'lgh, L'ham 9E 160
Turnpike Hill CB9: Wthfld 2H 7
Turnpike La. N8: Lon 3A 38
RM18: W Til 2F 156 (1H 47)
Turnpike Lane Station (Tube) 3A 38
Turnpike Pl. CM7: Brain 5J 193
Turnstone End CO4: Colc 7F 166
Turold Rd. SS17: Stan H 1N 147
Turp Av. RM16: Grays 9M 145
Turpin Av. RM5: Col R 3M 109
Turpin Cl. EN3: Enf 7A 76
Turpin La. DA8: Eri 4E 152
Turpins SS14: Bas 8D 116
Turpins Av. CO15: Clac S 8N 185
Turpins Cl. CO15: Clac S 8N 185
Turpins La. CO13: Kir S, Walt 6G 181
Turpin's La. IG8: Wfd G 2M 107
Turret Ct. CM5: Chip 8L 67
Turstan Rd. CM8: Wthm 7B 230
Tusser Cl. CM8: Riven 3G 25
Tusser Ct. CM2: Gt Bad 2E 72
Tusset M. CO3: S'way 8F 164
Tutors Way CM3: S Fer 1L 103
Tuttlebee La. IG9: Buck H 8G 91
Tuttleby Cotts. RM4: Abr 6K 93
Twain Ter. SS12: W'fd 2K 117
Twankhams All. CM16: Epp 9F 64
Tweed RM18: E Til 2L 157
Tweedale Ct. E15: Lon 7C 122
Tweed Cl. CO9: Hals 6J 207
Tweed Glen RM1: Romf 4B 110
Tweed Grn. RM1: Romf 4B 110
Tweed Way RM1: Romf 4B 110
Twelve Acres CM7: Brain 5M 193
Twentyman Cl. IG8: Wfd G 2G 107
Twickenham Rd. E11: Lon 4C 122
Twigg Cl. DA8: Eri 5C 152
Twine Cl. IG11: Bark 3G 141
Twining Rd. CO3: S'way 2F 172
Twin Oaks CM2: Chelm 7B 60
TWINSTEAD 7J 9
Twinstead SS12: W'fd 1M 117
TWINSTEAD GREEN 7H 9
Twin Tumps Way SE28: Lon 7F 140
Twitten La. CM2: Gall 8C 72
Twitty Fee CM3: Dan 1G 75 (2E 34)
(not continuous)
Twyford Av. SS3: Gt W 2L 139
Twyford Rd. IG1: Ilf 7B 124
Twyzel Rd. SS8: Can I 1J 151
Tyburn Hill CO6: Wak C, Whi C 6A 196 (4K 15)
Tyburns, The CM13: Hut 8M 97
Tycehurst Hill IG10: Lou 3M 91
Tydeman Cl. CO3: S'way 2D 172
TYE COMMON 8H 99 (1J 41)
Tye Comn. Rd. CM12: Bill, L Bur 1F 114 (1H 41)
Tyed Cft. CO3: S'way 9E 164
Tyefields SS13: Pits 8K 117 (3C 42)
TYE GREEN 5M 85 (5K 33)
Elsenham 3J 221 (6C 12)
Good Easter 5G 23
Great Sampford 1E 12
Harlow 5E 54 (7H 21)
Hawbush Green 2E 194 (1D 24)
Tye Grn. CM18: H'low 5D 54
CO10: Glem 1G 9
Tye Grn. Rd. CM22: Else 4L 199 (6B 12)
Tye Grn. Village CM18: H'low 6E 54
Tye Hall Chase CM1: Rox 2K 217
Tyehurst Cres. CO4: Colc 5C 166
Tyelands CM12: Bill 8H 99
Tye La. CO7: W'hoe 3L 175 (7H 17)
Tye Rd. CO7: A'lgh, Elms 8L 167 (6H 17)
Tye Rd., The CO7: Gt Ben 6N 177 (1B 28)
Tye, The CM3: E Han 2C 88 (4D 34)
CM4: Marg 3L 85 (4K 33)
Tyle Grn. RM11: Horn 8J 111
Tylehurst Gdns. IG1: Ilf 7B 124
Tyler Av. CO16: Clac S 1F 188
SS15: Lain 9L 115
Tyler Gro. DA1: Dart 9K 153
(not continuous)
Tylers CB10: Sew E 6D 6
Tylers Av. CM12: Bill 3K 99
SS1: Sth S 7M 137
TYLERS CAUSEWAY 1A 30
Tylers C'way. SG13: New S 1A 30
Tylers Cl. CM2: Chelm 4C 72
IG10: Lou 6L 91
Tylers Ct. *E17: Lon* *8A 106*
(off Westbury Rd.)
Tylers Cres. RM12: Horn 7G 127
TYLERSCROSS 8L 53
TYLER'S GREEN 3B 66 (2A 32)
Tylers Grn. Rd. BR8: Crock 7A 46
Tylers Ride CM3: S Fer 1L 103
Tylers Rd. CM19: Roy 7J 53 (1F 31)
Tyler St. CO12: Har 2H 209
Tyler Way CM14: Brtwd 7E 96
Tylewood SS7: Had 4J 135
Tylney Av. SS4: R'fd 4K 121
Tylney Cft. CM19: H'low 5A 54
(not continuous)
Tylney Rd. E7: Lon 6J 123 (5F 39)
Tylneys Rd. CO9: Hals 3M 207
Tymperleys Clock Mus. 8N 165
Tyms Way SS6: Ray 3L 119
Tyndale Cl. SS5: Hull 5K 103
Tyndale Dr. CO15: Jay 3E 188
Tyndales La. CM3: Dan 5H 75 (2E 34)
Tyndall Gdns. E10: Lon 4C 122
Tyndall Rd. E10: Lon 4C 122
Tyne RM18: E Til 2L 157
Tyne Cl. RM14: Upm 1A 128
Tynedale Ct. CO4: Colc 3B 166
Tynedale Sq. CO4: Colc 3B 166
Tyne Gdns. RM15: Ave 7N 143
Tynemouth Cl. E6: Lon 6A 140
Tyne Way CM1: Chelm 6F 58
Tyrell Pl. CM15: Shenf 7J 97
Tyrell Ri. CM14: War 2F 112
Tyrells SS5: Hock 2C 120
Tyrells Cl. CM2: Chelm 7N 59
RM14: Upm 4M 127
Tyrells, The SS17: Corr 2B 148
Tyrells Way CM2: Gt Bad 3G 73
Tyrone Cl. CM11: Bill 1L 115
Tyrone Rd. CM11: Bill 1L 115
SS1: Sth S 8E 138
Tyrrel Dr. SS1: Sth S 6N 137
Tyrrell Ct. SS13: Pits 9K 117
Tyrrell Rd. SS7: Ben 4B 134
Tyrrells Hall Cl. RM17: Grays 4N 155
Tyrrells Rd. CM11: Bill 1M 115
Tysea Cl. CM18: H'low 6E 54
TYSEA HILL 6D 94
Tysea Hill RM4: Noak H, Stap A 7D 94 (7A 32)
Tysea Rd. CM18: H'low 6E 54 (7H 21)
Tyssen Mead CM3: Bore 3F 60
Tyssen Pl. RM15: S Ock 3F 144
Tythe Barn Way CM3: S Fer 9J 89
Tythe Cl. CM1: Chelm 3N 59
Tythings, The CO9: Hals 6J 207

U

UCI Cinema 6C 116
Thurrock Lakeside 2C 154
Udall Gdns. RM5: Col R 3M 109
UGLEY 4A 12
UGLEY GREEN 1H 199 (5B 12)
Ullswater E18: Lon 6G 106
Ullswater Cl. CM77: Gt N 2C 204
Ullswater Rd. SS7: Thund 8E 118
Ullswater Way RM12: Horn 7E 126
Ulster Av. SS3: Shoe 8G 139
ULTING 7F 25
Ulting Hall Rd. CM9: Ult 7F 25
Ulting La. CM9: L'frd, Ult 7F 25
Ulting Rd. CM3: Hat P 3M 61 (6F 25)
Ulting Way SS11: W'fd 8A 102
Ulverston Ho. *RM3: Romf* *3J 111*
(off Kingsbridge Cir.)
Ulverston Rd. E17: Lon 6D 106
SS4: R'fd 7H 105
Una Rd. CO12: Har 3G 209
SS13: Pits 9N 117
Undercliff Gdns. SS9: Lgh S 6E 136
Undercliff Rd. E. IP11: Felix 1K 19
Undercliff Rd. W. IP11: Felix 1K 19
Underhill Rd. SS7: Ben 3E 134
Underwood Ct. *E10: Lon* *3B 122*
(off Leyton Grange Est.)
Underwood Rd. E4: Lon 2B 106
IG8: Wfd G 4J 107
Underwood Sq. SS9: Lgh S 4B 136
Union Cl. E11: Lon 6D 122
Union Cotts. E15: Lon 9E 122
Union La. SS4: R'fd 5K 121
Union Rd. CO15: Jay 4E 188
Union St. SE1: Lon 7A 38
Unity Cl. CO2: Colc 2B 174
Unity Trad. Est. IG8: Wfd G 6K 107
University of East London
Barking Campus 6F 124
Maryland Ho. *8E 122*
(off Manbey Pk. Rd.)
Stratford Campus *8E 122*
(off Water La.)
University of Essex 2F 174 (6G 17)
University of Essex Sports Cen. 2F 174
University Pl. DA8: Eri 5A 152
University Way DA1: Dart 9G 153 (3B 46)
(not continuous)
E16: Lon 7A 140
Unwin Pl. CM4: Stock 7N 85
Up.Chapel St. CO9: Hals 4K 207
Uphall Rd. IG1: Ilf 7A 124
Uphavering Ho. RM12: Horn 4G 126
Upland Cl. CM12: Bill 4J 99
Upland Ct. Rd. RM3: H Wood 6K 111
Upland Cres. CO5: W Mer 2C 228
Upland Dr. CM12: Bill 4H 99
CO4: Colc 5C 166 (5F 17)
Upland Rd. CM12: Bill 4H 99
CM16: Epp, Epp Up, Thorn 4C 64 (2H 31)
CO5: W Mer 2C 228
SS9: Lgh S 6F 136
Uplands Cl. SS5: Hock 2E 120
SS7: Ben 3B 134
Uplands Ct. CO15: Clac S 3H 189
Uplands Dr. CM1: Chelm 4M 59
Uplands End IG8: Wfd G 4L 107
Uplands Pk. Ct. SS6: Ray 4L 119
Uplands Pk. Rd. EN2: Enf 6A 30
SS6: Ray 3K 119
Uplands Rd. CM14: War 2H 113
CO15: Clac S 3H 189
IG8: Wfd G 4L 107
RM6: Chad H 7J 109
SS5: Hock 2E 120
SS7: Ben 3B 134
Uplands, The IG10: Lou 2M 91
UPMINSTER 4N 127 (4D 40)
Upminster Bridge Station (Tube) 4L 127 (4C 40)
Upminster Rd. RM11: Horn 4K 127 (4C 40)
RM12: Horn 4K 127 (4C 40)
RM14: Upm 4K 127 (4C 40)
Upminster Rd. Nth. RM13: Rain 3G 142 (6B 40)
Upminster Rd. Sth. RM13: Rain 4E 142 (6A 40)
Upminster Smockmill 4M 127 (4C 40)
Upminster Station (Rail & Tube) 4N 127 (4D 40)
Upminster Tithe Barn &
Agricultural Folk Mus. 2A 128 (4D 40)
Upminster Trad. Pk. RM14: Upm 2G 128
Upney Cl. RM12: Horn 7H 127
Upney La. IG11: Bark 8D 124 (5H 39)
Upney Station (Tube) 9E 124 (5H 39)
Uppark Dr. IG2: Ilf 1B 124
UPPEND 5J 11
Upper Acres CM8: Wthm 2C 230
Upper Av. SS13: Pits 6M 117
Up. Branston Rd. CO15: Clac S 9H 185
Up. Brentwood Rd. RM2: Romf 8G 110 (3B 40)
Up. Bridge Rd. CM2: Chelm 2B 72
Up. Chase CM2: Chelm 2B 72
Upper Chase CM3: Alth 2C 190
UPPER CLAPTON 4C 38
Up. Clapton Rd. E5: Lon 4C 38
Upper Cornsland CM14: Brtwd 9G 96
UPPER DOVERCOURT 5G 208 (3G 19)
UPPER EDMONTON 1C 38
Up. Farm Rd. CO9: Ashen 6F 216 (5C 8)
Up. Fenn Rd. CO9: Hals 4M 207
Up. Fourth Av. CO13: Frin S 9J 181
UPPER GREEN 1C 12
Clavering 1H 11
Great Sampford 1F 13
Upper Grn. CO6: Wak C 3K 15
CO8: Alph 1J 15
Up. Hall La. CO6: Gt Tey 6K 15
Up. Haye La. CO5: Fing 9E 174 (2F 27)
UPPER HOLLOWAY 4A 38
Upper Holloway Station (Rail) 4A 38
Up. Holt St. CO6: E Col 8D 198 (4J 15)
Upper Hook CM18: H'low 5E 54
Upper Ho's. CO10: Bulm 3J 195 (6G 9)
Up. Howe St. CM7: F'fld 1K 13
Up. Lambricks SS6: Ray 3L 119
Up. Market Rd. SS12: W'fd 8L 101
Up. Marsh La. EN11: Hod 6A 52
Upper Mayne SS15: Lain 6N 115 (3K 41)
Upper Mealines CM18: H'low 6F 54
Up. Mill Fld. CM6: Gt D 4M 203
Up. Moors CM3: Gt Walt 5H 57
Up. North St. CO10: Pos 1B 8
E14: Lon 7D 38
Upper Pk. CM20: H'low 2A 54
IG10: Lou 3K 91
Up. Park Rd. CO7: B'sea 6D 182
CO15: Clac S 1H 189
DA17: Belv 1A 46
SS12: W'fd 3L 117
Up. Pond St. CB11: Dun E 7H 5
Up. Rainham Rd. RM12: Horn 3D 126 (4A 40)
Upper Rd. CM11: Cray H 2E 116
CO10: L Cor 7K 9
E13: Lon 6E 38
Up. Roman Rd. CM2: Chelm 1C 72
Upper Ryle CM14: Brtwd 6E 96
Up. Second Av. CO13: Frin S 9H 181
Upper Sq. CB10: Saf W 3C 218
Upper Stonyfield CM19: H'low 3A 54
UPPER STREET 1C 18
Upper St. CO7: Strat M 1H 17
CO10: S'std 1H 9
N1: Lon 6A 38
Upper Swaines CM16: Epp 9E 64
Up. Thames St. EC4: Lon 7A 38
Up. Third Av. CO13: Frin S 9H 181
Up. Tollington Pk. N4: Lon 4A 38
Up. Trinity Rd. CO9: Hals 5K 207
UPPER WALTHAMSTOW 8D 106 (3E 38)
Up. Walthamstow Rd. E17: Lon 8C 106
Upsheres CB11: Saf W 5E 218
UPSHIRE 2K 77 (4F 31)
Upshirebury Grn. EN9: Wal A 3K 77
Upshire Rd. EN9: Wal A 2F 76 (4E 30)
UPTON 9G 123 (5F 39)
Upton Av. E7: Lon 9G 123
Upton Cl. CO6: W Ber 3E 164
SS17: Stan H 3M 147
Upton Ho. *RM3: Romf* *2H 111*
(off Barnstaple Rd.)
Upton La. E7: Lon 9G 123 (5F 39)
Upton Lodge E7: Lon 8G 123
UPTON PARK 6F 39
Upton Pk. Rd. E7: Lon 9H 123
Upton Pk. Stadium 6F 39
Upton Park Station (Tube) 6F 39
Upward Ct. RM1: Romf 8D 110
Upway SS6: Ray 4K 119
Upway, The SS14: Bas 8C 116
UPWICK GREEN 6H 11
Urban Av. RM12: Horn 5G 127
Urmond Rd. SS8: Can I 1G 150
Urswick Gdns. RM9: Dag 9K 125
Urswick Rd. E9: Lon 5C 38
RM9: Dag 9J 125
Usk Rd. RM15: Ave 5N 143
Usterdale Rd. CB10: Saf W 2D 218
Uttons Av. SS9: Lgh S 6C 136
Uvedale Rd. RM10: Dag 5M 125
Uxbridge Cl. SS11: W'fd 1N 117

V

Vaagen Rd. SS8: Can I 1H 151
Vadsoe Rd. SS8: Can I 9G 134
Valance Av. E4: Lon 7E 90
Valance Rd. CB11: Clav 2J 11
Vale Av. SS2: Sth S 4M 137
Vale Cl. CM15: Pil H 4C 96
CO4: Colc 5E 166
Vale End CM2: Gall 7D 72
Valence Av. RM8: Dag 3J 125 (4J 39)
Valence Cir. RM8: Dag 5J 125
Valence House Mus. & Gallery 5K 125 (4K 39)
Valence Rd. DA8: Eri 5B 152
Valence Way CO15: Clac S 9K 185
SS16: Lang H 1L 131
Valence Wood Rd. RM8: Dag 5J 125
Valens Cl. CO4: Colc 1A 166
Valenta Cl. CO1: Colc 9C 166
Valentine Ct. CM7: Brain 4G 193
Valentines CM4: Stock 7A 86
SS12: W'fd 1L 117
Valentines Dr. CO4: Colc 6C 166
Valentines Rd. IG1: Ilf 3A 124
Valentine's Way RM7: Rush G 4C 126
Valentine Vs. RM15: S Ock 5F 144
Valentine Way CM8: Sil E 8L 217
Valerie Ho. *SS9: Lgh S* *4D 136*
(off Station Rd.)
Vale Rd. DA11: N'fleet 4G 47
E7: Lon 8H 123
Vale Ter. CO8: Bures 8L 195
Vale, The CM4: Stock 1M 99
CM14: Brtwd 7F 96
IG8: Wfd G 4G 107
SS16: Van 3E 132
Valfreda Way CO7: W'hoe 5H 175
Valiant Cl. RM7: Maw 6N 109
Valkyrie Cl. CM9: Tol 7K 225
Valkyrie Rd. SS0: Wclf S 6J 137 (5J 43)
Vallance Cl. SS2: Sth S 3C 138
Vallance Rd. E2: Lon 6C 38
E1: Lon 6C 38
Vallentin Rd. E17: Lon 8C 106 (3E 38)
Valletta Cl. CM1: Chelm 8J 59
Valley Bri. CM1: Chelm 5K 59 (7A 24)
Valleybridge Rd. CO15: Clac S 8L 185
Valley Cl. CO3: S'way 3F 172
EN9: Wal A 2C 76
IG10: Lou 5M 91
Valley Cres. CO6: W Ber 4F 164
Valley Dr. DA12: Grav 5H 47
Valley Hill IG10: Lou 6L 91 (7G 31)
Valley Rd. CM7: Brain 4J 193
CM11: Bill 6K 99 (7K 33)
CO4: Colc 2F 174
CO7: W'hoe 6J 175
CO10: Gt Wal, New 4K 9
CO12: Har 5F 208
CO15: Clac S 8K 185 (3D 28)
DA3: Fawk 7E 46
DA8: Eri 2A 152
DA17: Belv 2A 152
Valley Side E4: Lon 8A 90
Valley Side Pde. E4: Lon 8A 90
Valley Vw. CM7: F'fld 3D 200
CO6: W Ber 4F 164
CO10: S'std 1H 9
Valley Vw. Cl. CO4: Colc 3A 166
Valley Wlk. CO14: Walt 7K 181
Valley Wash CO10: Pos 1B 8
Vallis Way *CO5: Tip* *5E 226*
(off Olley Wlk.)
Valmar Av. SS17: Stan H 4K 147
Vandenburg Circ. CM7: Weth 2A 14
Vanderbilt Av. SS6: Ray 8J 103
Vanderwalt Av. SS8: Can I 2K 151
Van Dieman's La. CM2: Chelm 2D 72
Van Dieman's Rd. CM2: Chelm 2D 72 (2A 34)
Van Diemens Pass SS8: Can I 2M 151
Van Dyck Rd. CO3: Colc 1H 173
Vane Ct. CM8: Wthm 2D 230
Vane La. CO6: Cogg 3L 197
Vanessa Dr. CO7: W'hoe 5H 175
VANGE 2G 132 (4B 42)
Vange Bells Cnr. SS17: Fob 5C 132
Vange By-Pass SS16: Pits 4E 132 (4A 42)
Vange Cnr. Dr. SS16: Van 5C 132
Vange Hill Ct. SS16: Van 3F 132
Vange Hill Dr. SS16: Van 1E 132
Vange Pk. Rd. SS16: Van 5C 132
Vange Riverview Cen. *SS16: Van* *2G 132*
(off High Rd.)
Vanguard Cl. RM7: Maw 6M 109

Vanguards, The SS3: Shoe 7K 139
(not continuous)
Vanguard Way CM7: Brain 4K 193
SS3: Shoe 7K 139
Vanguard Way Ind. Est. SS3: Shoe 7J 139
Vanryne Ho. IG10: Lou 2L 91
Vansittart Rd. E7: Lon 6F 122
Vansittart St. CO12: Har 2M 209
Vantorts Cl. CM21: Saw 2K 51
Vantorts Rd. CM21: Saw 3K 51
Varden Cl. CM1: Chelm 5H 59
Vardon Dr. SS9: Lgh S 3N 135
Vaughan Av. RM12: Horn 6H 127
SS2: Sth S 5B 138
Vaughan Cl. CM77: Rayne 6B 192
SS4: R'fd 2K 121
Vaughan Gdns. IG1: Ilf 2M 123
Vaughan Rd. E15: Lon 8F 122
Vaughan Williams Rd. SS15: Lain 7L 115
Vaughan Williams Way
CM14: Gt War, War 3D 112
Vaulx Rd. SS8: Can I 1H 151
Vaux Av. CO12: Har 6H 209
Vauxhall Av. CO15: Jay 6C 188
Vauxhall Dr. CM7: Brain 6F 192
Vega Cl. CO1: Colc 9C 166
Velizy Av. CM20: H'low 2C 54
Velizy Rdbt. CM20: H'low 2C 54
Vellacotts CM1: Chelm 4K 59
Venables Cl. RM10: Dag 6N 125
SS8: Can I 1J 151
Venables Ct. SS8: Can I 1J 151
Venette Cl. RM13: Rain 5F 142
Venlo Rd. SS8: Can I 9H 135
Venmore Dr. CM6: Gt D 3L 203
Venners Cl. DA7: Bexh 7C 152
Venta Way CM9: Mal 8D 214
Ventnor Dr. CO15: Clac S 5L 185
Ventnor Gdns. IG11: Bark 8D 124
Ventura Dr. CO1: Colc 9C 166
Veny Cres. RM12: Horn 7H 127
Vera Lynn Cl. E7: Lon 6G 123
Vera Rd. CM11: D'ham 6H 101
Verbena Cl. RM15: S Ock 6F 144
Verderers Rd. IG7: Chig 2F 108
Vere Rd. IG10: Lou 3B 92
Verlander Dr. SS6: Ray 9H 103
Vermeer Cres. SS3: Shoe 6L 139
Vermeer Ride CM1: Chelm 4A 60
Vermont Cl. CO15: Clac S 9L 185
SS13: Bas 7K 117
Verney Gdns. RM9: Dag 6K 125
Verney Rd. RM9: Dag 6K 125
(not continuous)
Vernon Av. E12: Lon 6M 123
IG8: Wfd G 4H 107
SS6: Ray 3H 119
Vernon Cnr. *CM4: Stock 7M 85*
(off Back La.)
Vernon Ct. SS9: Lgh S 5B 136
Vernon Cres. CM13: Brtwd 9K 97
Vernon Pl. WC1: Lon 7A 38
Vernon Rd. CM3: N Fam 5H 35
E11: Lon 3E 122
E15: Lon 9E 122
IG3: Ilf 3E 124
RM5: Col R 2A 110
SS9: Lgh S 5B 136
Vernon's Cl. CM22: Hen 8D 210
Vernons Rd.
CO6: Chap, For, Wak C 7D 196 (4A 16)
Vernons Wlk. SS14: Bas 7G 117
Vernon Way CM7: Brain 3L 193
Verona Ho. DA8: Eri 5D 152
Verona Rd. E7: Lon 9G 123
Veronica Cl. RM3: Romf 4G 111
Veronica Wlk. CO4: Colc 8E 166
Veronique Gdns. IG6: Ilf 9B 108
Vert Ho. RM17: Grays 5M 155
Vesta Cl. CO6: Cogg 3K 197
Vestry Cl. SS15: Lain 8L 115
Vestry House Mus. 8B 106 (3D 38)
Vestry Rd. E17: Lon 8B 106
Vexil Cl. RM19: Purf 2A 154
Veysey Gdns. RM10: Dag 5M 125
Viaduct Rd. CM1: Chelm 9J 59
SG12: Ware 4D 20
Viaduct, The E18: Lon 6G 107
Viborg Gdns. CM9: Mal 8A 214
Vicarage Av. CM8: Whi N 2E 24
Vicarage C'way. SG13: Hert H 6C 20
Vicarage Cl. CM6: Thax 7C 224
CM7: Gt Sal 6K 13
CM8: Whi N 3E 24
CM9: Tol D 3K 227
CM14: Brtwd 1B 112
DA8: Eri 4A 152
SS8: Can I 2D 150
SS15: Lain 9L 115
Vicarage Ct. CO9: Hals 4J 207
EN9: Wal A 4G 77
(off Horseshoe La.)
IG1: Ilf 7A 124
Vicarage Cres. CM3: Hat P 2M 61
Vicarage Dr. IG11: Bark 9B 124
Vicarage Fld. Shop. Cen. IG11: Bark 9B 124
Vicarage Gdns. CO15: Clac S 2H 189
Vicarage Hill SS7: Ben 5D 134 (4E 42)
Vicarage La. CM0: T'ham 2J 225 (3E 36)
CM2: Gt Bad 7G 72 (3B 34)
CM6: Thax 7C 224
CM9: Mun 3J 35
CM16: N Wea 3N 65 (2K 31)
(Rayley La.)
Vicarage La. CM16: N Wea 3A 66
(Weald Bri. Rd.)
CM22: Ugley 4A 12
CM23: Ber 4J 11
CO10: Act 3K 9
CO14: Walt 6M 181
CO16: T Sok 4K 179
DA12: Grav 4J 47
E15: Lon 9E 122 (5E 38)
IG1: Ilf 3C 124
IG7: Chig 8B 92 (1H 39)
SG14: Hart, W'frd 4A 20
Vicarage Mead CM6: Thax 7C 224
Vicarage Mdw. CM0: S'min 3D 222
CO9: Hals 5K 207
Vicarage M. CM2: Gt Bad 4G 73
Vicarage Rd. CM1: Rox 3N 217 (7H 23)
CM2: Chelm 3B 72
CM3: Ples 2A 56
CM7: F'fld 3D 200 (2K 13)
CM16: Coop 8H 65
CO10: Bel P 4E 8
DA5: Bex 4A 46
E10: Lon 2A 122
E15: Lon 9F 122
IG8: Wfd G 4L 107
RM10: Dag 9N 125
RM12: Horn 3E 126
SG9: Bunt, Wyd 4D 10
SG12: Ware 4D 20
Vicarage Sq. RM17: Grays 4K 155
Vicarage Wood CM20: H'low 2E 54
Vicars Orchard CO10: Bulm 1K 195
Vicars Wlk. RM8: Dag 5G 125
Viceroy Cl. CO2: Colc 3B 174
Viceroy Ct. SS0: Wclf S 7G 137
SS17: Horn H 2H 147
(off Gordon Rd.)
Vickers Rd. DA8: Eri 3B 152
SS2: Sth S 9J 121
Victor App. RM12: Horn 3H 127
Victor Av. SS13: Pits 9L 117
Victor Cl. RM12: Horn 3H 127
Victor Ct. *RM12: Horn 3H 127*
(off Victor Wlk.)
Victor Dr. SS9: Lgh S 6E 136
Victor Gdns. RM12: Horn 3H 127
SS5: Hock 2E 120
(not continuous)
Victoria Av. CB11: Saf W 5D 218
CO13: Kir S 6G 180
RM5: Col R 3N 109
RM16: Grays 9M 145
SS2: Sth S 3K 137 (4J 43)
SS6: Ray 3H 119
SS12: W'fd 8K 101
SS16: Bas 3L 131
Victoria Chase CO1: Colc 7M 165
Victoria Cl. CO7: W'hoe 4H 175
RM16: Grays 9M 145
SS15: Lain 8K 115
Victoria Ct. *CM7: Brain 6J 193*
(off Railway St.)
CM9: Mal 6D 214
CM14: War 1F 112
CM20: H'low 2D 54
CO12: Har 4L 209
CO15: Clac S 1J 189
E18: Lon 7H 107
RM1: Romf 9E 110
SS0: Wclf S 7K 137
(off Tower Ct. M.)
SS11: W'fd 2A 118
Victoria Cres. CM1: Chelm 8K 59
CO11: Law 4H 163
SS12: W'fd 9J 101
SS15: Lain 7K 115
Victoria Dock Rd. E16: Lon 7E 38
Victoria Dr. SS3: Gt W 4N 139
SS9: Lgh S 5D 136
Victoria Embkmt. SW1: Lon 7A 38
Victoria Esplanade CO5: W Mer 4D 228 (5F 27)
Victoria Gdns. CB11: Saf W 5D 218
CO4: Colc 4B 166
Victoria Ga. CM17: H'low 3H 55
Victoria Hill CM7: Gt Sal 5A 14
Victoria Ho. RM2: Romf 8G 111
Victoria Lanes Shop. Cen. SS1: Sth S 7M 137
Victoria Pk. Rd. E9: Lon 6C 38
Victoria Pl. CO1: Colc 9B 166
(Cannon St.)
CO1: Colc 8N 165
(Eld La.)
CO7: B'sea 7E 182
Victoria Plaza Shop. Cen. SS2: Sth S 6M 137
Victoria Rd. CM1: Chelm 8K 59 (1A 34)
(not continuous)
CM1: Writ 1G 70 (1J 33)
CM2: Chelm 8K 59
CM3: Cold N 8K 197
CM3: S Fer 2K 103
CM9: Mal 5C 214
CM14: War 1F 112
CO3: Colc 1K 173
CO14: Walt 6M 181
CO15: Clac S 1L 189
CO16: Wee H 9F 178
DA1: Dart 3C 46
DA8: Eri 4C 152
(not continuous)
E4: Lon 7E 90
E11: Lon 6E 122
E17: Lon 6C 106
E18: Lon 6H 107
Victoria Rd. EN9: Wal A 4C 76
IG9: Buck H 8K 91 (1F 39)
IG11: Bark 8A 124
N9: Lon 1B 38
N18: Lon 1B 38
RM1: Romf 1D 126 (3A 40)
RM10: Dag 7N 125
RM14: Bulp 6B 130
SS1: Sth S 6A 138
SS6: Ray 4L 119
SS9: Lgh S 6D 136
SS15: Lain 8J 115
SS16: Van 4E 132
SS17: Horn H 2H 147
SS17: Stan H 4L 147
Victoria Rd. Sth. CM1: Chelm 9K 59 (1A 34)
Victoria Road Stadium 7N 125 (5K 39)
Victoria Scott Ct. DA1: Cray 8D 152
Victoria St. CM7: Brain 6H 193 (7C 14)
CO12: Har 3M 209
E15: Lon 9E 122
SW1: Lon 7A 38
Victor M. Cl. SS12: W'fd 2L 117
Victor Rd. CO1: Colc 9B 166
Victor's Cres. CM13: Hut 8L 97
Victor Wlk. RM12: Horn 3H 127
Victory Cl. RM16: Chaf H 2F 154
SS11: W'fd 2A 118
Victory Ct. CO3: S'way 9F 164
DA8: Eri 5D 152
(off Frobisher Rd.)
Victory Gdns. CM7: Brain 4K 193
Victory La. SS4: R'fd 1J 121
Victory Path SS0: Wclf S 6G 136
Victory Rd. CO5: W Mer 3A 228
CO15: Clac S 1H 189
E11: Lon 8G 107
RM13: Rain 2E 142
Victory Way DA2: Dart 9N 153
RM7: Maw 6N 109
Vienna Cl. CO12: Har 6J 209
IG5: Ilf 6K 107
View Cl. IG7: Chig 2C 108
Vigerons Way RM16: Grays 2D 156
Vigilant Way DA12: Grav 5J 47
Vignoles Rd. RM7: Rush G 2M 125
Viking Bus. Cen. RM7: Rush G 2A 126
Viking Rd. CM9: Mal 8A 214
Vikings Way SS8: Can I 2D 150
Viking Way CM15: Pil H 5E 96
CO15: Hol S 7C 186
DA8: Eri 1A 152
RM13: Rain 4E 142
SS11: Runw 6L 101
Village Arc. E4: Lon 7D 90
Village Cl. CO13: Walt 7G 181
CO16: L Cla 4H 185
E4: Lon 2C 106
EN11: Rye P 3D 52
Village Ct. *E17: Lon 9B 106*
(off Eden Rd.)
Village Dr. SS8: Can I 2E 150
Village Ga. CM2: Chelm 8B 60
Village Grn. SS4: Cwdn 1M 105
Village Grn. Rd. DA1: Cray 9E 152
Village Hall Cl. SS8: Can I 2D 150
Village Hgts. IG8: Wfd G 2F 106
Village Rd. N9: Lon 7B 30
Village Sq. CM2: Chelm 8B 60
Village, The CM5: Will 1E 32
CM22: L Hall 2K 213
Village Way CO13: Walt 7G 181
Villa Rd. CO3: S'way 9D 164 (6C 16)
ME3: High 5K 47
SS7: Ben 2B 134
Villiers Cl. E10: Lon 4A 122
Villiers Pl. CM3: Bore 3F 60
Villiers-Sur-Marne Av. CM23: Bis S 1J 21
Villiers Way SS7: Thund 1F 134
Vince Cl. CO5: W Mer 3C 228
Vincent Av. SS17: Horn H 2H 147
Vincent Cl. IG6: Ilf 3B 108
SS3: Shoe 7J 139
SS17: Corr 2C 148
Vincent Lodge CM3: S Fer 2L 103
Vincent M. SS3: Shoe 7J 139
Vincent Rd. E4: Lon 3D 106
RM9: Dag 9K 125
RM13: Rain 4G 142
SS5: Hock 7G 104
Vincent Way CM12: Bill 3H 99
Vine Ct. SS14: Bas 9F 116
Vine Dr. CO7: W'hoe 3J 175
Vine Farm Rd. CO7: W'hoe 3J 175
Vinegar All. E17: Lon 8B 106
Vine Gdns. IG1: Ilf 7B 124
Vine Gro. CM20: Gil 7D 50
Vine Pde. CO7: W'hoe 3J 175
Vineries Cl. RM9: Dag 8L 125
Vine Rd. CO5: Tip 5C 226
E15: Lon 9F 122
Vinesse Rd.
CO6: L Hork, W Ber 5E 158 (3C 16)
Vine St. CM7: Gt Bar 2C 202 (3J 13)
RM7: Romf 8A 110
Vine Way CM14: Brtwd 7F 96
Vineway, The CO12: Har 3J 209
Vineyard Ga. CO2: Colc 9N 165
Vineyards Rd. EN6: N'thaw 3A 30
Vineyard Steps CO2: Colc 8N 165
Vineyards, The CM2: Gt Bad 3G 73
CM3: Hat P 1L 61
Vineyard St. CO2: Colc 9N 165
Vint Cres. CO3: Colc 9K 165
Vintners, The SS2: Temp I 1L 137
Vintry M. E17: Lon 8A 106
Viola Cl. RM15: S Ock 3F 144
Viola Wlk. CO4: Colc 8E 166
Violet Cl. CM1: Chelm 4N 59
Violet Rd. E17: Lon 1A 122
E18: Lon 6H 107
E3: Lon 6D 38
Virgil Rd. CM8: Wthm 2C 230
Virginia Cl. CO15: Clac S, Jay 3E 188
RM5: Col R 4A 110
SS7: Thund 8B 118
Virginia Gdns. IG6: Ilf 6B 108
Virley Cl. CM9: H'bri 4F 214
Viscount Dr. CO4: Colc 2C 166
Vista Av. CO13: Kir S 5G 180
Vista Dr. IG4: Ilf 9K 107
Vista Rd. CO15: Clac S 9K 185
SS11: W'fd 9N 101
Vitellus Cl. CO4: Colc 1B 166
Vivian Ct. CO14: Walt 6M 181
Voluntary Pl. E11: Lon 1G 122
Volwycke Av. CM9: Mal 8B 214
Voorburg Rd. SS8: Can I 2K 151
Voorne Av. SS8: Can I 3K 151
Vowler Rd. SS16: Lang H 2K 131
Voyagers Cl. SE28: Lon 6H 141
Voysey Gdns. SS13: Bas 6J 117

W

Waalwyk Dr. SS8: Can I 1J 151
Waarden Rd. SS8: Can I 1G 150
Waarem Av. SS8: Can I 1G 151
Waddesdon Rd. CO12: Har 3M 209
Waddington Rd. E15: Lon 7D 122
Waddington St. E15: Lon 8D 122
Wade Reach CO14: Walt 6L 181
Wade Rd. CO15: Clac S 5M 185
Wades Hill N21: Lon 7A 30
Wade's La. IP9: Holb 1G 19
WADESMILL 3C 20
Wadesmill Rd. SG12: Ware 4C 20
SG14: Hart, W'frd 4B 20
Wadeville Av. RM6: Chad H 1K 125
Wadham Av. E17: Lon 4B 106
Wadham Cl. CM4: Ing 5D 84
Wadham Pk. Av. SS5: Hock 7N 103
Wadham Rd. E17: Lon 4B 106 (2D 38)
Wadley Cl. CO5: Tip 6E 226
Wadley Rd. E11: Lon 2E 122
Wagon Mead CM22: Hat H 1E 210
Wagstaff Gdns. RM9: Dag 9H 125
Wagtail Dr. CM9: H'bri 3E 214
Wagtail Pl. CO5: K'dn 3K 211
Wainfleet Av. RM5: Col R 6A 110
Wainscott Northern By-Pass
ME2: High, Roch 6K 47
Wainsfield Vs. CM6: Thax 8D 224
Wainwright Av. CM13: Hut 5N 97
CM77: Gt N 8F 192
Wakefield Av. CM12: Bill 6J 99
Wakefield Cl. CB10: Gt Che 7D 202
CO1: Colc 7A 166
Wakefield Gdns. IG1: Ilf 1L 123
Wakelin Chase CM4: Ing 6C 84
Wakelin Way CM8: Wthm 5E 230
Wakerfield Cl. RM11: Horn 9K 111
Wakering Av. SS3: Shoe 7L 139
Wakering Rd. IG11: Bark 8B 124
(not continuous)
SS1: Gt W 4E 138 (4A 44)
SS3: Gt W 4E 138 (4A 44)
SS3: Shoe 6L 139 (5C 44)
Wakerings, The *IG11: Bark 8B 124*
(off Wakering Rd.)
Wake Rd. IG10: H Bee 8J 77 (5F 31)
WAKES COLNE 6C 196 (4K 15)
Wakescolne SS11: W'fd 1A 118
WAKES COLNE GREEN 3K 15
Wakeshall La. CO10: Bel P, Ovtn 5D 8
Wakes St. CO6: Wak C 6A 196 (4K 15)
Waldair Ct. E16: Lon 9A 140
Waldeck Ct. CB11: Saf W 7C 218
Waldegrave SS16: Bas 1C 132
Waldegrave Cl. CO11: Law 5G 163
Waldegrave Ct. IG11: Bark 1C 140
RM14: Upm 3M 127
Waldegrave Gdns. RM14: Upm 3M 127
Waldegrave Rd. RM8: Dag 4H 125
Waldegraves Farm Holiday Pk.
CO5: W Mer 5G 27
Waldegraves La. CO5: W Mer 1F 228 (5G 27)
Waldegraves, The CO8: Bures 8L 195
Waldegrave Way CO11: Law 5G 163
Walden Av. CB10: Wim 1D 12
RM13: Rain 2B 142
Walden Cl. CM9: Gt Tot 3M 229
Walden Ct. CM23: Bis S 9C 220
Walden Ho. Rd.
CM9: Gt Tot, W Bis 2M 229 (5H 25)
Walden Pl. CB10: Saf W 4C 218
Walden Rd. CB1: Hads 3C 6
CB10: A'dn, Saf W 9A 190 (5D 6)
CB10: Gt Che, L Ches 6D 202 (4A 6)
CB10: R'ter, Sew E 6E 6
CB10: Sew E 6D 6
CB11: Deb 1C 12
CB11: L'bry 1B 218 (6A 6)
CB11: Wen A 6L 227 (7B 6)
CM6: Thax 6B 224 (2F 13)
RM11: Horn 1H 127

Walden Way CO13: Frin S. 9J **181**
IG6: Ilf. 4D **108**
RM11: Horn 1H **127**
Waldgrooms CM6: Gt D 2K **203**
Waldingfield Rd. CO10: Act 3K **9**
CO10: Sud 5J **9**
Waldon RM18: E Til 1K **157**
Waldring Fld. SS14: Bas 8C **116**
Waldrist Way DA18: Eri 9L **141**
Waldstock Rd. SE28: Lon 7F **140**
WALES END. 1E 8
Walford Cl. CO6: Cogg 2L **197**
Walford Pl. CM2: Chelm 9A **60**
Walfords Cl. CM17: H'low 9H **51**
Walfords La. CM7: F'fld 2E **200**
Walford Way CO6: Cogg 3L **197**
Walfrey Gdns. RM9: Dag 9K **125**
Walkato Lodge IG9: Buck H 7J **91**
Walker Av. CM5: Fy'd 9C **200**
Walker Cl. DA1: Cray 8D **152**
Walker Dr. SS9: Lgh S 4N **135**
WALKERN 5A 10
Walkern Rd. SG2: B'tn 6A **10**
SG14: Wat S 1A **20**
Walkers Cl. CM1: Chelm 4M **59**
Walkers Sq. SS17: Stan H. 4M **147**
Walkey Way SS3: Shoe. 7L **139**
Walk, The CM7: Gt Bar. 3D **202**
CM12: Bill 7J **99**
CO6: Eig G. 7B **164**
RM11: Horn 4K **127**
SS5: Hull. 5K **103**
Walkways SS8: Can I 9F **134**
Wallace Binder Cl. CM9: Mal. 7B **214**
Wallace Cl. SE28: Lon 7J **141**
SS5: Hull. 5K **103**
Wallace Cres. CM2: Chelm 2D **72**
Wallace Dr. SS12: W'fd 2M **117**
Wallace La. CM3: Bore. 6C **24**
Wallace Rd. RM17: Grays 1K **155**
Wallace St. SS3: Shoe 7K **139**
Wallace Way RM1: Romf. 5B **110**
Wallasea Gdns. CM1: Chelm 6A **60**
Wall Ct. CM7: Gt N. 7H **193**
WALLEND 6G 39
Wall End Rd. E6: Lon. 9N **123**
Wallenger Av. RM2: Romf 7F **110**
Wallers Cl. IG8: Wfd G 3M **107**
RM9: Dag 1K **141**
Waller's Hoppet IG10: Lou 1M **91**
Wallers Way EN11: Hod. 2B **52**
Wallflower Ct. CM1: Chelm 5A **60**
Wallhouse Rd. DA8: Eri 5F **152**
Wallingford Ho. *RM3: Romf. 3J 111*
(off Kingsbridge Rd.)
WALLINGTON 2A 10
Wallington Rd. IG3: Ilf 2E **124**
SG7: Wall 2A **10**
Wallis Av. SS2: Sth S 4L **137**
Wallis Cl. RM11: Horn 3F **126**
Wallis Ct. CO3: S'way. 3F **172**
Wallis Rd. E9: Lon 8A **122**
Wall La. CO11: Wrab 3D **18**
Wall Rd. SS8: Can I. 2M **151**
WALL'S GREEN. 1F 33
Walls, The CO11: Mist. 4J **163** (3A **18**)
Wall St. CO16: Lee S 5A **28**
Wallwood Rd. E11: Lon 2D **122**
Walmer Cl. E4: Lon 8B **90**
RM7: Maw 6N **109**
Walnut Cl. IG6: Ilf. 8B **108**
Walnut Cotts. *CM21: Saw. 1K 51*
(off Station Rd.)
Walnut Ct. E17: Lon 8C **106**
SS5: Hock. 9D **104**
Walnut Dr. CM8: Wthm 3D **230**
Walnut Gdns. E15: Lon. 7E **122**
Walnut Gro. CM7: Brain 6G **192**
RM12: Horn 3H **127**
Walnut Hill Rd. DA13: Ist R, Meop 6G **47**
Walnut Rd. E10: Lon. 4A **122**
Walnut Tree Cl. EN11: Hod. 5A **52**
Walnut Tree Cres. CM21: Saw 1K **51**
WALNUTTREE GREEN 6H 11
Walnut Tree Ho. CO3: Colc 2J **173**
Walnut Tree Rd. DA8: Eri 3C **152**
RM8: Dag. 4K **125** (4J **39**)
Walnut Tree Way CO2: Colc 3J **173**
CO5: Tip 4C **226**
Walnut Way CO7: B'sea 6D **182**
CO15: Clac S. 1G **188**
IG9: Buck H. 9K **91**
Walpole Cl. RM17: Grays 2M **155**
Walpole Rd. E6: Lon. 9J **123**
E18: Lon 5F **106**
N17: Lon. 3B **38**
Walpole Wlk. *SS6: Ray 5N 119*
(off Bramfield Rd. E.)
Walsham Cl. SE28: Lon 7J **141**
Walsham Ent. Cen. RM17: Grays 3M **155**
Walsingham Cl. SS15: Lain 8L **115**
Walsingham Ho. E4: Lon 6D **90**
Walsingham Rd. CO2: Colc 9N **165**
SS2: Sth S 3N **137**
Walsingham Way CM12: Bill 3K **99**
Walter Hurford Pde. *E12: Lon 6N 123*
(off Walton Rd.)
Walter Radcliffe Way CO7: W'hoe 7J **175**
Walter Rodney Cl. E6: Lon 8M **123**
Walters Cl. CM2: Gall. 7D **72**
SS9: Lgh S 9D **120**
Walters Yd. CO1: Colc 8N **165**
Walter Way CM8: Sil E 7L **217**
WALTHAM ABBEY 4B 76 (4E 30)
Waltham Abbey 3C 76
Waltham Abbey Church & Gatehouse 3C 76
Waltham Abbey Sports Cen. 3E 76
Waltham Abbey Swimming Pool 4D 76
Waltham Cl. CM13: Hut. 5M **97**
Waltham Ct. SS0: Wclf S 6H **137**
Waltham Cres. SS2: Sth S 3N **137**
WALTHAM CROSS 3A 76 (4C 30)
Waltham Cross Station (Rail) 4D 30
Waltham Forest Pool & Track. 6B 106
Waltham Glen CM2: Chelm 3D **72**
Waltham Pk. Way E17: Lon 5A **106**
Waltham Rd. CM3: Bore. 1H **61** (5C **24**)
CM3: Terl. 4C **24**
EN9: Naze. 5E **62** (3E **30**)
IG8: Wfd G 3L **107**
SS6: Ray. 4H **119**
Walthams SS13: Pits. 8J **117**
WALTHAM'S CROSS. 2F 202 (3K 13)
Walthams Pl. SS13: Pits. 8J **117**
WALTHAMSTOW 7A 106 (3D 38)
Walthamstow Av. E4: Lon. 4A **106**
Walthamstow Bus. Cen. E17: Lon 6C **106**
Walthamstow Central Station (Rail & Tube)
. . . . . 9A 106 (3D 38)
Walthamstow Greyhound Stadium 4B 106
Walthamstow Queens Road Station (Rail)
. . . . . 9A 106 (3D 38)
Waltham Way CO13: Frin S 9K **181**
E4: Lon 8A **90** (1D **38**)
WALTON 1K 19
Walton Av. IP11: Felix. 1K **19**
Walton Ct. EN11: Rye P 3B **52**
SS15: Lain. 7L **115**
Walton Gdns. CM13: Hut. 4M **97**
EN9: Wal A 3B **76**
Walton Hall Farm Mus. 8J 147 (7J 41)
Walton Hall La. CM3: Pur. 8H **215** (3G **35**)
Walton High IP11: Felix 1K **19**
Walton Ho. *E4: Lon. 2A 106*
(off Chingford Mt. Rd.)
E17: Lon 7B 106
(off Drive, The)
Walton Maritime Mus. 5N 181 (7J 19)
WALTON-ON-THE-NAZE 6M 181 (1H 29)
Walton-on-the-Naze Station (Rail)
. . . . . 7M 181 (1H 29)
Walton Pier Ten Pin Bowling Cen. 6N 181
Walton Rd. CO13: Frin S 9J **181** (1G **29**)
CO13: Kir S 5D **180** (7F **19**)
(Sneating Hall La.)
CO13: Kir S, Walt. 6F **180** (1G **29**)
(Street, The)
CO14: Walt. 9J **181** (1H **29**)
CO15: Clac S. 1K **189**
CO16: T Sok 3M **179** (7E **18**)
E12: Lon 6N **123**
(not continuous)
EN11: Rye P 3B **52**
RM5: Col R 4L **109**
SS1: Sth S 8D **138**
Walton's Hall Rd. SS17: Stan H. 9J **147** (1J **47**)
Wambrook SS3: Shoe. 5H **139**
Wambrook Cl. CM13: Hut 7M **97**
Wamburg Rd. SS8: Can I 1L **151**
Wanderer Dr. IG11: Bark 3H **141**
Wangey Rd. RM6: Chad H 2J **125**
Wannock Gdns. IG6: Ilf. 4A **108**
Wansbeck Rd. E3: Lon. 9A **122**
Wansfell Gdns. SS1: Sth S. 5D **138**
Wansford Cl. CM14: Brtwd. 9C **96**
Wansford Rd. IG8: Wfd G 5J **107**
WANSTEAD. 1H 123 (4F 39)
Wanstead Gdns. IG4: Ilf 1K **123**
Wanstead La. IG1: Ilf 1K **123**
Wanstead Leisure Cen. 1J 123
Wanstead Pk. Av. E12: Lon 3K **123**
Wanstead Pk. Rd. IG1: Ilf. 1K **123**
Wanstead Park Station (Rail) 6H 123 (5F 39)
Wanstead Pl. E11: Lon. 1G **122**
Wanstead Station (Tube) 1H 123 (3F 39)
Wantz Chase CM9: Mal. 6C **214**
WANTZ CORNER. 4F 86
Wantz Haven CM9: Mal. 6C **214**
Wantz La. RM13: Rain 4F **142**
(not continuous)
Wantz Rd. CM4: Marg 9H **71** (4J **33**)
CM9: Mal. 6C **214** (1H **35**)
RM10: Dag 6N **125**
WAPPING 7C 38
Wapping High St. E1: Lon 7C **38**
Wapping La. CO7: B'sea 4A **182**
E1: Lon 7C **38**
Wapping Station (Tube) 7C 38
Wapping Way E1: Lon 7C **38**
Warboys Cres. E4: Lon. 2C **106**
Warburton Av. CO9: Sib H. 7J **219**
Warburtons SS17: Stan H. 2A **148**
Warburton Ter. E17: Lon. 6B **106**
Ward Av. RM17: Grays 2K **155**
Ward Cl. DA8: Eri 4B **152**
Warde Chase CO14: Walt 6L **181**
Warden Av. RM5: Col R 5N **109**
Warder Cl. CM6: Gt D 2M **203**
Ward Gdns. RM3: H Wood 5H **111**
Ward Hatch CM20: H'low 9F **50**
Wardle Way CM1: Chelm 4G **58**
Ward Path CM2: Chelm. 7C **60**
Wards Cft. CB11: Saf W 6C **218**
Wards Rd. IG2: Ilf. 2C **124**
WARE 4C 20
Warehouse Rd. CM6: Steb. 8E **222** (6J **13**)
Warehouse Vs. CM6: Steb 9F **222**
Waremead Rd. IG2: Ilf 9A **108**
Ware Mus. 4C 20
Warepoint Dr. SE28: Lon. 9C **140** (7H **39**)
Ware Priory & Gardens 4C 20
Ware Rd. EN11: Hail, Hod 1A **52**
SG12: Ton 3B **20**
SG12: Wid 4F **21**
SG13: Hail 1A **52** (6D **20**)
SG13: Hart 5B **20**
SG14: Wat S 2A **20**
Warescot Cl. CM15: Brtwd 6E **96**
Warescot Rd. CM15: Brtwd 6E **96**
WARESIDE. 4E 20
Wares Rd. CM1: Good E. 5G **23**
Ware Station (Rail) 5D 20
Wargrave Rd. CO15: Clac S 9H **185**
Warham Rd. CO12: Har 5G **209**
Warish Hall Rd. CM22: Tak. 2D **224** (1D **22**)
WARLEY. 2F 112 (1E 40)
Warley Av. RM8: Dag 2L **125**
Warley Cl. CM7: Brain 4L **193**
Warley Gap
CM13: Gt War, L War 4E **112** (2E **40**)
Warley Hall La. RM14: Upm 2J **129** (4F **41**)
Warley Hill CM13: Gt War, War 3E **112** (2E **40**)
CM14: War 3E **112** (1E **40**)
Warley Hill Bus. Pk., The CM13: Gt War 3F **112**
Warley Mt. CM14: War 1F **112**
Warley Rd. CM13: Gt War. 6N **111** (2D **40**)
IG5: Ilf. 5N **107**
IG8: Wfd G 4H **107**
RM14: Upm. 6N **111** (2D **40**)
Warley St. CM13: Gt War, Upm 8F **112** (3E **40**)
RM14: Upm 1F **128** (3E **40**)
Warley Way CO13: Frin S 8L **181**
Warleywoods Cres. CM14: War 1E **112**
Warlow Cl. EN3: Enf. 7A **76**
Warminster Ho. *RM3: Romf. 2K 111*
(off Redcar Rd.)
Warner Cl. CM11: Bill 7M **99**
CM77: Rayne. 7B **192**
E15: Lon 7E **122**
Warner Dr. CM7: Brain 4E **192**
Warner Pl. E2: Lon 6C **38**
Warners CM6: Gt D. 3L **203**
Warners Bri. Chase SS4: R'fd 9L **121**
Warners Cl. IG8: Wfd G 2G **106**
Warners Gdns. SS2: Sth S 9K **121**
(not continuous)
Warners Mill & Working Silk Mus.
. . . . . 6H 193 (7C 14)
Warners Path IG8: Wfd G. 2G **106**
Warner Village Cinema 1K 141
Thurrock Lakeside. 1D 154
Warnham Cl. CO16: Clac S 7F **184**
Warren Av. E10: Lon. 5C **122**
Warren Chase SS7: Thund. 2G **135**
Warren Cl. CM1: Broom. 9K **57**
CM22: Tak. 3D **224**
SS6: Ray 7J **119**
SS17: Stan H 4M **147**
Warren Ct. IG7: Chig. 1C **108**
Warren Dr. RM12: Horn 6E **126**
SS11: W'fd 8A **102**
SS14: Bas 9F **116**
Warren Dr., The E11: Lon. 2J **123**
Warren Farm Cotts. RM6: Chad H 8L **109**
Warren Fld. CM16: Epp. 2F **78**
Warren Gdns. E15: Lon 7D **122**
Warren Hgts. IG10: Lou 5J **91**
RM16: Chaf H. 2H **155**
Warren Hill IG10: Lou. 4J **91**
Warren La. CM15: Dodd, Kel H. 9C **82** (6D **32**)
CO3: S'way. 5C **172** (7C **16**)
RM16: Chaf H 2G **154** (1E **46**)
SG9: Cot 4A **10**
Warren Lingley Way CO5: Tip. 5E **226**
Warren Pond Rd. E4: Lon 7F **90**
(not continuous)
Warren Rd.
CM3: Ret C, Runw, S Han 2J **101** (6B **34**)
CM7: Brain 6L **193**
CO9: Hals. 5J **207**
DA13: Ludd. 7K **47**
DA13: S'fleet 5F **47**
E4: Lon 8C **90**
E10: Lon. 5C **122** (4E **38**)
E11: Lon 1J **123**
(not continuous)
IG6: Ilf. 9C **108**
ME2: Cux. 7K **47**
SS9: Lgh S 3N **135**
Warrens CO9: Hals 5J **207**
Warrenside CM7: Brain. 8J **193**
Warren Sports Cen. 9L 109
Warrens, The CM8: W Bis 2L **229**
CO13: Walt 8H **181**
Warren Street Station (Tube) 6A 38
Warren Ter. RM6: Chad H 8J **109**
(not continuous)
RM16: Chaf H. 9G **145**
Warren, The CM12: Bill 4G **99**
E12: Lon 6L **123**
SS17: Stan H 6N **147**
Warriner Av. RM12: Horn. 4H **127**
Warrington Gdns. RM11: Horn. 1G **127**
Warrington Rd. RM8: Dag. 4J **125**
Warrington Sq. CM12: Bill 5G **99**
RM8: Dag 4J **125**
Warrior Sq. E12: Lon 6N **123**
SS1: Sth S 6M **137**
Warrior Sq. E. SS1: Sth S 6M **137**
Warrior Sq. Nth. SS1: Sth S 6M **137**
Warrior Sq. Rd. SS3: Shoe. 9K **139**
Warriors Swimming Cen. 6M 137
Warton Rd. E15: Lon 9C **122**
Warwall E6: Lon 6A **140**
Warwick Bailey Cl. CO4: Colc 5L **165**
Warwick Cl. CM6: L Eas 6F **13**
CM7: Brain. 4J **193**
CM9: Mal. 7C **214**
SS6: Ray 6M **119**
SS7: Thund 8D **118**
SS8: Can I. 9G **135**
Warwick Ct. CM0: Bur C. 4D **196**
CO2: Colc 2C **174**
CO15: Clac S 1J **189**
DA8: Eri. 5D **152**
Warwick Cres. CM9: Mal 7C **214**
CO15: Clac S 9J **185**
Warwick Dr. CM9: Mal 7C **214**
SS4: R'fd 8L **121**
Warwick Gdns. IG1: Ilf 3A **124**
RM2: Romf 7G **111**
SS6: Ray 6M **119**
Warwick Grn. SS6: Ray 6N **119**
Warwick La. RM13: Ave, Rain. 3K **143** (6C **40**)
RM14: Ave, Upm 3K **143** (6C **40**)
Warwick Pde. CM3: S Fer. 9K **89**
Warwick Pl. CM14: Pil H 3N **95**
SS16: Lang H 2H **131**
Warwick Rd. CM6: L Can 2F **224**
CO15: Clac S. 1H **189**
E4: Lon 2A **106**
E11: Lon. 9H **107**
E12: Lon 7L **123**
E15: Lon 8F **122**
RM13: Rain. 4G **143**
SS1: Sth S 8D **138**
SS6: Ray 6L **119**
(not continuous)
Warwick Sq. CM1: Chelm. 7H **59**
Warwick Ter. *E10: Lon. 9D 106*
(off Lea Bri. Rd.)
Washall Dr. CM77: Gt N 8F **192**
WASHALL GREEN. 3H 11
Washford Gdns. CO15: Clac S 2H **189**
Washington Av. E12: Lon 6M **123**
SS15: Lain. 9J **115**
Washington Cl. CM9: Mal. 7A **214**
Washington Ct. CM9: Mal. 7A **214**
CO3: S'way 1F **172**
Washington Meads CM24: Stan M. 3D **220**
Washington Rd. CM9: Mal 7A **214**
CO12: Har. 5H **209**
E6: Lon 9J **123**
E18: Lon 6F **106**
Wash La. CM9: L Tot 6K **25**
CO15: Clac S 3H **189** (4D **28**)
(not continuous)
Wash Rd. CM13: Hut, Mount 5N **97** (7G **33**)
SS15: Bas, Lain 5L **115** (2K **41**)
(not continuous)
Watchfield La. SS6: Ray. 6J **119**
WATCH HOUSE GREEN 6M 199 (1K 23)
Watch Ho. Rd. CM6: Steb 9D **222** (6J **13**)
Watchouse Rd. CM2: Gall 8C **72** (3A **34**)
Waterbeach Rd. RM9: Dag 8H **125**
Waterden Cres. E15: Lon. 7A **122**
Waterdene SS8: Can I. 9E **134**
Waterden Rd. E15: Lon. 7A **122** (5D **38**)
WATER END. 5E 6
Waterfall Rd. N11: Lon 1A **38**
N14: Lon. 1A **38**
Waterfalls, The SS16: Lang H 3K **131**
Waterfield Cl. SE28: Lon 8G **140**
WATERFORD 4A 20
Waterford Rd. SS3: Shoe 8H **139**
Waterfront Wlk. SS14: Bas. 7C **116**
Waterglade Ind. Pk. RM20: W Thur. 4C **154**
Waterglade Retail Pk. CO15: Clac S 2J **189**
Waterhale SS1: Sth S. 5E **138**
WATERHALES. 4H 95 (7B 32)
Waterhall Av. E4: Lon. 1E **106**
Water Hall La. CM7: Shalf 4B **14**
Waterhall Meadows Nature Reserve. 8H 61
Waterhead Cl. DA8: Eri 5C **152**
Waterhouse La. CM1: Chelm 1N **71** (1K **33**)
CO7: A'gh 2N **167** (4J **17**)
Waterhouse Moor CM18: H'low 4E **54**
Waterhouse St. CM1: Chelm 2A **72**
Water La. CB9: Hel B, Hpstd 5H **7**
CB9: Stpl B. 3J **223** (5J **7**)
CB9: Stur 6K **223** (3K **7**)
CB10: R'ter 7F **7**
CB11: Deb. 1C **12**
CB11: Newp. 2L **215**
CM3: Ples 1B **56**
CM6: Broxt, Gt Eas 6E **12**
CM7: Shalf 5B **14**
CM19: H'low, Roy 7L **53** (1G **31**)
CM24: Stan M. 3D **220**
CM77: Tye G 6F **15**
CO3: Colc 7K **165**
CO4: L'ham 1E **160** (2G **17**)
CO6: L Hork, Nay 3F **158** (2D **16**)
CO8: Bures 7K **195**
CO9: Peb. 2H **15**
CO10: Caven 2F **9**
E15: Lon. 8E **122** (5E **38**)
IG3: Ilf 5D **124** (4H **39**)
RM19: Purf 2L **153**
Waterloo Bri. SE1: Lon. 7A **38**
Waterloo East Station (Rail) 7A 38
Waterloo Gdns. RM7: Romf. 1B **126**
Waterloo International Station (Rail) 7A 38
Waterloo La. CM1: Chelm 9K **59**
Waterloo Rd. CM14: Brtwd. 7F **96**
E6: Lon 9J **123**

Waterloo Rd. E7: Lon . . . 7F **122**
E10: Lon . . . 2A **122**
IG6: Ilf . . . 6B **108**
RM7: Romf, Rush G . . . 9C **110** (3A **40**)
SE1: Lon . . . 7A **38**
SS3: Shoe . . . 7H **139**
Waterloo Station (Rail, Tube) . . . 7A **38**
Watermans RM1: Romf . . . 9D **110**
Watermans Way CM16: N Wea . . . 6M **65**
Watermeadow Cl. DA8: Eri . . . 5F **152**
Watermead Way N17: Lon . . . 3C **38**
Watermill La. CM23: Farnh . . . 4A **220** (6K **11**)
CM24: Stan M . . . 4A **220** (6A **12**)
Watermill Rd. CO5: Fee . . . 1M **211**
Waters Edge SS0: Wclf S . . . 7J **137**
Waters Edge Ct. DA8: Eri . . . 3D **152**
Waters Gdns. RM10: Dag . . . 7M **125**
Waterside CM24: Stan M . . . 3D **220**
Water Side CO7: B'sea . . . 8E **182** (3K **27**)
Waterside SS1: Shoe . . . 8B **138**
Waterside Bus. Pk. CM8: Wthm . . . 3E **230**
Waterside Cl. IG11: Bark . . . 6F **124**
RM3: H Wood . . . 4L **111**
Waterside Farm Sports Cen. . . . 8E **134**
Waterside Ind. Est. EN11: Rye P . . . 6D **52**
Waterside Mead SS8: Can I . . . 8F **134**
Waterside Pl. CM21: Saw . . . 2M **51**
Waterside Rd. CM0: Brad S . . . 9B **194** (1E **36**)
SS4: Pag . . . 1C **44**
Waters Mead SS1: Sth S . . . 8E **138**
Watersmeet CM19: H'low . . . 7A **54**
Watersmeet Way SE28: Lon . . . 6H **141**
Waterson Rd. RM16: Grays . . . 2D **156**
Waterson Vale CM2: Chelm . . . 2D **72**
Waters Vs. CM22: Hat O . . . 7E **206**
Water Twr. Rd. CM14: Gt War . . . 2F **112**
Waterville Dr. SS16: Van . . . 2H **133**
Waterville M. CO2: Colc . . . 3B **174**
Waterways Bus. Cen. EN3: Enf . . . 8A **76**
Waterwick Hill CB11: Lang L . . . 2G **11**
WATERWORKS CORNER . . . 5E **106** (2E **38**)
Waterworks Dr. CO16: Clac S . . . 8F **184**
Waterworks La. SS17: Fob . . . 8D **132**
Waterworks Rd. CM9: Tol . . . 7K **225**
Watery La. CM5: H Lav, Mat G . . . 7B **22**
CM6: Gt D . . . 2F **23**
CM23: Man . . . 5J **11**
CO6: Cogg . . . 7G **15**
CO10: Gt Hen, L Hen . . . 7H **9**
SS11: Raw, Ray . . . 7H **103** (7E **34**)
Wates Way CM15: Brtwd . . . 7G **96**
Watford Ho. *RM3: Romf* . . . *2K **111***
(off Redruth Rd.)
Watkin M. EN3: Enf . . . 7A **76**
Watkins Cl. SS13: Bas . . . 6L **117**
Watkins Way SS3: Shoe . . . 5K **139**
Watling La. CM6: Thax . . . 6B **224**
Watling St. CM6: Thax . . . 7C **224**
DA1: Dart . . . 4C **46**
DA2: Bean, Dart, Grnh . . . 4D **46**
DA6: Bexh . . . 9A **152** (3A **46**)
DA11: Grav, N'fleet . . . 4F **47**
DA12: Cobh, Grav . . . 4F **47**
Watlington Rd. CM17: H'low . . . 8J **51**
SS7: Ben . . . 4B **134**
Watsham Pl. CO7: W'hoe . . . 3J **175**
Watson Av. E6: Lon . . . 9N **123**
Watson Cl. RM20: W Thur . . . 6D **154**
SS3: Shoe . . . 7H **139**
Watson Gdns. RM3: H Wood . . . 6H **111**
Watson Rd. CO15: Clac S . . . 1J **189**
Watsons Ct. CB10: Saf W . . . 3C **218**
WATTON AT STONE . . . 2A **20**
Watton-at-Stone Station (Rail) . . . 2A **20**
Watton Rd. SG12: Ware . . . 4C **20**
SG14: Wat S . . . 2A **20**
WATTON'S GREEN . . . 5F **94** (7B **32**)
Watts Bri. Rd. DA8: Eri . . . 4D **152**
Watts Cl. CM6: Barns . . . 3M **191**
Watt's Cres. RM19: Purf . . . 2N **153**
Watts La. SS4: R'fd . . . 6L **121**
Watts Rd. CO2: Colc . . . 4J **173**
Watts Yd. CM23: Man . . . 5K **11**
Wat Tyler Country Pk. . . . 5H **133**
Wat Tyler Wlk. *CO1: Colc* . . . *8N **165***
(off W. Stockwell St.)
Wavell Av. CO2: Colc . . . 2K **173**
Wavell Cl. CM1: Chelm . . . 3M **59**
Waveney Dr. CM1: Chelm . . . 5L **59**
Waverley Av. E17: Lon . . . 7D **106**
Waverley Bri. Ct. CM9: Mal . . . 4D **214**
Waverley Cl. E18: Lon . . . 5J **107**
Waverley Cres. RM3: Romf . . . 4G **111**
SS11: W'fd . . . 5K **101**
Waverley Gdns. IG6: Ilf . . . 6B **108**
IG11: Bark . . . 2D **140**
RM16: Grays . . . 9K **145**
Waverley Rd. E17: Lon . . . 7C **106**
E18: Lon . . . 5J **107**
RM13: Rain . . . 4F **142**
SS7: Thund . . . 1C **134**
SS15: Lain . . . 6N **115**
Waver Ter. CO5: Abb . . . 8B **174**
Wavertree Rd. E18: Lon . . . 6G **107**
SS7: Ben . . . 2B **134**
Wavring Av. CO13: Walt . . . 7H **181**
Waxwell Rd. SS5: Hull . . . 6L **103**
Wayback, The CB10: Saf W . . . 3D **218**
Way Bank La. CO10: Wixoe . . . 3B **8**
Waycross Rd. RM14: Upm . . . 2B **128**
Wayfarer Gdns. CM0: Bur C . . . 3C **196**
Wayfaring Grn. RM17: Grays . . . 3J **155**
Wayletts SS9: Lgh S . . . 9A **120**
SS15: Lain . . . 7J **115**
Wayre St. CM17: H'low . . . 8H **51**
Wayre, The CM17: H'low . . . 8H **51**
Wayside CM3: L Bad . . . 2E **74**
Wayside Av. RM12: Horn . . . 4H **127**
Wayside Cl. RM1: Romf . . . 7D **110**
Wayside Commercial Cen. IG11: Bark . . . 1E **140**
Wayside Gdns. RM10: Dag . . . 7M **125**
Wayside M. IG2: Ilf . . . 9N **107**
Waytemore Castle . . . 1K **21**
Weald Bri. Rd. CM16: N Wea . . . 3B **66** (2A **32**)
Weald Cl. CM14: Brtwd . . . 9D **96**
Weald Country Pk. . . . 6A **96**
WEALDGULLET . . . 5M **65**
Weald Hall La. CM16: Thorn . . . 4H **65** (2J **31**)
Weald Hall La. Ind. Est. CM16: Thorn . . . 4H **65**
Weald Pk. Way CM14: S Wea . . . 9B **96** (1D **40**)
Weald Rd. CM14: S Wea . . . 7L **95** (7C **32**)
Weald, The SS8: Can I . . . 1E **150**
Weald Way RM7: Romf . . . 1N **125**
Weale Rd. E4: Lon . . . 9D **90**
Wear Dr. CM1: Chelm . . . 5M **59**
(not continuous)
Weare Gifford SS3: Shoe . . . 6G **138**
Weathervane Cotts. CM7: Gt Bar . . . 3C **202**
Weaver Cl. E6: Lon . . . 7A **140**
Weaverdale SS3: Shoe . . . 5J **139**
Weaverhead Cl. CM6: Thax . . . 7C **224**
Weaverhead La. CM6: Thax . . . 7C **224**
Weavers SS16: Van . . . 2G **133**
Weavers Almshouses *E11:* . . . *1F **122***
(off Cambridge Rd.)
Weavers Cl. CM7: Brain . . . 5H **193**
CM11: Bill . . . 6K **99**
CO3: Colc . . . 1G **172**
Weavers Ct. CO9: Hals . . . 5K **207**
Weaversfield CM8: Sil E . . . 7K **217**
Weavers Grn. CO6: For . . . 1A **164**
Weavers Ho. *E11: Lon* . . . *1G **122***
(off New Wanstead)
Weavers Row CO9: Hals . . . 5L **207**
Webb Cl. CM2: Chelm . . . 8C **60**
Webb Ct. *SE28: Lon* . . . *7G **141***
(off Attlee Rd.)
Webber Cl. DA8: Eri . . . 5F **152**
Webb Ho. *RM10: Dag* . . . *5M **125***
(off Kershaw Rd.)
Webbscroft Rd. RM10: Dag . . . 6N **125**
WEBBS FARM INTERCHANGE . . . 9K **71** (3K **33**)
Webley Ct. *EN3: Enf* . . . *7A **76***
(off Sten Cl.)
Webster Cl. CO9: Sib H . . . 7J **219**
EN9: Wal A . . . 3F **76**
RM12: Horn . . . 5H **127**
Webster Pl. CM4: Stock . . . 7N **85**
Webster Rd. E11: Lon . . . 5C **122**
SS17: Stan H . . . 3N **147**
Websters Way SS6: Ray . . . 5K **119** (2F **43**)
Wedderburn Rd. IG11: Bark . . . 1D **140**
Wedds Way SS3: Gt W . . . 2M **139**
Wedgewood Cl. CM16: Epp . . . 9F **64**
Wedgewood Dr. CM17: H'low . . . 4K **55**
CO4: Colc . . . 5M **165**
Wedgwood Ct. SS4: R'fd . . . 1J **121**
Wedgwood Way SS4: R'fd . . . 1H **121**
Wedhey CM19: H'low . . . 3B **54**
Wedlake Cl. RM11: Horn . . . 3J **127**
Wedmore Av. IG5: Ilf . . . 5N **107**
Wednesbury Gdns. RM3: Romf . . . 4K **111**
Wednesbury Grn. RM3: Romf . . . 4K **111**
Wednesbury Rd. RM3: Romf . . . 4K **111**
Wedow Rd. CM6: Thax . . . 7C **224**
WEELEY . . . 5D **178** (7C **18**)
Weeley Bri. Holiday Pk. CO16: Wee . . . 6C **178**
Weeley By-Pass Rd. CO16: Wee . . . 5C **178** (7C **18**)
Weeley Crematorium
CO16: Wee . . . 4C **178** (7B **18**)
Weeleyhall Wood Nature Reserve . . . 7F **178**
WEELEY HEATH . . . 8E **178** (1C **28**)
Weeley Rd. CO7: Gt Ben . . . 9L **177** (1A **28**)
(Aingers Grn. Rd.)
CO7: Gt Ben . . . 6K **177** (1A **28**)
(Thorrington Rd.)
CO16: L Cla . . . 1G **184** (2D **28**)
Weeley Station (Rail) . . . 6D **178** (1C **28**)
Weelkes Cl. SS17: Stan H . . . 2L **147**
Weel Rd. SS8: Can I . . . 3K **151**
Weggs Willow CO4: Colc . . . 8C **166**
Weighbridge Ct. CB11: Saf W . . . 5C **218**
Weight Rd. CM2: Chelm . . . 9L **59**
Weind, The CM16: They B . . . 6D **78**
WEIR . . . 7J **119** (3F **43**)
Weirbrook SS6: Thund . . . 7H **119**
Weir Farm Rd. SS6: Ray . . . 7J **119**
Weir Gdns. SS6: Ray . . . 6J **119**
Weir La. CO2: B'hth . . . 7B **174** (1F **27**)
CO5: Fing . . . 7B **174** (1F **27**)
Weir Pond Rd. SS4: R'fd . . . 5L **121** (2J **43**)
Weir Wynd CM12: Bill . . . 7J **99**
Welbeck Cl. SS5: Hock . . . 3E **120**
Welbeck Dr. SS16: Lang H . . . 2J **131**
Welbeck Ri. SS16: Lang H . . . 2J **131**
Welbeck Rd. SS8: Can I . . . 3G **151**
Welch Cl. SS2: Sth S . . . 4C **138**
Welcome Ct. SS17: Stan H . . . 4K **147**
Welfare Rd. E15: Lon . . . 9E **122**
Welham Rd. RM18: E Til . . . 2L **157**
Welland Av. CM1: Chelm . . . 6E **58**
Welland Rd. CM0: Bur C . . . 2C **196**
Wellands CM8: W Bis . . . 2K **229**
Wellands Cl. CM8: W Bis . . . 2J **229**
Wellcome Av. DA1: Dart . . . 9J **153**
Well Cott. Cl. E11: Lon . . . 1J **123**
Weller Gro. CM1: Chelm . . . 4G **59**
Wellesley CM19: H'low . . . 8N **53**
Wellesley Rd. CM14: Brtwd . . . 7F **96**
CO3: Colc . . . 9M **165**
CO15: Clac S . . . 9J **185** (4D **28**)
E11: Lon . . . 9G **107**
E17: Lon . . . 1A **122**
IG1: Ilf . . . 4A **124**
Well Fld. CM1: Writ . . . 1J **71**
CO9: Hals . . . 6L **207**
Wellfields IG10: Lou . . . 2N **91**
Wellfield Way CO13: Walt . . . 8G **181**
Well Grn. Cl. CB11: Saf W . . . 6D **218**
Wellingborough Ho. *RM3: Romf* . . . *2K **111***
(off Redruth Rd.)
Wellingbury SS7: Ben . . . 1C **134**
Welling Rd. RM16: Ors . . . 6E **146**
Wellington Av. E4: Lon . . . 8A **90**
SS0: Lgh S . . . 5F **136**
SS5: Hull . . . 8K **103**
Wellington Cl. CM1: Chelm . . . 6F **58**
CM7: Brain . . . 4L **193**
RM10: Dag . . . 9A **126**
Wellington Ct. RM16: Grays . . . 8L **145**
Wellington Dr. RM10: Dag . . . 9A **126**
Wellington Hill IG10: H Bee, Lou . . . 7G **77** (5F **31**)
Wellingtonia Av. RM4: Hav . . . 1A **110**
Wellington Mans. E10: Lon . . . 3A **122**
Wellington M. CM12: Bill . . . 3J **99**
Wellington Pas. *E11: Lon* . . . *9G **107***
(off Wellington Rd.)
Wellington Pl. CM14: War . . . 2F **112**
Wellington Rd. CM9: Mal . . . 6B **214**
CM16: N Wea . . . 6M **65**
CO12: Har . . . 1N **209** (2J **19**)
E7: Lon . . . 6F **122**
E11: Lon . . . 9G **107**
RM18: Til . . . 7C **156**
SS5: Hock . . . 7E **104**
SS6: Ray . . . 3M **119**
Wellingtons, The CM0: S'min . . . 3D **222**
Wellington St. CO2: Colc . . . 9M **165**
CO7: B'sea . . . 7E **182**
DA12: Grav . . . 4H **47**
IG11: Bark . . . 1B **140**
WC2: Lon . . . 7A **38**
Well La. CM2: Gall . . . 8C **72**
CM3: Dan . . . 4C **74** (2D **34**)
CM4: Stock . . . 8N **85** (5K **33**)
CM15: Pil H . . . 2C **96**
CM19: H'low . . . 2N **53**
(not continuous)
CO5: Ethpe . . . 7J **171** (1A **26**)
CO10: Clare . . . 3D **8**
RM16: N Stif . . . 8H **145**
Well Mead CM12: Bill . . . 9L **99**
Wellmeads CM2: Chelm . . . 2C **72**
WELLPOND GREEN . . . 1F **21**
Well Row SG13: B'frd . . . 7A **20**
Wells Av. SS2: Sth S . . . 9J **121**
Wells Ct. CM1: Chelm . . . 6M **59**
CM6: Gt D . . . 2K **203**
Wellsfield SS6: Ray . . . 3L **119**
Wells Gdns. IG1: Ilf . . . 2L **123**
RM10: Dag . . . 7N **125**
RM13: Rain . . . 8D **126**
SS14: Bas . . . 7G **116**
Wells Hall Rd. CO10: Gt Cor . . . 5K **9**
Wells Ho. *IG11: Bark* . . . *9F **124***
(off Margaret Bondfield Av.)
Well Side CO6: M Tey . . . 3G **171**
Wells Mead CB11: Widd . . . 3B **12**
Wells Rd. CO1: Colc . . . 7A **166**
Wells St. CM1: Chelm . . . 8J **59**
Wellstead Gdns. SS0: Wclf S . . . 3G **136**
Well St. CO7: B'sea . . . 6D **182**
E8: Lon . . . 5C **38**
E15: Lon . . . 8E **122**
WELLSTYE GREEN . . . 2H **23**
Wellstye Grn. SS14: Bas . . . 7F **116**
Well Ter. CM9: Mal . . . 3D **214**
Wellwood Rd. IG3: Ilf . . . 3F **124**
Wellyard CB10: Hpstd . . . 7G **7**
WELSHWOOD PARK . . . 5E **166**
Welshwood Pk. Rd. CO4: Colc . . . 5E **166**
Welton Way SS4: R'fd . . . 6M **121**
Welwyn Rd. SG14: Hart, Pans . . . 5A **20**
Wembley Av. CM3: May . . . 8K **213**
Wendene SS16: Van . . . 2G **132**
Wenden Rd. CB11: A End, Saf W . . . 6A **218** (7B **6**)
CB11: A'den, Wen A . . . 1K **11**
WENDENS AMBO . . . 7K **227** (7A **6**)
Wendon Cl. SS4: R'fd . . . 3H **121**
Wendover Gdns. CM13: Brtwd . . . 8L **97**
Wendover Way RM12: Horn . . . 7G **127**
WENDY . . . 2B **4**
Wendy Rd. SG8: Shin W, Stpl M . . . 3A **4**
Wenham Dr. SS0: Wclf S . . . 4K **137**
Wenham Gdns. CM13: Hut . . . 5M **97**
Wenlock Rd. CO16: Wee . . . 8D **178**
Wenlock's La. CM4: B'more . . . 3G **82** (4E **32**)
WENNINGTON . . . 7J **143** (7C **40**)
Wennington Rd. RM13: Rain, Wen . 4E **142** (6B **40**)
Wensley Av. IG8: Wfd G . . . 4F **106**
Wensley Cl. RM5: Col R . . . 2M **109**
Wensleydale Av. IG5: Ilf . . . 6L **107**
Wensley Rd. SS7: Thund . . . 2H **135**
Wents Cl. CO7: Gt Ben . . . 5K **177**
Wentworth Cl. CM3: Hat P . . . 2M **61**
SE28: Lon . . . 6J **141**
Wentworth Cres. CM7: Brain . . . 3H **193**
Wentworth Mdws. CM9: Mal . . . 6B **214**
Wentworth Pl. RM16: Grays . . . 1N **155**
Wentworth Rd. E12: Lon . . . 6K **123**
SS2: Sth S . . . 3M **137**
Wentworth Way RM13: Rain . . . 3F **142**
Werneth Hall Rd. IG5: Ilf . . . 7M **107**
Wesel Av. IP11: Felix . . . 1K **19**
Wesley Av. CO4: Colc . . . 7C **166**
Wesley Ct. SS1: Sth S . . . 6N **137**
WESLEY END . . . 6A **8**
Wesley End Rd. CO9: Stamb . . . 6A **8**
Wesley Gdns. CM12: Bill . . . 3H **99**
Wesley Rd. E10: Lon . . . 2C **122**
SS1: Sth S . . . 7N **137**
Wessem Rd. SS8: Can I . . . 9H **135**
Wessex Cl. IG3: Ilf . . . 1D **124**
Wessex Dr. DA8: Eri . . . 7C **152**
Wessley Cl. CM0: T'ham . . . 2K **225**
Westall Rd. IG10: Lou . . . 2A **92**
West Av. CM1: Chelm . . . 6H **59**
CM3: Alth . . . 3B **190**
CM3: May . . . 7J **213**
CO15: Clac S . . . 2J **189**
E17: Lon . . . 8B **106**
SS5: Hull . . . 5J **103**
SS16: Lang H . . . 2G **131**
W. Avenue Rd. E17: Lon . . . 8A **106**
West Bank IG11: Bark . . . 1A **140**
W. Beech Av. SS11: W'fd . . . 9L **101**
W. Beech Cl. SS11: W'fd . . . 9M **101**
W. Beech M. SS11: W'fd . . . 9L **101**
West Belvedere CM3: Dan . . . 3F **74**
WEST BERGHOLT . . . 3F **164** (5C **16**)
WESTBOROUGH . . . 5K **137**
Westborough Rd. SS0: Wclf S . . . 4G **137**
Westbourne Cl. SS5: Hock . . . 9F **104**
SS7: Had . . . 1K **135**
Westbourne Dr. CM14: Brtwd . . . 1C **112**
Westbourne Gdns. CM12: Bill . . . 3K **99**
Westbourne Gro. CM2: Gt Bad . . . 3E **72**
SS0: Wclf S . . . 5G **137** (4H **43**)
Westbourne Rd. N7: Lon . . . 5A **38**
W. Bowers Rd. CM3: Wdhm W . . . 1E **34**
Westbrook CM19: H'low . . . 6M **53**
Westbury SS4: R'fd . . . 3H **121**
Westbury Av. N22: Lon . . . 3A **38**
Westbury Cl. CO6: Cop . . . 1M **171**
Westbury Ct. *IG11: Bark* . . . *1C **140***
(off Westbury Rd.)
Westbury Dr. CM14: Brtwd . . . 8F **96**
Westbury La. IG9: Buck H . . . 8H **91**
Westbury Ri. CM17: H'low . . . 4J **55**
Westbury Rd. CM14: Brtwd . . . 8F **96**
CO13: Gt Hol . . . 9D **180**
E7: Lon . . . 8H **123**
E17: Lon . . . 8A **106**
IG1: Ilf . . . 4N **123**
IG9: Buck H . . . 8J **91**
IG11: Bark . . . 1C **140**
SS2: Sth S . . . 4A **138**
W. Bury St. N9: Lon . . . 7B **30**
Westbury Ter. E7: Lon . . . 8H **123**
RM14: Upm . . . 4B **128**
West Chase CM9: Mal . . . 5B **214**
CM9: Mun . . . 3J **35**
Westcliff Av. SS0: Wclf S . . . 7K **137** (5J **43**)
Westcliff Dr. SS9: Lgh S . . . 5C **136**
Westcliff Gdns. SS8: Can I . . . 3L **151**
WESTCLIFF-ON-SEA . . . 7J **137** (5J **43**)
Westcliff Pde. SS0: Wclf S . . . 7K **137** (5J **43**)
Westcliff Pk. Dr. SS0: Wclf S . . . 5J **137**
Westcliff Station (Rail) . . . 6J **137** (5J **43**)
West Cliff Theatre . . . 2J **189**
West Cloister CM11: Bill . . . 6K **99**
West Cl. EN11: Hod . . . 3A **52**
RM13: Rain . . . 4F **142**
Westcott Cl. CO16: Clac S . . . 7H **185**
WESTCOURT . . . 4J **47**
West Ct. CM4: Ing . . . 6D **84**
CM21: Saw . . . 1K **51**
E17: Lon . . . 8A **106**
West Cres. SS8: Can I . . . 1F **150**
West Cft. CM11: Bill . . . 6K **99**
Westcroft Ct. EN10: Brox . . . 7A **52**
W. Dene Dr. RM3: Romf . . . 2H **111**
W. Dock Rd. CO12: Har . . . 2G **208**
Westdown Rd. E15: Lon . . . 6C **122**
West Dr. CM7: Weth . . . 8B **228**
Wested La. BR8: Crock . . . 7A **46**
West End CB2: Whitt . . . 2J **5**
W. End Av. E10: Lon . . . 9D **106**
W. End La. CB9: Ked . . . 2A **8**
CO12: Har . . . 6K **209**
W. End Rd. CO5: Tip . . . 8A **226** (4J **25**)
EN10: Brox . . . 1B **30**
Westerdale CM1: Chelm . . . 4M **59**
Westergreen Mdw. CM7: Brain . . . 7G **193**
Westerham Rd. E10: Lon . . . 2B **122**
Westerings CM3: Dan . . . 8F **74**
CM3: Pur . . . 8K **215**
Westerings, The CM2: Gt Bad . . . 5G **73**
SS5: Hock . . . 2D **120**
Westerland Av. SS8: Can I . . . 1K **151**
Westerlings, The CM77: Tye G . . . 2E **194**
Western Approaches
SS2: Lgh S, Sth S . . . 8F **120**
Western Av. CM14: Brtwd . . . 7F **96** (7E **32**)
CM16: Epp . . . 2E **78**
RM2: Romf . . . 6G **110**
RM10: Dag . . . 8A **126**
Western Cl. CM8: Sil E . . . 9M **217**
Western Ct. *RM1: Romf* . . . *9C **110***
(off Chandlers Way)
Western Esplanade SS0: Can I . . . 7H **137** (5J **43**)
SS1: Wclf S . . . 7H **137**
SS8: Can I . . . 3H **151** (6E **42**)
Western Gdns. CM14: Brtwd . . . 8F **96**
Western La. CM8: Sil E . . . 9M **217**
Western M. CM12: Bill . . . 6J **99**

Western Pathway RM12: Horn 9F 126
RM13: Rain 9F 126
Western Prom. CO7: B'sea 8C 182
CO16: P Bay 9D 182 (4K 27)
Western Rd. CM0: Bur C 4D 196 (7C 36)
CM8: Riven, Sil E 9M 217 (2F 25)
CM12: Bill 7H 99 (7J 33)
CM14: Brtwd 8F 96 (1E 40)
CM16: Epp 2E 78
CO7: B'sea 7D 182
E17: Lon 9C 106
EN9: Naze 1E 62
RM1: Romf 9C 110 (3A 40)
SS6: Ray 7H 119
SS7: Had 9L 119 (3F 43)
SS9: Lgh S 5N 135
Western Ter. EN11: Hod 2B 52
Westernville Gdns. IG2: Ilf 2B 124
Western Way SE28: Lon 9D 140 (7H 39)
Westferry Rd. E14: Lon 7D 38
Westferry Station (DLR) 7D 38
Westfield CM18: H'low 4D 54
IG10: Lou 4K 91
SS15: Lain 7J 115
Westfield Av. CM1: Chelm 7J 59
Westfield Cl. SS6: Ray 2H 119
SS11: W'fd 8N 101
Westfield Dr. CO6: Cogg 2L 197
Westfield Gdns. RM6: Chad H 1H 125
Westfield Ho. CM18: H'low 5C 54
Westfield Pk. Dr. IG8: Wfd G 3L 107
Westfield Rd. DA7: Bexh 8A 152
RM9: Dag 6K 125
Westfields CB11: Saf W 5D 218
Westfleet Trad. Est. SS11: W'fd 1N 117
West Ga. CM20: H'low 3B 54
(not continuous)
Westgate SS3: Shoe 8J 139
SS14: Bas 9B 116
Westgate Pk. SS14: Bas 1B 132
Westgate Rd. DA1: Dart 3B 46
(not continuous)
Westgate St. CO10: L Mel 2J 9
WEST GREEN 3B 38
West Grn. CB2: Barr 1E 4
SS7: Ben 1B 134
W. Green Rd. N15: Lon 3A 38
West Gro. IG8: Wfd G 3J 107
WEST HAM 6F 39
W. Ham La. E15: Lon 9D 122 (5E 38)
West Ham Station (Rail & Tube) 6E 38
West Ham United F.C. (Upton Pk.) 6F 39
WEST HANNINGFIELD 5H 87 (5B 34)
W. Hanningfield Rd.
CM2: Gt Bad, W Han 3F 86 (4B 34)
West Hayes CM22: Hat H 1E 210
West Hill DA1: Dart 3B 46
West Holme DA8: Eri 6A 152
West Hook SS16: Lang H 3H 131
WEST HORNDON 1N 129 (3G 41)
West Horndon Station (Rail) 1M 129 (3G 41)
West Ho. Est. CM0: S'min 2C 222
West House Wood Nature Reserve 4H 165
W. India Dock Rd. E14: Lon 7D 38
(not continuous)
West India Quay Station (DLR) 7D 38
Westlake Av. SS13: Pits 9M 117
Westlake Cres. CO7: W'hoe 4G 175
Westland Av. RM11: Horn 3J 127
WESTLAND GREEN 1G 21
Westland Vw. RM16: Grays 8K 145
West Lawn CM2: Gall 8D 72
Westleigh Av. SS9: Lgh S 4C 136
Westleigh Ct. E11: Lon 9G 107
SS9: Lgh S 5C 136
(off Westleigh Av.)
Westley CM0: Bur C 3E 196
Westley Heights Country Pk. 5K 131
Westley La. CB10: Saf W 5B 6
Westley Rd. SS16: Bas 4L 131
W. Lodge Rd. CO3: Colc 9L 165
Westlyn Cl. RM13: Rain 4G 143
West Mall *RM17: Grays 4K 155*
(in Mall, The)
W. Malling Way RM12: Horn 7G 126
Westman Rd. SS8: Can I 2L 151
Westmarch CM3: S Fer 2J 103
West Mayne SS15: Dun, Lain 7F 114 (3H 41)
Westmayne Ind. Pk. SS15: Lain 9G 115
Westmede IG7: Chig 3B 108
SS16: Lang H 2L 131
WEST MERSEA 3B 228 (5F 27)
West Mersea Yacht Club 2A 228
WESTMILL 5D 10
Westmill Rd. SG12: Ware, W'mll 4C 20
WESTMINSTER 7A 38
Westminster Bri. SW1: Lon 7A 38
Westminster Cl. IG6: Ilf 6C 108
Westminster Ct. CO2: Colc 2C 174
CO15: Clac S 1M 189
(off Connaught Gdns. E.)
E11: Lon 1G 123
(off Cambridge Pk.)
Westminster Dr. SS0: Wclf S 5G 137
SS5: Hock 1B 120
Westminster Gdns. CM7: Brain 4J 193
E4: Lon 7E 90
IG6: Ilf 6B 108
IG11: Bark 2D 140
Westminster Mans. SS0: Wclf S 4G 137
Westminster Station (Tube) 7A 38
Westmoreland Av. RM11: Horn 9G 111
Westmorland Cl. CO11: Mist 5M 163
E12: Lon 4K 123
Westmorland Rd. E17: Lon 1A 122
Weston Av. RM20: W Thur 4C 154 (1D 46)
Weston Chambers *SS1: Sth S 7M 137*
(off Weston Rd.)
Weston Cl. CM13: Hut 6M 97
Westone Mans. *IG11: Bark 9E 124*
(off Upney La.)
Weston Grn. RM9: Dag 6L 125
Weston Rd. CO2: Colc 1B 174
RM9: Dag 6K 125
SS1: Sth S 7M 137
W. Park Av. CM12: Bill 5J 99
W. Park Cl. RM6: Chad H 9J 109
W. Park Cres. CM12: Bill 6J 99
W. Park Dr. CM12: Bill 6J 99
W. Park Hill CM14: Brtwd 9D 96
W. Point Pl. SS8: Can I 2C 150
Westpole Av. EN2: Barn 6A 30
West Quay *CO7: W'hoe 7H 175*
(off Quay, The)
Westray Wlk. SS12: W'fd 2A 118
West Ridge CM12: Bill 8J 99
Westridge Way CO15: Clac S 7L 185
West Rd. CB11: Saf W 5C 218
CM20: H'low 8F 50
CM21: Saw 1G 50 (4J 21)
CM24: Stan M 4D 220
CO9: Hals 5K 207
CO15: Clac S, Jay 4E 188 (5C 28)
RM6: Chad H 1J 125
RM7: Rush G 2B 126
RM15: S Ock 3D 144 (6E 40)
SS0: Wclf S 5J 137 (4J 43)
SS3: Shoe 7H 139
Westrow Dr. IG11: Bark 7F 124
Westrow Gdns. IG3: Ilf 4E 124
Westside Cen. CO3: S'way 1C 172
West Smithfield EC4: Lon 7A 38
West Sq. CM1: Chelm 9K 59
CM9: Mal 5B 214
CM20: H'low 2B 54
W. Station Ind. Est. CM9: Mal 7A 214
W. Station Yd. CM9: Mal 7A 214
W. Stockwell St. CO1: Colc 8N 165
West St. CM9: Tol 8H 225 (6C 26)
CO2: Colc 9M 165
CO5: Rhdge 6F 174
CO6: Cogg 4H 197 (7G 15)
CO7: W'hoe 6H 175
CO12: Har 1M 209 (2J 19)
CO14: Walt 6M 181
DA8: Eri 2B 152 (1A 46)
DA11: Grav 3H 47
E11: Lon 5E 122
E17: Lon 9B 106
RM17: Grays 4K 155
SS2: Sth S 4K 137 (4J 43)
SS4: R'fd 5K 121 (2J 43)
SS9: Lgh S 6D 136
West Thorpe SS14: Bas 9D 116
WEST THURROCK 4D 154 (1D 46)
W. Thurrock Way
RM20: Chaf H, Grays, W Thur 1C 154 (1E 46)
WEST TILBURY 4G 156 (1J 47)
West Vw. CM22: Tak 2C 224
CO7: Ded 2M 161
IG10: Lou 2M 91
West Vw. Cl. CO4: Colc 4B 166
Westview Cl. RM13: Rain 3G 143
Westview Dr. IG8: Wfd G 6K 107
West Vw. Dr. SS6: Ray 6H 119
West Wlk. CM20: H'low 3B 54
Westward Deals CB9: Ked 2A 8
Westward Rd. E4: Lon 2A 106
(not continuous)
Westwater SS7: Ben 2B 134
Westway CM1: Chelm 3N 71 (2K 33)
CM3: S Fer 1J 103
West Way CM14: Brtwd 9D 96
Westway CO1: Colc 6M 165
CO3: Colc 7M 165 (5E 16)
SS3: Shoe 8J 139
WEST WICKHAM 1F 7
W. Wickham Rd. CB1: B'shm 1E 6
Westwood Av. CM14: Brtwd 1D 112
West Wood Cl. SS7: Had 2J 135
Westwood Ct. SS7: Had 2K 135
Westwood Dr. CO5: W Mer 3E 228
Westwood Gdns. SS7: Had 2K 135
Westwood Hill CO4: Colc 4J 165
Westwood Lodge SS7: Had 1J 135
Westwood Pk. Rd.
CO6: Gt Hork, W Ber 8E 158 (4C 16)
Westwood Rd. DA13: S'fleet 5E 46
IG3: Ilf 3E 124
SS8: Can I 2H 151
W. Wratting Comn. CB1: W Wra 1G 7
W. Wratting Rd. CB1: B'shm 1E 6
West Yd. CO9: Hals 6K 207
WEST YOKE 7E 46
West Yoke TN15: Ash 7E 46
W. Yoke Rd. TN15: Ash 7F 47
Wetherfield CM24: Stan M 2C 220
Wetherfield Rd. CO9: Sib H 2C 14
Wetherland SS16: Bas 1A 132
Wetherly Cl. CM17: H'low 8L 51
WETHERSFIELD 8B 228 (3A 14)
Wethersfield Cl. SS6: Ray 4G 118
Wethersfield Rd. CM7: F'fld 6A 228 (2K 13)
CO2: Colc 6A 174
CO9: Sib H 6H 219 (1D 14)
Wethersfield Way SS11: W'fd 2B 118
Wet La. CO4: Boxt 2M 159 (2E 16)
Wetzlar Ct. CO2: Colc 2B 174
Weybourne Cl. SS2: Sth S 3N 137
Weybourne Gdns. SS2: Sth S 3N 137
Weybridge Wlk. SS3: Shoe 5J 139
Weydale SS17: Corr 9C 132
Weylond Rd. RM8: Dag 5L 125
Weymarks SS15: Lain 8M 115
Weymouth Cl. CO15: Clac S 4H 189
E6: Lon 6A 140
Weymouth Rd. CM1: Chelm 5N 59
Whadden Chase CM4: Ing 6C 84
WHADDON 2C 4
Whaddon Rd. SG8: Meld 2D 4
Whalebone Av. RM6: Chad H 1L 125
Whalebone Gro. RM6: Chad H 1L 125
Whalebone La. E15: Lon 9E 122
Whalebone La. Nth.
RM6: Chad H, Col R 4K 109 (2K 39)
Whalebone La. Sth.
RM6: Chad H, Dag 2L 125 (4K 39)
RM8: Dag 2L 125 (4K 39)
Whales Yd. *E15: Lon 9E 122*
(off W. Ham La.)
Whaley Rd. CO4: Colc 8C 166
Wharf Cl. SS17: Stan H 4M 147
Wharfdale Rd. N1: Lon 6A 38
Wharfe Cl. CM8: Wthm 5B 230
Wharf La. CO8: Bures 8L 195
SS16: Pits 4G 132
Wharf Rd. CM2: Chelm 9L 59
CM14: Brtwd 9F 96
EN10: Wmly 3A 62 (2D 30)
RM17: Grays 4J 155
SS17: Fob 1E 148 (6A 42)
SS17: Stan H 4M 147 (6K 41)
(not continuous)
Wharf Rd. Sth. RM17: Grays 4J 155
Wharfside Cl. DA8: Eri 3D 152
Wharley Hook CM18: H'low 6E 54
Wharton Dr. CM1: Chelm 4B 60
Wheatear Ind. Est. CM8: Wthm 6E 230
Wheatear Pl. CM11: Bill 7L 99
Wheatfield Rd. CO3: S'way 9E 164
Wheatfields CM14: War 1F 112
CM17: H'low 6H 51
E6: Lon 6A 140
SS4: Stam 1K 43
Wheatfields Ct. *EN9: Wal A 4G 77*
(off Farthingale La.)
Wheatfield Way CM1: Chelm 8H 59
(not continuous)
SS16: Lang H 2J 131
Wheatlands CO7: Elms 9M 167
Wheatley Av. CM7: Brain 5L 193
Wheatley Cl. CM21: Saw 3H 51
RM11: Horn 9H 111
SS4: R'fd 3J 121
Wheatley Mans. *IG11: Bark 9F 124*
(off Bevan Av.)
Wheatley Rd. SS17: Corr 9C 132
Wheatley Ter. DA8: Eri 4D 152
Wheaton Av. SS16: Lang H 3J 131
Wheaton Rd. CM8: Wthm 5E 230
Wheatsheaf Cl. CO11: Wrab 3D 18
Wheatsheaf Ct. CO1: Colc 9B 166
Wheatsheaf La. CO11: Wrab 3D 18
Wheatsheaf Rd. RM1: Romf 1D 126
Wheatstone Rd. DA8: Eri 3B 152
Wheeler Cl. CO4: Colc 9E 166
IG8: Wfd G 3M 107
Wheelers CM16: Epp 8E 64
Wheelers Cl. EN9: Naze 1E 62
Wheelers Cross IG11: Bark 2C 140
Wheelers Farm Gdns. CM16: N Wea 5N 65
Wheeler's Hill CM3: L Walt 6L 57 (5A 24)
Wheelers La.
CM14: N'side, Pil H 3M 95 (6C 32)
SS17: Fob 9E 132
Wheel Farm Dr. RM10: Dag 5A 126
Wheelwrights, The SS2: Temp I 1M 137
WHEMPSTEAD 1B 20
Whempstead La. SG12: Wat S 1A 20
Whempstead Rd. SG2: B'tn 7A 10
SG2: B'tn, D End 1A 20
Whernside Av. SS8: Can I 9J 135
Whernside Cl. SE28: Lon 7H 141
Whieldon Grange CM17: H'low 4K 55
Whiffins Orchard CM16: Coop 8J 65
Whimbrel Cl. SE28: Lon 7H 141
Whinchat Rd. SE28: Lon 9C 140 (7H 39)
Whinfield Av. CO12: Har 6H 209
Whinhams Way CM12: Bill 5H 99
Whipletree Rd. CB2: Whitt 1J 5
Whipps Cross E17: Lon 9D 106
Whipps Cross Ho. *E17: Lon 9D 106*
(off Wood St.)
Whipps Cross Rd. E11: Lon 9D 106 (3E 38)
(not continuous)
Whist Av. SS11: W'fd 7N 101
Whistler M. *RM8: Dag 7G 125*
(off Fitzstephen Rd.)
Whistler Ri. SS3: Shoe 6L 139
Whiston Rd. E2: Lon 6B 38
Whitakers Way IG10: Lou 9M 77
Whitbreads Farm La. CM3: L Walt 4A 24
Whitby Av. CM13: Ingve 3N 113
Whitby Rd. CM0: S'min 4B 222
Whitchurch Rd. RM3: Romf 1H 111 (1B 40)
Whitcroft SS16: Lang H 3L 131
White Arch Pl. CO4: Boxt 2B 160
Whitear Wlk. E15: Lon 8D 122
WHITEASH GREEN 6N 201 (3E 14)
Whitebarn La. RM10: Dag 1M 141
White Barns CM3: Har E 3J 23
Whitebeam Cl. CM2: Chelm 3A 72
CO4: Colc 2L 165
Whitebeam Dr. RM15: S Ock 3F 144
White Bear CM24: Stan M 1D 220
WHITECHAPEL 7C 38
Whitechapel Rd. E1: Lon 7C 38
Whitechapel Station (Tube) 7C 38
White City SS3: Fou I 1G 45
WHITE COLNE 7E 198 (4J 15)
Whitecroft Rd. SG8: Meld 2D 4
Whiteditch La. CB11: Newp 1K 215 (1A 12)
White Elm Rd. CM3: Dan 8F 74 (3E 34)
Whitefield Ct. CM3: May 8L 213
Whitefriars Cres. SS0: Wclf S 6H 137
Whitefriars Way CO3: Colc 1H 173
White Gdns. RM10: Dag 8M 125
Whitegate Rd. CO7: B'sea 7F 182
SS1: Sth S 6M 137
White Gates RM12: Horn 4G 127
Whitegates Cl. CM77: Gt N 2C 204
White Hall RM4: Abr 2G 92
Whitehall SW1: Lon 7A 38
Whitehall Cl. CO2: Colc 2C 174
EN9: Naze 1E 62
IG7: Chig 9F 92
Whitehall Ct. CM8: Wthm 5D 230
Whitehall Est. CM19: H'low 4L 53
Whitehall Gdns. E4: Lon 7E 90
Whitehall Ind. Est. CO2: Colc 2D 174
Whitehall La. CO16: T Sok 3G 178 (7D 18)
DA8: Eri 7D 152 (2A 46)
IG9: Buck H 8G 90
RM17: Grays 3M 155
SS17: Fob 7D 132
Whitehall Pl. E7: Lon 7G 123
Whitehall Rd. CO2: Colc 3C 174 (7F 17)
E4: Lon 8E 90 (1E 38)
IG8: Wfd G 8G 90 (1F 39)
RM17: Grays 2M 155
White Hall Rd. SS3: Gt W 2M 139
Whitehall Rdbt. CM19: H'low 4M 53
White Hart La. CM1: Chelm 3N 59 (7B 24)
CM2: Chelm 3A 60
CM14: Brtwd 8F 96
CO6: W Ber 2E 164
CO12: Har 1M 209
N17: Lon 2A 38
N22: Lon 2A 38
RM7: Col R, Maw 5M 109 (2K 39)
SS5: Hock 2D 120
White Hart Lane Stadium 2C 38
White Hart Lane Station (Rail) 2B 38
Whitehead Cl. CM1: Writ 2K 71
White Hill SG2: Clot 5A 10
Whitehill La. DA12: Grav 4H 47
Whitehill Rd. DA3: Long 6E 46
DA12: Grav 4H 47
DA13: Meop 7H 47
DA13: S'fleet 6E 46
Whitehills Rd. IG10: Lou 2N 91
White Horse Av. CO9: Hals 6J 207
Whitehorse La. CB11: Newp 2L 215
White Horse La. CM8: Wthm 4C 230
CM9: Mal 6B 214
E1: Lon 6C 38
White Horse Rd. CO7: E Ber 1J 17
White Ho. Chase SS6: Ray 6L 119
Whitehouse Cl. CO4: L'ham 4D 160
Whitehouse Cres. CM2: Gt Bad 2E 72
White Ho. Dr. IG8: Wfd G 3F 106
Whitehouse Est. E10: Lon 1C 122
Whitehouse Hill
CM9: Salc, Tol D, Tol K 1N 227 (5C 26)
Whitehouse La. CM6: Steb 8E 222
CO6: W Ber 4E 164 (5C 16)
CO10: Bel O 4E 8
Whitehouse Mdws. SS9: Lgh S 9F 120
Whitehouse Rd. CM3: S Fer 9K 89
CM6: Steb 8E 222 (6J 13)
White Ho. Rd. SS9: Lgh S 3H 43
Whitehouse Rd. SS9: Lgh S, Sth S 9E 120
Whitelands CM15: Hook E 5G 83
Whitelands Cl. SS11: W'fd 7M 101
Whitelands Way RM3: H Wood 5H 111 (2C 40)
Whiteley La. SG9: Bkld 2C 10
White Lodge Cres. CO16: T Sok 5N 179
White Lyons Rd. CM14: Brtwd 8F 96
Whitemead CM1: Broom 1K 59
WHITE NOTLEY 4C 194 (2E 24)
White Notley Station (Rail) 2E 24
White Post Fld. CM6: Gt D 3M 203
CM21: Saw 2J 51
White Post La. DA13: Sole S 6H 47
E9: Lon 8A 122
White Rd. E15: Lon 9E 122
SS8: Can I 2C 150
WHITE RODING 5D 22
Whites Av. IG2: Ilf 1D 124
Whitesbridge La.
CM4: Chelm, Marg 8M 71
(not continuous)
White's Hill CM4: Stock 7A 86 (5K 33)
Whites Hill CM77: Cogg 7F 15
Whiteshott SS16: Bas 2B 132
Whiteshot Way CB10: Saf W 3E 218
Whites La. CM3: L L'gh 8J 203 (3B 24)
Whitesmith Dr. CM12: Bill 5G 99
White St. CM6: Gt D 3L 203
White Stubbs La. EN10: Brox 1A 30
SG13: B'frd, Brick, Brox, E Grn 1A 30
Whitethorn Gdns. CM2: Chelm 3D 72
RM11: Horn 1G 127
White Tree Ct. CM3: S Fer 2H 103
Whitewaites CM20: H'low 3D 54

Whiteways CB10: Gt Che 8C 202
CM11: Bill 6N 99
SS8: Can I 3K 151
SS9: Lgh S 9E 120
White Ways Ct. CM8: Wthm 4B 230
Whitewebbs La. EN2: Enf 5B 30
Whitewebbs Mus. of Transport & Industry, The 5A 30
Whitewebbs Rd. EN2: Enf 5A 30
Whitewell Rd. CO2: Colc 9N 165
Whitfield Ct. IG1: Ilf 2M 123
Whitfield Link CM2: Chelm 3E 72
Whitfield Rd. E6: Lon 9J 123
Whitfields SS17: Stan H 3A 148
Whiting Av. IG11: Bark 9A 124
Whitings IG2: Ilf 9D 108
Whitley Ct. EN11: Rye P 3B 52
Whitley Rd. EN11: Rye P 3B 52
Whitley's Chase CM7: Corn H 7K 7
Whitlock Dr. CO9: Gt Yel 3C 206
Whitmore Av. RM3: H Wood 6J 111
RM16: Grays 8L 145
Whitmore Cl. RM16: Ors 6G 146
Whitmore Ct. SS14: Bas 7F 116
Whitmore Cres. CM2: Chelm 8C 60
Whitmore Way SS14: Bas 8C 116 (3A 42)
Whitney Av. IG4: Ilf 8K 107
Whitney Rd. E10: Lon 2B 122
Whittaker Rd. E6: Lon 9J 123
Whittaker Way CO5: W Mer 2B 228
Whitta Rd. E12: Lon 6K 123
Whittingham Av. SS2: Sth S 4C 138
Whittingham Ho. SS2: Sth S 4C 138
Whittingstall Rd. EN11: Rye P 3B 52
Whittington Rd. CM13: Hut 5M 97
N22: Lon 2A 38
Whittington Way CM23: Bis S, Thor 2K 21
WHITTLESFORD 1J 5
Whittlesford Rd. CB2: L She 1H 5
CB2: New, Whitt 1H 5
Whittlesford Station (Rail) 2K 5
Whitworth Cen., The RM3: Romf 2G 110
Whitworth Cres. EN3: Enf 7A 76
Whybrews SS17: Stan H 3A 148
Whybridge Cl. RM13: Rain 1D 142
Whyteville Rd. E7: Lon 8H 123
Whytewaters SS16: Van 3G 132
Whyverne Cl. CM1: Chelm 5N 59
Wick Beech Av. SS11: W'fd 9M 101
Wick Cen., The SS12: W'fd 2N 117
Wick Chase SS2: Sth S 4D 138
Wick Cres. SS12: W'fd 2M 117
Wick Dr. SS12: W'fd 9L 101
(Nevendon Rd.)
SS12: W'fd 2M 117
(Wick Cres.)
WICKEN BONHUNT 2A 12
Wicken Rd. CB11: A'den 1K 11
CB11: Clav 2K 11
CB11: Newp 3J 215 (2A 12)
Wickets Way IG6: Ilf 3E 108
Wick Farm Rd. CM0: St La 1C 36
Wickfield Ash CM1: Chelm 5F 58
Wickfields IG7: Chig 3C 108
WICKFORD 9L 101 (1C 42)
Wickford Av. SS13: Pits 9H 117 (3B 42)
Wickford Bus. Pk. SS11: W'fd 1N 117
Wickford Cl. RM3: Romf 2K 111
Wickford Ct. SS13: Pits 9H 117
Wickford Dr. RM3: Romf 2K 111
Wickford M. SS13: Pits 9H 117
Wickford Pl. SS13: Pits 9H 117
Wickford Rd. CM3: S Fer 9G 89 (6E 34)
SS0: Wclf S 7K 137
Wickford Station (Rail) 8K 101 (1C 42)
Wickford Swimming Pool 8K 101
Wick Glen CM12: Bill 4H 99
WICKHAM BISHOPS 2L 229 (5G 25)
Wickham Bishops Rd.
CM3: Hat P 3N 61 (6F 25)
Wickham Cres. CM1: Chelm 5H 59
CM7: Brain 6J 193
Wickham Hall La. CM8: W Bis 4H 229 (6G 25)
WICKHAM HILL 8F 230
Wickham Pl. SS16: Bas 1D 132
Wickham Rd. CM8: Wthm 7C 230
CO3: Colc 1L 173
E4: Lon 4C 106
RM16: Grays 9E 146
WICKHAM ST PAUL 7G 9
Wickham's Chase CM3: Dan 8J 75
Wickhay SS15: Lain 1A 132
Wickhay Cotts. CM3: L Bad 6L 61
Wick La. CO5: Fing 2H 27
CO7: A'lgh 8F 160 (4G 17)
CO7: Gt Ben 1N 183
CO12: Har 6K 209 (3H 19)
CO16: Gt Ben 1N 183
E3: Lon 6D 38
SS11: W'fd 9M 101
(not continuous)
Wicklow Av. CM1: Chelm 5F 58
Wicklow Wlk. SS3: Shoe 7G 138
Wickmead Cl. SS2: Sth S 4C 138
Wick Rd. CM0: Bur C 4F 196
CO2: Colc 4D 174
CO4: L'ham 5F 160 (3G 17)
CO6: Stok 1F 17
CO7: Gt Ben 1M 183 (2B 28)
E9: Lon 5C 38
Wicks Cl. CM7: Brain 4E 192
Wick Ter. CO4: L'ham 5F 160
Widbrook CM15: Dodd 6F 82
Widbury Hill SG12: Ware 4D 20
Wid Cl. CM13: Hut 4N 97
WIDDINGTON 3C 12
Widdin St. E15: Lon 9E 122
Widecombe Cl. RM3: Romf 5H 111
Widecombe Gdns. IG4: Ilf 8L 107
WIDFORD 3A 72 (2K 33)
Ware 4G 21
Widford Chase CM2: Chelm 3A 72
Widford Cl. CM2: Chelm 3A 72
Widford Gro. CM2: Chelm 3A 72
Widford Hall La. *CM1: Chelm* *3N 71*
(off Tattersall Way)
Widford Ind. Est. CM1: Chelm 3N 71
(Hanbury Rd.)
CM1: Chelm 2N 71
(Westway)
Widford Pk. Pl. CM2: Chelm 3A 72
Widford Rd. CM2: Chelm 3A 72
SG12: Hun, Wid 4F 21
SG12: Wid 3G 21
Widgeon Pl. CO5: K'dn 3K 211
Widgeon Rd. DA8: Eri 5F 152
Widgeons SS13: Pits 9K 117
Widleybrook La. CM7: Bla E, Weth 8E 228
Wid Ter. CM15: Dodd 6F 82
Widworthy Hayes CM13: Hut 7L 97
Wigborough Rd.
CO5: Gt Wig, Lay B, Lay H 3D 26
(Layer-de-la-Haye)
CO5: Gt Wig, L Wig, Pel 4D 26
(Little Wigborough)
Wigboro Wick La. CO16: St O 4A 28
Wigeon Cl. CM77: Gt N 3C 204
WIGGENS GREEN 4J 7
Wiggin's La. CM12: Bill, L Bur 1G 114
Wightman Rd. N4: Lon 3A 38
N8: Lon 3A 38
Wigley Bush La.
CM14: Brtwd, S Wea 8B 96 (1D 40)
Wignall St. CO11: Law 5E 162 (3K 17)
Wigram Rd. E11: 1J 123
Wigram Sq. E17: Lon 7C 106
Wigton Rd. RM3: Romf 1J 111
Wigton Way RM3: Romf 1J 111
Wilbury Way N18: Lon 1B 38
Wilbye Cl. CO2: Colc 2J 173
Wild Boar Fld. CM7: Brain 5M 193
Wilde Cl. RM18: Til 7E 156
Wilfred Av. RM13: Rain 5E 142
Wilkes Rd. CM13: Hut 4N 97
Wilkin Ct. CO3: Colc 2H 173
SS9: Lgh S 4C 136
Wilkin Dr. CO5: Tip 6D 226
Wilkinson Cl. DA1: Dart 9K 153
(not continuous)
Wilkinson Gro. CM77: Bla N 3B 194
Wilkinsons Mead CM2: Chelm 7B 60
Willers Mill Wildlife Pk. 1E 4
Willett Rd. CO2: Colc 3J 173
Willetts Fld. CB10: Gt Sam 3K 205
William Boys Cl. CO4: Colc 7D 166
William Cl. CO7: W'hoe 2J 175
RM5: Col R 5A 110
William Cory Prom. DA8: Eri 3C 152
William De Ferrers Sports Cen. 1L 103
William Dr. CO15: Clac S 2H 189
William Grn. SS5: Hull 5L 103
William Groom Av. CO12: Har 5J 209
William Hunter Way CM14: Brtwd 8F 96
William Morris Gallery 7A 106 (2D 38)
William Pike Ho. *RM7: Romf* *1B 126*
(off Waterloo Gdns.)
William Rd. SS13: Pits 9N 117
Williams Dr. CM7: Brain 4H 193
Williamsons Way SS17: Corr 9A 132
William Sparrow Ct. CO7: W'hoe 4J 175
Williams Rd. CM1: Broom 2K 59
William St. E10: Lon 1B 122
IG11: Bark 9B 124
RM17: Grays 4L 155
(not continuous)
Williams Wlk. CO1: Colc 8N 165
WILLINGALE 1E 32
Willingale Av. SS6: Ray 4G 118
Willingale Cl. CM13: Hut 5A 98
IG8: Wfd G 3J 107
IG10: Lou 1B 92
Willingale Ct. CM16: They B 6D 78
Willingale Rd. CM4: Nor H 2G 68
CM5: Fy'd, Will 9D 200 (1D 32)
CM5: Nor H, Will 2G 68 (2E 32)
CM7: Brain 4M 193
IG10: Lou 9B 78 (6H 31)
Willingales, The SS15: Lain 9J 115
Willingale Way SS1: Sth S 5E 138
Willinghall Cl. EN9: Wal A 2D 76
Willingham Way CO4: Colc 8E 166
Willis Rd. DA8: Eri 2A 152
Willis's La. CB11: Quen, Rick G 2B 216
(not continuous)
Willmott Rd. SS2: Sth S 9J 121
Willoughby Av. CO5: W Mer 3D 228
Willoughby Dr. CM2: Chelm 9A 60
RM13: Rain 9C 126
Willoughby La. N17: Lon 2C 38
Willoughby's La. CM7: Brain 9L 191 (6D 14)
Willow Av. CO13: Walt 8G 180
Willow Bank CM2: Gall 7C 72
Willow Cl. CM0: Bur C 2D 196
CM1: Broom 2K 59
CM13: Hut 5L 97
CM15: Dodd 8G 82
CO7: A'lgh 1D 166
CO7: B'sea 7C 182
Willow Cl. IG9: Buck H 9K 91
RM12: Horn 5F 126
SS5: Hock 1E 120
SS6: Ray 3K 119
SS8: Can I 2F 150
SS9: Lgh S 9E 120
Willow Cotts. CM3: Bick 3G 88
Willow Ct. *E11: Lon* *4E 122*
(off Trinity Cl.)
Willow Cres. CM3: Hat P 3L 61
Willowdale Cen. SS12: W'fd 8L 101
Willowdene CM15: Pil H 4C 96
Willow Dene CO9: Sib H 5J 219
Willowdene Ct. CM14: War 1F 112
Willow Dr. SS6: Ray 3J 119
Willowfield CM18: H'low 5C 54
SS15: Lain 7L 115 (3K 41)
Willow Grn. CM4: Ing 5D 84
Willow Gro. CM3: S Fer 7G 88 (5E 34)
Willow Hall La. CO11: Wix 4D 18
Willowherb Wlk. RM3: Romf 4G 111
Willowhill SS17: Stan H 9N 131
Willowmead CM11: Rams H 3D 100
Willow Mead CM21: Saw 3K 51
IG7: Chig 9F 92
Willow Mdws. CO9: Sib H 7K 219
Willow Pde. RM14: Upm 3B 128
Willow Path EN9: Wal A 4E 76
Willow Pl. CM17: H'wd 7L 55
Willow Ri. CM8: Wthm 2D 230
Willow Rd. CM6: Gt D 2K 203
DA8: Eri 6E 152
E12: Lon 5M 123
EN1: Enf 6B 30
RM6: Chad H 1K 125
WILLOWS GREEN 2B 24
Willows, The CB10: Gt Che 7D 202
CM3: Bore 3F 60
CM11: Bill 9M 99
CO2: Colc 3A 174
E6: Lon 9M 123
IG10: Lou 5K 91
RM17: Grays 4N 155
SS1: Sth S 5E 138
SS7: Ben 2B 134
SS13: Pits 9K 117
Willow St. E4: Lon 6D 90
RM7: Romf 8A 110
Willow Tree Cl. RM4: Abr 2G 92
Willow Tree Ct. *CO4: Colc* *7E 166*
(off Hawthorn Av.)
Willow Tree Way CO6: E Col 8C 198
Willow Wlk. CM9: Mal 3E 214
CO5: Tip 4C 226
CO16: Wee 6D 178
DA1: Cray 9G 152
IG1: Ilf 4A 124
RM14: Upm 3B 128
SS4: Cwdn 2M 105
SS5: Hock 1E 120
SS7: Had 3K 135
Willow Way CO9: Hals 5J 207
CO12: Har 5H 209
CO15: Jay 5E 188
RM3: H Wood 3M 111
(not continuous)
Will Perrin Ct. RM13: Rain 1E 142
Will's Ayley La.
CB10: A'dn, Saf W, Sew E 6D 6
Wills Grn. CO5: Fee 8B 170
Wills Hill SS17: Stan H 2M 147
Wilmer Lea Cl. E15: Lon 9C 122
Wilmer Way N14: Lon 1A 38
WILMINGTON 5B 46
Wilmington Gdns. IG11: Bark 8C 124
Wilmington Rd. CO4: Colc 5C 166
Wilmot Grn. CM13: Gt War 3F 112
Wilmot Rd. E10: Lon 4B 122
Wilmslowe SS8: Can I 9K 135
Wilmslow Ho. *RM3: Romf* *2J 111*
(off Chudleigh Rd.)
Wilrich Av. SS8: Can I 2K 151
Wilshire Av. CM2: Chelm 8A 60
Wilsman Rd. RM15: S Ock 2F 144
Wilsner SS13: Pits 8K 117
Wilson Cl. CO7: W'hoe 4G 175
SS17: Stan H 5L 147
Wilson Ct. SS12: W'fd 1K 117
Wilson La. DA4: S Dar 6D 46
Wilson Marriage Rd. CO4: Colc 6C 166
Wilson Rd. IG1: Ilf 2M 123
SS1: Wclf S 7L 137
Wilsons Cnr. *CM14: Brtwd* *8G 96*
(off High St.)
Wilsons Ct. CM9: Mal 6D 214
Wilson's La. CO6: M Tey 3F 170
Wilson St. E17: Lon 9C 106
EC2: Lon 7B 38
Wilthorne Gdns. RM10: Dag 9N 125
Wilton Dr. RM5: Col R 4A 110
Wiltshire Av. RM11: Horn 8K 111
Wiltshire Ct. IG1: Ilf 8B 124
Wimarc Cres. SS6: Ray 3H 119
WIMBISH 7E 6
Wimbish Ct. SS13: Pits 8J 117
Wimbish End SS13: Pits 9J 117
WIMBISH GREEN 1F 13
Wimbish M. SS13: Pits 8J 117
Wimbish Wlk. CB10: Wim 1D 12
Wimborne Cl. CM21: Saw 2J 51
IG9: Buck H 8H 91
Wimborne Gdns. CO13: Frin S 7J 181
Wimborne Rd. SS2: Sth S 5N 137
Wimbourne SS15: Lain 8J 115
Wimhurst Cl. SS5: Hock 9D 104
Wimpole Hall 1B 4
Wimpole Rd. CO1: Colc 9B 166 (6F 17)
Wimsey Ct. CM8: Wthm 2D 230
Winbrook Cl. SS6: Ray 7L 119
Winbrook Rd. SS6: Ray 7L 119
Wincanton Gdns. IG6: Ilf 7A 108
Wincanton Rd. RM3: Romf 9H 95
Wincelow Hall Rd. CB10: Hpstd, R'ter 6G 7
Winchcombe Cl. SS9: Lgh S 3D 136
Winchelsea Dr. CM2: Gt Bad 3E 72
Winchelsea Pl. CO7: B'sea 5E 182
Winchelsea Rd. E7: Lon 5G 122
Winchester Av. RM14: Upm 3C 128
Winchester Cl. SS9: Lgh S 8E 120
Winchester Dr. SS6: Ray 1H 119
Winchester Gdns. SS15: Lain 6L 115
Winchester Ho. *IG11: Bark* *9F 124*
(off Keir Hardie Way)
Winchester Rd. CO2: Colc 1A 174
CO13: Frin S 9K 181
E4: Lon 4C 106 (2E 38)
IG1: Ilf 5C 124
N9: Lon 7B 30
WINCHMORE HILL 7A 30
Winchmore Hill CM1: Good E 5H 23
Winchmore Hill Rd. N14: Lon 7A 30
Winchmore Hill Station (Rail) 7A 30
Winckford Cl. CM3: L Walt 6K 57
Wincoat Cl. SS7: Ben 3C 134
Wincoat Dr. SS7: Ben 3C 134
Windermere Av. RM12: Horn 7E 126
SS5: Hull 6J 103
Windermere Ct. *CO15: Clac S* *1L 189*
(off Marine Pde. E.)
Windermere Dr. CM77: Gt N 1C 204
Windermere Gdns. IG4: Ilf 9L 107
Windermere Rd. CO15: Hol S 7N 185
DA7: Bexh 7A 152
SS1: Sth S 6A 138
SS7: Thund 8E 118
Wind Hill CM5: Mag L, M'ton 1A 32
Windhill CM23: Bis S 1K 21
(not continuous)
Winding Shott SG14: B'fld 4A 20
Winding Way RM8: Dag 5H 125
Windley Tye CM1: Chelm 8G 58
Windmill Cl. CM6: Gt D 2M 203
CM24: Stan M 3C 220
CO4: Boxt 4N 159
CO12: R'sy 6B 208
EN9: Wal A 4E 76
RM14: Upm 4L 127
Windmill Ct. CO4: Colc 3M 165
CO6: Cop 2M 171
Windmill Flds. CM17: H'low 8L 51
CO6: Cogg 2K 197
Windmill Gdns. CM7: Brain 9J 191
WINDMILL GREEN 5C 226
Windmill Hgts. CM12: Bill 8K 99
Windmill Hill CB10: Saf W 3B 218 (6B 6)
CM23: Man 5K 11
CO10: L Mel 2H 9
EN2: Enf 6A 30
Windmill La. E15: Lon 8D 122 (5E 38)
EN8: Chesh 3C 30
Windmill Mdws. CM6: Ayt R 1C 212 (4E 22)
Windmill Pk. CO15: Clac S 8K 185
Windmill Rd. CO9: Hals 5J 207
CO11: Brad, Mist 6N 163 (3B 18)
Windmills CO6: Gt Tey 2E 170
Windmill Steps *SS1: Sth S* *7A 138*
(off Kursaal Way)
Windmills, The CM1: Broom 9J 57
Windmill St. DA11: Grav 4H 47
(not continuous)
Windmill Vw. CO5: Tip 5C 226
Windmill Way CM15: Kel H 7B 82
Windrush SE28: Lon 8G 140
Windrush Dr. CM1: Chelm 5L 59
Windsor Av. CO15: Clac S 1H 189
RM16: Grays 9L 145
SS17: Corr 9B 132
Windsor Cl. CO2: Colc 4A 174
SS8: Can I 2H 151
SS9: Lgh S 3D 136
Windsor Ct. *CO1: Colc* *9C 166*
(off Hythe Hill)
CO7: B'sea 6E 182
Windsor Dr. SG14: Hart 5A 20
Windsor Gdns. CM7: Brain 4K 193
SS5: Hock 3G 121
SS7: Had 2J 135
SS11: W'fd 7L 101
Windsor Ho. *CO1: Colc* *9A 166*
(off Magdalen St.)
CO5: W Mer *2D 228*
(off Carrington Ct.)
Windsor M. SS6: Ray 6J 119
Windsor Rd. CM11: D'ham 3E 100
CM15: Pil H 5E 96
CO5: W Mer 2D 228
E4: Lon 1B 106
E7: Lon 7H 123
E10: Lon 4B 122
E11: Lon 3G 122
IG1: Ilf 6A 124
RM8: Dag 5K 125
RM11: Horn 2G 127
SS0: Wclf S 5K 137
SS13: Pits 7M 117
Windsor Rd. Folley CO5: W Mer 2D 228
Windsors, The IG9: Buck H 8L 91
Windsor Trad. Est. CM11: D'ham 4E 100

Windsor Way CM1: Chelm . . . 1N 71
SS6: Ray . . . 6L 119
Windsor Wharf E9: Lon . . . 8A 122
Windsor Wood EN9: Wal A . . . 3E 76
Windward Way CM3: S Fer . . . 2M 103
Windy Hill CM13: Hut . . . 7M 97
Winfields SS13: Pits . . . 8K 117
Wingate Cl. CM7: Brain . . . 4G 193
Wingate Rd. IG1: Ilf . . . 7A 124
Wing Cl. CM16: N Wea . . . 6M 65
Wingfield RM17: Grays . . . 3J 155
Wingfield Cl. CM13: Brtwd . . . 9K 97
Wingfield Gdns. RM14: Upm . . . 1B 128
Wingfield Rd. E15: Lon . . . 6E 122
E17: Lon . . . 9B 106
Winging Hill SG10: M Hud . . . 2G 21
Wingletye La. RM11: Horn . . . 8K 111 (4C 40)
Wingrave Cres. CM14: Brtwd . . . 1B 112
Wingrove E4: Lon . . . 6A 90
Wingrove Ct. CM1: Chelm . . . 5J 59
RM7: Romf . . . 9A 110
Wingrove Dr. RM19: Purf . . . 3M 153
Wing Way CM14: Brtwd . . . 7F 96
Winifred Av. RM12: Horn . . . 6H 127
Winifred Dell Ho. CM13: Gt War . . . 3F 112
Winifred Rd. DA8: Eri . . . 3C 152
RM8: Dag . . . 4K 125
SS13: Pits . . . 9J 117
Winifred Whittington Ho.
RM13: Rain . . . 5F 142
Winmill Rd. RM8: Dag . . . 5L 125
Winningales Ct. IG5: Ilf . . . 6L 107
Winnock Rd. CO1: Colc . . . 9A 166
(not continuous)
Winnowers Ct. SS4: R'fd . . . 5L 121
Winns Av. E17: Lon . . . 6A 106
Winns Ter. E17: Lon . . . 7A 106
Winsbeach E17: Lon . . . 6D 106
Winsey Chase CM7: F'fld . . . 3C 200
Winsford Gdns. SS0: Wclf S . . . 2F 136
Winsford Way CM2: Chelm . . . 4C 60
Winsley Rd. CO1: Colc . . . 9B 166
Winsley Sq. CO1: Colc . . . 1B 174
Winslow Gro. E4: Lon . . . 8E 90
WINSOR PARK . . . 5A 140
Winsor Ter. E6: Lon . . . 5A 140
Winstanley Rd. CB11: Saf W . . . 6D 218
Winstanley Way SS14: Bas . . . 7B 116
Winstead Gdns. RM10: Dag . . . 7A 126
Winston Av. CO3: Colc . . . 2J 173
CO5: Tip . . . 6E 226
Winston Cl. CM7: Brain . . . 2G 193
RM7: Maw . . . 8N 109
Winston Way CO9: Hals . . . 3M 207
IG1: Ilf . . . 5A 124 (4G 39)
Winstree SS13: Bas . . . 7J 117
Winstree Cl. CO2: Lay H . . . 9G 173
Winstree Rd. CM0: Bur C . . . 3D 196
CO3: S'way . . . 9E 164 (6C 16)
Winterbourne Rd. RM8: Dag . . . 4H 125
Winterbournes CO14: Walt . . . 7K 181
Winter Folly SS15: Lain . . . 1N 131
WINTER GARDENS . . . 8F 134 (5E 42)
Winter Gdns. Path SS8: Can I . . . 7E 134
Winter's Ct. E4: Lon . . . 9B 90
Winters Hill CO5: Lay M . . . 2B 26
Winters La. SG2: Walk . . . 5A 10
Winters Rd. CO5: Lay M . . . 2B 26
Winters Way EN9: Wal A . . . 3G 76
Winterswyk Av. SS8: Can I . . . 2L 151
Winton Av. SS0: Wclf S . . . 7K 137
SS12: W'fd . . . 8H 101
Winton Lodge SS0: Wclf S . . . 5H 137
Wiscombe Hill SS16: Lang H . . . 3L 131
Wisdoms Grn. CO6: Cogg . . . 2L 197
Wisdons Cl. RM10: Dag . . . 3N 125
Wiseman Rd. E10: Lon . . . 4A 122
Wisemans Gdns. CM21: Saw . . . 3H 51
Wissants CM19: H'low . . . 7A 54
WISSINGTON . . . 1D 158
Wistaria Cl. CM15: Pil H . . . 4F 96
Wistaria Pl. CO16: Clac S . . . 8G 185
Wisteria Cl. IG1: Ilf . . . 7A 124
Wisteria Ct. *CO4: Colc* . . . *8E 166*
(off Blackthorn Av.)
Wisteria Gdns. IG8: Wfd G . . . 2G 107
Wiston Rd. CO6: Nay . . . 2C 16
Witchards SS16: Bas . . . 1C 132
Witch Elm CO12: Har . . . 5H 209
Witch La. CO6: Cogg . . . 6H 15
Witchtree La. CB10: Hpstd . . . 6G 7
WITHAM . . . 5D 230 (4F 25)
Witham By-Pass CM8: Wthm . . . 9B 230 (5F 25)
Witham Cl. IG10: Lou . . . 5L 91
Witham Ct. E10: Lon . . . 5B 122
Witham Fossil Hall . . . 8L 217 (2F 25)
Witham Gdns. CM13: W H'dn . . . 1N 129
Witham Lodge CM8: Wthm . . . 7A 230
Witham Rd. CM3: Terl . . . 4E 24
CM8: Fau, Whi N . . . 3E 24
CM8: L Brax . . . 5F 230 (4G 25)
CM8: W Bis . . . 1J 229 (5G 25)
CM9: L'frd, Mal . . . 7G 25
CM9: Tol M . . . 9N 205 (5K 25)
CM77: Bla N, Whi N . . . 9J 193 (1D 24)
(not continuous)
CM77: Tye G . . . 8H 217 (1E 24)
RM2: Romf . . . 9F 110
RM10: Dag . . . 7M 125
Witham Rd. Sth. CM8: Whi N . . . 4C 194 (2D 24)
Witham Snooker & Bowl . . . 6E 230
WITHAM STH. INTERCHANGE . . . 9A 230 (5F 25)
Witham Station (Rail) . . . 4D 230 (4G 25)
Witherings, The RM11: Horn . . . 9J 111
WITHERMARSH GREEN . . . 1F 17
WITHERSFIELD . . . 2H 7
Withersfield Rd. CB9: H'hll . . . 2J 7
CB9: Thurl, Wthfld . . . 1J 7
Withies Grn. CM77: Tye G . . . 1E 24
Withrick Wlk. CO16: St O . . . 8M 183
Withy Mead E4: Lon . . . 9D 90
Withypool SS3: Shoe . . . 5H 139
Withywindle, The CM3: S Fer . . . 2J 103
Witney Rd. CM0: Bur C . . . 4E 196
Witneys, The CM22: L Hall . . . 2K 213
Wittem Rd. SS8: Can I . . . 9H 135
Wittenham Way E4: Lon . . . 9D 90
Witterings, The SS8: Can I . . . 9G 135
SS14: Bas . . . 1F 132
Wittering Wlk. RM12: Horn . . . 8G 126
Witting Cl. CO16: Clac S . . . 8H 185
Witton Wood La. CO13: Frin S . . . 9G 181
Witton Wood Rd. CO13: Frin S . . . 9H 181
WIVENHOE . . . 6H 175 (7H 17)
Wivenhoe Cross CO7: W'hoe . . . 4J 175 (7G 17)
Wivenhoe Pk. Cnr. CO7: Colc . . . 1G 175
Wivenhoe Rd. CO7: A'lgh, Elms . . . 6J 167 (6H 17)
CO7: Alr . . . 7L 175 (1H 27)
IG11: Bark . . . 2F 140
Wivenhoe Sailing Club . . . 7J 175
Wivenhoe Station (Rail) . . . 6H 175 (1G 27)
WIX . . . 4D 18
Wix By-Pass CO7: Gt Bro, L Ben . . . 8G 169 (6A 18)
CO7: Hor X, L Ben, L Bro . . . 5K 169 (6A 18)
CO11: Hor X . . . 5K 169
CO16: Hor X . . . 5K 169
WIXOE . . . 4A 8
Wix Rd. CO11: Brad . . . 3C 18
CO11: Sto G, Wix . . . 5D 18
CO12: Gt Oak . . . 8B 204 (5E 18)
CO12: R'sy . . . 6A 208 (3F 19)
RM9: Dag . . . 1J 141
Woburn Av. CM16: They B . . . 7D 78
CO13: Walt . . . 7G 180
RM12: Horn . . . 6E 126
Woburn Cl. SE28: Lon . . . 6J 141
Woburn Ct. E18: Lon . . . 6G 107
Woburn Pl. CM12: Bill . . . 3H 99
WC1: Lon . . . 6A 38
Wodehouse Rd. DA1: Dart . . . 9L 153
Wokindon Rd. RM16: Grays . . . 1D 156
Wolfe Av. CO2: Colc . . . 1A 174
Wolferton Rd. E12: Lon . . . 6M 123
Wolffe Gdns. E15: Lon . . . 8F 122
Wollaston Cres. SS13: Bas . . . 5L 117
Wollaston Way SS13: Bas . . . 5K 117
Wolmers Hey CM3: Gt Walt . . . 5H 57
Wolseley Av. CO15: Jay . . . 6D 188
Wolseley Rd. CM2: Chelm . . . 1B 72
E7: Lon . . . 9H 123
N8: Lon . . . 3A 38
RM7: Rush G . . . 2B 126
Wolsey Gdns. IG6: Ilf . . . 3A 108
Wolsleys Chase CM6: Dut H . . . 5F 13
Wolton Rd. CO2: Colc . . . 3J 173
Wolvercote Rd. SE2: Lon . . . 9J 141
Wolverton Ho. *RM3: Romf* . . . *2J 111*
(off Chudleigh Rd.)
Wolves Hall La. CO16: Ten . . . 5C 18
Wolves La. N13: Lon . . . 2A 38
N22: Lon . . . 2A 38
Wonston Rd. CM0: S'min . . . 2C 222
Wood Av. RM19: Purf . . . 2N 153
SS5: Hock . . . 8D 104
Wood Barn La. CO11: A'lgh, Law . . . 7C 162
Woodberry Cl. SS8: Can I . . . 8G 134
SS9: Lgh S . . . 1B 136
Woodberry Down CM16: Epp . . . 8F 64
Woodberry Gro. N4: Lon . . . 4B 38
Woodberry Rd. SS11: W'fd . . . 1A 118
Woodberry Way CO14: Frin S, Walt . . . 7L 181
E4: Lon . . . 6C 90
Woodbine Cl. CM19: H'low . . . 5B 54
EN9: Wal A . . . 5J 77
Woodbine Cl. Cvn. Pk. EN9: Wal A . . . 5J 77
Woodbine Pl. E11: Lon . . . 1G 123
Woodbridge Cl. RM3: Romf . . . 1H 111
Woodbridge Ct. IG8: Wfd G . . . 4L 107
Woodbridge Gro. CO16: Clac S . . . 9E 184
Woodbridge Ho. E11: Lon . . . 3F 122
Woodbridge La. RM3: Romf . . . 9H 95
Woodbridge Rd. IG11: Bark . . . 7E 124
Woodbrook Cres. CM12: Bill . . . 5H 99
Woodbrooke Way SS17: Corr . . . 9C 132
Woodbrook Gdns. EN9: Wal A . . . 3E 76
Woodburn Cl. SS7: Thund . . . 2J 135
(not continuous)
Woodbury Cl. E11: Lon . . . 8H 107
Woodbury Hill IG10: Lou . . . 2L 91
Woodbury Hollow IG10: Lou . . . 1L 91
Woodbury Rd. E17: Lon . . . 8B 106
Woodcock Cl. CO4: Colc . . . 9E 166
Woodcote App. SS7: Thund . . . 8B 118
Woodcote Av. RM12: Horn . . . 6E 126
Woodcote Cres. SS13: Pits . . . 9L 117
Woodcote M. IG10: Lou . . . 6K 91
Woodcote Rd. E11: Lon . . . 2G 122
SS9: Lgh S . . . 4F 136
Woodcotes SS3: Shoe . . . 5J 139
Woodcote Way SS7: Thund . . . 8B 118
Woodcroft CM18: H'low . . . 5B 54
Woodcroft Cl. SS7: Had . . . 2J 135
Woodcutters Av. RM16: Grays . . . 9M 145
SS9: Lgh S . . . 1C 136
Wood Dale CM2: Gt Bad . . . 4F 72
Woodedge Cl. E4: Lon . . . 7F 90
WOODEND . . . 6D 22
WOOD END . . . 6B 10
Wood End SS5: Hock . . . 2C 120
Wood End Cl. SS7: Had . . . 2J 135
WOODEND GREEN . . . 8E 210 (4C 12)
Woodend Rd. E17: Lon . . . 6C 106
Wooder Gdns. E7: Lon . . . 6G 122
Woodfall Dr. DA1: Cray . . . 9C 152
Wood Farm Cl. SS9: Lgh S . . . 2C 136
Woodfield SS12: W'fd . . . 1L 117
Woodfield Cl. CM24: Stan M . . . 3D 220
CO14: Walt . . . 7K 181
Woodfield Cotts. CM9: Mal . . . 2E 214
(not continuous)
Woodfield Dr. CO5: W Mer . . . 2B 228
RM2: Romf . . . 8E 110
Wood Fld. End CO2: Lay H . . . 9H 173
Woodfield Gdns. SS9: Lgh S . . . 6E 136
Woodfield Pk. Dr. SS9: Lgh S . . . 5F 136
Woodfield Rd. CM7: Brain . . . 5J 193
SS7: Had . . . 4M 135
SS9: Lgh S . . . 5F 136
Woodfields CM24: Stan M . . . 3D 220
Woodfield Ter. CM16: Thorn . . . 4H 65
CM24: Stan M . . . 3D 220
Woodfield Way CM3: Hat P . . . 2L 61
RM12: Horn . . . 3H 127
Woodfines, The RM11: Horn . . . 1H 127
WOODFORD . . . 3J 107 (2F 39)
Woodford Av. IG2: Ilf . . . 9M 107 (3G 39)
IG4: Ilf, Wfd G . . . 7K 107 (3G 39)
WOODFORD BRIDGE . . . 3L 107 (2G 39)
Woodford Bri. Rd. IG4: Ilf . . . 7K 107 (3G 39)
Woodford Cl. CO15: Clac S . . . 5K 185
Woodford Ct. EN9: Wal A . . . 3G 77
WOODFORD GREEN . . . 3G 107 (1F 39)
Woodford Hall Path E18: Lon . . . 5F 106
Woodford Ho. E18: Lon . . . 8G 106
Woodford New Rd. E17: Lon . . . 8E 106 (3E 38)
E18: Lon . . . 5E 106
IG8: Wfd G . . . 5E 106 (2E 38)
Woodford Rd. E7: Lon . . . 5H 123 (5F 39)
E18: Lon . . . 8G 106 (3E 38)
WOODFORD SIDE . . . 2F 106 (1E 38)
Woodford Station (Tube) . . . 3H 107 (2F 39)
Woodford Trad. Est. IG8: Wfd G . . . 6K 107
WOODFORD WELLS . . . 9H 91 (1F 39)
Woodgates End CM6: Broxt . . . 6D 12
Woodgates Rd. CO7: E Ber . . . 1J 17
Woodgrange Av. SS16: Lang H . . . 3L 131
Woodgrange Cl. SS1: Sth S . . . 6C 138
Woodgrange Ct. EN11: Hod . . . 6A 52
Woodgrange Dr. SS1: Sth S . . . 7A 138 (5K 43)
Woodgrange Park Station (Rail)
. . . 7K 123 (5F 39)
Woodgrange Rd. E7: Lon . . . 7H 123 (5F 39)
WOOD GREEN . . . 5J 77 (4F 31)
Hornsey . . . 2A 38
Wood Grn. SS13: Bas . . . 6J 117
Wood Grn. Est. CO7: Gt Ben . . . 9L 177
Woodgreen Rd. EN9: Wal A . . . 3H 77 (4F 31)
Wood Green Station (Tube) . . . 2A 38
Wood Hall CB11: A'den . . . 2K 11
Woodhall Cres. RM11: Horn . . . 2K 127
Woodhall Hill CM1: Chig S . . . 1E 58 (6K 23)
Woodhall Rd. CM1: Chelm . . . 4J 59
Woodham Ct. E18: Lon . . . 8F 106
Woodham Dr. CM3: Hat P . . . 2M 61
Woodham Fenn Nature Reserve . . . 1H 103
WOODHAM FERRERS . . . 6H 89 (5E 34)
Woodham Ferrers Station (Rail) . . . 9J 89 (6F 35)
Woodham Halt CM3: S Fer . . . 9J 89
WOODHAM MORTIMER . . . 4L 75 (2F 35)
Woodham Mortimer Rd.
CM9: Wdhm M, Wdhm W . . . 2L 75 (2F 35)
Woodham Pk. Dr. SS7: Ben . . . 4B 134
Woodham Rd.
CM3: S Fer, Stow M . . . 7N 89 (5F 35)
SS7: Ben . . . 4B 134
SS11: Bat, Ret C . . . 5C 102 (7D 34)
WOODHAM WALTER . . . 1F 35
WOODHATCH . . . 2A 80 (4A 32)
Woodhaven Gdns. IG6: Ilf . . . 8B 108
Woodhays SS13: Pits . . . 9K 117
WOODHILL . . . 5B 74 (2D 34)
Woodhill CM18: H'low . . . 6D 54
Wood Hill DA13: Meop . . . 7H 47
Woodhill Comn. Rd. CM3: Dan . . . 5B 74
Woodhill Rd. CM2: Dan, S'don . . . 4K 73 (2C 34)
CM3: Dan . . . 4M 73
Woodhouse Gro. E12: Lon . . . 8L 123
Woodhouse La. CM1: L Walt . . . 8H 57 (6K 23)
CM3: L Walt . . . 8H 57
CO6: Gt Hork . . . 1H 165
Woodhouse Rd. E11: Lon . . . 5F 122
Woodhurst Rd. SS8: Can I . . . 2E 150
Wooding Gro. CM19: H'low . . . 3A 54
Woodland Av. CM13: Hut . . . 4M 97 (7G 33)
E12: Lon . . . 5L 123
Woodland Chase CO3: S'way . . . 6A 164
Woodland Cl. CM3: Hat P . . . 1L 61
CM13: Hut . . . 4M 97
IG8: Wfd G . . . 9H 91
SS7: Had . . . 3M 135
Woodland Ct. *E11: Lon* . . . *1G 122*
(off New Wanstead)
Woodland Dr. CO3: Colc, S'way . . . 1G 172
Woodland Gro. CM16: Epp . . . 2F 78
Woodland Pk. Chase CM3: May . . . 9L 213
Woodland Pl. SS11: W'fd . . . 2B 118
Woodland Rd. CM1: Chelm . . . 7J 59
E4: Lon . . . 7C 90
IG10: Lou . . . 2L 91
Woodlands CM1: Broom . . . 8H 57
CM3: Alth . . . 2D 190
CM7: Brain . . . 5K 193
Woodlands CM16: Epp . . . 1F 78
CM23: Bis S . . . 9B 220
CO4: Colc . . . 6F 166
CO12: Gt Oak . . . 9B 204
CO16: Clac S . . . 3E 188
Woodlands Av. E11: Lon . . . 3H 123
RM6: Chad H . . . 1K 125
RM11: Horn . . . 9H 111 (3B 40)
SS6: Ray . . . 7L 119
SS16: Lang H . . . 3J 131
Woodlands Cl. CM4: Ing . . . 5E 84
CO15: Clac S . . . 5L 185
EN11: Hod . . . 6A 52
RM16: Grays . . . 1A 156
SS5: Hock . . . 2C 120
SS6: Ray . . . 7K 119
SS16: Van . . . 2G 133
Woodlands Ct. IG10: Lou . . . 4N 91
Woodlands Dr. EN11: Hod . . . 7A 52
SS17: Fob . . . 5D 132
Woodlands Gdns. E17: Lon . . . 8E 106
Woodlands La. DA12: Shorne . . . 5K 47
WOODLANDS PARK . . . 2J 203
Woodlands Pk. SS9: Lgh S . . . 3N 135
Woodlands Pk. Dr. CM6: Gt D . . . 2J 203
Woodlands Ri. CO16: Wee . . . 5D 178
Woodlands Rd. E11: Lon . . . 4E 122
E17: Lon . . . 7C 106
IG1: Ilf . . . 5B 124
RM1: Romf . . . 7D 110
RM3: H Wood . . . 5L 111
SS5: Hock . . . 2C 120
SS12: W'fd . . . 9L 101
Woodlands, The CO7: B'sea . . . 6D 182
SS3: Shoe . . . 6K 139
Woodlands Wlk. CM6: Gt D . . . 2J 203
Woodlands Way CM1: Broom . . . 9H 57
Woodland Way CM5: Chip . . . 9K 67
CM16: They B . . . 6C 78
CO7: W'hoe . . . 5H 175
CO9: Gosf . . . 8L 201
IG8: Wfd G . . . 9H 91
Wood La. CM5: Will . . . 1F 33
CM6: Ayt R . . . 2D 212
CM9: Mal . . . 3C 214
CM23: Bchgr . . . 7D 220
CO3: Eig G . . . 6A 164 (5B 16)
CO15: L Cla . . . 3N 185
CO16: L Cla . . . 3N 185
IG8: Wfd G . . . 1F 106
RM8: Dag . . . 6H 125 (5J 39)
RM9: Dag . . . 6H 125 (5J 39)
RM12: Horn . . . 7E 126 (5B 40)
SS5: Hock . . . 8D 104
Wood Lane Sports Cen. . . . 3N 125
Woodleigh E18: Lon . . . 5G 106
Woodleigh Av. SS9: Lgh S . . . 3C 136
Woodleys CM20: H'low . . . 2F 54
Woodley Wlk. SS3: Shoe . . . 4J 139
Woodlow SS7: Thund . . . 9H 119
Woodmanhurst Rd. SS17: Corr . . . 9A 132
Woodman La. E4: Lon . . . 4E 90
Woodman Path IG6: Ilf . . . 3D 108
Woodman Rd. CM14: War . . . 2F 112 (1E 40)
Woodman St. E16: Lon . . . 8A 140
(not continuous)
Wood Meads CM16: Epp . . . 8F 64
Woodmill M. EN11: Rye P . . . 3B 52
Woodpecker Cl. CO4: Colc . . . 7F 166
Woodpecker Rd. SE28: Lon . . . 7H 141
Woodpond Av. SS5: Hock . . . 2C 120
Woodredon Cl. CM19: Roy . . . 4H 53
Woodredon Farm La. EN9: Wal A . . . 5K 77
Woodredon Rd. EN9: Wal A . . . 5K 77
Woodridden Hill
EN9: Epp, They B, Wal A . . . 5K 77 (5F 31)
Woodriffe Rd. E11: Lon . . . 2D 122
Wood Rd. CM9: Mal . . . 2D 214
Woodroffe Cl. CM2: Chelm . . . 8B 60
Woodrolfe Farm La. CM9: Tol . . . 8L 225
Woodrolfe Pk. CM9: Tol . . . 7M 225
Woodrolfe Rd. CM9: Tol . . . 8L 225 (6D 26)
Woodrows La. CO16: Clac S . . . 7F 184
Woodrow Way CO4: Colc . . . 8E 166
Woodrush End CO3: S'way . . . 9C 164
Woodrush Way RM6: Chad H . . . 8J 109
Woods Cl. CB9: Stur . . . 6J 223
Woodshire Rd. RM10: Dag . . . 5N 125
Woodside CM0: S'min . . . 2C 222
CM3: L Bad . . . 1E 74
CM9: Gt Tot . . . 4N 229
CM16: N Wea, Thorn . . . 5H 65 (2J 31)
CM23: Bchgr . . . 9C 220
CO14: Walt . . . 8L 181
IG9: Buck H . . . 8J 91
SS9: Lgh S . . . 9A 120
Woodside Av. SS7: Thund . . . 7B 118
Woodside Chase SS5: Hock . . . 3D 120
Woodside Cl. CM13: Hut . . . 4N 97
CO4: Colc . . . 6E 166
DA7: Bexh . . . 9B 152
RM13: Rain . . . 4G 143
SS7: Lgh S . . . 9A 120
Woodside Cotts. CM11: Bill . . . 3M 99
Woodside Ct. E12: Lon . . . 3J 123
SS9: Lgh S . . . 1A 136
Woodside Gdns. E4: Lon . . . 3B 106
WOODSIDE GREEN . . . 2A 22
Woodside Pk. Stadium . . . 9C 220
Woodside Pk. Av. E17: Lon . . . 8D 106
Woodside Rd. DA7: Bexh . . . 9B 152
IG8: Wfd G . . . 1G 106
SS5: Hock . . . 7E 104
(Granville Rd.)

Woodside Rd. SS5: Hock 2A 120
(Hillside Rd.)
Woodside Vw. SS7: Thund 7C 118
Woodside Way CM6: Gt D 2H 203 (7F 13)
Woods Rd. CM3: Har E 3J 23
Woods, The SS7: Had 3M 135
Woodstock CO5: W Mer 2C 228
Woodstock Av. RM3: Romf 2M 111
Woodstock Cres. SS5: Hock 1C 120
SS15: Lain 9H 115
Woodstock Gdns. IG3: Ilf 4F 124
SS15: Lain 9H 115
Woodstock Pl. CM2: Gt Bad 5G 72
Woodstock Rd. E7: Lon 9J 123
E17: Lon 6D 106
WOOD STREET 6C 106 (2E 38)
Wood St. BR8: Swan 6B 46
CM2: Chelm 3A 72 (2A 34)
E17: Lon 7C 106 (3E 38)
RM17: Grays 4M 155
Wood Street Walthamstow Station (Rail) 8D 106 (3E 38)
Wood Vw. RM16: Grays 1N 155 (1G 47)
RM17: Grays 1N 155
Woodview SS16: Lang H 2G 131
Woodview Av. E4: Lon 1C 106
Woodview Cl. CO4: Colc 3D 166
Woodview Dr. CM3: Gt L 7L 203
Woodview Rd. CM6: Gt D 3K 203
Woodville Cl. SS4: R'fd 4J 121
Woodville Gdns. IG6: Ilf 7A 108
Woodville Rd. E11: Lon 3F 122
E18: Lon 6H 107
SS8: Can I 2K 151
Woodward Cl. RM17: Grays 2L 155
Woodward Gdns. RM9: Dag 9H 125
Woodward Hgts. RM17: Grays 2L 155
Woodward Rd. RM9: Dag 9G 124 (5J 39)
Woodwards CM19: H'low 5B 54
Woodway CM13: Hut 7K 97
CM15: Hut, Shenf 7K 97
Wood Way CM77: Gt N 2B 204
Woodyards CM0: Brad S 7B 194 (1E 36)
Woodyard, The CM16: Epp 7H 65
Woolards Way CM3: S Fer 1K 103
WOOLENSBROOK 7C 20
Woolf Cl. SE28: Lon 8G 140
Woolf Wlk. RM18: Til 7E 156
Woolhampton Way IG7: Chig 9G 92
Woolifers Av. SS17: Corr 1C 148
Woollard St. EN9: Wal A 4C 76
Woollard Way CM4: B'more 1H 83
WOOLLENSBROOK 7C 20
Woollett Cl. DA1: Cray 9E 152
Woolmergreen SS15: Lain 8M 115
(not continuous)
Woolmers Mead CM3: Ples 2B 56
Woolmonger's La. CM4: Nine A 1D 82 (4E 32)
Woolner Rd. CO16: Clac S 7H 185
Woolnough Cl. CB9: Stpl B 3K 223
Woolpack SS3: Shoe 7H 139
Woolpack La. CM7: Brain 3H 193
Woolpits Rd. CM7: Bar S 5K 13
Woolshots Cotts. CM11: Rams B 9F 100
Woolshots Rd. SS12: W'fd 9G 100
WOOLWICH 7G 39
Woolwich Mnr. Way E6: Lon 6A 140 (7G 39)
E16: Lon 9A 140
Woolwich Rd. CO16: Clac S 8G 184
DA7: Bexh 3A 46
DA17: 1A 46
Wootton Cl. RM11: Horn 9H 111
Worcester Av. RM14: Upm 4C 128
Worcester Cl. CM3: May 7L 213
CM7: Brain 7J 193
DA9: Grnh 9E 154
SS16: Lang H 1H 131
SS17: Stan H 2M 147
Worcester Ct. CM2: Gt Bad 5G 73
Worcester Cres. CO7: Alr 6A 176
IG8: Wfd G 1H 107
Worcester Dr. SS6: Ray 6M 119
Worcester Gdns. IG1: Ilf 2L 123
Worcester Rd. CM0: Bur C 2E 196
CO1: Colc 7A 166
E12: Lon 6M 123
Wordsworth Av. CM9: Mal 8C 214
E12: Lon 9L 123
E18: Lon 7F 106
Wordsworth Cl. RM3: Romf 5G 110
RM18: Til 7E 156
SS2: Sth S 4N 137
Wordsworth Ct. CM1: Chelm 6J 59
Wordsworth Rd. CM7: Brain 1H 193
CO3: Colc 9G 165
Wordsworths Way CO16: Clac S 8E 184
Wordsworth Way DA1: Dart 9L 153
(not continuous)
Workers Rd. CM5: H Lav 7A 22
CM17: H'low, H Lav 4N 55 (7A 22)
WORKHOUSE GREEN 7K 9
WORKHOUSE HILL 4M 159 (3E 16)
Workhouse Hill CO4: Boxt 4M 159 (3E 16)
Workhouse La. CM3: Ret C 8B 88
CM3: S Fer, Wdhm F 7G 89 (5E 34)
Workhouse Rd.
CO6: L Hork 6D 158 (3C 16)
Worland Rd. E15: Lon 9E 122
WORLD'S END 6A 30
Worlds End La. CO5: Fee 2L 211
World's End La. N21: Lon 7A 30
WORMINGFORD 8L 229 (3B 16)
WORMINGFORD GROVE 6B 158
Wormingford Rd. CO6: Wmgfd 3B 16
WORMLEY 2D 30
Broxbourne 2D 30
Wormley Ct. EN9: Wal A 3G 77
WORMLEY WEST END 1B 30
Wormyngford Ct. EN9: Wal A 3G 76
Worrin Cl. CM15: Shenf 7J 97
Worrin Rd. CM6: Fels 9E 212
CM15: Shenf 8J 97
Worsdell Way CO4: Colc 5N 165
Worship St. EC2: Lon 6B 38
Worsley Rd. E11: Lon 6E 122
Worsted La.
SG9: Gt Hor, Hare S, L Hor 4E 10
Worthing Cl. RM17: Grays 4H 155
Worthing M. CO15: Clac S 4G 189
Worthing Rd. SS15: Lain 9J 115
Worthington Way CO3: Colc 2G 172
Wortley Rd. E6: Lon 9K 123
Wouldham Rd. RM20: Grays 4H 155
WRABNESS 3E 18
Wrabness Rd. CO12: R'sy 5C 208 (3F 19)
(Orchard Cl.)
CO12: R'sy, Wrab 4A 208 (3E 18)
(Ray La.)
Wrabness Station (Rail) 3D 18
Wrackhall Ct. *SS8: Can I 3L 151*
(off Gafzelle Dr.)
Wragby Rd. E11: Lon 5E 122
Wrangley Ct. EN9: Wal A 3G 77
Wratting Rd. CB9: Gt Wra, Thurl 1J 7
CB9: H'hll 3J 7
Wray Av. IG5: Ilf 7N 107
Wray Cl. RM11: Horn 2G 127
Wraysbury Dr. SS15: Lain 6M 115
Wren Av. SS9: Lgh S 8C 120
Wren Cl. CM11: Bill 6L 99
CO3: S'way 2D 172
CO7: Gt Ben 6J 177
SS7: Thund 9B 118
SS9: Lgh S 8C 120
Wrendale CO15: Clac S 7K 185
Wren Dr. EN9: Wal A 4G 76
Wren Gdns. RM9: Dag 7J 125
RM12: Horn 3D 126
Wren Ho. *CO3: Colc 1G 173*
(off Christine Chase)
Wren Pl. CM14: Brtwd 9G 96
Wren Rd. RM9: Dag 7J 125
Wrens, The CM19: H'low 3A 54
Wren Ter. IG10: Lou 9A 78
Wren Wlk. RM18: Til 5D 156
Wrexham Rd. RM3: Romf 9H 95
SS15: Lain 1K 131
Wright Mead CM2: Chelm 7C 60
Wright's Av. CM77: Tye G 2E 194
Wrightsbridge Rd.
CM14: S Wea 7K 95 (7C 32)
Wrights Cl. RM10: Dag 6N 125
Wrights Ct. CM17: H'low 5H 55
WRIGHT'S GREEN 3M 213 (3A 22)
Wright's Grn. La.
CM22: L Hall 3L 213 (3A 22)
Wrights La. CM15: Wy G 6G 83
Wright's Piece CM22: Hen 7E 210
Wrigley Cl. E4: Lon 2D 106
Wrington Ho. *RM3: Romf 2K 111*
(off Redruth Rd.)
WRITTLE 1K 71 (1J 33)
Writtle Cl. CO16: Clac S 9F 184
Writtle Rd. CM1: Chelm 1N 71 (1K 33)
CM2: Chelm 1N 71
CM4: Marg 9H 71 (3J 33)
Writtle Wlk. RM13: Rain 1C 142
SS14: Bas 8F 116
Wrotham Rd. DA13: Ist R, Meop 7H 47
Wroth's Path IG10: Lou 9M 77
(not continuous)
Wroxall Rd. RM9: Dag 8H 125
Wroxham Cl. CO3: Colc 9J 165
SS9: Lgh S 9A 120
Wroxham Rd. SE28: Lon 7J 141
Wroxham Way IG6: Ilf 5A 108
Wryneck Cl. CO4: Colc 4N 165
Wulvesford CM8: Wthm 7A 230
Wyatt Point *SE28: Lon 9B 140*
(off Erebus Dr.)
Wyatt Rd. DA1: Cray 8D 152
E7: Lon 8G 123
Wyatts Dr. SS1: Sth S 7C 138
WYATT'S GREEN 6G 83 (5F 33)
Wyatts Grn. La.
CM15: Wy G 6G 83
Wyatt's Grn. Rd.
CM15: Dodd, Wy G 6G 82 (5E 32)
Wyatts La. CO10: L Cor 7K 9
E17: Lon 7C 106
Wyburn Rd. SS7: Had 9K 119
Wyburns Av. SS6: Ray 7L 119
Wyburns Av. E. SS6: Ray 7L 119
Wych Elm CM20: H'low 2B 54
CO2: Colc 3A 174
Wych Elm Cl. RM11: Horn 2L 127
Wych Elm Rd. RM11: Horn 1L 127
Wychford Dr. CM21: Saw 3H 51
Wych M. SS15: Lain 6M 115
Wychwood Gdns. IG5: Ilf 8M 107
Wycke Hill CM9: Mal 7A 214 (2G 35)
Wycke Hill Bus. Pk.
CM9: Mal 8A 214
Wycke La. CM9: Tol 8L 225
Wycliffe Gro. CO1: Colc 6M 165
Wycombe Av. SS7: Thund 9A 118
Wycombe Rd. IG2: Ilf 9M 107
WYDDIAL 3D 10
Wyddial Rd. SG9: Bunt 4D 10
Wyedale Dr. CO3: S'way 1F 172
Wyemead Cres. E4: Lon 8E 90
Wyfields IG5: Ilf 5A 108
Wyfold Ho. *SE2: Lon 9J 141*
(off Wolvercote Rd.)
Wyhill Wlk. RM10: Dag 8A 126
Wykeham Av. RM9: Dag 8H 125
RM11: Horn 1H 127
Wykeham Grn. RM9: Dag 8H 125
Wykeham Rd. CM1: Writ 9D 58
SS13: Pits 7L 117
Wyke Rd. E3: Lon 9A 122
Wykes Grn. SS14: Bas 8E 116
Wyldwood Cl. CM17: H'low 6H 51
Wymans Way E7: Lon 6J 123
Wymark Cl. RM13: Rain 2E 142
Wyncolls Rd. CO4: Colc 1C 166 (4F 17)
Wyndham Cl. CO2: Colc 6B 174
Wyndham Cres. CO15: Clac S 9L 185
Wyndham Rd. E6: Lon 9K 123
Wynn Bri. Cl. IG8: Wfd G 5K 107
Wynndale Rd. E18: Lon 5H 107
Wynters SS16: Bas 2C 132
Wynyard Rd. CB10: Saf W 2D 218
Wyseman Pl. CO11: Law 1H 163
Wyse's Rd.
CM1: Cook G, Hghwd 3B 70 (2G 33)
Wythams SS13: Pits 8K 117
Wythefield SS13: Pits 1H 133
Wythenshawe Rd. RM10: Dag 5M 125
Wyvern Ho. *RM17: Grays 4L 155*
(off Bridge Rd.)

Y

Yale M. CO4: Colc 3B 166
Yale Way RM12: Horn 6E 126
Yamburg Rd. SS8: Can I 2K 151
Yardeley SS15: Lain 9N 115
(not continuous)
Yardley Bus. Pk. SS14: Bas 7A 116
Yardley Cl. E4: Lon 4B 90
Yardley Hall La. CM6: Thax 2E 12
Yardley La. E4: Lon 4B 90
Yard, The CM7: Brain 6J 193
Yare Av. CM8: Wthm 4A 230
Yarmouth Cl. CO16: Clac S 7H 185
Yarnacott SS3: Shoe 6G 139
Yarnton Way DA18: Belv, Eri 9H 141
SE2: Lon 9H 141 (7J 39)
Yarwood Rd. CM2: Chelm 9N 59
Yeldham Lock CM2: Chelm 9B 60
Yeldham Rd.
CO9: Cas H, Gt Yel, Sib H 2H 219 (7D 8)
CO9: Stamb 6B 8
CO10: Bel W 6E 8
Yellowpine Way IG7: Chig 1G 108
Yelverton Cl. RM3: Romf 5H 111
Yeoman Cl. E6: Lon 7A 140
Yeoman Lodge CM2: Chelm 8A 60
Yeomen Way IG6: Ilf 3B 108
Yeovil Chase SS0: Wclf S 2G 136
Yevele Way RM11: Horn 2J 127
Yew Cl. CM8: Wthm 2E 230
IG9: Buck H 8K 91
SS15: Lain 6M 115
Yewlands CM21: Saw 3K 51
EN11: Hod 6A 52
Yew Tree Cl. CM3: Hat P 1L 61
CM13: Hut 5L 97
CO4: Colc 7E 166
Yew Tree Gdns. CM2: Chelm 4D 72
RM6: Chad H 9K 109
RM7: Romf 9B 110
Yew Tree Lodge *RM1: Romf 9B 110*
(off Yew Tree Gdns.)
Yew Wlk. EN11: Hod 6A 52
Yew Way CO15: Jay 6D 188
Yonge Cl. CM3: Bore 2F 60
Yorick Av. CO5: W Mer 3C 228
Yorick Rd. CO5: W Mer 3C 228 (5F 27)
York Av. SS17: Corr 9B 132
York Cl. CM15: Shenf 6J 97
SS6: Ray 7N 119
York Cres. IG10: Lou 2L 91
Yorkes CM18: H'low 6E 54
York Gdns. CM7: Brain 4K 193
York Hill IG10: Lou 2L 91
(not continuous)
York Lodge CM15: Hook E 5E 82
York Mans. CO15: Hol S 8B 186
York M. IG1: Ilf 5N 123
York Pl. CO1: Colc 7A 166
IG1: Ilf 4N 123
RM10: Dag 8A 126
York Ri. SS6: Ray 7N 119
York Rd. CM0: Bur C 4E 196
CM2: Chelm 2B 72
CM12: Bill 3J 99
CM15: Shenf 6J 97
CM16: N Wea 6M 65
CO6: E Col 8C 198
CO7: B'sea 7D 182
CO15: Hol S 7A 186 (3E 28)
E4: Lon 1A 106
(not continuous)
E7: Lon 8G 122
E10: Lon 5C 122 (4E 38)
IG1: Ilf 5N 123
RM13: Rain 9B 126
SE1: Lon 7A 38
SS1: Sth S 7M 137
SS4: R'fd 9H 105
SS6: Ray 7N 119
SS17: Horn H 1H 147
York St. CO11: Mist 4J 163
IG11: Bark 1B 140
York Ter. DA8: Eri 6A 152
York Way N7: Lon 5A 38
Young Cl. CO16: Clac S 8G 185
SS9: Lgh S 9F 120
YOUNGSBURY 2D 20
YOUNG'S END 4B 204 (2C 24)
Youngs Rd. IG2: Ilf 9C 108
Yoxley App. IG2: Ilf 1B 124
Yoxley Dr. IG2: Ilf 1B 124
Ypres Rd. CO2: Colc 3L 173
Yunus Khan Cl. E17: Lon 9A 106

Z

Zandi Rd. SS8: Can I 3K 151
Zealand Dr. SS8: Can I 2L 151
Zelham Dr. SS8: Can I 2M 151
Zider Pass SS8: Can I 2M 151
Zinnia M. CO16: Clac S 9G 184

HOSPITALS and HOSPICES covered by this atlas.

N.B. Where Hospitals and Hospices are not named on the map, the reference given is for the road in which they are situated.

BARKING HOSPITAL .9E **124**
Upney La.
BARKING
IG11 9LX
Tel: 0208 9838000

BASILDON HOSPITAL .3B **132**
Nether Mayne
BASILDON
SS16 5NL
Tel: 01268 533911

BECONTREE DAY HOSPITAL .4K **125**
508 Becontree Av.
DAGENHAM
RM8 3HR
Tel: 0208 2767288

BRENTWOOD COMMUNITY HOSPITAL .7H **97**
Crescent Dr.
Shenfield
BRENTWOOD
CM15 8DR
Tel: 01708 465000

BROOMFIELD HOSPITAL .9J **57**
Hospital App.
CHELMSFORD
CM1 7ET
Tel: 01245 440761

CHELMSFORD PRIORY HOSPITAL .7M **59**
Stump La.
CHELMSFORD
CM1 7SJ
Tel: 01245 345345

CLACTON & DISTRICT HOSPITAL .3J **189**
Tower Rd.
CLACTON-ON-SEA
CO15 1LH
Tel: 01255 201717

COLCHESTER GENERAL HOSPITAL .4M **165**
Turner Rd.
COLCHESTER
CO4 5JL
Tel: 01206 747474

ERITH & DISTRICT HOSPITAL .4B **152**
Park Cres.
ERITH
DA8 3EE
Tel: 020 83083131

ESSEX COUNTY HOSPITAL .9L **165**
Lexden Rd.
COLCHESTER
CO3 3NB
Tel: 01206 747474

ESSEX NUFFIELD HOSPITAL, THE .7H **97**
Shenfield Rd.
Shenfield
BRENTWOOD
CM15 8EH
Tel: 01277 695695

FAIR HAVENS HOSPICE .6G **137**
126 Chalkwell Av.
WESTCLIFFE-ON-SEA
SS0 8HN
Tel: 01702 344879

FARLEIGH HOSPICE .2B **72**
212 New London Rd.
CHELMSFORD
CM2 9AE
Tel: 01245 358130

GABLES DAY HOSPITAL, THE .5H **193**
17 Bocking End
BRAINTREE
CM7 9AE
Tel: 01376 555700

GOODMAYES HOSPITAL .9F **108**
Barley La.
ILFORD
IG3 8XJ
Tel: 020 89838000

HALSTEAD HOSPITAL .3K **207**
78 Hedingham Rd.
HALSTEAD
CO9 2DL
Tel: 01206 747474

HAROLD WOOD HOSPITAL .5J **111**
Gubbins La.
ROMFORD
RM3 0BE
Tel: 01708 345533

HARTSWOOD BUPA HOSPITAL .3E **112**
Eagle Way
Great Warley
BRENTWOOD
CM13 3LE
Tel: 01277 232525

HARWICH & DISTRICT HOSPITAL .4J **209**
419 Main Rd.
HARWICH
CO12 4EX
Tel: 01255 201201

HIGHWOOD HOSPITAL .7F **96**
Ongar Rd.
BRENTWOOD
CM15 9DY
Tel: 01708 465000

HOLLY HOUSE HOSPITAL .8H **91**
High Rd.
BUCKHURST HILL
IG9 5HX
Tel: 0208 5053311

KING GEORGE HOSPITAL .9F **108**
Barley La.
ILFORD
IG3 8YB
Tel: 020 89838000

LINDEN CENTRE, THE .8H **57**
Woodland Way, Broomfield
CHELMSFORD
CM1 7LF
Tel: 01245 318800

LITTLE HAVEN CHILDRENS HOSPICE .8K **119**
Daws Heath Rd., Hadleigh
BENFLEET
SS7 2LH
Tel: 01702 556645

LITTLE HIGHWOOD HOSPITAL .6E **96**
Ongar Rd.
BRENTWOOD
CM15 9DY
Tel: 01708 465000

MASCALLS PARK .3E **112**
Mascalls La.
Great Warley
BRENTWOOD
CM14 5HQ
Tel: 01708 465000

MAYFIELD CENTRE 1K **189**
93 Station Rd.
CLACTON-ON-SEA
CO15 1TW
Tel: 01255 207040

MORLAND ROAD DAY HOSPITAL 9M **125**
Morland Rd.
DAGENHAM
RM10 9HU
Tel: 0208 2767933

OAKS HOSPITAL 4M **165**
Oaks Pl.
Mile End Rd.
COLCHESTER
CO4 5XR
Tel: 01206 752121

OLDCHURCH HOSPITAL 1C **126**
Oldchurch Rd.
ROMFORD
RM7 0BE
Tel: 01708 345533

ONGAR WAR MEMORIAL HOSPITAL 5L **67**
Fyfield Rd.
ONGAR
CM5 0AL
Tel: 01277 362629

ORSETT HOSPITAL 5C **146**
Rowley Rd.
Orsett
GRAYS
RM16 3EU
Tel: 01268 533911

PRINCESS ALEXANDRA HOSPITAL, THE 2B **54**
Hamstel Rd.
HARLOW
CM20 1QX
Tel: 01279 444455

RIVERS HOSPITAL, THE 3H **51**
High Wych Rd.
SAWBRIDGEWORTH
CM21 0HH
Tel: 01279 600282

ROCHFORD HOSPITAL 5K **121**
Union La.
ROCHFORD
SS4 1RH
Tel: 01702 578000

RODING BUPA HOSPITAL 7K **107**
Roding La. Sth.
ILFORD
IG4 5PZ
Tel: 020 85511100

RUNWELL HOSPITAL 4A **102**
Runwell Chase
Runwell
WICKFORD
SS11 7QE
Tel: 01268 366000

SAFFRON WALDEN COMMUNITY HOSPITAL 3F **218**
Radwinter Rd.
SAFFRON WALDEN
CB11 3HY
Tel: 01799 522464

ST ANDREW'S CLARE HOUSE 5N **117**
Pound La.
North Benfleet
WICKFORD
SS12 9JP
Tel: 01268 723800

ST CLARE HOSPICE 8J **55**
Hastingwood Rd.
Hastingwood
HARLOW
CM17 9JX
Tel: 01279 413590

ST CLARE'S DAY HOSPICE 3D **214**
Bentalls Complex
Colchester Rd.
MALDON
CM9 4NW
Tel: 01621 857727

ST FRANCIS HOSPICE 9C **94**
The Hall
Broxhill Rd.
Havering-atte-Bower
ROMFORD
RM4 1QH
Tel: 01708 753319

ST GEORGES HOSPITAL (HORNCHURCH) 7J **127**
117 Suttons La.
HORNCHURCH
RM12 6RS
Tel: 01708 465000

ST HELENA HOSPICE (CLACTON) 2J **189**
Jackson Rd.
CLACTON-ON-SEA
CO15 1JP
Tel: 01255 221222

ST HELENA HOSPICE (COLCHESTER) 4B **166**
Barncroft Clo.
Highwoods
COLCHESTER
CO4 9JU
Tel: 01206 845566

ST JOHN'S HOSPITAL 3A **72**
Wood St.
CHELMSFORD
CM2 9BG
Tel: 01245 440761

ST LUKE'S HOSPICE 2B **132**
Fobbing Farm
Nethermayne
BASILDON
SS16 5NJ
Tel: 01268 524973

ST MARGARET'S HOSPITAL 8G **65**
The Plain
EPPING
CM16 6TN
Tel: 01992 561666

ST MICHAEL'S HOSPITAL 5G **192**
Rayne Rd.
BRAINTREE
CM7 2QU
Tel: 01245 440761

ST PETER'S HOSPITAL 6B **214**
Spital Rd.
MALDON
CM9 6EG
Tel: 01376 551221

SOUTHEND HOSPITAL 3H **137**
Prittlewell Chase
WESTCLIFF-ON-SEA
SS0 0RY
Tel: 01702 435555

SPRINGFIELD HOSPITAL 5M **59**
Lawn La.
CHELMSFORD
CM1 7GU
Tel: 01245 234000

THORPE COOMBE HOSPITAL 7C **106**
714 Forest Rd.
LONDON
E17 3HP
Tel: 0208 5395522

THURROCK COMMUNITY HOSPITAL 8M **145**
Long Lane
GRAYS
RM16 2PX
Tel: 01375 364650

WELLESLEY BUPA HOSPITAL 3A **138**
Eastern Av.
SOUTHEND-ON-SEA
SS2 4XH
Tel: 01702 462944

WHIPPS CROSS UNIVERSITY HOSPITAL 1D **122**
Whipps Cross Rd.
LONDON
E11 1NR
Tel: 020 85395522

WILLIAM JULIAN COURTAULD HOSPITAL 6G **193**
London Rd.
BRAINTREE
CM7 2LJ
Tel: 01245 440761

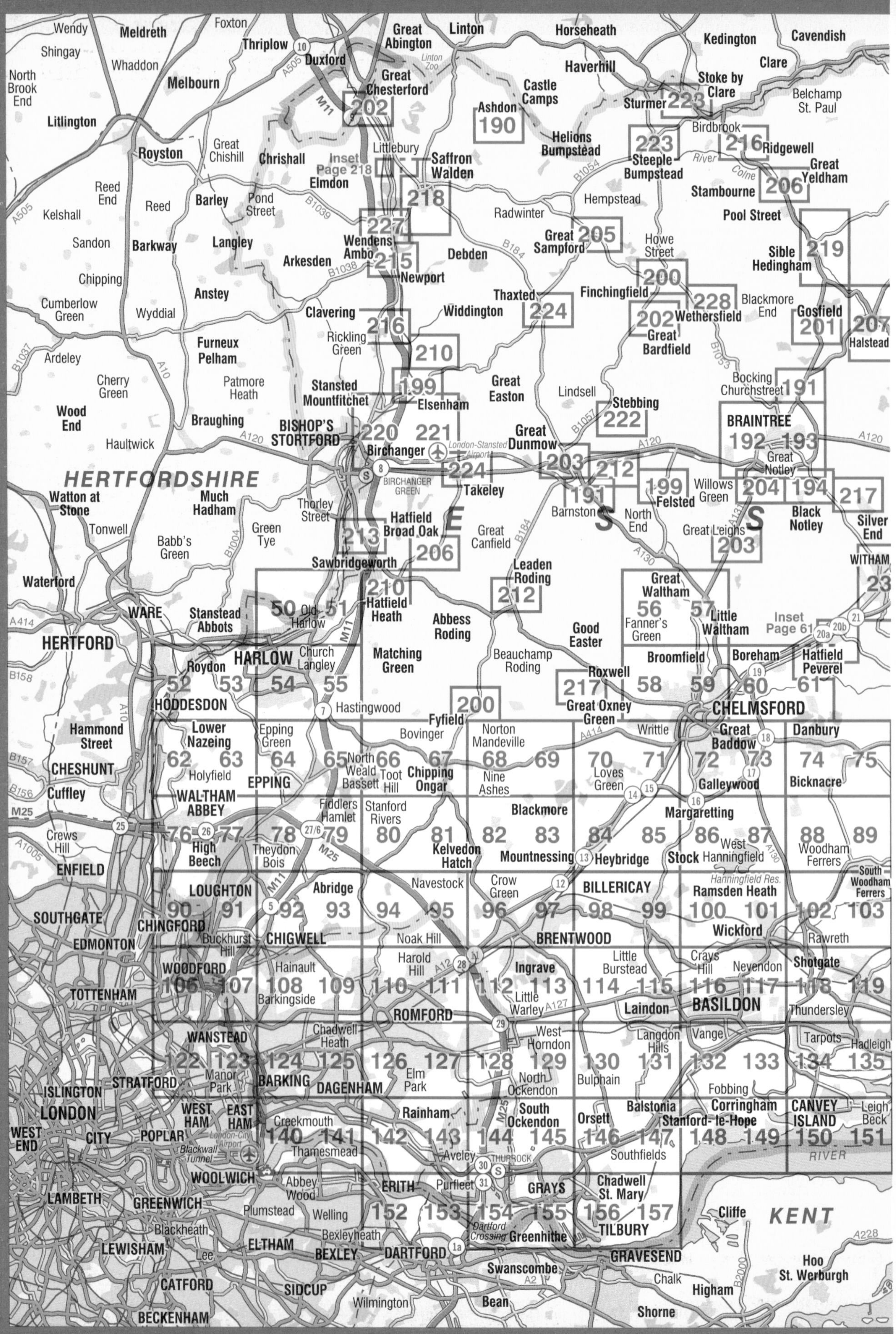

HERTFORDSHIRE
ESSEX
KENT
LONDON
CHELMSFORD
BRAINTREE
HARLOW
BISHOP'S STORTFORD
HERTFORD
BASILDON
BRENTWOOD
BILLERICAY
ROMFORD
Saffron Walden
Great Dunmow
Inset Page 218
Inset Page 61

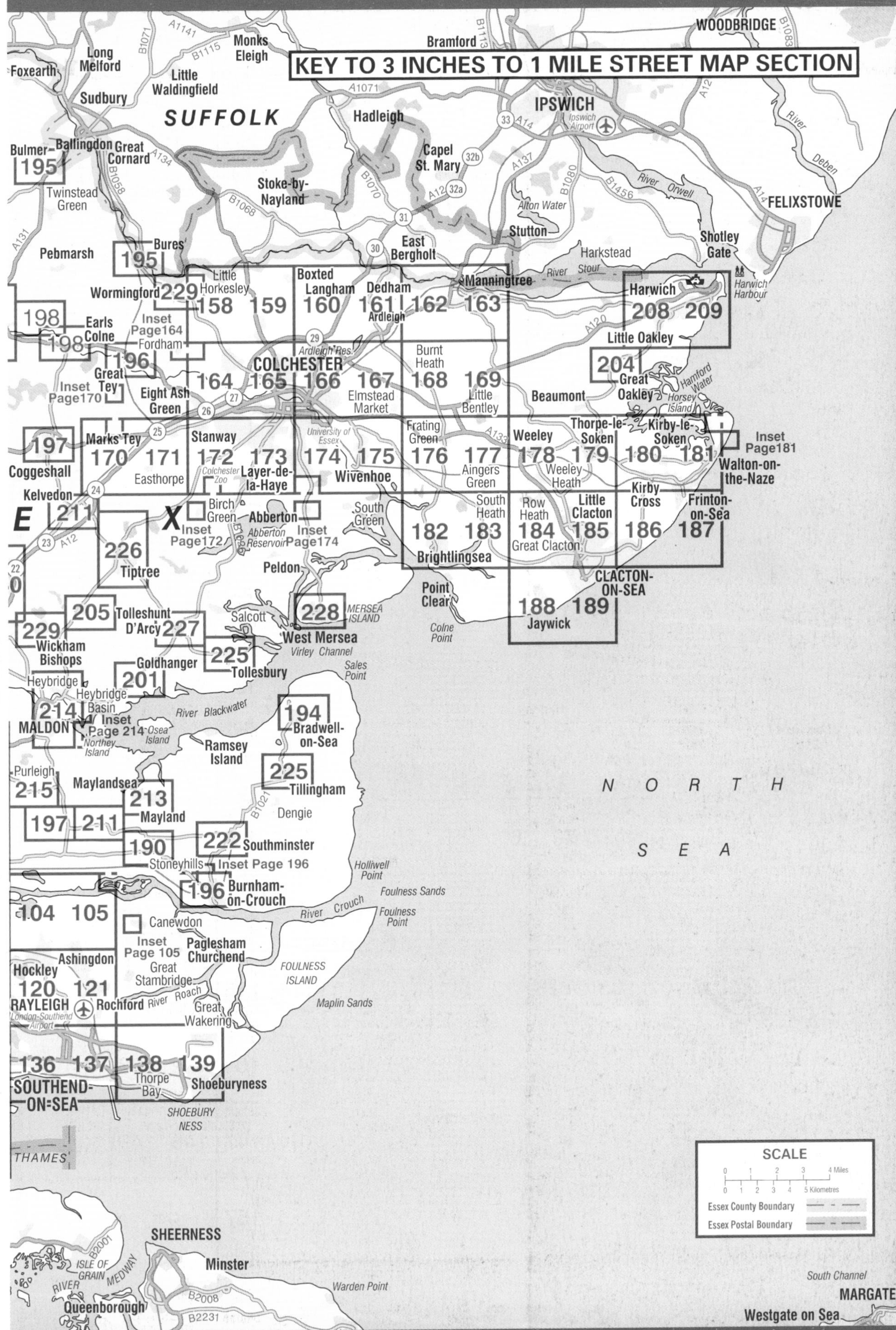

KEY TO 3 INCHES TO 1 MILE STREET MAP SECTION
SUFFOLK
IPSWICH
WOODBRIDGE
FELIXSTOWE
Harwich
COLCHESTER
Manningtree
Sudbury
Hadleigh
Dedham
Wivenhoe
Brightlingsea
CLACTON-ON-SEA
Jaywick
Frinton-on-Sea
Walton-on-the-Naze
West Mersea
Tollesbury
Tiptree
Coggeshall
Kelvedon
MALDON
Burnham-on-Crouch
Southminster
Bradwell-on-Sea
Tillingham
Dengie
FOULNESS ISLAND
Rochford
RAYLEIGH
Hockley
SOUTHEND-ON-SEA
Shoeburyness
SHEERNESS
Minster
Queenborough
MARGATE
Westgate on Sea
NORTH SEA
THAMES
SCALE
Essex County Boundary
Essex Postal Boundary